Cisco IOS 12.0 Bridging and IBM Network Solutions

Cisco Systems, Inc.

CISCO SYSTEMS

CISCO PRESS

Cisco Press
201 W 103rd Street
Indianapolis, IN 46290 USA

Cisco IOS 12.0 Bridging and IBM Network Solutions

Cisco Systems, Inc.

Copyright© 1999 Cisco Systems, Inc.

Cisco Press logo is a trademark of Cisco Systems, Inc.

Published by:
Cisco Press
201 West 103rd Street
Indianapolis, IN 46290 USA

Printed in the United States of America 1 2 3 4 5 6 7 8 9 0

Library of Congress Cataloging-in-Publication Number: 99-61690

ISBN: 1-57870-162-7

Warning and Disclaimer

This book is designed to provide information about **Cisco IOS 12.0 Bridging and IBM Network Solutions**. Every effort has been made to make this book as complete and as accurate as possible, but no warranty or fitness is implied.

The information is provided on an "as is" basis. The author, Cisco Press, and Cisco Systems, Inc., shall have neither liability nor responsibility to any person or entity with respect to any loss or damages arising from the information contained in this book or from the use of the discs or programs that may accompany it.

The opinions expressed in this book belong to the author and are not necessarily those of Cisco Systems, Inc.

Trademark Acknowledgments

All terms mentioned in this book that are known to be trademarks or service marks have been appropriately capitalized. Cisco Press or Cisco Systems, Inc., cannot attest to the accuracy of this information. Use of a term in this book should not be regarded as affecting the validity of any trademark or service mark.

Feedback Information

At Cisco Press, our goal is to create in-depth technical books of the highest quality and value. Each book is crafted with care and precision, undergoing rigorous development that involves the unique expertise of members from the professional technical community.

Readers' feedback is a natural continuation of this process. If you have any comments regarding how we could improve the quality of this book or otherwise alter it to better suit your needs, you can contact us through email at ciscopress@mcp.com. Please make sure to include the book title and ISBN in your message.

We greatly appreciate your assistance.

Publisher	John Wait
Executive Editor	Alicia Buckley
Cisco Systems Program Manager	Jim LeValley
Managing Editor	Patrick Kanouse
Acquisitions Editor	Tracy Hughes
Copy Editor	Michael Hughes
Team Coordinator	Amy Lewis
Book Designer	Scott Cook
Cover Designer	Karen Ruggles
Proofreader	Sheri Replin
Layout Technician	Jeannette McKay
Indexer	Tim Wright

Acknowledgments

The Cisco IOS Reference Library is the result of collaborative efforts of many Cisco technical writers and editors over the years. This bookset represents the continuing development and integration of user documentation for the ever-increasing set of Cisco IOS networking features and functionality.

The current team of Cisco IOS technical writers and editors includes Katherine Anderson, Hugh Bussell, Melanie Cheng, Christy Choate, Sue Cross, Meredith Fisher, Tina Fox, Sheryl Kelly, Marsha Kinnear, Doug MacBeth, Lavanya Mandavilli, Mary Mangone, Andy Mann, Bob Marburg, Greg McMillan, Madhu Mitra, Vicki Payne, Jeremy Pollock, Patricia Rohrs, Teresa Oliver Schick, Wink Schuetz, Grace Tai, Brian Taylor, Jamianne Von-Prudelle, and Amanda Worthington.

The writing team wants to acknowledge the many engineering, customer support, and marketing subject-matter experts for their participation in reviewing draft documents and, in many cases, providing source material from which this bookset is developed.

Contents at a Glance

Table of Contents

Bridging and IBM Networking Overview

This introduction discusses the following software components:

- Transparent and SRT Bridging
- SRB
- RSRB
- DLSw+
- STUN and BSTUN
- LLC2 and SDLC Parameters
- IBM Network Media Translation
- QLLC Conversion
- DSPU and SNA Service Point
- SNA FRAS
- APPN
- NCIA
- CMCC
- TRISL
- ALPS

This introduction gives a high-level description of each technology. For configuration information, refer to the appropriate chapter in this book.

NOTE   All commands supported on the Cisco 7500 series are also supported on the Cisco 7000 series.

Transparent and SRT Bridging

Cisco IOS software supports transparent bridging for Ethernet, Fiber Distributed Data Interface (FDDI), and serial media, and supports source-route transparent bridging (SRT) for Token Ring media. In addition, Cisco supports all the mandatory Management Information Base (MIB) variables specified for transparent bridging in RFC 1286.

Transparent Bridging Features

Cisco transparent bridging software implementation has the following features:

- Complies with the IEEE 802.1D standard.

- Provides the ability to logically segment a transparently bridged network into virtual local-area networks (LANs).

- Provides two spanning-tree protocols—an older bridge protocol data unit (BPDU) format that is compatible with Digital and other LAN bridges for backward compatibility and the IEEE standard BPDU format. In addition to features standard with these spanning-tree protocols, Cisco proprietary software provides for multiple domains for spanning trees. The spanning-tree parameters are configurable.

- Allows frame filtering based on Media Access Control (MAC) address, protocol type, or the vendor code. Additionally, the bridging software can be configured to selectively filter local-area transport (LAT) multicast service announcements.

- Provides deterministic load distribution while maintaining a loop-free spanning tree.

- Provides the ability to bridge over Asynchronous Transfer Mode (ATM), dial-on-demand routing (DDR), FDDI, Frame Relay, multiprotocol Link Access Procedure, Balanced (LAPB), Switched Multimegabit Data Service (SMDS), and X.25 networks.

- Provides concurrent routing and bridging, which is the ability to bridge a given protocol on some interfaces in a router and concurrently route that protocol on other interfaces in the same router.

- Provides integrated routing and bridging, which is the ability to route a given protocol between routed interfaces and bridge groups, or to route a given protocol between bridge groups.

- Provides fast-switched transparent bridging for Frame Relay encapsulated serial and High-Speed Serial Interface (HSSI) interfaces, according to the format specified in RFC 1490.

- Provides fast-switched transparent bridging for the ATM interface on the Cisco 7000, according to the format specified in RFC 1483.

- Provides for compression of LAT frames to reduce LAT traffic through the network.

- Provides both bridging and routing of virtual LANS (VLANs).

Cisco access servers and routers can be configured to serve as both multiprotocol routers and MAC-level bridges, bridging any traffic that cannot otherwise be routed. For example, a router routing the Internet Protocol (IP) can also bridge Digital's LAT protocol or NetBIOS traffic.

Cisco routers also support remote bridging over synchronous serial lines. As with frames received on all other media types, dynamic learning and configurable filtering applies to frames received on serial lines.

Transit bridging of Ethernet frames across FDDI media is also supported. The term transit refers to the fact that the source or destination of the frame cannot be on the FDDI media itself. This allows FDDI to act as a highly efficient backbone for the interconnection of many bridged networks. The configuration of FDDI transit bridging is identical to the configuration of transparent bridging on all other media types.

Integrated Routing and Bridging

While concurrent routing and bridging makes it possible to both route and bridge a specific protocol on separate interfaces within a router, the protocol is not switched between bridged and routed interfaces. Routed traffic is confined to the routed interfaces; bridged traffic is confined to bridged interfaces. A specified protocol may be either routed or bridged on a given interface, but not both.

Integrated routing and bridging makes it possible to route a specific protocol between routed interfaces and bridge groups, or route a specific protocol between bridge groups. Local or unroutable traffic can be bridged among the bridged interfaces in the same bridge group, while routable traffic can be routed to other routed interfaces or bridge groups. Figure I-1 illustrates how integrated routing and bridging in a router interconnects a bridged network with a routed network.

Figure I-1   *Integrated Routing and Bridging Interconnecting a Bridged Network with a Routed Network*

You can configure Cisco IOS software to route a specific protocol between routed interfaces and bridge groups or to route a specific protocol between bridge groups. Specifically, local or unroutable traffic is bridged among the bridged interfaces in the same bridge group, while routable traffic is routed to other routed interfaces or bridge groups. Using integrated routing and bridging, you can do the following:

- Switch packets from a bridged interface to a routed interface
- Switch packets from a routed interface to a bridged interface
- Switch packets within the same bridge group

Bridge-Group Virtual Interface

Because bridging operates in the data link layer and routing operates in the network layer, they follow different protocol configuration models. Taking the basic IP model as an example, all bridged interfaces would belong to the same network, while each routed interface represents a distinct network.

In integrated routing and bridging, the bridge-group virtual interface is introduced to avoid confusing the protocol configuration model when a specific protocol is both bridged and routed in a bridge group. Figure I-2 illustrates the bridge-group virtual interface as a user-configured virtual interface residing within a router.

Figure I-2   *Bridge-Group Virtual Interface in the Router*

The bridge-group virtual interface is a normal routed interface that does not support bridging, but does represent its corresponding bridge group to the routed interface. It has all the network layer attributes (such as a network layer address and filters) that apply to the corresponding bridge group. The interface number assigned to this virtual interface corresponds to the bridge group that this virtual interface represents. This number is the link between the virtual interface and the bridge group.

When you enable routing for a given protocol on the bridge-group virtual interface, packets coming from a routed interface but destined for a host in a bridged domain are routed to the bridge-group virtual interface and are forwarded to the corresponding bridged interface. All traffic routed to the bridge-group virtual interface is forwarded to the corresponding bridge group as bridged traffic. All routable traffic received on a bridged interface is routed to other routed interfaces as if it is coming directly from the bridge-group virtual interface.

To be able to receive routable packets arriving on a bridged interface but destined for a routed interface or to receive routed packets, the bridge-group virtual interface must also have the appropriate addresses. MAC addresses and network addresses are assigned to the bridge-group virtual interface as follows:

- The bridge-group virtual interface "borrows" the MAC address of one of the bridged interfaces in the bridge group associated with the bridge-group virtual interface.

- To route and bridge a given protocol in the same bridge group, you must configure the network layer attributes of the protocol on the bridge-group virtual interface. No protocol attributes should be configured on the bridged interfaces, and no bridging attributes can be configured on the bridge-group virtual interface.

Because there can be only one bridge-group virtual interface representing a bridge group and the bridge group can be made up of different media types configured for several different encapsulation methods, you may need to configure the bridge-group virtual interface with the particular encapsulation methods required to switch packets correctly.

For example, the bridge-group virtual interface has default data link and network layer encapsulations that are the same as those available on Ethernet interfaces, but you can configure the bridge-group virtual interface with encapsulations that are not supported on an Ethernet interface. In some cases, the default encapsulations provide appropriate results; in other cases, they do not. For example, with default encapsulation, Advanced Research Projects Agency (ARPA) packets from the bridge-group virtual interface are translated to Subnetwork Access Protocol (SNAP) when bridging IP to a Token Ring or FDDI bridged interface. But for Internetwork Packet Exchange (IPX), Novell-ether encapsulation from the bridge-group virtual interface is translated to raw-token or raw-FDDI when bridging IPX to a Token Ring or FDDI bridged interface. Because this behavior is usually not what you want, you must configure IPX SNAP or Service Advertisement Protocol (SAP) encapsulation on the bridge-group virtual interface.

Other Considerations

The following are additional facts regarding the support of integrated routing and bridging.

- Integrated routing and bridging is not supported on ciscoBus platforms (AGS+ and Cisco 7000 series).

- Integrated routing and bridging is supported for transparent bridging, but not for source-route bridging (SRB).

- Integrated routing and bridging is supported on all media interfaces except X.25 and Integrated Services Digital Network (ISDN) bridged interfaces.

- Integrated routing and bridging supports three protocols: IP, IPX, and AppleTalk in both fast-switching and process-switching modes.

- Integrated routing and bridging and concurrent routing and bridging cannot operate at the same time.

SRT Bridging Features

Cisco routers support transparent bridging on Token Ring interfaces that support SRT bridging. Both transparent and SRT bridging are supported on all Token Ring interface cards that can be configured for either 4- or 16-MB transmission speeds.

As with other media, all the features that use bridge-group commands can be used on Token Ring interfaces. As with other interface types, the bridge group can be configured to run either the IEEE or Digital spanning-tree protocols. When configured for the IEEE Spanning-Tree Protocol, the bridge cooperates with other SRT bridges and constructs a loop-free topology across the entire extended LAN.

You can also run the Digital Spanning-Tree Protocol over Token Ring. Use it when you have other non-IEEE bridges on other media and you do not have any SRT bridges on Token Ring. In this configuration, all the Token Ring transparent bridges must be Cisco routers. This is because the Digital Spanning-Tree Protocol has not been standardized on Token Ring.

As specified by the SRT bridging specification, only packets without a routing information field (RIF) (RII = 0 in the SA field) are transparently bridged. Packets with a RIF (RII = 1) are passed to the SRB module for handling. An SRT-capable Token Ring interface can have both SRB and transparent bridging enabled at the same time. However, with SRT bridging, frames that did not have a RIF when they were produced by their generating host never gain a RIF, and frames that did have a RIF when they were produced never lose that RIF.

NOTE   Because bridges running only SRT bridging never add or remove RIFs from frames, they do not integrate SRB with transparent bridging. A host connected to a source-route bridge that expects RIFs can never communicate with a device across a bridge that does not understand RIFs. SRT bridging cannot tie in existing source-route bridges to a transparent bridged network. To tie in existing bridges, you must use source-route translational bridging (SR/TLB) instead. SR/TLB is described in Chapter 3, "Configuring Source-Route Bridging."

Bridging between Token Ring and other media requires certain packet transformations. In all cases, the MAC addresses are bit-swapped because the bit ordering on Token Ring is different from that on other media. In addition, Token Ring supports one packet format, logical link control (LLC), while Ethernet supports two formats (LLC and Ethernet).

The transformation of LLC frames between media is simple. A length field is either created (when the frame is transmitted to non-Token Ring) or removed (when the frame is transmitted to Token Ring). When an Ethernet format frame is transmitted to Token Ring, the frame is translated into an LLC-1 SNAP packet. The destination service access point (DSAP) value is AA, the source service access point (SSAP) value is AA, and the organizational unique identifier (OUI) value is 0000F8. Likewise, when a packet in LLC-1 format is bridged onto Ethernet media, the packet is translated into Ethernet format.

CAUTION	Bridging between dissimilar media presents several problems that can prevent communication from occurring. These problems include bit order translation (or using MAC addresses as data), maximum transmission unit (MTU) differences, frame status differences, and multicast address usage. Some or all these problems might be present in a multimedia bridged LAN. Because of differences in the way end nodes implement Token Ring, these problems are most prevalent when bridging between Token Ring and Ethernet or between Ethernet and FDDI LANs.

Problems currently occur with the following protocols when bridged between Token Ring and other media: Novell IPX, DECnet Phase IV, AppleTalk, Banyan VINES, Xerox Network Systems (XNS), and IP. Further, problems can occur with the Novell IPX and XNS protocols when bridged between FDDI and other media. We recommend that these protocols be routed whenever possible.

SRB

Cisco IOS bridging software includes source-route bridging (SRB) capability. A source-route bridge connects multiple physical Token Rings into one logical network segment. If the network segment bridges only Token Ring media to provide connectivity, the technology is termed SRB. If the network bridges Token Ring and non-Token Ring media is introduced into the bridged network segment, the technology is termed remote source-route bridging (RSRB).

SRB enables routers to simultaneously act as a Level 3 router and a Level 2 source-route bridge. Thus, protocols such as Novell's IPX or XNS can be routed on Token Rings, while other protocols such as Systems Network Architecture (SNA) or NetBIOS are source-route bridged.

SRB technology is a combination of bridging and routing functions. A source-route bridge can make routing decisions based on the contents of the MAC frame header. Keeping the routing function at the MAC, or Level 2, layer allows the higher-layer protocols to execute their tasks more efficiently and allows the LAN to be expanded without the knowledge of the higher-layer protocols.

As designed by IBM and the IEEE 802.5 committee, source-route bridges connect extended Token Ring LANs. A source-route bridge uses the RIF in the IEEE 802.5 MAC header of a datagram (see Figure I-3) to determine which rings or Token Ring network segments the packet must transit.

Figure I-3   *IEEE 802.5 Token Ring Frame Format*

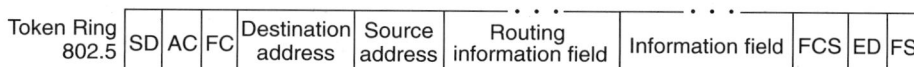

Token Ring 802.5	SD	AC	FC	Destination address	Source address	Routing information field	Information field	FCS	ED	FS

The source station inserts the RIF into the MAC header immediately following the source address field in every frame, giving this style of bridging its name. The destination station reverses the routing field to reach the originating station.

The information in a RIF is derived from explorer packets generated by the source node. These explorer packets traverse the entire source-route bridge network, gathering information on the possible paths the source node might use to send packets to the destination.

Transparent spanning-tree bridging requires time to recompute a topology in the event of a failure; SRB, which maintains multiple paths, allows fast selection of alternate routes in the event of failure. Most importantly, SRB allows the end stations to determine the routes the frames take.

SRB Features

Cisco SRB implementation has the following features:

- Provides configurable fast-switching software for SRB.

- Provides for a local source-route bridge that connects two or more Token Ring networks.

- Provides *ring groups* to configure a source-route bridge with more than two network interfaces. A ring group is a collection of Token Ring interfaces in one or more routers that are collectively treated as a *virtual ring*.

- Provides two types of explorer packets to collect RIF information—an *all-routes* explorer packet, which follows all possible paths to a destination ring, and a *spanning-tree* explorer packet, which follows a statically configured limited route (spanning tree) when looking for paths.

- Provides a dynamically determined RIF cache based on the protocol. The software also allows you to add entries manually to the RIF cache.

- Provides for filtering by MAC address, link service access point (LSAP) header, and protocol type.

- Provides for filtering of NetBIOS frames either by station name or by a packet byte offset.

- Provides for translation into transparently bridged frames to allow source-route stations to communicate with nonsource-route stations (typically on Ethernet).

- Provides support for the SRB MIB variables as described in the IETF draft "Bridge MIB" document, "Definition of Managed Objects for Bridges," by E. Decker, P. Langille, A. Rijsinghani, and K. McCloghrie, June 1991. Only the SRB component of the Bridge MIB is supported.

- Provides support for the Token Ring MIB variables as described in RFC 1231, "IEEE 802.5 Token Ring MIB," by K. McCloghrie, R. Fox, and E. Decker, May 1991. Cisco implements the mandatory tables (Interface Table and Statistics Table) but not the optional table (Timer Table) of the Token Ring MIB. The Token Ring MIB has been implemented for the 4/16-Mb Token Ring cards that can be user adjusted for either 4- or 16-Mb transmission speeds (CSC-1R, CSC-2R, CSC-R16M, or CSC-C2CTR).

- SRB is supported over FDDI on Cisco 7200 series routers.

- Particle-based switching is supported (over FDDI and Token Ring) by default on Cisco 7200 series routers.

RSRB

In contrast to SRB, which involves bridging between Token Ring media only, RSRB is the first Cisco technique for connecting Token Ring networks over non-Token Ring network segments. (DLSw+ is Cisco's strategic method for providing this function.)

Cisco RSRB software implementation includes the following features:

- Provides for multiple routers separated by non-Token Ring segments. Three options are available:

  — Encapsulate the Token Ring traffic inside IP datagrams passed over a Transmission Control Protocol (TCP) connection between two routers.

  — Use Fast-Sequenced Transport (FST) to transport RSRB packets to their peers without TCP or User Datagram Protocol (UDP) header or processor overhead.

  — Use data link layer encapsulations over a single serial line, Ethernet, Token Ring, or FDDI ring connected between two routers attached to Token Ring networks.

- Provides for configurable limits to the size of the TCP backup queue.

Figure I-4 shows an RSRB topology. The virtual ring can extend across any non-Token Ring media supported by RSRB, such as serial, Ethernet, FDDI, and WANs. The type of media you select determines the way you set up RSRB.

Figure I-4   *RSRB Topology*

NOTE   If you bridge across Token Ring media, it is recommended that you do not use RSRB. Use SRB instead. Refer to Chapter 3, "Configuring Source-Route Bridging."

DLSw+

Data-link switching plus (DLSw+) is a method of transporting SNA and NetBIOS. It complies with the DLSw standard documented in RFC 1795 as well as the DLSw Version 2 standard. DLSw+ is an alternative to RSRB that addresses several inherent problems that exist in RSRB, such as:

- SRB hop-count limits (SRB's limit is seven)
- Broadcast traffic (including SRB explorer frames or NetBIOS name queries)
- Unnecessary traffic (acknowledgments and keepalives)
- Data-link control timeouts

DLSw Standard

The DLSw standard, documented in RFC 1795, defines the switch-to-switch protocol between DLSw routers. The standard also defines a mechanism to terminate data-link control connections locally and multiplex the traffic from the data-link control connections to a TCP connection. The standard always calls for the transport protocol to be TCP and always requires that data-link control connections be locally terminated (the equivalent of Cisco's local acknowledgment option). The standard also requires that the SRB RIF be terminated at the DLSw router. The standard describes a means for prioritization and flow control and defines error recovery procedures that ensure data-link control connections are appropriately disabled if any part of their associated circuits breaks.

The DLSw standard does not specify when to establish TCP connections. The capabilities exchange allows compliance to the standard, but at different levels of support. The standard does not specify how to cache learned information about MAC addresses, RIFs, or NetBIOS names. It also does not describe how to track both capable or preferred DLSw partners for either backup or load-balancing purposes. The standard does not provide the specifics of media conversion, but leaves the details up to the implementation. It does not define how to map switch congestion to the flow control for data-link control. Finally, the MIB is documented under a separate RFC.

DLSw Version 2 Standard

In the Version 1 standard, the network design was required to be fully meshed so that all peers were connected to every other peer. This design created unnecessary broadcast traffic because an explorer was sent to every peer for every broadcast.

DLSw Version 2 addresses this problem and improves scalability in DLSw networks with the following enhancements:

- UDP/IP Multicast Service
- Enhanced Peer-on-Demand Routing Feature
- Expedited TCP Connection

UDP/IP Multicast Service

IP multicast service reduces the amount of network overhead because it avoids the need to maintain TCP Switch-to-Switch Protocol (SSP) connections between two DLSw peers when no circuits are available and it ensures that each broadcast results in only a single explorer over every link. Furthermore, multicast service avoids duplication and excessive bandwidth of broadcast traffic because it replicates and propagates messages only as necessary to its multicast members. This functionality is a subset of Cisco's existing DLSw+ border peering feature. In a border peer network, address resolution packets are sent via the border peer network and can take advantage of border peer caching to minimize bandwidth usage. DLSw Version 2 is for customers who run a multicast IP network and do not need the advantages of border peering.

With UDP Unicast, explorer frames and unnumbered information frames are sent via UDP rather than TCP. This feature eliminates retransmission of explorers and unnumbered information frames that could occur during congestion. Cisco's DLSw+ introduced the UDP Unicast feature prior to the release of DLSw Version 2 in Cisco IOS Release 11.2(6)F. One difference between the two enhancements is that the Release 11.2(6)F UDP Unicast feature requires that a TCP connection exist before packets are sent via UDP. Because the TCP session is up and capabilities have been exchanged, the peers know exclusive reachability information which will permit them to further reduce the explorer load on the network. DLSw Version 2, on the other hand, sends UDP/IP multicast and unicast before the TCP connection exists. Although DLSw Version 2 employs IP multicast service when address resolution packets (CANUREACH_EX, NETBIOS_NQ_ex, NETBIOS_ANQ, and DATAFRAME) are sent to multiple destinations; the response frames (ICANREACH_ex and NAME_RECOGNIZED_ex), are sent via UDP unicast.

Enhanced Peer-on-Demand Routing Feature

DLSw Version 2 now establishes TCP connections only when necessary and the TCP connections are brought down when there are no circuits to a DLSw peer for a specified amount of time. This method, known as peer-on-demand routing, was recently introduced in DLSw Version 2, but has been implemented in Cisco DLSw+ border peer technology since Cisco IOS Release 10.3.

Expedited TCP Connection

DLSw Version 2 more efficiently establishes TCP connections. Previously, DLSw created two unidirectional TCP connections and then disconnected one after the capabilities exchange took place. With DLSw Version 2, a single bidirectional TCP connection is established if the associated peer is known to support DLSw Version 2.

DLSw+ Features

DLSw+ is the Cisco version of DLSw and it supports several additional features and enhancements. DLSw+ is fully compatible with any vendor's RFC 1795 implementation and the following features are available when both peers are using DLSw+:

- Peer groups and border peers.

- Backup peers.

- Promiscuous and on-demand peers.

- Scalability enhancements through explorer firewalls and location learning.

- NetBIOS dial-on-demand routing feature support.

- UDP unicast support.

- Border peer caching and load balancing.

- Support for LLC1 circuits.

- Support for multiple bridge groups.

- Support for RIF Passthru.

- A choice of transport options, including TCP, FST, and direct encapsulation in High-Level Data Link Control (HDLC) or Frame Relay.

- SNA type of service feature support.

- Local acknowledgment for Ethernet-attached devices and media conversion for SNA PU 2.1 and PU 2.0 devices.

- Conversion between LLC2 to SDLC between Physical Unit (PU) 4 devices.

- Local or remote media conversion between LANs and either Synchronous Data Link Control (SDLC) Protocol or Qualified Logical Link Control (QLLC).

- SNA View, Blue Maps, and IBM's LAN Network Manager (LNM) support.

- MIB enhancements that allow DLSw+ features to be managed by the CiscoWorks Blue products, SNA Maps, and SNA View. Also, new traps alert network management stations of peer or circuit failures. For more information, refer to the current Cisco IOS release notes for the location of the Cisco MIB Web site.

DLSw+ Enhancements

DLSw+ goes beyond the standard to include additional functionality in the following areas:

- Modes of Operation—Ability to determine the capabilities of the participating router and to operate according to those capabilities.

- Improved Scalability—Ability to construct IBM internetworks in a way that reduces the amount of broadcast traffic and therefore enhances their scalability.

- Improved Performance—Ability to offer higher-performance transport options when the line speeds and traffic conditions do not require local acknowledgment.

- Enhanced Availability—Overall availability of an end-to-end connection between a pair of SNA and NetBIOS end systems.

Modes of Operation

DLSw+ operates in two modes:

- Standards compliance mode—DLSw+ can automatically detect (through the DLSw+ capabilities exchange) that the participating router is manufactured by another vendor. DLSw+ then operates in DLSw standard mode.

- Enhanced mode—DLSw+ can automatically detect that the participating router is another DLSw+ router. DLSw+ then operates in enhanced mode, providing the additional features of DLSw+ to the SNA and NetBIOS end systems.

NOTE   DLSw+ does not interoperate with prestandard implementations such as RFC 1434.

Some enhanced DLSw+ features are also available when a Cisco router is operating in standards compliance mode with another vendor's router. In particular, enhancements that are locally controlled options on a router can be accessed even though the remote router does not have DLSw+. These include reachability caching, explorer firewalls and media conversion.

Improved Scalability

One significant factor that limits the size of Token Ring internetworks is the amount of explorer traffic that traverses the WAN. DLSw+ includes the following features to reduce the number of explorers:

- Peer groups—The large Token Ring internetworks that Cisco has helped to build over the last several years have all followed a similar structure. That structure is a hierarchical grouping of routers based upon the usual flow of broadcasts through the network. A cluster of routers in a region or a division of a company is combined into a peer group.

- Border peers—Within a peer group, one or more routers are designated as border peers. When a DLSw+ router receives a test frame or NetBIOS name query, it sends a single explorer frame to its border peer. The border peer takes complete responsibility for forwarding the explorer on behalf of the peer group member. This arrangement eliminates duplicate explorers on the access links and minimizes the processing required in access routers.

- On-demand peers—On-demand peers greatly reduce the number of peers that must be configured. As Figure I-5 shows, you can use on-demand peers to establish an end-to-end circuit even though the DLSw+ routers servicing the end systems have no specific configuration information about the peers. This configuration permits casual, any-to-any connection without the burden of configuring the connection in advance. It also allows any-to-any switching in large internetworks where persistent TCP connections would not be possible.

Figure I-5 *Scalability with DLSw+*

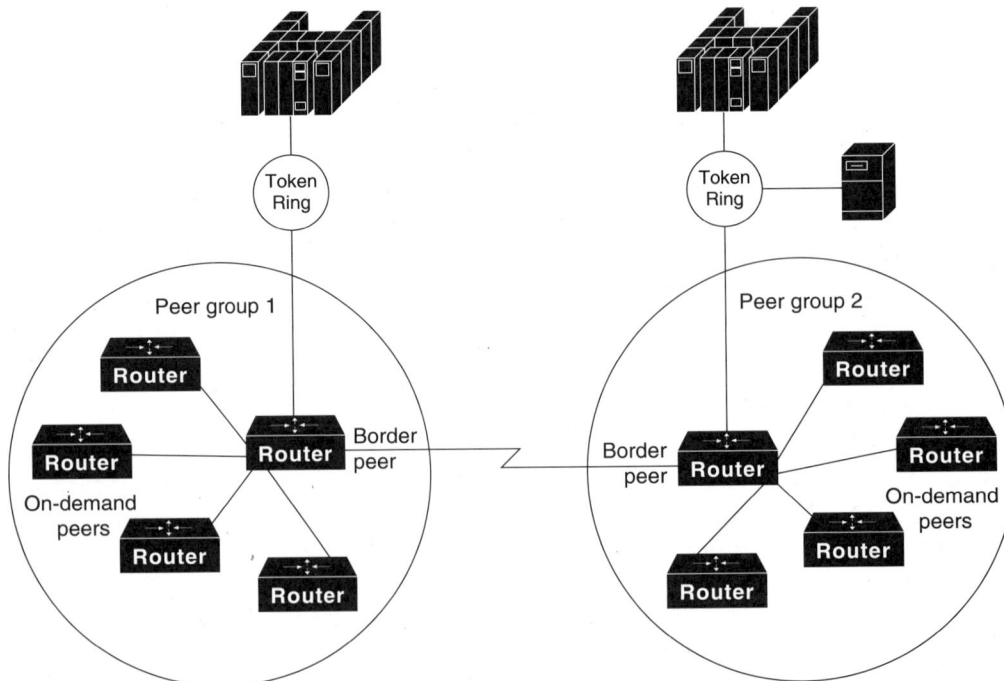

- Explorer firewalls—An explorer firewall permits only a single explorer for a particular destination MAC address or NetBIOS name to be sent across the WAN. While an explorer is outstanding and awaiting a response from the destination, subsequent explorers for that MAC address or NetBIOS name are merely stored. When the explorer response is received at the originating DLSw+, all explorers receive an immediate local response. This eliminates the start-of-day explorer storm that many networks experience.

- NetBIOS dial-on-demand routing—This feature allows you to transport NetBIOS in a dial-on-demand routing (DDR) environment by filtering NetBIOS Session Alive packets from the WAN. NetBIOS periodically sends Session Alive packets as LLC2 I-frames. These packets do not require a response and are superfluous to the function of proper data flow. Furthermore, these packets keep dial-on-demand interfaces up and this up time causes unwanted per-packet charges in DDR networks. By filtering these NetBIOS Session Alive packets, you reduce traffic on the WAN as well as some costs that are associated with dial-on-demand routing.

- UDP unicast enhancement—The SSP address resolution packets are sent via UDP unicast service rather than TCP. SSP packets include: CANUREACH_EX, NETBIOS_NQ_ex, NETBIOS_ANQ, and DATAFRAME. UDP unicast enhances the scalability of TCP peer networks because it allows DLSw+ to better control address resolution packets and unnumbered information frames during periods of congestion. Previously, these frames were carried over TCP. TCP retransmits frames that get lost or delayed in transit, and hence aggravate congestion. Because address resolution packets and unnumbered information frames are not sent on a reliable transport on the LAN, sending them reliably over the WAN is unnecessary. By using UDP for these frames, DLSw+ minimizes network congestion.

NOTE   UDP unicast enhancement does not affect FST or direct peer encapsulations.

- Border peer caching—Border peer caching increases the scalability of DLSw+ by minimizing broadcast traffic, bandwidth requirements, and the requirement for border peers to replicate explorers. Previously, border peers did not learn reachability information from the broadcasts that they forwarded. Now, border peers learn reachability information based on relay responses and store it in their remote and group caches. After the first search when a peer is found, every subsequent explorer is forwarded to the known destination, rather than forwarded as a broadcast. As a result, the network has fewer broadcasts.

- LLC1 circuits—Support for LLC1 circuits more efficiently transports LLC1 UI traffic across a DLSw+ cloud. With LLC1 circuit support, the LLC1 unnumbered information frames (UI) are no longer subject to input queuing and are guaranteed to traverse the same path for the duration of the flow. This feature improves transportation of LLC1 UI traffic because there is no longer the chance of having a specifically routed LLC1 UI frame broadcasted to all remote peers. The circuit establishment process has not changed except that the circuit is established as soon as the specifically routed LLC1 UI frame is received and the DLSw+ knows of reachability for the destination MAC address. Furthermore, the connection remains in the CIRCUIT_ESTABLISHED state (rather than proceeding to the CONNECT state) until there is no UI frame flow for a MAC/SAP pair for 10 minutes.

- Multiple bridge groups—This feature allows you to assign more than one bridge group for different physical Ethernet segments. See the dlsw bridge-group command for more information.

- RIF Passthru—This feature gives you the option to configure DLSw+ without RIF termination. By default, DLSw+ terminates the RIF to increase a network's scalability; however, some environments do not function properly if the RIF is terminated.

Improved Performance

DLSw+ improves performance by offering higher-performance transport options in the following areas:

- Transport Connection Type

- SNA Type of Service

Transport Connection Type

The transport connection between DLSw+ routers can vary according to the needs of the network and is not necessarily tied to TCP/IP as the DLSw standard is. Three different transport protocols are supported between DLSw+ devices:

- TCP for transport of SNA and NetBIOS traffic across WANs where bandwidth is limited and termination of data-link control sessions is required. This transport option is required when DLSw+ is operating in standards compliance mode.

- FST for transport across IP WANs with an arbitrary topology with sufficient bandwidth to accommodate SNA and NetBIOS.

- Direct encapsulation for transport across a point-to-point connection where the benefits of an arbitrary topology are not important.

SNA Type of Service

Performance is further enhanced with the SNA type of service (ToS) feature. Although DLSw+ priority queuing provides prioritization on the output queue of the interface, the priority characteristics are lost once the packet leaves the DLSw+ router and traverses the network. SNA ToS sets IP precedence in all DLSw+ frames, either setting all DLSw+ to a high precedence, or building multiple pipes for different priority traffic and setting each one appropriately. Also, when running Advanced Peer-to-Peer Networking (APPN) over DLSw+, APPN Class of Service (CoS) characteristics are lost once the packet is delivered to the DLSw+ router for bridging over an IP network. With the new DLSw+ SNA ToS feature, however, SNA ToS works in conjunction with weighted fair queuing to reduce the response time for SNA sessions and, therefore, ensures that DLSw+ gets more bandwidth. DLSw+ traffic is prioritized and APPN CoS characteristics are preserved across the network.

With SNA ToS feature, DLSw+ sets the precedence bits in the IP header of outbound DLSw+ packets. When DLSw+ is used in conjunction with APPN, SNA ToS maps APPN CoS to IP ToS, and preserves SNA CoS across an IP backbone. If priority queuing is not configured on DLSw+, the IP precedence value of "Network" is used for all DLSw+ packets. This default value ensures more bandwidth for DLSw+ packets than for other types of packets.

Table I-1 describes the various IP precedence values that map to the TCP ports.

Table I-1 *IP Precedence Values*

TCP Ports	Priority Queue Level	IP Precedence APPN Value	IP Precedence DLSw+ Value
2065	High	Network	Network control
1981	Medium	High	Internetwork control
1982	Normal	Medium	Critical
1983	Low	Low	Flash override

If you configure the **priority** option in the **dlsw remote-peer** command, DLSw+ automatically activates four TCP ports to that remote peer (ports 2065, 1981, 1982 and 1983) and assigns traffic to specific ports according to the rules defined in Table I-2. Alternately, SAP prioritization, LOCADDR prioritization, or APPN CoS can be used to customize how traffic is assigned to these ports.

Table I-2 *Port Number Priority Values*

TCP Ports	DLSw+ Queue Priority	Type of Traffic (Default)
2065	High	Circuit administration frames
		Peer keepalives
		Capabilities exchange
1981	Medium	None
1982	Normal	Information frames
1983	Low	Broadcast traffic

If you do not configure the **priority** option in the **dlsw remote-peer** command, then all DLSw+ traffic defaults to port 2065 and is assigned IP precedence "network." The default ToS settings can be changed by using policy routing based on the TCP ports that the DLSw+ router uses.

Please note the following design considerations with the SNA ToS feature:

- APPN CoS-to-IP ToS mapping occurs only if DLSw+ and APPN are running in the same router and a **priority** is specified on the remote peer statement.

- SNA ToS applies only to TCP or FST encapsulation types.

- When using FST encapsulation, SNA ToS marks all DLSw+ traffic with IP precedence "network."

Enhanced Availability

DLSw+ offers enhanced availability by caching a table of multiple paths to a given MAC address or NetBIOS name (where a path is either a remote peer or a local port). Furthermore, with the Border Peer Caching feature, border peers build an additional cache (group), which is checked before forwarding explorers for other routers.

Maintaining multiple paths per destination is especially attractive in SNA networks. A common technique used in the hierarchical SNA environment is assigning the same MAC address to different Token Ring interface couplers (TICs) on the IBM front-end processors (FEPs). DLSw+ ensures that duplicate TIC addresses are found, and, if multiple DLSw+ peers can be used to reach the FEPs, they are cached.

The way that multiple capable peers are handled with DLSw+ can be configured to meet either of the following network needs:

- Fault tolerance—To rapidly reconnect if a data-link connection is lost. If load balancing is not enabled, Cisco IOS software maintains a preferred path and one or more capable paths to each destination. The preferred peer is either the peer that responds first to an explorer frame or the peer with the least cost. The preferred port is always the port over which the first positive response to an explorer was received. If the preferred peer to a given destination is unavailable, the next available capable peer is promoted to the new preferred peer. No additional broadcasts are required, and recovery through an alternate peer is immediate. Maintaining multiple cache entries facilitates a timely reconnection after session outages.

- Load balancing—To distribute the network traffic over multiple DLSw+ peers in the network. Cisco IOS software can be configured to perform load balancing, in which case circuits are established in round-robin fashion using the list of capable routers. When used for load balancing, this technique improves overall SNA performance.

Figure I-6 shows a peer table of preferred (pref) and capable (cap) routes.

Figure I-6   *Enhanced Availability and Performance*

In addition to supporting multiple active peers, DLSw+ supports backup peers for all encapsulation types (including direct, FST, and TCP), which are connected only when the primary peer cannot be reached.

DLSw+ Support for Other SNA Features

DLSw+ can be used as a transport for SNA features such as LNM, DSPU, SNA service point, and APPN through a Cisco IOS feature called virtual data-link control (VDLC).

LNM over DLSw+ allows DLSw+ to be used in Token Ring networks that are managed by IBM's LNM software. Using this feature, LNM can be used to manage Token Ring LANs, control access units, and Token Ring attached devices over a DLSw+ network. All management functions continue to operate as they would in a source-route bridged network or an RSRB network.

DSPU over DLSw+ allows Cisco's DSPU feature to operate in conjunction with DLSw+ in the same router. DLSw+ can be used either upstream (toward the mainframe) or downstream (away from the mainframe) of DSPU. DSPU concentration consolidates the appearance of multiple physical units (PUs) into a single PU appearance to VTAM, minimizing memory and cycles in central site resources (VTAM, NCP, and routers) and speeding network startup.

SNA service point over DLSw+ allows Cisco's SNA service point feature to be used in conjunction with DLSw+ in the same router. Using this feature, SNA service point can be configured in remote routers, and DLSw+ can provide the path for the remote service point PU to communicate with NetView. This allows full management visibility of resources from a NetView 390 console, while concurrently offering the value-added features of DLSw+ in an SNA network.

APPN over DLSw+ allows Cisco's APPN feature to be used in conjunction with DLSw+ in the same router. With this feature, DLSw+ can be used to access an APPN backbone or APPN in the data center. DLSw+ can also be used as a transport for APPN, providing nondisruptive recovery from failures and high-speed intermediate routing. The DLSw+ network can appear as a connection network to the APPN network nodes.

Using DLSw+ as a transport for other Cisco IOS SNA features requires a feature called VDLC. Cisco IOS data-link users (such as LNM, DSPU, SNA service point, and APPN) write to a virtual data-link control interface. DLSw+ then reads from this interface and sends out the traffic. Similarly, DLSw+ can receive traffic destined for one of these Dependent LU Server (DLUS) and write it to the virtual data-link control interface, from which the appropriate Dependent LU (DLU) will read it.

In Figure I-7, APPN and DLSw+ use Token Ring and Ethernet, respectively, as "real" data-link controls, and use virtual data-link control to communicate between themselves. When one of the high-layer protocols passes data to the virtual data-link control, the virtual data-link control must pass it to a higher-layer protocol; nothing leaves the virtual data-link control without going through a data-link user.

Figure I-7   *VDLC Interaction with Higher-Layer Protocols*

The higher-layer protocols make no distinction between the VDLC and any other data-link control, but they do identify the VDLC as a destination. In the example shown in Figure I-7, APPN has two ports: a physical port for Token Ring and a logical (virtual) port for the VDLC. In the case of the APPN VDLC port, when you define the APPN VDLC port, you can also specify the MAC address assigned to it. That means data going from DLSw+ to APPN by way of the VDLC is directed to the VDLC MAC address. The type of higher-layer protocol you use determines how the VDLC MAC address is assigned.

STUN and BSTUN

Cisco IOS software supports serial tunnel (STUN) and block serial tunnel (BSTUN). Cisco's BSTUN implementation enhances Cisco 2500, 4000, 4500, 4700, 7200 series routers to support devices that use the Binary Synchronous Communication (Bisync) data-link protocol and asynchronous security protocols that include Adplex, ADT Security Systems, Inc., Diebold, and asynchronous generic traffic. BSTUN implementation is also supported on the 4T network interface module (NIM) on the Cisco series 4000 and 4500. Cisco's support of the bisync protocol enables enterprises to transport Bisync traffic and SNA multiprotocol traffic over the same network.

STUN Networks

STUN operates in two modes: passthrough and local acknowledgment. Figure I-8 shows the difference between passthrough mode and local acknowledgment mode.

The upper half of Figure I-8 shows STUN configured in passthrough mode. In passthrough mode, the routers act as a wire and the SDLC session remains between the end stations. In this mode, STUN provides a straight pass-through of all SDLC traffic, including control frames.

The lower half of Figure I-8 shows STUN configured in local acknowledgment mode. In local acknowledgment mode, the routers terminate the SDLC sessions and send only data across the WAN. Control frames no longer travel the WAN backbone networks.

Figure I-8   *Comparison of STUN in Passthrough Mode and Local Acknowledgment Mode*

NOTE	To enable STUN local acknowledgment, you first enable the routers for STUN and configure them to appear on the network as primary or secondary SDLC nodes. TCP/IP encapsulation must be enabled. Cisco's STUN local acknowledgment feature also provides priority queuing for TCP-encapsulated frames.

STUN Features

Cisco STUN implementation provides the following features:

- Encapsulates SDLC frames in either the Transmission Control Protocol/Internet Protocol (TCP/IP) or the HDLC protocol.

- Allows two devices using SDLC- or HDLC-compliant protocols that are normally connected by a direct serial link to be connected through one or more Cisco routers, reducing leased-line costs.

   When you replace direct serial links with routers, serial frames can be propagated over arbitrary media and topologies to another router with a STUN link to an appropriate end point. The intervening network is not restricted to STUN traffic, but rather, is multiprotocol. For example, instead of running parallel backbones for DECnet and SNA/SDLC traffic, this traffic now can be integrated into an enterprise backbone network.

- Supports local acknowledgment for direct Frame Relay connectivity between routers, without requiring TCP/IP.

- Allows networks with IBM mainframes and communications controllers to share data using Cisco routers and existing network links. As an SDLC function, STUN fully supports the IBM SNA and allows IBM SDLC frames to be transmitted across the network media and shared serial links. Figure I-9 illustrates a typical network configuration without STUN and the same network configured with STUN.

- Encapsulates SDLC frame traffic packets and routes them over any of the supported network media (serial, FDDI, Ethernet, and Token Ring, X.25, SMDS, and T1/T3) using TCP/IP encapsulation. Because TCP/IP encapsulation is used, you can use any of the Cisco routing protocols to route the packets.

- Copies frames to destinations based on address. STUN in passthrough mode does not modify the frames in any way or participate in SDLC windowing or retransmission; these functions are left to the communicating hosts. However, STUN in local acknowledgment mode does participate in SDLC windowing and retransmission through local termination of the SDLC session.

- Ensures reliable data transmission across serial media having minimal or predictable time delays. With the advent of STUN and WAN backbones, serial links now can be separated by wide geographic distances spanning countries and continents. As a result, these serial links have time delays that are longer than SDLC allows for bidirectional communication between hosts. The STUN local acknowledgment feature addresses the problems of unpredictable time delays, multiple retransmissions, or loss of sessions.

- Allows for configuration of redundant links to provide transport paths if part of the network goes down.

Figure I-9   *IBM Network Configuration Without STUN and with STUN*

BSTUN Networks

The Bisync feature enables your Cisco 2500, 3600, 4000, 4500, or 7200 series router to support devices that use the Bisync data-link protocol. This protocol enables enterprises to transport Bisync traffic over the same network that supports their SNA and multiprotocol traffic, eliminating the need for separate Bisync facilities.

At the access router, traffic from the attached Bisync device is encapsulated in IP. The Bisync traffic can then be routed across arbitrary media to the host site where another router supporting Bisync will remove the IP encapsulation headers and present the Bisync traffic to the Bisync host or controller over a serial connection. HDLC can be used as an alternative encapsulation method for point-to-point links.

BSTUN Features

Cisco implementation of BSTUN provides the following features:

- Encapsulates Bisync, Adplex, ADT Security Systems, Inc., Diebold, asynchronous generic, and Monitor Dynamics Inc., traffic for transfer over router links. The tunneling of asynchronous security protocols feature enables your Cisco 2500, 3600, 4000, 4500, or 7200 series router to support devices that use the following asynchronous security protocols:

    — adplex

    — adt-poll-select

    — adt-vari-poll

    — diebold

    — async-generic

    — mdi

- Provides a tunnel mechanism for BSTUN over Frame Relay, without using TCP/IP encapsulation.

- Supports legacy Bisync devices and host applications without modification.

- Uses standard synchronous serial interfaces on Cisco 2500 series and the 4T network interface module (NIM) on the Cisco 4000 series and Cisco 4500 series.

- Supports point-to-point, multidrop, and virtual multidrop configurations.

LLC2 and SDLC Parameters

The Logical Link Control, type 2 (LLC2) and SDLC protocols provide data link layer support for higher-layer network protocols and features such as SDLC Logical Link Control (SDLLC) and RSRB with local acknowledgment. The features that are affected by LLC2 parameter settings are listed in the next section, "Cisco Implementation of LLC2." The features that require SDLC configuration and use SDLC parameters are listed in the section "Cisco Implementation of SDLC" later in this chapter.

LLC2 and SDLC package data in frames. LLC2 and SDLC stations require acknowledgments from receiving stations after a set amount of frames have been sent before sending further data. The tasks described in this chapter modify default settings regarding the control field of the data frames. By modifying the control field parameters, you can determine the number of acknowledgments sent for frames received and the level of polling used to determine available stations. In this manner, you can set the amount of resources used for frame checking and optimize the network load.

SDLC is used as the primary SNA link-layer protocol for WAN links. SDLC defines two types of network nodes: primary and secondary. Primary nodes poll secondary nodes in a predetermined order. Secondary nodes then transmit any outgoing data. When configured as primary and secondary nodes, Cisco's routers are established as SDLC stations.

Cisco Implementation of LLC2

Cisco LLC2 implementation supports the following features:

- Local acknowledgment for RSRB

  This feature is used in Cisco's implementation of RSRB as described in Chapter 3, "Configuring Source-Route Bridging."

  Because LANs are now connected through RSRB and WAN backbones, the delays that occur are longer than LLC2 allows for bidirectional communication between hosts. Cisco's local acknowledgment feature addresses the problem of delays, retransmissions, and loss of user sessions.

- IBM LNM support

  Routers using 4- or 16-Mbps Token Ring interfaces configured for SRB support LNM and provide all IBM bridge program functions. With LNM, a router appears as an IBM source-route bridge, and can manage or monitor any connected Token Ring interface.

  LNM support is described in Chapter 3, "Configuring Source-Route Bridging."

- SDLLC media translation

  The SDLLC feature provides media translation between the serial lines running SDLC and Token Rings running LLC2. SDLLC consolidates the IBM SNA networks running SDLC into a LAN-based, multiprotocol, multimedia backbone network.

  SDLLC is described in Chapter 15, "Configuring IBM Network Media Translation."

- ISO Connection-Mode Network Service (CMNS)

  Cisco CMNS implementation runs X.25 packets over LLC2 so that X.25 can be extended to Ethernet, FDDI, and Token Ring media.

Cisco Implementation of SDLC

Cisco SDLC implementation supports the following features:

- Frame Relay Access Support (FRAS)

  With FRAS, a router functions as a Frame Relay Access Device (FRAD) for SDLC, Token Ring, and Ethernet-attached devices over a Frame Relay Boundary Network Node (BNN) link.

  Frame Relay access support is described in Chapter 19, "Configuring SNA Frame Relay Access Support."

- SDLLC media translation

  The SDLLC feature provides media translation between the serial lines running SDLC and Token Rings running LLC2. SDLLC consolidates the IBM SNA networks running SDLC into a LAN-based, multiprotocol, multimedia backbone network.

  SDLLC is described in Chapter 15, "Configuring IBM Network Media Translation."

- SDLC local acknowledgment

  SDLC local acknowledgment is used with SDLC STUN. TCP/IP must be enabled. With local acknowledgment, STUN SDLC connections can be terminated locally at the router, eliminating the need for acknowledgments to be sent across a WAN.

  SDLC local acknowledgment is described in the section "Establish the Frame Encapsulation Method" in Chapter 11, "Configuring Serial Tunnel and Block Serial Tunnel."

IBM Network Media Translation

Cisco IOS software includes the following media translation features that enable network communications across heterogeneous media:

- SDLLC media translation enables a device on a Token Ring to communicate with a device on a serial link.

- QLLC conversion enables an IBM device to communicate with an X.25 network without having to install the X.25 software on local IBM equipment.

SDLLC is a Cisco Systems proprietary software feature that enables a device on a Token Ring to communicate with a device on a serial link by translating between LLC2 and SDLC at the link layer.

SNA uses SDLC and LLC2 as link layer protocols to provide a reliable connection. The translation function between these industry-standard protocols takes place in the proprietary Cisco software.

Figure I-10 illustrates how SDLLC provides data link layer support for SNA communication.

Figure I-10 *SNA Data Link Layer Support*

SDLLC Media Translation Features

The SDLLC feature allows a PU 4, PU 2.1, or PU 2 to communicate with a PU 2 SDLC device as follows:

● SDLLC with direct connection—A 37x5 FEP on a Token Ring and the 3x74 cluster controller connected to a serial line are each connected to an interface on the same router configured with SDLLC.

● SDLLC with RSRB—A 37x5 FEP on a Token Ring and a 3x74 cluster controller connected to a serial line are connected to different routers. Only the device to which the 3x74 is connected is configured with SDLLC. The routers communicate via RSRB using direct encapsulation, RSRB over an FST connection, or RSRB over a TCP connection.

● SDLLC with RSRB and local acknowledgment—A 37x5 FEP on a Token Ring and a 3x74 cluster controller connected to a serial line are connected to different routers. Only the device to which the 3x74 is connected is configured with SDLLC. The routers communicate via RSRB over a TCP connection that has local acknowledgment enabled.

In all these topologies, each IBM end node (the FEP and cluster controller) has no indication that its counterpart is connected to a different medium running a different protocol. The 37x5 FEP responds as if the 3x74 cluster controller were communicating over a Token Ring, whereas the 3x74 responds as though the 37x5 FEP were communicating over a serial line. That is, the SDLLC software makes translation between the two media transparent to the end nodes.

Virtual Token Ring Concept

Central to Cisco's SDLLC feature is the concept of a virtual Token Ring device residing on a virtual Token Ring. Because the Token Ring device expects the node with which it is communicating also to be on a Token Ring, each SDLLC device on a serial line must be assigned an SDLLC virtual Token Ring address (SDLLC VTRA). Like real Token Ring addresses, SDLLC VTRAs must be unique across the network.

In addition to the SDLLC VTRA, an SDLLC virtual ring number must be assigned to each SDLLC device on a serial line. (The SDLLC virtual ring number differs from the virtual ring group numbers that are used to configure RSRB and multiport bridging.)

As part of its virtual telecommunications access method (VTAM) configuration, the IBM node on the Token Ring has knowledge of the SDLLC VTRA of the serial device with which it communicates. The SDLC VTRA and the SDLLC virtual ring number are a part of the SDLLC configuration for the router's serial interface. When the Token Ring host sends out explorer packets with the SDLLC VTRA as the destination address in the MAC headers, the router configured with that SDLLC VTRA intercepts the frame, fills in the SDLLC virtual ring number address and the bridge number in the RIF, then sends the response back to the Token Ring host. A route is then established between the Token Ring host and the router. After Cisco IOS software performs the appropriate frame conversion, the system uses this route to forward frames to the serial device.

Resolving Differences in LLC2 and SDLC Frame Size

IBM nodes on Token Ring media normally use frame sizes greater than 1 KB, whereas the IBM nodes on serial lines normally limit frame sizes to 265 or 521 bytes. To reduce traffic on backbone networks and provide better performance, Token Ring nodes should send frames that are as large as possible. As part of the SDLLC configuration on the serial interface, the largest frame size the two media can support should be selected. Cisco IOS software can fragment the frames it receives from the Token Ring device before forwarding them to the SDLC device, but it does not assemble the frames it receives from the serial device before forwarding them to the Token Ring device.

Maintaining a Dynamic RIF Cache

SDLLC maintains a dynamic RIF cache and caches the entire RIF; that is, the RIF from the source station to destination station. The cached entry is based on the best path at the time the session begins. SDLLC uses the RIF cache to maintain the LLC2 session between the router and the host FEP. SDLLC does not age these RIF entries. Instead, SDLLC places an entry in the RIF cache for a session when the session begins and flushes the cache when the session terminates. You cannot flush these RIFs because if you flush the RIF entries randomly, Cisco IOS software cannot maintain the LLC2 session to the host FEP.

Other Considerations

The following are additional facts regarding SDLC and SDLLC:

- As part of Cisco's SDLC implementation, only modulus 8 Normal Response Mode (NRM) sessions are maintained for the SDLC session.

- SDLC sessions are always locally acknowledged. LLC2 sessions can be optionally configured for local acknowledgment.

- SDLLC does not apply to SNA subarea networks, such as 37x5 FEP-to 37x5 FEP communication.

- Parameters such as the maximum number of information frames (I-frames) outstanding before acknowledgment, frequency of polls, and response time to poll frames can be modified per interface. If local acknowledgment is not enabled, these parameters are modified on the SDLC interface. If local acknowledgment is enabled, these parameters are modified on the Token Ring interface.

- Local acknowledgment only applies when the remote peer is defined for RSRB using IP encapsulation over a TCP connection. If no local acknowledgment is used, the remote peer can be defined for RSRB using direct encapsulation, RSRB using IP encapsulation over an FST connection, or RSRB using IP encapsulation over a TCP connection.

QLLC Conversion

Qualified Logical Link Control (QLLC) is a data-link protocol defined by IBM that allows SNA data to be transported across X.25 networks. (Although IBM has defined other protocols for transporting SNA traffic over an X.25 network, QLLC is the most widely used.) Figure I-11 illustrates how QLLC conversion provides data link layer support for SNA communication.

Figure I-11 *SNA Data Link Layer Support*

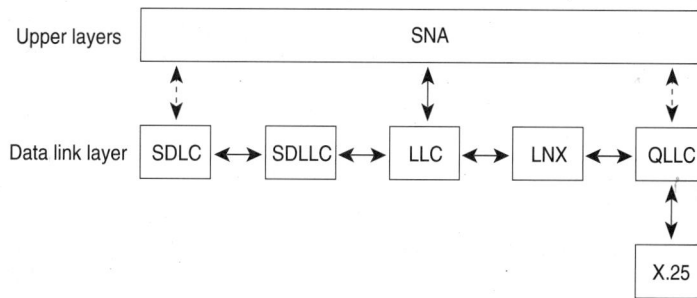

As shown in Figure I-12, any devices in the SNA communication path that use X.25, whether end systems or intermediate systems, require a QLLC implementation.

Figure I-12 *SNA Devices Running QLLC*

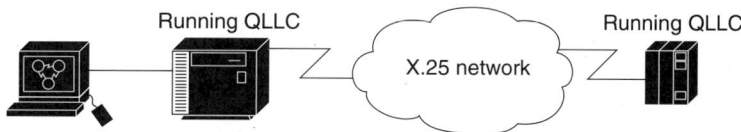

As shown in Figure I-13, the QLLC conversion feature eliminates the need to install the X.25 software on local IBM equipment. A device attached locally to a Token Ring network can communicate through a router running the QLLC Conversion feature with a remote device attached to an X.25 network using QLLC. Typically, the locally attached device is an FEP, an AS 400, or a PS/2, and the remote device is a terminal controller or a PS/2. In this case, only the remote device needs an X.25 interface and the FEP can communicate with the terminal controller as if it were directly attached via a Token Ring network.

Figure I-13 *Router Running QLLC Conversion Feature*

More elaborate configurations are possible. The router that implements QLLC conversion need not be on the same Token Ring network as the FEP. As shown in Figure I-14, QLLC/LLC2 conversion is possible even when an intermediate IP WAN exists between the router connected to the X.25 network and the router connected to the Token Ring.

Figure I-14 *QLLC Conversion Running on a Router with an Intermediate IP Network*

Cisco Implementation of QLLC Conversion

SNA uses QLLC and X.25 as link layer protocols to provide a reliable connection. QLLC itself processes QLLC control packets. In a Token Ring environment, SNA uses LLC to provide a reliable connection. The LAN-to-X.25 (LNX) software provides a QLLC conversion function to translate between LLC and QLLC.

Figure I-15 shows the simplest QLLC conversion topology: a single Token Ring device (for example, a 37x5 FEP) communicates with a single remote X.25 device (in this case a 3x74 cluster controller). In this example, a router connects the Token Ring network to the X.25 network.

Figure I-15   *QLLC Conversion Between a Single 37x5 and a Single 3x74*

In Figure I-15, each IBM end node has no indication that its counterpart is connected to a different medium running a different protocol. The 37x5 FEP responds as if the 3x74 cluster controller were communicating over a Token Ring, whereas the 3x74 responds as though the 37x5 FEP were communicating over an X.25 network. This is accomplished by configuring the router's X.25 interface as a virtual Token Ring, so that the X.25 virtual circuit appears to the Token Ring device (and to the router itself) as if it were a Token Ring to which the remote X.25 device is attached.

Also in this figure, the LLC2 connection extends from the 37x5 FEP across the Token Ring network to the router. The QLLC/X.25 session extends from the router across the X.25 network to the 3x74 cluster controller. Only the SNA session extends across the Token Ring and X.25 networks to provide an end-to-end connection from the 37x5 FEP to the 3x74 cluster controller.

As Figure I-16 shows, a router need not directly connect the two IBM end nodes; instead, some type of backbone WAN can connect them. Here, RSRB transports packets between Router A and Router B, while Router B performs all conversion between the LLC2 and X.25 protocols. Only the router attached to the serial line (Router B) needs to be configured for QLLC conversion. Both Router A and Router B are configured for normal RSRB.

Figure I-16   *QLLC Conversion Between a Single 37x5 and Multiple 3x74s Across an Arbitrary WAN*

How communication sessions are established over the communication link varies depending on whether or not LLC2 local acknowledgment has been configured on Router A's Token Ring interface. In both cases, the SNA session extends end-to-end and the QLLC/X.25 session extends from Router B to the 3x74 cluster controller. If LLC2 local acknowledgment has not been configured, the LLC2 session extends from the 37x5 FEP across the Token Ring network and the arbitrary WAN to Router B. In contrast, when LLC2 local acknowledgment has been configured, the LLC2 session extends from the 37x5 FEP Router A, where it is locally terminated. A TCP session is then used across the arbitrary WAN to Router B.

Comparing QLLC Conversion to SDLLC

Although the procedures you use to configure QLLC are similar to those used to configure SDLLC, there are structural and philosophical differences between the point-to-point links that SDLC uses and the multiplexed virtual circuits that X.25 uses.

The most significant structural difference between QLLC conversion and SDLLC is the addressing. To allow a device to use LLC2 to transfer data, both SDLLC and QLLC provide virtual MAC addresses. In SDLLC, the actual MAC address is built by combining the defined virtual MAC (whose last byte is 0x00) with the secondary address used on the SDLC link; in this way, SDLLC supports multidrop. In QLLC conversion, multidrop is meaningless, so the virtual MAC address represents just one session and is defined as part of the X.25 configuration. Because one physical X.25 interface can support many simultaneous connections for many different remote devices, you only need one physical link to the X.25 network. The different connections on different virtual circuits all use the same physical link.

The most significant difference between QLLC conversion and SDLLC is the fact that a typical SDLC/SDLLC operation uses a leased line. In SDLC, dial-up connections are possible, but the maximum data rate is limited. In QLLC, both switched virtual circuits (SVCs) and permanent virtual circuits (PVCs) are available, but the favored use is SVC. While the router maintains a permanent connection to the X.25 network, a remote device can use each SVC for some bounded period of time and then relinquish it for use by another device. Using a PVC is very much like using a leased line.

Table I-3 shows how the QLLC commands correspond to the SDLLC commands.

Table I-3   *QLLC and SDLLC Command Comparison*

QLLC Command	Analogous SDLLC Command
qllc largest-packet	sdllc ring-largest-frame, sdllc sdlc-largest-frame
qllc partner	sdllc partner
qllc sap	sdllc sap
qllc srb, x25 map qllc, x25 pvc qllc	sdllc traddr
qllc xid	sdllc xid
source-bridge qllc-local-ack	source-bridge sdllc-local-ack

Other Implementation Considerations

Consider the following when implementing QLLC conversion:

- To use the QLLC conversion feature, a router must have a physical link to an X.25 public data network (PDN). It must also have an SRB/RSRB path to an IBM FEP. This link could be a Token Ring or Ethernet interface, or even FDDI, if RSRB is being used.

- QLLC conversion can run on any router with at least one serial interface configured for X.25 communication and at least one other interface configured for SRB or RSRB.

- QLLC conversion security depends upon access control in SRB/RSRB and X.25 and upon XID validation.

You can configure DLSw+ for QLLC connectivity, which enables the following scenarios:

- Remote LAN-attached devices (physical units) or SDLC-attached devices can access an FEP or an AS/400 over an X.25 network.

- Remote X.25-attached SNA devices can access an FEP or an AS/400 over a Token Ring or over SDLC.

For information on configuring DLSw+ for QLLC conversion, refer to Chapter 9, "Configuring Data-Link Switching Plus."

You can configure DSPUs for QLLC. For more information on this configuration, refer to Chapter 17, "Configuring DSPU and SNA Service Point Support."

DSPU and SNA Service Point

Downstream physical unit (DSPU) is a software feature that enables the router to function as a physical unit (PU) concentrator for SNA PU type 2 nodes. PU concentration at the device simplifies the task of PU definition at the upstream host while providing additional flexibility and mobility for downstream PU devices.

The DSPU feature allows you to define downstream PU type 2 devices in Cisco IOS software. DSPU reduces the complexity of host configuration by letting you replace multiple PU definitions that represent each downstream device with one PU definition that represents the router.

Because you define the downstream PUs at the router rather than the host, you isolate the host from changes in the downstream network topology. Therefore, you can insert and remove downstream PUs from the network without making any changes on the host.

The concentration of downstream PUs at the router also reduces network traffic on the WAN by limiting the number of sessions that must be established and maintained with the host. The termination of downstream sessions at the router ensures that idle session traffic does not appear on the WAN.

SNA service point support in Cisco IOS software assumes that NetView or an equivalent product is available at the SNA host. The user interacts with the network management feature in the router and at the SNA host. In Cisco IOS software, you can configure the host connection and show the status of this connection. At the SNA host, you can use the NetView operator's console to view alerts and to send and receive Cisco syntax commands to the Cisco device.

Figure I-17 shows a router functioning as a DSPU concentrator.

Figure I-17   *Router Acting as a DSPU Concentrator*

Typically, a router establishes one or more upstream connections with one or more hosts and many downstream connections with PU type 2 devices. From an SNA perspective, the router appears as a PU type 2 device to the upstream host and assumes the role of a system services control point (SSCP) appearing as a PU type 5 device to its downstream PUs.

The SSCP sessions established between the router and its upstream host are completely independent of the SSCP sessions established between the router and its downstream PUs. SNA traffic is routed at a logical unit (LU) level using a routing algorithm that maps downstream LUs onto upstream LUs.

Figure I-18 illustrates the SNA perspective of DSPU.

Figure I-18   *SNA Perspective of DSPU*

SNA FRAS

Using FRAS, Cisco IOS software allows branch SNA devices to connect directly to a central site FEP over a Frame Relay network. FRAS converts LAN or SDLC protocols to a Frame Relay format understood by the Network Control Program (NCP) that runs in an FEP. Cisco IOS software and the NCP support two frame formats:

- RFC 1490 routed format for LLC2, specified in the FRF.3 Agreement from the Frame Relay Forum and known in NCP literature as Frame Relay Boundary Network Node (BNN) support. Support for this feature requires NCP 7.1 or higher.

- RFC 1490 802.5 source-route bridged format, known in NCP literature as Frame Relay Boundary Access Node (BAN) support. Support for this feature requires NCP 7.3 or higher.

Management service point support in FRAS allows the SNA network management application, NetView, to manage Cisco routers over the Frame Relay network as if it were an SNA downstream PU.

FRAS provides dial backup over RSRB in case the Frame Relay network is down. While the backup Public Switched Telephone Network (PSTN) is being used, the Frame Relay connection is tried periodically. As soon as the Frame Relay network is up, it will be used.

RFC 1490 Routed Format for LLC2 (BNN)

RFC 1490 specifies a standard method of encapsulating multiprotocol traffic with data-link (Level 2 of the OSI model) framing. The encapsulation for SNA data is specified in the FRF.3 Agreement.

The Frame Relay encapsulation method is based on the RFC 1490 frame format for "user-defined" protocols using Q.933 NLPID, as illustrated in Figure I-19.

Figure I-19   *Frame Relay Encapsulation Based on RFC 1490*

DLCI Q.922 Address	Control 0x30	NLPID Q.933 0x08	L2 Protocol ID 0x4c (802.2) 0x08	L3 Protocol ID	DSAP SSAP	Control	F C S

NOTE   The protocol ID for SNA subarea FID4 is 0x81. The protocol ID for SNA subarea FID2 is 0x82. The protocol ID for APPN FID2 is 0x83.

FRAS allows the router acting as a FRAD to take advantage of the SNA BNN support for Frame Relay provided by ACF/NCP 7.1 and OS/400 V2R3. Downstream PU 2.0 and PU 2.1 devices can be attached to the router through SDLC, Token Ring, or Ethernet links. The router acting as a FRAD is connected to the Network Control Program (NCP) or AS/400 through a public or private Frame Relay network, as illustrated in Figure I-20.

Figure I-20   *SNA BNN Support for Frame Relay*

The frame format that communicates across the Frame Relay BNN link is defined in RFC 1490 for routed SNA traffic. From the perspective of the SNA host (for example an NCP or AS/400), the Frame Relay connection is defined as a switched resource similar to a Token Ring BNN link. Because the frame format does not include link addresses to allow the NCP to distinguish among SNA devices on the same permanent virtual circuit, Cisco supports SAP multiplexing, which allows you to configure unique LLC2 SAPs for each downstream SNA device so that they can share a single permanent virtual circuit to an FEP.

Cisco IOS software is responsible for terminating the local data-link control frames (such as SDLC and Token Ring frames) and for modifying the data-link control frames to 802.2 compliant LLC frames. The LLC provides a reliable connection-oriented link layer transport required by SNA. (For example, 802.2 LLC is used to provide link layer acknowledgment, sequencing, and flow control.)

Cisco IOS software encapsulates these 802.2 LLC frames according to the RFC 1490 format for SNA traffic. The frames are then forwarded to the SNA host on a Frame Relay permanent virtual circuit (PVC). In the reverse direction, the software is responsible for de-encapsulating the data from the Frame Relay PVC, and for generating and transmitting the appropriate local data-link control frames to the downstream devices.

RFC 1490 Bridged Format for LLC2 (BAN)

BAN provides functionality similar to BNN except that it uses a bridged frame format, as illustrated in Figure I-21.

Figure I-21 *RFC 1490 Bridged Frame Format*

Q.922 Address			
Control	0x03	pad	0x00
NLPID	SNAP 0x80	OUI	00x0
OUI 0x80-C2 (bridged)			
PID 0x00-09			
pad 0x00		Frame Control	
Destination/Source MAC (12 bytes)			
DSAP		SSAP	
Control			
SNA Data			
PCS			

Because it includes the MAC header information in every frame, BAN supports multiple SNA devices sharing a single PVC without requiring SAP multiplexing. BAN also supports load balancing across duplicate data-link connection identifiers to the same or different FEPs at the data center to enhance overall availability. BAN works for devices attached by either Token Ring or Ethernet.

APPN

Advanced Peer-to-Peer Networking (APPN) is the second generation of SNA. APPN provides support for client/server applications and offers more dynamics than traditional hierarchical SNA, such as dynamic directory and routing services.

Cisco APPN implementation includes the following features:

- Implements High Performance Routing (HPR), the next step in the evolution of SNA networking. HPR replaced the APPN routing technique called intermediate session routing (ISR) with two elements that provide significant performance improvements:

  — Rapid Transport Protocol (RTP) provides functions including error recovery, packet resequencing, segmentation, selective retransmissions, flow control, and congestion control. RTP incorporates a new congestion avoidance algorithm, Adaptive Rate-Based (ARB) congestion control.

  — Automatic Network Routing provides a low-level routing mechanism that minimizes cycles and storage requirements for routing packets through intermediate nodes.

- Supports a wide variety of media: Token Ring, Ethernet, FDDI, Frame Relay, QLLC over X.25, and SDLC. APPN also enables interoperability with local and remote source route bridging via APPN ports that can connect directly to source-route bridge ring groups.

- Supports APPN connection networks over RSRB and DLSw+.

- Enables existing APPN products, such as IBM's Communications Manager/2 (CM/2), Application System/400 (AS/400), System/36 (S/36), and Advanced Communication Facility/Virtual Telecommunications Access Method (ACF/VTAM), to connect as network nodes (NNs) or end nodes (ENs) over a network of Cisco routers.

- Implements APPN across the channel. Cisco routers with Channel Interface Processors (CIPs) can replace FEPs and other channel-attached controllers, enabling ACF/VTAM definition either as an EN or NN that uses the Cisco network for session routing. Both APPN and CIP offer the ability to communicate through the source route bridging mechanism in the Cisco router.

- Implements the Dependent Logical Unit Requester (DLUR) feature. Enables Dependent Logical Units (DLUs) that support only legacy applications (such as those using 3270 data streams) to traverse the APPN network to access those applications.

- Allows prioritization of traffic and bandwidth based on user selected criteria.

- Implements scalability enhancement features, including Locate Throttling and Negative Caching, which allow you to conserve network resources.

- Supports SNMP management via APPN MIB (RFC 1593), an informational RFC provided by IBM.

- Supports a new MIB definition approved by the APPN Implementors Workshop (AIW). The new MIB provides better manageability of APPN network nodes across implementations and adds objects for supporting connection networks. Cisco supports both the current and new MIBs to allow for migration of Cisco's application customers from the current version which supports RFC 1593 to a new version for this new MIB.

- Supports IBM's distributed relational database architecture (DRDA) level 3 over the Transmission Control Protocol/Internet Protocol (TCP/IP). The Cisco router with Database Connection exists in the TCP/IP network, and clients use the Database Connection IP address and port on the router to connect to the IBM host system that exists in the Systems Network Architecture (SNA) network.When Database Connection is configured on a router, client-based Open Database Connectivity (ODBC) applications can connect to IBM's family of IBM D2 relational databases. The router with Database Connection converts DRDA packets over TCP/IP to DRDA packets over Advanced Program-to-Program Communications (APPC, LU 6.2) and then routes them to DB2 databases.SNA Terminology.

The basic component of an SNA network, subarea or APPN, is the network addressable unit (NAU). A NAU is assigned a unique eight-character name and an eight-character network identifier. Examples of NAUs are LUs, PUs, control points (CPs) and system services control points (SSCPs).

Logical Unit

A Logical Unit (LU) is an interface that enables end users to gain access to network resources and communicate with each other. Examples of LUs are printers, terminals, and applications. LUs communicate with each other via LU-LU sessions. The LU-LU session is the basis of communication in SNA; all end-user data traffic communicates through this session type.

To participate in an SNA network, a Dependent LU (DLU) requires the services of a VTAM host acting as an SSCP. The SSCP must establish connections with each DLU before the DLU is able to participate in the network. Dependent LUs, such as 3270 terminals, are only capable of maintaining a single LU-LU session at any one time.

An Independent LU (ILU) does not require the services of an SSCP to participate in an SNA network. In addition, an ILU can establish sessions to more than one partner in the network, and can have multiple parallel sessions with the same partner LU. Applications implementing Advanced Program-to-Program Communications (APPC) are examples of independent LUs.

Physical Unit

SNA defines a Physical Unit (PU) as the representation of the physical device. The PU manages and monitors the resources (such as attached links and adjacent link stations) associated with an SNA node.

Physical Unit Type 2 (PU2), the legacy physical unit, only supports dependent LUs, and requires the services from a VTAM host to perform network functions.

Physical Unit Type 2.1 (PU2.1), also known as a type 2.1 node, offers peer node capabilities in an SNA environment. A PU2.1 can support both dependent and independent LUs. In addition, a PU2.1 can support a control point, which is central to APPN networking.

APPN extends the PU T2.1 architecture to provide dynamic discovery and definition of resources and routing capabilities for large, complex networks.

Control Point

A control point (CP) identifies the networking components of a PU Type 2.1 node. In APPN, CPs are able to communicate with logically adjacent CPs by way of CP-CP sessions. Almost all APPN functions, including searches for network resources and discovery of network topology, use CP-CP sessions as the means of communication between nodes.

APPN Node Types

In an APPN network, different node types distinguish different levels of networking capabilities. This section describes APPN node types.

Low-Entry Networking Node

A low-entry networking (LEN) node, sometimes called a LEN end node (EN), is a PU 2.1 without APPN enhancements. The following are some of the characteristics of a LEN node:

- A LEN node does not support control point-to-control point (CP-CP) sessions. The CP does not communicate with other nodes.

- The LEN node participates in the APPN network by using the services of an adjacent Network Node (NN).

- Destination LUs in an attached APPN network must be defined to the LEN node, and destination LUs on the LEN must be defined on the attached NN.

LEN nodes predate APPN, but are able to interoperate with an APPN network. Because there is no CP-CP session between a LEN node and its NN, resources at the LEN node must be defined at the NN, reducing dynamic resource discovery capabilities.

End Node

An EN is a PU 2.1 that includes the APPN support necessary to gain full access to an APPN network. An EN is not capable of performing in an intermediate role when routing APPN sessions. The following are the characteristics of an EN:

- Contains a CP to manage its resources.

- Uses the services of an adjacent NN to access the network.

- Provides partial network services.

- May connect to multiple NNs.

- Is always a session end point.

Because an EN lacks full APPN routing capability, it may be thought of as an application host or point of user access. The EN establishes CP-CP sessions with its NN server, so topology and directory information can be exchanged dynamically, eliminating the need to define resources on the NN. The EN may connect to multiple network nodes and LU-LU sessions can be established through any of the connected network nodes, although only one network node can be its network node server at any one time.

Network Node

An NN implements the APPN extensions to the PU 2.1 architecture that allow it to provide intermediate routing services to LEN nodes and ENs. An NN contains a CP to manage it own resources and the ENs and LEN nodes in its domain.

An NN provides the following network services:

- Connectivity

- Location of resources in the network

- Route selection

- Intermediate session routing

- Data transport

- Network management

An NN may be a session end point or an intermediate system.

An NN Server is a network node that provides resource location and route selection services for the LEN nodes, ENs, and LUs it serves. The nodes served, ENs or LEN nodes, are defined as being in the network node server's domain.

APPN Components

This section describes the basic components of APPN and how they interact to provide APPN networking functions.

APPN Connections

The configuration services (CS) component of an APPN node manages local interfaces and connections to the APPN network. CS controls the ports and link stations on the node. A port defines a connection to a transport media accessible to APPN, while a link station identifies the addressing information and characteristics of a connection with another node.

APPN Network: Connection Phase

When two APPN nodes connect, the following activities occur:

- An APPN port is activated, allowing the node to access an interface and its corresponding transport media.

- A link station is activated, initiating a connection-oriented link with the partner node.

- If the CP is APPN capable, and there is no CP-CP session already between these two nodes over a different link, a pair of CP-CP sessions may be established between adjacent CPs. EN-NN and NN-NN CP-CP sessions can be established. Although EN-EN APPN connections can be defined, an EN will not establish CP-CP sessions with another EN. LEN nodes are not capable of establishing CP-CP sessions.

The entire connection phase may be configured to occur automatically, or the connection can be initiated manually via EXEC commands.

A link is defined as both the link stations within the two nodes it connects and the link connection between the nodes. A link station is the hardware or software within a node that enables the node to attach to, and provide control over, a link connection. A link connection is the physical medium over which data is transmitted. In legacy SNA, a transmission group may consist of one or more links between two nodes, but in the APPN architecture, transmission groups are limited to a single link. It is therefore common in APPN to use the terms link and transmission groups interchangeably.

Details of Link Activation

The connection phase in APPN begins with link activation, which initiates communication between nodes. It is independent of the DLC chosen, and may not be required for some DLC types. For switched connections, the connection phase is similar to "dial" and "answer" procedures. In an X.25 network, the connection phase would be the establishment of a virtual circuit. When the connect phase is complete, the two nodes can exchange and establish node characteristics through exchange identification (XID).

The exchange of XIDs allows a node to determine whether the adjacent station is active and to verify the identity of the adjacent node. Node identification fields, including the CP name, will be exchanged. This information exchange allows, for example, a node to correlate an incoming connection with a link station definition on the node.

During XID exchange, primary and secondary link stations are determined. The two link stations compare the XID node identifier values (block number plus ID number). If the link stations are defined as negotiable, then the higher node ID becomes primary. If the nodes have the same node ID, each generates a random number and the node with the higher random number becomes primary. The result of the primary-secondary role negotiation determines which node will send the mode-setting command—Set Normal Response Mode (SNRM) for SDLC, Set Asynchronous Balanced mode (SABM) for X.25, and so on.

After the link activation XID exchange is complete, CS creates a new path control and instructs the Address Space Manager (ASM) to activate a new address space. Then CS notifies Topology and Routing Services (TRS) that a transmission group (TG) has become active so the APPN topology can be updated. Finally, if a CP-CP session is to be activated, CS notifies SS. SS then activates the CP-CP session.

CP-CP Session Activation

After a link is established, the nodes determine whether CP-CP sessions should be established. Between network nodes, CP-CP sessions are normally activated on the first link to become active between the nodes. An EN determines which of the NNs will be used for a CP-CP session. The EN indicates which NN is the server by sending a request to activate a session, known as a BIND, to the CP on the adjacent NN. The NN accepts by sending BIND for a second LU 6.2 session, completing the CP-CP session pair. Each node uses one session to send CP-CP communication data, while the other is reserved for receiving data from the partner node.

CPSVCMG is the Class of Service (CoS) used for CP-CP sessions. It indicates a transmission priority of network, which is the highest of the four transmission priorities in APPN.

When the CP-CP session is established, the CPs exchange capabilities, and, in the case of EN to NN CP-CP sessions, register the local LUs.

APPN Topology

APPN maintains a map of the APPN network as known to a particular node. TRS is the APPN component responsible for maintaining the topology database.

There are two types of information in a topology database: local topology and network topology.

- Local topology, found in both ENs and NNs, describes the local links attached to a particular node, and the partner control points to which it is connected.

- Network topology, found only in NNs, describes all the NNs in the network and the links that interconnect them.

An EN uses the information in its local topology database to send local TG information to the NN server on APPN search requests and replies. The TG information is passed to the NN server when a route is requested, so the NN can select the best TG from the EN to one of its adjacent NNs. In a NN, the local topology database includes information about the attached ENs and TGs.

Figure I-22 shows the local topology as it is known to EN A, NN2, and EN B.

Figure I-22   *APPN Local Topology*

Network topology contains information on all network nodes in the APPN network and the TGs interconnecting them. Every NN maintains a fully replicated copy of the network topology database. Figure I-23 illustrates an APPN network topology.

Figure I-23   *Network Topology*

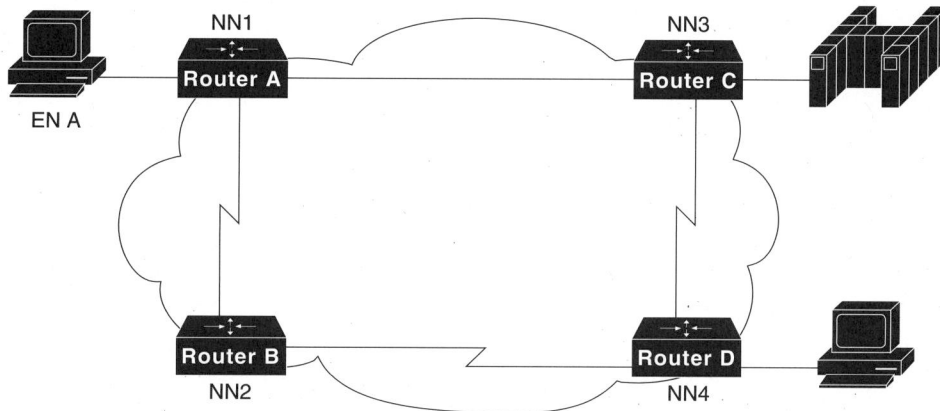

The network topology database is built from information about the local NN and its TGs to other NNs, and from Topology Database Updates (TDUs) received from adjacent NNs. TDUs are exchanged whenever NNs establish CP-CP sessions with each other. As updates occur in NNs or TGs between NNs, the owning NN sends a TDU to its adjacent NNs, which propagates the TDU to its adjacent NNs until the network topology database is again replicated.

For each NN, certain properties are specified in the topology database. Each node and TG in a network topology database is assigned a unique resource sequence number. These numbers are incremented to the next even value whenever the owning network node creates a TDU for that resource. TG database entries include whether CP-CP sessions are supported, and include the TG weight, TG status (operative or inoperative), TG number, partner node information, and TG characteristics such as cost per byte, cost per connect time, and security level.

TDUs provide updated information to NNs about the node itself and information about all locally owned TGs to other network nodes. TDUs can be triggered by changes in node or TG characteristics.

TRS broadcasts TDUs containing local node information every 5 days to prevent other network nodes from discarding valid information, which occurs after 15 days with no update. This 15-day cleanup of the database is called garbage collection.

In Figure I-24, NN3 adds itself to the network. NN3 forwards information about itself to NN1. NN1 forwards the information to NN2 and NN4. NN2 and NN4 then forward a second TDU to each other. Because they will have the same RSN and information, the second TDUs will be discarded.

Figure I-24 *Topology Database Update: Adding a Node*

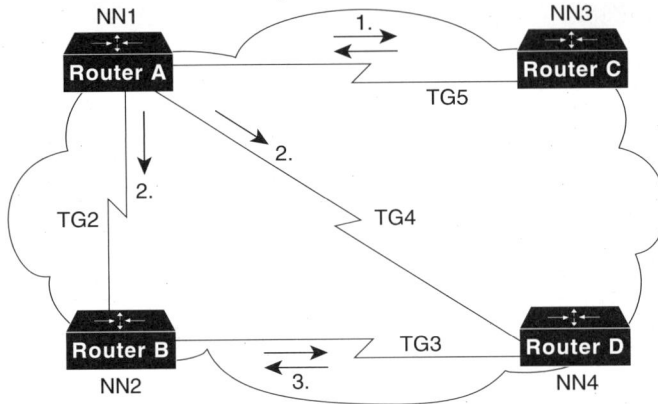

In Figure I-25, TG6 is activated between NN4 and NN3. TDUs are exchanged between the two nodes, so each node can build a new topology database. New information is propagated to adjacent nodes once NN4 and NN3 have updated topology databases. TG6 could be active, but with no CP-CP session established. The TG will still be included in the network topology and forwarded so that path can be used for sessions.

Figure I-25 *Topology Database Update: Adding a Transmission Group*

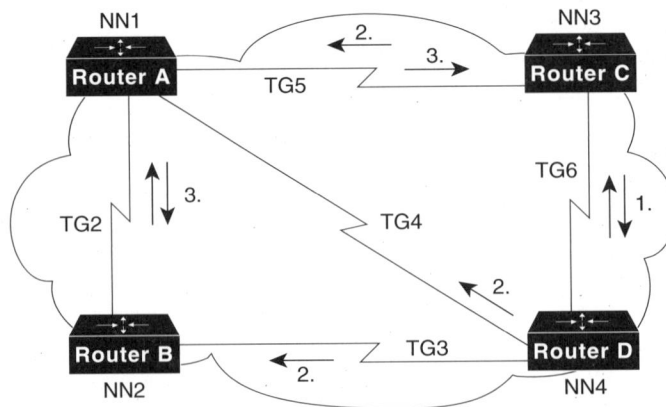

APPN Directory and APPN Searches

Directory services is the APPN component responsible for managing the directory database and searching for network resources throughout the APPN network. The directory database should not be confused with the topology database. The directory database maintains information about resource names and their owners, while the topology database maintains a network map of NNs and TGs. Directory services locates a session partner. Topology service computes an optimal route to the session partner when it has been located.

At a minimum, each APPN network resource must be defined on the node where the resource exists. When the resource is defined, it can be found through network searches. Optionally, the resource location may be defined in other nodes to optimize directory services search logic.

Registered directory entries are created dynamically in the local directory of the NN. These entries represent local LUs of an adjacent EN for which the NN is providing network node server function.

Cached directory entries are added dynamically and are based on the results of previous searches. A cache entry allows the node to attempt a directed search straight to the destination resource. If a cache entry does not exist, or the entry is incorrect, a broadcast search is issued to query each NN in the network for the destination resource. Each cache entry is verified before use to make sure the resource is still available. If the resource is not found, a broadcast search is attempted.

Some implementations, including Cisco's, support safe store of the directory cache. The cache entries in a network node's directory database are periodically written to a permanent storage medium. Safe store permits faster access (after a network node failure or initial power-on) by eliminating network broadcast searches for safe-stored resources.

The central resource registration feature implements the registration requester function of the APPN options set 1107, Central Resource Registration of LUs.

An EN registers its local resources at its NN server. The NN server, in turn, registers those resources at a central directory server. This feature significantly reduces the number of network broadcast searches in an APPN network. If every resource is registered, then all network nodes can query the central directory server, which eliminates the need for broadcast searches.

APPN Route Selection

Each APPN session is assigned a route on which the data path for this session will travel. APPN TRS is responsible for computing a route for an LU-LU session. A route is an ordered sequence of nodes and TGs that represents a path from an origin node to a destination node. TRS uses the topology database and its CoS definitions to obtain the information necessary to perform a route computation.While multiple routes may be available between an origin node and a destination node, the lowest-cost path that provides the desired level of service is selected (see Figure I-26). When a session is requested, the directory services function locates the target resource, and TRS selects a route.

Figure I-26 *An APPN Network: Selecting the Best Path*

When the origin LU requests a session, it either specifies a mode or uses a default mode for the session. The mode determines a CoS for this session request. Acceptable CoS characteristics are compared to node and TG characteristics to select the best route.

A CoS table entry specifies transmission priority, CoS name and one or multiple rows of CoS characteristics that are acceptable for that CoS. Note that traffic on sessions with the same CoS can only flow at the same transmission priority. You need a separately named entry to achieve a different priority on the same route.

TG characteristics include link speed, cost per connect time, cost per byte, security class (7 levels), propagation delay, and three user-defined fields.

Node properties include route additional resistance (RAR) and a congestion indicator.

The CoS table can contain multiple entries meeting the criteria. Some entries are more acceptable than others. The CoS table lets you assign weight to each entry to differentiate the value of each entry. For each possible route, compare the characteristics of the component nodes and transmission groups to the ranges of acceptable characteristics as defined in the CoS table for that CoS. For each NN or TG the characteristics are compared to see if they are within the range of tolerance. If so, a weight is assigned to each node and each TG and is added to the total weight for that particular route.

When all routes are weighed, the one with the lowest weight is selected. Ties are broken by random selection.

Route selection is a complex process and, where multiple routes are available, may involve considerable overhead. To reduce this overhead, TRS uses routing trees to store the best route path to each node in the network for a specific CoS. You may configure the number of routing trees the node will maintain at any one time.

Connection Networks

Connection networks provide extensions to the APPN route calculation algorithm to simplify definitions and enhance connectivity on shared transport media. If you specify a node as a member of a connection network, that node can establish a direct connection, when needed, between itself and any other member of the connection network.

For example, on one Token Ring, there may be 50 end nodes with links and a CP-CP session active to the same network node. The end nodes may communicate with each other through the network node, but this data path, which routes data through the network node then back on the same media to the target end node, is an inefficient use of both the network node and the transmission media.

Alternatively, APPN links can be configured between each end node in a mesh fashion, but this would require over 1000 link definitions. Instead, each end node can be configured as a member of the same connection network. This allows APPN route calculation to calculate a route through the connection network between the two end nodes. The resulting data path is a direct connection between end nodes without a corresponding link definition on either node.

APPN Intermediate Session Routing

After a route is selected, a BIND session command flows from the origin LU to the destination LU over the specified route. The BIND includes:

- A route selection control vector (RSCV), the route for this session.

- A fully qualified procedure correlation identifier (FQPCID), which uniquely identifies the session.

- A transmission priority that indicates the relative priority for frames traveling on this session relative to frames on other sessions. There are four priority levels: network, high, medium, and low. The transmission priority is assigned based on the session CoS. In SNA, transmission priority provides the mechanism for delivering high priority traffic, such as interactive traffic, ahead of lower priority traffic, such as batch jobs and file transfers.

- A pacing indicator that indicates the maximum window size (the maximum number of messages that can be transmitted prior to receiving a SNA response). It also indicates whether fixed window size or adaptive pacing is supported.

- A segmenting indicator that identifies the capabilities of adjacent nodes to perform segmentation of data frames received on this session.

As the BIND passes through each NN, the NN records the inbound session identifier or local form session identifier (LFSID), and assigns a new session identifier to be used on the outbound port. It also builds a "session connector" that connects the inbound session identifier with the outbound session identifier, so that it knows how to forward subsequent packets on this session. The session connector also stores information carried in the BIND, such as segmentation values and transmission priority, so that other components, such as path control, will be able to use the information on session traffic.

No subsequent data packets contain any routing information—they contain only the local form session identifier. Packets are forwarded based on information in session connectors, including port and outbound LFSID. LFSIDs are swapped at each NN because they have only local significance.

DLUR/DLUS

A dependent LU (DLU) is an LU that depends on the SSCP in VTAM to provide services for establishing sessions. Common DLU types are DLU 0, 1, 2, and 3.

DLUs originated in subarea SNA. In early APPN environments, only LU 6.2 independent LUs were supported. The PU supporting DLUs still required a logical link directly to a subarea network boundary function (VTAM or NCP) in order to operate. DLU Requester (DLUR) provides the extensions to APPN necessary to allow DLUs to interoperate in an APPN network and removes the restriction that DLUs must have a direct connection to a subarea network boundary function.

DLUR is the client half of Dependent LU Requester/Server (DLUR/DLUS). The Dependent LU Server (DLUS) is currently implemented in IBM's VTAM version 4.2.

There are three main concepts in DLUR/DLUS:

- Control flows to the DLUs from VTAM, such as active logical unit (ACTLU) and active physical unit (ACTPU), and session requests flow on a pair of LU 6.2 session between the DLUR and the DLUS.

- Upon receiving a session request from the LU over control session, the VTAM acting as DLUS notifies the VTAM owning the target application that a session is requested.

- The application initiates the session, and its serving network node selects the best route over the APPN network to the DLUR and destination LU.

The DLUR function resides on an EN or NN that owns the dependent LUs. In addition, the DLUR exists in a network node that offers its DLUR services to PU type 2.0 and PU type 2.1 nodes which connect to the DLUR. This arrangement consolidates the LU6.2 control sessions (only one pair is needed for all downstream PUs that the DLUR serves). In addition, this arrangement provides considerable cost savings over upgrading each device that owns dependent LUs to be APPN and DLUR capable.

The DLUR function does not have to be active in all APPN nodes—only in those nodes with DLUs directly attached. Once encapsulated in the LU 6.2 session, the DLUR control traffic (encapsulated SSCP-PU and SSCP-LU control flows) looks like regular APPN traffic.

By providing DLUS support in VTAM, SSCP support is extended to LUs residing on nodes that are nonadjacent to the VTAM or NCP boundary function. Traditional SSCP-PU and SSCP-LU session flows are multiplexed in LU 6.2 sessions between the DLUR and DLUS.

The benefits of using the DLUS/DLUR function include:

- The ability to use dynamic definition of the dependent LUs in VTAM, providing the served PU supports it, to reduce system definition and allow nodes to be moved in the network. All DLUR attached resources appear as switched resources that are not associated with a particular communications line or port.

- The SSCP owns resources that are non-adjacent to a VTAM or NCP.

- Dependent LUs are fully visible as VTAM resources for network management purposes.

- APPN routing can be used to select an optimal route for the session path, even though the secondary logical unit (SLU) is not APPN-capable. A key advantage of DLUR over SNA gateway functions is that the LU-LU session path from the application host to the dependent LU can differ from the path between the DLUR to the DLUS. SNA gateway and PU concentration devices are restricted to having their LU-LU session data paths identical to the path over which the SSCP-PU and SSCP-LU traffic flows.

- Because DLUR offers the ability to separate the control functions for dependent LUs from the session traffic, you can interrupt and recover, or even change, DLUS nodes without interrupting currently active LU-LU sessions to the dependent LUs.

- No changes to end user systems or applications are required.

- Network consolidation—combining the dependent LU traffic with other multiprotocol traffic—provides cost savings.

NCIA

Native Client Interface Architecture (NCIA) is a new software architecture introduced by Cisco Systems to make accessing IBM SNA applications over routed internetworks more scalable and flexible. NCIA is a component of Cisco IOS software. The architecture is intended to combine the benefits of the native SNA interface at end stations and mainframes with those of TCP/IP across the network backbone.

NCIA extends the use of the TCP/IP protocol all the way to the SNA end station. Because of the wide range of media supported by TCP/IP, including dialup telephone lines for remotely located users, NCIA makes multiprotocol access to corporate backbone networks much more flexible for SNA users.

NCIA allows SNA end stations such as PCs or workstations to encapsulate SNA traffic in TCP/IP, rather than requiring the traffic to travel through routers. The first phase of NCIA (NCIA I), used Cisco RSRB encapsulation. The current phase (NCIA Server) uses a new client/server model. NCIA Server is not backward compatible to NCIA I.

NCIA I

Using Cisco RSRB technology, NCIA I encapsulates the Token Ring traffic inside IP datagrams passed over a TCP connection between a router and a client. A virtual ring is created to allow the router to interconnect any client. The virtual ring acts as a logical Token Ring in the router, so that all the Token Rings connected to the router are treated as if they are all on the same Token Ring. The virtual ring is called a ring group. The ring group number is used just like a physical ring number and shows up in any route descriptors contained in packets being bridged. A ring group must be assigned a ring number that is unique throughout the network.

An NCIA I client acts as both an RSRB router and an end station. It must have a "fake" ring number and a "fake" bridge number so that it looks like an end station sitting on a real Token Ring. The fake ring and bridge numbers are visible to both the RSRB router and the NCIA client. The client must also have an LLC2 so that it can handle the LLC2 sessions.

NCIA Server

The NCIA Server feature extends the scalability of NCIA I, enhances its functionality, and provides support for both the installed base of RSRB routers and the growing number of DLSw+ routers. The NCIA Server feature includes the following enhancements:

- You do not need to configure a ring number on the client.
- You do not need to configure each client on the router.
- The MAC address can be dynamically assigned by the NCIA server running on the router.
- SNA is directly on top of TCP/IP; LLC2 is no longer required at end station.
- A client is a true end station, not a router peer.
- The NCIA Server communicates with other components in router, such as RSRB, APPN, DLSw+, and DSPU.
- Supports both connect-in and connect-out.
- The NCIA client/server model is independent of the upstream implementation.
- It is an efficient protocol between client and server.

NCIA Client/Server Model

The NCIA Server feature uses a client/server model, where the NCIA server is a software module on a Cisco router and the NCIA client is a PC or workstation (see Figure I-27). The NCIA server performs two major functions:

- Establishes TCP to NCIA Data-Link Control (NDLC) sessions with clients for the purpose of sending and receiving data.

- Uses the Cisco link services interface (CLSI) to communicate with other software modules in the router, such as APPN, DLSw+, and DSPU, and acts as the data intermediary between them and NCIA clients. The NCIA server's role as an intermediary is transparent to the client.

Figure I-27 *NCIA Server Client/Server Model*

NDLC is the protocol used between clients and servers. NDLC serves two purposes:

- Establishes the peer connection.
- Establishes the circuit between the client and the server.

The peer session must be established before an end-to-end circuit can be set up. During the set up period for the peer session, the MAC address representing a client is defined. The MAC address can be defined by the client or by the server when the client does not have a MAC address.

The NCIA Server feature supports connect-in and connect-out (from the server's perspective), but connect-out is not supported if the client station does not listen for the incoming connection. For a server to connect-out, clients must connect to the server first. After registering itself by providing its own MAC address, the client can then optionally disconnect from the server. When a server receives an explorer, and its destination MAC address is registered, an NCIA server will connect to that client if it is not connected. For NetBIOS explorers (addressed to functional address 0xC00000000080), the TCP session must remain up so that the server can broadcast the explorers to the client. If the TCP session is down, the server will not send the NetBIOS explorers to a client, even when the client is registered.

After the peer session has been established, the NDLC protocol establishes the circuit between the client and server. This circuit is used to transfer end-user data between the client and the server. Because the client and its target station are not on the same transport, they cannot form a direct, end-to-end circuit.

Each client must form a circuit between the client and server, and the server must form another circuit between the server and the target station. The server links those two circuits to form an end-to-end circuit. The server acts as a mediator between the client and the target station so that packets can be transferred between them.

In the NCIA server only peer keepalive is maintained. There is no keepalive at circuit level.

The NCIA server acts as a data-link provider, like Token Ring or Ethernet, in the router. It uses CLSI to communicate with other software modules, just as other data-link providers do. The network administrator configures the router to communicate with specific modules. For data-link users, such as APPN, DLSw+, and DSPU, the NCIA server can interface to them directly. For other data-link providers, the NCIA server must go through a DLSw+ local peer to communicate with them. The DLSw+ local peer passes packets back and forth among different data-link providers.

Advantages of the Client/Server Model

The client/server model used in the NCIA Server feature extends the scalability of NCIA. In addition, it provides support for both the installed base of RSRB routers and the growing number of DLSw+ routers.

Extended Scalability

The client/server model minimizes the number of central site RSRB or DLSw+ peer connections required to support a large network of NCIA clients (see Figure I-28). Rather than each client having a peer connection to a central site router, the clients attach to an IP backbone through an NCIA server that, in turn, has a single peer connection to a central site router. This scheme can greatly reduce the number of central site peer connections required. For example, in a network with 1000 clients and 10 NCIA servers, there would be only 10 central site peer connections. Note that there would still be 1000 LLC2 connections that must be locally acknowledged at the central site router, but this can easily be handled in a single central site router. When the number of LLC2 connections (or the number of clients) is in the tens of thousands, NCIA servers can take advantage of downstream PU concentration to minimize the number of LLC2 connections that must be supported by the central site routers.

Figure I-28 *NCIA Server Provides Extended Scalability to Support Large Networks*

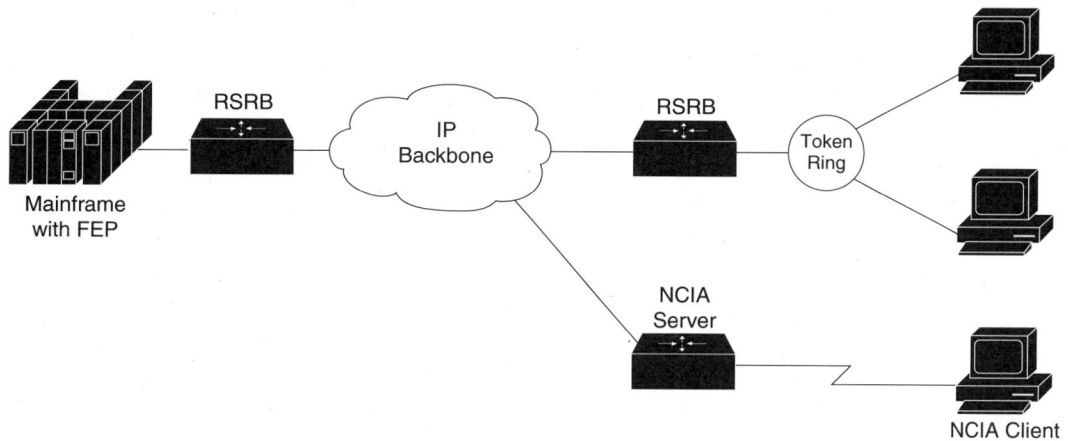

Migration Support

Using a client/server model allows the NCIA Server feature to be independent of the upstream implementation, allowing it to be implemented in a network that is still using RSRB, as well as in a DLSw+ network. It also greatly simplifies migration from RSRB to DLSw+, because it requires no changes at the client. A single NCIA server can support either approach (but not both). As Figure I-29 illustrates, a central site router can support RSRB and DLSw+ concurrently, allowing a portion of the NCIA servers to communicate using RSRB and another portion to communicate using DLSw+.

Figure I-29 *NCIA Server Provides Independence from the Upstream Network Implementation*

CMCC

Cisco Mainframe Channel Connection (CMCC) family of adapters includes the CIP for Cisco 7500 and Cisco 7000 series routers, and the ESCON Channel Port Adapter (ECPA) and the Parallel Channel Port Adapter (PCPA) for Cisco 7200 series routers.

NOTE   In this chapter, references to Channel Port Adapter (CPA) correspond to both the ECPA and the PCPA.

All CMCC adapters support the full range of channel software applications available in Cisco IOS software.

CIP

The CIP for the Cisco 7000 and Cisco 7500 series is designed for high-end network environments that demand high-performance, high-port density, high-capacity solutions.

The CIP provides support for the IBM ESCON Channel Adapter (ECA) and Bus-and-Tag Parallel Channel Adapter (PCA) channel-attached interfaces from Cisco 7000 series routers to IBM mainframes and in most cases, it eliminates the need for a separate FEP.

A single CIP can support up to two physical channel interfaces in any combination of either PCA or ECA. The CIP's Parallel channel interface is provided by the PCA, and the ESCON channel interface is provided by the ECA. Each CIP is preconfigured with the appropriate channel adapters at manufacturing time.

The Cisco 7000 and Cisco 7500 series routers support online insertion and removal (OIR), which allows you to install or remove CIPs while the system is operating. Figure I-30 shows the use of the CIP and CPA.

Figure I-30   *Cisco Mainframe Channel Connection Adapters*

CPA

The CPA is available for the Cisco 7200 series routers. The CPA expands the value of Cisco IBM channel solution by providing channel connectivity to mid-range mainframe configurations. The CPA is a standard single-width port adapter supporting ESCON or Parallel channel interfaces to IBM mainframes.

The only differences between CMCC software applications running on the CIP and a CPA are performance and capacity. The performance difference is based upon differences in the internal bus architecture of a CIP vs. a CPA, and the capacity difference is based on the difference in maximum memory configurations (128 MB for CIP and 32 MB for CPA).

Each CPA provides a single channel interface for Cisco 7200-series routers. In some situations, this eliminates the need for a separate FEP. The CPA contains a single I/O connector.

The Cisco 7200-series router supports online insertion and removal (OIR), which allows you to install or remove port adapters while the system is operating.

ECPA

An ECPA is classified as a high-speed port adapter providing a single ESCON physical channel interface. Current Cisco 7200 configuration guidelines recommend using no more than three high-speed port adapters in a single Cisco 7200 router.

PCPA

A PCPA provides a single Parallel channel physical interface supporting both 3.0 and 4.5 MBps data transfer rates.

Differences Between the CIP and CPA

Table I-4 illustrates the differences between the CMCC adapters.

Table I-4 *Differences Between the CIP and the CPA*

Product Differences	CIP	ECPA	PCPA
Router Platform	Cisco 7500 Cisco 7000 with RSP7000	Cisco 7200	Cisco 7200
Channel Interfaces	ESCON Parallel	ESCON	Parallel
Maximum Number of Interfaces	2	1	1
Maximum Memory	128 MB	32 MB	32 MB
Cisco IOS Release Support	Cisco IOS 10.2 and above	Cisco IOS 11.3(3)T and above	Cisco IOS 11.3(3)T and above
Virtual Port Adapter	2	0	0

Supported Environments

The CMCC adapters provide support for the environments discussed in the following sections:

- TCP/IP Environments Using CLAW
- TCP/IP Offload Environments
- IP Host Backup Environment
- TN3270 Server Environments
- Cisco SNA Environments
- Cisco MultiPath Channel Environments

TCP/IP Environments Using CLAW

Cisco IOS implements the Common Link Access to Workstation (CLAW) channel protocol to transport data between the mainframe and a CMCC adapter in TCP/IP environments. Each CLAW connection requires two devices out of a maximum of 256. Although this allows for a maximum of 128 CLAW connections per interface, a maximum of 32 CLAW connections per interface is recommended.

The CLAW packing feature enables the transport of multiple IP packets in a single channel operation and significantly increases throughput performance between a mainframe and a CMCC adapter. Currently, IBM's TCP/IP stack does not support the CLAW packing feature.

The CLAW packing feature requires changes to the mainframe CLAW driver support. In partnership with Cisco Systems, Interlink Computer Science has made the corresponding CLAW driver change to Cisco IOS for S/390 Release 2 and Interlink TCPaccess 5.2. Customers must make the necessary changes to their host configurations in order to enable the CLAW packing feature.

TCP/IP Offload Environments

TCP/IP mainframe protocol environments for IBM operating systems MVS, VM, and Transaction Processing Facility (TPF) are supported.

The TCP/IP offload feature for CMCC adapters delivers the same function as the TCP/IP offload function on the 3172 Interconnect Controller (Model 3), but with increased performance.

IP Host Backup Environment

You can connect multiple mainframes to a single CMCC adapter using a ESCON. Often, these mainframes run using the ESCON Multiple Image Facility (EMIF), which permits the physical machine to be divided into multiple logical partitions (LPARs). By defining an unused partition on another mainframe, a user can move the operating system from a failed mainframe or mainframe partition to the unused partition. By having multiple paths to each device, the move is accomplished without changing the mainframe software. This function also permits moving an IP stack between multiple operating system images.

On the CMCC adapter, each IP connection is treated as a physical device. The CMCC adapter does not support multiple active paths to a single IP connection (or device). Prior to IP Host Backup, the router configuration had to be changed whenever the mainframe operating system was moved from one mainframe or LPAR to another. The IP Host Backup feature permits the mainframe operating system to be moved from one mainframe to another without requiring a change to the router configuration at the time of the move.

NOTE   IP Host Backup does not provide single system image or automatic failover to a waiting backup application. Host operator action on the mainframe is required in these instances.

TN3270 Server Environments

The TN3270 server feature on a CMCC adapter card provides mapping between an SNA 3270 host and a TN3270 client connected to a TCP/IP network as shown in Figure I-31. Functionally, it is useful to view the TN3270 server from two different perspectives: SNA functions and Telnet Server functions.

- SNA Functions

  From the perspective of an SNA 3270 host connected to the CMCC adapter, the TN3270 server is an SNA device that supports multiple PUs, with each PU supporting up to 255 logical units (LUs). The LU can be Type 1, 2, or 3. The SNA host is unaware of the existence of the TCP/IP extension on the implementation of these LUs.

  The LUs implemented by TN3270 server are dependent LUs. To route these dependent LU sessions to multiple VTAM hosts connected to the TN3270 server in the CMCC adapter card, rather than routing in the VTAM hosts, the TN3270 server implements a SNA session switch with end node dependent LU requester (DLUR) function. Using the DLUR is optional so that the TN3270 server can be used with VTAM versions prior to version 4.2, which provide no Advanced Peer-to-Peer Networking (APPN) support.

  SNA session switch allows you to eliminate SNA subarea routing between hosts of TN3270 traffic by establishing APPN links with the primary LU hosts directly.

- Telnet Server Functions

  From the perspective of a TN3270 client, the TN3270 server is a high-performance Telnet server that supports Telnet connections, negotiation and data format. The server on the CMCC adapter card supports Telnet connection negotiation and data format as specified in RFC 1576 (referred to as "traditional TN3270") and RFC 1647 (referred to as "TN3270E").

Figure I-31   *TN3270 Implementation*

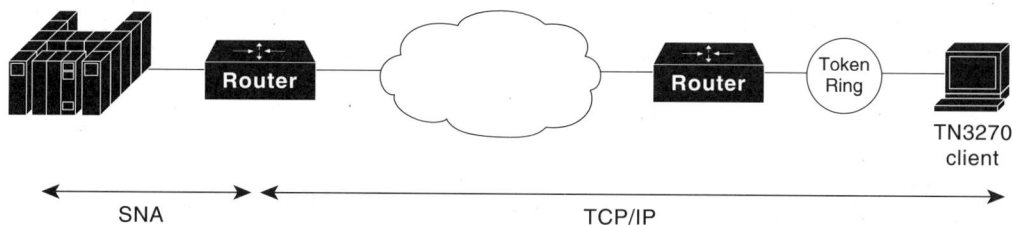

Unless the TN3270 server uses a Token Ring connection to an FEP as its host connection, it will require CSNA or CMPC support.

NOTE   To enable the TN3270 server feature, you must have a CMCC adapter installed in a Cisco 7000 with RSP7000, Cisco 7500 series router, or a Cisco 7200 router.

Cisco SNA Environments

The CSNA feature provides support for SNA protocols over both ESCON and Parallel interfaces to the IBM mainframe. As an IBM 3172 replacement, a CMCC adapter supports the External Communications Adapter (XCA) feature of Virtual Telecommunications Access Method (VTAM), which allows VTAM to define Token Ring devices attached to the 3172 as switched devices.

In SNA environments, support for the XCA feature of VTAM allows the CMCC adapter to provide an alternative to FEPs at sites where NCP is not required for SNA routing functions.

By providing CLS and the LLC2 protocol stack on the CMCC adapter card, all frames destined to the CMCC adapter or from the CMCC adapter card are switched by the router. The presentation of LAN media types allows the CSNA feature to take advantage of current SRB, RSRB, DLSw+, SR/TLB, SDLLC, QLLC services, and APPN.

The CSNA feature supports the following communication through a Cisco 7000 with RSP7000, Cisco 7500, and Cisco 7200 series router:

- Communication between a channel-attached mainframe running VTAM and a LAN/WAN attached Physical Unit (PU) 2.0 SNA node

- Communication between a channel-attached mainframe running VTAM and a LAN/WAN attached PU 2.1 SNA node

- Communication between a channel-attached mainframe running VTAM and a LAN/WAN attached PU 5/4 SNA node

- Communication between two mainframes running VTAM channel-attached to the same CMCC adapter card or different CMCC adapter cards in a Cisco 7000 with RSP7000, Cisco 7500 series router, or a Cisco 7200 router

The CSNA feature provides SNA connectivity through Media Access Control (MAC) addresses configured for internal MAC adapters on the Cisco 7000 with RSP7000, Cisco 7500 series router and the Cisco 7200 series router. These internal MAC adapters correspond to XCA major node definitions in VTAM, providing access points (LAN gateway) to VTAM for SNA network nodes. The internal MAC adapters are configured to exist on internal LANs located on a CMCC adapter card. Each CMCC adapter card can be configured with multiple internal Token Ring LANs. Each internal Token Ring LAN must be configured to participate in source-route bridging. There is a maximum limit of 18 internal MAC adapters per CMCC adapter. The internal MAC adapter is an emulation of LAN adapters in an IBM 3172 Interconnect Controller.

Cisco MultiPath Channel Environments

The CMPC feature provides support for APPN connections using both High Performance Routing (HPR) and Intermediate Session Routing (ISR). It supports the VTAM Transport Resource List (TRL) major node and the VTAM Local SNA major node.

The CMPC feature can be used to establish an APPN connection between VTAM and the following APPN nodes:

- Another VTAM channel attached to the same CMCC adapter.

- Another VTAM channel attached to a different CMCC adapter in the same router.

- TN3270 server DLUR in the same CMCC adapter.

- An APPN network node (NN) in the router with the CMCC adapter.

- Other APPN nodes external to the CMCC adapter and router with the CMCC adapter: CS/2, AS/400, other LAN or WAN attached VTAM nodes.

The CMPC feature isolates VTAM from the actual network topology. The MPC protocol is terminated on the CMCC adapter and converted to LLC protocols. Once converted to LLC protocols other Cisco features are used to connect VTAM to other APPN nodes in the network. CMPC can be used with DLSw+, RSRB, SR/TLB, SRB, SDLLC, QLLC, ATM LAN emulation, and FRAS host to provide connectivity to VTAM.

TRISL

Inter-Switch Link (ISL) is a layer 2 protocol that enables switches and routers to transport Ethernet frames from multiple VLANs across Fast Ethernet or Gigabit Ethernet links. Cisco's Token Ring Inter-Switch Link (TRISL) protocol extends the ISL model to include the transport of Token Ring frames from multiple VLANS across these same links.

TRISL support on Cisco routers provides inter-VLAN routing and bridging across a 100 Mb Fast Ethernet link. ISL and TRISL together provide routing and bridging between Token Ring and Ethernet LANs, ELANS, and VLANs.

TRISL is supported on Cisco 7500 or Cisco 7200 routers installed with any one of the following port adapters:

- Two-port Fast Ethernet/ISL 100BaseTX

- Two-port Fast Ethernet/ISL 100BaseFX

- One-port Fast Ethernet 100BaseTX

- One-port Fast Ethernet 100BaseFX

NOTE   The two-port Fast Ethernet/ISL port adapters support frame sizes up to 17,800 bytes and the one-port Fast Ethernet port adapters support a frame size of up to 1500 bytes.

The TRISL feature provides the following new capabilities and features:

- IP routing for source routed and non-source-routed frames between TRISL VLANs and any LAN, ELAN, or VLAN.

- IPX routing for source routed and non-source-routed frames between TRISL VLANs and any LANs, ELANs, or VLANs.

- Source-Route Bridging (SRB) between TRISL VLANs and SRB-capable LANs, ELANs, or VLANs.

- Source-Route Transparent Bridging (SRT) between TRISL VLANs and SRT-capable LANs, ELANs, or VLANs.

- Source-Route Translational Bridging (SR/TLB) between TRISL VLANs and Ethernet LANs, ELANs, or VLANs.

- Duplicate Ring Protocol (DRiP), which prevents external loops that could result if the router's virtual ring number were duplicated elsewhere in the network.

NOTE   VLAN Trunk Protocol (VTP) is currently not supported for TRISL on the routers.

ALPS

The Airline Product Set (ALPS) is a tunneling mechanism that transports airline protocol data across a Cisco router-based TCP/IP network to an X.25-attached mainframe. This feature provides connectivity between agent set control units (ASCUs) and a mainframe host that runs the airline reservation system.

Figure I-32 shows the basic ALPS topology and the protocols implemented in the feature. Three major components provide the end-to-end transportation of airline protocol traffic across the network: the Airline Control (ALC) protocol, the TCP-based transport protocol, and the access to the mainframe, Airline X.25 (AX.25) or exchange of mixed traffic over X.25 (EMTOX).

Figure I-32 *ALPS Architecture*

ASCU – agent set control unit
EMTOX – exchange of mixed traffic over X.25
CPE – customer premises equipment
AX.25 – Airline X.25

Cisco ALPS feature provides an end-to-end solution for airlines and central reservation systems.The ALPS feature is integrated in Cisco IOS software and allows airlines to replace their existing hardware and software with Cisco routers. For customers who already use Cisco routers, this feature allows them to consolidate networking overhead and functionality.

About the Cisco IOS 12.0 Reference Library

The Cisco IOS 12.0 Reference Library books are Cisco documentation that describe the tasks and commands necessary to configure and maintain your Cisco IOS network.

The Cisco IOS software bookset is intended primarily for users who configure and maintain access servers and routers, but are not necessarily familiar with the tasks, the relationship between tasks, or the commands necessary to perform particular tasks.

Cisco IOS Reference Library Organization

The Cisco IOS 12.0 Reference Library consists of 11 books. Each book contains technology-specific configuration chapters with corresponding command reference chapters. Each configuration chapter describes Cisco's implementation of protocols and technologies, related configuration tasks, and contains comprehensive configuration examples. Each command reference chapter complements the organization of its corresponding configuration chapter and provides complete command syntax information.

Books Available in the Cisco IOS 12.0 Reference Library

- *Cisco IOS 12.0 Network Protocols*, Vol I, IP, 1-57870-154-6

  This book is a comprehensive guide detailing available IP and IP routing alternatives. It describes how to implement IP addressing and IP services and how to configure support for a wide range of IP routing protocols including BGP for ISP networks and basic and advanced IP Multicast functionality.

- *Cisco IOS 12.0 Configuration Fundamentals*, 1-57870-155-4

  This comprehensive guide details Cisco IOS software configuration basics. It offers thorough coverage of router and access server configuration and maintenance techniques. In addition to hands-on implementation and task instruction, this book also presents the complete syntax for router and access server commands, and individual examples for each command.

- *Cisco IOS 12.0 Interface Configuration*, 1-57870-156-2

  This book is a comprehensive guide detailing how to configure physical and virtual interfaces--the two types of interfaces supported on Cisco routers. It provides readers with the most current router task and commands information for their network environments and teaches how to effectively implement these techniques and commands on their networks.

- *Cisco IOS 12.0 Wide Area Networking Solutions*, 1-57870-158-9

  This book offers thorough, comprehensive coverage of internetworking technologies, particularly ATM, Frame Relay, SMDS, LAPB, and X.25, teaching the reader how to configure the technologies in a LAN/WAN environment.

- *Cisco IOS 12.0 Switching Services*, 1-57870-157-0

  This book is a comprehensive guide detailing available Cisco IOS switching alternatives. Cisco's switching services range from fast switching and Netflow switching to LAN Emulation. This book describes how to configure routing between virtual LANs (VLANs) and teach how to effectively configure and implement VLANs on switches.

- *Cisco IOS 12.0 Multiservice Applications*, 1-57870-159-7

  This book shows you how to configure your router or access server to support voice, video, and broadband transmission. Cisco's voice and video support are implemented using voice packet technology, In voice packet technology, voice signals are packetized and transported in compliance with ITU-T specification H.323, which is the ITU-T specification for transmitting multimedia 9voice, video, and data) across a local-area network (LAN).

- *Cisco IOS 12.0 Network Security*, 1-57870-160-0

  This book documents security configuration from a remote site and for a central enterprise or service provider network. It describes AAA, Radius, TACACS+, and Kerberos network security features. It also explains how to encrypt data across enterprise networks. The book includes many illustrations that show configurations and functionality, along with a discussion of network security policy choices and some decision-making guidelines.

- *Cisco IOS 12.0 Quality of Service*, 1-57870-161-9

  Cisco IOS 12.0 Quality of Service is a comprehensive guide detailing available Cisco IOS quality of service (QoS) features. This book suggests benefits you can gain from implementing Cisco IOS QoS features, and describes how to effectively configure and implement the various QoS features. Some of the features described in this book include Committed Access Rate (CAR), weighted fair queuing (WFQ), and Weighted Random Early Detection (WRED), as well as many other features.

- *Cisco IOS 12.0 Network Protocols*, Volume II, IPX, AppleTalk, and More, 1-57870-164-3

  This book is a comprehensive guide detailing available network protocol alternatives. It describes how to implement various protocols in your network. This book includes documentation of the latest functionality for the IPX and AppleTalk desktop protocols as well as the following network protocols: Apollo Domain, Banyan VINES, DECNet, ISO CLNS, and XNS.

- *Cisco IOS 12.0 Bridging and IBM Networking Solutions*, 1-57870-162-7

  This book describes Cisco support for networks in IBM and bridging environments. Support includes: transparent and source-route transparent bridging, source-route bridging (SRB), remote source-route bridging (RSRB), data link switching plus (DLS+), serial tunnel and block serial tunnel, SDLC and LLC2 parameter, IBM network media translation, downstream physical unit and SNA service point, SNA Frame Relay access support, Advanced Peer-to-Peer Networking, and native client interface architecture (NCIA).

- *Cisco IOS 12.0 Dial Solutions*, 1-57870-163-5

  This book provides readers with real-world solutions and how to implement them on a network. Customers interested in implementing dial solutions across their network environment include remote sites dialing in to a central office, Internet service providers (ISPs), ISP customers at home offices, and enterprise WAN system administrators implementing dial-on-demand routing (DDR).

Book Conventions

The Cisco IOS documentation set uses the following conventions:

Convention	Description
^ or Ctrl	Represents the Control key. For example, when you read ^D or *Ctrl-D*, you should hold down the Control key while you press the D key. Keys are indicated in capital letters but are not case sensitive.
string	A string is defined as a nonquoted set of characters. For example, when setting an SNMP community string to public, do not use quotation marks around the string; otherwise, the string will include the quotation marks.

Examples use the following conventions:

Convention	Description
`screen`	Shows an example of information displayed on the screen.
`boldface screen`	Shows an example of information that you must enter.
< >	Nonprinting characters, such as passwords, appear in angled brackets.
!	Exclamation points at the beginning of a line indicate a comment line. They are also displayed by Cisco IOS software for certain processes.
[ ]	Default responses to system prompts appear in square brackets.

The following conventions are used to attract the reader's attention:

CAUTION Means *reader be careful*. In this situation, you might do something that could result in equipment damage or loss of data.

NOTE Means *reader take note*. Notes contain helpful suggestions or references to materials not contained in this manual.

TIMESAVER Means the *described action saves time*. You can save time by performing the action described in the paragraph.

Within the Cisco IOS12.0 Reference Library, the term *router* is used to refer to both access servers and routers. When a feature is supported on the access server only, the term *access server* is used.

Within examples, routers and access servers are alternately shown. These products are used only for example purposes; that is, an example that shows one product does not indicate that the other product is not supported.

Command Syntax Conventions

Command descriptions use the following conventions:

Convention	Description
boldface	Indicates commands and keywords that are entered literally as shown.
italics	Indicates arguments for which you supply values; in contexts that do not allow italics, arguments are enclosed in angle brackets (< >).
[**x**]	Keywords or arguments that appear within square brackets are optional.
{**x** | **y** | **z**}	A choice of required keywords (represented by **x**, **y**, and **z**) appears in braces separated by vertical bars. You must select one.
[**x** {**y** | **z**}]	Braces and vertical bars within square brackets indicate a required choice within an optional element. You do not need to select one. If you do, you have some required choices.

Cisco Connection Online

Cisco Connection Online (CCO) is Cisco Systems' primary, real-time support channel. Maintenance customers and partners can self-register on CCO to obtain additional information and services.

Available 24 hours a day, 7 days a week, CCO provides a wealth of standard and value-added services to Cisco's customers and business partners. CCO services include product information, product documentation, software updates, release notes, technical tips, the Bug Navigator, configuration notes, brochures, descriptions of service offerings, and download access to public and authorized files.

CCO serves a wide variety of users through two interfaces that are updated and enhanced simultaneously: a character-based version and a multimedia version that resides on the World Wide Web (WWW). The character-based CCO supports Zmodem, Kermit, Xmodem, FTP, and Internet e-mail, and it is excellent for quick access to information over lower bandwidths. The WWW version of CCO provides richly formatted documents with photographs, figures, graphics, and video, and hyperlinks to related information.

You can access CCO in the following ways:

- WWW: http://www.cisco.com

- WWW: http://www-europe.cisco.com

- WWW: http://www-china.cisco.com

- Telnet: cco.cisco.com

- Modem: From North America, 408 526-8070; from Europe, 33 1 64 46 40 82. Use the following terminal settings: VT100 emulation; databits: 8; parity: none; stop bits: 1; and connection rates up to 28.8 kbps.

Using Cisco IOS Software

This section provides helpful tips for understanding and configuring Cisco IOS software using the command-line interface (CLI).

Getting Help

Entering a question mark (**?**) at the system prompt displays a list of commands available for each command mode. You can also get a list of any command's associated keywords and arguments with the context-sensitive help feature.

To get help specific to a command mode, a command, a keyword, or an argument, use one of the following commands:

Command	Purpose
help	Obtains a brief description of the help system in any command mode.
*abbreviated-command-entry***?**	Obtains a list of commands that begin with a particular character string. (No space between command and question mark.)
abbreviated-command-entry<**Tab**>	Completes a partial command name.
?	Lists all commands available for a particular command mode.
command **?**	Lists a command's associated keywords. (Space between command and question mark.)
command keyword **?**	Lists a keyword's associated arguments. (Space between the keyword and question mark.)

Example: How to Find Command Options

This section provides an example of how to display syntax for a command. The syntax can consist of optional or required keywords. To display keywords for a command, enter a question mark (**?**) at the configuration prompt, or after entering part of a command followed by a space. Cisco IOS software displays a list of keywords available along with a brief description of the keywords. For example, if you were in global configuration mode, typed the command **arap**, and wanted to see all the keywords for that command, you would type **arap ?**.

Table I-5 shows examples of how you can use the question mark (**?**) to assist you in entering commands. It steps you through entering the following commands:

- **controller t1 1**

- **cas-group 1 timeslots 1-24 type e&m-fgb dtmf**

Table I-5 *How to Find Command Options*

Command	Comment
`Router> `**`enable`** `Password: `*`<password>`* `Router#`	Enters the **enable** command and password to access privileged EXEC commands.
	You have entered privileged EXEC mode when the prompt changes to `Router#`.

`Router# `**`config terminal`**
`Enter configuration commands, one per line. End with Ctrl-Z.`
`Router(config)#`
	Enters global configuration mode.

	You have entered global configuration mode when the prompt changes to `Router(config)#`.

`Router(config)# `**`controller t1 ?`**
`  <0-3>  Controller unit number`
`Router(config)# `**`controller t1 1`**
`Router(config-controller)#`
	Enters controller configuration mode by specifying the T1 controller that you want to configure using the **controller t1** global configuration command.

	Enters a **?** to display what you must enter next on the command line. In this example, you must enter a controller unit number from 0 to 3.
	You have entered controller configuration mode when the prompt changes to `Router(config-controller)#`.

Table I-5 *How to Find Command Options (Continued)*

Command	Comment
| ```
Router(config-controller)# ?
Controller configuration commands:
  cablelength    Specify the cable length for a DS1 link
  cas-group      Configure the specified timeslots for CAS
                 (Channel Associate Signals)
  channel-group  Specify the timeslots to channel-group
                 mapping for an interface
  clock          Specify the clock source for a DS1 link
  default        Set a command to its defaults
  description    Controller specific description
  ds0            ds0 commands
  exit           Exit from controller configuration mode
  fdl            Specify the FDL standard for a DS1 data
                 link
  framing        Specify the type of Framing on a DS1 link
  help           Description of the interactive help system
  linecode       Specify the line encoding method for a DS1
                 link
  loopback       Put the entire T1 line into loopback
  no             Negate a command or set its defaults
  pri-group      Configure the specified timeslots for PRI
  shutdown       Shut down a DS1 link (send Blue Alarm)
Router(config-controller)#
``` | Enters a **?** to display a list of all the controller configuration commands available for the T1 controller. |
| ```
Router(config-controller)# cas-group ?
  <0-23>          Channel number
Router(config-controller)# cas-group
``` | Enters the command that you want to configure for the controller. In this example, the **cas-group** command is used.

Enters a **?** to display what you must enter next on the command line. In this example, you must enter a channel number from 0 to 23.

Because a <cr> is not displayed, it indicates that you must enter more keywords to complete the command. |

Continues

Table I-5 *How to Find Command Options (Continued)*

Command	Comment

`Router(config-controller)# `**`cas-group 1 ?`**
`  timeslots      List of timeslots in the cas-group`
`Router(config-controller)# cas-group 1`
	After you enter the channel number, enter a **?** to display what you must enter next on the command line. In this example, you must enter the **timeslots** keyword.
	
	Because a <cr> is not displayed, it indicates that you must enter more keywords to complete the command.

`Router(config-controller)# `**`cas-group 1 timeslots ?`**
`  <1-24>         List of timeslots which comprise the`
`                 cas-group`
`Router(config-controller)# cas-group 1 timeslots`
	After you enter the **timeslots** keyword, enter a **?** to display what you must enter next on the command line. In this example, you must enter a list of timeslots from 1 to 24.
	
	You can specify timeslot ranges (for example, 1-24), individual timeslots separated by commas (for example 1, 3, 5), or a combination of the two (for example 1-3, 8, 17-24). The 16th time slot is not specified in the command line, because it is reserved for transmitting the channel signaling.
	
	Because a <cr> is not displayed, it indicates that you must enter more keywords to complete the command.

`Router(config-controller)# `**`cas-group 1 timeslots 1-24 ?`**
`  service    Specify the type of service`
`  type       Specify the type of signaling`
`Router(config-controller)# cas-group 1 timeslots 1-24`
	After you enter the timeslot ranges, enter a **?** to display what you must enter next on the command line. In this example, you must enter the **service** or **type** keyword.
	
	Because a <cr> is not displayed, it indicates that you must enter more keywords to complete the command.

Table I-5 *How to Find Command Options (Continued)*

Command	Comment

`Router(config-controller)# cas-group 1 timeslots 1-24 type ?`
`  e&m-fgb              E & M Type II FGB`
`  e&m-fgd              E & M Type IIFGD`
`  e&m-immediate-start  E & M Immediate Start`
`  fxs-ground-start     FXS Ground Start`
`  fxs-loop-start       FXS Loop Start`
`  sas-ground-start     SAS Ground Start`
`  sas-loop-start       SAS Loop Start`
`Router(config-controller)# cas-group 1 timeslots 1-24 type`
	In this example, the **type** keyword is entered. After you enter the **type** keyword, enter a **?** to display what you must enter next on the command line. In this example, you must enter one of the signaling types.
	
	Because a <cr> is not displayed, it indicates that you must enter more keywords to complete the command.

`Router(config-controller)# cas-group 1 timeslots 1-24 type`
`e&m-fgb ?`
`  dtmf      DTMF tone signaling`
`  mf        MF tone signaling`
`  service   Specify the type of service`
`  <cr>`
`Router(config-controller)# cas-group 1 timeslots 1-24 type`
`e&m-fgb`
	In this example, the **e&m-fgb** keyword is entered. After you enter the **e&m-fgb** keyword, enter a **?** to display what you must enter next on the command line. In this example, you can enter the **dtmf**, **mf**, or **service** keyword to indicate the type of channel-associated signaling available for the **e&m-fgb** signaling type.
	
	Because a <cr> is displayed, it indicates that you can enter more keywords or press <cr> to complete the command.

`Router(config-controller)# cas-group 1 timeslots 1-24 type`
`e&m-fgb dtmf ?`
`  dnis      DNIS addr info provisioned`
`  service   Specify the type of service`
`  <cr>`
`Router(config-controller)# cas-group 1 timeslots 1-24 type`
`e&m-fgb dtmf`
	In this example, the **dtmf** keyword is entered. After you enter the **dtmf** keyword, enter a **?** to display what you must enter next on the command line. In this example, you can enter the **dnis** or **service** keyword to indicate the options available for **dtmf** tone signaling.
	
	Because a <cr> is displayed, it indicates that you can enter more keywords or press <cr> to complete the command.

`Router(config-controller)# cas-group 1 timeslots 1-24 type`
`e&m-fgb dtmf`
`Router(config-controller)#`
	In this example, enter a <cr> to complete the command.

Continues

Understanding Command Modes

The Cisco IOS user interface is divided into many different modes. The commands available to you at any given time depend on which mode you are currently in. Entering a question mark (**?**) at the system prompt allows you to obtain a list of commands available for each command mode.

When you start a session on the router, you begin in user mode, often called EXEC mode. Only a limited subset of the commands are available in EXEC mode. In order to have access to all commands, you must enter privileged EXEC mode. Normally, you must enter a password to enter privileged EXEC mode. From privileged mode, you can enter any EXEC command or enter global configuration mode. Most of the EXEC commands are one-time commands, such as **show** commands, which show the current status of something, and **clear** commands, which clear counters or interfaces. The EXEC commands are not saved across reboots of the router.

The configuration modes allow you to make changes to the running configuration. If you later save the configuration, these commands are stored across router reboots. In order to get to the various configuration modes, you must start at global configuration mode. From global configuration mode, you can enter interface configuration mode, subinterface configuration mode, and a variety of protocol-specific modes.

ROM Monitor mode is a separate mode used when the router cannot boot properly. If your router or access server does not find a valid system image when it is booting, or if its configuration file is corrupted at startup, the system might enter read-only memory (ROM) Monitor mode.

Summary of Main Command Modes

Table I-6 summarizes the main command modes of Cisco IOS software.

Table I-6 *Summary of Main Command Modes*

Command Mode	Access Method	Prompt	Exit Method
User EXEC	Log in.	`Router>`	Use the **logout** command.
Privileged EXEC	From user EXEC mode, use the **enable** EXEC command.	`Router#`	To exit back to user EXEC mode, use the **disable** command. To enter global configuration mode, use the **configure terminal** privileged EXEC command.
Global configuration	From privileged EXEC mode, use the **configure terminal** privileged EXEC command.	`Router(config)#`	To exit to privileged EXEC mode, use the **exit** or **end** command or press **Ctrl-Z**. To enter interface configuration mode, enter an **interface** configuration command.

Table I-6 *Summary of Main Command Modes (Continued)*

Command Mode	Access Method	Prompt	Exit Method
Interface configuration	From global configuration mode, enter by specifying an interface with an **interface** command.	`Router(config-if)#`	To exit to global configuration mode, use the **exit** command. To exit to privileged EXEC mode, use the **exit** command or press **Ctrl-Z**. To enter subinterface configuration mode, specify a subinterface with the **interface** command.
Subinterface configuration	From interface configuration mode, specify a subinterface with an **interface** command.	`Router(config-subif)#`	To exit to global configuration mode, use the **exit** command. To enter privileged EXEC mode, use the **end** command or press **Ctrl-Z**.
ROM Monitor	From privileged EXEC mode, use the **reload** EXEC command. Press the Break key during the first 60 seconds while the system is booting.	`>`	To exit to user EXEC mode, type **continue**.

Using the No and Default Forms of Commands

Almost every configuration command also has a **no** form. In general, use the **no** form to disable a function. Use the command without the keyword **no** to reenable a disabled function or to enable a function that is disabled by default. For example, IP routing is enabled by default. To disable IP routing, specify the **no ip routing** command and specify **ip routing** to reenable it. Cisco IOS software command references provide the complete syntax for the configuration commands and describes what the **no** form of a command does.

Configuration commands can also have a **default** form. The **default** form of a command returns the command setting to its default. Most commands are disabled by default, so the **default** form is the same as the **no** form. However, some commands are enabled by default and have variables set to certain default values. In these cases, the **default** command enables the command and sets variables to their default values. Cisco IOS software command references describe what the **default** form of a command does if the command is not the same as the **no** form.

Saving Configuration Changes

Enter the **copy system:running-config nvram:startup-config** command to save your configuration changes to your startup configuration so that they will not be lost if there is a system reload or power outage. For example:

```
Router# copy system:running-config nvram:startup-config
Building configuration...
```

It might take a minute or two to save the configuration. After the configuration has been saved, the following output appears:

```
[OK]
Router#
```

On most platforms, this step saves the configuration to nonvolatile random-access memory (NVRAM). On the Class A Flash file system platforms, this step saves the configuration to the location specified by the CONFIG_FILE environment variable. The CONFIG_FILE variable defaults to NVRAM.

Bridging

CHAPTER 1

Configuring Transparent Bridging

Cisco IOS software bridging functionality combines the advantages of a spanning-tree bridge and a full multiprotocol router. This combination provides the speed and protocol transparency of an adaptive spanning-tree bridge, along with the functionality, reliability, and security of a router.

This chapter describes how to configure transparent bridging and source-route transparent (SRT) bridging. This chapter also describes the concepts of virtual networking, transparent bridging of virtual LANs (VLANs), and routing between VLANs. For a complete description of the transparent bridging commands mentioned in this chapter, refer to Chapter 2, "Transparent Bridging Commands." To locate documentation of other commands that appear in this chapter, you can search online at www.cisco.com.

Transparent and SRT Bridging Configuration Task List

To configure transparent bridging or SRT bridging on your router, complete one or more of the tasks in the following sections:

- Configure Transparent Bridging and SRT Bridging
- Transparently Bridged VLANs for ISL
- Routing Between ISL VLANs
- Configure a Subscriber Bridge Group
- Configure Transparent Bridging over WANs
- Configure Concurrent Routing and Bridging
- Configure Integrated Routing and Bridging
- Configure Transparent Bridging Options
- Filter Transparently Bridged Packets
- Adjust Spanning-Tree Parameters
- Tune the Transparently Bridged Network
- Monitor and Maintain the Transparent Bridge Network

See the "Transparent and SRT Bridging Configuration Examples" section for configuration examples.

Configure Transparent Bridging and SRT Bridging

To configure transparent and SRT bridging, you must perform the following tasks:

● Assign a Bridge Group Number and Define the Spanning-Tree Protocol

● Assign Each Network Interface to a Bridge Group

● Choose the Organizational Unit Identifier for Ethernet Type II Frames

Assign a Bridge Group Number and Define the Spanning-Tree Protocol

The first step in setting up your transparent bridging network is to define a spanning-tree protocol and assign a bridge group number. You can choose either the IEEE 802.1D Spanning-Tree Protocol or the earlier Digital protocol upon which this IEEE standard is based.

To assign a bridge group number and define a spanning-tree protocol, use the following command in global configuration mode:

Command	Purpose
bridge *bridge-group* **protocol** {**ieee** | **dec**}	Assigns a bridge group number and defines a spanning-tree protocol as either IEEE 802.1D standard or Digital.

The IEEE 802.1D Spanning-Tree Protocol is the preferred way of running the bridge. Use the Digital Spanning-Tree Protocol only for backward compatibility.

Assign Each Network Interface to a Bridge Group

A bridge group is an internal organization of network interfaces on a router. Bridge groups cannot be used outside the router on which it is defined to identify traffic switched within the bridge group. Bridge groups within the same router function as distinct bridges; that is, bridged traffic and bridge protocol data units (BPDUs) cannot be exchanged between different bridge groups on a router. Furthermore, bridge groups cannot be used to multiplex or demultiplex different streams of bridged traffic on a LAN. An interface can be a member of only one bridge group. Use a bridge group for each separately bridged (topologically distinct) network connected to the router. Typically, only one such network exists in a configuration.

The purpose of placing network interfaces into a bridge group is twofold:

- To bridge all nonrouted traffic among the network interfaces making up the bridge group. If the packet's destination address is known in the bridge table, it is forwarded on a single interface in the bridge group. If the packet's destination is unknown in the bridge table, it is flooded on all forwarding interfaces in the bridge group. The bridge places source addresses in the bridge table as it learns them during the process of bridging.

- To participate in the spanning-tree algorithm by receiving, and in some cases transmitting, BPDUs on the LANs to which they are attached. A separate spanning process runs for each configured bridge group. Each bridge group participates in a separate spanning tree. A bridge group establishes a spanning tree based on the BPDUs it receives on only its member interfaces.

For SRT bridging, if the Token Ring and serial interfaces are in the same bridge group, changing the serial encapsulation method causes the state of the corresponding Token Ring interface to be reinitialized. Its state will change from "up" to "initializing" to "up" again within a few seconds.

After you assign a bridge group number and define a spanning-tree protocol, assign each network interface to a bridge group by using the following command in interface configuration mode:

Command	Purpose
bridge-group *bridge-group*	Assigns a network interface to a bridge group.

Choose the Organizational Unit Identifier for Ethernet Type II Frames

For SRT bridging networks, you must choose the organizational unit identifier (OUI) code that will be used in the encapsulation of Ethernet Type II frames across Token Ring backbone networks. To choose the OUI, use the following command in interface configuration mode:

Command	Purpose
ethernet-transit-oui [**90-compatible** | **standard** | **cisco**]	Selects the Ethernet Type II OUI encapsulation code.

Transparently Bridged VLANs for ISL

Traditionally, a bridge group is an independently bridged subnetwork. In this definition, bridge groups cannot exchange traffic with other bridge groups, nor can they multiplex or demultiplex different streams of bridged traffic. Cisco's transparently bridged VLAN feature permits a bridge group to extend outside the router to identify traffic switched within the bridge group.

While bridge groups remain internal organizations of network interfaces functioning as distinct bridges within a router, transparent bridging on subinterfaces permits bridge groups to be used to multiplex different streams of bridged traffic on a LAN or HDLC serial interface. In this way, bridged traffic may be switched out of one bridge group on one router, multiplexed across a subinterface, and demultiplexed into a second bridge group on a second router. Together, the first bridge group and the second bridge group form a transparently bridged VLAN. This approach can be extended to impose logical topologies upon transparently bridged networks.

The primary application of transparently bridged VLANs constructed in this way is to separate traffic between bridge groups of local network interfaces, to multiplex bridged traffic from several bridge groups on a shared interface (LAN or HDLC serial), and to form VLANs composed of collections of bridge groups on several routers. These VLANs improve performance because they reduce the propagation of locally bridged traffic and they improve security benefits because they completely separate traffic.

In Figure 1-1, different bridge groups on different routers are configured into three VLANs that span the bridged network. Each bridge group consists of conventionally bridged local interfaces and a subinterface on the backbone FDDI LAN. Bridged traffic on the subinterface is encapsulated and "colored" with a VLAN identifier known as a *security association identifier* common to all bridge groups participating in the VLAN. In addition, bridges only accept packets bearing security association identifiers for which they have a configured subinterface. Thus, a bridge group is configured to participate in a VLAN if it contains a subinterface configured with the VLAN's characteristic security association identifier. See the section "Complex Integrated Routing and Bridging Example" later in this chapter for an example configuration of the topology shown in Figure 1-1.

NOTE	The 802.10 encapsulation used to "color" transparently bridged packets on subinterfaces might increase the size of a packet so that it exceeds the MTU size of the LAN from which the packet originated. To avoid MTU violations on the shared network, the originating LANs must either have a smaller native MTU than the shared network (as is the case from Ethernet to FDDI), or the MTU on all packet sources on the originating LAN must be configured to be at least 16 bytes less than the MTU of the shared network.

Figure 1-1   *Transparently Bridged VLANs on an FDDI Backbone*

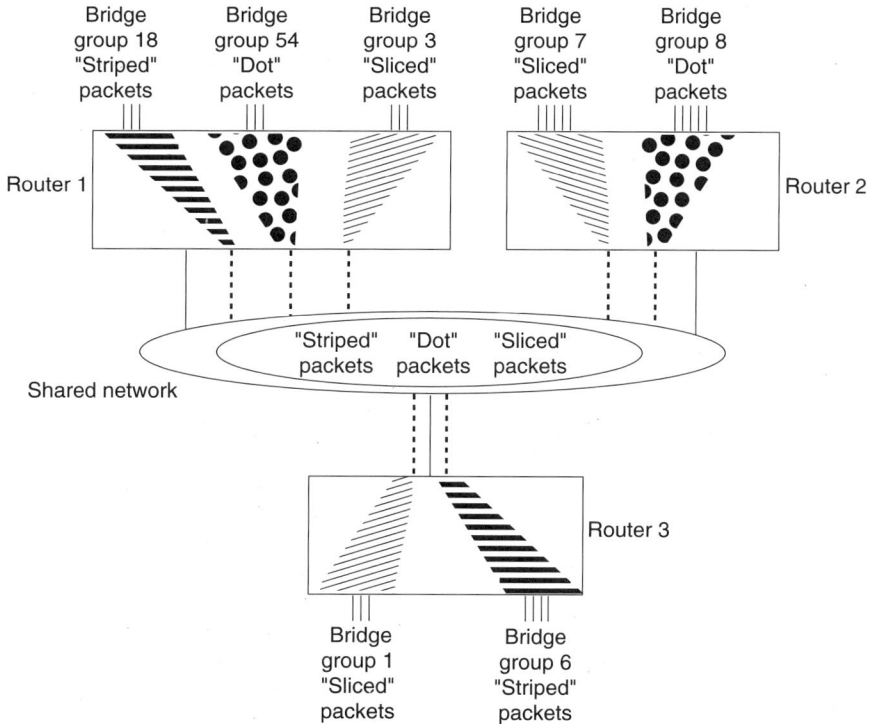

To configure a VLAN on a transparently bridged network, enter the following commands, beginning in interface configuration mode:

Step	Command	Purpose
1	**interface** *type slot/port.subinterface-number*	Specifies a subinterface.
2	**encapsulation sde** *said*	Specifies the IEEE 802.10 Security data exchange security association identifier. (In other words, specify the "color.")
3	**bridge-group** *bridge-group*	Associates the subinterface with an existing bridge group.

Transparently bridged VLANs are supported in conjunction with only the IEEE Spanning-Tree Protocol. When you logically segment a transparently bridged network into VLANs, each VLAN computes its own spanning-tree topology. Configuring each VLAN to compute its own spanning-tree topology provides much greater stability than running a single spanning tree throughout. Traffic bridged within one VLAN is unaffected by physical topology changes occurring within another VLAN.

NOTE	The current implementation of SDE encapsulation is not recommended for serial or Ethernet media.

Routing Between ISL VLANs

Cisco VLAN Routing implementation is designed to operate across all router platforms. However, the Inter-Switch Link (ISL) VLAN trunking protocol currently is defined on 100 BaseTX/FX Fast Ethernet interfaces only and, therefore, is appropriate to Cisco 7000 and higher-end platforms only. The IEEE 802.10 protocol can run over any LAN or HDLC serial interface. VLAN traffic is fast switched. The actual format of these VLAN encapsulations are detailed in the *IEEE Standard 802.10-1992 Secure Data Exchange* and in the *Inter-Switch Link (ISL) Protocol Specification.*

Cisco VLAN Routing implementation treats the ISL and 802.10 protocols as encapsulation types. On a physical router interface that receives and transmits VLAN packets, you can select an arbitrary subinterface and map it to the particular VLAN "color" embedded within the VLAN header. This mapping allows you to selectively control how LAN traffic is routed or switched outside of its own VLAN domain. In the VLAN routing paradigm, a switched VLAN corresponds to a single routed subnet and the network address is assigned to the subinterface.

To route a received VLAN packet, Cisco IOS software VLAN switching code first extracts the VLAN ID from the packet header (this is a 10-bit field in the case of ISL and a 4-byte entity known as the security association identifier in the case of IEEE 802.10), then demultiplexes the VLAN ID value into a subinterface of the receiving port. If the VLAN color does not resolve to a subinterface, Cisco IOS software can transparently bridge the foreign packet natively (without modifying the VLAN header) on the condition that Cisco IOS software is configured to bridge on the subinterface itself. For VLAN packets that bear an ID corresponding to a configured subinterface, received packets are then classified by protocol type before running the appropriate protocol specific fast switching engine. If the subinterface is assigned to a bridge group then non-routed packets are de-encapsulated before they are bridged. This is termed "fall-back bridging" and is most appropriate for nonroutable traffic types.

In Figure 1-2, Router A provides inter-VLAN connectivity between multiple Cisco switching platforms where there are three distinct virtual topologies present. For example, for VLAN 300 across the two Catalyst 1200A segments, traffic originating on LAN interface 1 is "tagged" with a VLAN ID of 300 as it is switched onto the FDDI ring. This ID allows the remote Catalyst 1200A to make an intelligent forwarding decision and only switch the traffic to local interfaces configured as belonging to the same VLAN broadcast domain. Router A provides an inter-VLAN mechanism that lets Router A function as a gateway for stations on a given LAN segment by transmitting VLAN encapsulated traffic to and from other switched VLAN domains or simply transmitting traffic in native (non-VLAN) format.

Figure 1-2   *Inter-VLAN Connectivity Between Multiple Switching Platforms*

Figure 1-2 illustrates the following scenarios:

- Clients on VLAN 300 want to establish sessions with a server attached to a port in a different VLAN (600). In this scenario, packets originating on LAN interface 3 of the Catalyst 1200B switch are tagged with an 802.10 header with a security association identifier of 300 as they are forwarded onto the FDDI ring. Router A can accept these packets because it is configured to route VLAN 300, classify and make a layer 3 forwarding decision based on the destination network address and the route out (in this case Fast Ethernet 3/1), and adding the ISL VLAN header (color 200) appropriate to the destination subnet as the traffic is switched.

- There is a network requirement to bridge two VLANs together through the system rather than selectively route certain protocols. In this scenario, the two VLAN IDs are placed in the same bridge group. Note that they form a single broadcast domain and spanning tree, effectively forming a single VLAN.

See the section "Routing Between VLANs Configuration Example" later in this chapter for an example configuration of the topology, shown in Figure 1-2.

To configure routing between VLANs, enter the following commands, beginning in interface configuration mode:

Step	Command	Purpose
1	**interface** *type slot/port.subinterface-number*	Specifies a subinterface.

Step	Command	Purpose
2	**encapsulation** {**sde** | **isl**} *domain*	Specifies the encapsulation type (either ISL or SDE) and the VLAN domain.
3	**bridge-group** *bridge-group*	Associates the subinterface with the VLAN.

Configure a Subscriber Bridge Group

The x digital subscriber line bridge support feature enables you to configure a router for intelligent bridge flooding for x digital subscriber line and other bridge applications. To configure a subscriber bridge group, use the following commands, beginning in global configuration mode:

Step	Command	Purpose
1	**bridge** *bridge-group* **protocol** {**ieee** | **dec**}	Defines the bridge spanning tree protocol.
2	**bridge** *bridge-group* **subscriber-policy** *policy*	Defines a subscriber bridge group and specifies the subscriber policy for the group.
3	**subscriber-policy** *policy* [[**no**] [**default**] *packet* [**permit**] [**deny**]]	Defines or modifies the forward and filter decisions of the subscriber policy.
4	**interface** *type number*	Configures a subinterface.
5	**bridge-group** *bridge-group* [**subscriber-trunk**]	Assigns a subscriber bridge group and indicates whether the interface is upstream or downstream from the traffic flow.

NOTE   Standard access lists can coexist with the subscriber policy. However, subscriber policy will take precedence over the access list by being checked first. A packet permitted by the subscriber policy will be checked against the access list if it is specified. A packet denied by subscriber policy will be dropped with no further access list checking.

Configure Transparent Bridging over WANs

You can configure transparent bridging over a variety of networks, as described in the following sections:

- Configure Fast-Switched Transparent Bridging over ATM
- Configure Transparent Bridging over DDR
- Configure Transparent Bridging over Frame Relay
- Configure Transparent Bridging over Multiprotocol LAPB

- Configure Transparent Bridging over SMDS

- Configure Transparent Bridging over X.25

Configure Fast-Switched Transparent Bridging over ATM

Cisco bridging implementation supports IEEE 802.3 frame formats and IEEE 802.10 frame formats. Cisco implementation can transparently bridge ARPA style ethernet packets (also known as Ethernet version 2).

Fast-switched transparent bridging over Asynchronous Transfer Mode (ATM) supports AAL5-SNAP encapsulated packets only. All bridged AAL5-SNAP encapsulated packets are fast switched. Fast-switched transparent bridging supports Ethernet, Fiber Distributed Data Interface (FDDI), and Token Ring packets sent in AAL5-SNAP encapsulation over ATM. See the section "Fast-Switched Transparent Bridging over ATM Example (Cisco 7000)" for an example configuration of fast-switched transparent bridging over ATM.

Configure Transparent Bridging over DDR

Cisco IOS software supports transparent bridging over dial-on-demand routing (DDR) and provides you some flexibility in controlling access and configuring the interface.

To configure DDR for bridging, complete the tasks in the following sections:

- Define the Protocols to Bridge

- Specify the Bridging Protocol

- Determine Access for Bridging

- Configure an Interface for Bridging

For an example of configuring transparent bridging over DDR, see the section "Transparent Bridging over DDR Examples" section.

Define the Protocols to Bridge

IP packets are routed by default unless they are explicitly bridged; all others are bridged by default unless they are explicitly routed.

To bridge IP packets, use the following command in global configuration mode:

Command	Purpose
no ip routing	Disables IP routing.

If you choose not to bridge another protocol, use the relevant command to enable routing of that protocol.

Specify the Bridging Protocol

You must specify the type of spanning-tree bridging protocol to use and also identify a bridge group. To specify the Spanning-Tree Protocol and a bridge group number, use the following command in global configuration mode:

Command	Purpose
bridge *bridge-group* **protocol** {**ieee**	**dec**}	Defines the type of spanning tree protocol and identifies a bridge group.

The bridge-group number is used when you configure the interface and assign it to a bridge group. Packets are bridged only among members of the same bridge group.

Determine Access for Bridging

You can determine access by either permitting all bridge packets or by controlling access according to Ethernet type codes.

To permit all transparent bridge packets, use the following command in global configuration mode:

Command	Purpose
dialer-list *dialer-group* **protocol bridge permit**	Defines a dialer list that permits all transparent bridge packets.

To control access by Ethernet type codes, use the following commands in global configuration mode:

Step	Command	Purpose
1	**access-list** *access-list-number* {**permit**	**deny**} *type-code* [*mask*]	Permits packets according to Ethernet type codes (access list numbers must be in the range 200–299).
2	**dialer-list** *dialer-group* **protocol bridge list** *access-list-number*	Defines a dialer list for the specified access list.

For a table of some common Ethernet types codes, see Appendix A, "Ethernet Type Codes."

Configure an Interface for Bridging

You can configure serial interfaces or Integrated Services Digital Network (ISDN) interfaces for DDR bridging. To configure an interface for DDR bridging, use the following commands, starting in global configuration mode:

Step	Command	Purpose
1	**interface** *type number*	Specifies the serial or ISDN interface and enters interface configuration mode.
2	**dialer string** *dial-string* **dialer map bridge** [**name** *hostname*] [**broadcast**] *dial-string*[:*isdn-subaddress*]	Configures the dial string to call. or Configures a dialer bridge map.
3	**bridge-group** *bridge-group*	Assigns the specified interface to a bridge group.

Configure Transparent Bridging over Frame Relay

The transparent bridging software supports bridging of packets over Frame Relay networks. This ability is useful for such tasks as transmitting packets from proprietary protocols across a Frame Relay network. Bridging over a Frame Relay network is supported both on networks that support a multicast facility and those that do not. Both cases are described in this section.

Fast-Switched Transparent Bridging

The transparent bridging software provides fast-switched transparent bridging for Frame Relay encapsulated serial and High-Speed Serial Interface (HSSI) networks.

Switched virtual vircuits (SVCs) are not supported for transparent bridging in this release. All the permanent virtual vircuits (PVCs) configured on a subinterface must belong to the same bridge group.

Bridging in a Frame Relay Network with No Multicasts

The Frame Relay bridging software uses the same spanning-tree algorithm as the other bridging functions, but allows packets to be encapsulated for transmission across a Frame Relay network. You specify IP-to-DLCI (data-link connection identifier) address mapping and the system maintains a table of both the Ethernet address and the DLCIs.

To configure bridging in a network that does not support a multicast facility, define the mapping between an address and the DLCI used to connect to the address. To bridge with no multicasts, use the following command in interface configuration mode:

Command	Purpose
frame-relay map bridge *dlci* **broadcast**	Defines the mapping between an address and the DLCI used to connect to the address.

An example configuration is provided in the section "Frame Relay Transparent Bridging Examples" at the end of this chapter.

Bridging in a Frame Relay Network with Multicasts

The multicast facility is used to learn about the other bridges on the network, eliminating the need for you to specify any mappings with the **frame-relay map bridge broadcast** command. An example configuration is provided in the section "Frame Relay Transparent Bridging Examples" at the end of the chapter for use as a configuration guide.

Configure Transparent Bridging over Multiprotocol LAPB

Cisco software implements transparent bridging over multiprotocol Link Access Protocol-Balanced (LAPB) encapsulation on serial interfaces. To configure transparent bridging over multiprotocol LAPB, use the following commands, beginning in global configuration mode:

Step	Command	Purpose
1	**interface serial** *number*	Specifies the serial interface.
2	**no ip address**	Specifies no IP address to the interface.
3	**encapsulation lapb multi**	Configures multiprotocol LAPB encapsulation.
4	**bridge-group** *bridge-group*	Assigns the interface to a bridge group.
5	**bridge** *bridge-group* **protocol** {**ieee**	**dec**}	Specifies the type of spanning tree protocol.

NOTE   Transparent bridging over multiprotocol LAPB requires use of the **encapsulation lapb multi** command. You cannot use the **encapsulation lapb protocol** command with a **bridge** keyword to configure this feature.

For an example of configuring transparent bridging over multiprotocol LAPB, see the section "Transparent Bridging over Multiprotocol LAPB Example" later in this chapter.

Configure Transparent Bridging over SMDS

We support fast-switched transparent bridging for Switched Multimegabit Data Service (SMDS) encapsulated serial and HSSI networks. Standard bridging commands are used to enable bridging on an SMDS interface.

To enable transparent bridging over SMDS, use the following commands, beginning in interface configuration mode:

Step	Command	Purpose
1	**interface serial** *number*	Specifies the serial interface.
2	**encapsulation smds**	Configures SMDS encapsulation on the serial interface.
3	**bridge-group** *bridge-group*	Associates the interface with a bridge group.
4	**smds multicast bridge** *smds-address*	Enables transparent bridging of packets across an SMDS network.

Broadcast Address Resolution Protocol (ARP) packets are treated differently in transparent bridging over an SMDS network than in other encapsulation methods. For SMDS, two packets are sent to the multicast address. One is sent using a standard (SMDS) ARP encapsulation; the other is sent with the ARP packet encapsulated in an 802.3 MAC header. The native ARP is sent as a regular ARP broadcast.

Cisco implementation of IEEE 802.6i transparent bridging for SMDS supports 802.3, 802.5, and FDDI frame formats. The router can accept frames with or without frame check sequence (FCS). Fast-switched transparent bridging is the default and is not configurable. If a packet cannot be fast switched, it is process switched.

An example configuration is provided in the section "Fast-Switched Transparent Bridging over SMDS Example" later in this chapter.

Configure Transparent Bridging over X.25

The transparent bridging software supports bridging of packets in X.25 frames. This ability is useful for such tasks as transmitting packets from proprietary protocols across an X.25 network.

The X.25 bridging software uses the same spanning-tree algorithm as the other bridging functions, but allows packets to be encapsulated in X.25 frames and transmitted across X.25 media. You specify the IP-to-X.121 address mapping, and the system maintains a table of both the Ethernet and X.121

addresses. To configure X.25 transparent bridging, use the following command in interface configuration mode:

Command	Purpose
x25 map bridge *x.121-address* **broadcast** [options-keywords]	Specifies IP-to-X.121 mapping.

Configure Concurrent Routing and Bridging

You can configure Cisco IOS software to route a given protocol among one group of interfaces and concurrently bridge that protocol among a separate group of interfaces, all within one router. The given protocol is not switched between the two groups. Rather, routed traffic is confined to the routed interfaces and bridged traffic is confined to the bridged interfaces. A protocol may be either routed or bridged on a given interface, but not both.

The concurrent routing and bridging capability is, by default, disabled. While concurrent routing and bridging is disabled, Cisco IOS software absorbs and discards bridgeable packets in protocols that are configured for routing on any interface in the router.

When concurrent routing and bridging is first enabled in the presence of existing bridge groups, it will generate a bridge route configuration command for any protocol for which any interface in the bridge group is configured for routing. This is a precaution that applies only when concurrent routing and bridging is not already enabled, bridge groups exist, and the **bridge crb** command is encountered.

To enable concurrent routing and bridging in Cisco IOS software, use the following command in global configuration mode:

Command	Purpose
bridge crb	Enables concurrent routing and bridging.

Information about which protocols are routed and which are bridged is stored in a table, which can be displayed with the **show interfaces crb** privileged EXEC command.

When concurrent routing and bridging has been enabled, you must configure an explicit bridge route command for any protocol that is to be routed on the interfaces in a bridge group in addition to any required protocol-specific interface configuration.

To configure specific protocols to be routed in a bridge group, use the following command in interface configuration mode:

Command	Purpose
bridge *bridge-group* **route** *protocol*	Specifies a protocol to be routed on a bridge group.

Configure Integrated Routing and Bridging

Perform one or more of the following tasks to configure integrated routing and bridging on your router:

- Assign a Bridge Group Number and Define the Spanning-Tree Protocol
- Configure Interfaces
- Enable Integrated Routing and Bridging
- Configure the Bridge-Group Virtual Interface
- Configure Protocols for Routing or Bridging

Assign a Bridge Group Number and Define the Spanning-Tree Protocol

Prior to configuring the router for integrated routing and bridging, you must enable bridging by setting up a bridge group number and specifying a Spanning-Tree Protocol. You can choose either the IEEE 802.1D Spanning-Tree Protocol or the earlier Digital protocol upon which this IEEE standard is based.

To assign a bridge group number and define a spanning tree protocol, use the following command in global configuration mode:

Command	Purpose
bridge *bridge-group* **protocol** {**ieee** | **dec**}	Assigns a bridge group number and defines a spanning tree protocol as either IEEE 802.1D standard or Digital.

The IEEE 802.1D Spanning-Tree Protocol is the preferred way of running the bridge. Use the Digital Spanning-Tree Protocol only for backward compatibility.

Configure Interfaces

To configure a router interface in Cisco IOS software, use the following commands, starting in global configuration mode:

Step	Command	Purpose
1	**interface** *type number*	Specifies the interface and enter interface configuration mode.
2	**port**	Specifies concentrator port operation.
3	**bridge-group** *bridge-group*	Assigns bridge-groups to appropriate interfaces.

Enable Integrated Routing and Bridging

After you have set up the interfaces in the router, you can enable integrated routing and bridging.

To enable integrated routing and bridging in Cisco IOS software, use the following command in global configuration mode:

Command	Purpose
bridge irb	Enables integrated routing and bridging.

Use the **show interfaces irb** privileged EXEC command to display the protocols that a given bridged interface can route to the other routed interface when the packet is routable, and to display the protocols that a given bridged interface bridges.

Configure the Bridge-Group Virtual Interface

The bridge-group virtual interface resides in the router. It acts like a normal routed interface that does not support bridging, but represents the entire corresponding bridge group to routed interfaces within the router. The bridge-group virtual interface is assigned the number of the bridge group that it represents. The bridge-group virtual interface number is the link between the bridge-group virtual interface and its bridge group. Because the bridge-group virtual interface is a virtual routed interface, it has all the network layer attributes, such as a network address and the ability to perform filtering. Only one bridge-group virtual interface is supported for each bridge group.

When you enable routing for a given protocol on the bridge-group virtual interface, packets coming from a routed interface but destined for a host in a bridged domain are routed to the bridge-group virtual interface, and are forwarded to the corresponding bridged interface. All traffic routed to the bridge-group virtual interface is forwarded to the corresponding bridge group as bridged traffic. All routable traffic received on a bridged interface is routed to other routed interfaces as if it is coming directly from the bridge-group virtual interface.

To create a bridge-group virtual interface, use the following command in interface configuration mode:

Command	Purpose
interface bvi *bridge-group*	Enables a bridge-group virtual interface.

When you intend to bridge and route a given protocol in the same bridge group, you must configure the network-layer attributes of the protocol on the bridge-group virtual interface. Do not configure protocol attributes on the bridged interfaces. No bridging attributes can be configured on the bridge-group virtual interface.

Although it is generally the case that all bridged segments belonging to a bridge group are represented as a single segment or network to the routing protocol, there are situations where several individual networks coexist within the same bridged segment. To make it possible for the routed domain to learn about the other networks behind the bridge-group virtual interface, configure a secondary address on the bridge-group virtual interface to add the corresponding network to the routing process.

Configure Protocols for Routing or Bridging

When integrated routing and bridging is enabled, the default route/bridge behavior in a bridge group is to bridge all packets.

You could then explicitly configure the bridge group to route a particular protocol so that routable packets of this protocol are routed, while nonroutable packets of this protocol or packets for protocols for which the bridge group is not explicitly configured to route will be bridged.

You could also explicitly configure the bridge group so that it does not bridge a particular protocol so that routable packets of this protocol are routed when the bridge is explicitly configured to route this protocol, and nonroutable packets are dropped because bridging is disabled for this protocol.

NOTE   Packets of nonroutable protocols, such as LAT, are only bridged. You cannot disable bridging for the nonroutable traffic.

To configure specific protocols to be routed or bridged in a bridge group, use one or more of the following commands in global configuration mode:

Command	Purpose
bridge *bridge-group* **route** *protocol*	Specifies a protocol to be routed in a bridge group.
no bridge *bridge-group* **route** *protocol*	Specifies that a protocol is not to be routed in a bridge group.
bridge *bridge-group* **bridge** *protocol*	Specifies that a protocol is to be bridged in the bridge group.
no bridge *bridge-group* **bridge** *protocol*	Specifies that a protocol is not to be bridged in the bridge group.

For example, to bridge AppleTalk, bridge and route IPX, and route IP in the same bridge group, you would do the following:

● Bridge AppleTalk—Because integrated routing and bridging bridges everything by default, no configuration is required to bridge AppleTalk.

● Bridge and route IPX—After using the **bridge irb** command to enable integrated routing and bridging, and the **interface bvi** command to create the bridge-group virtual interface for the bridge group, you would use the **bridge route** command to both bridge and route IPX (bridging is already enabled by default; the **bridge route** command enables routing).

● Route IP—Use the **bridge route** command to enable routing and then use the **no bridge bridge** command to disable bridging.

NOTE   When integrated routing and bridging is not enabled, routing a given protocol means that protocol is not bridged, and bridging a protocol means that protocol is not routed. When integrated routing and bridging is enabled, the disjunct relationship between routing and bridging is broken down and a given protocol can be switched between routed and bridged interfaces on a selective, independent basis.

Configure Transparent Bridging Options

You can configure one or more transparent bridging options. To configure transparent bridging options, perform one or more of the tasks in the following sections:

● Disable IP Routing

● Enable Autonomous Bridging

● Configure LAT Compression

● Establish Multiple Spanning-Tree Domains

● Prevent the Forwarding of Dynamically Determined Stations

● Forward Multicast Addresses

● Configure Bridge Table Aging Time

Disable IP Routing

If you want to bridge IP, you must disable IP routing because IP routing is enabled by default on Cisco IOS software. You can enable IP routing when you decide to route IP packets. To disable or enable IP routing, use one of the following commands in global configuration mode:

Command	Purpose
no ip routing	Disables IP routing.
ip routing	Enables IP routing.

All interfaces in the bridge group that are bridging IP should have the same IP address. However, if you have more than one bridge group, each bridge group should have its own IP address.

Enable Autonomous Bridging

Normally, bridging takes place on the processor card at the interrupt level. When autonomous bridging is enabled, bridging takes place entirely on the ciscoBus2 controller, significantly improving performance. Autonomous bridging is a high-speed switching feature that allows bridged traffic to be forwarded and flooded on the ciscoBus2 controller between resident interfaces. If you are using the ciscoBus2 controller, you can maximize performance by enabling autonomous bridging on the following ciscoBus2 interfaces:

- MEC
- FCIT transparent
- HSSI HDLC

Although performance improvements will be seen most in the resident interfaces, the autonomous bridging feature can also be used in bridge groups that include interfaces that are not on the ciscoBus2 controller. These interfaces include the CTR, FCI with encapsulation bridging, and HSSI with encapsulation other than HDLC, such as X.25, Frame Relay, or SMDS, MCI, STR, or SBE16.

If you enable autonomous bridging for a bridge group that includes a combination of interfaces that are resident on the ciscoBus2 controller and some that are not, the ciscoBus2 controller forwards only packets between resident interfaces. Forwarding between nonresident and resident interfaces is done in either the fast or process paths. Flooding between resident interfaces is done by the ciscoBus2 controller. Flooding between nonresident interfaces is done conventionally. If a packet is forwarded from a nonresident to a resident interface, the packet is conventionally forwarded. If packets are flooded from a nonresident interface to a resident interface, the packet is autonomously flooded.

To enable autonomous bridging on a per-interface basis, use the following command in interface configuration mode:

Command	Purpose
bridge-group *bridge-group* **cbus-bridging**	Enables autonomous bridging (if using the ciscoBus2 controller).

NOTE   You can filter by MAC-layer address on an interface only when autonomous bridging is enabled on that interface. If any filters or priority queuing is configured, autonomous bridging is automatically disabled.

Configure LAT Compression

The local-area transport (LAT) protocol used by Digital and Digital-compatible terminal servers is one of the common protocols that lacks a well-defined network layer (Layer 3) and so always must be bridged.

To reduce the amount of bandwidth that LAT traffic consumes on serial interfaces, you can specify a LAT-specific form of compression. Doing so applies compression to LAT frames being sent out by Cisco IOS software through the interface in question. To configure LAT compression, use the following command in interface configuration mode:

Command	Purpose
bridge-group *bridge-group* **lat-compression**	Reduces the amount of bandwidth that LAT traffic consumes on a serial interface.

LAT compression can be specified only for serial interfaces. For the most common LAT operations (user keystrokes and acknowledgment packets), LAT compression reduces LAT's bandwidth requirements by nearly a factor of two.

Establish Multiple Spanning-Tree Domains

Cisco IEEE 802.1D bridging software supports spanning-tree domains of bridge groups. Domains are a feature specific to Cisco. This feature is only available if you have specified IEEE as the Spanning-Tree Protocol. A domain establishes an external identification of the BPDUs sent from a bridge group. The purpose of this identification is as follows:

- Bridge groups defined within the domain can recognize that BPDU as belonging to them.

- Two bridged subnetworks in different domains that are sharing a common connection can use the domain identifier to identify and then ignore the BPDUs that belong to another domain. Each bridged subnetwork establishes its own spanning tree based on the BPDUs that it receives. The BPDUs it receives must contain the domain number to which the bridged subnetwork belongs. Bridged traffic is not domain identified.

NOTE   Domains do not constrain the propagation of bridged traffic. A bridge bridges nonrouted traffic received on its interfaces regardless of domain.

You can place any number of routers or bridges within the domain. Only the devices within a domain share spanning-tree information.

When multiple routers share the same cable and you want to use only certain discrete subsets of those routers to share spanning-tree information with each other, establish spanning-tree domains. This function is most useful when running other applications, such as IP User Datagram Protocol (UDP) flooding, that use the IEEE spanning tree. You also can use this feature to reduce the number of global reconfigurations in large bridged networks.

To establish multiple spanning-tree domains, use the following command in global configuration mode:

Command	Purpose
bridge *bridge-group* **domain** *domain-number*	Establishes a multiple spanning-tree domain.

For an example of how to configure domains, see the "Complex Transparent Bridging Network Topology Example" section later in this chapter.

Prevent the Forwarding of Dynamically Determined Stations

Normally, the system forwards any frames for stations that it has learned about dynamically. By disabling this activity, the bridge will only forward frames whose address have been statically configured into the forwarding cache. To prevent or allow forwarding of dynamically determined stations, use one of the following commands in global configuration mode:

Command	Purpose
no bridge *bridge-group* **acquire**	Filters out all frames except those whose addresses have been statically configured into the forwarding cache.
bridge *bridge-group* **acquire**	Removes the ability to filter out all frames except those whose addresses have been statically configured into the forwarding cache.

Forward Multicast Addresses

A packet with a routing information field (RIF), indicated by a source address with the multicast bit turned on, is not usually forwarded. However, you can configure bridging support to allow the forwarding of frames that would otherwise be discarded because they have a RIF. Although you can forward these frames, the bridge table will not be updated to include the source addresses of these frames.

To forward frames with multicast addresses, use the following command in global configuration mode:

Command	Purpose
bridge *bridge-group* **multicast-source**	Allows the forwarding of frames with multicast source addresses.

Configure Bridge Table Aging Time

A bridge forwards, floods, or drops packets based on the bridge table. The bridge table maintains both static entries and dynamic entries. Static entries are entered by the network manager or by the bridge itself. Dynamic entries are entered by the bridge learning process. A dynamic entry is automatically removed after a specified length of time, known as *aging time*, from the time the entry was created or last updated.

If hosts on a bridged network are likely to move, decrease the aging time to enable the bridge to adapt to the change quickly. If hosts do not transmit continuously, increase the aging time to record the dynamic entries for a longer time and thus reduce the possibility of flooding when the hosts transmit again.

To set the aging time, use the following command in global configuration mode:

Command	Purpose
bridge-group *bridge-group* **aging-time** *seconds*	Sets the bridge table aging time.

Filter Transparently Bridged Packets

A bridge examines frames and transmits them through the internetwork according to the destination address; a bridge will not forward a frame back to its originating network segment. The bridge software allows you to configure specific administrative filters that filter frames based upon information other than paths to their destinations. You can perform administrative filtering by performing one of the tasks in the following sections:

● Set Filters at the MAC Layer

● Filter LAT Service Announcements

NOTE   When setting up administrative filtering, remember that there is virtually no performance penalty in filtering by Media Access Control (MAC) address or vendor code, but there can be a significant performance penalty when filtering by protocol type.

When configuring transparent bridging access control, keep the following points in mind:

- You can assign only one access list to an interface.

- The conditions in the access list are applied to all outgoing packets not sourced by Cisco IOS software.

- Access lists are scanned in the order you enter them; the first match is used.

- An implicit deny everything entry is automatically defined at the end of an access list unless you include an explicit permit everything entry at the end of the list.

- All new entries to an existing list are placed at the end of the list. You cannot add an entry to the middle of a list. This means that if you have previously included an explicit permit everything entry, new entries will never be scanned. The solution is to delete the access list and retype it with the new entries.

- You can create extended access lists to specify more detailed filters, such as address match only.

- You should not use extended access lists on FDDI interfaces doing transit bridging as opposed to translational bridging.

- Configuring bridging access lists of type 700 may cause a momentary interruption of traffic flow.

Set Filters at the MAC Layer

You can filter transmission of frames at the MAC layer by performing tasks in one of the following sections:

- Filter by Specific MAC Address

- Filter by Vendor Code

- Filter by Protocol Type

When filtering by a MAC-layer address, you can use two kinds of access lists: standard access lists that specify a simple address and extended access lists that specify two addresses. You can also further restrict access by creating filters for these lists. After you have completed one of the preceding tasks, perform the task in the following section:

- Define and Apply Extended Access Lists

NOTE	MAC addresses on Ethernets are "bit swapped" when compared with MAC addresses on Token Ring and FDDI. For example, address 0110.2222.3333 on Ethernet is 8008.4444.CCCC on Token Ring and FDDI. Access lists always use the canonical Ethernet representation. When using different media and building access lists to filter on MAC addresses, keep this point in mind. Note that when a bridged packet traverses a serial link, it has an Ethernet-style address.

Filter by Specific MAC Address

You can filter frames with a particular MAC-layer station source or destination address. Any number of addresses can be configured into the system without a performance penalty. To filter by MAC-layer address, use the following command in global configuration mode:

Command	Purpose
bridge *bridge-group* **address** *mac-address* {**forward** | **discard**} [*interface*]	Filters particular MAC-layer station addresses.

When filtering specific MAC destination addresses, allow for multicast or broadcast packets that are required by the bridged network protocols. Refer to the example in the section "Multicast or Broadcast Packets Bridging Example" later in this chapter to guide you in building your configuration to allow for multicast or broadcast packets.

Filter by Vendor Code

The bridging software allows you to create access lists to administratively filter MAC addresses. These access lists can filter groups of MAC addresses, including those with particular vendor codes. There is no noticeable performance loss in using these access lists, and the lists can be of indefinite length. You can filter groups of MAC addresses with particular vendor codes by performing the first task and one or both of the other tasks that follow:

● Establish a vendor code access list.

● Filter source addresses.

● Filter destination addresses.

To establish a vendor code access list, use the following command in global configuration mode:

Command	Purpose
access-list *access-list-number* {**permit** | **deny**} *address mask*	Prepares access control information for filtering of frames by canonical (Ethernet-ordered) MAC address.

The vendor code is the first three bytes of the MAC address (left to right). For an example of how to filter by vendor code, see "Multicast or Broadcast Packets Bridging Example" later in this chapter.

NOTE	Remember that, as with any access list using MAC addresses, Ethernets swap their MAC address bit ordering, while Token Rings and FDDI do not. Therefore, an access list that works for one medium might not work for others.

Once you have defined an access list to filter by a particular vendor code, you can assign an access list to a particular interface for filtering on the MAC source addresses of packets received on that interface or the MAC destination addresses of packets that would ordinarily be forwarded out that interface. To filter by source or destination addresses, use one of the following commands in interface configuration mode:

Command	Purpose
bridge-group *bridge-group* **input-address-list** *access-list-number*	Assigns an access list to an interface for filtering by MAC source addresses.
bridge-group *bridge-group* **output-address-list** *access-list-number*	Assigns an access list to an interface for filtering by the MAC destination addresses.

Filter by Protocol Type

You can filter by protocol type by using the access-list mechanism and specifying a protocol type code. To filter by protocol type, perform the first task and one or more of the other tasks that follow:

● Establish a protocol type access list

● Filter Ethernet- and SNAP-encapsulated packets on input

● Filter Ethernet- and SNAP-encapsulated packets on output

● Filter IEEE 802.2-encapsulated packets on input

● Filter IEEE 802.2-encapsulated packets on output

NOTE	It is a good idea to have both input and output type code filtering on different interfaces.

The order in which you enter **access-list** commands affects the order in which the access conditions are checked. Each condition is tested in succession. A matching condition is then used to execute a permit or deny decision. If no conditions match, a "deny" decision is reached.

NOTE   Protocol type access lists can have an impact on system performance; therefore, keep the lists as short as possible and use wildcard bit masks whenever possible.

Access lists for Ethernet- and IEEE 802.2-encapsulated packets affect only bridging functions. It is not possible to use such access lists to block frames with protocols that are being routed.

You can establish protocol type access lists. Specify either an Ethernet type code for Ethernet-encapsulated packets or a DSAP/SSAP pair for 802.3 or 802.5-encapsulated packets. Ethernet type codes are listed in Appendix A, "Ethernet Type Codes."

To establish protocol type access lists, use the following command in global configuration mode:

Command	Purpose
access-list *access-list-number* {**permit** | **deny**} *type-code wild-mask*	Prepares access control information for filtering frames by protocol type.

You can filter Ethernet- and SNAP-encapsulated packets on input. For SNAP-encapsulated frames, the access list you create is applied against the two-byte TYPE field given after the DSAP/SSAP/OUI fields in the frame. The access list is applied to all Ethernet and SNAP frames received on that interface prior to the bridge learning process. SNAP frames also must pass any applicable IEEE 802.2 DSAP/SSAP access lists.

You can also filter Ethernet- and SNAP-encapsulated packets on output. The access list you create is applied just before sending out a frame to an interface.

To filter these packets on input or output, use either or both of the following commands in interface configuration mode:

Command	Purpose
bridge-group *bridge-group* **input-type-list** *access-list-number*	Adds a filter for Ethernet- and SNAP-encapsulated packets on input.
bridge-group *bridge-group* **output-type-list** *access-list-number*	Adds a filter for Ethernet- and SNAP-encapsulated packets on output.

You can filter IEEE 802-encapsulated packets on input. The access list you create is applied to all IEEE 802 frames received on that interface prior to the bridge-learning process. SNAP frames also must pass any applicable Ethernet type-code access list.

You can also filter IEEE 802-encapsulated packets on output. SNAP frames also must pass any applicable Ethernet type-code access list. The access list you create is applied just before sending out a frame to an interface.

To filter these packets on input or output, use one or both of the following commands in interface configuration mode:

Command	Purpose
bridge-group *bridge-group* **input-lsap-list** *access-list-number*	Adds a filter for IEEE 802-encapsulated packets on input.
bridge-group *bridge-group* **output-lsap-list** *access-list-number*	Adds a filter for IEEE 802-encapsulated packets on output.

Access lists for Ethernet- and IEEE 802-encapsulated packets affect only bridging functions. You cannot use such access lists to block frames with protocols that are being routed.

Define and Apply Extended Access Lists

If you are filtering by the MAC-layer address, whether it is by a specific MAC address, vendor code, or protocol type, you can define and apply extended access lists. Extended access lists allow finer granularity of control. They allow you to specify both source and destination addresses and arbitrary bytes in the packet.

To define an extended access list, use the following command in global configuration mode:

Command	Purpose
access-list *access-list-number* {**permit**	**deny**} *source source-mask destination destination-mask offset size operator operand*	Defines an extended access list for finer control of bridged traffic.

To apply an extended access list to an interface, use one or both of the following commands in interface configuration mode:

Command	Purpose
bridge-group *bridge-group* **input-pattern-list** *access-list-number*	Applies an extended access list to the packets being received by an interface.

Command	Purpose
bridge-group *bridge-group* **output-pattern-list** *access-list-number*	Applies an extended access list to the packet being sent by an interface.

After an access list is created initially, any subsequent additions (possibly entered from the terminal) are placed at the end of the list. In other words, you cannot selectively add or remove access list command lines from a specific access list.

CAUTION Because of their complexity, only use extended access lists if you are very familiar with Cisco IOS software. Further, do not specify an offset value that is greater than the size of the packet.

Filter LAT Service Announcements

The bridging software allows you to filter LAT frames. LAT bridge filtering allows the selective inclusion or exclusion of LAT multicast service announcements on a per-interface basis.

NOTE The LAT filtering commands are not implemented for Token Ring interfaces.

In the LAT protocol, a *group code* is defined as a decimal number in the range 0 to 255. Some of the LAT configuration commands take a list of group codes; this is referred to as a *group code list*. The rules for entering numbers in a group code list follow:

- Entries can be individual group code numbers separated with a space. (The Digital LAT implementation specifies that a list of numbers be separated by commas; however, Cisco implementation expects the numbers to be separated by spaces.)

- Entries can also specify a range of numbers. This is done by separating an ascending order range of group numbers with hyphens.

- Any number of group codes or group code ranges can be listed in one command; just separate each with a space.

In LAT, each node transmits a periodic service advertisement message that announces its existence and availability for connections. Within the message is a group code list; this is a mask of up to 256 bits. Each bit represents a group number. In the traditional use of LAT group codes, a terminal server only will connect to a host system when there is an overlap between the group code list of the user on the terminal server and the group code list in the service advertisement message. In an environment with many bridges and many LAT hosts, the number of multicast messages that each system has to deal with becomes unreasonable. The 256 group codes might not be enough to allocate local assignment policies, such as giving each DECserver 200 device its own group code in large bridged networks. LAT group code filtering allows you to have very fine control over which multicast messages actually get bridged. Through a combination of input and output permit and deny lists, you can implement many different LAT control policies.

You can filter LAT service advertisements by performing any of the tasks in the following sections:

- Enable LAT Group Code Service Filtering
- Specify Deny or Permit Conditions for LAT Group Codes on Input
- Specify Deny or Permit Conditions for LAT Group Codes on Output

Enable LAT Group Code Service Filtering

You can specify LAT group-code filtering to inform the system that LAT service advertisements require special processing. To enable LAT group-code filtering, use the following command in global configuration mode:

Command	Purpose
bridge *bridge-group* **lat-service-filtering**	Enables LAT service filtering.

Specify Deny or Permit Conditions for LAT Group Codes on Input

You can specify the group codes by which to deny or permit access upon input. Specifying deny conditions causes the system to not bridge any LAT service advertisement that contain any of the specified groups. Specifying permit conditions causes the system to bridge only those service advertisements that match at least one group in the specified group list.

To specify deny or permit conditions for LAT groups on input, use one of the following commands in interface configuration mode:

Command	Purpose
bridge-group *bridge-group* **input-lat-service-deny** *group-list*	Specifies the group codes with which to deny access upon input.
bridge-group *bridge-group* **input-lat-service-permit** *group-list*	Specifies the group codes with which to permit access upon input.

If a message specifies group codes in both the deny and permit list, the message is not bridged.

Specify Deny or Permit Conditions for LAT Group Codes on Output

You can specify the group codes by which to deny or permit access upon output. Specifying deny conditions causes the system to not bridge onto the output interface any LAT service advertisements that contain any of the specified groups. Specifying permit conditions causes the system to bridge onto the output interface only those service advertisements that match at least one group in the specified group list.

To specify deny or permit conditions for LAT groups on output, use one of the following commands in interface configuration mode:

Command	Purpose
bridge-group *bridge-group* **output-lat-service-deny** *group-list* or	Specifies the group codes with which to deny access upon output.
bridge-group *bridge-group* **output-lat-service-permit** *group-list*	Specifies the group codes with which to permit access upon output.

If a message matches both a deny and a permit condition, it will not be bridged.

Adjust Spanning-Tree Parameters

You might need to adjust certain spanning-tree parameters if the default values are not suitable for your bridge configuration. Parameters affecting the entire spanning tree are configured with variations of the **bridge** global configuration command. Interface-specific parameters are configured with variations of the **bridge-group** interface configuration command.

You can adjust spanning-tree parameters by performing any of the tasks in the following sections:

- Set the Bridge Priority
- Set an Interface Priority
- Assign Path Costs
- Adjust BPDU Intervals
- Disable the Spanning Tree on an Interface

NOTE   Only network administrators with a good understanding of how bridges and the Spanning-Tree Protocol work should make adjustments to spanning-tree parameters. Poorly planned adjustments to these parameters may have a negative impact on performance. A good source on bridging is the IEEE 802.1d specification.

Set the Bridge Priority

You can globally configure the priority of an individual bridge when two bridges tie for position as the root bridge, or you can configure the likelihood that a bridge will be selected as the root bridge. This priority is determined by default; however, you can change it. To set the bridge priority, use the following command in global configuration mode:

Command	Purpose
bridge *bridge-group* **priority** *number*	Sets the bridge priority.

Set an Interface Priority

You can set a priority for an interface. When two bridges tie for position as the root bridge, you configure an interface priority to break the tie. The bridge with the lowest interface value is elected. To set an interface priority, use the following command in interface configuration mode:

Command	Purpose
bridge-group *bridge-group* **priority** *number*	Establishes a priority for a specified interface.

Assign Path Costs

Each interface has a path cost associated with it. By convention, the path cost is 1000/data rate of the attached LAN, in Mbps. You can set different path costs. To assign path costs, use the following command in interface configuration mode:

Command	Purpose
bridge-group *bridge-group* **path-cost** *cost*	Sets a path cost different from the defaults.

Adjust BPDU Intervals

You can adjust BPDU intervals as described in the following sections:

- Adjust the Interval Between Hello BPDUs
- Define the Forward Delay Interval
- Define the Maximum Idle Interval

NOTE   Each bridge in a spanning tree adopts the interval between hello BPDUs, the forward delay interval, and the maximum idle interval parameters of the root bridge, regardless of what its individual configuration might be.

Adjust the Interval Between Hello BPDUs

You can specify the interval between hello BPDUs. To adjust this interval, use the following command in global configuration mode:

Command	Purpose
bridge *bridge-group* **hello-time** *seconds*	Specifies the interval between hello BPDUs.

Define the Forward Delay Interval

The forward delay interval is the amount of time spent listening for topology change information after an interface has been activated for bridging and before forwarding actually begins. To change the default interval setting, use the following command in global configuration mode:

Command	Purpose
bridge *bridge-group* **forward-time** *seconds*	Sets the default of the forward delay interval.

Define the Maximum Idle Interval

If a bridge does not hear BPDUs from the root bridge within a specified interval, it assumes that the network has changed and recomputes the spanning-tree topology. To change the default interval setting, using the following command in global configuration mode:

Command	Purpose
bridge *bridge-group* **max-age** *seconds*	Changes the amount of time a bridge will wait to hear BPDUs from the root bridge.

Disable the Spanning Tree on an Interface

When a *loop-free* path exists between any two bridged subnetworks, you can prevent BPDUs generated in one transparent bridging subnetwork from impacting nodes in the other transparent bridging subnetwork, yet still permit bridging throughout the bridged network as a whole. For example, when transparently bridged LAN subnetworks are separated by a WAN, BPDUs can be prevented from traveling across the WAN link.

To disable the spanning tree on an interface, use the following command in interface configuration mode:

Command	Purpose
bridge-group *bridge-group* **spanning-disabled**	Disables the spanning tree on an interface.

Tune the Transparently Bridged Network

The following sections describe how to configure features that enhance network performance by reducing the number of packets that traverse the backbone network:

- Configure Circuit Groups
- Configure Constrained Multicast Flooding

Configure Circuit Groups

In the process of loop elimination, the spanning-tree algorithm always blocks all but one of a group of parallel network segments between two bridges. When those segments are of limited bandwidth, it might be preferable to augment the aggregate bandwidth between two bridges by forwarding across multiple parallel network segments. Circuit groups can be used to group multiple parallel network segments between two bridges to distribute the load while still maintaining a loop-free spanning tree.

Deterministic load distribution distributes traffic between two bridges across multiple parallel network segments grouped together into a single circuit group. As long as one port of the circuit group is in the forwarding state, all ports in that circuit group will participate in load distribution regardless of their spanning-tree port states. This process guarantees that the computed spanning tree is still adaptive to any topology change and the load is distributed among the multiple segments. Deterministic load distribution guarantees packet ordering between source-destination pairs and always forwards traffic for a source-destination pair on the same segment in a circuit group for a given circuit-group configuration.

NOTE   You should configure all parallel network segments between two bridges into a single circuit group. Deterministic load distribution across a circuit group adjusts dynamically to the addition or deletion of network segments and to interface state changes.

If a circuit-group port goes down and up as a result of configuration or a line protocol change, the spanning-tree algorithm will bypass port transition and will time out necessary timers to force the eligible circuit-group ports to enter the forwarding state. This avoids the long disruption time caused by spanning-tree topology recomputation and therefore resumes the load distribution as quickly as possible.

To tune the transparently bridged network, perform the following tasks:

Step 1	Define a circuit group.
Step 2	Optionally, configure a transmission pause interval.
Step 3	Modify the load distribution strategy.

To define a circuit group, use the following command in interface configuration mode:

Command	Purpose
bridge-group *bridge-group* **circuit-group** *circuit-group*	Adds a serial interface to a circuit group.

For circuit groups of mixed-bandwidth serial interfaces, it might be necessary to configure a pause interval during which transmission is suspended to avoid misordering packets following changes in the composition of a circuit group. Changes in the composition of a circuit group include the addition or deletion of an interface and interface state changes. To configure a transmission pause interval, use the following command in global configuration mode:

Command	Purpose
bridge *bridge-group* **circuit-group** *circuit-group* **pause** *milliseconds*	Configures a transmission pause interval.

For applications that depend on the ordering of mixed unicast and multicast traffic from a given source, load distribution must be based upon the source MAC address only. To modify the load distribution strategy to accommodate such applications, use the following command in global configuration mode:

Command	Purpose
bridge *bridge-group* **circuit-group** *circuit-group* **source-based**	Bases load distribution on the source MAC address only.

For an example of how to configure a circuit group, see the "Complex Transparent Bridging Network Topology Example" section later in this chapter.

Configure Constrained Multicast Flooding

In a transparent bridge, multicast packets are flooded on all forwarding ports on the bridge. For some protocols, it is possible for a bridge to determine the membership of multicast groups, and constrain the flooding of multicasts to a subset of the forwarding ports. Constrained multicast flooding enables a bridge to determine group membership of IP multicast groups dynamically and flood multicast packets only on those ports that reach group members.

To enable constrained multicast flooding, use the following command in global configuration mode:

Command	Purpose
bridge cmf	Enables constrained multicast flooding for all configured bridge groups.

Monitor and Maintain the Transparent Bridge Network

This section describes how to monitor and maintain activity on the bridged network. You can use one or more of the following commands in privileged EXEC mode:

Command	Purpose
clear bridge *bridge-group*	Removes any learned entries from the forwarding database and clears the transmit and receives counts for any statically configured forwarding entries.
clear bridge [*bridge-group*] **multicast** [**router-ports** | **groups** | **counts**] [*group-address*] [*interface-unit*] [**counts**]	Removes multicast-group state information and clears the transmit and receive counts.
clear sse	Reinitializes the Silicon Switch Processor (SSP) on the Cisco 7000 series.
clear vlan statistics	Removes VLAN statistics from any statically or system configured entries.
show bridge [*bridge-group*] [*interface*]	Displays details of the bridge group.
show bridge [*bridge-group*] [*interface*] [*address* [*mask*]] [**verbose**]	Display sclasses of entries in the bridge forwarding database.
show bridge [*bridge-group*] **circuit-group** [*circuit-group*] [*src-mac-address*] [*dst-mac-address*]	Displays the interfaces configured in each circuit group and show whether they are participating in load distribution.
show bridge [*bridge-group*] **multicast** [**router-ports** | **groups**] [*group-address*]	Displays transparent bridging multicast state information.
show bridge group [**verbose**]	Displays information about configured bridge groups.

Command	Purpose
show bridge vlan	Displays IEEE 802.10 transparently bridged VLAN configuration.
show interfaces crb	Displays the configuration for each interface that has been configured for routing or bridging.
show interfaces [*interface*] **irb**	Displays the protocols that can be routed or bridged for the specified interface.
show span	Displays the spanning-tree topology known to the router, including whether or not filtering is in effect.
show sse summary	Displays a summary of SSP statistics.
show subscriber-policy *policy*	Displays the details of the subscriber policy.
show vlans	Displays a summary of VLAN subinterfaces.

Transparent and SRT Bridging Configuration Examples

The following sections provide example configurations that you can use as a guide to configuring your bridging environment:

- Basic Bridging Example

- Concurrent Routing and Bridging Example

- Basic Integrated Routing and Bridging Example

- Complex Integrated Routing and Bridging Example

- Integrated Routing and Bridging with Multiple Bridge Groups Example

- Transparently Bridged VLANs Configuration Example

- Routing Between VLANs Configuration Example

- Ethernet-to-FDDI Transparent Bridging Example

- Ethernet Bridging Example

- SRT Bridging Example

- Multicast or Broadcast Packets Bridging Example

- X.25 Transparent Bridging Example

- Frame Relay Transparent Bridging Examples

- Transparent Bridging over Multiprotocol LAPB Example

- Fast-Switched Transparent Bridging over ATM Example (Cisco 7000)

- Transparent Bridging over DDR Examples

- Fast-Switched Transparent Bridging over SMDS Example

- Complex Transparent Bridging Network Topology Example

- Fast Ethernet Subscriber Port, Frame Relay Trunk Example

- ATM Subscriber Ports, ATM Trunk Example

Basic Bridging Example

Figure 1-3 is an example of a basic bridging configuration. The system has two Ethernets, one Token Ring, one FDDI port, and one serial line. IP traffic is routed and everything else is bridged. The Digital-compatible bridging algorithm with default parameters is being used.

Figure 1-3 *Example of Basic Bridging*

The configuration file for the router depicted in Figure 1-3 would be as follows:

```
interface tokenring 0
 ip address 131.108.1.1 255.255.255.0
 bridge-group 1
!
interface fddi 0
 ip address 131.108.2.1 255.255.255.0
 bridge-group 1
!
```

```
interface ethernet 0
 ip address 192.31.7.26 255.255.255.240
 bridge-group 1
!
interface serial 0
 ip address 192.31.7.34 255.255.255.240
 bridge-group 1
!
interface ethernet 1
 ip address 192.31.7.65 255.255.255.240
 bridge-group 1
!
bridge 1 protocol dec
```

Concurrent Routing and Bridging Example

In the following example DECnet and IPX are concurrently routed and bridged. IP and AppleTalk are routed on all interfaces, DECnet and IP are routed on all interfaces not in the bridge group, and all protocols other than IP and AppleTalk are bridged on all interfaces in the bridge group:

```
!
ipx routing 0000.0c36.7a43
appletalk routing
!
decnet routing 9.65
decnet node-type routing-iv
!
interface Ethernet0/0
 ip address 172.19.160.65 255.255.255.0
 ipx network 160
 appletalk address 160.65
 decnet cost 7
!
interface Ethernet0/1
 ip address 172.19.161.65 255.255.255.0
 ipx network 161
 appletalk address 161.65
 decnet cost 7
!
interface Ethernet0/2
 ip address 172.19.162.65 255.255.255.0
 appletalk address 162.65
 bridge-group 1
!
interface Ethernet0/3
 ip address 172.19.14.65 255.255.255.0
 appletalk address 14.65
 appletalk zone california
 bridge-group 1
!
router igrp 666
network 172.19.0.0
!
```

```
bridge crb
bridge 1 protocol ieee
bridge 1 route appletalk
bridge 1 route ip
!
```

Basic Integrated Routing and Bridging Example

Figure 1-4 is an example of integrated routing and bridging that uses bridge group 1 to bridge and route IP. The router has three bridged Ethernet interfaces and one routed Ethernet interface.

Figure 1-4   *Basic IP Routing Using Integrated Routing and Bridging*

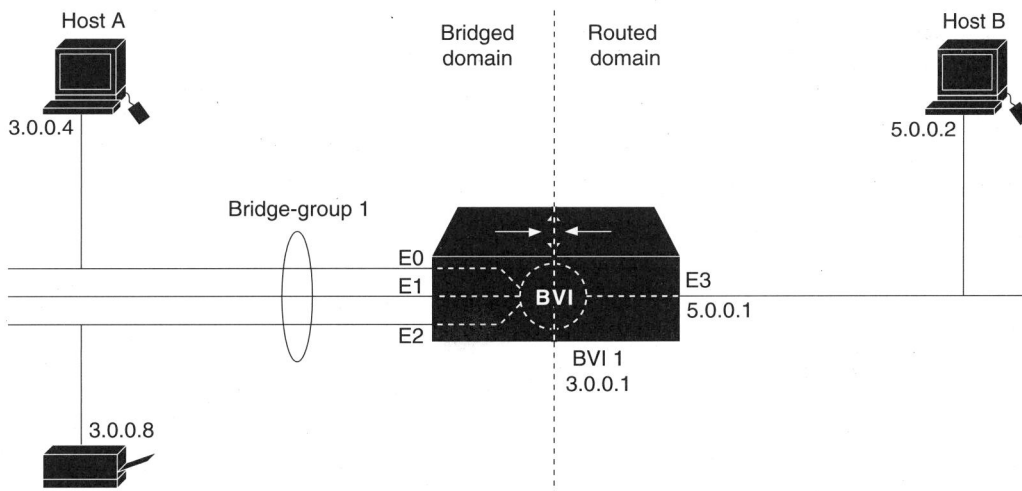

The following example shows the relevant portions of the configuration for the router:

```
interface Ethernet 0
 bridge-group 1
!
interface Ethernet 1
 bridge-group 1
!
interface Ethernet 2
 bridge-group 1
!
interface Ethernet 3
 ip address 5.0.0.1 255.0.0.0
!
interface BVI 1
 ip address 3.0.0.1 255.0.0.0
!
bridge irb
bridge 1 protocol ieee
 bridge 1 route ip
```

Complex Integrated Routing and Bridging Example

Figure 1-5 is a more complex example of integrated routing and bridging, where bridge group 1 is used to route IP traffic, bridge IPX traffic, and bridge and route AppleTalk traffic.

Figure 1-5   *Complex Integrated Routing and Bridging Example*

The following example shows the relevant portions of the configuration for the router:

```
appletalk routing
!
interface Ethernet 1
 ip address 5.0.0.1 255.0.0.0
 appletalk cable-range 35-35 35.1
 appletalk zone Engineering
!
interface Ethernet 2
 ip address 3.0.0.1 255.0.0.0
 bridge-group 1
!
interface Ethernet 3
 ip address 7.0.0.1 255.0.0.0
 bridge-group 1
!
interface BVI 1
 no ip address
 appletalk cable-range 33-33 33.1
 appletalk zone Accounting
!
bridge irb
bridge 1 protocol ieee
 bridge 1 route appletalk
 bridge 1 route ip
 no bridge 1 bridge ip
```

Integrated Routing and Bridging with Multiple Bridge Groups Example

In the example illustrated in Figure 1-6, integrated routing and bridging is used to route and bridge IP between two bridge groups.

Figure 1-6   *Integrated Routing and Bridging with Multiple Bridge Groups*

The following example shows the relevant portions of the configuration for the router:

```
interface Ethernet 1
 bridge-group 1
!
interface Ethernet 2
 bridge-group 1
!
interface Ethernet 3
 bridge-group 2
!
interface Ethernet 4
 bridge-group 2
!
interface BVI 1
 ip address 3.0.0.1 255.0.0.0
!
interface BVI 2
 ip address 5.0.0.1 255.0.0.0
!
bridge irb
bridge 1 protocol ieee
 bridge 1 route ip
bridge 2 protocol ieee
 bridge 2 route ip
```

Transparently Bridged VLANs Configuration Example

The "striped" VLAN is identified as security association identifier 45; the "dot" VLAN is identified as security association identifier 1008; the "sliced" VLAN is identified as security association identifier 4321. Note that the assignment of bridge group, interface, and subinterface numbers is of local significance only. You must coordinate only the configuration of a common Security Association Identifier across bridges.

Router One

```
bridge 18 protocol ieee
interface ethernet 0/1
 bridge-group 18
 !
interface ethernet 0/2
 bridge group 18
 !
interface ethernet 0/3
 bridge-group 18
 !
interface fddi 4/0.8
 encapsulation sde 45
 bridge-group 18
 !
 bridge 54 protocol ieee

interface ethernet 1/1
 bridge group 54
 !
interface ethernet 1/2
 bridge group 54
 !
interface ethernet 1/3
 bridge group 54
 !
interface fddi 4/0.13
 encapsulation sde 1008
 bridge group 54
 !
bridge 3 protocol ieee
 !
interface ethernet 2/1
 bridge-group 3
 !
interface ethernet 2/2
 bridge-group 3
 !
interface ethernet 2/3
 bridge-group 3
 !
interface fddi 4/0.30
 encapsulation sde 4321
 bridge-group 3
```

Router Two

```
bridge 7 protocol ieee
interface ethernet 0/1
 bridge-group 7
 !
interface ethernet 0/2
 bridge-group 7
```

```
interface ethernet 0/3
 bridge-group 7
!
interface ethernet 0/4
 bridge-group 7
!
interface fddi 2/0.11
 encapsulation sde 4321
 bridge-group 7
!
bridge 8 protocol ieee
interface ethernet 1/1
 bridge-group 8
!
interface ethernet 1/2
 bridge-group 8
!
interface ethernet 1/3
 bridge-group 8
!
interface ethernet 1/4
 bridge-group 8
!
interface fddi 2/0.14
 encapsulation sde 1008
 bridge-group 8
```

Router Three

```
bridge 1 protocol ieee
interface ethernet 0/1
 bridge-group 1
!
interface ethernet 0/2
 bridge-group 1
!
interface ethernet 0/3
 bridge-group 1
!
interface fddi 2/0.5
 encapsulation sde 4321
 bridge-group 1
!
bridge 6 protocol ieee
interface ethernet 1/1
 bridge-group 6
!
interface ethernet 1/2
 bridge-group 6
!
interface ethernet 1/3
 bridge-group 6
!
interface fddi 2/0.3
 encapsulation sde 45
 bridge-group 6
```

Routing Between VLANs Configuration Example

The following example shows the configuration for the topology, previously shown in Figure 1-2. IP traffic is routed to and from switched VLAN domains 300, 400, and 600 to any other IP routing interface, as is IPX for VLANs 500 and 600. Because Fast Ethernet interfaces 2/1.20 and 3/1.40 are combined in bridge group 50, all other nonrouted traffic is bridged between these two subinterfaces.

```
interface FDDI 1/0.10
 ip address 131.108.1.1 255.255.255.0
 encap sde 300
!
interface FastEthernet 2/1.20.
 ip address 171.69.2.2 255.255.255.0
 encap isl 400
 bridge-group 50
!
interface FastEthernet 2/1.30
 ipx network 1000
 encap isl 500
!
interface FastEthernet 3/1.40
 ip address 198.92.3.3 255.255.255.0
 ipx network 1001
 encap isl 600
 bridge-group 50
!
bridge 50 protocol ieee
```

Ethernet-to-FDDI Transparent Bridging Example

The following configuration example shows the configuration commands that enable transparent bridging between Ethernet and FDDI interfaces. Transparent bridging on an FDDI interface is allowed only on the CSC-C2FCIT interface card.

```
hostname tester
!
buffers small min-free 20
buffers middle min-free 10
buffers big min-free 5
!
no ip routing
!
interface ethernet 0
 ip address 131.108.7.207 255.255.255.0
 no ip route-cache
 bridge-group 1
!
interface ethernet 2
 ip address 131.108.7.208 255.255.255.0
 no ip route-cache
 bridge-group 1
!
```

```
interface Fddi 0
 ip address 131.108.7.209 255.255.255.0
 no ip route-cache
 no keepalive
 bridge-group 1
!
bridge 1 protocol ieee
```

If the other side of the FDDI ring were an FDDI interface running in encapsulation mode rather than in transparent mode, the following additional configuration commands would be needed:

```
interface fddi 0
 fddi encapsulate
```

Ethernet Bridging Example

In the following example, two buildings have networks that must be connected via a T1 link. For the most part, the systems in each building use either IP or DECnet, and therefore, should be routed. There are some systems in each building that must communicate, but they can use only a proprietary protocol.

The example places two Ethernets in each building. One of the Ethernets is attached to the hosts that use a proprietary protocol, and the other is used to attach to the rest of the building network running IP and DECnet. The Ethernet attached to the hosts using a proprietary protocol is enabled for bridging to the serial line and to the other building.

Figure 1-7 shows an example configuration. The interfaces marked with an asterisk (*) are configured as part of spanning tree 1. The routers are configured to route IP and DECnet. This configuration permits hosts on any Ethernet to communicate with hosts on any other Ethernet using IP or DECnet. In addition, hosts on Ethernet 1 in either building can communicate using protocols not supported for routing.

Figure 1-7   *Ethernet Bridging Configuration Example*

Router/Bridge in Building 1

The configuration file for the router in Building 1 would be as follows. Note that no bridging takes place over Ethernet 0. Both IP and DECnet routing are enabled on all interfaces.

```
decnet address 3.34
interface ethernet 0
 ip address 128.88.1.6 255.255.255.0
 decnet cost 10
!
interface serial 0
 ip address 128.88.2.1 255.255.255.0
 bridge-group 1
 decnet cost 10
!
interface ethernet 1
 ip address 128.88.3.1 255.255.255.0
 bridge-group 1
 decnet cost 10
!
bridge 1 protocol dec
```

Router/Bridge in Building 2

The configuration file for the router in Building 2 is similar:

```
decnet address 3.56
!
interface ethernet 0
 ip address 128.88.11.9 255.255.255.0
 decnet cost 10
!
interface serial 0
 ip address 128.88.2.2 255.255.255.0
 bridge-group 1
 decnet cost 10
!
interface ethernet 1
 ip address 128.88.16.8 255.255.255.0
 bridge-group 1
 decnet cost 10
!
bridge 1 protocol dec
```

SRT Bridging Example

In Figure 1-8, a Token Ring and an Ethernet at a remote sales site in New York City must be configured to pass unroutable bridged traffic across a satellite link to the backbone Token Ring at the corporate headquarters in Thule, Greenland. IP is the only routed protocol. They are running the IEEE Spanning-Tree Protocol to comply with the SRT bridging standard.

If there were source-routed traffic to bridge, the **source-bridge** command would also be used to configure source routing.

Figure 1-8   *Network Configuration Example*

New York City MGS   Thule, Greenland AGS+

Configuration for the New York City Router

```
interface tokenring 0
 ip address 150.136.1.1 255.255.255.128
 bridge-group 1
!
interface ethernet 0
 ip address 150.136.2.1 255.255.255.128
 bridge-group 1
!
interface serial 0
 ip address 150.136.3.1 255.255.255.128
 bridge-group 1
!
bridge 1 protocol ieee
```

Configuration for the Thule, Greenland, Router

```
interface tokenring 0
 ip address 150.136.10.1 255.255.255.128
 bridge-group 1
!
interface serial 0
 ip address 150.136.11.1 255.255.255.128
 bridge-group 1
!
bridge 1 protocol ieee
```

Multicast or Broadcast Packets Bridging Example

When filtering specific MAC destination addresses, allow for multicast or broadcast packets that are required by the bridged network protocols.

Assume you are bridging IP in your network as illustrated in Figure 1-9.

Figure 1-9   *Network Demonstrating Output Address List Filtering*

The MAC address of Host A is 0800.0907.0207 and the MAC address of Host B is 0260.8c34.0864. The following configuration would work as expected, because input addresses work on the source address on the incoming interface:

```
access-list 700 permit 0260.8c34.0864 0000.0000.0000
access-list 700 deny 0000.0000.0000 FFFF.FFFF.FFFF
interface ethernet 0
 bridge-group 1 input-address-list 700
```

However, the following configuration might work initially but will eventually fail. The failure occurs because the configuration does not allow for an ARP broadcast with a destination address of FFFF.FFFF.FFFF, even though the destination address on the output interface is correct:

```
access-list 700 permit 0260.8c34.0864 0000.0000.0000
access-list 700 deny 0000.0000.0000 FFFF.FFFF.FFFF
interface ethernet 0
 bridge-group 1 output-address-list 700
```

The correct access list would be as follows:

```
access-list 700 permit 0260.8c34.0864 0000.0000.0000
access-list 700 permit FFFF.FFFF.FFFF 0000.0000.0000
access-list 700 deny 0000.0000.0000 FFFF.FFFF.FFFF
interface ethernet 0
 bridge-group 1 output-address-list 700
```

X.25 Transparent Bridging Example

Figure 1-10 is an example configuration illustrating three bridges connected to each other through an X.25 network.

Figure 1-10 *X.25 Bridging Examples*

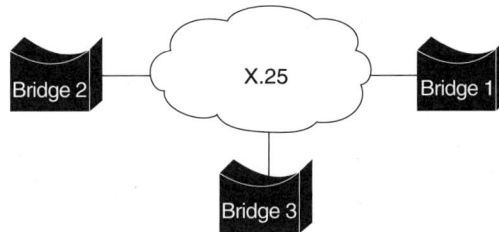

Following are the configuration commands for each of the bridges depicted in Figure 1-10.

Configuration for Bridge 1

```
interface ethernet 2
 bridge-group 5
 ip address 128.88.11.9 255.255.255.0
!
interface serial 0
 encapsulation x25
 x25 address 31370019027
 bridge-group 5
 x25 map bridge 31370019134 broadcast
 x25 map bridge 31370019565 broadcast
!
bridge 5 protocol ieee
```

Configuration for Bridge 2

```
interface serial 1
 encapsulation x25
 x25 address 31370019134
 bridge-group 5
 x25 map bridge 31370019027 broadcast
 x25 map bridge 31370019565 broadcast
!
bridge 5 protocol ieee
```

Configuration for Bridge 3

```
interface serial 0
 encapsulation x25
 x25 address 31370019565
 bridge-group 5
 x25 map bridge 31370019027 broadcast
 x25 map bridge 31370019134 broadcast
!
bridge 5 protocol ieee
```

Frame Relay Transparent Bridging Examples

Figure 1-11 illustrates three bridges connected to each other through a Frame Relay network.

Figure 1-11 *Frame Relay Bridging Example*

Bridging in a Frame Relay Network with No Multicasts

The Frame Relay bridging software uses the same spanning-tree algorithm as the other bridging functions, but allows packets to be encapsulated for transmission across a Frame Relay network. The command specifies IP-to-DLCI address mapping and maintains a table of both the Ethernet and DLCIs. Following are the configuration commands for each of the bridges in a network that does not support a multicast facility.

Configuration for Bridge 1

```
interface ethernet 2
 bridge-group 5
 ip address 128.88.11.9 255.255.255.0
!
interface serial 0
 encapsulation frame-relay
 bridge-group 5
 frame-relay map bridge 134 broadcast
 frame-relay map bridge 565 broadcast
!
bridge 5 protocol ieee
```

Configuration for Bridge 2

```
interface serial 1
 encapsulation frame-relay
 bridge-group 5
 frame-relay map bridge 27 broadcast
 frame-relay map bridge 565 broadcast
!
bridge 5 protocol ieee
```

Configuration for Bridge 3

```
interface serial 0
 encapsulation frame-relay
 bridge-group 5
 frame-relay map bridge 27 broadcast
 frame-relay map bridge 134 broadcast
!
bridge 5 protocol ieee
```

Bridging in a Frame Relay Network with Multicasts

The multicast facility is used to learn about the other bridges on the network, eliminating the need for the **frame-relay map** commands.

Following are the configuration commands for each of the bridges in a network that supports a multicast facility.

Configuration for Bridge 1

```
interface ethernet 2
 bridge-group 5
 ip address 128.88.11.9 255.255.255.0
!
interface serial 0
 encapsulation frame-relay
 bridge-group 5
!
bridge 5 protocol ieee
```

Configuration for Bridge 2

```
interface serial 1
 encapsulation frame-relay
 bridge-group 5
!
bridge 5 protocol ieee
```

Configuration for Bridge 3

```
interface serial 0
 encapsulation frame-relay
 bridge-group 5
!
bridge 5 protocol ieee
```

Transparent Bridging over Multiprotocol LAPB Example

The following example illustrates a router configured for transparent bridging over multiprotocol LAPB encapsulation:

```
!
no ip routing
!
interface ethernet 1
 no ip address
 no mop enabled
 bridge-group 1
!
interface serial 0
 no ip address
 encapsulation lapb multi
 bridge-group 1
!
 bridge 1 protocol ieee
```

Fast-Switched Transparent Bridging over ATM Example (Cisco 7000)

The following configuration example enables fast-switched transparent bridging over ATM:

```
interface atm 4/0
 ip address 1.1.1.1 255.0.0.0
 atm pvc 1 1 1 aal5snap
 atm pvc 2 2 2 aal5snap
 atm pvc 3 3 3 aal5snap
 bridge-group 1
!
bridge 1 protocol dec
```

Transparent Bridging over DDR Examples

The following two examples differ only in the packets that cause calls to be placed. The first example specifies by protocol (any bridge packet is permitted to cause a call to be made); the second example allows a finer granularity by specifying the Ethernet type codes of bridge packets.

The first example configures the serial 1 interface for DDR bridging. Any bridge packet is permitted to cause a call to be placed.

```
no ip routing
!
interface Serial1
 no ip address
 encapsulation ppp
 dialer in-band
 dialer enable-timeout 3
 dialer map bridge name urk broadcast 8985
```

```
 dialer hold-queue 10
 dialer-group 1
 ppp authentication chap
 bridge-group 1
 pulse-time 1
!
dialer-list 1 protocol bridge permit
bridge 1 protocol ieee
bridge 1 hello 10
```

The second example also configures the serial 1 interface for DDR bridging. However, this example includes an **access-list** command that specifies the Ethernet type codes that may cause calls to be placed and a **dialer list protocol list** command that refers to the specified access list.

```
no ip routing
!
interface Serial1
 no ip address
 encapsulation ppp
 dialer in-band
 dialer enable-timeout 3
 dialer map bridge name urk broadcast 8985
 dialer hold-queue 10
 dialer-group 1
 ppp authentication chap
 bridge-group 1
 pulse-time 1
!
access-list 200 permit 0x0800 0xFFF8
!
dialer-list 1 protocol bridge list 200
bridge 1 protocol ieee
bridge 1 hello 10
```

Fast-Switched Transparent Bridging over SMDS Example

The following configuration example enables fast-switched transparent bridging over SMDS:

```
interface serial 0
 encapsulation smds
 bridge group 1
 smds multicast bridge c141.5797.1313.ffff
```

Complex Transparent Bridging Network Topology Example

Figure 1-12 shows a network topology made up of four bridged subnetworks. Each bridged subnetwork is defined by the scope of a spanning tree. However, the scope of each spanning tree is not shown in detail because it is unnecessary for purposes of this discussion. Instead, it is shown by a half cloud labeled "To other parts of BSN."

Figure 1-12   *Bridged Subnetworks with Domains*

For proper bridging operation, the bridged subnetworks cannot have connections between them, but they can be connected to the same backbone. In Figure 1-12, three of the four bridged subnetworks are connected to the FDDI backbone and each belongs to a separate domain.

Domains used in this topology allow the bridged subnetworks to be independent of one another while still bridging traffic onto the backbone destined for other connected bridged subnetworks. Domains can be used in this manner only if the bridged subnetworks have a single point of attachment to one another. In this case, the connection to the FDDI backbone is that single point of attachment.

Each router on which a domain is configured and that has a single point of attachment to the other bridged subnetworks, checks whether a BPDU on the backbone is its own. If the BPDU does not belong to the bridged subnetwork, Cisco IOS software ignores the BPDU.

Separate bridged subnetworks, as in this example, allow spanning-tree reconfiguration of individual bridged subnetworks without disrupting bridging among the other bridged subnetworks.

To get spanning-tree information by bridge group, use the **show span** command. Included in this information is the root bridge of the spanning tree. The root bridge for each spanning tree can be any router in the spanning tree.

The routers in this network are configured for bridging and demonstrate some of the bridging features available.

Configuration for Router A

Router A demonstrates multiple bridge groups in one router for bridged traffic separation.

In Router A, the Token Ring interfaces are bridged together entirely independently of the other bridged interfaces in the router and belong to bridge group 1. Bridge group 1 does not use a bridge domain because the interfaces are bridged independently of other bridged subnetworks in the network topology and it has no connection to the FDDI backbone.

Also in Router A, the Ethernet interfaces belong to bridge group 3. Bridge group 3 has a connection to the FDDI backbone and has a domain defined for it so that it can ignore BPDUs for other bridged subnetworks.

```
interface ethernet 0
 bridge-group 3
!
interface ethernet 1
 bridge-group 3
!
interface ethernet 2
 bridge-group 3
!
interface ethernet 3
 bridge-group 3
!
interface fddi 0
 bridge-group 3
!
interface tokenring 1
 bridge-group 1
!
interface tokenring 2
 bridge-group 1
!
bridge 1 protocol ieee
bridge 3 domain 1
bridge 3 protocol ieee
```

Configuration for Router B

Router B demonstrates a simple bridge configuration. It is connected to the FDDI backbone and has domain 2 defined. As such, it can bridge traffic with the other FDDI-connected BSNs. Note that bridge group 1 has no relationship to bridge group 1 in Router A; bridge groups are an organization internal to each router.

```
interface ethernet 1
 bridge-group 1
!
interface ethernet 2
 bridge-group 1
!
interface fddi 0
 bridge-group 1
!
bridge 1 domain 2
bridge 1 protocol ieee
```

Configuration for Router C

Router C and Router D combine to demonstrate load balancing by means of circuit groups. Circuit groups are used to load balance across multiple parallel serial lines between a pair of routers. The router on each end of the serial lines must have a circuit group defined. The circuit group number can be the same or can be different. In this example, they are different.

Router C and Router D are configured with the same domain because they must understand one another's BPDUs. If they were configured with separate domains, Router D would ignore Router C's BPDUs (and vice versa).

```
interface fddi 0
 bridge-group 2
!
interface serial 0
 bridge-group 2
 bridge-group 2 circuit-group 7
!
interface serial 1
 bridge-group 2
 bridge-group 2 circuit-group 7
!
interface serial 2
 bridge-group 2
 bridge-group 2 circuit-group 7
!
bridge 2 domain 3
bridge 2 protocol ieee
```

Configuration for Router D

```
interface ethernet 4
 bridge-group 5
!
interface ethernet 5
 bridge-group 5
!
interface serial 0
 bridge-group 5
 bridge-group 5 circuit-group 4
!
interface serial 1
 bridge-group 5
 bridge-group 5 circuit-group 4
!
interface serial 2
 bridge-group 5
 bridge-group 5 circuit-group 4
!
bridge 5 domain 3
bridge 5 protocol ieee
```

Fast Ethernet Subscriber Port, Frame Relay Trunk Example

The following example uses the Fast Ethernet subinterface as the subscriber port and Frame Relay as the trunk:

```
bridge 1 protocol ieee

# Form a subscriber bridge group using policy 1
#
bridge 1 subscriber-policy 1
bridge 1 protocol ieee
interface fast0.1
encapsulation isl 1
#
# Put fast0.1 into subscriber group 1
#
bridge-group 1
interface fast0.2
encapsulation isl 2
#
# put fast0.2 into subscriber group 1
#
bridge-group 1
interface serial0
encapsulation frame-relay
int s0.1 point-to-point
#
# Use PVC 155 as the signal channel for setting up connections with the access-server
#
frame-relay interface-dlci 155
#
```

```
# Set the trunk to go upstream
#
bridge-group 1 trunk
```

ATM Subscriber Ports, ATM Trunk Example

The following example uses ATM subinterfaces as the subscriber ports and the ATM as the trunk:

```
bridge 1 protocol ieee
#
# Use subscriber policy 3
#
bridge 1 subscriber-policy 3
#
# Change the ARP behavior from permit to deny
#
subscriber-policy 3 arp deny
#
# Change the multicast from permit to deny
#
subscriber-policy 3 multicast deny

int atm0
int atm0.1 point-to-point
#
# Use AAL5 SNAP encapsulation
#
atm pvc 1 0 101 aal5snap
bridge group 1
int atm0.2
#
# Use AAL5 SNAP encapsulation
#
atm pvc 2 0 102 aal5snap
bridge-group 1

#
# Configure ATM trunk port
#
int atm1.1
#
# Use AAL5 SNAP encapsulation
#
atm pvc 1 0 101 aal5snap
#
# Specify trunk
#
bridge-group 1 trunk
```

Transparent Bridging Commands

Use the commands in this chapter to configure and monitor transparent bridging networks. For transparent bridging configuration information and examples, refer to Chapter 1, "Configuring Transparent Bridging."

access-list (extended)

Use the **access-list** global configuration command to provide extended access lists that allow more detailed access lists. These lists allow you to specify both source and destination addresses and arbitrary bytes in the packet.

> **access-list** *access-list-number* {**permit** | **deny**} *source source-mask destination destination-mask offset size operator operand*

Syntax	Description
access-list-number	Integer from 1100 to 1199 that you assign to identify one or more **permit/deny** conditions as an extended access list. Note that a list number in the range 1100 to 1199 distinguishes an extended access list from other access lists.
permit	Allows a connection when a packet matches an access condition. Cisco IOS software stops checking the extended access list after a match occurs. All conditions must be met to make a match.
deny	Disallows a connection when a packet matches an access condition. The software stops checking the extended access list after a match occurs. All conditions must be met to make a match.
source	Media Access Control (MAC) Ethernet address in the form *xxxx.xxxx.xxxx*.
source-mask	Mask of MAC Ethernet source address bits to be ignored. The software uses the *source* and *source-mask* arguments to match the source address of a packet.
destination	MAC Ethernet value used for matching the destination address of a packet.
destination-mask	Mask of MAC Ethernet destination address bits to be ignored. The software uses the *destination* and *destination mask* arguments to match the destination address of a packet.

Syntax	Description
offset	Range of values that must be satisfied in the access list. Specified in decimal or in hexadecimal format in the form 0x*nn*. The offset is the number of bytes from the destination address field; it is not an offset from the start of the packet. The number of bytes you need to offset from the destination address varies depending on the media encapsulation type you are using.
size	Range of values that must be satisfied in the access list. Must be an integer 1 to 4.
operator	Compares arbitrary bytes within the packet. Can be one of the following keywords: **lt**—less than **gt**—greater than **eq**—equal **neq**—not equal **and**—bitwise and **xor**—bitwise exclusive or **nop**—address match only
operand	Compares arbitrary bytes within the packet. The value to be compared to or masked against.

Default

No extended access lists are established.

Command Mode

Global configuration

Usage Guidelines

This command first appeared in Cisco IOS Release 10.0.

After an access list is initially created, any subsequent additions (possibly entered from the terminal) are placed at the end of the list. In other words, you cannot selectively add or remove access list command lines from a specific access list.

An extended access list should not be used on FDDI interfaces that provide transit bridging.

NOTE	Due to their complexity, extended access lists should only be used by those who are very familiar with Cisco IOS software. For example, to use extended access lists, it is important to understand how different encapsulations on different media would generally require different offset values to access particular fields.

CAUTION	Do not specify offsets into a packet that are greater than the size of the packet.

Examples

The following example permits packets from MAC addresses 000c.1b*xx.xxxx* to any MAC address if the packet contains a value less than 0x55AA in the 2 bytes that begin 0x1e bytes into the packet:

```
interface ethernet 0
 bridge-group 3 output-pattern 1102
access-list 1102 permit 000c.1b00.0000 0000.00ff.ffff
0000.0000.0000 ffff.ffff.ffff 0x1e 2 lt 0x55aa
```

The following example permits an NOP operation:

```
interface ethernet 0
 bridge-group 3 output-pattern 1102
access-list 1101 permit 0000.0000.0000 ffff.ffff.ffff 0000.0000.0000 ffff.ffff.ffff
```

Related Commands

To locate documentation of related commands, you can search online at www.cisco.com.

access-list (standard)
access-list (type-code)
bridge-group output-pattern-list

access-list (standard)

Use the **access-list** global configuration command to establish MAC address access lists. Use the **no** form of this command to remove a single access-list entry.

> **access-list** *access-list-number* {**permit** | **deny**} *address mask*
> **no access-list** *access-list-number*

Syntax   Description

Syntax	Description
access-list-number	Integer from 700 to 799 that you select for the list.

Syntax	Description
permit	Permits the frame.
deny	Denies the frame.
address mask	48-bit MAC addresses written in dotted triplet form. The ones bits in the *mask* argument are the bits to be ignored in *address*.

Default

No MAC address access lists are established.

Command Mode

Global configuration

Usage Guidelines

This command first appeared in Cisco IOS Release 10.0.

Configuring bridging access lists of type 700 may cause a momentary interruption of traffic flow.

Example

The following example assumes that you want to disallow the bridging of Ethernet packets of all Sun workstations on Ethernet interface 1. Software assumes that all such hosts have Ethernet addresses with the vendor code 0800.2000.0000. The first line of the access list denies access to all Sun workstations, while the second line permits everything else. You then assign the access list to the input side of Ethernet interface 1.

```
access-list 700 deny 0800.2000.0000 0000.00FF.FFFF
access-list 700 permit 0000.0000.0000 FFFF.FFFF.FFFF
interface ethernet 1
 bridge-group 1 input-address-list 700
```

Related Commands

To locate documentation of related commands, you can search online at www.cisco.com.

access-list (extended)
access-list (type-code)

access-list (type-code)

Use the **access-list** global configuration command to build type-code access lists. Use the **no** form of this command to remove a single access list entry.

> **access-list** *access-list-number* {**permit** | **deny**} *type-code wild-mask*
> **no access-list** *access-list-number*

Syntax	Description
access-list-number	User-selectable number between 200 and 299 that identifies the list.
permit	Permits the frame.
deny	Denies the frame.
type-code	16-bit hexadecimal number written with a leading "0x"; for example, 0x6000. You can specify either an Ethernet type code for Ethernet-encapsulated packets, or a DSAP/SSAP pair for 802.3 or 802.5-encapsulated packets. Ethernet type codes are listed in Appendix A, "Ethernet Type Codes."
wild-mask	16-bit hexadecimal number whose ones bits correspond to bits in the *type-code* argument that should be ignored when making a comparison. (A mask for a DSAP/SSAP pair should always be at least 0x0101. This is because these two bits are used for purposes other than identifying the SAP codes.)

Default

No type-code access lists are built.

Command Mode

Global configuration

Usage Guidelines

This command first appeared in Cisco IOS Release 10.0.

Type-code access lists can have an impact on system performance; therefore, keep the lists as short as possible and use wildcard bit masks whenever possible.

Access lists are evaluated according to the following algorithm:

- If the packet is Ethernet Type II or SNAP, the type-code field is used.
- If the packet is another type, then the LSAP is used.

If the length/type field is greater than 1500, the packet is treated as an LSAP packet unless the DSAP and SSAP fields are AAAA. If the latter is true, the packet is treated using type-code filtering.

If the LSAP-code filtering is used, all SNAP and Ethernet Type II packets are bridged without obstruction. If type-code filtering is used, all LSAP packets are bridged without obstruction.

If you have both Ethernet Type II and LSAP packets on your network, you should set up access lists for both.

Examples

The following example permits only LAT frames (type 0x6004) and filters out all other frame types:

```
access-list 201 permit 0x6004 0x0000
```

The following example filters out only type codes assigned to Digital (0x6000 to 0x600F) and lets all other types pass:

```
access-list 202 deny 0x6000 0x600F
access-list 202 permit 0x0000 0xFFFF
```

Use the last item of an access list to specify a default action; for example, permit everything else or deny everything else. If nothing else in the access list matches, the default action is normally to deny access; that is, filter out all other type codes.

Related Commands

To locate documentation of related commands, you can search online at www.cisco.com.

access-list (extended)
access-list (standard)

bridge acquire

Use the **bridge acquire** global configuration command to forward any frames for stations that the system has learned about dynamically. Use the **no** form of this command to disable the behavior.

>**bridge** *bridge-group* **acquire**
>**no bridge** *bridge-group* **acquire**

Syntax	Description
bridge-group	Bridge group number specified in the **bridge protocol** command.

Default
Enabled

Command Mode
Global configuration

Usage Guidelines
This command first appeared in Cisco IOS Release 10.0.

When using the command default, Cisco IOS software forwards any frames from stations that it has learned about dynamically. If you use the **no** form of this command, the bridge stops forwarding frames to stations it has dynamically learned about through the discovery process and limits frame forwarding to statically configured stations. That is, the bridge filters out all frames except those whose sourced-by or destined-to addresses have been statically configured into the forwarding cache. The **no** form of this command prevents the forwarding of a dynamically learned address.

Example
The following example prevents the forwarding of dynamically determined source and destination addresses:

```
no bridge 1 acquire
```

Related Commands
To locate documentation of related commands, you can search online at www.cisco.com.

bridge address
bridge protocol

bridge address

Use the **bridge address** global configuration command to filter frames with a particular MAC-layer station source or destination address. Use the **no** form of this command to disable the forwarding ability.

> **bridge** *bridge-group* **address** *mac-address* {**forward** | **discard**} [*interface*]
> **no bridge** *bridge-group* **address** *mac-address*

Syntax	Description
bridge-group	Bridge group number. It must be the same number specified in the **bridge protocol** command.

Syntax	Description
mac-address	48-bit dotted-triplet hardware address such as that displayed by the EXEC **show arp** command, for example, 0800.cb00.45e9. It is either a station address, the broadcast address, or a multicast destination address.
forward	Frame sent from or destined to the specified address is forwarded as appropriate.
discard	Frame sent from or destined to the specified address is discarded without further processing.
interface	(Optional) Interface specification, such as Ethernet 0. It is added after the **forward** or **discard** keyword to indicate the interface on which that address can be reached.

Default
Disabled

Command Mode
Global configuration

Usage Guidelines
This command first appeared in Cisco IOS Release 10.0.

Any number of addresses can be configured into the system without a performance penalty.

NOTE   MAC addresses on Ethernets are "bit swapped" when compared with MAC addresses on Token Ring and FDDI. For example, address 0110.2222.3333 on Ethernet is 8008.4444.CCCC on Token Ring and FDDI. Access lists always use the canonical Ethernet representation. When using different media and building access lists to filter on MAC addresses, keep this point in mind. Note that when a bridged packet traverses a serial link, it has an Ethernet-style address.

Examples
The following example enables frame filtering with MAC address 0800.cb00.45e9. The frame is forwarded through Ethernet interface 1:

```
bridge 1 address 0800.cb00.45e9 forward ethernet 1
```

The following example disables the ability to forward frames with MAC address 0800.cb00.45e9:

```
no bridge 1 address 0800.cb00.45e9
```

Related Commands

To locate documentation of related commands, you can search online at www.cisco.com.

bridge acquire
bridge-group input-address-list
bridge-group output-address-list
bridge protocol

bridge bridge

Use the **bridge bridge** global configuration command to enable the bridging of a specified protocol in a specified bridge group. Use the **no** form of this command to disable the bridging of a specified protocol in a specified bridge group.

> **bridge** *bridge-group* **bridge** *protocol*
> **no bridge** *bridge-group* **bridge** *protocol*

Syntax / Description

Syntax	Description
bridge-group	Bridge-group number. It must be the same number specified in the **bridge protocol** command.
protocol	Any of the supported routing protocols. The default is to bridge all these protocols.

Default

Bridge every protocol.

Command Mode

Global configuration

Usage Guidelines

This command first appeared in Cisco IOS Release 11.2.

When IRB is enabled, the default route/bridge behavior in a bridge group is to bridge all protocols. You do not have to use the **bridge bridge** command to enable bridging.

You can use the **no bridge bridge** command to disable bridging in a bridge group so that it does not bridge a particular protocol. When you disable bridging for a protocol in a bridge group, routable packets of this protocol are routed when the bridge is explicitly configured to route this protocol, and nonroutable packets are dropped because bridging is disabled for this protocol.

NOTE   Packets of nonroutable protocols such as LAT are only bridged. You cannot disable bridging for the nonroutable traffic.

Example

The following example disables bridging of IP in bridge group 1:

```
no bridge 1 bridge ip
```

Related Commands

To locate documentation of related commands, you can search online at www.cisco.com.

bridge irb
bridge protocol
bridge route

bridge circuit-group pause

Use the **bridge circuit-group pause** global configuration command to configure the interval during which transmission is suspended in a circuit group after circuit group changes take place.

bridge *bridge-group* **circuit-group** *circuit-group* **pause** *milliseconds*

Syntax   Description

Syntax	Description
bridge-group	Bridge group number specified in the **bridge protocol** command.
circuit-group	Number of the circuit group to which the interface belongs.
milliseconds	Forward delay interval. It must be a value in the range 0 to 10,000 ms.

Default

0 ms pause

Command Mode

Global configuration

Usage Guidelines

This command first appeared in Cisco IOS Release 10.3.

Circuit-group changes include the addition or deletion of an interface and interface state changes.

Example

The following example sets the circuit group pause to 5000 ms:

```
bridge 1 circuit-group 1 pause 5000
```

Related Commands

To locate documentation of related commands, you can search online at www.cisco.com.

bridge circuit-group source-based
bridge-group circuit-group
bridge protocol
show bridge circuit-group

bridge circuit-group source-based

Use the **bridge circuit-group source-based** global configuration command to use just the source MAC address for selecting the output interface. Use the **no** form of this command to remove the interface from the bridge group.

> **bridge** *bridge-group* **circuit-group** *circuit-group* **source-based**
> **no bridge** *bridge-group* **circuit-group** *circuit-group* **source-based**

Syntax	Description
bridge-group	Bridge group number specified in the **bridge protocol** command.
circuit-group	Number of the circuit group to which the interface belongs.

Default

No bridge-group interface is assigned.

Command Mode

Global configuration

Usage Guidelines

This command first appeared in Cisco IOS Release 10.3.

For applications that depend on the ordering of mixed unicast and multicast traffic from a given source, load distribution must be based on the source MAC address only. The **bridge circuit-group source-based** command modifies the load distribution strategy to accommodate such applications.

Example

The following example uses the source MAC address for selecting the output interface to a bridge group:

```
bridge 1 circuit-group 1 source-based
```

Related Commands

To locate documentation of related commands, you can search online at www.cisco.com.

bridge circuit-group pause
bridge-group circuit-group
bridge protocol
show bridge circuit-group

bridge cmf

Use the **bridge cmf** global configuration command to enable constrained multicast flooding (CMF) for all configured bridge groups. Use the **no** form of this command to disable constrained multicast flooding.

> **bridge cmf**
> **no bridge cmf**

Syntax Description

This command has no arguments or keywords.

Default

CMF is disabled.

Command Mode

Global configuration

Usage Guidelines

This command first appeared in Cisco IOS Release 11.2.

Example

The following example enables constrained multicast flooding for all configured bridge groups:

```
bridge cmf
```

Related Commands

To locate documentation of related commands, you can search online at www.cisco.com.

clear bridge multicast
show bridge multicast

bridge crb

Use the **bridge crb** global configuration command to enable Cisco IOS software to both route and bridge a given protocol on separate interfaces within a single router. Use the **no** form of this command to disable the feature.

> **bridge crb**
> **no bridge crb**

Syntax Description

This command has no arguments or keywords.

Defaults

Concurrent routing and bridging is disabled.

When concurrent routing and bridging has been enabled, the default behavior is to bridge all protocols that are not explicitly routed in a bridge group.

Command Mode

Global configuration

Usage Guidelines

This command first appeared in Cisco IOS Release 11.0.

When concurrent routing and bridging is first enabled in the presence of existing bridge groups, it generates a **bridge route** configuration command for any protocol for which any interface in the bridge group is configured for routing. This is a precaution that applies only when concurrent routing and bridging is not already enabled, bridge groups exist, and the **bridge crb** command is encountered.

Once concurrent routing and bridging has been enabled, you must configure an explicit **bridge route** command for any protocol that is to be routed on interfaces in a bridge group (in addition to any required protocol-specific interface configuration).

Example

The following command enables concurrent routing and bridging:

```
bridge crb
```

Related Commands

To locate documentation of related commands, you can search online at www.cisco.com.

bridge route

bridge domain

Use the **bridge domain** global configuration command to establish a domain by assigning it a decimal value between 1 and 10. Use the **no** form of this command to return it to a single bridge domain by choosing domain zero (0).

> **bridge** *bridge-group* **domain** *domain-number*
> **no bridge** *bridge-group* **domain**

Syntax	Description
bridge-group	Bridge group number specified in the **bridge protocol ieee** command. The **dec** keyword is not valid for this command.
domain-number	Domain ID number you choose. The default domain number is zero; this is the domain number required when communicating to IEEE bridges that do not support this domain extension.

Default

Single bridge domain

Command Mode

Global configuration

Usage Guidelines

This command first appeared in Cisco IOS Release 10.0.

Cisco has implemented a proprietary extension to the IEEE spanning-tree software in order to support multiple spanning-tree domains. You can place any number of routers within the domain. The routers in the domain, and only those routers, will then share spanning-tree information.

Use this feature when multiple routers share the same cable, and you wish to use only certain discrete subsets of these routers to share spanning-tree information with each other. This function is most useful when running other applications, such as IP UDP flooding, that use the IEEE Spanning-Tree Protocol. It can also be used to reduce the number of global reconfigurations in large bridged networks.

CAUTION	Use multiple spanning-tree domains with care. Because bridges in different domains do not share spanning-tree information, bridge loops can be created if the domains are not carefully planned.

NOTE	This command works only when the bridge group is running the IEEE Spanning-Tree Protocol.

Example

The following example places bridge group 1 in bridging domain 3. Only other routers that are in domain 3 will accept spanning-tree information from this router:

```
bridge 1 domain 3
```

Related Commands

To locate documentation of related commands, you can search online at www.cisco.com.

bridge protocol

bridge forward-time

Use the **bridge forward-time** global configuration command to specify the forward delay interval for Cisco IOS software. Use the **no** form of this command to return the default interval.

> **bridge** *bridge-group* **forward-time** *seconds*
> **no bridge** *bridge-group* **forward-time** *seconds*

Syntax | Description

Syntax	Description
bridge-group	Bridge group number specified in the **bridge protocol** command.
seconds	Forward delay interval. It must be a value in the range 10 to 200 seconds.

Default

30-second delay

Command Mode

Global configuration

Usage Guidelines

This command first appeared in Cisco IOS Release 10.0.

The forward delay interval is the amount of time the software spends listening for topology change information after an interface has been activated for bridging and before forwarding actually begins.

Each bridge in a spanning tree adopts the **hello-time**, **forward-time**, and **max-age** parameters of the root bridge, regardless of what its individual configuration might be.

Example

The following example sets the forward delay interval to 60 seconds:

```
bridge 1 forward-time 60
```

Related Commands

To locate documentation of related commands, you can search online at www.cisco.com.

bridge-group subscriber-trunk
bridge max-age
bridge protocol

bridge-group

Use the **bridge-group** interface configuration command to assign each network interface to a bridge group. Use the **no** form of this command to remove the interface from the bridge group.

> **bridge-group** *bridge-group*
> **no bridge-group** *bridge-group*

Syntax

Syntax	Description
bridge-group	Number of the bridge group to which the interface belongs. It must be a number in the range 1 to 63.

Default

No bridge group interface is assigned.

Command Mode

Interface configuration

Usage Guidelines

This command first appeared in Cisco IOS Release 10.0.

You can bridge on any interface, including any serial interface, regardless of encapsulation. Bridging can be configured between interfaces on different cards, although the performance is lower compared with interfaces on the same card. Also note that serial interfaces must be running with HDLC, X.25, or Frame Relay encapsulation.

NOTE   Several modifications to interfaces in bridge groups, including adding interfaces to bridge groups, will result in any Token Ring or FDDI interfaces in that bridge group being reinitialized.

Example

In the following example, Ethernet interface 0 is assigned to bridge-group 1 and bridging is enabled on this interface:

```
interface ethernet 0
 bridge-group 1
```

Related Commands

To locate documentation of related commands, you can search online at www.cisco.com.

bridge-group cbus-bridging
bridge-group circuit-group
bridge-group input-pattern-list
bridge-group output-pattern-list
bridge-group spanning-disabled

bridge-group aging-time

Use the **bridge-group aging-time** global configuration command to set the length of time that a dynamic entry can remain in the bridge table from the time the entry was created or last updated. Use the **no** form of this command to return to the default aging-time interval.

> **bridge-group** *bridge-group* **aging-time** *seconds*
> **no bridge-group** *bridge-group* **aging-time**

Syntax   Description

Syntax	Description
bridge-group	Number of the bridge group to which the interface belongs. It must be a number in the range 1 to 63.
seconds	Aging time, in the range 0 to 1,000,000 seconds. The default is 300 seconds.

Default

300 seconds

Command Mode

Global configuration

Usage Guidelines

This command first appeared in Cisco IOS Release 10.3.

If hosts on a bridged network are likely to move, decrease the aging-time to enable the bridge to adapt quickly to the change. If hosts do not transmit continuously, increase the aging time to record the dynamic entries for a longer time and thus reduce the possibility of flooding when the hosts transmit again.

Example

The following example sets the aging time to 200 seconds:

```
bridge-group 1 aging-time 200
```

Related Commands

To locate documentation of related commands, you can search online at www.cisco.com.

bridge-group

bridge-group cbus-bridging

Use the **bridge-group cbus-bridging** interface configuration command to enable autonomous bridging on a ciscoBus2 controller. Use the **no** form of this command to disable autonomous bridging.

> **bridge-group** *bridge-group* **cbus-bridging**
> **no bridge-group** *bridge-group* **cbus-bridging**

Syntax	Description
bridge-group	Number of the bridge group to which the interface belongs. It must be a number in the range 1 to 63.

Default

Autonomous bridging is disabled.

Command Mode

Interface configuration

Usage Guidelines

This command first appeared in Cisco IOS Release 10.0.

Normally, bridging takes place on the processor card at interrupt level. When autonomous bridging is enabled, bridging takes place entirely on the ciscoBus2 controller, significantly improving performance.

You can enable autonomous bridging on Ethernet, FDDI (FCIT) and HSSI interfaces that reside on a ciscoBus2 controller. Autonomous bridging is not supported on Token Ring interfaces, regardless of the type of bus in use.

To enable autonomous bridging on an interface, that interface must first be defined as part of a bridge group. When a bridge group includes both autonomously and normally bridged interfaces, packets are autonomously bridged in some cases, but bridged normally in others. For example, when packets are forwarded between two autonomously bridged interfaces, those packets are autonomously bridged. But, when packets are forwarded between an autonomously bridged interface and one that is not, the packet must be normally bridged. When a packet is flooded, the packet is autonomously bridged on autonomously bridged interfaces, but must be normally bridged on any others.

NOTE	In order to maximize performance when using a ciscoBus2 controller, use the **bridge-group cbus-bridging** command to enable autonomous bridging on any Ethernet, FDDI, or HSSI interface.

NOTE	You can only filter by MAC-level address on an interface when autonomous bridging is enabled on that interface; autonomous bridging disables all other filtering, as well as priority queuing.

Example

In the following example, autonomous bridging is enabled on Ethernet interface 0:

```
interface ethernet 0
 bridge-group 1
 bridge-group 1 cbus-bridging
```

Related Commands

To locate documentation of related commands, you can search online at www.cisco.com.

bridge-group

bridge-group circuit-group

Use the **bridge-group circuit-group** interface configuration command to assign each network interface to a bridge group. Use the **no** form of this command to remove the interface from the bridge group.

bridge-group *bridge-group* **circuit-group** *circuit-group*
no bridge-group *bridge-group* **circuit-group** *circuit-group*

Syntax   Description

bridge-group   Number of the bridge group to which the interface belongs. It must be a number in the range 1 to 63.

Syntax	Description
circuit-group	Circuit group number. The range is 1 to 9.

Default

No bridge group interface is assigned.

Command Mode

Interface configuration

Usage Guidelines

This command first appeared in Cisco IOS Release 10.3.

Circuit groups are primarily intended for use with HDLC-encapsulated serial interfaces. They are not supported for packet-switched networks such as X.25 or Frame Relay. Circuit groups are best applied to groups of serial lines of equal bandwidth, but can accommodate mixed bandwidths as well.

NOTE   You must configure bridging before you configure a circuit group on an interface.

Example

In the following example, Ethernet interface 0 is assigned to circuit group 1 of bridge group 1:

```
interface ethernet 0
 bridge-group 1 circuit-group 1
```

Related Commands

To locate documentation of related commands, you can search online at www.cisco.com.

bridge circuit-group pause
bridge circuit-group source-based
show bridge circuit-group

bridge-group input-address-list

Use the **bridge-group input-address-list** interface configuration command to assign an access list to a particular interface. This access list is used to filter packets received on that interface based on their MAC source addresses. Use the **no** form of this command to remove an access list from an interface.

bridge-group *bridge-group* **input-address-list** *access-list-number*
no bridge-group *bridge-group* **input-address-list** *access-list-number*

Syntax	Description
bridge-group	Number of the bridge group to which the interface belongs. It must be a number in the range 1 to 63.
access-list-number	Access list number you assigned with the **access-list** command. It must be in the range 700 to 799.

Default

No access list is assigned.

Command Mode

Interface configuration

Usage Guidelines

This command first appeared in Cisco IOS Release 10.0.

Example

The following example assumes you want to disallow the bridging of Ethernet packets of all Sun workstations on Ethernet interface 1. Software assumes that all such hosts have Ethernet addresses with the vendor code 0800.2000.0000. The first line of the access list denies access to all Sun workstations, while the second line permits everything else. You then assign the access list to the input side of Ethernet interface 1.

```
access-list 700 deny 0800.2000.0000 0000.00FF.FFFF
access-list 700 permit 0000.0000.0000 FFFF.FFFF.FFFF
interface ethernet 1
 bridge-group 1 input-address-list 700
```

Related Commands

To locate documentation of related commands, you can search online at www.cisco.com.

access-list (extended)
access-list (standard)
bridge address
bridge-group output-address-list

bridge-group input-lat-service-deny

Use the **bridge-group input-lat-service-deny** interface configuration command to specify the group codes by which to deny access upon input. Use the **no** form of this command to remove this access condition.

> **bridge-group** *bridge-group* **input-lat-service-deny** *group-list*
> **no bridge-group** *bridge-group* **input-lat-service-deny** *group-list*

Syntax	Description
bridge-group	Number of the bridge group to which the interface belongs. It must be a number in the range 1 to 63.
group-list	List of LAT service groups. Single numbers and ranges are permitted. Specify a zero (0) to disable the LAT group code for the bridge group.

Default

No group codes are specified.

Command Mode

Interface configuration

Usage Guidelines

This command first appeared in Cisco IOS Release 10.0.

Autonomous bridging must be disabled to use this command.

This command prevents the system from bridging any LAT service advertisement that has any of the specified groups set.

Example

The following example causes any advertisements with groups 6, 8, and 14 through 20 to be dropped:

```
interface ethernet 0
 bridge-group 1 input-lat-service-deny 6 8 14-20
```

Related Commands

To locate documentation of related commands, you can search online at www.cisco.com.

bridge-group
bridge-group input-lat-service-permit
bridge-group output-lat-service-deny

bridge-group input-lat-service-permit

Use the **bridge-group input-lat-service-permit** interface configuration command to specify the group codes by which to permit access upon input. Use the **no** form of this command to remove this access condition.

> **bridge-group** *bridge-group* **input-lat-service-permit** *group-list*
> **no bridge-group** *bridge-group* **input-lat-service-permit** *group-list*

Syntax	Description
bridge-group	Number of the bridge group to which the interface belongs. It must be a number in the range 1 to 63.
group-list	LAT service groups. Single numbers and ranges are permitted. Specify a zero (0) to disable the LAT group code for the bridge group.

Default

No group codes are specified.

Command Mode

Interface configuration

Usage Guidelines

This command first appeared in Cisco IOS Release 10.0.

Autonomous bridging must be disabled to use this command.

This command causes the system to bridge only those service advertisements that match at least one group in the group list specified by the *group-list* argument.

If a message specifies group codes in both the deny and permit list, the message is not bridged.

Example

The following example bridges any advertisements from groups 1, 5, and 12 through 14:

```
interface ethernet 1
 bridge-group 1 input-lat-service-permit 1 5 12-14
```

Related Commands

To locate documentation of related commands, you can search online at www.cisco.com.

bridge-group input-lat-service-deny
bridge-group output-lat-service-permit

bridge-group input-lsap-list

Use the **bridge-group input-lsap-list** interface configuration command to filter IEEE 802.2-encapsulated packets on input. Use the **no** form of this command to disable this capability.

> **bridge-group** *bridge-group* **input-lsap-list** *access-list-number*
> **no bridge-group** *bridge-group* **input-lsap-list** *access-list-number*

Syntax	Description
bridge-group	Number of the bridge group to which the interface belongs. It must be a number in the range 1 to 63.
access-list-number	Access list number you assigned with the standard **access-list** command. Specify a zero (0) to disable the application of the access list on the bridge group.

Default

Disabled

Command Mode

Interface configuration

Usage Guidelines

This command first appeared in Cisco IOS Release 10.0.

Autonomous bridging must be disabled to use this command.

This access list is applied to all IEEE 802.2 frames received on that interface prior to the bridge-learning process. SNAP frames must also pass any applicable Ethernet type-code access list.

Example

The following example specifies access list 203 on Ethernet interface 1:

```
interface ethernet 1
 bridge-group 3 input-lsap-list 203
```

Related Commands

To locate documentation of related commands, you can search online at www.cisco.com.

access-list (extended)
access-list (standard)
bridge-group
bridge-group output-lsap-list

bridge-group input-pattern-list

Use the **bridge-group input-pattern-list** interface configuration command to associate an extended access list with a particular interface in a particular bridge group. Use the **no** form of this command to disable this capability.

> **bridge-group** *bridge-group* **input-pattern-list** *access-list-number*
> **no bridge-group** *bridge-group* **input-pattern-list** *access-list-number*

Syntax	Description
bridge-group	Number of the bridge group to which the interface belongs. It must be a number in the range 1 to 63.
access-list-number	Access list number you assigned using the standard **access-list** command. Specify a zero (0) to disable the application of the access list on the interface.

Default

Disabled

Command Mode

Interface configuration

Usage Guidelines

This command first appeared in Cisco IOS Release 10.0.

Autonomous bridging must be disabled to use this command.

Example

The following command applies access list 1 to bridge group 3 using the filter defined in group 1:

```
interface ethernet 0
 bridge-group 3 input-pattern-list 1
```

Related Commands

To locate documentation of related commands, you can search online at www.cisco.com.

access-list (extended)
access-list (standard)
bridge-group
bridge-group output-pattern-list

bridge-group input-type-list

Use the **bridge-group input-type-list** interface configuration command to filter Ethernet- and SNAP-encapsulated packets on input. Use the **no** form of this command to disable this capability.

> **bridge-group** *bridge-group* **input-type-list** *access-list-number*
> **no bridge-group** *bridge-group* **input-type-list** *access-list-number*

Syntax	Description
bridge-group	Number of the bridge group to which the interface belongs. It must be a number in the range 1 to 63.
access-list-number	Access list number you assigned with the standard **access-list** command. Specify a zero (0) to disable the application of the access list on the bridge group.

Default
Disabled

Command Mode
Interface configuration

Usage Guidelines
This command first appeared in Cisco IOS Release 10.0.

Autonomous bridging must be disabled to use this command.

For SNAP-encapsulated frames, the access list is applied against the 2-byte TYPE field given after the DSAP/SSAP/OUI fields in the frame.

This access list is applied to all Ethernet and SNAP frames received on that interface prior to the bridge learning process. SNAP frames must also pass any applicable IEEE 802 DSAP/SSAP access lists.

Example
The following example shows how to configure a Token Ring interface with an access list that allows only the LAT protocol to be bridged:

```
interface tokenring 0
 ip address 131.108.1.1 255.255.255.0
 bridge-group 1
 bridge-group 1 input-type-list 201
```

Related Commands
To locate documentation of related commands, you can search online at www.cisco.com.

access-list (extended)
access-list (standard)
bridge-group
bridge-group output-type-list

bridge-group lat-compression

Use the **bridge-group lat-compression** interface configuration command to reduce the amount of bandwidth that LAT traffic consumes on the serial interface by specifying a LAT-specific form of compression. Use the **no** form of this command to disable LAT compression on the bridge group.

bridge-group *bridge-group* **lat-compression**
no bridge-group *bridge-group* **lat-compression**

Syntax

Syntax	Description
bridge-group	Number of the bridge group to which the interface belongs. It must be a number in the range 1 to 63.

Default

Disabled

Command Mode

Interface configuration

Usage Guidelines

This command first appeared in Cisco IOS Release 10.0.

Autonomous bridging must be disabled to use this command.

Compression is applied to LAT frames being sent out the router through the interface in question.

LAT compression can be specified only for serial interfaces. For the most common LAT operations (user keystrokes and acknowledgment packets), LAT compression reduces LAT's bandwidth requirements by nearly a factor of two.

Example

The following example compresses LAT frames on the bridge assigned to group 1:

```
bridge-group 1 lat-compression
```

Related Commands

To locate documentation of related commands, you can search online at www.cisco.com.

bridge-group

bridge-group output-address-list

Use the **bridge-group output-address-list** interface configuration command to assign an access list to a particular interface for filtering the MAC destination addresses of packets that would ordinarily be forwarded out that interface. Use the **no** form of this command to remove an access list from an interface.

> **bridge-group** *bridge-group* **output-address-list** *access-list-number*
> **no bridge-group** *bridge-group* **output-address-list** *access-list-number*

Syntax | Description

Syntax	Description
bridge-group	Number of the bridge group to which the interface belongs. It must be a number in the range 1 to 63.
access-list-number	Access list number you assigned with the standard **access-list** command.

Default

No access list is assigned.

Command Mode

Interface configuration

Usage Guidelines

This command first appeared in Cisco IOS Release 10.0.

Example

The following example assigns access list 703 to Ethernet interface 3:

```
interface ethernet 3
 bridge-group 5 output-address-list 703
```

Related Commands

To locate documentation of related commands, you can search online at www.cisco.com.

access-list (extended)
access-list (standard)
bridge address

bridge-group
bridge-group input-address-list

bridge-group output-lat-service-deny

Use the **bridge-group output-lat-service-deny** interface configuration command to specify the group codes by which to deny access upon output. Use the **no** form of this command to cancel the specified group codes.

> **bridge-group** *bridge-group* **output-lat-service-deny** *group-list*
> **no bridge-group** *bridge-group* **output-lat-service-deny** *group-list*

Syntax | Description

Syntax	Description
bridge-group	Number of the bridge group to which the interface belongs. It must be a number in the range 1 to 63.
group-list	List of LAT groups. Single numbers and ranges are permitted.

Default

No group codes are assigned.

Command Mode

Interface configuration

Usage Guidelines

This command first appeared in Cisco IOS Release 10.0.

Autonomous bridging must be disabled to use this command.

This command causes the system to not bridge onto this output interface any service advertisements that contain groups matching any of those in the group list.

Example

The following example prevents bridging of LAT service announcements from groups 12 through 20:

```
interface ethernet 0
 bridge-group 1
 bridge-group 1 output-lat-service-deny 12-20
```

Related Commands

To locate documentation of related commands, you can search online at www.cisco.com.

access-list (extended)
access-list (standard)
bridge-group
bridge-group input-lat-service-deny
bridge-group output-lat-service-permit

bridge-group output-lat-service-permit

Use the **bridge-group output-lat-service-permit** interface configuration command to specify the group codes by which to permit access upon output. Use the **no** form of this command to cancel specified group codes.

> **bridge-group** *bridge-group* **output-lat-service-permit** *group-list* ·
> **no bridge-group** *bridge-group* **output-lat-service-permit** *group-list*

Syntax	Description
bridge-group	Number of the bridge group to which the interface belongs. It must be a number in the range 1 to 63.
group-list	LAT service advertisements.

Default

No group codes are specified.

Command Mode

Interface configuration

Usage Guidelines

This command first appeared in Cisco IOS Release 10.0.

Autonomous bridging must be disabled to use this command.

This command causes the system to bridge onto this output interface only those service advertisements that match at least one group in the specified group code list.

NOTE	If a message matches both a deny and a permit condition, it will not be bridged.

Example

The following example allows only LAT service announcements from groups 5, 12, and 20 on this bridge:

```
interface ethernet 0
 bridge-group 1 output-lat-service-permit 5 12 20
```

Related Commands

To locate documentation of related commands, you can search online at www.cisco.com.

bridge-group input-lat-service-permit
bridge-group output-lat-service-deny

bridge-group output-lsap-list

Use the **bridge-group output-lsap-list** interface configuration command to filter IEEE 802-encapsulated packets on output. Use the **no** form of this command to disable this capability.

> **bridge-group** *bridge-group* **output-lsap-list** *access-list-number*
> **no bridge-group** *bridge-group* **output-lsap-list** *access-list-number*

Syntax	Description
bridge-group	Number of the bridge group to which the interface belongs. It must be a number in the range 1 to 63.
access-list-number	Access list number you assigned with the standard **access-list** command. Specify a zero (0) to disable the application of the access list on the bridge group.

Default

Disabled

Command Mode

Interface configuration

Usage Guidelines

This command first appeared in Cisco IOS Release 10.0.

Autonomous bridging must be disabled to use this command.

SNAP frames must also pass any applicable Ethernet type-code access list. This access list is applied just before sending out a frame to an interface.

For performance reasons, specify both input and output type code filtering on the same interface.

Access lists for Ethernet- and IEEE 802-encapsulated packets affect only bridging functions. It is not possible to use such access lists to block frames with protocols that are being routed.

Packets bearing an 802.2 LSAP of 0xAAAA qualify for LSAP filtering since they are inherently in 802.3 format. However, because they also carry a Type field, they are matched against any Type filters. Therefore, if you use LSAP filters on an interface that may bear SNAP encapsulated packets you must explicitly permit 0xAAAA.

Example

The following example specifies access list 204 on Ethernet interface 0:

```
interface ethernet 0
 bridge-group 4 output-lsap-list 204
```

Related Commands

To locate documentation of related commands, you can search online at www.cisco.com.

access-list (extended)
access-list (standard)
bridge-group
bridge-group input-lsap-list

bridge-group output-pattern-list

Use the **bridge-group output-pattern-list** interface configuration command to associate an extended access list with a particular interface. Use the **no** form of this command to disable this capability.

> **bridge-group** *bridge-group* **output-pattern-list** *access-list-number*
> **no bridge-group** *bridge-group* **output-pattern-list** *access-list-number*

Syntax	Description
bridge-group	Number of the bridge group to which the interface belongs. It must be a number in the range 1 to 63.

Syntax	Description
access-list-number	Extended access list number you assigned using the extended **access-list** command. Specify a zero (0) to disable the application of the access list on the interface.

Default

Disabled

Command Mode

Interface configuration

Usage Guidelines

This command first appeared in Cisco IOS Release 10.0.

Autonomous bridging must be disabled to use this command.

Example

The following example filters all packets sent by bridge group 3 using the filter defined in access-list 1102:

```
interface ethernet 0
 bridge-group 3 output-pattern-list 1102
```

Related Commands

To locate documentation of related commands, you can search online at www.cisco.com.

access-list (extended)
bridge-group
bridge-group input-pattern-list

bridge-group output-type-list

Use the **bridge-group output-type-list** interface configuration command to filter Ethernet- and SNAP-encapsulated packets on output. Use the **no** form of this command to disable this capability.

> **bridge-group** *bridge-group* **output-type-list** *access-list-number*
> **no bridge-group** *bridge-group* **output-type-list** *access-list-number*

Syntax

Syntax	Description
bridge-group	Number of the bridge group to which the interface belongs. It must be a number in the range 1 to 63.
access-list-number	Access list number you assigned with the standard **access-list** command. Specify a zero (0) to disable the application of the access list on the bridge group. This access list is applied just before sending out a frame to an interface.

Default

Disabled

Command Mode

Interface configuration

Usage Guidelines

This command first appeared in Cisco IOS Release 10.0.

Autonomous bridging must be disabled to use this command.

Example

The following example specifies access-list 202 on Ethernet interface 0:

```
interface ethernet 0
 bridge-group 2 output-type-list 202
```

Related Commands

To locate documentation of related commands, you can search online at www.cisco.com.

access-list (extended)
access-list (standard)
bridge-group
bridge-group input-type-list

bridge-group path-cost

Use the **bridge-group path-cost** interface configuration command to set a different path cost. Use the **no** form of this command to choose the default path cost for the interface.

> **bridge-group** *bridge-group* **path-cost** *cost*
> **no bridge-group** *bridge-group* **path-cost** *cost*

Syntax   Description

bridge-group   Number of the bridge group to which the interface belongs. It must be a number in the range 1 to 63.

cost   Path cost can range from 1 to 65,535, with higher values indicating higher costs. This range applies regardless of whether the IEEE or Digital Spanning-Tree Protocol has been specified.

Defaults

The default path cost is computed from the interface's bandwidth setting. The following are IEEE default path cost values. The Digital path cost default values are different.

Ethernet—100
16-Mb Token Ring—62
FDDI—10
HSSI—647
MCI/SCI Serial—647

Command Mode

Interface configuration

Usage Guidelines

This command first appeared in Cisco IOS Release 10.0.

By convention, the path cost is 10,000/data rate of the attached LAN (IEEE), or 100,000/data rate of the attached LAN (Digital), in megabits per second.

Example

The following example changes the default path cost for Ethernet interface 0:

```
interface ethernet 0
 bridge-group 1 path-cost 250
```

Related Commands

To locate documentation of related commands, you can search online at www.cisco.com.

bridge-group

bridge-group priority

Use the **bridge-group priority** interface configuration command to set an interface priority.
The interface priority is used to select the designated port for this bridge-group on the connected media.
One designated port on each media is needed to compute the spanning tree.

bridge-group *bridge-group* **priority** *number*

Syntax   Description

Syntax	Description
bridge-group	Number of the bridge group to which the interface belongs. It must be a number in the range 1 to 63.
number	Priority number ranging from 0 to 255 (Digital), or 0 to 64,000 (IEEE).

Defaults

When the IEEE Spanning-Tree Protocol is enabled on the router: 32,768

When the Digital Spanning-Tree Protocol is enabled on the router: 128

Command Mode

Interface configuration

Usage Guidelines

This command first appeared in Cisco IOS Release 10.0.

The lower the number, the more likely it is that the bridge on the interface will be chosen as the root.

Example

The following example increases the likelihood that the root bridge will be the one on Ethernet interface 0 in bridge group 1:

```
interface ethernet 0
 bridge-group 1 priority 0
```

Related Commands

To locate documentation of related commands, you can search online at www.cisco.com.

bridge-group
bridge priority

bridge-group spanning-disabled

Use the **bridge-group spanning-disabled** interface configuration command to disable the spanning tree on a given interface.

> **bridge-group** *bridge-group* **spanning-disabled**
> **no bridge-group** *bridge-group* **spanning-disabled**

Syntax   Description

bridge-group   Number of the bridge group to which the interface belongs. It must be a
                          number in the range 1 to 63.

Default

Spanning tree enabled

Command Mode

Interface configuration

Usage Guidelines

This command first appeared in Cisco IOS Release 10.0.

To enable transparent bridging on an interface, use the **bridge protocol** command to specify the type of Spanning-Tree Protocol to be used. The **bridge-group spanning-disabled** command can be used to disable that spanning tree on that interface.

When a *loop-free* path exists between any two bridged subnetworks, you can prevent BPDUs generated in one transparent bridging subnetwork from impacting nodes in the other transparent bridging subnetwork, yet still permit bridging throughout the bridged network as a whole.

For example, when transparently bridged LAN subnetworks are separated by a WAN, you can use this command to prevent BPDUs from traveling across the WAN link. You would apply this command to the serial interfaces connecting to the WAN in order to prevent BPDUs generated in one domain from impacting nodes in the remote domain. Because these BPDUs are prevented from traveling across the WAN link, using this command also has the secondary advantage of reducing traffic across the WAN link.

NOTE	In order to disable the spanning tree, you must make sure that no parallel paths exist between transparently bridged interfaces in the network.

Example

In the following example, the spanning tree for the serial interface 0 is disabled:

```
interface serial 0
 bridge-group 1 spanning-disabled
```

Related Commands

To locate documentation of related commands, you can search online at www.cisco.com.

bridge-group
bridge protocol

bridge-group sse

Use the **bridge-group sse** interface configuration command to enable the Cisco silicon switching engine (SSE) switching function. Use the **no** form of this command to disable SSE switching.

> **bridge-group** *bridge-group* **sse**
> **no bridge-group** *bridge-group* **sse**

Syntax   Description

bridge-group   Number of the bridge group to which the interface belongs. It must be a number in the range 1 to 63.

Default

Disabled

Command Mode

Interface configuration

Usage Guidelines

This command first appeared in Cisco IOS Release 10.3.

Example

The following example enables SSE switching:

```
bridge-group 1 sse
```

Related Commands

To locate documentation of related commands, you can search online at www.cisco.com.

source-bridge

bridge-group subscriber-trunk

To specify that an interface is at the upstream point of traffic flow, use the **bridge-group subscriber-trunk** interface configuration command. Use the **no** form of this command to remove the specification and reset the interface to a nontrunking port.

> **bridge-group** *bridge-group* **subscriber-trunk**
> **no bridge-group** *bridge-group* **subscriber-trunk**

Syntax	Description
bridge-group	Bridge group number, in the range from 1 to 256, specified in the **bridge protocol** command.

Default

The interface is set to a nontrunking port.

Command Mode

Interface configuration

Example

The following example sets bridge-group 1 as the upstream point of traffic flow:

```
bridge-group 1 subscriber-trunk
```

Related Commands

To locate documentation of related commands, you can search online at www.cisco.com.

bridge protocol
bridge subscriber-policy
show subscriber-policy
subscriber-policy

bridge hello-time

Use the **bridge hello-time** global configuration command to specify the interval between hello bridge protocol data units (BPDUs). Use the **no** form of this command to return the default interval.

> **bridge** *bridge-group* **hello-time** *seconds*
> **no bridge** *bridge-group* **hello-time**

Syntax	Description
bridge-group	Bridge group number. It must be the same number specified in the **bridge protocol** command.
seconds	Interval between 1 and 10 seconds.

Default

1 second

Command Mode

Global configuration

Usage Guidelines

This command first appeared in Cisco IOS Release 10.0.

Each bridge in a spanning tree adopts the **hello-time**, **forward-time**, and **max-age** parameters of the root bridge, regardless of what its individual configuration might be.

Example

The following example sets the interval to 5 seconds:

```
bridge 1 hello-time 5
```

Related Commands

To locate documentation of related commands, you can search online at www.cisco.com.

bridge forward-time
bridge max-age
bridge protocol

bridge irb

Use the **bridge irb** global configuration command to enable Cisco IOS software to route a given protocol between routed interfaces and bridge groups or to route a given protocol between bridge groups. Use the **no** form of this command to disable the feature.

> **bridge irb**
> **no bridge irb**

Syntax Description

This command has no arguments or keywords.

Default

Integrated routing and bridging (IRB) is disabled.

Command Mode

Global configuration

Usage Guidelines

This command first appeared in Cisco IOS Release 10.0.

IRB is supported for transparent bridging, but not for source-route bridging. IRB is supported on all interface media types except X.25 and ISDN bridged interfaces.

Example

The following example enables integrated routing and bridging:

```
bridge irb
```

Related Commands

To locate documentation of related commands, you can search online at www.cisco.com.

bridge bridge
bridge route
interface bvi
show interfaces irb

bridge lat-service-filtering

Use the **bridge lat-service-filtering** global configuration command to specify LAT group-code filtering. Use the **no** form of this command to disable the use of LAT service filtering on the bridge group.

> **bridge** *bridge-group* **lat-service-filtering**
> **no bridge** *bridge-group* **lat-service-filtering**

Syntax   Description

bridge-group   Bridge group number specified in the **bridge protocol** command.

Default

LAT service filtering is disabled.

Command Mode

Global configuration

Usage Guidelines

This command first appeared in Cisco IOS Release 10.0.

This command informs the system that LAT service advertisements require special processing.

Example

The following example specifies that LAT service announcements traveling across bridge group 1 require some special processing:

```
bridge 1 lat-service-filtering
```

Part
I

Command Reference

Related Commands

To locate documentation of related commands, you can search online at www.cisco.com.

bridge protocol

bridge max-age

Use the **bridge max-age** global configuration command to change the interval the bridge will wait to hear BPDUs from the root bridge. If a bridge does not hear BPDUs from the root bridge within this specified interval, it assumes that the network has changed and will recompute the spanning-tree topology. Use the **no** form of this command to return the default interval.

> **bridge** *bridge-group* **max-age** *seconds*
> **no bridge** *bridge-group* **max-age**

Syntax   Description

bridge-group   Bridge group number specified in the **bridge protocol** command.

seconds   Interval the bridge will wait to hear BPDUs from the root bridge. It must be a value in the range 10 to 200 seconds.

Default

15 seconds

Command Mode

Global configuration

Usage Guidelines

This command first appeared in Cisco IOS Release 10.0.

Each bridge in a spanning tree adopts the **hello-time**, **forward-time**, and **max-age** parameters of the root bridge, regardless of what its individual configuration might be.

Example

The following example increases the maximum idle interval to 20 seconds:

```
bridge 1 max-age 20
```

Related Commands

To locate documentation of related commands, you can search online at www.cisco.com.

bridge forward-time
bridge-group subscriber-trunk
bridge protocol

bridge multicast-source

Use the **bridge multicast-source** global configuration command to configure bridging support to allow the forwarding, but not the learning, of frames received with multicast source addresses. Use the **no** form of this command to disable this function on the bridge.

> **bridge** *bridge-group* **multicast-source**
> **no bridge** *bridge-group* **multicast-source**

Syntax

Syntax	Description
bridge-group	Bridge group number specified in the **bridge protocol** command.

Default

Disabled

Command Mode

Global configuration

Usage Guidelines

This command first appeared in Cisco IOS Release 10.0.

If you need to bridge Token Ring over another medium, RSRB is recommended.

Example

The following example allows the forwarding, but not the learning, of frames received with multicast source addresses:

```
bridge 2 multicast-source
```

Related Commands

To locate documentation of related commands, you can search online at www.cisco.com.

bridge protocol

bridge priority

Use the **bridge priority** global configuration command to configure the priority of an individual bridge, or the likelihood that it will be selected as the root bridge.

bridge *bridge-group* **priority** *number*

Syntax	Description
bridge-group	Bridge group number specified in the **bridge protocol** command.
number	The lower the number, the more likely the bridge will be chosen as root. When the IEEE Spanning-Tree Protocol is enabled, *number* ranges from 0 to 65,535 (default is 32,768). When the Digital Spanning-Tree Protocol is enabled, *number* ranges from 0 to 255 (default is 128).

Defaults

When the IEEE Spanning-Tree Protocol is enabled on the router: 32,768

When the Digital Spanning-Tree Protocol is enabled on the router: 128

Command Mode

Global configuration

Usage Guidelines

This command first appeared in Cisco IOS Release 10.0.

When two bridges tie for position as the root bridge, an interface priority determines which bridge will serve as the root bridge. Use the **bridge-group priority** interface configuration command to control an interface priority.

Example

The following example establishes this bridge as a likely candidate to be the root bridge:

```
bridge 1 priority 100
```

Related Commands

To locate documentation of related commands, you can search online at www.cisco.com.

bridge-group priority
bridge protocol

bridge protocol

Use the **bridge protocol** global configuration command to define the type of Spanning-Tree Protocol. Use the **no** form of this command with the appropriate keywords and arguments to delete the bridge group.

> **bridge** *bridge-group* **protocol** {**ieee** | **dec**}
> **no bridge** *bridge-group* **protocol** {**ieee** | **dec**}

Syntax

Syntax	Description
bridge-group	Number in the range 1 to 63 that you choose to refer to a particular set of bridged interfaces. Frames are bridged only among interfaces in the same group. You will use the group number you assign in subsequent bridge configuration commands.
ieee	IEEE Ethernet Spanning-Tree Protocol.
dec	Digital Spanning-Tree Protocol.

Default

No Spanning-Tree Protocol is defined.

Command Mode

Global configuration

Usage Guidelines

This command first appeared in Cisco IOS Release 10.0.

The routers support two Spanning-Tree Protocols: the IEEE 802.1 standard and the earlier Digital Spanning-Tree Protocol upon which the IEEE standard is based. Multiple domains are supported for the IEEE 802.1 Spanning-Tree Protocol.

NOTE	The IEEE 802.1D Spanning-Tree Protocol is the preferred way of running the bridge. Use the Digital Spanning-Tree Protocol only for backward compatibility.

Example

The following example shows bridge 1 as using the Digital Spanning-Tree Protocol:

```
bridge 1 protocol dec
```

Related Commands

To locate documentation of related commands, you can search online at www.cisco.com.

bridge domain
bridge-group

bridge route

Use the **bridge route** global configuration command to enable the routing of a specified protocol in a specified bridge group. Use the **no** form of this command to disable the routing of a specified protocol in a specified bridge group.

> **bridge** *bridge-group* **route** *protocol*
> **no bridge** *bridge-group* **route** *protocol*

Syntax

Syntax	Description
bridge-group	Bridge-group number. It must be the same number specified in the **bridge protocol** command.
protocol	One of the following protocols: **apollo**, **appletalk**, **clns**, **decnet**, **ip**, **ipx**, **vines**, **xns**.

Default

No default bridge group or protocol is specified.

Command Mode

Global configuration

Usage Guidelines

This command first appeared in Cisco IOS Release 10.3.

Example

In the following example, AppleTalk and IP are routed on bridge group 1:

```
bridge crb
bridge 1 protocol ieee
bridge 1 route appletalk
bridge 1 route ip
```

Related Commands

To locate documentation of related commands, you can search online at www.cisco.com.

bridge crb
bridge protocol

bridge subscriber-policy

To bind a bridge group with a subscriber policy, use the **bridge subscriber-policy** global configuration command. Use the **no** form of this command to disable the subscriber bridge group feature.

> **bridge** *bridge-group* **subscriber-policy** *policy*
> **no bridge** *bridge-group* **subscriber-policy** *policy*

Syntax	Description
bridge-group	Bridge group number, in the range of 1 to 256, specified in the **bridge protocol** command.
policy	Subscriber policy number in the range of 1 to 100.

Default

If no forward or filter decisions have been specified for the subscriber policy, the following defaults are applied:

Packet	Upstream
ARP	Permit
Broadcast	Deny
CDP	Deny/Disable

Packet	Upstream
Multicast	Permit
STP	Deny/Disable
Unknown Unicast	Deny

Command Mode
Global configuration

Usage Guidelines
Standard access lists can coexist with the subscriber policy. However, subscriber policy will take precedence over the access list by being checked first. A packet permitted by the subscriber policy will be checked against the access list if it is specified. A packet denied by subscriber policy will be dropped with no further access list checking.

Example
The following example forms a subscriber bridge group using policy 1:

```
bridge 1 subscriber-policy 1
```

Related Commands
To locate documentation of related commands, you can search online at www.cisco.com.

bridge protocol
show subscriber-policy
subscriber-policy

clear bridge
Use the **clear bridge** privileged EXEC command to remove any learned entries from the forwarding database and to clear the transmit and receive counts for any statically or system configured entries.

clear bridge *bridge-group*

Syntax   Description

bridge-group   Bridge group number specified in the **bridge protocol** command.

Command Mode
Privileged EXEC

Usage Guidelines
This command first appeared in Cisco IOS Release 10.0.

Example
The following example shows the use of the **clear bridge** command:

```
clear bridge 1
```

Related Commands
To locate documentation of related commands, you can search online at www.cisco.com.

bridge address
bridge protocol

clear bridge multicast

Use the **clear bridge multicast** EXEC command to clear transparent bridging multicast state information.

> **clear bridge** [*bridge-group*] **multicast** [**router-ports** | **groups** | **counts**]
> [*group-address*] [*interface-unit*] [**counts**]

Syntax	Description
bridge-group	(Optional) Bridge group number specified in the **bridge protocol** command.
router-ports	(Optional) Clears multicast router ports.
groups	(Optional) Clears multicast groups.
counts	(Optional) Clears RX and TX counts.
group-address	(Optional) Multicast IP address associated with a specific multicast group.
interface-unit	(Optional) Specific interface, such as Ethernet 0.

Command Mode
EXEC

Usage Guidelines

This command first appeared in Cisco IOS Release 11.2.

If you do not specify arguments or keywords as part of the command, the command clears router ports, group ports, and counts for all configured bridge groups.

Use the **show bridge multicast** command to list transparent bridging multicast state information, then use specific pieces of state information in the **clear bridge multicast** command.

Examples

The following example clears router ports, group ports, and counts for bridge group 1:

```
clear bridge 1 multicast
```

The following example clears the group and count information for the group identified as 235.145.145.223, interface Ethernet 0/3 for bridge group 1:

```
clear bridge 1 multicast groups 235.145.145.223 Ethernet0/3 counts
```

Related Commands

To locate documentation of related commands, you can search online at www.cisco.com.

bridge cmf
show bridge multicast

clear sse

Use the **clear sse** privileged EXEC command to reinitialize the Silicon Switch Processor (SSP) on the Cisco 7000 series routers with RSP7000.

clear sse

Syntax Description

This command has no arguments or keywords.

Command Mode

Privileged EXEC

Usage Guidelines

This command first appeared in Cisco IOS Release 10.3.

Example

The following example reinitializes the SSP:

```
clear sse
```

clear vlan statistics

Use the **clear vlan statistics** privileged EXEC command to remove virtual LAN statistics from any statically or system configured entries.

> **clear vlan statistics**

Syntax Description

This command has no arguments or keywords.

Command Mode

Privileged EXEC

Usage Guidelines

This command first appeared in Cisco IOS Release 11.2.

Example

The following example clears VLAN statistics:

```
clear vlan statistics
```

encapsulation isl

Use the **encapsulation isl** subinterface configuration command to enable the Inter-Switch Link (ISL), a Cisco proprietary protocol for interconnecting multiple switches and maintaining VLAN information as traffic goes between switches.

> **encapsulation isl** *domain*

Syntax	Description
domain	VLAN domain number.

Default

Disabled

Command Mode

Subinterface configuration

Usage Guidelines

This command first appeared in Cisco IOS Release 11.1.

ISL encapsulation adds a 30-byte header to the beginning of the Ethernet frame. The header contains a 2-byte VLAN identifier that maintains VLAN identities between switches.

Example

The following example enables ISL on FDDI subinterface 2/1.20:

```
interface FastEthernet 2/1.20.
 ip address 171.69.2.2 255.255.255.0
 encapsulation isl 400
 bridge-group 50
```

Related Commands

To locate documentation of related commands, you can search online at www.cisco.com.

bridge-group
show bridge vlan
show interfaces
show span

encapsulation sde

Use the **encapsulation sde** subinterface configuration command to enable IEEE 802.10 Secure Data Exchange (SDE) encapsulation of transparently bridged traffic on a specified interface within an assigned bridge group.

> **encapsulation sde** *said*

Syntax	Description
said	Security association identifier. The valid range is 0 through 0xFFF.

Default

Disabled

Command Mode

Subinterface configuration

Usage Guidelines

This command first appeared in Cisco IOS Release 10.3.

SDE encapsulation is only applicable to transparently bridged traffic and is configurable on the following interface types:

- Ethernet

- Nonencapsulated FDDI

- Token Ring (except MultiBus Token Ring)

- HDLC serial

NOTE   The current implementation of SDE encapsulation is not recommended for serial or Ethernet media.

Example

The following example enables SDE on FDDI subinterface 2/0.1 and assigns a security association identifier of 9999:

```
interface fddi 2/0.1
 encapsulation sde 9999
```

Related Commands

To locate documentation of related commands, you can search online at www.cisco.com.

bridge-group
show bridge vlan
show interfaces
show span

ethernet-transit-oui

Use the **ethernet-transit-oui** interface configuration command to choose the Organizational Unique Identifier (OUI) code to be used in the encapsulation of Ethernet Type II frames across Token Ring backbone networks. Various versions of this OUI code are used by Ethernet/Token Ring translational bridges. The default OUI form is **90-compatible**, which can be chosen with the **no** form of this command.

ethernet-transit-oui [90-compatible | standard | cisco]
no ethernet-transit-oui

Syntax	Description
90-compatible	(Optional) Default OUI form.
standard	(Optional) Standard OUI form.
cisco	(Optional) Cisco OUI form.

Default

90-compatible

Command Mode

Interface configuration

Usage Guidelines

This command first appeared in Cisco IOS Release 10.0.

This command replaces and extends the **bridge old-oui** command in Software Release 9.0.

The actual OUI codes that are used, when they are used, and how they compare to Software Release 9.0-equivalent commands is shown in Table 2-1.

Table 2-1 *Bridge OUI Codes*

Keyword	OUI Used	When Used/Benefits	9.0 Command Equivalent
90-compatible	0000F8	By default, when talking to other Cisco routers. Provides the most flexibility.	**no bridge old-oui**
cisco	00000C	Provided for compatibility with future equipment.	None

Continues

Table 2-1 *Bridge OUI Codes (Continued)*

Keyword	OUI Used	When Used/Benefits	9.0 Command Equivalent
standard	000000	When talking to IBM 8209 bridges and other vendor equipment. Does not provide for as much flexibility as the other two choices.	**bridge old-oui**

Do not use the keyword **standard** unless you are forced to interoperate with other vendor equipment, such as the IBM 8209, in providing Ethernet and Token Ring mixed media bridged connectivity. The use of the **standard** OUI of 000000 in the encapsulation of Ethernet Type II frames creates encapsulated frames on Token Rings that have formats identical to SNAP-encapsulated frames. The router receiving such a frame on a Token Ring for delivery on the Ethernet cannot distinguish between the two and, therefore, must make an arbitrary choice between presenting the frame on the Ethernet as a SNAP-encapsulated frame or as an Ethernet Type II frame. The choice has been made to present all such frames as Ethernet Type II. Therefore, it is impossible to use the **standard** keyword if you wish to bridge SNAP-encapsulated frames between Token Rings and Ethernets. Using either the **cisco** or **90-compatible** keywords does not present such a restriction because SNAP frames and Ethernet Type II-encapsulated frames have different OUI codes on Token Ring networks.

NOTE   Prior to Cisco IOS Software Release 11.1, the default OUI for SNAP on Token Ring for high-end routers was hexadecimal 000F8. and for low-end routers was hexadecimal 00000. If you combine Cisco IOS Software Release 11.1 or later with any earlier high-end release on adjacent routers that are bridging over a token ring, you must use the **ethernet-transit-oui standard** command to bring the two software versions into agreement.

Example

The following example specifies Cisco OUI form:

```
interface tokenring 0
 ethernet-transit-oui cisco
```

Related Commands

To locate documentation of related commands, you can search online at www.cisco.com.

bridge-group
bridge protocol

frame-relay map bridge broadcast

Use the **frame-relay map bridge broadcast** interface configuration command to bridge over a Frame Relay network. Use the **no** form of this command to delete the mapping entry.

frame-relay map bridge *dlci* **broadcast**
no frame-relay map bridge *dlci*

Syntax	Description
dlci	DLCI number. The valid range is 16 to 1007.

Default

No mapping entry is established.

Command Mode

Interface configuration

Usage Guidelines

This command first appeared in Cisco IOS Release 10.0.

Bridging over a Frame Relay network is supported both on networks that support a multicast facility and those that do not.

Example

The following example allows bridging over a Frame Relay network:

```
frame-relay map bridge 144 broadcast
```

Related Commands

To locate documentation of related commands, you can search online at www.cisco.com.

encapsulation frame-relay

interface bvi

Use the **interface bvi** interface configuration command to create the bridge-group virtual interface (BVI) that represents the specified bridge group to the routed world and links the corresponding bridge group to the other routed interfaces. Use the **no** form of this command to delete the BVI.

> **interface bvi** *bridge-group*
> **no interface bvi** *bridge-group*

Syntax

Description

bridge-group   Bridge-group number. It must be the same number specified in the **bridge protocol** command.

Default

No BVI is created.

Command Mode

Interface configuration

Usage Guidelines

This command first appeared in Cisco IOS Release 11.2.

You must enable IRB before attempting to create a BVI.

When you intend to bridge and route a given protocol in the same bridge group, you must configure the network-layer attributes of the protocol on the BVI. Do not configure protocol attributes on the bridged interfaces. No bridging attributes can be configured on the BVI.

Example

The following example creates a bridge-group virtual interface and associates it with bridge group 1:

```
interface bvi 1
```

Related Commands

To locate documentation of related commands, you can search online at www.cisco.com.

bridge irb

ip routing

Use the **ip routing** command to enable IP routing. Use the **no** form of this command to disable IP routing so that you can then bridge IP.

> **ip routing**
> **no ip routing**

Syntax Description

This command has no arguments or keywords.

Default

IP routing is enabled.

Command Mode

Global configuration

Usage Guidelines

This command first appeared in Cisco IOS Release 10.0.

All protocols except IP are bridged by a router unless their routing is explicitly enabled. IP is normally routed by the router.

Also, note that bridging and routing are done on a per-system basis. If a protocol is being routed, it must be routed on all interfaces that are handling that protocol. This is similar for bridging. You cannot route IP on one interface and bridge it on another interface.

Assign the same IP address to all network interfaces to manage the system with Telnet, TFTP, SNMP, ICMP (**ping**), and so forth. Once bridging is enabled, all IP and ARP frames are forwarded or flooded by the router according to standard bridging and spanning-tree rules. IP routing processes, such as IGRP or RIP, must not be running.

Example

The following example disables IP routing:

```
no ip routing
```

show bridge

Use the **show bridge** privileged EXEC command to view classes of entries in the bridge forwarding database.

show bridge [*bridge-group*] [*interface*] [*address* [*mask*]] [**verbose**]

Syntax	Description
bridge-group	(Optional) Number that specifies a particular spanning tree.
interface	(Optional) Specific interface, such as Ethernet 0.
address	(Optional) 48-bit canonical (Ethernet ordered) MAC address. This can be entered with an optional mask of bits to be ignored in the address, which is specified with the *mask* argument.
mask	(Optional) Bits to be ignored in the address. You must specify the *address* argument if you want to specify a mask.
verbose	(Optional) Shows additional detail, including any Frame Relay DLCI associated with a station address.

Command Mode

Privileged EXEC

Usage Guidelines

This command first appeared in Cisco IOS Release 10.0. The **verbose** keyword first appeared in Cisco IOS Release 11.0.

The following are possible variations of the **show bridge** command:

```
show bridge ethernet 0
show bridge 0000.0c00.0000   0000.00FF.FFFF
show bridge 0000.0c00.0e1a
show bridge
show bridge verbose
```

In the sample output, the first command would display all entries for hosts reachable via Ethernet interface 0, the second command would display all entries with the vendor code of 0000.0c00.0000, and the third command would display the entry for address 0000.0c00.0e1a. In the fourth command, all entries in the forwarding database would be displayed. The fifth command provides additional detail. In all five lines, the bridge-group number has been omitted.

Sample Displays

The following is sample output from the **show bridge** command. The second display is output from the **show bridge** command with the **verbose** argument.

```
Router# show bridge

Total of 300 station blocks, 280 free
Codes: P - permanent, S - self

Bridge Group 32:Bridge Group 32:

    Address        Action   Interface    Age   RX count   TX count
0180.c200.0000   receive    -            S        0          0
ffff.ffff.ffff   receive    -            S        0          0
0900.2b01.0001   receive    -            S        0          0
0300.0c00.0001   receive    -            S        0          0
0000.0c05.1000   forward    Ethernet0/1  4        1          0
0000.0c04.4b5b   receive    -            S        0          0
0000.0c04.4b5e   receive    -            S        0          0
0000.0c04.4b5d   receive    -            S        0          0
0000.0c04.4b5c   receive    -            S        0          0
0000.0c05.4a62   forward    Ethernet0/1  4        1          0
aa00.0400.2108   forward    Ethernet0/1  0       42          0
0000.0c12.b888   forward    Ethernet0/2  4        1          0
0000.0c12.b886   forward    Ethernet0/1  4        1          0
aa00.0400.4d09   forward    Ethernet0/1  4        1          0
0000.0c06.fb9a   forward    Ethernet0/1  4        1          0
0000.0c04.b039   forward    Ethernet0/1  4        1          0


router# show bridge verbose

Total of 300 station blocks, 287 free
Codes: P - permanent, S - self

BG Hash      Address      Action Interface    DLCI  Age RX count   TX count
32 00/0   0180.c200.0000 receive   -            -    S      0          0
32 00/1   ffff.ffff.ffff receive   -            -    S      0          0
32 01/0   0900.2b01.0001 receive   -            -    S      0          0
32 01/1   0300.0c00.0001 receive   -            -    S      0          0
32 10/0   0000.0c04.4b5b receive   -            -    S      0          0
32 15/0   0000.0c04.4b5e receive   -            -    S      0          0
32 16/0   0000.0c04.4b5d receive   -            -    S      0          0
32 17/0   0000.0c04.4b5c receive   -            -    S      0          0
32 29/0   aa00.0400.2108 forward   Ethernet0/1  -    0     48          0
32 30/0   0000.0c12.b888 forward   Ethernet0/2  -    0      1          0
32 A4/0   0800.2002.ff5b forward   Ethernet0/1  -    0      6          0
32 E2/0   aa00.0400.e90b forward   Ethernet0/1  -    0     65          0
32 F2/0   0000.0c04.b042 forward   Ethernet0/2  -    3      2          0
```

Table 2-2 describes significant fields shown in the display.

Table 2-2 *show bridge Field Descriptions*

Field	Description
Total of 300 station blocks	Total number of forwarding database elements in the system. The memory to hold bridge entries is allocated in blocks of memory sufficient to hold 300 individual entries. When the number of free entries falls below 25, another block of memory sufficient to hold another 300 entries is allocated. Therefore, the size of the bridge forwarding database is limited to the amount of free memory in the router.
295 free	Number in the free list of forwarding database elements in the system. The total number of forwarding elements is expanded dynamically, as needed.
BG	Bridging group to which the address belongs.
Hash	Hash key/relative position in the keyed list.
Address	Canonical (Ethernet ordered) MAC address.
Action	Action to be taken when that address is looked up; choices are to discard or forward the datagram.
Interface	Interface, if any, on which that address was seen.
Age	Number of minutes since a frame was received from or sent to that address. The letter "P" indicates a permanent entry. The letter "S" indicates the system as recorded by the router. On the modular systems, this is typically the broadcast address and the router's own hardware address; on the IGS, this field will also include certain multicast addresses.
RX count	Number of frames received from that address.
TX count	Number of frames forwarded to that address.

show bridge circuit-group

Use the **show bridge circuit-group** EXEC command to display the interfaces configured in each circuit group and show whether they are currently participating in load distribution.

> **show bridge** [*bridge-group*] **circuit-group** [*circuit-group*] [*src-mac-address*] [*dst-mac-address*]

Syntax	Description
bridge-group	(Optional) Number that specifies a particular bridge group.
circuit-group	(Optional) Number that specifies a particular circuit group.
src-mac-address	(Optional) 48-bit canonical (Ethernet ordered) source MAC address.
dst-mac-address	(Optional) 48-bit canonical (Ethernet ordered) destination MAC address.

Command Mode
EXEC

Usage Guidelines
This command first appeared in Cisco IOS Release 10.3.

Sample Displays
The following is sample output from various **show bridge circuit-group** command strings:

```
RouterA> show bridge circuit-group

Bridge group 1 Circuit group 1:
Interface Serial0 : inserted, learning, forwarding
Interface Serial3 : inserted, learning, forwarding
Bridge group 1 Circuit group 2:
Interface Serial2 : inserted, learning, forwarding

RouterA> show bridge 1 circuit-group 1

Bridge group 1 Circuit group 1:
Interface Serial0 : inserted, learning, forwarding
Interface Serial3 : inserted, learning, forwarding

RouterA> show bridge 1 circuit-group 2

Bridge group 1 Circuit group 2:
Interface Serial2 : inserted, learning, forwarding

RouterA> show bridge 1 circuit-group 1 0000.6502.23EA 0000.1234.4567

Output circuit group interface is Serial3

RouterA> show bridge 1 circuit-group 1 0000.6502.23EA

%Destination MAC address required

RouterB> show bridge 1 circuit-group 1

Bridge group 1 Circuit group 1:
Transmission pause interval is 250ms
Output interface selection is source-based
Interface Serial0 : inserted, learning, forwarding
Interface Serial3 : inserted, learning, forwarding
Interface Serial2 is unavailable

RouterB> show bridge 1 circuit-group 1 0000.6502.23EA 0000.1234.4567

%Please enter source MAC address only
```

Table 2-3 describes significant fields shown in the display.

Table 2-3 *show bridge circuit-group Field Descriptions*

Field	Description
inserted/not inserted	Indicates whether interface is included or not included in circuit-group operation. If the interface is administratively down, or if line protocol is not up, the interface is not included in the circuit-group operation.
learning/not learning	Indicates whether this interface is in Spanning-Tree Protocol (IEEE or Digital) learning or not learning state.
forwarding/not forwarding	Indicates whether this port is in Spanning-Tree Protocol (IEEE or Digital) forwarding or not forwarding state.

show bridge group

Use the **show bridge group** privileged EXEC command to display the status of each bridge group.

> **show bridge group** [**verbose**]

Syntax   Description

verbose   (Optional) Displays detailed information.

Command Mode
Privileged EXEC

Usage Guidelines
This command first appeared in Cisco IOS Release 10.3.

Sample Display
The following is sample output from the **show bridge group** command:

```
Router# show bridge group

Bridge Group 1 is running the DEC compatible Spanning Tree protocol

   Port 7 (ATM0.1 LANE Ethernet) of bridge group 1 is down
   Port 4 (TokenRing0) of bridge group 1 is forwarding
```

Forwarding and down indicate the port state as determined by the spanning-tree algorithm or via configuration.

show bridge multicast

Use the **show bridge multicast** EXEC command to display transparent bridging multicast state information.

> **show bridge** [*bridge-group*] **multicast** [**router-ports** | **groups**] [*group-address*]

Syntax   Description

Syntax	Description
bridge-group	(Optional) Bridge group number specified in the **bridge protocol** command.
router-ports	(Optional) Display information for multicast router ports.
groups	(Optional) Display information for multicast groups.
group-address	(Optional) Multicast IP address associated with a specific multicast group.

Command Mode

EXEC

Usage Guidelines

This command first appeared in Cisco IOS Release 11.2.

Sample Display

The following is sample output from the **show bridge multicast** command:

```
Router# show bridge multicast

Multicast router ports for bridge group 1:

 2 multicast router ports
  Fddi2/0        R
  Ethernet0/4    R

Multicast groups for bridge group 1:

  235.145.145.223          RX count    TX count
   Fddi2/0        R            0           2
   Ethernet0/4    R            0           3
   Ethernet0/3    G            1           0

  235.5.5.5                RX count    TX count
   Fddi2/0        R            0           2
   Ethernet0/4    R            0           3
   Ethernet0/3    G            1           0
```

```
235.4.4.4                    RX count    TX count
  Fddi2/0         R               0           2
  Ethernet0/4     R               0           3
  Ethernet0/3     G               1           0
```

Table 2-4 describes significant fields shown in the display.

Table 2-4 *show bridge multicast Field Descriptions*

Field	Description
Multicast router ports for…	List of the multicast router ports by bridge group. Within the bridge group cluster, the display lists the number of multicast router ports and then lists the ports by interface.
Multicast groups for…	List of the multicast groups by bridge group.
	Within each multicast group, identified by a unique address, the display lists each port by interface name and indicates whether that port is a group member ("G"), a multicast router port ("R"), or both.
	The RX and TX counts show the number of multicast packets that have constrained to the multicast group by the bridge.

show bridge vlan

Use the **show bridge vlan** privileged EXEC command to view virtual LAN subinterfaces.

> **show bridge vlan**

Syntax Description

This command has no arguments or keywords.

Command Mode

Privileged EXEC

Usage Guidelines

This command first appeared in Cisco IOS Release 10.3.

Sample Display

The following is sample output from the **show bridge vlan** command:

```
Router# show bridge vlan

Bridge Group: 50

Virtual LAN Trunking Interface(s):   vLAN Protocol:      vLAN ID:  State

Fddi2/0.1000                         IEEE 802.10         1000      forwarding
FastEthernet4/0.500                  Inter Switch Link   500       listening

Virtual LAN Native Interface(s):     State

Ethernet0/1                          forwarding
Serial1/1                            down
```

Table 2-5 describes the fields shown in the display.

Table 2-5 *show bridge vlan Field Description*

Field	Description
Bridge Group	Bridge group to which these interfaces belong.
Virtual LAN Trunking Interface(s)	VLAN interface.
vLAN Protocol	IEEE 802.10 or Cisco ISL encapsulation.
vLAN ID	VLAN identifier that maintains VLAN identities between switches.
State	Spanning-tree port state of the interface.
Virtual LAN Native Interface(s)	Interfaces whose transparently bridged traffic will be propagated only to other LAN segments within the same virtual LAN.

show interfaces crb

Use the **show interfaces crb** privileged EXEC command to display the configuration for each interface that has been configured for routing or bridging.

show interfaces crb

Syntax Description

This command has no arguments or keywords.

Command Mode

Privileged EXEC

Usage Guidelines

This command first appeared in Cisco IOS Release 11.0.

Sample Display

The following is sample output from the **show interfaces crb** command:

```
Router# show interfaces crb

Ethernet0/0

Routed protocols on Ethernet0/0:
appletalk decnet ip novell

Ethernet0/1

Routed protocols on Ethernet0/1:
appletalk  decnet  ip  novell

Ethernet0/2

Routed protocols on Ethernet0/2:
appletalk  ip

Bridged protocols on Ethernet0/2:
clns  decnet  vines  apollo
novell  xns

Software MAC address filter on Ethernet0/2
Hash Len   Address         Matches   Act   Type
0x00: 0    ffff.ffff.ffff  0         RCV   Physical broadcast
0x00: 1    ffff.ffff.ffff  0         RCV   Appletalk zone
0x2A: 0    0900.2b01.0001  0         RCV   DEC spanning tree
0x49: 0    0000.0c36.7a45  0         RCV   Interface MAC address
0xc0: 0    0100.0ccc.cccc  20        RCV   CDP
0xc2: 0    0180.c200.0000  0         RCV   IEEE spanning tree
0xF8: 0    0900.07ff.ffff  0         RCV   Appletalk broadcast

Ethernet0/3

Routed protocols on Ethernet0/3:
appletalk  ip

Bridged protocols on Ethernet0/3:
clns  decnet  vines  apollo
novell  xns
```

```
Software MAC address filter on Ethernet0/3
Hash Len   Address          Matches  Act   Type
0x00: 0    ffff.ffff.ffff   0        RCV   Physical broadcast
0x00: 1    ffff.ffff.ffff   0        RCV   Appletalk zone
0x2A: 0    0900.2b01.0001   0        RCV   DEC spanning tree
0x49: 0    0000.0c36.7a45   0        RCV   Interface MAC address
0xc0: 0    0100.0ccc.cccc   48       RCV   CDP
0xc2: 0    0180.c200.0000   0        RCV   IEEE spanning tree
0xF8: 0    0900.07ff.ffff   0        RCV   Appletalk broadcast
```

Table 2-6 describes significant fields shown in the display.

Table 2-6 *show interfaces crb* Field Descriptions

Field	Description
Routed protocols on…	List of the routed protocols configured for the specified interface.
Bridged protocols on…	List of the bridged protocols configured for the specified interface.
Software MAC address filter on…	Table of software MAC address filter information for the specified interface.
Hash	Hash key/relative position in the keyed list for this MAC-address entry.
Len	Length of this entry to the beginning element of this hash chain.
Address	Canonical (Ethernet ordered) MAC address.
Matches	Number of received packets matched to this MAC address.
Act	Action to be taken when that address is looked up; choices are to receive or discard the packet.
Type	MAC address type.

show interfaces irb

Use the **show interfaces irb** privileged EXEC command to display the configuration for each interface that has been configured for integrated routing or bridging.

> **show interfaces** [*interface*] **irb**

Syntax

interface

Description

(Optional) Specific interface, such as Ethernet 0.

Command Mode
Privileged EXEC

Usage Guidelines

This command first appeared in Cisco IOS Release 11.2.

Sample Display

The following is sample output from the **show interfaces irb** command:

```
Router# show interfaces ethernet 2 irb

Ethernet 2

Routed protocols on Ethernet 2:
appletalk ip

Bridged protocols on Ethernet 2:
appletalk   clns    decnet   vines
apollo      ipx     xns

Software MAC address filter on Ethernet 2
Hash Len  Address         Matches  Act  Type
0x00: 0   ffff.ffff.ffff  4886     RCV  Physical broadcast
0x1F: 0   0060.3e2b.a221  7521     RCV  Appletalk zone
0x1F: 1   0060.3e2b.a221  0        RCV  Bridge-group Virtual Interface
0x2A: 0   0900.2b01.0001  0        RCV  DEC spanning tree
0x05: 0   0900.0700.00a2  0        RCV  Appletalk zone
0xC2: 0   0180.c200.0000  0        RCV  IEEE spanning tree
0xF8: 0   0900.07ff.ffff  2110     RCV  Appletalk broadcast
```

Table 2-7 describes significant fields shown in the display.

Table 2-7   *show interfaces irb Field Descriptions*

Field	Description
Routed protocols on…	List of the routed protocols configured for the specified interface.
Bridged protocols on…	List of the bridged protocols configured for the specified interface.
Software MAC address filter on…	Table of software MAC address filter information for the specified interface.
Hash	Hash key/relative position in the keyed list for this MAC-address entry.
Len	Length of this entry to the beginning element of this hash chain.
Address	Canonical (Ethernet ordered) MAC address.
Matches	Number of received packets matched to this MAC address.
Act	Action to be taken when that address is looked up; choices are to receive or discard the packet.
Type	MAC address type.

show span

Use the **show span** privileged EXEC command to display the spanning-tree topology known to the router. The display indicates whether LAT group code filtering is in effect.

show span

Syntax Description

This command has no arguments or keywords.

Command Mode

Privileged EXEC

Usage Guidelines

This command first appeared in Cisco IOS Release 10.0.

Sample Display

The following is sample output from the **show span** command:

```
RouterA# show span

Bridge Group 1 is executing the DEC compatible Spanning Tree protocol
  Bridge Identifier has priority 128, address 0000.304c.f686
  Configured hello time 1, max age 15, forward delay 30
  We are the root of the spanning tree
  Topology change flag not set, detected flag not set
  Times:  hold 1, topology change 30, notification 30
          hello 1, max age 15, forward delay 30, aging 300
  Timers: hello 1, topology change 0, notification 0

Port 7 (ATM0.1 LANE Ethernet) of bridge group 1 is down
  Port path cost 0, Port priority 128
  Designated root has priority 128, address 0000.304c.f686
  Designated bridge has priority 128, address 0000.304c.f686
  Designated port is 7, path cost 0
  Timers: message age 0, forward delay 0, hold 0
```

show sse summary

Use the **show sse summary** EXEC command to display a summary of Silicon Switch Processor (SSP) statistics:

show sse summary

Syntax Description

This command has no arguments or keywords.

Command Mode

EXEC

Usage Guidelines

This command first appeared in Cisco IOS Release 10.3.

Sample Display

The following is sample output from the **show sse summary** command:

```
Router# show sse summary

SSE utilization statistics

                Program words  Rewrite bytes  Internal nodes  Depth
Overhead            499              1              8
IP                    0              0              0           0
IPX                   0              0              0           0
SRB                   0              0              0           0
CLNP                  0              0              0           0
IP access lists       0              0              0
Total used          499              1              8
Total free        65037         262143
Total available   65536         262144

Free program memory
 [499..65535]
Free rewrite memory
 [1..262143]

Internals
 75032 internal nodes allocated, 75024 freed
 SSE manager process enabled, microcode enabled, 0 hangs
 Longest cache computation 4ms, longest quantum 160ms at 0x53AC8
```

show subscriber-policy

To display the details of a subscriber policy, use the **show subscriber-policy** EXEC command.

> **show subscriber-policy** *range*

Syntax

range

Description

Range of subscriber policy numbers (range 1 to 100).

Command Mode
EXEC

Sample Display
The following is sample output from the **show subscriber-policy** command:

```
Router# show subscriber-policy 1

ARP: Permit
Broadcast: Deny
Multicast: Permit
Unknown: Deny
STP: Disable
CDP: Disable
```

Related Commands
To locate documentation of related commands, you can search online at www.cisco.com.

bridge protocol
bridge subscriber-policy
show bridge
subscriber-policy

subscriber-policy

To define or modify the forward and filter decisions of the subscriber policy, use the **subscriber-policy** global configuration command. Use the **no** or **default** form of this command to restore the default forward and filter values.

subscriber-policy *policy* [[**no** | **default**] *packet* [**permit** | **deny**]]

Syntax

policy

no

Description

Subscriber policy number in the range 1 to 100.

(Optional) Turn off the permit for the packet (this is an equivalent of the **deny** keyword).

Syntax	Description
default	(Optional) Deny forwarding of the packet (this is an equivalent of the **deny** keyword).
packet	One of the following packets:

- *arp*
- *broadcast*
- *cdp*
- *multicast*
- *stp*
- *unknown unicast*

permit	(Optional) Permit forwarding of the packet.
deny	(Optional) Deny forwarding of the packet.

Default

If no forward or filter decisions have been specified for the subscriber policy, the following defaults are applied:

Packet	Upstream
ARP	Permit
Broadcast	Deny
CDP	Deny/Disable
Multicast	Permit
STP	Deny/Disable
Unknown Unicast	Deny

Command Mode

Global configuration

Usage Guidelines

As an alternative to the command syntax described above, you can enter **subscriber-policy** *policy*, followed by the specific forward or filter decisions for each packet.

Examples

The following example changes the ARP behavior and the multicast behavior from permit to deny, using the command syntax shown in the section, "Command Syntax":

```
subscriber-policy 3 arp deny
subscriber-policy 3 multicast deny
```

The following example changes the ARP behavior and the multicast behavior from permit to deny, using the alternative syntax shown in the section, "Usage Guidelines":

```
subscriber-policy 3
arp deny
multicast deny
```

Related Commands

To locate documentation of related commands, you can search online at www.cisco.com.

bridge protocol
bridge subscriber-policy
show subscriber-policy

show vlans

Use the **show vlans** privileged EXEC command to view virtual LAN subinterfaces.

> **show vlans**

Syntax Description

This command has no arguments or keywords.

Command Mode

Privileged EXEC

Usage Guidelines

This command first appeared in Cisco IOS Release 11.0.

Sample Display

The following is sample output from the **show vlans** command:

```
RouterC7xxx# show vlans

Virtual LAN ID:300 (IEEE 802.10 Encapsulation)

   vLAN Trunk Interface: FDDI 1/1.10

   Protocols Configured:    Address:          Received:        Transmitted:
IP          31.108.1.1 642645

Virtual LAN ID:400 (ISL Encapsulation)

   vLAN Trunk Interface: FastEthernet 2/1.20

   Protocols Configured:    Address:          Received:        Transmitted:
IP          171.69.2.2 123456654321
Bridge Group50 51908234

Virtual LAN ID:500 (ISL Encapsulation)

   vLAN Trunk Interface: FastEthernet 2/1.30

   Protocols Configured:    Address:          Received:        Transmitted:
IPX         1000 987654456789

Virtual LAN ID:600 (ISL Encapsulation)

   vLAN Trunk Interface: FastEthernet 2/1.30

   Protocols Configured:    Address:          Received:        Transmitted:
IP          198.92.3.381144508
IPX         10012 3
Bridge Group5082345190
```

Table 2-8 describes the fields shown in the display.

Table 2-8 *show vlan Field Descriptions*

Field	Description
Virtual LAN ID	The domain number of the virtual LAN.
vLAN Trunk Interface	The subinterface that carries the VLAN traffic.
Protocols Configured	The protocols configured on the VLAN.
Address	The network address.
Received	Packets received.
Transmitted	Packets transmitted.

x25 map bridge

Use the **x25 map bridge** interface configuration command to configure the bridging of packets in X.25 frames. Use the **no** form of this command to disable the Internet-to-X.121 mapping.

> **x25 map bridge** *x.121-address* **broadcast** [*options-keywords*]
> **no x25 map bridge**

Syntax | Description

Syntax	Description
x.121-address	The X.121 address.
broadcast	Required keyword for bridging over X.25.
options-keywords	(Optional) Additional functionality that can be specified for originated calls. Can be any of the options listed in Table 2-9.

Default

Disabled

Command Mode

Interface configuration

Usage Guidelines

This command first appeared in Cisco IOS Release 10.0.

X.25 bridging software uses the same spanning-tree algorithm as the other bridging functions, but allows packets to be encapsulated in X.25 frames and transmitted across X.25 media. This command specifies IP-to-X.121 address mapping and maintains a table of both the Ethernet and X.121 addresses.

The X.25 bridging implementation supports the map options listed in Table 2-9.

Table 2-9 *X.25 Map Options*

Option	Description
compress	Specifies that X.25 payload compression be used for mapping the traffic to this host. Each virtual circuit established for compressed traffic uses a significant amount of memory (for a table of learned data patterns) and for computation (for compression and decompression of all data). Cisco recommends that compression be used with careful consideration to its impact on overall performance.

Continues

Table 2-9 *X.25 Map Options (Continued)*

Option	Description
method {**cisco** | **ietf** | **snap** | **multi**}D	Specifies the encapsulation method. The choices are as follows: • **cisco**—Cisco proprietary encapsulation; not available if more than one protocol is to be carried. • **ietf**—Default RFC 1356 operation: protocol identification of single-protocol virtual circuits and protocol identification within multiprotocol virtual circuits uses the standard encoding, which is compatible with RFC 877. Multiprotocol virtual circuits are used only if needed. • **snap**—RFC 1356 operation where IP is identified with SNAP rather than the standard IETF method (the standard method is compatible with RFC 877). • **multi**—Forces a map that specifies a single protocol to set up a multiprotocol virtual circuit when a call is originated; also forces a single-protocol PVC to use multiprotocol data identification methods for all datagrams sent and received.
no-incoming	Uses the map only to originate calls.
no-outgoing	Does not originate calls when using the map.
idle *minutes*	Specifies an idle timeout for calls other than the interface default; 0 minutes disables the idle timeout.
reverse	Specifies reverse charging for outgoing calls.
accept-reverse	Causes Cisco IOS software to accept incoming reverse-charged calls. If this option is not present, Cisco IOS software clears reverse-charged calls unless the interface accepts all reverse-charged calls.
broadcast	Causes Cisco IOS software to direct any broadcasts sent through this interface to the specified X.121 address. This option also simplifies the configuration of OSPF.
cug *group-number*	Specifies a closed user group number (from 1 to 99) for the mapping in an outgoing call.
nvc *count*	Sets the maximum number of virtual circuits for this map or host. The default *count* is the **x25 nvc** setting of the interface. A maximum number of eight virtual circuits can be configured for each map. Compressed TCP may use only 1 virtual circuit.
packetsize *in-size out-size*	Proposes maximum input packet size (*in-size*) and maximum output packet size (*out-size*) for an outgoing call. Both values typically are the same and must be one of the following values: 16, 32, 64, 128, 256, 512, 1024, 2048, or 4096.
windowsize *in-size out-size*	Proposes the packet count for input window (*in-size*) and output window (*out-size*) for an outgoing call. Both values typically are the same, must be in the range 1 to 127, and must be less than the value set by the **x25 modulo** command.

Table 2-9 *X.25 Map Options (Continued)*

Option	Description
throughput *in out*	Sets the requested throughput class values for input (*in*) and output (*out*) throughput across the network for an outgoing call. Values for *in* and *out* are in bits per second (bps) and range from 75 to 48,000 bps.
transit-delay *milliseconds*	Specifies the transit delay value in milliseconds (0 to 65,534) for an outgoing call, for networks that support transit delay.
nuid *username password*	Specifies that a network user ID (NUID) facility be sent in the outgoing call with the specified Terminal Access Controller Access Control System (TACACS) username and password (in a format defined by Cisco). This option should be used only when connecting to another Cisco router. The combined length of the username and password should not exceed 127 characters.
nudata *string*	Specifies the network user identification in a format determined by the network administrator (as allowed by the standards). This option is provided for connecting to non-Cisco equipment that requires an NUID facility. The string should not exceed 130 characters and must be enclosed in quotation marks (" ") if there are any spaces present.
rpoa *name*	Specifies the name defined by the **x25 roa** command for a list of transit Recognized Operating Agencies (ROAs) to use in outgoing Call Request packets.
passive	Specifies that the X.25 interface should send compressed outgoing TCP datagrams only if they were already compressed when they were received. This option is available only for compressed TCP maps.

Example

The following example allows bridging over an X.25 network:

```
x25 map bridge 31370054065 broadcast
```

Related Commands

To locate documentation of related commands, you can search online at www.cisco.com.

x25 address
x25 map

Configuring Source-Route Bridging

This chapter describes source-route bridging (SRB) configuration tasks. For a discussion of remote source-route bridging (RSRB) configuration tasks, refer to Chapter 7, "Configuring Remote Source-Route Bridging."

For a complete description of the SRB commands mentioned in this chapter, refer to Chapter 4, "Source-Route Bridging Commands." To locate documentation of other commands that appear in this chapter, you can search online at www.cisco.com.

SRB Configuration Task List

Perform the tasks in the following sections to configure SRB:

- Configure SRB
- Configure Bridging of Routed Protocols
- Configure Translation Between SRB and Transparent Bridging Environments
- Configure NetBIOS Support
- Configure LNM Support
- Secure the SRB Network
- Tune the SRB Network
- Establish SRB Interoperability with Specific Token Ring Implementations
- Monitor and Maintain the SRB Network

See the end of this chapter for the section "SRB Configuration Examples."

WARNING Cisco IOS software issues a warning if a duplicate bridge definition exists in a router. You must remove an old bridge definition before adding a new bridge definition to a router configuration.

Configure SRB

Cisco implementation of SRB enables you to connect two or more Token Ring networks using either Token Ring or Fiber Distributed Data Interface (FDDI) media.

Cisco IOS software offers the ability to encapsulate SRB traffic using RFC 1490 Bridged 802.5 encapsulation. This encapsulation provides SRB over Frame Relay functionality.

You can configure Cisco IOS software for SRB by performing the tasks in one of the first three sections and, optionally, the tasks in the last section:

- Configure a Dual-Port Bridge
- Configure a Multiport Bridge Using a Virtual Ring
- Configure SRB over FDDI
- Configure Fast-Switching SRB over FDDI
- Configure SRB over Frame Relay
- Enable the Forwarding and Blocking of Spanning-Tree Explorer Packets
- Enable the Automatic Spanning-Tree Function
- Limit the Maximum SRB Hops

Configure a Dual-Port Bridge

A dual-port bridge is the simplest source-route bridging configuration. When configured as a dual-port bridge, the access server or router serves to connect two Token Ring LANs. One LAN is connected through one port (Token Ring interface), and the other LAN is connected through the other port (also a Token Ring interface). Figure 3-1 shows a dual-port bridge.

Figure 3-1   *Dual-Port Bridge*

To configure a dual-port bridge that connects two Token Rings, you must enable SRB on each of the Token Ring interfaces that connect to the two Token Rings. To enable SRB, use the following command in interface configuration mode for each of the Token Ring interfaces:

Command	Purpose
source-bridge *local-ring bridge-number target-ring*	Enables local SRB on a Token Ring interface.

NOTE	Ring numbers need to be unique across interfaces and networks so, when you enable source-route bridging over an interface, the local and target rings are defined. Each node on the network will know if it is the target of explorer packets sent on the network.

A dual-port bridge is a limitation imposed by IBM Token Ring chips; the chips can process only two ring numbers. If you have a router with two or more Token Ring interfaces, you can work around the two-ring number limitation. You can configure your router as multiple dual-port bridges or as a multiport bridge using a virtual ring.

You can define several separate dual-port bridges in the same router. However, the routers on the LANs cannot have any-to-any connectivity; that is, they cannot connect to every other router on the bridged LANs. Only the routers connected to the dual-port bridge can communicate with one another. Figure 3-2 shows two separate dual-port bridges (T0-T2 and T1-T3) configured on the same router.

Figure 3-2   *Mtultiple Dual-Port Bridges*

To configure multiple dual-port source-route bridges, use the following command in interface configuration mode for each Token Ring interface that is part of a dual-port bridge:

Command	Purpose
source-bridge *local-ring bridge-number target-ring*	Enables local SRB on a Token Ring interface.

If you want your network to use only SRB, you can connect as many routers as you need via Token Rings. Remember, source-route bridging requires you to bridge only Token Ring media.

Configure a Multiport Bridge Using a Virtual Ring

A better solution for overcoming the two-ring number limitation of IBM Token Ring chips is to configure a multiport bridge using a virtual ring. A virtual ring on a multiport bridge allows the router to interconnect three or more LANs with any-to-any connectivity; that is, connectivity between any of the routers on each of the three LANs is allowed. A virtual ring creates a logical Token Ring internal to Cisco IOS software, which causes all the Token Rings connected to the router to be treated as if they are all on the same Token Ring. The virtual ring is called a ring group. Figure 3-3 shows a multiport bridge using a virtual ring.

Figure 3-3 *Multiport Bridge Using a Virtual Ring*

To take advantage of this virtual ring feature, each Token Ring interface on the router must be configured to belong to the same ring group. For information about configuring a multiport bridge using a virtual ring, see the "Configure a Multiport Bridge Using a Virtual Ring" section later in this chapter.

To configure a source-route bridge to have more than two network interfaces, you must perform the following tasks:

>   **Step 1** Define a ring group.
>
>   **Step 2** Enable SRB and assign a ring group to a Token Ring interface.

Once you have completed these tasks, the router acts as a multiport bridge not as a dual-port bridge.

NOTE Ring numbers need to be unique across interfaces and networks.

Define a Ring Group in SRB Context

Because all IBM Token Ring chips can process only two ring numbers, we have implemented the concept of a ring group or virtual ring. A ring group is a collection of Token Ring interfaces in one or more routers that share the same ring number. This ring number is used just like a physical ring number, showing up in any route descriptors contained in packets being bridged. Within the context of a multi-port bridge that uses SRB rather than RSRB, the ring group resides in the same router. See Chapter 7, "Configuring Remote Source-Route Bridging" to compare ring groups in the SRB and RSRB context.

A ring group must be assigned a ring number that is unique throughout the network. It is possible to assign different Token Ring interfaces on the same router to different ring groups, if, for example, you plan to administer them as interfaces in separate domains.

To define or remove a ring group, use one of the following commands in global configuration mode:

Command	Purpose
source-bridge ring-group *ring-group* [*virtual-mac-address*]	Defines a ring group.
no source-bridge ring-group *ring-group* [*virtual-mac-address*]	Removes a ring group.

Enable SRB and Assign a Ring Group to an Interface

After you have defined a ring group, you must assign that ring group to those interfaces you plan to include in that ring group. An interface can only be assigned to one ring group. To enable any-to-any connectivity among the end stations connected through this multiport bridge, you must assign the same target ring number to all Token Ring interfaces on the router.

To enable SRB and assign a ring group to an interface, use the following command in interface configuration mode:

Command	Purpose
source-bridge *local-ring bridge-number target-ring*	Enables SRB and assigns a ring group to a Token Ring interface.

Configure SRB over FDDI

Cisco implementation of SRB expands the basic functionality to allow autonomous switching of SRB network traffic for FDDI interfaces, adding counters to SRB accounting statistics, and implementing process-level switching of SRB over FDDI. This functionality provides a significant increase in performance for Token Rings interconnected across an FDDI backbone (see Figure 3-4).

SRB over FDDI is supported on the Cisco 4000-M, Cisco 4500-M, Cisco 4700-M, Cisco 7000 series, Cisco 7200 series, and Cisco 7500 routers.

Figure 3-4   *Autonomous FDDI SRB*

To configure autonomous FDDI SRB, use the following commands, beginning in global configuration mode:

Step	Command	Purpose
1	**interface fddi** *slot/port*	Configures an FDDI interface.
2	**source-bridge** *local-ring bridge-number target-ring*	Enables SRB.
3	**source-bridge route-cache cbus**	Enables autonomous switching.

Configure Fast-Switching SRB over FDDI

Fast-Switching SRB over FDDI enhances performance. For example, if you want to use access-lists, fast-switching SRB over FDDI provides fast performance and access-list filters capability.

To configure fast-switching SRB over FDDI, use the following commands, beginning in global configuration mode:

Step	Command	Purpose
1	**interface fddi** *slot/port*	Configures an FDDI interface.
2	**source-bridge** *local-ring bridge-number target-ring*	Enables SRB.
3	**source-bridge spanning**	Enables source-bridge spanning.
4	**source-bridge route-cache**	Enables fast-switching.
5	**multiring** *protocol-keyword*	Enables the collection and use of RIF information.

Configure SRB over Frame Relay

Cisco IOS software offers the ability to encapsulate SRB traffic using RFC 1490 Bridged 802.5 encapsulation. This provides SRB over Frame Relay functionality that is interoperable with other vendors' implementations of SRB over Frame Relay and with some vendors' implementations of FRAS BAN.

NOTE	In the initial release, SRB over Frame Relay does not support Cisco IOS software proxy explorer, automatic spanning-tree, or LAN Network Manager functions.

To configure SRB over Frame Relay, use the following commands in interface configuration mode:

Step	Command	Purpose
1	**interface serial** *number*	Specifies the serial port.
2	**encapsulation frame-relay**	Enables Frame Relay encapsulation.
3	**interface serial** *slot/port.subinterface-number* **point-to-point**	Configures a Frame Relay point-to-point subinterface.
4	**frame-relay interface-dlci** *dlci* **ietf**	Configures a DLCI number for the point-to-point subinterface.
5	**source-bridge** *source-ring-number bridge-number target-ring-number* **conserve-ring**	Assigns a ring number to the Frame Relay permanent virtual circuit.

Enable the Forwarding and Blocking of Spanning-Tree Explorer Packets

When trying to determine the location of remote destinations on a source-route bridge, the source device will need to send explorer packets. Explorer packets are used to collect routing information field (RIF) information. The source device can send spanning-tree explorers or all-routes explorers. Note that some older IBM devices generate only all-routes explorer packets, but many newer IBM devices are capable of generating spanning-tree explorer packets.

A spanning-tree explorer packet is an explorer packet that is sent to a defined group of nodes that comprise a statically configured spanning tree in the network. In contrast, an all-routes explorer packet is an explorer packet that is sent to every node in the network on every path.

Forwarding all-routes explorer packets is the default. However, in complicated SRB topologies, using this default can generate an exponentially large number of explorers that are traversing the network. The number of explorer packets becomes quite large because duplicate explorer packets are sent across the network to every node on every path. Eventually, each explorer packet will reach the destination device.

The destination device will respond to each of these explorer packets. It is from these responses that the source device will collect the RIF and determine which route it will use to communicate with the destination device. Usually, the route contained in the first returned response will be used.

The number of explorer packets traversing the network can be reduced by sending spanning-tree explorer packets. Spanning-tree explorer packets are sent to specific nodes; that is, to only the nodes on the spanning tree, not to all nodes in the network. You must manually configure the spanning-tree topology over which the spanning-tree explorers are sent. You do this by configuring which interfaces on the routers will forward spanning-tree explorers and which interfaces will block them.

To enable forwarding of spanning-tree explorers on an outgoing interface, use the following command in interface configuration mode:

Command	Purpose
source-bridge spanning	Enables the forwarding of spanning-tree explorer packets on an interface.

NOTE	While enabling the forwarding of spanning-tree explorer packets is not an absolute requirement, it is strongly recommended for complex topologies. Configuring an interface to block or forward spanning-tree explorers has no effect on how that interface handles all-routes explorer packets. All-routes explorers can always traverse the network.

To block forwarding of spanning tree explorers on an outgoing interface, use the following command in interface configuration mode:

Command	Purpose
no source-bridge spanning	Blocks spanning-tree explorer packets on an interface.

Enable the Automatic Spanning-Tree Function

The automatic spanning-tree function supports automatic resolution of spanning trees in SRB networks, which provides a single path for spanning explorer frames to traverse from a given node in the network to another. Spanning explorer frames have a single-route broadcast indicator set in the RIF. Port identifiers consist of ring numbers and bridge numbers associated with the ports. The spanning-tree algorithm for SRB does not support Topology Change Notification bridge protocol data unit (BDPU).

NOTE   Although the automatic spanning-tree function can be configured with source-route translational bridging (SR/TLB), the SRB domain and transparent bridging domain have separate spanning trees. Each Token Ring interface can belong to only one spanning tree. Only one bridge group can run the automatic spanning-tree function at a time.

To create a bridge group that runs an automatic spanning-tree function compatible with the IBM SRB spanning-tree implementation, use the following command in global configuration mode:

Command	Purpose
bridge *bridge-group* **protocol ibm**	Creates a bridge group that runs the automatic spanning-tree function.

To enable the automatic spanning-tree function for a specified group of bridged interfaces, use the following command in interface configuration mode:

Command	Purpose
source-bridge spanning *bridge-group*	Enables the automatic spanning-tree function on a group of bridged interfaces.

To assign a path cost for a specified interface, use the following command in interface configuration mode:

Command	Purpose
source-bridge spanning *bridge-group* **path-cost** *path-cost*	Assigns a path cost for a specified group of bridged interfaces.

NOTE   Ports running IEEE and IBM protocols form a spanning tree together on the LAN, but they do not mix in the router itself. Make sure the configurations are correct and that each LAN runs only one protocol.

See the end of this chapter for an example of SRB with the automatic spanning-tree function enabled.

Limit the Maximum SRB Hops

You can minimize explorer storms if you limit the maximum number of source-route bridge hops. For example, if the largest number of hops in the best route between two end stations is six, it might be appropriate to limit the maximum SRB hops to six to eliminate unnecessary traffic. This setting affects spanning-tree explorers and all-routes explorers sent from source devices.

To limit the number of SRB hops, use one of the following commands in interface configuration mode:

Command	Purpose
source-bridge max-hops *count*	Controls the forwarding or blocking of all-routes explorer frames received on this interface.
source-bridge max-in-hops *count*	Controls the forwarding or blocking of spanning-tree explorer frames received on this interface.
source-bridge max-out-hops *count*	Controls the forwarding or blocking of spanning-tree explorer frames sent from this interface.

Configure Bridging of Routed Protocols

Source-route bridges use Media Access Control (MAC) information, specifically the information contained in the RIF, to bridge packets. A RIF contains a series of ring and bridge numbers that represent the possible paths the source node might use to send packets to the destination. Each ring number in the RIF represents a single Token Ring in the source-route bridged network and is designated by a unique 12-bit ring number. Each bridge number represents a bridge that is between two Token Rings in the SRB network and is designated by a unique 4-bit bridge number. The information in a RIF is derived from explorer packets traversing the source-route bridged network. Without the RIF information, a packet could not be bridged across a source-route bridged network.

Unlike source-route bridges, Level 3 routers use protocol-specific information (for example, Novell Internetwork Packet Exchange (IPX) or Xerox Network Systems (XNS) headers) rather than MAC information to route datagrams. As a result, Cisco IOS software default for routed protocols is to not collect RIF information and to not be able to bridge routed protocols. However, if you want the software to bridge routed protocols across a source-route bridged network, the software must be able to collect and use RIF information to bridge packets across a source-route bridged network. You can configure the software to append RIF information to routed protocols so that routed protocols can be bridged. Figure 3-5 shows a network topology in which you would want to use this feature.

Figure 3-5   *Topology for Bridging Routed Protocols Across a Source-Route Bridged Network*

To configure Cisco IOS software to bridge routed protocols, you must perform the task in the first section and, optionally, one or both of the tasks in the other sections as follows:

● Enable Use of the RIF

● Configure a Static RIF Entry

● Configure the RIF Timeout Interval

Enable Use of the RIF

You can configure Cisco IOS software so that it will append RIF information to the routed protocols. This allows routed protocols to be bridged across a source-route bridged network. The routed protocols that you can bridge are as follows:

● Apollo Domain

● AppleTalk

● ISO Connectionless Network Service (CLNS)

● DECnet

● IP

● IPX

● VINES

● XNS

Enable use of the RIF only on Token Ring interfaces on the router.

To configure Cisco IOS software to append RIF information, use the following command in interface configuration mode:

Command	Purpose
multiring {*protocol-keyword* [**all-routes**	**spanning**]	**all**	**other**}	Enables collection and use of RIF information.

For an example of how to configure the software to bridge routed protocols, see the "SRB and Routing Certain Protocols Example" section later in this chapter.

Configure a Static RIF Entry

If a Token Ring host does not support the use of IEEE 802.2 TEST or XID datagrams as explorer packets, you might need to add static information to the RIF cache of the router.

To configure a static RIF entry, use the following command in global configuration mode:

Command	Purpose
rif *mac-address rif-string* {*interface-name*	**ring-group** *ring*}	Enters static source-route information into the RIF cache.

Configure the RIF Timeout Interval

RIF information that can be used to bridge routed protocols is maintained in a cache whose entries are aged.

NOTE	The **rif validate enable** commands have no effect on remote entries learned over RSRB.

To configure the number of minutes an inactive RIF entry is kept in the cache, use the following commands in global configuration mode:

Step	Command	Purpose
1	**rif timeout** *minutes*	Specifies the number of minutes an inactive RIF entry is kept.
2	**rif validate-enable**	Enables RIF validation for entries learned on an interface (Token Ring or FDDI).
3	**rif validate-enable-age**	Enables RIF validation on an SRB that is malfunctioning.
4	**rif validate-enable-route-cache**	Enables synchronization of the RIF cache with the protocol route cache.

Configure Translation Between SRB and Transparent Bridging Environments

SR/TLB is a Cisco IOS software feature that allows you to combine SRB and transparent bridging networks without the need to convert all of your existing source-route bridges to source-route transparent (SRT) nodes. As such, it provides a cost-effective connectivity path between Ethernets and Token Rings, for example.

When a router is configured for SR/TLB, the router operates in fast-switching mode by default, causing packets to be processed in the interrupt handler when the packets first arrive, rather than queuing them for scheduled processing. You can also use the **no source-bridge transparent fastswitch** command to disable fast-switched SR/TLB, causing the router to handle packets by process switching. For more information on disabling fast-switched SR/TLB, refer to the "Disable Fast-Switched SR/TLB" section in this chapter.

NOTE	When you are translationally bridging, you will have to route routed protocols and translationally bridge all others, such as local-area transport (LAT).

Overview of SR/TLB

You can bridge packets between an SRB domain and a transparent bridging domain. Using this feature, a software "bridge" is created between a specified virtual ring group and a transparent bridge group. To the source-route station, this bridge looks like a standard source-route bridge. There is a ring number and a bridge number associated with a ring that actually represents the entire transparent bridging domain. To the transparent bridging station, the bridge represents just another port in the bridge group.

When bridging from the SRB (typically, Token Ring) domain to the transparent bridging (typically, Ethernet) domain, the source-route fields of the frames are removed. RIFs are cached for use by subsequent return traffic.

When bridging from the transparent bridging domain to the SRB domain, the router checks the packet to see if it has a multicast or broadcast destination or a unicast (single host) destination. If it is multicast, the packet is sent as a spanning-tree explorer. If it is a unicast destination, the router looks up the path to the destination in the RIF cache. If a path is found, it will be used; otherwise, the router will send the packet as a spanning-tree explorer.

An example of a simple SR/TLB topology is shown in Figure 3-6.

Figure 3-6   *Example of a Simple SR/TLB Topology*

Transparent bridging "ring"

Source-route bridged domain

Transparent bridging domain

Token Ring

Router running SR/TLB

Frames lose RIFs in this direction

Frames gain RIFs in this direction

NOTE   The Spanning-Tree Protocol messages used to prevent loops in the transparent bridging domain are not passed between the SRB domain and the transparent bridging domain. Therefore, you must not set up multiple paths between the SRB and transparent bridging domains.

The following notes and caveats apply to all uses of SR/TLB:

- Multiple paths cannot exist between the source-route bridged domain and the transparent bridged domain. Such paths can lead to data loops in the network, because the spanning-tree packets used to avoid these loops in transparent bridging networks do not traverse the SRB network.

- Some devices, notably PS/2s under certain configurations running OS/2 Extended Edition Version 1.3, do not correctly implement the "largest frame" processing on RIFs received from remote source-route bridged hosts. The maximum Ethernet frame size is smaller than that allowed for Token Ring. As such, bridges allowing for communication between Ethernet and Token Ring will tell the Token Ring hosts, through the RIF on frames destined to the Token Ring, that hosts on the Ethernet cannot receive frames larger than a specified maximum, typically 1472 bytes. Some machines ignore this run-time limit specification and send frames larger than the Ethernet can accept. The router and any other Token Ring/Ethernet bridge has no choice but to drop these frames. To allow such hosts to successfully communicate across or to an Ethernet, you must configure their maximum frame sizes manually. For the PS/2, this can be done through Communications Manager.

- Any access filters applied on any frames apply to the frames as they appear on the media to which the interface with the access filter applies. This is important because in the most common use of SR/TLB (Ethernet and Token Ring connectivity), the bit ordering of the MAC addresses in the frame is swapped. Refer to the SR/TLB examples in the "SRB Configuration Examples" section of this chapter.

CAUTION   Bridging between dissimilar media presents several problems that can prevent communication from occurring. These problems include bit order translation (or usage of MAC addresses as data), maximum transmission unit (MTU) differences, frame status differences, and multicast address usage. Some or all of these problems might be present in a multimedia bridged LAN and prevent communication from taking place. Because of differences in the way end nodes implement Token Ring, these problems are most prevalent when bridging between Token Rings and Ethernets or between Token Ring and FDDI LANs.

We currently know that problems occur with the following protocols when bridged between Token Ring and other media: Novell IPX, DECnet Phase IV, AppleTalk, VINES, XNS, and IP. Further, problems can occur with the Novell IPX and XNS protocols when bridged between FDDI and other media. We recommend that these protocols be routed whenever possible.

To enable SR/TLB, you must perform the task in the following section:

- Enable Bridging Between Transparent Bridging and SRB

In addition, you can also perform the tasks in the following sections:

- Disable Fast-Switched SR/TLB

- Enable Translation Compatibility with IBM 8209 Bridges

- Enable Token Ring LLC2-to-Ethernet Conversion

Enable Bridging Between Transparent Bridging and SRB

Before enabling bridging, you must have completely configured your router using multiport SRB and transparent bridging. Once you have done this, establish bridging between transparent bridging and source-route bridging by using the following command in global configuration mode:

Command	Purpose
source-bridge transparent *ring-group pseudo-ring bridge-number tb-group* [*oui*]	Enables bridging between transparent bridging and SRB.

Disable Fast-Switched SR/TLB

To disable fast-switched SR/TLB and cause the router to handle packets by process switching, use the following command in global configuration mode:

Command	Purpose
no source-bridge transparent *ring-group* **fastswitch**	Disables fast-switched SR/TLB.

Enable Translation Compatibility with IBM 8209 Bridges

To transfer data between IBM 8209 Ethernet/Token Ring bridges and routers running the SR/TLB software (to create a Token Ring backbone to connect Ethernets), use the following command on each Token Ring interface in interface configuration mode:

Command	Purpose
ethernet-transit-oui [90-compatible | standard | cisco]	Moves data between IBM 8209 Ethernet/Token Ring bridges and routers running translational bridging software.

Enable Token Ring LLC2-to-Ethernet Conversion

Cisco IOS software supports the following types of Token Ring-to-Ethernet frame conversions using Logical Link Control, type 2 (LLC2) Protocol:

● Token Ring LLC2 to Ethernet Type II (0x80d5 processing)

● Token Ring LLC2 to Ethernet 802.3 LLC2 (standard)

For most non-IBM hosts, Token Ring LLC2 frames can be translated in a straightforward manner into Ethernet 802.3 LLC2 frames. This is the default conversion in Cisco IOS software.

However, many Ethernet-attached IBM devices use nonstandard encapsulation of LLC2 on Ethernet. Such IBM devices, including PS/2s running OS/2 Extended Edition and RT-PCs, do not place their LLC2 data inside an 802.3 format frame, but rather place it into an Ethernet Type 2 frame whose type is specified as *0x80d5*. This nonstandard format is called *0x80d5*, named after the type of frame. This format is also sometimes called *RT-PC Ethernet format* because these frames were first widely seen on the RT-PC. Hosts using this nonstandard 0x80d5 format cannot read the standard Token Ring LLC2 to Ethernet 802.2 LLC frames.

To enable Token Ring LLC2 to Ethernet LLC2 conversion, you can perform one or both of the following tasks:

● Enable 0x80d5 Processing

● Enable Standard Token Ring LLC2-to-Ethernet LLC2 Conversion

Enable 0x80d5 Processing

You can change Cisco IOS software's default translation behavior of translating Token Ring LLC to Ethernet 802.3 LLC to translate Token Ring LLC2 frames into Ethernet 0x80d5 format frames. To enable this nonstandard conversion, use the following command in global configuration mode:

Command	Purpose
source-bridge enable-80d5	Changes the Ethernet/Token Ring translation behavior to translate Token Ring LLC2 frames into Ethernet 0x80d5 format frames.

Enable Standard Token Ring LLC2-to-Ethernet LLC2 Conversion

After you change the translation behavior to perform Token Ring LLC2 frames into Ethernet 0x80d5 format frames, some of the non-IBM hosts in your network topology might use the standard Token Ring conversion of Token Ring LLC2 to 802.3 LLC2 frames. If this is the case, you can change the translation method of those hosts to use the standard translation method on a per-DSAP basis. The translation method for all the IBM hosts would still remain as Token Ring LLC2 to Ethernet 0x80d5 translation.

To define non-IBM hosts in your network topology to use the standard translation method while the IBM hosts use the nonstandard method, use the following command in global configuration mode:

Command	Purpose
source-bridge sap-80d5 *dsap*	Allows some other devices to use normal LLC2/IEEE 802.3 translation on a per-DSAP basis.

Configure NetBIOS Support

NetBIOS is a nonroutable protocol that was originally designed to transmit messages between stations, typically IBM PCs, on a Token Ring network. NetBIOS allows messages to be exchanged between the stations using a name rather than a station address. Each station knows its name and is responsible for knowing the names of other stations on the network.

NOTE   In addition to this type of NetBIOS, which runs over LLC2, we have implemented another type of NetBIOS that runs over IPX.

NetBIOS name caching allows Cisco IOS software to maintain a cache of NetBIOS names, which avoids the high overhead of transmitting many of the broadcasts used between client and server NetBIOS PCs (IBM PCs or PS/2s) in an SRB environment.

When NetBIOS name caching is enabled, the software performs the following actions:

● Notices when any hosts send a series of duplicated "query" frames and reduces them to one frame per period. The time period is configurable.

● Keeps a cache of mappings between NetBIOS server and client names and their MAC addresses. By watching NAME_QUERY and NAME_RECOGNIZED request and response traffic between clients and servers, Cisco IOS software can forward broadcast requests sent by clients to find servers (and by servers in reply to their clients) directly to their needed destinations, rather than forwarding them for broadcast across the entire bridged network.

The software will time out the entries in the NetBIOS name cache after a specific interval of their initial storage. The timeout value is a user-configurable value. You can configure the timeout value for a particular Token Ring if the NetBIOS name cache is enabled on the interface connecting to that Token Ring. In addition, you can configure static name cache entries that never time out for frequently accessed servers whose locations or paths typically do not change. Static RIF entries are also specified for such hosts.

Generally, NetBIOS name caching is most useful when a large amount of NetBIOS broadcast traffic creates bottlenecks on WAN media connecting distant locations, and the WAN media is overwhelmed with this traffic. However, when two high-speed LAN segments are directly interconnected, the packet savings of NetBIOS name caching is probably not worth the processor overhead associated with it.

NOTE   NetBIOS name caching is not recommended to be turned on in backbone routers, particularly if you have it enabled in all the routers connected to the backbone. NetBIOS caching should be distributed among multiple routers. NetBIOS name caching can be used only between Cisco routers that are running Software Release 9.1 or later.

To enable NetBIOS name caching, you must perform the tasks in the following sections:

● Enable the Proxy Explorers Feature on the Appropriate Interface

● Specify Timeout and Enable NetBIOS Name Caching

In addition, you can configure NetBIOS name caching as described in the following sections:

● Configure the NetBIOS Cache Name Length

● Enable NetBIOS Proxying

● Create Static Entries in the NetBIOS Name Cache

● Specify Dead-Time Intervals for NetBIOS Packets

Enable the Proxy Explorers Feature on the Appropriate Interface

In order to enable NetBIOS name caching on an interface, the proxy explorers feature must first be enabled on that interface. This feature must either be enabled for response to all explorer packets or for response to NetBIOS packets only.

To determine whether the proxy explorers feature has been enabled, use the following command in EXEC mode:

Command	Purpose
show startup-config	Determines whether or not the proxy explorers feature has been enabled.

To determine whether proxy explorers has been configured for response to all explorer packets, look in the configuration file for the **source-bridge proxy-explorer** entry for the appropriate interface. For example, if the appropriate interface is Token Ring 0, look for an entry similar to the following:

```
interface tokenring 0
source-bridge proxy-explorer
```

If that entry does not exist, look for the **source-bridge proxy-netbios-only** entry for the appropriate interface.

If neither entry exists, proxy explorers has not yet been enabled for the appropriate interface. To enable proxy explorers for response to all explorer packets, refer to the section "Configure Proxy Explorers" later in this chapter.

Otherwise, enable proxy explorers only for the NetBIOS name caching function by using the following command in global configuration mode:

Command	Purpose
source-bridge proxy-netbios-only	Enables use of proxy explorers only for the NetBIOS name caching function and not for their general local response to explorers.

Specify Timeout and Enable NetBIOS Name Caching

After you have ensured that the proxy explorers feature has been enabled for the appropriate interface, you can specify a cache timeout and enable NetBIOS name caching. To do this, use the following commands:

Step	Command	Purpose
1	**netbios name-cache timeout** *minutes*	Specifies the timeout for entries in the NetBIOS name cache.

Step	Command	Purpose
2	**netbios enable-name-cache**	Enables NetBIOS name caching for the appropriate interfaces.

Configure the NetBIOS Cache Name Length

To specify how many characters of the NetBIOS type name that the name cache will validate, enter the following command in global configuration mode:

Command	Purpose
netbios name-cache name-len *length*	Specifies the number of characters of the NetBIOS type name to cache.

Enable NetBIOS Proxying

Cisco IOS software can act as a proxy and send NetBIOS datagram type frames. To enable this capability, use the following global configuration command:

Command	Purpose
netbios name-cache proxy-datagram *seconds*	Enables NetBIOS proxying.

To define the validation time when the software is acting as a proxy for NetBIOS NAME_QUERY command or for explorer frames, use the following global configuration command:

Command	Purpose
rif validate-age *seconds*	Defines validation time.

Create Static Entries in the NetBIOS Name Cache

If the router communicates with one or more NetBIOS stations on a regular basis, adding static entries to the NetBIOS name cache for these stations can reduce network traffic and overhead. You can define a static NetBIOS name cache entry that associates the server with the NetBIOS name and the MAC address. If the router acts as a NetBIOS server, you can specify that the static NetBIOS name cache is available locally through a particular interface. If a remote router acts as the NetBIOS server, you can specify that the NetBIOS name cache is available remotely. To do this, use one of the following commands in global configuration mode:

Command	Purpose
netbios name-cache *mac-address netbios-name interface-name*	Defines a static NetBIOS name cache entry and specifies that it is available locally through a particular interface.
netbios name-cache *mac-address netbios-name* **ring-group** *group-number*	Defines a static NetBIOS name cache entry and specifies that it is available remotely.

If you have defined a NetBIOS name cache entry, you must also define a RIF entry. For an example of how to configure a static NetBIOS entry, see the "NetBIOS Support with a Static NetBIOS Cache Entry Example" section later in this chapter.

Specify Dead-Time Intervals for NetBIOS Packets

When NetBIOS name caching is enabled and default parameters are set on the router (as well as the NetBIOS name server and the NetBIOS name client), approximately 20 broadcast packets per logon are kept on the local ring where they are generated. The broadcast packets are of the type ADD_NAME_QUERY, ADD_GROUP_NAME, and STATUS_QUERY.

Cisco IOS software also converts pairs of FIND_NAME and NAME_RECOGNIZED packets received from explorers, which traverse all rings, to specific route frames that are sent only between the two machines that need to see these packets.

You can specify a query-timeout, or dead-time interval, to prevent repeat or duplicate broadcast of these type of packets for the duration of the interval.

To specify dead-time intervals, use one or both of the following commands in global configuration mode:

Command	Purpose
netbios name-cache query-timeout *seconds*	Specifies a dead-time interval during which Cisco IOS software drops any broadcast (NetBIOS ADD_NAME_QUERY, ADD_GROUP_NAME, or STATUS_QUERY) frames if they are duplicate frames sent by the same host.
netbios name-cache recognized-timeout *seconds*	Specifies a dead-time interval during which the software drops FIND_NAME and NAME_RECOGNIZED frames if they are duplicate frames sent by the same host.

Configure LNM Support

LAN Network Manager (LNM), formerly called LAN Manager, is an IBM product for managing a collection of source-route bridges. Using either a proprietary protocol or the Simple Network Management Protocol (SNMP), LNM allows you to monitor the entire collection of Token Rings that comprise your source-route bridged network. You can use LNM to manage the configuration of source-route bridges, monitor Token Ring errors, and gather information from Token Ring parameter servers.

NOTE	LNM is supported on the 4/16-Mb Token Ring cards that can be configured for either 4- or 16-Mb transmission speeds. LNM support is not provided on CSC-R16M cards with SBEMON 2.0.

LNM is not limited to managing locally attached Token Ring networks. It also can manage any other Token Rings in your source-route bridged network that are connected through non-Token Ring media. To accomplish this task, LNM works in conjunction with the IBM Bridge Program. The IBM Bridge Program gathers data about the local Token Ring network and relays it back to LNM. In this manner, the bridge program becomes a proxy for information about its local Token Ring. Without this ability, you would require direct access to a device on every Token Ring in the network. This process would make managing an SRB environment awkward and cumbersome.

Figure 3-7 shows some Token Rings attached through a cloud and one LNM linking to a source-route bridge on each local ring.

Figure 3-7   *LNM Linking to a Source-Route Bridge on Each Local Ring*

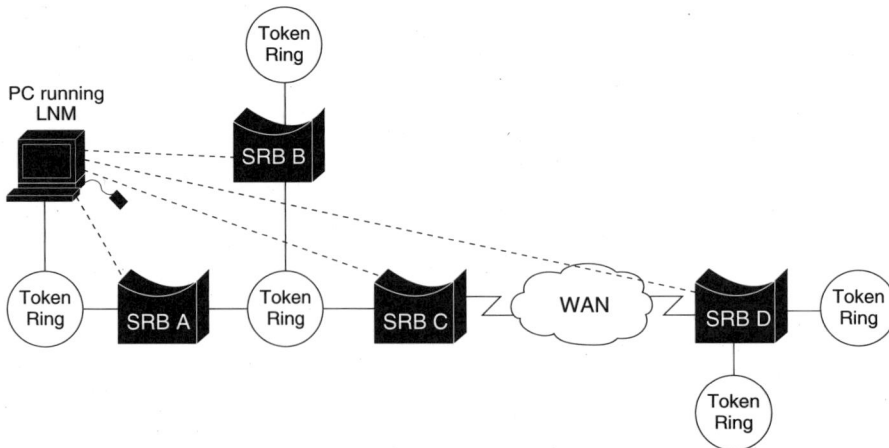

If LNM requires information about a station somewhere on a Token Ring, it uses a proprietary IBM protocol to query to one of the source-route bridges connected to that ring. If the bridge can provide the requested information, it simply responds directly to LNM. If the bridge does not have the necessary information, it queries the station using a protocol published in the IEEE 802.5 specification. In either case, the bridge uses the proprietary protocol to send a valid response back to LNM, using the proprietary protocol.

As an analogy, consider a language translator who sits between a French-speaking diplomat and a German-speaking diplomat. If the French diplomat asks the translator a question in French for the German diplomat and the translator knows the answer, he or she simply responds without translating the original question into German. If the French diplomat asks a question the translator does not know how to answer, the translator must first translate the question to German, wait for the German diplomat to answer, and then translate the answer back to French.

Similarly, if LNM queries a source-route bridge in the proprietary protocol and the bridge knows the answer, it responds directly using the same protocol. If the bridge does not know the answer, it must first translate the question to the IEEE 802.5 protocol, query the station on the ring, and then translate the response back to the proprietary protocol to send to LNM.

Figure 3-8 illustrates requests from the LNM originating in an IBM proprietary protocol and then translated into IEEE 802.5 MAC-level frames.

Figure 3-8   *LAN Network Manager Monitoring and Translating*

Notice that the proprietary protocol LNM uses to communicate with the source-route bridge is an LLC2 connection. Although its protocol cannot be routed, LNM can monitor or manage anything within the SRB network.

How a Router Works with LNM

As of Software Release 9.0, Cisco routers using 4/16-Mbps Token Ring interfaces configured for SRB support the proprietary protocol that LNM uses. These routers provide all functions the IBM Bridge Program currently provides. Thus LNM can communicate with a router as if it were an IBM source-route bridge, such as the IBM 8209, and can manage or monitor any Token Ring connected to the router.

Through IBM Bridge support, LNM provides three basic services for the SRB network:

- The Configuration Report Server (CRS) monitors the current logical configuration of a Token Ring and reports any changes to LNM. CRS also reports various other events, such as the change of an active monitor on a Token Ring.

- The Ring Error Monitor (REM) monitors errors reported by any station on the ring. In addition, REM monitors whether the ring is in a functional or a failure state.

- The Ring Parameter Server (RPS) reports to LNM when any new station joins a Token Ring and ensures that all stations on a ring are using a consistent set of reporting parameters.

IBM Bridge support for LNM also allows asynchronous notification of some events that can occur on a Token Ring. Examples of these events include notification of a new station joining the Token Ring or of the ring entering failure mode, known as *beaconing*. Support is also provided for LNM to change the operating parameters in the bridge. For a complete description of LNM, refer to the IBM product manual supplied with the LNM program.

LNM support in Cisco source-route bridges is a powerful tool for managing SRB networks. Through the ability to communicate with LNM and to provide the functionality of the IBM Bridge Program, Cisco device appears as part of the IBM network. You therefore gain from the interconnectivity of Cisco products without having to learn a new management product or interface.

When SRB is enabled on the router, configuring Cisco IOS software to perform the functions of an IBM Bridge for communication with LNM occurs automatically. Therefore, if SRB has been enabled, you do not need to perform any tasks to enable LNM support. However, the LNM software residing on a management station on a Token Ring on the network should be configured to properly communicate with the router.

There are several options for modifying LNM parameters in Cisco IOS software, but none are required for basic functionality. For example, because users can now modify the operation of Cisco IOS software through SNMP as well as through LNM, there is an option to exclude a user from modifying Cisco IOS software configuration through LNM. You also can specify which of the three LNM services (CRS, REM, RPS) the source-route bridge will perform.

To configure LNM support, perform the tasks in the following sections:

- Configure LNM Software on the Management Stations to Communicate with the Router

- Disable LNM Functionality

- Disable Automatic Report Path Trace Function

- Prevent LNM Stations from Modifying Cisco IOS Software Parameters
- Enable Other LRMs to Change Router Parameters
- Apply a Password to an LNM Reporting Link
- Enable LNM Servers
- Change Reporting Thresholds
- Change an LNM Reporting Interval
- Enable the RPS Express Buffer Function
- Monitor LNM Operation

Configure LNM Software on the Management Stations to Communicate with the Router

Because configuring an LNM station is a fairly simple task and is well covered in the LNM documentation, it is not covered in depth here. However, it is important to mention that you must enter the MAC addresses of the interfaces comprising the ports of the bridges as adapter addresses. When you configure the router as a multiport bridge, configuring an LNM station is complicated by the virtual ring that is involved. The basic problem extends from the fact that LNM is designed to only understand the concept of a two-port bridge, and the router with a virtual ring is a *multiport* bridge. The solution is to configure a virtual ring into the LNM Manager station as a series of dual-port bridges.

Disable LNM Functionality

Under some circumstances, you can disable all LNM server functions on the router without having to determine whether to disable a specific server, such as the RPS or the REM on a given interface.

To disable LNM functionality, use the following command in global configuration mode:

Command	Purpose
lnm disabled	Disables LNM functionality.

The command can be used to terminate all LNM server input and reporting links. In normal circumstances, this command should not be necessary because it is a superset of the functions normally performed on individual interfaces by the **no lnm rem** and **no lnm rps** commands.

Disable Automatic Report Path Trace Function

Under some circumstances, such as when new hardware has been introduced into the network and is causing problems, the automatic report path trace function can be disabled. The new hardware may be setting bit-fields B1 or B2 (or both) of the routing control field in the RIF embedded in a source-route bridged frame. This condition may cause the network to be flooded by report path trace frames if the condition is persistent. The **lnm pathtrace-disabled** command, along with its options, allows you to alleviate network congestion that may be occurring by disabling all or part of the automatic report path trace function within LNM.

To disable the automatic report path trace function, use the following command in global configuration mode:

Command	Purpose
**lnm pathtrace-disabled [all	origin]**	Disables LNM automatic report path trace function.

Prevent LNM Stations from Modifying Cisco IOS Software Parameters

Because there is now more than one way to remotely change parameters in a router (either using SNMP or the proprietary IBM protocol), some method is needed to prevent such changes from detrimentally interacting with each other. You can prevent any LNM station from modifying parameters in Cisco IOS software. It does not affect the ability of LNM to monitor events, only to change parameters on the router.

To prevent the modification of Cisco IOS software parameters by an LNM station, use the following command in global configuration mode:

Command	Purpose
lnm snmp-only	Prevents LNM stations from modifying LNM parameters in Cisco IOS software.

Enable Other LRMs to Change Router Parameters

LNM has a concept of reporting links and reporting link numbers. A reporting link is simply a connection (or potential connection) between a LAN Reporting Manager (LRM) and a bridge. A reporting link number is a unique number used to identify a reporting link. An IBM bridge allows four simultaneous reporting links numbered 0 through 3. Only the LRM attached on the lowest-numbered connection is allowed to change LNM parameters in the router, and then only when that connection number falls below a certain configurable number. In the default configuration, the LRM connected through link 0 is the only LRM that can change LNM parameters.

To enable other LRMs to change router parameters, use the following command in interface configuration mode:

Command	Purpose
lnm alternate *number*	Enables a LRM other than that connected through link 0 to change router parameters.

Apply a Password to an LNM Reporting Link

Each reporting link has its own password that is used not only to prevent unauthorized access from an LRM to a bridge but to control access to the different reporting links. This is important because it is possible to change parameters through some reporting links.

To apply a password to an LNM reporting link, use the following command in interface configuration mode:

Command	Purpose
lnm password *number string*	Applies a password to an LNM reporting link.

Enable LNM Servers

As in an IBM bridge, the router provides several functions that gather information from a local Token Ring. All of these functions are enabled by default, but also can be disabled. The LNM servers are explained in the section "How a Router Works with LNM" earlier in this chapter.

To enable LNM servers, use one or more of the following commands in interface configuration mode:

Command	Purpose
lnm crs	Enables the LNM Configuration Report Server (CRS).
lnm rem	Enables the LNM Ring Error Monitor (REM).
lnm rps	Enables the LNM Ring Parameter Server (RPS).

Change Reporting Thresholds

Cisco IOS software sends a message to all attached LNMs whenever it begins to drop frames. The threshold at which this report is generated is based on a percentage of frames dropped compared with those forwarded. This threshold is configurable, and defaults to a value of 0.10 percent. You can configure the threshold by entering a single number, expressing the percentage loss rate in hundredths of a percent. The valid range is 0 to 9999.

To change reporting thresholds, use the following command in interface configuration mode:

Command	Purpose
lnm loss-threshold *number*	Changes the threshold at which Cisco IOS software reports the frames-lost percentage to LNM.

Change an LNM Reporting Interval

All stations on a Token Ring notify the REM when they detect errors on the ring. In order to prevent excessive messages, error reports are not sent immediately, but are accumulated for a short interval and then reported. A station learns the duration of this interval from a router (configured as a source-route bridge) when it first enters the ring. This value is expressed in tens of milliseconds between error messages. The default is 200, or 2 seconds. The valid range is 0 to 65,535.

To change an LNM reporting interval, use the following command in interface configuration mode:

Command	Purpose
lnm softerr *milliseconds*	Sets the time interval during which stations report ring errors to the REM.

Enable the RPS Express Buffer Function

The RPS express buffer function allows the router to set the express buffer bit to ensure priority service for frames required for ring station initiation. When this function is enabled, the router sets the express buffer bit in its initialize ring station response. This allows Token Ring devices to insert into the ring during bursty conditions.

To enable LNM to use the RPS express buffer function, use the following command in interface configuration mode:

Command	Purpose
lnm express-buffer	Enables the RPS express buffer function.

Monitor LNM Operation

Once LNM support is enabled, you can monitor LNM operation. To observe the configuration of the LNM bridge and its operating parameters, use the following commands in EXEC mode:

Step	Command	Purpose
1	**show lnm bridge**	Displays all configured bridges and their global parameters.
2	**show lnm config**	Displays the logical configuration of all bridges configured in the router.
3	**show lnm interface** [*type number*]	Displays LNM information for an interface or all interfaces of the router.
4	**show lnm ring** [*ring-number*]	Displays LNM information about a Token Ring or all Token Rings on the network.
5	**show lnm station** [*address*]	Displays LNM information about a station or all stations on the network.

Secure the SRB Network

This section describes how to configure three features that are used primarily to provide network security: NetBIOS access filters, administrative filters, and access expressions that can be combined with administrative filters. In addition, these features can be used to increase network performance because they reduce the number of packets that traverse the backbone network.

Configure NetBIOS Access Filters

NetBIOS packets can be filtered when transmitted across a Token Ring bridge. Two types of filters can be configured:

● Host access list

Used for source and destination station names

● Byte offset access list

Used for arbitrary byte patterns in the packet itself.

As you configure NetBIOS access filters, keep the following issues in mind:

● The access lists that apply filters to an interface are scanned in the order they are entered.

● There is no way to put a new access list entry in the middle of an access list. All new additions to existing NetBIOS access lists are placed at the end of the existing list.

- Access list arguments are case sensitive. The software makes a literal translation, so that a lowercase "a" is different from an uppercase "A." (Most nodes are named in uppercase letters.)

- A host NetBIOS access list and byte NetBIOS access list can each use the same name. The two lists are identified as unique and bear no relationship to each other.

- The station names included in the access lists are compared with the source name field for NetBIOS commands 00 and 01 (ADD_GROUP_NAME_QUERY and ADD_NAME_QUERY), as well as the destination name field for NetBIOS commands 08, 0A, and 0E (DATAGRAM, NAME_QUERY, and NAME_RECOGNIZED).

- If an access list does not contain a particular station name, the default action is to deny the access to that station.

To minimize any performance degradation, NetBIOS access filters do not examine all packets. Rather, they examine certain packets that are used to establish and maintain NetBIOS client/server connections, thereby effectively stopping new access and load across the router. However, applying a new access filter does not terminate existing sessions immediately. All new sessions will be filtered, but existing sessions could continue for some time.

There are two ways you can configure NetBIOS access filters:

- Configure NetBIOS Access Filters Using Station Names

- Configure NetBIOS Access Filters Using a Byte Offset

Configure NetBIOS Access Filters Using Station Names

To configure access filters using station names, you must do the following:

Step 1 Assign the station access list name.

Step 2 Specify the direction of the message to be filtered on the interface.

The NetBIOS station access list contains the station name to match, along with a permit or deny condition. You must assign the name of the access list to a station or set of stations on the network.

To assign a station access list name, use the following command in global configuration mode:

Command	Purpose
netbios access-list host *name* {**permit** | **deny**} *pattern*	Assigns the name of an access list to a station or set of stations on the network.

When filtering by station name, you can choose to filter either incoming or outgoing messages on the interface. To specify the direction, use one of the following commands in interface configuration mode:

Command	Purpose
netbios input-access-filter host *name*	Defines an access list filter for incoming messages.
netbios output-access-filter host *name*	Defines an access list filter for outgoing messages.

Configure NetBIOS Access Filters Using a Byte Offset

To configure access filters you must do the following:

Step 1   Assign a byte offset access list name.

Step 2   Specify the direction of the message to be filtered on the interface.

Keep the following notes in mind while configuring access filters using a byte offset:

● When an access list entry has an offset plus the length of the pattern that is larger than the packet's length, the entry will not make a match for that packet.

● Because these access lists allow arbitrary byte offsets into packets, these access filters can have a significant impact on the amount of packets per second transiting across the bridge. They should be used only when situations absolutely dictate their use.

The NetBIOS byte offset access list contains a series of offsets and hexadecimal patterns with which to match byte offsets in NetBIOS packets. To assign a byte offset access list name, use the following command in global configuration mode:

Command	Purpose
netbios access-list bytes *name* {**permit** | **deny**} *offset* *pattern*	Defines the byte offsets and patterns within NetBIOS messages to match with access list parameters.

NOTE   Using NetBIOS Byte Offset access filters disables the autonomous or fast switching of SRB frames.

When filtering by byte offset, you can filter either incoming or outgoing messages on the interface. To specify the direction, use one of the following commands in interface configuration mode:

Command	Purpose
netbios input-access-filter bytes *name*	Specifies a byte-based access filter on incoming messages.
netbios output-access-filter bytes *name*	Specifies a byte-based access filter on outgoing messages.

Configure Administrative Filters for Token Ring Traffic

Source-route bridges normally filter frames according to the routing information contained in the frame. That is, a bridge will not forward a frame back to its originating network segment or any other network segment that the frame has already traversed. This section describes how to configure another type of filter—the administrative filter.

Administrative filters can filter frames based on the following methods:

- Protocol type—IEEE 802 or Subnetwork Access Protocol (SNAP)

- Token Ring vendor code

- Source address

- Destination address

Whereas filtering by Token Ring address or vendor code causes no significant performance penalty, filtering by protocol type significantly affects performance. A list of SNAP (Ethernet) type codes is provided in Appendix A, "Ethernet Type Codes."

Filter Frames by Protocol Type

You can configure administrative filters by protocol type by specifying protocol type codes in an access list. You then apply that access list to either IEEE 802.2 encapsulated packets or to SNAP-encapsulated packets on the appropriate interface.

The order in which you specify these elements affects the order in which the access conditions are checked. Each condition is tested in succession. A matching condition is then used to execute a permit or deny decision. If no conditions match, a deny decision is reached.

NOTE	If a single condition is to be denied, there must be an **access-list** command that permits everything as well or all access is denied.

To filter frames by protocol type, use the following command in global configuration mode:

Command	Purpose
access-list *access-list-number* {**permit** | **deny**} {*type-code wild-mask* | *address mask*}	Creates an access list for filtering frames by protocol type.

You can filter IEEE 802-encapsulated packets on either input or output. The access list you specify is the one you created that includes the protocol type codes.

To enable filtering on input or output, use one of the following commands in interface configuration mode:

Command	Purpose
source-bridge input-lsap-list *access-list-number*	Enables filtering of IEEE 802-encapsulated packets on input by type code.
source-bridge output-lsap-list *access-list-number*	Enables filtering of IEEE 802-encapsulated packets on output by type code.

You can filter SNAP-encapsulated packets on either input or output. The access list you specify is the one you created that includes the protocol type codes.

To enable filtering on input or output, use one of the following commands in interface configuration mode:

Command	Purpose
source-bridge input-type-list *access-list-number*	Filters SNAP-encapsulated packets on input by type code.
source-bridge output-type-list *access-list-number*	Filters SNAP-encapsulated frames on output by type code.

Filter Frames by Vendor Code

To configure administrative filters by vendor code or address, define access lists that look for Token Ring addresses or for particular vendor codes for administrative filtering. To do so, use the following command in global configuration mode:

Purpose	Command
access-list *access-list-number* {**permit** | **deny**} *address mask*	Configures vendor code access lists.

Filter Source Addresses

To configure filtering on IEEE 802 source addresses, assign an access list to a particular input interface for filtering the Token Ring or IEEE 802 source addresses. To do so, use the following command in interface configuration mode:

Command	Purpose
source-bridge input-address-list *access-list-number*	Enables filtering on IEEE 802 source addresses.

Filter Destination Addresses

To configure filtering on IEEE 802 destination addresses, assign an access list to a particular output interface. To do so, use the following command in interface configuration mode:

Command	Purpose
source-bridge output-address-list *access-list-number*	Enables filtering on IEEE 802 destination addresses.

Configure Access Expressions that Combine Administrative Filters

You can use access expressions to combine access filters to establish complex conditions under which bridged frames can enter or leave an interface. Using access expressions, you can achieve levels of control on the forwarding of frames that otherwise would be impossible when using only simple access filters. Access expressions are constructed from individual access lists that define administrative filters for the following fields in packets:

- LSAP and SNAP type codes
- MAC addresses
- NetBIOS station names
- NetBIOS arbitrary byte values

NOTE   For any given interface, an access expression cannot be used if an access list has been defined for a given direction. For example, if an input access list is defined for MAC addresses on an interface, no access expression can be specified for the input side of that interface.

In Figure 3-9, two routers each connect a Token Ring to an FDDI backbone. On both Token Rings, SNA and NetBIOS bridging support is required. On Token Ring A, NetBIOS clients must communicate with any NetBIOS server off Token Ring B or any other, unpictured router. However, the two 3174 cluster controllers off Token Ring A must only communicate with the one FEP off of Token Ring B, located at MAC address 0110.2222.3333.

Without access expressions, this scenario cannot be achieved. A filter on Router A that restricted access to only the FEP would also restrict access of the NetBIOS clients to the FEP. What is needed is an access expression that would state "If it is a NetBIOS frame, pass through, but if it is an SNA frame, only allow access to address 0110.2222.3333."

Figure 3-9   *Access Expression Example*

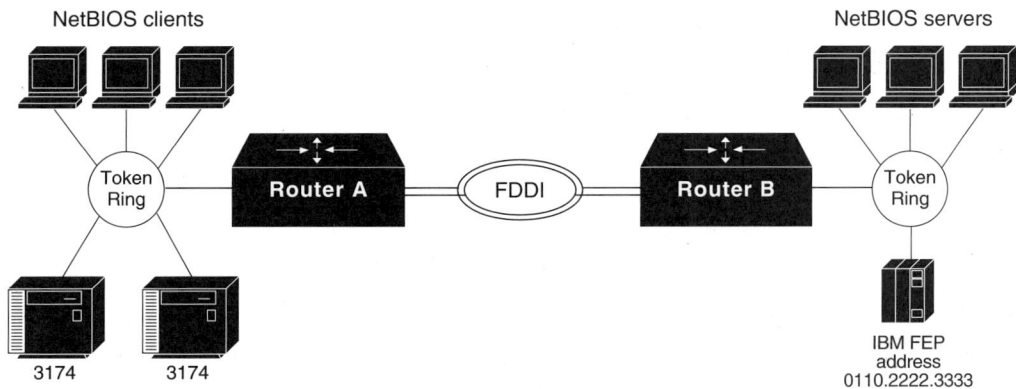

NOTE   Using access-expressions that combine access filters disables the autonomous or fast switching of SRB frames.

Configure Access Expressions

To configure an access expression perform the following tasks:

- Design the access expression.
- Configure the access lists used by the expression.
- Configure the access expression into the router.

When designing an access expression, you must create some phrase that indicates, in its entirety, all the frames that will pass the access expression. This access expression is designed to apply on frames coming from the Token Ring interface on Router A in Figure 3-9:

"Pass the frame if it is a NetBIOS frame or if it is an SNA frame destined to address 0110.2222.3333."

In Boolean form, this phrase can be written as follows:

"Pass if 'NetBIOS or (SNA and destined to 0110.2222.3333).'"

The preceding statement requires three access lists to be configured:

- An access list that passes a frame if it is a NetBIOS frame (SAP = 0xF0F0)

- An access list that passes a frame if it is an SNA frame (SAP = 0x0404)

- An access list that passes a MAC address of 0110.2222.3333

The following configuration allows for all these conditions:

```
! Access list 201 passes NetBIOS frames (command or response)
access-list 201 permit 0xF0F0 0x0001
!
access-list 202 permit 0x0404 0x0001 ! Permits SNA frames (command or response)
access-list 202 permit 0x0004 0x0001 ! Permits SNA Explorers with NULL DSAP
!
! Access list 701 will permit the FEP MAC address
! of 0110.2222.3333
access-list 701 permit 0110.2222.3333
```

The 0x0001 mask allows command and response frames to pass equally.

To apply the access expression to the appropriate interface, enter the following command in interface configuration mode:

Command	Purpose
access-expression {in | out} *expression*	Defines a per-interface access expression.

Optimize Access Expressions

It is possible to combine access expressions. Suppose you wanted to transmit SNA traffic through to a single address, but allow other traffic through the router without restriction. The phrase could be written as follows:

"Allow access if the frame is not an SNA frame, or if it is going to host 0110.2222.3333."

More tersely, this would be:

"Not SNA or destined to 0110.2222.3333."

The access lists defined in the previous section create the following configuration:

```
interface tokenring 0
 access-expression in ~lsap(202) ¦ dmac(701)
!
access-list 202 permit 0x0404 0x0001 ! Permits SNA frames (command or response)
access-list 202 permit 0x0004 0x0001 ! Permits SNA Explorers with NULL DSAP
!
! Access list 701 will permit the FEP MAC address
! of 0110.2222.3333
 access-list 701 permit 0110.2222.3333
```

This is a better and simpler access list than the one originally introduced and will probably result in better run-time execution as a result. Therefore, it is best to simplify your access expressions as much as possible before configuring them into Cisco IOS software.

NOTE   An "access-expression" type filter cannot exist with a "source-bridge" type filter on the same interface. The two types of filters are mutually exclusive.

Alter Access Lists Used in Access Expressions

Because access expressions are composed of access lists, special care must be taken when deleting and adding access lists that are referenced in these access expressions.

If an access list that is referenced in an access expression is deleted, the access expression merely ignores the deleted access list. However, if you want to redefine an access list, you can create a new access list with the appropriate definition and use the same name as the old access list. The newly defined access list replaces the old one of the same name.

For example, if you want to redefine the NetBIOS access list named MIS that was used in the preceding example, you would use the following sequence of configuration commands:

```
!  Replace the NetBIOS access list
interface tokenring 0
 access-expression in (smac(701) & netbios-host(accept))
 no netbios access-list host accept permit CISCO*
```

Tune the SRB Network

The following sections describe how to configure features that enhance network performance by reducing the number of packets that traverse the backbone network:

● Enable or Disable the Source-Route Fast-Switching Cache

● Enable or Disable the Source-Route Autonomous-Switching Cache

● Enable or Disable the Silicon Switching Engine

● Establish the Connection Timeout Interval

- Optimize Explorer Processing

- Configure Proxy Explorers

NOTE   In some situations, you might discover that default settings for LLC2 configurations are not acceptable. In such a case, you can configure LLC2 for optimal use. Chapter 13, "Configuring LLC2 and SDLC Parameters" describes how you can use them to optimize your network performance.

Enable or Disable the Source-Route Fast-Switching Cache

Rather than processing packets at the process level, the fast-switching feature enables Cisco IOS software to process packets at the interrupt level. Each packet is transferred from the input interface to the output interface without copying the entire packet to main system memory. Fast switching allows for faster implementations of local SRB between 4/16-MB Token Ring cards in the same router, or between two routers using the 4/16-Mb Token Ring cards and direct encapsulation.

By default, fast-switching software is enabled when SRB is enabled. To enable or disable source-route fast-switching, use one of the following commands in interface configuration mode:

Command	Purpose
source-bridge route-cache	Enables fast-switching.
no source-bridge route-cache	Disables fast-switching.

NOTE   Using either NetBIOS Byte Offset access filters or access expressions that combine access filters disables the fast switching of source-route bridging frames.

Enable or Disable the Source-Route Autonomous-Switching Cache

Autonomous switching is a feature that enables Cisco IOS software to transmit packets from the input ciscoBus card to the output ciscoBus card without any involvement on the part of the router processor.

Autonomous switching is available for local SRB between ciscoBus Token Ring (CTR) cards in the same router. Autonomous switching provides higher switching rates than does fast switching between 4/16-Mb Token Ring cards. Autonomous switching works for both two-port bridges and multiport bridges that use ciscoBus Token Ring cards.

In a virtual ring that includes both ciscoBus Token Ring and 4/16-Mb Token Ring interfaces, frames that flow from one CTR interface to another are autonomously switched and the remainder of the frames are fast switched. The switching that occurs on the CTR interface takes advantage of the high-speed ciscoBus controller processor.

To enable or disable source-route autonomous switching, use one of the following commands in interface configuration mode:

Command	Purpose
source-bridge route-cache cbus	Enables autonomous switching.
no source-bridge route-cache cbus	Disables autonomous switching.

NOTE   Using either NetBIOS Byte Offset access filters or access-expressions that combine access filters disables the autonomous switching of SRB frames.

Enable or Disable the Silicon Switching Engine

The silicon switching engine (SSE) acts as a programmable cache to speed the switching of packets. To enable or disable the SSE, use one of the following commands in interface configuration mode:

Command	Purpose
source-bridge route-cache sse	Enables the SSE function.
no source-bridge route-cache sse	Disables the SSE function.

Establish the Connection Timeout Interval

It may be necessary to adjust timeout intervals in a complex topology such as a large multihop WAN with virtual rings or satellite links. The timeout interval is used when a connection to a remote peer is attempted. If the timeout interval expires before a response is received, the connection attempt is aborted.

To set the connection timeout interval, use the following command in global configuration mode:

Command	Purpose
source-bridge connection-timeout *seconds*	Sets the connection timeout interval.

Optimize Explorer Processing

Efficient explorer processing is vital to the operation of SRB. The default configuration is satisfactory for most situations. However, there might be circumstances that create unexpected broadcast storms. You can optimize the handling of explorer frames, thus reducing processor overhead and increasing explorer packet throughput. Optimizing explorer processing enables the router to perform substantially better during explorer broadcast storms.

In networks with redundant topologies—two or more routers connected to the same set of Token Rings and doing source-route bridging—a station on one Token Ring trying to get to a station on another Token Ring may choose a less than optimal route through unnecessary routers, causing explorer storms due to excessive forwarding of explorer frames. For example, in the redundant topology example shown in Figure 3-10, if Station X on Token Ring 1 attempts to get to Station Z on Token Ring 4 by going through Router A, Token Ring 2, and Router B—a less than optimal route, excessive forwarding of explorer frames may cause explorer storms.

Figure 3-10 *Controlling Explorer Storms in Redundant Network Topologies*

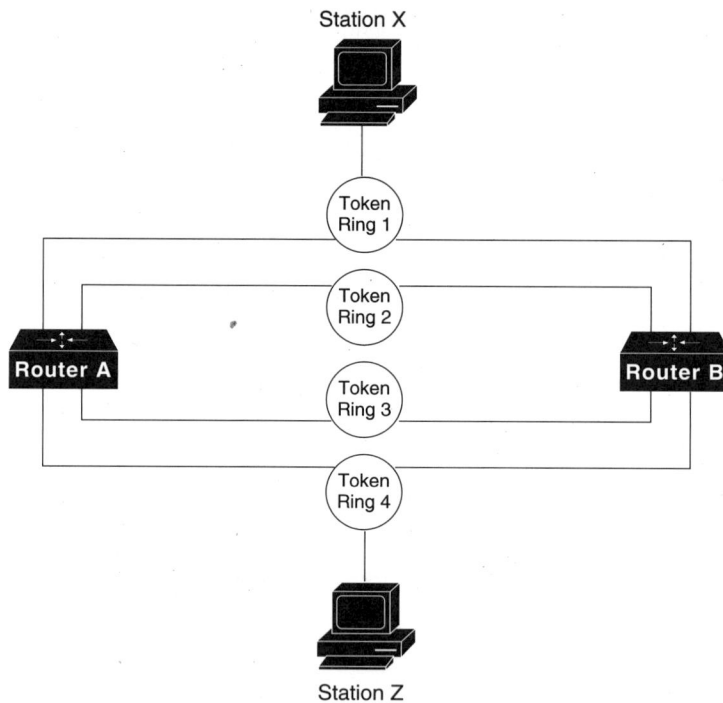

The **source-bridge explorer-dup-ARE-filter** command can be used to reduce explorer traffic by filtering explorer frames.

To optimize explorer processing, use one or more of the following commands in global configuration mode:

Command	Purpose
source-bridge explorerq-depth *depth*	Sets the maximum explorer queue depth.
source-bridge explorer-dup-ARE-filter	Prevents explorer storms in redundant network topologies by filtering explorers that have already been forwarded once.

Command	Purpose
source-bridge explorer-maxrate *maxrate*	Sets the maximum byte rate of explorers per ring.

You must also disable explorer fast-switching which is, by default, enabled. To disable explorer fast-switching, use the following command in global configuration mode:

Command	Purpose
no source-bridge explorer-fastswitch	Disables explorer fast switching.

To enable explorer fast-switching after it has been disabled, use the following command in global configuration mode:

Command	Purpose
source-bridge explorer-fastswitch	Enables explorer fast switching.

Configure Proxy Explorers

You can use the proxy explorers feature to limit the amount of explorer traffic propagating through the source-bridge network.

To configure proxy explorers, use the following command in interface configuration mode:

Command	Purpose
source-bridge proxy-explorer	Enables the interface to respond to any explorer packets that meet certain conditions necessary for a proxy response to occur.

Cisco IOS software does not propagate proxy responses for a station. Instead, the software obtains the RIF path from the RIF cache, changes the explorer to a specific frame, and forwards this frame to the destination. If a response is not received before the validation timer expires, the RIF entry is marked as invalid. The invalid RIF entry is flushed from the cache table when another explorer for this station is received and an explorer is forwarded to discover a path to this station.

Establish SRB Interoperability with Specific Token Ring Implementations

This section describes how you can establish interoperability between routers and specific Token Ring implementations. It includes the following sections:

- Establish SRB Interoperability with IBM PC/3270 Emulation Software

- Establish SRB Interoperability with TI MAC Firmware

- Report Spurious Frame-Copied Errors

Establish SRB Interoperability with IBM PC/3270 Emulation Software

You can establish interoperability with the IBM PC/3270 emulation program Version 3.0, even though it does not properly send packets over a source-route bridge.

Cisco SRB implementation rewrites the RIF headers of the explorer packets that the PC/3270 emulation program sends to go beyond the local ring, thus confusing the IBM implementation into not looking beyond the local ring for the remote host.

To rewrite RIF headers, use the following command in interface configuration mode:

Command	Purpose
source-bridge old-sna	Rewrites the RIF headers of explorer packets sent by the PC/3270 emulation program to go beyond the local ring.

Establish SRB Interoperability with TI MAC Firmware

You can use a workaround to establish interoperability with Texas Instruments MAC firmware.

There is a known defect in earlier versions of the Texas Instruments Token Ring MAC firmware. This implementation is used by Proteon, Apollo, and IBM RTs. A host using a MAC address whose first two bytes are zeros (such as a Cisco router) will not properly communicate with hosts using that version of Texas Instruments firmware.

There are two solutions. The first involves installing a static RIF entry for every faulty node with which the router communicates. If there are many such nodes on the ring, this may not be practical.

You also can set the MAC address of Cisco Token Ring to a value that works around the problem. Resetting the MAC address forces the use of a different MAC address on the specified interface, thereby avoiding the TI MAC firmware problem. However, you must ensure that no other host on the network is using that MAC address.

To reset the MAC address, use the following command in interface configuration mode:

Command	Purpose
mac-address *ieee-address*	Resets the MAC address of the Token Ring interface to a value that provides a workaround to a problem in Texas Instruments Token Ring MAC firmware.

Report Spurious Frame-Copied Errors

An IBM 3174 cluster controller can be configured to report frame-copied errors to IBM LAN Network Manager software. These errors indicate that another host is responding to the MAC address of the 3174 cluster controller. Both the 3174 cluster controller and the IBM LNM software can be configured to ignore frame-copied errors.

Monitor and Maintain the SRB Network

You can display a variety of information about the SRB network. To display the information you require, use one or more of the following commands in EXEC mode:

Command	Purpose
show controllers token	Displays internal state information about the Token Ring interfaces in the system.
show interfaces token	Provides high-level statistics for a particular interface.
show interfaces	Provides high-level statistics about the state of source bridging for a particular interface.
show lnm bridge	Displays all currently configured bridges and all parameters that are related to the bridge as a whole and not to one of its interfaces.
show lnm config	Displays the logical (multiport bridge) configuration of Cisco IOS software.
show lnm interface [*type number*]	Displays all LNM-relevant information about a specific interface.
show lnm ring [*ring-number*]	Displays all LNM-relevant information about a specific ring number.
show lnm station [*address*]	Displays all LNM-relevant information about a specific station or about all known stations on the ring.

Command	Purpose
show local-ack	Shows the current state of any current local acknowledgment for both LLC2 and SDLLC connections.
show netbios-cache	Displays the contents of the NetBIOS cache.
show rif	Displays the contents of the RIF cache.
show source-bridge	Displays the current source bridge configuration and miscellaneous statistics.
show span	Displays the spanning-tree topology for the router.
show sse summary	Displays a summary of Silicon Switch Processor (SSP) statistics.

To maintain the SRB network, use any of the following commands in privileged EXEC mode:

Command	Purpose
clear netbios-cache	Clears the entries of all dynamically learned NetBIOS names.
clear rif-cache	Clears the entire RIF cache.
clear source-bridge	Clears the SRB statistical counters.
clear sse	Reinitializes the SSP on the Cisco 7000 series.

In addition to the EXEC-mode commands to maintain the SRB network, you can use the following command in global configuration mode:

Command	Purpose
source-bridge tcp-queue-max *number*	Limits the size of the backup queue for RSRB to control the number of packets that can wait for transmission to a remote ring before they start being thrown away.

SRB Configuration Examples

The following sections provide SRB configuration examples:

- Basic SRB with Spanning-Tree Explorers Example

- SRB with Automatic Spanning-Tree Function Configuration Example

- Optimized Explorer Processing Configuration Example
- SRB-Only Example
- SRB and Routing Certain Protocols Example
- Multiport SRB Example
- SRB with Multiple Virtual Ring Groups Example
- SRB over FDDI Configuration Examples
- SRB over FDDI Fast-Switching Example
- SRB over Frame Relay Configuration Example
- Adding a Static RIF Cache Entry Example
- Adding a Static RIF Cache Entry for a Two-Hop Path Example
- SR/TLB for a Simple Network Example
- SR/TLB with Access Filtering Example
- NetBIOS Support with a Static NetBIOS Cache Entry Example
- LNM for a Simple Network Example
- LNM for a More Complex Network Example
- NetBIOS Access Filters Example
- Filtering Bridged Token Ring Packets to IBM Machines Example
- Administrative Access Filters—Filtering SNAP Frames on Output Example
- Creating Access Filters Example
- Access Filters Example
- Fast-Switching Example
- Autonomous Switching Example

Basic SRB with Spanning-Tree Explorers Example

Figure 3-11 illustrates a simple two-port bridge configuration. Token Rings 129 and 130 are connected through the router.

Figure 3-11 *Dual-Port Source-Route Bridge Configuration*

The example that follows routes IP, but source-route bridges all other protocols using spanning-tree explorers:

```
interface tokenring 0
 ip address 131.108.129.2 255.255.255.0
 source-bridge 129 1 130
 source-bridge spanning
 multiring all
!
interface tokenring 1
 ip address 131.108.130.2 255.255.255.0
 source-bridge 130 1 129
 source-bridge spanning
! use RIFs, as necessary, with IP routing software
 multiring all
```

SRB with Automatic Spanning-Tree Function Configuration Example

The following example of a Cisco series 7000 router configuration illustrates how to enable the automatic spanning-tree function on an SRB network:

```
source-bridge ring-group 100

interface tokenring 0/0
 no ip address
 ring-speed 16
 multiring all
 source-bridge active 1 10 100
 source-bridge spanning 1
!
interface tokenring 0/1
 no ip address
 ring-speed 16
 multiring all
 source-bridge active 2 10 100
 source-bridge spanning 1
!
bridge 1 protocol ibm
```

Optimized Explorer Processing Configuration Example

The following configuration example improves the handling of explorer frames, enabling Cisco IOS software to perform substantially better during explorer broadcast storms. In this configuration, the maximum byte rate of explorers is set to 100,000.

```
source-bridge explorer-maxrate 100000
source-bridge explorerQ-depth 100
no source-bridge explorer-fastswitch
```

SRB-Only Example

The following example shows that all protocols are bridged, including IP. Because IP is being bridged, the system has only one IP address.

```
no ip routing
!
interface tokenring 0
 ip address 131.108.129.2 255.255.255.0
 source-bridge 129 1 130
 source-bridge spanning
!
interface tokenring 1
 ip address 131.108.129.2 255.255.255.0
 source-bridge 130 1 129
 source-bridge spanning
!
interface ethernet 0
 ip address 131.108.129.2 255.255.255.0
```

SRB and Routing Certain Protocols Example

In the following configuration, IP, XNS, and IPX are routed, while all other protocols are bridged between rings. While not strictly necessary, the Novell IPX and XNS network numbers are set consistently with the IP subnetwork numbers. This makes the network easier to maintain.

```
xns routing 0000.0C00.02C3
!
novell routing 0000.0C00.02C3
!
interface tokenring 0
 ip address 131.108.129.2 255.255.255.0
 xns network 129
 novell network 129
 source-bridge 129 1 130
 source-bridge spanning
 multiring all
!
interface tokenring 1
 ip address 131.108.130.2 255.255.255.0
 xns network 130
```

```
novell network 130
source-bridge 130 1 129
source-bridge spanning
multiring all
!
interface ethernet 0
 ip address 131.108.2.68 255.255.255.0
 xns network 2
 novell network 2
```

Multiport SRB Example

Figure 3-12 shows an example configuration of a four-port Token Ring source-route bridge.
Rings 1000, 1001, 1002, and 1003 are all source-route bridged to each other across ring group 7.

Figure 3-12   *Four-Port Source-Route Bridge*

The following is a sample configuration file:

```
source-bridge ring-group 7
!
interface tokenring 0
 source-bridge 1000 1 7
 source-bridge spanning
!
interface tokenring 1
 source-bridge 1001 1 7
 source-bridge spanning
!
interface tokenring 2
 source-bridge 1002 1 7
 source-bridge spanning
!
interface tokenring 3
 source-bridge 1003 1 7
 source-bridge spanning
```

SRB with Multiple Virtual Ring Groups Example

Two virtual ring groups can only be connected through an actual Token Ring. Figure 3-13 shows
Virtual Rings 100 and 200 connected through Token Ring 3.

Figure 3-13 *Two Virtual Rings Connected by an Actual Token Ring*

Configuration for Router A

```
source-bridge ring-group 100
!
interface tokenring 0
 source-bridge 3 4 100
 source-bridge spanning
!
interface tokenring 1
 source-bridge 1 4 100
 source-bridge spanning
```

Configuration for Router B

```
source-bridge ring-group 200
!
interface tokenring 0
 source-bridge 3 1 200
 source-bridge spanning
!
interface tokenring 2
 source-bridge 2 1 200
 source-bridge spanning
```

SRB over FDDI Configuration Examples

The following examples show the configuration for SRB over FDDI as illustrated in Figure 3-14.

Router A

```
dlsw local-peer peer-id 132.11.11.2
dlsw remote-peer 0 tcp 132.11.11.3
interface Fddi0
 no ip address
 multiring all
 source-bridge 26 1 10
 source-bridge spanning
```

Router B

```
dlsw local-peer peer-id 132.11.11.2
dlsw remote-peer 0 tcp 132.11.11.3
interface TokenRing0
 no ip address
 ring-speed 16
 multiring all
 source-bridge 25 1 10
 source-bridge spanning
```

Figure 3-14 *SRB over FDDI Configuration*

SRB over FDDI Fast-Switching Example

The following example shows SRB over FDDI fast-switching:

```
interface fddi 2/0
 source-bridge 1 10 2
 source-bridge spanning
 source-bridge route-cache
 multiring ip
```

SRB over Frame Relay Configuration Example

Figure 3-15 illustrates a network with the following characteristics:

- Virtual Ring Number of Router A = 100

- Virtual Ring Number of FRAD B = 200

- Virtual Ring Number of FRAD C = 300

- DLCI number for PVC between Router A and FRAD B = 30

- DLCI number for PVC between Router A and FRAD C = 31

Figure 3-15 *FRAD Using SRB over Frame Relay to Connect to a Cisco Router*

In this example, we configure a new option, **conserve-ring**, on the **source-bridge** interface configuration command. When this option is configured, the SRB software does not add the ring number associated with the Frame Relay PVC (the partner's virtual ring) to outbound explorer frames. This option is permitted for Frame Relay subinterfaces only.

The router configures the partner FRAD's virtual ring number as the ring number for the PVC.

This approach does not require a separate ring number per DLCI. The router configures the partner FRAD's virtual ring number as the ring number for the PVC.

FRAD B would configure its virtual ring as 200 and the ring for the PVC as 100. FRAD C would configure its virtual ring as 300 and the ring for the PVC as 100.

Configuration of Router A

```
source-bridge ring-group 100
!
interface Serial1
 encapsulation frame-relay
!
```

```
interface Serial1.1 point-to-point
 frame-relay interface-dlci 30 ietf
 source-bridge 200 1 100 conserve-ring
 source-bridge spanning
!
interface Serial1.2 point-to-point
 frame-relay interface-dlci 31 ietf
 source-bridge 300 1 100 conserve-ring
 source-bridge spanning
!
interface TokenRing0
source-bridge 500 1 100
```

Configuration on Router B

```
source-bridge ring-group 200
!
interface Serial0
 encapsulation frame-relay
!
interface Serial0.30 point-to-point
 frame-relay interface-dlci 30 ietf
 source-bridge 100 1 200 conserve-ring
 source-bridge spanning
!
interface TokenRing0
source-bridge 600 1 200
```

Configuration on Router C

```
source-bridge ring-group 300
!
interface Serial0
 encapsulation frame-relay
!
interface Serial0.31 point-to-point
 frame-relay interface-dlci 31 ietf
 source-bridge 100 1 300 conserve-ring
 source-bridge spanning
!
interface TokenRing0
source-bridge 900 1 300
```

Adding a Static RIF Cache Entry Example

In the example configuration in Figure 3-16, the path between rings 8 and 9 connected via Bridge 1 is described by the route descriptor 0081.0090. A full RIF, including the route control field, would be 0630.0081.0090.

Figure 3-16 *Assigning a RIF to a Source-Route Bridge*

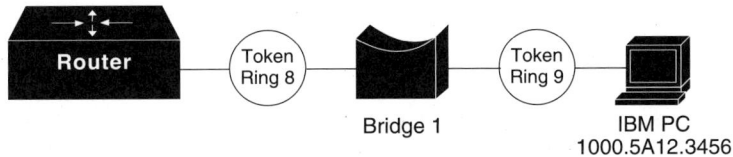

The static RIF entry would be submitted to the router on the left as follows:

```
rif 1000.5A12.3456 0630.0081.0090
```

Adding a Static RIF Cache Entry for a Two-Hop Path Example

In Figure 3-17, assume that a datagram was sent from a router on ring 21 (15 hexadecimal), across Bridge 5 to ring 256 (100 hexadecimal), and then across Bridge 10 (A hexadecimal) to ring 1365 (555 hexadecimal) for delivery to a destination host on that ring.

Figure 3-17 *Assigning a RIF to a Two-Hop Path*

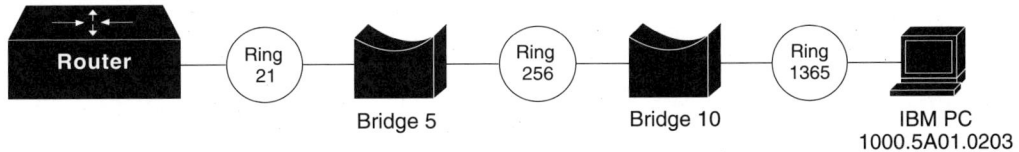

The RIF in the router on the left describing this two-hop path is 0830.0155.100a.5550 and is entered as follows:

```
rif 1000.5A01.0203 0830.0155.100a.5550
```

SR/TLB for a Simple Network Example

In the simple example illustrated in Figure 3-18, a four-port router with two Ethernets and two Token Rings is used to connect transparent bridging on the Ethernets to SRB on the Token Rings.

Figure 3-18 *Example of a Simple SR/TLB Configuration*

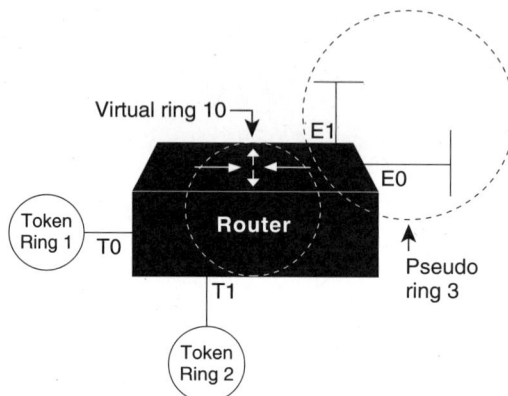

Assume that the following configuration for SRB and transparent bridging existed before you wanted to enable SR/TLB:

```
interface tokenring 0
 source-bridge 1 1 2
!
interface tokenring 1
 source-bridge 2 1 1
!
interface ethernet 0
 bridge-group 1
!
interface ethernet 0
 bridge-group 1
!
bridge 1 protocol dec
```

To enable SR/TLB, one aspect of this configuration must change immediately—a third ring must be configured. Before SR/TLB, the two Token Ring interfaces were communicating with two-port local source-route bridging; after SR/TLB, these two interfaces must be reconfigured to communicate through a virtual ring, as follows:

```
source-bridge ring-group 10
!
interface tokenring 0
 source-bridge 1 1 10
!
interface tokenring 1
 source-bridge 2 1 10
!
interface ethernet 0
 bridge-group 1
!
interface ethernet 1
 bridge-group 1
!
bridge 1 protocol dec
```

Now you are ready to determine two things:

- A ring number for the pseudo-ring that is unique throughout the source-route bridged network. For the preceding example configuration, use the number 3.

- A bridge number for the path to the pseudo-ring. For the preceding example configuration, use the number 1.

Once you have determined the ring number and the bridge number, you can add the **source-bridge transparent** command to the file, including these two values as parameters for the command. The following partial configuration includes this **source-bridge transparent** entry:

```
!
source-bridge ring-group 10
source-bridge transparent 10 3 1 1
!
interface tokenring 0
 source-bridge 1 1 10
!
interface tokenring 1
 source-bridge 2 1 10
!
interface ethernet 0
 bridge-group 1
!
interface ethernet 1
 bridge-group 1
!
bridge 1 protocol dec
```

SR/TLB with Access Filtering Example

In the example shown in Figure 3-19, you want to connect only a single machine, Host E, on an Ethernet to a single machine, Host R, on the Token Ring.

Figure 3-19 *Example of a Bit-Swapped Address*

You want to allow only these two machines to communicate across the router. Therefore, you might create the following configuration to restrict the access. However, this configuration will not work, as explained in the paragraph following the sample configuration file.

NOTE   For readability, the commands that control bridging are not shown here, just the commands that control the filtering.

```
interface tokenring 0
 access-expression output smac(701)
!
interface ethernet 0
 bridge-group 1 input-address-list 701
!
 access-list 701 permit 0110.2222.3333
```

The command for the Token Ring interface specifies that the access list 701 be applied on the source address of frames going out to the Token Ring, and the command for the Ethernet interface specifies that this access list be applied on the source address frames entering the interface from Ethernet. This would work if both interfaces used the same bit ordering, but Token Rings and Ethernets use opposite (swapped) bit orderings in their addresses in relationship to each other. Therefore, the address of Host E on the Token Ring is not 0110.2222.3333, but rather 8008.4444.cccc, resulting in the following configuration. The following configuration is better. This example shows that access lists for Token Ring and Ethernet should be kept completely separate from each other.

```
interface tokenring 0
 source-bridge input-address-list 702
!
interface ethernet 0
 bridge-group 1 input-address-list 701
!
 access-list 701 permit 0110.2222.3333
!!
 access-list 702 permit 0110.1234.5678
```

NetBIOS Support with a Static NetBIOS Cache Entry Example

Figure 3-20 shows a NetBIOS client on a Token Ring connected through a cloud to a NetBIOS server on another Token Ring.

Figure 3-20 *Specifying a Static Entry*

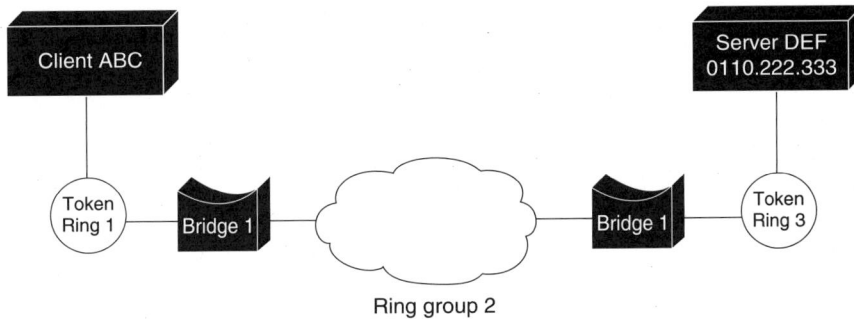

In Figure 3-20, a static entry is created in the router attached to ring 1 on the client side of the ring group. The static entry is to the server DEF, which is reached through the router attached to ring 3. If server DEF has the MAC address 0110.2222.3333, the configuration for the static entry on the client side is as follows:

```
rif 0110.2222.3333 0630.0021.0030 ring-group 2
netbios name-cache 0110.2222.3333 DEF ring-group 2
```

LNM for a Simple Network Example

Figure 3-21 shows a router with two Token Rings configured as a local source-route bridge.

Figure 3-21 *Router with Two Token Rings Configured as a Local Source-Route Bridge*

The associated configuration file follows:

```
interface tokenring 0
 source-bridge 1 2 3
!
interface tokenring 1
 source-bridge 3 2 1
```

The **show lnm config** command displays the logical configuration of this bridge, including the LNM configuration information that needs to be entered at the LNM Station. A sample **show lnm config** display follows:

```
Wayfarer# show lnm config

Bridge(s) currently configured:
From      ring 001, address 0000.3000.abc4
Across bridge 002
To        ring 003, address 0000.3000.5735
```

In this example, the MAC addresses 0000.3000.abc4 and 000.3000.5735 must be configured as Adapter Addresses at the LNM Station.

LNM for a More Complex Network Example

Figure 3-22 shows a router with three Token Rings configured as a multiport bridge, thus employing the concept of the virtual ring.

Figure 3-22 *Router with Three Token Rings Configured as a Multiport Bridge*

The associated configuration file follows:

```
source-bridge ring-group 8
!
interface tokenring 0
 source-bridge 1 1 8
!
interface tokenring 1
 source-bridge 2 2 8
!
interface tokenring 2
 source-bridge 3 3 8
```

The **show lnm config** command displays the logical configuration of this bridge, including all the pertinent information for configuring this router into LNM:

```
Wayfarer# show lnm config
Bridge(s) currently configured:

          From     ring 001, address 0000.0028.abcd
          Across bridge 001
          To       ring 008, address 4000.0028.abcd

          From     ring 002, address 0000.3000.abc4
          Across bridge 002
          To       ring 008, address 4000.3000.abc4

          From     ring 003, address 0000.3000.5735
          Across bridge 003
          To       ring 008, address 4000.3000.5735
```

In this example, six station definitions must be entered at the LNM Station, one for each of the MAC addresses listed in this sample **show lnm config** display.

NetBIOS Access Filters Example

The following command permits packets that include the station name ABCD to pass through the router, but denies passage to packets that do not include the station name ABCD:

```
netbios access-list host marketing permit ABCD
```

The following command specifies a prefix where the pattern matches any name beginning with the characters DEFG. Note that the string DEFG itself is included in this condition.

```
netbios access-list host marketing deny DEFG*
```

The following command permits any station name with the letter W as the first character and the letter Y as the third character in the name. The second and fourth letters in the name can be any character. This example would allow stations named WXYZ and WAYB; however, stations named WY and WXY would not be included in this statement, because the question mark must match some specific character in the name.

```
netbios access-list host marketing permit W?Y?
```

The following command illustrates how to combine wildcard characters:

```
netbios access-list host marketing deny AC?*
```

The command specifies that the marketing list deny any name beginning with AC that is at least three characters in length (the question mark would match any third character). The string ACBD and ACB would match, but the string AC would not.

The following command removes the entire marketing NetBIOS access list:

```
no netbios access-list host marketing
```

To remove single entries from the list, use a command such as the following:

```
no netbios access-list host marketing deny AC?*
```

This example removes only the list that filters station names with the letters AC at the beginning of the name.

Access lists are scanned in order. In the following example, the first list denies all entries beginning with the letters ABC, including one named ABCD. This voids the second command, because the entry permitting a name with ABCD comes after the entry denying it.

```
netbios access-list host marketing deny ABC*
netbios access-list host marketing permit ABCD
```

Filtering Bridged Token Ring Packets to IBM Machines Example

The example in Figure 3-23 disallows the bridging of Token Ring packets to all IBM workstations on Token Ring 1.

Figure 3-23 *Router Filtering Bridged Token Ring Packets to IBM Machines*

This example assumes that all hosts on Token Ring 1 have Token Ring addresses with the vendor code 1000.5A00.0000. The first line of the access list denies access to all IBM workstations, while the second line permits everything else. The access list is assigned to the input side of Token Ring 1.

```
! deny access to all IBM workstations
access-list 700 deny 1000.5A00.0000    8000.00FF.FFFF
! permit all other traffic
access-list 700 permit 0000.0000.0000    FFFF.FFFF.FFFF
!
interface token ring 1
! apply access list 700 to the input side of Token Ring 1
source-bridge input-address-list 700
```

Administrative Access Filters—Filtering SNAP Frames on Output Example

Figure 3-24 shows a router connecting four Token Rings.

Figure 3-24 *Router Filtering SNAP Frames on Output*

The following example allows only AppleTalk Phase 2 packets to be source-route bridged between Token Rings 0 and 1, and allows Novell packets only to be source-route bridged between Token Rings 2 and 3.

```
source-bridge ring-group 5
!
interface tokenring 0
 ip address 131.108.1.1 255.255.255.0
 source-bridge 1000 1 5
 source-bridge spanning
 source-bridge input-type-list 202
!
interface tokenring 1
 ip address 131.108.11.1 255.255.255.0
 source-bridge 1001 1 5
 source-bridge spanning
 source-bridge input-type-list 202
!
```

```
interface tokenring 2
 ip address 131.108.101.1 255.255.255.0
 source-bridge 1002 1 5
 source-bridge spanning
 source-bridge input-lsap-list 203
!
interface tokenring 3
 ip address 131.108.111.1 255.255.255.0
 source-bridge 1003 1 5
 source-bridge spanning
 source-bridge input-lsap-list 203
!
! SNAP type code filtering
! permit ATp2 data (0x809B)
! permit ATp2 AARP (0x80F3)
access-list 202 permit 0x809B 0x0000
access-list 202 permit 0x80F3 0x0000
access-list 202 deny 0x0000 0xFFFF
!
! LSAP filtering
! permit IPX (0xE0E0)
access-list 203 permit 0xE0E0 0x0101
access-list 203 deny 0x0000 0xFFFF
```

Note that it is not necessary to check for an LSAP of 0xAAAA when filtering SNAP-encapsulated AppleTalk packets, because for SRB, the use of type filters implies SNAP encapsulation.

Creating Access Filters Example

In math, you have the following:

```
3 x 4 + 2 = 14 but 3 x (4 + 2) = 18
```

Similarly, the following access expressions would return TRUE if lsap(201) and dmac(701) returned TRUE or if smac(702) returned TRUE:

```
lsap(201) & dmac(701) ¦ smac(702)
```

However, the following access expression would return TRUE only if lsap(201) returned TRUE and either of dmac(701) or smac(702) returned TRUE:

```
lsap(201) & (dmac(701) ¦ smac(702))
```

Referring to the earlier example, "An Example Using NetBIOS Access Filters," we had the phrase:

"Pass the frame if it is NetBIOS, or if it is an SNA frame destined to address 0110.2222.3333."

This phrase was converted to a simpler form:

Pass if "NetBIOS or (SNA and destined to 0110.2222.3333)."

So, for the following configuration:

```
! Access list 201 passes NetBIOS frames (command or response)
access-list 201 permit 0xF0F0 0x0001
!
access-list 202 permit 0x0404 0x0001 ! Permits SNA frames (command or response)
access-list 202 permit 0x0004 0x0001 ! Permits SNA Explorers with NULL DSAP
!
! Access list 701 will permit the FEP MAC address
! of 0110.2222.3333
access-list 701 permit 0110.2222.3333
```

The following access expression would result:

```
access-expression in lsap(201) | (lsap(202) & dmac(701))
```

Access Filters Example

Figure 3-25 shows two routers connecting two Token Rings to an FDDI backbone.

Figure 3-25 *Network Configuration Using NetBIOS Access Filters*

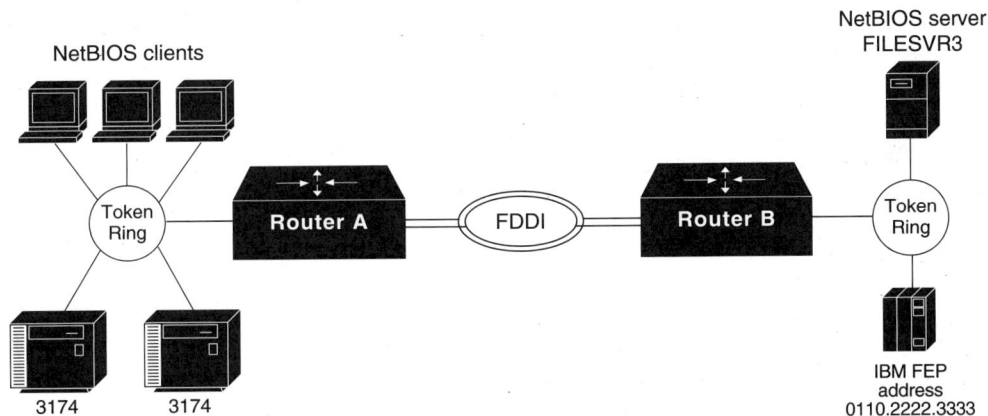

Suppose you want to permit the IBM 3174 cluster controllers to access the FEP at address 0110.2222.3333 and want the NetBIOS clients to access the NetBIOS server named FILESVR3. The following set of router configuration commands would meet this need:

```
netbios access-list host MIS permit FILESVR3
netbios access-list host MIS deny *
!
access-list 202 permit 0x0404 0x0001 ! Permits SNA frames (command or response)
access-list 202 permit 0x0004 0x0001 ! Permits SNA Explorers with NULL DSAP
!
access-list 701 permit 0110.2222.3333
!
interface tokenring 0
access-expression in (lsap(202) & dmac(701)) | netbios-host(MIS)
```

Fast-Switching Example

The following example disables fast switching between two Token Ring interfaces in the same router. Frames entering Token Ring interfaces 0 or 1 will not be fast switched to the other interface.

```
! global command establishing the ring group for the interface configuration commands
source-bridge ring-group 2
!
! commands that follow apply to interface token 0
interface tokenring 0
! enable srb between local ring 1, bridge 1, and target ring 2
source-bridge 1 1 2
!disable source-route fast-switching cache on interface token 0
no source-bridge route-cache
!
interface token 1
! enable srb between local ring 2, bridge 1, and target ring 1
source-bridge 2 1 1
no source-bridge route-cache
```

Autonomous Switching Example

The following example enables use of autonomous switching between two ciscoBus Token Ring interfaces in the same router. Frames entering Token Ring interfaces 0 or 1 will be autonomously switched to the other interface.

```
! global command to apply interface configuration commands to the ring group
source-bridge ring-group 2
!
! commands that follow apply to interface token 0
interface tokenring 0
! enable srb between local ring 1, bridge 1, and target ring 2
source-bridge 1 1 2
! enable autonomous switching for interface token 0
source-bridge route-cache cbus
!
interface tokenring 1
! enable srb between local ring 2, bridge 1, and target ring 1
source-bridge 2 1 1
source-bridge route-cache cbus
```

Source-Route Bridging Commands

Use the commands in this chapter to configure and monitor source-route bridging (SRB) networks. For SRB configuration information and examples, refer to Chapter 3, "Configuring Source-Route Bridging."

access-expression

Use the **access-expression** interface configuration command to define an access expression. Use the **no** form of this command to remove the access expression from the given interface. You use this command in conjunction with the **access-list** interface configuration command.

> **access-expression** {**in** | **out**} *expression*
> **no access-expression** {**in** | **out**} *expression*

Syntax	Description
in | **out**	Either **in** or **out** is specified to indicate whether the access expression is applied to packets entering or leaving this interface.
	You can specify both an input and an output access expression for an interface, but only one of each.
expression	Boolean access list expression, built as explained in the "Usage Guidelines" section.

Default

No access expression is defined.

Command Mode

Interface configuration

Usage Guidelines

This command first appeared in Cisco IOS Release 10.0.

An access expression consists of a list of terms, separated by Boolean operators, and optionally grouped in parentheses.

An access expression term specifies a type of access list, followed by its name or number. The result of the term is either true or false, depending on whether the access list specified in the term permits or denies the frame. Table 4-1 describes the terms that can be used.

Table 4-1   *Access Expression Terms*

Access Expression Term	Definition
lsap(2nn)	The LSAP access list to be evaluated for this frame (200 series).
type(2nn)	The SNAP type access list to be evaluated for this frame (200 series).
smac(7nn)	The access list to match the source MAC address of the frame (700 series).
dmac(7nn)	The access list to match the destination MAC address of the frame (700 series).
netbios-host(name)	The netbios-host access list to be applied on NetBIOS frames traversing the interface.
netbios-bytes(name)	The netbios-bytes access list to be applied on NetBIOS frames traversing the interface.

NOTE   The *netbios-host* and *netbios-bytes* access expression terms always will return FALSE for frames that are not NetBIOS frames.

Access expression terms are separated by Boolean operators as listed in Table 4-2.

Table 4-2   *Boolean Operators for Access Expression Terms*

Boolean Operators	Definitions
~ (called "not")	Negates, or reverses, the result of the term or group of terms immediately to the right of the ~. Example: "~lsap (201)" returns FALSE if "lsap (201)" itself were TRUE.
& (called "and")	Returns TRUE if the terms or parenthetical expressions to the left and right of the & both return TRUE. Example: "lsap (201) & dmac (701)" returns TRUE if both the lsap (201) and dmac (701) terms return TRUE.
| (called "or")	Returns TRUE if the terms or parenthetical expressions to the left or right of the | either or both of return TRUE. Example: "lsap (201) | dmac (701)" returns TRUE if either the lsap (201) or dmac (701) terms return TRUE, as well as if both return TRUE.

Terms can be grouped in parenthetical expressions. Any of the terms and operators can be placed in parentheses, similar to what is done in arithmetic expressions, to affect order of evaluation.

An "access-expression" type filter cannot exist with a "source-bridge" type filter on the same interface. The two types of filters are mutually exclusive.

NOTE	The incorrect use of parentheses can drastically affect the result of an operation because the expression is read left to right.

Related Commands

To locate documentation of related commands, you can search online at www.cisco.com.

access-list

access-list

Use the **access-list** global configuration command to configure the access list mechanism for filtering frames by protocol type or vendor code. Use the **no** form of this command to remove the single specified entry from the access list.

> **access-list** *access-list-number* {**permit** | **deny**} {*type-code wild-mask* | *address mask*}
> **no access-list** *access-list-number* {**permit** | **deny**} {*type-code wild-mask* |
>   *address mask*}

Syntax	Description
access-list-number	Integer that identifies the access list. If the *type-code wild-mask* arguments are included, this integer ranges from 200 to 299, indicating that filtering is by protocol type. If the *address* and *mask* arguments are included, this integer ranges from 700 to 799, indicating that filtering is by vendor code.
permit	Permits the frame.
deny	Denies the frame.
type-code	16-bit hexadecimal number written with a leading 0x; for example, 0x6000. Specify either a link service access point (LSAP) type code for 802-encapsulated packets or a SNAP type code for SNAP-encapsulated packets. (LSAP, sometimes called SAP, refers to the type codes found in the DSAP and SSAP fields of the 802 header.)

Syntax	Description
wild-mask	16-bit hexadecimal number whose ones bits correspond to bits in the *type-code* argument. The *wild-mask* indicates which bits in the *type-code* argument should be ignored when making a comparison. (A mask for a DSAP/SSAP pair should always be 0x0101 because these two bits are used for purposes other than identifying the SAP code.)
address	48-bit Token Ring address written in dotted triplet form. This field is used for filtering by vendor code.
mask	48-bit Token Ring address written in dotted triplet form. The ones bits in *mask* are the bits to be ignored in *address*. This field is used for filtering by vendor code.

NOTE   For source address filtering, the mask always should have the high-order bit set. This is because the IEEE 802 standard uses this bit to indicate whether a RIF is present, not as part of the source address.

Default

No access list is configured.

Command Mode

Global configuration

Usage Guidelines

This command first appeared in Cisco IOS Release 10.0.

For a list of type codes, refer to Appendix A, "Ethernet Type Codes."

Examples

In the following example, the access list permits only Novell frames (LSAP 0xE0E0) and filters out all other frame types. This set of access lists would be applied to an interface via the **source-bridge input-lsap list** or **source-bridge input-lsap list** commands (described later in this chapter).

```
access-list 201 permit 0xE0E0 0x0101
access-list 201 deny  0x0000 0xFFFF
```

Combine the DSAP/LSAP fields into one number to do LSAP filtering; for example, 0xE0E0—not 0xE0. Note that the deny condition specified in the preceding example is not required; access lists have an implicit deny as the last statement. Adding this statement can serve as a useful reminder, however.

The following access list filters out only SNAP type codes assigned to DEC (0x6000 to 0x6007) and lets all other types pass. This set of access lists would be applied to an interface using the **source-bridge input-type-list** or **source-bridge output-type-list** commands (described later in this chapter).

```
access-list 202 deny     0x6000 0x0007
access-list 202 permit   0x0000 0xFFFF
```

NOTE	Use the last item of an access list to specify a default action; for example, to permit everything else or to deny everything else. If nothing else in the access list matches, the default action is to deny access; that is, filter out all other type codes.

Type code access lists will negatively affect system performance by greater than 30 percent. Therefore, it is recommended that you keep the lists as short as possible and use wildcard bit masks whenever possible.

Related Commands

To locate documentation of related commands, you can search online at www.cisco.com.

access-expression
source-bridge input-address-list
source-bridge input-lsap-list
source-bridge input-type-list
source-bridge output-address-list
source-bridge output-lsap-list
source-bridge output-type-list

bridge protocol ibm

Use the **bridge protocol ibm** global configuration command to create a bridge group that runs the automatic spanning-tree function. Use the **no** form of this command to cancel the previous assignment.

> **bridge** *bridge-group* **protocol ibm**
> **no bridge** *bridge-group* **protocol ibm**

Syntax | Description

Syntax	Description
bridge-group	Number in the range 1 to 9 that you choose to refer to a particular set of bridged interfaces.

Default

No bridge group is defined.

Command Mode

Global configuration

Usage Guidelines

This command first appeared in Cisco IOS Release 10.3.

Example

The following example specifies bridge 1 to use the automatic spanning-tree function:

```
bridge 1 protocol ibm
```

Related Commands

To locate documentation of related commands, you can search online at www.cisco.com.

show source-bridge
source-bridge spanning (automatic)
source-bridge spanning (manual)

clear netbios-cache

Use the **clear netbios-cache** privileged EXEC command to clear the entries of all dynamically learned NetBIOS names. This command will not remove statically defined name cache entries.

clear netbios-cache

Syntax Description

This command has no arguments or keywords.

Command Mode

Privileged EXEC

Usage Guidelines

This command first appeared in Cisco IOS Release 10.0.

Cisco IOS software automatically learns NetBIOS names. This command clears those entries.

Example

The following example clears all dynamically learned NetBIOS names:

```
clear netbios-cache
```

Related Commands

To locate documentation of related commands, you can search online at www.cisco.com.

netbios enable-name-cache
netbios name-cache timeout
show netbios-cache

clear rif-cache

Use the clear rif-cache privileged EXEC command to clear the entire RIF cache.

clear rif-cache

Syntax Description

This command has no arguments or keywords.

Command Mode

Privileged EXEC

Usage Guidelines

This command first appeared in Cisco IOS Release 10.0.

Some entries in the RIF cache are dynamically added and others are static.

Example

The following example clears the entire RIF cache:

```
clear rif-cache
```

Related Commands

To locate documentation of related commands, you can search online at www.cisco.com.

rif
rif timeout
show rif

clear source-bridge

Use the **clear source-bridge** privileged EXEC command to clear the source-bridge statistical counters.

> **clear source-bridge**

Syntax Description

This command has no arguments or keywords.

Command Mode

Privileged EXEC

Usage Guidelines

This command first appeared in Cisco IOS Release 10.0.

Example

The following example clears the source-bridge statistical counters:

```
clear source-bridge
```

Related Commands

To locate documentation of related commands, you can search online at www.cisco.com.

clear bridge

clear sse

Use the **clear sse** privileged EXEC command to reinitialize the Silicon Switch Processor (SSP) on the Cisco 7000 series routers with RSP7000.

> **clear sse**

Syntax Description

This command has no arguments or keywords.

Default

Disabled

Command Mode

Privileged EXEC

Usage Guidelines

This command first appeared in Cisco IOS Release 10.3.

The silicon switching engine (SSE) is on the SSP board in the Cisco 7000 series routers with RSP7000.

Example

The following example reinitializes the SSP:

```
clear sse
```

ethernet-transit-oui

Use the **ethernet-transit-oui** interface configuration command to choose the Organizational Unique Identifier (OUI) code to be used in the encapsulation of Ethernet Type II frames across Token Ring backbone networks. Various versions of this OUI code are used by Ethernet/Token Ring translational bridges. Use the **no** form of this command to return the default OUI code.

> **ethernet-transit-oui [90-compatible | standard | cisco]**
> **no ethernet-transit-oui**

Syntax	Description
90-compatible	(Optional) Default OUI form.
standard	(Optional) Standard OUI form.
cisco	(Optional) Cisco OUI form.

Default

The default OUI form is 90-compatible.

Command Mode

Interface configuration

Usage Guidelines

This command first appeared in Cisco IOS Release 10.0.

This command replaces and extends the **bridge old-oui** command in Software Release 9.0.

Before using this command, you must have completely configured your router using multiport source-bridging and transparent bridging.

The **standard** keyword is used when you are forced to interoperate with other vendor equipment, such as the IBM 8209, in providing Ethernet and Token Ring mixed media bridged connectivity.

The actual OUI codes that are used, when they are used, and how they compare to Software Release 9.0-equivalent commands are shown in Table 4-3.

Table 4-3 *Bridge OUI Codes*

Keyword	OUI Used	When Used/Benefits	Software Release 9.0 Command Equivalent
90-compatible	0000F8	By default, when talking to other Cisco routers. Provides the most flexibility.	**no bridge old-oui**
cisco	00000C	Provided for compatibility with future equipment.	None
standard	000000	When talking to IBM 8209 bridges and other vendor equipment. Does not provide for as much flexibility as the other two choices.	**bridge old-oui**

Specify the **90-compatible** keyword when talking to Cisco routers. This keyword provides the most flexibility. When **90-compatible** is specified or the default is used, Token Ring frames with an OUI of 0x0000F8 are translated into Ethernet Type II frames while Token Ring frames with the OUI of 0x000000 are translated into SNAP-encapsulated frames. Specify the **standard** keyword when talking to IBM 8209 bridges and other vendor equipment. This OUI does not provide for as much flexibility as the other two choices. The **cisco** OUI is provided for compatibility with future equipment.

Do not use the **standard** keyword unless you are forced to interoperate with other vendor equipment, such as the IBM 8209, in providing Ethernet and Token Ring mixed media bridged connectivity. Only use the **standard** keyword when you are transferring data between IBM 8209 Ethernet/Token Ring bridges and routers running the SR/TLB software (to create a Token Ring backbone to connect Ethernets).

Use of the **standard** keyword causes the OUI code in Token Ring frames to always be 0x000000. In the context of the **standard** keyword, an OUI of 0x000000 identifies the frame as an Ethernet Type II frame. (Compare with 90-compatible, where 0x000000 OUI means SNAP-encapsulated frames.)

If you use the **90-compatible** keyword, the router, acting as an SR/TLB, can distinguish immediately on Token Ring interfaces between frames that started on an Ethernet Type II frame and those that started on an Ethernet as a SNAP-encapsulated frame. The distinction is possible because the router uses the 0x0000F8 OUI when converting Ethernet Type II frames into Token Ring SNAP frames, and leaves the OUI as 0x000000 for Ethernet SNAP frames going to a Token Ring. This distinction in OUIs leads to efficiencies in the design and execution of the SR/TLB product; no tables need to be kept to know which Ethernet hosts use SNAP encapsulation and which hosts use Ethernet Type II.

The IBM 8209 bridges, however, by using the 0x000000 OUI for all the frames entering the Token Ring, must take extra measures to perform the translation. For every station on each Ethernet, the 8209 bridges attempt to remember the frame format used by each station, and assume that once a station sends out a frame using Ethernet Type II or 802.3, it will always continue to do so. It must do this because in using 0x000000 as an OUI, there is no way to distinguish between SNAP and Type II frame types. Because the SR/TLB router does not need to keep this database, when 8209 compatibility is enabled with the **standard** keyword, the SR/TLB chooses to translate all Token Ring SNAP frames into Ethernet Type II frames as described earlier in this discussion. Because every nonroutable protocol on Ethernet uses either non SNAP 802.3 (which traverses fully across a mixed IBM 8209/ router Token Ring backbone) or Ethernet Type II, this results in correct interconnectivity for virtually all applications.

Do not use the **standard** OUI if you want SR/TLB to output Ethernet SNAP frames. Using either the **90-compatible** or **cisco** OUI does not present such a restriction because SNAP frames and Ethernet Type II-encapsulated frames have different OUI codes on Token Ring networks.

Example

The following example specifies standard OUI form:

```
interface tokenring 0
 ethernet-transit-oui standard
```

Related Commands

To locate documentation of related commands, you can search online at www.cisco.com.

ethernet-transit-oui
source-bridge transparent

lnm alternate

Use the **lnm alternate** interface configuration command to specify the threshold reporting link number. In order for a LAN Reporting Manager (LRM) to change parameters, it must be attached to the reporting link with the lowest reporting link number, and that reporting link number must be lower than this threshold reporting link number. Use the **no** form of this command to restore the default of 0.

> **lnm alternate** *number*
> **no lnm alternate**

Syntax

Syntax	Description
number	Threshold reporting link number. It must be in the range 0 to 3.

Default

0

Command Mode

Interface configuration

Usage Guidelines

This command first appeared in Cisco IOS Release 10.0.

LAN Network Manager (LNM) employs the concepts of reporting links and reporting link numbers. A reporting link is simply a connection (or potential connection) between an LRM and a bridge. A reporting link number is a unique number used to identify a reporting link. An IBM bridge allows four simultaneous reporting links numbered 0 to 3. Only the LRM attached to the lowest number connection is allowed to change any parameters, and then only when that connection number falls below a certain configurable number. In the default configuration, the LRM connected through link 0 is the only LRM allowed to change parameters.

NOTE   Setting the threshold reporting link number on one interface in a source-route bridge will cause it to appear on the other interface of the bridge because the command applies to the bridge itself and not to either of the interfaces.

Examples

The following example permits LRMs connected through links 0 and 1 to change parameters:

```
! provide appropriate global configuration command if not currently in your config.
!
! permit 0 and 1
lnm alternate 1
```

The following example permits all LRMs to change parameters in Cisco IOS software:

```
! provide appropriate global configuration command if not currently in your config.
!
! permit 0, 1, 2, and 3
lnm alternate 3
```

Related Commands

To locate documentation of related commands, you can search online at www.cisco.com.

lnm password

lnm crs

Use the **lnm crs** interface configuration command to monitor the current logical configuration of a Token Ring. Use the **no** form of this command to disable this function.

> **lnm crs**
> **no lnm crs**

Syntax Description

This command has no arguments or keywords.

Default

Enabled

Command Mode

Interface configuration

Usage Guidelines

This command first appeared in Cisco IOS Release 10.0.

The Configuration Report Server service keeps track of the current logical configuration of a Token Ring and reports any changes to LNM. It also reports on various other activities such as the change of the Active Monitor on a Token Ring.

For more information about the Active Monitor, refer to the *IBM Token Ring Architecture Reference Manual* or the IEEE 802.5 specification.

Example

The following example disables monitoring of the current logical configuration of a Token Ring:

```
interface tokenring 0
 no lnm crs
```

Related Commands

To locate documentation of related commands, you can search online at www.cisco.com.

lnm rem
lnm rps

lnm disabled

Use the **lnm disabled** global configuration command to disable LNM functionality. Use the **no** form of this command to restore LNM functionality.

> **lnm disabled**
> **no lnm disabled**

Syntax Description

This command has no arguments or keywords.

Default

Enabled

Command Mode

Global configuration

Usage Guidelines

This command first appeared in Cisco IOS Release 11.2.

Under some circumstances, you can disable all LNM server functions on the router without having to determine whether to disable a specific server, such as the ring parameter server or the ring error monitor on a given interface.

This command can be used to terminate all LNM server input and reporting links. In normal circumstances, this command should not be necessary because it is a superset of the functions normally performed on individual interfaces by the **no lnm rem** and **no lnm rps** commands.

Example

The following example disables LNM functionality:

```
lnm disabled
```

Related Commands

To locate documentation of related commands, you can search online at www.cisco.com.

lnm pathtrace-disabled
lnm rem
lnm rps
lnm snmp-only
show lnm bridge

lnm express-buffer

Use the **lnm express-buffer** interface configuration command to enable the LNM RPS express buffer function. Use the **no** form of this command to disable the function.

> **lnm express-buffer**
> **no lnm express-buffer**

Syntax Description

This command has no arguments or keywords.

Default

Disabled

Command Mode

Interface configuration

Usage Guidelines

This command first appeared in Cisco IOS Release 10.3.

The RPS express buffer function allows the router to set the express buffer bit to ensure priority service for frames required for ring station initiation. When this function is enabled, the router sets the express buffer bit in its initialize ring station response. This allows Token Ring devices to insert into the ring during bursty conditions.

Example

The following example enables the LNM RPS express buffer function:

```
lnm express-buffer
```

lnm loss-threshold

Use the **lnm loss-threshold** interface configuration command to set the threshold at which Cisco IOS software sends a message informing all attached LNMs that it is dropping frames. Use the **no** form of this command to return to the default value.

> **lnm loss-threshold** *number*
> **no lnm loss-threshold**

Syntax	Description
number	A single number expressing the percentage loss rate in hundredths of a percent. The valid range is 0 to 9999.

Default

10 (.10 percent)

Command Mode

Interface configuration

Usage Guidelines

This command first appeared in Cisco IOS Release 10.0.

The software sends a message to all attached LNMs whenever it begins to drop frames. The point at which this report is generated (threshold) is a percentage of the number of frames dropped compared with the number of frames forwarded.

When setting this value, remember that 9999 would mean 100 percent of your frames could be dropped before the message is sent. A value of 1000 would mean 10 percent of the frames could be dropped before sending the message. A value of 100 would mean 1 percent of the frames could be dropped before the message is sent.

Example

In the following example, the loss threshold is set to 0.02 percent:

```
interface tokenring 0
 lnm loss-threshold 2
```

lnm password

Use the **lnm password** interface configuration command to set the password for the reporting link. Use the **no** form of this command to return the password to its default value of 00000000.

lnm password *number string*
no lnm password *number*

Syntax   Description

number   Number of the reporting link to which to apply the password. This value should be in the range 0 to 3.

string   Password you enter at the keyboard. In order to maintain compatibility with LNM, the parameter *string* should be a six- to eight-character string of the type listed in the "Usage Guidelines" section.

Default

00000000

Command Mode

Interface configuration

Usage Guidelines

This command first appeared in Cisco IOS Release 10.0.

LNM employs the concepts of reporting links and reporting link numbers. A reporting link is simply a connection (or potential connection) between a LAN Reporting Manager (LRM) and a bridge. A reporting link number is a unique number used to identify a reporting link. An IBM bridge allows four simultaneous reporting links numbered 0 to 3. Only the LRM attached to the lowest number connection is allowed to change any parameters, and then only when that connection number falls below a certain configurable number. In the default configuration, the LRM connected through link 0 is the only LRM allowed to change parameters.

Each reporting link has its own password. Passwords are used not only to prevent unauthorized access from an LRM to a bridge, but to control access to the different reporting links. This is important because of the different abilities associated with the various reporting links.

Characters allowable in the *string* are the following:

- Letters

- Numbers

- Special characters @, #, $, or %

Passwords are displayed only through use of the privileged EXEC **show running-config** command.

NOTE There are two parameters in an IBM bridge that have no corresponding parameter in Cisco IOS software. This means that any attempt to modify these parameters from LNM will fail and display an error message. The LNM names of these two parameters are *route active status* and *single route broadcast mode*.

Example

In the following example, the password *Zephyr@* is assigned to reporting link 2:

```
! provide appropriate global configuration command if not currently in your config.
!
lnm password 2 Zephyr@
```

Related Commands

To locate documentation of related commands, you can search online at www.cisco.com.

lnm alternate

lnm pathtrace-disabled

Use the **lnm pathtrace-disabled** global configuration command to disable pathtrace reporting to LNM stations. Use the **no** form of this command to restore pathtrace reporting functionality.

lnm pathtrace-disabled [all | origin]
no lnm pathtrace-disabled

Syntax	Description
all	(Optional) Disable pathtrace reporting to the LNM and originating stations.
origin	(Optional) Disable pathtrace reporting to originating stations only.

Default

Enabled

Command Mode

Global configuration

Usage Guidelines

This command first appeared in Cisco IOS Release 11.2.

Under some circumstances, such as when new hardware has been introduced into the network and is causing problems, the automatic report path trace function can be disabled. The new hardware may be setting bit-fields B1 or B2 (or both) of the routing control field in the routing information field embedded in a source-route bridged frame. This condition may cause the network to be flooded by report path trace frames if the condition is persistent. The **lnm pathtrace-disabled** command, along with its options, allows you to alleviate network congestion that may be occurring by disabling all or part of the automatic report path trace function within LNM.

Example

The following example disables all pathtrace reporting:

```
lnm pathtrace-disabled
```

Related Commands

To locate documentation of related commands, you can search online at www.cisco.com.

lnm disabled
lnm pathtrace-disabled
show lnm bridge

lnm rem

Use the **lnm rem** interface configuration command to monitor errors reported by any station on the ring. Use the **no** form of this command to disable this function.

> **lnm rem**
> **no lnm rem**

Syntax Description

This command has no arguments or keywords.

Default

Enabled

Command Mode

Interface configuration

Usage Guidelines

This command first appeared in Cisco IOS Release 10.0.

The Ring Error Monitor (REM) service monitors errors reported by any station on the ring. It also monitors whether the ring is in a functional state or in a failure state.

Example

The following example shows the use of the **lnm rem** command:

```
interface tokenring 0
  lnm rem
```

Related Commands

To locate documentation of related commands, you can search online at www.cisco.com.

lnm crs
lnm rps

lnm rps

Use the **lnm rps** interface configuration command to ensure that all stations on a ring are using a consistent set of reporting parameters. Use the **no** form of this command to disable this function.

> **lnm rps**
> **no lnm rps**

Syntax Description

This command has no arguments or keywords.

Default

Enabled

Command Mode

Interface configuration

Usage Guidelines

This command first appeared in Cisco IOS Release 10.0.

The Ring Parameter Server (RPS) service ensures that all stations on a ring are using a consistent set of reporting parameters and are reporting to LNM when any new station joins a Token Ring.

Example

The following example shows the use of the **lnm rps** command:

```
interface tokenring 0
 lnm rps
```

Related Commands

To locate documentation of related commands, you can search online at www.cisco.com.

lnm crs
lnm rem

lnm snmp-only

Use the **lnm snmp-only** global configuration command to prevent any LNM stations from modifying parameters in Cisco IOS software. Use the **no** form of this command to allow modifications.

> **lnm snmp-only**
> **no lnm snmp-only**

Syntax Description

This command has no arguments or keywords.

Default

Enabled

Command Mode

Global configuration

Usage Guidelines

This command first appeared in Cisco IOS Release 10.0.

Configuring a router for LNM support is very simple. It happens automatically as a part of configuring the router to act as a source-route bridge. There are several commands available to modify the behavior of the LNM support, but none of them are necessary for it to function.

Because there is now more than one way to remotely change parameters in Cisco IOS software, this command was developed to prevent them from detrimentally interacting with each other.

This command does not affect the ability of LNM to monitor events, only to modify parameters in Cisco IOS software.

Example

The following command prevents any LNM stations from modifying parameters in the software:

```
lnm snmp-only
```

lnm softerr

Use the **lnm softerr** interface configuration command to set the time interval in which Cisco IOS software will accumulate error messages before sending them. Use the **no** form of this command to return to the default value.

> **lnm softerr** *milliseconds*
> **no lnm softerr**

Syntax   Description

milliseconds   Time interval in tens of milliseconds between error messages.
                        The valid range is 0 to 65,535.

Default

200 ms (2 seconds)

Command Mode

Interface configuration

Usage Guidelines

This command first appeared in Cisco IOS Release 10.0.

All stations on a Token Ring notify the REM when they detect errors on the ring. To prevent an excessive number of messages, error reports are not sent immediately, but are accumulated for a short period of time and then reported. A station learns this value from a router (configured as a source-route bridge) when it first enters the ring.

Example

The following example changes the error-reporting frequency to once every 5 seconds:

```
lnm softerr 500
```

Related Commands

To locate documentation of related commands, you can search online at www.cisco.com.

lnm rem

mac-address

Use the **mac-address** interface configuration command to set the MAC layer address of Cisco Token Ring.

> **mac-address** *ieee-address*

Syntax   Description

ieee-address   48-bit IEEE MAC address written as a dotted triplet of four-digit hexadecimal numbers.

Default

No MAC layer address is set.

Command Mode

Interface configuration

Usage Guidelines

This command first appeared in Cisco IOS Release 10.0.

There is a known defect in earlier forms of this command when using the Texas Instruments Token Ring MAC firmware. This implementation is used by Proteon, Apollo, and IBM RTs. A host using a MAC address whose first two bytes are zeros (such as a Cisco router) will not properly communicate with hosts using that form of this command of TI firmware.

There are two solutions. The first involves installing a static RIF entry for every faulty node with which the router communicates. If there are many such nodes on the ring, this may not be practical. The second solution involves setting the MAC address of the Cisco Token Ring to a value that works around the problem.

This command forces the use of a different MAC address on the specified interface, thereby avoiding the Texas Instrument MAC firmware problem. It is up to the network administrator to ensure that no other host on the network is using that MAC address.

Example

The following example sets the MAC layer address, where *xx.xxxx* is an appropriate second half of the MAC address to use:

```
interface tokenring 0
 mac-address 5000.5axx.xxxx
```

multiring

Use the **multiring** interface configuration command to enable collection and use of RIF information. Use the **no** form of this command to disable the use of RIF information for the protocol specified.

> **multiring** {*protocol-keyword* [**all-routes** | **spanning**] | **all** | **other**}
> **no multiring** {*protocol-keyword* [**all-routes** | **spanning**] | **all** | **other**}

Syntax	Description
protocol-keyword	Specifies a protocol; see the keyword list under the "Usage Guidelines" section.
all-routes	Uses all-routes explorers.
spanning	Uses spanning-tree explorers.
all	Enables the multiring for all frames.
other	Enables the multiring for any routed frame not included in the previous list of supported protocols.

Default

Disabled

Command Mode

Interface configuration

Usage Guidelines

This command first appeared in Cisco IOS Release 10.0. The keywords **all-routes** and **spanning** first appeared in Cisco Release 11.1.

Level 3 routers that use protocol-specific information (for example, Novell IPX or XNS headers) rather than MAC information to route datagrams also must be able to collect and use RIF information to ensure that they can transmit datagrams across a source-route bridge. The software default is to not collect and use RIF information for routed protocols. This allows operation with software that does not understand or properly use RIF information.

The current software allows you to specify a protocol. This is specified by the argument *protocol-keyword*. The protocols supported and the keywords you can enter include the following:

- **apollo**—Apollo Domain
- **appletalk**—AppleTalk Phase 1 and 2
- **clns**—ISO CLNS
- **decnet**—DECnet Phase IV
- **ip**—IP
- **ipx**—Novell IPX
- **vines**—Banyan VINES
- **xns**—XNS

NOTE   When you are configuring DLSw+ over FDDI, the **multiring** command supports only IP and IPX.

The **multiring** command was extended in Software Release 8.3 to allow for per-protocol specification of the interface's ability to append RIFs to routed protocols. When it is enabled for a protocol, the router will source packets that include information used by source-route bridges. This allows a router with Token Ring interfaces, for the protocol or protocols specified, to connect to a source-bridged Token Ring network. If a protocol is not specified for multiring, the router can only route packets to nodes directly connected to its local Token Ring.

NOTE   Previous to Software Release 8.3, the **multiring** command enabled multiring protocols, in particular, the use of explorers and RIFs, for all routable protocols. This sometimes caused problems when multiring-capable devices speaking one particular protocol were attached to the same ring as a nonmultiring-capable device speaking a different network protocol. If the earlier **multiring** command (pre-8.3 release) was not specified, nodes speaking one particular protocol would be able to communicate through the router, but nodes speaking other protocols could not. The reverse was true when the multiring capability was specified on the interface. In 8.3 or later releases of the software, the command **multiring all** is equivalent to the 8.2 and earlier forms of the **multiring** command.

Example

The following example enables IP and Novell IPX bridging on a Token Ring interface. RIFs will be generated for IP frames, but not for the Novell IPX frames.

```
! commands that follow apply to interface token 0
interface tokenring 0
! generate RIFs for IP frames
 multiring ip
! enable the Token Ring interface for IP
 ip address 131.108.183.37 255.255.255.0
! enable the Token Ring interface for Novell IPX
 novell network 33
```

Related Commands

To locate documentation of related commands, you can search online at www.cisco.com.

clear rif-cache
rif
rif timeout
show rif
xns encapsulation

netbios access-list bytes

Use the **netbios access-list bytes** global configuration command to define the offset and hexadecimal patterns with which to match byte offsets in NetBIOS packets. Use the **no** form of this command to remove an entire list or the entry specified with the *pattern* argument.

netbios access-list bytes *name* {**permit** | **deny**} *offset pattern*
no netbios access-list bytes *name* {**permit** | **deny**} *offset pattern*

Syntax	Description
name	Name of the access list being defined.
permit	Permits the condition.
deny	Denies the condition.
offset	Decimal number indicating the number of bytes into the packet where the byte comparison should begin. An *offset* of zero points to the very beginning of the NetBIOS header. Therefore, the NetBIOS delimiter string (0xFFEF), for example, begins at offset 2.
pattern	Hexadecimal string of digits representing a byte pattern. The argument *pattern* must conform to certain conventions. These conventions are listed under the "Usage Guidelines" section.

Default
No offset or pattern is defined.

Command Mode
Global configuration

Usage Guidelines
This command first appeared in Cisco IOS Release 10.0.

For offset pattern matching, the byte pattern must be an even number of hexadecimal digits in length.

The byte pattern must be no more than 16 bytes (32 hexadecimal digits) in length.

As with all access lists, the NetBIOS access lists are scanned in order.

You can specify a wildcard character in the byte string indicating that the value of that byte does not matter in the comparison. This is done by specifying two asterisks (**) in place of digits for that byte. For example, the following command would match *0xabaacd*, *0xab00cd*, and so on:

```
netbios access-list bytes marketing permit 3 0xab**cd
```

Examples
The following example shows how to configure for offset pattern matching:

```
netbios access-list bytes marketing permit 3 0xabcd
```

In the following example, the byte pattern would not be accepted because it must be an even number of hexadecimal digits:

```
netbios access-list bytes marketing permit 3 0xabc
```

In the following example, the byte pattern would not be permitted because the byte pattern is longer than 16 bytes in length:

```
netbios access-list bytes marketing permit 3 00112233445566778899aabbccddeeff00
```

The following example would match 0xabaacd, 0xab00cd, and so on:

```
netbios access-list bytes marketing permit 3 0xab**cd
```

The following example deletes the entire marketing NetBIOS access list named marketing:

```
no netbios access-list bytes marketing
```

The following example removes a single entry from the list:

```
no netbios access-list bytes marketing deny 3 0xab**cd
```

In the following example, the first line serves to deny all packets with a byte pattern starting in *offset* 3 of 0xab. However, this denial would also include the pattern 0xabcd because the entry permitting the pattern 0xabcd comes after the first entry:

```
netbios access-list bytes marketing deny 3 0xab
netbios access-list bytes marketing permit 3 0xabcd
```

Related Commands

To locate documentation of related commands, you can search online at www.cisco.com.

netbios input-access-filter bytes
netbios output-access-filter bytes

netbios access-list host

Use the **netbios access-list host** global configuration command to assign the name of the access list to a station or set of stations on the network. The NetBIOS station access list contains the station name to match, along with a permit or deny condition. Use the **no** form of this command to remove either an entire list or just a single entry from a list, depending upon the argument given for *pattern*.

> **netbios access-list host** *name* {**permit** | **deny**} *pattern*
> **no netbios access-list host** *name* {**permit** | **deny**} *pattern*

Syntax	Description
name	Name of the access list being defined.
permit	Permits the condition.
deny	Denies the condition.
pattern	A set of characters. The characters can be the name of the station or a combination of characters and pattern-matching symbols that establish a pattern for a set of NetBIOS station names. This combination can be especially useful when stations have names with the same characters, such as a prefix. The table in the "Usage Guidelines" section explains the pattern-matching symbols that can be used.

Default

No access list is assigned.

Command Mode

Global configuration

Usage Guidelines

This command first appeared in Cisco IOS Release 10.0.

Table 4-4 explains the pattern-matching characters that can be used.

Table 4-4 *Station Name Pattern-Matching Characters*

Character	Description
*	Used at the end of a string to match any character or string of characters.
?	Matches any single character. If this wildcard is used as the first letter of the name, you must precede it with a CNTL-V key sequence. Otherwise, it will be interpreted by the router as a request for help.

Examples

The following example specifies a full station name to match:

```
netbios access-list host marketing permit ABCD
```

The following example specifies a prefix where the pattern matches any name beginning with the characters DEFG:

```
!The string DEFG itself is included in this condition.
netbios access-list host marketing deny DEFG*
```

The following example permits any station name with the letter W as the first character and the letter Y as the third character in the name. The second and fourth character in the name can be any character. This example would allow stations named WXYZ and WAYB; however, stations named WY and WXY would not be allowed because the question mark (?) must match specific characters in the name:

```
netbios access-list host marketing permit W?Y?
```

The following example illustrates how to combine wildcard characters. In this example the marketing list denies any name beginning with AC that is not at least three characters in length (the question mark [?] would match any third character). The string ACBD and ACB would match, but the string AC would not:

```
netbios access-list host marketing deny AC?
```

In the following example, a single entry in the marketing NetBIOS access list is removed:

```
no netbios access-list host marketing deny AC?*
```

In the following example, the entire marketing NetBIOS access list is removed:

```
no netbios access-list host marketing
```

Related Commands

To locate documentation of related commands, you can search online at www.cisco.com.

netbios input-access-filter host
netbios output-access-filter host

netbios enable-name-cache

Use the **netbios enable-name-cache** interface configuration command to enable NetBIOS name caching. Use the **no** form of this command to disable the name-cache behavior.

> **netbios enable-name-cache**
> **no netbios enable-name-cache**

Syntax Description

This command has no arguments or keywords.

Default

Disabled

Command Mode

Interface configuration

Usage Guidelines

This command first appeared in Cisco IOS Release 10.0.

This command enables the NetBIOS name cache on the specified interface. By default, the name cache is disabled for the interface. Proxy explorers must be enabled on any interface that is using the NetBIOS name cache.

Example

The following example enables NetBIOS name caching for Token Ring interface 0:

```
interface tokenring 0
 source-bridge proxy-explorer
 netbios enable-name-cache
```

Related Commands

To locate documentation of related commands, you can search online at www.cisco.com.

clear netbios-cache
netbios name-cache timeout
show netbios-cache

netbios input-access-filter bytes

Use the **netbios input-access-filter bytes** interface configuration command to define a byte access list filter on incoming messages. The actual access filter byte offsets and patterns used are defined in one or more **netbios-access-list bytes** commands. Use the **no** form of this command with the appropriate name to remove the entire access list.

> **netbios input-access-filter bytes name**
> **no netbios input-access-filter bytes name**

Syntax	Description
name	Name of a NetBIOS access filter previously defined with one or more of the **netbios access-list bytes** global configuration commands.

Default

No access list is defined.

Command Mode

Interface configuration

Usage Guidelines

This command first appeared in Cisco IOS Release 10.0.

Example

The following example applies a previously defined filter named *marketing* to packets coming into Token Ring 1:

```
interface tokenring 1
 netbios input-access-filter bytes marketing
```

Related Commands

To locate documentation of related commands, you can search online at www.cisco.com.

netbios access-list bytes
netbios input-access-filter bytes

netbios input-access-filter host

Use the **netbios input-access-filter host** interface configuration command to define a station access list filter on incoming messages. The access lists of station names are defined in **netbios access-list host** commands. Use the **no** form of this command with the appropriate argument to remove the entire access list.

> **netbios input-access-filter host** *name*
> **no netbios input-access-filter host** *name*

Syntax   Description

name   Name of a NetBIOS access filter previously defined with one or more of the
                netbios access-list host global configuration commands.

Default

No access list is defined.

Command Mode

Interface configuration

Usage Guidelines

This command first appeared in Cisco IOS Release 10.0.

Example

The following example filters packets coming into tokenring1 using the NetBIOS access list named marketing:

```
interface tokenring 1
 netbios access-list host marketing permit W?Y?
 netbios input-access-filter host marketing
```

Related Commands

To locate documentation of related commands, you can search online at www.cisco.com.

netbios access-list host
netbios output-access-filter host

netbios name-cache

Use the **netbios name-cache** global configuration command to define a static NetBIOS name cache entry, tying the server with the name *netbios-name* to the *mac-address*, and specifying that the server is accessible either locally via the *interface-name* specified, or remotely, via the **ring-group** *group-number* specified. Use the **no** form of this command to remove the entry.

> **netbios name-cache** *mac-address netbios-name {interface-name |*
> **ring-group** *group-number}*
> **no netbios name-cache** *mac-address netbios-name*

Syntax	Description
mac-address	The MAC address.
netbios-name	Server name linked to the MAC address.
interface-name	Name of the interface by which the server is accessible locally.
ring-group	Specifies that the link is accessible remotely.
group-number	Number of the ring group by which the server is accessible remotely. This ring group number must match the number you have specified with the **source-bridge ring-group** command. The valid range is 1 to 4095.

Default

No entry is defined.

Command Mode

Global configuration

Usage Guidelines

This command first appeared in Cisco IOS Release 10.0.

To specify an entry in the static name cache, first specify a routing information field (RIF) that leads to the server's MAC address. Cisco IOS software displays an error message if it cannot find a static RIF entry for the server when the NetBIOS name-cache entry is attempted or if the server's type conflicts with that given for the static RIF entry.

NOTE	The names are case sensitive; therefore "Cc" is not the same as "cC".

Examples

The following example indicates the syntax usage of this command if the NetBIOS server is accessed locally:

```
source-bridge ring-group 2
rif 0220.3333.4444 00c8.042.0060 tokenring 0
netbios name-cache 0220.3333.4444 DEF tokenring 0
```

The following example indicates the syntax usage of this command if the NetBIOS server is accessed remotely:

```
source-bridge ring-group 2
 rif 0110.2222.3333 0630.021.0030 ring group 2
 netbios name-cache 0110.2222.3333 DEF ring-group 2
```

Related Commands

To locate documentation of related commands, you can search online at www.cisco.com.

show netbios-cache

netbios name-cache name-len

Use the **netbios name-cache name-len** global configuration command to specify how many characters of the NetBIOS type name the name cache will validate.

netbios name-cache name-len *length*

Syntax	Description
length	Length of the NetBIOS type name. The range is 8 to 16 characters.

Default

15 characters

Command Mode

Global configuration

Usage Guidelines

This command first appeared in Cisco IOS Release 10.0.

Example

The following example specifies that the name cache will validate 16 characters of the NetBIOS type name:

```
netbios name-cache name-len 16
```

Related Commands

To locate documentation of related commands, you can search online at www.cisco.com.

netbios enable-name-cache
netbios name-cache
netbios name-cache proxy-datagram
netbios name-cache query-timeout
netbios name-cache recognized-timeout
netbios name-cache timeout

netbios name-cache proxy-datagram

Use the **netbios name-cache proxy-datagram** global configuration command to enable Cisco IOS software to act as a proxy and send NetBIOS datagram type frames.

netbios name-cache proxy-datagram *seconds*

Syntax	Description
seconds	Time interval, in seconds, that the software forwards a route broadcast datagram type packet. The valid range is any number greater than 0.

Default

There is no default time interval.

Command Mode

Global configuration

Usage Guidelines

This command first appeared in Cisco IOS Release 10.0.

Example

The following example specifies that the software will forward a NetBIOS datagram type frame in 20-second intervals:

```
netbios name-cache proxy-datagram 20
```

Related Commands

To locate documentation of related commands, you can search online at www.cisco.com.

netbios enable-name-cache
netbios name-cache
netbios name-cache query-timeout
netbios name-cache recognized-timeout
netbios name-cache timeout

netbios name-cache query-timeout

Use the **netbios name-cache query-timeout** global configuration command to specify the "dead" time, in seconds, that starts when a host sends any ADD_NAME_QUERY, ADD_GROUP_NAME, or STATUS_QUERY frame. During this dead time, Cisco IOS software drops any repeat, duplicate ADD_NAME_QUERY, ADD_GROUP_NAME, or STATUS_QUERY frame sent by the same host. This timeout is only effective at the time of the login negotiation process. Use the **no** form of this command to bring the time back to the default of 6 seconds.

> **netbios name-cache query-timeout** *seconds*
> **no netbios name-cache query-timeout**

Syntax	Description
seconds	Dead time period in seconds. Default is 6 seconds.

Default

6 seconds

Command Mode

Global configuration

Usage Guidelines

This command first appeared in Cisco IOS Release 10.0.

Example

The following example sets the timeout to 15 seconds:

```
netbios name-cache query-timeout 15
```

Related Commands

To locate documentation of related commands, you can search online at www.cisco.com.

netbios name-cache recognized-timeout

netbios name-cache recognized-timeout

Use the **netbios name-cache recognized-timeout** global configuration command to specify the "dead" time, in seconds, that starts when a host sends any FIND_NAME or NAME_RECOGNIZED frame. During this dead time, Cisco IOS software drops any repeat, duplicate FIND_NAME or NAME_RECOGNIZED frame sent by the same host. This timeout is only effective at the time of the login negotiation process. Use the **no** form of this command to bring the time back to the default of 6 seconds.

> **netbios name-cache recognized-timeout** *seconds*
> **no netbios name-cache recognized-timeout**

Syntax	Description
seconds	Dead time period in seconds. Default is 6 seconds.

Default

6 seconds

Command Mode

Global configuration

Usage Guidelines

This command first appeared in Cisco IOS Release 10.0.

Example

The following example sets the timeout to 15 seconds:

```
netbios name-cache recognized-timeout 15
```

Related Commands

To locate documentation of related commands, you can search online at www.cisco.com.

netbios name-cache query-timeout

netbios name-cache timeout

Use the **netbios name-cache timeout** global configuration command to enable NetBIOS name caching and to set the time that entries can remain in the NetBIOS name cache. Use the **no** form of this command to bring the time back to the default of 15 minutes.

> **netbios name-cache timeout** *minutes*
> **no netbios name-cache timeout** *minutes*

Syntax   Description

minutes   Time, in minutes, that entries can remain in the NetBIOS name cache. Once
                         the time expires, the entry will be deleted from the cache. Default is 15
                         minutes.

Default

15 minutes

Command Mode

Global configuration

Usage Guidelines

This command first appeared in Cisco IOS Release 10.0.

This command allows you to establish NetBIOS name caching. NetBIOS name caching can be used only between routers that are running Software Release 9.1 or later. NetBIOS name-caching does not apply to static entries.

Example

The following example sets the timeout to 10 minutes:

```
interface tokenring 0
 netbios name-cache timeout 10
```

Related Commands

To locate documentation of related commands, you can search online at www.cisco.com.

show netbios-cache

netbios output-access-filter bytes

Use the **netbios output-access-filter bytes** interface configuration command to define a byte access list filter on outgoing messages. Use the **no** form of this command to remove the entire access list.

netbios output-access-filter bytes *name*
no netbios output-access-filter bytes *name*

Syntax   Description

name   Name of a NetBIOS access filter previously defined with one or more of the **netbios access-list bytes** global configuration commands.

Default

No access list is defined.

Command Mode

Interface configuration

Usage Guidelines

This command first appeared in Cisco IOS Release 10.0.

Example

The following example filters packets leaving Token Ring 1 using the NetBIOS access list named engineering:

```
interface tokenring 1
 netbios access-list bytes engineering permit 3 0xabcd
 netbios output-access-filter bytes engineering
```

Related Commands

To locate documentation of related commands, you can search online at www.cisco.com.

netbios access-list bytes
netbios input-access-filter bytes

netbios output-access-filter host

Use the **netbios output-access-filter host** interface configuration command to define a station access list filter on outgoing messages. Use the **no** form of this command to remove the entire access list.

> **netbios output-access-filter host** *name*
> **no netbios output-access-filter host** *name*

Syntax
Description

name   Name of a NetBIOS access filter previously defined with one or more of the
                  netbios access-list host global configuration commands.

Default

No access list filter is defined.

Command Mode

Interface configuration

Usage Guidelines

This command first appeared in Cisco IOS Release 10.0.

Example

The following example filters packets leaving Token Ring 1 using the NetBIOS access list named engineering:

```
interface tokenring 1
 netbios access-list host engineering permit W?Y?
 netbios output-access-filter host engineering
```

Related Commands

To locate documentation of related commands, you can search online at www.cisco.com.

netbios access-list host
netbios input-access-filter host

rif

Use the **rif** global configuration command to enter static source-route information into the routing information field (RIF) cache. If a Token Ring host does not support the use of IEEE 802.2 TEST or XID datagrams as explorer packets, you may need to add static information to the RIF cache of the router. Use the **no** form of this command to remove an entry from the cache.

> **rif** *mac-address rif-string* {*interface-name* | **ring-group** *ring*}
> **no rif** *mac-address* {*interface-name* | **ring-group** *ring*}

Syntax	Description
mac-address	12-digit hexadecimal string written as a dotted triplet; for example, 0010.0a00.20a6.
rif-string	Series of 4-digit hexadecimal numbers separated by a period (.). This RIF string is inserted into the packets sent to the specified MAC address.
interface-name	Interface name (for example, Token Ring 0) that indicates the origin of the RIF.
ring-group	Specifies the origin of the RIF is a ring group.
ring	Ring group number that indicates the origin of the RIF. This ring group number must match the number you have specified with the **source-bridge ring-group** command. The valid range is 1 to 4095.

Default

No static source-route information is entered.

Command Mode

Global configuration

Usage Guidelines

This command first appeared in Cisco IOS Release 10.0.

You must specify either an interface name or a ring group number to indicate the origin of the RIF. You specify an interface name (for example, tokenring 0) with the *interface-name* argument and you specify a ring group number with the **ring-group** *ring* argument. The ring group number must match the number you specified with the **source-bridge ring-group** command.

Using the command **rif** *mac-address* without any other arguments puts an entry into the RIF cache indicating that packets for this MAC address should not have RIF information.

Do not configure a static RIF with any of the *all rings* type codes. Doing so causes traffic for the configured host to appear on more than one ring and leads to unnecessary congestion.

NOTE   Input to the **source-bridge** interface configuration command is in decimal format. RIF displays and input are in hexadecimal format and IBM source-route bridges use hexadecimal for input. It is essential that bridge and ring numbers are consistent for proper network operation. This means you must explicitly declare the numbers to be hexadecimal by preceding the number with 0x, or you must convert IBM hexadecimal numbers to a decimal equivalent when entering them. For example, IBM hexadecimal bridge number 10 would be entered as hexadecimal number 0x10 or decimal number 16 in the configuration commands. In the displays, these commands always will be in decimal.

Example

The following example configuration sets up a static RIF:

```
! insert entry with MAC address 1000.5A12.3456 and RIF of
! 0630.0081.0090 into RIF cache
rif 1000.5A12.3456 0630.0081.0090 tokenring 0
```

Related Commands

To locate documentation of related commands, you can search online at www.cisco.com.

multiring
source-bridge ring-group

rif timeout

Use the **rif timeout** global configuration command to determine the number of minutes an inactive RIF entry is kept. RIF information is maintained in a cache whose entries are aged. Use the **no** form of this command to restore the default.

rif timeout *minutes*
no rif timeout

Syntax

Description

minutes

Number of minutes an inactive RIF entry is kept. The value must be greater than 0. Default is 15 minutes.

Default

15 minutes

Command Mode

Global configuration

Usage Guidelines

This command first appeared in Cisco IOS Release 10.0.

A RIF entry is cached based on the MAC address and the interface.

A RIF entry can be aged out even if there is active traffic, but the traffic is fast or autonomously switched.

A RIF entry is refreshed only if a RIF field of an incoming frame is identical to the RIF information of the RIF entry in the cache.

Until a RIF entry is removed from the cache, no new information is accepted for that RIF entry.

Example

The following example changes the timeout period to 5 minutes:

```
rif timeout 5
```

Related Commands

To locate documentation of related commands, you can search online at www.cisco.com.

clear rif-cache
rif validate-enable
show rif

rif validate-age

Use the **rif validate-age** global configuration command to define the validation time when Cisco IOS software is acting as a proxy for NetBIOS NAME_QUERY packet or for explorer frames.

> **rif validate-age** *seconds*

Syntax	Description
seconds	Interval, in seconds, at which a proxy is sent. The valid range is any number greater than 0. Default is 2 seconds.

Default

2 seconds

Command Mode

Global configuration

Usage Guidelines

This command first appeared in Cisco IOS Release 10.0.

If the timer expires before the response is received, the RIF entry or the NetBIOS cache entry is marked as invalid and is flushed from the cache table when another explorer or NAME_QUERY packet is received.

Example

The following example specifies the interval at which a proxy is sent to be 3 seconds:

```
rif validate-age 3
```

Related Commands

To locate documentation of related commands, you can search online at www.cisco.com.

rif
rif timeout

rif validate-enable

Use the **rif validate-enable** global configuration command to enable RIF validation for entries learned on an interface (Token Ring or FDDI). Use the **no** form of this command to disable the specification.

> **rif validate-enable**
> **no rif validate-enable**

Syntax Description

This command has no arguments or keywords.

Default

RIF validation is enabled.

Command Mode

Global configuration

Usage Guidelines

This command first appeared in Cisco IOS Release 11.0.

A RIF validation algorithm is used for the following cases:

● To decrease convergence time to a new source route path when an intermediate bridge goes down.

● To keep a valid RIF entry in a RIF cache even if a RIF entry is not refreshed either because traffic is fast or autonomously switched, or because there is no traffic.

A directed IEEE TEST command is sent to the destination MAC address. If a response received in the time specified by rif validate-age, the entry is refreshed and is considered valid. Otherwise, the entry is removed from the cache. To prevent sending too many TEST commands, any entry that has been refreshed in less than 70 seconds is considered valid.

Validation is triggered as follows:

- When a RIF entry is found in the cache.

- When a RIF field of an incoming frame and the RIF information of the RIF entry is not identical. If, as the result of validation, the entry is removed from the cache, the RIF field of the next incoming frame with the same MAC address is cached.

- When the RIF entry is not refreshed for the time specified in the **rif timeout** command.

NOTE   If the RIF entry has been in the RIF cache for 6 hours, and has not been refreshed for the time specified in the **rif timeout** command, the entry is removed unconditionally from the cache.

NOTE   The **rif validate-enable** commands have no effect on remote entries learned over RSRB.

Example

The following example enables RIF validation:

```
rif validate-enable
```

Related Commands

To locate documentation of related commands, you can search online at www.cisco.com.

rif timeout
rif validate-age
rif validate-enable-age
rif validate-enable-route-cache

rif validate-enable-age

Use the **rif validate-enable-age** global configuration command to enable RIF validation for stations on a source-route bridge network that do not respond to an IEEE TEST command. Use the **no** form of this command to disable the specification.

> **rif validate-enable-age**
> **no rif validate-enable-age**

Syntax Description

This command has no arguments or keywords.

Default

RIF validation is enabled.

Command Mode

Global configuration

Usage Guidelines

This command first appeared in Cisco IOS Release 11.0.

You must first issue the **rif validate-enable** command.

When this command is enabled, a RIF entry is not removed from the cache even if it becomes invalid. If the entry is refreshed, it becomes valid again.

If a RIF field of an incoming frame and the RIF information of the invalid RIF entry are not identical, the old RIF information is replaced by the new information.

NOTE   The **rif validate-enable** commands have no effect on remote entries learned over RSRB.

Example

The following example enables RIF validation:

```
rif validate-enable-age
```

Related Commands

To locate documentation of related commands, you can search online at www.cisco.com.

rif validate-enable

rif validate-enable-route-cache

Use the **rif validate-enable-route-cache** global configuration command to enable synchronization of the RIF cache with the protocol route cache. Use the **no** form of this command to disable the specification.

rif validate-enable-route-cache
no rif validate-enable-route-cache

Syntax Description

This command has no arguments or keywords.

Default

Disabled

Command Mode

Global configuration

Usage Guidelines

This command first appeared in Cisco IOS Release 11.0.

When a RIF entry is removed from the RIF cache, or the RIF information in the RIF entry is changed, the protocol route caches are synchronized with the RIF cache.

NOTE   The **rif validate-enable** commands have no effect on remote entries learned over RSRB.

Example

The following example synchronizes the RIF cache with the protocol route cache:

```
rif validate-enable-route-cache
```

Related Commands

To locate documentation of related commands, you can search online at www.cisco.com.

rif validate-enable

show controllers token

Use the **show controllers token** privileged EXEC command to display information about memory management, error counters, and the board itself. Depending on the board being used, the output can vary. This command also displays proprietary information. Thus, the information that **show controllers token** displays is of primary use to Cisco technical personnel. Information that is useful to users can be obtained with the **show interfaces tokenring** command, described later.

show controllers token

Syntax Description

This command has no arguments or keywords.

Command Mode

Privileged EXEC

Usage Guidelines

This command first appeared in Cisco IOS Release 10.0.

Sample Displays

The following is sample output from the **show controllers token** command of a CSC-IR or CSC-2R card:

```
Router# show controllers token

TR Unit 0 is board 0 - ring 0

  state 3, dev blk: 0x1D2EBC, mailbox: 0x2100010, sca: 0x2010000
    current address: 0000.3080.6f40, burned in address: 0000.3080.6f40
    current TX ptr: 0xBA8, current RX ptr: 0x800

  Last Ring Status: none

  Stats: soft:0/0, hard:0/0, sig loss:0/0
        tx beacon: 0/0, wire fault 0/0, recovery: 0/0
        only station: 0/0, remote removal: 0/0
    Bridge: local 3330, bnum 1, target 3583
      max_hops 7, target idb: 0x0, not local
    Interface failures: 0   -- Bkgnd Ints: 0
    TX shorts 0, TX giants 0
```

```
    Monitor state: (active)
       flags 0xC0, state 0x0, test 0x0, code 0x0, reason 0x0
f/w ver: 1.0, chip f/w: '000000.ME31100', [bridge capable]
       SMT form of this command s: 1.01 kernel, 4.02 fastmac
       ring mode: F00, internal enables:  SRB REM RPS CRS/NetMgr
       internal functional: 0000011A (0000011A), group: 00000000 (00000000)
       if_state: 1, ints: 0/0, ghosts: 0/0, bad_states: 0/0
       t2m fifo purges: 0/0
       t2m fifo current: 0, t2m fifo max: 0/0, proto_errs: 0/0
       ring: 3330, bridge num: 1, target: 3583, max hops: 7

Packet counts:
       receive total:  298/6197, small: 298/6197, large 0/0
              runts: 0/0, giants: 0/0
              local: 298/6197, bridged: 0/0, promis: 0/0
            bad rif: 0/0, multiframe: 0/0
       ring num mismatch 0/0, spanning violations 0
       transmit total: 1/25, small: 1/25, large 0/0
              runts: 0/0, giants: 0/0, errors 0/0
bad fs: 0/0, bad ac: 0
congested: 0/0, not present: 0/0
       Unexpected interrupts: 0/0,  last unexp. int: 0

       Internal controller counts:
       line errors:  0/0, internal errors: 0/0
       burst errors: 0/0, ari/fci errors:  0/0
       abort errors: 0/0, lost frame: 0/0
       copy errors:  0/0, rcvr congestion: 0/0
       token errors: 0/0, frequency errors: 0/0
       dma bus errors: -/-, dma parity errors: -/-
       Internal controller smt state:
       Adapter MAC:      0000.3080.6f40, Physical drop:      00000000
       NAUN Address:     0000.a6e0.11a6, NAUN drop:          00000000
       Last source:      0000.a6e0.11a6, Last poll:          0000.3080.6f40
       Last MVID:        0006,           Last attn code:     0006
       Txmit priority:   0006,           Auth Class:         7FFF
       Monitor Error:    0000,           Interface Errors:   FFFF
       Correlator:       0000,           Soft Error Timer:   00C8
       Local Ring:       0000,           Ring Status:        0000
       Beacon rcv type:  0000,           Beacon txmit type:  0000
       Beacon type:      0000,           Beacon NAUN:        0000.a6e0.11a6
```

Table 4-5 describes the fields shown in the first line of sample output.

Table 4-5 *show controllers token Field Descriptions—Part 1*

Field	Description
TR Unit 0	Unit number assigned to the Token Ring interface associated with this output.
is board 0	Board number assigned to the Token Ring controller board associated with this interface.
ring 0	Number of the Token Ring associated with this board.

Continues

In the following line, state 3 indicates the state of the board. The rest of this output line displays memory mapping that is of primary use to Cisco engineers.

```
state 3, dev blk: 0x1D2EBC, mailbox: 0x2100010, sca: 0x2010000
```

The following line also appears in **show interface token** output as the address and burned in address (bia), respectively:

```
current address: 0000.3080.6f40, burned in address: 0000.3080.6f40
```

The following line displays buffer management pointers that change by board:

```
current TX ptr: 0xBA8, current RX ptr: 0x800
```

The following line indicates the ring status from the controller chip set. This information is used by LAN Network Manager (LNM):

```
Last Ring Status: none
```

The following line displays Token Ring statistics:

```
Stats: soft:0/0, hard:0/0, sig loss:0/0
       tx beacon: 0/0, wire fault 0/0, recovery: 0/0
       only station: 0/0, remote removal: 0/0
```

The following line indicates that Token Ring communication has been enabled on the interface. If this line of output appears, the message "Source Route Bridge capable" should appear in the **show interfaces tokenring** display.

```
Bridge: local 3330, bnum 1, target 3583
```

Table 4-6 describes the fields shown in the following line of sample output:

```
max_hops 7, target idb: 0x0, not local
```

Table 4-6 *show controllers token Field Descriptions—Part 2*

Field	Description
max_hops 7	Maximum number of bridges.
target idb: 0x0	Destination interface definition.
not local	Interface has been defined as a remote bridge.

The following line is specific to the hardware:

```
Interface failures: 0   -- Bkgnd Ints: 0
```

In the following line, TX shorts are the number of packets the interface transmits that are discarded because they are smaller than the medium's minimum packet size. TX giants are the number of packets the interface transmits that are discarded because they exceed the medium's maximum packet size.

```
TX shorts 0, TX giants 0
```

The following line indicates the state of the controller. Possible values include active, failure, inactive, and reset.

```
Monitor state: (active)
```

The following line displays detailed information relating to the monitor state shown in the previous line of output. This information relates to the firmware on the controller. This information is relevant to Cisco engineers only if the monitor state is something other than active.

```
flags 0xC0, state 0x0, test 0x0, code 0x0, reason 0x0
```

Table 4-7 describes the fields in the following line or output:

```
f/w ver: 1.0 expr 0, chip f/w: '000000.ME31100', [bridge capable]
```

Table 4-7 *show controllers token Field Descriptions—Part 3*

Field	Description
f/w ver: 1.0	Version of Cisco firmware on the board.
chip f/w: '000000.ME31100'	Firmware on the chip set.
[bridge capable]	Interface has not been configured for bridging, but it has that capability.

The following line displays the version numbers for the kernel and the accelerator microcode of the Madge firmware on the board; this firmware is the LLC interface to the chip set:

```
SMT form of this command s: 1.01 kernel, 4.02 fastmac
```

The following line displays LAN Network Manager information that relates to ring status:

```
ring mode: F00, internal enables:  SRB REM RPS CRS/NetMgr
```

The following line corresponds to the functional address and the group address shown in **show interfaces tokenring** output:

```
internal functional: 0000011A (0000011A), group: 00000000 (00000000)
```

The following line displays interface board state information that is proprietary:

```
if_state: 1, ints: 0/0, ghosts: 0/0, bad_states: 0/0
```

The following lines display information that is proprietary. Cisco engineers use this information for debugging purposes:

```
t2m fifo purges: 0/0
t2m fifo current: 0, t2m fifo max: 0/0, proto_errs: 0/0
```

Each of the fields in the following line maps to a field in the **show source bridge** display, as follows: ring maps to srn; bridge num maps to bn; target maps to trn; and max hops maps to max.

```
ring: 3330, bridge num: 1, target: 3583, max hops: 7
```

In the following lines of output, the number preceding the slash (/) indicates the count since the value was last displayed; the number following the slash (/) indicates count since the system was last booted:

```
Packet counts:
        receive total:  298/6197, small: 298/6197, large 0/0
```

In the following line, the number preceding the slash (/) indicates the count since the value was last displayed; the number following the slash (/) indicates count since the system was last booted. The runts and giants values that appear here correspond to the runts and giants values that appear in **show interfaces tokenring** output:

```
runts: 0/0, giants: 0/0
```

The following lines are receiver-specific information that Cisco engineers can use for debugging purposes:

```
local: 298/6197, bridged: 0/0, promis: 0/0
bad rif: 0/0, multiframe: 0/0
ring num mismatch 0/0, spanning violations 0
transmit total: 1/25, small: 1/25, large 0/0
runts: 0/0, giants: 0/0, errors 0/0
```

The following lines include very specific statistics that are not relevant in most cases, but exist for historical purposes. In particular, the internal errors, burst errors, ari/fci, abort errors, copy errors, frequency errors, dma bus errors, and dma parity errors fields are not relevant.

```
Internal controller counts:
 line errors: 0/0,  internal errors: 0/0
 burst errors: 0/0,  ari/fci errors: 0/0
 abort errors: 0/0, lost frame: 0/0
 copy errors: 0/0, rcvr congestion: 0/0
 token errors: 0/0, frequency errors: 0/0
 dma bus errors: -/-, dma parity errors: -/-
```

The following lines are low-level Token Ring interface statistics relating to the state and status of the Token Ring with respect to all other Token Rings on the line:

```
Internal controller smt state:
Adapter MAC:     0000.3080.6f40, Physical drop:     00000000
NAUN Address:    0000.a6e0.11a6, NAUN drop:         00000000
Last source:     0000.a6e0.11a6, Last poll:         0000.3080.6f40
Last MVID:       0006,           Last attn code:    0006
Txmit priority:  0006,           Auth Class:        7FFF
Monitor Error:   0000,           Interface Errors:  FFFF
Correlator:      0000,           Soft Error Timer:  00C8
Local Ring:      0000,           Ring Status:       0000
Beacon rcv type: 0000,           Beacon txmit type: 0000
```

show interfaces tokenring

Use the **show interfaces tokenring** privileged EXEC command to display information about the Token Ring interface and the state of source-route bridging.

show interfaces tokenring [*number*]

Syntax	Description
number	(Optional) Interface number. If you do not provide a value, the command will display statistics for all Token Ring interfaces.

Command Mode

Privileged EXEC

Usage Guidelines

This command first appeared in Cisco IOS Release 10.0.

Sample Display

The following is sample output from the **show interfaces tokenring** command:

```
Router# show interfaces tokenring

TokenRing 0 is up, line protocol is up
Hardware is 16/4 Token Ring, address is 5500.2000.dc27 (bia 0000.3000.072b)
    Internet address is 150.136.230.203, subnet mask is 255.255.255.0
    MTU 8136 bytes, BW 16000 Kbit, DLY 630 usec, rely 255/255, load 1/255
    Encapsulation SNAP, loopback not set, keepalive set (10 sec)
    ARP type: SNAP, ARP Timeout 4:00:00
    Ring speed: 16 Mbps
    Single ring node, Source Route Bridge capable
    Group Address: 0x00000000, Functional Address: 0x60840000
    Last input 0:00:01, output 0:00:01, output hang never
    Output queue 0/40, 0 drops; input queue 0/75, 0 drops
    Five minute input rate 0 bits/sec, 0 packets/sec
    Five minute output rate 0 bits/sec, 0 packets/sec
    16339 packets input, 1496515 bytes, 0 no buffer
        Received 9895 broadcasts, 0 runts, 0 giants
        0 input errors, 0 CRC, 0 frame, 0 overrun, 0 ignored, 0 abort
    32648 packets output, 9738303 bytes, 0 underruns
0 output errors, 0 collisions, 2 interface resets, 0 restarts
    5 transitions
```

Table 4-8 describes significant fields shown in the display.

Table 4-8   *show interfaces tokenring Field Descriptions*

Field	Description
Token Ring is up/down	Interface is currently active and inserted into ring (up) or inactive and not inserted (down).
Token Ring is Reset	Hardware error has occurred. This is not in the sample output; it is informational only.
Token Ring is Initializing	Hardware is up, in the process of inserting the ring. This is not in the sample output; it is informational only.
Token Ring is Administratively Down	Hardware has been taken down by an administrator. This is not in the sample output; it is informational only. "Disabled" indicates Cisco IOS software has received over 5000 errors in a keepalive interval, which is 10 seconds by default.
line protocol is {up | down | administratively down}	Indicates whether the software processes that handle the line protocol believe the interface is usable (that is, whether keepalives are successful).
Hardware	Specifies the hardware type. "Hardware is ciscoBus Token Ring" indicates that the board is a CSC-C2CTR board. "Hardware is 16/4 Token Ring" indicates that the board is a CSC-1R, CSC-2R, or a CSC-R16M board. Also shows the address of the interface.
Internet address	Lists the Internet address followed by subnet mask.
MTU	Maximum transmission unit of the interface.
BW	Bandwidth of the interface in kilobits per second (kps).
DLY	Delay of the interface in microseconds.
rely	Reliability of the interface as a fraction of 255 (255/255 is 100 percent reliability), calculated as an exponential average over 5 minutes.
load	Load on the interface as a fraction of 255 (255/255 is completely saturated), calculated as an exponential average over 5 minutes.
Encapsulation	Encapsulation method assigned to interface.
loopback	Indicates whether loopback is set or not.
keepalive	Indicates whether keepalives are set or not.
ARP type	Type of Address Resolution Protocol assigned.
Ring speed	Speed of Token Ring—4 or 16 Mbps.
{Single ring | multiring node}	Indicates whether a node is enabled to collect and use source RIF for routable Token Ring protocols.

Table 4-8 *show interfaces tokenring* *Field Descriptions (Continued)*

Field	Description
Group Address	Interface's group address, if any. The group address is a multicast address; any number of interfaces on the ring may share the same group address. Each interface may have at most one group address.
Functional Address	Bit-significant group address. Each "on" bit represents a function performed by the station.
Last input	Number of hours, minutes, and seconds since the last packet was successfully received by an interface. Useful for knowing when a dead interface failed.
output hang	Number of hours, minutes, and seconds (or never) since the interface was last reset because of a transmission that took too long. When the number of hours in any of the "last" fields exceeds 24 hours, the number of days and hours is printed. If that field overflows, asterisks are printed.
Output queue, drops Input queue, drops	Number of packets in output and input queues. Each number is followed by a slash, the maximum size of the queue, and the number of packets dropped due to a full queue.
Five minute input rate, Five minute output rate	Average number of bits and packets transmitted per second in the last 5 minutes.
packets input	Total number of error-free packets received by the system.
broadcasts	Total number of broadcast or multicast packets received by the interface.
runts	Number of packets that are discarded because they are smaller than the medium's minimum packet size.
giants	Number of packets that are discarded because they exceed the medium's maximum packet size.
CRC	Cyclic redundancy check generated by the originating LAN station or far-end device does not match the checksum calculated from the data received. On a LAN, this usually indicates noise or transmission problems on the LAN interface or the LAN bus itself. A high number of CRCs is usually the result of a station transmitting bad data.
frame	Number of packets received incorrectly having a CRC error and a noninteger number of octets.
overrun	Number of times the serial receiver hardware was unable to hand received data to a hardware buffer because the input rate exceeded the receiver's ability to handle the data.

Continues

Table 4-8 *show interfaces tokenring Field Descriptions (Continued)*

Field	Description
ignored	Number of received packets ignored by the interface because the interface hardware ran low on internal buffers. These buffers are different than the system buffers mentioned previously in the buffer description. Broadcast storms and bursts of noise can cause the ignored count to be increased.
packets output	Total number of messages transmitted by the system.
bytes	Total number of bytes, including data and MAC encapsulation, transmitted by the system.
underruns	Number of times that the far-end transmitter has been running faster than the near-end router's receiver can handle. This may never be reported on some interfaces.
output errors	Sum of all errors that prevented the final transmission of datagrams out of the interface being examined. Note that this may not balance with the sum of the enumerated output errors, as some datagrams may have more than one error, and others may have errors that do not fall into any of the specifically tabulated categories.
collisions	Since a Token Ring cannot have collisions, this statistic is nonzero only if an unusual event occurred when frames were being queued or dequeued by the system software.
interface resets	Number of times an interface has been reset. The interface may be reset by the administrator or automatically when an internal error occurs.
Restarts	Should always be zero for Token Ring interfaces.
transitions	Number of times the ring made a transition from up to down or vice versa. A large number of transitions indicates a problem with the ring or the interface.

show lnm bridge

Use the **show lnm bridge** privileged EXEC command to display all currently configured bridges and all parameters that are related to the bridge as a whole, not to one of its interfaces.

> **show lnm bridge**

Syntax Description

This command has no arguments or keywords.

Command Mode
Privileged EXEC

Usage Guidelines
This command first appeared in Cisco IOS Release 10.0.

Sample Display
The following is sample output from the **show lnm bridge** command:

```
Router# show lnm bridge

Bridge 001-2-003, Ports 0000.3000.abc4, 0000.0028.abcd
Active Links:   0000.0000.0000   0000.0000.0000   0000.0000.0000   0000.0000.0000
Notification: 0 min, Threshold 00.10%
```

Table 4-9 describes significant fields shown in the display.

Table 4-9   *show lnm bridge Field Descriptions*

Field	Description
Bridge 001-2-003	Ring and bridge numbers of this bridge.
Ports 0000.3000.abc4....	MAC addresses of the two interfaces of this bridge.
Active Links:	Any LNM stations that are currently connected to this bridge. An entry preceded by an asterisk is the controlling LNM.
Notification: 0 min	Current counter notification interval in minutes.
Threshold 00.10%	Current loss threshold that will trigger a message to LNM.

show lnm config

Use the **show lnm config** privileged EXEC command to display the logical configuration of all bridges configured in a router. This information is needed to configure an LNM Management Station to communicate with a router. This is especially important when the router is configured as a multiport bridge, thus employing the concept of a virtual ring.

> **show lnm config**

Syntax Description
This command has no arguments or keywords.

Command Mode

Privileged EXEC

Usage Guidelines

This command first appeared in Cisco IOS Release 10.0.

Sample Displays

The following is sample output from the **show lnm config** command for a simple two-port bridge:

```
Router# show lnm config

Bridge(s) currently configured:

        From     ring 001, address 0000.3000.abc4
        Across bridge 002
        To       ring 003, address 0000.0028.abcd
```

The following is sample output from the **show lnm config** command for a multiport bridge:

```
Router# show lnm config

Bridge(s) currently configured:

        From     ring 001, address 0000.0028.abc4
        Across bridge 001
        To       ring 008, address 4000.0028.abcd

        From     ring 002, address 0000.3000.abc4
        Across bridge 002
        To       ring 008, address 4000.3000.abcd

        From     ring 003, address 0000.3000.5735
        Across bridge 003
        To       ring 008, address 4000.3000.5735
```

Table 4-10 describes significant fields shown in the display.

Table 4-10 *show lnm config Field Descriptions*

Field	Description
From ring 001	Ring number of the first interface in the two-port bridge.
address 0000.3000.abc4	MAC address of the first interface in the two-port bridge.
Across bridge 002	Bridge number assigned to this bridge.
To ring 003	Ring number of the second interface in the two-port bridge.
address 0000.0028.abcd	MAC address of the second interface in the two-port bridge.

show lnm interface

Use the **show lnm interface** privileged EXEC command to display all LNM-related information about a specific interface or all interfaces.

> **show lnm interface** [*type number*]

Syntax

Description

type   (Optional) Interface type.

number   (Optional) Interface number.

Command Mode

Privileged EXEC

Usage Guidelines

This command first appeared in Cisco IOS Release 10.0.

This command is for all types of interfaces, including Token Ring interfaces. If you want information specific to Token Ring, use the **show lnm ring** command.

Sample Display

The following is sample output from the **show lnm interface** command:

```
router# show lnm interface
 nonisolating error counts
interface  ring   Active Monitor  SET   dec   lost  cong.  fc    freq.token
TokenRing1 0001*  1000.5a98.23a0  00200 00001 00000 00000  00000 0000000002

Notification flags: FE00, Ring Intensive: FFFF, Auto Intensive: FFFF
Active Servers: LRM LBS REM RPS CRS
Last NNIN:   never, from 0000.0000.0000.
Last Claim:  never, from 0000.0000.0000.
Last Purge:  never, from 0000.0000.0000.
Last Beacon: never, 'none' from 0000.0000.0000.
Last MonErr: never, 'none' from 0000.0000.0000.

            isolating error counts
station        int ring   loc.   weight line   inter burst ac    abort
1000.5a98.23a0 T1  0001   0000   00 - N00000   00000 00000 00000 00000
1000.5a98.239e T1  0001   0000   00 - N00000   00000 00000 00000 00000
1000.5a6f.bc15 T1  0001   0000   00 - N00000   00000 00000 00000 00000
0000.3000.abc4 T1  0001   0000   00 - N00000   00000 00000 00000 00000
1000.5a98.239f T1  0001   0000   00 - N00000   00000 00000 00000 00000
```

Table 4-11 describes significant fields shown in the display. See the **show lnm station** command for a description of the fields in the bottom half of the sample output.

Table 4-11   *show lnm interface Field Descriptions*

Field	Description
interface	Interface about which information was requested.
ring	Number assigned to that Token Ring. An asterisk following the ring number indicates that there are stations with nonzero error counters present on that ring.
Active Monitor	Address of the station that is currently providing "Active Monitor" functions to the ring. The description of this server can be found in the *IBM Token Ring Architecture Reference Manual.*
SET	Current soft error reporting time for the ring in units of tens of milliseconds.
dec	Rate at which the various counters of nonisolating errors are being decreased. This number is in errors per 30 seconds.
other nonisolating error counts: lost, cong., fc, and freq.token	Current values of the five nonisolating error counters specified in the 802.5 specification. These are Lost Frame errors, Receiver Congestion errors, FC errors, Frequency errors, and Token errors.
Notification flags:	Representation of which types of ring errors are being reported to LNM. The description of this number can be found in the *IBM Token Ring Architecture Reference Manual.*
Ring Intensive:	Representation of which specific ring error messages are being reported to LNM when in the "Ring Intensive" reporting mode. The description of this number can be found in the *IBM Token Ring Architecture Reference Manual.*
Auto Intensive:	Representation of which specific ring error messages are being reported to LNM when in the "Auto Intensive" reporting mode. The description of this number can be found in the *IBM Token Ring Architecture Reference Manual.*

Table 4-11 *show lnm interface Field Descriptions (Continued)*

Field	Description
Active Servers:	A list of which servers are currently active on this Token Ring. The possible acronyms and their meanings are as follows: • CRS—Configuration Report Server • LRM—LAN Reporting Manager • LBS—LAN Bridge Server • REM—Ring Error Monitor • RPS—Ring Parameter Server The description of these servers can be found in the *IBM Token Ring Architecture Reference Manual.*
Last NNIN:	Time since the last "Neighbor Notification Incomplete" frame was received, and the station that sent this message.
Last Claim:	Time since the last "Claim Token" frame was received, and the station that sent this message.
Last Purge:	Time since the last "Purge Ring" frame was received, and the station that sent this message.
Last Beacon:	Time since the last "Beacon" frame was received, the type of the last beacon frame, and the station that sent this message.
Last Mon Err:	Time since the last "Report Active Monitor Error" frame was received, the type of the last monitor error frame, and the station that sent this message.

Related Commands

To locate documentation of related commands, you can search online at www.cisco.com.

show lnm ring
show lnm station

show lnm ring

Use the **show lnm ring** privileged EXEC command to display all LNM information about a specific Token Ring or all Token Rings. If a specific interface is requested, it also displays a list of all currently active stations on that interface.

> **show lnm ring** [*ring-number*]

Syntax	Description
ring-number	(Optional) Number of a specific Token Ring. It can be a value in the range 1 to 4095.

Command Mode

Privileged EXEC

Usage Guidelines

This command first appeared in Cisco IOS Release 10.0.

The output of this command is the same as the output of the **show lnm interface** command. See the **show lnm interface** and **show lnm station** commands for sample output and a description of the fields. The same information can be obtained by using the **show lnm interface** command, but instead of specifying an interface number, you specify a ring number as an argument.

Related Commands

To locate documentation of related commands, you can search online at www.cisco.com.

show lnm interface
show lnm station

show lnm station

Use the **show lnm station** privileged EXEC command to display LNM-related information about a specific station or all known stations on all rings. If a specific station is requested, it also displays a detailed list of that station's current MAC-level parameters.

> **show lnm station** [*address*]

Syntax	Description
address	(Optional) Address of a specific LNM station.

Command Mode

Privileged EXEC

Usage Guidelines

This command first appeared in Cisco IOS Release 11.0.

Sample Display

The following is sample output from the **show lnm station** command when a particular address (in this case, 1000.5abc15) has been specified:

```
Router# show lnm station 1000.5a6f.bc15

                                     isolating error counts
    station       int  ring  loc.  weight  line  inter burst   ac   abort
1000.5a6f.bc15     T1  0001  0000   00 - N  00000 00000 00000 00000 00000

Unique ID:  0000.0000.0000          NAUN: 0000.3000.abc4
Functional: C000.0000.0000         Group: C000.0000.0000
Physical Location:    00000      Enabled Classes:   0000
Allowed Priority:     00000      Address Modifier: 0000
Product ID:      00000000.00000000.00000000.00000000.0000
Ucode Level:     00000000.00000000.0000
Station Status: 00000000.0000
Last transmit status: 00
```

Table 4-12 describes significant fields shown in the display.

Table 4-12 *show lnm station Field Descriptions*

Field	Description
station	MAC address of the given station on the Token Ring.
int	Interface used to reach the given station.
ring	Number of the Token Ring where the given station is located.
loc.	Physical location number of the given station.
weight	Weighted accumulation of the errors of the given station, and of its NAUN. The three possible letters and their meanings are as follows:[1]
	• N—not in a reported error condition.
	• P—in a "pre-weight" error condition.
	• W—in a "pre-weight" error condition.
isolating error counts	Current values of the five isolating error counters specified in the 802.5 specification. These are Line errors, Internal errors, Burst errors, AC errors, and Abort errors.
Values below this point will be zero unless LNM has previously requested this information.	
Unique ID:	Uniquely assigned value for this station.

Continues

Table 4-12 *show lnm station Field Descriptions (Continued)*

Field	Description
NAUN:	MAC address of this station's "upstream" neighbor.
Functional:	MAC-level functional address currently in use by this station.
Group:	MAC-level group address currently in use by this station.
Physical Location:	Number assigned to this station as its "Physical Location" identifier.
Enabled Classes:	Functional classes that the station is allowed to transmit.
Allowed Priority:	Maximum access priority that the station may use when transmitting onto the Token Ring.
Address Modifier:	Reserved field.
Product ID:	Encoded 18-byte string used to identify what hardware/software combination is running on this station.
Ucode Level:	10-byte EBCDIC string indicating the microcode level of the station.
Station Status:	Implementation-dependent vector that is not specified anywhere.
Last transmit status:	Contains the strip status of the last "Report Transmit Forward" MAC frame forwarded by this interface.

1. The description of these error conditions can be found in the *IBM Architecture Reference Manual*.

show netbios-cache

Use the **show netbios-cache** privileged EXEC command to display a list of NetBIOS cache entries.

> **show netbios-cache**

Syntax Description

This command has no arguments or keywords.

Command Mode

Privileged EXEC

Usage Guidelines

This command first appeared in Cisco IOS Release 10.0.

Part
I

Command Reference

Sample Display

The following is sample output from the **show netbios-cache** command:

```
Router# show netbios-cache

HW Addr          Name          How       Idle      NetBIOS Packet Savings
1000.5a89.449a   IC6W06_B      TR1       6         0
1000.5a8b.14e5   IC_9Q07A      TR1       2         0
1000.5a25.1b12   IC9Q19_A      TR1       7         0
1000.5a25.1b12   IC9Q19_A      TR1       10        0
1000.5a8c.7bb1   BKELSA1       TR1       4         0
1000.5a8b.6c7c   ICELSB1       TR1       -         0
1000.5a31.df39   ICASC_01      TR1       -         0
1000.5ada.47af   BKELSA2       TR1       10        0
1000.5a8f.018a   ICELSC1       TR1       1         0
```

Table 4-13 describes significant fields shown in the display.

Table 4-13 *show netbios-cache Field Descriptions*

Field	Description
HW Addr	MAC address mapped to the NetBIOS name in this entry.
Name	NetBIOS name mapped to the MAC address in this entry.
How	Interface through which this information was learned.
Idle	Period of time (in seconds) since this entry was last accessed. A hyphen in this column indicates it is a static entry in the NetBIOS name cache.
NetBIOS Packet Savings	Number of packets to which local replies were made (thus preventing transmission of these packets over the network).

Related Commands

To locate documentation of related commands, you can search online at www.cisco.com.

netbios name-cache
netbios name-cache timeout

show rif

Use the **show rif** privileged EXEC command to display the current contents of the RIF cache.

show rif

Syntax Description

This command has no arguments or keywords.

Command Mode

Privileged EXEC

Usage Guidelines

This command first appeared in Cisco IOS Release 10.0.

Sample Display

The following is sample output from the **show rif** command:

```
Router# show rif

Codes: * interface, - static, + remote
Hardware Addr  How    Idle (min)   Routing Information Field
5C02.0001.4322 rg5                 0630.0053.00B0
5A00.0000.2333 TR0         3       08B0.0101.2201.0FF0
5B01.0000.4444 -           -       -
0000.1403.4800 TR1         0       -
0000.2805.4C00 TR0         *       -
0000.2807.4C00 TR1         *       -
0000.28A8.4800 TR0         0       -
0077.2201.0001 rg5         10      0830.0052.2201.0FF0
```

In the display, entries marked with an asterisk (*) are the router's interface addresses. Entries marked with a dash (–) are static entries. Entries with a number denote cached entries. If the RIF timeout is set to something other than the default of 15 minutes, the timeout is displayed at the top of the display. Table 4-14 describes significant fields shown in the display.

Table 4-14 *show rif Field Descriptions*

Field	Description
Hardware Addr	Lists the MAC-level addresses.
How	Describes how the RIF has been learned. Possible values include a ring group (rg), or interface (TR).
Idle (min)	Indicates how long, in minutes, since the last response was received directly from this node.
Routing Information Field	Lists the RIF.

Part
I

Command Reference

Related Commands

To locate documentation of related commands, you can search online at www.cisco.com.

multiring

show source-bridge

Use the **show source-bridge** privileged EXEC command to display the current source bridge configuration and miscellaneous statistics.

> **show source-bridge**

Syntax Description

This command has no arguments or keywords.

Command Mode

Privileged EXEC

Usage Guidelines

This command first appeared in Cisco IOS Release 10.0.

Sample Displays

The following is sample output from the **show source-bridge** command:

```
Router# show source-bridge

Local Interfaces:                          receive     transmit
            srn bn  trn r p s n  max hops    cnt          cnt          drops
TR0           5  1   10 *   *          7    39:1002     23:62923

Ring Group 10:
  This peer: TCP 150.136.92.92
  Maximum output TCP queue length, per peer: 100
  Peers:                    state   lv  pkts_rx  pkts_tx  expl_gn   drops TCP
    TCP 150.136.92.92         -       2     0        0         0       0   0
    TCP 150.136.93.93        open    2*    18       18         3       0   0
Rings:
    bn: 1 rn: 5   local   ma: 4000.3080.844b TokenRing0        fwd: 18
    bn: 1 rn: 2   remote  ma: 4000.3080.8473 TCP 150.136.93.93 fwd: 36

Explorers: ------- input -------       ------- output -------
        spanning  all-rings    total      spanning  all-rings    total
    TR0        0         3         3             3          5         8
```

The following is sample output from the **show source-bridge** command when Token Ring LANE is configured:

```
Router# show source-bridge

Local Interfaces:                             receive      transmit
           srn bn  trn r p s n  max hops        cnt          cnt       drops
AT2/0.1   2048  5  256 *   f   7  7  7         5073         5072         0
To3/0/0      1  1  256 *   f   7  7  7         4719         4720         0

Global RSRB Parameters:
 TCP Queue Length maximum: 100

Ring Group 256:
  No TCP peername set, TCP transport disabled
   Maximum output TCP queue length, per peer: 100
  Rings:
    bn: 5  rn: 2048 local  ma: 4000.0ca0.5b40 ATM2/0.1          fwd: 5181
    bn: 1  rn: 1    local  ma: 4000.3005.da06 TokenRing3/0/0    fwd: 5180

Explorers: ------- input -------        ------- output -------
          spanning all-rings    total   spanning all-rings    total
AT2/0.1         9         1        10         10        0        10
To3/0/0        10         0        10          9        1        10

   Local: fastswitched 20        flushed 0        max Bps 38400

            rings      inputs       bursts      throttles    output drops
          To3/0/0         10            0              0               0
```

Table 4-15 describes significant fields shown in the displays.

Table 4-15 *show source-bridge* Field Descriptions

Field	Description
Local Interfaces:	Description of local interfaces.
srn	Ring number of this Token Ring.
bn	Bridge number of this router for this ring.
trn	Group in which the interface is configured. Can be the target ring number or virtual ring group.
r	Ring group is assigned. An asterisk (*) in this field indicates that a ring group has been assigned for this interface.
p	Interface can respond with proxy explorers. An asterisk (*) in this field indicates the interface can respond to proxy explorers.
s	Spanning-tree explorers enabled on the interface. An asterisk (*) indicates that this interface will forward spanning-tree explorers.

Table 4-15   *show source-bridge* *Field Descriptions (Continued)*

Field	Description
n	Interface has NetBIOS name caching enabled. An asterisk (*) in this field indicates the interface has NetBIOS name caching enabled.
max hops	Maximum number of hops.
receive cnt	Bytes received on interface for source bridging.
transmit cnt	Bytes transmitted on interface for source bridging.
drops	Number of dropped packets.
Ring Group *n*:	Describes ring group *n*, where *n* is the number of the ring group.
This peer:	Address and address type of this peer.
Maximum output TCP queue length, per peer:	Maximum number of packets queued on this peer before Cisco IOS software starts dropping packets.
Peers:	Addresses and address types of the ring group peers.
state	Current state of the peer, open or closed. A hyphen indicates this router.
lv	Indicates local acknowledgment.
pkts_rx	Number of packets received.
pkts_tx	Number of packets transmitted.
expl_gn	Explorers generated.
drops	Number of packets dropped.
TCP	Lists the current TCP backup queue length.
Rings:	Describes the ring groups. Information displayed includes the bridge groups, ring groups, whether each group is local or remote, the MAC address, the network address or interface type, and the number of packets forwarded. A type shown as "locvrt" indicates a local virtual ring used by SDLLC or SR/TLB; a type shown as "remvrt" indicates a remote virtual ring used by SDLLC or SR/TLB.
Explorers:	This section describes the explorer packets that Cisco IOS software has transmitted and received.
input	Explorers received by Cisco IOS software.
output	Explorers generated by Cisco IOS software.
TR0	Interface on which explorers were received.
spanning	Spanning-tree explorers.
all-rings	All-rings explored.
total	Summation of spanning and all-rings.

Continues

Table 4-15 *show source-bridge Field Descriptions (Continued)*

Field	Description
fastswitched	Number of fast-switched packets.
flushed	Number of flushed packets.
max Bps	Maximum bytes per second.
rings	Interface for the particular ring.
inputs	Number of inputs.
bursts	Number of bursts.
throttles	Number of throttles.
output drops	Number of output drops.

show span

Use the **show span** EXEC command to display the spanning-tree topology known to the router.

> **show span**

Syntax Description

This command has no arguments or keywords.

Command Mode

EXEC

Usage Guidelines

This command first appeared in Cisco IOS Release 10.3.

Sample Display

The following is sample output from the **show span** command:

```
RouterA> show span

Bridge Group 1 is executing the IBM compatible spanning tree protocol
  Bridge Identifier has priority 32768, address 0000.0c0c.f68b
  Configured hello time 2, max age 6, forward delay 4
  Current root has priority 32768, address 0000.0c0c.f573
  Root port is 001A (TokenRing0/0), cost of root path is 16
  Topology change flag not set, detected flag not set
```

```
     Times:  hold 1, topology change 30, notification 30
             hello 2, max age 6, forward delay 4, aging 300
     Timers: hello 0, topology change 0, notification 0
Port 001A (TokenRing0/0) of bridge group 1 is forwarding. Path cost 16
    Designated root has priority 32768, address 0000.0c0c.f573
    Designated bridge has priority 32768, address 0000.0c0c.f573
    Designated port is 001B, path cost 0, peer 0
    Timers: message age 1, forward delay 0, hold 0
Port 002A (TokenRing0/1) of bridge group 1 is blocking. Path cost 16
    Designated root has priority 32768, address 0000.0c0c.f573
    Designated bridge has priority 32768, address 0000.0c0c.f573
    Designated port is 002B, path cost 0, peer 0
    Timers: message age 0, forward delay 0, hold 0
Port 064A (spanRSRB) of bridge group 1 is disabled. Path cost 250
    Designated root has priority 32768, address 0000.0c0c.f573
    Designated bridge has priority 32768, address 0000.0c0c.f68b
    Designated port is 064A, path cost 16, peer 0
    Timers: message age 0, forward delay 0, hold 0
```

A port (spanRSRB) is created with each virtual ring group. The port will be disabled until one or more peers go into open state in the ring group.

show sse summary

Use the **show sse summary** EXEC command to display a summary of Silicon Switch Processor (SSP) statistics:

> **show sse summary**

Syntax Description

This command has no arguments or keywords.

Command Mode

EXEC

Usage Guidelines

This command first appeared in Cisco IOS Release 11.0.

Sample Display

The following is sample output from the **show sse summary** command:

```
Router# show sse summary

SSE utilization statistics
```

```
                 Program words  Rewrite bytes  Internal nodes  Depth
Overhead                   499              1               8
IP                           0              0               0      0
IPX                          0              0               0      0
SRB                          0              0               0      0
CLNP                         0              0               0      0
IP access lists              0              0               0
Total used                 499              1               8
Total free               65037         262143
Total available          65536         262144

Free program memory
  [499..65535]
Free rewrite memory
  [1..262143]

Internals
  75032 internal nodes allocated, 75024 freed
  SSE manager process enabled, microcode enabled, 0 hangs
  Longest cache computation 4ms, longest quantum 160ms at 0x53AC8
```

source-bridge

Use the **source-bridge** interface configuration command to configure an interface for source-route bridging (SRB). Use the **no** form of this command to disable source-route bridging on an interface.

> **source-bridge** *source-ring-number bridge-number target-ring-number*
> [**conserve-ring**]
> **no source-bridge** *source-ring-number bridge-number target-ring-number*
> [**conserve-ring**]

Syntax	Description
source-ring-number	Ring number for the interface's Token Ring or FDDI ring. It must be a decimal number in the range 1 to 4095 that uniquely identifies a network segment or ring within the bridged Token Ring or FDDI network.
bridge-number	Number that uniquely identifies the bridge connecting the source and target rings. It must be a decimal number in the range 1 to 15.
target-ring-number	Ring number of the destination ring on this router. It must be unique within the bridged Token Ring or FDDI network. The target ring can also be a ring group. Must be a decimal number.

Syntax

conserve-ring

Description

(Optional) Keyword to enable SRB over Frame Relay. When this option is configured, the SRB software does not add the ring number associated with the Frame Relay PVC (the partner's virtual ring) to outbound explorer frames. This option is permitted for Frame Relay subinterfaces only.

Default

SRB is disabled.

Command Mode

Interface configuration

Usage Guidelines

This command first appeared in Cisco IOS Release 10.0. The revised version of the **source-bridge** command to enable SRB over Frame Relay first appeared in Cisco IOS Release 11.3.

The parser automatically displays the word "active" in the **source-bridge** command in configurations that have SRB enabled. You do not need to enter the **source-bridge** command with the **active** keyword.

Examples

In the following example, Token Ring 129 and Token Ring 130 are connected via a router:

```
interface tokenring 0
 source-bridge 129 1 130
 !
interface tokenring 1
 source-bridge active 130 1 129
```

In the following example, an FDDI ring on one router is connected to a Token Ring on a second router across a DLSw+ link:

```
dlsw local-peer peer-id 132.11.11.2
dlsw remote-peer 0 tcp 132.11.11.3
interface fddi 0
 no ip address
 multiring all
 source-bridge active 26 1 10
 !
dlsw local-peer peer-id 132.11.11.3
dlsw remote-peer 0 tcp 132.11.11.2
interface tokenring 0
 no ip address
 multiring all
 source-bridge active 25 1 10
```

In the following example, a router forwards frames from a locally attached Token Ring over the Frame
Relay using SRB:

```
source-bridge ring-group 200
!
interface Serial0
 encapsulation frame-relay
!
interface Serial0.30 point-to-point
 frame-relay interface-dlci 30 ietf
 source-bridge 100 1 200 conserve-ring
 source-bridge spanning
!
interface TokenRing0
 source-bridge 600 1 200
```

Related Commands

To locate documentation of related commands, you can search online at www.cisco.com.

debug frame-relay packet
debug source bridge
debug source error
debug source event
encapsulation frame-relay
frame-relay interface-dlci
source-bridge ring-group
source-bridge transparent

source-bridge connection-timeout

Use the **source-bridge connection-timeout** global configuration command to establish the interval of
time between first attempt to open a connection until a timeout is declared. Use the **no** form of this
command to disable this feature.

> **source-bridge connection-timeout** *seconds*
> **no source-bridge connection-timeout** *seconds*

Syntax   Description

seconds   Interval of time, in seconds, before a connection attempt to a remote peer is
                   aborted.

Default

The default connection-timeout interval is 10 seconds.

Command Mode
Global configuration

Usage Guidelines
This command first appeared in Cisco IOS Release 10.3.

The **source-bridge connection-timeout** command is used for setting timeout intervals in a complex topology such as a large multihop WAN with virtual rings or satellite links. The timeout interval is used when a connection to a remote peer is attempted. If the timeout interval expires before a response is received, the connection attempt is aborted.

Example
The following example sets the connection timeout interval to 60 seconds:

```
source-bridge connection-timeout 60
```

Related Commands
To locate documentation of related commands, you can search online at www.cisco.com.

source-bridge ring-group

source-bridge enable-80d5

Use the **source-bridge enable-80d5** global configuration command to change the router's Token Ring to Ethernet translation behavior. Use the **no** form of this command to disable this function.

> **source-bridge enable-80d5**
> **no source-bridge enable-80d5**

Syntax Description
This command has no arguments or keywords.

Default
Disabled

Command Mode
Global configuration

Usage Guidelines

This command first appeared in Cisco IOS Release 10.0.

Cisco IOS software supports two types of Token Ring LLC2 to Ethernet conversion.
They are as follows:

● Token Ring LLC2 to Ethernet 802.3 LLC2

● Token Ring LLC2 to Ethernet 0x80d5

Use this global configuration command to change the translation behavior. By default, Cisco IOS software translates Token Ring LLC2 to Ethernet 802.3 LLC2. This command allows you to configure the software to translate Token Ring LLC2 frames into Ethernet 0x80d5 format frames.

This command is useful when you have a non-IBM device attached to an IBM network with devices that are using the nonstandard Token Ring LLC2 to Ethernet 80d5 translation. If you do not configure your router to enable 80d5 processing, the non-IBM and IBM devices will not be able to communicate.

The parameters specifying the current parameters for the processing of 0x80d5 frames are given at the end of the output of the **show span** command.

NOTE   The 80d5 frame processing option is available only with SR/TLB. It is not available when source-route transparent bridging (SRT) is used.

Use the **show span** to check whether 80d5 processing is enabled. If it is, the following line displays in the output:

```
Translation between LLC2 and Ethernet Type II 80d5 is enabled
```

Example

The following example enables 0x80d5 processing, removes the translation for SAP 08, and adds the translation for SAP 1c:

```
source-bridge enable-80d5
 no source-bridge sap-80d5 08
 source-bridge sap-80d5 1c
```

Related Commands

To locate documentation of related commands, you can search online at www.cisco.com.

show span
source-bridge sap-80d5

source-bridge explorer-dup-ARE-filter

Use the **source-bridge explorer-dup-ARE-filter** global configuration command to prevent excessive forwarding of explorers in networks with redundant topologies. Use the **no** form of this command to disable this feature.

source-bridge explorer-dup-ARE-filter
no source-bridge explorer-dup-ARE-filter

Syntax Description

This command has no arguments or keywords.

Default

Duplicate explorer filtering is disabled.

Command Mode

Global configuration

Usage Guidelines

This command first appeared in Cisco IOS Release 11.2.

Example

The following example enables duplicate explorer filtering:

```
source-bridge explorer-dup-ARE-filter
```

source-bridge explorer-fastswitch

Use the **source-bridge explorer-fastswitch** global configuration command to enable explorer fast switching. To disable explorer fast switching, use the **no** form of this command.

source-bridge explorer-fastswitch
no source-bridge explorer-fastswitch

Syntax Description

This command has no arguments or keywords.

Default
Fast switching is enabled.

Command Mode
Global configuration

Usage Guidelines
This command first appeared in Cisco IOS Release 10.3.

Use the **no** form of this command in conjunction with the **source-bridge explorerq-depth** and the **source-bridge explorer-maxrate** command to optimize explorer processing.

Example
The following example enables explorer fast switching after it has been previously disabled:

```
source-bridge explorer-fastswitch
```

Related Commands
To locate documentation of related commands, you can search online at www.cisco.com.

source-bridge explorer-maxrate
source-bridge explorerq-depth

source-bridge explorer-maxrate

Use the **source-bridge explorer-maxrate** global configuration command to set the maximum byte rate of explorers per ring. To reset the default rate, use the **no** form of this command.

> **source-bridge explorer-maxrate** *maxrate*
> **no source-bridge explorer-maxrate** *maxrate*

Syntax	Description
maxrate	Number in the range 100 to 1,000,000,000 (in bytes per second). The default maximum byte rate is 38,400 bytes per second.

Default
The default maximum byte rate is 38,400 bytes per second.

Command Mode

Global configuration

Usage Guidelines

This command first appeared in Cisco IOS Release 10.3.

Given the number of different explorer packet types and sizes and the bandwidth limits of the various interfaces, the bus data rate (as opposed to the packet rate) is the common denominator used to decide when to flush incoming explorers. The packets are dropped by the interface before any other processing.

Example

The following command sets the maximum byte rate of explorers on a ring:

```
source-bridge explorer-maxrate 100000
```

source-bridge explorerq-depth

Use the **source-bridge explorerq-depth** global configuration command to set the maximum explorer queue depth. To reset the default value, use the **no** form of this command.

> **source-bridge explorerq-depth** *depth*
> **no source-bridge explorerq-depth** *depth*

Syntax   Description

depth   The maximum number of incoming packets. The valid range is 1 to 500.

Default

The default maximum depth is 30.

Command Mode

Global configuration

Usage Guidelines

This command first appeared in Cisco IOS Release 10.0.

In this implementation, the limit is on a per-interface basis such that each interface can have up to the maximum (default 30) outstanding packets on the queue before explorers from that particular interface are dropped.

Example

The following example sets the maximum explorer queue depth:

```
source-bridge explorerq-depth 100
```

source-bridge input-address-list

Use the **source-bridge input-address-list** interface configuration command to apply an access list to an interface configured for source-route bridging (SRB). This command filters source-routed packets received from the router interface based upon the source mac address. Use the **no** form of this command to remove the application of the access list.

> **source-bridge input-address-list** *access-list-number*
> **no source-bridge input-address-list** *access-list-number*

Syntax	Description
access-list-number	Number of the access list. The value must be in the range 700 to 799.

Default

No access list is assigned.

Command Mode

Interface configuration

Usage Guidelines

This command first appeared in Cisco IOS Release 10.3.

Example

The following example assigns access list 700 to Token Ring 0:

```
interface tokenring 0
 source-bridge input-address-list 700
!
access-list 700 deny 1000.5A00.0000  8000.00FF.FFFF
access-list 700 permit 0000.0000.0000  FFFF.FFFF.FFFF
```

Related Commands

To locate documentation of related commands, you can search online at www.cisco.com.

access-list
source-bridge output-address-list

source-bridge input-lsap-list

Use the **source-bridge input-lsap-list** interface configuration command to filter, on input, FDDI and IEEE 802-encapsulated packets that include the destination service access point (DSAP) and source service access point (SSAP) fields in their frame formats. The access list specifying the type codes to be filtered is given by this variation of the **source-bridge** interface configuration command.

source-bridge input-lsap-list *access-list-number*

Syntax

access-list-number

Description

Number of the access list. This access list is applied to all IEEE 802 or FDDI frames received on that interface prior to the source-routing process. Specify zero (0) to disable the filter. The value must be in the range 200 to 299.

Default

Disabled

Command Mode

Interface configuration

Usage Guidelines

This command first appeared in Cisco IOS Release 10.0.

Example

The following example specifies access list 203:

```
interface tokenring 0
 source-bridge input-lsap-list 203
```

Related Commands

To locate documentation of related commands, you can search online at www.cisco.com.

access-list
source-bridge output-lsap-list

source-bridge input-type-list

Use the **source-bridge input-type-list** interface configuration command to filter SNAP-encapsulated packets on input.

source-bridge input-type-list access-list-number

Syntax	Description
access-list-number	Number of the access list. This access list is applied to all SNAP frames received on that interface prior to the source-routing process. Specify zero (0) to disable the application of the access list on the bridge group. The value must be in the range 200 to 299.

Default

Disabled

Command Mode

Interface configuration

Usage Guidelines

This command first appeared in Cisco IOS Release 10.0.

Use the **access list** command to specify type code when using the **source-bridge input-type-list** command.

Example

The following example specifies access list 202:

```
interface tokenring 0
 source-bridge input-type-list 202
 !
access-list 202 deny 0x6000 0x0007
access-list 202 permit 0x0000 0xFFFF
```

Related Commands

To locate documentation of related commands, you can search online at www.cisco.com.

access-list
source-bridge output-type-list

source-bridge max-hops

Use the **source-bridge max-hops** interface configuration command to control the forwarding or blocking of all-routes explorer frames received on an interface. Use the **no** form of this command to reset the count to the maximum value.

> **source-bridge max-hops** *count*
> **no source-bridge max-hops**

Syntax	Description
count	Determines the number of bridges an explorer packet can traverse. Typically, the maximum number of bridges for interoperability with IBM equipment is seven.

Default

The maximum number of bridge hops is seven.

Command Mode

Interface configuration

Usage Guidelines

This command first appeared in Cisco IOS Release 11.2.

Frames are forwarded only if the number of hops in the routing information field (RIF) of the input frame plus hops appended by the router is less than or equal to the specified count. If the interface is connected to a destination interface, the router appends one hop. If the interface is tied to a virtual ring, the router appends two hops. This applies only to all-routes explorer frames on input to this interface.

Example

The following example limits the maximum number of source-route bridge hops to 5:

```
source-bridge max-hops 5
```

Related Commands

To locate documentation of related commands, you can search online at www.cisco.com.

source-bridge
source-bridge max-in-hops
source-bridge max-out-hops

source-bridge max-in-hops

Use the **source-bridge max-in-hops** interface configuration command to control the forwarding or blocking of spanning-tree explorer frames received on an interface. Use the **no** form of this command to reset the count to the maximum value.

> **source-bridge max-in-hops** *count*
> **no source-bridge max-in-hops**

Syntax   Description

count   Determines the number of bridges an explorer packet can traverse. Typically, the maximum number of bridges for interoperability with IBM equipment is 7.

Default

The maximum number of bridge hops is 7.

Command Mode

Interface configuration

Usage Guidelines

This command first appeared in Cisco IOS Release 11.2.

Frames are forwarded only if the number of hops in the routing information field (RIF) of the input frame is less than or equal to the specified count. This applies only to spanning-tree explorer frames input to the specified interface.

Example

The following example limits the maximum number of source-route bridge hops to 3:

```
source-bridge max-in-hops 3
```

Related Commands

To locate documentation of related commands, you can search online at www.cisco.com.

source-bridge
source-bridge max-hops
source-bridge max-out-hops

source-bridge max-out-hops

Use the **source-bridge max-out-hops** interface configuration command to control the forwarding or blocking of spanning-tree explorer frames sent from this interface. Use the **no** form of this command to reset the count to the maximum value.

> **source-bridge max-out-hops** *count*
> **no source-bridge max-out-hops**

Syntax

Syntax	Description
count	Determines the number of bridges an explorer packet can traverse. Typically, the maximum number of bridges for interoperability with IBM equipment is 7.

Default

The maximum number of bridge hops is 7.

Command Mode

Interface configuration

Usage Guidelines

This command first appeared in Cisco IOS Release 11.2.

Frames are forwarded only if the number of hops in the routing information field (RIF) of the frame (including the hops appended by the router) is less than or equal to the specified count. This applies only to spanning-tree explorer frames output from the specified interface.

Example

The following example limits the maximum number of source-route bridge hops to 5:

```
source-bridge max-out-hops 5
```

Related Commands

To locate documentation of related commands, you can search online at www.cisco.com.

source-bridge
source-bridge max-hops
source-bridge max-in-hops

source-bridge output-address-list

Use the **source-bridge output-address-list** interface configuration command to apply an access list to an interface configured for source-route bridging. This command filters source-routed packets sent to the router interface based upon the destination mac address. Use the **no** form of this command to remove the application of the access list.

> **source-bridge output-address-list** *access-list-number*
> **no source-bridge output-address-list** *access-list-number*

Syntax   Description

access-list-number   Number of the access list. The value must be in the range 700 to 799.

Default
No access list is assigned.

Command Mode
Interface configuration

Usage Guidelines
This command first appeared in Cisco IOS Release 10.0.

Example
To disallow the bridging of Token Ring packets of all IBM workstations on Token Ring 1, use this sample configuration. The software assumes that all such hosts have Token Ring addresses with the vendor code 1000.5A00.0000. The vendor portion of the MAC address is the first three bytes (left to right) of the address. The first line of the access list denies access to all IBM workstations, while the second line permits access to all other devices on the network. Then, the access list can be assigned to the input side of Token Ring 1.

```
access-list 700 deny 1000.5A00.0000   8000.00FF.FFFF
access-list 700 permit 0000.0000.0000   FFFF.FFFF.FFFF
interface tokenring 1
 source-bridge output-address-list 700
```

Related Commands

To locate documentation of related commands, you can search online at www.cisco.com.

access-list
source-bridge input-address-list

source-bridge output-lsap-list

Use the **source-bridge output-lsap-list** interface configuration command to filter, on output, FDDI and IEEE 802-encapsulated packets that have destination service access point (DSAP) and source service access point (SSAP) fields in their frame formats.

source-bridge output-lsap-list *access-list-number*

Syntax	Description
access-list-number	Number of the access list. This access list is applied just before sending out a frame to an interface. Specify zero (0) to disable the filter. The value must be in the range 200 to 299.

Default

No filters are applied.

Command Mode

Interface configuration

Usage Guidelines

This command first appeared in Cisco IOS Release 10.0.

The access list specifying the type codes to be filtered is given by this command.

Example

The following example specifies access list 251:

```
interface tokenring 0
 source-bridge output-lsap-list 251
access-list 251 permit 0xE0E0 0x0101
access-list 251 deny 0x0000 0xFFFF
```

Related Commands

To locate documentation of related commands, you can search online at www.cisco.com.

access-list
source-bridge input-lsap-list

source-bridge output-type-list

Use the **source-bridge output-type-list** interface configuration command to filter SNAP-encapsulated frames by type code on output.

source-bridge output-type-list *access-list-number*

Syntax   Description

access-list-number   Number of the access list. This access list is applied just before
                              sending out a frame to an interface. Specify zero (0) to disable the
                              application of the access list on the bridge group. The value must
                              be in the range 200 to 299.

Default

No filters are applied.

Command Mode

Interface configuration

Usage Guidelines

This command first appeared in Cisco IOS Release 10.0.

Input and output type code filtering on the same interface reduces performance and is not recommended.

Access lists for Token Ring- and IEEE 802-encapsulated packets affect only SRB functions. Such access lists do not interfere with protocols that are being routed.

Use the access list specifying the types codes in this command.

Example

The following example filters SNAP-encapsulated frames on output:

```
! apply interface configuration commands to interface tokenring 0
interface tokenring 0
! filter SNAP-encapsulated frames on output using access list 202
 source-bridge output-type-list 202
!
access-list 202 deny 0x6000 0x0007
access-list 202 permit 0x0000 0xFFFF
```

Related Commands

To locate documentation of related commands, you can search online at www.cisco.com.

access-list
source-bridge input-type-list

source-bridge proxy-explorer

Use the **source-bridge proxy-explorer** interface configuration command to configure the interface to respond to any explorer packets from a source node that meet the conditions described below. Use the **no** form of this command to cancel responding to explorer packets with proxy explorers.

> **source-bridge proxy-explorer**
> **no source-bridge proxy-explorer**

Syntax Description

This command has no arguments or keywords.

Default

Disabled

Command Mode

Interface configuration

Usage Guidelines

This command first appeared in Cisco IOS Release 10.0.

The proxy explorer function allows the source-route bridge interface to respond to a source node on behalf of a particular destination node. The interface responds with proxy explorers. The following conditions must be met in order for the interface to respond to a source node with proxy explorers on behalf of a destination node:

● The destination node must be in the RIF cache.

● The destination node must not be on the same ring as the source node.

● The explorer packet must be an IEEE 802.2 XID or TEST packet.

● The packet cannot be from the IBM Token Ring LAN Network Manager source SAP.

If all of the above conditions are met, the source-route bridge interface will turn the packet around, append the appropriate RIF, and reply to the source node.

Use proxy explorers to limit the amount of explorer traffic propagating through the source-bridge network, especially across low-bandwidth serial lines. The proxy explorer is most useful for multiple connections to a single node.

Example

The following example configures the router to use proxy explorers on Token Ring 0:

```
interface tokenring 0
 source-bridge proxy-explorer
```

source-bridge proxy-netbios-only

Use the **source-bridge proxy-netbios-only** global configuration command to enable proxy explorers for the NetBIOS name-caching function. Use the **no** form of this command to disable the NetBIOS name-caching function.

> **source-bridge proxy-netbios-only**
> **no source-bridge proxy-netbios-only**

Syntax Description

This command has no arguments or keywords.

Default

Disabled

Command Mode
Global configuration

Usage Guidelines
This command first appeared in Cisco IOS Release 10.0.

Example ·
The following example configures the router to use proxy explorers:

```
source-bridge proxy-netbios-only
```

source-bridge ring-group

Use the **source-bridge ring-group** global configuration command to define or remove a ring group from the configuration. Use the **no** form of this command to cancel previous assignments.

> **source-bridge ring-group** *ring-group* [*virtual-mac-address*]
> **no source-bridge ring-group** *ring-group* [*virtual-mac-address*]

Syntax	Description
ring-group	Ring group number. The valid range is 1 to 4095.
virtual-mac-address	(Optional) 12-digit hexadecimal string written as a dotted triplet (for example, 0010.0a00.20a6).

Default
No ring group is defined.

Command Mode
Global configuration

Usage Guidelines
This command first appeared in Cisco IOS Release 10.0.

To configure a source-route bridge with more than two network interfaces, the *ring group* concept is used. A ring group is a collection of Token Ring interfaces in one or more routers that are collectively treated as a virtual ring. The ring group is denoted by a ring number that must be unique for the network.

The ring group's number is used just like a physical ring number, showing up in any route descriptors contained in packets being bridged.

To configure a specific interface as part of a ring group, its target ring number parameter is set to the ring group number specified in this command. Do not use the number 0; it is reserved to represent the local ring.

To avoid an address conflict on the virtual MAC address, use a locally administered address in the form 4000.*xxxx.xxxx*.

Example

In the following example, multiple Token Rings are source-route bridged to one another through a single router. These Token Rings are all part of ring group 7.

```
! all token rings attached to this bridge/router are part of ring group 7
source-bridge ring-group 7
!
interface tokenring 0
 source-bridge 1000 1 7
!
interface tokenring 1
 source-bridge 1001 1 7
!
interface tokenring 2
 source-bridge 1002 1 7
!
interface tokenring 3
 source-bridge 1003 1 7
```

Related Commands

To locate documentation of related commands, you can search online at www.cisco.com.

source-bridge

source-bridge route-cache

Use the **source-bridge route-cache** interface configuration command to enable fast switching. Use the **no** form of this command to disable fast switching.

> **source-bridge route-cache**
> **no source-bridge route-cache**

Syntax Description

This command has no arguments or keywords.

Default
Enabled

Command Mode
Interface configuration

Usage Guidelines
This command first appeared in Cisco IOS Release 10.0.

By default, fast-switching software is enabled in the source-route bridging (SRB) software. Fast switching allows for faster implementations of local SRB between 4/16-Mb Token Ring cards in the same router. This feature also allows for faster implementations of local SRB between two routers using the 4/16-Mb Token Ring cards and the direct interface encapsulation.

Example
The following example disables use of fast switching between two 4/16-Mb Token Ring interfaces:

```
interface token 0
 source-bridge 1 1 2
 no source-bridge route-cache
!
interface token 1
 source-bridge 2 1 1
 no source-bridge route-cache
```

Related Commands
To locate documentation of related commands, you can search online at www.cisco.com.

source-bridge

source-bridge route-cache cbus

Use the **source-bridge route-cache cbus** interface configuration command to enable autonomous switching. Use the **no** form of this command to disable autonomous switching.

> **source-bridge route-cache cbus**
> **no source-bridge route-cache cbus**

Syntax Description

This command has no arguments or keywords.

Default

Disabled

Command Mode

Interface configuration

Usage Guidelines

This command first appeared in Cisco IOS Release 10.0.

Autonomous switching in source-route bridging (SRB) software is available for local SRB between ciscoBus Token Ring cards in the same router. Autonomous switching provides higher switching rates than does fast-switching between 4/16-Mb Token Ring cards. Autonomous switching works for both two-port bridges and multiport bridges that use ciscoBus Token Ring cards.

In a virtual ring that includes both ciscoBus Token Ring and 4/16-MbToken Ring interfaces, frames that flow from one ciscoBus Token Ring interface to another are autonomously switched, and the remainder of the frames are fast switched. The switching that occurs on the ciscoBus Token Ring interface takes advantage of the high-speed ciscoBus controller processor.

NOTE	Using either NetBIOS byte offset access lists or the access-expression capability to logically combine the access filters disables the autonomous or fast switching of SRB frames.

Example

The following example enables use of autonomous switching between two ciscoBus Token Ring interfaces:

```
interface token 0
 source-bridge 1 1 2
 source-bridge route-cache cbus
 !
interface token 1
 source-bridge 2 1 1
 source-bridge route-cache cbus
```

Related Commands

To locate documentation of related commands, you can search online at www.cisco.com.

source-bridge

source-bridge route-cache sse

Use the **source-bridge route-cache sse** interface configuration command to enable Cisco silicon switching engine (SSE) switching function. Use the **no** form of this command to disable SSE switching.

> **source-bridge route-cache sse**
> **no source-bridge route-cache sse**

Syntax Description

This command has no arguments or keywords.

Default

Disabled

Command Mode

Interface configuration

Usage Guidelines

This command first appeared in Cisco IOS Release 10.0.

Example

The following example enables use of SSE switching between two 4/16-Mb Token Ring interfaces:

```
interface token 0
 source-bridge 1 1 2
 source-bridge route-cache sse
!
interface token 1
 source-bridge 2 1 1
 source-bridge route-cache sse
```

Related Commands

To locate documentation of related commands, you can search online at www.cisco.com.

source-bridge

source-bridge sap-80d5

Use the **source-bridge sap-80d5** global configuration command to allow non-IBM hosts (attached to a router with 80d5 processing enabled) to use the standard Token Ring to Ethernet LLC2 translation instead of the nonstandard Token Ring to Ethernet 80d5 translation. This command allows you to set the translation on a per-DSAP basis. Use the **no** form of this command to disable this feature.

> **source-bridge sap-80d5** *dsap*
> **no source-bridge sap-80d5** *dsap*

Syntax

Syntax	Description
dsap	Destination service access point (DSAP).

Default

Enabled

Command Mode

Global configuration

Usage Guidelines

This command first appeared in Cisco IOS Release 10.0.

By default, the following DSAPs are enabled for 0x80d5 translation simply by specifying the **source-bridge enable-80d5** command:

- For SNA—04, 08, 0C, 00
- For NetBIOS—F0

Any of these DSAPs can be disabled with the **no** form of this command.

The parameters specifying the current parameters for the processing of 0x80d5 frames are given at the end of the output of the **show span** command.

NOTE	The 80d5 frame processing option is available only with SR/TLB. It is not available when source-route transparent bridging (SRT) is used.

Use the **show span** to check whether 80d5 processing is enabled for a particular DSAP. The following line displays in the output if 80d5 processing is enabled, listing each DSAP for which it is enabled:

```
Translation is enabled for the following DSAPs:
 04 0C 1C F0
```

Example

The following example enables 0x80d5 processing, removes the translation for SAP 08, and adds the translation for SAP 1c:

```
source-bridge enable-80d5
 no source-bridge sap-80d5 08
 source-bridge sap-80d5 1c
```

Related Commands

To locate documentation of related commands, you can search online at www.cisco.com.

show span
source-bridge enable-80d5

source-bridge spanning (automatic)

Use the automatic version of the **source-bridge spanning** interface configuration command to enable the automatic spanning-tree function for a specified group of bridged interfaces. Use the **no source-bridge spanning** command to return to the default disabled state. Use the **no source-bridge spanning path-cost** command to return an assigned path cost to the default path cost of 16.

> **source-bridge spanning** *bridge-group* [**path-cost** *path-cost*]
> **no source-bridge spanning** *bridge-group* [**path-cost** *path-cost*]

Syntax	Description
bridge-group	Number in the range 1 to 9 that you choose to refer to a particular group of bridged interfaces. This must be the same number as assigned in the **bridge protocol ibm** command.
path-cost	(Optional) Assign a path cost for a specified interface.

Syntax	Description
path-cost	(Optional) Path cost for the interface. The valid range is 0 to 65,535.

Defaults

The automatic spanning-tree function is disabled. The default path cost is 16.

Command Mode

Interface configuration

Usage Guidelines

This command first appeared in Cisco IOS Release 10.3.

Example

The following example adds Token Ring 0 to bridge group 1 and assigns a path cost of 12 to Token Ring 0:

```
interface tokenring 0
 source-bridge spanning 1 path-cost 12
```

Related Commands

To locate documentation of related commands, you can search online at www.cisco.com.

bridge protocol ibm
show source-bridge

source-bridge spanning (manual)

Use the **source-bridge spanning** interface configuration command to enable use of spanning explorers. The **no** form of this command disables their use. Only spanning explorers will be blocked; everything else will be forwarded.

> **source-bridge spanning**
> **no source-bridge spanning**

Syntax Description

This command has no arguments or keywords.

Default

Disabled

Command Mode

Interface configuration

Usage Guidelines

This command first appeared in Cisco IOS Release 10.0.

Use of the **source-bridge spanning** command is recommended. This command puts the interface into a forwarding or active state with respect to the spanning tree. There are two types of explorer packets used to collect RIF information:

- All-rings, all-routes explorer packets follow all possible paths to a destination ring. In a worst case scenario, the number of all-rings explorers generated may be exponentially large.

- Spanning or limited-route explorer packets follow a spanning tree when looking for paths, greatly reducing the number of explorer packets required. There is currently no dynamic spanning-tree algorithm to establish that spanning tree; it must be manually configured.

Example

The following example enables use of spanning explorers:

```
! Global configuration command establishing the ring group for the interface
configuration commands
 source-bridge ring-group 48
!
! commands that follow apply to interface token 0
interface tokenring 0
! configure interface tokenring 0 to use spanning explorers
 source-bridge spanning
```

Related Commands

To locate documentation of related commands, you can search online at www.cisco.com.

source-bridge

source-bridge transparent

Use the **source-bridge transparent** global configuration command to establish bridging between transparent bridging and source-route bridging (SRB). Use the **no** form of this command to disable a previously established link between a source-bridge ring group and a transparent bridge group.

> **source-bridge transparent** *ring-group pseudo-ring bridge-number tb-group* [*oui*]
> **no source-bridge transparent** *ring-group pseudo-ring bridge-number tb-group*

Syntax	Description
ring-group	Virtual ring group created by the **source-bridge ring-group** command. This is the source-bridge virtual ring to associate with the transparent bridge group. This ring group number must match the number you have specified with the **source-bridge ring-group** command. The valid range is 1 to 4095.
pseudo-ring	Ring number used to represent the transparent bridging domain to the source-route bridged domain. This number must be a unique number, not used by any other ring in your source-route bridged network.
bridge-number	Bridge number of the bridge that leads to the transparent bridging domain.
tb-group	Number of the transparent bridge group that you want to tie into your source-route bridged domain. The **no** form of this command disables this feature.
oui	(Optional) Organizational unique identifier. Possible values include the following: • **90-compatible** • **standard** • **cisco**

Default
Not established

Command Mode
Global configuration

Usage Guidelines

This command first appeared in Cisco IOS Release 10.0.

Before using this command, you must have completely configured your router using multiport source-bridging and transparent bridging.

Specify the **90-compatible** OUI when talking to Cisco routers. This OUI provides the most flexibility. Specify the **standard** OUI when talking to IBM 8209 bridges and other vendor equipment. This OUI does not provide for as much flexibility as the other two choices. The **cisco** OUI is provided for compatibility with future equipment.

Do not use the **standard** OUI unless you are forced to interoperate with other vendor equipment, such as the IBM 8209, in providing Ethernet and Token Ring mixed media bridged connectivity. Only use the **standard** keyword when you are transferring data between IBM 8209 Ethernet/Token Ring bridges and routers running the SR/TLB software (to create a Token Ring backbone to connect Ethernets). Use of the **standard** keyword causes the OUI code in Token Ring frames to always be 0x000000. In the context of the **standard** keyword, an OUI of 0x000000 identifies the frame as an Ethernet Type II frame. If the OUI in Token Ring frame is 0x000000 SR/TLB will output an Ethernet Type II frame.

When 8209 compatibility is enabled with the **ethernet transit-oui standard** command, the SR/TLB chooses to translate all Token Ring SNAP frames into Ethernet Type II frames, as described earlier in this chapter.

Example

The following example establishes bridging between a transparent-bridge network and a source-route network:

```
source-bridge ring-group 9
source-bridge transparent 9 6 2 2
!
interface tokenring 0
 source-bridge 5 2 9
!
interface token ring 1
source bridge 4 2 9
!
interface ethernet 0
bridge-group 2
!
interface ethernet 1
bridge-group 2

bridge 2 protocol ieee
```

Related Commands

To locate documentation of related commands, you can search online at www.cisco.com.

bridge-group
source-bridge
source-bridge ring-group

source-bridge transparent fastswitch

Use the **source-bridge transparent fastswitch** global configuration command to enable fast switching of packets between the SRB and transparent domains. Use the **no** form of this command to disable fast switching of packets.

> **source-bridge transparent** *ring-group* **fastswitch**
> **no source-bridge transparent** *ring-group* **fastswitch**

Syntax   Description

ring-group   Virtual ring group created by the **source-bridge ring-group** command. This is the source-bridge virtual ring to associate with the transparent bridge group. This ring group number must match the number you have specified with the **source-bridge ring-group** command. The valid range is 1 to 4095.

fastswitch   Fast-switched SR/TLB enables Cisco IOS software to process packets at the interrupt level.

Default

Fast-switched SR/TLB is enabled.

Command Mode

Global configuration

Usage Guidelines

This command first appeared in Cisco IOS Release 11.2.

Because fast-switched SR/TLB is enabled by default when the router is configured for SR/TLB, there are no user-specified changes to the operation of the router, and the enabling command does not appear in the configuration.

The **no source-bridge transparent** *ring-group* **fastswitch** command is provided to disable fast-switched SR/TLB, causing the router to handle packets by process switching. When fast-switched SR/TLB is disabled, the **no** form of the command appears on a separate line of the configuration, immediately below the parent **source-bridge transparent** command.

If fast-switch SR/TLB has been disabled, it can enabled using the **source-bridge transparent** *ring-group* **fastswitch** command, but the enabling form of the command will not appear in the configuration.

Example

The following example disables fast-switched SR/TLB between a transparent-bridge network and a source-route network:

```
source-bridge ring-group 9
source-bridge transparent 9 6 2 2
no source-bridge transparent 9 fastswitch
!
interface tokenring 0
 source-bridge 5 2 9
interface token ring 1
 source bridge 4 2 9
!
interface ethernet 0
 bridge-group 2
!
interface ethernet 1
 bridge-group 2

bridge 2 protocol ieee
```

Related Commands

To locate documentation of related commands, you can search online at www.cisco.com.

bridge-group
source-bridge
source-bridge ring-group

Configuring Token Ring Inter-Switch Link

This chapter explains how to configure Token Ring Inter-Switch Link (TRISL) on Cisco routers. The chapter describes TRISL in the context of the Inter-Switch Link (ISL) protocol and the Token Ring virtual LAN (VLAN) concept.

For a complete description of the Token Ring Inter-Switch Link commands in this chapter, refer to Chapter 6, "Token Ring Inter-Switch Link Commands." To locate documentation of other commands that appear in this chapter, use the command reference master index or search online.

Cisco's TRISL Implementation

This section contains information related to Cisco's implementation of TRISL that you should understand before you proceed to the "TRISL Configuration Tasks" section.

ISL and TRISL

ISL is a Layer 2 protocol that enables switches and routers to transport Ethernet frames from multiple VLANs across Fast Ethernet or Gigabit Ethernet links. Cisco's TRISL protocol extends the ISL model to include the transport of Token Ring frames from multiple VLANs across these same links.

TRISL support on Cisco routers provides inter-VLAN routing and bridging across a 100 Mb Fast Ethernet link. ISL and TRISL together provide routing and bridging between Token Ring and Ethernet LANs, emulated LANs (ELANs), and VLANs.

TRISL is supported on Cisco 7500 or Cisco 7200 routers installed with any one of the following port adapters:

- Two-port Fast Ethernet/ISL 100BaseTX
- Two-port Fast Ethernet/ISL 100BaseFX
- One-port Fast Ethernet 100BaseTX
- One-port Fast Ethernet 100BaseFX

NOTE	The two-port Fast Ethernet/ISL port adapters support frame sizes up to 17,800 bytes and the one-port Fast Ethernet port adapters support a frame size of up to 1500 bytes.

The TRISL feature provides the following new capabilities and features, which will be described in the "TRISL Configuration Tasks" and "TRISL Configuration Examples" sections later in the chapter:

- IP routing for source-routed and non-source–routed frames between TRISL VLANs and any LAN, ELAN, or VLAN.

- IPX routing for source-routed and non-source–routed frames between TRISL VLANs and any LANs, ELANs, or VLANs.

- Source-route bridging (SRB) between TRISL VLANs and SRB-capable LANs, ELANs, or VLANs.

- Source-route transparent bridging (SRT) between TRISL VLANs and SRT-capable LANs, ELANs, or VLANs.

- Source-route translational bridging (SR/TLB) between TRISL VLANs and Ethernet LANs, ELANs, or VLANs.

- Duplicate Ring Protocol (DRiP), which prevents external loops that could result if the router's virtual ring number were duplicated elsewhere in the network.

NOTE   VLAN Trunking Protocol (VTP) is currently not supported for TRISL on the routers.

Token Ring VLANs

A VLAN is essentially a broadcast domain. In transparent bridging, there is only one type of broadcast frame and, therefore, only one level of broadcast domain and one level of VLAN. In source routing, however, there are two types of broadcast frames:

- Those that are confined to a single ring

- Those that traverse the bridged domain

Therefore, there are two levels of VLANs in a Token Ring switched network.

The first level is the Token Ring Concentrator Relay Function (TrCRF). At this level, the VLAN is a logical ring and, as such, is assigned a ring number. On a Token Ring switch, the logical ring (TrCRF) contains one or more physical ports. On a router, the logical ring (TrCRF) does not contain any physical ports, but is used only in processing source-routed traffic to terminate the RIF.

The second level is the Token Ring Bridge Relay Function (TrBRF). This is the parent VLAN to which TrCRF VLANs are assigned. At this level, the VLAN is a logical bridge and, as such, is assigned a bridge number. The logical bridge (TrBRF) contains the virtual ports that establish a connection between the TrBRF and its TrCRFs. The TrBRF can be extended across a network of switches and routers via ISL, as shown in Figure 5-1.

Figure 5-1 *Physical View of Switches Interconnected via ISL*

When you extend the TrBRF across an ISL link, you are essentially extending the bridge across devices, as shown in Figure 5-2.

Figure 5-2 *Logical View of Switches Interconnected via ISL*

Therefore, if you use source-route bridging between the TrCRFs that belong to the TrBRF, only one hop appears in the routing information field (RIF).

Traffic is switched between the ports in a TrCRF and bridged via SRB or SRT between the TrCRFs in a TrBRF.

Figure 5-3 illustrates a TrBRF that contains TrCRFs on both a router and a switch.

Figure 5-3 *TrCRFs in a TrBRF*

TRISL Configuration Tasks

To configure and monitor TRISL in your network, perform one or more of the following tasks:

- Configure IP Routing over TRISL
- Configure Hot Standby Router Protocol over TRISL
- Configure IPX Routing over TRISL
- Configure Source-Route Bridging over TRISL
- Configure Source-Route Transparent Bridging over TRISL
- Configure Source-Route Translational Bridging over TRISL
- Monitor TRISL Statistics

Configure IP Routing over TRISL

The IP routing over TRISL VLANs feature extends IP routing capabilities to include support for routing IP frame types in VLAN configurations. To configure IP routing over TRISL, use the following commands, beginning in global configuration mode:

Step	Command	Purpose
1	**ip routing**	Enables IP routing on the router.
2	**interface** *type slot/port.subinterface-number*	Specifies the subinterface on which TRISL will be used.
3	**encapsulation tr-isl trbrf-vlan** *vlanid* **bridge-num** *bridge-number*	Defines the encapsulation format, and specify the VLAN identifier.
4	**ip address** *ip-address mask*	Sets a primary IP address for an interface.

You can configure TRISL to route source-routed traffic by enabling the collection and use of RIF information on a TRISL subinterface. This creates a "pseudo-ring" to terminate the RIF path on a ring. Without RIF information, a packet could not be bridged across a source-route bridged network connected to this interface.

To route source-routed traffic, use the following additional commands in interface configuration mode:

Step	Command	Purpose
1	**multiring trcrf-vlan** *vlanid* **ring** *ring-number*	Creates a pseudo-ring to terminate the RIF and assigns it to a VLAN.
2	**multiring** {*protocol-keyword* [**all-routes** | **spanning** | **all** | **other**]}	Enables collection and use of RIF information with routed protocols.

NOTE	TRISL encapsulation must be specified for a subinterface before an IP address can be assigned to that subinterface.

Configure Hot Standby Router Protocol over TRISL

The Hot Standby Router Protocol (HSRP) provides fault tolerance and enhanced routing performance for IP networks. HSRP allows Cisco routers to monitor each other's operational status and very quickly assume packet forwarding responsibility in the event the current forwarding device in the HSRP group fails or is taken down for maintenance. The standby mechanism remains transparent to the attached hosts and can be deployed on any LAN type. With multiple hot-standby groups, routers can simultaneously provide redundant backup and perform load-sharing across different IP subsets.

To configure HSRP over TRISL between VLANs, use the following commands in interface configuration mode:

Step	Command	Purpose
1	**interface** *type slot/port.subinterface-number*	Specifies the subinterface on which ISL will be used.
2	**encapsulation tr-isl trbrf-vlan** *vlanid* **bridge-num** *bridge-number*	Defines the encapsulation format, and specifies the VLAN identifier.
3	**ip address** *ip-address mask* [**secondary**]	Specifies the IP address for the subnet on which ISL will be used.
4	**standby** [*group-number*] **ip** [*ip-address* [**secondary**]]	Enables HSRP.

To customize hot standby group attributes, use one or more of the following commands in interface configuration mode:

Command	Purpose
standby [*group-number*] **timers** *hellotime holdtime*	Configures the time between hello packets and the hold time before other routers declare the active router to be down.
standby [*group-number*] **priority** *priority*	Sets the hot standby priority used to choose the active router.
standby [*group-number*] **preempt**	Specifies that if the local router has priority over the current active router, the local router should attempt to take its place as the active router.

Command	Purpose
standby [*group-number*] **track** *type-number* [*interface-priority*].	Configures the interface to track other interfaces, so that if one of the other interfaces goes down, the hot standby priority for the device is lowered.
standby [*group-number*] **authentication** *string*	Enables the automatic spanning-tree function on a group of bridged interfaces.

Configure IPX Routing over TRISL

The IPX Routing over ISL VLANs feature extends Novell NetWare routing capabilities to include support for routing all standard IPX encapsulations for Token Ring frame types in VLAN configurations. Users with Novell NetWare environments can configure either SAP or SNAP encapsulations to be routed using the TRISL encapsulation across VLAN boundaries.

Netware users can now configure consolidated VLAN routing over a single VLAN trunking interface. With configurable Token Ring encapsulation protocols on a per VLAN basis, users have the flexibility of using VLANs regardless of their NetWare Token Ring encapsulation. Encapsulation types and corresponding framing types are described in the "Configuring Novell IPX" chapter of the *Network Protocols Configuration Guide, Part II.*

NOTE	Only one type of IPX encapsulation can be configured per VLAN (subinterface). The IPX encapsulation used must be the same within any particular subnet. A single encapsulation must be used by all NetWare systems that belong to the same LAN.

To configure Cisco IOS software to route IPX on a router with connected VLANs, use the following commands, beginning in global configuration mode:

Step	Command	Purpose
1	**ipx routing** [*node*]	Enables IPX routing globally.
2	**interface** *type slot/port.subinterface-number*	Specifies the subinterface on which TRISL will be used.
3	**encapsulation tr-isl trbrf-vlan** *vlanid* **bridge-num** *bridge-number*	Defines the encapsulation for TRISL.
4	**ipx encapsulation** *encapsulation type*	Specifies the IPX encapsulation.
5	**ipx network** *network number*	Specifies the IPX network.

NOTE	The default IPX encapsulation format for Token Ring in Cisco IOS routers is SAP. Therefore, you only need to explicitly configure the IPX encapsulation type if your Token Ring network requires SNAP encapsulation instead of SAP.

When routing source-routed traffic for specific VLANs, use the following additional commands in interface configuration mode:

Step	Command	Purpose
1	**multiring trcrf-vlan** *vlanid* **trcrf-ring** *ring-number*	Creates a pseudo-ring to terminate the RIF and assigns it to a VLAN.
2	**multiring** {*protocol-keyword* [**all-routes** | **spanning** | **all** | **other**]}	Enables collection and use of RIF information with routed protocols.

Configure Source-Route Bridging over TRISL

To configure source-route bridging over TRISL, use the following commands, starting in global configuration mode:

Step	Command	Purpose
1	**source-bridge ring-group** *vring-num*	Configures a virtual ring for the router.
2	**interface** *type slot/port.subinterface-number*	Specifies the subinterface on which TRISL will be used.
3	**encapsulation tr-isl trbrf-vlan** *vlanid* **bridge-num** *bridge-number*	Defines the encapsulation for TRISL.
4	**source-bridge trcrf-vlan** *vlanid* **ring-group** *ring-number*	Attaches a TrCRF VLAN identifier to the router's virtual ring.

Configure Source-Route Transparent Bridging over TRISL

To configure transparent bridging over TRISL, use the following command, starting in global configuration mode:

Step	Command	Purpose
1	**interface** *type slot/port.subinterface-number*	Specifies the subinterface on which TRISL will be used.

Step	Command	Purpose
2	**encapsulation tr-isl trbrf-vlan** *vlanid* **bridge-num** *bridge-number*	Defines the encapsulation for TRISL.
3	**bridge-group** *bridge-group number*	Specifies the bridge group to which the TRISL subinterface belongs.

Configure Source-Route Translational Bridging over TRISL

To configure source-route translational bridging over TRISL, use the following commands, starting in global configuration mode:

Step	Command	Purpose
1	**source-bridge ring-group** *vring-num*	Configures a virtual ring for the router.
2	**source-bridge transparent** *ring-group pseudo-ring bridge-number tb-group* [*oui*]	Enables bridging between transparent bridging and source-route bridging.
3	**interface** *type slot/port.subinterface-number*	Specifies the subinterface on which TRISL will be used.
4	**encapsulation tr-isl trbrf-vlan** *vlanid* **bridge-num** *bridge-number*	Defines the encapsulation for TRISL.
5	**source-bridge trcrf-vlan** *vlanid* **ring-group** *ring-number*	Assigns a VLAN ID to the router's virtual ring.

NOTE   For a complete description of SR/TLB, including configuring translation compatibility with IBM 8209 bridges and configuring Token Ring LLC2 to Ethernet Type II (0x80d5) and Token Ring LLC2 to Ethernet 802.3 LLC2 (standard) translations, please refer to Chapter 3, "Configuring Source-Route Bridging" and Chapter 4, "Source-Route Bridging Commands."

Configure Automatic Spanning Tree

The automatic spanning-tree function supports automatic resolution of spanning trees in SRB networks, which provides a single path for spanning explorer frames to traverse from a given node in the network to another. Spanning explorer frames have a single-route broadcast indicator set in the routing information field. Port identifiers consist of ring numbers and bridge numbers associated with the ports. The spanning-tree algorithm for SRB does not support Topology Change Notification bridge protocol data unit (BPDU).

Although the automatic spanning-tree function can be configured with SR/TLB, the SRB domain and transparent bridging domain have separate spanning trees. Each Token Ring interface can belong to only one spanning tree. Only one bridge group can run the automatic spanning-tree function at a time.

To create a bridge group that runs an automatic spanning-tree function compatible with the IBM SRB spanning-tree implementation, use the following command in global configuration mode:

Command	Purpose
bridge *bridge-group* **protocol ibm**	Creates a bridge group that runs the automatic spanning-tree function.

To enable the automatic spanning-tree function for a specified group of bridged interfaces in SRB or SR/TLB, use the following command in interface configuration mode:

Command	Purpose
source-bridge spanning *bridge-group*	Enables the automatic spanning-tree function on a group of bridged interfaces.

Monitor TRISL Statistics

You can collect, clear, and display statistical information about the network.

The Duplicate Ring Protocol (DRiP) runs on Cisco routers and switches that support switched VLAN networking and is used to identify active Token Ring VLANs (TrCRFs).

DRiP maintains the status of TrCRFs and uses this information to determine whether there are multiple TrCRFs active in a TrBRF.

DRiP information is used for the following:

- All-routes explorer filtering

  DRiP information is used in conjunction with the local configuration to determine which of the TrCRFs configured within a TrBRF have active ports. This information is used on the base switch to correctly filter all-routes explorers and on the ISL module to discard AREs that have already been on an attached ring.

- Detecting the configuration of duplicate TrCRFs across routers and switches, which would cause a TrCRF to be distributed across ISL trunks

  DRiP information is used in conjunction with the local configuration information to determine which TrCRFs are already active on the switches. If a TrCRF is enabled on more than one switch or router, the ports associated with the TrCRF are disabled on all switches. A router will not disable the internal ring used for SRB and for routing source-routed traffic. Instead, the router generates the following error message to indicate that two identical TrCRFs exist:

```
DRIP conflict with CRF <vlan-id>
```

To show or clear DRiP or VLAN statistics, use one or all the following commands in privileged EXEC mode:

Command	Purpose
clear drip counters	Clears DRiP counters.
clear vlan statistics	Removes VLAN statistics from any statically configured or system configured entries.
show drip	Displays DRiP information.
show vlans	Displays a summary of VLAN subinterfaces.

NOTE   When DRiP counters are cleared, the counter is reset to 0. Incrementing of DRiP counters indicates that the router is receiving packets across the TrBRF.

TRISL Configuration Examples

The following sections provide TRISL configuration examples:

- IP Routing Non-Source–Routed Frames Between a TRISL VLAN and a Token Ring Interface Example

- IP Routing Source-Routed Frames Between a TRISL VLAN and a Token Ring Interface Example

- IP Routing Source-Route Frames Between a TRISL VLAN and an Ethernet ISL VLAN Example

- IP Routing Source-Routed Frames Between TRISL VLANs Example

- IPX Routing Non-Source–Routed Frames Between a TRISL VLAN and a Token Ring Interface Example

- IPX Routing Source-Routed Frames Between a TRISL VLAN and a Token Ring Interface Example

- IPX Routing Source-Route Frames Between a TRISL VLAN and an Ethernet ISL VLAN Example

- IPX Routing Source-Routed Frames Between TRISL VLANs Example

- SRB Between Token Ring and TRISL VLAN Example

- SRB Between TRISL VLANs Example

- Transparent Bridging Between Token Ring and TRISL VLAN Example

- SR/TLB Between a TRISL VLAN and an Ethernet Interface Example

- SR/TLB Between a TRISL VLAN and an Ethernet ISL VLAN Example

NOTE	Because the VLAN Trunk Protocol (VTP) is not supported on the router configured with TRISL, the TrCRF configuration on the router must also be specified in the Catalyst 5000 switch configuration.

IP Routing Non-Source–Routed Frames Between a TRISL VLAN and a Token Ring Interface Example

Figure 5-4 illustrates IP routing between a TRISL VLAN and a Token Ring interface.

Figure 5-4   *IP Routing Between a TRISL VLAN and a Token Ring Interface*

The following is the configuration for the router:

```
ip routing
interface TokenRing 3/1
 ip address 4.4.4.1 255.255.255.0
!
interface FastEthernet4/0.1
 ip address 5.5.5.1 255.255.255.0
 encapsulation tr-isl trbrf 999 bridge-num 14
```

The following is the configuration for the Catalyst 5000 switch with the Token Ring switch module in slot 5. In this configuration, the Token Ring port 1 is assigned to the TrCRF VLAN 40.

```
#vtp
set vtp domain trisl
set vtp mode server
set vtp v2 enable
#drip
set tokenring reduction enable
```

```
set tokenring distrib-crf disable
#vlans
set vlan 999 name trbrf type trbrf bridge 0xe stp ieee
set vlan 40 name trcrf40 type trcrf parent 999 ring 0x1 mode srt
#add token port to trcrf 40
set vlan 40    5/1
set trunk 1/2 on
```

IP Routing Source-Routed Frames Between a TRISL VLAN and a Token Ring Interface Example

Figure 5-5 illustrates IP routing source-routed frames between a TRISL VLAN and a Token Ring interface.

Figure 5-5 *Routing Source-Routed Frames Between a TRISL VLAN and a Token Ring Interface*

The following is the configuration for the router:

```
ip routing
interface TokenRing 3/1
 ip address 4.4.4.1 255.255.255.0
!
interface FastEthernet4/0.1
 ip address 5.5.5.1 255.255.255.0
 encapsulation tr-isl trbrf 999 bridge-num 14
 multiring trcrf-vlan 200 ring 100
 multiring all
```

The following is the configuration for the Catalyst 5000 switch with the Token Ring switch module in slot 5. In this configuration, the Token Ring port 5/1 is assigned to the TrCRF VLAN 40.

```
#vtp
set vtp domain trisl
```

```
set vtp mode server
set vtp v2 enable
#drip
set tokenring reduction enable
set tokenring distrib-crf disable
#vlans
set vlan 999 name trbrf type trbrf bridge 0xe stp ibm
set vlan 200 name trcrf200 type trcrf parent 999 ring 0x64 mode srb
set vlan 40 name trcrf40 type trcrf parent 999 ring 0x1 mode srb
#add token port to trcrf 40
set vlan 40   5/1
set trunk 1/2 on
```

IP Routing Source-Route Frames Between a TRISL VLAN and an Ethernet ISL VLAN Example

Figure 5-6 illustrates IP routing source-route frames between a TRISL VLAN and an Ethernet ISL VLAN.

Figure 5-6   *IP Routing Source-Routed Frames Between a TRISL VLAN and an Ethernet ISL VLAN*

The following is the configuration for the router:

```
interface FastEthernet4/0.1
 ip address 5.5.5.1 255.255.255.0
 encapsulation tr-isl trbrf-vlan 999 bridge-num 14
 multiring trcrf-vlan 200 ring 100
 multiring all
!
interface FastEthernet4/0.2
 ip address 4.4.4.1 255.255.255.0
 encapsulation isl 12
```

The following is the configuration for the Catalyst 5000 switch with the Ethernet module in slot 2 and a Token Ring switch module in slot 5. In this configuration, the Token Ring port is assigned with TrCRF VLAN 100 and the Ethernet port is assigned with VLAN 12.

```
#vtp
set vtp domain trisl
set vtp mode server
set vtp v2 enable
#drip
set tokenring reduction enable
set tokenring distrib-crf disable
#vlans
set vlan 999 name trbrf type trbrf bridge 0xe stp ibm
set vlan 100 name trcrf100 type trcrf parent 999 ring 0x1 mode srb
set vlan 200 name trcrf200 type trcrf parent 999 ring 0x64 mode srb
set vlan 12 name eisl12 type ethernet
#add token port to trcrf 100
set vlan 100 5/1
#add ethernet
set vlan 12 2/1
set trunk 1/2 on
```

IP Routing Source-Routed Frames Between TRISL VLANs Example

Figure 5-7 illustrates IP routing source-routed frames between two TrBRF VLANs.

Figure 5-7   *IP Routing Source-Routed Frames Between TrBRF VLANs*

The following is the configuration for the router:

```
interface FastEthernet4/0.1
 ip address 5.5.5.1 255.255.255.0
 encapsulation tr-isl trbrf-vlan 999 bridge-num 14
 multiring trcrf-vlan 200 ring 100
 multiring all
!
interface FastEthernet4/0.2
 ip address 4.4.4.1 255.255.255.0
 encapsulation tr-isl trbrf-vlan 998 bridge-num 13
 multiring trcrf-vlan 300 ring 101
 multiring all
```

The following is the configuration for the Catalyst 5000 switch with the Token Ring switch module in slot 5. In this configuration, the Token Ring port attached to ring 102 is assigned with TrCRF VLAN 40 and the Token Ring port attached to ring 103 is assigned with TrCRF VLAN 50.

```
#vtp
set vtp domain trisl
set vtp mode server
set vtp v2 enable
#drip
set tokenring reduction enable
set tokenring distrib-crf disable
#vlans
set vlan 999 name trbrf type trbrf bridge 0xe stp ibm
set vlan 200 name trcrf200 type trcrf parent 999 ring 0x64 mode srb
set vlan 40 name trcrf40 type trcrf parent 999 ring 0x66 mode srb
set vlan 998 name trbrf type trbrf bridge 0xd stp ibm
set vlan 300 name trcrf300 type trcrf parent 998 ring 0x65 mode srb
set vlan 50 name trcrf50 type trcrf parent 998 ring 0x67 mode srb
#add token port to trcrf 40
set vlan 40   5/1
#add token port to trcrf 50
set vlan 50   5/2
set trunk 1/2 on
```

IPX Routing Non-Source–Routed Frames Between a TRISL VLAN and a Token Ring Interface Example

Figure 5-8 shows IPX routing non-source–routed frames between a TRISL VLAN and a Token Ring interface.

Figure 5-8 *IPX Routing Non-Source–Routed Frames Between a TRISL VLAN and a Token Ring Interface Example*

The following is the configuration for the router:

```
ipx routing
interface TokenRing 3/1
 ipx network 1
!
interface FastEthernet4/0.1
 ipx network 10
 encapsulation tr-isl trbrf 999 bridge-num 14
```

The following is the configuration for the Catalyst 5000 switch with the Token Ring switch module in slot 5. In this configuration, the Token Ring port attached to ring 1 is assigned to the TrCRF VLAN 40.

```
#vtp
set vtp domain trisl
set vtp mode server
set vtp v2 enable
#drip
set tokenring reduction enable
set tokenring distrib-crf disable
#vlans
set vlan 999 name trbrf type trbrf bridge 0xe stp ieee
set vlan 40 name trcrf40 type trcrf parent 999 ring 0x1 mode srt
#add token port to trcrf 40
set vlan 40    5/1
set trunk 1/2 on
```

IPX Routing Source-Routed Frames Between a TRISL VLAN and a Token Ring Interface Example

Figure 5-9 shows IPX routing source-routed frames between a TRISL VLAN and a Token Ring interface.

Figure 5-9   *IPX Routing Source-Routed Frames Between a TRISL VLAN and a Token Ring Interface*

The following is the configuration for the router:

```
ipx routing
!
interface TokenRing 3/1
 ipx network 1
 multiring all
!
interface FastEthernet4/0.1
 ipx network 10
 encapsulation tr-isl trbrf 999 bridge-num 14
 multiring trcrf-vlan 200 ring 100
 multiring all
```

The following is the configuration for the Catalyst 5000 switch with the Token Ring switch module in slot 5. In this configuration, the Token Ring port attached to ring 1 is assigned to the TrCRF VLAN 40.

```
#vtp
set vtp domain trisl
set vtp mode server
set vtp v2 enable
#drip
set tokenring reduction enable
set tokenring distrib-crf disable
#vlans
set vlan 999 name trbrf type trbrf bridge 0xe stp ibm
```

```
set vlan 200 name trcrf200 type trcrf parent 999 ring 0x64 mode srb
set vlan 40 name trcrf40 type trcrf parent 999 ring 0x1 mode srb
#add token port to trcrf 40
set vlan 40    5/1
set trunk 1/2 on
```

IPX Routing Source-Route Frames Between a TRISL VLAN and an Ethernet ISL VLAN Example

Figure 5-10 shows IPX routing source-route frames between a TRISL VLAN and an Ethernet ISL VLAN.

Figure 5-10 *IPX Routing Source-Routed Frames Between a TRISL VLAN and an Ethernet ISL VLAN*

The following is the configuration for the router:

```
ipx routing
interface FastEthernet4/0.1
 ipx network 10
 encapsulation tr-isl trbrf-vlan 999 bridge-num 14
 multiring trcrf-vlan 20 ring 100
 multiring all
!
interface FastEthernet4/0.2
 ipx network 30
 encapsulation isl 12
```

The following is the configuration for the Catalyst 5000 switch with the Ethernet module in slot 2 and a Token Ring switch module in slot 5. In this configuration, the Token Ring port is assigned with TrCRF VLAN 100 and the Ethernet port is assigned with VLAN 12.

```
#vtp
set vtp domain trisl
set vtp mode server
set vtp v2 enable
#drip
set tokenring reduction enable
set tokenring distrib-crf disable
```

```
#vlans
set vlan 999 name trbrf type trbrf bridge 0xe stp ibm
set vlan 100 name trcrf100 type trcrf parent 999 ring 0x1 mode srb
set vlan 20 name trcrf20 type trcrf parent 999 ring 0x64 mode srb
set vlan 12 name default type eisl12
#add token port to trcrf 100
set vlan 100 5/1
#add ethernet
set vlan 12 2/1
set trunk 1/2 on
```

IPX Routing Source-Routed Frames Between TRISL VLANs Example

Figure 5-11 shows IPX source-routed frames between TRISL VLANs.

Figure 5-11 *IPX Routing Source-Routed Frames Between TRISL VLANs*

The following is the configuration for the router:

```
ipx routing
interface FastEthernet4/0.1
 ipx network 10
 encapsulation tr-isl trbrf-vlan 999 bridge-num 14
 multiring trcrf-vlan 200 ring 100
 multiring all
!
interface FastEthernet4/0.2
 ipx network 20
 encapsulation tr-isl trbrf-vlan 998 bridge-num 13
 multiring trcrf-vlan 300 ring 101
 multiring all
```

The following is the configuration for the Catalyst 5000 switch with the Token Ring switch module in slot 5. In this configuration, the Token Ring port attached to ring 102 is assigned with TrCRF VLAN 40 and the Token Ring port attached to ring 103 is assigned with TrCRF VLAN 50.

```
#vtp
set vtp domain trisl
set vtp mode server
set vtp v2 enable
#drip
set tokenring reduction enable
set tokenring distrib-crf disable
#vlans
set vlan 999 name trbrf type trbrf bridge 0xe stp ibm
set vlan 200 name trcrf200 type trcrf parent 999 ring 0x64 mode srb
set vlan 40 name trcrf40 type trcrf parent 999 ring 0x66 mode srb
set vlan 998 name trbrf type trbrf bridge 0xd stp ibm
set vlan 300 name trcrf300 type trcrf parent 998 ring 0x65 mode srb
set vlan 50 name trcrf50 type trcrf parent 998 ring 0x67 mode srb
#add token port to trcrf 40
set vlan 40    5/1
#add token port to trcrf 50
set vlan 50    5/2
set trunk 1/2 on
```

SRB Between Token Ring and TRISL VLAN Example

Figure 5-12 illustrates SRB between a Token Ring interface on a router and a TRISL VLAN.

Figure 5-12 *SRB Between a Token Ring Interface and TRISL VLAN*

The following is the configuration for the router with the Token Ring interface:

```
source-bridge ring-group 100
!
interface TokenRing3/1
 ring speed 16
 source-bridge 10 1 100
 source-bridge spanning
!
interface FastEthernet4/0.1
 encapsulation tr-isl trbrf-vlan 999 bridge-num 14
 source-bridge trcrf-vlan 40 ring-group 100
 source-bridge spanning
!
```

The following is the configuration for the Catalyst 5000 switch:

```
#vtp
set vtp domain trisl
set vtp mode server
set vtp v2 enable
#drip
set tokenring reduction enable
set tokenring distrib-crf disable
#vlans
set vlan 999 name trbrf type trbrf bridge 0xe stp ibm
set vlan 40 name trcrf40 type trcrf parent 999 ring 0x64 mode srb
set vlan 50 name trcrf50 type trcrf parent 999 ring 0x14 mode srb
#add token port to trcrf 50
set vlan 50    5/1
```

SRB Between TRISL VLANs Example

Figure 5-13 illustrates SRB between two TrCRF VLANs.

Figure 5-13 *SRB Between TRISL VLANs*

The following is the configuration for the router:

```
source-bridge ring-group 101
!
interface FastEthernet4/0.1
 encapsulation tr-isl trbrf 999 bridge-num 14
 source-bridge trcrf-vlan 100 ring-group 101
 source-bridge spanning
!
interface FastEthernet4/0.2
 encapsulation tr-isl trbrf 998 bridge-num 13
 source-bridge trcrf-vlan 102 ring-group 101
 source-bridge spanning
```

The following is the configuration for the Catalyst 5000 switch with the Token Ring switch module in slot 5. The Token Ring port on 5/1 is assigned to TrCRF VLAN 40 and the Token Ring port on 5/2 is assigned to TrCRF VLAN 50.

In this configuration, the keyword name is optional and srb is the default mode.

```
#vtp
set vtp domain trisl
set vtp mode server
set vtp v2 enable
#drip
set tokenring reduction enable
set tokenring distrib-crf disable
#vlans
set vlan 999 name trbrf type trbrf bridge 0xe stp ibm
set vlan 100 name trcrf100 type trcrf parent 999 ring 0x65 mode srb
set vlan 40 name trcrf40 type trcrf parent 999 ring 0x1 mode srb
set vlan 998 name trbrf type trbrf bridge 0xd stp ibm
set vlan 102 name trcrf102 type trcrf parent 998 ring 0x65 mode srb
set vlan 50 name trcrf50 type trcrf parent 998 ring 0xa mode srb
#add token port to trcrf 40
set vlan 40    5/1
#add token port to trcrf 50
set vlan 50    5/2
#enable trunk
set trunk 1/2 on
```

Transparent Bridging Between Token Ring and TRISL VLAN Example

Figure 5-14 illustrates transparent bridging between a router's Token Ring interface and a TRISL VLAN.

Figure 5-14 *Transparent Bridging Between Token Ring and TRISL VLAN*

The following is the configuration for the router:

```
bridge 1 protocol ieee
!
interface Tokenring0
 bridge-group 1
!
interface FastEthernet0/0.1
 encapsulation tr-isl trbrf-vlan 50 bridge-num 11
 bridge-group 1
```

The following is the configuration for the Catalyst 5000 switch with a Token Ring switch module in slot 5:

```
#vtp
set vtp domain trisl
set vtp mode server
set vtp v2 enable
#drip
set tokenring reduction enable
set tokenring distrib-crf disable
#vlans
set vlan 50 name trbrf50 type trbrf bridge 0xb stp ieee
set vlan 100 name trcrf100 type trcrf ring 0x14 parent 50 mode srt
#enable trunk
set trunk 1/2 on
#add token port to trcrf 100
set vlan 100 5/1
```

SR/TLB Between a TRISL VLAN and an Ethernet Interface Example

Figure 5-15 illustrates SR/TLB between a TRISL VLAN and an Ethernet interface.

Figure 5-15 *SR/TLB Between a TRISL VLAN and an Ethernet Interface*

The following is the configuration for the router:

```
source-bridge ring-group 100
source-bridge transparent 100 101 6 1
!
interface Ethernet2/0
 bridge-group 1
!
interface FastEthernet4/0.1
 encapsulation tr-isl trbrf-vlan 999 bridge-num 14
 source-bridge trcrf-vlan 200 ring-group 100
 source-bridge spanning
!
bridge 1 protocol ieee
!
```

The following is the configuration for the Catalyst 5000 switch with an Ethernet card in module 5 and using port 1. The Token Ring port on 5/1 is assigned to TrCRF VLAN 40.

```
#vtp
set vtp domain trisl
set vtp mode server
set vtp v2 enable
#drip
set tokenring reduction enable
set tokenring distrib-crf disable
#vlans
set vlan 999 name trbrf999 type trbrf bridge 0xe stp ibm
set vlan 200 name trcrf200 type trcrf parent 999 ring 0x64 mode srb
```

```
set vlan 40 name trcrf40 type trcrf parent 999 ring 0x1 mode srb
#add token port to trcrf 40
set vlan 40    5/1
#enable trunk
set trunk 1/2 on
```

SR/TLB Between a TRISL VLAN and an Ethernet ISL VLAN Example

Figure 5-16 illustrates SR/TLB between a TRISL VLAN and an Ethernet ISL VLAN.

Figure 5-16 *SR/TLB Between a TRISL VLAN and an Ethernet ISL VLAN*

The following is the configuration for the router:

```
source-bridge ring-group 100
source-bridge transparent 100 101 6 1
!
interface FastEthernet4/0.1
 encapsulation tr-isl trbrf-vlan 999 bridge-num 14
 source-bridge trcrf-vlan 20 ring-group 100
 source-bridge spanning
!
interface FastEthernet4/0.2
 encapsulation isl 12
 bridge-group 1
!
bridge 1 protocol ieee
```

The following is the configuration for the Catalyst 5000 switch with an Ethernet module in slot 2 and a Token Ring switch module in slot 5. In this configuration, the Token Ring port attached to ring 101 is assigned to TrCRF VLAN 21, and the router's virtual ring is assigned to TrCRF VLAN 20.

```
#vtp
set vtp domain trisl
set vtp mode server
```

```
set vtp v2 enable
#drip
set tokenring reduction enable
set tokenring distrib-crf disable
#vlans
set vlan 999 type trbrf bridge 0xe stp ibm
set vlan 20 type trcrf parent 999 ring 0x64 mode srb
set vlan 21 type trcrf parent 999 ring 0x65 mode srb
#add token port to trcrf 21
set vlan 21 5/1
#add ethernet
set vlan 12 type ethernet
set vlan 12 2/1
set trunk 1/2 on
```

Token Ring Inter-Switch Link Commands

Use the commands in this chapter to configure Token Ring Inter-Switch Link (TRISL) on Cisco routers. To locate documentation of related commands, you can search online at www.cisco.com. For TRISL configuration task information and examples, refer to Chapter 5, "Configuring Token Ring Inter-Switch Link."

For hardware technical descriptions and for information about installing the router interfaces, refer to the hardware installation and maintenance publication for your particular product.

clear drip counters

Use the **clear drip counters** privileged EXEC command to clear DRiP counters.

> **clear drip counters**

Syntax Description

This command has no arguments or keywords.

Command Mode

Privileged EXEC

Usage Guidelines

This command first appeared in Cisco IOS Release 11.3(4)T.

Use the **clear drip counters** command if you want to check whether the router is receiving any packets. The counters will start at 0. If the counters are incrementing, DRiP is active on the router.

Example

The following example clears DRiP counters:

```
router# clear drip counters
```

Related Commands

To locate documentation of related commands, you can search online at www.cisco.com.

encapsulation tr-isl trbrf-vlan
show drip

encapsulation tr-isl trbrf-vlan

Use the **encapsulation tr-isl** subinterface configuration command to enable TRISL, a Cisco protocol for interconnecting multiple routers and switches and maintaining Token Ring VLAN information as traffic travels between switches.

> **encapsulation tr-isl trbrf-vlan** *vlanid* **bridge-num** *bridge-number*

Syntax	Description
vlanid	Number identifying the VLAN.
bridge-num *bridge-number*	Keyword and bridge number assigned to the ISL trunk. Possible values are 01 to 15.

Command Mode

Subinterface configuration

Usage Guidelines

This command first appeared in Cisco IOS Release 11.3(4)T.

Examples

The following example enables TRISL is on a Fast Ethernet subinterface:

```
interface FastEthernet4/0.2
encapsulation tr-isl trbrf-vlan 999 bridge-num 14
```

Related Commands

To locate documentation of related commands, you can search online at www.cisco.com.

clear drip counters
clear vlan statistics
multiring
multiring trcrf-vlan
show drip
show vlan
source-bridge trcrf-vlan

multiring trcrf-vlan

Use the **multiring trcrf-vlan** interface configuration command to create a pseudo-ring to terminate the RIF for source routed traffic and assign it to a VLAN. Use the **no** form of this command to disable the caching of RIFs on the subinterface.

> **multiring trcrf-vlan** *vlanid* **ring** *ring-number*
> **no multiring trcrf-vlan** *vlanid* **ring** *ring-number*

Syntax

Description

Syntax	Description
vlanid	VLAN ID number.
ring *ring-number*	Keyword and the logical ring number for Token Ring VLANs. Possible values are 01 to 4095.

Default

Disabled

Command Mode

Interface configuration

Usage Guidelines

This command first appeared in Cisco IOS Release 11.3(4)T.

When you use this command, you must also use the **multiring** command to enable the collection and caching of RIFs with routed protocols. The **multiring trcrf-vlan** command must be issued before the **multiring** command.

Example

In the following example, the **multiring trcrf-vlan** command is used to configure a pseudo-ring for the subinterface:

```
interface FastEthernet4/0.1
  ip address 5.5.5.1 255.255.255.0
  encapsulation tr-isl trbrf-vlan 999 bridge-num 14
  multiring trcrf-vlan 1000 ring 100
  multiring all
```

Related Commands

To locate documentation of related commands, you can search online at www.cisco.com.

clear drip counters
multiring
show drip
show rif
show vlan

show drip

Use the **show drip** privileged EXEC command to display the status of the DRiP database.

> **show drip**

Syntax Description

This command has no arguments or keywords.

Command Mode

Privileged EXEC

Usage Guidelines

This command first appeared in Cisco IOS Release 11.3(4)T.

Sample Display

The following is sample output from the **show drip** command:

```
Router# show drip

DRIP Database for Mgmt Domain FastEthernet4/0
-------------------------------------------------
Mac Address 0010-A6AE-B440
Vlan     100    Status   30 : l-active, l-config,

Mac Address 0010-2F72-C800
Vlan      20    Status   0C : r-active, r-config,
Vlan    1003    Status   0C : r-active, r-config,

Statistics:
Advertisements received          126
Advertisements processed         1
Advertisements transmitted       131
Last revision transmitted        0x84
Last changed revision transmitted  0x2
```

Related Commands

To locate documentation of related commands, you can search online at www.cisco.com.

encapsulation tr-isl trbrf-vlan
clear drip counters
show vlan

source-bridge trcrf-vlan

Use the **source-bridge trcrf-vlan** privileged EXEC command to attach a TrCRF VLAN to the router's virtual ring. Use the **no** form of the command to disable the attachment of a VLAN to the router's virtual ring.

source-bridge trcrf-vlan *vlanid* **ring-group** *ringnum*

Syntax	Description
vlanid	VLAN ID number.
ring-group *ringnum*	Keyword and ring number of the virtual ring.

Command Mode

Privileged EXEC

Usage Guidelines

This command first appeared in Cisco IOS Release 11.3(4)T.

The **source-bridge trcrf-vlan** command is required for SRB traffic across a TRISL trunk. Use the **encapsulation tr-isl** command for the subinterface, prior to attaching a TrCRF VLAN to the router's ring.

Example

Following is an example of the **source-bridge trcrf-vlan** command for an interface where the VLAN ID number and ring group number is specified:

```
interface FastEthernet4/0.2
encapsulation tr-isl trbrf-vlan 999 bridge-num 14
source-bridge trcrf-vlan 100 ring-group 101
```

Related Commands

To locate documentation of related commands, you can search online at www.cisco.com.

show source-bridge
source-bridge ring-group
encapsulation tr-isl trbrf-vlan

PART II

IBM Networking

Configuring Remote Source-Route Bridging

This chapter describes how to configure remote source-route bridging (RSRB). For a complete descrip–tion of the RSRB commands mentioned in this chapter, refer to Chapter 8, "Remote Source-Route Bridging Commands." To locate documentation of other commands that appear in this chapter, you can search online at www.cisco.com.

Configuration Considerations

Only use IP encapsulation over a Transmission Control Protocol (TCP) connection within complex meshed networks to support connections between peers that are separated by multiple hops and can potentially use multiple paths, and where performance is not an issue. Use direct encapsulation in point-to-point connections. In a point-to-point configuration, using TCP adds unnecessary processing overhead. Multiple peer types, however, can be combined to in a single router by following the directions for each peer type. For example, in order for a peer to support both TCP and Fast Sequenced Transport (FST) remote-peers, you would need to define both a **source-bridge fst** peername and a **source-bridge remote-peer** command for the local router, using the same local IP address.

FST is fast-switched when it receives or sends frames from Ethernet, Token Ring, or FDDI interfaces. It is also fast-switched when it sends and receives from serial interfaces configured with the High-Level Data Link Control (HDLC) encapsulation. In all other cases, FST is slow-switched.

In cases where FST is fast-switched, in either the Cisco routers configured for FST or in the routers contained within the IP "cloud" between a pair of FST peers, only one path is used at a given time between the two FST peers. A single path greatly decreases the likelihood that frames arrive out of sequence. In the rare cases where frames do arrive out of sequence, the FST code on the receiving peer discards the out-of-order frame. Thus, the Token Ring end hosts rarely lose a frame over the FST router cloud and performance levels remain adequate.

The same conditions are true for any slow-switched topology that provides only a single path (for example, a single X.25 network cloud) between the peers. Similarly, if two slow-switched paths are of very different costs such that one always will be chosen over the other, the chances of having frames received out of sequence are also rare.

However, if two or more slow-switched paths of equal cost exist between the two routers (such as two parallel X.25 networks), the routers alternate in sending packets between the two or more equal-cost paths. This results in a high probability of frames arriving out of sequence at the receiver. In such cases, the FST code disposes of every out-of-sequence packet, leading to a large number of drops. This requires that the end hosts retransmit frames, greatly reducing overall throughput.

When parallel paths exist, we strongly recommend choosing one as the preferred path. Choose a preferred path by specifying a higher bandwidth for the path that contains the direct connections to the two or more parallel paths on the router.

Do not use FST when the probability exists for frames to lose their order in your network. If you have a network where frames are routinely reordered, it is better to use the TCP protocol for remote source-route bridging. TCP provides the overhead necessary to bring frames back in order on the receiving router. FST, to remain fast, does not provide for such a mechanism and will discard out-of-order frames.

LLC2 local acknowledgment can only be enabled with TCP remote peers (as opposed to LAN or direct serial interface remote peers) because Cisco IOS software needs the reliable transmission of TCP to provide the same reliability that an LLC2 LAN end-to-end connection provides. Therefore, the direct media encapsulation options for the **source-bridge remote-peer** command cannot be used.

If the LLC2 session between the local host and the router terminates on either side of the connection, the other device will be informed to terminate its connection to its local host.

If the TCP queue length of the connection between the two routers reaches 90 percent of its limit, they send Receiver-not-Ready (RNR) messages to the local hosts until the queue limit is reduced to below this limit.

The configuration of the LLC2 parameters for the local Token Ring interfaces can affect overall performance. Refer to Chapter 13, "Configuring LLC2 and SDLC Parameters" for more details about fine-tuning your network through the LLC2 parameters.

NOTE   As previously stated, local acknowledgment for LLC2 is meant only for extreme cases in which communication is not possible otherwise. Because the router must maintain a full LLC2 session, the number of simultaneous sessions it can support before performance degrades depends on the mix of other protocols and their loads.

The routers at each end of the LLC2 session execute the full LLC2 protocol, which can result in some overhead. The decision to turn on local acknowledgment for LLC2 should be based on the speed of the backbone network in relation to the Token Ring speed. For LAN segments separated by slow-speed serial links (for example, 56 kbps), the T1 timer problem could occur more frequently. In such cases, it may be wise to turn on local acknowledgment for LLC2. For LAN segments separated by a FDDI backbone, backbone delays will be minimal; in such cases, local acknowledgment for LLC2 should not be turned on. Speed mismatch between the LAN segments and the backbone network is one criterion to be used in the decision to use local acknowledgment for LLC2.

There are some situations (such as Host B failing between the time Host A sends data and the time Host B receives it) in which Host A would behave as if, at the LLC2 layer, data was received when it actually was not, because the device acknowledges that it received data from Host A before it confirms that Host B can actually receive the data. But, because both NetBIOS and SNA have error recovery in situations where an end device goes down, these higher-level protocols will resend any missing or lost data. These transaction request/confirmation protocols exist above LLC2, so they are not affected by tight timers, as is LLC2. They also are transparent to local acknowledgment.

If you are using NetBIOS applications, note that there are two NetBIOS timers—one at the link level and one at the next higher level. Local acknowledgment for LLC2 is designed to solve session timeouts at the link level only. If you are experiencing NetBIOS session timeouts, you have two options:

- Experiment with increasing your NetBIOS timers.

- Avoid using NetBIOS applications on slow serial lines.

RSRB Configuration Task List

To configure RSRB, perform the tasks in one of the following sections:

- Configure RSRB Using Direct Encapsulation

- Configure RSRB Using IP Encapsulation over an FST Connection

- Configure RSRB Using IP Encapsulation over a TCP Connection

- Configure RSRB Using IP Encapsulation over a Fast-Switched TCP Connection

- Configure RSRB Using TCP and LLC2 Local Acknowledgment

- Configure Direct Frame Relay Encapsulation Between RSRB Peers

After you configure RSRB, you can establish service access point (SAP) prioritization by performing the tasks described in the "Establish SAP Prioritization" section later in this chapter.

To tune and maintain the RSRB network, perform the tasks in the following sections:

- Tune the RSRB Network

- Monitor and Maintain the RSRB Network

See the end of this chapter for the section "RSRB Configuration Examples."

Configure RSRB Using Direct Encapsulation

Configuring RSRB using the direct encapsulation method uses a HDLC (High-Level Data Link)-like encapsulation to pass frames over a single physical network connection between two routers attached to Token Rings. Use this method when you run source-route bridge traffic over point-to-point, single-hop, serial, or LAN media. Although this method does not have the flexibility of the TCP method, it provides better performance because it involves less overhead. To configure a remote source-route bridge to use a point-to-point serial line or a single Ethernet, or single Fiber Distributed Data Interface (FDDI) hop, perform the tasks in the following sections:

● Define a Ring Group in RSRB Context

● Identify the Remote Peers (Direct Encapsulation)

● Enable SRB on the Appropriate Interfaces

Define a Ring Group in RSRB Context

In Cisco's implementation of RSRB, whenever you connect Token Rings using non-Token Ring media, you must treat that non-Token Ring media as a virtual ring by assigning it to a ring group. Every router with which you wish to exchange Token Ring traffic must be a member of this same ring group. These routers are referred to as remote peer bridges. Therefore, the ring group is made up of interfaces that reside on separate routers.

A ring group must be assigned a ring number that is unique throughout the network. It is possible to assign different interfaces on the same router to different ring groups, if, for example, you plan to administer them as interfaces in separate domains.

To define or remove a ring group, use one of the following commands in global configuration mode:

Command	Purpose
source-bridge ring-group *ring-group* [*virtual-mac-address*]	Defines a ring group.
no source-bridge ring-group *ring-group* [*virtual-mac-address*]	Removes a ring group.

Identify the Remote Peers (Direct Encapsulation)

The interfaces that you identify as remote peer bridges must be serial, Ethernet, FDDI, or Token Ring interfaces. On a serial interface, you must use HDLC encapsulation. To identify remote-peer bridges, use the following command in global configuration mode:

Command	Purpose
source-bridge remote-peer *ring-group* **interface** *interface-name* [*mac-address*] [**lf** *size*]	Defines the ring group and identify the interface over which to send SRB traffic to another router in the ring group.

Configure a **source-bridge remote peer** command for each peer router that is part of the virtual ring. When using direct encapsulation, you do not need to configure a local router ID.

NOTE   If the medium being used for the direct connection is a multipoint medium (for example, Ethernet or FDDI), then you may have to specify a target Media Access Control (MAC) address for the remote peer. If so, this MAC address should be the MAC address of the interface on the remote peer that is connected to the transport medium (the medium shared by the local and remote peers).

You can assign a keepalive interval to the remote source-bridging peer. Use the following command in interface configuration mode:

Command	Purpose
source-bridge keepalive *seconds*	Defines the keepalive interval of the remote source-bridging peer.

Enable SRB on the Appropriate Interfaces

Enable source-route bridging (SRB) on each interface through which SRB traffic will pass. The value you specify in the target ring parameter should be the ring group number you have assigned to the interface. To enable SRB on an interface, use the following command in interface configuration mode:

Command	Purpose
source-bridge *local-ring bridge-number target-ring*	Enables SRB on an interface.

Configure RSRB Using IP Encapsulation over an FST Connection

Encapsulating the source-route bridged traffic inside IP datagrams passed over a Fast-Sequenced Transport (FST) connection between two routers is not as fast as using direct encapsulation. It does, however, outperform IP encapsulation over a TCP connection because it has lower overhead. However, this method is fast-switched and does not support any IP-level functions, including local acknowledgment or fragmentation. Nor is it suitable for use in networks that tend to reorder frame sequences.

To configure a remote source-route bridge to use IP encapsulation over an FST connection, you must perform the tasks in the following sections:

- Set Up an FST Peer Name and Assign an IP Address
- Identify the Remote Peers (FST Connection)
- Enable SRB on the Appropriate Interfaces

NOTE	FST encapsulation preserves the dynamic media-independent nature of IP routing to support SNA and NetBIOS applications.

For an example of how to configure RSRB over an FST connection, see the "RSRB Using IP Encapsulation over an FST Connection Example" section later in this chapter.

Set Up an FST Peer Name and Assign an IP Address

To set up an FST peer name and provide an IP address to be used by the local router, use the following command in global configuration mode:

Command	Purpose
source-bridge fst-peername *local-interface-address*	Sets up an FST peer name and provides the local router with an IP address.

In Cisco's implementation of RSRB, whenever you connect Token Rings using non-Token Ring media, you must treat that non-Token Ring media as a virtual ring by assigning it to a ring group. Every router with which you want to exchange Token Ring traffic must be a member of this same ring group. Therefore, after you set up an FST peer name, define a ring group. For more information about defining a ring group, see the "Define a Ring Group in SRB Context" section of Chapter 3, "Configuring Source-Route Bridging."

Identify the Remote Peers (FST Connection)

All the routers with which you want to exchange Token Ring traffic are referred to as remote peer bridges. The remote peers can be at the other end of an FST connection. To identify the remote peers, use the following command in global configuration mode:

Command	Purpose
source-bridge remote-peer *ring-group* **fst** *ip-address* [**lf** *size*]	Identifies your peers and specifies an FST connection.

Specify one **source bridge remote peer** command for each peer router that is part of the virtual ring. Also, specify one **source bridge remote peer** command to identify the IP address of the local router. The IP address you specify should be the IP address you want the router to reach.

You can assign a keepalive interval to the RSRB peer. Use the following command in interface configuration mode:

Command	Purpose
source-bridge keepalive *seconds*	Defines the keepalive interval of the RSRB peer.

Enable SRB on the Appropriate Interfaces

Enable SRB on each interface through which SRB traffic passes. Make the value of the target ring parameter you specify the ring group number you assigned to the interface. To enable SRB on an interface, use the following command in interface configuration mode:

Command	Purpose
source-bridge *local-ring bridge-number target-ring*	Enables local SRB on a Token Ring interface.

Configure RSRB Using IP Encapsulation over a TCP Connection

Encapsulating the source-route bridged traffic inside IP datagrams passed over a TCP connection between two routers offers lower performance, but is the appropriate method to use under the following conditions:

- You plan to connect Token Ring networks across arbitrary media including Ethernet, FDDI, serial interfaces, X.25 networks, and so forth.

- You plan to connect Token Ring networks across a multiprotocol backbone network.

- You plan to load balance over multiple, redundant paths. Using this topology, when a path fails there is no need for hosts to retransmit explorer packets. IP routing handles the network reconfiguration transparently to the Token Ring hosts.

To configure a remote source-route bridge to use IP encapsulation over a TCP connection, you must perform the tasks in the following sections:

- Identify the Remote Peer (TCP Connection)
- Enable SRB on the Appropriate Interfaces

Identify the Remote Peer (TCP Connection)

In Cisco's implementation, whenever you connect Token Rings using non-Token Ring media, you must treat that non-Token Ring media as a virtual ring by assigning it to a ring group. Every router with which you want to exchange Token Ring traffic must be a member of this same ring group. For more infor–mation about defining a ring group, see the "Define a Ring Group in SRB Context" section of Chapter 3, "Configuring Source-Route Bridging."

To identify the remote peers, use the following command in global configuration mode:

Command	Purpose
source-bridge remote-peer *ring-group* **tcp** *ip-address* [**lf** *size*] [**tcp-receive-window** *wsize*] [**local-ack**] [**priority**]	Identifies the IP address of a peer in the ring group with which to exchange source-bridge traffic using TCP.

Specify one **source-bridge remote peer** command for each peer router that is part of the virtual ring. Configure an additional **source-bridge remote peer** command to identify the IP address to be used by the local router.

You can assign a keepalive interval to the RSRB peer. Use the following command in interface configuration mode:

Command	Purpose
source-bridge keepalive *seconds*	Defines the keepalive interval of the remote source-bridging peer.

Enable SRB on the Appropriate Interfaces

To enable SRB on an interface, use the following command in interface configuration mode:

Command	Purpose
source-bridge *local-ring bridge-number target-ring*	Enables local source-route bridging on a Token Ring interface.

The value of the target ring parameter you specify should be the ring group number.

Configure RSRB Using IP Encapsulation over a Fast-Switched TCP Connection

The fast-switched TCP (FTCP) encapsulation type speeds up Token Ring-to-Token Ring RSRB over TCP by fast-switching Token Ring frames to and from the TCP pipe. FTCP encapsulation supports the same options as TCP, with the exception of priority queuing.

In Cisco's implementation, whenever you connect Token Rings using non-Token Ring media, you must treat that non-Token Ring media as a virtual ring by assigning it to a ring group. Every router with which you wish to exchange Token Ring traffic must be a member of this same ring group. For more information about defining a ring group, see the "Define a Ring Group in SRB Context" section of Chapter 3, "Configuring Source-Route Bridging."

To configure RSRB fast switching, you must perform the tasks in the following sections:

● Identify the Remote Peer (FTCP Connection)

● Enable SRB on the Appropriate Interfaces

Identify the Remote Peer (FTCP Connection)

Identify the remote peer with which the router communicates. To identify the remote peers, use the following command in global configuration mode:

Command	Purpose
source-bridge remote-peer *ring-group* **ftcp** *ip-address* [**lf** *size*] [**tcp-receive-window** *wsize*] [**local-ack**]	Identifies the IP address of a peer in the ring group with which to exchange source-bridge traffic using TCP.

Identify the IP address of a remote peer for each interface you configure for RSRB. The IP address you specify is the IP address the router tries to reach.

To assign a keepalive interval to the remote peer, use the following command in interface configuration mode:

Command	Purpose
source-bridge keepalive *seconds*	Defines the keepalive interval of the remote peer.

Enable SRB on the Appropriate Interfaces

To enable SRB on an interface, use the following command in interface configuration mode:

Command	Purpose
source-bridge *local-ring bridge-number target-ring*	Enables local SRB on a Token Ring interface.

The value of the target ring parameter you specify should be the ring group number.

Configure RSRB Using TCP and LLC2 Local Acknowledgment

Encapsulating source-route bridged traffic inside IP datagrams that traverse a TCP connection between two routers with local acknowledgment enabled is appropriate when you have LANs separated by wide geographic distances and you want to avoid time delays, multiple retransmissions, or loss of user sessions.

Logical Link Control–Type 2 (LLC2) is an ISO standard data-link level protocol used in Token Ring networks. LLC2 was designed to provide reliable transmission of data across LAN media and to cause minimal or at least predictable time delays. However, RSRB and WAN backbones created LANs that are separated by wide, geographic distances spanning countries and continents. As a result, LANs have time delays that are longer than LLC2 allows for bidirectional communication between hosts. Local acknowledgment addresses the problem of unpredictable time delays, multiple retransmissions, and loss of user sessions.

In a typical LLC2 session, when one host sends a frame to another host, the sending host expects the receiving host to respond positively or negatively in a predefined period of time commonly called the *T1 time*. If the sending host does not receive an acknowledgment of the frame it sent within the T1 time, it retries a few times (normally 8 to 10). If there is still no response, the sending host drops the session.

Figure 7-1 illustrates an LLC2 session. A 37x5 on a LAN segment can communicate with a 3x74 on a different LAN segment separated via a wide-area backbone network. Frames are transported between Router A and Router B using RSRB. However, the LLC2 session between the 37x5 and the 3x74 is still end-to-end; that is, every frame generated by the 37x5 traverses the backbone network to the 3x74, and the 3x74, on receipt of the frame, acknowledges it.

Figure 7-1   *LLC2 Session Without Local Acknowledgment*

On backbone networks consisting of slow serial links, the T1 timer on end hosts could expire before the frames reach the remote hosts, causing the end host to retransmit. Retransmission results in duplicate frames reaching the remote host at the same time as the first frame reaches the remote host. Such frame duplication breaks the LLC2 protocol, resulting in the loss of sessions between the two IBM machines.

One way to solve this time delay is to increase the timeout value on the end nodes to account for the maximum transit time between the two end machines. However, in networks consisting of hundreds or even thousands of nodes, every machine would need to be reconfigured with new values. With local acknowledgment for LLC2 enabled, the LLC2 session between the two end nodes would not be end-to-end, but instead, would terminate at two local routers. Figure 7-2 shows the LLC2 session with the 37x5 ending at Router A and the LLC2 session with the 3x74 ending at Router B. Both Router A and Router B execute the full LLC2 protocol as part of local acknowledgment for LLC2.

Figure 7-2   *LLC2 Session with Local Acknowledgment*

With local acknowledgment for LLC2 enabled in both routers, Router A acknowledges frames received from the 37x5. The 37x5 still operates as if the acknowledgments it receives are from the 3x74. Router A looks like the 3x74 to the 37x5. Similarly, Router B acknowledges frames received from the 3x74. The 3x74 operates as if the acknowledgments it receives are from the 37x5. Router B looks like the 3x74 to 37x5. The end stations do not time out and lose sessions because the frames no longer have to travel the WAN backbone networks to be acknowledged. Instead, they are locally acknowledged by routers.

Enabling local acknowledgment for LLC2 has the following advantages:

- Local acknowledgment for LLC2 solves the T1 timer problem without having to change any configuration on the end nodes. The end nodes are unaware that the sessions are locally acknowledged. In networks consisting of hundreds or even thousands of machines, this is a definite advantage. All the frames acknowledged by Cisco IOS software appear to the end hosts to be coming from the remote IBM machine. In fact, by looking at a trace from a protocol analyzer, one cannot say whether a frame was acknowledged by the local router or by a remote IBM machine. The MAC addresses and the RIFs generated by Cisco IOS software are identical to those generated by the remote IBM machine. The only way to find out whether a session is locally acknowledged is to use either a **show local-ack** command or a **show source-bridge** command on the router.

- All the supervisory (RR, RNR, REJ) frames that are locally acknowledged go no farther than the router. Without local acknowledgment for LLC2, every frame traverses the backbone. With local acknowledgment, only data (I-frames) traverse the backbone, resulting in less traffic on the backbone network. For installations in which customers pay for the amount of traffic passing through the backbone, this could be a definite cost-saving measure. A simple protocol exists between the two peers to bring up or down a TCP session.

To configure a remote source-route bridge to use IP encapsulation over a TCP connection, perform the tasks in the following sections:

- Enable LLC2 Local Acknowledgment Between Two Remote Peer Bridges
- Enable SRB on the Appropriate Interfaces

Enable LLC2 Local Acknowledgment Between Two Remote Peer Bridges

In Cisco's implementation, whenever you connect Token Rings using non-Token Ring media, you must treat that non-Token Ring media as a virtual ring by assigning it to a ring group. Every router with which you wish to exchange Token Ring traffic must be a member of this same ring group. For more information about defining a ring group, see the "Define a Ring Group in SRB Context" section of Chapter 3, "Configuring Source-Route Bridging."

To enable LLC2 local acknowledgment, use the following command in global configuration mode:

Command	Purpose
source-bridge remote-peer *ring-group* **tcp** *ip-address* **local-ack**	Enables LLC2 local acknowledgment on a per-remote-peer basis.

Use one instance of the **source-bridge remote-peer** command for each interface you configure for RSRB.

Enable SRB on the Appropriate Interfaces

To enable SRB on an interface, use the following command in interface configuration mode:

Command	Purpose
source-bridge *local-ring bridge-number target-ring*	Enables local SRB on a Token Ring interface.

The value of the target ring parameter you specify should be the ring group number.

For an example of how to configure RSRB with local acknowledgment, see the "RSRB with Local Acknowledgment Example" section later in this chapter.

Enable Local Acknowledgment and Passthrough

To configure some sessions on a few rings to be locally acknowledged while the remaining sessions are passed through, use the following command in global configuration mode:

Command	Purpose
source-bridge passthrough *ring-group*	Configures Cisco IOS software for passthrough.

Configure Direct Frame Relay Encapsulation Between RSRB Peers

You can configure direct Frame Relay encapsulation to allow the RSRB peers to send RSRB protocol packets on a Frame Relay PVC. This configuration eliminates the overhead introduced by TCP/IP encapsulated Frame Relay packets.

Figure 7-3 illustrates direct Frame Relay encapsulation between RSRB peers.

Figure 7-3   *RSRB Direct Frame Relay Encapsulation*

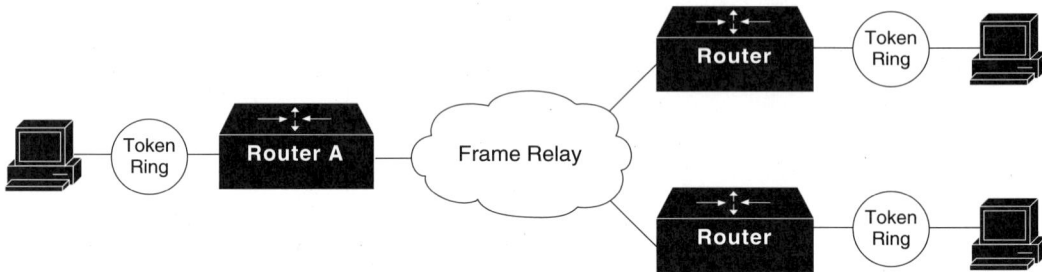

The RSRB direct encapsulation design can use RFC 1490 format or Cisco Frame Relay encapsulation for routed packets.

To configure RSRB direct Frame Relay encapsulation, use the following commands, starting in interface configuration mode:

Step	Command	Purpose
1	**source-bridge remote-peer** *ring-group* **frame-relay interface** *name* [mac-address] [*dlci-number*] [**lf** *size*]	Specifies the serial interface on which Frame Relay is configured.
2	**frame-relay map rsrb** *dlci-number*	Specifies the DLCI number onto which the RSRB traffic is to be mapped.

Establish SAP Prioritization

The SAP prioritization feature allows you to use SAP priority lists and filters to specify the priority of one protocol over another across an RSRB or SDLLC WAN.

Define a SAP Priority List

To establish a SAP priority list, use the following commands in interface configuration mode:

Step	Command	Purpose
1	**sap-priority-list** *number queue-keyword* [**dsap** *ds*] [**ssap** *ss*] [**dmac** *dm*] [**smac** *sm*]	Defines the priority list.
2	**sap-priority** *list-number*	Defines the priority on an interface.
3	**priority-group** *list-number*	Applies the priority list to an interface.

Define SAP Filters

You can define SAP filters and NetBIOS filters on Token Ring and Ethernet interfaces.

To filter by local service access point (LSAP) address on the RSRB WAN interface, use the following global configuration commands as appropriate:

Command	Purpose
rsrb remote-peer *ring-group* **tcp** *ip-address* **lsap-output-list** *access-list-number*	Filters by LSAP address (TCP encapsulation).
rsrb remote-peer *ring-group* **fst** *ip-address* **lsap-output-list** *access-list-number*	Filters by LSAP address (FST encapsulation).
rsrb remote-peer *ring-group* **interface** *name* **lsap-output-list** *access-list-number*	Filters by LSAP address (direct encapsulation).

To filter packets by NetBIOS station name on an RSRB WAN interface, use one of the following global configuration commands as appropriate:

Command	Purpose
rsrb remote-peer *ring-group* **tcp** *ip-address* **netbios-output-list** *name*	Filters by NetBIOS station name (TCP encapsulation).
rsrb remote-peer *ring-group* **fst** *ip-address* **netbios-output-list** *name*	Filters by NetBIOS station name (FST encapsulation).
rsrb remote-peer *ring-group* **interface** *type* **netbios-output-list** *host*	Filters by NetBIOS station name (direct encapsulation).

Tune the RSRB Network

The following sections describe how to configure features that enhance network performance by reducing the number of packets that traverse the backbone network:

- Prioritize Traffic Based on SNA Local LU Addresses
- Enable Class of Service
- Assign a Priority Group to an Input Interface
- Configure the Largest Frame Size

Prioritize Traffic Based on SNA Local LU Addresses

You can prioritize Systems Network Architecture (SNA) traffic on an interface configured for either serial tunnel (STUN) or RSRB communication. The SNA local logical unit (LU) address prioritization feature allows SNA traffic to be prioritized according to the address of the LUs on the FID2 transmission headers. Currently, only dependent LUs are supported. The prioritization takes place on LU-LU traffic between an SNA Node type 5 or Node type 4, and Node type 2.

Figure 7-4 shows how SNA local address prioritization can be used.

Figure 7-4   *SNA Local Address Prioritization*

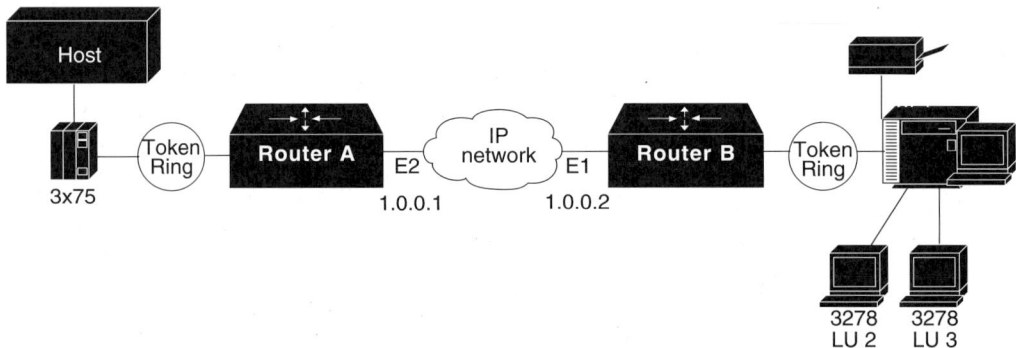

In Figure 7-4, the IBM mainframe is channel-attached to a 3x75 FEP, which is connected to a cluster controller via RSRB. Multiple 3270 terminals and printers, each with a unique local LU address, are then attached to the cluster controller. By applying SNA local LU address prioritization, each LU associated with a terminal or printer can be assigned a priority; that is, certain users can have terminals that have better response time than others, and printers can have lowest priority.

NOTE	Both local acknowledgment and TCP priority features for STUN or RSRB must be turned on for SNA local address prioritization to take effect.

With the SNA local LU address prioritization feature, you can establish queuing priorities based on the address of the logical unit. To prioritize traffic, use the following commands in global configuration mode:

Step	Command	Purpose
1	**locaddr-priority-list** *list-number address-number queue-keyword* [**dsap** *ds*] [**dmac** *dm*] [**ssap** *ss*] [**smac** *sm*]	Maps LUs to TCP port numbers.

Step	Command	Purpose
2	**priority-list** *list-number* **protocol** *protocol-name* *queue-keyword*	Sets the priority of TCP port numbers.

Enable Class of Service

To prioritize SNA traffic across the SNA backbone network, you can enable the class of service (CoS) feature. This feature is useful only between FEP-to-FEP (PU4-to-PU4) communication across the non-SNA backbone. It allows important FEP traffic to flow on high-priority queues.

To enable CoS, IP encapsulation over a TCP connection and LLC2 local acknowledgment must be enabled.

To enable CoS, use the following command in global configuration mode:

Command	Purpose
source-bridge cos-enable	Enables CoS.

Assign a Priority Group to an Input Interface

To assign a priority group to an input interface, use the following command in interface configuration mode:

Command	Purpose
locaddr-priority *list-number*	Assigns a priority group to an input interface.

Configure the Largest Frame Size

You can configure the largest frame size that is used to communicate with any peers in the ring group.

Generally, the router and the LLC2 device with which it communicates should support the same maximum SDLC I-frame size. The larger this value, the more efficiently the line is used, thus increasing performance.

Faster screen updates to 3278-style terminals often result by configuring the Token Ring FEP to send as large an I-frame as possible and then allowing Cisco IOS software to segment the frame into multiple SDLC I-frames.

After you configure the Token Ring FEP to send the largest possible I-frame, configure the software to support the same maximum I-frame size. The default is 516 bytes.and the maximum value is 8144 bytes.

To configure the largest frame size, use the following command in global configuration mode:

Command	Purpose
source-bridge largest-frame *ring-group size*	Specifies the largest frame size used to communicate with any peers in the ring group.

Monitor and Maintain the RSRB Network

To display a variety of information about the RSRB network, use one or more of the following commands in EXEC mode:

Command	Purpose
show controllers token	Displays internal state information about the Token Ring interfaces in the system.
show interfaces	Provides high-level statistics about the state of source bridging for a particular interface.
show local-ack	Shows the current state of any current local acknowledgment for both LLC2 and SDLLC connections.

In addition to the EXEC-mode commands to maintain the RSRB network, you can use the following command in global configuration mode:

Command	Purpose
source-bridge tcp-queue-max *number*	Limits the size of the backup queue for RSRB to control the number of packets that can wait for transmission to a remote ring before they start being discarded.

RSRB Configuration Examples

The following sections provide RSRB configuration examples:

- RSRB Direct Frame Relay Encapsulation Example

- RSRB Using IP Encapsulation over a TCP Connection Example

- RSRB/TCP Fast-Switching Configuration Example

- RSRB Using IP Encapsulation over an FST Connection Example

- RSRB Using All Types of Transport Methods Example

- RSRB with Local Acknowledgment Example

- RSRB with Local Acknowledgment and Passthrough Example

- Local Acknowledgment for LLC2 Example

- IP for Load Sharing over RSRB Example

- Configuring Priority for Locally Terminated Token Ring Interfaces in RSRB Example

- SNA Traffic Prioritization by LU Address Example

RSRB Direct Frame Relay Encapsulation Example

The following is the configuration file for direct Frame Relay encapsulation between RSRB peers:

```
source-bridge ring-group 200
source-bridge remote-peer 200 frame-relay interface serial0 30
!
interface serial 0
 mtu 3000
 no ip address
 encapsulation frame-relay
 clockrate 56000
 frame-relay lmi-type ansi
 frame-relay map rsrb 30
!
!
interface TokenRing 0
 ip address 10.10.10.1 255.255.255.0
 ring-speed 16
 multiring all
 source-bridge active 102 1 200
 source-bridge spanning
```

RSRB Using IP Encapsulation over a TCP Connection Example

Figure 7-5 illustrates two routers configured for RSRB using TCP as a transport. Each router has two Token Rings. They are connected by an Ethernet segment over which the source-route bridged traffic will pass. The first router configuration is a source-route bridge at address 131.108.2.29.

Figure 7-5 *RSRB Using TCP as a Transport*

Using TCP as the transport, the configuration for the source-route bridge at address 131.108.2.29 as depicted in Figure 7-5 is as follows:

```
source-bridge ring-group 5
source-bridge remote-peer 5 tcp 131.108.2.29
source-bridge remote-peer 5 tcp 131.108.1.27
!
interface ethernet 0
 ip address 131.108.4.4 255.255.255.0
!
interface tokenring 0
 ip address 131.108.2.29 255.255.255.0
 source-bridge 1000 1 5
 source-bridge spanning
!
interface tokenring 1
 ip address 131.108.128.1 255.255.255.0
 source-bridge 1001 1 5
 source-bridge spanning
```

The configuration of the source-route bridge at 131.108.1.27 is as follows:

```
source-bridge ring-group 5
source-bridge remote-peer 5 tcp 131.108.2.29
source-bridge remote-peer 5 tcp 131.108.1.27
!
interface ethernet 0
 ip address 131.108.4.5 255.255.255.0
!
interface tokenring 0
 ip address 131.108.1.27 255.255.255.0
 source-bridge 10 1 5
 source-bridge spanning
!
interface tokenring 1
 ip address 131.108.131.1 255.255.255.0
 source-bridge 11 1 5
 source-bridge spanning
```

RSRB/TCP Fast-Switching Configuration Example

The following configuration enables RSRB/TCP fast switching:

```
source-bridge ring group 100
source-bridge remote-peer 100 ftcp 198.92.88.138
source-bridge remote-peer 100 ftcp 198.92.88.145
```

RSRB Using IP Encapsulation over an FST Connection Example

Figure 7-6 shows two routers connecting IBM hosts on Token Rings through an Ethernet backbone.

Figure 7-6   *RSRB Using FST as a Transport*

This configuration example enables IP encapsulation over an FST connection. In this configuration, the **source-bridge fst-peername** global configuration command is used to provide an IP address for the local router. The **source-bridge ring-group** global configuration command is used to define a ring group. The **source-bridge remote peer** command with the **fst** option is used to associate the remote peer's IP address with the router's ring group and specify the remote peer's RSRB protocol version number. Because all FST peers support version 2 RSRB, the **version** keyword is always specified.

The configuration of the source-route bridge at 131.108.2.29 is as follows:

```
source-bridge fst-peername 131.108.2.29
source-bridge ring-group 5
source-bridge remote-peer 5 fst 131.108.1.27
!
interface ethernet 0
 ip address 131.108.4.4 255.255.255.0
!
interface tokenring 0
 ip address 131.108.2.29 255.255.255.0
 source-bridge 1000 1 5
 source-bridge spanning
!
interface tokenring 1
 ip address 131.108.128.1 255.255.255.0
 source-bridge 1001 1 5
 source-bridge spanning
```

The configuration of the source-route bridge at 131.108.1.27 is as follows:

```
source-bridge fst-peername 131.108.1.27
source-bridge ring-group 5
source-bridge remote-peer 5 fst 131.108.2.29
!
interface ethernet 0
 ip address 131.108.4.5 255.255.255.0
!
interface tokenring 0
 ip address 131.108.1.27 255.255.255.0
 source-bridge 10 1 5
 source-bridge spanning
!
interface tokenring 1
 ip address 131.108.131.1 255.255.255.0
 source-bridge 11 1 5
 source-bridge spanning
```

RSRB Using All Types of Transport Methods Example

Figure 7-7 shows a router configured for RSRB using all types of transport methods.

Figure 7-7   *RSRB Using All Types of Transport Methods*

The configuration for the network in Figure 7-7 is as follows:

```
source-bridge fst-peername 131.108.251.1
source-bridge ring-group 5
source-bridge remote-peer 5 interface serial0
source-bridge remote-peer 5 interface serial1
source-bridge remote-peer 5 interface Ethernet0 0000.0c00.1234
source-bridge remote-peer 5 tcp 131.108.251.1
source-bridge remote-peer 5 fst 131.108.252.4
source-bridge remote-peer 5 tcp 131.108.253.5
!
interface tokenring 0
 source-bridge 1 1 5
 source-bridge spanning
!
interface ethernet 0
 ip address 131.108.251.1 255.255.255.0
```

The two peers using the serial transport method only function correctly if routers at the other end of the serial line have been configured to use the serial transport. The peers must also belong to the same ring group.

RSRB with Local Acknowledgment Example

In Figure 7-8, a triangular configuration provides the maximum reliability with minimal cost, and one of the links is doubled to gain better bandwidth. In addition to IP and SRB traffic, AppleTalk is also routed between all the sites. In this configuration, all the sessions between Router C and Router D are locally acknowledged. All the sessions between Router C and Router E are not locally acknowledged and are configured for normal remote source-route bridging. This example shows that not every peer must be locally acknowledged and that local acknowledgment can be turned on or off at the customer's discretion.

Figure 7-8 *RSRB with Local Acknowledgment—Simple Configuration*

The configuration for each of the routers in Figure 7-8 follows.

Router C

```
appletalk routing
!
source-bridge ring-group 5
source-bridge remote-peer 5 tcp 132.21.1.1
source-bridge remote-peer 5 tcp 132.21.2.6 local-ack
source-bridge remote-peer 5 tcp 132.21.10.200
!
interface tokenring 0
 ip address 132.21.1.1 255.255.255.0
 source-bridge 1 1 5
 source-bridge spanning
 multiring all
!
interface ethernet 0
 ip address 132.21.4.25 255.255.255.0
 appletalk address 4.25
 appletalk zone Twilight
!
interface serial 0
 ip address 132.21.16.1 255.255.255.0
```

```
 appletalk address 16.1
 appletalk zone Twilight
!
interface serial 1
 ip address 132.21.17.1 255.255.255.0
 appletalk address 17.1
 appletalk zone Twilight
!
interface serial 2
 ip address 132.21.18.1 255.255.255.0
 appletalk address 18.1
 appletalk zone Twilight
!
 router igrp 109
 network 132.21.0.0
!
 hostname RouterC
```

Router D

```
appletalk routing
!
source-bridge ring-group 5
source-bridge remote-peer 5 tcp 132.21.1.1 local-ack
source-bridge remote-peer 5 tcp 132.21.2.6
source-bridge remote-peer 5 tcp 132.21.10.200
!
interface tokenring 0
 ip address 132.21.2.6 255.255.255.0
 source-bridge 2 1 5
 source-bridge spanning
 multiring all
!
interface ethernet 0
 ip address 132.21.5.1 255.255.255.0
 appletalk address 5.1
 appletalk zone Twilight
!
interface serial 0
 ip address 132.21.16.2 255.255.255.0
 appletalk address 16.2
 appletalk zone Twilight
!
interface serial 1
 ip address 132.21.19.1 255.255.255.0
 appletalk address 19.1
 appletalk zone Twilight
!
router igrp 109
 network 132.21.0.0
!
hostname RouterD
```

Router E

```
appletalk routing
!
source-bridge ring-group 5
source-bridge remote-peer 5 tcp 132.21.1.1
source-bridge remote-peer 5 tcp 132.21.2.6
source-bridge remote-peer 5 tcp 132.21.10.200
!
interface tokenring 0
 ip address 132.21.10.200 255.255.255.0
 source-bridge 10 1 5
 source-bridge spanning
 multiring all
!
interface ethernet 0
 ip address 132.21.7.1 255.255.255.0
 appletalk address 7.1
 appletalk zone Twilight
!
interface serial 0
 ip address 132.21.19.2 255.255.255.0
 appletalk address 19.2
 appletalk zone Twilight
!
interface serial 1
 ip address 132.21.17.2 255.255.255.0
 appletalk address 17.2
 appletalk zone Twilight
!
interface serial 2
 ip address 132.21.18.2 255.255.255.0
 appletalk address 18.2
 appletalk zone Twilight
!
 router igrp 109
 network 132.21.0.0
!
hostname RouterE
```

RSRB with Local Acknowledgment and Passthrough Example

Figure 7-9 shows two routers configured for RSRB with local acknowledgment and passthrough over the three serial lines that connect these routers. In the example, five Token Rings connect to each of these routers.

Figure 7-9   *Network Topology for RSRB with Local Acknowledgment and Passthrough*

The configuration files for each of these routers follows.

Router A

```
source-bridge ring-group 2048
source-bridge remote-peer 2048 tcp 159.76.1.250 local-ack version 2
source-bridge remote-peer 2048 tcp 159.76.7.250 version 2
source-bridge passthrough 1281
source-bridge passthrough 1282
source-bridge passthrough 1283
source-bridge passthrough 1284
!
interface tokenring 0
 ip address 159.76.7.250 255.255.255.0
 llc2 ack-max 1
 llc2 t1-time 1800
 llc2 idle-time 29000
 llc2 ack-delay-time 5
 source-bridge 1024 1 2048
 source-bridge spanning
 early-token-release
 multiring all
!
interface tokenring 1
 ip address 159.76.8.250 255.255.255.0
 clns-speed 4
 clns mtu 464
 source-bridge 1281 1 2048
 source-bridge spanning
 multiring all
!
interface tokenring 2
 ip address 159.76.9.250 255.255.255.0
 ring-speed 4
```

```
 clns mtu 4464
 source-bridge 1282 1 2048
 source-bridge spanning
 multiring all
!
interface tokenring 3
 ip address 159.76.10.250 255.255.255.0
 ring speed 4
 clns mtu 4464
 source-bridge 1283 1 2048
 source-bridge spanning
 multiring all
!
interface tokenring 4
 ip address 159.78.11.250 255.255.255.0
 ring speed 4
 clns mtu 4464
 source-bridge 1284 1 2048
 source-bridge spanning
 multiring all
!
interface serial 0
 ip address 159.76.20.2 255.255.255.0
!
interface serial 1
 ip address 159.76.21.4 255.255.255.0
!
interface serial 2
 ip address 159.76.22.6 255.255.255.0
 shutdown
! interface serial 3
 no ip address
 shutdown
```

Router B

```
source-bridge ring-group 2048
source-bridge remote-peer 2048 tcp 159.76.1.250 version 2
source-bridge remote-peer 2048 tcp 159.76.7.250 local-ack version 2
!
interface tokenring 0
 ip address 159.76.1.250 255.255.255.0
 llc2 ack-max 2
 llc2 t1-time 1900
 llc2 idle-time 29000
 llc2 ack-delay-time 5
 source-bridge 512 1 2048
 source-bridge spanning
 early-token-release
 multiring all
!!
interface tokenring 1
 ip address 159.76.2.250 255.255.255.0
 ring-speed 16
```

```
 clns mtu 8136
!
 source-bridge 513 1 2048
 source-bridge spanning
 early-token-release
 multiring all
!
interface tokenring 2
 ip address 159.76.3.250 255.255.255.0
 ring speed 16
 clns mtu 8136
 source-bridge 514 1 2048
 source-bridge spanning
 early-token-release
 multiring all
!
interface tokenring 3
 ip address 159.76.4.250 255.255.255.0
 ring-speed 4
 clns mtu 4464
 source-bridge 519 2 2043
 source-bridge spanning
 multiring all
!
interface tokenring 4
 ip address 159.76.5.250 255.255.255.0
 ring-speed 4
 clns mtu 4464
 source-bridge 272 2 2048
 source-bridge spanning
 multiring all
!
interface serial 0
 ip address 159.76.20.1 255.255.255.0
!
interface serial 1
 ip address 159.76.21.3 255.255.255.0
!
interface serial 2
 ip address 159.76.22.5 255.255.255.0
!
interface serial 3
 no ip address
 shutdown
```

Local Acknowledgment for LLC2 Example

Figure 7-10 shows an IBM FEP located in San Francisco communicating with IBM 3174 cluster controller hosts in Sydney, Paris, and Los Angeles. The session between the FEP and the IBM 3174 system in Los Angeles is not locally terminated because the distance is great enough to cause timeouts on the line. However, the sessions to Paris and Sydney are locally terminated.

Figure 7-10 *RSRB with Local Acknowledgment—Complex Configuration*

The configuration for each of these routers follows.

Router/Bridge 4 in San Francisco

```
source-bridge ring-group 100
! use direct encapsulation across serial link to Los Angeles
 source-bridge remote-peer 100 direct 131.108.32.2
 ! use fast sequenced transport with local termination to Paris
 source-bridge remote-peer 100 tcp 131.108.18.48 local-ack
 ! use tcp encapsulation with local termination to Sydney
 source-bridge remote-peer 100 tcp 131.108.141.4 local-ack
 !
interface tokenring 0
 ! source ring 1, bridge 4, destination ring 100
source-bridge 1 4 100
! receive up to seven frames before sending an acknowledgment
llc2 ack-max 7
! allow a 30 msec delay before I-frames must be acknowledged
llc2 ack-delay-time 30
!
interface tokenring 1
! source ring 100, bridge 4, destination ring 1
source-bridge 100 4 1
```

Router/Bridge 7 in Sydney

```
source-bridge ring-group 100
 ! use tcp encapsulation with local termination from Sydney
 source-bridge remote-peer 100 tcp 131.108.6.88 local-ack
 interface tokenring 0
 ! source ring 1, bridge 7, destination ring 100
 source-bridge 1 7 100
 ! receive up to seven frames before sending an acknowledgment
 llc2 ack-max 7
 ! allow a 30 msec delay before I-frames must be acknowledged
 llc2 ack-delay-time 30
 !
 interface tokenring 1
 ! source ring 100, bridge 7, destination ring 1
 source-bridge 100 7 1
```

Router/Bridge 6 in Paris

```
source-bridge ring-group 100
 ! use fast sequenced transport with local termination from Paris
 source-bridge remote-peer 100 tcp 131.108.6.88 local-ack
 interface tokenring 0
 ! source ring 1, bridge 6, destination ring 100
 source-bridge 1 6 100
 ! receive up to seven frames before sending an acknowledgment
 llc2 ack-max 7
 ! allow a 30 msec delay before I-frames must be acknowledged
 llc2 ack-delay-time 30
 !
 interface tokenring 1
 ! source ring 100, bridge 6, destination ring 1
 source-bridge 100 6 1
```

Router/Bridge 5 in Los Angeles

```
source-bridge ring-group 100
 ! use direct encapsulation across serial link from Los Angeles
 source-bridge remote-peer 100 direct 131.108.6.88

 interface tokenring 0
 ! source ring 1, bridge 5, destination ring 100
 source-bridge 1 5 100
 ! receive up to seven frames before sending an acknowledgment
 llc2 ack-max 7
 ! allow a 30 msec delay before I-frames must be acknowledged
 llc2 ack-delay-time 30
 !
 interface tokenring 1
 ! source ring 100, bridge 5, destination ring 1
 source-bridge 100 5 1
```

NOTE   Both peers need to be configured for LLC2 local acknowledgment. If only one is so configured, undesirable results occur.

IP for Load Sharing over RSRB Example

As Figure 7-11 shows, two routers are connected by two serial lines. Each is configured as a basic remote dual-port bridge, but extended to include both reliability and IP load sharing. When both serial lines are up, traffic is split between them, effectively combining the bandwidth of the connections. If either serial line goes down, all traffic is routed to the remaining line with no disruption. This happens transparently with respect to the end connections, unlike other source-route bridges that would abort those connections.

Figure 7-11 *RSRB—Simple Reliability*

The sample configuration files that enable this configuration follow.

Configuration for Router/Bridge A

```
source-bridge ring-group 5
source-bridge remote-peer 5 tcp 204.31.7.1
source-bridge remote-peer 5 tcp 204.31.8.1
!
interface tokenring 0
 ip address 204.31.7.1 255.255.255.0
 source-bridge 1 1 5
 source-bridge spanning
 multiring all
!
interface serial 0
 ip address 204.31.9.1 255.255.255.0
!
interface serial 1
 ip address 204.31.10.1 255.255.255.0
!
 router igrp 109
 network 204.31.7.0
 network 204.31.9.0
 network 204.31.10.0
!
hostname RouterA
```

Configuration for Router/Bridge B

```
source-bridge ring-group 5
source-bridge remote-peer 5 tcp 204.31.7.1
source-bridge remote-peer 5 tcp 204.31.8.1
!
interface tokenring 0
 ip address 204.31.8.1 255.255.255.0
 source-bridge 2 1 5
 source-bridge spanning
 multiring all
!
interface serial 0
 ip address 204.31.9.2 255.255.255.0
!
interface serial 1
 ip address 204.31.10.2 255.255.255.0
!
 router igrp 109
 network 204.31.8.0
 network 204.31.9.0
 network 204.31.10.0
!
 hostname RouterB
```

Configuring Priority for Locally Terminated Token Ring Interfaces in RSRB Example

Figure 7-12 shows a network that uses RSRB to bridge Token Ring traffic.

Figure 7-12 *RSRB Configuration Example*

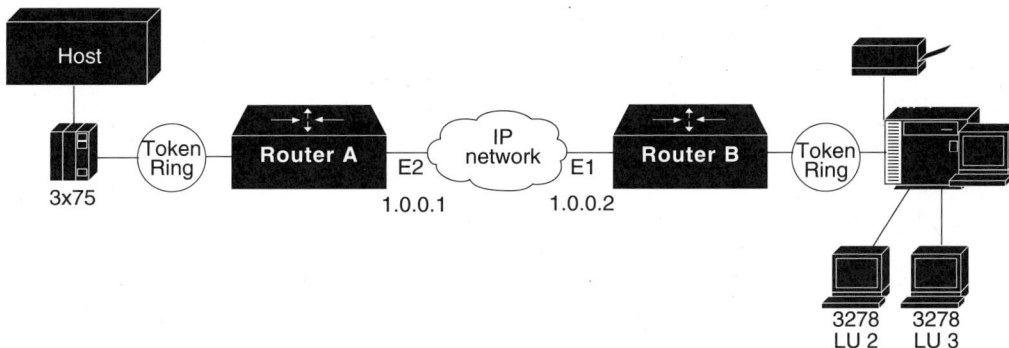

The configuration for each of the routers in Figure 7-12 follows.

Router/Bridge A

```
source-bridge ring-group 2624
source-bridge remote-peer 2624 tcp 1.0.0.1
source-bridge remote-peer 2624 tcp 1.0.0.2 local-ack priority
!
interface tokenring 0
 source-bridge 2576 8 2624
 source-bridge spanning
 multiring all
 locaddr-priority 1
!
interface ethernet 0
 ip address 1.0.0.1 255.255.255.0
 priority-group 1
!
 locaddr-priority-list 1 02 high
 locaddr-priority-list 1 03 high
 locaddr-priority-list 1 04 medium
 locaddr-priority-list 1 05 low
!
 priority-list protocol ip high tcp 1996
 priority-list protocol ip medium tcp 1987
 priority-list protocol ip normal tcp 1988
 priority-list protocol ip low tcp 1989
```

Router/Bridge B

```
source-bridge ring-group 2624
source-bridge remote-peer 2624 tcp 1.0.0.2
source-bridge remote-peer 2624 tcp 1.0.0.1 local-ack priority
!
interface tokenring 0
 source-bridge 2626 8 2624
 source-bridge spanning
 multiring all
 locaddr-priority 1
!
interface ethernet 0
 ip address 1.0.0.2 255.255.255.0
 priority-group 1
!
 locaddr-priority-list 1 02 high
 locaddr-priority-list 1 03 high
 locaddr-priority-list 1 04 medium
 locaddr-priority-list 1 05 low
!
 priority-list protocol ip high tcp 1996
 priority-list protocol ip medium tcp 1987
 priority-list protocol ip normal tcp 1988
 priority-list protocol ip low tcp 1989
```

SNA Traffic Prioritization by LU Address Example

The following example enables SNA traffic prioritization by LU address:

```
locaddr-priority-list 1 01 medium
locaddr-priority-list 1 02 normal
locaddr-priority-list 1 03 low
locaddr-priority-list 1 04 high
!
priority-list 2 protocol ip low tcp 1996
priority-list 2 protocol ip high tcp 1987
priority-list 2 protocol ip medium tcp 1988
priority-list 2 protocol ip normal tcp 1989
!
interface tokenring 0
source-bridge 123
locaddr-priority 1

interface serial 0
priority-group 2
```

Remote Source-Route Bridging Commands

Use the commands in this chapter to configure remote source-route bridging (RSRB) networks. For RSRB configuration information and examples, refer to Chapter 7, "Configuring Remote Source-Route Bridging."

locaddr-priority

Use the **locaddr-priority** interface configuration command to assign a remote source-route bridging (RSRB) priority group to an input interface. Use the **no** form of this command to remove the RSRB priority group assignment from the interface.

> **locaddr-priority** *list-number*
> **no locaddr-priority** *list-number*

Syntax	Description
list-number	Priority list number of the input interface.

Default
No RSRB priority group is assigned.

Command Mode
Interface configuration

Usage Guidelines
This command first appeared in Cisco IOS Release 10.0.

You must use the **priority-list** command to assign priorities to the ports, as shown in Table 8-1.

Table 8-1 *Common RSRB Services and Their Port Numbers*

Service	Port
RSRB high priority	1996
RSRB medium priority	1987
RSRB normal priority	1988
RSRB low priority	1989

Example

In the following example, Token Ring interface 0 is assigned the RSRB priority group 1:

```
source-bridge ring-group 2624
source-bridge remote-peer 2624 tcp 1.0.0.1
source-bridge remote-peer 2624 tcp 1.0.0.2 local-ack priority
!
interface tokenring 0
 source-bridge 2576 8 2624
 locaddr-priority 1
```

Related Commands

To locate documentation of related commands, you can search online at www.cisco.com.

locaddr-priority-list
priority-list

locaddr-priority-list

Use the **locaddr-priority-list** global configuration command to map logical units (LUs) to queuing priorities as one of the steps to establishing queuing priorities based on LU addresses. Use the **no** form of this command to remove that RSRB priority queuing assignment. You use this command in conjunction with the **priority list** command.

> **locaddr-priority-list** *list-number address-number queue-keyword* [**dsap** *ds*] [**dmac** *dm*][**ssap** *ss*] [**smac** *sm*]
> **no locaddr-priority-list** *list-number address-number queue-keyword* [**dsap** *ds*] [**dmac** *dm*][**ssap** *ss*] [**smac** *sm*]

Syntax	Description
list-number	Arbitrary integer between 1 and 10 that identifies the LU address priority list selected by the user.

Syntax	Description
address-number	Value of the LOCADDR= parameter on the LU macro, which is a one-byte address of the LU in hexadecimal.
queue-keyword	Priority queue name; one of **high**, **medium**, **normal**, or **low**.
dsap *ds*	(Optional) Indicates that the next argument, *ds*, represents the destination service access point address. The argument *ds* is a hexadecimal value.
dmac *dm*	(Optional) Indicates that the next argument, *dm*, is the destination MAC address. The argument *dm* is a dotted triple of four-digit hexadecimal numbers.
ssap *ss*	(Optional) Indicates that the next argument, *ss*, is the source service access point address. If this is not specified, the default is all source service access point addresses.
smac *sm*	(Optional) Indicates that the next argument, *sm*, is the source MAC address, written as a dotted triple of four-digit hexadecimal numbers. If this is not specified, the default is all source MAC addresses.

Default

No mapping

Command Mode

Global configuration

Usage Guidelines

This command first appeared in Cisco IOS Release 10.0. The keywords **ssap** and **smac** first appeared in Cisco IOS Release 11.0.

Use this command to map LUs to queuing priorities. Once you establish the priority for each LU, you can assign a priority to a TCP port. Hence, you establish a mapping between the LUs and queuing priorities, and queuing priorities and TCP ports.

It is preferable to prioritize NetBIOS traffic below SNA traffic but, by default, NetBIOS traffic is assigned the high priority on TCP port 1996.

Example

In the following example, LU 01 is assigned a medium priority and maps to TCP port 1996; LU 02 has been assigned a normal priority and maps to TCP port 1987; LU 03 has been assigned a low priority and maps to TCP port 1988; LU 04 has been assigned high priority and maps to TCP port 1989.

```
locaddr-priority-list 1 01 medium
locaddr-priority-list 1 02 normal
locaddr-priority-list 1 03 low
locaddr-priority-list 1 04 high

priority-list 1 protocol ip low tcp 1996
priority-list 1 protocol ip high tcp 1987
priority-list 1 protocol ip medium tcp 1988
priority-list 1 protocol ip normal tcp 1989
```

Related Commands

To locate documentation of related commands, you can search online at www.cisco.com.

locaddr-priority
priority-list

priority-group

Use the **priority-group** interface configuration command to assign a specified priority list to an interface. Use the **no** form of this command to disable priority queuing on this interface.

> **priority-group** *list-number*
> **no priority-group** *list-number*

Syntax	Description
list-number	Priority list number assigned to the interface.

Default

No priority list number is established.

Command Mode

Interface configuration

Usage Guidelines

This command first appeared in Cisco IOS Release 10.0.

Example

The following is an example of a priority-group assignment:

```
interface ethernet 0
 ip address 1.0.0.1 255.255.255.0
 priority-group 1
```

Related Commands

To locate documentation of related commands, you can search online at www.cisco.com.

locaddr-priority-list
priority-list

priority-list

Use the **priority-list** global configuration command to establish queuing priorities based upon the protocol type as one of the steps to establishing queuing priorities based on logical unit (LU) addresses. Use the **no** form of this command to remove the priority list. Use this command in conjunction with the **locaddr-priority-list** command.

> **priority-list** *list-number* **protocol** *protocol-name queue-keyword*
> **no priority-list** *list-number address-number queue-keyword*

Syntax	Description
list-number	Arbitrary integer between 1 and 10 that identifies the LU address priority list selected by the user.
protocol	Keyword indicating you want the priority list to be based on a protocol type.
protocol-name	Protocol you are using. In most cases, this will be **ip.**
queue-keyword	Priority queue name; one of **high, medium, normal,** or **low.**

Default

No queuing priorities are established.

Command Mode

Global configuration

Usage Guidelines

This command first appeared in Cisco IOS Release 10.0.

Use this command to assign the priority level defined to TCP segments originating from or destined to a specified TCP port. Assign priorities to the ports as shown in Table 8-2.

Table 8-2   *Common RSRB Services and Their Port Numbers*

Service	Port
RSRB high priority	1996
RSRB medium priority	1987
RSRB normal priority	1988
RSRB low priority	1989

Once you establish the priority for each LU using the **locaddr-priority-list** command, you can assign a priority to a TCP port using the **priority-list** command. By using both commands, you establish a mapping between the LUs and queuing priorities, and between the queuing priorities and TCP ports.

It is preferable to prioritize NetBIOS traffic below SNA traffic but, by default, NetBIOS traffic is assigned the high priority on TCP port 1996.

Example

In the following example, LU 01 has been assigned a medium priority and maps to TCP port 1996; LU 02 has been assigned a normal priority and maps to TCP port 1987; LU 03 has been assigned a low priority and maps to TCP port 1988; LU 04 has been assigned high priority and maps to TCP port 1989.

```
locaddr-priority-list 1 01 medium
locaddr-priority-list 1 02 normal
locaddr-priority-list 1 03 low
locaddr-priority-list 1 04 high

priority-list 1 protocol ip low tcp 1996
priority-list 1 protocol ip high tcp 1987
priority-list 1 protocol ip medium tcp 1988
priority-list 1 protocol ip normal tcp 1989
```

Related Commands

To locate documentation of related commands, you can search online at www.cisco.com.

locaddr-priority
locaddr-priority-list

rsrb remote-peer lsap-output-list

Use the **rsrb remote-peer lsap-output-list** global configuration command to define service access point (SAP) filters by local SAP (LSAP) address on the remote source-route bridging WAN interface.

> **rsrb remote-peer** *ring-group* **tcp** *ip-address* **lsap-output-list** *access-list-number*
> **rsrb remote-peer** *ring-group* **fst** *ip-address* **lsap-output-list** *access-list-number*
> **rsrb remote-peer** *ring-group* **interface** *name* **lsap-output-list** *access-list-number*

Syntax

Syntax	Description
ring-group	Virtual ring number of the remote peer.
tcp	TCP encapsulation.
fst	FST encapsulation.
ip-address	IP address.
interface	Direct encapsulation.
name	Interface name.
access-list-number	Number of the access list.

Default

No filters are assigned.

Command Mode

Global configuration

Usage Guidelines

This command first appeared in Cisco IOS Release 10.0.

Example

The following example specifies SAP filters by LSAP address:

```
rsrb remote-peer 1000 tcp 131.108.2.30 lsap-output-list 201
```

Related Commands

To locate documentation of related commands, you can search online at www.cisco.com.

priority-list
sap-priority
sap-priority-list

rsrb remote-peer netbios-output-list

Use the **rsrb remote-peer netbios-output-list** global configuration command to filter packets by NetBIOS station name on a remote source-route bridging WAN interface.

rsrb remote-peer *ring-group* **tcp** *ip-address* **netbios-output-list** *name*
rsrb remote-peer *ring-group* **fst** *ip-address* **netbios-output-list** *name*
rsrb remote-peer *ring-group* **interface** *type* **netbios-output-list** *host*

Syntax	Description
ring-group	Virtual ring number of the remote peer.
tcp	TCP encapsulation.
fst	FST encapsulation.
ip-address	IP address.
interface	Direct encapsulation.
type	Interface name.
name	Name of a NetBIOS access filter previously defined with one or more **netbios access-list host** global configuration commands.
host	Host name.

Default

No filter is assigned.

Command Mode

Global configuration

Usage Guidelines

This command first appeared in Cisco IOS Release 10.0.

Example

The following example filters packets by NetBIOS station name:

```
rsrb remote-peer 1000 tcp 131.108.2.30 netbios-output-list host engineering
```

Related Commands

To locate documentation of related commands, you can search online at www.cisco.com.

netbios access-list host
priority-list
sap-priority
sap-priority-list

sap-priority

Use the **sap-priority** interface configuration command to define a priority list on an interface.

sap-priority *list-number*

Syntax	Description
list-number	Priority list number you specified in the **sap-priority-list** command.

Default

No priority list is defined.

Command Mode

Interface configuration

Usage Guidelines

This command first appeared in Cisco IOS Release 10.0.

Example

The following example specifies priority list number 1:

```
sap-priority 1
```

Related Commands

To locate documentation of related commands, you can search online at www.cisco.com.

sap-priority-list
source-bridge

sap-priority-list

Use the **sap-priority-list** global configuration command to define a priority list.

> **sap-priority-list** *list-number queue-keyword* [**dsap** *ds*] [**ssap** *ss*] [**dmac** *dm*]
> [**smac** *sm*]

Syntax	Description
list-number	Arbitrary integer between 1 and 10 that identifies the priority list.
queue-keyword	Priority queue name or a remote source-route bridge TCP port name.
dsap	(Optional) Indicates that the next argument, *ds*, represents the destination service access point address. The argument *ds* is a hexadecimal number.
ssap	(Optional) Indicates that the next argument, *ss*, represents the source service access point address. The argument *ss* is a hexadecimal number.
dmac	(Optional) Indicates that the next argument, *dm*, represents the destination MAC address. The argument *dm* is written as a dotted triplet of four-digit hexadecimal numbers.
smac	(Optional) Indicates that the next argument, *sm*, represents the source MAC address. The argument *sm* is written as a dotted triplet of four-digit hexadecimal numbers.

Default

No priority list is defined.

Command Mode

Global configuration

Usage Guidelines

This command first appeared in Cisco IOS Release 10.0.

To give precedence to traffic on a particular LLC2 session, you must specify all four keywords (**dsap**, **ssap**, **dmac**, and **smac**) to uniquely identify the LLC2 session.

Example

The following example defines priority list 1 and specifies SSAP and DSAP addresses:

```
sap-priority-list 1 high dsap 04 ssap 04
```

show local-ack

Use the **show local-ack** privileged EXEC command to display the current state of any current local acknowledgment for both LLC2 and SDLLC connections, as well as for any configured pass through rings.

show local-ack

Syntax Description

This command has no arguments or keywords.

Command Mode

Privileged EXEC

Usage Guidelines

This command first appeared in Cisco IOS Release 10.0.

Sample Display

The following is sample output from the **show local-ack** command:

```
Router# show local-ack

local 1000.5a59.04f9, lsap 04, remote 4000.2222.4444, dsap 04
llc2 = 1798136, local ack state = connected
Passthrough Rings: 4 7
```

Table 8-3 describes significant fields shown in the display.

Table 8-3 *show local-ack Field Descriptions*

Field	Description
local	MAC address of the local Token Ring station with which the route has the LLC2 session.
lsap	Local service access point (LSAP) value of the Token Ring station with which the router has the LLC2 session.
remote	MAC address of the remote Token Ring on whose behalf the router is providing acknowledgments. The remote Token Ring station is separated from the device via the TCP backbone.
dsap	Destination SAP value of the Token Ring station on whose behalf the router is providing acknowledgments.
llc2	Pointer to an internal data structure used by the manufacturer for debugging.
local ack state	State of the local acknowledgment for both LLC2 and SDLC connections. The possible states are as follows: • disconnected—No session between the two end nodes. • connected—Full data transfer possible between the two. • awaiting connect—Cisco IOS software is waiting for the other end to confirm a session establishment with the remote host.
Passthrough Rings	Ring numbers of the virtual rings that have been defined as passthroughs using the **source-bridge passthrough** command. If a ring is not a passthrough, it is locally terminated.

source-bridge connection-timeout

Use the **source-bridge connection-timeout** global configuration command to establish the interval of time between first attempt to open a connection until a timeout is declared. Use the **no** form of this command to disable this feature.

> **source-bridge connection-timeout** *seconds*
> **no source-bridge connection-timeout** *seconds*

Syntax	Description
seconds	Interval of time, in seconds, before a connection attempt to a remote peer is aborted.

Default

The default connection-timeout interval is 10 seconds.

Command Mode

Global configuration

Usage Guidelines

This command first appeared in Cisco IOS Release 10.3.

The **source-bridge connection-timeout** command is used for setting timeout intervals in a complex topology, such as a large multihop WAN with virtual rings or satellite links. The timeout interval is used when a connection to a remote peer is attempted. If the timeout interval expires before a response is received, the connection attempt is aborted.

Example

The following example sets the connection timeout interval to 60 seconds:

```
source-bridge connection-timeout 60
```

Related Commands

To locate documentation of related commands, you can search online at www.cisco.com.

source-bridge ring-group

source-bridge cos-enable

Use the **source-bridge cos-enable** global configuration command to force the Cisco IOS software to read the contents of the format identification (FID) frames to prioritize traffic when using TCP. Use the **no** form of this command to disable prioritizing.

> **source-bridge cos-enable**
> **no source-bridge cos-enable**

Syntax Description

This command has no arguments or keywords.

Default
Enabled

Command Mode
Global configuration

Usage Guidelines
This command first appeared in Cisco IOS Release 10.0.

Use this command to prioritize your SNA traffic across the backbone network. All your important FEP traffic can flow on high-priority queues. This is useful only between FEP-to-FEP (PU4-to-PU4) communications (across the non-SNA backbone).

NOTE   LLC2 local acknowledgment must be turned on for the Class of Service (CoS) feature to take effect and the **source-bridge remote-peer tcp** command with the **priority** keyword must be issued.

Example
The following example enables CoS for prioritization of SNA traffic across a network:

```
source-bridge cos-enable
```

Related Commands
To locate documentation of related commands, you can search online at www.cisco.com.

source-bridge remote-peer tcp

source-bridge fst-peername

Use the **source-bridge fst-peername** global configuration command to set up a Fast-Sequenced Transport (FST) peer name. Use the **no** form of this command to disable the IP address assignment.

> **source-bridge fst-peername** *local-interface-address*
> **no source-bridge fst-peername** *local-interface-address*

Syntax   Description

local-interface-address   IP address to assign to the local router.

Default
Disabled

Command Mode
Global configuration

Usage Guidelines
This command first appeared in Cisco IOS Release 10.0.

This command is the first step to configuring a remote source-route bridge to use FST.

Example
The following example sets up an FST peer name:

```
source-bridge fst-peername 150.136.64.98
```

Related Commands
To locate documentation of related commands, you can search online at www.cisco.com.

source-bridge remote-peer fst

source-bridge keepalive

Use the **source-bridge keepalive** interface configuration command to assign the keepalive interval of the remote source-bridging peer. Use the **no** form of this command to cancel previous assignments.

> **source-bridge keepalive** *seconds*
> **no source-bridge keepalive**

Syntax   Description

seconds   Keepalive interval in seconds. The valid range is 10 to 300.
                             The default value is 30 seconds.

Default
30 seconds

Command Mode

Interface configuration

Usage Guidelines

This command first appeared in Cisco IOS Release 10.0.

Example

The following example sets the keepalive interval to 60 seconds:

```
source-bridge keepalive 60
```

Related Commands

To locate documentation of related commands, you can search online at www.cisco.com.

show interface
source-bridge
source-bridge remote-peer fst
source-bridge remote-peer tcp

source-bridge largest-frame

Use the **source-bridge largest-frame** global configuration command to configure the largest frame size that is used to communicate with any peers in the ring group. Use the **no** form of this command to cancel previous assignments.

> **source-bridge largest-frame** *ring-group size*
> **no source-bridge largest-frame** *ring-group*

Syntax	Description
ring-group	Ring group number. This ring group number must match the number you have specified with the **source-bridge ring-group** command. The valid range is 1 to 4095.
size	Maximum frame size.

Default

No frame size is assigned.

Command Mode
Global configuration

Usage Guidelines
This command first appeared in Cisco IOS Release 10.0.

Cisco IOS software negotiates all transit routes down to the specified size or lower. Use the *size* argument with this command to prevent timeouts in end hosts by reducing the amount of data they have to transmit in a fixed interval. For example, in some networks containing slow links, it would be impossible to transmit an 8 K frame and receive a response within a few seconds. These are fairly standard defaults for an application on a 16-Mb Token Ring. If the frame size is lowered to 516 bytes, then only 516 bytes must be transmitted and a response received in 2 seconds. This feature is most effective in a network with slow links. The legal values for this argument are 516, 1500, 2052, 4472, 8144, 11,407, and 17,800 bytes.

Example
The following example sets the largest frame that can be transmitted through a ring group to 1500 bytes:

```
source-bridge largest-frame 8 1500
```

Related Commands
To locate documentation of related commands, you can search online at www.cisco.com.

source-bridge ring-group

source-bridge passthrough

Use the **source-bridge passthrough** global configuration command to configure some sessions on a few rings to be locally acknowledged and the remaining to passthrough. Use the **no** form of this command to disable passthrough on all the rings and allow the session to be locally acknowledged.

> **source-bridge passthrough** *ring-group*
> **no source-bridge passthrough** *ring-group*

Syntax	Description
ring-group	Ring group number. This ring is either the start ring or destination ring of the two IBM end machines for which the passthrough feature is to be configured. This ring group number must match the number you specified with the **source-bridge ring-group** command. The valid range is 1 to 4095.

Default
Disabled

Command Mode
Global configuration

Usage Guidelines
This command first appeared in Cisco IOS Release 10.0.

Use this command in conjunction with the **source-bridge remote-peer tcp** command that has the **local-ack** keyword specified, which causes every new LLC2 session to be locally terminated. If a machine on the Token Ring attempts to start an LLC2 session to an end host that exists on the *ring-number* specified in the **source-bridge passthrough** command, the session will "pass through" and not use local acknowledgment for LLC2.

If you specify passthrough for a ring, LLC2 sessions will never be locally acknowledged on that ring. This is true even if a remote peer accessing the ring has set the **local-ack** keyword in the **source-bridge remote-peer tcp** command. The **source-bridge passthrough** command overrides any setting in the **source-bridge remote-peer tcp** command.

You can define more than one **source-bridge passthrough** command in a configuration.

Example
The following example configures the router to use local acknowledgment on remote peer at 1.1.1.2 but pass through on rings 9 and 4:

```
source-bridge ring-group 100
source-bridge remote-peer 100 tcp 1.1.1.1
source-bridge remote-peer 100 tcp 1.1.1.2 local-ack
source-bridge passthrough 9
source-bridge passthrough 4
```

Related Commands
To locate documentation of related commands, you can search online at www.cisco.com.

source-bridge remote-peer tcp
source-bridge ring-group

source-bridge remote-peer frame-relay (direct encapsulation)

Use the **source-bridge remote-peer frame-relay** global configuration command when specifying a point-to-point direct encapsulation connection. Use the **no** form of this command to disable previous interface assignments.

> **source-bridge remote-peer** *ring-group* **frame-relay interface** *name*
> [*mac-address*][*dlci-number*] [**If** *size*]
> **no source-bridge remote-peer** *ring-group* **frame-relay interface** *name*

Syntax	Description
ring-group	Ring group number. This ring group number must match the number you specified with the **source-bridge ring-group** command. The valid range is 1 to 4095.
name	Name of the interface over which to send source-route bridged traffic.
mac-address	(Optional) MAC address for the interface on the other side of the virtual ring. This argument is required for nonserial interfaces. You can obtain the value of this MAC address by using the **show interface** command and then scanning the display for the interface specified by *name*.
dlci-number	(Optional) Data-link connection identifier (DLCI) number for Frame Relay encapsulation.
If *size*	(Optional) Maximum-sized frame to be sent to this remote peer. The Cisco IOS software negotiates all transit routes down to this size or lower. This argument is useful in preventing timeouts in end hosts by reducing the amount of data they have to transmit in a fixed interval. The legal values for this argument are 516, 1500, 2052, 4472, 8144, 11,407 and 17,800 bytes.

Default

No point-to-point direct encapsulation connection is specified.

Command Mode

Global configuration

Usage Guidelines

This command first appeared in Cisco IOS Release 11.2.

Use this command to identify the interface over which to send source-route bridged traffic to another router in the ring group. A serial interface does not require that you include a MAC-level address; all other types of interfaces do require MAC addresses.

You must specify one **source-bridge remote-peer** command for each peer router that is part of the virtual ring. You must also specify one **source-bridge remote-peer** command to identify the IP address of the local router.

It is possible to mix all types of transport methods within the same ring group.

NOTE   The two peers using the serial-transport method will only function correctly if there are routers at the end of the serial line that have been configured to use the serial transport. The peers must also belong to the same ring group.

Example

The following example sends source-route bridged traffic over serial interface 0 and Ethernet interface 0:

```
! send source-route bridged traffic over serial 0
source-bridge remote-peer 5 frame-relay interface serial 0
! specify MAC address for source-route bridged traffic on Ethernet 0
source-bridge remote-peer 5 interface Ethernet 0 0000.0c00.1234
```

Related Commands

To locate documentation of related commands, you can search online at www.cisco.com.

show interface
source-bridge
source-bridge remote-peer fst
source-bridge remote-peer tcp

source-bridge remote-peer fst

Use the **source-bridge remote-peer fst** global configuration command to specify a Fast-Sequenced Transport (FST) encapsulation connection. Use the **no** form of this command to disable the previous assignments.

> **source-bridge remote-peer** *ring-group* **fst** *ip-address* **[lf** *size*]
> **no source-bridge remote-peer** *ring-group* **fst** *ip-address*

Syntax	Description
ring-group	Ring group number. This ring group number must match the number you specified with the **source-bridge ring-group** command. The valid range is 1 to 4095.
ip-address	IP address of the remote peer with which the router will communicate.
If *size*	(Optional) Maximum-sized frame to be sent to this remote peer. Cisco IOS software negotiates all transit routes down to this size or lower. Use this argument to prevent timeouts in end hosts by reducing the amount of data they have to transmit in a fixed interval. The legal values for this argument are 516, 1500, 2052, 4472, 8144, 11,407, and 17,800 bytes.

Default

No FST encapsulation connection is specified.

Command Mode

Global configuration

Usage Guidelines

This command first appeared in Cisco IOS Release 10.0.

The two peers using the serial-transport method will only function correctly if there are routers at the end of the serial line that have been configured to use the serial transport. The peers must also belong to the same ring group.

You must specify one **source-bridge remote-peer** command for each peer router that is part of the virtual ring. You must also specify one **source-bridge remote-peer** command to identify the IP address of the local router.

Example

In the following example, the **source-bridge-fst-peername** command specifies an IP address of 150.136.64.98 for the local router. The **source-bridge ring-group** command assigns the device to a ring group. The **source-bridge remote-peer fst** command specifies ring group number 100 for the remote peer at IP address 150.136.64.97.

```
source-bridge fst-peername 150.136.64.98
source-bridge ring-group 100
source-bridge remote-peer 100 fst 150.136.64.97
```

Related Commands

To locate documentation of related commands, you can search online at www.cisco.com.

source-bridge
source-bridge fst-peername
source-bridge remote-peer frame-relay (direct encapsulation)
source-bridge remote-peer tcp

source-bridge remote-peer ftcp

Use the **source-bridge remote-peer ftcp** global configuration command to enable fast switching of Token Ring frames over TCP/IP. Use the **no** form of this command to remove a remote peer from the specified ring group.

> **source-bridge remote-peer** *ring-group* **ftcp** *ip-address* [**lf** *size*] [**tcp-receive-window** *wsize*][**local-ack**]
> **no source-bridge remote-peer** *ring-group* **ftcp** *ip-address*

Syntax	Description
ring-group	Ring-group number. This ring-group number must match the number you have specified with the **source-bridge ring-group** command. The valid range is 1 to 4095.
ip-address	IP address of the remote peer with which the router will communicate.
lf *size*	(Optional) Maximum-sized frame to be sent to this remote peer. Cisco IOS software negotiates all transit routes down to this size or lower.
tcp-receive-window *wsize*	(Optional) The TCP receive window size in bytes. The range is 10,240 to 65,535 bytes. The default window size is 10,240 bytes.
local-ack	(Optional) LLC2 sessions destined for a specific remote peer are locally terminated and acknowledged. Use local acknowledgment for LLC2 sessions going to this remote peer.

Default

No IP address is identified. The default window size is 10,240 bytes.

Command Mode

Global configuration

Usage Guidelines

This command first appeared in Cisco IOS Release 10.3.

Use this argument to prevent timeouts in end hosts by reducing the amount of data they have to transmit in a fixed interval. The default value for this argument is 516 bytes.

If you change the default TCP receive window size on one peer, you must also change the receive window size on the other peer. Both sides of the connection should have the same window size.

If you configure one peer for LLC2 local acknowledgment, you need to configure both peers for LLC2 local acknowledgment. If only one peer is so configured, unpredictable (and undesirable) results will occur.

Two peers using the serial-transport method will only function correctly if there are routers at the end of the serial line that have been configured to use the serial transport. The peers must also belong to the same ring group.

Examples

In the following example, the remote peer with IP address 131.108.2.291 belongs to ring group 5. It also uses LLC2 local acknowledgment and enables prioritization over a TCP network:

```
source-bridge ring-group 5
source-bridge remote-peer 5 ftcp 131.108.2.291 local-ack priority
```

The following example shows how to locally administer and acknowledge LLC2 sessions destined for a specific remote peer:

```
! identify the ring group as 100
source-bridge ring-group 100
! remote peer at IP address 1.1.1.1 does not use local acknowledgment
source-bridge remote-peer 100 ftcp 1.1.1.1
! remote peer at IP address 1.1.1.2 uses local acknowledgment
source-bridge remote-peer 100 ftcp 1.1.1.2 local-ack
!
interface tokenring 0
source-bridge 1 1 100
```

Sessions between a device on Token Ring 0 that must go through remote peer 1.1.1.2 use local acknowledgment for LLC2, but sessions that go through remote peer 1.1.1.1 do not use local acknowledgment (that is, they "pass through").

Related Commands

To locate documentation of related commands, you can search online at www.cisco.com.

source-bridge
source-bridge remote-peer fst
source-bridge remote-peer frame-relay (direct encapsulation)

source-bridge remote-peer tcp

Use the **source-bridge remote-peer tcp** global configuration command to identify the IP address of a peer in the ring group with which to exchange source-bridge traffic using TCP. Use the **no** form of this command to remove a remote peer for the specified ring group.

> **source-bridge remote-peer** *ring-group* **tcp** *ip-address* [**lf** *size*]
> [**tcp-receive-window** *wsize*][**local-ack**] [**priority**]
> **no source-bridge remote-peer** *ring-group* **tcp** *ip-address*

Syntax	Description
ring-group	Ring group number. This ring group number must match the number you specified with the **source-bridge ring-group** command. The valid range is 1 to 4095.
ip-address	IP address of the remote peer with which the router will communicate.
lf *size*	(Optional) Maximum-sized frame to be sent to this remote peer. Cisco IOS software negotiates all transit routes down to this size or lower. Use this argument to prevent timeouts in end hosts by reducing the amount of data they have to transmit in a fixed interval. The valid values for this argument are 516, 1500, 2052, 4472, 8144, 11,407, and 17,800 bytes.
tcp-receive-window *wsize*	(Optional) The TCP receive window size in bytes. The range is 10,240 to 65,535 bytes. The default window size is 10,240 bytes.
local-ack	(Optional) LLC2 sessions destined for a specific remote peer are locally terminated and acknowledged. Use local acknowledgment for LLC2 sessions going to this remote peer.
priority	(Optional) Enables prioritization over a TCP network. You must specify the keyword **local-ack** earlier in the same **source-bridge remote-peer** command. The keyword **priority** is a prerequisite for features such as Systems Network Architecture (SNA) Class of Service (CoS) and SNA LU address prioritization over a TCP network.

Default

No IP address is identified. The default window size is 10,240 bytes.

Command Mode

Global configuration

Usage Guidelines

This command first appeared in Cisco IOS Release 10.0. The **tcp-receive-window** keyword and *wsize* argument first appeared in Cisco IOS Release 11.1.

If you change the default TCP receive window size on one peer, you must also change the receive window size on the other peer. Both sides of the connection should have the same window size.

If you configure one peer for LLC2 local acknowledgment, you need to configure both peers for LLC2 local acknowledgment. If only one peer is so configured, unpredictable results occur.

You must specify one **source-bridge remote-peer** command for each peer router that is part of the virtual ring. You must also specify one **source-bridge remote-peer** command to identify the IP address of the local router.

The two peers using the serial-transport method will only function correctly if there are routers at the end of the serial line that have been configured to use the serial transport. The peers must also belong to the same ring group.

Examples

In the following example, the remote peer with IP address 131.108.2.291 belongs to ring group 5. It also uses LLC2 local acknowledgment, priority, and RSRB protocol version 2.

```
! identify the ring group as 5
source-bridge ring-group 5
! remote peer at IP address 131.108.2.291 belongs to ring group 5, uses
! tcp as the transport, is set up for local acknowledgment, and uses priority
source-bridge remote-peer 5 tcp 131.108.2.291 local-ack priority
```

The following example shows how to locally administer and acknowledge LLC2 sessions destined for a specific remote peer:

```
! identify the ring group as 100
source-bridge ring-group 100
! remote peer at IP address 1.1.1.1 does not use local acknowledgment
source-bridge remote-peer 100 tcp 1.1.1.1
! remote peer at IP address 1.1.1.2 uses local acknowledgment
source-bridge remote-peer 100 tcp 1.1.1.2 local-ack
!
interface tokenring 0
 source-bridge 1 1 100
```

Sessions between a device on Token Ring 0 that must go through remote peer 1.1.1.2 use local acknowledgment for LLC2, but sessions that go through remote peer 1.1.1.1 do not use local acknowledgment (that is, they "pass through").

Related Commands

To locate documentation of related commands, you can search online at www.cisco.com.

source-bridge
source-bridge remote-peer fst
source-bridge remote-peer frame-relay (direct encapsulation)

source-bridge tcp-queue-max

Use the **source-bridge tcp-queue-max** global configuration command to modify the size of the backup queue for remote source-route bridging. This backup queue determines the number of packets that can wait for transmission to a remote ring before packets start being thrown away. Use the **no** form of this command to return to the default value.

> **source-bridge tcp-queue-max** *number*
> **no source-bridge tcp-queue-max**

Syntax

Syntax	Description
number	Number of packets to hold in any single outgoing TCP queue to a remote router. The default is 100 packets.

Default

The default number of packets is 100.

Command Mode

Global configuration

Usage Guidelines

This command first appeared in Cisco IOS Release 10.3.

Example

If, for example, your network experiences temporary bursts of traffic using the default packet queue length, the following command raises the limit from 100 to 150 packets:

```
source-bridge tcp-queue-max 150
```

Configuring Data-Link Switching Plus

This chapter describes how to configure data-link switching plus (DLSw+), Cisco's implementation of the DLSw standard for Systems Network Architecture (SNA) and NetBIOS devices. For a complete description of the DLSw+ commands mentioned in this chapter, refer to Chapter 10, "DLSw+ Configuration Commands." To locate documentation of other commands that appear in this chapter, search online at www.cisco.com.

DLSw+ Configuration Task List

DLSw+ supports local or remote media conversion between LANs and Synchronous Data Link Control (SDLC) or Qualified Logical Link Control (QLLC). For clarity, the configuration task list below describes configuration in a Token Ring environment. The only differences for SDLC and Ethernet are the specific commands needed to configure those media, plus a media-specific command to associate the interface with DLSw+.

To configure DLSw+, complete the tasks in the following sections:

- Define a Source-Bridge Ring Group for DLSw+

- Define a DLSw+ Local Peer for the Router

- Define a DLSw+ Ring List or Port List

- Define a DLSw+ Bridge Group List

- Define DLSw+ Remote Peers

- Enable DLSw+ over Frame Relay

- Enable DLSw+ on a Token Ring or FDDI Interface

- Enable DLSw+ on an Ethernet Interface

- Enable DLSw+ on an SDLC Interface

- Enable DLSw+ over QLLC

- Enable NetBIOS DDR

- Enable NetBIOS DDR

- Tune the DLSw+ Configuration

- Monitor and Maintain the DLSw+ Network

See the end of this chapter for the section "DLSw+ Configuration Examples." Media-specific configuration examples for Ethernet and SDLC are also provided. For details of SDLC commands in the sample SDLC configuration, refer to Chapter 14, "LLC2 and SDLC Commands."

Define a Source-Bridge Ring Group for DLSw+

The source-bridge ring can be shared between DLSw+ and source-route bridging /remote source-route bridging (SRB/RSRB). In DLSw+, the source-bridge ring group specifies the virtual ring that will appear to be the last ring in the routing information field (RIF). Because RIFs are terminated at the router, there is no correlation between the ring-group number specified in DLSw+ peers. The numbers can be the same for management simplicity, but they do not have to be. To define a source-bridge ring group for DLSw+, use the following command in global configuration mode:

Command	Purpose
source-bridge ring-group *ring-group* [*virtual-mac-address*]	Defines a ring group.

Refer to the section "DLSw+ Using TCP Encapsulation and LLC2 Local Acknowledgment—Basic Configuration Example" for a sample configuration file.

Define a DLSw+ Local Peer for the Router

Defining a DLSw+ local peer for a router enables DLSw+. You specify all local DLSw+ parameters as part of the local peer definition. To define a local peer, use the following command in global configuration mode:

Command	Purpose
dlsw local-peer [**peer-id** *ip-address*] [**group** *group*] [**border**] [**cost** *cost*] [**lf** *size*] [**keepalive** *seconds*] [**passive**] [**promiscuous**] [**init-pacing-window** *size*] [**max-pacing-window** *size*][**biu-segment**]	Defines the DLSw+ local peer.

Refer to the section "DLSw+ Using TCP Encapsulation and LLC2 Local Acknowledgment—Basic Configuration Example" for a sample configuration.

Define a DLSw+ Ring List or Port List

DLSw+ ring lists map traffic on a local interface to remote peers. You can create a ring list of local ring numbers and apply the list to remote peer definitions. Traffic received from a remote peer is only forwarded to the rings specified in the ring list. Traffic received from a local interface is only forwarded to peers if the input ring number appears in the ring list applied to the remote peer definition. The definition of a ring list is optional. If you want all peers and all rings to receive all traffic, you do not have to define a ring list. Simply specify 0 for the list number in the remote peer statement.

To define a ring list, use the following command in global configuration mode:

Command	Purpose
dlsw ring-list *list-number* **rings** *ring-number*	Defines a ring list.

DLSw+ port lists map traffic on a local interface (either Token Ring or serial) to remote peers. Port lists do not work with Ethernet interfaces, or any other interface types connected to DLSw+ by means of a bridge group. You can create a port list of local ports and apply the list to remote peer definitions. Traffic received from a remote peer is only forwarded to peers if the input port number appears in the port list applied to the remote peer definition. The port list command provides a single command to specify both serial and Token Ring interfaces. Figure 9-1 shows how port lists are used to map traffic.

Figure 9-1   *Mapping Traffic Using Port Lists*

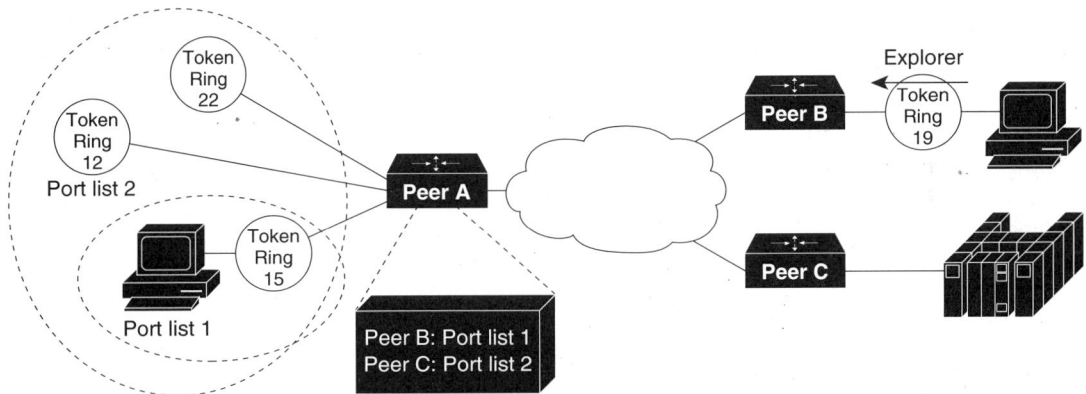

The definition of a port list is optional. If you want all peers and all interfaces to receive all traffic, you do not have to define a port list. Simply specify 0 for the list number in the remote peer statement.

To define a port list, use the following command in global configuration mode:

Command	Purpose
dlsw port-list *list-number type number*	Defines a port list.

NOTE Either the ring list or the port list command can be used to associate rings with a given ring list. The ring list command is easier to type in if you have a large number of rings to define.

Define a DLSw+ Bridge Group List

DLSw+ bridge group lists map traffic on the local Ethernet bridge group interface to remote peers. You can create a bridge group list and apply the list to remote peer definitions. Traffic received from a remote peer is only forwarded to the bridge group specified in the bridge group list. Traffic received from a local interface is only forwarded to peers if the input bridge group number appears in the bridge group list applied to the remote peer definition. The definition of a bridge group list is optional. Because each remote peer has a single list number associated with it, if you want traffic to go to a bridge group and to either a ring list or port list, you should specify the same list number in each definition.

To define a bridge-group list, use the following command in global configuration mode:

Command	Purpose
dlsw bgroup-list *list-number* **bgroups** *number*	Defines a ring list.

Define DLSw+ Remote Peers

You can define three types of encapsulation on a remote peer by performing the tasks in the following sections:

- Configure TCP Encapsulation

- Configure FST Encapsulation

- Configure Direct Encapsulation

The configuration commands for each of the encapsulation methods share some optional parameters that permit support for specific features, such as backup peers. There are some command options for Transmission Control Protocol (TCP) encapsulation support features that are not available with other encapsulation types: SNA dial-on-demand routing (DDR) and configured dynamic peers. The configuration combinations for each of the encapsulation methods and features are described in greater detail following the command tables.

Configure TCP Encapsulation

To configure TCP encapsulation on a remote peer, use the following command in global configuration mode:

Command	Purpose
dlsw remote-peer *list-number* **tcp** *ip-address* [**backup-peer** [*ip-address* | **frame-relay interface serial** *number dlci-number* | **interface** *name*]] [**bytes-netbios-out** *bytes-list-name*] [**cost** *cost*] [**dest-mac** *mac-address*] [**dmac-output-list** *access-list-number*] [**dynamic**] [**host-netbios-out** *host-list-name*] [**keepalive** *seconds*] [**lf** *size*] [**linger** *minutes*] [**lsap-output-list** *list*] [**no-llc** *minutes*] [**priority**] [**tcp-queue-max** *size*] [**timeout** *seconds*]	Defines a TCP encapsulation remote peer.

Table 9-1 is a list of valid port numbers used for TCP connections when the **priority** keyword is used with the **dlsw remote-peer** command:

Table 9-1   *Valid Port Numbers for TCP Connections*

Priority	Port
High	2065
Medium	1981
Normal	1982
Low	1983

Backup Peers

The **backup-peer** option is common to all encapsulation types (direct, FST, and TCP) on a remote peer and specifies that this remote peer is a backup peer for the router with the specified IP-address, Frame Relay data-link connection identifier (DLCI) number, or interface name. When the primary peer fails, all circuits over this peer are disconnected and the user can start a new session via their backup peer. Prior to Cisco IOS Release 11.2(6)F, you could configure backup peers only for primary FST and TCP.

Also, when you specify the **backup-peer** option in a **dlsw remote-peer tcp** command, the backup peer is activated only when the primary peer becomes unreachable. Once the primary peer is reactivated, all new sessions use the primary peer and the backup peer remains active only as long as there are LLC2 connections using it. You can use the **linger** option to specify a period, in minutes, that the backup peer remains connected after the connection to the primary peer is reestablished. When the linger period expires, the backup peer connection is taken down.

NOTE   Because the expiration of the linger period may cause active LLC2 sessions to be terminated, you should not use the **linger** option unless you want active LLC2 sessions over the backup peer to be terminated. If the linger option is not specified, the backup peer will remain active as long as circuits remain. It will not, however, pass explorers and will not create any new circuits while the primary is up.

SNA DDR

In TCP encapsulation, you can use the **keepalive** and **timeout** options to run DLSw+ over a switched line and have the Cisco IOS software take the switched line down dynamically when it is not in use. Utilizing these options gives the IP Routing table more time to converge when a network problem hinders a remote peer connection. In small networks with good IP convergence time and ISDN lines that start quickly, it is not as necessary to use the **keepalive** option. To use this feature, you must set the **keepalive** value to 0, and you may need to use a lower value for the **timeout** option than the default, which is 90 seconds.

Configured Dynamic Peers

In TCP encapsulation, the **dynamic** option and its suboptions **no-llc** and **inactivity** allow you to specify and control the activation of dynamic peers, which are configured peers that are activated only when required. Dynamic peer connections are established only when there is DLSw+ data to send. The dynamic peer connections are taken down when the last LLC2 connection using them terminates and the time period specified in the **no-llc** option expires. You can also use the **inactivity** option to take down dynamic peers when the circuits using them are inactive for a specified number of minutes.

NOTE   Because the **inactivity** option may cause active LLC2 sessions to be terminated, you should not use this option unless you want active LLC2 sessions to be terminated.

The **dest-mac** and **dmac-output-list** options allow you to specify filter lists as part of the **dlsw remote-peer** command to control access to remote peers. For static peers in direct, FST, or TCP encapsulation, these filters control which explorers are sent to remote peers. For dynamic peers in TCP encapsulation, these filters also control the activation of the dynamic peer. For example, you can specify at a branch office that a remote peer is activated only when there is an explorer frame destined for the Media Access Control (MAC) address of an front-end processor (FEP).

The **dest-mac** option permits the connection to be established only when there is an explorer frame destined for the specified MAC address. The **dmac-output-list** option permits the connection to be established only when the explorer frame passes the specified access list. To permit access to a single

MAC address, use the **dest-mac** option because it is a configuration "short-cut" compared to the **dmac-output-list** option.

Refer to the section "DLSw+ Using TCP Encapsulation and LLC2 Local Acknowledgment—Basic Configuration Example" at the end of this chapter for a sample configuration.

Local Acknowledgment

When you have LANs separated by wide geographic distances and you want to avoid multiple retransmissions or loss of user sessions that can occur with time delays, encapsulate the source-route bridged traffic inside IP datagrams passed over a TCP connection between two routers with local acknowledgment enabled.

Logical Link Control, type 2 (LLC2) is an ISO standard data-link level protocol used in Token Ring networks. LLC2 was designed to provide reliable transmission of data across LAN media and to cause minimal or at least predictable time delays. However, RSRB and WAN backbones created LANs that are separated by wide, geographic distances-spanning countries and continents. As a result, LANs have time delays that are longer than LLC2 allows for bidirectional communication between hosts. Local acknowledgment addresses the problem of unpredictable time delays, multiple retransmissions, and loss of user sessions.

In a typical LLC2 session, when one host sends a frame to another host, the sending host expects the receiving host to respond positively or negatively in a predefined period of time, commonly called the *T1 time*. If the sending host does not receive an acknowledgment of the frame it sent within the T1 time, it retries a few times (normally 8 to 10). If there is still no response, the sending host drops the session.

Figure 9-2 illustrates an LLC2 session in which a 37x5 on a LAN segment communicates with a 3x74 on a different LAN segment separated via a wide-area backbone network. Frames are transported between Router A and Router B by means of DLSw+. However, the LLC2 session between the 37x5 and the 3x74 is still end-to-end; that is, every frame generated by the 37x5 traverses the backbone network to the 3x74, and the 3x74, on receipt of the frame, acknowledges it.

Figure 9-2 *LLC2 Session Without Local Acknowledgment*

On backbone networks consisting of slow serial links, the T1 timer on end hosts could expire before the frames reach the remote hosts, causing the end host to retransmit. Retransmission results in duplicate frames reaching the remote host at the same time as the first frame reaches the remote host. Such frame duplication breaks the LLC2 protocol, resulting in the loss of sessions between the two IBM machines.

One way to solve this time delay is to increase the timeout value on the end nodes to account for the maximum transit time between the two end machines. However, in networks consisting of hundreds or even thousands of nodes, every machine would need to be reconfigured with new values. With local acknowledgment for LLC2 enabled, the LLC2 session between the two end nodes would not be not end-to-end, but instead, would terminate at two local routers. Figure 9-3 shows the LLC2 session with the 37x5 ending at Router A and the LLC2 session with the 3x74 ending at Router B. Both Router A and Router B execute the full LLC2 protocol as part of local acknowledgment for LLC2.

Figure 9-3 *LLC2 Session with Local Acknowledgment*

With local acknowledgment for LLC2 enabled in both routers, Router A acknowledges frames received from the 37x5. The 37x5 still operates as if the acknowledgments it receives are from the 3x74. Router A looks like the 3x74 to the 37x5. Similarly, Router B acknowledges frames received from the 3x74. The 3x74 operates as if the acknowledgments it receives are from the 37x5. Router B looks like the 3x74 to 37x5. Because the frames do not have to travel the WAN backbone networks to be acknowledged, but are locally acknowledged by routers, the end machines do not time out, resulting in no loss of sessions.

Enabling local acknowledgment for LLC2 has the following advantages:

- Local acknowledgment for LLC2 solves the T1 timer problem without having to change any configuration on the end nodes. The end nodes are unaware that the sessions are locally acknowledged. In networks consisting of hundreds or even thousands of machines, this is a definite advantage. All the frames acknowledged by Cisco IOS software appear to the end hosts to be coming from the remote IBM machine. In fact, by looking at a trace from a protocol analyzer, one cannot say whether a frame was acknowledged by the local router or by a remote IBM machine. The MAC addresses and the RIFs generated by Cisco IOS software are identical to those generated by the remote IBM machine. The only way to find out whether a session is locally acknowledged is to use either a **show local-ack** command or a **show source-bridge** command on the router.

- All the supervisory (RR, RNR, REJ) frames that are locally acknowledged go no farther than the router. Without local acknowledgment for LLC2, *every* frame traverses the backbone. With local acknowledgment, only data (I-frames) traverse the backbone, resulting in less traffic on the backbone network. For installations in which customers pay for the amount of traffic passing through the backbone, this could be a definite cost-saving measure. A simple protocol exists between the two peers to bring up or down a TCP session.

Notes on Using LLC2 Local Acknowledgment

LLC2 local acknowledgment is enabled with TCP and DLSw+ Lite remote peers.

If the LLC2 session between the local host and the router terminates in either router, the other will be informed to terminate its connection to its local host.

If the TCP queue length of the connection between the two routers reaches the high-water mark, the routers sends Receiver-Not-Ready (RNR) messages to the local hosts until the queue limit is reduced to below this limit. It is possible, however, to prevent the RNR messages from being sent by using the **dlsw llc2 nornr** command.

The configuration of the LLC2 parameters for the local Token Ring interfaces can affect overall performance. Refer to Chapter 13, "Configuring LLC2 and SDLC Parameters" in this manual for more details about fine-tuning your network through the LLC2 parameters.

The routers at each end of the LLC2 session execute the full LLC2 protocol, which could result in some overhead. The decision to use local acknowledgment for LLC2 should be based on the speed of the backbone network in relation to the Token Ring speed. For LAN segments separated by slow-speed serial links (for example, 56 kbps), the T1 timer problem could occur more frequently. In such cases, it might be wise to turn on local acknowledgment for LLC2. For LAN segments separated by a T1, backbone delays will be minimal; in such cases, FST or direct should be considered. Speed mismatch between the LAN segments and the backbone network is one criterion to help you decide to use local acknowledgment for LLC2.

There are some situations (such as the receiving host failing between the time the sending host sends data and the time the receiving host receives it), in which the sending host would determine, at the LLC2 layer, that data was received when it actually was not. This error occurs because the router acknowledges that it received data from the sending host before it determines that the receiving host can actually receive the data. But because both NetBIOS and SNA have error recovery in situations where an end device goes down, these higher-level protocols will resend any missing or lost data. Because these transaction request/confirmation protocols exist above LLC2, they are not affected by tight timers, as is LLC2. They also are transparent to local acknowledgment.

If you are using NetBIOS applications, note that there are two NetBIOS timers—one at the link level and one at the next higher level. Local acknowledgment for LLC2 is designed to solve link timeouts only. If you are experiencing NetBIOS session timeouts, you have two options:

● Experiment with increasing your NetBIOS timers and decreasing your maximum NetBIOS frame size.

● Avoid using NetBIOS applications on slow serial lines.

Configure FST Encapsulation

To configure (FST) encapsulation on a remote peer, use the following command in global configuration mode:

Command	Purpose
dlsw remote-peer *list-number* **fst** *ip-address* [**backup-peer** [*ip-address*	**frame-relay interface serial** *number dlci-number*	**interface** *name*]] [**bytes-netbios-out** *bytes-list-name*] [**cost** *cost*] [**dest-mac** *mac-address*] [**dmac-output-list** *access-list-number*] [**host-netbios-out** *host-list-name*] [**keepalive** *seconds*] [**lf** *size*] [**linger** *minutes*] [**lsap-output-list** *list*]	Defines an FST encapsulation remote peer.

Configure Direct Encapsulation

Direct encapsulation is supported over High-Level Data Link Control (HDLC) and Frame Relay. Direct encapsulation over Frame Relay comes in two forms: DLSw Lite (LLC2 encapsulation) and Passthru. To configure direct encapsulation, use the following commands in global configuration mode.

Step	Command	Purpose
1	**dlsw remote-peer** *list-number* **frame-relay interface serial** *number dlci-number* [**backup-peer** [*ip-address* | **frame-relay interface serial** *number dlci-number* | **interface** *name*]] [**bytes-netbios-out** *bytes-list-name*] [**cost** *cost*] [**dest-mac** *mac-address*] [**dmac-output-list** *access-list-number*] [**host-netbios-out** *host-list-name*] [**keepalive** *seconds*] [**lf** *size*] [**linger** *minutes*] [**lsap-output-list** *list*] **pass-thru**	Defines a direct encapsulation in Frame Relay for the remote peer.
2	**dlsw remote-peer** *list-number* **interface serial** *number* [**backup-peer** [*ip-address* | **frame-relay interface serial** *number dlci-number* | **interface** *name*]] [**bytes-netbios-out** *bytes-list-name*] [**cost** *cost*] [**dest-mac** *mac-address*] [**dmac-output-list** *access-list-number*] [**host-netbios-out** *host-list-name*] [**keepalive** *seconds*] [**lf** *size*] [**linger** *minutes*] [**lsap-output-list** *list*] **pass-thru**	Defines a direct encapsulation in HDLC for the remote peer.

NOTE   To distinguish between DLSw Lite and Passthru, use the **pass-thru** option in the **dlsw remote peer** command.

Enable DLSw+ over Frame Relay

You can configure Cisco IOS software for direct encapsulation of DLSw+ in Frame Relay according to RFC 1490. DLSw+ direct encapsulation over RFC 1490 supports either pass-through or local acknowledgment (data-link control termination). DLSw+ supports transport for both SNA and NetBIOS data. SNA physical unit (PU) 2.0 and PU 2.1 are supported.

The configuration requires a minimum number of Permanent Virtual Circuits (PVCs) (since multiple protocols can share a single PVC). A minimum number of PVCs simplifies configuration because multiple PUs can share a PVC without requiring configuration of multiple service access points (SAPs).

The **pass-thru** option adds the smallest amount of link overhead and requires minimal processing cycles in the attaching routers when compared to TCP/IP encapsulation.

The local acknowledgment option prevents data-link control timeouts during periods of WAN congestion. It also minimizes WAN traffic by keeping data-link control acknowledgments and keepalives off the WAN.

No controller or FEP upgrades are required to take advantage of this feature (if already Token Ring attached), reducing costs and simplifying migration to Frame Relay.

To enable DLSw+ over Frame Relay with passthru, use the following commands, beginning in global configuration mode:

Step	Command	Purpose
1	**interface serial** *number*	Specifies the serial port.
2	**encapsulation frame-relay**	Enables Frame Relay encapsulation.
3	**frame-relay map dlsw** *dlci-number*	Defines the mapping between DLSw+ and the DLCI.
4	**dlsw remote-peer** *list-number* **frame-relay interface serial** *number dlci-number* **pass-thru**	Defines direct encapsulation in Frame Relay.

NOTE	The DLSw+ remote peer statement should specify **pass-thru**.

To enable DLSw+ over Frame Relay with local acknowledgment (also known as DLSw Lite), use the following commands, beginning in global configuration mode:

Step	Command	Purpose
1	**interface serial** *number*	Specifies the serial port.
2	**encapsulation frame-relay**	Enables Frame Relay encapsulation.
3	**frame-relay map llc2** *dlci-number*	Defines the mapping between DLSw+ and the DLCI.
4	**fdlsw remote-peer** *list-number* **frame-relay interface serial** *number dlci-number*	Defines direct encapsulation in Frame Relay.

Enable DLSw+ on a Token Ring or FDDI Interface

To enable DLSw+ on a Token Ring or FDDI interface, use the following command in interface configuration mode:

Command	Purpose
source-bridge *local-ring bridge-number ring-group*	Enables DLSw+ on a Token Ring or FDDI interface.

By default, DLSw+ receives traffic from all defined source-bridge ring-groups in the router. By configuring SRB on the interface, it permits DLSw+ to communicate on that interface.

NOTE   The *ring-group* number specified in the **source-bridge** command must be the number of a defined source-bridge ring-group or DLSw+ will not see this interface.

Enable DLSw+ on an Ethernet Interface

To enable DLSw+ on certain Ethernet interfaces, use the following command in global configuration mode:

Command	Purpose
dlsw bridge-group *group-number*	Enables DLSw+ on an Ethernet interface.
bridge group *bridge group*	Number of the bridge group to which the interface belongs.

In interface mode, the interfaces must also be put into the bridge-group.

NOTE   By default, Cisco IOS software translates Token Ring LLC2 to Ethernet 802.3 LLC2. To configure the router to translate Token Ring LLC2 frames into Ethernet 0x80d5 format frames, refer to the section "Enable Token Ring LLC2-to-Ethernet Conversion" in Chapter 3, "Configuring Source-Route Bridging."

Enable DLSw+ on an SDLC Interface

To establish devices as SDLC stations, use the following commands in interface configuration mode:

Step	Command	Purpose
1	**encapsulation sdlc**	Sets the encapsulation type of the serial interface to SDLC.
2	**sdlc role {none | primary | secondary | prim-xid-poll}**	Establishes the role of the interface.
3	**sdlc vmac** *mac-address*[1]	Configures a MAC address for the serial interface.

Step	Command	Purpose
4	**sdlc address** *hexbyte* [**echo**]	Assigns a set of secondary stations attached to the serial link.
5	**sdlc partner** *mac-address sdlc-address*	Specifies the destination address with which an LLC session is established for the SDLC station.

1. The last byte of the MAC address must be 00.

To enable DLSw+ on an SDLC interface, use the following command in interface configuration mode:

Command	Purpose
sdlc dlsw {*sdlc-address* | **default** | **partner** *mac-address* [**inbound** | **outbound**]}	Enables DLSw+ on an SDLC interface.

Use the **default** option if you have more than 10 SDLC devices to attach to the DLSw+ network. To configure an SDLC multidrop line downstream, you configure the SDLC role as either **primary** or **prim-xid-poll**. SDLC role **primary** specifies that any PU without the **xid-poll** parameter in the **sdlc address** command is a PU 2.0 device. SDLC role **prim-xid-poll** specifies that every PU is type 2.1. We recommend that you specify **sdlc role primary** if all SDLC devices are type PU 2.0 or a mix of PU 2.0 and PU 2.1. Specify **sdlc role prim-xid-poll** if all devices are type PU 2.1

To configure DLSw+ to support LLC2-to-SDLC conversion for PU 4 or PU 5 devices, specify the echo option in the **sdlc address** command. A PU 4-to-PU 4 configuration requires that **none** be specified in the **sdlc role** command.

Refer to the sections "DLSw+ with SDLC Multidrop Support Configuration Examples" and "DLSw+ with LLC2-to-SDLC Conversion Between PU 4-to-PU 4 Communication" for sample configurations.

Enable DLSw+ over QLLC

You can configure DLSw+ for QLLC connectivity, which enables both of the following scenarios:

● Remote LAN-attached devices (PUs) or SDLC-attached devices can access an FEP or an AS/400 over an X.25 network.

Cisco QLLC support allows remote X.25-attached SNA devices to access an FEP without requiring X.25 NCP Packet Switching Interface (NPSI) in the FEP. This may eliminate the requirement for NPSI (if GATE and DATE are not required), thereby eliminating the recurring license cost. In addition, because the QLLC attached devices appear to be Token Ring-attached to the Network Control Program (NCP), they require no preconfiguration in the FEP. Remote X.25-attached SNA devices can also connect to an AS/400 over Token Ring using this support.

● Remote X.25-attached SNA devices can access an FEP or an AS/400 over a Token Ring or over SDLC.

For environments just beginning to migrate to LANs, Cisco QLLC support allows deployment of LANs in remote sites while maintaining access to the FEP over existing NPSI links. Remote LAN-attached devices (PUs) or SDLC-attached devices can access a FEP over an X.25 network without requiring X.25 hardware or software in the LAN-attached devices. Cisco IOS software supports direct attachment to the FEP over X.25 without the need for routers at the data center for SNA traffic.

To enable QLLC connectivity for DLSw+, use the following commands in interface configuration mode:

Step	Command	Purpose
1	**encapsulation x.25**	Specifies an interface as an X.25 device.
2	**x25 address** *subaddress*	Activates X.25 subaddresses.
3	**x25 map qllc** *x121-addr* [*x25-map-options*]	Associates a virtual MAC address with the X.121 address of the remote X.25 device.
4	**qllc dlsw** {**subaddress** *subaddress* | **pvc** *pvc-low* [*pvc-high*]} [**vmac** *vmacaddr* [*poolsize*]] [**partner** *partner-macaddr*] [**sap** *ssap dsap*] [**xid** *xidstring*] [**npsi-poll**]	Enables DLSw+ over QLLC.

Enable NetBIOS DDR

DLSw+ can filter NetBIOS Session Alive packets from the WAN. NetBIOS periodically sends Session Alive packets as LLC2 I-frames. These packets do not require a response and are superfluous to the function of proper data flow. Furthermore, these packets keep dial-on-demand interfaces up and this up time causes unwanted per-packet charges in DDR networks. By filtering these NetBIOS Session Alive packets, you reduce traffic on the WAN, as well as some costs that are associated with DDR.

To enable NetBIOS DDR, use the following command in global configuration mode:

Command	Purpose
dlsw netbios keepalive-filter	Enables NetBIOS DDR.

Tune the DLSw+ Configuration

To modify an existing configuration parameter, perform one or more of the tasks in the following sections:

- Configure DLSw+ Timers

- Configure Maximum Entries in Group Cache

- Configure Peer-on-Demand Defaults

- Configure Promiscuous Peer Defaults

- Configure Static Resources Capabilities Exchange

- Configure Static Paths

- Configure Duplicate Path Handling

- Disable Border Peer Caching

- Disable UDP Unicast

- Enable RIF Passthru

Configure DLSw+ Timers

To configure DLSw+ timers (including group cache entries), use the following command in global configuration mode:

Command	Purpose
dlsw timer {**icannotreach-block-time** | **netbios-cache-timeout** | **netbios-explorer-timeout** | **netbios-group-cache** | **netbios-retry-interval** | **netbios-verify-interval** | **sna-cache-timeout** | **sna-explorer-timeout** | **sna-group-cache** | **sna-retry-interval** | **sna-verify-interval**} *time*	Configures DLSw+ timers.

Configure Maximum Entries in Group Cache

To define the maximum entries in a group cache, use the following command in global configuration mode:

Command	Purpose
dlsw group-cache max-entries *number*	Defines the maximum entries in a group cache.

Configure Peer-on-Demand Defaults

To configure peer-on-demand defaults, use the following command in global configuration mode:

Command	Purpose
dlsw peer-on-demand-defaults [**fst**] [**bytes-netbios-out** *bytes-list-name*] [**cost** *cost*] [**dest-mac** *destination mac-address*] [**dmac-output-list** *access-list-number*] [**host-netbios-out** *host-list-name*] [**inactivity** *minutes*] [**keepalive** *seconds*] [**lf** *size*] [**lsap-output-list** *list*] [**port-list** *port-list-number*] [**priority**] [**tcp-queue-max**]	Configures peer-on-demand defaults.

Configure Promiscuous Peer Defaults

To configure promiscuous peer defaults, use the following command in global configuration mode:

Command	Purpose
dlsw prom-peer-defaults [**bytes-netbios-out** *bytes-list-name*] [**cost** *cost*] [**dest-mac** *destination-mac-address*] [**dmac-output-list** *access-list-number*] [**host-netbios-out** *host-list-name*] [**keepalive** *seconds*] [**lf** *size*] [**lsap-output-list** *list*] [**tcp-queue-max** *size*]	Configures promiscuous peer defaults.

Configure Static Resources Capabilities Exchange

To reduce explorer traffic destined for this peer, the peer can send other peers a list of resources for which it has information (**icanreach**) or does not have information (**icannotreach**). This information is exchanged as part of a capabilities exchange. To configure static resources that will be exchanged as part of a capabilities exchange, use one of the following commands in global configuration mode:

Command	Purpose
dlsw icannotreach saps *sap* [*sap...*]	Configures a resource not locally reachable by the router.
or	or
dlsw icanreach {**mac-exclusive**	**netbios-exclusive**	**mac-address** *mac-addr* [**mask** *mask*]	**netbios-name** *name*	**saps**}	Configures a resource locally reachable by the router.

Configure Static Paths

To configure static paths to minimize explorer traffic originating in this peer, use one of the following commands in global configuration mode:

Command	Purpose
dlsw mac-addr *mac-addr* {**ring** *ring number* | **remote-peer** {**interface serial** *number* | **ip-address** *ip-address*} | **rif** *rif string* | **group** *group*}	Configures the location or path of a static MAC address.
or	or
dlsw netbios-name *netbios-name* {**ring** *ring number* | **remote-peer** {**interface serial** *number* | **ip-address** *ip-address*} | **rif** *rif string* | **group** *group*}	Configures a static NetBIOS name.

Configure Duplicate Path Handling

To configure duplicate path handling, use the following command in global configuration mode:

Command	Purpose
dlsw duplicate-path-bias [load-balance]	Configures duplicate path handling.

Disable Border Peer Caching

To disable the border peer caching feature, use the following command in global configuration mode:

Command	Purpose
dlsw group-cache disable	Disables the border peer caching feature.

Disable UDP Unicast

To disable User Datagram Protocol (UDP) Unicast, use the following command in global configuration mode:

Command	Purpose
dlsw udp-disable	Disables UDP Unicast.

Enable RIF Passthru

By default, DLSw+ terminates the routing information field (RIF) for Token Ring, terminates the LLC for all media types, and forwards data only across a WAN with DLSw+ and TCP/IP headers. The RIF is a field in source-route bridged frames that indicates the SRB path the frame should take when traversing a Token Ring network. In the case of an explorer packet, the RIF is a field in the source-route bridged frame that indicates the SRB path that the SRB explorer has traversed so far. The RIF is limited to seven hop counts by the IBM standards. Because DLSw+ terminates the RIF at the virtual ring, the network's scalability increases because the hop count of the packet starts over and the packet can traverse seven additional hops. Also, RIF termination simplifies network design because ring numbers no longer have to be unique throughout an entire enterprise.

Some environments do not function properly if the RIF is terminated. For that reason, DLSw+ now supports the RIF Passthru feature, in which the entire source-route bridged path appears in the RIF.

The RIF Passthru feature enables two key functions when DLSw+ is used between FEPs (PU 4s). First, RIF Passthru is required to allow multiple active paths between FEPs. Second, RIF Passthru is required to remotely load an NCP (in other words, set initialization mode/request initialization mode support). See the **dlsw remote-peer tcp** command for further usage guidelines.

To enable RIF Passthru, use the following command in global configuration mode:

Command	Purpose
dlsw remote-peer tcp [**rif-passthru** *virtual-ring-number*]	Enables RIF Passthru.

Monitor and Maintain the DLSw+ Network

To monitor and maintain activity on the DLSw+ network, use one or more of the following commands in privileged EXEC mode:

Command	Purpose
clear dlsw circuit	Closes all the DLSw+ circuits.[1]
clear dlsw reachability	Removes all entries from the DLSw+ reachability cache.
clear dlsw statistics	Resets to zero the number of frames that have been processed in the local, remote, and group caches.
show dlsw capabilities interface *type number*	Displays capabilities of a direct-encapsulated remote peer.
show dlsw capabilities ip-address *ip-address*	Displays capabilities of a TCP/FST remote peer.
show dlsw capabilities local	Displays capabilities of the local peer.

Command	Purpose
show dlsw circuits	Displays DLSw+ circuit information.
show dlsw fastcache	Displays the fast cache for FST and direct-encapsulated peers.
show dlsw peers	Displays DLSw+ peer information.
show dlsw reachability	Displays DLSw+ reachability information.
dlsw disable	Disables and reenable DLSw+ without altering the configuration.
show dlsw statistics [border-peers]	Displays the number of frames that have been processed in the local, remote, and group caches.

1. Issuing the **clear dlsw circuits** command will cause the loss of any associated LLC2 sessions.

DLSw+ Configuration Examples

The following sections provide DLSw+ configuration examples:

- DLSw+ Using TCP Encapsulation and LLC2 Local Acknowledgment—Basic Configuration Example

- DLSw+ Using TCP Encapsulation with Local Acknowledgment—Peer Group Configuration Example 1

- DLSw+ Using TCP Encapsulation with Local Acknowledgment—Peer Group Configuration Example 2

- DLSw+ with SDLC Multidrop Support Configuration Examples

- DLSw+ with LLC2-to-SDLC Conversion Between PU 4-to-PU 4 Communication

- DLSw+ Translation Between Ethernet and Token Ring Configuration Example

- DLSw+ Translation Between FDDI and Token Ring Configuration Example

- DLSw+ Translation Between SDLC and Token Ring Media Example

- DLSw+ over Frame Relay Configuration Example

- DLSw+ over QLLC Configuration Examples

- DLSw+ with RIF Passthru Configuration Example

DLSw+ Using TCP Encapsulation and LLC2 Local Acknowledgment—Basic Configuration Example

This sample configuration requires the following tasks, which are described in earlier sections of this document:

● Define a Source-Bridge Ring Group for DLSw+

● Define a DLSw+ Local Peer for the Router

● Define DLSw+ Remote Peers

● Enable DLSw+ on the Appropriate LAN Interface

Figure 9-4 illustrates a DLSw+ configuration with local acknowledgment.

Figure 9-4   *DLSw+ with Local Acknowledgment—Simple Configuration*

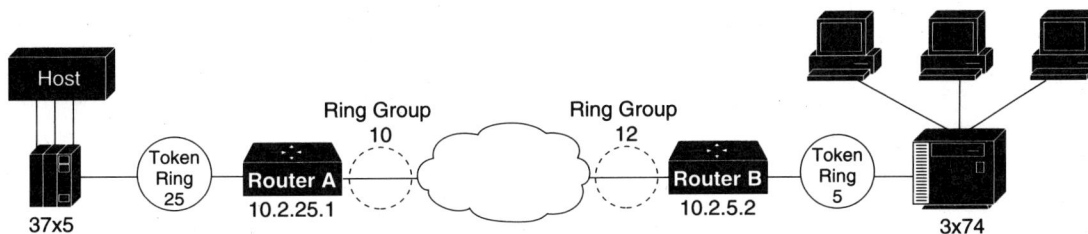

Router A

```
source-bridge ring-group 10
!
dlsw local-peer peer-id 10.2.25.1
dlsw remote-peer 0 tcp 10.2.5.2
 interface loopback 0
 ip address 10.2.25.1 255.255.255.0
 .
 .
 .
interface tokenring 0
 no ip address
 ring-speed 16
 source-bridge active 25 1 10
 source-bridge spanning
```

Router B

```
source-bridge ring-group 12
dlsw local-peer peer-id 10.2.5.2
dlsw remote-peer 0 tcp 10.2.25.1
 interface loopback 0
 ip address 10.2.5.2 255.255.255.0
 .

 .
interface tokenring 0
 no ip address
 ring-speed 16
 source-bridge active 5 1 12
 source-bridge spanning
```

DLSw+ Using TCP Encapsulation with Local Acknowledgment— Peer Group Configuration Example 1

Figure 9-5 illustrates border peers with TCP encapsulation, showing circuits to each other. Router A is configured to operate in promiscuous mode, and border peers Routers B and C forward broadcasts. This configuration reduces processing requirements in Router A (the access router) and still supports any-to-any networks.

Figure 9-5 *DLSw+ with Peer Groups Specified (Example 1)*

Router A

```
hostname RouterA
!
source-bridge ring group 31
dlsw local-peer peer-id 128.207.152.5 group 70 promiscuous
dlsw remote peer 0 tcp 128.207.150.8
!
interface serial 0
 ip unnumbered tokenring
 clockrate 56000
!
interface tokenring 0
 ip address 128.207.152.5 255.255.255.0
 ring-speed 16
 source-bridge 200 13 31
 source-bridge spanning
!
.
.
.
router igrp 777
network 128.207.0.0
```

Router B

```
hostname RouterB
!
.
.
.
source-bridge ring-group 31
dlsw local-peer peer-id 128.207.150.8 group 70 border promiscuous
dlsw remote-peer 0 tcp 128.207.169.3
!
.
.
.
interface serial 0
 ip unnumbered tokenring 0
 bandwidth 56
!
.
.
.
interface tokenring 0
 ip address 128.207.150.8 255.255.255.0
 ring-speed 16
source-bridge 3 14 31
 source-bridge spanning
!
router igrp 777
network 128.207.0.0
```

Router C

```
hostname RouterC
!
.
.
.
source-bridge ring-group 69
dlsw local-peer peer-id 128.207.169.3 group 69 border promiscuous
dlsw remote-peer 0 tcp 128.207.150.8
!
.
.
.
interface tokenring 3/0
description fixed to flashnet
 ip address 128.207.2.152 255.255.255.0
 ring-speed 16
 multiring all
!
interface tokenring 3/1
 ip address 128.207.169.3 255.255.255.0
 ring-speed 16
source-bridge 33 2 69
 source-bridge spanning
!
.
.
.
router igrp 777
network 128.207.0.0
```

DLSw+ Using TCP Encapsulation with Local Acknowledgment—Peer Group Configuration Example 2

Figure 9-6 illustrates a peer group configuration that allows any-to-any connection except for Router B. Router B has no connectivity to anything except router C because the **promiscuous** keyword is omitted.

Figure 9-6 *DLSw+ with Peer Groups Specified (Example 2)*

Router A

```
hostname Router A
!
.
.
.
source-bridge ring-group 2000
dlsw local-peer peer-id 150.150.99.1 group 2 promiscuous
dlsw remote-peer 0 tcp 150.150.100.1
!
interface loopback 0
 ip address 150.150.99.1 255.255.255.192
!
!
.
.
.
interface tokenring 0
 no ip address
 ring-speed 16
```

```
source-bridge 99 1 2000
 source-bridge spanning
!
.
.
.
router eigrp 202
network 150.150.0.0
```

Router B

```
hostname RouterB
!
.
.
.
source-bridge ring-group 2000
dlsw local-peer peer-id 150.150.98.1 group 2
dlsw remote-peer 0 tcp 150.150.100.1
!
interface loopback 0
 ip address 150.150.98.1 255.255.255.192
!
.
.
.
interface serial 1
 no ip address
 encapsulation sdlc
 no keepalive
 clockrate 9600
 sdlc role primary
 sdlc vmac 4000.8888.0100
 sdlc address 01
 sdlc xid 01 05d20006
 sdlc partner 4000.1020.1000 01
 sdlc dlsw 1
!
interface tokenring 0
 no ip address
 ring-speed 16
source-bridge 98 1 2000
 source-bridge spanning
!
.
.
.
router eigrp 202
network 150.150.0.0
```

Router C

```
hostname RouterC
!
.
.
.
source-bridge ring-group 2000
dlsw local-peer peer-id 150.150.100.1 group 2 border promiscuous
dlsw remote-peer 0 tcp 150.150.96.1
!
interface loopback 0
 ip address 150.150.100.1 255.255.255.192
!
.
.
.
!
interface tokenring 0
 no ip address
 ring-speed 16
 source-bridge 500 1 2000
!
router eigrp 202
network 150.150.0.0
```

Router D

```
hostname RouterD
!
.
.
.
source-bridge ring-group 2000
dlsw local-peer peer-id 150.150.96.1 group 1 border promiscuous
dlsw remote-peer 0 tcp 150.150.100.1
!
interface loopback 0
 ip address 150.150.96.1 255.255.255.192
!
.
.
!
.
.
.
interface tokenring 0/0
 no ip address
 ring-speed 16
 source-bridge 96 1 2000
 source-bridge spanning
!
interface tokenring 0/1
 no ip address
```

```
 ring-speed 16
 source-bridge 92 1 2000
 source-bridge spanning
!
.
.
.
router eigrp 202
network 150.150.0.0
```

Router E

```
hostname RouterE
!
.
.
.
source-bridge ring-group 2000
dlsw local-peer peer-id 150.150.97.1 group 1 promiscuous
dlsw remote-peer 0 tcp 150.150.96.1
!
interface loopback 0
 ip address 150.150.97.1 255.255.255.192
!
!
.
.
.
interface tokenring 0
 no ip address
 ring-speed 16
 source-bridge 97 1 2000
 source-bridge spanning
!
.
.
.
router eigrp 202
network 150.150.0.0
```

DLSw+ with SDLC Multidrop Support Configuration Examples

In the following example, all devices are type PU 2.0,

```
interface serial 2
 mtu 4400
 no ip address
 encapsulation sdlc
 no keepalive
 clockrate 19200
 sdlc role primary
 sdlc vmac 4000.1234.5600
 sdlc address C1
```

```
sdlc xid C1 05DCCCC1
sdlc partner 4001.3745.1088 C1
sdlc address C2
sdlc xid C2 05DCCCC2
sdlc partner 4001.3745.1088 C2
sdlc dlsw C1 C2
```

The following example shows mixed PU 2.0 (device using address C1) and PU 2.1
(device using address C2) devices:

```
interface serial 2
 mtu 4400
 no ip address
 encapsulation sdlc
 no keepalive
 clockrate 19200
 sdlc role primary
 sdlc vmac 4000.1234.5600
 sdlc address C1
 sdlc xid C1 05DCCCC1
 sdlc partner 4001.3745.1088 C1
 sdlc address C2 xid-poll
 sdlc partner 4001.3745.1088 C2
 sdlc dlsw C1 C2
```

In the following example, all devices are type PU 2.1 (Method 1):

```
interface serial 2
 mtu 4400
 no ip address
 encapsulation sdlc
 no keepalive
 clockrate 19200
 sdlc role primary
 sdlc vmac 4000.1234.5600
 sdlc address C1 xid-poll
 sdlc partner 4001.3745.1088 C1
 sdlc address C2 xid-poll
 sdlc partner 4001.3745.1088 C2
 sdlc dlsw C1 C2
```

In the following example, all devices are type PU 2.1 (Method 2):

```
interface serial 2
 mtu 4400
 no ip address
 encapsulation sdlc
 no keepalive
 clockrate 19200
 sdlc role prim-xid-poll
 sdlc vmac 4000.1234.5600
 sdlc address C1
 sdlc partner 4001.3745.1088 C1
 sdlc address C2
 sdlc xid C2 05DCCCC2
 sdlc partner 4001.3745.1088 C2
 sdlc dlsw C1 C2
```

DLSw+ with LLC2-to-SDLC Conversion Between PU 4-to-PU 4 Communication

The following example is a sample configuration for LLC2-to-SDLC conversion for PU 4-to-PU 4 communication as shown in Figure 9-7:

Figure 9-7   *LLC2-to-SDLC Conversion for PU 4-to-PU 4 Communication*

Router A

```
interface serial 0
 mtu 4096
 ip address 10.4.21.2 255.255.255.0
 encapsulation frame-relay IETF
 keepalive 12
 frame-relay map llc2  46
 frame-relay map llc2  45
 frame-relay map ip 10.4.21.1 43 broadcast
 frame-relay map ip 10.4.21.3 45 broadcast
 frame-relay map ip 10.4.21.4 46 broadcast
 frame-relay lmi-type ansi

interface TokenRing 0
 mac-address 4000.1250.1001
 no ip address
 ring-speed 16
 fras map llc 4000.1060.1000 4 4 Serial0 frame-relay 45 4 4
```

Router B

```
interface serial 0
 mtu 4096
 ip address 10.4.21.3 255.255.255.0
 encapsulation frame-relay IETF
 keepalive 12
 no fair-queue
 frame-relay map llc2  53
 frame-relay map llc2  54
 frame-relay map llc2  56
 frame-relay map ip 10.4.21.1 53 broadcast
 frame-relay map ip 10.4.21.2 54 broadcast
 frame-relay map ip 10.4.21.4 56 broadcast
 frame-relay lmi-type ansi

interface serial 1
 no ip address
```

```
encapsulation sdlc
no keepalive
clockrate 9600
sdlc address 01 echo
fras map sdlc 1 Serial0 frame-relay 54 4 4 fid4
```

DLSw+ Translation Between Ethernet and Token Ring Configuration Example

DLSw+ also supports Ethernet media. The configuration is similar to other DLSw+ configurations, except for configuring for a specific media. The following example shows Ethernet media (see Figure 9-8).

Figure 9-8   *DLSw+ Translation Between Ethernet and Token Ring*

Router A

```
hostname RouterA
!
.
.
.
source-bridge ring-group 31
dlsw local-peer peer-id 128.207.111.1
dlsw remote-peer 0 tcp 128.207.1.145 lf 1500
 dlsw bridge-group 5
!
interface Ethernet 0
 ip address 128.207.111.1 255.255.255.0
 bridge-group 5
!
.
.
.
bridge 5 protocol ieee
!
.
```

Router B

```
hostname RouterB
!
.
.
.
source-bridge ring-group 500
dlsw local-peer peer-id 128.207.1.145
dlsw remote-peer 0 tcp 128.207.111.1 lf 1500
 dlsw bridge-group 5
.
.
.
interface ethernet 1/2
 ip address 128.207.1.145 255.255.255.0
 bridge-group 5

.

.
interface tokenring 2/0
 no ip address
 ring-speed 16
 source-bridge 7 1 500
 source-bridge spanning
!
.
.
.
bridge 5 protocol ieee
```

DLSw+ Translation Between FDDI and Token Ring Configuration Example

DLSw+ also supports FDDI media. The configuration is similar to other DLSw+ configurations except for configuring for a specific media type. The following example shows FDDI media (see Figure 9-9).

Figure 9-9   *DLSw+ Translation Between FDDI and Token Ring*

In the following configuration, an FDDI ring on Router A is connected to a Token Ring on Router B across a DLSw+ link.

Router A

```
source-bridge ring-group 10
dlsw local-peer peer-id 132.11.11.2
dlsw remote-peer 0 tcp 132.11.11.3
interface fddi 0
 no ip address
s ource-bridge active 26 1 10
 source-bridge spanning
```

Router B

```
source-bridge ring-group 10
dlsw local peer peer-id 132.11.11.3
dlsw remote-peer 0 tcp 132.11.11.2
interface tokenring 0
 no ip address
 source-bridge active 25 1 10
 source-bridge spanning
```

DLSw+ Translation Between SDLC and Token Ring Media Example

DLSw+ provides media conversion between local or remote LANs and SDLC. For additional information about configuring SDLC parameters, refer to Chapter 13, "Configuring LLC2 and SDLC Parameters."

Figure 9-10 illustrates DLSw+ with SDLC encapsulation. In this example, 4000.1020.1000 is the MAC address of the FEP host (PU 4.0). The MAC address of the AS/400 host is 1000.5aed.1f53, which is defined as Node Type 2.1. Router B serves as the primary station for the remote secondary station 01. Router B can serve as either primary station or secondary station to remote station D2.

Figure 9-10 *DLSw+ Translation Between SDLC and Token Ring Media*

Router A

```
hostname RouterA
!
.
.
.
source-bridge ring-group 2000
dlsw local-peer peer-id 150.150.10.2
dlsw remote-peer 0 tcp 150.150.10.1
!
.
.
.
interface serial 8
 ip address 150.150.10.2 255.255.255.192
 clockrate 56000
!
.
.
.
interface tokenring 0
 no ip address
 ring-speed 16
 source-bridge 500 1 2000
 source-bridge spanning
!
.
.
.
```

```
router eigrp 202
 network 150.150.0.0
```

Router B

```
hostname RouterB
!
 .
 .
 .
source-bridge ring-group 2000
dlsw local-peer peer-id 150.150.10.1
dlsw remote-peer 0 tcp 150.150.10.2
!
 .
 .
 .
interface serial 0
 ip address 150.150.10.1 255.255.255.192
!
interface serial 1
 description PU2 with SDLC station role set to secondary
 no ip address
 encapsulation sdlc
 no keepalive
 clockrate 9600
 sdlc role primary
 sdlc vmac 4000.9999.0100
 sdlc address 01
 sdlc xid 01 05d20006
 sdlc partner 4000.1020.1000 01
 sdlc dlsw 1
!
interface serial 2
 description Node Type 2.1 with SDLC station role set to negotiable or primary
 encapsulation sdlc
 sdlc role none
 sdlc vmac 1234.3174.0000
 sdlc address d2
 sdlc partner 1000.5aed.1f53 d2
 sdlc dlsw d2
!
interface tokenring 0
 no ip address
 ring-speed 16
 source-bridge 100 1 2000
 source-bridge spanning
!
interface tokenring 1
 no ip address
 ring-speed 16
 source-bridge 400 1 2000
 source-bridge spanning
!
router eigrp 202
 network 150.150.0.0
```

DLSw+ over Frame Relay Configuration Example

Frame Relay support extends the DLSw+ capabilities to include Frame Relay in direct mode. Frame Relay support includes permanent virtual circuit capability. DLSw+ runs over Frame Relay with or without local acknowledgement. It supports the Token Ring-to-Token Ring connections similar to Fast-Sequenced Transport and other direct data link controls. Figure 9-11 illustrates a DLSw+ configuration over Frame Relay with RIF passthrough.

Figure 9-11   *DLSw+ over Frame Relay*

The following configuration examples are based on Figure 9-11. The Token Rings in the illustration are in Ring 2.

Router A

```
source-bridge ring-group 100
dlsw local-peer
dlsw remote-peer 0 frame-relay interface serial 0 30 passthru
!
interface tokenring 0
 ring-speed 16
 source-bridge active 1 1 100
!
interface serial 0
 mtu 3000
 no ip address
 encapsulation frame-relay
 frame-relay lmi-type ansi
 frame-relay map llc2 30
```

Router B

```
source-bridge ring-group 100
dlsw local-peer
dlsw remote-peer 0 frame-relay interface serial 0 30 passthru
!
interface tokenring 0
 ring-speed 16
 source-bridge active 2 1 100
!
```

```
interface serial 0
 mtu 3000
 no ip address
 encapsulation frame-relay
 frame-relay lmi-type ansi
 frame-relay map llc2 30
```

DLSw+ over QLLC Configuration Examples

The following three examples describe QLLC support for DLSw+.

Example 1

In this configuration, DLSw+ is used to allow remote devices to connect to a DLSw+ network over an X.25 public packet-switched network.

In this example, all QLLC traffic is addressed to destination address 4000.1161.1234, which is the MAC address of the FEP.

The remote X.25-attached IBM 3174 cluster controller is given a virtual MAC address of 1000.0000.0001. This virtual MAC address is mapped to the X.121 address of the 3174 (31104150101) in the X.25 attached router.

```
interface serial 0
 encapsulation x25
 x25 address 3110212011
 x25 map qllc 1000.0000.0001 31104150101
 qllc dlsw partner 4000.1611.1234
```

Example 2

In this configuration, a single IBM 3174 cluster controller needs to communicate with both an AS/400 and a FEP. The FEP is associated with subaddress 150101 and the AS/400 is associated with subaddress 151102.

If an X.25 call comes in for 33204150101, the call is mapped to the FEP and forwarded to MAC address 4000.1161.1234. The IBM 3174 appears to the FEP as a Token Ring-attached resource with MAC address 1000.0000.0001. The IBM 3174 uses a source SAP of 04 when communicating with the FEP, and a source SAP of 08 when communicating with the AS/400.

```
interface serial 0
 encapsulation x25
 x25 address 31102
 x25 map qllc 1000.0000.0001 33204
 qllc dlsw subaddress 150101 partner 4000.1161.1234
 qllc dlsw subaddress 150102 partner 4000.2034.5678 sap 04 08
```

Example 3

In this example, two different X.25 resources want to communicate over X.25 to the same FEP.

In the router attached to the X.25 network, every X.25 connection request for X.121 address 31102150101 is directed to DLSw+. The first SVC to be established will be mapped to virtual MAC address 1000.0000.0001. The second SVC to be established will be mapped to virtual MAC address 1000.0000.0002.

```
interface serial 0
 encapsulation x25
 x25 address 31102
 x25 map qllc 33204
 x25 map qllc 35765
 qllc dlsw subaddress 150101 vmacaddr 1000.0000.0001 2 partner 4000.1611.1234
```

DLSw+ with RIF Passthru Configuration Example

Figure 9-12 is a sample configuration for DLSw+ using the RIF Passthru feature.

Figure 9-12 *Network Configuration with RIF Passthru*

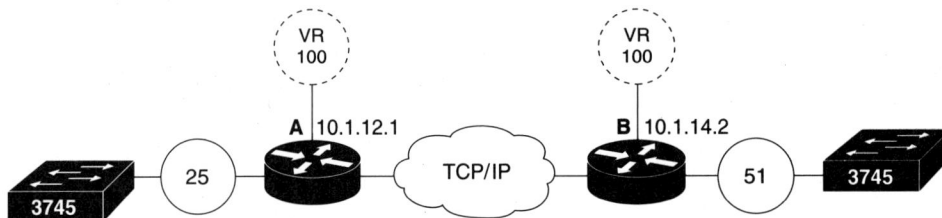

Router A

```
source-bridge ring-group 100
dlsw local-peer peer id 10.1.12.1
dlsw remote-peer 0 tcp 10.1.14.2 rif-passthru 100

interface tokenring 0
  ring-speed 16
  source-bridge 25 1 100
  source-bridge spanning
```

Router B

```
source-bridge ring-group 100
dlsw local-peer peer id 10.1.14.2
dlsw remote-peer 0 tcp 10.1.12.1 rif-passthru 100

interface tokenring 0
  ring-speed 16
  source-bridge 51 1 100
  source-bridge spanning
```

DLSw+ Configuration Commands

This chapter describes the commands to configure data-link switching plus (DLSw+), our implementation of the DLSw standard. For DLSw+ configuration tasks and examples, refer to Chapter 9, "Configuring Data-Link Switching Plus." For specific SDLC commands to configure DLSw+ for SDLC, refer to Chapter 14, "LLC2 and SDLC Commands."

clear dlsw circuit

Use the **clear dlsw circuit** privileged EXEC command to cause all DLSw+ circuits to be closed.

   clear dlsw circuit [*circuit id*]

Syntax	Description
circuit-id	Circuit ID for a specific remote circuit. The valid range is 0 to 4,294,967,295.

Command Mode
Privileged EXEC

Usage Guidelines
This command first appeared in Cisco IOS Release 11.2 F.

A user can specify a circuit ID of a specific circuit to clear rather than clearing all circuits.

CAUTION   This command also drops the associated LLC2 session. The command usage should be used with caution and under the advice of a Cisco engineer.

Example
The following example closes all DLSw+ circuits:

```
clear dlsw circuit
```

clear dlsw reachability

Use the **clear dlsw reachability** privileged EXEC command to remove all entries from the DLSw+ reachability cache.

> **clear dlsw reachability**

Syntax Description

This command has no arguments or keywords.

Command Mode

Privileged EXEC

Usage Guidelines

This command first appeared in Cisco IOS Release 11.2 F.

This command does not affect existing sessions.

Example

The following example removes all entries from the DLSw+ reachability cache:

```
clear dlsw reachability
```

clear dlsw statistics

Use the **clear dlsw statistics** privileged EXEC command to reset to zero the number of frames that have been processed in the local, remote, and group cache.

> **clear dlsw statistics**

Syntax Description

This command has no arguments or keywords.

Command Mode

Privileged EXEC

Usage Guidelines

This command first appeared in Cisco IOS Release 11.2 F.

Example

The following example resets to zero the number of frames in the local, remote, and group cache:

```
clear dlsw statistics
```

dlsw allroute-netbios

Use the **dlsw allroute-netbios** global configuration command to change the single-route explorer to an all-route broadcast for NetBIOS. Use the **no** form of this command to return to the default single-route explorer.

> **dlsw allroute-netbios**
> **no dlsw allroute-netbios**

Syntax Description

This command has no arguments or keywords.

Default

Single-route explorer

Command Mode

Global configuration

Usage Guidelines

This command first appeared in Cisco IOS Release 11.1.

Example

The following example specifies all-route broadcasts for NetBIOS:

```
dlsw allroute-netbios
```

dlsw allroute-sna

Use the **dlsw allroute-sna** global configuration command to change the single-route explorer to an all-route broadcast for SNA. Use the **no** form of this command to return to the default single-route explorer.

> **dlsw allroute-sna**
> **no dlsw allroute-sna**

Syntax Description

This command has no arguments or keywords.

Default

Single-route explorer

Command Mode

Global configuration

Usage Guidelines

This command first appeared in Cisco IOS Release 11.1.

Example

The following example specifies all-route broadcasts for SNA:

```
dlsw allroute-sna
```

dlsw bgroup-list

Use the **dlsw bgroup-list** global configuration command to map traffic on the local Ethernet bridge group interface to remote peers. Use the **no** form of this command to cancel the map.

> **dlsw bgroup-list** *list-number* **bgroups** *number*
> **no dlsw bgroup-list**

Syntax	Description
list-number	The ring list number. This number is subsequently used in the **dlsw remote-peer** command to define the segment to which the bridge-group should be applied. The valid range is 1 to 255.

Syntax

number

Description

The transparent bridge group list number. The valid range is 1 to 63.

Default

There is no default setting.

Command Mode

Global configuration

Usage Guidelines

This command first appeared in Cisco IOS Release 11.0.

Traffic received from a remote peer is forwarded only to the bridge group specified in the bridge group list. Traffic received from a local interface is forwarded to peers if the input bridge group number appears in the bridge group list applied to the remote peer definition. The definition of a bridge group list is optional. Each remote peer has a single list number associated with it; therefore, if you want traffic to go to a bridge group and to either a ring list or port list, you should specify the same list number in each definition.

Example

The following example configures bridge-group list 1:

```
dlsw bgroup-list 1 bgroups 33
```

Related Commands

To locate documentation of related commands, you can search online at www.cisco.com.

dlsw bridge-group
dlsw ring-list

dlsw bridge-group

Use the **dlsw bridge-group** global configuration command to link DLSw+ to the bridge group of the Ethernet LANs. Use the **no** form of this command to disable the link.

> **dlsw bridge-group** *group-number* [**llc2** [**N2** *number*] [**ack-delay-time** *milliseconds*]
> [**ack-max** *number*] [**idle-time** *milliseconds*] [**local-window** *number*]
> [**t1-time** *milliseconds*] [**tbusy-time** *milliseconds*] [**tpf-time** *milliseconds*]
> [**trej-time** *milliseconds*] [**txq-max** *number*] [**xid-neg-val-time** *milliseconds*]
> [**xid-retry-time** *milliseconds*]] [**locaddr-priority** *lu address priority list number*]
> [**sap-priority** *priority list number*]
>
> **no dlsw bridge-group** *group-number* [**llc2** [**N2** *number*] [**ack-delay-time**
> *milliseconds*] [**ack-max** *number*] [**idle-time** *milliseconds*] [**local-window**
> *number*] [**t1-time** *milliseconds*] [**tbusy-time** *milliseconds*] [**tpf-time**
> *milliseconds*] [**trej-time** *milliseconds*] [**txq-max** *number*] [**xid-neg-val-time**
> *milliseconds*] [**xid-retry-time** *milliseconds*]] [**locaddr-priority** *lu address
> priority list number*] [**sap-priority** *priority list number*]

Syntax	Description
group-number	The transparent bridge group to which DLSw+ will be attached. The valid range is 1 to 63.
llc2	(Optional) LLC2 interface subcommands.
N2 *number*	(Optional) Number of times router should retry various operations. The valid range is 1 to 255.
ack-delay-time *milliseconds*	(Optional) Max time the router allows incoming I-frames to stay unacknowledged. The valid range is 1 to 60,000.
ack-max *number*	(Optional) Max number of I-frames received before an acknowledgment must be sent. The valid range is 1 to 255.
idle-time *milliseconds*	(Optional) Frequency of polls during periods of idle traffic. The valid range is 1 to 60,000.
local-window *number*	(Optional) Max number of I-frames to send before waiting for an acknowledgment. The valid range is 1 to 127.
t1-time *milliseconds*	(Optional) How long router waits for an acknowledgment to transmitted I-frames. The valid range is 1 to 60,000.
tbusy-time *milliseconds*	(Optional) Amount of time router waits while the other LLC2 station is in a busy state before attempting to poll the remote station. The valid range is 1 to 60,000.
tpf-time *milliseconds*	(Optional) Amount of time router waits for a final response to a poll frame before resending the original poll frame. The valid range is 1 to 60,000.

Syntax	Description
trej-time *milliseconds*	(Optional) Amount of time router waits for a resend of a rejected frame before sending the reject command. The valid range is 1 to 60,000.
txq-max *number*	(Optional) Queue for holding LLC2 information frames. The valid range is 20 to 200.
xid-neg-val-time *milliseconds*	(Optional) Frequency of exchange identification (XID). The valid range is 1 to 60,000.
xid-retry-time *milliseconds*	(Optional) How long router waits for reply to XID. The valid range is 1 to 60,000.
locaddr-priority *lu address priority list number*	(Optional) Assign an input SNA LU Addr priority list to this bridge group. The valid range is 1 to 10.
sap-priority *priority list number*	(Optional) Assign an input sap priority list to this bridge group. The valid range is 1 to 10.

Part II

Command Reference

Default

There is no default setting.

Command Mode

Global configuration

Usage Guidelines

This command first appeared in Cisco IOS Release 11.0.

More than one bridge group can be attached to DLSw+ by using this command multiple times. Multiple bridge group support is available in Cisco IOS Release 11.3.

Example

The following example links DLSw+ to bridge group 1, 2, and 3:

```
dlsw local-peer peer-id 1.1.1.1
dlsw remote-peer 0 tcp 2.2.2.2
dlsw bridge-group 1
dlsw bridge-group 2
dlsw bridge-group 3
```

```
interface Ethernet0
 bridge-group 1

interface Ethernet1
 bridge-group 2

interface Ethernet2
 bridge-group 3

bridge 1 protocol ieee
bridge 2 protocol ieee
bridge 3 protocol ieee
```

Related Commands

To locate documentation of related commands, you can search online at www.cisco.com.

dlsw bgroup-list

dlsw disable

Use the **dlsw disable** global configuration command to disable DLSw+ without altering the configuration. Use the **no** form of this command to reenable DLSw+.

> **dlsw disable**
> **no dlsw disable**

Syntax Description

This command has no arguments or keywords.

Default

There is no default setting.

Command Mode

Global configuration

Usage Guidelines

This command first appeared in Cisco IOS Release 11.0.

Example

The following example reenables DLSw+:

```
no dlsw disable
```

dlsw duplicate-path-bias

Use the **dlsw duplicate-path-bias** global configuration command to specify how DLSw+ handles duplicate paths to the same Media Access Control (MAC) address or NetBIOS name. Use the **no** form of this command to return to the default (fault-tolerance).

> **dlsw duplicate-path-bias [load-balance]**
> **no dlsw duplicate-path-bias [load-balance]**

Syntax	Description
load-balance	(Optional) Specifies that sessions are load-balanced across duplicate paths.

Default

Fault-tolerance is the default logic used to handle duplicate paths.

Command Mode

Global configuration

Usage Guidelines

This command first appeared in Cisco IOS Release 11.0.

A path is either a remote peer or a local port.

In full-tolerance mode, the preferred path is always used unless it is unavailable. The preferred path is either the path over which the first response to an explorer was received, or, in the case of remote peers, the peer with the least cost.

Example

The following example specifies load balancing to resolve duplicate paths:

```
dlsw duplicate-path-bias load-balance
```

dlsw group-cache disable

Use the **dlsw group cache disable global** configuration command to disable the border peer caching feature. Use the **no** form of this command to return to the default peer caching feature.

> **dlsw group-cache disable**
> **no dlsw group-cache disable**

Syntax Description

This command has no arguments or keywords.

Default

Border peer caching is enabled.

Command Mode

Global configuration

Usage Guidelines

This command first appeared in Cisco IOS Release 11.2 F.

If a border peer becomes a nonborder peer, then the group cache is automatically deleted.

This command prevents a border peer from learning reachability information from relay responses. This command also prevents a border peer from using local or remote caches to make forwarding decisions.

Example

The following example disables the group cache:

```
dlsw group-cache disable
```

Related Commands

To locate documentation of related commands, you can search online at www.cisco.com.

dlsw group-cache max-entries

dlsw group-cache max-entries

Use the **dlsw group-cache max entries** global configuration command to limit the number of entries in the group cache. Use the **no** form of this command to return to the default.

> **dlsw group-cache max-entries** *number*
> **no dlsw group-cache max entries**

Syntax	Description
number	Maximum number of entries allowed in the group cache. The valid range is 0 through 12,000. If the value is set to 0, then there is no limit to the number of entries. The default is 2000.

Default

The default setting is 2000.

Command Mode

Global configuration

Usage Guidelines

This command first appeared in Cisco IOS Release 11.2 F.

Once the number of entries has reached the maximum number specified, if a new entry needs to be added an entry will be removed to make room.

The value set for *number* applies to both the NetBIOS and SNA group cache.

Example

The following configuration defines the maximum number of entries allowed in the NetBIOS or SNA group cache as 1800:

```
dlsw group-cache max-entries 1800
```

Related Commands

To locate documentation of related commands, you can search online at www.cisco.com.

dlsw group-cache disable

dlsw icannotreach saps

Use the **dlsw icannotreach saps** global configuration command to configure a list of service access points (SAPs) not locally reachable by the router. Use the **no** form of this command to remove the list.

> **dlsw icannotreach saps** *sap* [*sap...*]
> **no dlsw icannotreach saps** *sap* [*sap...*]

Syntax	Description
sap [*sap...*]	One or more SAPs.

Default

No lists are configured.

Command Mode

Global configuration

Usage Guidelines

This command first appeared in Cisco IOS Release 10.3

The **dlsw icannotreach saps** command causes the local router to send a control vector to its peers during the capabilities exchange, which tells the peers not to send canureach messages to the local router for sessions using those DSAPs. (They are DSAPs from the peer's perspective and SSAPs from the perspective of the devices attached to the local router.) The effect is that devices attached to the peer will not be able to initiate sessions to devices attached to the local router using the listed DSAPs. Devices attached to the local router, however, will still be able to start sessions with devices on its peers using the listed saps as SSAPs. The reason is that the local router can still send **canureach** requests to its peers, since no filtering is actually done on the local router. The filtering done by the peers does not prohibit the peers from responding to **canureach** requests from the local router sending the control vector, only sending **canureach** requests to the local router.

Example

The following example specifies that NetBIOS traffic will be denied:

```
dlsw icannotreach saps F0
```

dlsw icanreach

Use the **dlsw icanreach** global configuration command to configure a resource that is locally reachable by this router. Use the **no** form of this command to remove the resource.

> **dlsw icanreach** {**mac-exclusive** | **netbios-exclusive** [**remote**] | **mac-address**
> *mac-addr* [**mask** *mask*] | **netbios-name** *name* | **saps**}
> **no dlsw icanreach** {**mac-exclusive** | **netbios-exclusive** [**remote**] | **mac-address**
> *mac-addr* [**mask** *mask*] | **netbios-name** *name* | **saps**}

Syntax	Description
mac-exclusive	Router can reach only the MAC addresses that are user configured.
netbios-exclusive	Router can reach only the NetBIOS names that are user configured.
remote	Gives the NetBIOS workstations (that are local to the router and that are not already defined in the **dlsw icanreach netbios-name** *name* statement) access to remote servers.
mac-address *mac-addr*	Configures a MAC address that this router can locally reach.

Syntax	Description
mask *mask*	(Optional) MAC address mask in hexadecimal *h.h.h.* The "f" value represents the "don't care" bit and the "0" value represents the "care" bit. The mask indicates which bits in the MAC address are relevant.
netbios-name *name*	Configures a NetBIOS name that this router can locally reach. Wildcards (*) are allowed at the end of the name. Trailing white spaces are ignored when comparing against an actual name in a NetBIOS frame.
saps	(Optional) Array of SAPs.

Default

No resources are configured.

Command Mode

Global configuration

Usage Guidelines

This command first appeared in Cisco IOS Release 11.0.

This command can be entered at any time. It causes a capabilities exchange to relay the information to all active peers. By specifying resource names or MAC addresses in this command, you can avoid broadcasts from remote peers that are looking for this resource. By specifying "exclusive," you can avoid broadcasts to this router or any resources. For example, you could configure the front-end processor (FEP) MAC address or corporate site LAN servers in central site routers to avoid any broadcasts over the WAN for these resources.

Configuring the **remote** keword allows roving workstations to access remote servers. With the **remote** keyword specified, all local NetBIOS stations will be able to make outgoing connections regardless of whether their own NetBIOS name is configured in the **icanreach netbios-name** list. Incoming connections will be limited to those with a destination name that is specified in the list.

In the default case (where the remote keyword is not specified), a local NetBIOS station that is not configured in the **icanreach netbios-name** list will not be able to make a connection in this router over DLSw+, whether incoming or outgoing.

NOTE	Because the configuration of the **mac-address** and **netbios-name** keywords prevents the DLSw+ peer from exploring, a misconfiguration could prevent DLSw+ from being able to find a resource actually available elsewhere in the network.

Example

The following example indicates that this peer only has information about a single NetBIOS server, and that no peers should send this peer explorers searching for other NetBIOS names. Because the **remote** option is also configured, NetBIOS workstations that are connected to the NetBIOS server lanserv will be able to establish a DLSw+ connection:

```
dlsw icanreach netbios-exclusive
dlsw icanreach netbios-name lanserv
```

Related Commands

To locate documentation of related commands, you can search online at www.cisco.com.

show dlsw capabilities

dlsw llc2 nornr

Use the **dlsw llc2 nornr** global configuration command to prevent the Receiver-Not-Ready (RNR) message from being sent while establishing an LLC2 connection. Use the **no** form of this command to return to the default.

> **dlsw llc2 nornr**
> **no dlsw llc2 nornr**

Default

The command is disabled by default.

Command Mode

Global configuration

Usage Guidelines

This command first appeared in Cisco IOS Release 11.0.

This command is used when any device does not handle the LLC2 RNR frames.

Examples

The following example keeps the receiver not ready message from being sent when establishing an LLC2 connection:

```
dlsw llc2 nornr
```

The following is output from a Sniffer trace showing when it would be appropriate to use the **dlsw llc2 nornr** command because the RNR message is being rejected from the FEP when the router is trying to establish an LLC2 connection:

```
SUMMARY  Delta T    From 400020401003             From 400023491026
8     0.173                                  LLC C D=00 S=04 TEST P
9     0.003    LLC R D=04 S=00 TEST F
10    0.002                                  SNA XID Fmt 2 T4
11    0.059    SNA XID Fmt 2 T4
12    0.004                                  SNA XID Fmt 2 T4
13    0.065    SNA XID Fmt 2 T4
14    0.005                                  SNA XID Fmt 2 T4
16    0.054    LLC C D=04 S=04 SABME P
17    0.003                                  LLC R D=04 S=04 UA
```

The router sends a receiver not ready message.

```
18    0.001    LLC C D=04 S=04 RNR NR=0
```

From frames 19 to 35, the FEP does not respond.

```
19    0.002    LLC C D=04 S=04 RR NR=0
20    0.048    SNA  C NC  NC-ER-OP
21    0.997    LLC C D=04 S=04 RR NR=0 P
22    1.000    LLC C D=04 S=04 RR NR=0 P
24    1.000    LLC C D=04 S=04 RR NR=0 P
25    1.000    LLC C D=04 S=04 RR NR=0 P
31    1.000    LLC C D=04 S=04 RR NR=0 P
32    1.000    LLC C D=04 S=04 RR NR=0 P
34    1.000    LLC C D=04 S=04 RR NR=0 P
35    1.000    LLC C D=04 S=04 RR NR=0 P
```

The router disconnects the circuit.

```
37    1.000    LLC C D=04 S=04 DISC P
38    0.002                                  LLC R D=04 S=04 UA F
```

The sequence repeats.

```
39    0.179                                  LLC C D=00 S=04 TEST P
41    0.767    SNA XID Fmt 2 T4
42    0.634    SNA XID Fmt 2 T4
43    0.173                                  LLC C D=00 S=04 TEST
44    0.003    LLC R D=04 S=00 TEST F
45    0.002                                  SNA XID Fmt 2 T4
46    0.060    SNA XID Fmt 2 T4
47    0.004                                  SNA XID Fmt 2 T4
48    0.063    SNA XID Fmt 2 T4
49    0.005                                  SNA XID Fmt 2 T4
```

dlsw local-peer

Use the **dlsw local-peer** global configuration command to define the parameters of the DLSw+ local peer. Use the **no** form of this command to cancel the definitions.

dlsw local-peer [**peer-id** *ip-address*] [**group** *group*] [**border**] [**cost** *cost*]
[**lf** *size*] [**keepalive** *seconds*] [**passive**] [**promiscuous**] [**biu-segment**]
[**init-pacing-window** *size*] [**max-pacing-window** *size*]
no dlsw local-peer [**peer-id** *ip-address*] [**group** *group*] [**border**] [**cost** *cost*]
[**lf** *size*] [**keepalive** *seconds*] [**passive**] [**promiscuous**] [**biu-segment**]
[**init-pacing-window** *size*] [**max-pacing-window** *size*]

Syntax	Description
peer-id *ip-address*	(Optional) Local peer IP address; required for Fast-Sequenced Transport (FST) and TCP.
group *group*	(Optional) Peer group number for this router. The valid range is 1 to 255.
border	(Optional) Enables as a border peer. Group option must be specified in order to use the border peer option.
cost *cost*	(Optional) Peer cost advertised to remote peers in the capabilities exchange. The valid range is 1 to 5.
lf *size*	(Optional) Largest frame size for this local peer. Valid sizes are the following: 516-516 byte maximum frame size 1470-1470 byte maximum frame size 1500-1500 byte maximum frame size 2052-2052 byte maximum frame size 4472-4472 byte maximum frame size 8144-8144 byte maximum frame size 11,407-11,407 byte maximum frame size 11,454-11,454 byte maximum frame size 17,800-17,800 byte maximum frame size
keepalive *seconds*	(Optional) Default remote peer keepalive interval in seconds. The valid range is 0 to 1200 seconds. The default is 30 seconds. The value 0 means no keepalives.
passive	(Optional) Specifies that this router will not initiate remote peer connections to configured peers.
promiscuous	(Optional) Accepts connections from nonconfigured remote peers.

Syntax	Description
biu-segment	(Optional) Causes DLSw+ to spoof the maximum receivable I-frame size in XID so that each end station sends the largest frame it can.
init-pacing-window *size*	(Optional) Size of the initial pacing window, as defined in RFC 1795. The valid range is 1 to 2000.
max-pacing-window *size*	(Optional) Maximum size of the pacing window, as defined in RFC 1795. The valid range is 1 to 2000.

Default

No parameters are defined.

Command Mode

Global configuration

Usage Guidelines

This command first appeared in Cisco IOS Release 10.3.

When there are multiple peers to a given destination, use the **cost** keyword to determine which router is preferred and which is capable. The **cost** keyword only applies in fault tolerance mode.

The **biu-segment** option is a performance/utilization improvement. If a frame that arrives from a remote peer is too large for the destination station to handle, DLSw+ segments the frame. If you choose to implement this option, you must add the option to both DLSw peer partners.

Example

The following command defines the local peer IP address and specifies the peer group number for this router:

```
dlsw local-peer peer-id 10.2.17.1 group 2
```

Related Commands

To locate documentation of related commands, you can search online at www.cisco.com.

dlsw duplicate-path-bias
show dlsw capabilities

dlsw mac-addr

Use the **dlsw mac-addr** global configuration command to configure a static MAC address. Use the **no** form of this command to cancel the configuration.

> **dlsw mac-addr** *mac-addr* {**ring** *ring -number*| **remote-peer** {**interface serial** *number* | **ip-address** *ip-address*}| **rif** *rif-string* | **group** *group*}
>
> **no dlsw mac-addr** *mac-addr* {**ring** *ring -number*| **remote-peer** {**interface serial** *number* | **ip-address** *ip-address*}| **rif** *rif-string* | **group** *group*}

Syntax	Description
mac-addr	Specifies the MAC address.
ring *ring-number*	Maps the MAC address to a ring number or ring group number. The valid range is 1 to 4095.
remote-peer	Maps the MAC address to a specific remote peer.
interface serial *number*	Specifies the remote peer by direct serial interface.
ip-address *ip-address*	Specifies the remote peer by IP address.
rif *rif-string*	Maps the MAC address to a local interface using a RIF string. The RIF string describes a source-routed path from the router to the MAC address. It starts at the router's ring-group and ends on the ring where the MAC address is located. The direction should be from the router toward the MAC address. See IEEE 802.5 standard for details.
group *group*	Maps the MAC address to a specified peer group. Valid numbers are in the range 1 to 255.

Default

No static MAC address is configured.

Command Mode

Global configuration

Usage Guidelines

This command first appeared in Cisco IOS Release 11.0.

You can statically define resources to prevent Cisco IOS software from sending explorer frames for the specified resource. For example, you can include the MAC address of a FEP in the configuration for each remote router to eliminate any broadcasts that are searching for a FEP. Alternatively, you can specify a single **dlsw icanreach** statement in the router attached to the FEP indicating the MAC address of the FEP. This information is sent to all remote routers as part of the capabilities exchange.

NOTE	Because the configuration of this command prevents the DLSw+ peer from exploring, a misconfiguration could prevent DLSw+ from being able to find a resource actually available elsewhere in the network.

Example

The following example maps the static MAC address 1000.5A12.3456 to the remote peer at IP address 10.17.3.2:

```
dlsw mac-addr 1000.5A12.3456 remote-peer ip-address 10.17.3.2
```

Related Commands

To locate documentation of related commands, you can search online at www.cisco.com.

show dlsw reachability

dlsw max-multiple-rifs

Use the **dlsw max-multiple-rifs global** configuration command to enable caching of multiple RIFs per interface. Use the **no** form of this command to turn off the feature.

> **dlsw max-multiple-rifs** *multiple-rifs-per-port*
> **no dlsw max-multiple-rifs** *multiple-rifs-per-port*

Syntax / Description

Syntax	Description
multiple-rifs-per-port	Number of multiple RIF entries per interface. The valid range is 1 to 4.

Default

The default value is 1.

Command Mode

Global configuration

Usage Guidelines

This command first appeared in Cisco IOS Release 11.3.

A MAC address or NetBIOS name can have several RIF entries. Prior to this command, DLSw+ could cache only one of these RIF entries per local Token Ring port. With the **dlsw max-multiple-rifs** command configured, however, DLSw+ can cache multiple RIF entries (up to four) for a specific MAC address or NetBIOS name on one Token Ring port.

If the value 1 is specified, multiple RIF caching is not enabled.

Example

The following example enables the router to cache up to 2 RIFs per interface:

```
dlsw max-multiple-rifs 2
```

dlsw netbios-keepalive-filter

Use the **dlsw netbios-keepalive-filter global** configuration command to enable the NetBIOS dial-on-demand routing (DDR) feature. Use the **no** form of this command to turn off the feature.

> **dlsw netbios-keepalive-filter**
> **no dlsw netbios-keepalive-filter**

Syntax Description

This command has no arguments or keywords.

Default

Disabled

Command Mode

Global configuration

Usage Guidelines

This command first appeared in 11.2 F.

Refer to the Introduction, "Bridging and IBM Networking Overview" for more details on the NetBIOS DDR feature.

Example

The following example enables NetBIOS DDR:

```
dlsw netbios-keepalive-filter
```

dlsw netbios-name

Use the **dlsw netbios-name** global configuration command to configure a static NetBIOS name. Use the **no** form of this command to cancel the configuration.

> **dlsw netbios-name** *netbios-name* {**ring** *ring-number* | **remote-peer**
> {**interface serial** *number* | **ip-address** *ip-address*}| **rif** *rif-string* | **group** *group*}
> **no dlsw netbios-name** *netbios-name* {**ring** *ring-number* | **remote-peer**
> {**interface serial** *number* | **ip-address** *ip-address*}| **rif** *rif-string* | **group** *group*}

Part
II

Command Reference

Syntax	Description
netbios-name	Specifies the NetBIOS name. Wildcards are allowed.
ring *ring number*	Maps the NetBIOS name to a ring number or ring group number. Test frames for this name will only be sent to LAN ports in this ring group.
remote-peer	Maps the NetBIOS name to a specific remote peer.
interface serial *number*	Specifies the remote peer by direct interface.
ip-address *ip-address*	Specifies the remote peer by IP address.
rif *rif- string*	Maps the MAC address to a local interface using a RIF string. The RIF string describes a source-routed path from the router to the MAC address. It starts at the router's ring-group and ends on the ring where the MAC address is located. The direction should be from the router towards the MAC address. See IEEE 802.5 standard for details.
group *group*	Maps the NetBIOS name to a specified peer group. Valid numbers are in the range 1 to 255.

Default

No static NetBIOS name is configured.

Command Mode

Global configuration

Usage Guidelines

This command first appeared in Cisco IOS Release 11.0.

NOTE   Because the configuration of this command prevents the DLSw+ peer from exploring, a misconfiguration could prevent DLSw+ from being able to find a resource actually available elsewhere in the network.

Example

The following example configures a static NetBIOS name and links it to group 3:

```
dlsw netbios-name netname group 3
```

Related Commands

To locate documentation of related commands, you can search online at www.cisco.com.

show dlsw reachability

dlsw peer-on-demand-defaults

Use the **dlsw peer-on-demand-defaults** global configuration command to configure defaults for peer-on-demand transport. Use the **no** form of this command to disable the previous assignment.

> **dlsw peer-on-demand-defaults** [**fst**] [**bytes-netbios-out** *bytes-list-name*] [**cost** *cost*]
> [**dest-mac** *destination-mac-address*] [**dmac-output-list** *access-list-number*]
> [**host-netbios-out** *host-list-name*] [**inactivity** *minutes*] [**keepalive** *seconds*]
> [**lf** size] [**lsap-output-list** *list*] [**port-list** *port-list-number*] [**priority**]
> [**tcp-queue-max**]
> **no dlsw peer-on-demand-defaults** [**fst**] [**bytes-netbios-out** *bytes-list-name*]
> [**cost** *cost*] [**dest-mac** *destination-mac-address*] [**dmac-output-list**
> *access-list-number*] [**host-netbios-out** *host-list-name*] [**inactivity** *minutes*]
> [**keepalive** *seconds*] [**lf** size] [**lsap-output-list** *list*] [**port-list** *port-list-number*]
> [**priority**] [**tcp-queue-max**]

Syntax	Description
fst	(Optional) Use FST encapsulation for all peers-on-demand being established by this router.

Syntax	Description
bytes-netbios-out *bytes-list-name*	(Optional) Configures NetBIOS bytes output filtering for peer-on-demand peers. The *bytes-list-name* is the name of the previously defined netbios bytes access list filter.
cost *cost*	(Optional) Specifies the cost to reach peer-on-demand peers. The valid range is 1 to 5. The default cost is 3.
dest-mac *destination-mac-address*	(Optional) Specifies the exclusive destination MAC address for peer-on-demand peers.
dmac-output-list *access-list-number*	(Optional) Specifies the filter output destination MAC addresses.
host-netbios-out *host-list-name*	(Optional) Configures NetBIOS host output filtering for peer-on-demand peers. The *host-list-name* is the name of the previously defined NetBIOS host access list filter.
inactivity *minutes*	(Optional) Configures the length of time after the peer's circuit count is zero that the peer-on-demand is disconnected. The valid range is 0 to 1440 seconds. The default is 10 minutes.
keepalive *seconds*	(Optional) Configures the peer-on-demand keepalive interval. The valid range is 0 to 1200 seconds. The default is 30 seconds.
lf *size*	(Optional) Largest frame size for this remote peer. Valid maximum frame sizes are the following: 516-516 bytes 1470-1470 bytes 1500-1500 bytes 2052-2052 bytes 4472-4472 bytes 8144-8144 bytes 11,407-11,407 bytes 11,454-11,454 bytes 17,800-17,800 bytes
lsap-output-list *list*	(Optional) Configures local service access point (LSAP) output filtering for peer-on-demand peers. Valid numbers are in the range 200 to 299.
port-list *port-list-number*	(Optional) Configures a port list for peer-on-demand peers. Valid numbers are in the range 0 to 4095.
priority	(Optional) Configures prioritization for peer-on-demand peers. The default state is off.

Syntax	Description
tcp-queue-max	(Optional) Configures the maximum output TCP queue size for peer-on-demand peers.

Default

The default peer-on-demand transport is TCP.

Command Mode

Global configuration

Usage Guidelines

This command first appeared in Cisco IOS Release 11.0.

A peer-on-demand peer is a non-configured remote-peer that was connected because of an LLC2 session established through a Border Peer DLSw+ network.

Example

The following example configures FST for peer-on-demand transport:

```
dlsw peer-on-demand-defaults fst
```

Related Commands

To locate documentation of related commands, you can search online at www.cisco.com.

show dlsw peers

dlsw port-list

Use the **dlsw port-list** global configuration command to map traffic on a local interface (Token Ring or serial) to remote peers. Use the **no** form of this command to disable the previous map assignment.

> **dlsw port-list** *list-number type number*
> **no dlsw port-list** *list-number type number*

Syntax	Description
list-number	Port list number. The valid range is 1 to 255.
type	Interface type.
number	Interface number.

Default
No port list is configured.

Command Mode
Global configuration

Usage Guidelines
This command first appeared in Cisco IOS Release 11.0.

Traffic received from a remote peer is forwarded only to the ports specified in the port list. Traffic received from a local interface is forwarded to peers if the input port number appears in the port list applied to the remote peer definition. The definition of a port list is optional.

Example
The following example configures a DLSw peer port list for Token Ring interface 1:

```
dlsw port-list 3 token ring 1
```

Related Commands
To locate documentation of related commands, you can search online at www.cisco.com.

dlsw bgroup-list
dlsw ring-list

dlsw prom-peer-defaults

Use the **dlsw prom-peer-defaults** global configuration command to configure defaults for promiscuous transport. Use the **no** form of this command to disable the previous assignment.

> **dlsw prom-peer-defaults** [**fst**] [**bytes-netbios-out** *bytes-list-name*] [**cost** *cost*]
> [**dest-mac** *destination-mac-address*] [**dmac-output-list** *access-list-number*]
> [**host-netbios-out** *host-list-name*] [**keepalive** *seconds*] [**lf** *size*]
> [**lsap-output-list** *list*] [**tcp-queue-max** *size*]

Part II

Command Reference

no dlsw prom-peer-defaults [**fst**] [**bytes-netbios-out** *bytes-list-name*] [**cost** *cost*]
[**dest-mac** *destination-mac-address*] [**dmac-output-list** *access-list-number*]
[**host-netbios-out** *host-list-name*] [**keepalive** *seconds*] [**lf** *size*]
[**lsap-output-list** *list*] [**tcp-queue-max** *size*]

Syntax	Description
bytes-netbios-out *bytes-list-name*	(Optional) Configures NetBIOS bytes output filtering for promiscuous peers. The *bytes-list-name* is the name of the previously defined NetBIOS bytes access list filter.
cost *cost*	(Optional) Specifies the cost to reach promiscuous peers. The valid range is 1 to 5. The default cost is 3.
dest-mac *destination-mac-address*	(Optional) Specifies the exclusive destination MAC address for promiscuous peers.
dmac-output-list *access-list-number*	(Optional) Specifies the filter output destination MAC addresses.
fst	(Optional) Uses FST encapsulation for all prom peers being established by this router.
host-netbios-out *host-list-name*	(Optional) Configures NetBIOS host output filtering for promiscuous peers. The *host-list-name* is the name of the previously defined NetBIOS host access list filter.
keepalive *seconds*	(Optional) Configures the promiscuous keepalive interval. The valid range is 0 to 1200 seconds. The default is 30 seconds.
lf *size*	(Optional) Largest frame size for this promiscuous peer. Valid maximum frame sizes are the following: 516-516 bytes 1470-1470 bytes 1500-1500 bytes 2052-2052 bytes 4472-4472 bytes 81,44-81,44 bytes 11,407-11,407 bytes 11,454-11,454 bytes 17,800-17,800 bytes
lsap-output-list *list*	(Optional) Configures LSAP output filtering for promiscuous peers. Valid numbers are in the range 200 to 299.
tcp-queue-max *size*	(Optional) Configures the maximum output TCP queue size for promiscuous peers.

Default

The default prom-peer transport is TCP.

Command Mode

Global configuration

Usage Guidelines

This command first appeared in Cisco IOS Release 11.0.

A prom-peer is a peer not configured as a remote-peer on this DLSw+ device, but which initiated a peer connection that was accepted because promiscuous peering was enabled.

Example

The following example configures cost for promiscuous peers:

```
dlsw prom-peer-defaults cost 4
```

Related Commands

To locate documentation of related commands, you can search online at www.cisco.com.

show dlsw capabilities

dlsw remote-peer frame-relay

Use the **dlsw remote-peer frame-relay** global configuration command to specify the remote peer with which the router will connect. Use the **no** form of this command to disable the previous assignments.

> **dlsw remote-peer** *list-number* **frame-relay interface serial** *number dlci-number*
> **[backup-peer** [*ip-address* | **frame-relay interface serial** *number dlci-number* |
> **interface** *name*]] **[bytes-netbios-out** *bytes-list-name*] **[cost** *cost*]
> **[dest-mac** *mac-address*] **[dmac-output-list** *access-list-number*]
> **[host-netbios-out** *host-list-name*] **[keepalive** *seconds*] **[lf** *size*] **[linger** *minutes*]
> **[lsap-output-list** *list*] **[passive] pass-thru**
> **no dlsw remote-peer** *list-number* **frame-relay interface serial** *number dlci-number*
> **[backup-peer** [*ip-address* | **frame-relay interface serial** *number dlci-number* |
> **interface** *name*]] **[bytes-netbios-out** *bytes-list-name*] **[cost** *cost*]
> **[dest-mac** *mac-address*] **[dmac-output-list** *access-list-number*]
> **[host-netbios-out** *host-list-name*] **[keepalive** *seconds*] **[lf** *size*] **[linger** *minutes*]
> **[lsap-output-list** *list*] **[passive] pass-thru**

Part
II

Command Reference

Syntax	Description
list-number	Ring list number. The valid range is 1 to 255. The default is 0, which means DLSw+ forwards explorers over all ports or bridge groups on which DLSw+ is enabled.
interface serial *number*	Serial interface number of the remote peer with which the router is to communicate.
dlci-number	DLCI number of the remote peer.
backup-peer *ip-address*	(Optional) IP address of the existing TCP/FST peer for which this peer is the backup peer.
backup-peer frame-relay interface serial *number* *dlci-number*	(Optional) Serial interface and DLCI number of the existing Direct /LLC2 frame-relay peer for which this peer is the backup peer.
backup-peer interface *name*	(Optional) Interface name of the existing direct peer for which this peer is the backup peer.
bytes-netbios-out *bytes-list-name*	(Optional) Configures NetBIOS bytes output filtering for this peer. The *bytes-list-name* argument is the name of the previously defined NetBIOS bytes access list filter.
cost *cost*	(Optional) Cost to reach this remote peer. The valid range is 1 to 5.
dest-mac *mac-address*	(Optional) Permits the connection to be established only when there is an explorer frame destined for the specified 48-bit MAC address written in dotted triplet form.
dmac-output-list *access-list-number*	(Optional) Permits the connection to be established only when the explorer frame passes the specified access list. The *access-list-number* is the list number specified in the **access-list** command.
host-netbios-out *host-list-name*	(Optional) Configures NetBIOS host output filtering for this peer. The *host-list-name* is the name of the previously defined NetBIOS host access list filter.
keepalive *seconds*	(Optional) Sets the keepalive interval for this remote peer. The range is 0 to 1200 seconds.
lf *size*	(Optional) Largest frame size, in bytes, this local peer will use on a circuit to avoid segmented frames. Valid sizes are 516, 1470, 1500, 2052, 4472, 8144, 11,407, 11,454, and 17,800 bytes.

Syntax

linger *minutes*	(Optional) Configures length of time the backup peer remains connected after the primary peer connection is reestablished. The valid range is 1 to 300 minutes. The default is 5 minutes.
lsap-output-list *list*	(Optional) Filters output IEEE 802.5 encapsulated packets. Valid access list numbers are in the range 200 to 299.
passive	(Optional) Designates this remote peer as passive.
pass-thru	Selects pass through mode. The default is local acknowledgment mode.

Description

Part
II

Command Reference

Default

No remote peers are specified.

Command Mode

Global configuration

Usage Guidelines

This command first appeared in Cisco IOS Release 11.0. The following keywords and arguments first appeared in Cisco IOS Release 11.2: **dest-mac** *mac-address*, **dmac-output-list** *access-list-number*, and **linger** *minutes*.

The **cost** keyword specified in a remote peer statement takes precedence over the cost learned as part of the capabilities exchange with the remote peer. The **cost** keyword is relevant only in fault tolerance mode.

When you need to permit access to only a single MAC address, the **dest-mac** option is a shortcut over the **dmac-output-list** option.

When **pass-thru** is not specified, traffic will be locally acknowledged and reliably transported in LLC2 across the WAN.

Examples

The following example specifies a DLSw+ Lite peer as a backup to a primary direct peer:

```
dlsw remote-peer 0 frame-relay interface serial 1 40 pass-thru
dlsw remote-peer 0 frame-relay interface serial 0 30 backup-peer frame-relay interface
serial 1 40
```

The following example specifies Frame Relay encapsulation connection for remote peer transport:

```
dlsw remote-peer 0 frame-relay interface 0 30
```

Related Commands
To locate documentation of related commands, you can search online at www.cisco.com.

show dlsw peers

dlsw remote-peer fst

Use the **dlsw remote-peer fst** global configuration command to specify an FST encapsulation connection for remote peer transport. Use the **no** form of this command to disable the previous FST assignments.

> **dlsw remote-peer** *list-number* **fst** *ip-address* [**backup-peer** [*ip-address* | **frame-relay**
> **interface serial** *number dlci-number* | **interface** *name*]]
> [**bytes-netbios-out** *bytes-list-name*] [*cost cost*] [**dest-mac** *mac-address*]
> [**dmac-output-list** *access-list-number*] [**host-netbios-out** *host-list-name*]
> [**keepalive** *seconds*] [**lf** *size*] [**linger** *minutes*] [**lsap-output-list** *list*] [**passive**]
> **no dlsw remote-peer** *list-number* **fst** *ip-address* [**backup-peer** [*ip-address* |
> **frame-relay interface serial** *number dlci-number* | **interface** *name*]]
> [**bytes-netbios-out** *bytes-list-name*] [**cost** *cost*] [**dest-mac** *mac-address*]
> [**dmac-output-list** *access-list-number*] [**host-netbios-out** *host-list-name*]
> [**keepalive** *seconds*] [**lf** *size*] [**linger** *minutes*] [**lsap-output-list** *list*] [**passive**]

Syntax	Description
list-number	Ring list number. The valid range is 1 to 255. The default is 0, which means DLSw+ forwards explorers over all ports or bridge groups on which DLSw+ is enabled.
ip-address	IP address of the remote peer with which the router is to communicate.
backup-peer *ip-address*	(Optional) IP address of the existing TCP/FST peer for which this peer is the backup peer.
backup-peer frame-relay-interface serial *number dlci-number*	(Optional) Serial interface and DLCI number of the existing Direct /LLC2 frame-relay peer for which this peer is the backup peer.
backup-peer interface *name*	(Optional) Interface name of the existing direct peer for which this peer is the backup peer.

Syntax	Description
bytes-netbios-out *bytes-list-name*	(Optional) Configures NetBIOS bytes output filtering for this peer. The *bytes-list-name* argument is the name of the previously defined NetBIOS bytes access list filter.
cost *cost*	(Optional) Cost to reach this remote peer. The valid range is 1 to 5.
dest-mac *mac-address*	(Optional) Permits the connection to be established only when there is an explorer frame destined for the specified 48-bit MAC address written in dotted triplet form.
dmac-output-list *access-list-number*	(Optional) Permits the connection to be established only when the explorer frame passes the specified access list. The *access-list-number* is the list number specified in the **access-list** command.
host-netbios-out *host-list-name*	(Optional) Configures NetBIOS host output filtering for this peer. The *host-list-name* is the name of the previously defined NetBIOS host access list filter.
keepalive *seconds*	(Optional) Sets the keepalive interval for this remote peer. The range is 0 to 1200 seconds.
lf *size*	(Optional) Largest frame size this local peer will use on a circuit to avoid segmented frames. Valid sizes are 516, 1470, 1500, 2052, 4472, 8144, 11,407, 11,454, and 17,800 bytes.
linger *minutes*	(Optional) Configures length of time the backup peer remains connected after the primary peer connection is reestablished. The valid range is 1 to 300 minutes. The default is 5 minutes.
lsap-output-list *list*	(Optional) Filters output IEEE 802.5 encapsulated packets. Valid access list numbers are in the range 200 to 299.
passive	(Optional) Designates this remote peer as passive.

Default

No FST encapsulation connection is specified.

Command Mode

Global configuration

Usage Guidelines

This command first appeared in Cisco IOS Release 10.3. The following keywords and arguments first appeared in Cisco IOS Release 11.2: **dest-mac** *mac-address*, **dmac-output-list** *access-list-number*, and **linger** *minutes*.

The **cost** keyword specified in a remote peer statement takes precedence over the cost learned as part of the capabilities exchange with the remote peer. The **cost** keyword is relevant only in fault tolerance mode.

When you need to permit access to a single MAC address, the **dest-mac** option is a shortcut over the **dmac-output-list** option.

Examples

The following example specifies an FST peer as backup to a primary TCP peer:

```
dlsw remote-peer 0 tcp 10.2.18.1
dlsw remote-peer 1 fst 10.2.17.8 backup-peer 10.2.18.1
```

The following example specifies an FST encapsulation connection for remote peer transport:

```
dlsw remote-peer 1 fst 10.2.17.8
```

Related Commands

To locate documentation of related commands, you can search online at www.cisco.com.

show dlsw peers

dlsw remote-peer interface

Use the **dlsw remote-peer interface** global configuration command when specifying a point-to-point direct encapsulation connection. Use the **no** form of this command to disable previous interface assignments.

> **dlsw remote-peer** *list-number* **interface serial** *number* [**backup-peer** [*ip-address* |
> **frame-relay interface serial** *number dlci-number* | **interface** *name*]]
> [**bytes-netbios-out** *bytes-list-name*] [**cost** *cost*] [**dest-mac** *mac-address*]
> [**dmac-output-list** *access-list-number*] [**host-netbios-out** *host-list-name*]
> [**keepalive** *seconds*] [**lf** *size*] [**linger** *minutes*] [**lsap-output-list** *list*] [**passive**]
> [**pass-thru**]

no dlsw remote-peer *list-number* **interface serial** *number* [**backup-peer** [*ip-address* |
frame-relay interface serial *number dlci-number* | **interface** *name*]]
[**bytes-netbios-out** *bytes-list-name*] [**cost** *cost*] [**dest-mac** *mac-address*]
[**dmac-output-list** *access-list-number*] [**host-netbios-out** *host-list-name*]
[**keepalive** *seconds*] [**lf** *size*] [**linger** *minutes*] [**lsap-output-list** *list*] [**passive**]
[**pass-thru**]

Syntax

Description

list-number

Ring list number. The valid range is 1 to 255. The default is 0, which means all.

serial *number*

Specifies the remote peer by direct serial interface.

backup-peer *ip-address*

(Optional) IP address of the existing TCP/FST peer for which this peer is the backup peer.

backup-peer frame-relay interface serial *number dlci-number*

(Optional) Serial interface and DLCI number of the existing Direct /LLC2 frame-relay peer for which this peer is the backup peer.

backup-peer interface *name*

(Optional) Interface name of the existing direct peer for which this peer is the backup peer.

bytes-netbios-out *bytes-list-name*

(Optional) Configures NetBIOS bytes output filtering for this peer. The *bytes-list-name* argument is the name of the previously defined NetBIOS bytes access list filter.

cost *cost*

(Optional) Cost to reach this remote peer. The valid range is 1 to 5.

dest-mac *mac-address*

(Optional) Permits the connection to be established only when there is an explorer frame destined for the specified 48-bit MAC address written in dotted triplet form.

dmac-output-list *access-list-number*

(Optional) Permits the connection to be established only when the explorer frame passes the specified access list. The *access-list-number* is the list number specified in the **access-list** command.

host-netbios-out *host-list-name*

(Optional) Configures NetBIOS host output filtering for this peer. The *host-list-name* is the name of the previously defined NetBIOS host access list filter.

keepalive *seconds*

(Optional) Sets the keepalive interval for this remote peer. The range is 0 to 1200 seconds.

Syntax	Description
lf *size*	(Optional) Largest frame size, in bytes, this local peer will use on a circuit to avoid segmented frames. Valid sizes are 516, 1470, 1500, 2052, 4472, 8144, 11,407, 11,454, and 17,800 bytes.
linger *minutes*	(Optional) Configures length of time the backup peer remains connected after the primary peer connection is reestablished. The valid range is 1 to 300 minutes. The default is 5 minutes.
lsap-output-list *list*	(Optional) Filters output IEEE 802.5 encapsulated packets. Valid access list numbers are in the range 200 to 299.
passive	(Optional) Designates this remote peer as passive.
pass-thru	(Optional) Selects passthrough mode. The default is local acknowledgment mode.

Default

No point-to-point direct encapsulation connection is specified.

Command Mode

Global configuration

Usage Guidelines

This command first appeared in Cisco IOS Release 10.3. The following keywords and arguments first appeared in Cisco IOS Release 11.2: **dest-mac** *mac-address*, **dmac-output-list** *access-list-number*, and **linger** *minutes*.

The **cost** keyword specified in a remote peer statement takes precedence over the cost learned as part of the capabilities exchange with the remote peer. The **cost** keyword is relevant only in fault tolerance mode.

When you need to permit access to a single MAC address only, the **dest-mac** option is a shortcut over the **dmac-output-list** option.

Examples

The following example specifies a point-to-point direct peer backup to a primary direct peer:

```
dlsw remote-peer 0 interface serial 1 pass-thru
dlsw remote-peer 1 interface serial 2 pass-thru backup-peer interface serial 1
```

The following example specifies a point-to-point direct encapsulation connection for remote peer transport:

```
dlsw remote-peer 1 interface serial 2 pass-thru
```

Related Commands
To locate documentation of related commands, you can search online at www.cisco.com.

show dlsw peers

dlsw remote-peer tcp

Use the **dlsw remote-peer tcp** global configuration command to identify the IP address of a peer with which to exchange traffic using TCP. Use the **no** form of this command to remove a remote peer.

> **dlsw remote-peer** *list-number* **tcp** *ip-address* [**backup-peer** [*ip-address* | **frame-relay interface serial** *number dlci-number* | **interface** *name*]] [**bytes-netbios-out** *bytes-list-name*] [**cost** *cost*] [**dest-mac** *mac-address*] [**dmac-output-list** *access-list-number*] [**dynamic**] [**host-netbios-out** *host-list-name*] [**inactivity** *minutes*] [**dynamic**] [**keepalive** *seconds*] [**lf** *size*] [**linger** *minutes*] [**lsap-output-list** *list*] [**no-llc** *minutes*] [**passive**] [**priority**] [**rif-passthru** *virtual-ring-number*] [**tcp-queue-max** *size*] [**timeout** *seconds*]
>
> **no dlsw remote-peer** *list-number* **tcp** *ip-address* [**backup-peer** [*ip-address* | **frame-relay interface serial** *number dlci-number* | **interface** *name*]] [**bytes-netbios-out** *bytes-list-name*] [**cost** *cost*] [**dest-mac** *mac-address*] [**dmac-output-list** *access-list-number*] [**dynamic**] [**host-netbios-out** *host-list-name*] [**inactivity** *minutes*] [**dynamic**] [**keepalive** *seconds*] [**lf** *size*] [**linger** *minutes*] [**lsap-output-list** *list*] [**no-llc** *minutes*] [**passive**] [**priority**] [**rif-passthru** *virtual-ring-number*] [**tcp-queue-max** *size*] [**timeout** *seconds*]

Syntax	Description
list-number	Remote peer ring group list number. This ring group list number default is 0. Otherwise, this value must match the number you specify with the **dlsw ring-list**, **dlsw port-list** or **dlsw bgroup-list** command.
tcp *ip-address*	IP address of the remote peer with which the router is to communicate.
backup-peer *ip-address*	(Optional) IP address of the existing TCP/FST peer for which this peer is the backup peer.

Syntax	Description
backup-peer frame-relay interface serial *number dlci-number*	(Optional) Serial interface and DLCI number of the existing Direct /LLC2 frame-relay peer for which this peer is the backup peer.
backup-peer interface *name*	(Optional) Interface name of the existing direct peer for which this peer is the backup peer.
bytes-netbios-out *bytes-list-name*	(Optional) Configures NetBIOS bytes output filtering for this peer. The *bytes-list-name* argument is the name of the previously defined NetBIOS bytes access list filter.
cost *cost*	(Optional) The cost to reach this remote peer. The valid range is 1 to 5.
dest-mac *mac-address*	(Optional) Permits the TCP connection to be established only when there is an explorer frame destined for the specified 48-bit MAC address written in dotted triplet form.
dmac-output-list *access-list-number*	(Optional) Permits the TCP connection to be established only when the explorer frame passes the specified access list. The *access-list-number* is the list number specified in an **access-list** command.
dynamic	(Optional) Permits the TCP connection to be established only when there is DLSw+ data to send.
host-netbios-out *host-list-name*	(Optional) Configures NetBIOS host output filtering for this peer. The *host-list-name* is the name of the previously defined NetBIOS host access list filter.
inactivity *minutes*	(Optional) Configures the length of time a connection can be idle before closing the dynamic remote peer connection. The valid range is 1 to 300 minutes. The default is 5 minutes.
keepalive *seconds*	Sets the keepalive interval for this remote peer. The range is 0 to 1200 seconds.
lf *size*	(Optional) Largest frame size, in bytes, this local peer will use on a circuit to avoid segmented frames. Valid sizes are 516, 1470, 1500, 2052, 4472, 8144, 11,407, 11,454, and 17,800 bytes.
linger *minutes*	(Optional) Configures length of time the backup peer remains connected after the primary peer connection is reestablished. The valid range is 1 to 300 minutes. The default is 5 minutes.
lsap-output-list *list*	(Optional) Filters output IEEE 802.5 encapsulated packets. Valid access list numbers are in the range 200 to 299.

Syntax	Description
no-llc *minutes*	(Optional) Configures the length of time a remote peer remains connected after all LLC2 connections are gone. The valid range is 1 to 300 minutes. The default is 5 minutes.
passive	(Optional) Designates this remote peer as passive.
priority	(Optional) Enables prioritization features for this remote peer. Valid TCP port numbers are the following: • High: 2065 • Medium: 1981 • Normal: 1982 • Low: 1983
rif-passthru *virtual-ring-number*	(Optional) Configures the remote peer as RIF-passthru. The *virtual-ring-number* value is the same number as the *ring number* value assigned in the **source-bridge ring-group** commands of the DLSw+ Passthru peers.
tcp-queue-max *size*	(Optional) Maximum output TCP queue size for this remote peer. The valid maximum TCP queue size is a number in the range 10 to 2000.
timeout *seconds*	(Optional) Configures the retransmit time limit for TCP. The valid range is 5 to 1200 seconds. The default is 90 seconds.

Defaults

No peer IP address is identified.

The **linger** option is inactive. If the **linger** option is added with no minutes specified, the default is 5 minutes.

The **dynamic** option is not on by default. If the **dynamic** option is added without either the **inactivity** or **no-llc** argument specified, the default is to terminate the TCP connection to the remote peer after 5 minutes of no active LLC2 connection.

Command Mode

Global configuration

Part II

Command Reference

Usage Guidelines

This command first appeared in Cisco IOS Release 10.3. The following keywords and arguments first appeared in Cisco IOS Release 11.1: **dynamic**, **inactivity** *minutes*, **linger** *minutes*, **no-llc** *minutes,* and **timeout** *seconds*. The following keywords and arguments first appeared in Cisco IOS Release 11.2: **dest-mac** *mac-address*, **dmac-output-list** *access-list-number*, **linger** *minutes*.

SNA DDR technology allows switched links to be closed during idle periods. To enable this feature, set the **keepalive** option to 0 and configure the **timeout** option. When the **dynamic** option is configured, the **keepalive** option is automatically set to 0.

To enhance DDR cost-savings, you can configure the TCP connection to a remote peer to be dynamically established (that is, established only when there is DLSw data to send). You can further configure the TCP connection to terminate after a specified period of idle time on the peer or after a specified period of no active LLC sessions on the peer.

You cannot use both **no-llc** and **inactivity** in a command specifying a dynamic peer.

When you need to permit access to a single MAC address, the **dest-mac** option is a shortcut over the **dmac-output-list** option.

Use the **linger** option to specify that a backup peer will remain connected for a specified period of time after the primary connection is gone.

When the **priority** option on the **dlsw remote-peer** command is configured, DLSw+ automatically activates four TCP ports to that remote peer (ports 2065, 1981, 1982 and 1983) and assigns traffic to specific ports. Furthermore, if APPN is running with DLSw+ and you specify the **priority** option on the **dlsw remote-peer** command, then the SNA ToS will map APPN Class of Service (CoS) to TCP TOS and will preserve the APPN CoS characteristics throughout the network.

The **rif passthru** option works only on Token Ring LANs via SRB. Other LAN types, such as SDLC and QLLC, are not supported. The RIF Passthru feature is supported with TCP encapsulation and it disables local acknowledgment.

The following features are not supported with the DLSw+ RIF Passthru feature:

- Border peers
- Peer-on-demand peers
- Dynamic peers
- Backup peers

Examples

The following example specifies a TCP encapsulation connection for remote peer transport:

```
dlsw remote-peer 0 tcp 10.2.17.8
```

The following example specifies a TCP peer as backup to a primary FST peer:

```
dlsw remote-peer 0 fst 10.2.18.9
dlsw remote-peer 0 tcp 10.2.17.8 backup-peer 10.2.18.9
```

Related Commands

To locate documentation of related commands, you can search online at www.cisco.com.

show dlsw peers

dlsw ring-list

Use the **dlsw ring-list** to configure a ring list, mapping traffic on a local interface to remote peers. Use the **no** form of this command to cancel the definition.

> **dlsw ring-list** *list-number* **rings** *ring-number*
> **no dlsw ring-list** *list-number* **rings** *ring-number*

Syntax	Description
list-number	Ring list number. The valid range is 1 to 255.
rings	Specifies one or more physical or virtual rings.
ring-number	Physical or virtual ring number. The valid range is 1 to 4095.

Default

There is no default setting.

Command Mode

Global configuration

Usage Guidelines

This command first appeared in Cisco IOS Release 11.0.

Traffic received from a remote peer is forwarded only to the rings specified in the ring list. Traffic received from a local interface is forwarded to peers if the input ring number appears in the ring list applied to the remote peer definition. The definition of a ring list is optional.

Example

The following example configures a DLSw ring list, assigning rings 1, 2, and 3 to ring list 3:

```
dlsw ring-list 3 rings 1 2 3
```

Related Commands

To locate documentation of related commands, you can search online at www.cisco.com.

dlsw port-list
dlsw remote-peer frame-relay
show dlsw capabilities

dlsw timer

Use the **dlsw timer** global configuration command to tune an existing configuration parameter. Use the **no** form of this command to restore the default parameters.

> **dlsw timer** {**icannotreach-block-time** | **netbios-cache-timeout** | **netbios-explorer-timeout** | **netbios-group-cache** | **netbios-retry-interval** | **netbios-verify-interval** | **sna-cache-timeout** | **explorer-delay-time** | **sna-explorer-timeout** | **explorer-wait-time** | **sna-group-cache** | **sna-retry-interval** | **sna-verify-interval**} *time*
>
> **no dlsw timer** {**icannotreach-block-time** | **netbios-cache-timeout** | **netbios-explorer-timeout** | **netbios-group-cache** | **netbios-retry-interval** | **netbios-verify-interval** | **sna-cache-timeout** | **explorer-delay-time** | **sna-explorer-timeout** | **explorer-wait-time** | **sna-group-cache** | **sna-retry-interval** | **sna-verify-interval**} *time*

Syntax	Description
icannotreach-block-time	Cache life of unreachable resource; during this time searches for the resource are blocked. The valid range is 1 to 86,400 seconds. The default is 0 (disabled).
netbios-cache-timeout	Cache life of NetBIOS name location for the local and remote reachability caches. The valid range is 1 to 86,400 seconds. The default is 960 seconds (16 minutes).
netbios-explorer-timeout	Length of time that Cisco IOS software waits for an explorer response before marking a resource unreachable (on both a LAN and a WAN). The valid range is 1 to 86,400 seconds. The default is 6 seconds.
netbios-group-cache	Cache life of NetBIOS entries in the group cache. The valid range is 1 to 86,000 seconds. The default is 240 seconds (4 minutes).

Syntax	Description
netbios-retry-interval	NetBIOS explorer retry interval (on a LAN only). The valid range is 1 to 86,400 seconds. The default is 1 second.
netbios-verify-interval	Number of seconds between a cache entry's creation and its marking as stale. If a search request comes in for a stale cache entry, a directed verify query is sent to ensure the cache still exists. The valid range is 1 to 86,400 seconds. The default is 240 seconds (4 minutes).
sna-cache-timeout	Length of time that an SNA MAC/service access point (SAP) location cache entry exists before it is discarded (for local and remote caches). The valid range is 1 to 86,400 seconds. The default is 960 seconds (16 minutes).
explorer-delay-time	Time to wait before sending or accepting explorers. The valid range is 1 to 5 minutes. The default is 0.
sna-group-cache	Cache life of SNA entries in the group cache. The valid range is 1 to 86,000 seconds. The default is 240 seconds (4 minutes).
sna-explorer-timeout	Length of time that Cisco IOS software waits for an explorer response before marking a resource unreachable (on a LAN and WAN). The valid range is 1 to 86,400 seconds. The default is 180 seconds (3 minutes).
explorer-wait-time	Time to wait for all stations to respond to explorers. The valid range is 1 to 86,400 seconds. The default is 0.
sna-retry-interval	Interval between SNA explorer retries (on a LAN). The valid range is 1 to 86,400 seconds. The default is 30 seconds.
sna-verify-interval	Number of seconds between a cache entry's creation and its marking as stale. If a search request comes in for a stale cache entry, a directed verify query is sent to ensure that the cache still exists. The valid range is 1 to 86,400 seconds. The default is 240 seconds (4 minutes).

Default

The default settings of each timer option is described in the "Syntax Description" section of the **dlsw timer** command.

Command Mode

Global configuration

Usage Guidelines

This command first appeared in Cisco IOS Release 10.3.

The **netbios-group-cache** and **sna-group-cache** options were added to this command for the border peer caching feature.

Examples

The following configuration defines the length of time that an entry will stay in the group cache as 120 seconds (2 minutes):

```
dlsw timers sna-group-cache 120
```

The following example configures the length of time that an SNA MAC location cache entry exists before it is discarded:

```
dlsw timer sna-cache-timeout 3
```

dlsw tos disable

Use the **dlsw tos disable global** configuration command to disable any ToS bits in DLSw+ generated packets.

> **dlsw tos disable**

Syntax Description

This command has no arguments or keywords.

Default

There is no default setting.

Command Mode

Global configuration

Usage Guidelines

This command first appeared in Cisco IOS Release 12.0.

Example

The following example disables the tos bits in DLSw+ generated packets:

```
dlsw tos disable
```

dlsw tos map

Use the **dlsw tos map global** configuration command to associate a ToS value for priority peers. Use the **no** form of this command to return to the default setting.

dlsw tos map [**high** *value* [**medium** *value* | **normal** *value* | **low** *value*]]
no dlsw tos map [**high** *value* [**medium** *value* | **normal** *value* | **low** *value*]]

Part
II

Command Reference

Syntax

value

Description

The type of service (ToS) bit value. Valid ranges are 0 to 7.

Default

The default setting, with priority peers configured, is defined in Table 10-1.

Command Mode

Global configuration

Usage Guidelines

By default, DLSw+ peer traffic is set to Critical-ECP. When the **priority** keyword is specified in the dlsw remote peer tcp command, DLSw+ automatically activates four TCP ports to that remote peer (ports 2065, 1981, 1982 and 1983) and associates a priority level. This command enables the user to customize the prioritization of DLSw+ traffic within the network. If priority peers are not configured, however, high is the only option. See Table 10-1 for corresponding priority levels and options.

Table 10-1 *Priority Levels and Options*

ToS Bit Value	DLSw+ Translation Value	ToS Bit Value Meaning	TCP Port Numbers
0	Routine		
1	Priority		
2	Immediate	Low	1983

Continues

Table 10-1   *Priority Levels and Options (Continued)*

ToS Bit Value	DLSw+ Translation Value	ToS Bit Value Meaning	TCP Port Numbers
3	Flash	Normal	1982
4	Flash Override	Medium	1981
5	Critical ECP	High	2065
6	Internetwork Control		
7	Network Control		

ToS bit values 6 and 7 are not recommended for usage because of potential interference with critical network infrastructure flows. Although using ToS bit values 0 and 1 will not cause negative impact to the network, the values do not prioritize the traffic.

Examples

The following example changes the default setting on IP packets generated by DLSw+ from high to low:

```
dlsw tos map low 2
```

The following is an example policy routing configuration that shows how to modify the default setting of TCP port 2065. The configuration changes the default setting on IP packets from network control priority to routine priority.

```
ip local policy route-map test
access-list 101 permit tcp any eq 2065 any
access-list 101 permit tcp any any eq 2065
route-map test permit 20
 match ip address 101
set ip precedence routine
```

dlsw udp-disable

Use the **dlsw udp-disable** global configuration command to disable the UDP unicast feature. Use the **no** form of this command to return to the default UDP unicast feature.

> **dlsw udp-disable**
> **no dlsw udp-disable**

Syntax Description

This command has no arguments or keywords.

Default

The UDP unicast feature is enabled.

Command Mode

Global configuration

Usage Guidelines

This command first appeared in Cisco IOS Release 11.2 F.

If the **dlsw udp-disable** command is configured, then a DLSw+ node will not send packets via UDP Unicast and will not advertise UDP Unicast support in its capabilities exchange message.

Refer to the Introduction, "Bridging and IBM Networking Overview" for more information on the UDP Unicast feature.

Example

The following example disables the UDP unicast feature:

```
dlsw udp-disable
```

qllc dlsw

Use the **qllc dlsw** interface configuration command to enable DLSw+ over Qualified Logical Link Control (QLLC). Use the **no** form of this command to cancel the configuration.

> **qllc dlsw** {**subaddress** *subaddress* | **pvc** *pvc-low* [*pvc-high*]} [**vmac** *vmacaddr*
> [*poolsize*]] [**partner** *partner-macaddr*] [**sap** *ssap dsap*] [**xid** *xidstring*]
> [**npsi-poll**]
> **no qllc dlsw** {**subaddress** *subaddress* | **pvc** *pvc-low* [*pvc-high*]} [**vmac** *vmacaddr*
> [*poolsize*]] [**partner** *partner-macaddr*] [**sap** *ssap dsap*] [**xid** *xidstring*]
> [**npsi-poll**]

Syntax	Description
subaddress *subaddress*	An X.121 subaddress.
pvc	Maps one or more permanent virtual circuits (PVCs) to a particular QLLC service (in this case, DLSw+). QLLC will attempt to reach the partner by sending and ID.STN.IND to DLSw+.

Syntax	Description
pvc-low	Lowest logical channel number (LCN) for a range of X.25 PVCs. Acceptable values for PVCs are decimal numbers between 1 and 4095. There is no default value.
pvc-high	(Optional) Highest LCN. If not specified the range of PVCs consists of just one PVC.
vmac *vmacaddr*	(Optional) Defines either the only virtual MAC address used for DLSw+ or the lowest virtual MAC address in a pool of virtual MAC addresses.
poolsize	(Optional) Specifies the number of contiguous virtual MAC addresses that have been reserved for DLSw+. If the parameter is not present, then just one virtual MAC address is available.
partner *partner-macaddr*	Virtual MAC address to which an incoming call wishes to connect. The **qllc dlsw** command must be repeated for each different partner. Each partner is identified by a unique subaddress.
sap *ssap dsap*	Overrides the default SAP values (04) for a Token Ring connection. *dsap* refers to the partner's SAP address; *ssap* applies to the virtual MAC address that corresponds to the X.121 device.
xid *xidstring*	XID format 0 type 2 string.
npsi-poll	Inhibits forwarding a null XID on the X.25 link. Instead, Cisco IOS software will send a null XID response back to the device that sent the null XID command.

Default

No defaults are specified.

Command Mode

Interface configuration

Usage Guidelines

This command first appeared in Cisco IOS Release 11.0.

Any incoming call whose X.121 destination address matches the router's X.121 address and this subaddress will be dispatched to DLSw+ (with an ID.STN IND). If a router is providing several QLLC services different subaddresses must be used to discriminate between them. Subaddresses can be used even if a remote X.25 device is not explicitly mapped to a specific virtual MAC address. This is most useful when PU 2.1 devices are connecting to a host because the X.25 device's control point name and network name are used to validate the connection, rather than some virtual MAC address. The subaddress is optional. If no subaddress is provided, any incoming call that matches the router's X.121 address will be dispatched to DLSw+. On outgoing calls, the subaddress is concatenated to the interface's X.121 address.

When DLSw+ receives a Can You Reach inquiry about a virtual MAC address in the pool, the QLLC code will attempt to set up a virtual circuit to the X.121 address that maps to the virtual MAC address specified. If an incoming call is received, QLLC sends an ID.STN.IND with a virtual MAC address from the pool to DLSw+. If there is no virtual MAC address, then the **x25 map qllc** or **x25 pvc qllc** command must provide a virtual MAC address.

The **npsi-poll** parameter is needed to support PU 2.0 on the partner side that wishes to connect to a FEP on the X.25 side. In a Token Ring or DLSw+ environment the PU 2.0 will send a null XID to the FEP. If the software forwards this null XID to an X.25 attached FEP, the FEP will assume that it is connecting to PU2.1 and will break off the connection when the PU 2.0 next send an XID Format 0 Type 2.

Part II

Command Reference

Example

The following commands assign virtual MAC address 1000.0000.0001 to a remote X.25-attached 3174, which is then mapped to the X.121 address of the 3174 (31104150101) in an X.25-attached router:

```
interface serial 0
 x25 address 3110212011
 x25 map qllc 1000.000.0001 31104150101
 qllc dlsw partner 4000.1161.1234
```

sdlc dlsw

Use the **sdlc dlsw** interface configuration command to attach SDLC addresses to DLSw+. Use the **no** form of this command to cancel the configuration.

> **sdlc dlsw** {*sdlc-address* | **default** | **partner** *mac-address* [**inbound** | **outbound**]}
> **no sdlc dlsw** {*sdlc-address* | **default** | **partner** *mac-address* [**inbound** | **outbound**]}

Syntax	Description
sdlc-address	SDLC addresses are in hexadecimal. The valid range is 1 to FE.
default	Allows the user to configure an unlimited number of SDLC addresses to DLSw+.
partner *mac-address*	MAC address for default partner.
inbound	(Optional) Partner will initiate connection.
outbound	(Optional) Initiate connection to partner.

Default

No correspondence is defined between SDLC addresses and DLSw+.

Command Mode

Interface configuration

Usage Guidelines

This command first appeared in Cisco IOS Release 11.0.

Examples

The following command attaches SDLC address d2 to DLSw+:

```
sdlc dlsw d2
```

The following command attaches SDLC addresses d2, d5, e3, e4, e6, b1, c3, d4, a1, and a5:

```
sdlc dlsw d2 d5 e3 e4 e6 b1 c3 d4 a1 a5
```

Related Commands

To locate documentation of related commands, you can search online at www.cisco.com.

encapsulation sdlc
sdlc address
sdlc role

show dlsw capabilities

Use the **show dlsw capabilities** privileged EXEC command to display the configuration of a specific peer or all peers.

> **show dlsw capabilities** [**interface** *type number* | **ip-address** *ip-address* | **local**]

Syntax	Description
interface *type number*	(Optional) Specifies the interface type and number for which the DLSw+ capabilities are to be displayed.
ip-address *ip-address*	(Optional) Specifies a peer by its IP address.
local	(Optional) Specifies the local DLSw+ peer.

Command Mode

Privileged EXEC

Usage Guidelines

This command first appeared in Cisco IOS Release 10.3.

Sample Display

The following is sample output from the **show dlsw capabilities** command:

```
Router# show dlsw capabilities

DLSw: Capabilities for peer 1.1.1.6(2065)
            vendor id (OUI)        : '00C' (cisco)
   version number        : 1
   release number        : 0
   init pacing window     : 20
   unsupported saps       : none
   num of tcp sessions    : 1
   loop prevent support   : no
   icanreach mac-exclusive : no
   icanreach netbios-excl. : no
   reachable mac addresses : none
   reachable netbios names : none
   cisco version number   : 1
   peer group number      : 0
   border peer capable    : no
   peer cost              : 3
   biu-segment configured : no
   UDP Unicast support    : yes
   local-ack configured   : yes
   priority configured    : no
   configured ip address  : 1.1.1.6
   peer type              : conf
   version string         :
Cisco Internetwork Operating System Software
IOS (tm) RSP Software (RSP-JSV-M), Version 11.3(4), RELEASE SOFTWARE (fc1)
Copyright (c) 1986-1998 by cisco Systems, Inc.
Compiled Tue 16-Jun-98 04:29 by phanguye
```

Table 10-2 describes significant fields shown from the **show dlsw capabilities** command.

Table 10-2 *show dlsw capabilities Field Descriptions*

Field	Description
vendor id (OUI)	Vendor ID.
version number	RFC 1795 version of SSP protocol.

Continues

Part II

Command Reference

Table 10-2 *show dlsw capabilities* Field Descriptions (Continued)

Field	Description
release number	RFC 1795 release of SSP protocol.
init pacing window	Initial pacing window. ·
unsupported saps	Unsupported SAPs.
num of tcp sessions	Number of TCP sessions.
loop prevent support	No loop prevent support.
icanreach mac-exclusive	Configured MAC addresses that the router can reach.
icanreach netbios-excl.	Configured NetBIOS names that the router can reach.
reachable mac addresses	Reachable MAC addresses.
reachable netbios name	Reachable NetBIOS names.
cisco version number	Cisco version number.
peer group number	Peer group member number.
border peer capable	Border peer capability.
peer cost	Peer cost.
biu-segment configured	BIU segment configured.
UDP Unicast support	UDP unicast support.
local-ack configured	Local acknowledgment capable.
priority configured	Priority capability.
configured ip address	Configured IP address.
peer type	Peer type can be peer-on-demand or promiscuous.
version string	Cisco IOS software version information.

show dlsw circuits

Use the **show dlsw circuits** privileged EXEC command to display the state of all circuits involving this MAC address as a source and destination.

> **show dlsw circuits** [**detail**] [**mac-address** *address* | **sap-value** *value* | **circuit id**]

Syntax	Description
detail	(Optional) Displays circuit state information in expanded format.
mac-address *address*	(Optional) Specifies the MAC address to be used in the circuit search.

Syntax	Description
sap-value *value*	(Optional) Specifies the SAP to be used in the circuit search.
circuit id	(Optional) Specifies the circuit ID of the circuit index.

Command Mode

Privileged EXEC

Part
II

Command Reference

Usage Guidelines

This command first appeared in Cisco IOS Release 10.3.

Sample Displays

The following is sample output from the **show dlsw circuits** command:

```
Router# show dlsw circuits

Index           local addr(lsap)   remote addr(dsap)  state      uptime
4060086272      4000.0000.0056(F0) 4001.0000.0049(F0) CONNECTED  00:00:13
Total number of circuits connected: 1
```

The following is sample output from the **show dlsw circuits** command with the **detail** argument:

```
Router# show dlsw circuits detail

Index   local addr(lsap)     remote addr(dsap)     state uptime
194 0800.5a9b.b3b2(F0)  0800.5ac1.302d(F0)   CONNECTED 00:00:13
        PCEP: 995AA4     UCEP: A52274
        Port: To0/0      peer 172.18.15.166(2065)
        Flow-Control-Tx CW:20, Permitted:28; Rx CW:22, Granted:25
        RIF = 0680.0011.0640
Total number of circuits connected: 1
```

Table 10-3 describes significant fields shown in the display.

Table 10-3 *show dlsw circuits* Field Descriptions

Field	Description
Index	Number the software uses to reference an individual circuit.
local addr (lsap)	MAC address and SAP value used by end station closest to this DLSw+ peer.
remote addr (dsap)	MAC address and SAP value used by end station that is across the peer connection (remote).
state	Indicates whether circuit has completed establishment.
uptime	Length of time a circuit has been connected.

Continues

Table 10-3 *show dlsw circuits Field Descriptions*

Field	Description
total number of circuits connected	Number of total connected circuits. If a circuit has not completed connection, it will not show a value.

show dlsw fastcache

Use the **show dlsw fastcache** privileged EXEC command to display the fast cache for FST and direct-encapsulated peers.

show dlsw fastcache

Syntax Description

This command has no arguments or keywords.

Command Mode

Privileged EXEC

Usage Guidelines

This command first appeared in Cisco IOS Release 11.0.

Sample Display

The following is sample output from the **show dlsw fastcache** command with an FST peer:

```
Router# show dlsw fastcache

    peer              local-mac      remote-mac   l/r sap rif
FST 10.2.32.1        0800.5a8f.881c 0800.5a8f.8822  04/04  0680.02D5.1360
```

The following is sample output from the **show dlsw fastcache** command:

```
Router# show dlsw fastcache

    peer              local-mac      remote-mac   l/r sap rif
IF Se1 0800.5a8f.881c  0800.5a8f.8822 F0/F0 0680.02D5.1360
```

Table 10-4 describes significant fields shown in the display.

Table 10-4 *show dlsw fastcache Field Descriptions*

Field	Description
peer	The peer in which the router is connected. Could represent either an IP address or interface.
local-mac	Local MAC address.
remote-mac	Remote MAC address.
l/r sap	Local/remote SAP value.
rif	RIF value.

show dlsw peers

Use the **show dlsw peers** privileged EXEC command to display DLSw peer information.

show dlsw peers [**interface** *type number* | **ip-address** *ip-address* | **udp**]

Syntax	Description
interface *typenumber*	(Optional) Specifies the interface type and number for which the DLSw+ peer information is to be displayed.
ip-address *ip-address*	(Optional) Specifies a remote peer by its IP address.
udp	(Optional) Shows UDP frame forwarding statistics for specified peers.

Command Mode

Privileged EXEC

Usage Guidelines

This command first appeared in Cisco IOS Release 11.0.

Sample Displays

The following is sample output from the **show dlsw peers** command:

```
Router# show dlsw peers udp

Peers:      tot-Q'd    total-rx  total-tx   tot-retx  tot-drop curr-Q'd TCP uptime
1.1.1.        0          23         0          0         0        0        0 00:01:02
Total number of connected peers: 2
Total number of connections:     8
```

The following is sample output from the **show dlsw peers** command with a TCP connection:

```
Router# show dlsw peers

Peers:              state     pkts_rx   pkts_tx  type  drops ckts TCP    uptime
 TCP 1.1.91.1
       High priority   CONNECT      43        40  conf     0    1   0 00:01:02
     Medium priority   CONNECT       0         0  conf     0    -   0 00:01:02
     Normal priority   CONNECT       4        41  conf     0    -   5 00:01:02
        Low priority   CONNECT       1         0  conf     0    -   0 00:01:02
 TCP 1.1.93.1
       High priority   CONNECT       3         3  conf     0    0   0 00:00:58
     Medium priority   CONNECT       0         0  conf     0    -   0 00:00:58
     Normal priority   CONNECT       0         0  conf     0    -   0 00:00:58
        Low priority   CONNECT       0        39  conf     0    -   0 00:00:58
Total number of connected peers: 2
Total number of connections:     8
```

The following is sample output from the **show dlsw peers** command with a Direct Frame Relay connection:

```
Router # show dlsw peers

Peers:                 state    pkts_rx pkts_tx  type  drops ckts TCP     uptime
IF SE1      16connect652597conf0--00:04:09
Total number of connected peers: 2
Total number of connections:     8
```

The following is sample output from the **show dlsw peers** command with a Direct Frame Relay with local acknowledgment (LLC2) connection:

```
Router # show dlsw peers

Peers:                 state pkts_rx pkts_tx  type   drops ckts TCP uptime
LLC2 SE116connect1179108conf01-00:04:09
Total number of connected peers: 2
Total number of connections:     8
```

Table 10-5 describes the significant fields shown in the **show dlsw peers** command display.

Table 10-5   *show dlsw peers Field Descriptions*

Field	Description
Peers	Information related to the remote peer, including encapsulation type, IP address (if using FST or TCP), and interface number (if using direct encapsulation).
tot-Q'd	Number of UDP packets that have been queued because of TCP congestion.
total-rx	Number UDP packets received from the peer.
total-tx	Number of UDP packets transmitted to the peer.
tot-retx	Number of reachability retransmits (for example, DLSw+ retries NQ_ex and CUR_ex) when originally sent via UDP.
tot-drop	Number of queued UDP packets that were dropped because of persistent TCP congestion.
curr-Q'd	Number of current UDP packets queued because of TCP congestion.
TCP	Number of packets currently on TCP output queue.
state	State of the peer: CONNECT: Normal working peer. DISCONN: Peer is not connected. CAP_EXG: Capabilities exchange mode. Waiting for capabilities response. WAIT_RD: TCP write pipe (local port 2065) is open and peer is waiting for remote peer to open the read port (local port 2067). This field applies only to TCP peers. WAN_BUSY: TCP outbound queue is full. This field applies only to TCP peers.
pkts_rx	Number of received packets.
pkts_tx	Number of transmitted packets.
type	Type of remote peer: conf : configured prom : promiscuous pod : peer on demand

Continues

Table 10-5 *show dlsw peers Field Descriptions (Continued)*

Field	Description
drops	The number of drops done by this peer. Reasons for the counter to increment: • WAN interface not up for a direct peer. • DLSW tries to send a packet before the peer is fully connected (waiting for TCP event or capabilities event). • Outbound TCP queue full. • FST sequence number count mismatch. • Cannot get buffer to "slow switch" FST packet. • CiscoBus controller failure on high end (cannot move packet from receive buffer to transmit buffer, or vice versa). • Destination IP address of FST packet does not match local peer-ID. • WAN interface not up for an FST peer. • No SRB route cache command configured. • Madge ring buffer is full on low end systems (WAN feeding LAN too fast).
uptime	How long the connection has been established to this peer.
ckts	Number of active circuits through this peer. This field applies only to TCP and LLC2 transport peer types.
total number of connected peers	Total number of currently connected peers.
total number of connections	Total number of active cicuit connections.

show dlsw reachability

Use the **show dlsw reachability** privileged EXEC command to display DLSw+ reachability information.

> **show dlsw reachability** [[**group** [*value*] | **local** | **remote**] | [**mac-address** [*address*] [**netbios-names** [*name*]]

Syntax	Description
group	(Optional) Displays contents of group reachability cache only.
value	(Optional) Specifies the group number for the reachability check. Only displays group cache entries for the specified group. The valid range is 1 to 255.
local	(Optional) Displays contents of local reachabilty cache only.

Syntax	Description
remote	(Optional) Displays contents of remote reachabilty cache only.
mac-address	(Optional) Displays DLSw reachability for MAC addresses only.
address	(Optional) Specifies the MAC address for which to search in the reachability cache.
netbios-names	(Optional) Displays DLSw reachability for NetBIOS names only.
name	(Optional) Specifies the NetBIOS name for which to search in the reachability cache.

Command Mode

Privileged EXEC

Usage Guidelines

This command first appeared in Cisco IOS Release 11.0.

If none of the group, local, or remote options are specified, then the caches will be displayed in the following order: local, remote, and group.

Sample Displays

The following is sample output from the **show dlsw reachability group** command:

```
Router# show dlsw reachability group

DLSw Group MAC address reachability cache list
Mac Addr Group
0000.3072.1070     10
DLSW Group NetBIOS Name reachability cache list
NetBIOS Name    Group
```

The following is sample output from the **show dlsw reachability** command:

```
Router# show dlsw reachability

DLSw MAC address reachability cache list
Mac Addr        status      Loc.    peer/port           rif
0000.f641.91e8  SEARCHING   LOCAL
0006.7c9a.7a48  FOUND       LOCAL   TokenRing0/0    0CB0.0011.3E71.A041.0DE5.0640
0800.5a4b.1cbc  SEARCHING   LOCAL
0800.5a54.ee59  SEARCHING   LOCAL
0800.5a8f.9c3f  FOUND       LOCAL   TokenRing0/0    08B0.A041.0DE5.0640
4000.0000.0050  FOUND       LOCAL   TokenRing0/0    0CB0.0011.3E71.A041.0DE5.0640
4000.0000.0306  FOUND       LOCAL   TokenRing0/0    0CB0.0011.3E71.A041.0DE5.0640
4000.0000.0307  SEARCHING   LOCAL
```

```
4000.0000.0308  SEARCHING  LOCAL
4000.1234.56c1  FOUND      LOCAL    Serial3/7      --no rif--
4000.1234.56c2  FOUND      LOCAL    Serial3/7      --no rif--
4000.3000.0100  FOUND      LOCAL    TokenRing0/0   08B0.A041.0DE5.0640
4000.4000.ff40  SEARCHING  LOCAL
4000.7470.00e7  SEARCHING  LOCAL
4000.ac0b.0001  FOUND      LOCAL    TokenRing0/0   08B0.A041.0DE5.0640
4001.0000.0064  FOUND      LOCAL    TokenRing0/0   0CB0.0011.3E71.A041.0DE5.0640
4001.3745.1088  FOUND      LOCAL    TokenRing0/0   08B0.A041.0DE5.0640
4100.0131.1030  FOUND      LOCAL    TokenRing0/0   08B0.A041.0DE5.0640
10B0.FFF1.4041.0041.3E71.A041.0DE5.0640

DLSw NetBIOS Name reachability cache list
NetBIOS Name    status     Loc.     peer/port       rif
APPNCLT2        FOUND      LOCAL    TokenRing0/0   08B0.A041.0DE5.0640
```

The following is sample output from the **show dlsw reachability** command with the **mac-address** argument:

```
Router# show dlsw reachability mac-address 4000.00000306

DLSw MAC address reachability cache list
Mac Addr        status     Loc.     peer/port       rif
4000.0000.0306  FOUND      LOCAL    TokenRing0/0   0CB0.0011.3E71.A041.0DE5.0640
```

The following is sample output from the **show dlsw reachability** command with the **netbios-names** argument:

```
Router# show dlsw reachability netbios-names

DLSw NetBIOS Name reachability cache list
NetBIOS Name    status     Loc.     peer/port       rif
APPNCLT2        FOUND      LOCAL    TokenRing0/0   08B0.A041.0DE5.0640
```

Table 10-6 describes the significant fields shown in the **show dlsw reachability** command.

Table 10-6 *show dlsw reachability Field Descriptions*

Field	Description
Mac Addr	MAC address of station being sought (destination MAC address of canureach_ex packet).
NetBIOS Name	NetBIOS name of station being sought (destination MAC address of NQ_ex packet).

Table 10-6 *show dlsw reachability Field Descriptions (Continued)*

Field	Description
status	Result of station search. The status can be one of the following: • FOUND: Station has recently sent a broadcast or responded to a broadcast. • SEARCHING: Router has sent broadcast to this station and is waiting for a response. • NOT_FOUND: Negative caching is on and the station has not responded to queries. • UNCONFIRMED: Station is configured, but DLSw has not verified it. • VERIFY: Cache information is being verified because cache is going stale or the user configuration is being verified.
Loc.	Location of station. LOCAL indicates that the station is on the local network. REMOTE indicates that the station is on the remote network.
peer/port	Peer/port number. If the Loc. field lists a REMOTE station, the peer/port field indicates the peer through which the remote station is reachable. If the Loc. field lists a LOCAL station, the peer/port field indicates the port through which the local station is reachable. For ports, the port number and slot number are given. Pxxx-Syyy denotes port xxx slot yyy. If the station is reachable through a bridge group, it is shown by TBridge-xxx.
rif	Shows the RIF in the cache. This column applies only to LOCAL stations. If the station was reached through a medium that does not support RIFs (such as SDLC or Ethernet), then "--no rif--" is shown.

show dlsw statistics

Use the **show dlsw statistics** privileged EXEC command to display the number of frames that have been processed in the local, remote, and group cache.

show dlsw statistics [**border-peers**]

Syntax	Description
border-peers	(Optional) Displays the number of frames processed in the local, remote, and group caches.

Command Mode
Privileged EXEC

Part
II

Command Reference

Usage Guidelines

This command first appeared in Cisco IOS Release 11.2 F.

Sample Display

The following sample is a sample output from the **show dlsw statistics** command. The output displays the number of frames processed in the local, remote, and group cache:

```
router# show dlsw statistics border-peers

100 Border Peer Frames processed
10 Border frames found Local
20 Border frames found Remote
17 Border frames found Group Cache
```

Configuring Serial Tunnel and Block Serial Tunnel

Cisco's serial tunnel (STUN) implementation allows Synchronous Data Link Control (SDLC) Protocol devices and High-Level Data Link Control (HDLC) devices to connect to one another through a multi-protocol internetwork rather than through a direct serial link. STUN encapsulates SDLC frames in either the Transmission Control Protocol/Internet Protocol (TCP/IP) or the HDLC protocol. STUN provides a straight passthrough of all SDLC traffic (including control frames, such as Receiver Ready) end-to-end between Systems Network Architecture (SNA) devices.

Cisco's SDLC local acknowledgment provides local termination of the SDLC session so that control frames no longer travel the WAN backbone networks. This means end nodes do not time out and a loss of sessions does not occur. You can configure your network with STUN, or with STUN and SDLC local acknowledgment. To enable SDLC local acknowledgment, Cisco IOS software must first be enabled for STUN and routers configured to appear on the network as primary or secondary SDLC nodes. TCP/IP encapsulation must be enabled. Cisco SDLC Transport feature also provides priority queuing for TCP encapsulated frames.

Cisco block serial tunnel (BSTUN) implementation enables Cisco series 2500, 4000, 4500, 4700 and 7200 series routers to support devices that use the Binary Synchronous Communications (Bisync) data-link protocol and asynchronous security protocols that include Adplex, ADT Security Systems, Inc., Diebold, and asynchronous generic traffic. BSTUN implementation is also supported on the 4T network interface module (NIM) on the Cisco series 4000 and 4500. Cisco support of the Bisync protocol enables enterprises to transport Bisync traffic and SNA multiprotocol traffic over the same network.

This chapter describes how to configure STUN and BSTUN. For a complete description of the STUN and BSTUN commands mentioned in this chapter, refer to Chapter 12, "Serial Tunnel and Block Serial Tunnel Commands." To locate documentation of other commands, you can search online at www.cisco.com.

STUN Configuration Task List

To configure and monitor STUN or STUN local acknowledgment, complete the tasks in the following sections:

- Enable STUN
- Configure SDLC Broadcast
- Specify STUN Protocol Group
- Enable STUN Keepalive

- Enable STUN Remote Keepalive

- Enable STUN Interfaces

- Establish the Frame Encapsulation Method

- Configure STUN with Multilink Transmission Groups

- Set Up STUN Traffic Priorities

- Monitor STUN Network Activity

The "STUN Configuration Examples" section follows these configuration tasks.

Enable STUN

To enable STUN, use the following command in global configuration mode:

Command	Purpose
stun peer-name *ip-address*	Enables STUN for a particular IP address.

When configuring redundant links, ensure that the STUN peer names you choose on each router are the IP addresses of the most stable interfaces on each device, such as a loopback or Ethernet interface. See the section "STUN Configuration Examples" later in this chapter.

Configure SDLC Broadcast

The SDLC broadcast feature allows SDLC broadcast address FF to be replicated for each of the STUN peers, so each of the end stations receives the broadcast frame. For example, in Figure 11-1, the FEP views the end stations 1, 2, and 3 as if they are on an SDLC multidrop link. Any broadcast frame sent from the FEP to Router A is duplicated and sent to each of the downstream routers (B and C).

Figure 11-1 *SDLC Broadcast Across Virtual Multidrop Lines*

To enable SDLC broadcast, use the following command in interface configuration mode:

Command	Purpose
sdlc virtual-multidrop	Enables SDLC broadcast.

Only enable SDLC broadcast on the device that is configured to be the secondary station on the SDLC link (Router A in Figure 11-1).

You must also configure SDLC address FF on Router A for each of the STUN peers. To do so, use the following command in interface configuration mode:

Command	Purpose
stun route address *address-number* **tcp** *ip-address* [**local-ack**] [**priority**] [**tcp-queue-max**]	Configures SDLC address FF on Router A for each STUN peer.

Specify STUN Protocol Group

Place each STUN interface in a group that defines the ISO 3309-compliant framed protocol running on that link. Packets will only travel between STUN interfaces that are in the same protocol group.

There are three predefined STUN protocols:

● Basic

● SDLC

● SDLC transmission group

You can also specify a custom STUN protocol.

If you want to use the STUN Local Acknowledgment feature, you must specify either the SDLC protocol or the SDLC transmission group protocol.

NOTE   Before you can specify a custom protocol, you must first define the protocol; see the section "Create and Specify a Custom STUN Protocol" later in this chapter for the procedure.

Specify a Basic STUN Group

The basic STUN protocol does not depend on the details of serial protocol addressing and is used when addressing is unimportant. Use this when your goal is to replace one or more sets of point-to-point (not multidrop) serial links by using a protocol other than SDLC. Use the following command in global configuration mode:

Command	Purpose
stun protocol-group *group-number* **basic**	Specifies a basic protocol group and assigns a group number.

Specify an SDLC Group

You can specify SDLC protocol groups to associate interfaces with the SDLC protocol. Use the SDLC STUN protocol to place the routers in the midst of either point-to-point or multipoint (multidrop) SDLC links. To define an SDLC protocol group, enter the following command in global configuration mode:

Command	Purpose
stun protocol-group *group-number* **sdlc**	Specifies an SDLC protocol group and assigns a group number.

If you specify an SDLC protocol group, you cannot specify the **stun route all** command on any interface of that group.

For an example of how to configure an SDLC protocol group, see the section "Configuring Serial Link Address Prioritization Using STUN TCP/IP Encapsulation Example" later in this chapter.

Specify an SDLC Transmission Group

An SNA transmission group is a set of lines providing parallel links to the same pair of SNA front-end-processor (FEP) devices. This provides redundancy of paths for fault tolerance and load sharing. To define an SDLC transmission group, use the following command in global configuration mode:

Command	Purpose
stun protocol-group *group-number* **sdlc sdlc-tg**	Specifies an SDLC protocol group, assigns a group number, and creates an SNA transmission group.

All STUN connections in a transmission group must connect to the same IP address and use the SDLC local acknowledgment feature.

Create and Specify a Custom STUN Protocol

To define a custom protocol and tie STUN groups to the new protocol, use the following commands in global configuration mode:

Step	Command	Purpose
1	**stun schema** *name* **offset** *constant-offset* **length** *address-length* **format** *format-keyword*	Creates a custom protocol.
2	**stun protocol-group** *group-number* **schema**	Specifies the custom protocol group and assigns a group number.

Enable STUN Keepalive

To define the number of times to attempt a peer connection before declaring the peer connection to be down, use the following command in global configuration mode:

Command	Purpose
stun keepalive-count	Specifies the number of times to attempt a peer connection.

Enable STUN Remote Keepalive

To enable detection of the loss of a peer, use the following command in global configuration mode:

Command	Purpose
stun remote-peer-keepalive *seconds*	Enables detection of the loss of a peer.

Enable STUN Interfaces

You must enable STUN on serial interfaces and place these interfaces in the protocol groups you have defined. To enable STUN on an interface and to place the interface in a STUN group, use the following commands in interface configuration mode:

Step	Command	Purpose
1	**encapsulation stun**	Enables STUN function on a serial interface.
2	**stun group** *group-number*	Places the interface in a previously defined STUN group.

When a given serial link is configured for the STUN function, it is no longer a shared multiprotocol link. All traffic that arrives on the link will be transported to the corresponding peer as determined by the current STUN configuration.

Establish the Frame Encapsulation Method

To allow SDLC frames to travel across a multimedia, multiprotocol network, you must encapsulate them using one of the methods in the following sections:

- Configure HDLC Encapsulation Without Local Acknowledgment

- Configure TCP Encapsulation Without Local Acknowledgment

- Configure TCP Encapsulation with SDLC Local Acknowledgment and Priority Queuing

- Configure Local Acknowledgment for Direct Frame Relay Connectivity

Configure HDLC Encapsulation Without Local Acknowledgment

You can encapsulate SDLC or HDLC frames using the HDLC protocol. The outgoing serial link can still be used for other kinds of traffic. The frame is not TCP encapsulated. To configure HDLC encapsulation, use one of the following commands in interface configuration mode:

Command	Purpose
stun route all interface serial *number*	Forwards all HDLC or SDLC traffic of the identified interface number.
or	or
stun route all interface serial *number* **direct**	Forwards all HDLC or SDLC traffic on a direct STUN link.
or	or
stun route address *address-number* **interface serial** *number*	Forwards HDLC or SDLC traffic of the identified address.
or	or
stun route address *address-number* **interface serial** *number* **direct**	Forwards HDLC or SDLC traffic of the identified address across a direct STUN link.

Use the **no** forms of these commands to disable HDLC encapsulation.

NOTE   You can forward all traffic only when you are using basic STUN protocol groups.

Configure TCP Encapsulation Without Local Acknowledgment

If you do not want to use SDLC local acknowledgment and only need to forward all SDLC frames encapsulated in TCP, use the following commands in interface configuration mode:

Step	Command	Purpose
1	.**stun route all tcp** *ip-address*	Forwards all TCP traffic for this IP address.
2	**stun route address** *address-number* **tcp** *ip-address* [**local-ack**] [**priority**] [**tcp-queue-max**]	Specifies TCP encapsulation.

Use the **no** form of these commands to disable forwarding of all TCP traffic.

This configuration is typically used when two routers can be connected via an IP network as opposed to a point-to-point link.

Configure TCP Encapsulation with SDLC Local Acknowledgment and Priority Queuing

You configure SDLC local acknowledgment using TCP encapsulation. When you configure SDLC local acknowledgment, you also have the option to enable support for priority queuing.

NOTE   To enable SDLC local acknowledgment, you must specify an SDLC or SDLC transmission group.

SDLC local acknowledgment provides local termination of the SDLC session so that control frames no longer travel the WAN backbone networks. This means that time-outs are less likely to occur.

Figure 11-2 illustrates an SDLC session. IBM 1, using a serial link, can communicate with IBM 2 on a different serial link separated by a wide-area backbone network. Frames are transported between Router A and Router B using STUN, but the SDLC session between IBM 1 and IBM 2 is still end-to-end. Every frame generated by IBM 1 traverses the backbone network to IBM 2, which, upon receipt of the frame, acknowledges it.

Figure 11-2 *SDLC Session Without Local Acknowledgment*

With SDLC local acknowledgment, the SDLC session between the two end nodes is not end-to-end, but instead terminates at the two local routers, as shown in Figure 11-3. The SDLC session with IBM 1 ends at Router A and the SDLC session with IBM 2 ends at Router B. Both Router A and Router B execute the full SDLC protocol as part of SDLC Local Acknowledgment. Router A acknowledges frames received from IBM 1. The node IBM 1 treats the acknowledgments it receives as if they are from IBM 2. Similarly, Router B acknowledges frames received from IBM 2. The node IBM 2 treats the acknowledgments it receives as if they are from IBM 1.

Figure 11-3 *SDLC Session with Local Acknowledgment*

To configure TCP encapsulation with SDLC local acknowledgment and priority queuing, perform the tasks in the following sections:

● Assign the Router an SDLC Primary or Secondary Role

● Enable the SDLC Local Acknowledgment Feature

● Establish Priority Queuing Levels

Assign the Router an SDLC Primary or Secondary Role

To establish local acknowledgment, the router must play the role of an SDLC primary or secondary node. Primary nodes poll secondary nodes in a predetermined order. Secondaries then transmit if they have outgoing data.

For example, in an IBM environment, an FEP is the primary station and cluster controllers are secondary stations. If the router is connected to an FEP, the router should appear as a cluster controller and must be assigned the role of a secondary SDLC node. If the router is connected to a cluster controller, the router should appear as an FEP and must be assigned the role of a primary SDLC node. Devices connected to SDLC primary end-stations must play the role of an SDLC secondary and routers attached to SDLC secondary end stations must play the role of an SDLC primary station.

To assign the router a primary or secondary role, use one of the following commands in interface configuration mode:

Command	Purpose
stun sdlc-role primary	Assigns the STUN-enabled router an SDLC primary role.
or	or
stun sdlc-role secondary	Assigns the STUN-enabled router an SDLC secondary role.

Enable the SDLC Local Acknowledgment Feature

To enable SDLC local acknowledgment, use the following command in interface configuration mode:

Command	Purpose
stun route address *address-number* **tcp** *ip-address* [**local-ack**] [**priority**] [**tcp-queue-max**]	Establishes SDLC local acknowledgment using TCP encapsulation.

The **stun route address 1 tcp local-ack priority tcp-queue-max** interface configuration command enables local acknowledgment and TCP encapsulation. Both options are required to use transmission groups. You should specify the SDLC address with the echo bit turned off for transmission group interfaces. The SDLC broadcast address 0xFF is routed automatically for transmission group interfaces. The **priority** keyword creates multiple TCP sessions for this route. The **tcp-queue-max** keyword sets the maximum size of the outbound TCP queue for the SDLC. The default TCP queue size is 100. The value for **hold-queue in** should be greater than the value for **tcp-queue-max**.

You can use the **priority** keyword (to set up the four levels of priorities to be used for TCP encapsulated frames) at the same time you enable local acknowledgment. The **priority** keyword is described in the following section. Use the **no** form of this command to disable SDLC Local Acknowledgment. For an example of how to enable local acknowledgment, see the section "Configuring Serial Link Address Prioritization Using STUN TCP/IP Encapsulation Example" later in this chapter.

Establish Priority Queuing Levels

With SDLC local acknowledgment enabled, you can establish priority levels used in priority queuing for serial interfaces. The priority levels are as follows:

- Low

- Medium

- Normal

- High

To set the priority queuing level, use the following command in interface configuration mode:

Command	Purpose
stun route address *address number* **tcp** *ip-address* [**local-ack**] **priority** [**tcp-queue-max**]	Establishes the four levels of priorities to be used in priority queuing.

Use the **no** form of this command to disable priority settings. For an example of how to establish priority queuing levels, see the section "Configuring Serial Link Address Prioritization Using STUN TCP/IP Encapsulation Example" later in this chapter.

Configure Local Acknowledgment for Direct Frame Relay Connectivity

To implement STUN with local acknowledgment using direct Frame Relay encapsulation, use the following command in interface configuration mode:

Command	Purpose
stun route address *sdlc-addr* **interface** *frame-relay-port* **dlci** *number localsap* **local-ack cls**	Configures Frame Relay encapsulation between STUN peers with local acknowledgment.

Configure STUN with Multilink Transmission Groups

You can configure multilink SDLC transmission groups across STUN connections between IBM communications controllers, such as IBM 37x5s. Multilink transmission groups allow you to collapse multiple WAN leased lines into one leased line.

SDLC multilink transmission groups provide the following features:

- Network Control Program (NCP) SDLC address allowances, including echo and broadcast addressing.

- Remote NCP load sequence. After a SIM/RIM exchange but before a SNRM/UA exchange, NCPs send numbered I-frames. During this period, I-frames are not locally acknowledged, but instead are passed through. After the SNRM/UA exchange, local acknowledgment occurs.

- Rerouting of I-frames sent by Cisco IOS software to the NCP if a link is lost in a multilink transmission group.

- Flow control rate tuning causes a sending NCP to "feel" WAN congestion and hold frames that would otherwise be held by Cisco IOS software waiting to be transmitted on the WAN. This allows the NCP to perform its class of service (CoS) algorithm more efficiently based on a greater knowledge of network congestion.

STUN connections that are part of a transmission group must have local acknowledgment enabled. Local acknowledgment keeps SDLC poll traffic off the WAN and reduces store-and-forward delays through the router. It also might minimize the number of NCP timers that expire due to network delay. Also, these STUN connections must go to the same IP address. This is because SNA transmission groups are parallel links between the same pair of IBM communications controllers.

Design Recommendations

This section provides some recommendations that are useful in configuring SDLC multilink transmission groups.

The bandwidth of the WAN should be larger than or equal to the aggregate bandwidth of all serial lines to avoid excessive flow control and to ensure response timed does not degrade. If other protocols are also using the WAN, ensure that the WAN bandwidth is significantly greater than the aggregate SNA serial line bandwidth to ensure that the SNA traffic does not monopolize the WAN.

When you use a combination of routed transmission groups and directly connected NCP transmission groups, you need to plan the configuration carefully to ensure that SNA sessions do not stop unexpectedly. Assuming that hardware reliability is not an issue, single-link routed transmission groups are as reliable as direct NCP-to-NCP single-link transmission groups. This is true because neither the NCP nor Cisco IOS software can reroute I-frames when a transmission group has only one link. Additionally, a multilink transmission group directed between NCPs and a multilink transmission group through a router are equally reliable. Both can perform rerouting.

However, you might run into problems if you have a configuration in which two NCPs are directly connected (via one or more transmission group links) and one link in the transmission group is routed. The NCPs treat this as a multilink transmission group. However, Cisco IOS software views the transmission group as a single-link transmission group.

A problem can arise in the following situation: Assume that an I-frame is being transmitted from NCP A (connected to router A) to NCP B (connected to router B) and that all SDLC links are currently active. Router A acknowledges the I-frame sent from NCP A and sends it over the WAN. If, before the I-frame reaches Router B, the SDLC link between router B and NCP B goes down, Router B attempts to reroute the I-frame on another link in the transmission group when it receives the I-frame. However, because this is a single-link transmission group, there are no other routes and Router B drops the I-frame. NCP B never receives this I-frame because Router A acknowledges its receipt and NCP A marks it as transmitted and deletes it. NCP B detects a gap in the transmission group sequence numbers and waits to receive the missing I-frame. NCP B waits forever for this I-frame and does not send or receive any other frames. NCP B is technically not operational and all SNA sessions through NCP B are lost.

Finally, consider a configuration in which one or more lines of an NCP transmission group are connected to a router and one or more lines are directly connected between NCPs. If the network delay associated with one line of an NCP transmission group is different from the delay of another line in the same NCP transmission group, the receiving NCP spends additional time resequencing PIUs.

Set Up STUN Traffic Priorities

Use the methods described in the following sections to determine the order in which traffic should be handled on the network:

- Assign Queuing Priorities
- Prioritize STUN Traffic over All Other Traffic

Assign Queuing Priorities

You can assign queuing priorities by one of the following:

- Serial interface address or TCP port
- Logical unit (LU) address

Prioritize by Serial Interface Address or TCP Port

You can prioritize traffic on a per-serial-interface address or TCP port basis. You might want to do this so that traffic between one source-destination pair is always sent before traffic between another source-destination pair.

NOTE   You must first enable local acknowledgment and priority levels as described earlier in this chapter.

To prioritize traffic, use one of the following commands in global configuration mode:

Command	Purpose
priority-list *list-number* **stun** *queue* **address** *group-number address-number*	Assigns a queuing priority to the address of the STUN serial interface.
or	or
priority-list *list-number* **protocol ip** *queue* **tcp** *tcp-port-number*	Assigns a queuing priority to a TCP port.

You must also use the following command in interface configuration mode:

Command	Purpose
priority-group *list-number*	Assigns a priority list to a priority group.

Figure 11-4 illustrates serial link address prioritization. Device A communicates with Device C and Device B communicates with Device D. With the serial link address prioritization, you can choose to give A-C a higher priority over B-D across the serial tunnel.

Figure 11-4 *Serial Link Address Prioritization*

To disable priorities, use the **no** forms of these commands.

For an example of how to prioritize traffic according to serial link address, see the section "Configuring Serial Link Address Prioritization Using STUN TCP/IP Encapsulation Example" later in this chapter.

Prioritize by Logical Unit Address

SNA local logical unit (LU) address prioritization is specific to IBM SNA connectivity and is used to prioritize SNA traffic on either STUN or remote source-route bridging (RSRB). To set the queuing priority by LU address, use the following command in interface configuration mode:

Command	Purpose
locaddr-priority-list *list-number address-number queue-keyword*	Assigns a queuing priority based on the logical unit address.

In Figure 11-5, LU address prioritization can be set so that particular LUs receive data in preference to others or so that LUs have priority over the printer, for example.

Figure 11-5 *SNA LU Address Prioritization*

To disable this priority, use the **no** form of this command.

For an example of how to prioritize traffic according to logical unit address, see "Configuring LOCADDR Priority Groups for STUN Example" later in this chapter.

Prioritize STUN Traffic over All Other Traffic

You can prioritize STUN traffic to be routed first before all other traffic on the network. To give STUN traffic this priority, use the following command in global configuration mode:

Command	Purpose
priority-list *list-number* **stun** *queue* **address** *group-number address-number*	Prioritizes STUN traffic in your network over that of other protocols.

To disable this priority, use the **no** form of this command.

For an example of how to prioritize STUN traffic over all other traffic, see the section "Configuring Serial Link Address Prioritization Using STUN TCP/IP Encapsulation Example" later in this chapter.

Monitor STUN Network Activity

You can list statistics regarding STUN interfaces, protocol groups, number of packets sent and received, local acknowledgment states, and more. To get activity information, use the following command in EXEC mode:

Command	Purpose
show stun	Lists the status display fields for STUN interfaces.

STUN Configuration Examples

The following sections provide STUN configuration examples:

- Configuring STUN Priorities Using HDLC Encapsulation Example

- Configuring SDLC Broadcast Example

- Configuring Serial Link Address Prioritization Using STUN TCP/IP Encapsulation Example

- Configuring STUN Multipoint Implementation Using a Line-Sharing Device Example

- Configuring STUN Local Acknowledgment for SDLC Example

- Configuring STUN Local Acknowledgment for Frame Relay Example

- Configuring LOCADDR Priority Groups—Simple Example

- Configuring LOCADDR Priority Groups for STUN Example

Configuring STUN Priorities Using HDLC Encapsulation Example

Assume that the link between Router A and Router B in Figure 11-6 is a serial tunnel that uses the simple serial transport mechanism. Device A communicates with Device C (SDLC address C1) with a high priority. Device B communicates with Device D (SDLC address A7) with a normal priority.

Figure 11-6 *STUN Simple Serial Transport*

The following configurations set the priority of STUN hosts A, B, C, and D.

Router A

```
stun peer-name 1.0.0.1
stun protocol-group 1 sdlc
stun protocol-group 2 sdlc
!
interface serial 0
 no ip address
 encapsulation stun
 stun group 1
 stun route address C1 interface serial 2
!
interface serial 1
 no ip address
 encapsulation stun
 stun group 2
 stun route address A7 interface serial 2
!
interface serial 2
 ip address 1.0.0.1 255.0.0.0
 priority-group 1
!
priority-list 1 stun high address 1 C1
priority-list 1 stun low address 2 A7
```

Router B

```
stun peer-name 1.0.0.2
stun protocol-group 1 sdlc
stun protocol-group 2 sdlc
!
interface serial 0
 no ip address
 encapsulation stun
 stun group 1
 stun route address C1 interface serial 1
!
interface serial 1
 ip address 1.0.0.2 255.0.0.0
 priority-group 1
!
interface serial 2
 no ip address
 encapsulation stun
 stun group 2
 stun route address A7 interface serial 1
!
priority-list 1 stun high address 1 C1
priority-list 1 stun low address 2 A7
```

Configuring SDLC Broadcast Example

In the following example, an FEP views end stations 1, 2, and 3 as if they were on an SDLC multidrop link. Any broadcast frame sent from the FEP to Router A is duplicated and sent to each of the downstream routers (B and C).

```
stun peer-name xxx.xxx.xxx.xxx
stun protocol-group 1 sdlc
interface serial 1
encapsulation stun
 stun group 1
 stun sdlc-role secondary
 sdlc virtual-multidrop
 sdlc address 1
 sdlc address 2
 sdlc address 3
 stun route address 1 tcp yyy.yyy.yyy.yyy local-ack
 stun route address 2 tcp zzz.zzz.zzz.zzz local-ack
 stun route address 3 tcp zzz.zzz.zzz.zzz local-ack
 stun route address FF tcp yyy.yyy.yyy.yyy
 stun route address FF tcp zzz.zzz.zzz.zzz
```

Configuring Serial Link Address Prioritization Using STUN TCP/IP Encapsulation Example

Assume that the link between Router A and Router B is a serial tunnel that uses the TCP/IP encapsulation as shown in Figure 11-7. Device A communicates with Device C (SDLC address C1) with a high priority. Device B communicates with Device D (SDLC address A7) with a normal priority. The configuration file for each router follows the figure.

Figure 11-7   *STUN TCP/IP Encapsulation*

Router A

```
stun peer-name 1.0.0.1
stun protocol-group 1 sdlc
stun protocol-group 2 sdlc
!
interface serial 0
 no ip address
 encapsulation stun
```

```
 stun group 1
 stun route address C1 tcp 1.0.0.2 local-ack priority
 priority-group 1
!
interface serial 1
 no ip address
 encapsulation stun
 stun group 2
 stun route address A7 tcp 1.0.0.2 local-ack priority
 priority-group 2
!
interface ethernet 0
 ip address 1.0.0.1 255.0.0.0
!
interface ethernet 1
 ip address 1.0.0.3 255.0.0.0
!
priority-list 1 protocol ip high tcp 1994
priority-list 1 protocol ip medium tcp 1990
priority-list 1 protocol ip normal tcp 1991
priority-list 1 protocol ip low tcp 1992
priority-list 1 stun high address 1 C1
!
priority-list 2 protocol ip high tcp 1994
priority-list 2 protocol ip medium tcp 1990
priority-list 2 protocol ip normal tcp 1991
priority-list 2 protocol ip low tcp 1992
priority-list 2 stun normal address 2 A7
!
hostname routerA
router igrp
network 1.0.0.0
```

Router B

```
stun peer-name 1.0.0.2
stun protocol-group 1 sdlc
stun protocol-group 2 sdlc
!
interface serial 0
 no ip address
 encapsulation stun
 stun group 1
 stun route address C1 tcp 1.0.0.1 local-ack priority
 priority-group 1
!
interface serial 2
 no ip address
 encapsulation stun
 stun group 2
 stun route address A7 tcp 1.0.0.1 local-ack priority
 priority-group 2
!
```

```
interface ethernet 0
 ip address 1.0.0.2 255.0.0.0
!
interface ethernet 1
 ip address 1.0.0.4 255.0.0.0
!
priority-list 1 protocol ip high tcp 1994
priority-list 1 protocol ip medium tcp 1990
priority-list 1 protocol ip normal tcp 1991
priority-list 1 protocol ip low tcp 1992
priority-list 1 stun high address 1 C1
!
priority-list 2 protocol ip high tcp 1994
priority-list 2 protocol ip medium tcp 1990
priority-list 2 protocol ip normal tcp 1991
priority-list 2 protocol ip low tcp 1992
priority-list 2 stun normal address 2 A7
!
hostname routerB
router igrp 109
network 1.0.0.0
```

Configuring STUN Multipoint Implementation Using a Line-Sharing Device Example

In Figure 11-8, four separate PS/2 computers are connected to a line-sharing device off of Router B. Each PS/2 computer has four sessions open on an AS/400 device attached to Router A. Router B functions as the primary station, while Router A functions as the secondary station. Both routers locally acknowledge packets from the IBM PS/2 systems.

Figure 11-8   *STUN Communication Involving a Line-Sharing Device*

The configuration file for the routers shown in Figure 11-8 follows.

Router A

```
! enter the address of the stun peer
stun peer-name 150.136.134.86
! specify that group 4 uses the SDLC protocol
stun protocol-group 4 sdlc
stun remote-peer-keepalive

interface ethernet 1
! enter the IP address for the Ethernet interface
 ip address 150.136.134.86 255.255.255.0
 !
! description of IBM AS/400 link
interface serial 2
! description of IBM AS/400 link; disable the IP address on a serial interface
 no ip address
! enable STUN encapsulation on this interface
 encapsulation stun
! apply previously defined stun group 4 to serial interface 2
 stun group 4
! establish this router as a secondary station
stun sdlc-role secondary
! wait up to 63000 msec for a poll from the primary before timing out
 sdlc poll-wait-timeout 63000
! list addresses of secondary stations (PS/2 systems) attached to link
sdlc address C1
sdlc address C2
sdlc address C3
sdlc address C4
! use tcp encapsulation to send frames to SDLC stations C1, C2, C3, or
! C4 and locally terminate sessions with these stations
stun route address C1 tcp 150.136.134.58 local-ack
stun route address C2 tcp 150.136.134.58 local-ack
stun route address C3 tcp 150.136.134.58 local-ack
stun route address C4 tcp 150.136.134.58 local-ack
```

Router B

```
! enter the address of the stun peer
stun peer-name 150.136.134.58
! this router is part of SDLC group 4
stun protocol-group 4 sdlc
stun remote-peer-keepalive
!
interface ethernet 1
! enter the IP address for the Ethernet interface
ip address 150.136.134.58 255.255.255.0
!
! description of PS/2 link
interface serial 4
! disable the IP address on a serial interface
 no ip address
! enable STUN encapsulation on this interface
 encapsulation stun
```

```
! apply previously defined stun group 4 to serial interface 2
stun group 4
! establish this router as a primary station
stun sdlc-role primary
sdlc line-speed 9600
! wait 2000 milliseconds for a reply to a frame before resending it
sdlc t1 2000
! resend a frame up to four times if not acknowledged
sdlc n2 4
! list addresses of secondary stations (PS/2 systems) attached to link
sdlc address C1
sdlc address C2
sdlc address C3
sdlc address C4
! use tcp encapsulation to send frames to SDLC stations C1, C2, C3, or
! C4 and locally terminate sessions with these stations
stun route address C3 tcp 150.136.134.86 local-ack
stun route address C1 tcp 150.136.134.86 local-ack
stun route address C4 tcp 150.136.134.86 local-ack
stun route address C2 tcp 150.136.134.86 local-ack
! set the clockrate on this interface to 9600 bits per second
clockrate 9600
```

Configuring STUN Local Acknowledgment for SDLC Example

The following example shows a sample configuration for a pair of routers performing SDLC local acknowledgment.

Router A

```
stun peer-name 150.136.64.92
stun protocol-group 1 sdlc
stun remote-peer-keepalive
!
interface Serial 0
 no ip address
 encapsulation stun
 stun group 1
 stun sdlc-role secondary
 sdlc address C1
 stun route address C1 tcp 150.136.64.93 local-ack
 clockrate 19200
```

Router B

```
stun peer-name 150.136.64.93
stun protocol-group 1 sdlc
stun remote-peer-keepalive
!
interface Serial 0
 no ip address
```

```
encapsulation stun
stun group 1
stun sdlc-role primary
sdlc line-speed 19200
sdlc address C1
stun route address C1 tcp 150.136.64.92 local-ack
clockrate 19200
```

Configuring STUN Local Acknowledgment for Frame Relay Example

The following example describes an interface configuration for Frame Relay STUN with local acknowledgment:

```
stun peer-name 10.1.21.1 cls 4
stun protocol-group 120 sdlc
!
interface Serial1
 no ip address
 encapsulation frame-relay
 frame-relay lmi-type ansi
 frame-relay map llc2 22
!
interface Serial4
 no ip address
 encapsulation stun
 clockrate 9600
 stun group 120
 stun sdlc-role secondary
 sdlc address C1
 sdlc address C2
 stun route address C1 interface Serial1 dlci 22 04 local-ack
 stun route address C2 interface Serial1 dlci 22 08 local-ack
!
```

Configuring LOCADDR Priority Groups—Simple Example

The following example shows how to establish queuing priorities on a STUN interface based on an LU address:

```
! sample stun peer-name global command
stun peer-name 131.108.254.6
! sample protocol-group command for reference
stun protocol-group 1 sdlc
!
interface serial 0
! disable the ip address for interface serial 0
 no ip address
! enable the interface for STUN
 encapsulation stun
! sample stun group command
```

```
 stun group 2
! sample stun route command
 stun route address 10 tcp 131.108.254.8 local-ack priority
!
! assign priority group 1 to the input side of interface serial 0
locaddr-priority 1
priority-group 1
!
interface Ethernet 0
! give locaddr-priority-list 1 a high priority for LU 02
 locaddr-priority-list 1 02 high
! give locaddr-priority-list 1 a low priority for LU 05
 locaddr-priority-list 1 05 low
```

Configuring LOCADDR Priority Groups for STUN Example

The following configuration example shows how to assign a priority group to an input interface:

Router A

```
stun peer-name 1.0.0.1
stun protocol-group 1 sdlc
!
interface serial 0
 no ip address
 encapsulation stun
 stun group 1
 stun route address C1 tcp 1.0.0.2 local-ack priority
 clockrate 19200
 locaddr-priority 1
 priority-group 1
!
interface Ethernet 0
 ip address 1.0.0.1 255.255.255.0
!
 locaddr-priority-list 1 02 high
 locaddr-priority-list 1 03 high
 locaddr-priority-list 1 04 medium
 locaddr-priority-list 1 05 low
!
 priority-list 1 protocol ip high tcp 1994
 priority-list 1 protocol ip medium tcp 1990
 priority-list 1 protocol ip normal tcp 1991
 priority-list 1 protocol ip low tcp 1992
```

Router B

```
stun peer-name 1.0.0.2
stun protocol-group 1 sdlc
!
interface serial 0
```

```
 no ip address
 encapsulation stun
 stun group 1
 stun route address C1 tcp 1.0.0.1 local-ack priority
 clockrate 19200
 locaddr-priority 1
 priority-group 1
!
interface Ethernet 0
 ip address 1.0.0.2 255.255.255.0
!
 locaddr-priority-list 1 02 high
 locaddr-priority-list 1 03 high
 locaddr-priority-list 1 04 medium
 locaddr-priority-list 1 05 low
!
 priority-list 1 protocol ip high tcp 1994
 priority-list 1 protocol ip medium tcp 1990
 priority-list 1 protocol ip normal tcp 1991
 priority-list 1 protocol ip low tcp 1992
```

Block Serial Tunneling

Cisco's implementation of Block Serial Tunneling (BSTUN) provides the following features:

● Encapsulates Bisync, Adplex, ADT Security Systems, Inc., Diebold, and asynchronous generic
   traffic for transfer over router links. The tunneling of asynchronous security protocols (ASP)
   feature enables your Cisco 2500, 3600, 4000, 4500, or 7200 series router to support devices that
   use the following asynchronous security protocols:

   — adplex

   — adt-poll-select

   — adt-vari-poll

   — diebold

   — async-generic

   — mdi

● Provides a tunnel mechanism for BSTUN over Frame Relay without using TCP/IP encapsulation.

● Supports legacy Bisync devices and host applications without modification.

● Uses standard synchronous serial interfaces on Cisco 2500 series and the 4T network interface
   module (NIM) on the Cisco 4000 series and Cisco 4500 series.

● Supports point-to-point, multidrop, and virtual multidrop configurations.

NOTE	The async-generic item, listed above, is not a protocol name. It is a command keyword used to indicate generic support of other asynchronous security protocols that are not explicitly supported.

Bisync Network Overview

The Bisync feature enables your Cisco 2500, 3600, 4000, 4500, 4700, and 7200 series router to support devices that use the Bisync datalink protocol. This protocol enables enterprises to transport Bisync traffic over the same network that supports their SNA and multiprotocol traffic, eliminating the need for separate Bisync facilities.

At the access router, traffic from the attached Bisync device is encapsulated in IP. The Bisync traffic can then be routed across arbitrary media to the host site where another router supporting Bisync will remove the IP encapsulation headers and present the Bisync traffic to the Bisync host or controller over a serial connection. HDLC can be used as an alternative encapsulation method for point-to-point links. Figure 11-9 shows how you can reconfigure an existing Bisync link between two devices and provide the same logical link without any changes to the existing Bisync devices.

Figure 11-9   *Routers Consolidating Bisync Traffic by Encapsulation in IP or HDLC*

The routers transport all Bisync blocks between the two devices in pass-through mode using BSTUN as encapsulation. BSTUN uses the same encapsulation architecture as STUN, but is implemented on an independent tunnel.

Point-to-Point and Multidrop Support

The Bisync feature supports point-to-point, multidrop, and virtual multidrop Bisync configurations.

In point-to-point operation, the Bisync blocks between the two point-to-point devices are received and forwarded transparently by Cisco IOS software. The contention to acquire the line for transmission is handled by the devices themselves.

Cisco Bisync multipoint operation is provided as a logical multipoint configuration. Figure 11-10 shows how a multipoint Bisync link is reconfigured using Cisco routers. Router A is configured as Bisync secondary. It monitors the address field of the polling or selection block and uses this address information to put into the BSTUN frame for BSTUN to deliver to the correct destination router. To simulate the Bisync multidrop, an EOT block is sent by the Bisync primary router before a poll or selection block. This ensures that Bisync tributary stations are in control mode before being polled or selected.

Figure 11-10 *Multipoint Bisync Link Reconfigured Using Routers*

Multidrop configurations are common in Bisync networks where up to 8 or 10 Bisync devices are frequently connected to a Bisync controller port over a single low-speed link. Bisync devices from different physical locations in the network appear as a single multidrop line to the Bisync host or controller. Figure 11-11 illustrates a multidrop Bisync configuration before and after implementing routers.

Figure 11-11 *Integrating Bisync Devices over a Multiprotocol Network*

Asynchronous Network Overview

These protocols enable enterprises to transport polled asynchronous traffic over the same network that supports their SNA and multiprotocol traffic, eliminating the need for separate facilities. Figure 11-12 shows how you can reconfigure an existing asynchronous link between two security devices and provide the same logical link without any changes to the existing devices.

Figure 11-12 *Routers Consolidate Polled Asynchronous Traffic Using Encapsulation in IP or HDLC*

Router A is configured as the secondary end of the BSTUN asynchronous link and is attached to the security control station; Router B is configured as the primary end of the BSTUN asynchronous link and has one or more alarm panels attached to it.

At the downstream router, traffic from the attached alarm panels is encapsulated in IP. The asynchronous (alarm) traffic can be routed across arbitrary media to the host site where the upstream router supporting these protocols removes the IP encapsulation headers and presents the original traffic to the security control station over a serial connection. HDLC can be used as an alternative encapsulation method for point-to-point links.

The routers transport all asynchronous (alarm) blocks between the two devices in passthru mode using BSTUN for encapsulation. BSTUN uses the same encapsulation architecture as STUN, but is implemented on an independent tunnel. As each asynchronous frame is received from the line, a BSTUN header is added to create a BSTUN frame and then BSTUN is used to deliver the frame to the correct destination router.

Cisco routers do not perform any local acknowledgment or cyclic redundancy check (CRC) calculations on the asynchronous alarm blocks. The two end devices are responsible for error recovery in the asynchronous alarm protocol.

Virtual Multidrop Support for Multipoint Security Network Configurations

Multipoint configurations are common in security networks where a number of alarm panels are frequently connected to a security control station over a single low-speed link. Cisco virtual multidrop support allows alarm panels from different physical locations in the network to appear as a single multidrop line to the security control station. Both Adplex and ADT are virtual multidropped protocols.

Multidrop operation is provided as a logical multipoint configuration. Figure 11-13 shows how a multipoint security network is reconfigured using Cisco routers. Router A is configured as an alarm secondary node, routers B and C are configured as alarm primary nodes. Router A monitors the address field of the polling or selection block and puts this address information in the BSTUN frame so BSTUN can deliver the frame to the correct downstream node.

Figure 11-13 *Multipoint Asynchronous Security Protocol Link Reconfigured Using Routers*

Frame Sequencing

Both Bisync and asynchronous alarm protocols are half-duplex protocols; transmission can occur in either direction, but only in one direction at a time. Each block of transmission is acknowledged explicitly by the remote end. To avoid the problem associated with simultaneous transmisssion, there is an implicit role of primary and secondary station.

Frame Sequencing in Bisync Networks

In a multidrop setup in Bisync networks, the Bisync control station is primary and the tributary stations are secondary. In a point-to-point configuration, the primary role is assumed by the Bisync device that has successfully acquired the line for transmission through the ENQ bidding sequence. The primary role stays with this station until it sends EOT.

To protect against occasional network latency, which causes the primary station to time out and resend the block before the Bisync block sent by the secondary is received, the control byte of the encapsulating frame is used as a sequence number. This sequence number is controlled and monitored by the primary Bisync router. This allows the primary Bisync router to detect and discard "late" Bisync blocks sent by the secondary router and ensure integrity of the Bisync link.

NOTE	Frame sequencing is implemented in passthru mode only.

Frame Sequencing in Asynchronous Networks

Network delays in asynchronous networks make it possible for a frame to arrive "late," meaning that the poll-cycling mechanism at the security control station has already moved on to poll the next alarm panel in sequence when it receives the poll response from the previous alarm panel.

To protect against this situation, routers configured for adplex or for adt-poll-select protocols use a sequence number built into the encapsulating frame to detect and discard late frames. The upstream router (connected to the security control station) inserts a frame sequence number into the protocol header, which is shipped through BSTUN and bounced back by the downstream router (connected to the alarm panel). The upstream router maintains a frame-sequence count for the line, and checks the incoming frame-sequence number from the downstream router. If the two frame-sequence numbers do not agree, the frame is considered late (out of sequence) and is discarded.

Because the adt-vari-poll option allows the transmission of unsolicited messages from the alarm panel, frame sequencing is not supported for this protocol.

NOTE	Polled asynchronous (alarm) protocols are implemented only in passthrough mode. There is no support for local acknowledgment.

BSTUN Configuration Task List

The Bisync feature is configured similar to SDLC STUN, but is configured as a protocol within a BSTUN feature. To configure and monitor Bisync with BSTUN, complete the tasks in the following sections:

- Enable BSTUN
- Define the Protocol Group
- Enable STUN Keepalive
- Enable STUN Remote Keepalive
- Enable Frame Relay Encapsulation
- Define Mapping Between BSTUN and DLCI
- Configure BSTUN on the Serial Interface
- Place a Serial Interface in a BSTUN Group
- Specify How Frames Are Forwarded
- Set Up BSTUN Traffic Priorities
- Configure Protocol Group Options on a Serial Interface
- Configure Direct Serial Encapsulation for Passthrough Peers
- Configure Local Acknowledgment Peers
- Monitor the Status of BSTUN

The "BSTUN Configuration Examples" section follows these tasks.

Enable BSTUN

To enable BSTUN in IP networks, use the following commands in global configuration mode:

Step	Command	Purpose
1	**bstun peer-name** *ip-address*	Enables BSTUN.
2	**bstun lisnsap** *sap-value*	Enables BSTUN for Frame Relay transport.

The IP address in the **bstun peer-name** command defines the address by which this BSTUN peer is known to other BSTUN peers that are using the TCP transport. If this command is unconfigured or the **no** form of this command is specified, all BSTUN routing commands with IP addresses are deleted. BSTUN routing commands without IP addresses are not affected by this command.

The **bstun lisnsap** command specifies a SAP on which to detect incoming calls.

Define the Protocol Group

Define a BSTUN group and specify the protocol it uses. To define the protocol group, use the following command in global configuration mode:

Command	Purpose
bstun protocol-group *group-number* {**bsc** | **bsc-local-ack** | **adplex** | **adt-poll** | **adt-poll-select** | **adt-vari-poll** | **diebold** | **async-generic** | **mdi**}	Defines the protocol group.

The **bsc-local-ack** protocol option only works for 3270 Bisync uses.

The block serial protocols include bsc, bsc-local-ack, adplex, adt-poll-select, adt-vari-poll, diebold, async-generic, and mdi.

Traditionally, the adt-poll-select protocol is used over land-based links, while the adt-vari-poll protocol is used over satellite (VSAT) links. The adt-vari-poll protocol typically uses a much slower polling rate when alarm consoles poll alarm panels because adt-vari-poll allows alarm panels to send unsolicited messages to the alarm console. In an adt-vari-poll configuration, alarm panels do not have wait for the console to poll them before responding with an alarm, they automatically send the alarm.

Interfaces configured to run the adplex protocol have their baud rate set to 4800 bps, use even parity, 8 data bits, 1 start bit, and 1 stop bit.

Interfaces configured to run the adt-poll-select and adt-vari-poll protocols have their baud rate set to 600 bps, use even parity, 8 data bits, 1 start bit, and 1.5 stop bits. If different line configurations are required, use the **rxspeed**, **txspeed**, **databits**, **stopbits**, and **parity** line configuration commands to change the line attributes.

Interfaces configured to run the diebold protocol have their baud rate set to 300 bps, use even parity, 8 data bits, 1 start bit, and 2 stop bits. If different line configurations are required, use the **rxspeed**, **txspeed**, **databits**, and **parity** line configuration commands to change the line attributes.

Interfaces configured to run the async-generic protocol have their baud rate set to 9600 bps, use no parity, 8 data bits, 1 start bit, and 1 stop bit. If different line configurations are required, use the **rxspeed**, **txspeed**, **databits**, **stopbits**, and **parity** line configuration commands to change the line attributes.

Interfaces configured to run the mdi protocol have their baud rate set to 600 bps, use even parity, 8 data bits, 1 start bit, and 1.5 stop bits. If different line configurations are required, use the **rxspeed**, **txspeed**, **databits**, **stopbits**, and **parity** line configuration commands to change the line attributes. The mdi protocol allows alarm panels to be sent to the MDI alarm console.

Enable BSTUN Keepalive

To define the number of times to attempt a peer connection before declaring the peer connection be down, use the following command in global configuration mode:

Command	Purpose
bstun keepalive-count	Specifies the number of times to attempt a peer connection.

Enable BSTUN Remote Keepalive

To enable detection of the loss of a peer, use the following command in global configuration mode:

Command	Purpose
bstun remote-peer-keepalive *seconds*	Enables detection of the loss of a peer.

Enable Frame Relay Encapsulation

To enable Frame Relay encapsulation, use the following commands, beginning in global configuration mode:

Step	Command	Purpose
1	**interface serial** *number*	Specifies a serial port.
2	**encapsulation frame-relay**	Enables Frame Relay encapsulation on the serial port.

Define Mapping Between BSTUN and DLCI

To configure the mapping between BSTUN and the DLCI, use one of the following commands in interface configuration mode:

Command	Purpose
frame-relay map bstun *dlci*	Defines the mapping between BSTUN and the DLCI when using BSC passthrough.
frame-relay map llc2 *dlci*	Defines the mapping between BSTUN and the DLCI when using BSC local acknowledgment.

Configure BSTUN on the Serial Interface

Configure BSTUN on the serial interface before issuing any further BSTUN or protocol configuration commands for the interface. To configure the BSTUN function on a specified interface, use the following commands in interface configuration mode:

Step	Command	Purpose
1	**interface serial** *number*	Specifies a serial port.
2	**encapsulation bstun**[1]	Configures BSTUN on an interface.

1. This command must be configured on an interface before any other BSTUN commands are configured for this interface.

Place a Serial Interface in a BSTUN Group

Each BSTUN-enabled interface on a router must be placed in a previously defined BSTUN group. Packets will only travel between BSTUN-enabled interfaces that are in the same group. To assign a serial interface to a BSTUN group, use the following command in interface configuration mode:

Command	Purpose
bstun group *group-number*	Assigns a serial interface to a BSTUN group.

Specify How Frames Are Forwarded

To specify how frames are forwarded when received on a BSTUN interface, use one of the following commands in interface configuration mode:

Command	Purpose
bstun route address *address-number* **interface serial** *number*	Propagates the serial frame that contains a specific address. HDLC encapsulation is used to propagate the serial frames.
bstun route all interface serial *number*	Propagates all BSTUN traffic received on the input interface, regardless of the address contained in the serial frame. HDLC encapsulation is used to propagate the serial frames.
bstun route address *address-number* **tcp** *ip-address*	Propagates the serial frame that contains a specific address. TCP encapsulation is used to propagate frames that match the entry.

Command	Purpose
bstun route all tcp *ip-address*[1]	Propagates all BSTUN traffic received on the input interface, regardless of the address contained in the serial frame. TCP encapsulation is used to propagate frames that match the entry.
bstun route address *cu-address* **interface serial** *serial-int* **dlci** *dlci*	Propagates the serial frame that contains a specific address. Specify the control unit address for the Bisync end station. Frame Relay encapsulation is used to propagate the serial frames.
bstun route all interface serial *serial-int* **dlci** *dlci*	Propagates all frames, regardless of the control unit address for the Bisync end station. Frame Relay encapsulation is used to propagate the serial frames in bisync passthrough mode.
bstun route address *cu-address* **interface serial** *serial-int* **dlci** *dlci* *rsap* **priority** *priority*	Propagates the serial frame that contains a specific address. Specifies the control unit address for the bisync end station. Frame Relay encapsulation is used to propagate the serial frames for Bisync local acknowledgment mode.
bstun route all interface serial *serial-int* **dlci** *dlci* *rsap* **priority** *priority*	Propagates all BSTUN traffic received on the input interface, regardless of the address contained in the serial frame. Frame Relay encapsulation is used to propagate the serial frames.

1. The **bstun route all tcp** command functions in either passthru or local acknowledgment mode.

For Bisync local acknowledgment, we recommend that you use the **bstun route all tcp** command. This command reduces the amount of duplicate configuration detail that would otherwise be needed to specify devices at each end of the tunnel.

Set Up BSTUN Traffic Priorities

You can assign BSTUN traffic priorities based on either the BSTUN header or the TCP port. To prioritize traffic, use one of the following commands in global configuration mode:

Command	Purpose
priority-list *list-number* **protocol bstun** *queue* [**gt** *packetsize*] [**lt** *packetsize*] **address** *bstun-group bsc-addr*	Establishes BSTUN queuing priorities based on the BSTUN header.
priority-list *list-number* **protocol ip** *queue* **tcp** *tcp-port-number*	Assigns a queuing priority to TCP port.

You can customize BSTUN queuing priorities based on either the BSTUN header or TCP port. To customize priorities, use one of the following commands in global configuration mode:

Command	Purpose
queue-list *list-number* **protocol bstun** *queue* [**gt** *packetsize*] [**lt** *packetsize*] **address** *bstun-group bsc-addr*	Customizes BSTUN queuing priorities based on the BSTUN header.
queue-list *list-number* **protocol ip** *queue* **tcp** *tcp-port-number*	Customizes BSTUN queuing priorities based on the TCP port.

NOTE	Because the asynchronous security protocols share the same tunnels with Bisync when configured on the same routers, any traffic priorities configured for the tunnel apply to both Bisync and the various asynchronous security protocols.

Configure Protocol Group Options on a Serial Interface

Depending on the selected block serial protocol group, you must configure one or more options for that protocol group. The options for each of these protocol groups are explained in the following sections:

● Configure Bisync Options on a Serial Interface

● Configure Asynchronous Security Protocol Options on a Serial Interface

Configure Bisync Options on a Serial Interface

To configure Bisync options on a serial interface, use one of the following commands in interface configuration mode:

Command	Purpose
bsc char-set {**ascii**	**ebcdic**}	Specifies the character set used by the Bisync support feature.
bsc contention *address*	Specifies an address on a contention interface.
bsc dial-contention *time-out*	Specifies that the router at the central site will behave as a central router with dynamic allocation of serial interfaces. The timeout value is the length of time an interface can be idle before it is returned to the idle interface pool.
bsc extended-address *poll-address select-address*	Specifies a nonstandard Bisync address.

Command	Purpose
full-duplex	Specifies that the interface can run Bisync in full-duplex mode.
bsc pause *time*	Specifies the amount of time between the start of one polling cycle and the next.
bsc poll-timeout *time*	Specifies the timeout for a poll or a select sequence.
bsc host-timeout *time*	Specifies the timeout for a nonreception of poll or a select sequence from the host. If the frame is not received within this time the remote connection will be deactivated.
bsc primary	Specifies that the router is acting as the primary end of the Bisync link.
bsc retries *retry-count*	Specifies the number of retries before a device is considered to have failed.
bsc secondary	Specifies that the router is acting as the secondary end of the Bisync link.
bsc spec-poll	Specifies specific polls, rather than general polls, used on the host-to-router connection.
bsc servlim *servlim-count*	Specifies the number of cycles of the active poll list that are performed between polls to control units in the inactive poll list.

Configure Asynchronous Security Protocol Options on a Serial Interface

To configure asynchronous security protocol options on a serial interface, use one or more of the following commands in interface configuration mode:

Command	Purpose
asp role primary	Specifies that the router is acting as the primary end of the polled asynchronous link.
asp role secondary	Specifies that the router is acting as the secondary end of the polled asynchronous link.
asp addr-offset *address-offset*	For asynchronous-generic configurations, specifies the location of the address byte within the polled asynchronous frame being received.

Command	Purpose
asp rx-ift *interframe-timeout*	For asynchronous-generic configurations, specifies the timeout period between frames to delineate the end of one frame being received from the start of the next frame.

Configure Direct Serial Encapsulation for Passthrough Peers

To configure direct serial encapsulation for passthrough peers, use the following command in interface configuration mode:

Command	Purpose
frame relay map bstun	Configures the Frame Relay interface for passthrough.

Configure Local Acknowledgment Peers

To configure local acknowledgment peers, use the following command in interface configuration mode:

Command	Purpose
frame-relay map llc2 *dlci*	Configures the Frame Relay interface for local acknowledgment.

Monitor the Status of BSTUN

To list statistics for BSTUN interfaces, protocol groups, number of packets sent and received, local acknowledgment states, and other activity information, use the following commands in EXEC mode:

Command	Purpose
show bstun [**group** *bstun-group-number*] [**address** *address-list*]	Lists the status display fields for BSTUN interfaces.
show bsc [**group** *bstun-group-number*] [**address** *address-list*]	Displays status of the interfaces on which Bisync is configured.

BSTUN Configuration Examples

The following sections provide BSTUN configuration examples:

- Simple Bisync Configuration Example
- Bisync Addressing on Contention Interfaces
- Nonstandard Bisync Addressing Example
- Priority Queuing: with Priority Based on BSTUN Header Example
- Priority Queuing: with Priority Based on BSTUN Header and Packet Sizes Example
- Priority Queuing: with Priority Based on BSTUN Header and Bisync Address Example
- Priority Queuing: with Priority Based on BSTUN TCP Ports Example
- Priority Queuing: with Priority Based on BSTUN TCP Ports and Bisync Address Example
- Custom Queuing: with Priority Based on BSTUN Header Example
- Custom Queuing: with Priority Based on BSTUN Header and Packet Size Example
- Custom Queuing: with Priority Based on BSTUN Header and Bisync Address Example
- Custom Queuing: with Priority Based on BSTUN TCP Ports Example
- Custom Queuing: with Priority Based on BSTUN TCP Ports and Bisync Address Example
- Asynchronous Configuration Example
- BSTUN over Frame Relay Configuration with Local Acknowledgment Example
- BSTUN over Frame Relay Configuration with Passthrough Example

Simple Bisync Configuration Example

Figure 11-14 shows a simple Bisync configuration example.

Figure 11-14 *Simple Bisync Configuration*

The configuration files for the routers shown in Figure 11-14 follows.

Router 45ka

```
version 10.2
!
hostname 45ka
!
no ip domain-lookup
!
bstun peer-name 150.10.254.201
bstun protocol-group 1 bsc
!
interface ethernet 0
 ip address 198.92.0.201 255.255.255.0
 media-type 10BaseT
!
interface ethernet 1
 no ip address
 shutdown
 media-type 10BaseT
!
interface serial 0
 no ip address
 encapsulation bstun
 clockrate 19200
 bstun group 1
 bsc char-set ebcdic
 bsc secondary
 bstun route address C9 tcp 150.10.254.210
bstun route address C8 tcp 150.10.254.210
bstun route address C7 tcp 150.10.254.208
```

```
bstun route address C6 tcp 150.10.254.208
bstun route address C5 tcp 150.10.254.208
bstun route address C4 tcp 150.10.254.208
bstun route address C3 tcp 150.10.254.207
bstun route address C2 tcp 150.10.254.207
bstun route address C1 tcp 150.10.254.207
bstun route address 40 tcp 150.10.254.207
!
interface serial 1
no ip address
shutdown
!
interface serial 2
 no ip address
 shutdown
!
interface serial 3
 no ip address
 shutdown
!
interface tokenring 0
 no ip address
 shutdown
!
interface tokenring 1
 ip address 150.10.254.201 255.255.255.0
 ring-speed 16
!
line con 0
line aux 0
line vty 0 4
login
!
end
```

Router 25ka

```
version 10.2
!
hostname 25ka
!
no ip domain-lookup
!
bstun peer-name 150.10.254.207
bstun protocol-group 1 bsc
!
interface serial 0
 no ip address
 shutdown
!
interface serial 1
 no ip address
 encapsulation bstun
 clockrate 19200
```

```
 bstun group 1
 bsc char-set ebcdic
 bsc primary
 bstun route address C3 tcp 150.10.254.201
 bstun route address C2 tcp 150.10.254.201
 bstun route address C1 tcp 150.10.254.201
 bstun route address 40 tcp 150.10.254.201
!
interface tokenring 0
 ip address 150.10.254.207 255.255.255.0
 ring-speed 16
!
interface bri 0
 no ip address
 shutdown
!
line con 0
line aux 0
line vty 0 4
login
!
end
```

Configuration for Router 4kc

```
version 10.2
!
hostname 4kc
!
no ip domain-lookup
!
bstun peer-name 150.10.254.210
bstun protocol-group 1 bsc
!
interface ethernet 0
 ip address 198.92.0.210 255.255.255.0
 media-type 10BaseT
!
interface serial 0
 no ip address
 encapsulation bstun
 clockrate 19200
 bstun group 1
 bsc char-set ebcdic
 bsc primary
 bstun route address C9 tcp 150.10.254.201
 bstun route address C8 tcp 150.10.254.201
!
interface serial 1
 no ip address
 shutdown
!
```

```
interface serial 2
 no ip address
 shutdown
!
interface serial 3
 no ip address
 shutdown
!
interface tokenring 0
 ip address 150.10.254.210 255.255.255.0
 ring-speed 16
!
interface tokenring 1
 no ip address
 shutdown!
line con 0
line aux 0
line vty 0 4
login
!
end
```

Router 25kb

```
version 10.2
!
hostname 25kb
!
no ip domain-lookup
!
bstun peer-name 150.10.254.208
bstun protocol-group 1 bsc
!
interface serial 0
 no ip address
 encapsulation bstun
 no keepalive
 clockrate 19200
 bstun group 1
 bsc char-set ebcdic
 bsc primary
 bstun route address C7 tcp 150.10.254.201
 bstun route address C6 tcp 150.10.254.201
 bstun route address C5 tcp 150.10.254.201
 bstun route address C4 tcp 150.10.254.201
!
interface serial 1
 no ip address
 shutdown
!
interface tokenring 0
 ip address 150.10.254.208 255.255.255.0
 ring-speed 16
!
!
```

```
line con 0
line aux 0
line vty 0 4
login
!
end
```

Bisync Addressing on Contention Interfaces

The following examples show user-configurable addressing on contention interfaces:

Remote Devices

```
bstun peer-name 1.1.1.20
bstun protocol-group 1 bsc
interface serial 0
 bstun group 1
 bsc contention 20
 bstun route address 20 tcp 1.1.1.1
```

Host Device

```
bstun peer-name 1.1.1.1
bstun protocol-group 1 bsc
interface serial 0
 bstun group 1
 bsc dial-contention 100
 bstun route address 20 tcp 1.1.1.20
 bstun route address 21 tcp 1.1.1.21
```

Nonstandard Bisync Addressing Example

This example specifies an extended address on serial interface 0:

```
bstun peer-name 1.1.1.1
bstun protocol-group 1 bsc
!
interface serial 0
 bstun group 1
 bsc extended-address 23 83
 bsc extended-address 87 42
 bsc primary
 bstun route address 23 tcp 1.1.1.20
```

Priority Queuing: with Priority Based on BSTUN Header Example

In the following example, the output interface examines header info and places packets with the BSTUN header on specified output queue:

```
priority-list 1 protocol bstun normal
interface serial 0
 priority-group 1
interface serial 1
 encapsulation bstun
 bstun group 1
 bsc char-set ebcdic
 bstun route all interface serial 0
                ...or...
bstun route address C1 interface serial 0
```

Priority Queuing: with Priority Based on BSTUN Header and Packet Sizes Example

In the following example, the output interface examines header information and packet size and places packets with the BSTUN header that match criteria (*gt* or *lt* specified packet size) on specified output queue:

```
priority-list 1 protocol bstun low gt 1500
priority-list 1 protocol bstun hi lt 500
interface serial 0
 priority-group 1
interface serial 1
 encapsulation bstun
 bstun group 1
 bsc char-set ebcdic
 bstun route all interface serial 0
                ...or...
bstun route address C1 interface serial 0
```

Priority Queuing: with Priority Based on BSTUN Header and Bisync Address Example

In the following example, the output interface examines header information and Bisync address and places packets with the BSTUN header that match Bisync address on specified output queue:

```
priority-list 1 protocol bstun normal address 1 C1
interface serial 0
 priority-group 1
interface serial 1
 encapsulation bstun
 bstun group 1
 bsc char-set ebcid
 bstun route address C1 interface serial 0
```

Priority Queuing: with Priority Based on BSTUN TCP Ports Example

In the following example, the output interface examines TCP port number and places packets with the BSTUN port number (1976) on specified output queue:

```
priority-list 1 protocol ip high tcp 1976
interface serial 0
 priority-group 1
interface serial 1
 encapsulation bstun
 bstun group 1
 bstun route all tcp 200.190.30.1
```

Priority Queuing: with Priority Based on BSTUN TCP Ports and Bisync Address Example

In the following example, four TCP/IP sessions (high, medium, normal, and low) are established with BSTUN peers using BSTUN port numbers. The input interface examines the Bisync address and uses the specified output queue definition to determine which BSTUN TCP session to use for sending the packet to the BSTUN peer.

The output interface examines the TCP port number and places packets with the BSTUN port numbers on the specified output queue.

```
priority-list 1 protocol ip high   tcp 1976
priority-list 1 protocol ip medium tcp 1977
priority-list 1 protocol ip normal tcp 1978
priority-list 1 protocol ip low    tcp 1979
!
priority-list 1 protocol bstun normal address 1 C1
!
interface serial 0
 priority-group 1
!
interface serial 1
 encapsulation bstun
 bstun group 1
 bsc char-set ebcdic
 bstun route address C1 tcp 200.190.30.1 priority
 priority-group 1
```

Custom Queuing: with Priority Based on BSTUN Header Example

In the following example, the output interface examines header info and places packets with the BSTUN header on specified output queue:

```
queue-list 1 protocol bstun normal
!
interface serial 0
 custom-queue-list 1
!
```

```
interface serial 1
 encapsulation bstun
 bstun group 1
 bstun route all interface serial 0
```

Custom Queuing: with Priority Based on BSTUN Header and Packet Size Example

In the following example, the output interface examines header information and packet size and places packets with the BSTUN header that match criteria (*gt* or *lt* specified packet size) on specified output queue:

```
queue-list 1 protocol bstun low gt 1500
queue-list 1 protocol bstun high lt 500
!
interface serial 0
 custom-queue-list 1
!
interface serial 1
 encapsulation bstun
 bstun group 1
 bstun route all interface serial 0
```

Custom Queuing: with Priority Based on BSTUN Header and Bisync Address Example

In the following example, the output interface examines header info and Bisync address and places packets with the BSTUN header that match Bisync address on specified output queue:

```
queue-list 1 protocol bstun normal address 1 C1
!
interface serial 0
 custom-queue-list 1
!
interface serial 1
 encapsulation bstun
 bstun group 1
 bsc char-set ebcdic
 bstun route address C1 interface serial 0
```

Custom Queuing: with Priority Based on BSTUN TCP Ports Example

In the following example, the output interface examines the TCP port number and places packets with the BSTUN port number (1976) on specified output queue:

```
queue-list 1 protocol ip high tcp 1976
!
```

```
interface serial 0
 custom-queue-list 1
!
interface serial 1
 encapsulation bstun
 bstun group 1
 bstun route all tcp 200.190.30.1
```

Custom Queuing: with Priority Based on BSTUN TCP Ports and Bisync Address Example

In the following example, four TCP/IP sessions (high, medium, normal, and low) are established with BSTUN peers using BSTUN port numbers. The input interface examines the Bisync address and uses the specified output queue definition to determine which BSTUN TCP session to use.

The output interface examines the TCP port number and places packets with the BSTUN port numbers on the specified output queue.

For Bisync addressing, output queues map as shown in Table 11-1:

Table 11-1 *Bisync Addressing Output Queues*

Output Queue	Session Mapped	BSTUN Port
1	Medium	1977
2	Normal	1978
3	Low	1979
4–10	High	1976

```
queue-list 1 protocol ip high tcp 1976
queue-list 1 protocol ip medium tcp 1977
queue-list 1 protocol ip normal tcp 1978
queue-list 1 protocol ip low tcp 1979
!
priority-list 1 protocol bstun normal address 1 C1
!
interface serial 0
 custom-queue-list 1
!
interface serial 1
 encapsulation bstun
 bstun group 1
 bsc char-set ebcdic
 bstun route address C1 tcp 200.190.30.1 priority
 custom-queue-list 1
```

Asynchronous Configuration Example

In the following example, Router A and Router B are configured for both Adplex and Bisync across the same BSTUN as shown in Figure 11-15.

Figure 11-15 *Combined Adplex and Bisync Configuration Example*

The configuration files for the routers in Figure 11-15 follow.

Router A

```
version 11.0
!
hostname router-a
!
bstun peer-name 172.28.1.190
bstun protocol-group 1 bsc
bstun protocol-group 2 adplex
bstun protocol-group 3 adplex
!
interface serial 0
 no ip address
!
interface serial 1
 no ip address
!
interface serial 2
 physical-layer async
 description Connection to 1st Security Alarm Console.
 no ip address
 encapsulation bstun
```

```
 no keepalive
 bstun group 2
 bstun route address 2 tcp 172.28.1.189
 bstun route address 3 tcp 172.28.1.189
 adplex secondary
!
interface serial 3
 description Connection to BSC 3780 host.
 no ip address
 encapsulation bstun
 no keepalive
 clockrate 9600
 bstun group 1
 bstun route all tcp 172.28.1.189
 bsc char-set ebcdic
 bsc contention
!
interface serial 4
 physical-layer async
 description Connection to 2nd Security Alarm Console.
 no ip address
 encapsulation bstun
 no keepalive
 bstun group 3
 bstun route address 2 tcp 172.28.1.189
 bstun route address 3 tcp 172.28.1.189
 adplex secondary
!
interface serial 5
 no ip address
!
interface serial 6
 no ip address
!
interface serial 7
 no ip address
!
interface serial 8
 no ip address
!
interface serial 9
 no ip address
!
interface tokenring 0
 ip address 172.28.1.190 255.255.255.192
 ring-speed 16
!
interface BRI0
 ip address
 shutdown
!
ip host ss10 172.28.0.40
ip host s2000 172.31.0.2
ip route 0.0.0.0 0.0.0.0 172.28.1.129
!
```

```
snmp-server community public RO
!
line con 0
 exec-timeout 0 0
line 2
 no activation-character
 transport input-all
 parity even
 stopbits 1
 rxspeed 4800
 txspeed 4800
line 4
 transport input all
 parity even
 stopbits 1
 rxspeed 4800
 txspeed 4800
line aux 0
 transport input all
line vty 0 4
 password mango
 login
!
end
```

Router B

```
version 11.0
!
hostname router-b
!
bstun peer-name 172.28.1.189
bstun protocol-group 1 bsc
bstun protocol-group 2 adplex
bstun protocol-group 3 adplex
source-bridge ring-group 100
!
interface serial 0
 no ip address
!
interface serial 1
 no ip address
!
interface serial 2
 physical-layer async
 description Connection to Security Alarm Panel.
 no ip address
 encapsulation bstun
 no keepalive
 bstun group 2
 bstun route all tcp 172.28.1.190
 adplex primary
!
```

```
interface serial 3
 description Connection to BSC 3780 device.
 no ip address
 encapsulation bstun
 no keepalive
 clockrate 9600
 bstun group 1
 bstun route all tcp 172.28.1.190
 bsc char-set ebcdic
 bsc contention
!
interface serial 4
 physical-layer async
 description Connection to async port on NCD (VT100 terminal emulation).
 no ip address
!
interface serial 5
 no ip address
 encapsulation sdlc-primary
 no keepalive
 nrzi-encoding
 clockrate 9600
 sdllc traddr 4000.0000.4100 222 2 100
 sdlc address C1
 sdllc xid C1 05D40003
 sdllc partner 4000.0000.0307 C1
!
interface serial 6
 description Connection to alarm panel.
 physical-layer async
 no ip address
 encapsulation bstun
 no keepalive
 bstun group 3
 bstun route all tcp 172.28.1.190
 adplex primary
!interface serial 7
 no ip address
!
interface serial 8
 no ip address
!
interface serial 9
 no ip address
!
interface tokenring 0
 ip address 172.28.1.189 255.255.255.192
 ring-speed 16
 source-bridge 4 1 100
!
interface BRI0
 ip address
 shutdown
!
```

```
ip host ss10 172.28.0.40
ip host s2000 172.31.0.2
ip route 0.0.0.0 0.0.0.0 172.28.1.129
!
snmp-server community public RO
!
line con 0
 exec-timeout 0 0
line 2
 no activation-character
 transport input-all
 parity even
 stopbits 1
 rxspeed 4800
 txspeed 4800
line 4
 transport input all
 stopbits 1
line 6
 transport input all
 parity even
 stopbits 1
 rxspeed 4800
 txspeed 4800
line 7
 transport input all
line aux 0
 transport input all
line vty 0 4
 password mango
 login
!
end
```

BSTUN over Frame Relay Configuration with Local Acknowledgment Example

The following example configures BSTUN over Frame Relay with Local Acknowledgment configured:

```
bstun protocol-group 1 bsc-local-ack

interface Serial1
 encapsulation frame-relay ietf
 clockrate 125000
 frame-relay map llc2 16

interface Serial4
 no ip address
encapsulation bstun
bstun group 1
bsc secondary
bstun route address C3 interface Serial1 dlci 16 C
bstun route address C2 interface Serial1 dlci 16 8
bstun route address C1 interface Serial1 dlci 16 4
```

BSTUN over Frame Relay Configuration with Passthrough Example

The following example configures BSTUN over Frame Relay with Passthrough configured:

```
bstun protocol-group 1 bsc

interface Serial1
 encapsulation frame-relay
 clockrate 125000
 frame-relay map bstun 16

interface Serial4
 no ip address
encapsulation bstun
bstun group 1
bsc secondary
bstun route address C3 interface Serial1 dlci 16
bstun route address C2 interface Serial1 dlci 16
bstun route address C1 interface Serial1 dlci 16
```

Serial Tunnel and Block Serial Tunnel Commands

Cisco's serial tunnel (STUN) feature allows Synchronous Data Link Control (SDLC) or High-Level Data Link Control (HDLC) devices to connect to one another through a multiprotocol internetwork rather than through a direct serial link. STUN encapsulates SDLC frames in either the Transmission Control Protocol/Internet Protocol (TCP/IP) or the HDLC protocol. STUN provides a straight passthrough of all SDLC traffic (including control frames, such as Receiver Ready) end-to-end between Systems Network Architecture (SNA) devices.

Cisco's SDLC local acknowledgment provides local termination of the SDLC session so that control frames no longer travel the WAN backbone networks. This means end nodes do not time out, and a loss of sessions does not occur. You can configure your network with STUN, or with STUN and SDLC local acknowledgment. To enable SDLC local acknowledgment, Cisco IOS software must first be enabled for STUN and routers configured to appear on the network as primary or secondary SDLC nodes. TCP/IP encapsulation must be enabled. Cisco's SDLC transport feature also provides priority queuing for TCP encapsulated frames.

Cisco's block serial tunnel (BSTUN) implementation enables Cisco 2500, 3600, 4000, 4500, 4700 and 7200 series routers to support devices that use the Binary Synchronous Communications (Bisync) data-link protocol and asynchronous security protocols that include Adplex, ADT Security Systems, Inc., Diebold, asynchronous generic, and mdi traffic. Cisco's support of the Bisync protocol enables enterprises to transport Bisync traffic and SNA multiprotocol traffic over the same network.

Use the commands in this chapter to configure BSTUN, Bisync, STUN, and SDLC local acknowledgment networks. For STUN and BSTUN configuration information and examples, refer to Chapter 11, "Configuring Serial Tunnel and Block Serial Tunnel." To locate documentation of related commands, you can search online at www.cisco.com.

asp addr-offset

Use the **asp addr-offset** interface configuration command to configure an asynchronous port to transmit and receive polled asynchronous traffic through a BSTUN tunnel. Use the **no** form of this command to cancel the specification.

> **asp addr-offset** *address-offset*
> **no asp addr-offsetn**

Syntax	Description
address-offset	Location of the address byte within the polled asynchronous frame being received.

Default
No default is specified.

Command Mode
Interface configuration

Usage Guidelines
This command first appeared in Cisco IOS Release 11.2 F.

This command is used to specify the offset from the start of the frame where the address byte is located. This command only applies when the asynchronous-generic protocol has been specified on an interface using a combination of the **bstun protocol-group** global configuration command and the **bstun group** interface configuration command.

Interfaces configured to run the asynchronous-generic protocol have their baud rate set to 9600 bps, use 8 data bits, no parity, 1 start bit, and 1 stop bit. If different line configurations are required, use the **rxspeed**, **txspeed**, **databits**, **stopbits**, and **parity** line configuration commands to change the line attributes.

The addresses of the alarm panels should be used in the address field of the **bstun route address** interface configuration command.

Example
The following example specifies that the first byte in the polled asynchronous frame contains the device address:

```
asp addr-offset 0
```

Related Commands
To locate documentation of related commands, you can search online at www.cisco.com.

asp role
asp rx-ift
bstun protocol-group
bstun route

asp role

Use the **asp role** interface configuration command to specify whether the router is acting as the primary end of the polled asynchronous link or as the secondary end of the polled asynchronous link connected to the serial interface and the attached remote device is a security alarm control station. Use the **no** form of this command to cancel the specification.

> **asp role** {**primary** | **secondary**}
> **no asp role** {**primary** | **secondary**}

Syntax	Description
primary	Router is the primary end of the polled asynchronous link connected to the serial interface, and the attached remote devices are alarm panels.
secondary	Router is the secondary end of the polled asynchronous link connected to the serial interface, and the attached remote device is a security alarm control station.

Default

No default is specified.

Command Mode

Interface configuration

Usage Guidelines

This command first appeared in Cisco IOS Release 11.2 F.

This command enables the interface on which ASP is configured. Configure the interface connected to the alarm console as a secondary router and the interface connected to the alarm panel as a primary router.

The addresses of the alarm panels should be used in the address field of the **bstun route address** interface configuration command.

Example

The following example specifies the router as the primary end of the link:

```
asp role primary
```

Related Commands

To locate documentation of related commands, you can search online at www.cisco.com.

bstun route

asp rx-ift

Use the **asp rx-ift** interface configuration command to specify a time period that, by expiring, signals the end of one frame being received and the start of the next. Use the **no** form of this command to cancel the specification.

>   **asp rx-ift** *interframe-timeout*
>   **no asp rx-ift**

Syntax	Description
interframe-timeout	Number of milliseconds between the end of one frame being received and the start of the next frame.

Default

The default timeout value is 40 ms.

Command Mode

Interface configuration

Usage Guidelines

This command first appeared in Cisco IOS Release 11.2 F.

The interframe timeout is useful when different baud rates are used between the router and the alarm console or alarm panel. For example, you might set an interframe timeout of 6 ms if the polled asynchronous protocol is running at 9600 bps, but set the value to 40 ms if the protocol is running at 300 bps.

This command applies only when the asynchronous-generic protocol has been specified on an interface using a combination of the **bstun protocol-group** global configuration command and the **bstun group** interface configuration command.

Interfaces configured to run the asynchronous-generic protocol have their baud rate set to 9600 bps, use 8 data bits, no parity, 1 start bit, and 1 stop bit. If different line configurations are required, use the **rxspeed**, **txspeed**, **databits**, **stopbits**, and **parity** line configuration commands to change the line attributes.

The addresses of the alarm panels should be used in the address field of the **bstun route address** interface configuration command.

Example
The following example sets the interframe timeout value to 6 ms because the polled asynchronous protocol is running at 9600 bps:

```
asp rx-ift 6
```

Related Commands
To locate documentation of related commands, you can search online at www.cisco.com.

asp addr-offset
asp role
bstun protocol-group
bstun route

bsc char-set

Use the **bsc char-set** interface configuration command to specify the character set used by the Bisync support feature in this serial interface as either EBCDIC or ASCII. Use the **no** form of this command to cancel the character set specification.

bsc char-set {ascii | ebcdic}
no bsc char-set {ascii | ebcdic}

Syntax	Description
ascii	ASCII character set
ebcdic	EBCDIC character set

Default
EBCDIC

Command Mode
Interface configuration

Usage Guidelines

This command first appeared in Cisco IOS Release 11.0.

Example

The following command specifies that the ASCII character set will be used:

```
bsc char-set ascii
```

bsc contention

Use the **bsc contention** interface configuration command to specify an address on a contention interface. Use the **no** form of this command to cancel the specification.

> **bsc contention** *address*
> **no bsc contention**

Syntax   Description

address   Address assigned to contention interface. The range is 1 to 255.
                             The default is 0x01.

Default

The default address is 0x01 to accommodate backward compatibility to the previous point-to-point contention implementation.

Command Mode

Interface configuration

Usage Guidelines

This command first appeared in Cisco IOS Release 11.0.

Example

The following command specifies address 20 on the remote device:

```
bsc contention 20
```

Related Commands

To locate documentation of related commands, you can search online at www.cisco.com.

bsc dial-contention

bsc dial-contention

Use the **bsc dial-contention** interface configuration command to specify a router at the central site as a central router with dynamic allocation of serial interfaces. Use the **no** form of this command to cancel the specification. A timeout value is configurable to ensure that an interface does not get locked out because of a device outage during transmission.

> **bsc dial-contention** *time-out*
> **no bsc dial-contention**

Syntax

Description

time-out	Amount of time interface can sit idle before it is returned to the idle interface pool. The range is 2 to 30 seconds. The default is 5 seconds.

Default

5 seconds

Command Mode

Interface configuration

Usage Guidelines

This command first appeared in Cisco IOS Release 11.2 F.

Example

The following command defines a dial-in interface at the central site with an idle timeout of 10 seconds:

```
bsc dial-contention 10
```

Related Commands

To locate documentation of related commands, you can search online at www.cisco.com.

bsc contention

bsc host-timeout

Use the **bsc host-timeout** interface configuration command to detect deactivation of devices at the host. Use the **no** form of this command to cancel the configuration.

> **bsc host-timeout** *interval*
> **no bsc host-timeout** *interval*

Syntax   Description

interval   Timeout interval within which a poll or select for a control unit must be received. If this interval expires, the remote router is sent a teardown peer signal. The range is 30 to 3000 deciseconds. The default is 60 seconds.

Default

The default interval is 60 seconds.

Command Mode

Interface configuration

Usage Guidelines

This command first appeared in Cisco IOS Release 11.2 F.

This command is used to detect deactivation of devices at the host. If the host is told to deactivate or not poll a device it will take time for the signal to propagate the network and get the remote end from polling. The timeout can be used to fine tune the delay in detecting the host outage. The remote peer will stop polling the control unit that has timed out in the interval one to two times the configured timeout value.

Example

The following example configures a timeout of 50 seconds:

```
bsc host-timeout 500
```

Related Commands

To locate documentation of related commands, you can search online at www.cisco.com.

bsc secondary
bstun group
bstun protocol-group

bsc pause

Use the **bsc pause** interface configuration command to specify the interval to the tenth of a second, between starts of the polling cycle. Use the **no** form of this command to cancel the specification.

> **bsc pause** *time*
> **no bsc pause** *time*

Syntax

Syntax	Description
time	Interval in tenths of a second. The default value is 10 (1 second). The maximum time is 25.5 seconds.

Default

10 (1 second)

Command Mode

Interface configuration

Usage Guidelines

This command first appeared in Cisco IOS Release 11.0.

Example

The following command sets the interval to 2 seconds:

```
bsc pause 20
```

bsc poll-timeout

Use the **bsc poll-timeout** interface configuration command to specify the timeout, in tenths of a second, for a poll or select sequence. Use the **no** form of this command to cancel the specification.

> **bsc poll-timeout** *time*
> **no bsc poll-timeout** *time*

Syntax

Syntax	Description
time	Time in tenths of a second. The default value is 10 (1 second).

Default
10 (1 second)

Command Mode
Interface configuration

Usage Guidelines
This command first appeared in Cisco IOS Release 11.0.

Example
The following command sets the interval to 2 seconds:

```
bsc poll-timeout 20
```

bsc primary

Use the **bsc primary** interface configuration command to specify that the router is acting as the primary end of the Bisync link connected to the serial interface, and that the attached remote devices are Bisync tributary stations. Use the **no** form of this command to cancel the specification.

> **bsc primary**
> **no bsc primary**

Syntax Description
This command has no arguments or keywords.

Default
No default is specified.

Command Mode
Interface configuration

Usage Guidelines
This command first appeared in Cisco IOS Release 11.0.

The Bisync support feature in the serial interface uses the address of the incoming encapsulation for reply.

Example

The following example specifies the router as the primary role:

```
bsc primary
```

Related Commands

To locate documentation of related commands, you can search online at www.cisco.com.

bstun route

bsc retries

Use the **bsc retries** interface configuration command to specify the number of retries performed before a device is considered to have failed. Use the **no** form of this command to cancel the specification.

bsc retries *retries*
no bsc retries *retries*

Syntax   Description

retries   Number of retries before a device fails. The default is 5.

Default

5 retries

Command Mode

Interface configuration

Usage Guidelines

This command first appeared in Cisco IOS Release 11.0.

Example

The following command sets the retry count to 10:

```
bsc retries 10
```

bsc secondary

Use the **bsc secondary** interface configuration command to specify that the router is acting as the secondary end of the Bisync link connected to the serial interface, and the attached remote device is a Bisync control station. Use the **no** form of this command to cancel the specification.

> **bsc secondary**
> **no bsc secondary**

Syntax Description

This command has no arguments or keywords.

Default

No default is specified.

Command Mode

Interface configuration

Usage Guidelines

This command first appeared in Cisco IOS Release 11.0.

The Bisync support feature in this serial interface uses the address of the poll or selection block in the framing encapsulation. It also generates an end of transmission (EOT) frame preceding each Bisync poll and selection.

Example

The following example specifies the router as the secondary role:

```
bsc secondary
```

Related Commands

To locate documentation of related commands, you can search online at www.cisco.com.

bstun route

bsc servlim

Use the **bsc servlim** interface configuration command to specify the number of cycles of the active poll list that are performed between polls to control units in the inactive poll list. Use the **no** form of this command to cancel the specification.

> **bsc servlim** *servlim-count*
> **no bsc servlim** *servlim-count*

Syntax
servlim-count

Description
Number of cycles. The range is 1 to 50. The default is 3.

Default
3 cycles

Command Mode
Interface configuration

Usage Guidelines
This command first appeared in Cisco IOS Release 11.0.

Example
The following command sets the number of cycles to 2:

```
bsc servlim 2
```

bsc spec-poll

Use the **bsc spec-poll** interface configuration command to set specific polls, rather than general polls, used on the host-to-router connection. Use the **no** form of this command to cancel the specification.

> **bsc spec-poll**
> **no spec-poll**

Syntax Description
This command has no arguments or keywords.

Default

No default is specified.

Command Mode

Interface configuration

Usage Guidelines

This command first appeared in Cisco IOS Release 11.1.

Use the **bsc spec-poll** command when a router is connected to a host, and only when that host issues specific polls rather than general polls. Tandem hosts that poll ATM cash machines are typically configured to use specific polls rather than general polls.

Configuring a downstream (control-unit/device connected) router to support specific polling has no effect.

Example

The following commands configure serial interface 0 to use specific poll:

```
interface serial 0
 description Connection to host.
 encapsulation bstun
 bstun group 1
 bsc secondary
 bsc spec-poll
 bsc char-set ebcdic
 bstun route all tcp 10.10.14.122
```

bstun group

Use the **bstun group** interface configuration command to specify the BSTUN group to which the interface belongs. Use the **no** form of this command to remove the interface from the BSTUN group.

> **bstun group** *group-number*
> **no bstun group** *group-number*

Syntax	Description
group-number	BSTUN group to which the interface belongs.

Default

No default is specified.

Command Mode

Interface configuration

Usage Guidelines

This command first appeared in Cisco IOS Release 11.0.

Each BSTUN-enabled interface must be placed in a BSTUN group that was previously defined by the **bstun protocol-group** command. Packets only travel between BSTUN-enabled interfaces that are in the same group.

Example

The following example specifies that serial interface 1 belongs to the previously defined protocol group 1:

```
interface serial 1
 encapsulation bstun
 bstun group 1
```

Related Commands

To locate documentation of related commands, you can search online at www.cisco.com.

bstun protocol-group
encapsulation bstun

bstun keepalive-count

Use the **bstun keepalive-count** global configuration command to define the number of times to attempt a peer connection before declaring the peer connection to be down. Use the **no** form of this command to cancel the definition.

> **bstun keepalive-count** *count*
> **no bstun keepalive-count**

Syntax	Description
count	Number of connection attempts. The range is between 2 and 10 retries.

Default
No default is specified.

Command Mode
Global configuration

Usage Guidelines
This command first appeared in Cisco IOS Release 11.1.

Example
The following example sets the number of times to retry a connection to a peer to 4:

```
bstun keepalive-count 4
```

Related Commands
To locate documentation of related commands, you can search online at www.cisco.com.

bstun remote-peer-keepalive

bstun lisnsap

Use the **bstun lisnsap** global configuration command to configure a SAP on which to listen for incoming calls. Use the **no** form of this command to cancel the SAP on which to listen.

> **bstun lisnsap** *sap-value*
> **no bstun lisnsap**

Syntax	Description
sap-value	SAP on which to listen for incoming calls. The default is 04.

Default
The default SAP value is 04.

Command Mode
Global configuration

Usage Guidelines

This command first appeared in Cisco IOS Release 11.2 F.

Changes to the **bstun lisnsap** command configuration will not take effect until after the router has been reloaded.

Example

The following example configures a SAP for listening:

```
bstun lisnsap
```

Related Commands

To locate documentation of related commands, you can search online at www.cisco.com.

bstun route (Frame Relay)
frame-relay map bstun
frame-relay map llc2

bstun peer-name

Use the **bstun peer-name** global configuration command to enable the BSTUN function. Use the **no** form of this command to disable the function.

> **bstun peer-name** *ip-address*
> **no bstun peer-name** *ip-address*

Syntax	Description
ip-address	Address by which this BSTUN peer is known to other BSTUN peers that are using the TCP transport.

Default

No default is specified.

Command Mode

Global configuration

Usage Guidelines

This command first appeared in Cisco IOS Release 11.0.

The IP address defines the address by which this BSTUN peer is known to other BSTUN peers that are using the TCP transport. If this command is unconfigured or the **no** form of this command is specified, all BSTUN routing commands with IP addresses are deleted. BSTUN routing commands without IP addresses are not affected by this command.

Example

The following example enables the BSTUN function:

```
bstun peer-name 150.10.254.201
```

Related Commands

To locate documentation of related commands, you can search online at www.cisco.com.

bstun protocol-group

bstun protocol-group

Use the **bstun protocol-group** global configuration command to define a BSTUN group and the protocol it uses. Use the **no** form of this command to delete the BSTUN group.

> **bstun protocol-group** *group-number protocol*
> **no bstun protocol-group** *group-number protocol*

Syntax	Description
group-number	BSTUN group number. Valid numbers are decimal integers in the range 1 to 255.
protocol	Block serial protocol, selected from the following: **adplex** **adt-poll-select** **adt-vari-poll** **async-generic** **bsc** **bsc-local-ack** **diebold** **mdi**

Default

No defaults are specified.

Command Mode

Global configuration

Usage Guidelines

This command first appeared in Cisco IOS Release 11.0.

Interfaces configured to run the Adplex protocol have their baud rate set to 4800 bps, use even parity, 8 data bits, 1 start bit, and 1 stop bit.

Interfaces configured to run the adt-vari-poll and adt-poll-select protocols have their baud rate set to 600 bps, use even parity, 8 data bits, 1 start bit, and 1.5 stop bits. If different line configurations are required, use the **rxspeed**, **txspeed**, **databits**, **stopbits**, and **parity** line configuration commands to change the line attributes.

Interfaces configured to run the asynchronous-generic protocol have their baud rate set to 9600 bps, use no parity, 8 data bits, 1 start bit, and 1 stop bit. If different line configurations are required, use the **rxspeed**, **txspeed**, **databits**, **stopbits**, and **parity** line configuration commands to change the line attributes.

Interfaces configured to run the mdi protocol have their baud rate set to 600 bps, use even parity, 8 data bits, 1 start bit, and 1.5 stop bits. If different line configurations are required, use the **rxspeed**, **txspeed**, **databits**, **stopbits**, and **parity** line configuration commands to change the line attributes. The mdi protocol allows alarm panels to be sent to the MDI alarm console.

Example

The following example defines BSTUN group 1, specifies that it uses the Bisync protocol, and indicates that frames will be locally acknowledged:

```
bstun protocol-group 1 bsc-local-ack
```

Related Commands

To locate documentation of related commands, you can search online at www.cisco.com.

bstun group

Part
II

Command Reference

bstun remote-peer-keepalive

Use the **bstun remote-peer-keepalive** global configuration command to enable detection of the loss of a peer. Use the **no** form of this command to disable detection.

bstun remote-peer-keepalive *seconds*
no bstun remote-peer-keepalive

Syntax

Description

seconds

Keepalive interval, in seconds. The range is 1 to 300 seconds.
The default is 30 seconds.

Default

30 seconds

Command Mode

Global configuration

Usage Guidelines

This command first appeared in Cisco IOS Release 11.1.

Example

In the following example, the remote-peer-keepalive interval is set to 60 seconds:

```
bstun remote-peer-keepalive 60
```

Related Commands

To locate documentation of related commands, you can search online at www.cisco.com.

bstun keepalive-count

bstun route

Use the **bstun route** interface configuration command to define how frames will be forwarded from a BSTUN interface to a remote BSTUN peer. Use the **no** form of this command to cancel the definition.

bstun route {**all** | **address** *address-number*} {**tcp** *ip-address* | **interface serial** *number*} [**direct**]

no bstun route {**all** | **address** *address-number*} {**tcp** *ip-address* | **interface serial** *number*} [**direct**]

Syntax	Description
all	All BSTUN traffic received on the input interface is propagated, regardless of the address contained in the serial frame.
address	Serial frame that contains a specific address is propagated.
address-number	Poll address, a hexadecimal number from 01 to FF (but not all values are valid). The reply address to be used on the return leg is calculated from the configured poll address.
tcp	TCP encapsulation is used to propagate frames that match the entry.
ip-address	IP address of the remote BSTUN peer.
interface serial	HDLC encapsulation is used to propagate the serial frames.
number	Serial line to an appropriately configured router on the other end.
direct	(Optional) Specified interface is also a direct BSTUN link, rather than a serial connection to another peer.

Default

No defaults are specified.

Command Mode

Interface configuration

Usage Guidelines

This command first appeared in Cisco IOS Release 11.0.

When the ADplex protocol is specified in the **bstun protocol-group** command, ADplex device addresses are limited to the range 1 to 127 because ADplex alarm panels invert the device address in the ADplex frame when responding to alarm console commands.

When the adt-poll-select protocol is specified in the **bstun protocol-group** command, routes for specific addresses cannot be specified on the downstream router (connected to the alarm panel), because no address field is provided within frames that are sent back to the alarm console. The only way to route traffic back to the alarm console is to use the **bstun route all** form of the **bstun route** command. This is also true for the diebold protocol and any other protocol supported by the asynchronous-generic protocol group that does not include a device address in the frame.

When the adt-vari-poll protocol is specified in the **bstun protocol-group** command, ADT device addresses are limited to the range 0 to 255, and address 0 is reserved for use as a broadcast address for adt-vari-poll only. If address 0 is specified in the **bstun route address** form of the **bstun route** command, the address is propagated to all configured BSTUN peers.

It is possible to use both the **all** and the **address** keywords on different **bstun route** commands on the same serial interface. When this is done, the **address** specifications take precedence; if none of these match, then the **all** specification is used to propagate the frame.

Example

In the following example, all BSTUN traffic received on serial interface 0 is propagated, regardless of the address contained in the serial frame:

```
bstun route all interface serial 0
```

bstun route (Frame Relay)

Use the **bstun route** interface configuration command to define how frames will be forwarded from a BSTUN interface to a remote BSTUN peer over Frame Relay. Use the **no** form of this command to cancel the definition.

> **bstun route** {**all** | **address** *cu-address*} **interface serial** *number* **dlci** *dlci rsap*
> **priority** *priority*
> **no bstun route** {**all** | **address** *cu-address*} **interface serial** *number* **dlci** *dlci rsap*
> **priority** *priority*]

Syntax	Description
all	All BSTUN traffic received on the input interface is propagated, regardless of the address contained in the serial frame.
address	Serial frames that contain a specific address are propagated.
cu-address	Control unit address for the Bisync end station.
interface serial *number*	Specify a serial interface on which Frame Relay encapsulation is used to propagate serial frames.

Syntax	Description
dlci *dlci*	Data-link connection identifier to be used on the Frame Relay interface.
rsap	Remote SAP, to be used when initiating an LLC2 session. This argument is configurable only if the interface group number supports local acknowledgment.
priority *priority*	Priority port to be used for this LLC2 session. Configurable only if the interface group number supports local acknowledgment.

Default

No defaults are specified.

Command Mode

Interface configuration

Usage Guidelines

This command first appeared in Cisco IOS Release 11.1.

Example

The following example configures BSTUN over Frame Relay. All BSTUN traffic is propagated to serial interface 0 regardless of the address contained in the serial frame:

```
bstun route all interface serial 0 dlci 16
```

encapsulation bstun

Use the **encapsulation bstun** interface configuration command to configure BSTUN on a particular serial interface. Use the **no** form of this command to disable the BSTUN function on the interface.

> **encapsulation bstun**
> **no encapsulation bstun**

Syntax Description

This command has no arguments or keywords.

Default

No default is specified.

Command Mode

Interface configuration

Usage Guidelines

This command first appeared in Cisco IOS Release 11.0.

The **encapsulation bstun** command must be configured on an interface before any further BSTUN or Bisync commands are configured for the interface.

You must use this command to enable BSTUN on an interface. Before using this command, complete the following two tasks:

- Enable BSTUN on a global basis by identifying BSTUN on IP addresses. The command is **bstun peer-name**.

- Define a protocol group number to be applied to the interface. Packets only travel between interfaces that are in the same protocol group. The command is **bstun protocol-group**.

After using the **encapsulation bstun** command, use the **bstun group** command to place the interface in the previously defined protocol group.

Example

The following example configures the BSTUN function on serial interface 0:

```
interface serial 0
 no ip address
 encapsulation bstun
```

Related Commands

To locate documentation of related commands, you can search online at www.cisco.com.

bstun group
bstun peer-name
bstun protocol-group

encapsulation stun

Use the **encapsulation stun** interface configuration command to enable STUN encapsulation on a specified serial interface.

encapsulation stun

Syntax Description

This command has no arguments or keywords.

Default

STUN encapsulation is disabled.

Command Mode

Interface configuration

Usage Guidelines

This command first appeared in Cisco IOS Release 10.0.

Use this command to enable STUN on an interface. Before using this command, complete the following two tasks:

- Enable STUN on a global basis by identifying STUN on IP addresses. The command is **stun peer-name**.

- Define a protocol group number to be applied to the interface. Packets only travel between interfaces that are in the same protocol group. The command is **stun protocol-group**.

After using the **encapsulation stun** command, use the **stun group** command to place the interface in the previously defined protocol group.

Example

This partial configuration example shows how to enable serial interface 5 for STUN traffic:

```
! sample stun peer name and stun protocol-group global commands
stun peer-name 131.108.254.6
stun protocol-group 2 sdlc
!
interface serial 5
! sample ip address command
no ip address
! enable the interface for STUN; must specify encapsulation stun
```

```
! command to further configure the interface
encapsulation stun
! place interface serial 5 in previously defined STUN group 2
stun group 2
! enter stun route command
stun route 7 tcp 131.108.254.7
```

Related Commands

To locate documentation of related commands, you can search online at www.cisco.com.

stun group
stun peer-name
stun protocol-group

frame-relay map bstun

Use the **frame-relay map bstun** interface configuration command to configure BSTUN over Frame Relay for passthru. Use the **no** form of this command to cancel the configuration.

> **frame-relay map bstun** *dlci*
> **no frame-relay map bstun** *dlci*

Syntax   Description

dlci   Frame Relay DLCI number on which to support passthru.

Default

No default is specified.

Command Mode

Interface configuration

Usage Guidelines

This command first appeared in Cisco IOS Release 11.2 F.

Example

The following example maps BSTUN traffic to DLCI number 16:

```
frame-relay map bstun 16
```

Related Commands

To locate documentation of related commands, you can search online at www.cisco.com.

bstun lisnsap
bstun protocol-group
encapsulation frame-relay

frame-relay map llc2

Use the **frame-relay map llc2** interface configuration command to configure BSTUN over Frame Relay when using Bisync local acknowledgment. Use the **no** form of this command to cancel the configuration.

> **frame-relay map llc2** *dlci*
> **no frame-relay map llc2** *dlci*

Syntax	Description
dlci	Frame Relay DLCI number on which to support local acknowledgment.

Default

No default is specified.

Command Mode

Interface configuration

Usage Guidelines

This command first appeared in Cisco IOS Release 11.2 F.

Example

The following example maps BSTUN traffic to DLCI number 16:

```
frame-relay map DLCI 16
```

Related Commands

To locate documentation of related commands, you can search online at www.cisco.com.

bstun lisnsap
bstun protocol-group
encapsulation frame-relay

locaddr-priority-list

Use the **locaddr-priority-list** interface configuration command to establish queuing priorities based upon the address of the logical unit (LU). Use the **no** form of this command to cancel all previous assignments.

> **locaddr-priority-list** *list-number address-number queue-keyword*
> **no locaddr-priority-list**

Syntax	Description
list-number	Arbitrary integer between 1 and 10 that identifies the LU address priority list.
address-number	Value of the LOCADDR=parameter on the LU macro, which is a 1-byte address of the LU in hexadecimal.
queue-keyword	Enables a priority queue type: Valid queue-keyword values and their equivalent priority queue type level are: • **high**—Priority queue type is high. • **medium**—Priority queue type is medium. • **normal**—Priority queue type is normal. • **low**—Priority queue type is low.

Default

No queuing priorities are established.

Command Mode

Interface configuration

Usage Guidelines

This command first appeared in Cisco IOS Release 10.0.

Example

The following example shows how to establish queuing priorities based on the address of the serial link on a STUN connection. Note that you must use the **priority-group** interface configuration command to assign a priority group to an input interface.

```
stun peer-name 131.108.254.6
stun protocol-group 1 sdlc
!
interface serial 0
 no ip address
 encapsulation stun
 stun group 1
 stun route address 4 interface serial 0 direct
 locaddr priority 1
 priority-group 1
!
 locaddr-priority-list 1 02 high
 locaddr-priority-list 1 03 high
 locaddr-priority-list 1 04 medium
 locaddr-priority-list 1 05 low
```

Related Commands

To locate documentation of related commands, you can search online at www.cisco.com.

priority-group

priority-group

Use the **priority-group** interface configuration command to assign a priority group to an interface. Use the **no** form of this command to remove assignments.

> **priority-group** *list-number*
> **no priority-group** *list-number*

Syntax	Description
list-number	Priority list number assigned to the interface.

Default

No priority group is assigned.

Command Mode

Interface configuration

Usage Guidelines

This command first appeared in Cisco IOS Release 10.0.

Example

The following example shows how to establish queuing priorities based on the address of the serial link on a STUN connection. Note that you must use the **priority-group** interface configuration command to assign a priority group to an output interface.

```
! sample stun peer-name global command
stun peer-name 131.108.254.6
! sample protocol-group command for reference
stun protocol-group 1 sdlc
!
interface serial 0
! disable the ip address for interface serial 0
no ip address
! enable the interface for STUN
encapsulation stun
! sample stun group command
stun group 2
! sample stun route command
stun route address 10 tcp 131.108.254.8 local-ack priority
!
! assign priority group 1 to the input side of interface serial 0
priority-group 1
! assign a low priority to priority list 1 on serial link identified
! by group 2 and address A7
priority-list 1 stun low address 2 A7
```

Related Commands

To locate documentation of related commands, you can search online at www.cisco.com.

locaddr-priority-list
priority-list protocol ip tcp
priority-list stun address

priority-list protocol bstun

Use the **priority-list protocol bstun** global configuration command to establish BSTUN queuing priorities based on the BSTUN header. Use the **no** form of this command to revert to normal priorities.

> **priority-list** *list-number* **protocol bstun** *queue* [**gt** | **lt** *packetsize*]
> [**address** *bstun-group bsc-addr*]
> **no priority-list** *list-number* **protocol bstun** *queue* [**gt** | **lt** *packetsize*]
> [**address** *bstun-group bsc-addr*]

Syntax	Description
list-number	Arbitrary integer between 1 and 10 that identifies the priority list selected by the user.
queue	Priority queue type: **high**, **medium**, **normal**, or **low**.
gt | **lt** *packetsize*	(Optional) Output interface examines header information and packet size and places packets with the BSTUN header that match criteria (gt or lt specified packet size) on specified output.
address *bstun-group bsc-addr*	(Optional) Output interface examines header information and Bisync address and places packets with the BSTUN header that match Bisync address on the specified output queue.

Default

Prioritize based on BSTUN header.

Command Mode

Global configuration

Usage Guidelines

This command first appeared in Cisco IOS Release 11.0.

Example

In the following example, the output interface examines the header information and places packets with the BSTUN header on the output queue specified as medium:

```
priority-list 1 protocol bstun medium
```

Related Commands

To locate documentation of related commands, you can search online at www.cisco.com.

encapsulation bstun

priority-list protocol ip tcp

Use the **priority-list protocol ip tcp** global configuration command to establish BSTUN or STUN queuing priorities based on the TCP port. Use the **no** form of this command to revert to normal priorities.

> **priority-list** *list-number* **protocol ip** *queue* **tcp** *tcp-port-number*
> **no priority-list** *list-number* **protocol ip** *queue* **tcp** *tcp-port-number*

Syntax   Description

Syntax	Description
list-number	Arbitrary integer between 1 and 10 that identifies the priority list selected by the user.
queue	Priority queue type: **high**, **medium**, **normal**, or **low**.
tcp-port-number	BSTUN port and priority settings are as follows: High—BSTUN port 1976 Medium—BSTUN port 1977 Normal—BSTUN port 1978 Low—BSTUN port 1979 STUN port and priority settings are as follows: High—STUN port 1994 Medium—STUN port 1990 Normal—STUN port 1991 Low—STUN port 1992

Default

The default is normal queue.

Command Mode

Global configuration

Usage Guidelines

This command first appeared in Cisco IOS Release 10.0.

Use the **priority-list stun address** command first. Priority settings created with this command are assigned to SDLC ports.

NOTE	SDLC local acknowledgment with the priority option must be enabled using the **stun route address tcp** command.

Examples

In the following example, queuing priority for address C1 using priority list 1 is set to high. A priority queue of high is assigned to the SDLC port 1994.

```
priority-list 1 stun high address 1 c1
priority-list 1 protocol ip high tcp 1994
```

In the following example, queuing priority for address C1 using priority list 1 is set to high. A priority queue of high is assigned to BSTUN port 1976.

```
priority-list bstun high address 1 c1
priority-list 1 protocol ip high 1976
```

Related Commands

To locate documentation of related commands, you can search online at www.cisco.com.

bstun protocol-group
encapsulation bstun
encapsulation stun
priority-group
priority-list stun address
stun route address tcp

priority-list stun address

Use the **priority-list stun address** global configuration command to establish STUN queuing priorities based on the address of the serial link. Use the **no** form of this command to revert to normal priorities.

> **priority-list** *list-number* **stun** *queue* **address** *group-number address-number*
> **no priority-list** *list-number* **stun** *queue-keyword* **address** *group-number*
>   *address-number*

Syntax	Description
list-number	Arbitrary integer between 1 and 10 that identifies the priority list selected by the user.

Syntax	Description
queue	Enables a priority queue type: Valid queue values and their equivalent priority queue type level are: • **high**—Priority queue type is high. • **medium**—Priority queue type is medium. • **normal**—Priority queue type is normal. • **low**—Priority queue type is low.
group-number	Group number that is used in the **stun group** command.
address-number	Address of the serial link. For an SDLC link, the format is a 1-byte hex value (for example, C1). For a non-SDLC link, the address format can be specified by the **stun schema** command.

Default
The default is normal queue.

Command Mode
Global configuration

Usage Guidelines
This command first appeared in Cisco IOS Release 10.0.

NOTE   SDLC local acknowledgment with the priority option must be enabled using the **stun route address interface serial** command.

Example
In the following example, queuing priority for address C1 using priority list 1 is set to **high**:

```
priority-list 1 stun high address 1 c1
```

Related Commands

To locate documentation of related commands, you can search online at www.cisco.com.

priority-list protocol ip tcp
stun group
stun route address interface serial
stun schema offset length format

queue-list protocol bstun

Use the **queue-list protocol bstun** global configuration command to customize BSTUN queuing priorities based on the BSTUN header. Use the **no** form of this command to revert to normal priorities.

> **queue-list** *list-number* **protocol bstun** *queue* [**gt** | **lt** *packetsize*]
> [**address** *bstun-group bsc-addr*]
> **no queue-list** *list-number* **protocol bstun** *queue* [**gt** | **lt** *packetsize*]
> [**address** *bstun-group bsc-addr*]

Syntax	Description
list-number	Arbitrary integer between 1 and 10 that identifies the priority list selected by the user.
queue	Enables a priority queue type: Valid queue-keyword values and their equivalent priority queue type level are:
	• **high**—Priority queue type is high.
	• **medium**—Priority queue type is medium.
	• **normal**—Priority queue type is normal.
	• **low**—Priority queue type is low.
gt	**lt** *packetsize*	(Optional) Output interface examines header information and packet size and places packets with the BSTUN header that match criteria (gt or lt specified packet size) on specified output.
address *bstun-group bsc-addr*	(Optional) Output interface examines header information and Bisync address and places packets with the BSTUN header that match Bisync address on the specified output queue.

Default

Prioritize based on BSTUN header.

Command Mode
Global configuration

Usage Guidelines
This command first appeared in Cisco IOS Release 11.0.

Example
In the following example, the output interface examines the header information and places packets with the BSTUN header on the output queue specified as medium.

```
queue-list 1 protocol bstun medium
```

Related Commands
To locate documentation of related commands, you can search online at www.cisco.com.

encapsulation bstun

queue-list protocol ip tcp

Use the **queue-list protocol ip tcp** global configuration command to customize BSTUN queuing priorities based on the TCP port. Use the **no** form of this command to revert to normal priorities.

> **queue-list** *list-number* **protocol ip** *queue* **tcp** *tcp-port-number*
> **no queue-list** *list-number* **protocol ip** *queue* **tcp** *tcp-port-number*

Syntax	Description
list-number	Arbitrary integer between 1 and 10 that identifies the priority list selected by the user.
queue	Enables a priority queue type: Valid queue-keyword values and their equivalent priority queue type level are: • **high**—Priority queue type is high. • **medium**—Priority queue type is medium. • **normal**—Priority queue type is normal. • **low**—Priority queue type is low.

Syntax	Description
tcp-port-number	BSTUN port and priority settings are as follows: High—BSTUN port 1976 Medium—BSTUN port 1977 Normal—BSTUN port 1978 Low—BSTUN port 1979 STUN port and priority settings are as follows: High—STUN port 1994 Medium—STUN port 1990 Normal—STUN port 1991 Low—STUN port 1992

Default

The default is normal queue.

Command Mode

Global configuration

Usage Guidelines

This command first appeared in Cisco IOS Release 11.0.

Example

In the following example, queuing priority for address C1 using priority list 1 is set to high. A priority queue of high is assigned to BSTUN port 1976.

```
queue-list bstun high address 1 c1
queue-list 1 protocol ip high 1976
```

Related Commands

To locate documentation of related commands, you can search online at www.cisco.com.

encapsulation bstun

sdlc virtual-multidrop

Use the **sdlc virtual-multidrop** interface configuration command to allow SDLC broadcast address FF to be replicated for each of the STUN peers, so each of the end stations receive the broadcast frame. Use the **no** form of this command to disable the SDLC broadcast feature.

> **sdlc virtual-multidrop**
> **no sdlc virtual-multidrop**

Syntax Description

This command has no arguments or keywords.

Default

SDLC broadcast is disabled.

Command Mode

Interface configuration

Usage Guidelines

This command first appeared in Cisco IOS Release 10.3.

Example

The following example allows each STUN peer to receive a broadcast frame:

```
sdlc virtual-multidrop
```

Related Commands

To locate documentation of related commands, you can search online at www.cisco.com.

stun route address tcp

show bsc

Use the **show bsc** privileged EXEC command to display statistics about the interfaces on which Bisync is configured.

> **show bsc** [**group** *bstun-group-number*] [**address** *address-list*]

Syntax	Description
bstun-group-number	(Optional) BSTUN group number. Valid numbers are decimal integers in the range 1 to 255.
address-list	(Optional) List of poll addresses.

Command Mode

Privileged EXEC

Usage Guidelines

This command first appeared in Cisco IOS Release 11.0.

Sample Displays

The following is sample output from the **show bsc** command:

```
Router# show bsc

BSC pass-through on Serial4:
HDX enforcement state: IDLE.
Frame sequencing state: IDLE.
Total Tx Counts: 0 frames(total). 0 frames(data). 0 bytes.
Total Rx Counts: 0 frames(total). 0 frames(data). 0 bytes.

BSC local-ack on serial5:
Secondary state is CU_Idle.
Control units on this interface:

        Poll address: C2. Select address: E2.
        State is Active.
        Tx Counts: 1137 frames(total). 0 frames(data). 1137 bytes.
        Rx Counts: 1142 frames(total). 0 frames(data). 5710 bytes.

        Poll address: C3. Select address: E3 *CURRENT-CU*
        State is Active.
        Tx Counts: 1136 frames(total). 0 frames(data). 1136 bytes.
        Rx Counts: 1142 frames(total). 0 frames(data). 5710 bytes.

Total Tx Counts: 2273 frames(total). 0 frames(data). 2273 bytes.
Total Rx Counts: 2284 frames(total). 0 frames(data). 11420 bytes.
```

The following is sample output from the **show bsc** command specifying BSTUN group 50:

```
Router# show bsc group 50

BSC local-ack on serial5:
Secondary state is CU_Idle.
Control units on this interface:

        Poll address: C2. Select address: E2.
        State is Active.
        Tx Counts: 1217 frames(total). 0 frames(data). 1217 bytes.
        Rx Counts: 1222 frames(total). 0 frames(data). 6110 bytes.

        Poll address: C3. Select address: E3 *CURRENT-CU*
        State is Active.
        Tx Counts: 1214 frames(total). 0 frames(data). 1214 bytes.
        Rx Counts: 1220 frames(total). 0 frames(data). 6100 bytes.

Total Tx Counts: 2431 frames(total). 0 frames(data). 2431 bytes.
Total Rx Counts: 2442 frames(total). 0 frames(data). 12200 bytes.
```

The following is sample output from the **show bsc** command specifying BSTUN group 50 and poll address C2:

```
Router# show bsc group 50 address C2

BSC local-ack on serial5:
Secondary state is CU_Idle.
Control units on this interface:

        Poll address: C2. Select address: E2.
        State is Active.
        Tx Counts: 1217 frames(total). 0 frames(data). 1217 bytes.
        Rx Counts: 1222 frames(total). 0 frames(data). 6110 bytes.

Total Tx Counts: 1217 frames(total). 0 frames(data). 1217 bytes.
Total Rx Counts: 1222 frames(total). 0 frames(data). 6110 bytes.
```

The following is sample output from the **show bsc** command specifying poll address C2:

```
Router# show bsc address C2

BSC pass-through on Serial4:
HDX enforcement state: IDLE.
Frame sequencing state: IDLE.
Total Tx Counts: 0 frames(total). 0 frames(data). 0 bytes.
Total Rx Counts: 0 frames(total). 0 frames(data). 0 bytes.

BSC local-ack on serial5:
Secondary state is CU_Idle.
Control units on this interface:

        Poll address: C2. Select address: E2.
        State is Active.
```

```
    Tx Counts: 1137 frames(total). 0 frames(data). 1137 bytes.
    Rx Counts: 1142 frames(total). 0 frames(data). 5710 bytes.

Total Tx Counts: 1137 frames(total). 0 frames(data). 1137 bytes.
Total Rx Counts: 1142 frames(total). 0 frames(data). 5710 bytes.
```

Table 12-1 describes significant fields shown in the display.

Table 12-1 *show bsc Command Field Descriptions*

Field	Description
BSC *x* on *interface y*	Indicates whether the router is configured for passthru or local acknowledgment on the indicated interface.
Output queue depth	Packets queued on this interface. This field is only displayed when the value is not zero.
Frame builder state	Current frame building state. This field is only displayed when the state is not IDLE.
HDX enforcement state	Current half-duplex transmit enforcement state. The possible values are: • IDLE—Waiting for communication activity. • PND_COMP—Waiting for router to transmit. • PND_RCV—Waiting for attached device to respond to transmission.
Frame sequencing state	Frame sequencing state to protect against network latencies. When the router is configured as the primary end of the link, the possible values are: • IDLE—Waiting for a poll. • SEC—In a session with a device. When the router is configured as the secondary end of the link, the possible values are: • IDLE—Waiting for a poll. • PRI—In a session with a device. When the router is configured for point-to-point contention, the possible values are: • IDLE—Waiting for a poll. • PEND—Waiting for the first data frame. • PRI—Connected device is acting as a primary device. • SEC—Connected device is acting as a secondary device.

Continues

Part II

Command Reference

Table 12-1 *show bsc Command Field Descriptions (Continued)*

Field	Description
Total Tx Counts	Total transmit frame count for the indicated interface.
Total Rx Count	Total receive frame count for the indicated interface.
Primary state is …	The current state when the router is configured as the primary end of the link. The possible values are: • TCU_Down—Waiting for the line to become active. • TCU_EOFile—A valid block ending in ETX has been received. • TCU_Idle—Waiting for work or notification of completion of the transmission of EOT. • TCU_InFile—A valid block ending in ETB has been received. • TCU_Polled—A general poll has been issued. • TCU_Selected—A select has been issued. • TCU_SpecPolled—A specific poll has been sent. • TCU_TtdDelay—An ETB block was acknowledged, but the next block to be transmitted has not yet been received. • TCU_TtdSent—A TTD has been transmitted because no data was received by the time the timeout for sending Ttd expired. • TCU_TxEOFile—A block of data ending in ETX has been transmitted. • TCU_TxInFile—A block of data ending in ETB has been transmitted. • TCU_TxRetry—Trying to transmit a frame again.

Table 12-1 *show bsc Command Field Descriptions (Continued)*

Field	Description
Secondary state is …	The current state when the router is configured as the secondary end of the link. The possible values are: • CU_DevBusy—A select has been refused with WACK or RVI. • CU_Down—Waiting for the line to become active. • CU_EOFile—A valid block ending in ETX has been received. • CU_Idle—Waiting for a poll or select action. • CU_InFile—A valid block ending in ETB has been received. • CU_Selected—A select has been acknowledged. • CU_TtdDelay—An ETB block was acknowledged, but the next block to be transmitted has not yet been received. • CU_TtdSent—A TTD has been transmitted because no data was received by the time the timeout for sending Ttd expired. • CU_TxEOFile—A block of data ending in ETX has been transmitted. • CU_TxInFile—A block of data ending in ETB has been transmitted. • CU_TxRetry—Trying to transmit a frame again. • CU_TxSpecPollData—A data frame (typically S/S) has been used to answer a specific poll. • CU_TxStatus—Host has polled for device-specific status.
Poll address	Address used when the host wants to get device information.
Select address	Address used when the host wants to send data to the device.
State is …	Current initialization state of this control unit. The possible values are: • Active—The remote device is active. • Inactive—The remote device is dead. • Initializing—No response from remote device yet.
Tx Counts	Transmit frame count for this control unit.
Rx Counts	Receive frame count for this control unit.
Total Tx Counts	Total transmit frame count for the indicated interface.
Total Rx Counts	Total receive frame count for the indicated interface.

Part II

Command Reference

show bstun

Use the **show bstun** privileged EXEC command to display the current status of STUN connections.

show bstun [**group** bstun-group-number] [**address** address-list]

Syntax

group *bstun-group-number*

address *address-list*

Description

(Optional) BSTUN group number. Valid numbers are decimal integers in the range 1 to 255.

(Optional) List of poll addresses.

Command Mode

Privileged EXEC

Usage Guidelines

This command first appeared in Cisco IOS Release 11.0.

Sample Displays

The following is sample output from the **show bstun** command with no options:

```
Router# show bstun

This peer: 22.22.1.107
 *Serial0  (group 1 [bsc])
route   transport  address      state   rx_pkts   tx_pkts   drops
all     TCP        22.22.1.108 closed      0         0         0

  Serial4  (group 3 [bsc])
route   transport  address      state   rx_pkts   tx_pkts   drops
C2      TCP        22.22.2.108 closed      0         0         0
C1      TCP        22.22.2.108 closed      0         0         0
40      TCP        22.22.1.108 closed      0         0         0

  Serial5  (group 50 [bsc])
route   transport  address      state   rx_pkts   tx_pkts   drops
C2      TCP        22.22.2.108 open        4         4         0
C3      TCP        22.22.2.108 open        3         3         0
```

The following is sample output from the **show bstun** command specifying BSTUN group 3:

```
Router# show bstun group 3

This peer: 22.22.1.107
  Serial4  (group 3 [bsc])
```

```
route  transport  address       state   rx_pkts   tx_pkts   drops
C2     TCP        22.22.2.108 closed      0         0         0
C1     TCP        22.22.2.108 closed      0         0         0
40     TCP        22.22.1.108 closed      0         0         0
```

The following is sample output from the **show bstun** command specifying BSTUN group 3 and poll address C1:

```
Router# show bstun group 3 address C1

This peer: 22.22.1.107
  Serial4  (group 3 [bsc])
route  transport  address       state   rx_pkts   tx_pkts   drops
C1     TCP        22.22.2.108 closed      0         0         0
```

The following is sample output from the **show bstun** command specifying poll address C2:

```
Router# show bstun address C2

This peer: 22.22.1.107
  Serial4  (group 3 [bsc])
route  transport  address       state   rx_pkts   tx_pkts   drops
C2     TCP        22.22.2.108 closed      0         0         0

  Serial5  (group 50 [bsc])
route  transport  address       state   rx_pkts   tx_pkts   drops
C2     TCP        22.22.2.108 open        4         4         0
```

Table 12-2 describes significant fields shown in the output.

Table 12-2 *show bstun Command Field Descriptions*

Field	Description
This peer	Lists the peer name or address. The interface name (as defined by the **description** command), its BSTUN group number, and the protocol associated with the group are shown on the next header line.
route	Bisync control unit address.
transport	Description of link, either a serial interface using serial transport (indicated by IF followed by interface name), or a TCP connection to a remote router (TCP followed by IP address).
address	Address or the word *all* if the default forwarding entry is specified, followed by a repeat of the group number given for the interface.
state	State of the link: open is the normal, working state; direct indicates a direct link to another line, as specified with the **direct** keyword on the **bstun route** command.
rx_pkts	Number of received packets.
tx_pkts	Number of transmitted packets.
drops	Number of packets that had to be dropped for whatever reason.

show stun

Use the **show stun** privileged EXEC command to display the current status of STUN connections.

>**show stun**

Syntax Description

This command has no arguments or keywords.

Command Mode

Privileged EXEC

Usage Guidelines

This command first appeared in Cisco IOS Release 10.0.

Sample Display

The following is sample output from the **show stun** command:

```
Router# show stun

This peer: 131.108.10.1
Serial0 -- 3174 Controller for test lab (group 1 [sdlc])
                         state   rx-pkts  tx-pkts  drops  poll
   7[ 1] IF Serial1       open     20334    86440      5  8P
  10[1] TCP 131.108.8.1    open      6771     7331      0
 all[1] TCP 131.108.8.1    open    612301  2338550   1005
```

In the display, the first entry reports proxy polling is enabled for address 7 and serial 0 is running with modulus 8 on the primary side of the link. The link has received 20,334 packets, transmitted 86,440 packets, and dropped 5 packets.

Table 12-3 describes significant fields shown in the output.

Table 12-3 *show stun Command Field Descriptions*

Field	Description
This peer	Lists the peer name or address. The interface name (as defined by the **description** command), its STUN group number, and the protocol associated with the group are shown on the header line.
STUN address	Address or the word *all* if the default forwarding entry is specified, followed by a repeat of the group number given for the interface.

Table 12-3 *show stun Command Field Descriptions (Continued)*

Field	Description
Type of link	Description of link, either a serial interface using serial transport (indicated by IF followed by interface name), or a TCP connection to a remote router (TCP followed by IP address).
state	State of the link: open is the normal, working state; direct indicates a direct link to another line, as specified with the **direct** keyword on the **stun route** command.
rx_pkts	Number of received packets.
tx_pkts	Number of transmitted packets.
drops	Number of packets that for whatever reason had to be dropped.
poll	Report of the proxy poll parameters, if any. P indicates a primary and S indicates a secondary node. The number before the letter is the modulus of the link.

stun group

Use the **stun group** interface configuration command to place each STUN-enabled interface on a router in a previously defined STUN group. Use the **no** form of this command to remove an interface from a group.

> **stun group** *group-number*
> **no stun group** *group-number*

Syntax

Description

group-number   Integer in the range 1 to 255.

Default

Disabled

Command Mode

Interface configuration

Usage Guidelines

This command first appeared in Cisco IOS Release 10.0.

Before using this command, complete the following steps:

Step 1   Enable STUN on a global basis with the **stun peer-name** command.

Step 2   Define the protocol group in which you want to place this interface with the **stun protocol-group** command.

Step 3   Enable STUN on the interface using the **encapsulation stun** command.

Packets only travel between STUN-enabled interfaces that are in the same group. Once a given serial link is configured for the STUN function, it is no longer a shared multiprotocol link. All traffic that arrives on the link is transported to the corresponding peer as determined by the current STUN configuration.

Example

The following example places serial interface 0 in STUN group 2, which is defined to run the SDLC transport:

```
! sample stun peer-name global command
stun peer-name 131.108.254.6
! sample protocol-group command telling group 2 to use the SDLC protocol
stun protocol-group 2 sdlc
!
interface serial 0
! sample ip address subcommand
 no ip address
! sample encapsulation stun subcommand
 encapsulation stun
! place interface serial0 in previously defined STUN group 2
 stun group 2
! enter stun route command
 stun route 7 tcp 131.108.254.7
```

Related Commands

To locate documentation of related commands, you can search online at www.cisco.com.

encapsulation stun
priority-list stun address
stun peer-name
stun protocol-group

stun keepalive-count

Use the **stun keepalive-count** global configuration command to define the number of times to attempt a peer connection before declaring the peer connection to be down. Use the **no** form of this command to cancel the definition.

> **stun keepalive-count** *count*
> **no stun keepalive-count**

Syntax

Syntax	Description
count	Number of connection attempts. The range is between 2 and 10 retries.

Default

No default is specified.

Command Mode

Global configuration

Usage Guidelines

This command first appeared in Cisco IOS Release 10.0.

Example

The following example sets the number of times to retry a connection to a peer to 4:

```
stun keepalive-count 4
```

Related Commands

To locate documentation of related commands, you can search online at www.cisco.com.

stun remote-peer-keepalive

stun peer-name

Use the **stun peer-name** global configuration command to enable STUN for an IP address. Use the **no** form of this command to disable STUN for an IP address.

> **stun peer-name** *ip-address* **cls**
> **no stun peer-name** *ip-address* **cls**

Syntax	Description
ip-address	IP address by which this STUN peer is known to other STUN peers.

Default
STUN is disabled.

Command Mode
Global configuration

Usage Guidelines
This command first appeared in Cisco IOS Release 10.0.

Use this command to enable any further STUN features. After using this command, complete the following steps:

Step 1   Define the protocol group in which you want to place this interface with the **stun protocol-group** command.

Step 2   Enable STUN on the interface using the **encapsulation stun** command.

Step 3   Place the interface in a STUN group with the **stun group** command.

Example
The following example assigns IP address 131.108.254.6 as the STUN peer:

```
stun peer-name 131.108.254.6 cls
```

Related Commands
To locate documentation of related commands, you can search online at www.cisco.com.

encapsulation stun
stun group
stun protocol-group

stun protocol-group

Use the **stun protocol-group** global configuration command to create a protocol group. Use the **no** form of this command to remove an interface from the group.

> **stun protocol-group** *group-number* {**basic** | **sdlc** [**sdlc-tg**] | **schema**}
> **no stun protocol-group**

Syntax	Description
group-number	Integer in the range 1 to 255.
basic	Indicates a non-SDLC protocol.
sdlc	Indicates an SDLC protocol.
sdlc-tg	(Optional) Identifies the group as part of an SNA transmission group.
schema	Indicates a custom protocol.

Default

No protocol group established.

Command Mode

Global configuration

Usage Guidelines

This command first appeared in Cisco IOS Release 10.0.

Use the **sdlc** keyword to specify an SDLC protocol. You must specify either the **sdlc** or the **sdlc-tg** keyword before you can enable SDLC local acknowledgment. SDLC local acknowledgment is established with the **stun route address tcp** command.

Use the **basic** keyword to specify a non-SDLC protocol, such as HDLC.

Use the **schema** keyword to specify a custom protocol. The custom protocol must have been previously created with the **stun schema** command.

Use the optional **sdlc-tg** keyword, in conjunction with the **sdlc** keyword, to establish an SNA transmission group. A transmission group is a set of protocol groups providing parallel links to the same pair of IBM establishment controllers. This provides redundancy of paths. In case one or more links go down, an alternate path will be used. All STUN connections in a transmission group must connect to the same IP address. SDLC local acknowledgment must be enabled.

NOTE   If you specify the keyword **sdlc** in the **stun protocol group** command string, you cannot specify the **stun route all** command on that interface.

Examples

The following example specifies that group 7 will use the SDLC STUN protocol to route frames within that group:

```
stun protocol-group 7 sdlc
```

The following example specifies that group 5 use the basic protocol, wherein the serial addressing is unimportant and you have a point-to-point link:

```
stun protocol-group 5 basic
```

Related Commands

To locate documentation of related commands, you can search online at www.cisco.com.

encapsulation stun
stun route address interface serial
stun route address tcp
stun schema offset length format

stun remote-peer-keepalive

Use the **stun remote-peer-keepalive** global configuration command to enable detection of the loss of a peer. Use the **no** form of this command to disable detection.

> **stun remote-peer-keepalive** *seconds*
> **no stun remote-peer-keepalive**

Syntax   Description

seconds   Keepalive interval, in seconds. The range is 1 to 300 seconds. The default is 30 seconds.

Default

30 seconds

Command Mode

Global configuration

Usage Guidelines

This command first appeared in Cisco IOS Release 10.0.

Example

In the following example, the remote-peer-keepalive interval is set to 60 seconds:

```
stun remote-peer-keepalive 60
```

Related Commands

To locate documentation of related commands, you can search online at www.cisco.com.

stun keepalive-count

stun route address interface dlci

Use the **stun route address interface dlci** interface configuration command to configure direct Frame Relay encapsulation between STUN peers with SDLC local acknowledgment. Use the **no** form of this command to disable the configuration.

>**stun route address** *sdlc-addr* **interface** *frame-relay-port* **dlci** *number localsap*
>   **local-ack cls**
>**no stun route address** *sdlc-addr* **interface** *frame-relay-port* **dlci** *number localsap*
>   **local-ack cls**

Syntax	Description
sdlc-addr	Address of the serial interface.
frame-relay-port	Port number.
number	Data-link connection identifier (DLCI) number.

Syntax	Description
localsap	Local connecting SAP.
local-ack	Enable local acknowledgment.
cls	Use Cisco Link Services (CLS) to access the frame relay network.

Default
The configuration is disabled.

Command Mode
Interface configuration

Usage Guidelines
This command first appeared in Cisco IOS Release 11.0.

Example
The following command enables Frame Relay encapsulation between STUN peers with SDLC local acknowledgment:

```
stun route address c1 interface serial1 dlci 22 04 local-ack
```

Related Commands
To locate documentation of related commands, you can search online at www.cisco.com.

stun route all interface serial

stun route address interface serial

Use the **stun route address interface serial** interface configuration command to forward all HDLC traffic on a serial interface. Use the **no** form of this command to disable this method of HDLC encapsulation.

> **stun route address** *address-number* **interface serial** *number* [**direct**]
> **no stun route address** *address-number* **interface serial** *number*

Syntax / Description

Syntax	Description
address-number	Address of the serial interface.
number	Number assigned to the serial interface.
direct	(Optional) Forwards all HDLC traffic on a direct STUN link.

Default

The configuration is disabled.

Command Mode

Interface configuration

Usage Guidelines

This command first appeared in Cisco IOS Release 10.0.

Examples

In the following example, serial frames with a STUN route address of 4 are forwarded through serial interface 0 using HDLC encapsulation:

```
stun route address 4 interface serial 0
```

In the following example, serial frames with STUN route address 4 are propagated through serial interface 0 using STUN encapsulation:

```
stun route address 4 interface serial 0 direct
```

Related Commands

To locate documentation of related commands, you can search online at www.cisco.com.

stun route all interface serial

stun route address tcp

Use the **stun route address tcp** interface configuration command to specify TCP encapsulation and optionally establish SDLC local acknowledgment (SDLC transport) for STUN. Use the **no** form of this command to disable this method of TCP encapsulation.

> **stun route address** *address-number* **tcp** *ip-address* [**local-ack**] [**priority**]
> [**tcp-queue-max**]
> **no stun route address** *address-number* **tcp** *ip-address* [**local-ack**] [**priority**]
> [**tcp-queue-max**]

Syntax — Description

Syntax	Description
address-number	Number that conforms to SDLC addressing conventions.
ip-address	IP address by which this STUN peer is known to other STUN peers that are using the TCP as the STUN encapsulation.
local-ack	(Optional) Enables local acknowledgment for STUN.
priority	(Optional) Establishes the four levels used in priority queuing: low, medium, normal, and high.
tcp-queue-max	(Optional) Sets the maximum size of the outbound TCP queue for the SDLC link.

Defaults

TCP encapsulation is not established; TCP queue size default is 100.

Command Mode

Interface configuration

Usage Guidelines

This command first appeared in Cisco IOS Release 10.0. The **tcp-queue-max** keyword first appeared in Cisco IOS Release 11.1.

SDLC transport participates in SDLC windowing and retransmission through support of local acknowledgment. SDLC sessions require that end nodes send acknowledgments for a set amount of data frames received before allowing further data to be transmitted. Local acknowledgment provides local termination of the SDLC session, so that control frames no longer travel the WAN backbone networks. This means end nodes do not time out and a loss of sessions does not occur.

Example

In the following example, a frame with a source-route address of 10 is propagated using TCP encapsulation to a device with an IP address of 131.108.8.1:

```
stun route address 10 tcp 131.108.8.1
```

Related Commands

To locate documentation of related commands, you can search online at www.cisco.com.

sdlc address ff ack-mode
stun route all tcp

stun route all interface serial

Use the **stun route all interface serial** interface configuration command to encapsulate and forward all STUN traffic using HDLC encapsulation on a serial interface.

stun route all interface serial *number* [**direct**]

Syntax	Description
number	Number assigned to the serial interface.
direct	(Optional) Indicates that the specified interface is also a direct STUN link, rather than a serial connection to another peer.

Default

No default is specified.

Command Mode

Interface configuration

Usage Guidelines

This command first appeared in Cisco IOS Release 10.0.

An appropriately configured router must exist on the other end of the designated serial line. The outgoing serial link still can be used for other kinds of traffic (the frame is not TCP encapsulated). This mode is used when TCP/IP encapsulation is not needed or when higher performance is required. Enter the serial line number connected to the router for the *interface-number* argument.

Examples

In the following example, all traffic on serial interface 0 is propagated using STUN encapsulation:

```
stun route all interface serial 0
```

In the following example, serial interface 1 is a direct STUN link, not a serial connection to another peer:

```
stun route all interface serial 1 direct
```

Related Commands

To locate documentation of related commands, you can search online at www.cisco.com.

stun route address interface serial

stun route all tcp

Use the **stun route all tcp** interface configuration command with TCP encapsulation to forward all STUN traffic on an interface regardless of what address is contained in the serial frame.

> **stun route all tcp** *ip-address*

Syntax

Description

ip-address

IP address by which this remote STUN peer is known to other STUN peers. Use the address that identifies the remote STUN peer that is connected to the remote serial link.

Default

Disabled

Command Mode

Interface configuration

Usage Guidelines

This command first appeared in Cisco IOS Release 10.0.

TCP/IP encapsulation allows movement of serial frames across arbitrary media types and topologies. This is particularly useful for building shared, multiprotocol enterprise network backbones.

Example

In the following example, all STUN traffic received will be propagated through the bridge:

```
stun route all tcp 131.108.10.1
```

stun schema offset length format

Use the **stun schema offset length format** global configuration command to define a protocol other than SDLC for use with STUN. Use the **no** form of this command to disable the new protocol.

       stun schema *name* **offset** *constant-offset* **length** *address-length* **format**
          format-keyword
       no stun schema *name* **offset** *constant-offset* **length** *address-length* **format**
          format-keyword

Syntax	Description
name	Name that defines your protocol. It can be up to 20 characters in length.
constant-offset	Constant offset, in bytes, for the address to be found in the frame.
address-length	Length in one of the following formats: decimal (4 bytes), hexadecimal (8 bytes), or octal (4 bytes).
format-keyword	The allowable format keywords are **decimal** (0 to 9), **hexadecimal** (0 to F), and **octal** (0 to 7).
	Format to be used to specify and display addresses for routes on interfaces that use this STUN protocol. Valid format keyword values and their ranges are:

- **decimal**—0 to 9
- **hexadecimal**—0 to F
- **octal**—0 to 7

Default

No protocol is defined.

Command Mode

Global configuration

Usage Guidelines

This command first appeared in Cisco IOS Release 10.0.

Use this command before defining the protocol group (**stun protocol-group** command). The serial protocol you define must meet the following criteria:

- The protocol uses full-duplex conventions (RTS/CTS always high).

- The protocol uses standard HDLC checksum and framing (beginning and end of frames, data between frames).

- Addresses are contained in a constant location (offset) within the frame.

- Addresses are found on a byte boundary.

Example

In the following example, a protocol named new-sdlc is created. In the protocol frame structure, the constant offset is 0, the address length is 1 byte, and the address format is hexadecimal.

```
stun schema new-sdlc offset 0 length 1 format hexadecimal
```

Related Commands

To locate documentation of related commands, you can search online at www.cisco.com.

priority-list stun
stun protocol-group

stun sdlc-role primary

Use the **stun sdlc-role primary** interface configuration command to assign the router the role of SDLC primary node. Primary nodes poll secondary nodes in a predetermined order.

> **stun sdlc-role primary**

Syntax Description

This command has no arguments or keywords.

Default

No role is assigned.

Command Mode

Interface configuration

Usage Guidelines

This command first appeared in Cisco IOS Release 10.0.

If the router is connected to a cluster controller, for example a 3x74, it should appear as a front-end processor (FEP) such as a 37x5, and must be assigned the role of a primary node.

Example

The following example assigns the router the role of SDLC primary node:

```
stun sdlc-role primary
```

Related Commands

To locate documentation of related commands, you can search online at www.cisco.com.

encapsulation stun
stun sdlc-role secondary

stun sdlc-role secondary

Use the **stun sdlc-role secondary** interface configuration command to assign the router the role of SDLC secondary node. Secondary nodes respond to polls sent by the SDLC primary by transmitting any outgoing data they may have.

stun sdlc-role secondary

Syntax Description

This command has no arguments or keywords.

Default

No secondary role is assigned.

Command Mode

Interface configuration

Usage Guidelines

This command first appeared in Cisco IOS Release 10.0.

If the router is connected to a front-end processor (FEP), for example a 37x5, it should appear as a cluster controller such as a 3x74, and must be assigned the role of a secondary node.

Example

The following example assigns the router the role of SDLC secondary node:

```
stun sdlc-role secondary
```

Related Commands

To locate documentation of related commands, you can search online at www.cisco.com.

encapsulation stun
stun sdlc-role primary

Configuring LLC2 and SDLC Parameters

You do not need to configure Logical Link Control, type 2 (LLC2) because it is already enabled on Token Ring interfaces. This chapter describes how to modify the default settings of LLC2 parameters as needed.

To support the Synchronous Data Link Control (SDLC) protocol, you must configure the router to act as a primary or secondary SDLC station. You also can change default settings on any SDLC parameters. Configuration examples for both LLC2 and SDLC are given at the end of the chapter.

For a complete description of the LLC2 and SDLC commands mentioned in this chapter, refer to Chapter 14, "LLC2 and SDLC Commands." To locate documentation of other commands that appear in this chapter, you can search online at www.cisco.com.

LLC2 Configuration Task List

Because LLC2 is already enabled on a Token Ring, you do not need to enable it on the router. However, you can enhance LLC2 performance by completing the following tasks:

- Control Transmission of Information Frames
- Establish the Polling Level
- Set Up Exchange Identification Transmissions

To determine which LLC2 parameters need adjustment, you can perform the following task:

- Monitor LLC2 Stations

See the section "LLC2 Configuration Example" later in this chapter.

Control Transmission of Information Frames

Control the number of Information frames (I-frames) and acknowledgments sent on the LLC2 network by completing the tasks described in the following sections:

- Set the Maximum Number of I-Frames Received Before Sending an Acknowledgment
- Set the Maximum Delay for Acknowledgments
- Set the Maximum Number of I-Frames Sent Before Requiring Acknowledgment
- Set the Number of Retries Allowed
- Set the Time for Resending I-Frames
- Set the Time for Resending Rejected Frames

Set the Maximum Number of I-Frames Received Before Sending an Acknowledgment

You can reduce overhead on the network by increasing the maximum number of frames Cisco IOS software can receive at once before it must send the sender an acknowledgment. To do so, use the following command in interface configuration mode:

Command	Purpose
llc2 ack-max *packet-count*	Sets maximum number of I-frames the router can receive before it sends an acknowledgment.

Set the Maximum Delay for Acknowledgments

You can ensure timely receipt of acknowledgments so that transmission of data is not delayed. Even if the maximum amount of frames has not been reached, you can set a timer forcing the router to send an acknowledgment and reset the maximum amount counter to 0.

To set the maximum delay time, use the following command in interface configuration mode:

Command	Purpose
llc2 ack-delay-time *milliseconds*	Sets the I-frame acknowledgment time.

Set the Maximum Number of I-Frames Sent Before Requiring Acknowledgment

You can set the maximum number of I-frames that the router sends to an LLC2 station before the software requires an acknowledgment from the receiving end. A higher value reduces overhead on the network. Ensure that the receiving LLC2 station can handle the number of frames set by this value.

To set this value, use the following command in interface configuration mode:

Command	Purpose
llc2 local-window *packet-count*	Sets the maximum number of I-frames the router sends before it requires an acknowledgment.

Set the Number of Retries Allowed

You can set the number of times the router will resend a frame when the receiving station does not acknowledge the frame. Once this value is reached, the session is dropped. This value also is used to determine how often the software will retry polling a busy station. Use this command in conjunction with the **llc2 t1-time** command described in the section "Set the Time for Resending I-Frames." Using them together ensures that frame transmission is monitored at a reasonable level, while limiting the number of unsuccessful repeated tries.

To set the number of retries, use the following command in interface configuration mode:

Command	Purpose
llc2 n2 *retry-count*	Establishes the number of times the router will resend unacknowledged frames or try polling a busy station.

Set the Time for Resending I-Frames

You can set the amount of time the router waits before resending unacknowledged I-frames. This interval is called the *T1 time*. Use this command in conjunction with setting the number of retries and setting the transit poll-frame timer. Using these commands in conjunction with each other provides a balance of network monitoring and performance.

To set the T1 time, use the following command in interface configuration mode:

Command	Purpose
llc2 t1-time *milliseconds*	Controls how long the router waits for an acknowledgment of transmitted I-frames.

NOTE   Ensure that you allow enough time for the round trip between the router and its LLC2-speaking stations. Under heavy network loading conditions, resending I-frames every 3000 milliseconds (ms) is appropriate.

Set the Time for Resending Rejected Frames

You can set the amount of time that the router will wait for an expected frame before sending a reject command (REJ). Typically, when an LLC2 station sends an I-frame, a sequence number is included in the frame. The LLC2 station that receives these frames will expect to receive them in order. If it does not, it can reject a frame and indicate which frame it is expecting to receive instead. If the correct frame is not sent to the software before the reject timer expires, the software sends a REJ to the remote station and disconnects the LLC2 session.

To set the reject timer, use the following command in interface configuration mode:

Command	Purpose
llc2 trej-time *milliseconds*	Sets the time Cisco IOS software waits for a resend of a rejected frame before sending a reject command to the remote station.

Establish the Polling Level

You can control the amount of polling that occurs on the LLC2 network by completing the tasks described in the following sections:

- Set the Polling Frequency
- Set the Polling Interval
- Set the Transmit-Poll-Frame Timer

Set the Polling Frequency

You can set the optimum interval of time after which the router sends Receiver Ready messages or frames that tell other LLC2 stations that the router is available. These polls occur during periods of idle time on the network.

To set polling frequency, use the following command in interface configuration mode:

Command	Purpose
llc2 idle-time *milliseconds*	Controls the polling frequency during idle traffic.

Set the Polling Interval

The amount of time the router waits until repolling a busy station can also be set. Use this command in conjunction with setting the number of retries. Typically, you do not need to use this command unless an LLC2 station has unusually long busy periods before clearing the busy state. In this case, you should increase the value so that the station does not time out.

To set the polling interval, use the following command in interface configuration mode:

Command	Purpose
llc2 tbusy-time *milliseconds*	Sets the amount of time the router will wait before repolling a busy station.

Set the Transmit-Poll-Frame Timer

When the router sends a command that must receive a response, a poll bit is sent in the frame. When the software sends the poll bit, it cannot send any other frame with the poll bit set until the receiver replies to that poll frame with a frame containing a final bit set. When the timer expires, the software assumes that it can send another frame with a poll bit.

Set the transmit-poll-frame timer to reduce problems with receiving stations that are faulty and cannot send the frame with the final bit set by using the following command in interface configuration mode:

Command	Purpose
llc2 tpf-time *milliseconds*	Sets the amount of time the router waits for a final response to a poll frame before the resending it.

This value should be larger than the T1 time. The T1 time determines how long the software waits for receipt of an acknowledgment before sending the next set of frames. Refer to the section "Set the Time for Resending I-Frames" earlier in this chapter for more information.

Set Up Exchange Identification Transmissions

You can control the number of frames used for exchange identification (XID) on the LLC2 network by completing the tasks described in the following sections:

- Set the Frequency of XID Transmissions
- Set the Time for XID Retries

Set the Frequency of XID Transmissions

XID frames identify LLC2 stations at a higher level than the MAC address and contain information about the configuration of the stations. You can set how often the router sends an XID frame by using the following command in interface configuration mode:

Command	Purpose
llc2 xid-neg-val-time *milliseconds*	Sets the frequency of XID transmissions.

CAUTION   Do not change the value unless requested by your technical support representative.

Set the Time for XID Retries

You can set the amount of time the router waits for a reply to the XID frames it sends to remote stations. The value should be larger than the T1 time, which indicates how long the software waits for an acknowledgment before dropping the session.

To set the time for XID retries, use the following command in interface configuration mode:

Command	Purpose
llc2 xid-retry-time *milliseconds*	Sets how long the router waits for a reply to the XID frames it sends to remote stations.

Monitor LLC2 Stations

You can display the configuration of LLC2 stations to determine which LLC2 parameters need adjustment. Use the following command in EXEC mode:

Command	Purpose
show llc2	Displays the configuration of LLC2 stations.

SDLC Configuration Task List

The SDLC tasks described in this section configure the router as an SDLC station. (This is in contrast to a router configured for SDLC Transport, where the device is not an SDLC station, but passes SDLC frames between two SDLC stations across a mixed-media, multiprotocol environment.) The first task is required; you accomplish it with the appropriate set of commands for your network needs. The remaining tasks are optional: You can perform them as necessary to enhance SDLC performance.

- Enable the Router as a Primary or a Secondary SDLC Station
- Enable SDLC Two-Way Simultaneous Mode
- Determine the Use of Frame Rejects
- Set SDLC Timer and Retry Counts
- Set SDLC Frame and Window Sizes
- Control the Buffer Size
- Control Polling of Secondary Stations
- Configure an SDLC Interface for Half-Duplex Mode
- Specify the XID Value
- Set the Largest SDLC I-Frame Size

To determine which SDLC parameters need adjustment, you can perform the following task:

● Monitor SDLC Stations

See the end of this chapter for SDLC configuration examples.

Enable the Router as a Primary or a Secondary SDLC Station

SDLC defines two types of network nodes: primary and secondary. Primary nodes poll secondary nodes in a predetermined order. Secondaries then transmit if they have outgoing data. When configured as primary and secondary nodes, our devices are established as SDLC stations.

Depending on your particular network needs, perform the tasks in one of the following sections to enable the router as an SDLC station:

● Establish an SDLC Station for Frame Relay Access Support

● Establish an SDLC Station for DLSw+ Support

● Establish an SDLC Station for SDLLC Media Translation

Establish an SDLC Station for Frame Relay Access Support

You can establish the router to be any of the following:

● A primary SDLC station

● A secondary SDLC station

● Either primary or secondary, depending on the role of the end stations or on XID negotiations

● A primary Node Type 2.1 (NT2.1) node

To establish devices as SDLC stations when you plan to configure Frame Relay access support, use the following commands in interface configuration mode:

Step	Command	Purpose
1	**encapsulation sdlc**	Sets the encapsulation type of the serial interface to SDLC.
2	**sdlc role {none | primary | secondary | prim-xid-poll}**	Establishes the role of the interface.

If the interface does not play a role, the router can be either primary or secondary, depending on the end stations. The SDLC end station must be configured as negotiable or primary NT2.1. When the end stations are configured as physical unit (PU) type 2, you can set the role of the interface to primary or secondary. When the end station is configured as secondary NT2.1, you must set the role of the interface to poll the primary XID.

NOTE	Currently, Frame Relay access support does not support the secondary role.

Establish an SDLC Station for DLSw+ Support

To establish devices as SDLC stations when you plan to configure our DLSw+ feature, use the following commands in interface configuration mode:

Step	Command	Purpose
1	**encapsulation sdlc**	Sets the encapsulation type of the serial interface to SDLC.
2	**sdlc role {none	primary	secondary	prim-xid-poll}**	Establishes the role of the interface.
3	**sdlc vmac** *mac-address*	Configures a MAC address for the serial interface.
4	**sdlc partner** *mac-address sdlc-address*	Specifies the destination address with which an LLC session is established for the SDLC station.
5	**sdlc dlsw** {*sdlc-address* / **default**	**partner** *mac-address* [**inbound**	**outbound**]}	Attaches SDLC addresses to DLSw+.

To configure an SDLC multidrop line downstream, you configure the SDLC role as either **primary** or **prim-xid-poll**. SDLC role **primary** specifies that any PU without the xid-poll parameter in the **sdlc address** command is a PU 2.0 device. SDLC role **prim-xid-poll** specifies that every PU is type 2.1. We recommend that you specify **sdlc role primary** if all SDLC devices are type PU 2.0 or a mix of PU 2.0 and PU 2.1. Specify **sdlc role prim-xid-poll** if all devices are type PU 2.1

For additional DLSw+ configuration commands, refer to Chapter 10, "DLSw+ Configuration Commands."

Establish an SDLC Station for SDLLC Media Translation

To establish devices as SDLC stations when you plan to configure our SDLLC media translation feature, use the commands in the order listed in the following table. One serial interface can have two or more secondary stations attached to it through a modem sharing device. Each secondary station address must be assigned to the primary station. You must use the following commands in interface configuration mode for the serial interface:

Step	Command	Purpose
1	**encapsulation sdlc-primary**	Establishes a router as the primary SDLC station on the serial line.
2	**encapsulation sdlc-secondary**	Establishes other routers as secondary SDLC stations.
3	**sdlc address** *hexbyte* [*echo*]	Assigns secondary stations to a primary station.

Use the **show interfaces** command to list the configuration of the SDLC serial lines. Use the **no sdlc address** command to remove a secondary address assignment. Addresses are hexadecimal (base 16).

Enable SDLC Two-Way Simultaneous Mode

SDLC two-way simultaneous mode allows a primary SDLC link station to achieve more efficient use of a full-duplex serial line. With two-way simultaneous mode, the primary link station can send data to one secondary link station while there is a poll outstanding. Two-way simultaneous mode works on the SDLC primary side only. On a secondary link station, it responds to a poll from the primary station.

SDLC two-way simultaneous mode operates in either a multidrop link environment or point-to-point link environment.

In a multidrop link environment, a two-way simultaneous primary station is able to poll a secondary station and receive data from the station, and send data (I-frames) to other secondary stations.

In a point-to-point link environment, a two-way simultaneous primary station can send data (I-frames) to the secondary station although there is a poll outstanding, as long as the window limit is not reached.

To enable two-way simultaneous mode, use either of the following commands in interface configuration mode:

Command	Purpose
sdlc simultaneous full-datamode or	Enables the primary station to send data to and receive data from the polled secondary station.
sdlc simultaneous half-datamode	Prohibits the primary stations from sending data to the polled secondary station.

Determine the Use of Frame Rejects

You can specify that a secondary station does not send frame reject messages, or reject commands indicating frame errors. If you do so, the router drops an SDLC connection if the system receives an error from the secondary station. To determine handling of frame rejects, use the following command in interface configuration mode:

Command	Purpose
sdlc frmr-disable	Specifies that this secondary station does not support frame rejects.

To specify that the secondary station does support frame rejects, use the **no sdlc frmr-disable** command.

Set SDLC Timer and Retry Counts

When an SDLC station sends a frame, it waits for an acknowledgment from the receiver indicating that this frame has been received. You can modify the time the router allows for an acknowledgment before resending the frame. You can also determine the number of times that a software resends a frame before terminating the SDLC session. By controlling these values, you can reduce network overhead while continuing to check transmission of frames.

To set the SDLC timer and retry counts, use one or both of the following commands in interface configuration mode:

Command	Purpose
sdlc t1 *milliseconds*	Controls the amount of time Cisco IOS software waits for a reply.
sdlc n2 *retry-count*	Sets the number of times Cisco IOS software will retry an operation that has timed out.

Set SDLC Frame and Window Sizes

You can set the maximum size of an incoming frame and set the maximum number of I-frames (or window size) the router will receive before sending an acknowledgment to the sender. By using higher values, you can reduce network overhead.

To set SDLC frame and window sizes, use any of the following commands in interface configuration mode:

Command	Purpose
sdlc n1 *bit-count*	Sets the maximum size of an incoming frame.
sdlc k *window-size*	Sets the local window size of the router.

Command	Purpose
sdlc poll-limit-value *count*	Sets how many times a primary station will poll a secondary station.

Control the Buffer Size

You can control the buffer size on the router. The buffer holds data that is pending transmission to a remote SDLC station. This command is particularly useful in the case of the SDLLC media translator, which allows an LLC2-speaking SNA station on a Token Ring to communicate with an SDLC-speaking SNA station on a serial link. The frame sizes and window sizes on Token Rings are often much larger than those acceptable for serial links, and serial links are often slower than Token Rings.

To control backlogs that can occur during periods of high data transfer from the Token Ring to the serial line, use the following command in interface configuration mode on a per-address basis:

Command	Purpose
sdlc holdq *address queue-size*	Sets the maximum number of packets held in queue before transmitting.

Control Polling of Secondary Stations

You can control the intervals at which the router polls secondary stations, the length of time a primary station can send data to a secondary station, and how often the software polls one secondary station before moving on to the next station.

Keep the following points in mind when using these commands:

- Secondary stations cannot transmit data until they are polled by a primary station. Increasing the poll-pause timer increases the response time of the secondary stations. Decreasing the timer can flood the serial link with unneeded polls, requiring secondary stations to spend wasted CPU time processing them.

- Increasing the value of the poll limit allows for smoother transactions between a primary station and a single secondary station, but can delay polling of other secondary stations.

To control polling of secondary stations, use one or more of the following commands in interface configuration mode:

Command	Purpose
sdlc poll-pause-timer *milliseconds*	Sets the length of time the router pauses between sending each poll frame to secondary stations on a single serial interface.

Command	Purpose
sdlc poll-limit-value *count*	Sets how many times a primary station will poll a secondary station.

To retrieve default polling values for these operations, use the **no** forms of these commands.

Configure an SDLC Interface for Half-Duplex Mode

By default, SDLC interfaces operate in full-duplex mode. To configure an SDLC interface for half-duplex mode, use the following command in interface configuration mode:

Command	Purpose
half-duplex	Configures an SDLC interface for half-duplex mode.

On an interface that is in half-duplex mode and that has been configured for DCE, you can adjust the delay between the detection of a Request To Send (RTS) signal and the assertion of the Clear To Send (CTS) signal. To do so, use the following command in interface configuration mode:

Command	Purpose
half-duplex timer cts-delay *value*	Delays the assertion of a CTS.

On an interface that is in half-duplex mode and that has been configured for DTE, you can adjust the time the interface waits for the DCE to assert CTS before dropping an RTS. To do so, use the following command in interface configuration mode:

Command	Purpose
half-duplex timer rts-timeout *value*	Adjusts the amount of time before interface drops an RTS.

Specify the XID Value

The XID value you define on the router must match that of the IDBLK and IDNUM system generation parameters defined in VTAM on the Token Ring host to which the SDLC device will be communicating. To specify the XID value, use the following command in interface configuration mode:

Command	Purpose
sdlc xid *address xid*	Specifies the XID value to be associated with the SDLC station.

Set the Largest SDLC I-Frame Size

Generally, the router and the SDLC device with which it communicates should support the same maximum SDLC I-frame size. The larger this value, the more efficient the line usage, thus increasing performance.

After the SDLC device has been configured to send the largest possible I-frame, you must configure the router to support the same maximum I-frame size. The default is 265 bytes. The maximum value the software can support must be less than the value of the LLC2 largest frame value defined when setting the largest LLC2 I-frame size.

To set the largest SDLC I-frame size, use the following command in interface configuration mode:

Command	Purpose
sdlc sdlc-largest-frame *address size*	Sets the largest I-frame size that can be sent or received by the designated SDLC station.

Monitor SDLC Stations

To monitor the configuration of SDLC stations to determine which SDLC parameters need adjustment, use the following command in EXEC mode:

Command	Purpose
show interfaces	Displays SDLC station configuration information.

You determine the status of end stations by sending an SDLC test frame to a physical unit via its SDLC address and router interface. You can either send out the default information string or a predefined one. You can send a preset number of test frames a continuous stream that can later be halted. The **sdlc test serial** command precheck for correct interface and SDLC address of the end station. You can view the results of the test frames after the frames have been sent or a SDLC test frame stop has been executed. To send an SDLC test frame, use the following command in EXEC mode:

Command	Purpose
sdlc test serial *number address* [*iterations* | **continuous** | **stop** | **string** *string*]	Sends an SDLC test frame.

NOTE   Only a device configured as primary is allowed to send test frames.

Configuration Examples

The following sections provide LLC2 and SDLC configuration examples:

- LLC2 Configuration Example

- SDLC Two-Way Simultaneous Mode Configuration Example

- SDLC Encapsulation for Frame Relay Access Support Configuration Examples

- SDLC Configuration for DLSw+ Example

- Half-Duplex Configuration Example

LLC2 Configuration Example

You can configure the number of LLC2 frames received before an acknowledgment. For this example, assume that at time 0, two I-frames are received. The maximum amount of three has not been reached, so no acknowledgment for these frames is sent. If a third frame, which would force the router to send an acknowledgment, is not received within 800 ms, an acknowledgment is sent anyway because the delay timer alarm is activated.

```
interface tokenring 0
 llc2 ack-max 3
 llc2 ack-delay-time 800
```

At this point, because all frames are acknowledged, the counter for the maximum amount of I-frames will be reset to zero.

SDLC Two-Way Simultaneous Mode Configuration Example

The following configuration defines serial interface 0 as the primary SDLC station with two SDLC secondary stations, C1 and C2, attached to it through a modem-sharing device. Two-way simultaneous mode is enabled.

```
interface serial 0
 encapsulation sdlc-primary
 sdlc address c1
 sdlc address c2
 sdlc simultaneous full-datamode
```

The network for this configuration is shown in Figure 13-1.

Figure 13-1 *Two SDLC Secondary Stations Attached to a Single Serial Interface through a Modem Sharing Device*

SDLC Encapsulation for Frame Relay Access Support Configuration Examples

The following examples describe possible SDLC encapsulation configurations if you plan to configure Frame Relay access support.

The following configuration is appropriate if the SDLC station is a negotiable or primary Node Type 2.1 station:

```
interface serial 2/6
 no ip address
 encapsulation sdlc
 clockrate 9600
 fras map sdlc C1 serial 2/0 frame-relay 32 4 4
 sdlc address C1
```

The following configuration is appropriate if the SDLC station is a secondary Node Type 2.1 station:

```
interface serial 2/6
 no ip address
 encapsulation sdlc
 clockrate 9600
 fras map sdlc C1 serial 2/0 frame-relay 32 4 4
 sdlc role prim-xid-poll
 sdlc address C1
```

The following configuration is appropriate if the SDLC station is a secondary PU 2 station:

```
interface serial 2/6
 no ip address
 encapsulation sdlc
 clockrate 9600
 fras map sdlc C1 serial 2/0 frame-relay 32 4 4
 sdlc role primary
 sdlc address C1
 sdlc xid C1 01700001
```

SDLC Configuration for DLSw+ Example

The following example describes an SDLC configuration if you plan to implement DLSw+ support. In this example, 4000.3745.001 is the MAC address of the host. The router serves as the primary station for the remote secondary stations, c1 and c2. Both c1 and c2 are reserved for DLSw+ and cannot be used by any other data-link user.

```
interface serial 0
 encapsulation sdlc
 sdlc vmac 4000.3174.0000
 sdlc address c1
 sdlc xid c1 01712345
 sdlc partner 4000.3745.0001 c1
 sdlc address c2
 sdlc xid c2 01767890
 sdlc partner 4000.3745.0001 c2
 sdlc dlsw c1 c2
 sdlc role primary
```

Half-Duplex Configuration Example

In the following example, an SDLC interface has been configured for half-duplex mode:

```
encapsulation sdlc-primary
 half-duplex
```

LLC2 and SDLC Commands

Logical Link Control, type 2 (LLC2) Protocol provides connection-oriented service and is widely used in LAN environments, particularly among IBM communication systems connected by Token Ring. Cisco IOS software supports LLC2 connections over Ethernet, Token Ring, and Fiber Distributed Data Interface (FDDI).

The LLC2 commands provide operations that support the following features:

● Local acknowledgment in remote source-route bridging (RSRB)

● IBM LAN Network Manager (LNM) support used in source-route bridging (SRB)

● Synchronous Data Link Control (SDLC)/LLC2 Media Translation (SDLLC)

● ISO Connection-Mode Network Services (CMNS) running X.25 packets over LLC2

SDLC is used as the primary Systems Network Architecture (SNA) link-layer protocol for WAN links. SDLC defines two types of network nodes: primary and secondary. Primary nodes poll secondary nodes in a predetermined order. Secondaries then transmit if they have outgoing data. When configured as primary and secondary nodes, routers are established as SDLC stations.

The SDLC commands described in this chapter pertain to routers configured as SDLC stations. This is in contrast to a device configured for SDLC Transport where the router is not configured as an SDLC station, but acts as an intermediary, passing SDLC frames between two SDLC stations across a mixed-media, multiprotocol environment.

The SDLC commands support the following features:

● SDLLC SDLC/LLC2 media translation

● SDLC local acknowledgment for serial tunnel (STUN)-enabled interfaces

Use the commands in this chapter to adjust the LLC2 and SDLC parameters. For LLC2 and SDLC parameter configuration information and examples, refer to Chapter 13, "Configuring LLC2 and SDLC Parameters."

encapsulation sdlc

Use the **encapsulation sdlc** interface configuration command to configure an SDLC interface.

encapsulation sdlc

Syntax Description

This command has no arguments or keywords.

Default

Disabled

Command Mode

Interface configuration

Usage Guidelines

This command first appeared in Cisco IOS Release 10.3.

The **encapsulation sdlc** command must be used to configure an SDLC interface if you plan to implement DLSw+ or Frame Relay access support.

SDLC defines two types of network nodes: primary and secondary. Primary nodes poll secondary nodes in a predetermined order. Secondaries then transmit if they have outgoing data. When configured as primary and secondary nodes, Cisco routers are established as SDLC stations. Use the **sdlc role** interface configuration command to establish the role as primary or secondary.

In the IBM environment, a front-end processor (FEP) is the primary station and establishment controllers (ECs) are secondary stations. In a typical scenario, an EC may be connected to dumb terminals and to a Token Ring network at a local site. At the remote site, an IBM host connects to an IBM FEP, which can also have links to another Token Ring LAN. Typically, the two sites are connected through an SDLC leased line.

If a router is connected to an EC, it takes over the function of the FEP and must therefore be configured as a primary SDLC station. If the router is connected to a FEP, it takes the place of the EC and must therefore be configured as a secondary SDLC station.

Example

The following example configures an SDLC interface:

```
interface serial 2/6
 no ip address
 encapsulation sdlc
```

Related Commands

To locate documentation of related commands, you can search online at www.cisco.com.

sdlc role

encapsulation sdlc-primary

Use the **encapsulation sdlc-primary** interface configuration command to configure the router as the primary SDLC station if you plan to configure the SDLLC media translation feature.

> **encapsulation sdlc-primary**

Syntax Description

This command has no arguments or keywords.

Default

Disabled

Command Mode

Interface configuration

Usage Guidelines

This command first appeared in Cisco IOS Release 10.0.

The **encapsulation sdlc-primary** or **encapsulation sdlc-secondary** command must be used to configure an SDLC interface. To use the **encapsulation sdlc-primary** command, first select the interface on which you want to enable SDLC. Then, establish the router as a primary station. Next, assign secondary station addresses to the primary station using the **sdlc address** command.

SDLC defines two types of network nodes: primary and secondary. Primary nodes poll secondary nodes in a predetermined order. Secondaries then transmit if they have outgoing data. When configured as primary and secondary nodes, Cisco routers are established as SDLC stations.

In the IBM environment, a front-end processor (FEP) is the primary station and establishment controllers (ECs) are secondary stations. In a typical scenario, an EC may be connected to dumb terminals and to a Token Ring network at a local site. At the remote site, an IBM host connects to an IBM FEP, which can also have links to another Token Ring LAN. Typically, the two sites are connected through an SDLC leased line.

If a router is connected to an EC, it takes over the function of the FEP and must therefore be configured as a primary SDLC station. If the router is connected to an FEP, it takes the place of the EC and must therefore be configured as a secondary SDLC station.

Example

The following example shows configures serial interface 0 on your router to allow two SDLC secondary stations to attach through a modem-sharing device (MSD) with addresses C1 and C2:

```
! enter a global command if you have not already
interface serial 0
 encapsulation sdlc-primary
 sdlc address c1
 sdlc address c2
```

Related Commands

To locate documentation of related commands, you can search online at www.cisco.com.

encapsulation sdlc-secondary
sdlc address
show interfaces

encapsulation sdlc-secondary

Use the **encapsulation sdlc-secondary** interface configuration command to configure the router as a secondary SDLC station if you plan to configure the SDLLC media translation feature.

> **encapsulation sdlc-secondary**

Syntax Description

This command has no arguments or keywords.

Default

Disabled

Command Mode

Interface configuration

Usage Guidelines

This command first appeared in Cisco IOS Release 10.0.

An **encapsulation sdlc-primary** or **encapsulation sdlc-secondary** command must be used to configure an SDLC interface. To use the **encapsulation sdlc-secondary** command, first select the interface on which you want to enable SDLC. Then establish the router as a secondary station. Next, assign secondary station addresses to the primary station using the **sdlc address** command.

SDLC defines two types of network nodes: primary and secondary. Primary nodes poll secondary nodes in a predetermined order. Secondaries then transmit if they have outgoing data. When configured as primary and secondary nodes, Cisco devices are established as SDLC stations.

In the IBM environment, a front-end processor (FEP) is the primary station and establishment controllers (ECs) are secondary stations. In a typical scenario, an EC may be connected to dumb terminals and to a Token Ring network at a local site. At the remote site, an IBM host connects to an IBM FEP, which can also have links to another Token Ring LAN. Typically, the two sites are connected through an SDLC leased line.

If a router is connected to an EC, it takes over the function of the FEP and must therefore be configured as a primary SDLC station. If the router is connected to a FEP, it takes the place of the EC and must therefore be configured as a secondary SDLC station.

Example

The following example establishes the router as a secondary SDLC station:

```
interface serial 0
 encapsulation sdlc-secondary
```

Related Commands

To locate documentation of related commands, you can search online at www.cisco.com.

encapsulation sdlc-primary
sdlc address
show interfaces

llc2 ack-delay-time

Use the **llc2 ack-delay-time** interface configuration command to set the amount of time Cisco IOS software waits for an acknowledgment before sending the next set of information frames.

llc2 ack-delay-time *milliseconds*

Syntax   Description

milliseconds   Number of milliseconds the software allows incoming information frames to stay unacknowledged. The minimum is 1 millisecond and the maximum is 60,000 milliseconds. The default is 100 milliseconds.

Default

100 milliseconds

Command Mode

Interface configuration

Usage Guidelines

This command first appeared in Cisco IOS Release 10.0.

Upon receiving an information frame, each LLC2 station starts a timer. If the timer expires, an acknowledgment will be sent for the frame, even if the **llc2 ack-max** number of received frames has not been reached. Experiment with the value of the **llc2 ack-delay-time** command to determine the configuration that balances acknowledgment network overhead and quick response time (by receipt of timely acknowledgments).

Use this command in conjunction with the **llc2 ack-max** command to determine the maximum number of information frames Cisco IOS software can receive before sending an acknowledgment.

Example

In the following example, the software allows a 100-millisecond delay before I-frames must be acknowledged:

```
! enter a global command, if you have not already
interface tokenring 0
! sample ack-max command
 llc2 ack-max 3
! allow a 100 millisecond delay before I-frames must be acknowledged
 llc2 ack-delay-time 100
```

At time 0, two information frames are received. The llc2 ack-max amount of three has not been reached, so no acknowledgment for these frames is sent. If a third frame, which would force the software to send an acknowledgment, is not received in 100 milliseconds, an acknowledgment will be sent anyway because the llc2 ack-delay timer expires. At this point, because all frames are acknowledged, the counter for the ack-max purposes will be reset to 0.

Related Commands

To locate documentation of related commands, you can search online at www.cisco.com.

llc2 ack-max
show llc2

llc2 ack-max

Use the **llc2 ack-max** interface configuration command to control the maximum amount of information frames Cisco IOS software can receive before it must send an acknowledgment.

llc2 ack-max *packet-count*

Syntax

packet-count

Description

Maximum number of packets the software will receive before sending an acknowledgment. The minimum is 1 packet and the maximum is 127 packets. The default is 3 packets.

Default

3 packets

Command Mode

Interface configuration

Usage Guidelines

This command first appeared in Cisco IOS Release 10.0.

An LLC2-speaking station can send only a predetermined number of frames before it must wait for an acknowledgment from the receiver. If the receiver waits until receiving a large number of frames before acknowledging any of them, and then acknowledges them all at once, it reduces overhead on the network.

For example, an acknowledgment for five frames can specify that all five have been received, as opposed to sending a separate acknowledgment for each frame. To keep network overhead low, make this parameter as large as possible.

However, some LLC2-speaking stations expect this to be a low number. Some NetBIOS-speaking stations expect an acknowledgment to every frame. Therefore, for these stations, this number is best set to 1. Experiment with this parameter to determine the best configuration.

Example

In the following example, the software is configured to receive up to seven frames before it must send an acknowledgment. Seven frames is the maximum allowed by SNA before a reply must be received:

```
! enter a global command, if you have not already
interface tokenring 0
! receive up to seven frames before sending an acknowledgment
 llc2 ack-max 7
! sample delay-time command
 llc2 ack-delay-time 100
```

Related Commands

To locate documentation of related commands, you can search online at www.cisco.com.

llc2 ack-delay-time
llc2 local-window
show llc2

llc2 idle-time

Use the **llc2 idle-time** interface configuration command to control the frequency of polls during periods of idle time (no traffic).

> **llc2 idle-time** *milliseconds*

Syntax	Description
milliseconds	Number of milliseconds that can pass with no traffic before the LLC2 station sends a Receiver Ready frame. The minimum is 1 millisecond and the maximum is 60,000 milliseconds. The default is 10,000 milliseconds.

Default

10,000 milliseconds

Command Mode

Interface configuration

Usage Guidelines

This command first appeared in Cisco IOS Release 10.0.

Periodically, when no information frames are being transmitted during an LLC2 session, LLC2 stations are sent a Receiver Ready frame to indicate they are available. Set the value for this command low enough to ensure a timely discovery of available stations, but not too low, or you will create a network overhead with too many Receiver Ready frames.

Example

In the following example, Cisco IOS software waits 20,000 milliseconds before sending a Receiver Ready ("are you there") frame:

```
! enter a global command, if you have not already
interface tokenring 0
! wait 20000 milliseconds before sending receiver-ready frames
 llc2 idle-time 20000
```

Related Commands

To locate documentation of related commands, you can search online at www.cisco.com.

llc2 tbusy-time
llc2 tpf-time
show llc2

llc2 local-window

Use the **llc2 local-window** interface configuration command to control the maximum number of information frames Cisco IOS software sends before it waits for an acknowledgment.

llc2 local-window *packet-count*

Syntax	Description
packet-count	Maximum number of packets that can be sent before the software must wait for an acknowledgment. The minimum is 1 packet and the maximum is 127 packets. The default is 7 packets.

Default

7 packets

Command Mode

Interface configuration

Usage Guidelines

This command first appeared in Cisco IOS Release 10.0.

An LLC2-speaking station can send only a predetermined number of frames before it must wait for an acknowledgment from the receiver. Set this number to the maximum value that can be supported by the stations with which the router communicates. Setting this value too large can cause frames to be lost because the receiving station may not be able to receive all of them.

Example

In the following example, the software will send as many as 30 information frames through Token Ring interface 1 before it must receive an acknowledgment:

```
! enter a global command, if you have not already
interface tokenring 1
 llc2 local-window 30
```

Related Commands

To locate documentation of related commands, you can search online at www.cisco.com.

llc2 ack-max
show llc2

llc2 n2

Use the **llc2 n2** interface configuration command to control the amount of times Cisco IOS software retries sending unacknowledged frames or repolls remote busy stations.

llc2 n2 *retry-count*

Syntax	Description
retry-count	Number of times the software retries operations. The minimum is 1 retry and the maximum is 255 retries. The default is 8 retries.

Default

8 retries

Command Mode

Interface configuration

Usage Guidelines

This command first appeared in Cisco IOS Release 10.0.

An LLC2 station must have some limit to the number of times it will resend a frame when the receiver of that frame has not acknowledged it. After the software is told that a remote station is busy, it will poll again based on the *retry-count* value. When this retry count is exceeded, the LLC2 station terminates its session with the other station. Set this parameter to a value that balances between frame checking and network performance.

Example

In the following example, the software will resend a frame up to four times through Token Ring interface 1 before it must receive an acknowledgment. Because you generally do not need to change the retry limit, this example shows you how to reset the limit to the default of 8.

```
! enter a global command, if you have not already
interface tokenring 1
! retry value of 8
 llc2 n2 8
```

Related Commands

To locate documentation of related commands, you can search online at www.cisco.com.

llc2 t1-time
llc2 tbusy-time
llc2 trej-time
show llc2

llc2 t1-time

Use the **llc2 t1-time** interface configuration command to control the amount of time the Cisco IOS software will wait before resending unacknowledged information frames.

> **llc2 t1-time** *milliseconds*

Syntax

Description

Syntax	Description
milliseconds	Number of milliseconds the software waits before resending unacknowledged information frames. The minimum is 1 millisecond and the maximum is 60,000 milliseconds. The default is 1000 milliseconds.

Default

1000 milliseconds

Command Mode

Interface configuration

Usage Guidelines

This command first appeared in Cisco IOS Release 10.0.

Use this command in conjunction with the **llc2 n2** command to provide a balance of network monitoring and performance. Ensure that enough time is allowed to account for the round trip between the router and its LLC2-speaking stations under heavy network loading conditions.

Example

In the following example, the software will wait 4000 milliseconds before resending an unacknowledged frame through Token Ring interface 2:

```
! enter a global command, if you have not already
interface tokenring 2
! wait 4000 milliseconds before retransmitting a frame through tokenring 2
 llc2 t1-time 4000
```

Related Commands

To locate documentation of related commands, you can search online at www.cisco.com.

llc2 n2
llc2 tpf-time
llc2 xid-retry-time
show llc2

llc2 tbusy-time

Use the **llc2 tbusy-time** interface configuration command to control the amount of time Cisco IOS software waits until repolling a busy remote station.

> **llc2 tbusy-time** *milliseconds*

Syntax

milliseconds

Description

Number of milliseconds the software waits before repolling a busy remote station. The minimum is 1 millisecond and the maximum is 60,000 milliseconds. The default is 9600 milliseconds.

Default

9600 milliseconds

Command Mode

Interface configuration

Usage Guidelines

This command first appeared in Cisco IOS Release 10.0.

An LLC2 station has the ability to notify other stations that it is temporarily busy, so the other stations will not attempt to send any new information frames. The frames sent to indicate this are called Receiver-Not-Ready (RNR) frames. Change the value of this parameter only to increase the value for LLC2-speaking stations that have unusually long busy periods before they clear their busy status. Increasing the value will prevent the stations from timing out.

Example

In the following example, the software will wait up to 12,000 milliseconds before attempting to poll a remote station through Token Ring interface 0 to learn the station's status:

```
! enter a global command, if you have not already
interface tokenring 0
! wait 12000 milliseconds before polling a station through tokenring 0
 llc2 tbusy-time 12000
```

Related Commands

To locate documentation of related commands, you can search online at www.cisco.com.

llc2 n2
llc2 idle-time
show llc2

Part
II

Command Reference

llc2 tpf-time

Use the **llc2 tpf-time** interface configuration command to set the amount of time Cisco IOS software waits for a final response to a poll frame before resending the poll frame.

> **llc2 tpf-time** *milliseconds*

Syntax	Description
milliseconds	Number of milliseconds the software waits for a final response to a poll frame before resending the poll frame. The minimum is 1 millisecond and the maximum is 60,000 milliseconds. The default is 1000 milliseconds.

Default

1000 milliseconds

Command Mode

Interface configuration

Usage Guidelines

This command first appeared in Cisco IOS Release 10.0.

When sending a command that must receive a response, a poll bit is sent in the frame. This is the receiving station's clue that the sender is expecting some response from it, be it an acknowledgment of information frames or an acknowledgment of more administrative tasks, such as starting and stopping the session. Once a sender gives out the poll bit, it cannot send any other frame with the poll bit set until the receiver replies with a frame containing a final bit set. If the receiver is faulty, it may never return the final bit to the sender. Therefore, the sender could be waiting for a reply that will never come. To avoid this problem, when a poll-bit-set frame is sent, a transmit-poll-frame (TPF) timer is started. If this timer expires, the software assumes that it can send another frame with a poll bit.

Usually, you will not want to change this value. If you do, the value should be larger than the T1 time, set with the **llc2 t1-time** command. The T1 time determines how long the software waits for receipt of an acknowledgment before sending the next set of frames.

Example

While you generally will not want to change the transmit-poll-frame time, this example sets the TPF time to 3000 milliseconds. Because the TPF time should be larger than the LLC2 T1 time, this example shows the TPF time as double the LLC2 T1 time.

```
! enter a global command, if you have not already
interface tokenring 0
! send a poll bit set through tokenring 0 after a 3000 ms delay
 llc2 tpf-time 3000
! wait 1500 milliseconds for an acknowledgment before resending I-frames
 llc2 t1-time 1500
```

Related Commands

To locate documentation of related commands, you can search online at www.cisco.com.

llc2 idle-time
llc2 n2
llc2 t1-time
show llc2

llc2 trej-time

Use the **llc2 trej-time** interface configuration command to control the amount of time Cisco IOS software waits for a correct frame after sending a reject command to the remote LLC2 station.

llc2 trej-time *milliseconds*

Syntax	Description
milliseconds	Number of milliseconds the software waits for a resend of a rejected frame before sending a reject command to the remote station. The minimum is 1 millisecond and the maximum is 60,000 milliseconds. The default is 3200 milliseconds.

Default

3200 milliseconds

Command Mode

Interface configuration

Usage Guidelines

This command first appeared in Cisco IOS Release 10.0.

When an LLC2 station sends an information frame, a sequence number is included in the frame. The LLC2 station that receives these frames will expect to receive them in order. If it does not, it can reject a frame and indicate which frame it is expecting to receive instead. Upon sending a reject, the LLC2 station starts a reject timer. If the frames are not received before this timer expires, the session is disconnected.

Example

In the following example, the software will wait up to 1000 milliseconds to receive a previously rejected frame before resending its reject message to the station that sent the frame:

```
! enter a global command, if you have not already
interface tokenring 0
! wait 1000 milliseconds before resending a reject message through tokenring 0
 llc2 trej-time 1000
```

Related Commands

To locate documentation of related commands, you can search online at www.cisco.com.

llc2 n2
show llc2

llc2 xid-neg-val-time

Use the **llc2 xid-neg-val-tim** interface configuration command to control the frequency of exchange identification (XID) transmissions by Cisco IOS software.

llc2 xid-neg-val-time *milliseconds*

Syntax	Description
milliseconds	Number of milliseconds after which the software sends XID frames to other LLC2-speaking stations. The minimum is 0 milliseconds and the maximum is 60,000 milliseconds. The default is 0 milliseconds.

Default

0 milliseconds

Command Mode

Interface configuration

Usage Guidelines

This command first appeared in Cisco IOS Release 10.0.

Do not change the **llc2 xid-neg-val-time** parameter unless requested by your technical support representative.

LLC2-speaking stations can communicate exchange identification (XID) frames to each other. These frames identify the stations at a higher level than the MAC address and also can contain information about the configuration of the station. These frames are typically sent only during setup and configuration periods when it is deemed that sending them is useful. The greatest frequency at which this information is transferred is controlled by this timer.

Example

The following example shows how to reset the frequency of XID transmissions to the default of 0 milliseconds:

```
! enter a global command, if you have not already
interface tokenring 0
! set the frequency of XID transmissions to 0
 llc2 xid-neg-val-time 0
```

Related Commands

To locate documentation of related commands, you can search online at www.cisco.com.

llc2 xid-retry-time
show llc2

llc2 xid-retry-time

Use the **llc2 xid-retry-time** interface configuration command to set the amount of time Cisco IOS software waits for a reply to exchange identification (XID) frames before dropping the session.

> **llc2 xid-retry-time** *milliseconds*

Syntax

milliseconds

Description

Number of milliseconds the software waits for a reply to XID frames before dropping a session. The minimum is 1 millisecond and the maximum is 60,000 milliseconds. The default is 60,000 milliseconds.

Default

60,000 milliseconds

Command Mode

Interface configuration

Usage Guidelines

This command first appeared in Cisco IOS Release 10.0.

Set this value greater than the value of the T1 time, or the time the software waits for an acknowledgment before dropping the session. T1 time is set with the **llc2 t1-time** command.

Example

The following example sets the software to wait up to 60,000 milliseconds for a reply to XID frames it sent to remote stations (which resets the value to its default):

```
! enter a global command, if you have not already
interface tokenring 0
! wait 60000 milliseconds for a reply to XID frames
 llc2 xid-retry-time 60000
```

Related Commands

To locate documentation of related commands, you can search online at www.cisco.com.

llc2 t1-time
llc2 xid-neg-val-time
show llc2

sdlc address

Use the **sdlc address** interface configuration command to assign a set of secondary stations attached to the serial link. Use the **no** form of this command to remove an assigned secondary station.

> **sdlc address** *hexbyte* [**echo**]
> **no sdlc address** *hexbyte*

Syntax	Description
hexbyte	Hexadecimal number (base 16) indicating the address of the serial link.
echo	(Optional) Treats nonecho and echo SDLC addresses as the same address.

Default

No secondary stations are assigned.

Command Mode

Interface configuration

Usage Guidelines

This command first appeared in Cisco IOS Release 10.0.

Before using this command, first select the interface on which you want to enable SDLC. Then, establish the router as a primary station with the **encapsulation sdlc-primary** command. Next, assign secondary station addresses to the primary station using the **sdlc address** command. The addresses are given in hexadecimal (base 16) and are given one per line.

The optional keyword **echo** is valid only for TG interfaces. When you use the **echo** keyword, hexbyte is the nonecho SDLC address.

Example

The following example shows how to configure serial interface 0 to have two SDLC secondary stations attached to it through a modem-sharing device with addresses C1 and C2:

```
interface serial 0
 encapsulation sdlc-primary
 sdlc address c1
 sdlc address c2
```

Related Commands

To locate documentation of related commands, you can search online at www.cisco.com.

encapsulation sdlc-primary
encapsulation sdlc-secondary
show interfaces

sdlc address ff ack-mode

Use the **sdlc address ff ack-mode** interface configuration command to configure the IBM reserved address ff as a valid local address.

sdlc address ff ack-mode

Syntax Description

This command has no arguments or keywords.

Command Mode

Interface configuration

Usage Guidelines

This command first appeared in Cisco IOS Release 11.0.

The **sdlc address ff ack-mode** command is used to support applications that require local termination of an SDLC connection with address FF. This command should be used only if you use the SDLC address FF as a regular (not a broadcast) address.

Example

The following example enables local acknowledgment of SDLC address FF:

```
stun peer-name xxx.xxx.xxx.xxx
stun protocol-group 1 sdlc
interface serial 1
 encapsulation stun
 stun group 1
 stun sdlc-role secondary
 sdlc address c1
 sdlc address ff ack-mode
 stun route address c1 tcp yyy.yyy.yyy.yyy local-ack
 stun route address ff tcp yyy.yyy.yyy.yyy local-ack
```

Related Commands

To locate documentation of related commands, you can search online at www.cisco.com.

stun route address tcp

sdlc dlsw

Use the **sdlc dlsw** interface configuration command to attach SDLC addresses to DLSw+. Use the **no** form of this command to cancel the configuration.

> **sdlc dlsw** {*sdlc-address* | **default** | **partner** *mac-address* [**inbound** | **outbound**]}
> **no sdlc dlsw** {*sdlc-address* | **default** | **partner** *mac-address* [**inbound** | **outbound**]}

Syntax

Description

sdlc-address SDLC addresses are in hexadecimal. The valid range is 1 to FE.

default Allows the user to configure an unlimited number of SDLC addresses to DLSw+.

partner *mac-address* MAC address for default partner.

inbound (Optional) Partner will initiate connection.

outbound (Optional) Initiate connection to partner.

Default

No correspondence is defined between SDLC addresses and DLSw+.

Command Mode

Interface configuration

Usage Guidelines

This command first appeared in Cisco IOS Release 11.0.

Examples

The following command attaches SDLC address d2 to DLSw+:

```
sdlc dlsw d2
```

The following command attaches SDLC addresses d2, d5, e3, e4, e6, b1, c3, d4, a1, and a5:

```
sdlc dlsw d2 d5 e3 e4 e6 b1 c3 d4 a1 a5
```

Related Commands

To locate documentation of related commands, you can search online at www.cisco.com.

encapsulation sdlc
sdlc address
sdlc role

sdlc dte-timeout

Use the **sdlc dte-timeout** interface configuration command to adjust the amount of time a data terminal equipment (DTE) interface waits for the data circuit-terminating equipment (DCE) to assert a Clear To Send (CTS) signal before dropping a Request To Send (RTS).

sdlc dte-timeout *unit*

Syntax	Description
unit	Timeout wait interval in microseconds. The valid range is 10 to 64,000. Each unit is approximately 5 microseconds. The default is 10 units.

Default

10 units (approximately 50 microseconds)

Command Mode

Interface configuration

Usage Guidelines

This command first appeared in Cisco IOS Release 10.0.

Use this command on an interface that is in half-duplex mode and that has been configured for DTE.

Example

The following example sets the amount of time that the DTE waits for the DCE to assert a CTS to 100 units (approximately 500 microseconds):

```
sdlc dte-timeout 100
```

Related Commands

To locate documentation of related commands, you can search online at www.cisco.com.

half-duplex
half-duplex timer

sdlc frmr-disable

Use the **sdlc frmr-disable** interface configuration command to indicate that secondary stations on a particular serial link do not support Frame Rejects (FRMRs) or error indications. Use the **no** form of this command to specify that the secondary station does support FRMRs.

> **sdlc frmr-disable**
> **no sdlc framer-disable**

Syntax Description

This command has no arguments or keywords.

Default

Support of FRMRs or error indications

Command Mode

Interface configuration

Usage Guidelines

This command first appeared in Cisco IOS Release 10.0.

FRMRs are error indications that can be sent to an SDLC station indicating that a protocol error has occurred. Not all SDLC stations support FRMRs. If this command is enabled, when Cisco IOS software receives an error, it drops the line by sending a disconnect request to the remote station.

Example

In the following example, the software is set to drop the serial line when it receives a protocol error:

```
interface serial 0
 sdlc frmr-disable
```

Related Commands

To locate documentation of related commands, you can search online at www.cisco.com.

show interfaces

sdlc holdq

Use the **sdlc holdq** interface configuration command to control the maximum number of packets that can be held in a buffer before being transmitted to a remote SDLC station.

> **sdlc holdq** *address queue-size*

Syntax

Syntax	Description
address	SDLC address for which you are specifying a queue size.
queue-size	Local send window size. The minimum is 1 packet. No maximum value has been established. The default is 200 packets.

Default

200 packets

Command Mode

Interface configuration

Usage Guidelines

This command first appeared in Cisco IOS Release 10.0.

This command is particularly useful with the SDLLC feature that allows an LLC2-speaking SNA station on a Token Ring to communicate with an SDLC-speaking SNA station on a serial link. Frame sizes and window sizes on Token Rings are often much larger than those acceptable for serial links. The fact that serial links are often much slower than Token Rings often makes this problem worse. Therefore, temporary backlogs can exist in periods of high data transfer from the Token Ring station to the serial station. A buffer creates a holding place for backlogged frames awaiting transmission on the serial link. This command is specified for each SDLC address and, therefore, for each SDLC secondary station on the serial link.

Example

The following example shows how to change the output hold queue length to 30 frames on an SDLC station of address C1 off serial interface 0:

```
! enter a global command, if you have not already
interface serial 0
! use SDLC encapsulation
 encapsulation sdlc-primary
! establish address of SDLC station off serial 0 as c1
 sdlc address c1
! change the output hold queue length to 30 frames on the SDLC station
 sdlc holdq c1 30
```

Related Commands

To locate documentation of related commands, you can search online at www.cisco.com.

show interfaces

sdlc k

Use the **sdlc k** interface configuration command to set the window size in order to control the maximum number of information frames Cisco IOS software transmits before it must stop transmitting and wait for an acknowledgment from the receiving router.

sdlc k *window-size*

Syntax

Syntax	Description
window-size	Local send window size. The minimum is one frame. The maximum is seven frames, which is the default.

Default

Seven frames

Command Mode

Interface configuration

Usage Guidelines

This command first appeared in Cisco IOS Release 10.0.

When the Cisco IOS software is communicating with SDLC, it must have a parameter that controls the maximum number of information frames it will send before it must stop sending and wait for an acknowledgment. The **k** parameter controls this window of acceptable frames. Use this command in conjunction with the **sdlc n1** command to create a balance between frame checking and network performance.

Example

In the following example, the software can send up to five frames before it must receive an acknowledgment:

```
! enter a global command, if you have not already
interface tokenring 0
!send up to 5 frames, then wait for acknowledgment
 sdlc k 5
```

Part II

Command Reference

Related Commands

To locate documentation of related commands, you can search online at www.cisco.com.

sdlc n1
show interfaces

sdlc line-speed

Use the **sdlc line-speed** interface configuration command to enable adaptive SDLC T1.

> **sdlc line-speed** *rate*
> **no sdlc line-speed** *rate*

Syntax

rate

Description

Clockrate in bits per second.

Default

No default rate

Command Mode

Interface configuration

Usage Guidelines

This command first appeared in Cisco IOS Release 10.0.

This feature is used to calculate the adjusted SDLC T1 value. The adjusted T1 is used to compensate for the delay between the time the system software passes a packet to the microcode, and the time the packet is actually sent out on the line. For a DCE device, this should be equal to the clockrate on the interface. For a DTE device, it should be equal to the clockrate on the DCE device to which the DTE is connected.

Example

In the following example, the SDLC line-speed rate is set to *rate*:

```
sdlc line-speed rate
```

Related Commands

To locate documentation of related commands, you can search online at www.cisco.com.

sdlc n2
sdlc t1

sdlc n1

Use the **sdlc n1** interface configuration command to control the maximum size of an incoming frame.

      sdlc n1 *bit-count*

Syntax	Description
bit-count	Number indicating bit size. Frames that exceed this size are rejected. The minimum is 1 bit. The maximum is 12,000 bits, which is the default.

Default

12,000 bits

Command Mode

Interface configuration

Usage Guidelines

This command first appeared in Cisco IOS Release 10.0.

Use with the **sdlc k** command to reduce network overhead while continuing to check frame transmission.

Example

In the following example, Cisco IOS software rejects frames larger than 10,000 bits:

```
! enter a global command, if you have not already
interface tokenring 0
! reject frames larger than 10000 bits
 sdlc n1 10000
```

Related Commands

To locate documentation of related commands, you can search online at www.cisco.com.

sdlc k
show interfaces

sdlc n2

Use the **sdlc n2** interface configuration command to determine the number of times that Cisco IOS software resends a frame before terminating the SDLC session.

> **sdlc n2** *retry-count*

Syntax	Description
retry-count	Number of retry attempts. When this number is exceeded, the SDLC station terminates its session with the other station. The minimum is 1 and the maximum is 255. The default is 20 retries.

Default

20 retries

Command Mode

Interface configuration

Usage Guidelines

This command first appeared in Cisco IOS Release 10.0.

Use with the **sdlc t1** command to reduce network overhead while continuing to check transmission.

Example

In the following example, the software is set to drop an SDLC station after 5 unsuccessful attempts to receive an acknowledgment for a frame:

```
interface serial 0
 sdlc n2 5
```

Related Commands

To locate documentation of related commands, you can search online at www.cisco.com.

sdlc t1
show interfaces

sdlc partner

Use the **sdlc partner** interface configuration command to specify the destination address with which an LLC session is established for the SDLC station. Use the **no** form of this command to cancel the configuration.

sdlc partner *mac-address sdlc-address*
no sdlc partner *mac-address sdlc-address*

Syntax	Description
mac-address	The 48-bit Media Access Control (MAC) address of the Token Ring host.
sdlc-address	SDLC address of the serial device that will communicate with the Token Ring host. The valid range is 1 to FE.

Default

No partner is defined.

Command Mode

Interface configuration

Usage Guidelines

This command first appeared in Cisco IOS Release 11.0.

Example

The following example establishes the correspondence between an SDLC and QLLC connection:

```
sdlc partner 1000.5aed.1f53 d2
```

Related Commands

To locate documentation of related commands, you can search online at www.cisco.com.

encapsulation sdlc
sdlc dlsw
sdlc vmac

sdlc poll-limit-value

Use the **sdlc poll-limit-value** interface configuration command to control how many times a single secondary station can be polled for input before the next station must be polled. Use the **no** form of this command to retrieve the default value.

> **sdlc poll-limit-value** *count*
> **no sdlc poll-limit-value** *count*

Syntax   Description

count   Number of times Cisco IOS software can poll one secondary station before proceeding to the next station. The minimum is 1 time, which is the default. The maximum is 10 times.

Default

1 time

Command Mode

Interface configuration

Usage Guidelines

This command first appeared in Cisco IOS Release 10.0.

As is typical for the primary station of an SDLC connection, if a secondary station sends its full possible window of input to the primary router or access server, Cisco IOS software immediately will re-poll the same secondary for more data in an attempt to capture the complete transaction at one time. The **sdlc poll-limit-value** command indicates how many times this can happen before the next station in the poll loop must be polled.

Increasing the value allows for smoother transaction processing but can delay polling of other stations or giving output to other stations.

Example

The following example specifies that the router can be polled two times before the next station in the poll list must be polled:

```
! enter a global command, if you have not already
interface serial 4
 no ip address
! use stun encapsulation
encapsulation stun
! establish stun group 4 on interface serial 4
 stun group 4
 stun sdlc-role primary
! poll the router up to two times before polling the next station
 sdlc poll-limit-value 2
```

Related Commands

To locate documentation of related commands, you can search online at www.cisco.com.

sdlc poll-pause-timer
show interfaces

sdlc poll-pause-timer

Use the **sdlc poll-pause-timer** interface configuration command to control how long Cisco IOS software pauses between sending each poll frame to secondary stations on a single serial interface. Use the **no** form of this command to retrieve the default value.

sdlc poll-pause-timer *milliseconds*
no sdlc poll-pause-timer *milliseconds*

Syntax

Syntax	Description
milliseconds	Number of milliseconds that the software waits before sending the poll frame to a single serial interface. This is a number in the range 1 to 10,000. The default is 10 milliseconds.

Default

10 milliseconds

Command Mode

Interface configuration

Usage Guidelines

This command first appeared in Cisco IOS Release 10.0.

As is typical for the primary station of an SDLC connection, the software generates polls periodically to each of the secondary stations to solicit their input. After polling each station on a single serial interface, the software will pause before beginning to poll the next station.

Because the secondaries cannot transmit data until they are polled, increasing this timer can increase response time to the users. However, making this parameter too small can flood the serial link with unneeded polls and require the secondary stations to spend wasted CPU time processing them.

Example

In the following example, the software pauses 2000 milliseconds before sending a series of poll frames through serial interface 4:

```
! enter a global command, if you have not already
interface serial 4
no ip address
! use STUN encapsulation
 encapsulation stun
! establish stun group 4 on interface serial 4
 stun group 4
!
 stun sdlc-role primary
! wait 2000 milliseconds before sending each series of poll frames
 sdlc poll-pause-timer 2000
```

Related Commands

To locate documentation of related commands, you can search online at www.cisco.com.

sdlc poll-limit-value
show interfaces

sdlc poll-wait-timeout

Use the **sdlc poll-wait-timeout** interface configuration command when the router has been configured for local acknowledgment and some form of SDLC communication (SDLLC or STUN, for example) to specify the interval Cisco IOS software will wait for polls from a primary node before timing out that connection.

sdlc poll-wait-timeout *milliseconds*

Syntax   Description

milliseconds   Number of milliseconds the software will wait for a poll from the primary
station before timing out the connection to the primary station. The
minimum is 10 milliseconds and the maximum is 64,000 milliseconds.
The default is 10,000 milliseconds.

Default

10,000 milliseconds

Command Mode

Interface configuration

Usage Guidelines

This command first appeared in Cisco IOS Release 10.0.

This command can be used on an interface that has been configured as a secondary node, but is not to
be used on an interface that has been configured as a primary node.

In a locally acknowledged multidrop environment, the polls the primary node sends to the router can be
delayed because the primary node is busy polling other secondary nodes. In such situations, this
command can be used to extend the timeout, thus reducing the likelihood Cisco IOS software times out
the connection to the primary node.

Example

The following example specifies that the local software will wait an interval of 63,000 milliseconds for
a poll from a primary station before timing out:

```
! sample stun peer-name global command
stun peer-name 150.136.134.86
! sample protocol-group command
stun protocol-group 4 sdlc
!
interface serial 0
! sample ip address command
 no ip address
! sample encapsulation stun command
 encapsulation stun
! place interface serial0 in previously defined STUN group 4
 stun group 4
! must enter the next command to use the sdlc poll-wait-timeout command
 stun sdlc-role secondary
! set timeout period for polls from primary station to 63000 milliseconds.
```

```
sdlc poll-wait-timeout 63000
! list the addresses of the sdlc stations on the link
 sdlc address C1
 sdlc address C2
! provide stun route command
 stun route address C2 tcp 150.136.134.58
 stun route address C1 tcp 150.136.134.58
```

Related Commands

To locate documentation of related commands, you can search online at www.cisco.com.

sdlc poll-limit-value
sdlc poll-pause-timer

sdlc qllc-prtnr

To establish correspondence between an SDLC and QLLC connection, use the **sdlc qllc-prtnr** interface configuration command.

sdlc qllc-prtnr *virtual-mac-address sdlc-address*

Syntax	Description
virtual-mac-address	The virtual Media Access Control (MAC) address in the form *h.h.h.*
sdlc-address	SDLC address in hexadecimal. The valid range is 1 to FE.

Default

No correspondence is defined.

Command Mode

Interface configuration

Usage Guidelines

This command first appeared in Cisco IOS Release 10.3.

Example

The following example establishes the correspondence between an SDLC and QLLC connection:

```
sdlc qllc-prtnr 4000.0122.0001 c1
```

Related Commands

To locate documentation of related commands, you can search online at www.cisco.com.

show interfaces

sdlc role

Use the **sdlc role** interface configuration command to establish the router to be either a primary or secondary SDLC station. Use the **no** form of this command to cancel the designation.

> **sdlc role {none | primary | secondary | prim-xid-poll}**
> **no sdlc role {none | primary | secondary | prim-xid-poll}**

Syntax	Description
none	Establishes the router as either a primary or secondary station, depending on the end stations.
primary	Establishes the router as a primary station.
secondary	Establishes the router as a secondary station.
prim-xid-poll	Establishes the router as a primary station when the end station is configured as a secondary NT2.1.

Default

No default role is assigned.

Command Mode

Interface configuration

Usage Guidelines

This command first appeared in Cisco IOS Release 10.3.

If the role is **none**, the router can be either primary or secondary, depending on the end stations. The SDLC end station must be configured as negotiable or primary NT2.1. When the end stations are configured as physical unit, type 2 (PU 2), you can set the role of the interface to **primary** or **secondary**. When the end station is configured as secondary NT2.1, you must set the role of the interface to **prim-xid-poll**.

To configure an SDLC multidrop line (downstream), configure the SDLC role as follows:

● **primary** if all SDLC devices are type PU 2.0 or mixed PU 2.0 and 2.1

● **prim-xid-poll** if all devices are type PU 2.1

Example

The following example configures the router as a primary SDLC station:

```
interface serial 2/6
 no ip address
 encapsulation sdlc
 fras map sdlc c1 serial 2/0 frame-relay 32 4 4
 sdlc role primary
 sdlc address c1
 sdlc xid c1 01700001
```

Related Commands

To locate documentation of related commands, you can search online at www.cisco.com.

encapsulation sdlc

sdlc sdlc-largest-frame

Use the **sdlc sdlc-largest-frame** interface configuration command to indicate the largest information frame (I-frame) size that can be sent or received by the designated SDLC station. Use the **no** form of this command to return to the default value.

> **sdlc sdlc-largest-frame** *address size*
> **no sdlc sdlc-largest-frame** *address size*

Syntax   Description

address	Address of the SDLC station that will communicate with the router.
size	Largest frame size that can be sent or received. The default is 265 bytes.

Default

The default largest I-frame is 265 bytes.

Command Mode

Interface configuration

Usage Guidelines

This command first appeared in Cisco IOS Release 10.3.

Example

In the following example, Cisco IOS software can send or receive a frame as large as 265 bytes (the default) from the SDLC station at address C6. Any frames larger will be fragmented by the software.

```
interface serial 4
 sdlc sdlc-largest-frame c6 265
```

sdlc simultaneous

To enable an interface configured as a primary SDLC station to operate in two-way simultaneous mode, use the **sdlc simultaneous** interface configuration command.

sdlc simultaneous [full-datamode | half-datamode]

Syntax	Description
full-datamode	(Optional) Enables the primary station to send data to and receive data from the polled secondary station.
half-datamode	(Optional) Prohibits the primary station from sending data to the polled secondary station.

Default

Two-way simultaneous mode is disabled.

Command Mode

Interface configuration

Usage Guidelines

This command first appeared in Cisco IOS Release 10.3.

By default, the SDLC driver supports alternative mode. This means that in a multidrop environment, the primary station cannot send data to another secondary station until it receives a response (F bit) from the secondary station with which it is currently communicating.

In contrast, two-way simultaneous mode enables the interface configured as a primary SDLC station to send data to a second secondary station, even when it is receiving data from another secondary station. This capability improves utilization of a full-duplex serial line.

Examples

The following example enables all primary stations to send and receive data at the same time:

```
sdlc simultaneous full-datamode
```

The following example enables all secondary stations to send or receive data at the same time:

```
sdlc simultaneous half-datamode
```

Related Commands

To locate documentation of related commands, you can search online at www.cisco.com.

encapsulation sdlc-primary
show interfaces

sdlc slow-poll

Use the **sdlc slow-poll** interface configuration command to enable the slow-poll capability of the router as a primary SDLC station. Use the **no** form of this command to disable slow-poll capability.

> **sdlc slow-poll** *seconds*
> **no sdlc slow-poll**

Syntax   Description

seconds   Amount of time in seconds.

Default
10 seconds

Command Mode
Interface configuration

Usage Guidelines

This command first appeared in Cisco IOS Release 10.0.

You can use this command to improve the performance of a multidropped SDLC configuration when one or more of the secondary stations are inactive.

When slow-poll is enabled, if the router acting as a primary station detects that a secondary SDLC station is not responding, it polls that secondary SDLC station less frequently. The router spends less time waiting for the inactive secondary station to respond, thereby minimizing the performance degradation on the active secondary SDLC stations on the multidropped line.

Example

The following example enables the slow-poll capability:

```
interface serial 0
 sdlc slow-poll
```

Related Commands

To locate documentation of related commands, you can search online at www.cisco.com.

sdlc poll-limit-value
sdlc poll-pause-timer
show interfaces

sdlc t1

Use the **sdlc t1** interface configuration command to control the amount of time Cisco IOS software waits for an acknowledgment to a frame or sequence of frames.

sdlc t1 *milliseconds*

Syntax	Description
milliseconds	Number of milliseconds that the software waits. The minimum is 1 millisecond and the maximum is 64,000 milliseconds. The default is 3000 milliseconds.

Default

3000 milliseconds

Command Mode

Interface configuration

Usage Guidelines

This command first appeared in Cisco IOS Release 10.0.

When an SDLC station sends a frame, it waits for an acknowledgment from the receiver that the frame has been received. The sending station cannot wait indefinitely for a response. When the frame is sent, a timer is started. To be consistent with the original specification of SDLC, this timer is called the T1 timer and is controlled by this parameter. If this timer reaches its limit before the acknowledgment is received, the software will try again and resend the frame.

Example

In the following example, the software waits up to 4000 milliseconds for a reply to a frame or sequence of frames:

```
! enter a global command, if you have not already
interface tokenring 0
 sdlc t1 4000
```

Related Commands

To locate documentation of related commands, you can search online at www.cisco.com.

sdlc n2
show interfaces

sdlc test serial

Use the **sdlc test serial** EXEC command to determine the status of end stations. Use the **sdlc test serial** command with the **stop** keyword to halt the sending of the test frames.

> **sdlc test serial** *number address* [*iterations* | **continuous** | **stop** | **string** *string*]

Syntax	Description
serial *number*	Serial interface on which the test frame is to be sent out.
address	SDLC address (in hexadecimal) of the end station to receive the test frame.
iterations	(Optional) Number of test frames to be sent. The valid range is 1 to 25 frames. The default is 10 frames.
continuous	(Optional) Sends frames continuously until the **sdlc test serial** command is issued with the **stop** keyword.

Syntax	Description
stop	(Optional) Halts the sending of test frames.
string *string*	(Optional) Specifies a string of characters as data within the test frame. If this option is not specified, the default test string is ABCDEFGHIJKLMNOPQRSTUVWXYZ.

Defaults

The **sdlc test serial** command is not active.

The default test string is "ABCDEFGHIJKLMNOPQRSTUVWXYZ."

Command Mode

EXEC

Usage Guidelines

This command first appeared in Cisco IOS Release 11.2.

The command will precheck for correct interface and SDLC address. The results of the test frames sent can be viewed after the frames have been sent or an **sdlc test serial** command with the **stop** keyword has been issued.

Sample Displays

The following are variations of the **sdlc test serial** command, followed by the response for each:

```
Router# sdlc test serial 0 c1

SDLC Test for address C1 completed
Frames sent=10 Frames received=10

Router# sdlc test serial 0 c1 255

SDLC Test for address C1 completed
Frames sent=255 Frames received=255

Router# sdlc test serial 0 C1 stop

SDLC Test for address C1 completed
Frames sent=44 Frames received=44

Router# sdlc test serial 0 c1 string HeyMrPUareyouthere

SDLC Test for address C1 completed
Frames sent=10 Frames received=10
```

Related Commands

To locate documentation of related commands, you can search online at www.cisco.com.

show interfaces

sdlc vmac

Use the **sdlc vmac** interface configuration command to configure a MAC address for the serial interface. Use the **no** form of this command to disable the configuration.

> **sdlc vmac** *mac-address*
> **no sdlc vmac** *mac-address*

Syntax	Description
mac-address	48-bit MAC address of the Token Ring host.

Default

Disabled

Command Mode

Interface configuration

Usage Guidelines

This command first appeared in Cisco IOS Release 11.0.

This command must be configured if you plan to configure DLSw+. The last byte of the address must be 00.

Example

The following example specifies a MAC address for the serial interface:

```
sdlc vmac 1234.3174.0000
```

Related Commands

To locate documentation of related commands, you can search online at www.cisco.com.

encapsulation sdlc
sdlc dlsw

sdlc xid

Use the **sdlc xid** interface configuration command to specify an exchange identification (XID) value appropriate for the designated SDLC station associated with this serial interface. Use the **no** form of this command to disable XID processing for this address.

> **sdlc xid** *address xid*
> **no sdlc xid** *address xid*

Syntax   Description

address   Address of the SDLC station associated with this interface.

xid   XID the Cisco IOS software will use to respond to XID requests the router receives. This value must be 4 bytes (8 digits) in length and is specified with hexadecimal digits.

Default
Disabled

Command Mode
Interface configuration

Usage Guidelines
This command first appeared in Cisco IOS Release 10.3.

XID requests and responses are usually exchanged before sessions are started. Be sure that the XID value configured in the Cisco IOS software matches the IDBLK and IDNUM parameters configured on the host. The XID response to an XID request will contain the information you configured in the **sdlc xid** command. The host will check the XID response it receives with the IDBLK and IDNUM parameters (that are configured in the VTAM). If they match, the host will initiate a session with the router. If they do not match, the host will not initiate a session.

Example
The following example specifies an XID value of 01720002 at address C2:

```
interface serial 0
 sdlc xid c2 01720002
```

Related Commands

To locate documentation of related commands, you can search online at www.cisco.com.

encapsulation sdlc

show interfaces

Use the **show interfaces** privileged EXEC command to display the SDLC information for a given SDLC interface.

>> **show interfaces**

Syntax Description

This command has no arguments or keywords.

Command Mode

Privileged EXEC

Usage Guidelines

This command first appeared in Cisco IOS Release 10.0.

Sample Display

The following is sample output from the **show interfaces** command for an SDLC primary interface supporting the SDLLC function:

```
Router# show interfaces

Serial 0 is up, line protocol is up
 Hardware is MCI Serial
 MTU 1500 bytes, BW 1544 Kbit, DLY 20000 usec, rely 255/255, load 1/255
 Encapsulation SDLC-PRIMARY, loopback not set
      Timers (msec): poll pause 100 fair poll 500. Poll limit 1
      [T1 3000, N1 12016, N2 20, K 7] timer: 56608 Last polled device: none
      SDLLC [ma: 0000.0C01.14--, ring: 7 bridge: 1, target ring: 10
            largest token ring frame 2052]
SDLC addr C1 state is CONNECT
      VS 6, VR 3, RCNT 0, Remote VR 6, Current retransmit count 0
      Hold queue: 0/12 IFRAMEs 77/22 RNRs 0/0 SNRMs 1/0 DISCs 0/0
      Poll: clear, Poll count: 0, chain: p: C1 n: C1
      SDLLC [largest SDLC frame: 265, XID: disabled]
  Last input 00:00:02, output 00:00:01, output hang never
  Output queue 0/40, 0 drops; input queue 0/75, 0 drops
```

```
Five minute input rate 517 bits/sec, 30 packets/sec
Five minute output rate 672 bits/sec, 20 packets/sec
     357 packets input, 28382 bytes, 0 no buffer
     Received 0 broadcasts, 0 runts, 0 giants
     0 input errors, 0 CRC, 0 frame, 0 overrun, 0 ignored, 0 abort
     926 packets output, 77274 bytes, 0 underruns
     0 output errors, 0 collisions, 0 interface resets, 0 restarts
     2 carrier transitions
```

Table 14-1 shows the timer fields relevant to all SDLC connections.

Table 14-1 *Timer Fields and Descriptions When SDLC Is Enabled*

Field	Description
Timers (msec):	Lists the timers and their current values.
poll pause, fair poll, Poll limit	Current values of these timers, as described in the individual command sections in this chapter.
T1, N1, N2, K	Current values for these timers, as described in the individual command sections in this chapter.

Table 14-2 shows other data given for each SDLC secondary station configured to be attached to this interface.

Table 14-2 *SDLC Field Descriptions*

Field	Description
addr	Address of this secondary SDLC station.
state is	Current state of this connection. The possible values are: • DISCONNECT—No communication is being attempted to this secondary. • CONNECT—A normal connect state exists between this router and this secondary. • DISCSENT—This router has sent a disconnect request to this secondary and is awaiting its response. • SNRMSENT—This router has sent a connect request (SNRM) to this secondary and is awaiting its response. • THEMBUSY—This secondary has told this router that it is temporarily unable to receive any more information frames. • USBUSY—This router has told this secondary that it is temporarily unable to receive any more information frames. • BOTHBUSY—Both sides have told each other that they are temporarily unable to receive any more information frames. • ERROR—This router has detected an error and is waiting for a response from the secondary acknowledging this.

Continues

Table 14-2 *SDLC Field Descriptions (Continued)*

Field	Description
VS	Sequence number of the next information frame this station sends.
VR	Sequence number of the next information frame from this secondary that this station expects to receive.
Remote VR	Last frame transmitted by this station that has been acknowledged by the other station.
Current retransmit count	Number of times the current I-frame or sequence of I-frames has been retransmitted.
Hold queue:	Number of frames in hold queue/Maximum size of hold queue.
IFRAMEs, RNRs, SNRMs, DISCs	Sent/received count for these frames.
Poll:	"Set" if this router has a poll outstanding to the secondary; "clear" if it does not.
Poll count:	Number of polls, in a row, given to this secondary station at this time.
chain:	Shows the previous (p) and next (n) secondary address on this interface in the round robin loop of polled devices.

Related Commands

To locate documentation of related commands, you can search online at www.cisco.com.

encapsulation sdlc-primary
encapsulation sdlc-secondary
sdlc frmr-disable
sdlc holdq
sdlc n1
sdlc n2
sdlc poll-limit-value
sdlc poll-pause-timer

show llc2

Use the **show llc2** privileged EXEC command to display the LLC2 connections active in the router.

> **show llc2**

Syntax Description

This command has no arguments or keywords.

Command Mode

Privileged EXEC

Usage Guidelines

This command first appeared in Cisco IOS Release 10.0.

Sample Display

The following is sample output from the **show llc2** command:

```
Router# show llc2

TokenRing0 DTE=1000.5A59.04F9,400022224444 SAP=04/04, State=NORMAL
V(S)=5, V(R)=5, Last N(R)=5, Local window=7, Remote Window=127
ack-max=3, n2=8, Next timer in 7768
xid-retry timer 0/60000 ack timer 0/1000
p timer 0/1000 idle timer 7768/10000
rej timer 0/3200 busy timer 0/9600
ack-delay timer 0/3200
CMNS Connections to:
 Address 1000.5A59.04F9 via Ethernet2
 Protocol is up
 Interface type X25-DCE RESTARTS 0/1
 Timers: T10 1 T11 1 T12 1 T13 1
```

The display includes a CMNS addendum, indicating LLC2 is running with CMNS. When LLC2 is not running with CMNS, the **show llc2** command does not display a CMNS addendum.

Table 14-3 describes significant fields shown in the display.

Table 14-3 *show llc2 Field Descriptions*

Field	Description
TokenRing0	Name of interface on which the session is established.
DTE=1000.5A59.04F9, 400022224444	Address of the station to which the router is talking on this session. (The address is the MAC address of the interface on which the connection is established, except when Local Acknowledgment or SDLLC is used, in which case the address used by the Cisco IOS software is shown as in this example, following the DTE address and separated by a comma.)
SAP=04/04	Other station's and the router's (remote/local) service access point (SAP) for this connection. The SAP is analogous to a "port number" on the router and allows for multiple sessions between the same two stations.

Continues

Table 14-3 *show llc2 Field Descriptions (Continued)*

Field	Description
State=NORMAL	Current state of the LLC2 session. The possible values are:
	• ADM—Asynchronous Disconnect Mode—A connection is not established, and either end can begin one.
	• SETUP—Request to begin a connection has been sent to the remote station, and this station is waiting for a response to that request.
	• RESET—A previously open connection has been reset because of some error by this station, and this station is waiting for a response to that reset command.
	• D_CONN—This station has requested a normal, expected, end of communications with the remote, and is waiting for a response to that disconnect request.
	• ERROR—This station has detected an error in communications and has told the other station of this. This station is waiting for a reply to its posting of this error.
	• NORMAL—Connection between the two sides is fully established, and normal communication is occurring.
	• BUSY—Normal communication state exists, except busy conditions on this station make it such that this station cannot receive information frames from the other station at this time.
	• REJECT—Out-of-sequence frame has been detected on this station, and this station has requested that the other resend this information.
	• AWAIT—Normal communication exists, but this station has had a timer expire, and is trying to recover from it (usually by resending the frame that started the timer).
	• AWAIT_BUSY—A combination of the AWAIT and BUSY states.
	• AWAIT_REJ—A combination of the AWAIT and REJECT states.
V(S)=5	Sequence number of the next information frame this station will send.
V(R)=5	Sequence number of the next information frame this station expects to receive from the other station.
Last N (R)=5	Last sequence number of this station's transmitted frames acknowledged by the remote station.
Local Window=7	Number of frames this station may send before requiring an acknowledgment from the remote station.
Remote Window=127	Number of frames this station can accept from the remote.
ack-max=3, n2=8	Value of these parameters, as given in the previous configuration section.
Next timer in 7768	Number of milliseconds before the next timer, for any reason, goes off.

Table 14-3 *show llc2 Field Descriptions (Continued)*

Field	Description
xid-retry timer 0/60000....	Series of timer values in the form of next-time/time-between, where "next-time" is the next time, in milliseconds, that the timer will wake, and "time-between" is the time, in milliseconds, between each timer wakeup. A "next-time" of zero indicates that the given timer is not enabled, and will never wake.
CMNS Connections to:	List of values that affect the interface if CMNS is enabled.
Address 1000.5A59.04F9 via Ethernet2	MAC address of remote station.
Protocol is up	Up indicates the LLC2 and X.25 protocols are in a state where incoming and outgoing Call Requests can be made on this LLC2 connection.
Interface type X25-DCE	One of X25-DCE, X25-DTE, or X25-DXE (both DTE and DCE).
RESTARTS 0/1	Restarts sent/received on this LLC2 connection.
Timers:	T10, T11, T12, T13 (or T20, T21, T22, T23 for DTE); these are Request packet timers. These are similar in function to X.25 parameters of the same name.

Related Commands

To locate documentation of related commands, you can search online at www.cisco.com.

llc2 ack-delay-time
llc2 ack-max
llc2 idle-time
llc2 local-window
llc2 n2
llc2 t1-time
llc2 tbusy-time
llc2 tpf-time
llc2 trej-time
llc2 xid-neg-val-time
llc2 xid-retry-time

Configuring IBM Network Media Translation

This chapter describes how to configure Cisco IOS software for IBM network media translation with Synchronous Logical Data Link Control (SDLLC) or Qualified Logical Link Control (QLLC). For a complete description of the SDLLC and QLLC commands in this chapter, refer to Chapter 16, "IBM Network Media Translation Commands." To locate documentation of other commands that appear in this chapter, you can search online at www.cisco.com.

SDLLC Configuration Task List

To configure SDLLC, perform the tasks in the following sections:

- Configure SDLLC with Direct Connection
- Configure SDLLC with RSRB
- Configure SDLLC with RSRB and Local Acknowledgment
- Configure SDLLC with Ethernet and Translational Bridging
- Customize SDLLC Media Translation
- Monitor SDLLC Media Translation

NOTE Because data-link switching plus (DLSw+) contains its own media conversion, SDLLC is not required when using DLSw+.

To configure QLLC, see the section "QLLC Conversion Configuration Task List." See the end of this chapter for the sections "SDLLC Configuration Examples" and "QLLC Conversion Configuration Examples."

Configure SDLLC with Direct Connection

In the SDLLC configuration with direct connection, a 37x5 front-end processor (FEP) on a Token Ring and a 3x74 cluster controller connected to a serial line are each connected to an interface on the same router configured with SDLLC. In this configuration, the Logical Link Control, type 2 (LLC2) session extends from the 37x5 FEP across the Token Ring to the router. The SDLLC session extends from the router across the serial line to the 3x74 cluster controller. The Systems Network Architecture (SNA) session extends across the Token Ring and the serial line to provide an end-to-end connection. The router is configured with source-route bridging (SRB).

To configure SDLLC with direct connection, you must perform the tasks in the following sections:

● Enable SDLLC Media Translation

● Associate a SAP Value

● Specify the XID Value

● Initiate Connection to Token Ring Host

For an example of how to configure SDLLC with direct connection, see the section "SDLLC with Direct Connection Example" later in this chapter.

Enable SDLLC Media Translation

The interfaces you will configure for SDLLC media translation are the serial interfaces that connect to the serial lines linking the remote Synchronous Data Link Control (SDLC) devices. To configure them, use the following command in interface configuration mode:

Command	Purpose
sdllc traddr *xxxx.xxxx.xx00 lr bn tr*	Enables SDLLC media translation on a serial interface.

Associate a SAP Value

You can associate a service access point (SAP) value by using the following command in interface configuration mode:

Command	Purpose
sdllc sap *sdlc-address ssap dsap*	Associates a SAP value.

Specify the XID Value

The XID value you define in Cisco IOS software must match that of the IDBLK and IDNUM system generation parameters defined in VTAM of the Token Ring host to which the SDLC device will be communicating. To define XID, use the following command in interface configuration mode:

Command	Purpose
sdllc xid *address xxxxxxxx*	Specifies the XID value appropriate for the SDLC station to match VTAM values.

Initiate Connection to Token Ring Host

The Token Ring host is always kept in a state ready to accept a connection from the remote serial device. The remote serial device is responsible for initiating connections. The advantage of this scheme is that the serial device can communicate with the Token Ring host whenever it chooses without requiring personnel to be on the host site.

Cisco IOS software actually initiates the connection on behalf of the serial device. To initiate connections, both the Media Access Control (MAC) address of the Token Ring host and the SDLC line address are required. You must configure Cisco IOS software to define the Token Ring host as the partner of the serial device. To do so, use the following command in interface configuration mode:

Command	Purpose
sdllc partner *mac-address sdlc-address*	Enables connections for SDLLC.

Configure SDLLC with RSRB

A router need not directly connect the two IBM end nodes: a 37x5 FEP on a Token Ring and a 3x74 cluster controller connected to a serial line can be connected to different routers. However, the router to which the 3x74 is connected must be configured with SDLLC. They communicate via remote source-route bridging (RSRB) using direct encapsulation, RSRB over an FST connection, or RSRB over a TCP connection. RSRB transports packets between Router A and Router B, while Router B performs all conversion between the LLC2 and SDLC protocols by means of the SDLLC software.

To configure the router for SDLLC with RSRB, you must perform all the tasks in the "Configure SDLLC with Direct Connection" section earlier in this chapter. In addition, you must perform one of the sets of tasks in the following sections:

- Configure RSRB Using Direct Encapsulation

- Configure RSRB over an FST Connection

- Configure RSRB over a TCP Connection

For more information about configuring RSRB, see Chapter 3, "Configuring Source-Route Bridging" and Chapter 4, "Source-Route Bridging Commands."

NOTE	When you configure RSRB, you must include a **source-bridge remote peer** command on the router connected to the serial line and another **source-bridge remote peer** command on the one connected to the Token Ring. If you have more than one serial line connected to the same router, then you will have a **source-bridge remote peer** command for each interface in its configuration that will be using SDLLC with RSRB.

For an example of how to configure SDLLC with RSRB, see the section "SDLLC with RSRB (Multiple 3x74s) Example" later in this chapter.

Configure RSRB Using Direct Encapsulation

To configure SDLLC with RSRB using direct encapsulation, use the following commands in global configuration mode:

Step	Command	Purpose
1	**source-bridge ring-group** *ring-group* [*virtual-mac-address*]	Defines a ring group.
2	**source-bridge remote-peer** *ring-group* **interface** *interface-name* [*mac-address*]	Defines a remote peer.

Configure RSRB over an FST Connection

To configure SDLLC with RSRB over an FST connection, use the following commands in global configuration mode:

Step	Command	Purpose
1	**source-bridge ring-group** *ring-group* [*virtual-mac-address*]	Defines a ring group.
2	**source-bridge fst-peername** *local-interface-address*	For FST connection only, sets up an FST peer name.
3	**source-bridge remote-peer** *ring-group* **fst** *ip-address*	Defines a remote peer.

Configure RSRB over a TCP Connection

To configure SDLLC with RSRB over a TCP connection, use the following commands in global configuration mode:

Step	Command	Purpose
1	**source-bridge ring-group** *ring-group* [*virtual-mac-address*]	Defines a ring group.
2	**source-bridge remote-peer** *ring-group* **tcp** *ip-address*	Defines a remote peer.

Configure SDLLC with RSRB and Local Acknowledgment

RSRB can be configured for only local acknowledgment with RSRB using IP encapsulation over a TCP connection. Configuring SDLLC local acknowledgment can reduce time-outs and keepalive traffic on the connection.

If LLC2 local acknowledgment is configured, it must be configured on the serial interface of the router on the 3x74 cluster controller side of the connection and on the Token Ring interface of the router on the 37x5 FEP side of the connection. Whether or not local acknowledgment is configured, the SNA session extends end-to-end and the SDLC session extends from the router configured with the serial interface to the 3x74 cluster controller. However, the LLC2 session extends from the 37x5 FEP to the router with the Token Ring interface configured. The LLC2 session is locally terminated at that router. A TCP session is then established across the WAN to a router on the 3x74 side of the connection.

To configure Cisco IOS software for SDLLC with RSRB and local acknowledgment, you must perform all the tasks in the "Configure SDLLC with Direct Connection" section earlier in this chapter. In addition, you must use the following commands in global configuration mode:

Step	Command	Purpose
1	**source-bridge ring-group** *ring-group* [*virtual-mac-address*]	Defines a ring group.
2	**source-bridge remote-peer** *ring-group* **tcp** *ip-address* **local-ack**	Defines a remote peer with the local acknowledgment feature.
3	**source-bridge sdllc-local-ack**	Enables local acknowledgment for connections involving SDLLC media translation.

Local acknowledgment is not supported when the LLC2 device is attached to an Ethernet rather than to a Token Ring.

For an example of how to configure SDLLC with RSRB and local acknowledgment, see the section "SDLLC with RSRB and Local Acknowledgment Example" later in this chapter.

For more information about configuring RSRB and local acknowledgment, see Chapter 3, "Configuring Source-Route Bridging" and Chapter 4, "Source-Route Bridging Commands."

Configure SDLLC with Ethernet and Translational Bridging

SDLLC support over Ethernet combines translational bridging with Ethernet support of 37x5 FEP connections. Figure 15-1 shows SDLLC with Ethernet and translational bridging. The 3x75 FEP is attached to Router A through Ethernet. The same router is configured for translational bridging, which translates Ethernet packets into Token Ring packets and passes them across the WAN to Router B connected to the 3x74 cluster controller via a serial line. The LLC2 session terminates at Router B connected to the 3x74 cluster controller. In addition, Router B maintains an SDLC session from itself to the cluster controller.

Figure 15-1 *SDLLC with Ethernet and Translational Bridging*

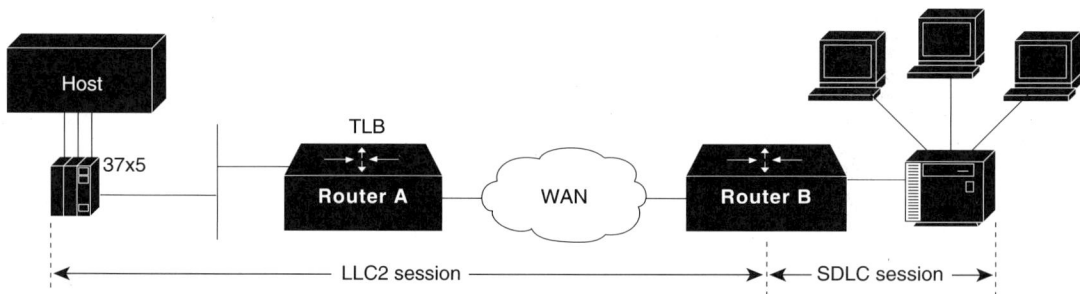

Customize SDLLC Media Translation

To increase performance on connections involving SDLLC media translation, perform the tasks in the following sections:

- Set the Largest LLC2 I-Frame Size

- Set the Largest SDLC I-Frame Size

- Increase the SDLC Line Speed

Refer to the section "Other Customizing Considerations" at the end of this chapter for additional information.

Set the Largest LLC2 I-Frame Size

Generally, the router and the LLC2 device with which it communicates should support the same maximum SDLC I-frame size. The larger this value, the better the line is used, thus increasing performance.

Faster screen updates to 3278-style terminals often result by configuring the Token Ring FEP to send as large an I-frame as possible and then allowing Cisco IOS software to segment the frame into multiple SDLC I-frames.

After the Token Ring FEP has been configured to send the largest possible I-frame, it is best to configure the software to support the same maximum I-frame size. The default is 516 bytes. The maximum value the software can support is 8144 bytes.

To set the largest LLC2 I-frame size, use the following command in interface configuration mode:

Command	Purpose
sdllc ring-largest-frame *value*	Specifies the largest I-frame size that can be sent or received by the designated LLC2 primary station.

Set the Largest SDLC I-Frame Size

Generally, the router and the SDLC device with which it communicates should support the same maximum SDLC I-frame size. The larger this value, the better the line is utilized, thus increasing performance.

After the SDLC device has been configured to send the largest possible I-frame, you must configure Cisco IOS software to support the same maximum I-frame size. The default is 265 bytes. The maximum value the software can support must be less than the value of the LLC2 largest frame value defined when setting the largest LLC2 I-frame size.

To set the largest SDLC I-frame size, use the following command in interface configuration mode:

Command	Purpose
sdllc sdlc-largest-frame *address value*	Sets the largest I-frame size that can be sent or received by the designated SDLC station.

Increase the SDLC Line Speed

You can increase the data transfer rate by increasing the SDLC line speed on the serial interface. If possible, increase the link speed of the 3x74 to 19.2 kbps on older units, or to 64 kbps on new units.

To increase the SDLC line speed, use the following command in interface configuration mode:

Command	Purpose
clock rate *bps*	Adjusts the clock rate on the serial interface of the SCI and MCI cards to an acceptable bit rate.

Other Customizing Considerations

In addition to adjusting the SDLLC parameters described in this section, you can improve performance on the connection by adjusting the LLC2 and SDLC parameters described in Chapter 13, "Configuring LLC2 and SDLC Parameters."

For IBM host configuration consider changing the default MAXOUT (window size) value. Widely used installation guides for IBM equipment show a MAXOUT value of 1 in the VTAM-switched major node for the IBM 3174 PU. Changing this value to 7 improves the performance, because VTAM can send seven frames before requiring an acknowledgment.

Monitor SDLLC Media Translation

To monitor connections using SDLLC media translation, use the following monitoring commands in privileged EXEC mode:

Step	Command	Purpose
1	**show interfaces**	Displays information about SDLC and LLC2 connections involving interfaces on which SDLLC media translation has been enabled.
2	**show sdllc local-ack**	Displays the current state of any connections using local acknowledgment for LLC2 and SDLLC connections.
3	**show llc2**	Displays information about LLC2 connections involving interfaces on which SDLLC media translation has been enabled.

In **show llc2** output, look for the LLC2 connections that correspond to the MAC addresses you assigned to the SDLLC interfaces using the **sdllc traddr** command. For information about these commands, see Chapter 14, "LLC2 and SDLC Commands" and Chapter 16, "IBM Network Media Translation Commands."

QLLC Conversion Configuration Task List

Perform the tasks in the following sections to configure QLLC conversion. The first task is required; all others are optional and depend on your specific needs.

● Enable QLLC Conversion on a Serial Interface

● Customize QLLC Conversion

● Monitor QLLC Conversion

See the end of this chapter for QLLC configuration examples.

Enable QLLC Conversion on a Serial Interface

The interfaces you configure for QLLC conversion are the serial interfaces that connect to the X.25 network linking the remote devices with which you plan to communicate.

To enable QLLC conversion, you must perform the first of the following tasks. Perform the remaining tasks as appropriate.

● Enable QLLC Conversion on the Appropriate Serial Interfaces

● Define the XID Value Associated with an X.25 Device

● Enable to Open a Connection to the Local Token Ring Device

Enable QLLC Conversion on the Appropriate Serial Interfaces

You can enable QLLC conversion on a serial interface to support either a switched virtual circuit (SVC) or a permanent virtual circuit (PVC). The tasks you perform differ somewhat depending on the type of virtual circuit you plan to support on the interface. In either case, first verify that RSRB is enabled by using the following command in privileged EXEC mode:

Command	Purpose
show configuration	Ensures that RSRB is enabled on the interfaces.

In the sections for the appropriate serial interfaces of the **show configuration** display, look for one or more **source-bridge remote-peer** entries and a **source-bridge** *rn* entry. For more information about configuring a serial interface for RSRB, see Chapter 14, "Configuring LLC2 and SDLC Parameters."

To enable QLLC conversion to support an SVC, use the following commands in interface configuration mode:

Step	Command	Purpose
1	**x25 map qllc** *virtual-mac-addr x121-addr* [*x25-map-options*]	Maps a virtual Token Ring MAC address for the interface to its X.121 address.
2	**qllc srb** *virtual-mac-addr srn trn*	Enables the use of QLLC conversion on the interface.

To enable QLLC conversion to support a PVC, use the following commands in interface configuration mode:

Step	Command	Purpose
1	**x25 pvc** *circuit* **qllc** *x121-address* [*x25-map-options*]	Sets up a PVC for QLLC conversion.
2	**qllc srb** *virtual-mac-addr srn trn*	Enables the use of QLLC conversion on the interface.

To configure QLLC to accept a call from any remote X.25 device, use the following command in interface configuration mode:

Command	Purpose
qllc accept-all-calls	Configures QLLC to accept a call from any remote X.25 device.

In a Token Ring or RSRB environment the LAN-attached devices initiate a connection by sending a null XID packet upstream. If Cisco IOS software forwards this null XID to an X.25-attached FEP, the FEP responds as if it were connecting to an PU2.1 device, and breaks the connection when the PU 2.0 next sends an XID Format 0 Type 2. To resolve this situation and to enable the connection, use the following command in interface configuration mode:

Command	Purpose
qllc npsi-poll *virtual-mac-addr*	Enables connection between a PU 2.0 on the LAN side and a FEP running NPSI on the X.25 side.

The **qllc npsi-poll** command intercepts any null XID packet that the router receives on the LAN interface, and returns a null XID response to the downstream device. It continues to allow XID Format 3 and XID Format 0 packets through the X.25 device.

Define the XID Value Associated with an X.25 Device

The XID serves as a password to ensure that only those devices that should communicate with the Token Ring host have that privilege. If the XID is defined in NCP on the host, you must enable Cisco IOS software to reply (on behalf of the X.25 device) to the Token Ring host's requests for an XID reply. Although the XID value is used to reply to XID requests received on the LLC2 side of the connection, you apply this command on the serial interface defined for X.25. This XID value must match that of IDBLK and IDNUM defined in the NCP.

NOTE   For most QLLC installations, you do not need to define the XID value. You only need to do so if the remote X.25 device is not configured to send its own XID. This is only possible for a device that is attached through a PVC, although most devices that are connected through X.25 send their own XIDs.

To define the XID value associated with an X.25 device, use the following command in interface configuration mode:

Command	Purpose
qllc xid *virtual-mac-addr xid*	Specifies the XID value appropriate for the X.25 device associated with the Token Ring interface.

Enable to Open a Connection to the Local Token Ring Device

If you plan to use SVCs rather than PVCs, you must enable Cisco IOS software to open a connection to the local Token Ring device on behalf of the remote X.25 device when an incoming call is received. When QLLC conversion is used over an SVC, the remote X.25 device typically initiates the X.25/QLLC session and the software in turn initiates the LLC2 session.

To enable the software to open a connection to the local Token Ring device, use the following command in interface configuration mode:

Command	Purpose
qllc partner *virtual-mac-addr mac-addr*	Enables the software to open a connection to the local Token Ring device.

Customize QLLC Conversion

To customize your configuration of QLLC conversion, you can perform one or more of the following tasks in the following sections:

- Specify the Largest Packet That Can Be Sent or Received on the X.25 Interface

- Specify SAP Values Other Than the Default IBM SAP Values

- Specify the Largest Packet That Can Be Sent or Received on the X.25 Interface

Enable QLLC Local Acknowledgment for RSRB Connections

Enable local acknowledgment when the round-trip time through the TCP/IP network is as large or larger than the LLC2 timeout period.

To enable QLLC local acknowledgment for RSRB connections, use the following global configuration command on the router connected to the X.25 interface and configure the remote peers for local acknowledgment:

Command	Purpose
source-bridge qllc-local-ack	Enables QLLC local acknowledgment for RSRB connections.

If, for example, Router B with X.25 interface has the IP address ip1, and the remote peer (Router A) has the address ip2, and they use a virtual ring group vrg, then both routers use the following configuration commands:

```
source-bridge ring-group vrg
source-bridge remote-peer vrg tcp ip1 local-ack
source-bridge remote-peer vrg tcp ip2
```

The configuration for Router B is as follows:

```
source-bridge ring-group vrg
source-bridge remote-peer vrg tcp ip1
source-bridge remote-peer vrg tcp ip2 local-ack
```

This will not affect Router A.

Specify SAP Values Other Than the Default IBM SAP Values

To use SAP values other than the default IBM SAP values, use the following command in interface configuration mode:

Command	Purpose
qllc sap *virtual-mac-addr ssap dsap*	Specifies a SAP value other than the default IBM SAP value.

Specify the Largest Packet That Can Be Sent or Received on the X.25 Interface

There are two ways for a packet to become segmented:

- The X.25 software performs the segmentation and the other X.25 station reassembles the packet.

- The QLLC conversion performs SNA header segmentation. In this case, QLLC does not reassemble, but passes smaller SNA segments to the IBM end station.

If the QLLC software does not perform SNA segmentation, then the X.25 software must be capable of performing X.25 segmentation of the largest packet that it can receive from the LLC2 side. This packet can be several thousand bytes long, whereas the typical size for X.25 packets is 1024 bytes or less. (The default is 128, but that can be overridden with larger values.) The X.25 software, especially in the X.25 attached IBM end station, might not be able to reassemble a very large packet. In this situation, specifying the largest QLLC packet can be useful.

By default, the maximum SNA data unit size established for the virtual circuit is the maximum packet size that can be sent or received on the X.25 interface. If packets received on the LLC2 interface are larger than the largest value allowed on the X.25 connection, they can be segmented by the X.25 software before being sent on the X.25 interface. Moreover, there is no reassembly on receiving packets on the X.25 interface before sending them on the LLC2 interface. Thus, you might need to reconfigure the maximum packet size for the X.25 interface to match that for the LLC2 interface.

When the remote X.25 device has a limit on the maximum total length of recombined X.25 segments it will support, you must ensure the length is not exceeded. For example, a device whose maximum SNA packet size is limited to 265 bytes might not be able to handle a series of X.25 packets that it has to recombine to make a 4, 8, or 17 KB SNA packet, such as one often encounters in an LLC2 environment.

You cannot configure the X.25 interface with a larger packet size than the LLC2 interface.

To specify the largest packet that can be sent or received on the X.25 interface, use the following command in interface configuration mode:

Command	Purpose
qllc largest-packet *virtual-mac-address max-size*	Specifies the largest packet that can be sent or received on the X.25 interface.

Monitor QLLC Conversion

To monitor connections using QLLC conversion, use the following commands in privileged EXEC mode:

Step	Command	Purpose
1	**show interfaces serial** *number*	Displays information about X.25 and LLC2 connections involving interfaces on which QLLC conversion has been enabled.

Step	Command	Purpose
2	**show qllc**	Displays the current state of any connections using QLLC local acknowledgment.
3	**show llc2**	Displays information about LLC2 connections involving interfaces on which QLLC conversion has been enabled.

SDLLC Configuration Examples

The following sections provide SDLLC configuration examples:

- SDLLC with Direct Connection Example

- SDLLC with Single Router Using RSRB Example

- SDLLC with RSRB (Single 3x74) Example

- SDLLC with RSRB (Multiple 3x74s) Example

- SDLLC with RSRB and Local Acknowledgment Example

In the "QLLC Conversion Configuration Examples" section, refer to the "NCP and VTAM Sysgen Parameters" section for sample NCP definitions that the 37x5 FEP in these topologies could use and for sample VTAM definitions that the IBM host in these topologies could use to reflect the routers in the communication path.

SDLLC with Direct Connection Example

Figure 15-2 shows a router configuration when the router directly connects the Token Ring and the serial line. Cisco IOS software is configured with SRB.

Figure 15-2 *SDLLC Communication Between a 37x5 and a 3x74 Connected to the Same Router (Direct Connection)*

A configuration file that enables direct connection follows:

```
source-bridge ring-group 100
!
interface tokenring 0
 source-bridge 111 1 100
!
interface serial 0
 encapsulation sdlc-primary
 sdlc address c1
 sdllc traddr 0110.2222.3300 222 2 100
 sdllc partner 4000.0122.0001 c1
 sdllc xid c1 1720001
```

SDLLC with Single Router Using RSRB Example

Figure 15-3 shows a software configuration in which the router directly connects the Token Ring and the serial line, but uses RSRB to create a virtual ring 100. This configuration has the following characteristics:

- The FEP (37x5) sees C1 3x74 at MAC address 0110.2222.3300

- The RIF from the FEP to the devices would appear as:

  ring 111—bridge 1—ring 100—bridge 1—ring 8

Figure 15-3 *SDLLC with Single Router Using RSRB*

The following sample configuration file is for SDLLC with a single router using RSRB:

```
source-bridge ring-group 100
source-bridge remote-peer 100 tcp 131.108.1.1
source-bridge remote-peer 100 tcp 131.108.2.2

interface tokenring 0
 ip address 131.108.2.2 255.255.255.0
 source-bridge 111 1 100
```

```
interface serial 0
 encapsulation sdlc-primary
 sdlc address c1
 sdllc traddr 0110.2222.3300 8 1 100
 sdllc partner 1000.5a7d.8123 c1
 sdllc xid c1 17200c1
```

SDLLC with RSRB (Single 3x74) Example

In Figure 15-4, SDLLC with RSRB connects a FEP (37x5) and a single 3x74 cluster controller. The host wants to communicate with a single 3174 that its FEP sees on a Token Ring. However, the 3x74 seen by the FEP is in fact SDLC device C1 connected by means of a serial link through a remote router.

Figure 15-4 *SDLLC with RSRB with a Single 3x74*

The configuration files for the network shown in Figure 15-4 follow.

Router A

```
source-bridge ring-group 100
source-bridge remote-peer 100 tcp 131.108.1.1
source-bridge remote-peer 100 tcp 131.108.2.2
!
interface tokenring 0
 ip address 131.108.1.1 255.255.255.0
 source-bridge 10 1 100
!
interface ethernet 0
 ip address 131.108.2.1 255.255.255.0
```

Router B

```
source-bridge ring-group 100
source-bridge remote-peer 100 tcp 131.108.1.1
source-bridge remote-peer 100 tcp 131.108.2.2
!
interface tokenring 0
 ip address 131.108.2.2 255.255.255.0
 source-bridge 1 1 100
!
interface serial 0
 encapsulation sdlc-primary
 sdlc address c1
 sdllc traddr 0110.2222.3300 8 1 100
 sdllc partner 1000.5a7d.8123 c1
 sdllc xid c1 17200c1
```

SDLLC with RSRB (Multiple 3x74s) Example

In the setup shown in Figure 15-5, Router A needs no SDLLC configuration, Router B has the SDLLC configuration and supports multipoint on the SDLC link with a modem-sharing device, and Router C is also configured with SDLLC. For information about the NCP and VTAM system generation (sysgen) parameters that are used in this configuration, see the "NCP and VTAM Sysgen Parameters" section later in this chapter.

Figure 15-5 *SDLLC with RSRB with Multiple 3x74s*

The following configuration files describe the network shown in Figure 15-5.

Router A

```
source-bridge ring-group 100
source-bridge remote-peer 100 tcp 131.108.2.1
source-bridge remote-peer 100 tcp 131.108.2.2
source-bridge remote-peer 100 tcp 131.108.2.3
!
interface tokenring 0
 ip address 131.108.1.1 255.255.255.0
 source-bridge 10 1 100
!
interface ethernet 0
 ip address 131.108.2.1 255.255.255.0
```

Router B

```
source-bridge ring-group 100
source-bridge remote-peer 100 tcp 11.108.2.1
source-bridge remote-peer 100 tcp 11.108.2.2
source-bridge remote-peer 100 tcp 11.108.2.3
!
interface ethernet 0
 ip address 131.108.2.2 255.255.255.0
!
interface serial 0
 encapsulation sdlc-primary
 sdlc address c1
 sdlc address c2
 sdllc traddr 0110.2222.3300 7 1 100
 sdllc partner 1000.5a7d.8123 c1
 sdllc partner 1000.5a7d.8123 c2
 sdllc xid c1 17200c1
 sdllc xid c2 17200c2
```

Router C

```
source-bridge ring-group 100
source-bridge remote-peer 100 tcp 131.108.2.1
source-bridge remote-peer 100 tcp 131.108.2.2
source-bridge remote-peer 100 tcp 131.108.2.3
!
interface ethernet 0
 ip address 131.108.2.3 255.255.255.0
!
interface serial 0
 encapsulation sdlc-primary
 sdlc address c3
 sdllc traddr 0110.2222.3300 9 1 100
 sdllc partner 1000.5a7d.8123 c3 MUST MATCH TIC LOCADD, NOTE 2
 sdllc xid c3 17200c3 MUST MATCH VTAM IDBLK/IDNUM, NOTE 4
```

SDLLC with RSRB and Local Acknowledgment Example

The configuration shown in Figure 15-6 enables local acknowledgment for Router B, which means that the LLC session terminates at Router A. However, the LLC2 session between Router A and Router C is not locally acknowledged and terminates at Router C.

For information about the NCP and VTAM system generation (sysgen) parameters that are used in this configuration, see the "NCP and VTAM Sysgen Parameters" section later in this chapter.

Figure 15-6 *SDLLC with RSRB and Local Acknowledgment*

The following sample configuration files describe the network shown in Figure 15-6. (The notes in the sample configuration files refer to the "Notes" section within the "NCP and VTAM Sysgen Parameters" section.)

Router A

```
source-bridge ring-group 100
source-bridge remote-peer 100 tcp 131.108.2.1
source-bridge remote-peer 100 tcp 131.108.2.2 local-ack
source-bridge remote-peer 100 tcp 131.108.2.3
!
interface tokenring 0
 ip address 131.108.1.1 255.255.255.0
 source-bridge 1 1 100
!
interface ethernet 0
 ip address 131.108.2.1 255.255.255.0
```

Router B

```
source-bridge ring-group 100
source-bridge remote-peer 100 tcp 131.108.2.1 local-ack
source-bridge remote-peer 100 tcp 131.108.2.2
source-bridge remote-peer 100 tcp 131.108.2.3

source-bridge sdllc local-ack
!
interface ethernet 0
 ip address 131.108.2.2 255.255.255.0
!
interface serial 0
 encapsulation sdlc-primary
 sdlc address c1
 sdllc traddr 4000.3174.0b0d 7 1 100
 sdllc partner 1000.5a7d.8123 c1
 !Must match TIC LOCADD [See NOTE 2]
 sdllc xid c1 017200c1
 !Must match VTAM IDBLK/IDNUM [See NOTE 4]
!
interface serial 1
 encapsulation sdlc-primary
 sdlc address c2
 sdllc traddr 0110.2222.3200 8 1 100
 sdllc partner 1000.5a7d.8123 c2
 !Must match TIC LOCADD [See NOTE 2]
 sdllc xid c2 017200c2
 !Must match VTAM IDBLK/IDNUM [See NOTE 4]
```

Router C

```
source-bridge ring-group 100
source-bridge remote-peer 100 tcp 131.108.2.1
source-bridge remote-peer 100 tcp 131.108.2.2
source-bridge remote-peer 100 tcp 131.108.2.3
!
interface ethernet 0
ip address 131.108.2.3 255.255.255.0
!
interface serial 0
 encapsulation sdlc-primary
 sdlc address c3
 sdllc traddr 4000.3174.0c00 9 1 100
 sdllc partner 1000.5a7d.8123 c3
 Must match TIC LOCADD [See NOTE 2]
 sdllc xid c3 017200c3
 !Must match VTAM IDBLK/IDNUM [See NOTE 4]
```

QLLC Conversion Configuration Examples

The following sections provide QLLC conversion configuration examples:

- QLLC Conversion Between a Single 37x5 and a Single 3x74 Example

- QLLC Conversion Between a Single 37x5 and Multiple 3x74s Example

- QLLC Conversion Between Multiple 37x5s and Multiple 3x74s Example

- QLLC Conversion Between a Single 37x5 and Multiple 3x74s Across an Arbitrary WAN Example

- NCP and VTAM Sysgen Parameters

The examples describe four increasingly complex QLLC conversion topologies and possible software configurations for each. Following the examples are sample NCP definitions that the 37x5 FEP in these topologies could use and VTAM definitions that the IBM host in these topologies could use to reflect the routers in the communication path.

QLLC Conversion Between a Single 37x5 and a Single 3x74 Example

Figure 15-6, shown previously, illustrates the simplest QLLC conversion topology—a single 37x5 FEP on a Token Ring communicating with a single 3x74 cluster controller across an X.25 network. A router connects the Token Ring to the X.25 network. In Figure 15-6, notice that the router's X.25 interface is treated as a virtual ring for configuration purposes.

The following configuration file configures Cisco IOS software to support the network topology shown in Figure 15-6:

```
source-bridge ring-group 100
!
interface serial 0
 encapsulation x25
 x25 address 31102120100
 x25 map qllc 0100.0000.0001 31104150101
 qllc srb 0100.0000.0001 201 100
!
 ! Allow the 3x74 to initiate the connection.
!
 qllc partner 0100.0000.0001 4000.0101.0132

interface tokenring 0
 source-bridge 1 1 100
```

In this configuration file, the **source-bridge ring-group** command defines a virtual ring number 100. The serial 0 interface that connects to the X.25 network is then configured for X.25 DTE operation using the **encapsulation x25** command and assigned the X.121 address of 31102120100 using the **x25 address** command. The **x25 map qllc** command associates the X.121 address of the remote X.25 device (31104150101) with a virtual Token Ring MAC address (0100.0000.0001) the Token Ring device will use to communicate with this remote X.25 device. The **qllc srb** command indicates that the virtual MAC address of the X.25 device will be used to communicate with the real MAC address of the Token Ring device.

The **qllc partner** command enables the software to open a connection to the local Token Ring device at MAC address 4000.0101.0132 on behalf of the remote X.25 device at virtual Token Ring MAC address 0100.0000.0001. The **source-bridge** command configures the router's Token Ring 0 interface for local source-route bridging by associating the router's virtual ring number 100 with the ring number (1) of the local Token Ring and the bridge number (1) that uniquely identifies this bridge interface.

QLLC Conversion Between a Single 37x5 and Multiple 3x74s Example

Figure 15-7 shows a slightly more complex QLLC conversion topology. The same 37x5 FEP on a Token Ring connects through a router to an X.25 network, but communicates with multiple 3x74 cluster controllers through X.25.

Figure 15-7 *QLLC Conversion Between a Single 37x5 and Multiple 3x74s*

The following configuration file configures Cisco IOS software to support the network topology shown in Figure 15-7:

```
source-bridge ring-group 100
!
interface serial 0
 encapsulation x25
 x25 address 3137005469
!
 ! configure the first 3174
!
 x25 map qllc 0000.0cff.0001 31370054111
!
```

```
! 1001 - virtual ring used by all qllc devices
! 100 - the virtual ring group
!
 qllc srb 0000.0cff.0001 1001 100
 qllc partner 0000.0cff.0001 4000.1160.0000
 qllc xid 0000.0cff.0001 01710017
!
! configure the second 3174
!
 x25 map qllc 0000.0cff.0002 313700543247
!
! 1001 - virtual ring used by all qllc devices
! 100 - the virtual ring group
!
 qllc srb 0000.0cff.0002 1001 100
 qllc partner 0000.0cff.0002 4000.1160.0000
 qllc xid 0000.0cff.0002 01710017
!
interface tokenring 0
!
! Since this is a real bridge, we have to define the way it
! bridges to the Qllc virtual ring.
!
 source-bridge 1 1 100
 source-bridge spanning
```

QLLC Conversion Between Multiple 37x5s and Multiple 3x74s Example

In the following example, two 3x74s on a Token Ring each attach to a different 37x5 on the other side of an X.25 network. Only one Token Ring interface is used. Do not create a bridge from the QLLC virtual ring (1001) to the physical Token Ring (1). Instead, define a virtual ring group (for example, 100).

```
interface serial 0
 encapsulation x25
 x25 address 3137005469
!
! configure the router for the first 3x74
!
 x25 map qllc 0000.0cff.0001 31370054111
!
! 1001 - virtual ring used by all qllc devices
! 1 - the local Token Ring number
!
 qllc srb 0000.0cff.0001 1001 1
 qllc partner 0000.0cff.0001 4000.1160.0000
!
! configure the router for the second 3x74
!
 x25 map qllc 0000.0cff.0002 31370053247
!
```

```
! 1001 - virtual ring used by all qllc devices
! 1 - the local Token Ring number
!
! Note that the partner's MAC address and XID are different from
! those in the first 3x74.
!
 qllc srb 0000.0cff.0001 1001 1
 qllc partner 0000.0cff.0002 4000.1161.1234
!
interface tokenring 0
!
! Since this is a real bridge, we have to define the way it bridges
! to the QLLC virtual ring.
!
 source-bridge 1 1 1001
 source-bridge spanning
```

QLLC Conversion Between a Single 37x5 and Multiple 3x74s Across an Arbitrary WAN Example

Figure 15-7, shown previously, includes an added arbitrary WAN in the communication path between the 37x5 FEP and the multiple 3x74 cluster controllers. The arbitrary WAN can be a multihop network, whereas QLLC conversion treats the X.25 network as a single-hop network.

In Figure 15-7, notice that the arbitrary WAN and the routers on either side of it form a single virtual ring, as configured using the **source-bridge ring-group** global configuration command.

In this configuration file, Router A uses an IP address of 131.108.2.2 and its Token Ring interface is attached to Token Ring 1. Because Router A connects to the Token Ring, it does not need to be configured for QLLC conversion. Router B, configured for QLLC conversion because it connects directly to the X.25 network through its serial interface, uses an X.121 address of 31102120100 and an IP address of 131.108.1.1. The 37x5 device uses a MAC address of 4000.0101.0132. The virtual MAC address of 0100.0000.0001 has been assigned to the 3x74 device.

Router A

The following configuration file configures the Router A in Figure 15-7:

```
source-bridge ring-group 100
source-bridge remote-peer 100 tcp 131.108.1.1 local-ack
source-bridge remote-peer 100 tcp 131.108.2.2 local-ack
!
interface ethernet 0
 ip address 131.108.3.3 255.255.255.0
!
interface tokenring 0
 ip address 131.108.2.2 255.255.255.0
 source-bridge 1 1 100
 source-bridge spanning
```

Router B

The following configuration file configures the Router B in Figure 15-7:

```
source-bridge ring-group 100
source-bridge remote-peer 100 tcp 131.108.1.1 local-ack
source-bridge remote-peer 100 tcp 131.108.2.2 local-ack
source-bridge qllc-local-ack
!
interface serial 0
 encapsulation x25
 x25 address 31102120100
 x25 map qllc 0100.0000.0001 31104150101
 x25 map qllc 0100.0000.0002 31104150102
 qllc srb 0100.0000.0001 201 100
 qllc srb 0100.0000.0002 201 100
!
 ! Allow the 3174 to initiate the connection.
!
 qllc partner 0100.0000.0001 4000.0101.0132
 qllc partner 0100.0000.0002 4000.0101.0132
!
interface ethernet 0
 ip address 131.108.1.1 255.255.255.0
```

NCP and VTAM Sysgen Parameters

The sample system generation (sysgen) parameters in this section show typical NCP and VTAM values that correspond with configurations for Router A, Router B, and Router C in Figure 15-5, Figure 15-6, and Figure 15-7. Figure 15-5 and Figure 15-6 show SDLLC media translation and Figure 15-7 shows QLLC conversion.

IBM's ACF/NCP uses a function called NTRI (NCP/Token Ring Interconnection) to support Token Ring-attached SNA devices. NTRI also provides translation from Token Ring-attached SNA devices (physical units) to switched (dial-up) devices. VTAM provides the resolution for these devices in a Switched Major Node. VTAM treats these devices on NTRI logical lines as switched devices. (For more information, consult IBM documentation *NCP/SSP/EP Resource Definition Reference*, SC30-3448-04.)

Using SDLLC, Cisco IOS software translates SDLC leased line protocol into Token Ring LLC2 protocol, then the NTRI function in ACF/NCP translates Token Ring LLC2 protocol into an SNA switched protocol.

NCP Generation Definitions

```
*********************************************************************
***               SAMPLES BASED ON ACF/NCP V5 R4.
***               NOT ALL NCP PARAMETERS ARE SHOWN
*********************************************************************
*
*********************************************************************
*   OPTIONS DEFINITION STATEMENT
*********************************************************************
NCPOPTOPTIONS   NEWDEFN=YESNTRI GENERATION, MUST BE FIRST STMT
*
*********************************************************************
*     BUILD MACRO
*********************************************************************
NCPBU BUILD     LOCALTO=1.5,NTRI ACK TIMER FOR LOCAL TOKEN RINGS
                REMOTTO=2.5,NTRI ACK TIMER FOR REMOTE TOKEN RINGS
                            USED IN SDLLC CONFIGURATIONS, NOTE 1
*
*********************************************************************
*     DYNAMIC RECONFIGURATION POOL SPACE
*********************************************************************
DRPOOLLUDRPOOL  NUMTYP2=50RESERVE 50 LUS ON PU. T2 PUS
*
*********************************************************************
*     PHYSICAL GROUP FOR NTRI TIC #1, DEFINITIONS FOR THE TOKEN RING
*     ADAPTER TO ESTABLISH PHYSICAL CONNECTIVITY
*********************************************************************
EPHYG GROUP     ECLTYPE=PHYSICAL
*
EPHYL LINE      ADAPTER=TIC2,          TYPE OF ADAPTER
                ADDRESS=(16,FULL),     INTERNAL FEP TIC ADDRESS
                PORTADD=0,
                LOCADD=10005a7d8123,TIC ADDRESS, NOTE 2
                RCVBUFC=1440,
                MAXTSL=2012,
                TRSPEED=16             TOKEN RING SPEED
*
EPHYPUPU
*
EPHYLULU        ISTATUS=INACTIVE
*
*********************************************************************
*     NTRI PERIPHERAL LOGICAL LINE GROUP, LINE AND PU PAIRS ARE
*     GENERATED BY THE AUTOGEN PARAMETER.
*********************************************************************
ELOGG GROUP     ECLTYPE=LOGICAL,
                PHYPORT=0,
                CALL=INOUT,
                AUTOGEN=3              ONE PER SDLLC CONTROLLER,
                                      NOTE 3
*********************************************************************
```

VTAM Definitions

```
********************************************************************
*            VTAM SWITCHED MAJOR NODE, BASED ON ACF/VTAM V3 R4.
*            THE CODING BELOW SUPPORTS DIAL IN OPERATION ONLY. TYPICALLY,
*            NTRI IMPLEMENTATIONS USE ONLY DIAL IN. IF DIAL OUT FROM AN
*            APPLICATION IS REQUIRED, PATH MACROS MUST BE USED. CONSULT
*            THE APPROPRIATE VTAM INSTALLATION REFERENCE MANUAL.
********************************************************************
VSWITCH     VBUILD              TYPE=SWNET
*
VPU1        PU                  ADDR=13,        COULD BE ANYTHING (NOT USED)
                                IDBLK=017,      XID PARM, NOTE 4
                                IDNUM=200c1,    XID PARM, NOTE 4
                                MAXOUT=7,
                                MAXDATA=265,
                                MODETAB=AMODETAB,
                                DLOGMOD=US327X,
                                PUTYPE=2,
                                USSTAB=USS327X
*
VLU1A       LU                  LOCADDR=2,
VLU1B       LU                  LOCADDR=3
*
VPU2        PU                  ADDR=13,        COULD BE ANYTHING (NOT USED)
                                IDBLK=017,      XID PARM, NOTE 4
                                IDNUM=200c2,    XID PARM, NOTE 4
                                MAXOUT=7,
                                MAXDATA=265,
                                MODETAB=AMODETAB,
                                DLOGMOD=US327X,
                                PUTYPE=2,
                                USSTAB=USS327X
*
VLU2A       LU                  LOCADDR=2,
VLU2B       LU                  LOCADDR=3
*
VPU3        PU                  ADDR=13,        COULD BE ANYTHING (NOT USED)
                                IDBLK=017,      XID PARM, NOTE 4
                                IDNUM=200c3,    XID PARM, NOTE 4
                                MAXOUT=7,
                                MAXDATA=265,
                                MODETAB=AMODETAB,
                                DLOGMOD=US327X,
                                PUTYPE=2,
                                USSTAB=USS327X
*
VLU3A       LU                  LOCADDR=2,
VLU3B       LU                  LOCADDR=3
*
```

Notes

In these sample definitions:

1 REMOTTO is the NCP's T1 timer for remote Token Rings. All connections use RIF information and therefore look like remote Token Ring devices. The default is 2.5 seconds, which is adequate for most situations; however, when slow-speed links are used, this parameter should be reviewed to ensure enough time for link-level acknowledgments.

2 The LOCADD parameter defines the locally administered address of the TIC in the NCP. Cisco IOS software, configured for SDLLC, will insert this address as the 802.5 destination address field in TEST and XID frames to establish connectivity and then in data frames during the session. The **sdllc partner** and **qllc partner** commands define this connection in Cisco IOS software. Each SDLC control unit is defined with an **sdllc partner** or **qllc partner** command.

3 The AUTOGEN parameter specifies the number of LINE and PU pairs that are automatically generated by NDF (Network Definition Facility). Each controller requires a LINE and PU definition in the ELCTYPE LOGICAL group. These represent control block space in the NCP simulating switched line as described earlier.

4 The IDBLK and IDNUM parameters in VTAM are used to identify incoming connection requests. IDBLK is typically unique for each type of IBM device. IDNUM is any five hexadecimal digit combination. Cisco routers configured for SDLLC or QLLC conversion must associate an IDBLK/IDNUM combination with a controller by using the **sdllc xid** or **qllc xid** command. If not using the **qllc xid** command, then IDBLK/IDNUM must agree with the values of the X.25 attached devices. During activation, an XID will be sent to the NCP containing the specific IDBLK/IDNUM. NCP will send these values to VTAM in an SNA command called REQCONT. VTAM will search its switched major nodes to find a match. If found, VTAM will establish sessions with the device by sending activation commands (ACTPU, ACTLUs).

CHAPTER 16

IBM Network Media Translation Commands

Use the commands in this chapter to configure and monitor Qualified Logical Link Control (QLLC) or SDLLC connections. SDLLC is a Cisco IOS software feature that provides translation between Synchronous Data Link Control (SDLC) and Logical Link Control, type 2 (LLC2). For QLLC conversion or SDLLC parameter configuration information and examples, refer to Chapter 15, "Configuring IBM Network Media Translation."

qllc accept-all-calls

Use the **qllc accept-all-calls** interface configuration command to enable the router to accept a call from any remote X.25 device. Use the **no** form of this command to cancel the request.

> **qllc accept-all-calls**
> **no qllc accept-all-calls**

Syntax Description

This command has no arguments or keywords.

Default

Disabled

Command Mode

Interface configuration

Usage Guidelines

This command first appeared in Cisco IOS Release 11.2 F.

This command allows QLLC to accept all inbound X.25 calls, provided that the QLLC Call User Data (CUD) is in the call packet and the destination X.121 address in the call packet matches the serial interface's configured destination X.121 address or subaddress. When using this command, the source X.121 address does not need to be configured via an **x25 map qllc** command for the call to be accepted.

This command is applicable to QLLC support for DLSw+, APPN, and DSPU. It is not applicable to QLLC support for SRB and RSRB.

Example

The following example enables QLLC connectivity for DLSw+ and allows QLLC to accept all inbound X.25 calls. Every X.25 connection request for X.121 address 0308 with QLLC CUD is directed to DLSw+. The first SVC to be established will be mapped to virtual MAC address 4000.0B0B.0001. If a call comes in with an X.121 address of 0308, the call will be forwarded to MAC address 4001.1161.1234.

```
interface serial 0
 encapsulation x25
 x25 address 0308
 qllc accept-all-calls
 qllc dlsw vmac 4000.0B0B.0001 500 partner 4001.1161.1234
```

Related Commands

To locate documentation of related commands, you can search online at www.cisco.com.

x25 map qllc

qllc largest-packet

Use the **qllc largest-packet** interface configuration command to indicate the maximum size of the Systems Network Architecture (SNA) packet that can be sent or received on an X.25 interface configured for QLLC conversion. Use the **no** form of this command to restore the default largest packet size.

> **qllc largest-packet** *virtual-mac-addr max-size*
> **no qllc largest-packet** *virtual-mac-addr max-size*

Syntax	Description
virtual-mac-addr	Virtual Media Access Control (MAC) address associated with the remote X.25 device, as defined using the **x25 map qllc** or **x25 pvc qllc** interface configuration commands. This address is written as a dotted triple of four-digit hexadecimal numbers.
max-size	Maximum size, in bytes, of the SNA packet that can be sent or received on the X.25 interface configured for QLLC conversion. This value agrees with the value configured in the remote SNA device. The valid range is 0 to 1024.

Default

Maximum size is 265 bytes.

Command Mode

Interface configuration

Usage Guidelines

This command first appeared in Cisco IOS Release 10.3.

SNA packets that are larger than the largest value allowed on the X.25 connection and are received on the LLC2 interface are segmented before being sent on the X.25 interface. When a segmented packet is received on the X.25 interface, it is passed immediately to the LLC2 interface and no effort is made to wait for the segment to be completed.

When the remote X.25 device has a limit on the maximum total length of recombined X.25 segments it will support, you can use the **qllc largest-packet** command to ensure the length is not exceeded. For example, a device whose maximum SNA packet size is limited to 265 bytes might not be able to handle a series of X.25 packets that it has to recombine to make a 4, 8, or 17 KM SNA packet, such as one often encounters in an LLC2 environment.

You use the **qllc largest-packet** command in conjunction with the **x25 map qllc** and **qllc srb** commands.

NOTE   Do not configure the maximum SNA packet size on an X.25 interface to be larger than the maximum SNA packet size allowed on the LLC2 interface.

Consult your IBM documentation to set the maximum packet size on the remote X.25 device.

Example

In the following example, the maximum packet size that has been established for the virtual circuit is used as the maximum packet size that can be sent or received on the X.25 interface:

```
interface serial 0
 encapsulation x25
 x25 address 31102120100
 x25 map qllc 0100.0000.0001 31104150101
 qllc srb 0100.0000.0001 201 100
!
 qllc partner 0100.0000.0001 4000.0101.0132
 qllc xid 0100.0000.0001 01720001
 qllc largest-packet 0100.0000.0001 521
```

Related Commands

To locate documentation of related commands, you can search online at www.cisco.com.

qllc srb
x25 map qllc
x25 pvc qllc

qllc npsi-poll

Use the **qllc npsi-poll** interface configuration command to enable a connection between a PU 2 on the LAN side and a front-end processor (FEP) running NPSI on the X.25 side. Use the **no** form of this command to disable this capability.

> **qllc npsi-poll** *virtual-mac-addr*
> **no qllc npsi-poll** *virtual-mac-addr*

Syntax   Description

virtual-mac-addr   MAC address associated with the remote X.25 device, as defined using the **x25 map qllc** or **x25 pvc qllc** interface configuration commands. This address is written as a dotted triple of four-digit hexadecimal numbers.

Default

Disabled

Command Mode

Interface configuration

Usage Guidelines

This command first appeared in Cisco IOS Release 11.1.

The **qllc npsi-poll** command is necessary only when the upstream device is a FEP running NPSI and the downstream device is a PU 2.

This command is necessary because in a Token Ring or RSRB environment the LAN attached devices start up by sending a null exchange ID packet upstream. If Cisco IOS software forwards this null XID to an X.25-attached FEP, the FEP responds as if it were connecting to an PU2.1 device, and breaks the connection when the PU 2 next sends an XID Format 0 Type 2. The **qllc npsi-poll** command intercepts any null XID packet that the software receives on the LAN interface and returns a null XID response to the downstream device. It continues to allow XID Format 3 and XID Format 0 packets through the X.25 device.

Example

The following example facilitates a connection between a FEP running NPSI and a downstream PU 2.0:

```
qllc npsi-poll 0100.0000.0001
```

Related Commands

To locate documentation of related commands, you can search online at www.cisco.com.

qllc srb
sdlc qllc-prtnr
x25 map qllc
x25 pvc qllc

qllc partner

Use the **qllc partner** interface configuration command to enable a router configured for QLLC conversion to open a connection to the local Token Ring device on behalf of the remote X.25 device when an incoming call is received. Use the **no** form of this command to disable this capability.

> **qllc partner** *virtual-mac-addr mac-addr*
> **no qllc partner** *virtual-mac-addr mac-addr*

Syntax	Description
virtual-mac-addr	MAC address associated with the remote X.25 device, as defined using the **x25 map qllc** or **x25 pvc qllc** interface configuration commands. This address is written as a dotted triple of four-digit hexadecimal numbers.
mac-addr	48-bit MAC address of the Token Ring host that will communicate with the remote X.25 device.

Default

Disabled

Command Mode

Interface configuration

Usage Guidelines

This command first appeared in Cisco IOS Release 10.3.

Part II

Command Reference

When Cisco IOS software receives an incoming call from the designated X.121 address, it opens an LLC2 connection with the device at the given MAC address. Both the MAC address of the Token Ring device and the virtual MAC address for the remote X.25 device with which it is to communicate are required in order for the software to initiate connections with the Token Ring device. This allows the Token Ring host to be permanently ready to accept a connection rather than requiring operator action at the host to initiate the connection with the X.25 device.

You must issue the **qllc partner** command for each remote X.25 device that will communicate with the local Token Ring host through this interface.

You use the **qllc partner** command in conjunction with the **x25 map qllc** and **qllc srb** commands.

Example

In the following example, the **qllc partner** command is used to associate the virtual MAC address 0100.0000.0001, as defined in the previous **x25 map qllc** entry, with the MAC address of the Token Ring host that will communicate with the remote X.25 device:

```
interface serial 0
 encapsulation x25
 x25 address 31102120100
 x25 map qllc 0100.0000.0001 31104150101
 qllc srb 0100.0000.0001 201 100
!
 qllc partner 0100.0000.0001 4000.0101.0132
 qllc xid 0100.0000.0001 01720001
```

Related Commands

To locate documentation of related commands, you can search online at www.cisco.com.

qllc srb
sdlc qllc-prtnr
x25 map qllc
x25 pvc qllc

qllc sap

Use the **qllc sap** interface configuration command to associate a service access point (SAP) value other than the default SAP value with a serial interface configured for X.25 communication and QLLC conversion. The **no** form of this command returns this SAP value to its default state.

> **qllc sap** *virtual-mac-addr ssap dsap*
> **no qllc sap** *virtual-mac-addr ssap dsap*

Syntax   Description

virtual-mac-addr	MAC address associated with the remote X.25 device, as defined using the **x25 map qllc** or **x25 pvc qllc** interface configuration commands. This address is written as a dotted triple of four-digit hexadecimal numbers.
ssap	Source SAP value. It can be a decimal number in the range 2 to 254. The default is 4.
dsap	Destination SAP value. It can be a decimal number in the range 2 to 254. The default is 4.

Defaults

The default source SAP value is 4.

The default destination SAP value is 4.

Command Mode

Interface configuration

Usage Guidelines

This command first appeared in Cisco IOS Release 10.3.

A SAP can be viewed as a port through which a higher-layer application can communicate with its counterpart (peer) operating on another system. While the standard SAP value for IBM devices is 4, other values are allowed.

You use the **qllc sap** command in conjunction with the **x25 map qllc** and **qllc srb** interface configuration commands.

Example

In the following example, source SAP and destination SAP values of 2 are specified for the remote X.25 device at the X.121 address 31370054065:

```
interface serial 0
 x25 map qllc 31370054065 4000.0122.0001
 qllc srb 9 100
 qllc sap 4000.0122.0001 02 02
```

Related Commands

To locate documentation of related commands, you can search online at www.cisco.com.

qllc srb
x25 map qllc
x25 pvc qllc

qllc srb

Use the **qllc srb** interface configuration command to enable QLLC conversion on a serial interface configured for X.25 communication. The **no** form of this command disables QLLC conversion on the interface.

> **qllc srb** *virtual-mac-addr srn trn*
> **no qllc srb** *srn trn*

Syntax	Description
virtual-mac-addr	MAC address associated with the remote X.25 device, as defined using the **x25 map qllc** or **x25 pvc qllc** interface configuration commands. It can be 1 to 15 digits long.
srn	Source ring number. This value defines a virtual ring for all of the remote X.25 devices attached to the QLLC interface.
trn	Target ring number. It must be a virtual ring group that has been defined with the **source-bridge ring-group** global configuration command.

Default

QLLC conversion is not enabled.

Usage Guidelines

Any number of QLLC conversion connections using the same X.25 serial interface can share a common source ring. However, this source ring must be a unique hexadecimal ring number within the source-bridged network.

If the router has only one Token Ring interface and is bridging from the remote X.25 devices to this interface, then *trn* is the number of the ring on that Token Ring interface. If the router has several Token Ring interfaces and interconnects them by means of the **source-bridge ring-group** command, then *trn* is the number of that virtual ring group, as assigned using the **source-bridge ring-group** global configuration command.

Command Mode

Interface configuration

Usage Guidelines

This command first appeared in Cisco IOS Release 10.3.

Use the **qllc srb** command to associate the ring number and bridge number that have been assigned to the interface with a virtual ring group of which the interface will be a part. The serial interface appears to be a ring, or source ring number, on a source-route bridge network, and ties in to the virtual ring group or target ring number. The target ring number provides access to other real rings that have been designated using the **source-bridge** global configuration command. Note that you can configure QLLC conversion on a router containing no Token Ring interface cards, such as a router connecting a serial-attached device to an X.25 public data network (PDN).

The **qllc srb** command automatically turns on the LLC2 process with default values. To change any of the LLC2 parameters (described in Chapter 14, "LLC2 and SDLC Commands"), apply their values to the serial interface that has been configured for QLLC conversion. This is done on the serial interface, even though LLC2 does not technically run on the serial interface, but on the virtual ring associated with the serial interface.

You use the **qllc srb** command in conjunction with the **x25 map qllc** command.

Example

In the following example, the **qllc srb** command is used to define a virtual ring number of 201 for the remote X.25 device, and an actual or virtual ring number of 100 for the Token Ring interface:

```
interface serial 0
 encapsulation x25
 x25 address 31102120100
 x25 map qllc 0100.0000.0001 31104150101
 qllc srb 0100.0000.0001 201 100
```

Related Commands

To locate documentation of related commands, you can search online at www.cisco.com.

source-bridge
source-bridge ring-group
x25 map qllc
x25 pvc qllc

qllc xid

Use the **qllc xid** interface configuration command to associate an exchange ID (XID) value with the remote X.25 device that communicates through Cisco IOS software using QLLC conversion. The **no** form of this command disables XID processing for this address.

> **qllc xid** *virtual-mac-addr xid*
> **no qllc xid** *virtual-mac-addr xid*

Syntax

Syntax	Description
virtual-mac-addr	MAC address associated with the remote X.25 device, as defined using the **x25 map qllc** or **x25 pvc qllc** interface configuration command. This address is written as a dotted triple of four-digit hexadecimal numbers.
xid	Combined XID IDBLK and XID IDNUM you are associating with the X.25 device at this X.121 address. This hexadecimal value must be 4 bytes (8 digits) in length.

Default

XID processing is not enabled.

Command Mode

Interface configuration

Usage Guidelines

This command first appeared in Cisco IOS Release 10.3.

Most QLLC installations do not need the **qllc xid** configuration command. It is only needed if the remote X.25 device is not configured to send its own XID. This is only possible for a device that is attached via a permanent virtual circuit (PVC). Even so, most devices that are connected via X.25 will send their own XIDs. Use the **qllc xid** command when the Token Ring host requires login validation for security purposes and the remote X.25 device does not send an XID. The XID value is used to reply to XID requests received on the Token Ring (LLC2) side of the connection. XID requests and responses are usually exchanged before sessions are started. The XID response to the XID request from the Token Ring host will contain the information you configure using the **qllc xid** command. The host will check the XID response it receives with the IDBLK and IDNUM parameters (configured in VTAM). If they match, the Token Ring host will initiate a session with the router. If they do not match, the host will not initiate a session with the router.

You use the **qllc xid** command in conjunction with the **x25 map qllc** and the **qllc srb** commands.

Example

In the following example, the X.25 device at X.121 address 31104150101 must use an XID IDBLK of 017 and XID IDNUM of 20001 to access the Token Ring host whose MAC address is associated with the remote X.25 device, as applied using the **sdllc partner** command:

```
interface serial 0
 encapsulation x25
 x25 address 31102120100
 x25 map qllc 0100.0000.0001 31104150101
 qllc srb 0100.0000.0001 201 100
!
 qllc partner 0100.0000.0001 4000.0101.0132
 qllc xid 0100.0000.0001 01720001
```

Related Commands

To locate documentation of related commands, you can search online at www.cisco.com.

qllc srb
sdllc partner
x25 map qllc
x25 pvc qllc

sdllc partner

Use the **sdllc partner** interface configuration command to enable device-initiated connections for SDLLC. This command must be specified for the serial interface that links to the serial line device. Use the **no** form of this command to cancel the original instruction.

> **sdllc partner** *mac-address sdlc-address*
> **no sdllc partner** *mac-address sdlc-address*

Syntax	Description
mac-address	MAC address of the Token Ring host.
sdlc-address	SDLC address of the serial device that will communicate with the Token Ring host.

Default

Disabled

Command Mode

Interface configuration

Usage Guidelines

This command first appeared in Cisco IOS Release 10.0.

Both the MAC address of the Token Ring host and the SDLC serial line address are required to initiate connections with the Token Ring host.

The Token Ring host and the serial device communicate with each other through Cisco IOS software. Although the device is said to initiate connections, the software actually initiates connections with the Token Ring host on behalf of the serial device. As part of Cisco SDLLC implementation, the serial device "thinks" that it is communicating with a host also on a serial line. It is actually the software that does all the frame and protocol conversions between serial and Token Ring devices.

There are two conditions under which Cisco IOS software will attempt to initiate a connection to a host on behalf of a serial device:

- When the serial device attached to the router is powered on. In this case, the router attached to the serial line detects a change in interface signals and initiates a connection with the Token Ring hosts by exchanging explorer and XID packets.

- When a previously shut down serial interface is brought back on line. When the **no shutdown** command is issued, the software will detect a change in the serial line state from down to up and initiate a session with the Token Ring host by exchanging explorer and XID packets.

Cisco IOS software will continue trying once a minute to initiate a connection whenever one of these two conditions is met, until the host responds to its requests. When you no longer want the software to initiate connections with a host, use the **no sdllc partner** command.

NOTE	For device-initiated sessions, the host will check the IDBLK and IDNUM parameters of the serial device it receives in the XID packet against the information configured on the host. If the information in the XID packet does not match with what is configured on the host, the host will drop the session. Therefore, for device-initiated connections, always specify the correct IDBLK and IDNUM parameters on the router serial interfaces with the **sdllc xid** command.

Example

In the following example, a serial device at SDLC address C2 wants to initiate a connection with a Token Ring host at MAC address 4000.0122.0001. The router initiates the connection on behalf of a serial device:

```
! sample global command
source-bridge ring-group 100
!
interface serial 0
! router initiates connections with Token Ring host at MAC address
! 4000.0122.0001 on behalf of serial device c2
sdllc partner 4000.0122.0001 c2
```

Related Commands

To locate documentation of related commands, you can search online at www.cisco.com.

sdllc xid

sdllc ring-largest-frame

Use the **sdllc ring-largest-frame** interface configuration command to indicate the largest I-frame size that can be sent to or received from the LLC2 primary station. Use the **no** form of this command to return to the default.

Part
II

Command Reference

> **sdllc ring-largest-frame** *value*
> **no sdllc ring-largest-frame** *value*

Syntax   Description

value   Frame size in bytes. Possible values include 516, 1500, 2052, 4472, 8144, 11,407, and 17,800.

Default

516 bytes

Command Mode

Interface configuration

Usage Guidelines

This command first appeared in Cisco IOS Release 10.0.

Possible values for the *value* argument match those that are possible for the **lf** *size* of the various **source-bridge remote-peer** commands. You must ensure that your remote peer connection can support this largest frame size. Possible values for the *value* argument include 516, 1500, 2052, 4472, 8144, 11,407, and 17,800.

Faster screen updates to 3278-style terminals often can be obtained by allowing the Token Ring FEP to send as large a frame as possible and by allowing Cisco IOS software to segment the frame into multiple SDLC I-frames.

Example

In the following example, the software can send or receive a frame as large as 11,407 bytes from the LLC2 primary station. Any frames larger will be fragmented by the software.

```
! sample global command
source-bridge ring-group 100
!
interface serial 3
! largest frame sent or received on serial 3 is 11407 bytes
sdllc ring-largest-frame 11407
```

Related Commands

To locate documentation of related commands, you can search online at www.cisco.com.

source-bridge remote-peer fst
source-bridge remote-peer interface
source-bridge remote-peer tcp

sdllc sap

Use the **sdllc sap** interface configuration command to associate a SAP value other than the default SAP value with a serial interface configured for SDLLC. Use the **no** form of this command to return this SAP value to its default state.

> **sdllc sap** *sdlc-address ssap dsap*
> **no sdllc sap** *sdlc-address ssap dsap*

Syntax	Description
sdlc-address	MAC address associated with the remote SDLC device.
ssap	Source SAP value. It must be in the range 1 to 254. The default is 4.
dsap	Destination SAP value. It must be in the range 1 to 254. The default is 4.

Default

The default SAP value for IBM SNA devices is 4.

Command Mode

Interface configuration

Usage Guidelines

This command first appeared in Cisco IOS Release 10.0.

You use the **sdllc sap** command in conjunction with the **sdllc traddr** interface configuration commands. A SAP can be viewed as a port through which a higher-layer application can communicate with its counterpart (peer) operating on another system. While the standard SAP value for IBM SNA devices is 4, and NetBIOS devices is xF0, other values are allowed.

Example

In the following example, source SAP and destination SAP values of 2 are specified for the remote SDLC device at the SDLC address C1 02 02:

```
interface serial 0
 sdllc sap c1 02 02
```

Related Commands

To locate documentation of related commands, you can search online at www.cisco.com.

sdllc traddr

sdllc sdlc-largest-frame

Use the **sdllc sdlc-largest-frame** interface configuration command to indicate the largest information frame (I-frame) size that can be sent or received by the designated SDLC station. Use the **no** form of this command to return to the default value.

> **sdllc sdlc-largest-frame** *address value*
> **no sdllc sdlc-largest-frame** *address value*

Syntax	Description
address	Address of the SDLC station that will communicate with the Token Ring host.
value	Largest frame size that can be sent or received by this SDLC station. The default is 265 bytes.

Default

265 bytes

Command Mode

Interface configuration

Usage Guidelines

This command first appeared in Cisco IOS Release 10.0.

Most SDLC devices are limited to frames of 265 bytes. I-frames received from the Token Ring station that are larger than this size will be properly fragmented.

Example

In the following example, Cisco IOS software can send or receive a frame as large as 265 bytes (the default) from the SDLC station at address C6. Any frames larger will be fragmented by the software.

```
! sample global command
source-bridge ring-group 100
!
interface serial 4
! largest frame sent or received on serial 4 is 265 bytes
 sdllc sdlc-largest-frame c6 265
```

sdllc traddr

Use the **sdllc traddr** interface configuration command to enable SDLLC media translation on a serial interface. The address specified is a MAC address to be assigned to the serial station. Use the **no** form of this command to disable SDLLC media translation on the interface.

> **sdllc traddr** *xxxx.xxxx.xx00 lr bn tr*
> **no sdllc traddr** *xxxx.xxxx.xx00 lr bn tr*

Syntax   Description

Syntax	Description
xxxx.xxxx.xx00	MAC address to be assigned to the serial interface.
lr	SDLLC virtual ring number.
bn	SDLLC bridge number.
tr	SDLLC target ring number.

Default

Disabled

Command Mode

Interface configuration

Usage Guidelines

This command first appeared in Cisco IOS Release 10.0.

Every control unit hooked off the serial line requires a virtual Token Ring address (VTRA). This is usually assigned by the system administrator as a locally administered MAC address (unique across the network).

When you enable SDLLC Media Translation by specifying the **sdllc traddr** command on a serial interface, you must specify a VTRA for each serial station attached to the serial line. The last two hexadecimal digits (that is, the last byte) of the VTRA must be 00. Cisco IOS software uses this byte to represent the SDLC address of a station on the serial link.

NOTE	Addresses in the range *xxxx.xxxx.xx00* to *xxxx.xxxx.xxFF* are reserved for use by Cisco IOS software. You must adhere to this addressing requirement. If you do not follow this addressing requirement, there may be a conflict between the VTRA and the addresses reserved by the software for the SDLC link.

The variables *lr*, *bn*, and *tr* represent the SDLLC virtual ring number, bridge number, and target ring number, respectively, that you assign to the interface. In design, the serial interface appears to be a ring, *lr*, on a source-route bridged network, and ties in through the bridge, *bn*, to the virtual ring-group, *tr*. This provides access to other, real rings through remote source-route bridging **source-bridge remote-peer** commands. Note that SDLLC can be configured on a router containing no Token Ring interface cards.

The **sdllc traddr** command automatically turns on the LLC2 process with default values. To change any of the LLC2 parameters, specify their values on the serial interface that is being enabled for SDLLC. This is done on the serial interface, even though LLC2 does not technically run on the serial interface, but on the SDLLC virtual ring associated with the serial interface. LLC2 commands can be configured after specifying the **sdllc traddr** command.

Part
II

Command Reference

Example

In the following example, SDLLC media translation is enabled off the serial 0 interface to a serial station at MAC address 0110.2222.3300. The SDLLC virtual ring number is 8, the bridge number is 1, and the target ring number is 100.

```
! global command to apply commands to the ring group
source-bridge ring-group 100
! remote peer at IP address 131.108.1.1 belongs to ring group 100 and uses
! tcp as the transport
source-bridge remote-peer 100 tcp 131.108.1.1
source-bridge remote-peer 100 tcp 131.108.2.2
!
interface serial 0
 encapsulation sdlc-primary
! establish address of SDLC station off serial-0 as c1
 sdlc address c1
! enable SDLLC media translation to serial station 0110.2222.3300
! on virtual ring 8, bridge 1, to target ring 100
 sdllc traddr 0110.2222.3300 8 1 100
```

Related Commands

To locate documentation of related commands, you can search online at www.cisco.com.

sdllc sap
source-bridge remote-peer fst
source-bridge remote-peer interface
source-bridge remote-peer tcp

sdllc xid

Use the **sdllc xid** interface configuration command to specify an XID value appropriate for the designated SDLC station associated with this serial interface. Use the **no** form of this command to disable XID processing for this address.

> **sdllc xid** *address xxxxxxxx*
> **no sdllc xid** *address xxxxxxxx*

Syntax	Description
address	Address of the SDLC station associated with this interface.
xxxxxxxx	XID the Cisco IOS software will use to respond to XID requests received on the Token Ring (LLC2) side of the connection. This value must be 4 bytes (8 digits) in length and is specified with hexadecimal digits.

Default
Disabled

Command Mode
Interface configuration

Usage Guidelines
This command first appeared in Cisco IOS Release 10.0.

XID requests and responses are usually exchanged before sessions are started. Be sure that the XID value configured on the router matches the IDBLK and IDNUM parameters configured on the host. The XID response to an XID request from the Token Ring host will contain the information you configured in the **sdllc xid** command. The host will check the XID response it receives with the IDBLK and IDNUM parameters (that are configured in virtual telecommunications access method (VTAM)). If they match, the Token Ring host will initiate a session with the router. If they do not match, the host will not initiate a session.

Example
The following example specifies an XID value of 01720002 at address C2:

```
! sample global command
source-bridge ring-group 100
!
interface serial 0
! sdllc exchange identification value of 01720002 at address c2
 sdllc xid c2 01720002
```

Related Commands
To locate documentation of related commands, you can search online at www.cisco.com.

sdllc partner

show interfaces

Use the **show interfaces** privileged EXEC command to display the SDLC information for a given SDLC interface.

show interfaces

Syntax Description

This command has no arguments or keywords.

Command Mode

Privileged EXEC

Usage Guidelines

This command first appeared in Cisco IOS Release 10.0.

Sample Display

The following is sample output from the **show interfaces** command for an SDLC primary interface supporting the SDLLC function:

```
Router# show interfaces

Serial 0 is up, line protocol is up
Hardware is MCI Serial
MTU 1500 bytes, BW 1544 Kbit, DLY 20000 usec, rely 255/255, load 1/255
Encapsulation SDLC-PRIMARY, loopback not set
          Timers (msec): poll pause 100 fair poll 500. Poll limit 1
          [T1 3000, N1 12016, N2 20, K 7] timer: 56608 Last polled device: none
          SDLLC [ma: 0000.0C01.14--, ring: 7 bridge: 1, target ring: 10
                    largest token ring frame 2052]
SDLC addr C1 state is CONNECT
     VS 6, VR 3, RCNT 0, Remote VR 6, Current retransmit count 0
     Hold queue: 0/12 IFRAMEs 77/22 RNRs 0/0 SNRMs 1/0 DISCs 0/0
     Poll: clear, Poll count: 0, chain: p: C1 n: C1
     SDLLC [largest SDLC frame: 265, XID: disabled]
Last input 00:00:02, output 00:00:01, output hang never
Output queue 0/40, 0 drops; input queue 0/75, 0 drops
Five minute input rate 517 bits/sec, 30 packets/sec
Five minute output rate 672 bits/sec, 20 packets/sec
               357 packets input, 28382 bytes, 0 no buffer
               Received 0 broadcasts, 0 runts, 0 giants
               0 input errors, 0 CRC, 0 frame, 0 overrun, 0 ignored, 0 abort
               926 packets output, 77274 bytes, 0 underruns
               0 output errors, 0 collisions, 0 interface resets, 0 restarts
               2 carrier transitions
```

Table 16-1 shows the fields relevant to all SDLC connections.

Table 16-1 *show interfaces* *Field Descriptions When SDLC Is Enabled*

Field	Description
Timers (msec)	List of timers in milliseconds.
poll pause, fair poll, Poll limit	Current values of these timers, as described in the individual commands in this chapter.
T1, N1, N2, K	Current values for these variables, as described in the individual commands in this chapter.

Table 16-2 shows other data given for each SDLC secondary configured to be attached to this interface.

Table 16-2 *SDLC Field Descriptions*

Field	Description
addr	Address of this secondary.
State	Current state of this connection. The possible values are:
	• DISCONNECT—No communication is being attempted to this secondary.
	• CONNECT—A normal connect state exists between this router and this secondary.
	• DISCSENT—This router has sent a disconnect request to this secondary and is awaiting its response.
	• SNRMSENT—This router has sent a connect request (SNRM) to this secondary and is awaiting its response.
	• THEMBUSY—This secondary has told this router that it is temporarily unable to receive any more information frames.
	• USBUSY—This router has told this secondary that it is temporarily unable to receive any more information frames.
	• BOTHBUSY—Both sides have told each other that they are temporarily unable to receive any more information frames.
	• ERROR—This router has detected an error and is waiting for a response from the secondary acknowledging this.
VS	Sequence number of the next information frame this station sends.
VR	Sequence number of the next information frame from this secondary that this station expects to receive.
RCNT	Number of correctly sequenced I-frames received when Cisco IOS software was in a state in which it is acceptable to receive I-frames.

Continues

Table 16-2 *SDLC Field Descriptions (Continued)*

Field	Description
Remote VR	Last frame transmitted by this station that has been acknowledged by the other station.
Current retransmit count	Number of times the current I-frame or sequence of I-frames has been retransmitted.
Hold queue	Number of frames in hold queue/Maximum size of hold queue.
IFRAMEs, RNRs, SNRMs, DISCs	Sent/received count for these frames.
Poll	"Set" if this router has a poll outstanding to the secondary; "clear" if it does not.
Poll count	Number of polls, in a row, given to this secondary at this time.
chain	Shows the previous (p) and next (n) secondary address on this interface in the round robin loop of polled devices.

show qllc

Use the **show qllc** EXEC command to display the current state of any QLLC connections.

> **show qllc**

Syntax Description

This command has no arguments or keywords.

Command Mode

Privileged EXEC

Usage Guidelines

This command first appeared in Cisco IOS Release 10.3.

Sample Display

The following is sample output from the **show qllc** command:

```
Router# show qllc

QLLC Connections:
Serial2: 1000.5a35.3a4f->1000.5a59.04f9. SAPs 4 4. Rings Src 200, Tgt 100.
State Connect
Remote DTE 1002. QLLC Protocol State NORMAL lci 1 (PVC)
```

In the display, the first two lines of the **show qllc** command show that there is a QLLC session between a Token Ring device and an X.25 remote device. The X.25 device has a virtual MAC address of 100.5a35.3a4f with a SAP of 04. It is using a PVC with logical channel number 1. The Token Ring device has a MAC address of 1000.5a59.04f9 with a SAP of 04. The state of the QLLC session is CONNECTED.

Table 16-3 describes the fields shown in the display.

Table 16-3 *show qllc Field Descriptions*

Field	Description
Serial2	Serial interface for the X.25 link.
1000.5a35.3a4f	Virtual MAC address for the X.25 attached device.
1000.5a59.04f9	MAC address of the Token Ring attached device with which the X.25 attached device is communicating. This device might be on a local Token Ring or attached via source-route bridging (SRB) or remote source-route bridging (RSRB).
SAPs 4 4	Source SAP value at the virtual MAC address and destination SAP value at the Token Ring station.
Rings Src 200	Ring number for the source virtual ring defined by the **qllc srb** command.
Tgt 100	Ring number for the target virtual ring defined by the **source-bridge ring-group** command.

Continues

Table 16-3 *show qllc Field Descriptions (Continued)*

Field	Description
State	State of the QLLC-LLC2 conversion. This can be any of the following:
	• DISCONNECT—No connection exists.
	• NET DISC WAIT—X.25 device is disconnecting. The QLLC conversion is waiting for the Token Ring device to disconnect.
	• QLLC DISC WAIT—The Token Ring device is disconnecting. The QLLC conversion is waiting for the X.25 device to disconnect.
	• QLLC PRI WAIT—Connection is being established. The Token Ring device is ready to complete the connection and Cisco IOS software is establishing the QLLC connection with the X.25 device.
	• NET CONTACT REPLY WAIT—Remote X.25 device is a FEP, and has made contact with Cisco IOS software. The software is attempting to reach Token Ring device.
	• QLLC SEC WAIT—Connection is being established.
	• NET UP WAIT—Connection is being established. QLLC connection to X.25 device has been established; awaiting completion on the connection to the Token Ring attached device.
	• CONNECT—Connections from the software to X.25 and Token Ring devices are established. Data can flow end to end.
Remote DTE 1002	X.121 address of X.25 connected device.
QLLC Protocol State	State of the QLLC protocol between the software and the X.25 attached device. These states are different from the state of the underlying X.25 virtual circuit. The following are possible values:
	• ADM—Asynchronous Disconnected Mode.
	• SETUP—Cisco IOS software has initiated QLLC connection, awaiting confirmation from the X.25 device.
	• RESET—Cisco IOS software has initiated QLLC Reset, awaiting confirmation from the X.25 device.
	• DISCONNECTING—Cisco IOS software has initiated QLLC Disconnect, awaiting confirmation from the X.25 device.
	• NORMAL—QLLC connection has been completed. SNA data can be transmitted and received.
lci 1 (PVC)	Logical channel number used on the X.25 interface.

show sdllc local-ack

Use the **show sdllc local-ack** privileged EXEC command to display the current state of any current local acknowledgment connections, as well as any configured passthrough rings.

> **show sdllc local-ack**

Syntax Description

This command has no arguments or keywords.

Command Mode

Privileged EXEC

Usage Guidelines

This command first appeared in Cisco IOS Release 10.0.

Sample Display

The following is sample output from the **show sdllc local-ack** command:

```
Router# show sdllc local-ack

local 1000.5a59.04f9, lsap 04, remote 4000.2222.4444, dsap 04
llc2 = 1798136, local act state = connected
Passthrough Rings: 4 7
```

In the display, the first two lines of the **show sdllc local-ack** command show that there is a local acknowledgment session between two Token Ring devices. The device on the local ring has a MAC address of 1000.5a59.04f9 with a SAP of 04. The remote device has a MAC address of 4000.2222.4444 with a SAP of 04. The state of the local acknowledgment session is connected.

The passthrough rings display is independent of the rest of the **show sdllc local-ack** command. The passthrough rings display indicates that there are two rings, 4 and 7, configured for passthrough. This means that stations on these rings will not have their sessions locally acknowledged but will instead have their acknowledgments end-to-end.

Table 16-4 describes significant fields shown in the display.

Table 16-4   *show sdllc local-ack Field Descriptions*

Field	Description
local	MAC address of the local Token Ring station with which the router has the LLC2 session.
lsap	Local SAP value of the Token Ring station with which the router has the LLC2 session.
remote	MAC address of the remote Token Ring station on whose behalf the router is providing acknowledgments. The remote Token Ring station is separated from the router via the TCP backbone.
dsap	Destination SAP value of the remote Token Ring station on whose behalf the router is providing acknowledgments.
llc2	Pointer to an internal data structure used by technical support staff for debugging.
local-ack state:	Current state. Possible values are as follows: • disconnected—No session between the two end hosts. • connected—Full data transfer possible between the two end hosts. • awaiting connect—This router is waiting for the other end to confirm a session establishment with the remote host.
Passthrough Rings	Ring number of the start ring and destination ring for the two IBM machines when you do not have local acknowledgment for LLC2 configured for your routers using RSRB.

source-bridge fst-peername

Use the **source-bridge fst-peername** global configuration command to set up a Fast-Sequenced Transport (FST) peer name. Use the **no** form of this command to disable the IP address assignment.

> **source-bridge fst-peername** *local-interface-address*
> **no source-bridge fst-peername** *local-interface-address*

Syntax   Description

local-interface-address   IP address to assign to the local router.

Default
Disabled

Command Mode

Global configuration

Usage Guidelines

This command first appeared in Cisco IOS Release 10.0.

Using this command is the first step to configuring a remote source-route bridge to use FST.

Example

The following example configures an FST peer for IP address 150.136.64.98:

```
source-bridge fst-peername 150.136.64.98
```

Related Commands

To locate documentation of related commands, you can search online at www.cisco.com.

source-bridge remote-peer fst

source-bridge qllc-local-ack

Use the **source-bridge qllc-local-ack** global configuration command to enable or disable QLLC local acknowledgment for all QLLC conversion connections. The **no** form of this command disables this capability.

> **source-bridge qllc-local-ack**
> **no source-bridge qllc-local-ack**

Syntax Description

This command has no arguments or keywords.

Default

QLLC local acknowledgment is disabled.

Command Mode

Global configuration

Part II

Command Reference

Usage Guidelines

This command first appeared in Cisco IOS Release 10.3.

In a remote source-route bridged topology, QLLC local acknowledgment is used to configure the QLLC conversion router (connecting the remote X.25 devices) to exchange local acknowledgment information with the Token Ring router (on the Token Ring side of the cloud). This Token Ring device has been configured for LLC2 local acknowledgment using the **source-bridge remote peer tcp local-ack** command.

You only have to issue the **source-bridge qllc-local-ack** command on the QLLC conversion router. When this command is issued, all of the QLLC conversion sessions are locally acknowledged at the Token Ring interface of the Token Ring router with which it is communicating using QLLC conversion.

Example

The following configuration indicates that the local router (131.108.2.2) QLLC conversion sessions will be locally acknowledged at the remote router:

```
source-bridge ring-group 100
source-bridge remote-peer 100 tcp 131.108.1.1 local-ack
source-bridge remote-peer 100 tcp 131.108.2.2
source-bridge qllc-local-ack
```

Related Commands

To locate documentation of related commands, you can search online at www.cisco.com.

source-bridge remote-peer tcp
source-bridge ring-group

source-bridge remote-peer fst

Use the **source-bridge remote-peer fst** global configuration command to specify a Fast-Sequenced Transport (FST) encapsulation connection. Use the **no** form of this command to disable the previous assignments.

> **source-bridge remote-peer** *ring-group* **fst** *ip-address* [**lf** *size*] [**version** *number*]
> **no source-bridge remote-peer** *ring-group* **fst** *ip-address*

Syntax	Description
ring-group	Ring group number. This ring group number must match the number you have specified with the **source-bridge ring-group** command. The valid range is 1 to 4095.
ip-address	IP address of the remote peer with which the router will communicate.

Syntax	Description
lf *size*	(Optional) Maximum size frame to be sent to this remote peer. Cisco IOS software negotiates all transit routes down to this size or lower. Use this argument to prevent timeouts in end hosts by reducing the amount of data they have to transmit in a fixed interval. The legal values for this argument are 516, 1500, 2052, 4472, 8144, 11,407, and 17,800 bytes.
version *number*	(Optional) Forces RSRB protocol version number for the remote peer. Because all FST peers support version 2 RSRB, the **version** keyword is always specified.

Default

No FST encapsulation connection is specified.

Command Mode

Global configuration

Usage Guidelines

This command first appeared in Cisco IOS Release 10.0. The **version** *number* option first appeared in Cisco IOS Release 10.3.

The two peers using the serial-transport method will only function correctly if there are routers at the end of the serial line that have been configured to use the serial transport. The peers must also belong to the same ring group.

Example

In the following example, the **source-bridge fst-peername** command specifies an IP address of 150.136.64.98 for the local router. The **source-bridge ring-group** command assigns the router to a ring group. The **source-bridge remote-peer fst** command specifies ring group number 100 for the remote peer at IP address 150.136.64.97.

```
source-bridge fst-peername 150.136.64.98
source-bridge ring-group 100
source-bridge remote-peer 100 fst 150.136.64.97 version 2 RSRB
```

Related Commands

To locate documentation of related commands, you can search online at www.cisco.com.

source-bridge
source-bridge fst-peername
source-bridge remote-peer interface
source-bridge remote-peer tcp

source-bridge remote-peer interface

Use the **source-bridge remote-peer interface** global configuration command when specifying a point-to-point direct encapsulation connection. Use the **no** form of this command to disable previous interface assignments.

> **source-bridge remote-peer** *ring-group* **interface** *interface-name* [*mac-address*]
> [**lf** *size*]
> **no source-bridge remote-peer** *ring-group* **interface** *interface-name*

Syntax	Description
ring-group	Ring group number. This ring group number must match the number you have specified with the **source-bridge ring-group** command. The valid range is 1 to 4095.
interface-name	Name of the serial interface over which to send source-route bridged traffic.
mac-address	(Optional) MAC address for the interface you specify using the *interface-name* argument. This argument is required for nonserial interfaces. You can obtain the value of this MAC address by using the **show interfaces** command, and then scanning the display for the interface specified by *interface-name*.
lf *size*	(Optional) Maximum size frame to be sent to this remote peer. Cisco IOS software negotiates all transit routes down to this size or lower. This argument is useful in preventing timeouts in end hosts by reducing the amount of data they have to transmit in a fixed interval. The legal values for this argument are 516, 1500, 2052, 4472, 8144, 11,407, and 17,800 bytes.

Default

No point-to-point direct encapsulation connection is specified.

Command Mode

Global configuration

Usage Guidelines

This command first appeared in Cisco IOS Release 10.0.

Use this command to identify the interface over which to send source-route bridged traffic to another router/bridge in the ring group. A serial interface does not require that you include a MAC-level address; all other types of interfaces do require MAC addresses.

It is possible to mix all types of transport methods within the same ring group.

NOTE	The two peers using the serial-transport method will only function correctly if there are routers at the end of the serial line that have been configured to use the serial transport. The peers must also belong to the same ring group.

Example

The following example shows how to send source-route bridged traffic over serial interface 0 and Ethernet interface 0:

```
! send source-route bridged traffic over serial 0
source-bridge remote-peer 5 interface serial 0
! specify MAC address for source-route bridged traffic on Ethernet 0
source-bridge remote-peer 5 interface ethernet 0 0000.0c00.1234
```

Related Commands

To locate documentation of related commands, you can search online at www.cisco.com.

show interfaces
source-bridge remote-peer tcp

source-bridge remote-peer tcp

Use the **source-bridge remote-peer tcp** global configuration command to identify the IP address of a peer in the ring group with which to exchange source-bridge traffic using TCP. Use the **no** form of this command to remove a remote peer for the specified ring group.

> **source-bridge remote-peer** *ring-group* **tcp** *ip-address* [**lf** *size*] [**local-ack**] [**priority**]
> **no source-bridge remote-peer** *ring-group* **tcp** *ip-address*

Syntax	Description
ring-group	Ring group number. This ring group number must match the number you have specified with the **source-bridge ring-group** command. The valid range is 1 to 4095.
ip-address	IP address of the remote peer with which the router will communicate.
lf *size*	(Optional) Maximum size frame to be sent to this remote peer. Cisco IOS software negotiates all transit routes down to this size or lower. Use this argument to prevent timeouts in end hosts by reducing the amount of data they have to transmit in a fixed interval. The valid values for this argument are 516, 1500, 2052, 4472, 8144, 11,407, and 17,800 bytes.
local-ack	(Optional) LLC2 sessions destined for a specific remote peer are to be locally terminated and acknowledged. Local acknowledgment should be used for LLC2 sessions going to this remote peer.
priority	(Optional) Enables prioritization over a TCP network. You must specify the keyword **local-ack** earlier in the same **source-bridge remote-peer** command. The keyword **priority** is a prerequisite for features such as SNA class of service (CoS) and SNA logical unit (LU) address prioritization over a TCP network.

Default
No IP address is identified.

Command Mode
Global configuration

Usage Guidelines
This command first appeared in Cisco IOS Release 10.0.

If you configure one peer for LLC2 local acknowledgment, you need to configure both peers for LLC2 local acknowledgment. If only one peer is so configured, unpredictable (and undesirable) results will occur.

The two peers using the serial-transport method will only function correctly if there are routers at the end of the serial line that have been configured to use the serial transport. The peers must also belong to the same ring group.

Examples

In the following example, the remote peer with IP address 131.108.2.291 belongs to ring group 5. It also uses LLC2 local acknowledgment, priority, and RSRB protocol version 2.

```
! identify the ring group as 5
source-bridge ring-group 5
! remote peer at IP address 131.108.2.291 belongs to ring group 5, uses
! tcp as the transport, is set up for local acknowledgment, uses
! priority, and uses RSRB protocol form of this command
source-bridge remote-peer 5 tcp 131.108.2.291 local-ack priority
```

The following example shows how to locally administer and acknowledge LLC2 sessions destined for a specific remote peer:

```
! identify the ring group as 100
source-bridge ring-group 100
! remote peer at IP address 1.1.1.1 does not use local acknowledgment
source-bridge remote-peer 100 tcp 1.1.1.1
! remote peer at IP address 1.1.1.2 uses local acknowledgment
source-bridge remote-peer 100 tcp 1.1.1.2 local-ack
!
interface tokenring 0
 source-bridge 1 1 100
```

Sessions between a device on Token Ring 0 that must go through remote peer 1.1.1.2 use local acknowledgment for LLC2, but sessions that go through remote peer 1.1.1.1 do not use local acknowledgment (that is, they "pass through").

Related Commands

To locate documentation of related commands, you can search online at www.cisco.com.

source-bridge remote-peer fst
source-bridge remote-peer interface

source-bridge ring-group

Use the **source-bridge ring-group** global configuration command to define or remove a ring group from the configuration. Use the **no** form of this command to cancel previous assignments.

> **source-bridge ring-group** *ring-group* [*virtual-mac-address*]
> **no source-bridge ring-group** *ring-group* [*virtual-mac-address*]

Syntax	Description
ring-group	Ring group number. The valid range is 1 to 4095.

Syntax	Description
virtual-mac-address	(Optional) 12-digit hexadecimal string written as a dotted triplet (for example, 0010.0a00.20a6).

Default

No ring group is defined.

Command Mode

Global configuration

Usage Guidelines

This command first appeared in Cisco IOS Release 10.0.

To configure a source-route bridge with more than two network interfaces, the *ring-group* concept is used. A ring group is a collection of Token Ring interfaces in one or more routers that are collectively treated as a virtual ring. The ring group is denoted by a ring number that must be unique for the network. The ring group's number is used just like a physical ring number, showing up in any route descriptors contained in packets being bridged.

To configure a specific interface as part of a ring group, its target ring number parameter is set to the ring group number specified in this command. Do not use the number 0. It is reserved to represent the local ring.

To avoid an address conflict on the virtual MAC address, use a locally administered address in the form 4000.*xxxx.xxxx*.

Example

In the following example, multiple Token Rings are source-route bridged to one another through a single router/bridge. These Token Rings are all part of ring group 7.

```
! all token rings attached to this bridge/router are part of ring group 7
source-bridge ring-group 7
!
interface tokenring 0
 source-bridge 1000 1 7
!
interface tokenring 1
 source-bridge 1001 1 7
!
interface tokenring 2
 source-bridge 1002 1 7
!
interface tokenring 3
 source-bridge 1003 1 7
```

Related Commands

To locate documentation of related commands, you can search online at www.cisco.com.

source-bridge

source-bridge sdllc-local-ack

Use the **source-bridge sdllc-local-ack** global configuration command to activate local acknowledgment for SDLLC sessions on a particular interface. Use the **no** form of this command to deactivate local acknowledgment for SDLLC sessions.

> **source-bridge sdllc-local-ack**
> **no source-bridge sdllc-local-ack**

Syntax Description

This command has no arguments or keywords.

Default

Disabled

Command Mode

Global configuration

Usage Guidelines

This command first appeared in Cisco IOS Release 10.0.

This command must be issued only on a router with a serial interface. Once the command is issued, all SDLLC sessions between the two devices will be locally acknowledged. You cannot selectively choose which SDLLC sessions are to be locally acknowledged and which are not. Also, local acknowledgment is not supported when the LLC2 station is attached to Ethernet rather than to Token Ring.

NOTE   You must use the TCP encapsulation option if you use local acknowledgment for SDLLC.

Example

The following example activates local acknowledgment for SDLLC sessions:

```
source-bridge ring-group 100
source-bridge remote-peer 100 tcp 131.108.1.1 local-ack
source-bridge remote-peer 100 tcp 131.108.2.2
source-bridge sdllc-local-ack
```

x25 map qllc

Use the **x25 map qllc** interface configuration command to specify the X.121 address of the remote X.25 device with which you plan to communicate using QLLC conversion. The **no** form of this command disables QLLC conversion to this X.121 address.

> **x25 map qllc** *virtual-mac-addr x121-addr* [*x25-map-options*]
> **no x25 map qllc** *virtual-mac-addr x121-addr* [*x25-map-options*]

Syntax	Description
virtual-mac-addr	Virtual MAC address.
x121-addr	X.121 address of the remote X.25 device you are associating with this virtual MAC address. It can be from 1 to 15 digits long.
x25-map-options	(Optional) Additional functionality that can be specified for originated calls. It can be any of the options listed in Table 16-5.

Default

No association is made.

Command Mode

Interface configuration

Usage Guidelines

This command first appeared in Cisco IOS Release 10.3.

The central notion that binds the QLLC conversion interface to the X.25 and SRB facilities is the X.25 address map. For each remote client, an X.121 address is associated with a virtual MAC address. The rest of the configuration is specified by using the virtual Token Ring address to refer to the connection.

When a Token Ring device wishes to open communications with another device, it will send the request to the address it knows, which is the MAC address. Cisco IOS software accepts this connection request and must transform it into a known X.121 address. The **x25 map qllc** command matches the MAC address with the X.121 address.

You must enter a mapping for each X.25 device with which the router will exchange traffic.

All QLLC conversion commands use the *virtual-mac-addr* parameter that you define with the **x25 map qllc** command to refer to the connection.

You use the **x25 map qllc** command in conjunction with the **qllc srb** command.

Table 16-5 shows the possible values for the *x25-map-options* argument.

Table 16-5 *X.25 Map Options*

Option	Description
compress	Specifies that X.25 payload compression be used for mapping the traffic to this host. Each virtual circuit established for compressed traffic uses a significant amount of memory (for a table of learned data patterns) and for computation (for compression and decompression of all data). Cisco recommends that compression be used with careful consideration to its impact on overall performance.
method {cisco | ietf | snap | multi}	Specifies the encapsulation method. The choices are as follows: • **cisco**—Cisco's proprietary encapsulation; not available if more than one protocol is to be carried. • **ietf**—Default RFC 1356 operation: protocol identification of single-protocol virtual circuits and protocol identification within multiprotocol virtual circuits uses the standard encoding, which is compatible with RFC 877. Multiprotocol virtual circuits are used only if needed. • **snap**—RFC 1356 operation where IP is identified with SNAP rather than the standard IETF method (the standard method is compatible with RFC 877). • **multi**—Forces a map that specifies a single protocol to set up a multiprotocol virtual circuit when a call is originated; also forces a single-protocol PVC to use multiprotocol data identification methods for all datagrams sent and received.
no-incoming	Uses the map only to originate calls.
no-outgoing	Does not originate calls when using the map.
idle *minutes*	Specifies an idle timeout for calls other than the interface default; 0 minutes disables the idle timeout.
reverse	Specifies reverse charging for outgoing calls.
accept-reverse	Causes Cisco IOS software to accept incoming reverse-charged calls. If this option is not present, Cisco IOS software clears reverse-charged calls unless the interface accepts all reverse-charged calls.

Continues

Table 16-5 *X.25 Map Options (Continued)*

Option	Description
broadcast	Causes Cisco IOS software to direct any broadcasts sent through this interface to the specified X.121 address. This option also simplifies the configuration of OSPF; see the section "Usage Guidelines" for more details.
cug *group-number*	Specifies a closed user group number (from 1 to 99) for the mapping in an outgoing call.
nvc *count*	Sets the maximum number of virtual circuits for this map or host. The default *count* is the **x25 nvc** setting of the interface. A maximum number of eight virtual circuits can be configured for each map. Compressed TCP may use only one virtual circuit.
packetsize *in-size out-size*	Proposes maximum input packet size (*in-size*) and maximum output packet size (*out-size*) for an outgoing call. Both values typically are the same and must be one of the following values: 16, 32, 64, 128, 256, 512, 1024, 2048, or 4096.
windowsize *in-size out-size*	Proposes the packet count for input window (*in-size*) and output window (*out-size*) for an outgoing call. Both values typically are the same, must be in the range 1 to 127, and must be less than the value set by the **x25 modulo** command.
throughput *in out*	Sets the requested throughput class values for input (*in*) and output (*out*) throughput across the network for an outgoing call. Values for *in* and *out* are in bits per second (bps) and range from 75 to 48,000 bps.
transit-delay *milliseconds*	Specifies the transit delay value in milliseconds (0 to 65,534) for an outgoing call, for networks that support transit delay.
nuid *username password*	Specifies that a network user ID (NUID) facility be sent in the outgoing call with the specified Terminal Access Controller Access Control System (TACACS) username and password (in a format defined by Cisco). This option should be used only when connecting to another Cisco router. The combined length of the username and password should not exceed 127 characters.
nudata *string*	Specifies the network user identification in a format determined by the network administrator (as allowed by the standards). This option is provided for connect–ing to non-Cisco equipment that requires an NUID facility. The string should not exceed 130 characters and must be enclosed in quotation marks (" ") if there are any spaces present.
roa *name*	Specifies the name defined by the **x25 roa** command for a list of transit Recognized Operating Agencies (ROAs) to use in outgoing Call Request packets.
passive	Specifies that the X.25 interface should send compressed outgoing TCP datagrams only if they were already compressed when they were received. This option is available only for compressed TCP maps.

Example

In the following example, the **x25 map qllc** command is used to associate the remote X.25 device at X.121 address 31104150101 with the virtual MAC address 0100.000.0001:

```
interface serial 0
 encapsulation x25
 x25 address 31102120100
 x25 map qllc 0100.0000.0001 31104150101
 qllc srb 0100.0000.0001 201 100
```

Related Commands

To locate documentation of related commands, you can search online at www.cisco.com.

qllc accept-all-calls
qllc srb

x25 pvc qllc

Use the **x25 pvc qllc** interface configuration command to associate a virtual MAC address with a PVC for communication using QLLC conversion. The **no** form of this command removes the association.

> **x25 pvc** *circuit* **qllc** *x121-address* [*x25-map-options*]
> **no x25 pvc** *circuit* **qllc** *x121-address* [*x25-map-options*]

Syntax	Description
circuit	PVC you are associating with the virtual MAC address. This must be lower than any number assigned to switched virtual circuits.
x121-address	X.121 address.
x25-map-options	(Optional) Additional functionality that can be specified for originated calls. It can be any of the options listed in Table 16-5.

Default

No association is made.

Command Mode

Interface configuration

Usage Guidelines

This command first appeared in Cisco IOS Release 11.0.

When a Token Ring device wishes to communicate with another device, it will send the request to the address it knows, which is the MAC address. Cisco IOS software accepts this connection request and transforms it into the known X.121 address and virtual circuit. You must use the **x25 map qllc** command to specify the required protocol-to-X.121 address mapping before you use the **x25 pvc qllc** command. The **x25 map qllc** command associates the MAC address with the X.121 address, and the **x25 pvc qllc** command further associates that address with a known PVC.

You use the **x25 pvc** command in conjunction with the **x25 map qllc** and **qllc srb** commands.

Example

In the following example, the **x25 pvc qllc** command associates the virtual MAC address 0100.0000.0001, as defined in the previous **x25 map qllc** command entry, with PVC 3:

```
interface serial 0
 encapsulation x25
 x25 address 31102120100
 x25 map qllc 0100.0000.0001 31104150101
 x25 pvc 3 qllc 0100.0000.0001
```

Related Commands

To locate documentation of related commands, you can search online at www.cisco.com.

qllc srb
x25 map qllc

Configuring DSPU and SNA Service Point Support

This chapter describes Cisco IOS support for Systems Network Architecture (SNA) downstream physical unit (DSPU) devices and SNA Service Point. For a complete description of the DSPU and SNA Service Point commands mentioned in this chapter, refer to Chapter 18, "DSPU and SNA Service Point Configuration Commands." To locate documentation of other commands that appear in this chapter, you can search online at www.cisco.com.

DSPU Configuration Task List

To configure DSPU, perform the tasks in the following sections. The last two tasks are optional.

- Define DSPU Upstream Hosts
- Define Downstream PUs
- Define DSPU LUs
- Configure DSPU to Use a Data-Link Control
- Define the Number of Outstanding, Unacknowledged Activation RUs
- Configure SNA Service Point Support
- Monitor DSPU and SNA Service Point Feature Status

See the end of this chapter for the section, "DSPU and SNA Service Point Configuration Examples."

Define DSPU Upstream Hosts

The upstream host provides logical units (LUs) that Cisco IOS software assigns for use by its downstream PUs. Because one upstream host can only provide a maximum of 255 LUs, the DSPU feature supports multiple hosts. Multiple upstream host support allows the DSPU router to provide more than 255 LUs for use by its downstream PUs.

To define a DSPU host over Token Ring, Ethernet, Fiber Distributed Data Interface (FDDI), remote source-route bridging (RSRB), or virtual data-link control connections, use the following command in global configuration mode:

Command	Purpose
dspu host *host-name* **xid-snd** *xid* **rmac** *remote-mac* [**rsap** *remote-sap*] [**lsap** *local-sap*] [**interface** *slot/port*] [**window** *window-size*] [**maxiframe** *max-iframe*] [**retries** *retry-count*] [**retry-timeout** *retry-timeout*] [**focalpoint**]	Defines a DSPU host over Token Ring, Ethernet, FDDI, RSRB, or virtual data-link control connections.

To define a DSPU host over a Synchronous Data Link Control (SDLC) connection, use the following command in global configuration mode:

Command	Purpose
dspu host *host-name* **xid-snd** *xid* **sdlc** *sdlc-addr* [**interface** *slot/port*] [**window** *window-size*] [**maxiframe** *max-iframe*] [**retries** *retry-count*] [**retry-timeout** *retry-timeout*] [**focalpoint**]	Defines a DSPU host over an SDLC connection.

To define a DSPU host over an X.25/Qualified Logical Link Control (QLLC) connection, use the following command in global configuration mode:

Command	Purpose
dspu host *host-name* **xid-snd** *xid* **x25** *remote-x121-addr* [**qllc** *local-x121-subaddr*] [**interface** *slot/port*] [**window** *window-size*] [**maxiframe** *max-iframe*] [**retries** *retry-count*] [**retry-timeout** *retry-timeout*] [**focalpoint**]	Defines a DSPU host over an X.25/QLLC connection.

To define a DSPU host over a Frame Relay connection, use the following command in global configuration mode:

Command	Purpose
dspu host *host-name* **xid-snd** *xid* **dlci** *dlci-number* [**rsap** *remote-sap*] [**lsap** *local-sap*] [**interface** *slot/port*] [**window** *window-size*] [**maxiframe** *max-iframe*] [**retries** *retry-count*] [**retry-timeout** *retry-timeout*] [**focalpoint**]	Defines a DSPU host over a Frame Relay connection.

Define Downstream PUs

To define the downstream PUs, perform either of the tasks in the following sections, depending on your circumstances:

● Explicitly Define a Downstream PU

● Enable the Default PU Option

Explicitly Define a Downstream PU

Explicitly define a downstream PU if you require Cisco IOS software to perform verification checking on incoming downstream connections or to initiate an outgoing downstream connection.

For Cisco IOS 11.3 and above, the number of DSPU PUs you can configure is 1024.

To explicitly define a downstream PU over Token Ring, Ethernet, FDDI, RSRB, virtual data-link control, or native client interface architecture (NCIA) connections, use the following command in global configuration mode:

Command	Purpose
dspu pu *pu-name* [**rmac** *remote-mac*] [**rsap** *remote-sap*] [**lsap** *local-sap*] [**xid-rcv** *xid*] [**interface** *slot/port*] [**window** *window-size*] [**maxiframe** *max-iframe*] [**retries** *retry-count*] [**retry-timeout** *retry-timeout*]	Explicitly defines a downstream PU over Token Ring, Ethernet, FDDI, RSRB, virtual data-link control, or NCIA connections.

To explicitly define a downstream PU over an SDLC connection, use the following command in global configuration mode:

Command	Purpose
dspu pu *pu-name* **sdlc** *sdlc-addr* [**xid-rcv** *xid*] [**interface** *slot/port*] [**window** *window-size*] [**maxiframe** *max-iframe*] [**retries** *retry-count*] [**retry-timeout** *retry-timeout*]	Explicitly defines a downstream PU over an SDLC connection.

To explicitly define a downstream PU over an X.25/QLLC connection, use the following command in global configuration mode:

Command	Purpose
dspu pu *pu-name* **x25** *remote-x121-addr* [**qllc** *local-x121-subaddr*] [**xid-rcv** *xid*] [**interface** *slot/port*] [**window** *window-size*] [**maxiframe** *max-iframe*] [**retries** *retry-count*] [**retry-timeout** *retry-timeout*]	Explicitly defines a downstream PU over an X.25/QLLC connection.

To explicitly define a downstream PU over a Frame Relay connection, use the following command in global configuration mode:

Command	Purpose
dspu pu *pu-name* **dlci** *dlci-number* [**rsap** *remote-sap*] [**lsap** *local-sap*] [**xid-rcv** *xid*] [**interface** *type slot/port*] [**window** *window-size*] [**maxiframe** *max-iframe*] [**retries** *retry-count*] [**retry-timeout** *retry-timeout*]	Explicitly defines a downstream PU over a Frame Relay connection.

If Cisco IOS software will perform verification checking on incoming downstream connections, there are several combinations of parameters that you can configure for verification matching:

- Match on xid-rcv value only.

  User may define a downstream PU using only the xid-rcv value so that any connecting PU that specifies the value of the configured XID will match that PU definition.

- Match on xid-rcv and interface values.

  User may define a downstream PU using the xid-rcv and interface values so that any PU connecting into the configured interface that specifies the value of the configured XID will match the PU definition.

- Match on addressing values only.

  User may define a downstream PU using only the addressing values (RMAC/RSAP/LSAP, SDLC, DLCI/RSAP/LSAP, or X25/QLLC) so that any connecting PU with addressing that matches the configured addressing will match that PU definition.

- Match on xid-rcv and addressing values.

  User may define a downstream PU using the xid-rcv and addressing values (RMAC/RSAP/LSAP, SDLC, DLCI/RSAP/LSAP, or X25/QLLC) so that any connecting PU with addressing that matches the configured addressing and specifies the value of the configured xid will match the PU definition.

- Match on addressing and interface values.

  User may define a downstream PU using the interface and addressing values (RMAC/RSAP/LSAP, SDLC, DLCI/RSAP/LSAP, or X25/QLLC) so that any PU connecting into the configured interface with addressing that matches the configured addressing will match the PU definition.

- Match on xid, addressing, and interface values.

  User may define a downstream PU using the xid, interface, and addressing parameters (RMAC/ RSAP/LSAP, SDLC, DLCI/RSAP/LSAP, or X25/QLLC) so that any PU connecting into the configured interface with addressing that matches the configured addressing and specifies the value of the configured xid will match the PU definition.

Cisco IOS software rejects any incoming downstream connections that do not match the parameters of a defined downstream PU unless the default PU option is also enabled.

Enable the Default PU Option

Configure the DSPU default PU option if you do not require Cisco IOS software to verify incoming downstream connections. The default PU option allows the software to accept incoming downstream connections without an explicit definition for the downstream PU.

To enable the default PU option, use the following command in global configuration mode:

Command	Purpose
dspu default-pu [**window** *window-size*] [**maxiframe** *max-iframe*]	Enables the default PU option.

Define DSPU LUs

Specify the LU routing algorithm used to map the upstream LUs to the downstream LUs and to define all LUs for each upstream and downstream PU.

The DSPU feature assigns upstream LUs to downstream LUs based on the selected LU routing algorithm and performs the mapping necessary for SNA data transfer.

The DSPU feature supports two alternative mapping algorithms that are described in the following sections:

- Define Dedicated LU Routing
- Define Pooled LU Routing

An upstream host PU or downstream PU can support up to 255 LU sessions. The DSPU feature allows each LU to be individually configured for either dedicated LU routing or pooled LU routing.

Define Dedicated LU Routing

You can configure an upstream LU so that it is reserved, or dedicated, for use by a specific downstream LU.

To define a dedicated LU or a range of dedicated LUs for an upstream host and downstream PU, use the following command in global configuration mode:

Command	Purpose
dspu lu *lu-start* [*lu-end*] {**host** *host-name host-lu-start* | **pool** *pool-name*} [**pu** *pu-name*]	Defines a dedicated LU or a range of dedicated LUs for a downstream PU.

See the "Dedicated LU Routing Example" section later in this chapter for an example of dedicated LU routing.

Define Pooled LU Routing

You can configure an upstream host LU so that it is a member of a pool of LUs. When a downstream connection is established and the downstream LU is configured as a pooled LU, Cisco IOS software selects an upstream LU from the pool for assignment to the downstream LU.

Pooled LU routing allows a limited number of upstream host LUs to be shared (at different times) among many downstream LUs.

To define a host LU or a range of host LUs in an LU pool, use the following command in global configuration mode:

Command	Purpose
dspu pool *pool-name* **host** *host-name* **lu** *lu-start* [*lu-end*] [**inactivity-timeout** *inactivity-minutes*]	Defines a host LU or a range of host LUs in an LU pool.

You can configure a downstream LU as a pooled LU. When a downstream connection is established and the downstream LU is configured as a pooled LU, the software selects an upstream LU from the specified pool for assignment to the downstream LU.

To define a pooled LU or a range of pooled LUs for a downstream PU, use the following command in global configuration mode:

Command	Purpose
dspu lu *lu-start* [*lu-end*] **pool** *pool-name* **pu** *pu-name*	Defines a pooled LU or a range of pooled LUs for a downstream PU.

See the "Pooled LU Routing Example" section later in this chapter for an example of pooled LU routing.

Configure DSPU to Use a Data-Link Control

The final step in configuring DSPU is to define the data-link controls that will be used for upstream host and downstream PU connections.

The DSPU feature supports the data-link controls described in the following sections:

- Configure DSPU to Use Token Ring, Ethernet, or FDDI

- Configure DSPU to Use RSRB

- Configure DSPU to Use RSRB with Local Acknowledgment

- Configure DSPU to Use Virtual Data-Link Control

- Configure DSPU to Use SDLC

- Configure DSPU to Use QLLC

- Configure DSPU to Use Frame Relay

- Configure DSPU to Use NCIA

Configure DSPU to Use Token Ring, Ethernet, or FDDI

You can configure DSPU to use the Token Ring, Ethernet, or FDDI data-link controls by enabling a service access point (SAP) address on the interface. Each interface can support up to 254 local SAPs enabled for either upstream or downstream connections; a local SAP cannot be enabled for both upstream and downstream connections on the same interface.

To enable a local SAP on the Token Ring, Ethernet, or FDDI interfaces for use by upstream hosts, use the following command in interface configuration mode:

Command	Purpose
dspu enable-host [**lsap** *local-sap*]	Enables local SAP for upstream hosts.

To enable a local SAP on the Token Ring, Ethernet, or FDDI interfaces for use by downstream PUs, use the following command in interface configuration mode:

Command	Purpose
dspu enable-pu [**lsap** *local-sap*]	Enables local SAP for downstream PUs.

Once a local SAP is enabled, it is ready to accept incoming connection attempts from the remote device (upstream host or downstream PU). Alternatively, initiate an outgoing connection to the remote device by using the following command in interface configuration mode:

Command	Purpose
dspu start {*host-name* | *pu-name*}	Initiates a connection with an upstream host or a downstream PU via Token Ring or Ethernet.

Configure DSPU to Use RSRB

To configure DSPU to use RSRB, you must create a DSPU/RSRB data-link control.

Cisco's implementation of DSPU/RSRB data-link control uses the concept of a virtual Token Ring device residing on a virtual Token Ring to represent Cisco IOS software to upstream hosts and downstream PUs across an RSRB network. This is similar to Cisco's implementation of SDLLC.

Because the upstream host and downstream PU expects its peer to also be on a Token Ring, you must assign a virtual Token Ring address (the DSPU virtual MAC address) to the DSPU/RSRB data-link control. Like real Token Ring addresses, the DSPU virtual MAC address must be unique across the network.

In addition to assigning the DSPU virtual MAC address, you must also assign a DSPU virtual ring number to the DSPU/RSRB data-link control. The DSPU virtual ring number must be unique across the network.

NOTE	The DSPU virtual ring number is a different number from the virtual ring group numbers that you use to configure RSRB and multiport bridging.

The combination of the DSPU virtual MAC address and the DSPU virtual ring number identifies the DSPU/RSRB data-link control interface to the rest of an RSRB network.

When an end station (either an upstream host or a downstream PU) attempts to connect with the DSPU software, the following events occur:

1   The end station sends explorer packets with the locally administered MAC address on the router interface to which the end station is connected.

2   The router configured with that locally administered MAC address or with the hardware MAC address intercepts the frame, fills in the DSPU virtual ring number and the DSPU bridge number in the routing information field (RIF), and sends a response to the end station.

3   The end station establishes a session with the DSPU router.

To define the DSPU/RSRB data-link control interface, use the following commands in global configuration mode:

Step	Command	Purpose
1	**source-bridge ring-group** *ring-group* [*virtual-mac-address*]	Defines an RSRB ring group.
2	**source-bridge remote-peer** *ring-group* **tcp** *ip-address* **local-ack**	Defines a remote peer with the local acknowledgment feature.

Step	Command	Purpose
3	**dspu rsrb** *local-virtual-ring bridge-number target-virtual-ring virtual-macaddr*	Defines the DSPU/RSRB interface.

After you define the DSPU RSRB data-link control, configure DSPU to use the RSRB data-link control by enabling a local SAP for either upstream or downstream connections.

To enable a local SAP on RSRB for use by upstream hosts, use the following command in global configuration mode:

Command	Purpose
dspu rsrb enable-host [**lsap** *local-sap*]	Enables local SAP for upstream hosts.

To enable a local SAP on RSRB for use by downstream PUs, use the following command in global configuration mode:

Command	Purpose
dspu rsrb enable-pu [**lsap** *local-sap*]	Enables local SAP for downstream PUs.

Once a local SAP is enabled, it is ready to accept incoming connection attempts from the remote device (upstream host or downstream PU) over RSRB. Alternatively, initiate an outgoing connection to the remote device by using the following command in global configuration mode:

Command	Purpose
dspu rsrb start {*host-name* | *pu-name*}	Initiates a connection with an upstream host or a downstream PU via RSRB.

Configure DSPU to Use RSRB with Local Acknowledgment

Configuring DSPU to use RSRB with local acknowledgment is identical to configuring RSRB with local acknowledgment. If you add the **local-ack** keyword to the source-bridge remote-peer configuration command, DSPU will use local acknowledgment for any end stations that connect to DSPU from that peer.

To configure DSPU to use RSRB with local acknowledgment, use the following commands in global configuration mode:

Step	Command	Purpose
1	**source-bridge ring-group** *ring-group* [*virtual-mac-address*]	Defines an RSRB ring group.
2	**source-bridge remote-peer** *ring-group* **tcp** *ip-address* **local-ack**	Defines a remote peer with the local acknowledgment feature.
3	**dspu rsrb** *local-virtual-ring bridge-number target-virtual-ring virtual-macaddr*	Defines the DSPU/RSRB interface.

Configure DSPU to Use Virtual Data-Link Control

To configure DSPU to use virtual data-link control, you must create a DSPU virtual data-link control interface.

Similar to our implementation of SDLLC, the DSPU virtual data-link control interface uses the concept of a virtual Token Ring device residing on a virtual Token Ring to represent Cisco IOS software to upstream hosts and downstream PUs across a network.

Because the upstream host and downstream PU expects its peer to also be on a Token Ring, you must assign a virtual Token Ring address (the DSPU virtual MAC address) to the DSPU virtual data-link control interface. Like real Token Ring addresses, the DSPU virtual MAC address must be unique across the network.

In addition to assigning the DSPU virtual MAC address, you must also identify the SRB virtual ring number with which the DSPU virtual MAC address will be associated. The SRB virtual ring number is set using the **source-bridge ring-group** command. This is documented in Chapter 4, "Source-Route Bridging Commands."

The combination of the DSPU virtual MAC address and the SRB virtual ring number identifies the DSPU virtual data-link control interface to the rest of the DLSw+ network.

When an end station (either an upstream host or a downstream PU) attempts to connect with the DSPU software, the following events occur:

1   The end station sends explorer packets with the locally administered MAC address on the router interface to which the end station is connected.

2   The router configured with that locally administered MAC address intercepts the frame, DLSw+ adjusts RIF, and sends a response to the end station.

3   The end station establishes a session with the DSPU router.

Prior to creating the DSPU virtual data-link control interface, you must also configure DLSw+ peers so that DLSw+ can provide the communication path. The commands for defining DLSw+ local and remote peers are documented in Chapter 10, "DLSw+ Configuration Commands."

To define the DSPU virtual data-link control interface, use the following command in global configuration mode:

Command	Purpose
dspu vdlc *ring-group virtual-mac-address*	Defines the DSPU virtual data-link control interface.

After you define the DSPU virtual data-link control interface, configure DSPU to use virtual data-link control by enabling a local SAP for either upstream or downstream connections.

To enable a local SAP on the virtual data-link control for use by upstream hosts, use the following command in global configuration mode:

Command	Purpose
dspu vdlc enable-host [**lsap** *local-sap*]	Enables local SAP for upstream hosts.

To enable a local SAP on the virtual data-link control for use by downstream PUs, use the following command in global configuration mode:

Command	Purpose
dspu vdlc enable-pu [**lsap** *local-sap*]	Enables local SAP for downstream PUs.

Once a local SAP is enabled, it is ready to accept incoming connection attempts from the remote device (upstream host or downstream PU) using virtual data-link control. Alternatively, initiate an outgoing connection to the remote device by using the following command in global configuration mode:

Command	Purpose
dspu vdlc start {*host-name*	*pu-name*}	Initiates a connection with an upstream host or a downstream PU via virtual data-link control.

Configure DSPU to Use SDLC

Before DSPU may be configured to use the SDLC data-link control, the serial interface must be defined for SDLC encapsulation and assigned an SDLC role.

To define the serial interface to use SDLC and specify the SDLC role, use the following commands in interface configuration mode:

Step	Command	Purpose
1	**encapsulation sdlc**	Enables SDLC encapsulation on the serial interface.
2	**sdlc role** {**none** | **primary** | **secondary** | **prim-xid-poll**}	Specifies the SDLC role of the router.

For the connection to be established without XID exchange, the SDLC role must be **primary** if DSPU will be initiating connections to the SDLC partner. The SDLC role must be **secondary** or **none** if the SDLC partner will be initiating connections with DSPU.

When an XID exchange is required, the SDLC role must be **prim-xid-poll** or **none** if DSPU will be initiating connections to the SDLC partner. The role must be **none** if the SDLC partner will be initiating connections with DSPU.

The SDLC address(es) used on the SDLC link must also be defined. If DSPU is configured to initiate the connection, then the SDLC address identifies the SDLC partner. If the remote SDLC device initiates the connection, then the SDLC address identifies the address for which a connection will be accepted.

To configure the SDLC address, use the following command in interface configuration mode:

Command	Purpose
sdlc address *hexbyte*	Defines the SDLC address.

Finally, the SDLC address must be enabled for use by DSPU. Each interface can support up to 255 SDLC addresses enabled for either upstream or downstream connections; an SDLC address cannot be enabled for both upstream and downstream connections on the same interface. If the SDLC role is **none**, there can be only one SDLC address on that interface.

To enable an SDLC address for use by upstream host connections, use the following command in interface configuration mode:

Command	Purpose
dspu enable-host sdlc *sdlc-address*	Enables the SDLC address for an upstream host.

To enable an SDLC address for use by downstream PU connections, use the following command in interface configuration mode:

Command	Purpose
dspu enable-pu sdlc *sdlc-address*	Enables the SDLC address for the downstream PU.

When the SDLC role is configured as **primary**, DSPU initiates a connection with the remote device by sending set normal response mode (SNRM) when the SDLC address is enabled for DSPU.

When the SDLC role is configured as **prim-xid-poll**, DSPU initiates a connection with the remote device by sending a NULL XID when the SDLC address is enabled for DSPU.

When the SDLC role is configured as **secondary**, DSPU will not be ready to respond to SNRM until a **dspu start** *pu-name* command is issued.

When the SDLC role is configured as **none**, DSPU is ready to respond to a received XID or SNRM when the SDLC address is enabled for DSPU; otherwise, the connection may be initiated by issuing the **dspu start** *pu-name* command.

To configure DSPU to respond to SNRM when the SDLC role is configured as **secondary**, or to initiate a connection when the SDLC role is configured as **none**, use the following command in interface configuration mode:

Command	Purpose
dspu start {*host-name* | *pu-name*}	Initiates a connection with a remote device when the SDLC role is configured as **secondary** or **none**.

Configure DSPU to Use QLLC

Before DSPU may be configured to use the QLLC data-link control, the serial interface must be defined for X.25 encapsulation and assigned an X.121 address.

To define the serial interface to use X.25, use the following commands in interface configuration mode:

Step	Command	Purpose
1	**encapsulation x25** [**dce**]	Enables X.25 encapsulation on the serial interface.
2	**x25 address** *x121-addr*	Defines an X.121 address.

X.25 routing must also be configured so that incoming calls to the local X.121 address can be appropriately routed to the serial interface and mapped into the QLLC data-link control.

To define X.25 routing, use the following commands in global configuration mode:

Step	Command	Purpose
1	**x25 routing**	Enables X.25 routing.
2	**x25 route** ^*local-x121-addr*.* **alias serial slot/port**	Enables routing of X.25 packets to the serial interface.

To define which calls get mapped into QLLC, use the following command in interface configuration mode:

Command	Purpose
x25 map qllc *x121-addr*	Defines the remote X.121 address for mapping into QLLC.

Finally, the local X.121 subaddress must be enabled for use by DSPU. An X.121 subaddress can be enabled for either upstream or downstream connections; an X.121 subaddress cannot be enabled for both upstream and downstream connections on the same interface.

To enable an X.121 subaddress for use by upstream host connections via QLLC, use the following command in interface configuration mode:

Command	Purpose
dspu enable-host qllc *x121-subaddress*	Enables an X.121 subaddress for an upstream host.

To enable an X.121 subaddress for use by downstream PU connections via QLLC, use the following command in interface configuration mode:

Command	Purpose
dspu enable-pu qllc *x121-subaddress*	Enables an X.121 subaddress for a downstream PU.

Once an X.121 subaddress is enabled, it is ready to accept incoming connection attempts from the remote device (upstream host or downstream PU) over QLLC. Alternatively, initiate an outgoing connection to the remote device by using the following command in interface configuration mode:

Command	Purpose
dspu start {*host-name*	*pu-name*}	Initiates a connection with an upstream host or a downstream PU via QLLC.

Configure DSPU to Use Frame Relay

Before DSPU may be configured to use the LLC2/Frame Relay data-link control, the serial interface must be defined for Frame Relay encapsulation.

To define the serial interface for Frame Relay encapsulation, use the following command in interface configuration mode:

Command	Purpose
encapsulation frame-relay ietf	Enables Frame Relay encapsulation on a serial interface.

The DLCI used on the Frame Relay link must be mapped into LLC2.

To configure the mapping of a DLCI into LLC2, use the following command in interface configuration mode:

Command	Purpose
frame-relay map llc2 *dlci-number*	Configures DLCI mapping into LLC2.

Finally, the local SAP address must be enabled for use by DSPU. A SAP address can be enabled for either upstream or downstream connections; a SAP address cannot be enabled for both upstream and downstream connections on the same interface.

To enable a local SAP on the LLC2/Frame Relay interface for use by upstream hosts, use the following command in interface configuration mode:

Command	Purpose
dspu enable-host [**lsap** *local-sap*]	Enables local SAP for upstream hosts.

To enable a local SAP for the LLC2/Frame Relay interface for use by downstream PUs, use the following command in interface configuration mode:

Command	Purpose
dspu enable-pu [**lsap** *local-sap*]	Enables local SAP for downstream PUs.

Once a local SAP is enabled, it is ready to accept incoming connection attempts from the remote device (upstream host or downstream PU) over Frame Relay. Alternatively, initiate an outgoing connection to the remote device by using the following command in interface configuration mode:

Command	Purpose
dspu start {*host-name*	*pu-name*}	Initiates a connection with an upstream host or a downstream PU via LLC2/Frame Relay.

Configure DSPU to Use NCIA

To configure DSPU to use NCIA, you must use the following commands:

● Configure the NCIA server as the underlying transport mechanism.

● Enable a local SAP on the NCIA server for use by downstream PUs.

To configure the NCIA server as the underlying transport mechanism, use the following command in global configuration mode:

Command	Purpose
dspu ncia *server-number*	Configures the NCIA server as the underlying transport mechanism.

To enable a local SAP on the NCIA server for use by downstream PUs, use the following command in global configuration mode:

Command	Purpose
dspu ncia enable-pu [**lsap** *local-sap*]	Enables local SAP for downstream PUs.

Define the Number of Outstanding, Unacknowledged Activation RUs

The DSPU feature allows you to define the number of activation request/response units (RUs), such as ACTLUs or DDDLU NMVTs, that can be sent by Cisco IOS software before waiting for responses from the remote PU.

The DSPU activation window provides pacing to avoid depleting the router buffer pool during PU activation. Increasing the window size allows more LUs to become active in a shorter amount of time (assuming the required buffers for activation RUs are available). Decreasing the window size limits the amount of buffers the DSPU may use during PU activation. Typically, you do not need to change the default window size.

To define the number of unacknowledged activation RUs that can be outstanding, use the following command in global configuration mode:

Command	Purpose
dspu activation-window *window-size*	Defines the number of unacknowledged activation RUs.

Configure SNA Service Point Support

Cisco implementation of SNA Service Point support includes support for three commands: Alerts, RUNCMD, and Vital Product Data support.

Alert support is provided as Cisco IOS software sends unsolicited Alerts to NetView (or an equivalent network management application) at the host. This function occurs at the various router interfaces and protocol layers within the device.

RUNCMD support enables you to send commands to the router from the NetView console using the NetView RUNCMD facility, and the router sends the relevant replies back to the RUNCMD screen.

Vital Product Data support allows you to request Vital Product Data from the NetView console. The router replies to NetView with the relevant information.

To configure SNA Service Point support, perform the tasks in the following sections:

- Define a Link to an SNA Host
- Configure Service Point Support to Use a Data-Link Control
- Specify Names for All Attached LANs
- Specify the Physical Location of the Router

NOTE	You do not need to perform the tasks in the next section if you have configured a DSPU host with the **focalpoint** parameter.

Define a Link to an SNA Host

To define a link to an SNA host over Token Ring, Ethernet, FDDI, RSRB, or virtual data-link control connections, use the following command in global configuration mode:

Command	Purpose
sna host *host-name* **xid-snd** *xid* **rmac** *remote-mac* [**rsap** *remote-sap*] [**lsap** *local-sap*] [**interface** *slot/port*] [**window** *window-size*] [**maxiframe** *max-iframe*] [**retries** *retry-count*] [**retry-timeout** *retry-timeout*] [**focalpoint**]	Defines a link to an SNA host over Token Ring, Ethernet, FDDI, RSRB, or virtual data-link control connections.

To define a link to an SNA host over an SDLC connection, use the following command in global configuration mode:

Command	Purpose
sna host *host-name* **xid-snd** *xid* **sdlc** *sdlc-addr* [**interface** *slot/port*] [**window** *window-size*] [**maxiframe** *max-iframe*] [**retries** *retry-count*] [**retry-timeout** *retry-timeout*] [**focalpoint**]	Defines a link to an SNA host over an SDLC connection.

To define a link to an SNA host over an X.25/QLLC connection, use the following command in global configuration mode:

Command	Purpose
sna host *host-name* **xid-snd** *xid* **x25** *remote-x121-addr* [**qllc** *local-x121-subaddr*] [**interface** *slot/port*] [**window** *window-size*] [**maxiframe** *max-iframe*] [**retries** *retry-count*] [**retry-timeout** *retry-timeout*] [**focalpoint**]	Defines a link to an SNA host over an X.25/ QLLC connection.

To define a link to an SNA host over a Frame Relay connection, use the following command in global configuration mode:

Command	Purpose
sna host *host-name* **xid-snd** *xid* **dlci** *dlci-number* [**rsap** *remote-sap*] [**lsap** *local-sap*] [**interface** *slot/port*] [**window** *window-size*] [**maxiframe** *max-iframe*] [**retries** *retry-count*] [**retry-timeout** *retry-timeout*] [**focalpoint**]	Defines a link to an SNA host over a Frame Relay connection.

Configure Service Point Support to Use a Data-Link Control

To configure Service Point to use a data-link control, perform the tasks in one of the following sections:

- Configure Service Point to Use Token Ring, Ethernet, or FDDI

- Configure Service Point to Use RSRB

- Configure Service Point to Use RSRB with Local Acknowledgment

- Configure Service Point to Use Virtual Data-Link Control

- Configure Service Point Support for Frame Relay

- Configure Service Point Support for SDLC

- Configure Service Point Support for X.25

NOTE   You do not need to perform this task if you have configured a DSPU host with the **focalpoint** parameter and have configured the DSPU host to use a data-link control.

Configure Service Point to Use Token Ring, Ethernet, or FDDI

To enable a local SAP on the Token Ring, Ethernet, or FDDI interfaces for use by SNA Service Point, use the following command in interface configuration mode:

Command	Purpose
sna enable-host [**lsap** *lsap-address*]	Enables local SAP for Service Point.

Once a local SAP is enabled, it is ready to accept incoming connection attempts from the remote host. Alternatively, initiate an outgoing connection to the remote host by using the following command in interface configuration mode:

Command	Purpose
sna start *host-name*	Initiates a connection with a host via Token Ring, Ethernet, or FDDI.

Configure Service Point to Use RSRB

To define the Service Point/RSRB data-link control interface, use the following commands in global configuration mode:

Step	Command	Purpose
1	**source-bridge ring-group** *ring-group* [*virtual-mac-address*]	Defines an RSRB ring group.
2	**sna rsrb** *local-virtual-ring bridge-number target-virtual-ring virtual-macaddr*	Defines the Service Point/RSRB interface.

To enable a local SAP on RSRB for use by hosts, use the following command in global configuration mode:

Command	Purpose
sna rsrb enable-host [**lsap** *local-sap*]	Enables local SAP for hosts.

Once a local SAP is enabled, it is ready to accept incoming connection attempts from the remote host over RSRB. Alternatively, initiate an outgoing connection to the remote host by using the following command in global configuration mode:

Command	Purpose
sna rsrb start *host-name*	Initiates a connection with a host via RSRB.

Configure Service Point to Use RSRB with Local Acknowledgment

To configure Service Point to use RSRB with local acknowledgment, use the following commands in global configuration mode:

Step	Command	Purpose
1	**source-bridge ring-group** *ring-group* [*virtual-mac-address*]	Defines an RSRB ring group.
2	**source-bridge remote-peer** *ring-group* **tcp** *ip-address* **local-ack**	Defines a remote peer with the local acknowledgment feature.
3	**sna rsrb** *local-virtual-ring bridge-number target-virtual-ring virtual-macaddr*	Defines the Service Point/RSRB interface.

Configure Service Point to Use Virtual Data-Link Control

To configure SNA Service Point to use virtual data-link control, you must create an SNA virtual data-link control interface.

Similar to our implementation of SDLLC, the SNA virtual data-link control interface uses the concept of a virtual Token Ring device residing on a virtual Token Ring to represent Cisco IOS software to upstream hosts and downstream PUs across a network.

Because the upstream host and downstream PU expect their peer to also be on a Token Ring, you must assign a virtual Token Ring address (the SNA virtual data-link control virtual MAC address) to the SNA virtual data-link control interface. Like real Token Ring addresses, the SNA virtual MAC address must be unique across the network.

You must also identify the SRB virtual ring number with which the SNA virtual MAC address will be associated. The SRB virtual ring number is set using the **source-bridge ring-group** command, which is documented in Chapter 4, "Source-Route Bridging Commands."

The combination of the SNA virtual MAC address and the SRB virtual ring number identifies the SNA virtual data-link control interface to the rest of the DLSw+ network.

When an end station (either an upstream host or a downstream PU) attempts to connect with the SNA Service Point software, the following events occur:

1 The end station sends explorer packets with the locally administered MAC address on the router interface to which the end station is connected.

2 The router configured with that locally administered MAC address intercepts the frame, DLSw+ adjusts the RIF and sends a response to the end station.

3 The end station establishes a session with the SNA Service Point router.

Prior to creating the SNA virtual data-link control interface, you must also configure DLSw+ peers so that DLSw+ can provide the communication path. The commands for defining DLSw+ local and remote peers are documented in Chapter 10, "DLSw+ Configuration Commands."

To define the Service Point virtual data-link control interface, use the following command in global configuration mode:

Command	Purpose
sna vdlc *ring-group virtual-mac-address*	Defines the Service Point virtual data-link control interface.

After you create the SNA virtual data-link control interface, configure SNA Service Point to use virtual data-link control by enabling a local SAP for upstream connections. To enable a local SAP on virtual data-link control for use by hosts, use the following command in global configuration mode:

Command	Purpose
sna vdlc enable-host [**lsap** *local-sap*]	Enables local SAP for hosts.

Once a local SAP is enabled, it is ready to accept incoming connection attempts from the remote host using virtual data-link control. Alternatively, initiate an outgoing connection to the remote host by using the following command in global configuration mode:

Command	Purpose
sna vdlc start *host-name*	Initiates a connection with a host via virtual data-link control.

Configure Service Point Support for Frame Relay

To configure Service Point support for Frame Relay, use the following commands in interface configuration mode:

Step	Command	Purpose
1	**frame-relay map llc2** *dlci-number*	Defines DLCI mapping into LLC2.
2	**sna enable-host lsap** *lsap-address*	Enables a local SAP for hosts.

Configure Service Point Support for SDLC

To configure Service Point support for SDLC, use the following commands in interface configuration mode:

Step	Command	Purpose
1	**sdlc role** {**none** | **primary** | **secondary** | **prim-xid-poll**}	Specifies the SDLC role of the router.
2	**sdlc address** *hexbyte*	Defines the SDLC address.
3	**sna enable-host sdlc** *sdlc-address*	Enables the SDLC address for the host.

Configure Service Point Support for X.25

To configure Service Point support for X.25, use the following commands in interface configuration mode:

Step	Command	Purpose
1	**x25 address** *x121-address*	Defines an X.121 address.
2	**x25 map qllc** *x121-addr*	Defines remote X.121 address for mapping to QLLC.
3	**sna enable-host qllc** *x121-subaddress*	Enables QLLC subaddress for host.
4	**x25 route** ^*x121-addr*.*** alias** *serial interface*	Enables routing of X.25 packets to serial interface.

Specify Names for All Attached LANs

You can specify names for all Token Ring or Ethernet LANs attached to the router. These names are used to identify the LAN when Cisco IOS software sends an Alert to the host. To specify names for all attached LANs, use the following command in interface configuration mode:

Command	Purpose
lan-name *lan-name*	Defines the name of an attached LAN.

Specify the Physical Location of the Router

You can specify the physical location of the router if you intend requesting vital product information from the router. To specify the physical location, use the following command in interface configuration mode:

Command	Purpose
location *location-description*	Defines the physical location of the router.

Monitor DSPU and SNA Service Point Feature Status

You can monitor the status of the DSPU and SNA Service Point features. To display information about the state of the DSPU and SNA Service Point features, use the following commands in EXEC mode:

Command	Purpose
show dspu	Shows the status of all DSPU resources.
show dspu pu {*host-name* | *pu-name*} [**all**]	Shows the status of DSPU hosts or downstream PUs.
show dspu pool *pool-name* [**all**]	Shows the status of a DSPU pool.
show sna	Shows the status of all SNA hosts.
show sna pu *host-name* [**all**]	Shows the status of an SNA host.

To control the reporting of DSPU notification events (DSPU-specific SNMP Traps and Unsolicited SNA Messages to Operator), use the following command in global configuration mode:

Command	Purpose
dspu notification-level {**off** | **low** | **medium** | **high**}	Specifies the level of notification event reporting.

DSPU and SNA Service Point Configuration Examples

The following sections provide DSPU and SNA Service Point configuration examples:

- Dedicated LU Routing Example
- Pooled LU Routing Example
- Upstream Host via RSRB DSPU Configuration Example
- DSPU over DLSw+ Using Virtual Data-Link Control Configuration Example
- Downstream PU via SDLC DSPU Configuration Example

- Upstream Host via SDLC DSPU Configuration Example

- Downstream PU via QLLC/X.25 DSPU Configuration Example

- Upstream Host via Frame Relay DSPU Configuration Example

- DSPU NCIA Configuration Example

- SNA Service Point Support Configuration Example

- SNA Service Point over DLSw+ Using Virtual Data-Link Control Configuration Example

Dedicated LU Routing Example

Figure 17-1 illustrates the use of dedicated LU routing. Each upstream host LU is dedicated for use by a specific downstream LU.

Figure 17-1 *Dedicated LU Routing*

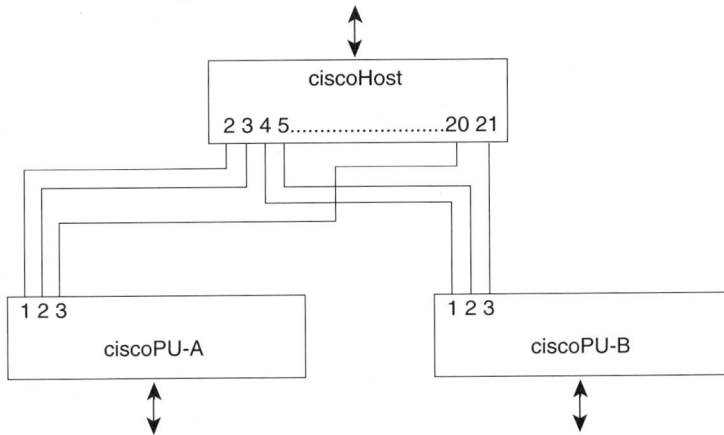

The following is a configuration file for the dedicated LU routing shown in Figure 17-1:

```
dspu host ciscohost xid-snd 06500001 rmac 4000.3745.0001
dspu pu ciscopu-a xid-rcv 05D00001 rmac 1000.5AED.0001
dspu lu 1 2 host ciscohost 2
dspu lu 3 3 host ciscohost 20
dspu pu ciscopu-b xid-rcv 05D00002 rmac 1000.5AED.0002
dspu lu 1 2 host ciscohost 4
dspu lu 3 3 host ciscohost 21
```

Pooled LU Routing Example

Figure 17-2 illustrates the use of pooled LU routing. Each upstream LU is configured in the LU pool and each downstream LU is configured as a pooled LU.

Figure 17-2   *Pooled LU Routing*

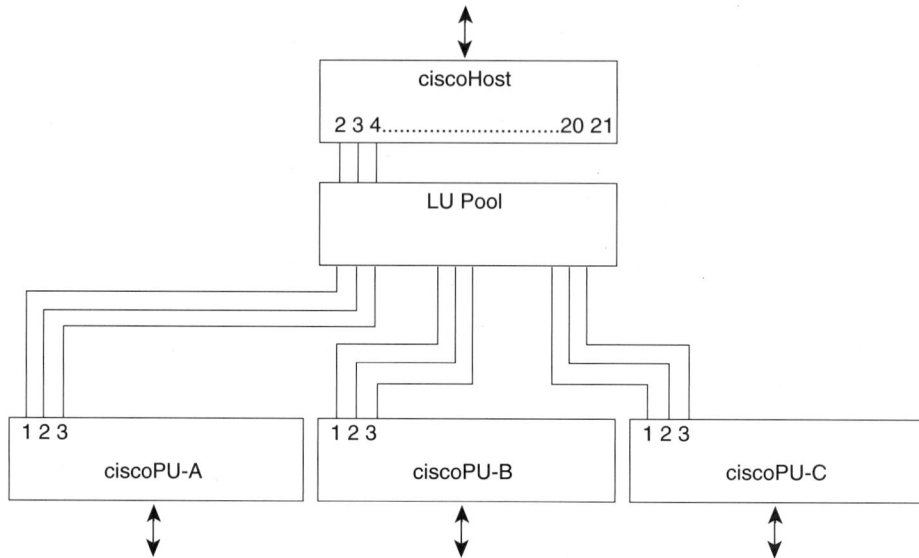

The following is a configuration file for the pooled LU routing shown in Figure 17-2:

```
dspu host ciscohost xid-snd 06500001 rmac 4000.3745.0001
dspu pool lupool host ciscohost lu 2 21
dspu pu ciscopu-a xid-rcv 05D00001 rmac 1000.5AED.0001
dspu lu 1 3 pool lupool
dspu pu ciscopu-b xid-rcv 05D00002 rmac 1000.5AED.0002
dspu lu 1 3 pool lupool
dspu pu ciscopu-c xid-rcv 05D00003 rmac 1000.5AED.0003
dspu lu 1 3 pool lupool
```

Upstream Host via RSRB DSPU Configuration Example

The following configuration example represents one possible definition for the network topology shown earlier in Figure 17-1. This example demonstrates the configuration of an upstream host via RSRB (with local acknowledgment) and downstream PUs via Token Ring.

```
source-bridge ring-group 99
source-bridge remote-peer 99 tcp 150.10.13.1
source-bridge remote-peer 99 tcp 150.10.13.2 local-ack

dspu rsrb 88 1 99 4000.ffff.0001
dspu rsrb enable-host lsap 4

dspu host ciscohost xid-snd 06500001 rmac 4000.3172.0001 rsap 4 lsap 4
dspu pool ciscopool host ciscohost lu 2 8
dspu rsrb start ciscohost
```

```
dspu pu ciscopu1 xid-rcv 05d00001
dspu lu 2 3 pool ciscopool

dspu pu ciscopu2 xid-rcv 05d00002
dspu lu 2 4 pool ciscopool

dspu pu ciscopu3 xid-rcv 05d00003
dspu lu 2 2 pool ciscopool

dspu pu ciscopu4 xid-rcv 05d00004
dspu lu 2 2 pool ciscopool
dspu lu 3 3 host ciscohost 9

interface tokenring 0
 description tokenring connection for downstream PUs
 ring-speed 16
 dspu enable-pu lsap 8
```

DSPU over DLSw+ Using Virtual Data-Link Control Configuration Example

The following example illustrates pooled LU routing over DLSw+ using virtual data-link control:

```
source-bridge ring-group 99
dlsw local-peer peer-id 150.10.16.2
dlsw remote-peer 0 tcp 150.10.16.1
!
dspu vdlc 99 4000.4500.01f0
dspu vdlc enable-pu lsap 8
dspu vdlc enable-host lsap 12
!
dspu host HOST-B xid-snd 065bbbb0 rmac 4000.7000.01f1 rsap 4 lsap 12 focalpoint
dspu pool pool-b host HOST-B lu 2 254
!
dspu pu PU3K-A xid-rcv 05d0000a rmac 4000.3000.0100 rsap 10 lsap 8
dspu lu 2 254 pool pool-b
!
dspu default-pu
dspu lu 2 5 pool pool3k-a
!
dspu vdlc start HOST-B
dspu vdlc start PU3K-A
!
interface serial 3
 description IP connection to dspu7k
 ip address 150.10.16.2 255.255.255.0
 clockrate 4000000
```

Downstream PU via SDLC DSPU Configuration Example

The following example demonstrates the configuration of downstream PUs via SDLC and an upstream host via Token Ring:

```
dspu host ciscohost xid-snd 06500001 rmac 4000.3172.0001 rsap 4 lsap 12
dspu pool ciscopool host ciscohost lu 2 11
!
dspu pu pu-sdlc0 sdlc C1 interface serial 0
dspu lu 2 6 pool ciscopool
!
dspu pu pu-sdlc1 sdlc C1 interface serial 1
dspu lu 2 6 pool ciscopool
!
interface serial 0
 description SDLC connection for pu-sdlc0
 encapsulation sdlc
 sdlc role primary
 sdlc address C1
 dspu enable-pu sdlc C1
 clockrate 56000
!
interface serial 1
 description SDLC connection for pu-sdlc1
 encapsulation sdlc
 sdlc role primary
 sdlc address C1
 dspu enable-pu sdlc C1
 clockrate 56000
!
interface tokenring 0
 description tokenring connection for ciscohost
 ring-speed 16
 dspu enable-host lsap 12
 dspu start ciscohost
```

Upstream Host via SDLC DSPU Configuration Example

The following example demonstrates the configuration of an upstream host via SDLC and downstream PUs via Token Ring and Ethernet:

```
dspu host ciscohost xid-snd 06500001 sdlc C1 interface serial 0
dspu pool ciscopool host ciscohost lu 2 11
!
dspu pu pu-token rmac 4000.4444.0001 rsap 4 lsap 8
dspu lu 2 6 pool ciscopool
!
dspu pu pu-ether rmac 0200.2222.0001 rsap 4 lsap 8
dspu lu 2 6 pool ciscopool
!
interface serial 0
 description SDLC connection for ciscohost
 encapsulation sdlc
```

```
 sdlc role secondary
 sdlc address C1
 dspu enable-host sdlc C1
 clockrate 56000
!
interface tokenring 0
 description tokenring connection for pu-token
 ring-speed 16
 dspu enable-pu lsap 8
!
interface ethernet 0
 description Ethernet connection for pu-ether
 dspu enable-pu lsap 8
```

Downstream PU via QLLC/X.25 DSPU Configuration Example

The following example demonstrates the configuration of a downstream PU via QLLC/X.25 and upstream host via Ethernet:

```
x25 routing
!
dspu host ciscohost xid-snd 06500001 rmac 0200.2222.0001 rsap 4 lsap 12
dspu pool ciscopool host ciscohost lu 2 11
!
dspu pu pu-qllc x25 320108 qllc 08
dspu lu 2 11 pool ciscopool
!
interface serial 0
 description QLLC connection for pu-qllc
 encapsulation x25
 x25 address 3202
 x25 map qllc 320108
 dspu enable-pu qllc 8
!
interface ethernet 0
 description Ethernet connection for pu-ether
 dspu enable-host lsap 12
 dspu start ciscohost
!
 x25 route ^3202.* alias serial 0
```

Upstream Host via Frame Relay DSPU Configuration Example

The following example demonstrates the configuration of an upstream host via Frame Relay and downstream PUs via Token Ring and Ethernet:

```
dspu host ciscohost xid-snd 06500001 dlci 200 rsap 4 lsap 12
dspu pool ciscopool host ciscohost lu 2 11
!
dspu pu pu-token rmac 4000.4444.0001 rsap 4 lsap 8
dspu lu 2 6 pool ciscopool
!
```

```
dspu pu pu-ether rmac 0200.2222.0001 rsap 4 lsap 8
dspu lu 2 6 pool ciscopool
!
interface serial 0
 description Frame Relay connection for ciscohost
 encapsulation frame-relay ietf
 frame-relay map llc2 200
 dspu enable-host lsap 12
 dspu start ciscohost
!
interface tokenring 0
 description tokenring connection for pu-token
 ring-speed 16
 dspu enable-pu lsap 8
!
interface ethernet 0
 description Ethernet connection for pu-ether
 dspu enable-pu lsap 8
```

DSPU NCIA Configuration Example

The following example illustrates an NCIA client/server session using DSPU:

```
ncia server 1 10.2.20.4 4000.3745.0001 1000.0000.0001 128
!
dspu ncia 1
dspu ncia enable-pu lsap 8
!
dspu host HOST-9370 xid-snd 11100001 rmac 4000.1060.1000 rsap 4 lsap 4
!
dspu pu CISCOPU-A xid-rcv 01700001
dspu lu 2 6 host HOST-9370 2
!
interface TokenRing 0
 ring-speed 16
 llc2 xid-retry-time 0
 dspu enable-host lsap 4
 dspu start HOST-9370
!
```

SNA Service Point Support Configuration Example

The following is an example of an RSRB configuration that implements SNA Service Point:

```
source-bridge ring-group 99
source-bridge remote-peer 99 tcp 150.10.13.2 local-ack
!
sna rsrb 88 1 99 4000.ffff.0001
!
sna host CNM02 xid-snd 05dbc000 rmac 4001.3745.1088 rsap 4 lsap 4 focalpoint
sna rsrb enable-host lsap 4
sna rsrb start CNM02
!
```

SNA Service Point over DLSw+ Using Virtual Data-Link Control Configuration Example

The following is an example of an SNA Service Point configuration that uses virtual data-link control over DLSw+:

```
source-bridge ring-group 99
dlsw local-peer peer-id 150.10.16.2
dlsw remote-peer 0 tcp 150.10.16.1
!
sna vdlc 99 4000.4500.01f0
sna vdlc enable-host lsap 12
!
sna host HOST-B xid-snd 065bbbb0 rmac 4000.7000.01f1 rsap 4 lsap 12 focalpoint
!
sna vdlc start HOST-B
!
interface serial 3
 description IP connection to dspu7k
 ip address 150.10.16.2 255.255.255.0
 clockrate 4000000
```

DSPU and SNA Service Point Configuration Commands

This chapter describes the commands you use to configure the downstream physical unit (DSPU) feature, which provides a gateway facility for downstream Systems Network Architecture (SNA) physical units (PUs), and SNA Service Point support. For DSPU and SNA Service Point configuration tasks and examples, refer to Chapter 17, "Configuring DSPU and SNA Service Point Support."

dspu activation-window

Use the **dspu activation-window** global configuration command to define the number of activation request/response units (RUs) and response messages (such as ACTLUs or DDDLU NMVTs) that can be sent without waiting for responses from the remote PU. Use the **no** form of this command to return to the default window size.

> **dspu activation-window** *window-size*
> **no dspu activation-window**

Syntax · Description

Syntax	Description
window-size	Number of outstanding unacknowledged activation RUs. The default is 5.

Default

The default window size is 5 outstanding unacknowledged activation RUs.

Command Mode

Global configuration

Usage Guidelines

This command first appeared in Cisco IOS Release 10.3.

You do not typically need to define the number of activation RUs, but doing so can enhance activation performance in some situations. Increasing the DSPU activation window allows more LUs to become active in a shorter amount of time (assuming the required buffers for activation RUs are available). Conversely, decreasing the DSPU activation window limits the amount of buffers the DSPU can use during PU/LU activation. This command provides pacing to avoid depleting the buffer pool during PU activation.

Example

In the following example, the DSPU activation window is configured to 10. The DSPU can send up to 10 activation RUs without a response from the remote PU. However, the DSPU cannot send any additional activation RUs until a response is received. The DSPU can only have 10 activation RUs awaiting response at any given time.

```
dspu activation-window 10
```

dspu default-pu

Use the **dspu default-pu** global configuration command to enable the default PU feature to be used when a downstream PU attempts to connect but does not match any of the explicit PU definitions. Use the **no** form of this command to disable the default PU feature.

> **dspu default-pu** [**window** *window-size*] [**maxiframe** *max-iframe*]
> **no dspu default-pu** [**window** *window-size*] [**maxiframe** *max-iframe*]

Syntax	Description
window *window-size*	(Optional) Sends and receives window sizes used across the link. The range is 1 to 127. The default is 7.
maxiframe *max-iframe*	(Optional) Maximum size (in bytes) of an I-frame that can be transmitted or received across the link. The range is 64 bytes to 18,432 bytes. The default is 1472.

Defaults

The default window size is 7.

The default maximum I-frame size is 1472.

Command Mode

Global configuration

Usage Guidelines

This command first appeared in Cisco IOS Release 10.3.

If the DSPU default PU is not defined, a connection attempt by a downstream PU that does not match any explicit PU definition is rejected.

The **dspu default-pu** command must be followed by at least one **dspu lu** command to define which pool the default LUs will be assigned from. Note that default LUs cannot be defined as dedicated LUs from a host.

The maximum I-frame size includes the SNA transmission header (TH), request header (RH), and request/response unit (RU), but does not include the DLC header. The DSPU feature segments frames being transmitted to fit within this frame size. If an XID is received from a remote PU, which indicates that it supports a different maximum I-frame size, then the smaller of the two values is used.

Example

In the following example, the default PU feature is enabled with a window size of 5 and a maximum I-frame size of 128. Each default PU can have up to 3 LUs assigned from the hostpool pool of LUs.

```
dspu pool hostpool host ibm3745 lu 2 254
dspu default-pu window 5 maxiframe 128
dspu lu 2 4 pool hostpool
```

Related Commands

To locate documentation of related commands, you can search online at www.cisco.com.

dspu lu
dspu pool

dspu enable-host (Token Ring, Ethernet, FDDI, Frame Relay)

Use the **dspu enable-host** interface configuration command to enable a local SAP on Token Ring, Ethernet, FDDI, or Frame Relay interfaces for use by upstream hosts. Use the **no** form of this command to cancel the definition.

> **dspu enable-host** [**lsap** *local-sap*]
> **no dspu enable-host** [**lsap** *local-sap*]

Syntax	Description
lsap	(Optional) Specifies that the local SAP will be activated as an upstream SAP for both receiving incoming connection attempts and for starting outgoing connection attempts.
local-sap	(Optional) Local SAP address. The default is 12.

Default

The default local SAP address is 12.

Command Mode

Interface configuration

Usage Guidelines

This command first appeared in Cisco IOS Release 10.3.

Example

In the following example, the local SAP address 10 on Token Ring interface 0 is enabled for use by upstream host connections:

```
interface tokenring 0
 dspu enable-host lsap 10
```

Related Commands

To locate documentation of related commands, you can search online at www.cisco.com.

dspu host (Frame Relay)
dspu host (Token Ring, Ethernet, FDDI, RSRB, VDLC)

dspu enable-host (QLLC)

Use the **dspu enable-host** interface configuration command to enable an X.121 subaddress for use by upstream host connections via QLLC. Use the **no** form of this command to disable the X.121 subaddress.

> **dspu enable-host qllc** *x121-subaddress*
> **no dspu enable-host qllc** *x121-subaddress*

Syntax	Description
qllc	Required keyword for QLLC data-link control.
x121-subaddress	X.121 subaddress.

Default

No default X.121 subaddress is specified.

Command Mode

Interface configuration

Usage Guidelines

This command first appeared in Cisco IOS Release 11.0.

Example

In the following example, X.121 subaddress 320108 is enabled for use by upstream host connections:

```
interface serial 0
 encapsulation x35
 x25 address 3202
 x25 map qllc 320112
 dspu enable-host qllc 320108
```

Related Commands

To locate documentation of related commands, you can search online at www.cisco.com.

dspu host (QLLC)
x25 map qllc

dspu enable-host (SDLC)

Use the **dspu enable-host** interface configuration command to enable an SDLC address for use by upstream host connections. Use the **no** form of this command to cancel the definition.

> **dspu enable-host sdlc** *sdlc-address*
> **no dspu enable-host sdlc** *sdlc-address*

Syntax	Description
sdlc	Required keyword for SDLC data-link control.
sdlc-address	SDLC address.

Default

No default SDLC address is specified.

Command Mode

Interface configuration

Usage Guidelines

This command first appeared in Cisco IOS Release 11.0.

Example

In the following example, SDLC address C1 is enabled for use by upstream host connections:

```
interface serial 0
 encapsulation sdlc
 sdlc role secondary
 sdlc address c1
 dspu enable-host sdlc c1
```

Related Commands

To locate documentation of related commands, you can search online at www.cisco.com.

dspu host (SDLC)
sdlc address
sdlc role

dspu enable-pu (Ethernet, Frame Relay, Token Ring, FDDI)

Use the **dspu enable-pu** interface configuration command to enable an Ethernet, Frame Relay, Token Ring, or FDDI address for use by downstream PU connections. Use the **no** form of this command to disable the connection.

> **dspu enable-pu** [**lsap** *local-sap*]
> **no dspu enable-pu** [**lsap** *local-sap*]

Syntax	Description
lsap *local-sap*	(Optional) Local SAP address used by the DSPU to establish connection with the remote host. The default local SAP address is 8.

Default

The default local SAP address is 8.

Command Mode

Interface configuration

Usage Guidelines

This command first appeared in Cisco IOS Release 10.3.

Example

The following example demonstrates the configuration of a downstream PU via Token Ring and Ethernet:

```
interface tokenring 0
 ring-speed 16
 dspu enable-pu lsap 8

interface ethernet 0
 dspu enable-pu lsap 8
```

Related Commands

To locate documentation of related commands, you can search online at www.cisco.com.

dspu pu (Frame Relay)
dspu pu (Token Ring, Ethernet, FDDI, RSRB, VDLC, NCIA)

dspu enable-pu (QLLC)

Use the **dspu enable-pu** interface configuration command to enable an X.121 subaddress for use by downstream PU connections via QLLC. Use the **no** form of this command to cancel the definition.

> **dspu enable-pu qllc** *x121-subaddress*
> **no dspu enable-pu qllc** *x121-subaddress*

Syntax	Description
qllc	Required keyword for QLLC data-link control.
x121-subaddress	Variable-length X.121 address. It is assigned by the X.25 network service provider.

Default

No default address is assigned.

Command Mode

Interface configuration

Usage Guidelines

This command first appeared in Cisco IOS Release 11.0.

Example

The following example enables an X.121 subaddress for use by downstream PU connections:

```
interface serial 0
 encapsulation x25
 x25 address 3201
 x25 map qllc 320208
 dspu enable-pu qllc 08
```

Related Commands

To locate documentation of related commands, you can search online at www.cisco.com.

dspu pu (QLLC)
x25 map qllc

dspu enable-pu (SDLC)

Use the **dspu enable-pu** interface configuration command to enable an SDLC address for use by downstream PU connections. Use the **no** form of this command to disable the connection.

> **dspu enable-pu sdlc** *sdlc-address*
> **no dspu enable-pu sdlc** *sdlc-address*

Syntax	Description
sdlc	Required keyword for SDLC data-link control.
sdlc-address	SDLC address.

Default

No default address is specified.

Command Mode

Interface configuration

Usage Guidelines

This command first appeared in Cisco IOS Release 11.0.

Example

The following example enables a DSPU downstream connection:

```
interface serial 0
 encapsulation x25
 sdlc role primary
 sdlc address c1
 dspu enable-pu sdlc c1
```

Related Commands

To locate documentation of related commands, you can search online at www.cisco.com.

dspu pu (SDLC)
sdlc address
sdlc role

dspu host (Frame Relay)

Use the **dspu host** global configuration command to define a DSPU host over a Frame Relay connection. Use the **no** form of this command to cancel the definition.

> **dspu host** *host-name* **xid-snd** *xid* **dlci** *dlci-number* [**rsap** *remote-sap*] [**lsap** *local-sap*]
> [**interface** *slot/port*] [**window** *window-size*] [**maxiframe** *max-iframe*]
> [**retries** *retry-count*] [**retry-timeout** *retry-timeout*] [**focalpoint**]
> **no dspu host** *host-name* **xid-snd** *xid* **dlci** *dlci-number* [**rsap** *remote-sap*]
> [**lsap** *local-sap*] [**interface** *slot/port*] [**window** *window-size*]
> [**maxiframe** *max-iframe*] [**retries** *retry-count*] [**retry-timeout** *retry-timeout*]
> [**focalpoint**]

Part
II

Command Reference

Syntax	Description
host-name	The specified DSPU host.
xid-snd *xid*	XID that is sent to the host during connection establishment. The XID value is 8 hexadecimal digits that include both block and ID numbers. For example, if the XID value is 05D00001, the block number is 05D and the ID number is 00001.
dlci *dlci-number*	Frame Relay data-link connection identifier (DLCI) number; a decimal number.
rsap *rsap-addr*	(Optional) Remote service access point (SAP) address.
lsap *lsap-addr*	(Optional) Local SAP address.
interface *slot/port*	(Optional) Slot and port number of the interface.
window *window-size*	(Optional) Sends and receives window sizes used for the host link. The range is 1 to 127.
maxiframe *max-iframe*	(Optional) Sends and receives maximum I-frame sizes used for the host link. The range is 64 to 18,432. The default is 1472.
retries *retry-count*	(Optional) Number of times the DSPU attempts to retry establishing connection with remote host PU. The range is 0 to 255 (0 = no retry attempts, 255 = infinite retry attempts). The default is 255.
retry-timeout *retry-timeout*	(Optional) Delay (in seconds) between DSPU attempts to retry establishing connection with remote host PU. The range is 1 to 600 seconds. The default is 30 seconds.
focalpoint	(Optional) Specifies that the host link will be used for the focal point support.

Defaults

The default remote SAP is 4.
The default local SAP is 12.
The default window size is 7.
The default maximum I-frame is 1472.
The default retry count is 255.
The default retry timeout is 30 seconds.

Command Mode

Global configuration

Usage Guidelines

This command first appeared in Cisco IOS Release 10.3.

The local SAP address must be enabled by a **dspu enable-host (Token Ring, Ethernet, FDDI, Frame Relay)** command.

If an XID is received from a remote PU that indicates it supports a different maximum I-frame size, then the smaller of the two values is used.

Alerts from downstream PUs are forwarded to the focalpoint host. The **focalpoint** parameter must be included in no more than one **dspu host** command.

Example

The following example defines a DSPU host for Frame Relay support:

```
dspu host rosebud xid-snd 06500001 dlci 200 rsap 4 lsap 12
```

Related Commands

To locate documentation of related commands, you can search online at www.cisco.com.

dspu enable-host (Token Ring, Ethernet, FDDI, Frame Relay)
dspu pool

dspu host (QLLC)

Use the **dspu host** global configuration command to define a DSPU host over an X.25/QLLC connection. Use the **no** form of this command to delete the DSPU host definition.

> **dspu host** *host-name* **xid-snd** *xid* **x25** *remote-x121-addr* [**qllc** *local-x121-subaddr*]
> [**interface** *slot/port*] [**window** *window-size*] [**maxiframe** *max-iframe*]
> [**retries** *retry-count*] [**retry-timeout** *retry-timeout*] [**focalpoint**]
> **no dspu host** *host-name* **xid-snd** *xid* **x25** *remote-x121-addr* [**qllc** *local-x121-subaddr*]
> [**interface** *slot/port*] [**window** *window-size*] [**maxiframe** *max-iframe*]
> [**retries** *retry-count*] [**retry-timeout** *retry-timeout*] [**focalpoint**]

Syntax	Description
host-name	The specified DSPU host.
xid-snd *xid*	XID that is sent to the host during connection establishment. The *xid* value is 8 hexadecimal digits that include both block and ID numbers. For example, if the *xid* value is 05D00001, the Block number is 05D and the ID number is 00001.

Syntax	Description
x25 *remote-x121-addr*	Remote X.121 address.
qllc *local-x121-subaddr*	(Optional) Local X.121 subaddress.
interface *slot/port*	(Optional) Slot and port number of the interface.
window *window-size*	(Optional) Sends and receives window sizes used for the host link. The range is 1 to 127. The default is 7.
maxiframe *max-iframe*	(Optional) Sends and receives maximum I-frame sizes used for the host link. The range is 64 to 18,432. The default is 1472.
retries *retry-count*	(Optional) Number of times the DSPU attempts to retry establishing connection with remote host PU. The range is 0 to 255 (0 = no retry attempts, 255 = infinite retry attempts). The default is 255.
retry-timeout *retry-timeout*	(Optional) Delay (in seconds) between DSPU attempts to retry establishing connection with remote host PU. The range is 1 to 600 seconds. The default is 30 seconds.
focalpoint	(Optional) Specifies that the host link will be used for the focal point support.

Defaults

The default window size is 7.
The default maximum I-frame is 1472.
The default retry count is 255.
The default retry timeout is 30 seconds.

Command Mode

Global configuration

Usage Guidelines

This command first appeared in Cisco IOS Release 11.0.

The X.121 subaddress must be enabled by a **dspu enable-host (QLLC)** command.

If an XID is received from a remote PU that indicates it supports a different maximum I-frame size, then the smaller of the two values is used.

Alerts from downstream PUs are forwarded to the focalpoint host. The **focalpoint** parameter must be included in no more than one **dspu host** command.

Example

The following example defines a DSPU host:

```
dspu host hosta xid-snd 065ffff0 x25 00000123005 qllc 12
```

Related Commands

To locate documentation of related commands, you can search online at www.cisco.com.

dspu enable-host (QLLC)
dspu pool
dspu start

dspu host (SDLC)

Use the **dspu host** global configuration command to define a DSPU host over an SDLC connection. Use the **no** form of this command to cancel the definition.

> **dspu host** *host-name* **xid-snd** *xid* **sdlc** *sdlc-addr* [**interface** *slot/port*]
> [**window** *window-size*] [**maxiframe** *max-iframe*] [**retries** *retry-count*]
> [**retry-timeout** *retry-timeout*] [**focalpoint**]
> **no dspu host** *host-name* **xid-snd** *xid* **sdlc** *sdlc-addr* [**interface** *slot/port*]
> [**window** *window-size*] [**maxiframe** *max-iframe*] [**retries** *retry-count*]
> [**retry-timeout** *retry-timeout*] [**focalpoint**]

Syntax	Description
host-name	The specified DSPU host.
xid-snd *xid*	XID that is sent to the host during connection establishment. The XID value is 8 hexadecimal digits that include both Block and ID numbers. For example, if the XID value is 05D00001, the Block number is 05D and the ID number is 00001.
sdlc *sdlc-addr*	SDLC hexadecimal address.
interface *slot/port*	(Optional) Slot and port number of the interface.
window *window-size*	(Optional) Sends and receives window sizes used for the host link. The range is 1 to 127. The default window size is 7.
maxiframe *max-iframe*	(Optional) Sends and receives maximum I-frame sizes used for the host link. The range is 64 to 18,432. The default is 1472.

Syntax	Description
retries *retry-count*	(Optional) Number of times the DSPU attempts to retry establishing connection with remote host PU. The range is 0 to 255 (0 = no retry attempts, 255 = infinite retry attempts). The default is 255.
retry-timeout *retry-timeout*	(Optional) Delay (in seconds) between DSPU attempts to retry establishing connection with remote host PU. The range is 1 to 600 seconds. The default is 30 seconds.
focalpoint	(Optional) Specifies that the host link will be used for the focal point support.

Defaults

The default window size is 7.
The default maximum I-frame is 1472.
The default number of retries is 255.
The default retry timeout is 30 seconds.

Command Mode

Global configuration

Usage Guidelines

This command first appeared in Cisco IOS Release 11.0.

The SDLC address must be enabled by a **dspu enable-host (SDLC)** command.

If an XID is received from a remote PU that indicates it supports a different maximum I-frame size, then the smaller of the two values is used.

Alerts from downstream PUs are forwarded to the focalpoint host. The **focalpoint** parameter must be included in no more than one **dspu host** command.

Example

The following example defines a DSPU host for SDLC:

```
dspu host hosta xid-snd 065ffff0 sdlc c1
```

Related Commands

To locate documentation of related commands, you can search online at www.cisco.com.

dspu enable-host (SDLC)
dspu pool

dspu host (Token Ring, Ethernet, FDDI, RSRB, VDLC)

Use the **dspu host** global configuration command to define a DSPU host over Token Ring, Ethernet, FDDI, RSRB, or virtual data-link control (VDLC) connections. Use the **no** form of this command to cancel the definition.

Part
II

Command Reference

> **dspu host** *host-name* **xid-snd** *xid* **rmac** *remote-mac* [**rsap** *remote-sap*]
> [**lsap** *local-sap*] [**interface** *slot/port*] [**window** *window-size*]
> [**maxiframe** *max-iframe*] [**retries** *retry-count*] [**retry-timeout** *retry-timeout*]
> [**focalpoint**]
>
> **no dspu host** *host-name* **xid-snd** *xid* **rmac** *remote-mac* [**rsap** *remote-sap*]
> [**lsap** *local-sap*] [**interface** *slot/port*] [**window** *window-size*]
> [**maxiframe** *max-iframe*] [**retries** *retry-count*] [**retry-timeout** *retry-timeout*]
> [**focalpoint**]

Syntax	Description
host-name	The specified DSPU host.
xid-snd *xid*	XID that is sent to the host during connection establishment. The XID value is 8 hexadecimal digits that include both Block and ID numbers. For example, if the XID value is 05D00001, the Block number is 05D and the ID number is 00001.
rmac *remote-mac*	MAC address of the remote host PU.
rsap *remote-sap*	(Optional) SAP address of the remote host PU. The default is 4.
lsap *local-sap*	(Optional) Local SAP address used by the DSPU to establish connection with the remote host. The default is 12.
interface *slot/port*	(Optional) Slot and port number of the interface.
window *window-size*	(Optional) Sends and receives window sizes used for the host link. The range is 1 to 127. The default is 7.
maxiframe *max-iframe*	(Optional) Sends and receives maximum I-frame sizes used for the host link. The range is 64 to 18,432. The default is 1472.
retries *retry-count*	(Optional) Number of times the DSPU attempts to retry establishing connection with remote host PU. The range is 0 to 255 (0 = no retry attempts, 255 = infinite retry attempts). The default is 255.

Syntax	Description
retry-timeout *retry-timeout*	(Optional) Delay (in seconds) between DSPU attempts to retry establishing connection with remote host PU. The range is 1 to 600 seconds. The default is 30 seconds.
focalpoint	(Optional) Specifies that the host link will be used for the focal point support.

Defaults

The default remote SAP address is 4.
The default local SAP address is 12.
The default window size is 7.
The default maximum I-frame is 1472.
The default number of retries is 255.
The default retry timeout is 30 seconds.

Command Mode

Global configuration

Usage Guidelines

This command first appeared in Cisco IOS Release 11.0.

The local SAP address must be enabled by one of the following commands: **dspu enable-host (Token Ring, Ethernet, FDDI, Frame Relay)**, **dspu rsrb enable-host**, or **dspu vdlc enable-host**.

If an XID is received from a remote PU that indicates it supports a different maximum I-frame size, then the smaller of the two values is used.

Alerts from downstream PUs are forwarded to the focalpoint host. The **focalpoint** parameter must be included in no more than one **dspu host** command.

Example

The following example shows the definition for a DSPU host with 252 LUs and a connection to be established across an RSRB link:

```
dspu rsrb 88 1 99 4000.ffff.0001
dspu rsrb enable-host lsap 10
dspu host ibm3745 xid 06500001 rmac 4000.3745.0001 lsap 10
dspu pool hostpool lu 2 253 host ibm3745
```

Related Commands

To locate documentation of related commands, you can search online at www.cisco.com.

dspu enable-host (Token Ring, Ethernet, FDDI, Frame Relay)
dspu pool
dspu rsrb enable-host
dspu rsrb start
dspu start
dspu vdlc enable-host

dspu lu

Use the **dspu lu** global configuration command to define a dedicated LU or a range of LUs for an upstream host and a downstream PU. Use the **no** form of this command to cancel the definition.

> **dspu lu** *lu-start* [*lu-end*] {**host** *host-name host-lu-start* / **pool** *pool-name*}
> [**pu** *pu-name*]
> **no dspu lu** *lu-start* [*lu-end*] {**host** *host-name host-lu-start* / **pool** *pool-name*}
> [**pu** *pu-name*]

Syntax	Description
lu-start	Starting LU address in the range of LUs to be assigned from a pool or dedicated to a host.
lu-end	(Optional) Ending LU address in the range of LUs to be assigned from a pool or dedicated to a host.
host *host-name host-lu-start*	Specifies that each LU in the range of LUs will be dedicated to a host LU *host-name*. The range of host LUs starts with the address *host-lu-start*.
pool *pool-name*	Specifies that each LU in the range of LUs will be assigned from the specified pool.
pu *pu-name*	(Optional) Downstream PU for which this range of LUs is being defined.

Default

There are no default specifications.

Command Mode

Global configuration

Usage Guidelines

This command first appeared in Cisco IOS Release 10.3.

If the **dspu lu** command immediately follows one of these commands:

dspu default-pu
dspu pu (Frame Relay)
dspu pu (QLLC)
dspu pu (SDLC)
dspu pu (Token Ring, Ethernet, FDDI, RSRB, VDLC, NCIA)

The **dspu lu** command is applied to that PU, and the **pu** keyword and *pu-name* are not required. If the keyword and argument are included, the LU defined by the **dspu lu** command will be applied to the named PU.

The pool and host parameters are mutually exclusive. You can define a range of LUs to be either assigned from a pool or dedicated to a host.

Example

The following example defines downstream LUs as dedicated LUs. The downstream PU, ciscopu, has three downstream LUs with addresses 2, 3, and 4. When ciscopu establishes a connection with the DSPU, the three downstream LUs (2, 3, and 4) are dedicated to LUs 22, 23, and 24, respectively, from the IBM 3745 host.

```
dspu host ibm3745 xid-snd 065000001 rmac 4000.3745.0001
dspu pu ciscopu xid-rcv 05D00001 rmac 1000.5AED.1F53
dspu lu 2 4 host ibm3745 22
```

Related Commands

To locate documentation of related commands, you can search online at www.cisco.com.

dspu default-pu
dspu host (Frame Relay)
dspu host (QLLC)
dspu host (SDLC)
dspu host (Token Ring, Ethernet, FDDI, RSRB, VDLC)
dspu pool
dspu pu (Frame Relay)
dspu pu (QLLC)
dspu pu (SDLC)
dspu pu (Token Ring, Ethernet, FDDI, RSRB, VDLC, NCIA)

dspu ncia

Use the **dspu ncia** global configuration command to configure the NCIA server as the underlying transport. Use the **no** form of this command to cancel the definition.

> **dspu ncia** [*server-number*]
> **no dspu ncia** [*server-number*]

Syntax

server-number	(Optional) Server number configured in the **ncia server** command. Currently, only one NCIA server is supported.

Default

There are no default settings.

Command Mode

Global configuration

Usage Guidelines

This command first appeared in Cisco IOS Release 11.2.

You must use the **ncia server** command to configure an NCIA server on the router before using the **dspu ncia** command to configure the NCIA server as the underlying transport.

Example

The following example configures the NCIA server as the underlying transport mechanism communicating directly with DSPU:

```
dspu ncia 1
```

Related Commands

To locate documentation of related commands, you can search online at www.cisco.com.

dspu ncia enable-pu
ncia server

dspu ncia enable-pu

Use the **dspu ncia enable-pu** global configuration command to enable a SAP on the NCIA server for use by downstream connections. Use the **no** form of this command to disable the SAP.

dspu ncia enable-pu [**lsap** *local-sap*]
no dspu ncia enable-pu [**lsap** *local-sap*]

Syntax   Description

lsap *local-sap*   (Optional) Specifies that the local SAP address will be activated as an upstream SAP for receiving incoming connection attempts. The default is 8.

Default
The default local SAP is 8.

Command Mode
Global configuration

Usage Guidelines
This command first appeared in Cisco IOS Release 11.2.

Example
In the following example, the local SAP address 8 is enabled for use by the downstream PU CISCOPU-A:

```
dspu ncia 1
dspu ncia enable-pu lsap 8
!
dspu host HOST-9370 xid-snd 11100001 rmac 4000.1060.1000 rsap 4 lsap 4
!
dspu pu CISCOPU-A xid-rcv 01700001
dspu lu 2 6 host HOST-9370 2
!
interface TokenRing 0
 ring-speed 16
 llc2 xid-retry-time 0
 dspu enable-host lsap 4
 dspu start HOST-9370
```

Related Commands

To locate documentation of related commands, you can search online at www.cisco.com.

dspu ncia
dspu pu (Token Ring, Ethernet, FDDI, RSRB, VDLC, NCIA)

dspu notification-level

Use the **dspu notification-level** global configuration command to specify the DSPU notifications to send to SNMP and SNA network management. Use the **no** form of this command to specify the default notification level, **low**.

Part
II

Command Reference

dspu notification-level {off | low | medium | high}
no dspu notification-level

Syntax	Description
off	Sends neither SNMP traps, nor unsolicited SNA messages for DSPU.
low	Sends PU and LU activation failures only.
medium	Sends PU state changes and PU and LU activation failures.
high	Sends both PU and LU state changes and activation failures.

Default

The default notification level is **low**.

Command Mode

Global configuration

Usage Guidelines

This command first appeared in Cisco IOS Release 11.1.

This command applies to both SNMP traps and unsolicited SNA messages to operator. Note that the upstream PU and LU notification events and the LU state change notification events are not sent as unsolicited SNA messages to operator. These events are sent as SNMP traps only.

Example

The following example sets the notification level to enable DSPU to send notifications to network management for both PU and LU state changes and activation failures:

```
dspu notification-level high
```

Related Commands

To locate documentation of related commands, you can search online at www.cisco.com.

snmp-server host

dspu pool

Use the **dspu pool** global configuration command to define a range of host LUs in an LU pool. Use the **no** form of this command to remove the definition.

> **dspu pool** *pool-name* **host** *host-name* **lu** *lu-start* [*lu-end*]
> [**inactivity-timeout** *minutes*]
> **no dspu pool** *pool-name* **host** *host-name* **lu** *lu-start* [*lu-end*]
> [**inactivity-timeout** *minutes*]

Syntax	Description
pool-name	Name identifier of the pool.
host *host-name*	Name of the host that owns the range of host LUs in the pool.
lu *lu-start*	Starting LU address in the range of host LUs in the pool.
lu-end	(Optional) Ending address (inclusive) of the range of host LUs in the pool. If no ending address is specified, only one LU (identified by *lu-start*) will be defined in the pool.
inactivity-timeout *minutes*	(Optional) Interval of inactivity (in minutes) on either the SSCP-LU or LU-LU sessions, which will cause the downstream LU to be disconnected from the upstream LU. The default is disabled.

Default

The inactivity-timeout is disabled.

Command Mode

Global configuration

Usage Guidelines

This command first appeared in Cisco IOS Release 10.3.

You can include multiple **dspu pool** commands that specify the same pool name. In this way, an LU pool can include several LU ranges from the one host PU, or it can include LUs from different host PUs. The LUs from host *host-name* starting at *lu-start* and ending with *lu-end*, inclusive, will be included in the pool *pool-name*. For the LUs in this pool, if there is no traffic on either the SSCP-LU or LU-LU sessions for the inactivity-timeout number of minutes, the downstream LU will be disconnected from the upstream LU, and the upstream LU will be allocated to any downstream LU waiting for a session. A value of zero for inactivity minutes means no timeouts. (Note that the inactivity-timeout applies to all LUs in this pool, not just the LUs defined by this **dspu pool** command. The last value configured will be used.)

Examples

The following example defines a pool of host LUs. A pool of 253 host LUs is defined with all LUs supplied from the ibm3745 host PU:

```
dspu host ibm3745 xid-snd 065000001 rmac 4000.3745.0001
dspu pool hostpool host ibm3745 lu 2 254
```

The following example defines multiple pools and defines a disjoint pool of host LUs. One pool with a total of 205 host LUs and second pool with a total of 48 host LUs are defined with all LUs supplied from the same ibm3745 host PU. Host LUs with addresses 2 to 201 and 250 to 254 are defined in hostpool1. Host LUs with addresses 202 to 249 are defined in hostpool2.

```
dspu host ibm3745 xid-snd 065000001 rmac 4000.3745.0001
dspu pool hostpool1 host ibm3745 lu 2 201
dspu pool hostpool2 host ibm3745 lu 202 249
dspu pool hostpool1 host ibm3745 lu 250 254
```

The following example defines a pool of LUs from multiple hosts. A pool of 506 host LUs is defined with 253 LUs supplied by the ibm3475 host PU and 253 supplied by the ibm3172 hostPU.

```
dspu host ibm3745 xid-snd 065000001 rmac 4000.3745.0001
dspu host ibm3172 xid 06500002 rmac 4000.3172.0001
dspu pool hostpool host ibm3745 lu 2 254
dspu pool hostpool host ibm3172 lu 2 254
```

Related Commands

To locate documentation of related commands, you can search online at www.cisco.com.

dspu host (Frame Relay)
dspu host (QLLC)
dspu host (Token Ring, Ethernet, FDDI, RSRB, VDLC)
dspu lu

dspu pu (Frame Relay)

Use the **dspu pu** global configuration command to define a DSPU host over a Frame Relay connection. Use the **no** form of this command to cancel the definition.

> **dspu pu** *pu-name* **dlci** *dlci-number* [**rsap** *remote-sap*] [**lsap** *local-sap*] [**xid-rcv** *xid*] [**interface** *slot/port*] [**window** *window-size*] [**maxiframe** *max-iframe*] [**retries** *retry-count*] [**retry-timeout** *retry-timeout*]
>
> **no dspu pu** *pu-name* **dlci** *dlci-number* [**rsap** *remote-sap*] [**lsap** *local-sap*] [**xid-rcv** *xid*] [**interface** *slot/port*] [**window** *window-size*] [**maxiframe** *max-iframe*] [**retries** *retry-count*] [**retry-timeout** *retry-timeout*]

Syntax	Description
pu-name	Name of the downstream PU.
dlci *dlci-number*	Frame Relay data-link connection identifier (DLCI) number; a decimal number.
rsap *remote-sap*	(Optional) SAP address of the downstream PU. The default is 4.
lsap *local-sap*	(Optional) Local SAP address used by the DSPU to establish connection with the downstream PU. The default is 8.
xid-rcv *xid*	(Optional) Specifies a match on XID.
interface *slot/port*	(Optional) Slot and port number of the interface.
window *window-size*	(Optional) Sends and receives sizes used for the downstream PU link. The range is 1 to 127. The default is 7.
maxiframe *max-iframe*	(Optional) Maximum I-frame that can be transmitted or received across the link. The range is 64 to 18,432. The default is 1472.
retries *retry-count*	Number of times the DSPU attempts to retry establishing connection with downstream PU. The range is 0 to 255 (0 = no retry attempts, 255 = infinite retry attempts). The default is 4.
retry-timeout *retry-timeout*	(Optional) Delay (in seconds) between DSPU attempts to retry establishing connection with downstream PU. The range is 1 to 600 seconds. The default is 30 seconds.

Defaults

The default remote SAP is 4.
The default local SAP is 8.
The default window size is 7.
The default maximum I-frame is 1472.

The default retry count is 4.
The default retry timeout is 30 seconds.

Command Mode

Global configuration

Usage Guidelines

This command first appeared in Cisco IOS Release 11.0.

Example

The following example defines a downstream PU:

```
dspu pu pub dlci 8
```

Related Commands

To locate documentation of related commands, you can search online at www.cisco.com.

dspu enable-pu (Ethernet, Frame Relay, Token Ring, FDDI)
dspu lu

dspu pu (QLLC)

Use the **dspu pu** global configuration command to explicitly define a downstream PU over an X.25 connection. Use the **no** form of this command to cancel the definition.

> **dspu pu** *pu-name* **x25** *remote-x121-addr* [**qllc** *local-x121-subaddr*] [**xid-rcv** *xid*]
> [**interface** *slot/port*] [**window** *window-size*] [**maxiframe** *max-iframe*]
> [**retries** *retry-count*] [**retry-timeout** *retry-timeout*]
> **no dspu pu** *pu-name* **x25** *remote-x121-addr* [**qllc** *local-x121-subaddr*] [**xid-rcv** *xid*]
> [**interface** *slot/port*] [**window** *window-size*] [**maxiframe** *max-iframe*]
> [**retries** *retry-count*] [**retry-timeout** *retry-timeout*]

Syntax	Description
pu-name	Name of the downstream PU.
x25 *remote-x121-addr*	Variable-length X.121 address. It is assigned by the X.25 network service provider.

Syntax	Description
qllc *local-x121-subaddr*	(Optional) Local X.121 subaddress.
xid-rcv *xid*	(Optional) Specifies a match on XID.
interface *slot/port*	(Optional) Slot and port number of the interface.
window *window-size*	(Optional) Sends and receives sizes used for the downstream PU link. The range is 1 to 127. The default is 7.
maxiframe *max-iframe*	(Optional) Maximum I-frame that can be transmitted or received across the link. The range is 64 to 18,432. The default is 1472.
retries *retry-count*	Number of times the DSPU attempts to retry establishing connection with downstream PU. The range is 0 to 255 (0 = no retry attempts, 255 = infinite retry attempts). The default is 4.
retry-timeout *retry-timeout*	(Optional) Delay (in seconds) between DSPU attempts to retry establishing connection with downstream PU. The range is 1 to 600 seconds. The default is 30 seconds.

Defaults

The default window size is 7.
The default maximum I-frame is 1472.
The default retry count is 4.
The default retry timeout is 30 seconds.

Command Mode

Global configuration

Usage Guidelines

This command first appeared in Cisco IOS Release 11.0.

Example

The following example defines a downstream PU:

```
dspu pu testpu xid-rcv 05d00001 x25 32012 qllc 12
```

Related Commands

To locate documentation of related commands, you can search online at www.cisco.com.

dspu enable-pu (QLLC)
dspu lu

dspu pu (SDLC)

Use the **dspu pu** global configuration command to define a DSPU host over an SDLC connection. Use the **no** form of this command to cancel the definition.

> **dspu pu** *pu-name* **sdlc** *sdlc-addr* [**xid-rcv** *xid*] [**interface** *slot/port*]
>   [**window** *window-size*] [**maxiframe** *max-iframe*] [**retries** *retry-count*]
>   [**retry-timeout** *retry-timeout*]
> **no dspu pu** *pu-name* **sdlc** *sdlc-addr* [**xid-rcv** *xid*] [**interface** *slot/port*]
>   [**window** *window-size*] [**maxiframe** *max-iframe*] [**retries** *retry-count*]
>   [**retry-timeout** *retry-timeout*]

Syntax	Description
pu-name	Name of the downstream PU.
sdlc *sdlc-addr*	SDLC address.
xid-rcv *xid*	(Optional) Specifies a match on XID.
interface *slot/ port*	(Optional) Slot and port number of the interface.
window *window-size*	(Optional) Sends and receives sizes used for the downstream PU link. The range is 1 to 127. The default is 7.
maxiframe *max-iframe*	(Optional) Maximum I-frame that can be transmitted or received across the link. The range is 64 to 18,432. The default is 1472.
retries *retry-count*	(Optional) Number of times the DSPU attempts to retry establishing connection with downstream PU. The range is 0 to 255 (0 = no retry attempts, 255 = infinite retry attempts). The default is 4.
retry-timeout *retry-timeout*	(Optional) Delay (in seconds) between DSPU attempts to retry establishing connection with downstream PU. The range is 1 to 600 seconds. The default is 30 seconds.

Defaults

The default window size is 7.
The default maximum I-frame is 1472.

The default retry count is 4.
The default retry timeout is 30 seconds.

Command Mode

Global configuration

Usage Guidelines

This command first appeared in Cisco IOS Release 11.0.

Example

The following example defines a downstream PU:

```
dspu pu testpu sdlc c1 interface serial 0
```

Related Commands

To locate documentation of related commands, you can search online at www.cisco.com.

dspu enable-pu (SDLC)
dspu lu

dspu pu (Token Ring, Ethernet, FDDI, RSRB, VDLC, NCIA)

Use the **dspu pu** global configuration command to define an explicit downstream PU over Token Ring, Ethernet, FDDI, RSRB, virtual data-link control, or NCIA connections. Use the **no** form of this command to cancel the definition.

> **dspu pu** *pu-name* [**rmac** *remote-mac*] [**rsap** *remote-sap*] [**lsap** *local-sap*]
> [**xid-rcv** *xid*] [**interface** *slot/port*] [**window** *window-size*]
> [**maxiframe** *max-iframe*] [**retries** *retry-count*] [**retry-timeout** *retry-timeout*]
> **no dspu pu** *pu-name* [**rmac** *remote-mac*] [**rsap** *remote-sap*] [**lsap** *local-sap*]
> [**xid-rcv** *xid*] [**interface** *slot/port*] [**window** *window-size*]
> [**maxiframe** *max-iframe*] [**retries** *retry-count*] [**retry-timeout** *retry-timeout*]

Syntax	Description
pu-name	Name of the downstream PU.
rmac *remote-mac*	(Optional) MAC address of the downstream PU.

Syntax	Description
rsap *remote-sap*	(Optional) SAP address of the downstream PU. The default is 4.
lsap *local-sap*	(Optional) Local SAP address used by the DSPU to establish connection with the downstream PU. The default is 8.
xid-rcv *xid*	(Optional) Specifies a match on XID.
interface *slot/port*	(Optional) Slot and port number of the interface.
window *window-size*	(Optional) Sends and receives sizes used for the downstream PU link. The range is 1 to 127. The default is 7.
maxiframe *max-iframe*	(Optional) Maximum I-frame that can be transmitted or received across the link. The range is 64 to 18,432. The default is 1472.
retries *retry-count*	Number of times the DSPU attempts to retry establishing connection with downstream PU. The range is 0 to 255 (0 = no retry attempts, 255 = infinite retry attempts). The default is 4.
retry-timeout *retry-timeout*	(Optional) Delay (in seconds) between DSPU attempts to retry establishing connection with downstream PU. The range is 1 to 600 seconds. The default is 30 seconds.

Defaults

The default remote SAP is 4.
The default local SAP is 8.
The default window size is 7.
The default maximum I-frame is 1472.
The default retry count is 4.
The default retry timeout is 30 seconds.

Command Mode

Global configuration

Usage Guidelines

This command first appeared in Cisco IOS Release 10.3.

The local SAP address must be enabled by one of the following commands:

- **dspu enable-pu (Ethernet, Frame Relay, Token Ring, FDDI) lsap**

- **dspu ncia enable-pu lsap**

- **dspu rsrb enable-pu lsap**

- **dspu vdlc enable-pu lsap**

The Sends and receives maximum I-frame size includes the SNA TH and RH, but does not include the data-link control header. The DSPU feature will segment frames being transmitted to fit within this frame size. If an XID is received from a remote PU which indicates that it supports a different maximum I-frame size, then the smaller of the two values is used.

If you want the DSPU to attempt a ConnectOut to the remote node using the **dspu start** command, you must configure the **rmac** keyword and argument. If you want this PU to match against a ConnectIn attempt, then several combinations of **rmac**, **rsap**, **xid-rcv** are possible. The matching algorithms are as follows:

- **rmac**—Match on remote MAC/SAP address of downstream PU.

- **xid-rcv**—Match on XID value received from downstream PU.

- **rmac/rsap, xid-rcv**—Match on remote MAC/SAP address of downstream PU and XID value received from downstream PU.

If an XID is received from a remote PU which indicates that it supports a different maximum I-frame size, then the smaller of the two values is used.

For Cisco IOS 11.3 and above, the number of DSPU PUs that can be configured is 1024.

Examples

In the following example, a downstream PU is defined with only the MAC address and SAP address specified. A downstream PU that attempts an incoming connection to the DSPU will only be accepted if the remote MAC/SAP address matches the configured values for this downstream PU (and the proper local SAP address is enabled).

```
dspu pu ciscopu rmac 1000.5AED.1F53 rsap 20
dspu lu 2 5 pool hostpool
interface tokenring 0
dspu enable-pu lsap 8
```

In the following example, a downstream PU is defined with only an **xid-rcv** value. Any downstream PU that attempts an incoming connection specifying the **xid-rcv** value, 05D00001, will be accepted without regard to remote MAC or SAP address (although the proper local SAP address must be enabled).

```
dspu pu ciscopu xid-rcv 05d00001
dspu lu 2 5 pool hostpool
interface tokenring 0
 dspu enable-pu lsap 8
```

In the following example, a downstream PU is defined with **xid-rcv**, **rmac**, and **rsap** keywords. Any downstream PU that attempts to ConnectIn to the DSPU must match all three configured values for the connection to be accepted (the proper local SAP address must also be enabled).

```
dspu pu ciscopu xid-rcv 05d00001 rmac 1000.5AED.1F53 rsap 20
dspu lu 2 5 pool hostpool
interface tokenring 0
 dspu enable-pu lsap 8
```

Related Commands

To locate documentation of related commands, you can search online at www.cisco.com.

dspu enable-pu (Ethernet, Frame Relay, Token Ring, FDDI)
dspu lu
dspu ncia enable-pu
dspu rsrb enable-pu
dspu rsrb start
dspu start
dspu vdlc enable-pu

dspu rsrb

Use the **dspu rsrb** global configuration command to define the local virtual ring, virtual bridge, target virtual ring, and virtual MAC address that the DSPU feature will simulate at the RSRB. Use the **no** form of this command to cancel the definition.

> **dspu rsrb** *local-virtual-ring bridge-number target-virtual-ring virtual-macaddr*
> **no dspu rsrb** *local-virtual-ring bridge-number target-virtual-ring virtual-macaddr*

Syntax	Description
local-virtual-ring	DSPU local virtual ring number.
bridge-number	Bridge number connecting the DSPU local virtual ring and the RSRB target virtual ring. The valid range is 1 to 15.
target-virtual-ring	RSRB target virtual ring number. The RSRB target virtual ring corresponds to the ring-number parameter defined by a **source-bridge ring-group** command.
virtual-macaddr	DSPU virtual MAC address.

Default

There are no default settings.

Command Mode

Global configuration

Usage Guidelines

This command first appeared in Cisco IOS Release 10.3.

The bridge number parameter can be specified only once in a configuration.

Use the **dspu rsrb** command to enable DSPU host and downstream connections to be established across an RSRB link.

If the **local-ack** parameter is specified on the **source-bridge remote-peer** statement, DSPU will establish host connections across RSRB using local acknowledgment. DSPU cannot support local acknowledgment for downstream PU connections across RSRB.

Examples

The following example defines DSPU to start a connection to the host across an RSRB link (without local acknowledgment). The DSPU is identified by its local ring number 88 and its virtual MAC address 4000.FFFF.0001. When the DSPU attempts an outgoing connection to the ibm3745 host, the connection will be established across the RSRB virtual ring 99.

```
source-bridge ring-group 99
source-bridge remote-peer 99 tcp 150.10.13.1
source-bridge remote-peer 99 tcp 150.10.13.2

dspu rsrb 88 1 99 4000.FFFF.0001
dspu rsrb enable-host lsap 10

dspu host ibm3745 xid-snd 06500001 rmac 4000.3745.0001 lsap 10
dspu rsrb start ibm3745
interface serial 0
 ip address 150.10.13.1 255.255.255.0
```

The following example defines DSPU to start a connection to the host across an RSRB link (with local acknowledgment). The DSPU is identified by its local ring number 88 and its virtual MAC address 4000.FFFF.0001. When the DSPU attempts an outward connection to the ibm3745 host, the connection will be established across the RSRB virtual ring 99 using RSRB local acknowledgment.

```
source-bridge ring-group 99
source-bridge remote-peer 99 tcp 150.10.13.1
source-bridge remote-peer 99 tcp 150.10.13.2 local-ack

dspu rsrb 88 1 99 4000.FFFF.0001
dspu rsrb enable-host lsap 10

dspu host ibm3745 xid-snd 06500001 rmac 4000.3745.0001 lsap 10
dspu rsrb start ibm3745

interface serial 0
 ip address 150.10.13.1 255.255.255.0
```

The following example defines DSPU to allow a connection from the downstream PU across an RSRB link. The DSPU is identified by its local ring number 88 and its virtual MAC address 4000.FFFF.0001. The downstream PU will specify the DSPU virtual MAC address 4000.FFFF.0001 and SAP address 20 in its host definitions. The DSPU will accept incoming connections from the downstream PU across the RSRB virtual ring 99.

```
source-bridge ring-group 99
source-bridge remote-peer 99 tcp 150.10.13.1
source-bridge remote-peer 99 tcp 150.10.13.2

dspu rsrb 88 1 99 4000.FFFF.0001
dspu rsrb enable-pu lsap 20

dspu pu ciscopu xid-rcv 05D00001 lsap 20

interface serial 0
 ip address 150.10.13.1 255.255.255.0
```

Part
II

Command Reference

Related Commands

To locate documentation of related commands, you can search online at www.cisco.com.

dspu rsrb enable-host
dspu rsrb enable-pu
dspu rsrb start
source-bridge ring-group
source-bridge remote-peer

dspu rsrb enable-host

Use the **dspu rsrb enable-host** global configuration command to enable an RSRB SAP for use by DSPU host connections. Use the **no** form of this command to disable the RSRB SAP.

> **dspu rsrb enable-host** [**lsap** *local-sap*]
> **no dspu rsrb enable-host** [**lsap** *local-sap*]

Syntax   Description

lsap *local-sap*   (Optional) Specifies that the local SAP address will be activated as an upstream SAP for both receiving incoming connections attempts and for starting outgoing connection attempts. The default is 12.

Default

The default local SAP is 12.

Command Mode
Global configuration

Usage Guidelines
This command first appeared in Cisco IOS Release 10.3.

Example
In the following example, the local SAP address 10 of the RSRB is enabled for use by the ibm3745 host PU:

```
source-bridge ring-group 99
source-bridge remote-peer 99 tcp 150.10.13.1
source-bridge remote-peer 99 tcp 150.10.13.2

dspu rsrb 88 1 99 4000.FFFF.0001
dspu rsrb enable-host lsap 10

dspu host ibm3745 xid-snd 06500001 rmac 4000.3745.0001 lsap 10

interface serial 0
 ip address 150.10.13.1 255.255.255.0
```

Related Commands
To locate documentation of related commands, you can search online at www.cisco.com.

dspu host (Token Ring, Ethernet, FDDI, RSRB, VDLC)
dspu rsrb

dspu rsrb enable-pu

Use the **dspu rsrb enable-pu** global configuration command to enable an RSRB SAP for use by DSPU downstream connections. Use the **no** form of this command to disable the SAP.

> **dspu rsrb enable-pu** [**lsap** *local-sap*]
> **no dspu rsrb enable-pu** [**lsap** *local-sap*]

Syntax	Description
lsap local-sap	(Optional) Specifies that the local SAP address will be activated as an upstream SAP for both receiving incoming connection attempts and for starting outgoing connection attempts.

Default
The default local SAP is 8.

Command Mode
Global configuration

Usage Guidelines
This command first appeared in Cisco IOS Release 10.3.

Example
In the following example, the local SAP address 20 of the RSRB is enabled for use by the ciscopu DSPU downstream PU:

```
source-bridge ring-group 99
source-bridge remote-peer 99 tcp 150.10.13.1
source-bridge remote-peer 99 tcp 150.10.13.2

dspu rsrb 88 1 99 4000.FFFF.0001
dspu rsrb enable-pu lsap 20

dspu pu ciscopu xid-rcv 05D00001 lsap 20
```

Related Commands
To locate documentation of related commands, you can search online at www.cisco.com.

dspu pu (Token Ring, Ethernet, FDDI, RSRB, VDLC, NCIA)
dspu rsrb

dspu rsrb start

Use the **dspu rsrb start** global configuration command to specify that an attempt will be made to connect to the remote resource defined by host name or PU name through the RSRB. Use the **no** form of this command to cancel the definition.

> **dspu rsrb start** {*host-name* | *pu-name*}
> **no dspu rsrb start** {*host-name* | *pu-name*}

Syntax	Description
host-name	Name of a host defined in a **dspu host (Token Ring, Ethernet, FDDI, RSRB, VDLC)** command.
pu-name	Name of a PU defined in a **dspu pu (Token Ring, Ethernet, FDDI, RSRB, VDLC, NCIA)** command.

Default

There are no default settings.

Command Mode

Global configuration

Usage Guidelines

This command first appeared in Cisco IOS Release 10.3.

Before issuing this command, you must enable the correct local SAP with the appropriate enable command (**dspu rsrb enable-host** for a host resource, and **dspu rsrb enable-pu** for a PU resource).

This command is only valid if the target MAC address has been defined in the resource. For a host resource, this not a problem because the MAC address is mandatory, but for a PU resource the MAC address is optional. The command will fail if the MAC address is missing.

Example

In the following example, the DSPU will initiate a connection with the ibm3745 host PU across the RSRB link:

```
source-bridge ring-group 99
source-bridge remote-peer 99 tcp 150.10.13.1
source-bridge remote-peer 99 tcp 150.10.13.2

dspu rsrb 88 1 99 4000.FFFF.0001
dspu rsrb enable-host lsap 10

dspu host ibm3745 xid-snd 06500001 rmac 4000.3745.0001 lsap 10
dspu rsrb start ibm3745

interface serial 0
 ip address 150.10.13.1 255.255.255.0
```

Related Commands

To locate documentation of related commands, you can search online at www.cisco.com.

dspu host (Token Ring, Ethernet, FDDI, RSRB, VDLC)
dspu pu (Token Ring, Ethernet, FDDI, RSRB, VDLC, NCIA)
dspu rsrb
dspu rsrb enable-host
dspu rsrb enable-pu

dspu start

Use the **dspu start** interface configuration command to specify that an attempt will be made to connect to the remote resource defined by host name or PU name. Use the **no** form of this command to cancel the definition.

> **dspu start** {*host-name* | *pu-name*}
> **no dspu start** {*host-name* | *pu-name*}

Syntax	Description
host-name	Name of a host defined in a **dspu host** command.
pu-name	Name of a PU defined in a **dspu pu** command.

Default

There are no default settings.

Command Mode

Interface configuration

Usage Guidelines

This command first appeared in Cisco IOS Release 10.3.

Before issuing this command, you must enable the correct address using the appropriate **dspu enable-host** or **dspu enable-pu** command.

This command is only valid if the target address (RMAC SDLC, DLCI, or X.25 parameter) has been defined for the resource. For a host resource, this not a problem because the address specification is mandatory, but for a PU resource, specifying the address is optional. The **dspu start** command will fail if the address is missing.

Example

In the following example, the DSPU will initiate a connection with the ciscopu downstream PU on Token Ring interface 0:

```
dspu pu ciscopu xid rcv 05D00001 rmac 1000.5AED.1F53 lsap 20
interface tokenring 0
 dspu enable-pu lsap 20
 dspu start ciscopu
```

Related Commands

To locate documentation of related commands, you can search online at www.cisco.com.

dspu enable-host (Token Ring, Ethernet, FDDI, Frame Relay)
dspu enable-host (QLLC)
dspu enable-host (SDLC)
dspu enable-pu (Ethernet, Frame Relay, Token Ring, FDDI)
dspu enable-pu (SDLC)
dspu enable-pu (QLLC)
dspu host (Frame Relay)
dspu host (QLLC)
dspu host (SDLC)
dspu host (Token Ring, Ethernet, FDDI, RSRB, VDLC)
dspu pu (Frame Relay)
dspu pu (QLLC)
dspu pu (SDLC)
dspu pu (Token Ring, Ethernet, FDDI, RSRB, VDLC, NCIA)

dspu vdlc

Use the **dspu vdlc** global configuration command to identify the local virtual ring and virtual MAC address that will be used to establish DSPU host and downstream connections over DLSw+ using virtual data-link control. Use the **no** form of this command to cancel the definition.

> **dspu vdlc** *ring-group virtual-mac-address*
> **no dspu vdlc** *ring-group virtual-mac-address*

Syntax   Description

ring-group   Local virtual ring number identifying the SRB ring group.

virtual-mac-address   Virtual MAC address that represents the DSPU virtual data-link control.

Default

There are no default settings.

Command Mode

Global configuration

Usage Guidelines

This command first appeared in Cisco IOS Release 11.2.

The virtual data-link control local virtual ring must have been previously configured using the **source-bridge ring-group** command.

The virtual data-link control virtual MAC address must be unique within the DLSw+ network.

To avoid an address conflict on the virtual MAC address, use a locally administered address in the form 4000.*xxxx.xxxx*.

Example

The following example defines DSPU to start a connection to the host using virtual data-link control. The DSPU virtual data-link control is identified by its virtual MAC address 4000.4500.01f0, existing on the SRB virtual ring 99. When the DSPU attempts an outgoing connection to the host HOST-B, the connection will be established across the virtual ring 99.

```
source-bridge ring-group 99
dlsw local-peer peer-id 150.10.16.2
dlsw remote-peer 0 tcp 150.10.16.1

dspu vdlc 99 4000.4500.01f0
dspu vdlc enable-host lsap 12

dspu host HOST-B xid-snd 065bbbb0 rmac 4000.7000.01f1 rsap 4 lsap 12 focalpoint

dspu vdlc start HOST-B

interface serial 3
 description IP connection to dspu7k
 ip address 150.10.16.2 255.255.255.0
 clockrate 4000000
```

Related Commands

To locate documentation of related commands, you can search online at www.cisco.com.

dlsw local-peer
dlsw remote-peer
dspu vdlc enable-host
dspu vdlc enable-pu
dspu vdlc start
source-bridge ring-group

dspu vdlc enable-host

Use the **dspu vdlc enable-host** global configuration command to enable a SAP for use by DSPU host connections. Use the **no** form of this command to disable the SAP.

> **dspu vdlc enable-host** [**lsap** *local-sap*]
> **no dspu vdlc enable-host** [**lsap** *local-sap*]

Syntax   Description

lsap *local-sap*   (Optional) Specifies that the local SAP address will be activated as an upstream SAP for both receiving incoming connections attempts and for starting outgoing connection attempts. The default is 12.

Default

The default local SAP is 12.

Command Mode

Global configuration

Usage Guidelines

This command first appeared in Cisco IOS Release 11.2.

Example

In the following example, the local SAP address 12 is enabled for use by the host PU HOST-B:

```
source-bridge ring-group 99
dlsw local-peer peer-id 150.10.16.2
dlsw remote-peer 0 tcp 150.10.16.1
```

```
dspu vdlc 99 4000.4500.01f0
dspu vdlc enable-pu lsap 8
dspu vdlc enable-host lsap 12

dspu host HOST-B xid-snd 065bbbb0 rmac 4000.7000.01f1 rsap 4 lsap 12 focalpoint
dspu pool pool-b host HOST-B lu 2 254

dspu host HOST3K-A xid-snd 05d0000a rmac 4000.3000.0100 rsap 8 lsap 12
dspu pool pool3k-a host HOST3K-A lu 2 254

dspu pu PU3K-A xid-rcv 05d0000a rmac 4000.3000.0100 rsap 10 lsap 8
dspu lu 2 254 pool pool-b

dspu default-pu
dspu lu 2 5 pool pool3k-a

dspu vdlc start HOST-B
dspu vdlc start HOST3K-A
dspu vdlc start PU3K-A

interface serial 3
 description IP connection to dspu7k
 ip address 150.10.16.2 255.255.255.0
 clockrate 4000000
```

Part II

Command Reference

Related Commands

To locate documentation of related commands, you can search online at www.cisco.com.

dspu host (Token Ring, Ethernet, FDDI, RSRB, VDLC)
dspu vdlc

dspu vdlc enable-pu

Use the **dspu vdlc enable-pu** global configuration command to enable a SAP for use by DSPU virtual data-link control downstream connections. Use the **no** form of this command to disable the SAP.

> **dspu vdlc enable-pu** [**lsap** *local-sap*]
> **no dspu vdlc enable-pu** [**lsap** *local-sap*]

Syntax   Description

lsap *local-sap*   (Optional) Specifies that the local SAP address will be activated as an upstream SAP for both receiving incoming connection attempts and for starting outgoing connection attempts. The default is 8.

Default

The default local SAP is 8.

Command Mode

Global configuration

Usage Guidelines

This command first appeared in Cisco IOS Release 11.2.

Example

In the following example, the local SAP address 8 is enabled for use by the downstream PU PU3K-A:

```
source-bridge ring-group 99
dlsw local-peer peer-id 150.10.16.2
dlsw remote-peer 0 tcp 150.10.16.1

dspu vdlc 99 4000.4500.01f0
dspu vdlc enable-pu lsap 8
dspu vdlc enable-host lsap 12

dspu host HOST-B xid-snd 065bbbb0 rmac 4000.7000.01f1 rsap 4 lsap 12 focalpoint
dspu pool pool-b host HOST-B lu 2 254

dspu host HOST3K-A xid-snd 05d0000a rmac 4000.3000.0100 rsap 8 lsap 12
dspu pool pool3k-a host HOST3K-A lu 2 254

dspu pu PU3K-A xid-rcv 05d0000a rmac 4000.3000.0100 rsap 10 lsap 8
dspu lu 2 254 pool pool-b

dspu default-pu
dspu lu 2 5 pool pool3k-a

dspu vdlc start HOST-B
dspu vdlc start HOST3K-A
dspu vdlc start PU3K-A

interface serial 3
 description IP connection to dspu7k
 ip address 150.10.16.2 255.255.255.0
 clockrate 4000000
```

Related Commands

To locate documentation of related commands, you can search online at www.cisco.com.

dspu pu (Token Ring, Ethernet, FDDI, RSRB, VDLC, NCIA)
dspu vdlc

dspu vdlc start

Use the **dspu vdlc start** global configuration command to specify that an attempt will be made to connect to the remote resource defined by host name or PU name through virtual data-link control. Use the **no** form of this command to cancel the definition.

> **dspu vdlc start** {*host-name* | *pu-name*}
> **no dspu vdlc start** {*host-name* | *pu-name*}

Syntax   Description

host-name   Name of a host defined in a **dspu host (Token Ring, Ethernet, FDDI, RSRB, VDLC)** command.

pu-name   Name of a PU defined in a **dspu pu (Token Ring, Ethernet, FDDI, RSRB, VDLC, NCIA)** command.

Default

There are no default settings.

Command Mode

Global configuration

Usage Guidelines

This command first appeared in Cisco IOS Release 11.2.

Before issuing this command, you must enable the correct local SAP with the appropriate enable command (**dspu vdlc enable-host** for a host resource, and **dspu vdlc enable-pu** for a PU resource).

This command is only valid if the target MAC address has been defined in the resource. For a host resource, this is not a problem because the MAC address is mandatory, but for a PU resource the MAC address is optional. The command will fail if the MAC address is missing.

Example

In the following example, DSPU attempts to initiate connections with host PU HOST-B, host PU HOST3k-A, and downstream PU PU3k-A over DLSw+ using virtual data-link control:

```
source-bridge ring-group 99
dlsw local-peer peer-id 150.10.16.2
dlsw remote-peer 0 tcp 150.10.16.1
```

```
dspu vdlc 99 4000.4500.01f0
dspu vdlc enable-pu lsap 8
dspu vdlc enable-host lsap 12

dspu host HOST-B xid-snd 065bbbb0 rmac 4000.7000.01f1 rsap 4 lsap 12 focalpoint
dspu pool pool-b host HOST-B lu 2 254

dspu host HOST3K-A xid-snd 05d0000a rmac 4000.3000.0100 rsap 8 lsap 12
dspu pool pool3k-a host HOST3K-A lu 2 254

dspu pu PU3K-A xid-rcv 05d0000a rmac 4000.3000.0100 rsap 10 lsap 8
dspu lu 2 254 pool pool-b

dspu default-pu
dspu lu 2 5 pool pool3k-a

dspu vdlc start HOST-B
dspu vdlc start HOST3K-A
dspu vdlc start PU3K-A

interface serial 3
 description IP connection to dspu7k
 ip address 150.10.16.2 255.255.255.0
 clockrate 4000000
```

Related Commands

To locate documentation of related commands, you can search online at www.cisco.com.

dspu host (Token Ring, Ethernet, FDDI, RSRB, VDLC)
dspu pu (Token Ring, Ethernet, FDDI, RSRB, VDLC, NCIA)
dspu vdlc
dspu vdlc enable-host
dspu vdlc enable-pu

lan-name

Use the **lan-name** interface configuration command to specify a name for the LAN that is attached to the interface. This name is included in any Alert sent to the SNA host when a problem occurs on this interface or LAN. Use the **no** form of this command to revert to the default name.

> **lan-name** *lan-name*

Syntax	Description
lan-name	Name used to identify the LAN when you send Alerts to the SNA host. The default LAN name is the name of the interface.

Default

The default name used for the LAN is the name of the interface, such as *tr0*.

Command Mode

Interface configuration

Usage Guidelines

This command first appeared in Cisco IOS Release 11.0.

Example

The following example identifies a LAN:

```
lan-name LAN1
```

Related Commands

To locate documentation of related commands, you can search online at www.cisco.com.

show sna

location

Use the **location** global configuration command to specify the physical location of the router or access server. This information is included in the vital product information when this information is requested from an SNA host. Use the **no** form of this command to remove the physical location information.

location *location-description*

Syntax	Description
location-description	A description of the physical location of the device. This can be up to 50 characters long and may include blanks.

Default

No default is specified.

Command Mode

Global configuration

Usage Guidelines

This command first appeared in Cisco IOS Release 11.0.

Example

The following example describes the location of a router:

```
location Building G, Level 4, Room 45
```

Related Commands

To locate documentation of related commands, you can search online at www.cisco.com.

show sna

show dspu

Use the **show dspu** privileged EXEC command to display the status of the DSPU feature.

show dspu [**pool** *pool-name* | [**pu** {*host-name* | *pu-name*} [**all**]]

Syntax	Description
pool *pool-name*	(Optional) Name of a pool of LUs (as defined by the **dspu pool** command).
pu	(Optional) Name of defined PU (as defined by either the **dspu pu** or the **dspu host** command).
host-name	Name of a host defined in a **dspu host** command.
pu-name	Name of a PU defined in a **dspu pu** command.
all	(Optional) Shows a detailed status.

Command Mode

Privileged EXEC

Usage Guidelines

This command first appeared in Cisco IOS Release 10.3.

Sample Displays

The following is sample output from the **show dspu** command. It shows a summary of the DSPU status:

```
Router# show dspu

dspu host HOST_NAMEA interface PU STATUS sssssss
FRAMES RECEIVED nnnnnn FRAMES SENT nnnnnn
LUs USED BY DSPU nnn LUs ACTIVE nnn
LUs USED BY API nnn LUs ACTIVE nnn
LUs ACTIVATED BY HOST BUT NOT USED nnn
dspu host HOST_NAMEB interface PU STATUS sssssss
FRAMES RECEIVED nnnnnn FRAMES SENT nnnnnn
LUs USED BY DSPU nnn LUs ACTIVE nnn
LUs USED BY API nnn LUs ACTIVE nnn
LUs ACTIVATED BY HOST BUT NOT USED nnn
dspu pu PU_NAMEE interface PU STATUS sssssss
FRAMES RECEIVED nnnnnn FRAMES SENT nnnnnn
LUs USED BY DSPU nnn LUs ACTIVE nnn
LUs USED BY API nnn LUs ACTIVE nnn
LUs ACTIVATED BY HOST BUT NOT USED nnn
dspu pu PU_NAMEF interface PU STATUS sssssss
FRAMES RECEIVED nnnnnn FRAMES SENT nnnnnn
LUs USED BY DSPU nnn LUs ACTIVE nnn
LUs USED BY API nnn LUs ACTIVE nnn
LUs ACTIVATED BY HOST BUT NOT USED nnn
```

The following is sample output from the **show dspu** command with the **pu** keyword:

```
Router# show dspu pu putest

dspu pu PUTEST interface PU STATUS sssssss
RMAC remote_mac RSAP remote_sap LSAP local_sap
XID xid RETRIES retry_count RETRY_TIMEOUT retry_timeout
WINDOW window_size MAXIFRAME max_iframe
FRAMES RECEIVED nnnnnn FRAMES SENT nnnnnn
LUs USED BY DSPU nnn LUs ACTIVE nnn
LUs USED BY API nnn LUs ACTIVE nnn
LUs ACTIVATED BY HOST BUT NOT USED nnn
```

The following is sample output from the **show dspu** command with the **all** keyword:

```
Router# show dspu pu putest all

dspu pu PUTEST interface PU STATUS sssssss
RMAC remote_mac RSAP remote_sap LSAP local_sap
XID xid RETRIES retry_count RETRY_TIMEOUT retry_timeout
WINDOW window_size MAXIFRAME max_iframe
FRAMES RECEIVED nnnnnn FRAMES SENT nnnnnn
LU nnn PEER PU HOST_NAMEA PEER LU nnn STATUS ttttttt
       FRAMES RECEIVED nnnnnn FRAMES SENT nnnnnn
LU nnn PEER PU HOST_NAMEA PEER LU nnn STATUS ttttttt
       FRAMES RECEIVED nnnnnn, FRAMES SENT nnnnnn
LU nnn PEER PU HOST_NAMEB PEER LU nnn STATUS ttttttt
       FRAMES RECEIVED nnnnnn, FRAMES SENT nnnnnn
```

Part II

Command Reference

The following shows a summary of the LUs in a pool:

```
Router# show dspu pool poolname

dspu pool poolname host HOST_NAMEA lu start-lu end-lu
```

The following shows the details of all the LUs in a pool:

```
Router# show dspu pool poolname all

dspu pool poolname host HOST_NAMEA lu start-lu end-lu
DSPU POOL poolname INACTIVITY_TIMEOUT timeout-value
lu nnn host HOST_NAMEA peer lu nnn pu PU_NAMEF status tttttttt
lu nnn host HOST_NAMEA peer lu nnn pu PU_NAMEF status tttttttt
lu nnn host HOST_NAMEA peer lu nnn pu PU_NAMEF status tttttttt
```

show sna

Use the **show sna** privileged EXEC command to display the status of the SNA Service Point feature.

show sna [pu *host-name* [**all**]]

Syntax	Description
pu	(Optional) Name of a host defined in an **sna host** command.
host-name	The name of a host defined in an **sna host** command.
all	(Optional) Shows detailed status.

Command Mode

Privileged EXEC

Usage Guidelines

This command first appeared in Cisco IOS Release 11.0.

Sample Displays

The following is sample output from the **show sna** command. It shows a summary of the SNA feature's status:

```
Router# show sna

sna host HOST_NAMEA TokenRing1 PU STATUS active
FRAMES RECEIVED 00450 FRAMES SENT 00010
LUs USED BY DSPU nnn LUs ACTIVE nnn
```

```
LUs USED BY API nnn LUs ACTIVE nnn
LUs ACTIVATED BY HOST BUT NOT USED nnn
```

The following is sample output from the **show sna** command with the **pu** keyword:

```
Router# show sna pu putest

sna host PUTEST TokenRing1 PU STATUS active
RMAC 400000000004 RSAP 04 LSAP 04
XID 05d00001 RETRIES 255 RETRY_TIMEOUT 30
WINDOW 7 MAXIFRAME 1472
FRAMES RECEIVED 0450 FRAMES SENT 0010
LUs USED BY DSPU nnn LUs ACTIVE nnn
LUs USED BY API nnn LUs ACTIVE nnn
LUs ACTIVATED BY HOST BUT NOT USED nnn
```

Because the **all** keyword refers to LUs under the PU, this has no significance for the Service Point host.

sna enable-host (QLLC)

Use the **sna enable-host** interface configuration command to enable an X.121 subaddress for use by the SNA Service Point on the interface. Use the **no** form of this command to disable SNA Service Point on the interface.

> **sna enable-host qllc** *x121-subaddress*
> **no sna enable-host qllc** *x121-subaddress*

Syntax

Syntax	Description
qllc	Required keyword for QLLC data-link control.
x121-subaddress	The X.121 subaddress.

Default

No default X.121 subaddress is specified.

Command Mode

Interface configuration

Usage Guidelines

This command first appeared in Cisco IOS Release 11.0.

Example

In the following example, X.121 subaddress 320108 is enabled for use by host connections:

```
sna enable-host qllc 320108
```

Related Commands

To locate documentation of related commands, you can search online at www.cisco.com.

sna host (QLLC)
x25 map qllc

sna enable-host (SDLC)

Use the **sna enable-host** interface configuration command to enable an SDLC address for use by host connections. Use the **no** form of this command to cancel the definition.

> **sna enable-host sdlc** *sdlc-address*
> **no sna enable-host sdlc** *sdlc-address*

Syntax   Description

sdlc   Required keyword for SDLC data-link control.

sdlc-address   SDLC address.

Default

No default SDLC address is specified.

Command Mode

Interface configuration

Usage Guidelines

This command first appeared in Cisco IOS Release 11.0.

Example

In the following example, SDLC address C1 is enabled for use by host connections:

```
encapsulation sdlc
sdlc role secondary
```

```
sdlc address c1
sna enable-host sdlc c1
```

Related Commands

To locate documentation of related commands, you can search online at www.cisco.com.

encapsulation sdlc
sna host (SDLC)

sna enable-host (Token Ring, Ethernet, Frame Relay, FDDI)

Use the **sna enable-host** interface configuration command to enable SNA on the interface. Use the **no** form of this command to disable SNA on the interface.

> **sna enable-host** [**lsap** *lsap-address*]
> **no sna enable-host** [**lsap** *lsap-address*]

Syntax	Description
lsap	(Optional) Activates a local SAP as an upstream SAP, for both receiving ConnectIn attempts and for starting ConnectOut attempts.
lsap-address	(Optional) Local SAP. The default is 12.

Default

The default LSAP parameter is 12.

Command Mode

Interface configuration

Usage Guidelines

This command first appeared in Cisco IOS Release 11.0.

Example

The following example enables SNA on the interface and specifies that the local SAP 10 will be activated as an upstream SAP:

```
sna enable-host lsap 10
```

Related Commands

To locate documentation of related commands, you can search online at www.cisco.com.

show sna
sna host (Frame Relay)
sna host (Token Ring, Ethernet, FDDI, RSRB, VDLC)

sna host (Frame Relay)

Use this form of the **sna host** global configuration command to define a link to an SNA host over a Frame Relay connection. Use the **no** form of this command to cancel the definition.

> **sna host** *host-name* **xid-snd** *xid* **dlci** *dlci-number* [**rsap** *remote-sap*] [**lsap** *local-sap*]
> [**interface** *slot/port*] [**window** *window-size*] [**maxiframe** *max-iframe*]
> [**retries** *retry-count*] [**retry-timeout** *retry-timeout*] [**focalpoint**]
> **no sna host** *host-name* **xid-snd** *xid* **dlci** *dlci-number* [**rsap** *remote-sap*]
> [**lsap** *local-sap*] [**interface** *slot/port*] [**window** *window-size*]
> [**maxiframe** *max-iframe*] [**retries** *retry-count*] [**retry-timeout** *retry-timeout*]
> [**focalpoint**]

Syntax	Description
host-name	The specified SNA host.
xid-snd *xid*	The XID that is sent to the host during connection establishment. The XID value is 8 hexadecimal digits that include both block and ID numbers. For example, if the XID value is 05D00001, the block number is 05D and the ID number is 00001.
dlci *dlci-number*	DLCI number.
rsap *remote-sap*	(Optional) SAP address of the remote host PU. The default is 4.
lsap *local-sap*	(Optional) Local SAP address used by the SNA Service Point to establish connection with the remote host. The default is 12.
interface *slot/ port*	(Optional) Slot and port number of the interface.

Syntax	Description
window *window-size*	(Optional) Sends and receives window sizes used for the host link. The range is 1 to 127. The default is 7.
maxiframe *max-iframe*	(Optional) Sends and receives maximum I-frame sizes used for the host link. The range is 64 to 18,432. The default is 1472.
retries *retry-count*	(Optional) Number of times the SNA Service Point attempts to retry establishing connection with remote host PU. The range is 0 to 255 (0 = no retry attempts, 255 = infinite retry attempts). The default is 255.
retry-timeout *retry-timeout*	(Optional) Delay (in seconds) between attempts to retry establishing connection with remote host PU. The range is 1 to 600 seconds. The default is 30 seconds.
focalpoint	(Optional) Host link to be used for the focal point support.

Defaults
The default remote SAP is 4.
The default local SAP is 12.
The default window size is 7.
The default maximum I-frame size is 1472.
The default retry count is 255.
The default retry timeout is 30 seconds.

Command Mode
Global configuration

Usage Guidelines
This command first appeared in Cisco IOS Release 11.0.

Example
The following example defines a link to an SNA host:

```
sna host CNM01 xid-snd 05d00001 dlci 200 rsap 4 lsap 4
```

Related Commands
To locate documentation of related commands, you can search online at www.cisco.com.

sna enable-host (Token Ring, Ethernet, Frame Relay, FDDI)
sna start

Part II

Command Reference

sna host (QLLC)

Use this form of the **sna host** global configuration command to define a link to an SNA host over an X.25/QLLC connection. Use the **no** form of this command to cancel the definition.

> **sna host** *host-name* **xid-snd** *xid* **x25** *remote-x121-addr* [**qllc** *local-x121-subaddr*]
> [**interface** *slot/port*] [**window** *window-size*] [**maxiframe** *max-iframe*]
> [**retries** *retry-count*] [**retry-timeout** *retry-timeout*] [**focalpoint**]
> **no sna host** *host-name* **xid-snd** *xid* **x25** *remote-x121-addr* [**qllc** *local-x121-subaddr*]
> [**interface** *slot/port*] [**window** *window-size*] [**maxiframe** *max-iframe*]
> [**retries** *retry-count*] [**retry-timeout** *retry-timeout*] [**focalpoint**]

Syntax	Description
host-name	SNA host.
xid-snd *xid*	XID that is sent to the host during connection establishment. The XID value is 8 hexadecimal digits that include both block and ID numbers. For example, if the XID value is 05D00001, the block number is 05D and the ID number is 00001.
x25 *remote-x121-addr*	SDLC address.
qllc *local-x121-subaddr*	(Optional) Specifies the SAP address of the remote host PU. The default is 4.
interface *slot/port*	(Optional) Slot and port number of the interface.
window *window-size*	(Optional) Sends and receives window sizes used for the host link. The range is 1 to 127. The default is 7.
maxiframe *max-iframe*	(Optional) Sends and receives maximum I-frame sizes used for the host link. The range is 64 to 18,432. The default is 1472.
retries *retry-count*	(Optional) Number of times the SNA Service Point attempts to retry establishing connection with remote host PU. The range is 0 to 255 (0 = no retry attempts, 255 = infinite retry attempts). The default is 255.
retry-timeout *retry-timeout*	(Optional) Delay (in seconds) between attempts to retry establishing connection with remote host PU. The range is 1 to 600 seconds. The default is 30 seconds.
focalpoint	(Optional) Host link to be used for the focal point support.

Defaults

The default remote SAP is 4.
The default window size is 7.

The default maximum I-frame size is 1472.
The default retry count is 255.
The default retry timeout is 30 seconds.

Command Mode

Global configuration

Usage Guidelines

This command first appeared in Cisco IOS Release 11.0.

Example

The following example defines a link to an SNA host:

```
sna host MLM1 xid-snd 05d00001 x25 320108 qllc 08
```

Related Commands

To locate documentation of related commands, you can search online at www.cisco.com.

sna enable-host (QLLC)
sna start

sna host (SDLC)

Use this form of the **sna host** global configuration command to define a link to an SNA host over an SDLC connection. Use the **no** form of this command to cancel the definition.

> **sna host** *host-name* **xid-snd** *xid* **sdlc** *sdlc-addr* [**rsap** *remote-sap*] [**lsap** *local-sap*]
> [**interface** *slot/port*] [**window** *window-size*] [**maxiframe** *max-iframe*]
> [**retries** *retry-count*] [**retry-timeout** *retry-timeout*] [**focalpoint**]
> **no sna host** *host-name* **xid-snd** *xid* **rmac** *remote-mac* [**rsap** *remote-sap*]
> [**lsap** *local-sap*] [**interface** *slot/port*] [**window** *window-size*] [**maxiframe**
> *max-iframe*] [**retries** *retry-count*] [**retry-timeout** *retry-timeout*] [**focalpoint**]

Syntax	Description
host-name	SNA host.
xid-snd *xid*	XID that is sent to the host during connection establishment. The XID value is 8 hexadecimal digits that include both block and ID numbers. For example, if the XID value is 05D00001, the block number is 05D and the ID number is 00001.

Syntax	Description
sdlc *sdlc-addr*	SDLC address.
rsap *remote-sap*	(Optional) SAP address of the remote host PU. The default is 4.
lsap *local-sap*	(Optional) Local SAP address used by the SNA Service Point to establish connection with the remote host. The default is 12.
interface *slot/port*	(Optional) Slot and port number of the interface.
window *window-size*	(Optional) Sends and receives window sizes used for the host link. The range is 1 to 127. The default is 7.
maxiframe *max-iframe*	(Optional) Sends and receives maximum I-frame sizes used for the host link. The range is 64 to 18,432. The default is 1472.
retries *retry-count*	(Optional) Number of times the SNA Service Point attempts to retry establishing connection with remote host PU. The range is 0 to 255 (0 = no retry attempts, 255 = infinite retry attempts). The default is 255.
retry-timeout *retry-timeout*	(Optional) Delay (in seconds) between attempts to retry establishing connection with remote host PU. The range is 1 to 600 seconds. The default is 30 seconds.
focalpoint	(Optional) Host link to be used for the focal point support.

Defaults

The default remote SAP is 4.
The default local SAP is 12.
The default window size is 7.
The default maximum I-frame size is 1472.
The default retry count is 255.
The default retry timeout is 30 seconds.

Command Mode

Global configuration

Usage Guidelines

This command first appeared in Cisco IOS Release 11.0.

Example

The following example defines a link to an SNA host:

```
sna host CNM01 xid-snd 05d00001 sdlc c1 rsap 4 lsap 4 focalpoint
```

Related Commands

To locate documentation of related commands, you can search online at www.cisco.com.

sna enable-host (SDLC)
sna start

sna host (Token Ring, Ethernet, FDDI, RSRB, VDLC)

Use this form of the **sna host** global configuration command to define a link to an SNA host over Token Ring, Ethernet, FDDI, RSRB, or virtual data-link control connections. Use the **no** form of this command to cancel the definition.

> **sna host** *host-name* **xid-snd** *xid* **rmac** *remote-mac* [**rsap** *remote-sap*] [**lsap** *local-sap*]
> [**interface** *slot/port*] [**window** *window-size*] [**maxiframe** *max-iframe*]
>   [**retries** *retry-count*] [**retry-timeout** *retry-timeout*] [**focalpoint**]
> **no sna host** *host-name* **xid-snd** *xid* **rmac** *remote-mac* [**rsap** *remote-sap*]
>   [**lsap** *local-sap*] [**interface** *slot/port*] [**window** *window-size*]
>   [**maxiframe** *max-iframe*] [**retries** *retry-count*] [**retry-timeout** *retry-timeout*]
>   [**focalpoint**]

Syntax	Description
host-name	SNA host.
xid-snd *xid*	XID that is sent to the host during connection establishment. The XID value is 8 hexadecimal digits that include both block and ID numbers. For example, if the XID value is 05D00001, the block number is 05D and the ID number is 00001.
rmac *remote-mac*	MAC address of the remote host PU.
rsap *remote-sap*	(Optional) SAP address of the remote host PU. The default is 4.
lsap *local-sap*	(Optional) Local SAP address used by the SNA Service Point to establish connection with the remote host. The default is 12.
interface *slot/ port*	(Optional) Slot and port number of the interface.
window *window-size*	(Optional) Sends and receives window sizes used for the host link. The range is 1 to 127. The default is 7.
maxiframe *max-iframe*	(Optional) Sends and receives maximum I-frame sizes used for the host link. The range is 64 to 18,432. The default is 1472.
retries *retry-count*	(Optional) Number of times the SNA Service Point attempts to retry establishing connection with remote host PU. The range is 0 to 255 (0 = no retry attempts, 255 = infinite retry attempts). The default is 255.

Syntax	Description
retry-timeout *retry-timeout*	(Optional) Delay (in seconds) between attempts to retry establishing connection with remote host PU. The range is 1 to 600 seconds. The default is 30 seconds.
focalpoint	(Optional) Host link to be used for the focal point support.

Defaults

The default remote SAP is 4.
The default local SAP is 12.
The default window size is 7.
The default maximum I-frame size is 1472.
The default retry count is 255.
The default retry timeout is 30 seconds.

Command Mode

Global configuration

Usage Guidelines

This command first appeared in Cisco IOS Release 11.0.

Example

The following example defines a link to an SNA host:

```
sna host CNM01 xid-snd 05d00001 rmac 4001.3745.1088 rsap 4 lsap 4 focalpoint
```

Related Commands

To locate documentation of related commands, you can search online at www.cisco.com.

sna enable-host (Token Ring, Ethernet, Frame Relay, FDDI)
sna rsrb enable-host
sna rsrb start
sna start
sna vdlc enable-host
sna vdlc start

sna rsrb

Use the **sna rsrb** interface configuration command to specify the entities that the SNA feature will simulate at the remote source-route bridge. Use the **no** form of this command to cancel the specification.

> **sna rsrb** *local-virtual-ring bridge-number target-virtual-ring virtual-macaddr*
> **no sna rsrb** *local-virtual-ring bridge-number target-virtual-ring virtual-macaddr*

Part
II

Command Reference

Syntax	Description
local-virtual-ring	Local virtual ring number.
bridge-number	Virtual bridge number. The valid range is 1 to 15.
target-virtual-ring	Target virtual ring number.
virtual-macaddr	Virtual MAC address.

Default
No defaults are specified.

Command Mode
Interface configuration.

Usage Guidelines
This command first appeared in Cisco IOS Release 11.0.

You can specify the bridge number no more than once in any configuration.

Example
The following example identifies a LAN:

```
sna rsrb 88 1 99 4000.FFFF.0001
```

Related Commands
To locate documentation of related commands, you can search online at www.cisco.com.

sna rsrb start

sna rsrb enable-host

Use the **sna rsrb enable-host** global configuration command to enable an RSRB SAP for use by SNA Service Point. Use the **no** form of this command to disable the RSRB SAP.

> **sna rsrb enable-host** [**lsap** *local-sap*]
> **no sna rsrb enable-host** [**lsap** *local-sap*]

Syntax

Description

lsap *local-sap*   (Optional) Specifies that the local SAP address will be activated as an upstream SAP for both receiving incoming connections attempts and for starting outgoing connection attempts. The default is 12.

Default

The default local SAP address is 12.

Command Mode

Global configuration

Usage Guidelines

This command first appeared in Cisco IOS Release 11.0.

Example

In the following example, the local SAP address 10 of the RSRB is enabled for use by the ibm3745 host PU:

```
source-bridge ring-group 99
source-bridge remote-peer 99 tcp 150.10.13.1
source-bridge remote-peer 99 tcp 150.10.13.2

sna rsrb 88 1 99 4000.FFFF.0001
sna rsrb enable-host lsap 10

sna host ibm3745 xid-snd 06500001 rmac 4000.3745.0001 lsap 10

interface serial 0
 ip address 150.10.13.1 255.255.255.0
```

Related Commands

To locate documentation of related commands, you can search online at www.cisco.com.

sna host (Token Ring, Ethernet, FDDI, RSRB, VDLC)

sna rsrb start

Use the **sna rsrb start** global configuration command to specify that an attempt will be made to connect to the remote resource defined by host name through the RSRB. Use the **no** form of this command to cancel the definition.

> **sna rsrb start** *host-name*
> **no sna rsrb start** *host-name*

Syntax   Description

host-name   The name of a host defined in an **sna host (Token Ring, Ethernet, FDDI, RSRB, VDLC)** or equivalent command.

Default

There are no default settings.

Command Mode

Global configuration

Usage Guidelines

This command first appeared in Cisco IOS Release 11.0.

Before issuing this command, you must enable the correct local SAP with the appropriate enable command (**sna rsrb enable-host**).

Example

In the following example, the SNA Service Point will initiate a connection with the ibm3745 host PU across the RSRB link:

```
source-bridge ring-group 99
source-bridge remote-peer 99 tcp 150.10.13.1
source-bridge remote-peer 99 tcp 150.10.13.2
```

```
sna rsrb 88 1 99 4000.FFFF.0001
sna rsrb enable-host lsap 10

sna host ibm3745 xid-snd 06500001 rmac 4000.3745.0001 lsap 10
sna rsrb start ibm3745

interface serial 0
 ip address 150.10.13.1 255.255.255.0
```

Related Commands

To locate documentation of related commands, you can search online at www.cisco.com.

sna host (Token Ring, Ethernet, FDDI, RSRB, VDLC)
sna rsrb

sna start

Use the **sna start** interface configuration command to initiate a connection to a remote resource. Use the **no** form of this command to cancel the connection attempt.

> **sna start** [*resource-name*]
> **no sna start** [*resource-name*]

Syntax	Description
resource-name	(Optional) Name of a host defined in an **sna host** command.

Default

No default is specified.

Command Mode

Interface configuration

Usage Guidelines

This command first appeared in Cisco IOS Release 11.0.

Before issuing this command, you must enable the correct address using the **sna enable-host** command.

Example

The following example initiates a connection to CNM01:

```
sna start CNM01
```

Related Commands

To locate documentation of related commands, you can search online at www.cisco.com.

sna host (Frame Relay)
sna host (QLLC)
sna host (SDLC)
sna host (Token Ring, Ethernet, FDDI, RSRB, VDLC)

sna vdlc

Use the **sna vdlc** global configuration command to identify the local virtual ring and virtual MAC address that will be used to establish SNA host connections over DLSw+ using virtual data-link control. Use the **no** form of this command to cancel the definition.

> **sna vdlc** *ring-group virtual-mac-address*
> **no sna vdlc** *ring-group virtual-mac-address*

Syntax	Description
ring-group	Local virtual ring number identifying the SRB ring group.
virtual-mac-address	Virtual MAC address that represents the SNA virtual data-link control.

Default

There are no default settings.

Command Mode

Global configuration

Usage Guidelines

This command first appeared in Cisco IOS Release 11.2.

The virtual data-link control local virtual ring must have been previously configured using the **source-bridge ring-group** command.

The virtual data-link control virtual MAC address must be unique within the DLSw+ network.

To avoid an address conflict on the virtual MAC address, use a locally administered address in the form 4000.*xxxx.xxxx*.

Example

The following is an example of an SNA Service Point configuration that uses virtual data-link control over DLSw+:

```
source-bridge ring-group 99
dlsw local-peer peer-id 150.10.16.2
dlsw remote-peer 0 tcp 150.10.16.1

sna vdlc 99 4000.4500.01f0
sna vdlc enable-host lsap 12

sna host HOST-B xid-snd 065bbbb0 rmac 4000.7000.01f1 rsap 4 lsap 12 focalpoint

sna vdlc start HOST-B

interface serial 3
 description IP connection to dspu7k
 ip address 150.10.16.2 255.255.255.0
 clockrate 4000000
```

Related Commands

To locate documentation of related commands, you can search online at www.cisco.com.

dlsw local-peer
dlsw remote-peer
sna vdlc start
source-bridge ring-group

sna vdlc enable-host

Use the **sna vdlc enable-host** global configuration command to enable a SAP for use by SNA Service Point. Use the **no** form of this command to disable the SAP.

> **sna vdlc enable-host** [**lsap** *local-sap*]
> **no sna vdlc enable-host** [**lsap** *local-sap*]

Syntax

lsap *local-sap*

Description

(Optional) Specifies that the local SAP address will be activated as an upstream SAP for both receiving incoming connection attempts and for starting outgoing connection attempts. The default is 12.

Default

The default local SAP address is 12.

Command Mode

Global configuration

Usage Guidelines

This command first appeared in Cisco IOS Release 11.2.

Example

In the following example, the local SAP address 12 is enabled for use by the host PU HOST-B:

```
source-bridge ring-group 99
dlsw local-peer peer-id 150.10.16.2
dlsw remote-peer 0 tcp 150.10.16.1

sna vdlc 99 4000.4500.01f0
sna vdlc enable-host lsap 12

sna host HOST-B xid-snd 065bbbb0 rmac 4000.7000.01f1 rsap 4 lsap 12 focalpoint

sna vdlc start HOST-B

interface serial 3
 description IP connection to dspu7k
 ip address 150.10.16.2 255.255.255.0
 clockrate 4000000
```

Related Commands

To locate documentation of related commands, you can search online at www.cisco.com.

sna host (Token Ring, Ethernet, FDDI, RSRB, VDLC)

sna vdlc start

Use the **sna vdlc start** global configuration command to specify that an attempt will be made to connect to the remote resource defined by host name through virtual data-link control. Use the **no** form of this command to cancel the definition.

> **sna vdlc start** *host-name*
> **no sna vdlc start** *host-name*

Syntax   Description

host-name   The name of a host defined in an **sna host (Token Ring, Ethernet, FDDI, RSRB, VDLC)** or equivalent command.

Default

There are no default settings.

Command Mode

Global configuration

Usage Guidelines

This command first appeared in Cisco IOS Release 11.2.

Before issuing this command, you must enable the correct local SAP with the **sna vdlc enable-host** command.

Example

In the following example, SNA Service Point uses virtual data-link control to initiate a connection with the host PU HOST-B:

```
source-bridge ring-group 99
dlsw local-peer peer-id 150.10.16.2
dlsw remote-peer 0 tcp 150.10.16.1

sna vdlc 99 4000.4500.01f0
sna vdlc enable-host lsap 12

sna host HOST-B xid-snd 065bbbb0 rmac 4000.7000.01f1 rsap 4 lsap 12 focalpoint

sna vdlc start HOST-B

interface serial 3
```

```
description IP connection to dspu7k
ip address 150.10.16.2 255.255.255.0
clockrate 4000000
```

Related Commands

To locate documentation of related commands, you can search online at www.cisco.com.

sna vdlc

Configuring SNA Frame Relay Access Support

This chapter describes Frame Relay Access Support (FRAS) for Systems Network Architecture (SNA) devices. It also explains how to configure FRAS and how to use a FRAS host to connect Cisco Frame Relay Access Devices (FRADs) to channel-attached mainframes, LAN-attached FEPs, and LAN-attached AS/400s through a Cisco router.

For a complete description of the FRAS commands in this chapter, refer to Chapter 20, "SNA Frame Relay Access Support Commands." To locate documentation of specific commands, you can search online at www.cisco.com.

SNA FRAS Configuration Task List

To configure FRAS, perform the tasks described in the following sections:

- Configure FRAS Boundary Network Node Statically
- Configure FRAS BNN Dynamically
- Configure FRAS Boundary Access Node Support
- Configure Source-Route Bridging over Frame Relay
- Configure FRAS Congestion Management
- Configure FRAS Data-Link Connection Identifier Backup
- Configure Frame Relay Remote Source-Route Bridging Dial Backup
- Configure Frame Relay Data-Link Switching Plus Dial Backup
- Monitor and Maintain FRAS

To configure the FRAS host, see the section "Configure FRAS Host." For configuration examples, see the section "FRAS and FRAS Host Configuration Examples" at the end of this chapter.

Configure FRAS Boundary Network Node Statically

To configure FRAS boundary network node (BNN) statically, use one of the following commands in interface configuration mode:

Command	Purpose
fras map llc *mac-address lan-lsap lan-rsap* **serial** *port* **frame-relay** d*lci fr-lsap fr-rsap* [**pfid2** | **afid2** | **fid4**]	Associates an LLC connection with a Frame Relay DLCI.
fras map sdlc *sdlc-address* **serial** *port* **frame-relay** *dlci fr-lsap fr-rsap* [**pfid2** | **afid2** | **fid4**]	Associates an SDLC link with a Frame Relay DLCI.

In this implementation, you configure and define each end station MAC and SAP address pair statically.

Because Frame Relay itself does not provide a reliable transport as required by SNA, the RFC 1490 support of SNA uses LLC2 as part of the encapsulation to provide link-level sequencing, acknowledgment, and flow control. The serial interface configured for Internet Engineering Task Force (IETF) encapsulation (that is, RFC 1490) accepts all LLC2 interface configuration commands.

Configure FRAS BNN Dynamically

To configure FRAS BNN dynamically, use one of the following commands in interface configuration mode:

Command	Purpose
fras map llc *lan-lsap* **serial** *interface* **frame-relay dlci** *dlci fr-rsap*	Associates an LLC connection with a Frame Relay DLCI.
fras map sdlc *sdlc-address* **serial** *port* **frame-relay** *dlci fr-lsap fr-rsap* [**pfid2** | **afid2** | **fid4**]	Associates an SDLC link with a Frame Relay DLCI.

When you associate an LLC connection with a Frame Relay DLCI, the router "learns" the MAC/SAP information as it forwards packets to the host. The FRAS BNN feature provides seamless processing at the router regardless of end station changes. End stations can be added or deleted without reconfiguring the router.

When you associate an SDLC link with a Frame Relay DLCI, you configure and define each end station MAC and SAP address pair statically.

Because Frame Relay itself does not provide a reliable transport as required by SNA, the RFC 1490 support of SNA uses LLC2 as part of the encapsulation to provide link-level sequencing, acknowledgment, and flow control. The serial interface configured for Internet Engineering Task Force (IETF) encapsulation (that is, RFC 1490) can take all LLC2 interface configuration commands.

Configure FRAS Boundary Access Node Support

To configure Frame Relay boundary access node (BAN), use the following command in interface configuration mode:

Command	Purpose
fras ban *local-ring bridge-number ring-group ban-dlci-mac* **dlci** *dlci#1* [*dlci#2 . . . dlci#5*] [**bni** *mac-addr*]	Associates a bridge to the Frame Relay BAN.

BAN simplifies router configuration when multiple LLC sessions are multiplexed over the same DLCI. By comparison, SAP multiplexing requires static definitions and maintenance overhead. By using BAN, the Token Ring MAC address is included in every frame to uniquely identify the LLC session. Downstream devices can be dynamically added and deleted with no configuration changes required on the router.

Configure Source-Route Bridging over Frame Relay

To configure source-route bridging (SRB) over Frame Relay, use the following commands in interface configuration mode:

Step	Command	Purpose
1	**interface serial** *number*	Specifies the serial port.
2	**encapsulation frame-relay**	Enables Frame Relay encapsulation.
3	**interface serial** *slot/port.subinterface-number* **point-to-point**	Configures a Frame Relay point-to-point subinterface.
4	**frame-relay interface-dlci** *dlci* **ietf**	Configures a DLCI number for the point-to-point subinterface.
5	**source-bridge** *source-ring-number bridge-number target-ring-number* **conserve-ring**	Assigns a ring number to the Frame Relay permanent virtual circuit.

Cisco IOS software offers the ability to encapsulate SRB traffic using RFC 1490 Bridged 802.5 encapsulation. This provides SRB over Frame Relay functionality. This SRB over Frame Relay feature is interoperable with other vendors' implementations of SRB over Frame Relay and with some vendors' implementations of FRAS BAN.

SRB over Frame Relay does not support the following Cisco IOS software functions:

- Proxy explorer
- Automatic spanning tree
- LAN Network Manager

Configure FRAS Congestion Management

FRAS provides a congestion control mechanism based on the interaction between congestion notification bits in the Frame Relay packet and the dynamic adjustment of the LLC2 send window. This window shows the number of frames Cisco IOS software can send before waiting for an acknowledgment. The window size decreases with the occurrence of backward explicit congestion notification (BECN) and increases when no BECN frames are received.

To configure congestion management, use the following commands in interface configuration mode:

Step	Command	Purpose
1	**llc2 local-window** *packet-count*	Specifies the maximum window size for each logical connection.
2	**llc2 dynwind** [**nw** *nw-number*] [**dwc** *dwc-number*]	Enables the dynamic window flow-control mechanism.

You can enable the dynamic window mechanism only if you are using Frame Relay IETF encapsulation.

Configure FRAS Data-Link Connection Identifier Backup

To configure FRAS data-link connection identifier (DLCI) backup, use the following command in interface configuration mode:

Command	Purpose
fras ddr-backup interface *interface dlci-number*	Specifies an interface to be used for the backup connection and indicates the DLCI number of the session.

FRAS DLCI backup is an enhancement to Cisco's FRAS implementation that lets you configure a secondary path to the host to be used when the Frame Relay network becomes unavailable. When the primary Frame Relay link to the Frame Relay WAN fails, the FRAS DLCI backup feature causes the router to reroute all sessions from the main Frame Relay interface to the secondary interface. The secondary interface can be either serial or ISDN and must have a DLCI configured.

Figure 19-1 illustrates Frame Relay backup over an ISDN connection.

Figure 19-1 *FRAS DLCI Backup over ISDN*

NOTE   This feature provides backup for the local end of the Frame Relay connection, not the complete end-to-end connection.

Configure Frame Relay Remote Source-Route Bridging Dial Backup

When the Frame Relay network is down, Cisco IOS software checks whether the dial backup feature is configured for the particular DLCI number. If it is configured, the software removes the FRAS to the downstream device connection and establishes the remote source-route bridging (RSRB) to this downstream device connection.

To configure RSRB dial backup, use the following command in interface configuration mode:

Command	Purpose
fras backup rsrb *vmacaddr local-ring-number target-ring-number host-mac-address*	Activates Frame Relay RSRB dial backup.

Configure Frame Relay Data-Link Switching Plus Dial Backup

The FRAS dial backup over data-link switching plus (DLSw+) feature provides a secondary path that is used when the Frame Relay network becomes unavailable. If preconfigured properly, when the primary link to the Frame Relay WAN fails, FRAS dial backup over DLSw+ feature moves existing sessions to the alternate link automatically. When the primary link is restored, existing sessions are kept on the backup connection so they can be moved non-disruptively to the primary link at the user's discretion.

To enable FRAS dial backup over DLSw+, use the following command in interface configuration mode:

Command	Purpose
fras backup dlsw *virtual-mac-address target-ring-number host-mac-address* [retry *number*]	Configures an auxiliary (backup) route between the end stations and the host for use when the DLCI connection to the Frame Relay network is lost.

Figure 19-2 shows a Frame Relay network with FRAS dial backup over DLSw+.

Figure 19-2   *FRAS Dial Backup over DLSw+*

Figure 19-3 shows the active FRAS dial backup over DLSw+ when the Frame Relay connection to the NCP is lost.

Figure 19-3   *FRAS Dial Backup over DLSw+ when Frame Relay Is Unavailable*

Monitor and Maintain FRAS

To display information about the state of FRAS, use the following command in privileged EXEC mode:

Command	Purpose
show fras	Displays the mapping and connection state of FRAS.

Configure FRAS Host

The FRAS Host provides a scalable and efficient solution for SNA FRAD access to channel-attached hosts and to LAN-attached hosts. The FRAS Host function operates in two modes, which are documented in the following sections:

- FRAS Host LLC2 Passthru—In this mode, the LLC2 sessions are not locally terminated in the router's LLC2 stack. This is the recommended solution if your scenario includes a Channel Interface Processor (CIP) interface to the mainframe.

- FRAS Host LLC2 Local Termination—In this mode, the LLC2 sessions are locally terminated in the router's LLC2 stack. This is the recommended solution if either of the following is true:

    — Your scenario includes a LAN-attached AS/400 or mainframe.

    — Your scenario includes conversion from RFC1490 encapsulation to DLSw+ encapsulation.

FRAS Host LLC2 Passthru

The FRAS Host LLC passsthru feature combines with a CIP-attached Cisco router's high-speed channel access to provide FEP-class performance at a fraction of what it would cost to achieve similar functionality using a FEP. If the CIP SNA feature is used to interface with the mainframe, then FRAS Host LLC2 passthru mode is the recommended solution. In this topology the LLC2 passthru solution to the CIP-SNA LLC2 stack provides better performance, is more robust, and responds well to different types of congestion.

To prevent LLC2 session timeout, LLC2 characteristics (windows and timers) may be tuned on the CIP internal LAN adapter. The CIP/SNA LLC2 stack reacts to congestion by dynamically adjusting its LLC2 transmit window for that LLC2 session in response to dropped frames.

With the FRAS Host LLC passthru feature, you gain performance benefits of a channel attachment without FEP upgrades such as the addition of a Frame Relay interface, an upgrade to NCP (with its associated increase in monthly charges), and a possible increase in system memory.

Figure 19-4 illustrates Cisco FRAD access to a mainframe through a channel-attached Cisco router.

Figure 19-4 *Cisco FRAD Access to a Mainframe through a Cisco 7500*

FRAS Host LLC2 Local Termination

If the FRAS Host feature is used to allow remote FRADs to communicate with a LAN-attached IBM 3745 or AS/400, then LLC2 termination via DLSw+ local switching is the recommended solution. With this approach, the LLC2 sessions are terminated at the Route Processor. To prevent LLC2 session timeout, LLC2 characteristics (windows and timers) may be tuned on the virtual Token Ring interface. If the dynamic window algorithm is enabled on the virtual Token Ring interface, LLC2 local termination will react to congestion by dynamically adjusting its LLC2 transmit window in response to occurrence of Frame Relay BECN.

When you use the FRAS Host LLC2 local termination feature on a Token Ring-attached FEP, the FRAS Host Cisco router shields the FEP from having to manage the interface to the Frame Relay network. This avoids interface, memory, and NCP upgrades. The FRAS Host Cisco router simply provides LLC2 sessions to the FEP over the LAN.

If used in an environment with AS/400s, FRAS Host LLC2 local termination provides an even more valuable function. The Cisco FRAS Host router offloads the management of the Frame Relay connections from the AS/400. This reduces AS/400 system hardware requirements and frees AS/400 CPU cycles for user applications.

Figure 19-5 illustrates Cisco FRAD access to a LAN-attached SNA host through a Cisco router.

Figure 19-5 *Cisco FRAD Access to a LAN-Attached AS/400 through a Cisco 4500*

Congestion Management

Both passthru and local acknowledgment environments support frame discard eligibility (DE) for additional congestion management. In both environments, you can further tune the interface to the Frame Relay network by taking advantage of Cisco IOS Frame Relay features. Taken together, these features increase overall throughput dramatically by comparison to generic FRADs, which typically cannot use the network with the same degree of efficiency.

FRAS Host Configuration Task List

To configure the FRAS Host migration feature, perform the tasks in the following sections:

- Create a Virtual Token Ring Interface
- Configure SRB on the Virtual Token Ring Interface
- Accept Default LLC2 Passthru or Enable LLC2 Local Termination
- Enable the FRAS Host Feature for BAN or BNN
- Monitor LLC2 Sessions Using FRAS Host

Create a Virtual Token Ring Interface

To configure a virtual Token Ring interface, use the following command in interface configuration mode:

Command	Purpose
interface virtual-tokenring *number*	Configures a virtual Token Ring interface.

Configure SRB on the Virtual Token Ring Interface

To configure SRB on the Token Ring interface, use the following commands, beginning in global configuration mode:

Step	Command	Purpose
1	**source-bridge ring-group** *ring-group virtual-mac-address*	Enables local SRB.
2	**source-bridge** *local-ring bridge-number target-ring*	Enables FRAS Host traffic to access the SRB domain.

NOTE	If you are using LLC2 passthru with an Ethernet-attached host, you must configure Cisco source-route translational bridging (SR/TLB) feature.

Accept Default LLC2 Passthru or Enable LLC2 Local Termination

LLC2 passthru is the default operational mode for all FRAS Host connections that use a virtual Token Ring interface. You do not need to perform any configuration to accept the default LLC2 passthru mode.

To enable LLC2 local termination for FRAS Host connections using the virtual Token Ring, use the following commands, beginning in global configuration mode:

Step	Command	Purpose
1	**dlsw local-peer**	Enables data-link local switching.
2	**fras-host dlsw-local-ack**	Enables LLC2 local termination for FRAS Host connections.

Enable the FRAS Host Feature for BAN or BNN

To enable the FRAS Host for BAN or BNN, use the following commands in interface configuration mode:

Step	Command	Purpose
1	**fras-host bnn** (*sub*)*interface* **fr-lsap** *sap* **vmac** *virt-mac* **hmac** *hmac* [**hsap** *hsap*]	Configures the FRAS host for BNN.
2	**fras-host ban** (*sub*)*interface* **hmac** *hmac* [**bni** *bni-mac*]	Configures the FRAS host for BAN.

Monitor LLC2 Sessions Using FRAS Host

To display the status of LLC2 sessions using FRAS Host, use the following command in privileged EXEC mode:

Command	Purpose
show fras-host [(*sub*)*interface*] [**dlci** *dlci-num*] [**detail**]	Displays the status of LLC2 sessions using FRAS Host.

FRAS and FRAS Host Configuration Examples

The following sections provide both FRAS and FRAS Host configuration examples:

- LAN-Attached SNA Devices Example
- SDLC-Attached SNA Devices Example
- FRAS BNN Topology Example
- FRAS BNN Example
- FRAS BAN Example
- SRB over Frame Relay Example

- FRAS DLCI Backup over Serial Interface Example
- FRAS Dial Backup over DLSw+ Example
- Cisco FRAD or FRAS Router Configuration Examples
- FRAS Host CIP Connection to VTAM Configuration Example
- FRAS Host Ethernet Connection to AS/400 Configuration Example

LAN-Attached SNA Devices Example

Figure 19-6 illustrates the configuration of SNA devices attached to a LAN.

Figure 19-6 *LAN-Attached SNA Devices*

The configuration for the network shown in Figure 19-6 is as follows:

```
interface tokenring 0
 no ip address
 no keepalive
 ring-speed 16
 fras map llc 0800.5a8f.8802 4 4 serial 0 frame-relay 200 4 4
!
interface serial 0
 mtu 2500
 no ip address
 encapsulation frame-relay IETF
 keepalive 12
 frame-relay lmi-type ansi
 frame-relay map llc2 200
```

SDLC-Attached SNA Devices Example

Figure 19-7 illustrates the configuration of SDLC-attached SNA devices.

Figure 19-7 *SDLC-Attached SNA Devices*

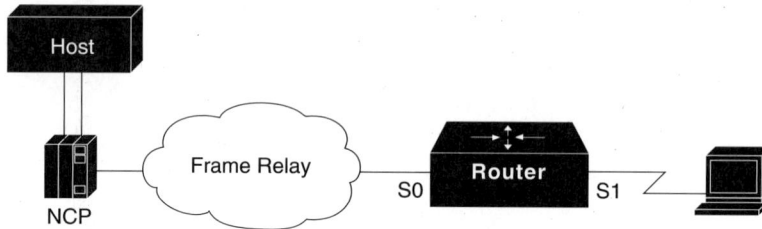

The configuration file for the network shown in Figure 19-7 is as follows:

```
interface serial 1
 no ip address
 encapsulation sdlc
 no keepalive
 clockrate 56000
 sdlc address C1
 sdlc xid C1 05D01501
 sdlc role primary
 fras map sdlc C1 serial 0 frame-relay 200 4 4
!
interface serial 0
 mtu 2500
 no ip address
 encapsulation frame-relay ietf
 keepalive 12
 frame-relay lmi-type ansi
 frame-relay map llc2 200
```

FRAS BNN Topology Example

FRAS BNN transports SNA traffic across different media through a Cisco router and then through a Frame Relay link to the host. SNA PU 2.0 and PU 2.1 devices may be attached to the remote router through Token Ring, SDLC, or Ethernet to access the Frame Relay network. The FRAS BNN topology is illustrated in Figure 19-8.

Figure 19-8 *FRAS BNN Topology*

The original Frame Relay BNN feature transports traffic from multiple PUs over a single DLCI. This function is called SAP multiplexing. The router uses a unique SAP address (fr-lsap) for each down-stream PU when communicating with the host. In this implementation, each end station's MAC/SAP address pair must be statically defined to the router. Consequently, the router must be reconfigured each time an end station is moved, added, or deleted. The configuration overhead for this implementation can be high.

The FRAS BNN feature, where the router "learns" the MAC/SAP information as it forwards packets to the host, offers several advantages over the original FRAS BNN implementation. The BNN enhancement alleviates the need to reconfigure the router when end stations are moved, added, or deleted. The configuration is simple: one map definition in the router is sufficient for multiple downstream devices. The router "learns" the addresses of the downstream devices in the normal course of communication (as shown in Figure 19-9).

Figure 19-9 illustrates the Frame Relay BNN configuration for both the original implementation and the enhanced implementation.

Figure 19-9 *Frame Relay BNN Support*

If the end station initiates the LLC session, the router acquires the Token Ring address and the SAP value of the end station from the incoming frame. Instead of mapping the end station's MAC/SAP address pair (as was done in the original FRAS BNN implementation), the destination MAC/SAP address pair of the incoming frame is mapped to the Frame Relay DLCI. If the destination SAP specified by the end station is equal to the lan-lsap address, the router associates the LLC (LAN) connection with the Frame Relay DLCI. The MAC address and the SAP address of the end station are no longer required in the router configuration. Thus, in the enhanced FRAS BNN implementation one configuration command achieves the same result for the end stations as did multiple configuration commands in the original FRAS BNN implementation.

NOTE   The new FRAS BNN feature, which provides seamless processing at the router regardless of end-station changes, is designed to coexist with the original FRAS BNN feature. In Cisco IOS Release 11.2, only LLC2 traffic will be supported. SDLC must be configured using the original BNN implementation.

FRAS BNN Example

The following configuration example enables the FRAS BNN feature. The topology is illustrated in Figure 19-10.

Figure 19-10 *FRAS BNN Configuration*

```
interface Serial0
 no ip address
 encapsulation frame-relay IETF
 frame-relay lmi-type ansi
 frame-relay map llc2 16
!
interface TokenRing0
 no ip address
 ring-speed 16
 fras map llc 0800.5aab.0856 04 04 Serial 0 frame-relay 16 04 04
 fras map llc 04 Serial 0 frame-relay dlci 16 04
```

NOTE	In this configuration example, the second to last line describes the old configuration for workstation A. The last line describes the configuration for the new workstations B and C.

FRAS BAN Example

The following configuration shows FRAS BAN support for Token Ring and serial interfaces. You must specify the **source-bridge ring-group** global command before you configure the **fras ban** interface command. When Token Ring is configured, the **source-bridge** interface command includes the *local-ring, bridge-number*, and the *target-ring* values. The **source-bridge** command enables local SRB on a Token Ring interface.

```
source-bridge ring-group 200
!
interface serial 0
 mtu 4000
 encapsulation frame-relay ietf
 frame-relay lmi-type ansi
 frame-relay map llc2  16
 frame-relay map llc2  17
 fras ban 120 1 200 4000.1000.2000 dlci 16 17
!
interface tokenring 0
 source-bridge 100 5 200
```

For SDLC connections, you must include SDLC configuration commands as follows:

```
!
interface Serial1
 description SDLC line PU2.0
 mtu 265
 no ip address
 encapsulation sdlc
 no keepalive
 clockrate 9600
 sdlc role primary
 sdlc vmac 4000.0000.0000
 sdlc address C2
 sdlc xid C2 05D01502
 sdlc partner 4000.0000.2345 C2
 sdlc address C8
 sdlc xid C8 05D01508
 sdlc partner 4000.0000.2345 C8
 sdlc address C9
 sdlc xid C9 05D01509
 sdlc partner 4000.0000.2345 C9
 fras ban frame-relay Serial0 4000.0000.2345 dlci 16
!
interface Serial2
 description SDLC line PU2.1
 no ip address
 encapsulation sdlc
 no keepalive
 clockrate 19200
 sdlc role prim-xid-poll
 sdlc vmac 2000.0000.0000
 sdlc address C6
 sdlc partner 1000.2000.3000 C6
 fras ban frame-relay serial0 1000.2000.3000 dlci 16
```

SRB over Frame Relay Example

Figure 19-11 illustrates the interoperability provided by SRB over Frame Relay. FRADs B and C forward frames from their locally attached Token Rings over the Frame Relay network using SRB.

Figure 19-11   *FRAD Using SRB over Frame Relay to Connect to a Cisco Router*

Figure 19-11 illustrates a network with the following characteristics:

- Virtual ring number of Router A = 100

- Virtual ring number of FRAD B = 200

- Virtual ring number of FRAD C = 300

- DLCI number for the partner's virtual ring (PVC) between Router A and FRAD B = 30

- DLCI number for PVC between Router A and FRAD C = 31

In this example, we configure a new option, **conserve-ring**, on the **source-bridge** interface configuration command. When this option is configured, the SRB software does not add the ring number associated with the Frame Relay PVC to outbound explorer frames. This option is permitted for Frame Relay subinterfaces only.

The router configures the partner FRAD's virtual ring number as the ring number for the PVC.

This approach does not require a separate ring number per DLCI. The router configures the partner FRAD's virtual ring number as the ring number for the PVC.

FRAD B configures its virtual ring as 200 and the ring for the PVC as 100. FRAD C configures its virtual ring as 300 and the ring for the PVC as 100.

FRAS DLCI Backup over Serial Interface Example

The following example shows a configuration for FRAS DLCI backup over a serial interface:

```
interface serial0
 mtu 3000
 no ip address
 encapsulation frame-relay IETF
 bandwidth 56
 keepalive 11
 frame-relay map llc2 277
 frame-relay map llc2 278
 frame-relay lmi-type ansi
 fras ddr-backup interface serial1 188
!
interface serial1
 mtu 3000
 no ip address
 encapsulation frame-relay IETF
 no cdp enable
 frame-relay map llc2 188
 frame-relay lmi-type ansi
!
interface serial2
 no ip address
 encapsulation sdlc
 no keepalive
 clock rate 19200
 sdlc role prim-xid-poll
 sdlc address D6
 fras map sdlc D6 s0 frame-relay 277 8 4
!
interface tokenring0
 no ip address
 ring-speed 16
 fras map llc 0000.f63a.2f70 4 4 serial0 frame-relay 277 4 4
```

Router A

```
source-bridge ring-group 100
!
interface Serial1
 encapsulation frame-relay
!
interface Serial1.1 point-to-point
 frame-relay interface-dlci 30 ietf
 source-bridge 200 1 100 conserve-ring
 source-bridge spanning
!
interface Serial1.2 point-to-point
 frame-relay interface-dlci 31 ietf
 source-bridge 300 1 100 conserve-ring
 source-bridge spanning
!
interface TokenRing0
 source-bridge 500 1 100
```

FRAS Dial Backup over DLSw+ Example

The following examples show configurations for FRAS dial backup over DLSw+.

FRAS Dial Backup on a Subinterface

```
source-bridge ring-group 200
dlsw local-peer peer-id 10.8.8.8
dlsw remote-peer 0 tcp 10.8.8.7 dynamic
interface ethernet0
 ip address 10.8.8.8 255.255.255.0
!
interface serial0
 no ip address
 encapsulation frame-relay IETF
 frame-relay lmi-type ansi
!
interface Serial0.1 point-to-point
 description fras backup dlsw+ listening on dlci 16 configuration example
 no ip address
 frame-relay interface-dlci 16
 fras backup dlsw 4000.1000.2000 200 1000.5aed.1f53
!
interface TokenRing0
 no ip address
 ring-speed 16
 fras map llc 0000.f63a.2f50 4 4 Serial0.1 frame-relay 16 4 4
```

FRAS Dial Backup on a Main Interface

```
source-bridge ring-group 200
dlsw local-peer peer-id 10.8.8.8
dlsw remote-peer 0 tcp 10.8.8.7 dynamic
interface ethernet0
 ip address 10.8.8.8 255.255.255.0
!
interface serial0
 no ip address
 encapsulation frame-relay IETF
 frame-relay lmi-type ansi
frame-relay map llc2 16
fras backup dlsw 4000.1000.2000 200 1000.5aed.1f53
!
interface Serial1
 ip address 10.8.8.8
!
interface tokening0
 no ip address
 ring-speed 16
 fras map llc 0000.f63a.2f50 4 4 Serial0 frame-relay 16 4 4
```

Cisco FRAD or FRAS Router Configuration Examples

This section provides the following configuration examples (see Figure 19-12):

- Cisco FRAD or FRAS Router A with BNN Configuration Example
- Cisco FRAD or FRAS Router B with BAN Configuration Example
- Cisco FRAD or FRAS Router C with BAN Configuration Example

Figure 19-12 *FRAS Host CIP Connection to VTAM*

Cisco FRAD or FRAS Router A with BNN Configuration Example

```
interface Serial0
 encapsulation frame-relay IETF
 frame-relay map llc2 16
!
interface TokenRing0
 fras map llc 4001.2222.0000 4 4 Serial0 frame-relay 16 4 4
```

Cisco FRAD or FRAS Router B with BAN Configuration Example

```
source-bridge ring-group 200
!
interface Serial0
 encapsulation frame-relay IETF
```

```
 frame-relay map llc2 37
 fras ban 10 1 200 4000.3745.0000 dlci 37
!
interface TokenRing0
 source-bridge 20 1 200
```

Cisco FRAD or FRAS Router C with BAN Configuration Example

```
source-bridge ring-group 400
!
interface Serial0
 encapsulation frame-relay IETF
 frame-relay map llc2 46
 fras ban 50 1 400 4000.3745.0220 dlci 46 bni 4001.3745.1088
!
interface TokenRing0
 source-bridge 60 1 400
```

FRAS Host CIP Connection to VTAM Configuration Example

The following example shows the configuration for the network shown in Figure 19-13:

```
source-bridge ring-group 100
!
interface Serial0/1
 encapsulation frame-relay IETF
 frame-relay map llc2 16
 frame-relay map llc2 46
!
interface Serial0/2
 encapsulation frame-relay IETF
!
interface Serial0/2.37 point-to-point
 frame-relay interface-dlci 37
!
interface Channel4/0
 no keepalive
!
interface Channel4/1
 no keepalive
 lan TokenRing 0
  source-bridge 104 1 100
  adapter 0 4001.3745.1008
!
interface Virtual-TokenRing0
 source-bridge 47 1 100
 source-bridge spanning
 fras-host bnn Serial 0/1 fr-lsap 04 vmac 4005.3003.0000 hmac 4001.3745.1088
 fras-host ban Serial 0/1 hmac 4001.3745.1088 bni 4001.3745.1088
 fras-host ban Serial 0/2.37 hmac 4001.3745.1088
```

FRAS Host Ethernet Connection to AS/400 Configuration Example

The configuration example in this section is shown in Figure 19-13.

Figure 19-13 *FRAS Host Ethernet Connection to AS/400*

```
source-bridge ring-group 226
dlsw local-peer
dlsw bridge-group 1
!
interface Ethernet0
 bridge-group 1
!
interface Serial2
 encapsulation frame-relay IETF
 frame-relay map llc2 502
 frame-relay lmi-type ansi
!
interface Virtual-TokenRing0
 no ip address
 ring-speed 16
 source-bridge 1009 1 226
 fras-host dlsw-local-ack
 fras-host bnn Serial2 fr-lsap 04 vmac 4000.1226.0000 hmac 0800.5ae1.151d
```

SNA Frame Relay Access Support Commands

This chapter describes the commands to configure Systems Network Architecture (SNA) Frame Relay Access Support (FRAS). For SNA FRAS configuration tasks and examples, refer to Chapter 19, "Configuring SNA Frame Relay Access Support."

NOTE   Because Frame Relay does not provide the reliable transport required by SNA, the RFC 1490 support of SNA uses Logical Link Control, type 2 (LLC2) as part of the encapsulation to provide link-level sequencing, acknowledgment, and flow control. The serial interface configured for Internet Engineering Task Force (IETF) encapsulation (RFC 1490) accepts all LLC2 interface configuration commands. For more information about LLC2 interface configuration commands, refer to Chapter 14, "LLC2 and SDLC Commands."

frame-relay map llc2

Use the **frame-relay map llc2** interface configuration command to map LLC2 traffic to a data-link connection identifier (DLCI). Use the **no** form of this command to cancel the LLC2 map.

frame-relay map llc2 *dlci-number*
no frame-relay map llc2

Syntax

dlci-number

Description

Frame Relay DLCI

Default

No defaults are defined.

Command Mode

Interface configuration

Usage Guidelines

This command first appeared in Cisco IOS Release 10.3.

Example

The following example maps LLC2 traffic to DLCI number 200:

```
frame-relay map llc2 200
```

frame-relay map rsrb

Use the **frame-relay map rsrb** interface configuration command to specify the DLCI number onto which the RSRB traffic is to be mapped. Use the **no** form of this command to cancel the RSRB map.

frame-relay map rsrb *dlci-number*
no frame-relay map rsrb

Syntax   Description

dlci-number   Frame Relay DLCI

Default

No defaults are defined.

Command Mode

Interface configuration

Usage Guidelines

This command first appeared in Cisco IOS Release 10.3.

Example

The following example shows RSRB traffic mapped to DLCI number 30:

```
frame-relay map rsrb 30
```

Related Commands

To locate documentation of related commands, you can search online at www.cisco.com.

encapsulation frame-relay

fras backup dlsw

Use the **fras backup dlsw** interface configuration command to configure an auxiliary route between the end stations and the host for use as a backup when the DLCI connection to the Frame Relay network is lost. Use the **no** form of this command to cancel the backup configuration.

> **fras backup dlsw** *virtual-mac-address target-ring-number host-mac-address*
> [**retry** *retry-number*]
> **no fras backup dlsw** *virtual-mac-address target-ring-number host-mac-address*
> [**retry** *retry-number*]

Part
II

Command Reference

Syntax	Description
virtual-mac-address	12-digit hexadecimal string used as a source MAC address for all packets going to the host.
target-ring-number	Number configured in the **source-bridge ring-group** command. This is a virtual ring. The valid range is 1 to 4095.
host-mac-address	Destination MAC address of the host.
retry *retry-number*	(Optional) Number of attempts by the end station to reconnect to the primary Frame Relay interface before activating the backup link. The range is 1 to 5 retries. If the **retry** option is not specified, the default number of retries is 5.

Default

FRAS dial backup over DLSw+ is disabled.

Command Mode

Interface configuration

Usage Guidelines

This command first appeared in Cisco IOS Release 11.2 F.

Configure DLSw+ as normally required. Specify the optional keyword **dynamic** at the end of the **dlsw remote-peer** configuration command to enable the peer relationship to be established only when needed (for example, when the **fras backup dlsw** command becomes active).

Example

The following example configures FRAS dial backup over DLSw+:

```
fras backup dlsw 4000.1000.2000 200 1000.5aed.1f53
```

Related Commands

To locate documentation of related commands, you can search online at www.cisco.com.

dlsw local-peer
dlsw remote-peer tcp
frame-relay lmi-type
frame-relay map llc2
fras map llc
show fras
source-bridge ring-group

fras ban

Use the **fras ban** interface configuration command to associate bridging over a Frame Relay network using boundary access node (BAN). Use the **no** form of this command to cancel each association.

> **fras ban** *local-ring bridge-number ring-group ban-dlci-mac* **dlci** *dlci#1*
>   [*dlci#2 … dlci#5*] [**bni** *mac-addr*]
> **no fras ban** *local-ring bridge-number ring-group ban-dlci-mac* **dlci** *dlci#1*
>   [*dlci#2 … dlci#5*] [**bni** *mac-addr*]

Syntax	Description
local-ring	Decimal number from 1 to 4095 describing the Token Ring interface.
bridge-number	Decimal number from 1 to 15 that uniquely identifies a bridge connecting two rings.
ring-group	Decimal number from 1 to 4095 representing a collection of Token Ring interfaces on one or more routers.
ban-dlci-mac	Frame Relay BAN PVC MAC address.

Syntax

dlci#1 [*dlci#2 ... dlci#5*]

bni *mac-addr*

Description

Frame Relay DLCI. Each DLCI number is unique and is a decimal within the range of 16 to 1007. The keyword **dlci** precedes the list of one or more DLCI numbers. If more than one DLCI number is needed for load balancing in the FRAS BAN configuration command, a maximum of five DLCI numbers are allowed.

(Optional) Boundary node identifier (BNI) MAC address of the NCP that receives frames from the router.

Default

No defaults are defined.

Command Mode

Interface configuration

Usage Guidelines

This command first appeared in Cisco IOS Release 11.1.

Multiple **fras ban** commands may be configured; however, each **fras ban** command must use a unique DLCI MAC address.

You must configure the **source-bridge ring-group** global configuration command prior to configuring the **fras ban** command.

Example

The following example shows FRAS BAN support for Token Ring and serial interfaces:

```
source-bridge ring-group 200
!
interface serial 0
 mtu 4000
 encapsulation frame-relay ietf
 frame-relay lmi-type ansi
 frame-relay map llc2  16
 frame-relay map llc2  17
 fras ban 120 1 200 4000.1000.2000 dlci 16 17
!
interface tokenring 0
 source-bridge 100 5 200
```

Related Commands

To locate documentation of related commands, you can search online at www.cisco.com.

source-bridge ring-group

fras ddr-backup

Use the **fras ddr-backup** interface configuration command to configure an auxiliary interface for use as a backup when the primary Frame Relay link to the Frame Relay WAN fails. Use the **no** form of this command to cancel the backup configuration.

> **fras ddr-backup interface** *interface dlci-number*
> **no fras ddr-backup**

Syntax	Description
interface *interface*	The interface over which the backup connection is made.
dlci-number	The DLCI number of the session.

Default

FRAS DLCI backup is disabled by default.

Command Mode

Interface configuration

Usage Guidelines

This command first appeared in Cisco IOS Release 11.2 F.

Example

The following example configures FRAS DLCI backup on serial interface 1:

```
fras ddr-backup interface serial1 188
```

Related Commands

To locate documentation of related commands, you can search online at www.cisco.com.

show llc2
show fr pvc
show fras

fras-host ban

Use the **fras-host ban** interface configuration command to enable the FRAS Host function for BAN.
Use the **no** form of this command to disable the FRAS Host BAN functionality.

> **fras-host ban** *(sub)interface* **hmac** *hmac* [**bni** *bni*]
> **no fras-host ban**

Syntax	Description
(sub)interface	Associated Frame Relay interface or subinterface.
hmac hmac	MAC address of the CIP adapter or LAN-attached host.
bni *bni*	(Optional) Boundary node identifier MAC address. The default *bni* is 4FFF.0000.0000.

Default

The FRAS Host function for BAN is disabled for the Frame Relay subinterface.

The default *bni* is 4FFF.0000.0000.

Command Mode

Interface configuration

Usage Guidelines

This command first appeared in Cisco IOS Release 11.2 F.

Example

The following example enables the FRAS Host function for BAN:

```
fras-host ban Serial0 hmac 4001.3745.0001
```

Related Commands

To locate documentation of related commands, you can search online at www.cisco.com.

fras ban
fras-host bnn
fras-host dlsw-local-ack
interface virtual-tokenring

fras-host bnn

Use the **fras-host bnn** interface configuration command to enable the FRAS Host function for BNN. Use the **no** form of this command to disable the FRAS Host function.

> **fras-host bnn** *(sub)interface* **fr-lsap** *sap* **vmac** *virt-mac* **hmac** *hmac* [**hsap** *hsap*]
> **no fras-host bnn**

Syntax	Description
(sub)interface	Associated Frame Relay interface or subinterface.
fr-lsap *sap*	LLC2 service access point (SAP). The destination SAP on inbound BNN frames received from Frame Relay.
vmac *virt-mac*	Used in combination with the DLCI number to form a unique MAC address. The first four bytes of the MAC address are formed by the VMAC while the last two bytes are formed from the DLCI number. The last two bytes of the VMAC must be configured as zeros.
hmac hmac	MAC address of the CIP adaptor or LAN-attached host.
hsap *hsap*	(Optional) Host SAP. If this parameter is not specified, the host SAP value used will match **fr-lsap**.

Default

FRAS Host for BNN is disabled for the Frame Relay subinterface.

Command Mode

Interface configuration

Usage Guidelines

This command first appeared in Cisco IOS Release 11.2 F.

Example

The following example enables the FRAS Host function for BNN:

```
fras-host bnn Serial0 fr-lsap 04 vmac 4005.3003.0000 hmac 4001.3745.0001
```

Related Commands

To locate documentation of related commands, you can search online at www.cisco.com.

fras-host ban
fras-host dlsw-local-ack
fras-map
interface virtual-tokenring

fras-host dlsw-local-ack

Use the **fras-host dlsw-local-ack** interface configuration command to enable LLC2 local termination for FRAS Host connections using the virtual Token-Ring. Use the **no** form of this command to disable LLC2 local termination.

> **fras-host dlsw-local-ack**
> **no fras-host dlsw-local-ack**

Syntax Description

This command has no arguments or keywords.

Default

The default state is FRAS Host LLC2 local termination disabled.

Command Mode

Interface configuration

Usage Guidelines

This command first appeared in Cisco IOS Release 11.2 F.

Example

The following example enables LLC2 local termination for FRAS Host connections using the virtual Token Ring:

```
fras-host dlsw-local-ack
```

Related Commands

To locate documentation of related commands, you can search online at www.cisco.com.

dlsw local-peer
fras-host ban
fras-host bnn
interface virtual-tokenring

fras map llc

Use the **fras map llc** interface configuration command to associate an LLC connection with a Frame Relay DLCI. Use the **no** form of this command to disable the association.

> **fras map llc** *lan-lsap* **serial** *interface* **frame-relay dlci** *dlci fr-rsap*
> **no fras map llc** *lan-lsap* **serial** *interface* **frame-relay dlci** *dlci fr-rsap*

Syntax	Description
lan-lsap	LLC2 LAN SAP that is the local SAP address of the router.
serial *interface*	Serial interface on which Frame Relay is configured.
frame-relay dlci *dlci*	Frame Relay DLCI.
fr-rsap	LLC2 Frame Relay SAP that is the destination SAP of the router on the Frame Relay side.

Default

The default state is FRAS BNN enhancement disabled.

Command Mode

Interface configuration

Part
II

Command Reference

Usage Guidelines

This revised version of the **fras map llc** command for the enhanced FRAS BNN functionality first appeared in Cisco IOS Release 11.2 F.

If the destination SAP specified by the end station is equal to *lan-lsap*, the router associates the LLC (LAN) connection with the Frame Relay DLCI.

The MAC address and the SAP address of the end station are no longer required for the BNN enhanced configuration.

Example

In the FRAS BNN enhancement, the revised **fras map llc** command achieves the same result as using multiple **fras map llc** commands in the original FRAS BNN implementation. The following example provides one map definition for both end stations:

```
fras map llc 4 Serial 0 frame-relay dlci 16 04
```

Related Commands

To locate documentation of related commands, you can search online at www.cisco.com.

show fras
show llc2

fras map sdlc

Use the **fras map sdlc** interface configuration command to associate an SDLC link with a Frame Relay DLCI. Use the **no** form of this command to cancel the association.

> **fras map sdlc** *sdlc-address* **serial** *port* **frame-relay** *dlci fr-lsap fr-rsap*
> [**pfid2** |**afid2** | **fid4**]
> **no fras map sdlc** *sdlc-address* **serial** *port* **frame-relay** *dlci fr-lsap fr-rsap*
> [**pfid2** |**afid2** | **fid4**]

Syntax	Description
sdlc-address	SDLC address of the downstream SNA device in hexadecimal.
serial *port*	Serial interface on which Frame Relay is configured.
frame-relay *dlci*	Frame Relay DLCI.
fr-lsap	Local SAP address of the logical link connection on the Cisco Frame Relay Access Device (CFRAD).
fr-rsap	Destination SAP address on the host.

Syntax	Description
pfid	(Optional) FID2 SNA transmission header for SNA peripheral traffic.
afid2	(Optional) FID2 transmission header for APPN traffic.
fid4	(Optional) Transmission header used on SNA subarea flows.

Default
No defaults are defined.

Command Mode
Interface configuration

Usage Guidelines
This command first appeared in Cisco IOS Release 10.3.

You can map multiple SDLC links to a DLCI.

Example
The following example associates an SDLC link with a Frame Relay DLCI:

```
fras map sdlc c1 serial 0 frame-relay 200 4 4
```

Related Commands
To locate documentation of related commands, you can search online at www.cisco.com.

frame-relay map llc2

interface virtual-tokenring

Use the **interface virtual-tokenring** command to create a virtual Token Ring interface. Use the **no** form of this command to cancel the configuration.

> **interface virtual-tokenring** *number*
> **no interface virtual-tokenring**

Syntax	Description
number	Number of the virtual Token Ring.

Default
No defaults are assigned.

Command Mode
Interface configuration

Usage Guidelines
This command first appeared in Cisco IOS Release 11.2 F.

Example
The following example configures the virtual Token Ring interface:

```
interface virtual-tokenring 0
```

Related Commands
To locate documentation of related commands, you can search online at www.cisco.com.

source bridge
fras ban
fras-host bnn

llc2 dynwind

Use the **llc2 dynwind** interface configuration command to enable dynamic window congestion management. Use the **no** form of this command to cancel the configuration.

> **llc2 dynwind** [**nw** *nw-number*] [**dwc** *dwc-number*]
> **no llc2 dynwind** [**nw** *nw-number*] [**dwc** *dwc-number*]

Syntax	Description
nw *nw-number*	(Optional) Specifies a number of frames that must be received to increment the working window value by 1. The default is 4.
dwc *dwc-number*	(Optional) Specifies the number by which the working window value is divided when BECN occurs. Valid numbers are 1, 2, 4, 8, and 16. 1 is a special value that indicates that the working window value should be set to 1 when BECN is indicated. The default is 1.

Defaults

The default *nw-number* value is 4.

The default *dwc-number* value is 1.

Command Mode

Interface configuration

Usage Guidelines

This command first appeared in Cisco IOS Release 10.3.

Example

The following example specifies that to increment the working window 6 frames must be received, and the working window value should be set to 1 when BECN occurs:

```
llc2 dynwind nw 6 dwc 1
```

show fras

Use the **show fras** privileged EXEC command to view notification that the FRAS dial backup over DLSw+ feature is active, to display information about the connection state in FRAS, and to display current BNN, BAN, and dial backup information.

show fras

Syntax Description

This command has no arguments or keywords.

Command Mode

Privileged EXEC

Usage Guidelines

This command first appeared in Cisco IOS Release 11.1.

Sample Display

The following is sample output from the **show fras** command:

```
Router# show fras

Boundary Network Node (BNN):
DLCI: 66
  Type    Destination      Int    LSap  RSap  Role  State
  fr                              4     4     S     ls_reset (Backup is enabled)
  llc     0000.f63a.2f50   To0    4     4     P     ls_contacted
```

Table 20-1 describes significant fields shown in the display.

Table 20-1 *show fras Field Descriptions*

Field	Description
Type	Connection type. The display example shows LLC and Frame Relay.
Destination	Destination MAC address from the perspective of the Cisco IOS software.
Int	Interface on which the connection resides.
LSap	Local SAP value.
RSap	Remote SAP value.
Role	Local link station role; P means primary and S means secondary.
State	Link station protocol machine state. This value may be one of the following states: • ls_reset—Initial state. • ls_RqOpnStnSent—TEST frame sent; request to open a connection endpoint. • ls_ExchgXid—XID negotiation taking place. • ls_ConnRqSent—SABME sent (connecting side). • ls_SigStnWait—Waiting for signal to clean up the congestion and respond to polling with an RNR. • ls_ConnRspWait—Wait for the other connection end point to bring up the link. • ls_ConnRspSent—A UA has been sent and the router is waiting for a RR to clear up the flow. • ls_Contacted—Everything is connected • ls_DiscWait—Wait for acknowledge to disconnect request.
Backup is enabled	Notification displayed when the FRAS dial backup feature is configured.

show fras-host

Use the **show fras-host** EXEC command to display the status of LLC2 sessions using FRAS Host.

show fras-host [*(sub)interface*] [**dlci** *dlci-num*] [**detail**]

Syntax	Description
(sub)interface	Only display LLC2 sessions from a specified Frame Relay interface or subinterface.
dlci *dlci-number*	Only display LLC2 sessions from a specified DLCI.
detail	Display additional information such as the routing information fields (RIFs) and statistics associated with the LLC2 sessions.

Command Mode

EXEC

Usage Guidelines

This command first appeared in Cisco IOS Release 11.2 F.

Sample Display

The following is sample output from the **show fras-host** command:

```
router# show fras-host

Number of Active Control Blocks = 2
Number of Available Control Blocks in Pool = 126

PortDLCITypeFrRsapFrLSapHostSapVMacHostMac
Se016 BNN0408044000.ABBA.001E4000.3000.2000
Se137 BAN0404044000.0223.00194000.3000.2000
```

Table 20-2 describes significant fields shown in the display.

Table 20-2 *show fras-host Field Descriptions*

Field	Description
Port	Frame Relay interface or subinterface associated with this LLC2 session.
DLCI	DLCI number associated with this LLC2 session.
Type	FRAS encapsulation type associated with this LLC2 session.
FrRsap	Frame Relay Remote LLC2 Sap associated with this LLC2 session. This SAP is the source sap on LLC2 frames sent by the remote FRAD.

Table 20-2 *show fras-host Field Descriptions (Continued)*

Field	Description
FrLSap	Frame Relay Local LLC2 SAP associated with this LLC2 session. This SAP is the destination SAP on LLC2 frames sent by the remote FRAD.
HostSap	Destination SAP on LLC2 frames sent to the CIP or LAN-attached AS/400. This SAP will be identical to FrLSap unless the **hsap** parameter is configured on the **fras-host bnn** command.
VMac	MAC address associated with the remote FRAD for this LLC2 session.
HostMac	MAC address associated with the host for this LLC2 session.

Related Commands

To locate documentation of related commands, you can search online at www.cisco.com.

fras-host ban
fras-host bnn
fras-host dlsw-local-ack

show fras map

Use the **show fras map** privileged EXEC command to display the mapping and connection state of FRAS.

show fras map

Syntax Description

This command has no arguments or keywords.

Command Mode

Privileged EXEC

Usage Guidelines

This command first appeared in Cisco IOS Release 10.3.

Sample Display

The following is sample output from the **show fras map** command:

```
Router# show fras map

Type Destination    Int   LSap   RSap   Role   State
tr   0800.5a8f.8802 tr0   4      4      P      ls_contacted
fr   200            s0    4      4      S      ls_contacted
```

Table 20-3 describes significant fields shown in the display.

Table 20-3   *show fras map Field Descriptions*

Field	Description
Type	Interface type.
Destination	Destination address.
Int	Interface.
LSap	Local SAP.
RSap	Remote SAP.
Role	Local link station role; P means primary, S means secondary.
State	Link station protocol machine state.

source-bridge

Use the **source-bridge** interface configuration command to configure an interface for source-route bridging (SRB). Use the **no** form of this command to disable source-route bridging on an interface.

> **source-bridge** *source-ring-number bridge-number target-ring-number*
> [**conserve-ring**]
> **no source-bridge** *source-ring-number bridge-number target-ring-number*
> [**conserve-ring**]

Syntax	Description
source-ring-number	Ring number for the interface's Token Ring or FDDI ring. It must be a decimal number in the range 1 to 4095 that uniquely identifies a network segment or ring within the bridged Token Ring or FDDI network.
bridge-number	Number that uniquely identifies the bridge connecting the source and target rings. It must be a decimal number in the range 1 to 15.

Syntax	Description
target-ring-number	Ring number of the destination ring on this router. The number must be unique within the bridged Token Ring or FDDI network. The target ring can also be a ring group. It must be a decimal number.
conserve-ring	(Optional) Keyword to enable SRB over Frame Relay. When this option is configured, the SRB software does not add the ring number associated with the Frame Relay partner's virtual ring (PVC) to outbound explorer frames. This option is permitted for Frame Relay subinterfaces only.

Default

SRB is disabled.

Command Mode

Interface configuration

Usage Guidelines

This revised version of the **source-bridge** command to enable SRB over Frame Relay first appeared in Cisco IOS Release 11.2 F.

The parser automatically displays the word "active" in the **source-bridge** command in configurations that have SRB enabled. You do not need to enter the **source-bridge** command with the **active** keyword.

Examples

In the following example, Token Rings 129 and 130 are connected via a router:

```
interface tokenring 0
 source-bridge 129 1 130
!
interface tokenring 1
 source-bridge active 130 1 129
```

In the following example, an FDDI ring on one router is connected to a Token Ring on a second router across a DLSw+ link:

```
dlsw local-peer peer-id 132.11.11.2
dlsw remote-peer 0 tcp 132.11.11.3
interface fddi 0
 no ip address
 multiring all
 source-bridge active 26 1 10
!
```

```
dlsw local-peer peer-id 132.11.11.3
dlsw remote-peer 0 tcp 132.11.11.2
interface tokenring 0
 no ip address
 multiring all
 source-bridge active 25 1 10
```

In the following example, a router forwards frames from a locally attached Token Ring over the Frame Relay using SRB:

```
source-bridge ring-group 200
!
interface Serial0
 encapsulation frame-relay
!
interface Serial0.30 point-to-point
 frame-relay interface-dlci 30 ietf
 source-bridge 100 1 200 conserve-ring
 source-bridge spanning
!
interface TokenRing0
 source-bridge 600 1 200
```

Related Commands

To locate documentation of related commands, you can search online at www.cisco.com.

debug frame-relay packet
debug source bridge
debug source error
debug source event
encapsulation frame-relay
frame-relay interface-dlci
source-bridge ring-group
source-bridge transparent

Configuring Advanced Peer-to-Peer Networking

Many enterprises today maintain two networks: a traditional, hierarchical Systems Network Architecture (SNA) subarea network and an interconnected LAN network, based on connectionless, dynamic protocols. The advantage of the subarea SNA network is that it is manageable and deterministic and provides guaranteed response time. The disadvantages are that it requires extensive system definition and does not take advantage of the capabilities of intelligent devices.

Cisco provides remote source-route bridging (RSRB) and data-link switching plus (DLSw+), which enable encapsulation of SNA traffic and consolidation of SNA with multiprotocol networks.

Advanced Peer-to-Peer Networking (APPN) gives the additional flexibility to route SNA natively, without encapsulation. You can use APPN by itself or in combination with RSRB and DLSw+ to provide the best solution for your networking needs.

High Performance Routing (HPR) is an enhancement to APPN that improves network performance and reliability. Considered the next step in the evolution of SNA networking, HPR provides two new elements: Rapid Transport Protocol (RTP) and Automatic Network Routing (ANR).

This chapter describes how to configure APPN. For a complete description of the APPN commands in this chapter, refer to Chapter 22, "APPN Configuration Commands." To locate documentation of other commands that appear in this chapter, you can search online at www.cisco.com.

APPN Command Modes

APPN offers the ability to define attributes of the APPN network that can become quite complex. To easily manage the capability to define the details of APPN, special configuration command modes and conventions have been developed.

Because APPN offers a large number of configuration options, specific configuration dialogues are used for each major APPN configuration task. When you define the major item, you will automatically enter the detailed configuration mode for that item. There are two options to exit the detailed mode. The **complete** command exits the detailed configuration mode and updates the APPN subsystem with the changes. The **exit** command leaves the definition in **no complete** state and does not update the APPN subsystem.

Completing APPN Definitions

No APPN definition is usable by the APPN subsystem until the definition is marked as complete. This is accomplished by using the **complete** command when you have finished defining items in the detailed configuration mode.

Changing APPN Definitions

To update a major definition item that is already known to APPN, enter the major item definition as it was originally defined. Then, to indicate that you wish to modify an existing definition, enter **no complete**. You will then be able to change the items in the detailed configuration mode for that major definition. Remember to enter **complete** when you have finished changing the configuration item to update the APPN subsystem with your changes.

APPN Configuration Task List

To configure APPN in your network, perform the tasks discussed in the following sections. Because of the hierarchical nature of APPN definitions, you should configure APPN by following the order specified below. Definition of an APPN control point and at least one APPN port are required. In addition, you must start the APPN subsystem to activate APPN routing. The other tasks in this list are optional and may or may not need to be configured, depending on your APPN network.

- Define an APPN Control Point
- Configure HPR Resources
- Define an APPN Port
- Define an APPN Link Station
- Define an APPN Connection Network
- Define an APPN Class of Service
- Define an APPN Mode
- Define an APPN Partner LU Location
- Start the APPN Subsystem
- Stop the APPN Subsystem
- Start and Stop APPN Ports and Link Stations
- Tune the APPN Network
- Monitor the APPN Network

See the end of this chapter for "APPN Configuration Examples."

Define an APPN Control Point

An APPN control point definition is required to use APPN. This definition adds the fully qualified control point name for the node, which is a combination of a network identifier and a control point name. The network identifier must be the same as other network nodes in the APPN subnetwork attached to this node. The control point name identifies this node uniquely within the particular subnetwork.

To define an APPN control point, use the following command in global configuration mode:

Command	Purpose
appn control-point *netid.cpname*	Defines an APPN control point.

Using this command takes you from global configuration mode into APPN control point configuration mode. From this mode, you can perform any of the following optional definition tasks, which identify various capabilities and attributes of the control point.

APPN offers configuration commands that allow you to limit the resources on the router that are consumed for APPN. You may configure both the maximum memory and maximum percentage of system buffers that APPN is permitted to use. APPN cached directory entries and cached topology routing trees can additionally be limited to a maximum number.

To configure these resources, use the following commands in APPN control point configuration mode:

Step	Command	Purpose
1	**maximum-memory** *bytes*	Specifies the maximum memory available to APPN.
2	**buffer-percent** *number*	Specifies the maximum percentage of system buffers available to APPN.
3	**max-cached-entries** *number*	Specifies the maximum number of cached directory entries.
4	**max-cached-trees** *number*	Specifies the maximum number of cached topology routing trees.

By default, the central resource registration function is enabled in the router so that registration of downstream resources in the central directory server will be attempted by the router when it receives a request from the control point that owns the resource. If there is unpredictable behavior related to the central resource registration function or central directory server, use the **no central-resource-registration** command to disable the central resource registration function. In normal circumstances, there should not be any reason to disable the central resource registration function.

To enable or disable the central resource registration function, use the following commands in APPN control point configuration mode:

Step	Command	Purpose
1	**central-resource-registration**	Enables the central resource registration function.
2	**no central-resource-registration**	Disables the central resource registration function.

If you plan to use Dependent LU Requestor (DLUR) to provide services for dependent LUs connected to this APPN node, you must indicate that this DLUR function is requested for this control point and may specify the number of PUs, from 1 to 100,000, that are served by this DLUR. If you do not specify the maximum number of PUs, there is no limit on the number of PUs served by this DLUR. In addition, you may configure node-wide defaults for the Dependent LU Server and Backup Dependent LU Server that this node will contact.

To specify DLUR or DLUS services for this control point, use the following commands in APPN control point configuration mode:

Step	Command	Purpose
1	**dlur [max-pus** *number*]	Specifies that the DLUR is supported on the control point and optionally specifies the maximum number of physical units (PUs) served by this DLUR.
2	**dlus** *netid.cpname*	Specifies the name of the default DLUS that provides SSCP services to the downstream PU.
3	**backup-dlus** *netid.cpname*	Specifies the default backup DLUS to perform SSCP services for downstream PUs if the default DLUS is unavailable.

You may configure the relative resistance you wish this node to have when being considered for APPN intermediate session routing (ISR). This is a number in the range 0 through 255 that specifies this node's relative resistance. The default resistance is 128.

To configure the relative resistance of the local node, use the following command in APPN control point configuration mode:

Command	Purpose
route-additional-resistance *number*	Specifies the resistance of the local node.

Cisco's APPN implementation allows you to save the APPN directory on a TFTP host. This feature allows the node to restore previously learned directory information when the node is restored to service or in the event of a failure.

To save the APPN directory, use the following commands in APPN control point configuration mode:

Step	Command	Purpose
1	**safe-store-host ip address** *address* **directory** *path*	Enables directory safe store and specify the IP host address and the file path for safe store.
2	**safe-store-cycle** *number*	Specifies the number of separate cache instances to save before overwriting previous instances.
3	**safe-store-interval** *interval*	Specifies how often the directory database is stored to permanent media.

The ID number and ID block combine to form the identifier for this node in the XID that is exchanged when the local node connects to other nodes.

To specify the ID number and ID block, use the following commands in APPN control point configuration mode:

Step	Command	Purpose
1	**xid-block-number** *number*	Specifies the ID block (the first three digits of the node identifier for the local node).
2	**xid-id-number** *number*	Specifies the ID number (the last five digits of the node identifier for the local node).

Configure HPR Resources

APPN HPR offers configuration commands that allow you to limit the resources on the router that are used for APPN HPR. To configure these resources, use the following commands in APPN control point configuration mode:

Step	Command	Purpose
1	**hpr**	Enables HPR.
2	**hpr max-sessions** *num-sessions*	Specifies the maximum number of sessions allowed over an RTP connection.
3	**hpr retries low-retries medium-retries high-retries networ***k-retries*	Specifies the maximum number of request packets to send before closing the RTP connection.

Step	Command	Purpose
4	**hpr timers liveness** *low-time medium-time high-time network-time*	Specifies how many seconds to wait for a packet to be received before initiating a path switch.
5	**hpr timers path-switch** *low-time medium-time high-time network-time*	Specifies the amount of time allowed to attempt a path switch for an RTP connection.

To add, remove, or complete configuration items within the APPN control point configuration mode, use one of the following commands:

Command	Purpose
no *command*	Negates or restores the default value for a configuration command.
complete	Completes the APPN control point definition, returns to global configuration mode, and updates the APPN subsystem.
no complete	Allows modifications to a previously completed APPN control point definition.
exit	Exits APPN control point definition dialog without completing the definition and without updating the APPN subsystem.

Configure Serial Interface Encapsulation

If you plan to use APPN over a serial interface, the interface must be configured as a serial encapsulation type supported by APPN. The following encapsulation types are supported:

- ATM
- Frame Relay
- PPP
- SDLC
- SMDS
- X25
- ISDN (via PPP)

Define an APPN Port

An APPN port definition is used to associate APPN capabilities with a specific interface APPN will use. Each interface that will be used for APPN communications requires an APPN port definition statement. A port can be associated with a specific interface by using the following command in global configuration mode:

Command	Purpose
appn port *portname interface*	Defines an APPN port associated with an interface.

A port may also be associated with a source-route bridge ring group to enable APPN to send and receive traffic to any local or remote source-route bridged station. To configure a virtual port that connects to a source-bridge ring-group, use the following command in global configuration mode:

Command	Purpose
appn port *portname* **rsrb**	Defines an APPN port associated with a source-route bridge group.

A port may also be associated with virtual data-link control to allow link stations using this port to connect over DLSw+ using virtual data-link control. To configure an APPN virtual data-link control port, use the following command in global configuration mode:

Command	Purpose
appn port *portname* **vdlc**	Defines an APPN port associated with virtual data-link control.

Using any of these commands takes you from global configuration mode into APPN port configuration mode. From this mode, you can perform one or more of the definition tasks that follow. These tasks define various capabilities and attributes of the port. Some tasks are required; others are optional.

Configure APPN HPR Port Definitions

You can specify the SAP value used for Automatic Network Routing frames. The SAP value is used by all link stations that use the port. To specify the SAP value, use the following command in APPN port configuration mode:

Command	Purpose
hpr sap *sap*	Specifies the SAP for Automatic Network Routing frames.

HPR is enabled at the control point configuration mode. To selectively disable HPR on a port definition, use the following command in APPN port configuration mode:

Command	Purpose
no hpr	Disables support for HPR on a port.

Each APPN link negotiates a maximum basic transmit unit size during the connection phase with an adjacent node. This value limits the size of an SNA frame that can be sent over the link. On a port, the maximum basic transmit unit that can be received on this port can be configured and will be enforced for every APPN link using this port. In addition, the desired maximum basic transmit unit that can be sent by this node can be specified. The maximum basic transmit unit must be smaller than the maximum transmission unit (MTU) for the interface associated with this port.

The maximum basic transmit unit for a link can affect APPN ISR performance. Larger maximum basic transmit units allow more data to be placed in each SNA frame, offering higher data throughput for APPN ISR.

The Basic Transmission Unit (BTU) specifies a maximum message size of all SNA control information and data, exclusive of DLC and LLC header information. BTU should be set lower than the MTU to allow for DLC control information such as station addresses, DLC control fields, and the routing information field (RIF), if present.

APPN, by default, uses a maximum BTU size which varies from 1280 to 4096, depending on the type of port being defined. Use the following commands in APPN port configuration mode if you wish APPN to use a different maximum BTU size.

Step	Command	Purpose
1	**max-rcv-btu-size** *size*	Specifies the desired maximum receive basic transmit unit.
2	**desired-max-send-btu-size** *size*	Specifies the maximum basic transmit unit size for transmission groups using this port.

APPN uses SAP 4 by default. If you wish APPN to use a different SAP on this port, use the following command in APPN port configuration mode:

Command	Purpose
local-sap *sap*	Specifies the local SAP to activate on the interface.

The maximum number of link stations that can use an APPN port at any one time is configurable. Also configurable is the number of this maximum that are reserved for link stations connecting in to this port and link stations connecting out from this port.

To specify the maximum number of link stations, use the following commands in APPN port configuration mode:

Step	Command	Purpose
1	**max-link-stations** *number*	Specifies the maximum number of active link stations allowed on this port.
2	**reserved-inbound** *number*	Specifies the number of link stations to be reserved for inbound links.
3	**reserved-outbound** *number*	Specifies the number of link stations to be reserved for outbound links.

A port is configured, by default, to accept connections from other APPN nodes dynamically without requiring a link station definition for that node. It is possible to configure a port so that it does not accept incoming connection requests unless a link station has been predefined for the partner node.

To configure a port so that it does not accept incoming connection requests, use the following command in APPN port configuration mode:

Command	Purpose
no service-any	Specifies that this port will not create dynamic link stations.

The **null-xid-poll** command permits PU 2.0 devices that connect in with XID0 to build a dynamic link station. It is no longer necessary to configure a link definition. When this command is used, the router expects its partner to reveal its identity first by responding with either XID3 or XID0.

This feature works in a mixed environment of PU 2.0 and PU 2.1 devices where the same APPN port is shared by both types of devices. By default, XID3 is used to poll the devices. When a PU 2.0 device responds with XID0, the link is created and established dynamically. PU 2.1 devices are not affected by this change and go through the XID3 negotiation as usual.

To configure **null-xid-poll**, use the following command in APPN port configuration mode:

Command	Purpose
null-xid-poll	Specifies that the null XID should be used to poll the remote node associated with this APPN port.

Care must be exercised when configuring **null-xid-poll**. If two Cisco APPN network node routers connect across ports configured with **null-xid-poll**, the APPN connection will fail because both routers expect the other to respond first using either XID0 or XID3. Similar behavior may occur when a port configured with **null-xid-poll** attempts communication with a front-end processor configured for XID polling. You only need to configure **null-xid-poll** when dealing with a PU 2.0 device that does not respond gracefully to the XID3 poll.

If the port defined is an RSRB virtual port, the port must be assigned a MAC address and must be associated with a source-route bridge ring group. To assign a MAC address and associate it with a source-route bridge ring group, use the following command in APPN port configuration mode:

Command	Purpose
rsrb-virtual-station *mac-address local-ring bridge-number target-ring*	Assigns a MAC address and ring number to an RSRB virtual port, and associates it with a source-route bridge ring group.

If the port defined is a virtual data-link control port, the port must be associated with a source-route bridge ring group and assigned a MAC address. To associate the port with a ring group and assign it a MAC address, use the following command in APPN port configuration mode:

Command	Purpose
vdlc *ring-group* [**vmac** *vdlc-mac-address*]	Associates the virtual data-link control port with a source-route bridge ring group, and assigns a MAC address.

If the port is defined as an SDLC port, the secondary SDLC address can be specified. For X.25, an X.121 address for this port may be configured. To specify the secondary SDLC address or the X.25 subaddress, enter one of the following commands in APPN port configuration mode:

Command	Purpose
sdlc-sec-addr *address*	Assigns a secondary SDLC address to this port.
x25-subaddress {**pvc** | **svc**} *address*	Assigns an X.121 address for a port on an X.25 interface.

Many APPN port configuration commands are used to assign link station parameters for dynamic links that use this port. In addition, these values can be used to establish default values for defined link stations associated with this port. For more information on these commands, see the section "Define an APPN Link Station."

Use the following configuration commands to configure default link station values for link stations associated with this port.

Commands	Purpose
cost-per-byte *cost*	Specifies the cost per byte transmission group characteristic for link stations on this port.
cost-per-connect-time *cost*	Specifies the cost per connect time transmission group characteristic for link stations on this port.

Commands	Purpose
effective-capacity *capacity*	Specifies the effective capacity transmission group characteristic for link stations on this port.
limited-resource	Specifies that the link stations on this port should be taken down when no sessions are using the link.
propagation-delay {**minimum** | **lan** | **telephone** | **packet-switched** | **satellite** | **maximum**}	Specifies the propagation delay transmission group characteristic for link stations on this port.
retry-limit {*retries* | **infinite**} [*interval*]	Specifies how many times a link-station will attempt activation and the interval between retries.
role {**negotiable** | **primary** | **secondary**}	Specifies the link station role used in XID negotiations.
security *security-level*	Specifies the security level transmission group characteristic for link stations on this port.
user-defined-1 *value*	Specifies the user-defined-1 transmission group characteristic for link stations on this port.
user-defined-2 *value*	Specifies the user-defined-2 transmission group characteristic for link stations on this port.
user-defined-3 *value*	Specifies the user-defined-3 transmission group characteristic for link stations on this port.

The following commands allow for the addition, removal, or completion of configuration items within the APPN port configuration mode.

Command	Purpose
no *command*	Negates or restores the default value for a configuration command.
complete	Completes the APPN port definition, returns to global configuration mode, and updates the APPN subsystem.
no complete	Allows modifications to a previously completed APPN port definition.
exit	Exits APPN port definition dialog without completing the definition and without updating the APPN subsystem.

Define an APPN Link Station

A link station is a representation of the connection or potential connection to another node. In many cases, if the partner node is initiating the connection, a link station definition is not necessary. It will be built dynamically when the partner node initiates the connection. You must define a link station if you want this node to initiate APPN connections with other nodes. In addition, you may define a link station to specify attributes of an APPN connection regardless of which node initiates the connection.

To define an APPN logical link, use the following command in global configuration mode:

Command	Purpose
appn link-station *linkname*	Defines an APPN logical link.

Defining an APPN logical link takes you from global configuration mode into APPN link station configuration mode. In the APPN link station configuration mode, you must associate the link station with an APPN port that it will use.

Command	Purpose
port *portname*	Associates a link station with the APPN port that it will use.

Configure APPN HPR Link Definitions

HPR is enabled at the control point configuration mode. To selectively disable HPR on a link definition, use the following command in APPN link station configuration mode:

Command	Purpose
no hpr	Disables support for HPR on a link.

When defining a link that can initiate a connection to a partner node, you must provide a destination address to allow this node to contact the partner. This address is also used for incoming connections to associate the appropriate link station with the incoming call. To specify a destination address, use one of the following commands in APPN link station configuration mode, depending on the media in use:

Command	Purpose
atm-dest-address *pvc*	Configures the remote address of a node across an ATM interface.
fr-dest-address *dlci* [*sap*]	Specifies the Frame Relay DLCI of the partner node for Frame Relay links.
lan-dest-address *mac-addr* [*sap*]	Specifies a destination address and destination SAP for LAN media that use a 6-byte hardware address. This includes Token Ring, Ethernet, FDDI, and connections through RSRB and virtual data-link control.
ppp-dest-address *sap*	Specifies the destination SAP across a PPP interface.

Command	Purpose
sdlc-dest-address *address*	Specifies the SDLC address for the partner node for SDLC links.
smds-dest-address *address sap*	Specifies the remote address of a node across an SMDS interface.
x25-dest-address *address*	Specifies the X.25 address for the partner node for X.25 links.

For most APPN connections, the adjacent control point name, transmission group number, and link station role can be learned or negotiated dynamically, so there is no reason to configure them. However, if necessary, use the following commands to configure these items:

Command	Purpose
adjacent-cp-name *netid.cpname*	Specifies the name of the partner node for the link station.[1]
tg-number *number*	Specifies the transmission group number for the link.
role {**negotiable** | **primary** | **secondary**}	Specifies the link station role.

1. If the partner node requests values that differ from those configured, the link activation will fail.

A link station defaults to attempt a connection with the adjacent node when the APPN subsystem starts. If you wish to define a link, but not have it automatically attempt to establish a connection with the partner node, use the following command in APPN link station configuration mode:

Command	Purpose
no connect-at-startup	Specifies that the link will not attempt to establish an APPN connection when the APPN subsystem is started.

APPN attempts to bring up CP-CP sessions on the first active link between network nodes. You can prevent CP-CP session establishment on a link by using the following command in APPN link station configuration mode:

Command	Purpose
no cp-cp-sessions-supported	Specifies that no CP-CP sessions will be established on this link.

By default, APPN accepts connections and learns the node type of the partner node during XID exchange. If you wish to enforce that only a certain node type is permitted to connect via this link station, use the following command in APPN link station configuration mode:

Command	Purpose
verify-adjacent-node-type {**learn**	**len**	**nn**}	Specifies that the adjacent node type must be verified as a requirement of link activation.

If you want this link to disconnect when no sessions are using it, you may indicate that the link is a limited resource by using the following command in APPN link station configuration mode:

Command	Purpose
limited-resource	Specifies that the link is to be taken down when no sessions are using the link.

When this node is attempting to establish a connection with an adjacent node, you can configure the number of times this node will attempt to initiate contact and the time interval between connection attempts. Each time the link station is started, the retry count is reset and the node will attempt connection until the retry limit is reached. To specify the retry limit, use the following command in APPN link station configuration mode:

Command	Purpose
retry-limit {*retries*	**infinite**} [*interval*]	Specifies how many times a link station will attempt activation, and the interval between retries.

APPN links can be configured to interoperate with priority or custom queuing mechanisms available in Cisco IOS software. To configure an APPN link for priority or custom queuing, enter one of the following commands in APPN link station configuration mode:

Command	Purpose
link-queuing custom *queue-number*	Specifies the custom queuing queue number for this link station.
link-queuing priority *level*	Specifies the priority queuing parameter for this link station.

If you are using dependent LU requestor (DLUR), you may configure the primary and backup dependent LU server (DLUS) for links on which this node is providing SSCP services via the DLUR function. These definitions override the node-wide defaults that may have been configured in APPN control point configuration mode.

To configure the primary and backup dependent LU server (DLUS), use the following commands in APPN link station configuration mode:

Step	Command	Purpose
1	**dlus** *netid.cpname*	Specifies the name of the DLUS node that provides SSCP services to the downstream PUs of the link.
2	**backup-dlus** *netid.cpname*	Specifies the backup DLUS node that will be used in the event the primary DLUS is unreachable.

Normally, DLUR will discover the capabilities of the adjacent node and will initiate the proper XID exchange for PU type 2.0 nodes. However, a node which sends null XID but cannot receive XID3 will require configuration as a type 2.0 device to allow the node to connect properly for DLUR services. In addition, if you wish to configure this node to establish the link to the downstream PU in cases where the DLUS is initiating the activation of the device, you must configure the downstream PU name as it is known to the DLUS. In most cases, the DLUR initiates activation of the device, so coding the PU name is not necessary.

To configure a node as a type 2.0 device and configure the downstream PU name, use the following commands in APPN link station configuration mode:

Step	Command	Purpose
1	**pu-type-20**	Specifies that the downstream PU whose dependent LU request is propagated through the link is a PU Type 2.0.
2	**dlur-dspu-name** *pu-name*	Specifies the downstream PU name.

APPN calculates routes for SNA sessions using a complex algorithm that compares various characteristics of an APPN transmission group with the acceptable range of these characteristics defined in the APPN class of service (CoS) requested. Cisco uses defaults for these values that offer basic APPN functionality without the need to customize transmission group characteristics. However, if you wish to configure transmission group characteristics for an APPN connection, use the configuration commands below.

To configure the transmission group characteristics for an APPN connection, enter one or more of the following commands in APPN link station configuration mode:

Commands	Purpose
cost-per-byte *cost*	Specifies the cost per byte transmission group characteristic for this link.
cost-per-connect-time *cost*	Specifies the relative cost per connection transmission group characteristic for the link.

Commands	Purpose
effective-capacity *capacity*	Specifies effective-capacity transmission group characteristic for the link.
propagation-delay {**minimum** | **lan** | **telephone** | **packet-switched** | **satellite** | **maximum**}	Specifies the propagation delay transmission group characteristic for the link.
security *security-level*	Specifies the security level transmission group characteristic for the link.
user-defined-1 *value*	Specifies the user-defined-1 transmission group characteristic for this link station.
user-defined-2 *value*	Specifies the user-defined-2 transmission group characteristic for this link station.
user-defined-3 *value*	Specifies the user-defined-3 transmission group characteristic for this link station.

The following commands allow for the addition, removal, or completion of configuration items within the APPN link station configuration mode:

Command	Purpose
no *command*	Negates or restores the default value for a configuration command.
complete	Completes the APPN link station definition, returns to global configuration mode, and updates the APPN subsystem.
no complete	Allows modifications to a previously completed APPN link station definition.
exit	Exits APPN link station definition dialog without completing the definition and without updating the APPN subsystem.

Define an APPN Connection Network

An APPN connection network allows nodes on the same shared media to connect directly, even if there is no APPN link defined between them. Connection networks can be used to provide any-to-any connectivity on shared media without the need to define any-to-any link station connectivity. When a route is calculated through a connection network, a dynamic link station will be built and a connection will be established between the nodes on each side of the connection network. You must configure the same connection network name at each node that will participate in the connection network.

To indicate that this node is a member of a specific connection network, use the following command from global configuration mode:

Command	Purpose
appn connection-network *netid.cnname*	Defines an APPN connection network.

Using this command takes you from global configuration mode into APPN connection network configuration mode.

From APPN connection network configuration mode, you can specify up to five ports that are visible to the connection network. Usually, only a single port definition is desired for each connection network. However, in some instances it may be desirable to have more than one port as a member of a connection network, especially if two ports are attached to the same physical media. APPN route selection may choose any of the listed ports when calculating routes to or from any other member of this connection network. Therefore, it is important to ensure that each port listed is accessible by means of hardware address from every member of the connection network.

Ensure the port you choose is on an interface type that supports APPN connection networks. Connection network definitions are supported on Token Ring, Ethernet, and FDDI interfaces, as well as RSRB and DLSw+ virtual ports.

To associate a port name with this connection network definition, use the following command in APPN connection network configuration mode:

Command	Purpose
port *portname*	Associates a port name with this connection network definition.

The following commands allow for the addition, removal, or completion of configuration items within the APPN connection network configuration mode.

Command	Purpose
no *command*	Negates or restores the default value for a configuration command.
complete	Completes the APPN connection network definition, returns to global configuration mode, and updates the APPN subsystem.
no complete	Allows modifications to a previously completed APPN connection network definition.

Command	Purpose
exit	Exits APPN connection network definition dialog without completing the definition and without updating the APPN subsystem.

Define an APPN Class of Service

Cisco provides standard predefined APPN CoS definitions that are commonly used in APPN networks. These are #BATCH, #BATCHSC, #CONNECT, #INTER, #INTERSC, SNASVCMG, CPSVCMG. You can define an APPN CoS or modify the predefined definitions. Each CoS definition must have between one and eight node rows, between one and eight transmission group rows, as well as a transmission priority to be used for this CoS.

Each node row defines the weight to be assigned to a node used in APPN route calculation which is within the range of values for this row. The first row should have the smallest weight and the most restrictive range of acceptable values. Subsequent rows should have higher weight and be less restrictive than the previous rows in the range of acceptable values. Note that if a node does not fit within the acceptable range for any of the node rows, it will not be considered for inclusion in a route with the CoS.

For each node row defined, specify maximum and minimum values for node congestion and route-additional-resistance. Node congestion is either yes or no; route-additional-resistance is a value between 0 and 255 with higher numbers indicating higher resistance to intermediate routes.

Similarly, each transmission group row defines the weight to be assigned to a link used in APPN route calculation which is within the acceptable range of values for this row. Like node rows, each subsequent row should increase in weight and be less restrictive than the previous in the range of acceptable values. If the transmission group characteristics do not lie within any the acceptable range for any of the transmission group rows, the link will not be considered when calculating a route with this CoS.

Each transmission group row allows you to specify the maximum and minimum values for cost per byte, cost per connect, link capacity, propagation delay, security, and three user defined characteristics. Each of these values is specified using a relative value between 0 and 255.

To define CoS, use the following command in global configuration mode:

Command	Purpose
appn class-of-service *cosname*	Defines an APPN CoS.

Using this command takes you from global configuration mode into APPN CoS configuration mode. From the CoS mode, you must use the following commands:

Step	Command	Purpose
1	**node-row** *index* **weight** *weight* **congestion** {**yes** | **no**} {**yes** | **no**} **route-additional-resistance** *min max*	Specifies a node row number, the weight for this row, and the minimum and maximum values that may be assigned this weight.
2	**tg-row** *index* **weight** *weight* **byte** *min max* **time** *min max* **capacity** *min max* **delay** *min max* **security** *min max* **user1** *min max* **user2** *min max* **user3** *min max*	Specifies a transmission group row number, the weight for this row, and the minimum and maximum values for transmission groups that may be assigned this weight.
3	**transmission-priority** *priority*	Specifies the transmission priority for the CoS.

The following commands allow for the addition, removal, or completion of configuration items within the APPN CoS configuration mode:

Command	Purpose
no *command*	Negates or restores the default value for a configuration command.
complete	Completes the APPN CoS definition, returns to global configuration mode, and updates the APPN subsystem.
no complete	Allows modifications to a previously completed APPN CoS definition.
exit	Exits APPN CoS definition dialog without completing the definition and without updating the APPN subsystem.

Define an APPN Mode

An APPN mode definition is used by a network node to associate a mode name received on an APPN search or session request with a CoS known to this node. Most APPN nodes will supply the CoS to their network node server, so mode definition may not be required in many APPN networks. However, if this node is providing network node services to an end node that does not supply CoS, or if this node is providing network node services for a LEN node, mode definitions may be required for each mode that is used by the partner node.

Cisco provides standard predefined mode definitions for modes that are commonly used in an APPN network. The predefined mode names are the blank mode, #BATCH, #BATCHSC, #INTER, #INTERSC, CPSVCMG, and SNASVCMG. You can change a predefined mode or define a new mode.

To define an APPN mode, use the following command in global configuration mode:

Command	Purpose
appn mode *modename*	Defines an APPN mode.

Using this command takes you from global configuration mode into APPN mode configuration mode. Within this mode, you must assign a CoS to the mode definition.

Command	Purpose
class-of-service *cosname*	Associates a CoS with the defined mode.

The following commands allow for the addition, removal, or completion of configuration items within the APPN mode configuration mode.

Command	Purpose
no *command*	Negates or restores the default value for a configuration command.
complete	Completes the APPN mode definition, returns to global configuration mode, and updates the APPN subsystem.
no complete	Allows modifications to a previously completed APPN mode definition.
exit	Exits APPN CoS definition dialog without completing the definition and without updating the APPN subsystem.

Define an APPN Partner LU Location

The APPN directory stores names of resources and their owners. Usually, this information is learned dynamically via APPN searches. However, you may wish to manually define the location of specific resources. Doing so can improve network performance by allowing directed APPN searches to travel straight to the owning control point, without the need for an initial broadcast search for the resource. However, APPN is known for its dynamic capabilities, not its need for system definition. For this reason, and for easier manageability, it is good practice to define location names only when necessary.

When a LEN node is attached to an APPN network node, all destination resources that reside on the LEN node must be defined on the network node to be reachable via the APPN network.

To define a partner LU location, use the following command in global configuration mode:

Command	Purpose
appn partner-lu-location *netid.luname*	Specifies the partner resource name.

Using this command takes you from the global configuration mode into the APPN partner LU location configuration mode.

You must configure an owning control point for each partner LU configured. The owning control point is the control point name for the LEN, end node, or network node on which the resource resides. To specify the name of the control point owning the partner LU, use the following command in APPN partner LU location configuration mode:

Command	Purpose
owning-cp *netid.cpname*	Specifies the name of the control point owning the partner LU.

If this node is not the network node server for the resource, you may also configure the network node server name. To reduce APPN searching, the network node server operand must be coded and must be the current server for the resource.

If this node is the network node server for the resource being defined, do not configure a network node server.

To specify the name of the network node server for the resource, use the following command in APPN partner LU location configuration mode:

Command	Purpose
serving-nn *netid.cpname*	Specifies the name of the network node server for the resource.

A partial name wildcard partner LU is a definition that applies to all resources that match a partial name. For example, a definition for location NETA.PE, which is specified as a wildcard definition, serves as a entry for NETA.PEANUT and NETA.PENNY, but not NETA.PUMKIN. Be careful when using partial name wildcards, as they can easily cause network problems if resources that match the partial name do not actually exist in the specified location.

A full wildcard partner LU definition is specified by defining a partner LU location without specifying a resource name and specifying the wildcard option. Full wildcards answer positively to any search for any resource in the network. Only one full wildcard definition can exist in an APPN network. Full wildcards are sometimes used when the APPN subnetwork is small and an attached LEN node is the gateway to a large connected network. Full wildcard definitions reduce APPN performance and can cause a variety of network problems. Hence, use of full wildcard definitions should be avoided.

To specify a partial name or full wildcard partner LU, use the following command in APPN partner LU location configuration mode:

Command	Purpose
wildcard	Specifies the entry as a partial-name wildcard or a full wildcard.

The following commands allow for the addition, removal, or completion of configuration items within the APPN partner LU location configuration mode.

Command	Purpose
no *command*	Negates or restores the default value for a configuration command.
complete	Completes the APPN partner LU definition, returns to global configuration mode, and updates the APPN subsystem.
no complete	Allows modifications to a previously completed APPN partner LU definition.
exit	Exits APPN partner LU definition dialog without completing the definition and without updating the APPN subsystem.

Start the APPN Subsystem

The APPN subsystem may be started via global configuration mode or privileged EXEC mode.

Command	Purpose
appn routing	Starts the APPN subsystem from global configuration mode. Provided this configuration is saved, the APPN subsystem will start each time the router is booted.
appn start	Starts the APPN subsystem from privileged EXEC mode without affecting the current configuration.

Stop the APPN Subsystem

The APPN subsystem may be stopped through global configuration mode or privileged EXEC mode commands.

Command	Purpose
no appn routing	Deactivates APPN routing from global configuration mode and removes it from the current configuration.
appn stop	Deactivates APPN routing from privileged EXEC mode without affecting the current configuration.

Start and Stop APPN Ports and Link Stations

APPN port and link station definitions are started automatically when the APPN subsystem starts. However, configuration commands will not take effect on an APPN port or link when it is active. The following privileged EXEC commands allow APPN ports and link stations to be stopped and started when making configuration changes or when resetting the APPN port or link is desired:

Command	Purpose
appn stop link-station *linkname*	Deactivates the specified APPN link.
appn stop port *portname*	Deactivates the specified APPN port.
appn start link-station *linkname*	Activates the specified APPN link.
appn start port *portname*	Activates the specified APPN port.

Tune the APPN Network

Two new APPN scalability enhancement features, Locate Throttling and Negative Caching, allow you to conserve network resources. Locate throttling reduces multiple network broadcasts for the same target resource when a broadcast request is already pending from the network node server (NNS). Negative caching prevents excess searches to unreachable resources. These two features significantly reduce network traffic, particularly in the event of an unexpected resource failure.

Locate Throttling

The locate throttling feature prevents multiple broadcast locate searches that can occur when more than one resource requests sessions with the same destination LU.

When more than one resource requests sessions with the same destination LU, APPN initiates searches for each request. This can consume large amounts of network resources, particularly if APPN broadcast searches are performed.

The locate throttling feature offers a way to regulate, or "throttle," locate searches to the same destination LU. For example, if the response to a locate request is pending, and another search request is issued for the same destination LU that the router has no knowledge of, then the subsequent search request for that LU is queued to wait for the response from the first search. The locate request is withheld only if it is a locate broadcast search. For a locate directed search, no queuing is necessary.

Negative Caching

The negative caching feature prevents excess searches to unreachable resources.

When a resource becomes unavailable in the network, either temporarily or for an extended period of time, there may be a great number of subsequent requests for that resource. This consumes network resources unnecessarily and quite often adversely affects network performance.

The negative caching feature offers a means of reducing the search broadcast by retaining searches to unreachable resources. If a resource is unreachable in the network, the router rejects requests to the resource. A configurable timer allows you to determine the length of time a resource is considered unreachable. During this period, requests for the resource are rejected. When the timer expires, a full search is performed upon receipt of the first search request for that resource. A configurable threshold allows you to determine the number of searches to be rejected before a full APPN search is performed. When either of the two thresholds expires, a full APPN search is performed.

Each APPN network resource must be defined on the node where the resource exists. When the resource is defined, it can be found through network searches. Optionally, the resource location may be defined in other nodes to optimize directory services search logic.

Registered directory entries are created dynamically in the local directory of the network node. These entries represent local LUs of an adjacent end node for which the network node is providing network node server function.

Cached directory entries are added dynamically and are based on the results of previous searches. A cache entry allows the node to attempt a directed search straight to the destination resource. If a cache entry does not exist, or the entry is incorrect, a broadcast search is issued to query each network node in the network for the destination resource. Each cache entry is verified before use to make sure the resource is still available. If the resource is not found, a broadcast search is attempted.

You can configure the APPN search function to conserve network resources by using either of the following commands in APPN control point configuration mode:

Command	Purpose
locate-queuing	Prevents multiple broadcast locate searches to the same destination LU.
negative-caching [**time**] *time* [**threshold**] *threshold-value*	Prevents multiple locate broadcast searches to unreachable resources.

Monitor the APPN Network

You can monitor the status and configuration of the APPN subsystem by issuing any of the following commands in EXEC mode:

Command	Purpose
show appn class-of-service [**brief**	**detail**]	Displays APPN classes of service that are defined to the local node.
show appn connection-network [**brief**	**detail**]	Displays APPN connection networks that are defined to the local node.
show appn directory [**name** *cp-name*] [**brief**	**detail**]	Displays the contents of the APPN directory database.
show appn dlur-lu [**pu** *pu-name*] [**brief**	**detail**]	Displays dependent LUs served by the DLUR function.
show appn dlur-pu [**dlus** *dlus-name*] [**brief**	**detail**]	Displays dependent PUs served by the DLUR function.
show appn dlus [**brief**	**detail**]	Displays the status of connections to dependent LU servers.
show appn intermediate-session [**pcid** *pcid*] [**name** *lu-name*] [**brief**	**detail**]	Displays information about the SNA sessions that are currently being routed through the local node.
show appn link-station [**name** *link-station-name*] [**port** *port-name*] [**brief**	**detail**]	Displays information about the APPN link stations that are active on or defined to the local node.
show appn mode	Displays information about the APPN modes defined to the local node.
show appn node	Displays information about the local APPN control point.
show appn port [**port** *port-name*] [**brief**	**detail**]	Displays information about the APPN ports that are active on the local node.
show appn rtp [**connection** *connection-id*] [**class-of-service** *cos-name*] [**name** *cp-name*] [**brief**	**detail**]	Displays information about RTP connections.
show appn session [**pcid** *pcid*] [**name** *lu-name*] [**brief**	**detail**]	Displays information about the SNA LU6.2 sessions, such as CP-CP sessions, that originate at the local node.
show appn topology [**name** *cp-name*] [**brief**	**detail**]	Displays the contents of the APPN topology database.

APPN Configuration Examples

The following sections provide example configurations that show how to configure various aspects of an APPN network:

- Locate Throttling Configuration Example
- Negative Caching Configuration Example
- APPN HPR Configuration Example
- APPN Link over Token Ring Configuration Example
- APPN Link over FDDI Configuration Example
- APPN Link over Frame Relay Configuration Example
- APPN Link over SDLC Configuration Example
- APPN Link over RSRB Using TCP Local Acknowledgment Configuration Example
- APPN Link over DLSw+ Using Virtual Data-Link Control Configuration Example
- APPN Connection Network over DLSw+ Using Virtual Data-Link Control Configuration Example
- APPN Link over QLLC Configuration Example
- APPN Link over ATM Configuration Example
- APPN Link over PPP Configuration Example
- APPN Link over SMDS Configuration Example
- APPN over Ethernet LAN Emulation Example

These examples specify proper configuration between two Cisco routers. If you are defining an APPN connection to a non-Cisco APPN platform, the configuration for Cisco IOS software will be similar to those shown here.

Locate Throttling Configuration Example

The following example enables the locate throttling feature, which is disabled by default:

```
interface tokenring 0
!
appn control-point neta.router1

 appn port tr0 tokenring 0
  complete

 locate-queuing
  complete
```

Negative Caching Configuration Example

The following example configures the negative caching feature to specify that requests for unreachable resources will be retained in the directory database for 90 seconds or until 25 locate search requests have been made:

```
interface tokenring 0
!
appn control-point neta.router1
!
 negative-caching time 90 threshold 25
  complete
```

APPN HPR Configuration Example

The following configuration connects two routers with a Frame Relay link and enables HPR.

Router A

```
interface Serial0
 encapsulation frame-relay IETF
 no keepalive
 clock rate 1000000
 frame-relay map llc2 141
 frame-relay map hpr 141
!
appn control cisco.routera
 hpr
 hpr timers liveness 1200 600 300 60
  complete
!
appn port FRAME0 Serial0
 complete
!
appn link-station routerb
 port FRAME0
 fr-dest-address 141
 effective-capacity 1000000
  complete
```

Router B

```
interface Serial0
 encapsulation frame-relay IETF
 no keepalive
 frame-relay map llc2 141
 frame-relay map hpr 141
!
appn control cisco.routerb
 hpr
 hpr timers liveness 1200 600 300 60
  complete
!
```

```
appn port FRAME0 Serial0
  complete
!
appn link-station routera
 port FRAME0
 fr-dest-address 141
 effective-capacity 1000000
  complete
```

APPN Link over Token Ring Configuration Example

The following example illustrates a basic APPN link over Token Ring media. In this example, Router 1 is configured to establish the connection, while Router 2 will wait for the connection from Router 1 and build a dynamic link station when Router 1 connects.

Router 1

```
interface tokenring 0
!
appn control-point neta.router1
  complete
!
appn port tr0 tokenring 0
  complete
!
appn link-station router2
 port tr0
 lan-dest-address 1111.1111.1112
  complete
```

Router 2

```
 ! tokenring 1 mac address is 1111.1111.1112
interface tokenring 1
!
appn control-point neta.router2
  complete
!
appn port tr1 tokenring 0
  complete
```

APPN Link over FDDI Configuration Example

The following example illustrates an APPN link over FDDI. In this example, each router is configured with a defined link station to the other. Both routers are configured to not accept dynamic APPN connection requests on the FDDI port. Router 1 is configured to attempt to connect to Router 2, retrying every minute if the connection is not established. Router 2 is configured to wait for an incoming call from Router 1 and not attempt to establish the connection.

Router 1

```
! FDDI0 mac address is 1111.1111.1111
interface Fddi 0
!
appn control-point neta.router1
  complete
!
appn port fd0 Fddi0
 no service-any
 complete
!
appn link-station router2
 port fd0
 lan-dest-address 1111.1111.1112
 retry-limit infinite 60
  complete
```

Router 2

```
! FDDI0 mac address is 1111.1111.1112
interface Fddi0
!
appn control-point neta.router1
  complete
!
appn port fd0 Fddi0
 no service-any
  complete
!
appn link-station router2
 port fd0
 lan-dest-address 1111.1111.1111
 no connect-at-startup
  complete
```

APPN Link over Frame Relay Configuration Example

The following example illustrates an APPN link over Frame Relay. Both routers are configured to attempt to establish the connection with the partner.

Router 1

```
interface serial 0
 encapsulation frame-relay IETF
 frame-relay map llc2 22
!
appn control-point neta.router1
  complete
!
appn port framerly serial 0
  complete
!
```

```
appn link-station router2
 port framerly
 fr-dest-address 22
  complete
```

Router 2

```
interface serial 3
 encapsulation frame-relay IETF
 frame-relay map llc2 21
!
appn control-point neta.router2
  complete
!
appn port frame serial 3
  complete
!
appn link-station router1
 port frame
 fr-dest-address 21
 complete
```

APPN Link over SDLC Configuration Example

The following example illustrates an APPN link over Synchronous Data Link Control (SDLC). In this example, Router 2 is configured without a link station—it will be built dynamically when contacted by Router 1.

Router 1

```
interface serial 0
 encapsulation sdlc
 sdlc address c1
!
appn control-point neta.router1
  complete
!
appn port sdlc serial 0
 sdlc-sec-addr c1
  complete
!
appn link-station router2
 port sdlc
 sdlc-dest-address c1
  complete
```

Router 2

```
interface serial 3
 encapsulation sdlc
 sdlc address c1
!
appn port sdlc serial 3
 sdlc-sec-addr c1
 complete
```

APPN Link over RSRB Using TCP Local Acknowledgment Configuration Example

The following example illustrates an APPN link using an RSRB virtual port. This configuration allows APPN links to span a routed IP multiprotocol network cloud as well as offering transport over interface encapsulation types not supported natively by APPN. In this example, the interface encapsulation is HDLC, the default for serial interfaces. Both routers are configured to attempt to initiate the connection with the other when their respective link stations are activated.

Router 1

```
source-bridge ring-group 33
source-bridge remote-peer 33 tcp 1.1.1.1
source-bridge remote-peer 33 tcp 1.1.1.2 local-ack
!
interface serial 0
 ip address 1.1.1.1 255.255.255.0
!
appn control-point neta.router1
  complete
!
appn port rsrbport rsrb
 rsrb-virtual-station 1111.1111.1111 13 1 33
  complete
!
appn link-station router2
 port rsrbport
 lan-dest-address 1111.1111.1112
  complete
```

Router 2

```
source-bridge ring-group 33
source-bridge remote-peer 33 tcp 1.1.1.2
source-bridge remote-peer 33 tcp 1.1.1.1 local-ack
!
interface serial 3
 ip address 1.1.1.2 255.255.255.0
!
```

```
appn control-point neta.router2
  complete
!
appn port rsrbport rsrb
 rsrb-virtual-station 1111.1111.1112 23 1 33
  complete
!
appn link-station router1
 port rsrbport
 lan-dest-address 1111.1111.1111
  complete
```

APPN Link over DLSw+ Using Virtual Data-Link Control Configuration Example

Figure 21-1 illustrates an example of an APPN link over DLSw+, where Node 1 has a link defined to Node 3. Node 3 merely has an APPN virtual data-link control port and will create a dynamic link station when Node 1 starts its link station.

Figure 21-1 *APPN Link over DLSw+ Using Virtual Data-Link Control*

The following examples provide the relevant portions of the configuration for each node.

Node 3 (Router 2)

```
source-bridge ring-group 100
dlsw local-peer peer-id 172.18.3.111
dlsw remote-peer 0 tcp 172.18.3.133
!
interface ethernet 0
 ip address 172.18.3.111 255.255.255.0
 loopback
 media-type 10BaseT
!
appn control-point NETA.BART
 complete
!
appn port VDLC vdlc
 vdlc 100 vmac 4000.4545.6969
 complete
!
```

Node 2 (Router 1)

```
!
source-bridge ring-group 100
source-bridge ring-group 33
dlsw local-peer peer-id 172.18.3.133
dlsw remote-peer 0 tcp 172.18.3.111
!
interface ethernet 0
 ip address 172.18.3.133 255.255.255.0
 loopback
 media-type 10BaseT
!
interface tokenring 0
 no ip address
 ring-speed 16
 source-bridge 1 1 100
!
```

Node 1 (End Node)

```
DEFINE_LOCAL_CP   FQ_CP_NAME(NETA.APU            )
                  CP_ALIAS(APU )
                  NAU_ADDRESS(INDEPENDENT_LU)
                  NODE_TYPE(EN)
                  NODE_ID(X'05D00000')
                  NW_FP_SUPPORT(NONE)
                  HOST_FP_SUPPORT(YES)
                  MAX_COMP_LEVEL(NONE)
                  MAX_COMP_TOKENS(0);

  DEFINE_LOGICAL_LINK   LINK_NAME(BART )
                  ADJACENT_NODE_TYPE(NN)
                  PREFERRED_NN_SERVER(NO)
                  DLC_NAME(IBMTRNET)
                  ADAPTER_NUMBER(0)
                  DESTINATION_ADDRESS(X'40004545696904')
                  ETHERNET_FORMAT(NO)
                  CP_CP_SESSION_SUPPORT(YES)
                  ACTIVATE_AT_STARTUP(no)
                  LIMITED_RESOURCE(NO)
                  LINK_STATION_ROLE(use_adapter_definition)
                  SOLICIT_SSCP_SESSION(NO)
                  MAX_ACTIVATION_ATTEMPTS(USE_ADAPTER_DEFINITION)
                  USE_PUNAME_AS_CPNAME(NO)
                  EFFECTIVE_CAPACITY(USE_ADAPTER_DEFINITION)
                  COST_PER_CONNECT_TIME(USE_ADAPTER_DEFINITION)
                  COST_PER_BYTE(USE_ADAPTER_DEFINITION)
                  SECURITY(USE_ADAPTER_DEFINITION)
                  PROPAGATION_DELAY(USE_ADAPTER_DEFINITION)
                  USER_DEFINED_1(USE_ADAPTER_DEFINITION)
                  USER_DEFINED_2(USE_ADAPTER_DEFINITION)
                  USER_DEFINED_3(USE_ADAPTER_DEFINITION);
```

APPN Connection Network over DLSw+ Using Virtual Data-Link Control Configuration Example

Figure 21-2 illustrates a connection network, NETA.CONN, over DLSw+ using virtual data-link control on the network nodes.

Figure 21-2 *APPN Connection Network over DLSw+ Using Virtual Data-Link Control*

The following example provides the relevant portions of the configuration for each network node.

End Node 1

```
DEFINE_LOCAL_CP   FQ_CP_NAME(NETA.EN1)
                  CP_ALIAS(EN1)
                  NAU_ADDRESS(INDEPENDENT_LU)
                  NODE_TYPE(EN)
                  NODE_ID(X'05D00000')
                  NW_FP_SUPPORT(NONE)
                  HOST_FP_SUPPORT(YES)
                  MAX_COMP_LEVEL(NONE)
                  MAX_COMP_TOKENS(0);
DEFINE_LOGICAL_LINK   LINK_NAME(TONN1)
                      ADJACENT_NODE_TYPE(NN)
                      PREFERRED_NN_SERVER(NO)
                      DLC_NAME(IBMTRNET)
                      ADAPTER_NUMBER(0)
                      DESTINATION_ADDRESS(X'40001111222204')
                      ETHERNET_FORMAT(NO)
```

```
                    CP_CP_SESSION_SUPPORT(YES)
                    ACTIVATE_AT_STARTUP(NO)
                    LIMITED_RESOURCE(NO)
                    LINK_STATION_ROLE(USE_ADAPTER_DEFINITION)
                    SOLICIT_SSCP_SESSION(NO)
                    MAX_ACTIVATION_ATTEMPTS(USE_ADAPTER_DEFINITION)
                    USE_PUNAME_AS_CPNAME(NO)
                    EFFECTIVE_CAPACITY(USE_ADAPTER_DEFINITION)
                    COST_PER_CONNECT_TIME(USE_ADAPTER_DEFINITION)
                    COST_PER_BYTE(USE_ADAPTER_DEFINITION)
                    SECURITY(USE_ADAPTER_DEFINITION)
                    PROPAGATION_DELAY(USE_ADAPTER_DEFINITION)
                    USER_DEFINED_1(USE_ADAPTER_DEFINITION)
                    USER_DEFINED_2(USE_ADAPTER_DEFINITION)
                    USER_DEFINED_3(USE_ADAPTER_DEFINITION);
```

Router 1

```
source-bridge ring-group 113
dlsw local-peer peer-id 10.2.17.1
dlsw remote-peer 0 tcp 10.2.17.2
!
interface TokenRing0/0
 no ip address
 ring-speed 16
!
interface TokenRing0/1
 ip address 10.2.17.1 255.255.255.0
 no ip address
 ring-speed 16
!
appn control-point NETA.NN1
  complete
!
appn port TR0 TokenRing0/0
  complete
!
appn port VDLC vdlc
 vdlc 113 vmac 4000.2222.3333
 source-bridge 1 1 113
  complete
!
appn connection-network NETA.CONN
 port VDLC
  complete
!
appn link-station T0NN2
 port VDLC
 lan-dest-address 4000.3333.4444
  complete
```

Router 2

```
source-bridge ring-group 113
dlsw local-peer peer-id 10.2.17.2
dlsw remote-peer 0 tcp 10.2.17.1
dlsw remote-peer 0 tcp 10.2.17.3
!
interface TokenRing0/0
 ip address 10.2.17.2 255.255.255.0
 no ip address
 ring-speed 16
!
appn control-point NETA.NN2
  complete
!
appn port VDLC vdlc
 vdlc 113 vmac 4000.3333.4444
 source-bridge 1 1 113
  complete
!
```

Router 3

```
source-bridge ring-group 113
dlsw local-peer peer-id 10.2.17.3
dlsw remote-peer 0 tcp 10.2.17.2
!
interface TokenRing0/0
 no ip address
 ring-speed 16
!
interface TokenRing0/1
 ip address 10.2.17.3 255.255.255.0
 no ip address
 ring-speed 16
!
appn control-point NETA.NN3
  complete
!
appn port TR0 TokenRing0/0
  complete
!
appn port VDLC vdlc
 vdlc 113 vmac 4000.4444.5555
 source-bridge 1 1 113
  complete
!
appn connection-network NETA.CONN
 port VDLC
  complete
!
appn link-station T0NN2
 port VDLC
 lan-dest-address 4000.3333.4444
  complete
!
```

End Node 2

```
DEFINE_LOCAL_CP  FQ_CP_NAME(NETA.EN2)
                 CP_ALIAS(EN2)
                 NAU_ADDRESS(INDEPENDENT_LU)
                 NODE_TYPE(EN)
                 NODE_ID(X'05D00000')
                 NW_FP_SUPPORT(NONE)
                 HOST_FP_SUPPORT(YES)
                 MAX_COMP_LEVEL(NONE)
                 MAX_COMP_TOKENS(0);
DEFINE_LOGICAL_LINK  LINK_NAME(TONN3)
                     ADJACENT_NODE_TYPE(NN)
                     PREFERRED_NN_SERVER(NO)
                     DLC_NAME(IBMTRNET)
                     ADAPTER_NUMBER(0)
                     DESTINATION_ADDRESS(X'40005555666604')
                     ETHERNET_FORMAT(NO)
                     CP_CP_SESSION_SUPPORT(YES)
                     ACTIVATE_AT_STARTUP(NO)
                     LIMITED_RESOURCE(NO)
                     LINK_STATION_ROLE(USE_ADAPTER_DEFINITION)
                     SOLICIT_SSCP_SESSION(NO)
                     MAX_ACTIVATION_ATTEMPTS(USE_ADAPTER_DEFINITION)
                     USE_PUNAME_AS_CPNAME(NO)
                     EFFECTIVE_CAPACITY(USE_ADAPTER_DEFINITION)
                     COST_PER_CONNECT_TIME(USE_ADAPTER_DEFINITION)
                     COST_PER_BYTE(USE_ADAPTER_DEFINITION)
                     SECURITY(USE_ADAPTER_DEFINITION)
                     PROPAGATION_DELAY(USE_ADAPTER_DEFINITION)
                     USER_DEFINED_1(USE_ADAPTER_DEFINITION)
                     USER_DEFINED_2(USE_ADAPTER_DEFINITION)
                     USER_DEFINED_3(USE_ADAPTER_DEFINITION);
```

APPN Link over QLLC Configuration Example

The following example illustrates an APPN link over QLLC to an AS400:

```
interface serial 1
 no ip address
 encapsulation x25 dce
 no keepalive
 x25 address 1024
 x25 map qllc 1234
 clockrate 19200
 no cdp enable
!
appn control-point NETA.APPN1
  complete
!
appn port QLLC1 serial 1
  complete
!
```

```
appn link-station AS400
 port QLLC1
 x25-dest-address svc 1234
  complete
```

APPN Link over ATM Configuration Example

The following example illustrates an APPN link over ATM:

```
interface ATM2/0
 atm pvc 1 1 12 aal5nlpid
 map-group atm-appn2
!
appn control-point NETA.APPN2
  complete
!
appn port ATM ATM2/0
  complete
!
appn link-station ATMLINK
 port ATM
 atm-dest-address 1
  complete
```

APPN Link over PPP Configuration Example

The following example illustrates an APPN link over PPP:

```
interface serial 1
 ip address 10.1.1.2 255.255.255.0
 encapsulation ppp
 no keepalive
 no fair-queue

appn control-point NETA.APPN2
  complete

appn port PPP serial 1
  complete

appn link-station PPPLINK
 port PPP
  complete
```

APPN Link over SMDS Configuration Example

The following example illustrates and APPN link over SMDS:

```
interface serial 0
 ip address 10.1.1.1 255.255.255.0
 encapsulation smds...
```

```
appn control-point NETA.APPN2
  complete

appn port SMDS serial 0
  complete

appn link-station SMDSLINK
 port SMDS
 smds-dest-address c120.0000.0002
  complete
```

APPN over Ethernet LAN Emulation Example

APPN over Ethernet LAN Emulation (LANE) is an enhancement to Cisco's APPN intermediate session routing (ISR) implementation that allows an APPN router to participate in an emulated LAN.

APPN over Ethernet LANE enables the APPN network node on the router to communicate with an end system on a switched LAN environment.

Figure 21-3 shows a typical scenario for the support of APPN over Ethernet LANE. The Catalyst 5000 is defined as the LAN Emulation Configuration Server (LECS), LAN Emulation Server (LES), broadcast and unknown server (BUS) and LEC. The network node router is a LEC using the Catalyst 5000 as the server and it is on the same emulated LAN as the Catalyst 5000. This feature allows a workstation that is attached to a legacy Ethernet segment to connect to the network node server, which is directly attached to an ATM network.

Figure 21-3 *Typical Topology Using APPN over Ethernet LANE*

In the following example, an enterprise is migrating their flat source-route bridged campus network to a switch-based ATM network. The new network has an ATM backbone that consists of ATM LS1010 switches and Catalyst 5000 switches. The campus network's Token Ring ports are replaced with Ethernet. The backbone protocol is TCP and APPN.

The following configuration reflects the network illustrated in Figure 21-4.

Configuration of the Primary DLUR Router

```
service internal
service udp-small-servers
service tcp-small-servers
!
hostname dlur1
!
!
interface ATM 1/0
 no ip address
 shutdown
!
interface TokenRing 4/0
 ip address 172.22.24.201 255.255.255.0
 ring-speed 16
 multiring all
!
interface ATM 9/0
 mtu 1500
 no ip address
 no ip mroute-cache
 no ip route-cache
 atm clock INTERNAL
 atm pvc 1 0 5 qsaal
 atm pvc 2 0 16 ilmi
 atm pvc 223 1 32 aal5nlpid
 atm pvc 224 1 34 aal5nlpid
!
interface ATM 9/0.1 multipoint
 ip address 10.10.10.1 255.255.255.0
 no ip mroute-cache
 no ip route-cache
 lane client ethernet RED
!
interface ATM 9/0.2 multipoint
 ip address 10.10.50.50 255.255.255.0
 no ip redirects
 no ip mroute-cache
 no ip route-cache
 lane client ethernet BLUE
 standby 1 priority 100
 standby 1 preempt
 standby 1 authentication usaa
 standby 1 ip 10.10.50.70
!
```

```
interface ATM 10/0
 mtu 1500
 no ip address
 atm clock INTERNAL
 atm pvc 1 0 5 qsaal
 atm pvc 2 0 16 ilmi
 atm pvc 60 1 36 aal5nlpid
!
interface ATM 10/0.1 multipoint
 lane client ethernet RED
!
interface ATM 10/0.2 multipoint
 lane client ethernet BLUE
!
!
appn control-point NETA.LATCP3
  dlus NETA.SJMVS1
  dlur
  complete
!
appn port BACK1483 ATM 10/0
  complete
!
appn port BACK1483 ATM 10/0
  complete
!
appn port REDLANE ATM 10/0.1
  complete
!
appn port BLUELANE ATM 10/0.2
  complete
!
appn port BLUELAN9 ATM 9/0.2
  complete
!
appn port REDLAN9 ATM 9/0.1
  complete
!
appn link-station TOCIP190
  port RFC1483
  atm-dest-address 223
  complete
!
appn link-station TOCIP191
  port RFC1483
  atm-dest-address 224
  complete
!
```

```
appn link-station BACKUP
 port BACK1483
 atm-dest-address 60
  complete
!
appn link-station DLUR2
 port BLUELANE
 lan-dest-address 0060.474a.2140
  complete
!
no ip classless
ip route 0.0.0.0 0.0.0.0 172.22.24.1
!
!
line con 0
 exec-timeout 0 0
line aux 0
 transport input all
line vty 0
 password lab
 login
 length 49
 width 126
line vty 1 4
 password lab
 login
!
scheduler heapcheck process
end
```

Configuration of the Secondary DLUR Router

```
!
version 11.2
service udp-small-servers
service tcp-small-servers
!
hostname dlur2
!
!
interface TokenRing 4/0
 ip address 172.22.24.202 255.255.255.0
 no ip mroute-cache
 no ip route-cache
 ring-speed 16
 multiring all
!
```

```
interface ATM 9/0
 mtu 1500
 no ip address
 no ip mroute-cache
 no ip route-cache
 atm clock INTERNAL
 atm pvc 1 0 5 qsaal
 atm pvc 2 0 16 ilmi
 atm pvc 223 1 33 aal5nlpid
 atm pvc 224 1 35 aal5nlpid
!
interface ATM 9/0.1 multipoint
 no ip mroute-cache
 no ip route-cache
 lane client ethernet RED
!
interface ATM 9/0.2 multipoint
 ip address 10.10.50.60 255.255.255.0
 no ip redirects
 no ip mroute-cache
 no ip route-cache
 lane client ethernet BLUE
 standby 1 priority 10
 standby 1 preempt
 standby 1 authentication usaa
 standby 1 ip 10.10.50.70
!
interface ATM 10/0
 mtu 1500
 no ip address
 atm clock INTERNAL
 atm pvc 1 0 5 qsaal
 atm pvc 2 0 16 ilmi
 atm pvc 60 1 36 aal5nlpid
!
interface ATM 10/0.1 multipoint
 lane client ethernet RED
!
interface ATM 10/0.2 multipoint
 lane client ethernet BLUE
!
!
appn control-point NETA.RISCP3
   dlus NETA.SJMVS1
   dlur
   complete
!
appn port RFC1483 ATM9/0
   complete
!
```

```
appn port BACK1483 ATM10/0
  complete
!
appn port REDLANE ATM10/0.1
  complete
!
appn port BLUELANE ATM10/0.2
  complete
!
appn port REDLAN9 ATM9/0.1
  complete
!
appn port BLUELAN9 ATM9/0.2
  complete
!
appn link-station TOCIP190
 port RFC1483
 atm-dest-address 223
  complete
!
appn link-station TOCIP191
 port RFC1483
 atm-dest-address 224
  complete
no ip classless
ip route 0.0.0.0 0.0.0.0 172.22.24.1
!
line con 0
 exec-timeout 0 0
line aux 0
 transport input all
line vty 0
 password lab
 login
 length 49
 width 126
line vty 1 4
 password lab
 login
```

Figure 21-4 *Migrating a Source-Route Bridged Network to a Switch-Based ATM Network*

In Figure 21-4, workstations are attached to an access Catalyst switch. The access Catalyst switch is connected to a distribution layer Catalyst switch over Fast Ethernet. The distribution Catalyst switch has an ATM link to the LS1010 switch. Using LANE, the Dependent LU Requester (DLUR) router and the distribution Catalyst switch appear to be on the same LAN.

No APPN configuration is required for the primary DLUR router in this example. The following examples show the configuration of the primary and secondary DLURs:

Primary DLUR Router Configuration of the Interface

```
interface ATM 9/0.2 multipoint
 ip address 10.10.50.50 255.255.255.0
 no ip redirects
 no ip mroute-cache
 no ip route-cache
 lane client ethernet BLUE
 standby 1 priority 100
 standby 1 preempt
 standby 1 authentication usaa
 standby 1 ip 10.10.50.70
```

Secondary DLUR Configuration of the Interface

```
interface ATM 9/0.2 multipoint
 ip address 10.10.50.60 255.255.255.0
 no ip redirects
 no ip mroute-cache
 no ip route-cache
 lane client ethernet BLUE
 standby 1 priority 10
 standby 1 preempt
 standby 1 authentication usaa
 standby 1 ip 10.10.50.70
```

Priority determines whether the router is primary or secondary. The router that has the higher priority is the primary and the other is the backup.

To access the host, the workstation uses the boundary functions of the DLUR router. The workstations define an Ethernet link to the DLUR router. The DLUR router defines an Ethernet emulated LAN link to the workstation. The advantage of using LANE is that existing LAN-based applications can run over an ATM-switched network without changes.

APPN Configuration Commands

Use the commands in this chapter to configure and monitor the Advanced Peer-to-Peer Networking (APPN) feature. For APPN configuration tasks and examples, refer to Chapter 21, "Configuring Advanced Peer-to-Peer Networking."

adjacent-cp-name

Use the **adjacent-cp-name** APPN link station configuration command to specify the name of the partner node for the link station. Use the **no** form of this command to delete the definition.

> **adjacent-cp-name** *netid.cpname*
> **no adjacent-cp-name**

Syntax

Syntax	Description
netid.cpname	Fully qualified network name of the remote control point. A fully qualified name is a string of one to eight characters, a period, and another string of one to eight characters. The following characters are acceptable: A–Z, a–z 0–9 $ # @ The first character of either string must not be a number. The default is that no partner nodes are specified.

Default

No partner nodes are specified.

Command Mode

APPN link station configuration

Usage Guidelines

This command first appeared in Cisco IOS Release 11.0.

If the name configured with this command does not match the remote node's control point (CP) name, the link will not come up. If the **no** form of the command is issues, or the command is not issued at all, no checking is done. This command must be specified if the adjacent node is LEN.

Example

The following example defines a link station that specifies the name of the partner node:

```
appn link-station APPN1
 port TR0
 lan-dest-address 1000.C4C1.E5C5
 adjacent-cp-name CISCO.APPN1
 complete
```

Related Commands

To locate documentation of related commands, you can search online at www.cisco.com.

appn link-station
show appn link-station

appn class-of-service

Use the **appn class-of-service** global configuration command to define an APPN class of service that is not an IBM-supplied default. Use the **no** form of this command to return to the default. This command begins the APPN class of service configuration command mode.

> **appn class-of-service** *cosname*
> **no appn class-of-service** *cosname*

Syntax

cosname

Description

Class of service (COS) name not among IBM default names. COS names must be a Type A character string. A Type A character string contains one to eight of the following characters:
A–Z, a–z
0–9
$ # @

Defaults

There is no default COS name.

If this command is not issued, an IBM default COS can be used. The IBM supplied default classes of service are #CONNECT, #BATCH, #INTER, #BATCHSC, #INTERSC, CPSVCMG, and SNASVCMG.

Command Mode

Global configuration

Usage Guidelines

This command first appeared in Cisco IOS Release 11.0.

COS is a definition of the transport network characteristics that should be used to establish a particular session. The COS definition assigns relative values to factors such as acceptable levels of security, cost per byte, cost per connect-time, propagation delay, and effective capacity. APPN network nodes use COS to select the best session routes between LUs.

If one of the IBM default classes of service does not meet the needs of a particular network, the **appn class-of-service** global configuration command can be used to create a user-defined definition.

Example

The following example defines a COS with one node row and one tg row:

```
appn class-of-service #SECURE
 node-row 1 weight 5 congestion no no route-additional-resistance 0 255
 tg-row 1 weight 30 byte 0 255 time 0 255 capacity 0 255 delay 0 255 security 200 255
 user1 0 255 user2 0 255 user3 0 255
 complete
```

Related Commands

To locate documentation of related commands, you can search online at www.cisco.com.

node-row
show appn class-of-service
tg-row
transmission-priority

appn connection-network

Use the **appn connection-network** global configuration command to specify the fully qualified network name for the connection network. Use the **no** form of this command to delete the definition. This command begins the APPN connection network configuration command mode.

> **appn connection-network** *netid.cnname*
> **no appn connection-network** *netid.cnname*

Syntax	Description
netid.cnname	Fully qualified network name for the connection network. *cnname* is the name of the virtual network node in the connection network. A fully qualified name is a string of one to eight characters, a period, and another string of one to eight characters. The following characters are acceptable: A–Z, a–z 0–9 $ # @ The first character of either string must not be a number.

Default

No default connection network name is assigned.

Command Mode

Global configuration

Usage Guidelines

This command first appeared in Cisco IOS Release 11.0.

The connection network name must be the same on all nodes that define the connection network, and must be different from any other connection network, LU, or control point in the total network.

Example

The following example defines a connection network using APPN port TR0:

```
appn connection-network CISCO.CAPPN1
 port TR0
 complete
```

Related Commands

To locate documentation of related commands, you can search online at www.cisco.com.

port (APPN connection network)
show appn connection-network

appn control-point

Use the **appn control-point** global configuration command to specify the fully qualified control point name for the node. Use the **no** form of this command to delete the name and clear all APPN definitions. This command begins the APPN control point configuration command mode.

appn control-point *netid.cpname*
no appn control-point *netid.cpname*

Part
II

Command Reference

Syntax

netid.cpname

Description

Fully qualified control point name for the local node.
A fully qualified name is a string of one to eight characters, a period, and another string of one to eight characters.
The following characters are acceptable:
A–Z, a–z
0–9
$ # @
The first character of either string must not be a number.

Default

No default control point name is assigned.

Command Mode

Global configuration

Usage Guidelines

This command first appeared in Cisco IOS Release 11.0.

You must issue the **appn control-point** command to activate APPN routing. There can be only one control point definition in the system. The control point name must be unique in the network.

Example

The following example defines a control point named CISCO.APPN1:

```
appn control-point CISCO.APPN1
 complete
```

Related Commands

To locate documentation of related commands, you can search online at www.cisco.com.

appn routing
appn start
appn stop
backup-dlus (APPN control point)
buffer-percent
dlur
dlus (APPN control point)
interrupt-switched
max-cached-entries
max-cached-trees
maximum-memory
route-additional-resistance
safe-store-cycle
safe-store-host
safe-store-interval
show appn node
xid-block-number
xid-id-number

appn link-station

Use the **appn link-station** global configuration command to assign the name of an adjacent link station. Use the **no** form of this command to delete the link station name. This command begins the APPN link station configuration command mode.

> **appn link-station** *linkname*
> **no appn link-station** *linkname*

Syntax

Description

linkname

Name that identifies the link station. The name must be a Type A string. A Type A character string contains one to eight of the following characters:
A–Z, a–z
0–9
$ # @

Default

No default link station name is assigned.

Command Mode
Global configuration

Usage Guidelines
This command first appeared in Cisco IOS Release 11.0.

A link represents a connection between a local link station and a link station in an adjacent node. The link can be considered a direct connection between two distinct Type 2.1 or Type 2.0 nodes. The link station provides a route over which local sessions or intermediate sessions can pass. Two link stations are required to build a link: one on each node.

A link station can be predefined with the **appn link-station** command, or dynamically defined. If you specify **service-any** in the associated **appn port** command, link stations can be dynamically defined when a connect request is received. In this case, the **appn link-station** command would not be required. You must define an APPN link station if you intend this node to initiate the connection to the adjacent node.

Example
The following example defines a link station using port TR0:

```
appn link-station CISCO1
 port TR0
 lan-destination-address 0200.0000.0001
 complete
```

Related Commands
To locate documentation of related commands, you can search online at www.cisco.com.

adjacent-cp-name
atm-dest-address
backup-dlus (APPN link station)
connect-at-startup
cost-per-byte (APPN link station)
cost-per-connect-time (APPN link station)
cp-cp-sessions-supported
dlur-dspu-name
dlus (APPN link station)
effective-capacity (APPN link station)
fr-dest-address
lan-dest-address
limited-resource (APPN link station)
link-queuing

port (APPN link station)
ppp-dest-address
propagation-delay (APPN link station)
pu-type-20
retry-limit (APPN link station)
role (APPN link station)
sdlc-dest-address
security (APPN link station)
show appn link-station
smds-dest-address
tg-number
user-defined-1 (APPN link station)
user-defined-2 (APPN link station)
user-defined-3 (APPN link station)
verify-adjacent-node-type
x25-dest-address

appn mode

Use the **appn mode** global configuration command to specify a new mode or to change an IBM-defined mode and identify the class of service (COS) associated with the mode name. Use the **no** form of this command to delete the previous definition. This command begins the APPN mode configuration command mode.

> **appn mode** *modename*
> **no appn mode** *modename*

Syntax   Description

modename   Name of the mode. A Type A character string. A Type A character
                             string contains one to eight of the following characters:
                             A–Z, a–z
                             0–9
                             $ # @

Default
IBM-defined [blank] mode

Command Mode
Global configuration

Usage Guidelines

This command first appeared in Cisco IOS Release 11.0.

The IBM-defined modes are #BATCH, #BATCHSC, #INTER, #INTERSC, #CPSVCMG, #SNASVCMG, #CPSVRMG, and [blank]. These definitions can not be changed.

This command is required when LEN nodes are using this node for network services. The LEN node will issue a BIND containing this mode name; this command will be used to associate the mode name with a COS name.

Example

The following example changes the IBM-defined mode #BATCH to use the #CONNECT class of service:

```
appn mode #BATCH
 class-of-service #CONNECT
 complete
```

Related Commands

To locate documentation of related commands, you can search online at www.cisco.com.

class-of-service
show appn mode

appn partner-lu-location

Use the **appn partner-lu-location** global configuration command to specify an LU that would be the destination LU for an LU-LU session request from an LU using this node for network services. Use the **no** form of this command to delete the previous definition. This command begins the APPN partner LU configuration command mode.

> **appn partner-lu-location** *netid.luname*
> **no appn partner-lu-location** *netid.luname*

Syntax

netid.luname

Description

Fully qualified name of the partner LU. A fully qualified name is a string of one to eight characters, a period, and another string of one to eight characters. The following characters are acceptable:
A–Z, a–z
0–9
$ # @
The first character of either string must not be a number.

Default

No default *netid.luname* is specified. You must supply a value; otherwise, the configuration will fail.

Command Mode

Global configuration

Usage Guidelines

This command first appeared in Cisco IOS Release 11.0.

Use this command to define an entry in the directory database. This command improves network performance by allowing directed LOCATE (because the partner name is known) instead of a broadcast. The disadvantage is that definitions must be created. Alternatively, partner names can be discovered dynamically and added to the database as they are learned. This process, however, requires either prior sessions to the node or broadcast traffic (which causes additional network traffic) sent to locate the node.

Example

The following example defines the location of an LU named CISCO.LU21:

```
appn partner-lu-location CISCO.LU21
 owning-cp CISCO.CP2
 complete
```

Related Commands

To locate documentation of related commands, you can search online at www.cisco.com.

owning-cp
serving-nn
show appn directory
wildcard

appn path-switch connection

Use the **appn path-switch connection** EXEC command to manually initiate a path switch if a better path exists.

> **appn path-switch connection** *rtp-connection-id*

Syntax   Description

rtp-connection-id   An RTP connection ID is a 16-byte hexadecimal number.

Command Mode

EXEC

Usage Guidelines

This command first appeared in Cisco IOS Release 11.3.

Example

The following example initiates a path switch:

```
appn path-switch connection 8000000000A06278
```

Related Commands

To locate documentation of related commands, you can search online at www.cisco.com.

show appn rtp

appn port

Use the **appn port** global configuration command to define an APPN port and relate it to a previously defined interface. Use the **no** form of this command to cancel the APPN port definition.

> **appn port** *portname* {*interface* | **rsrb** | **vdlc**}
> **no appn port** *portname*

Syntax	Description
portname	Port name to be associated with the interface.
interface	Previously defined interface type and number with which the port name is to be associated.
rsrb	Specify **rsrb** instead of an interface if this port will utilize RSRB as a transport protocol.
vdlc	Specify **vdlc** to allow link stations using this virtual port to connect over DLSw+, or any other higher-layer protocol that is CLSI-compliant, using virtual data-link control (VDLC).

Defaults

No default port name is specified. No default interface is provided. You must provide the port name and interface, or the configuration will fail.

Command Mode

Global configuration

Usage Guidelines

This command first appeared in Cisco IOS Release 11.0.

At least one APPN port must be defined for each interface that will participate in APPN routing. If more that one service access point (SAP) will be used over a particular port, then a port must be defined for each SAP.

If you configure APPN to run over DLSw+, you specify **vdlc**, and must also use the **vdlc** APPN port configuration command to identify which ring group the APPN VDLC port uses and, optionally, which virtual MAC address is used as the local MAC address identifying this APPN port.

Examples

The following example associates an APPN port named FDDI0 with FDDI interface 0:

```
appn port FDDI0 fddi0
 complete
```

In the following example, the **appn port vdlc** command creates an APPN VDLC port named "vdlcport," and the **vdlc** APPN port configuration command identifies the ring group (100) and VDLC virtual MAC address (4000.3745.000):

```
appn port VDLCPORT vdlc
 vdlc 100 vmac 4000.3745.0000
 complete
```

Related Commands

To locate documentation of related commands, you can search online at www.cisco.com.

appn start port
appn stop port
cost-per-byte (APPN port)
cost-per-connect-time (APPN port)
desired-max-send-btu-size
effective-capacity (APPN port)
interface
limited-resource (APPN port)
local-sap
max-link-stations
max-rcv-btu-size
propagation-delay (APPN port)

reserved-inbound
reserved-outbound
retry-limit (APPN port)
role (APPN port)
rsrb-virtual-station
sdlc-sec-addr
security (APPN port)
service-any
show appn port
user-defined-1 (APPN port)
user-defined-2 (APPN port)
user-defined-3 (APPN port)
vdlc
x25-subaddress

appn routing

Use the **appn routing** global configuration command to indicate that APPN routing should be activated. Use the **no** form of this command to deactivate APPN routing.

> **appn routing**
> **no appn routing**

Syntax Description

This command has no arguments or keywords.

Default

APPN routing is disabled.

Command Mode

Global configuration

Usage Guidelines

This command first appeared in Cisco IOS Release 11.0.

For **appn routing** to complete successfully, an APPN control point must be configured using the **appn control-point** global configuration command.

Example

The following example activates APPN routing:

```
appn routing
```

Related Commands

To locate documentation of related commands, you can search online at www.cisco.com.

appn control-point
appn start
appn stop

appn start

Use the **appn start** EXEC command to activate the APPN subsystem in this node.

       appn start

Syntax Description

This command has no arguments or keywords.

Default

The APPN subsystem is disabled.

Command Mode

EXEC

Usage Guidelines

This command first appeared in Cisco IOS Release 11.0.

Example

The following example activates APPN:

```
appn start
```

Related Commands

To locate documentation of related commands, you can search online at www.cisco.com.

appn routing
appn stop

appn start link-station

Use the **appn start link-station** EXEC command to activate a logical APPN link.

Part
II

Command Reference

appn start link-station *linkname*

Syntax	Description
linkname	Name of the link-station. Must be a Type A character string. A Type A character string contains one to eight of the following characters: A–Z, a–z 0–9 $ # @

Default

No logical APPN links are activated.

Command Mode

EXEC

Usage Guidelines

This command first appeared in Cisco IOS Release 11.0.

Example

The following example activates an APPN link station:

```
appn start link-station TR0
```

Related Commands

To locate documentation of related commands, you can search online at www.cisco.com.

appn link-station
appn stop link-station
show appn link-station

appn start port

Use the **appn start port** EXEC command to activate APPN routing over a particular port.

> **appn start port** *portname*

Syntax

Description

portname

Name of the port. Must be a Type A character string.
A Type A character string contains one to eight of the following characters:
A–Z, a–z
0–9
$ # @

Default

No APPN routing is activated.

Command Mode

EXEC

Usage Guideline

This command first appeared in Cisco IOS Release 11.0.

This command is also used when the APPN subsystem is already started and a port is added or a characteristic is changed by subcommand.

Example

The following example activates APPN routing over port TR0:

```
appn start port TR0
```

Related Commands

To locate documentation of related commands, you can search online at www.cisco.com.

appn port
appn stop port
show appn port

appn stop

Use the **appn stop** EXEC command to deactivate APPN routing without affecting the current configuration.

> **appn stop**

Syntax Description

This command has no arguments or keywords.

Default

This command has no default state.

Command Mode

EXEC

Usage Guidelines

This command first appeared in Cisco IOS Release 11.0.

Example

The following example deactivates APPN routing:

```
appn stop
```

Related Commands

To locate documentation of related commands, you can search online at www.cisco.com.

appn control-point
appn routing
appn start

appn stop link-station

Use the **appn stop link-station** EXEC command to deactivate an APPN connection between the local node and an adjacent node.

appn stop link-station *linkname*

Syntax

Syntax	Description
linkname	Name of the link station. The name must be a Type A character string. A Type A character string contains one to eight of the following characters: A–Z, a–z 0–9 $ # @

Default

This command has no default state.

Command Mode

EXEC

Usage Guidelines

This command first appeared in Cisco IOS Release 11.0.

Example

The following example deactivates an APPN link between the local node and an adjacent node:

```
appn stop link-station APPN1
```

Related Commands

To locate documentation of related commands, you can search online at www.cisco.com.

appn link-station
appn start link-station

appn stop port

Use the **appn stop port** EXEC command to deactivate APPN routing over a specified port.

appn stop port *portname*

Syntax	Description
portname	Name of the port. Must be a Type A character string. A Type A character string contains one to eight of the following characters: A–Z, a–z 0–9 $ # @

Default

This command has no default state.

Command Mode

EXEC

Usage Guidelines

This command first appeared in Cisco IOS Release 11.0.

For a port deactivation to be successful, no APPN link station can be active on that port.

Example

The following example deactivates APPN routing over port TR0:

```
appn stop port TR0
```

Related Commands

To locate documentation of related commands, you can search online at www.cisco.com.

appn port
appn start port

atm-dest-address

Use the **atm-dest-address** APPN link station configuration command to specify the address of the partner node for ATM links. Use the **no** form of this command to return to the default.

> **atm-dest-address** *pvc*
> **no atm-dest-address**

Syntax

pvc

Description

Permanent virtual circuit (PVC) of the remote node. Valid range is 1 to 4096.

Defaults

No default PVC or SAP are provided.

Command Mode

APPN link station configuration

Usage Guidelines

This command first appeared in Cisco IOS Release 11.1.

The command should be specified only if the APPN port used by the link station is an ATM port. Note that for the Cisco 4500, the default maximum number of PVCs allowed is 32.

Example

The following example specifies ATM destination address 1:

```
interface ATM2/0
 atm pvc 1 1 12 aal5nlpid
 map-group atm-appn2
 !
appn control-point NETA.APPN2
 complete
!
appn port ATM ATM2/0
 complete
!
appn link-station ATMLINK
 port ATM
 atm-dest-address 1
 complete
```

Related Commands

To locate documentation of related commands, you can search online at www.cisco.com.

appn link-station
lan-dest-address
sdlc-dest-address
show appn link-station

backup-dlus (APPN control point)

Use the **backup dlus** APPN control point configuration command to specify the name of the default backup DLUS, which performs SSCP services for downstream PUs if the default DLUS is unable to provide the services. Use the **no** form of this command to delete the definition.

> **backup-dlus** *netid.cpname*
> **no backup-dlus**

Syntax

Description

netid.cpname

Fully qualified network name. A fully qualified name is a string of one to eight characters, a period, and another string of one to eight characters. The following characters are acceptable:
A–Z, a–z
0–9
$ # @
The first character of either string must not be a number.

Default

No backup DLUS is specified.

Command Mode

APPN control point configuration

Usage Guidelines

This command first appeared in Cisco IOS Release 11.0.

You must specify **dlur** and **dlus** before you can specify **backup-dlus**. You can use the **backup-dlus** link station configuration command to override this command for a particular link station.

Example

The following example defines an APPN control point with a backup DLUS:

```
appn control-point CISCO.ROUTER
 dlur max-pus 100
 dlus CISCO.APPN1
 backup-dlus CISCO.APPN2
 complete
```

Related Commands

To locate documentation of related commands, you can search online at www.cisco.com.

appn control-point
backup-dlus (APPN link station)
dlur (APPN control point)

backup-dlus (APPN link station)

Use the **backup-dlus** APPN link station configuration command to specify the default backup DLUS node that provides SSCP services to the downstream PUs of the link in the event that the DLUS is unable to provide the DLUR function. Use the **no** form of this command to return to the default.

> **backup-dlus** *netid.cpname*
> **no backup-dlus**

Syntax	Description
netid.cpname	Fully qualified network name. A fully qualified name is a string of one to eight characters, a period, and another string of one to eight characters. The following characters are acceptable: A–Z, a–z 0–9 $ # @ The first character of either string must not be a number.

Default

The default state is **no backup-dlus.**

Command Mode

APPN link station configuration

Usage Guidelines

This command first appeared in Cisco IOS Release 11.0.

You must specify the **dlur** and **dlus** APPN control point commands before you can specify **backup-dlus**. You can use the **backup-dlus** link station configuration command on the link station to override this command for that particular link station.

Example

The following example specifies the backup DLUS node for a link station:

```
appn link-station CISCO.HOST
 port FDDI0
 lan-dest-address 0200.0000.1234
 dlus CISCO.APPN1
 backup-dlus CISCO.APPN3
 complete
```

Related Commands

To locate documentation of related commands, you can search online at www.cisco.com.

appn link-station
backup-dlus (APPN control point)
dlus (APPN control point)
dlus (APPN link station)

buffer-percent

Use the **buffer-percent** APPN control point configuration command to specify the percent of buffers that are reserved for use by APPN. Use the **no** form of this command to cancel the buffer reservation.

buffer-percent *number*
no buffer-percent

Syntax	Description
number	Maximum percentage of I/O memory that APPN is allowed to allocate for buffers. The valid range is 1 to 100 percent. The default is 100 percent.

Default

100 percent

Command Mode

APPN control point configuration

Usage Guidelines

This command first appeared in Cisco IOS Release 11.0.

Use the **buffer-percent** command to ensure that APPN will not monopolize the buffers. If other protocols are to be routed through the local node, this command can reserve buffers for protocols other than APPN.

Example

The following example limits APPN's buffer usage to 25 percent of the device's buffers:

```
appn control-point CISCO.ROUTER
 buffer-percent 25
 complete
```

Related Commands

To locate documentation of related commands, you can search online at www.cisco.com.

appn control-point
show buffers
show memory

central-resource-registration

Use the **central-resource-registration** APPN control point configuration command to enable the central resource registration function. Use the **no** form of this command to disable the central resource registration function.

> **central-resource-registration**
> **no central-resource-registration**

Syntax Description

This command has no arguments or keywords.

Default

The central resource registration function is enabled.

Command Mode
APPN control point configuration

Usage Guidelines
This command first appeared in Cisco IOS Release 11.2.

By default, the central resource registration function is enabled in the router so that registration of downstream resources in the central directory server will be attempted by the router when it receives a request from the control point that owns the resource. If there is unpredictable behavior related to the central resource registration or central directory server, use the **no central-resource-registration** command to disable the central resource registration function. In normal circumstances, there should not be any reason to disable the central resource registration function.

Example
The following example disables the central resource registration function:

```
appn control-point neta.router
 no central-resource-registration
 complete
```

Related Commands
To locate documentation of related commands, you can search online at www.cisco.com.

show appn directory

class-of-service

Use the **class-of-service** APPN mode configuration command to specify the class of service (CoS) that maps to a particular mode name. Use the **no** form of this command to return to the default.

> **class-of-service** *cosname*
> **no class-of-service**

Syntax	Description
cosname	Name of the class of service. Must be a Type A character string. A Type A character string contains one to eight of the following characters: A–Z, a–z 0–9 $ # @ The default is #CONNECT.

Default

The default **class-of-service** name is #CONNECT.

Command Mode

APPN mode configuration

Usage Guidelines

This command first appeared in Cisco IOS Release 11.0.

LEN nodes use this node for network services. The mode name is passed in the BIND and this command is used to correlate the mode name to a **class-of-service** name.

Example

The following example defines a mode with class of service #INTER:

```
appn mode MAPPN1
 class-of-service #INTER
 complete
```

Related Commands

To locate documentation of related commands, you can search online at www.cisco.com.

appn mode

connect-at-startup

Use the **connect-at-startup** APPN link station configuration command to specify that the link will call out to the partner and attempt to bring up the link when the link's definition is complete. Use the **no** form of this command to return to the default.

> **connect-at-startup**
> **no connect-at-startup**

Syntax Description

This command has no arguments or keywords.

Default

Connect-at-startup is enabled.

Command Mode

APPN link station configuration

Usage Guidelines

This command first appeared in Cisco IOS Release 11.0.

Example

The following example deactivates call out for APPN link station ETHER12:

```
appn link-station ETHER12
 appn port ETHER1
 lan-dest-address 0200.0000.4321
 no connect-at-startup
 complete
```

Related Commands

To locate documentation of related commands, you can search online at www.cisco.com.

appn link-station

cost-per-byte (APPN link station)

Use the **cost-per-byte** APPN link station configuration command to specify the cost per byte of transmitting a byte of data over this connection. Use the **no** form of this command to return to the default.

> **cost-per-byte** *cost*
> **no cost-per-byte**

Syntax | Description

Syntax	Description
cost	Number in the range 0 to 255. The default is the value specified in the **appn port** command.

Default

The value specified in the **appn port** command.

Command Mode

APPN link station configuration

Usage Guidelines

This command first appeared in Cisco IOS Release 11.0.

Use this command to specify the relative cost to transmit a byte over the link. The relative cost per byte is used in route selection. Cost per byte may be specified at the port level, in which case it applies to all link stations that connect through the port. Cost per byte specified at the link station level overrides the cost per byte specified at the port level, and relates to the defined link station only. This value is compared to the values specified for a class of service to determine if this link can be used to support the class of service.

Example

The following example sets the cost-per-byte value to 10:

```
appn link-station CISCO1
 port RSRB1
 lan-dest-address 1000.2020.0211
 cost-per-byte 10
 complete
```

Related Commands

To locate documentation of related commands, you can search online at www.cisco.com.

appn link-station
cost-per-byte (APPN port)
show appn link-station

cost-per-byte (APPN port)

Use the **cost-per-byte** APPN port configuration command to specify the cost per byte of transmitting a byte of data through this port. Use the **no** form of this command to return to the default.

> **cost-per-byte** *cost*
> **no cost-per-byte**

Syntax

Syntax	Description
cost	Number in the range 0 to 255. The default is 0.

Default

The default cost is 0.

Command Mode

APPN port configuration

Usage Guidelines

This command first appeared in Cisco IOS Release 11.0.

Specifying **cost-per-byte** at the port level applies to all link stations accessed through this port, unless **cost-per-byte** is specified on an individual **appn link-station** command. Specifying this value on the **appn link-station** command overrides the port value. The cost is used in route selection for a particular class of service. Cost per byte specified at the link station level overrides the cost per byte specified at the port level, and relates to the defined link station only. This value is compared to the values specified for a class of service to determine if this link can be used to support the class of service.

Example

The following example sets the cost per byte value to 10:

```
appn port FR0 serial 0
 cost-per-byte 100
 complete
```

Related Commands

To locate documentation of related commands, you can search online at www.cisco.com.

appn port
cost-per-byte (APPN link station)
show appn port

cost-per-connect-time (APPN link station)

Use the **cost-per-connect-time** APPN link station configuration command to specify the relative cost of the link. Use the **no** form of this command to return to the default.

> **cost-per-connect-time** *cost*
> **no cost-per-connect-time**

Syntax

Description

cost

Number in the range 0 to 255. The default is the value specified in the **appn port** command.

Default

The value specified in the **appn port** command.

Command Mode

APPN link station configuration

Usage Guidelines

This command first appeared in Cisco IOS Release 11.0.

The relative cost of the link, which typically reflects the tariff of the transmission facility, is used in route selection. Cost per connect time may be specified at the port level, in which case it applies to all link stations that connect through the port. Cost per connect time specified at the link station level overrides the cost per connect time specified at the port level, and relates to the defined link station only. This value is compared to the values specified for a class of service to determine if this link can be used to support the class of service.

Example

The following example sets the cost per connect time to 100:

```
appn link-station CISCO4
 port FDDI0
 cost-per-connect-time 100
 complete
```

Related Commands

To locate documentation of related commands, you can search online at www.cisco.com.

appn link-station
cost-per-connect-time (APPN port)
show appn link-station

cost-per-connect-time (APPN port)

Use the **cost-per-connect-time** APPN port configuration command to specify the cost per connect time. Use the **no** form of this command to return to the default.

>**cost-per-connect-time** *cost*
>**no cost-per-connect-time**

Syntax

cost

Description

Number in the range 0 to 255. The default is 0.

Default

The default cost is 0.

Command Mode

APPN port configuration

Usage Guidelines

This command first appeared in Cisco IOS Release 11.0.

Specifying **cost-per-connect-time** at the port level applies to all link stations accessed through this port, unless **cost-per-connect-time** is specified on an individual **appn link-station** command. Specifying this value on the **appn link-station** command overrides the port value. The cost is used in route selection for a particular class of service. Cost per connect time specified at the link station level overrides the cost per connect time specified at the port level, and relates to the defined link station only. This value is compared to the values specified for a class of service to determine if this link can be used to support the class of service.

Example

The following example sets the cost per connect time to 100:

```
appn port SDLC0 Serial1
 cost-per-connect-time 100
 complete
```

Related Commands

To locate documentation of related commands, you can search online at www.cisco.com.

appn port
cost-per-connect-time (APPN link station)
show appn port

cp-cp-sessions-supported

Use the **cp-cp-sessions-supported** APPN link station configuration command to specify that a control point-control point (CP-CP) session can be established over this connection. Use the **no** form of this command to specify that a CP-CP session cannot be established over this link.

> **cp-cp-sessions-supported**
> **no cp-cp-sessions-supported**

Syntax Description

This command has no arguments or keywords.

Default

CP-CP sessions are supported.

Command Mode

APPN link station configuration

Usage Guidelines

This command first appeared in Cisco IOS Release 11.0.

The **no** form of this command must be specified for a link to a LEN node.

CP sessions to additional NNs are optional. Having fewer CP-CP sessions reduces the number of topology update messages and memory required, while increasing convergence time (the time required to update all network nodes).

Example

The following example specifies that no CP-CP sessions are supported:

```
appn link-station FDDI41
 port FDDI1
 lan-dest-address 0400.0000.2323
 no cp-cp-sessions-supported
 complete
```

Related Commands

To locate documentation of related commands, you can search online at www.cisco.com.

appn link-station
show appn link-station
verify-adjacent-node-type

desired-max-send-btu-size

Use the **desired-max-send-btu-size** APPN port configuration command to specify the maximum BTU size on this link. Use the **no** form of this command to return to the default.

> **desired-max-send-btu-size** *size*
> **no desired-max-send-btu-size**

Syntax	Description
size	BTU size (in bytes) on this link, in the range 99 to 5107. The default is 1024 bytes.

Default

The default size is 1024 bytes.

Command Mode

APPN port configuration

Usage Guidelines

This command first appeared in Cisco IOS Release 11.0.

The MTU size must be big enough to accommodate the configured size of the BTU.

Example

The following example sets the maximum BTU size to 4000:

```
appn port TR0 tokenring 0/0
 desired-max-send-btu-size 4000
 complete
```

Related Commands

To locate documentation of related commands, you can search online at www.cisco.com.

appn port
mtu
show appn port

dlur

Use the **dlur** APPN control point configuration command to specify that the Dependent LU Requestor (DLUR) function is supported on this CP. Use the **no** form of this command to return to the default.

> **dlur** [**max-pus** *number*]
> **no dlur**

Syntax	Description
max-pus *number*	(Optional) Maximum number of physical units (PUs) served by this DLUR, in the range 1 to 100,000. There is no default. If **max-pus** is not specified, there is no limit on the number of PUs served by this DLUR.

Defaults

If the **dlur** command is not specified, the DLUR function is not supported on this CP. If **max-pus** is not specified, there is no limit on the number of PUs served by this DLUR.

Command Mode

APPN control point configuration

Usage Guidelines

This command first appeared in Cisco IOS Release 11.0.

Example

The following example specifies the DLUR function on the CP and specifies that the maximum number of PUs served by this DLUR is 100:

```
appn control-point CISCO.ROUTER
 dlur max-pus 100
 dlus CISCO.HOST
 complete
```

Related Commands

To locate documentation of related commands, you can search online at www.cisco.com.

appn control-point
dlus (APPN control point)
show appn dlur-lu
show appn dlur-pu
show appn dlus

dlur-dspu-name

Use the **dlur-dspu-name** APPN link station configuration command to specify the name of the downstream PU connected by this link. Use the **no** form of this command to delete the definition.

> **dlur-dspu-name** *pu-name*
> **no dlur-dspu-name**

Syntax	Description
pu-name	Type A character string. A Type A character string contains one to eight of the following characters: A–Z, a–z 0–9 $ # @

Default

No default name is specified.

Command Mode

APPN link station configuration

Usage Guidelines

This command first appeared in Cisco IOS Release 11.0.

The DLUR function requires the specification of the DSPU name for a PU 2.0 node. Specification is also required when the DLUR function must activate the link to a PU 2.1 or PU 2.0 node, when driven by a host-initiated PU activation, and when the link to the PU is not active.

Example

The following example specifies the DSPU name of a downstream node:

```
appn link-station LINK4
 port TR1
 lan-dest-address 1000.2020.0211
 dlur-dspu-name PU003334
 pu-type-20
 complete
```

Related Commands

To locate documentation of related commands, you can search online at www.cisco.com.

appn link-station
dlur
dlus (APPN link station)

dlus (APPN control point)

Use the **dlus** APPN control point configuration command to specify the name of the default Dependent LU Server (DLUS) that provides SSCP services to the downstream PUs. Use the **no** form of this command to delete the definition.

> **dlus** *netid.cpname*
> **no dlus**

Syntax

netid.cpname

Description

Fully qualified CP name. A fully qualified name is a string of one to eight characters, a period, and another string of one to eight characters. The following characters are acceptable:
A–Z, a–z
0–9
$ # @
The first character of either string must not be a number.

Default

No default DLUS is defined.

Command Mode

APPN control point configuration

Usage Guidelines

This command first appeared in Cisco IOS Release 11.0.

The **dlur** command must be specified if **dlus** is specified. The name of the node-default DLUS should be specified when supporting downstream PUs that request or require ACTPUs, when DLUR does not currently have an active session with the DLUS, and when no DLUS or back-up DLUS name has been provided on the APPN link station definition.

Example

The following example defines the DLUS:

```
appn control-point CISCO.ROUTER1
 dlur
 dlus CISCO.APPN1
 complete
```

Related Commands

To locate documentation of related commands, you can search online at www.cisco.com.

appn control-point
dlur
dlus (APPN link station)
show appn dlur-lu

dlus (APPN link station)

Use the **dlus** APPN link station configuration command to specify the name of the default Dependent LU Server (DLUS) node that provides SSCP services to the downstream PUs of this link station. Use the **no** form of this command to delete the definition.

> **dlus** *netid.cpname*
> **no dlus**

Syntax

Description

netid.cpname

Fully qualified CP name. A fully qualified name is a string of one to eight characters, a period, and another a string of one to eight characters. The following characters are acceptable:
A–Z, a–z
0–9
$ # @
The first character of either string must not be a number.

Default

No default DLUS is specified.

Command Mode

APPN link station configuration

Usage Guideline

This command first appeared in Cisco IOS Release 11.0.

The **dlus** command is used to override the value of *netid.cpname* specified in the control point definition.

Example

The following example specifies the DLUS for a specific APPN link station:

```
appn link-station LINK5
 port TR1
 lan-dest-address 0200.0000.5678
 dlus CISCO.APPN1
 complete
```

Related Commands

To locate documentation of related commands, you can search online at www.cisco.com.

appn control-point
dlur
dlus (APPN control point)
show appn dlus

effective-capacity (APPN link station)

Use the **effective-capacity** APPN link station configuration command to specify the bit rate for the connection. Use the **no** form of this command to return to the default.

> **effective-capacity** *capacity*
> **no effective-capacity**

Syntax	Description
capacity	Number of bits per second in the range 0 to 100,000,000. The default is the value specified in the **appn port** command.

Default

The value specified in the **appn port** command.

Command Mode

APPN link station configuration

Usage Guidelines

This command first appeared in Cisco IOS Release 11.0.

The bit rate is compared to the class of service requirements when selecting routes. This can be specified on the link station command to identify the bit rate for this link station only. This value overrides the value specified on the port command. Effective capacity is used by the node to determine the least cost route for APPN intermediate sessions.

Example

The following example defines the effective capacity:

```
appn link-station FRLINK44
 port FR0
 fr-dest-address 44
 effective-capacity 4000000
 complete
```

Related Commands

To locate documentation of related commands, you can search online at www.cisco.com.

appn link-station
effective-capacity (APPN port)
show appn link-station

effective-capacity (APPN port)

Use the **effective-capacity** APPN port configuration command to specify the effective capacity of a link. Use the **no** form of this command to return to the default.

> **effective-capacity** *capacity*
> **no effective-capacity**

Syntax   Description

capacity   Number of bits per second in the range 0 to 100,000,000.
                                The default is media dependent.

Default

The default is media dependent:

Ethernet—10,000,000 bps
FDDI—100,000,000 bps
Frame Relay—56,000 bps
QLLC—56,000 bps
RSRB—56,000 bps
SDLC—56,000 bps
Token Ring—16,000,000 bps

Command Mode

APPN port configuration

Usage Guidelines

This command first appeared in Cisco IOS Release 11.0.

Specifying this command at the port level identifies the capacity for all link stations accessed through this port. Specifying this command on the link station command overrides the port value. This command also specifies the value for dynamically created transmission groups. The cost is used in route selection for a particular class of service.

Example

The following example defines the effective capacity:

```
appn port FR0 serial 1/1
 effective-capacity 2000000
 complete
```

Related Commands

To locate documentation of related commands, you can search online at www.cisco.com.

appn port
effective-capacity (APPN link station)
show appn port

fr-dest-address

Use the **fr-dest-address** APPN link station configuration command to specify the address of the partner node for Frame Relay links. Use the **no** form of this command to return to the default.

> **fr-dest-address** *dlci* [*sap*]
> **no fr-dest-address**

Syntax	Description
dlci	Number in the range 16 to 1007 that represents the DLCI, or virtual circuit, for a Frame Relay connection.
sap	(Optional) 1-byte hexadecimal number in the range 04 to EC, and divisible by 4. The default value is 04 (hexadecimal).

Defaults

No default DLCI is provided.

The default SAP value is 04 (hexadecimal).

Part II

Command Reference

Command Mode

APPN link station configuration

Usage Guideline

This command first appeared in Cisco IOS Release 11.0.

The command should be specified only if the APPN port used by the link station is a Frame Relay port.

Example

The following example specifies DLCI 100:

```
appn link-station FRLNK100
 port FR0
 fr-dest-address 100
 complete
```

Related Commands

To locate documentation of related commands, you can search online at www.cisco.com.

appn link-station
lan-dest-address
sdlc-dest-address
show appn link-station

hpr (APPN control point)

Use the **hpr** APPN control point configuration command to specify that HPR is supported in this router. Use the **no** form of this command to disable HPR in this router.

> **hpr**
> **no hpr**

Syntax Description

This command has no arguments or keywords.

Default

HPR is not enabled.

Command Mode
APPN control point configuration

Usage Guidelines
This command first appeared in Cisco IOS Release 11.3.

Example
The following example enables HPR support for this router:

```
hpr
```

Related Commands
To locate documentation of related commands, you can search online at www.cisco.com.

show appn node
show appn rtp

hpr (APPN link station)

Use the **hpr** APPN link station configuration command to specify that HPR is supported over the indicated link station. Use the **no** form of this command to disable HPR over the link station.

> **hpr**
> **no hpr**

Syntax Description
This command has no arguments or keywords.

Default
If the **hpr** command is not specified at the link station, then the default is the value configured for the corresponding port definition.

Command Mode
APPN link station configuration

Usage Guidelines

This command first appeared in Cisco IOS Release 11.3.

Example

The following example disables HPR support on the link station:

```
no hpr
```

Related Commands

To locate documentation of related commands, you can search online at www.cisco.com.

hpr (APPN control point)
hpr (APPN port)
show appn link-station

hpr (APPN port)

Use the **hpr** APPN port configuration command to specify that HPR is supported over the indicated port. Use the **no** form of this command to disable HPR over the link station.

> **hpr**
> **no hpr**

Syntax Description

This command has no arguments or keywords.

Default

If this command is not specified for a port, the default is the value configured for the control point definition.

Command Mode

APPN port configuration

Usage Guidelines

This command first appeared in Cisco IOS Release 11.3.

Example
The following example disables HPR support on port:

```
no hpr
```

Related Commands
To locate documentation of related commands, you can search online at www.cisco.com.

hpr (APPN control point)
hpr (APPN port)
show appn link-station

hpr max-sessions
Use the **hpr max-sessions** APPN control point configuration command to specify the maximum number of sessions allowed over an RTP connection. Use the **no** form of this command to cancel the specification.

> **hpr max-sessions** *num-sessions*
> **no hpr max-sessions**

Syntax   Description

Syntax	Description
num-sessions	Maximum number of sessions allowed over an RTP connection. The valid range is 1 to 65,535. The default is 65,535.

Default
The default maximum number of sessions allowed is 65,535.

Command Mode
APPN control point configuration

Usage Guidelines
This command first appeared in Cisco IOS Release 11.3.

Example
The following example sets the maximum number of sessions allowed over an RTP session to 32:

```
hpr max-sessions 32
```

Related Commands

To locate documentation of related commands, you can search online at www.cisco.com.

show appn node
show appn rtp

hpr retries

Use the **hpr retries** APPN control point configuration command to specify the number of times to retry sending a packet before initiating a path switch of the RTP connection. Use the **no** form of this command to cancel the specification.

> **hpr retries** *low-retries medium-retries high-retries network-retries*
> **no hpr retries**

Syntax	Description
low-retries	Number of times to retry sending a low-priority packet before initiating a path switch. Valid values are 0 to 10. The default is 6.
medium-retries	Number of times to retry sending a medium-priority packet before initiating a path switch. Valid values are 0 to 10. The default is 6.
high-retries	Number of times to retry sending a high-priority packet before initiating a path switch. Valid values are 0 to 10. The default is 6.
network-retries	Number of times to retry sending a network-priority packet before initiating a path switch. Valid values are 0 to 10. The default is 6.

Defaults

The default for all four retry values is 6.

Command Mode

APPN control point configuration

Usage Guidelines

This command first appeared in Cisco IOS Release 11.3.

Example

The following example sets the HPR retry values:

```
hpr retries 10 6 4 2
```

Related Commands

To locate documentation of related commands, you can search online at www.cisco.com.

hpr timers liveness
show appn node
show appn rtp

hpr sap

Use the **hpr sap** APPN port configuration command to specify the SAP for automatic network routing frames. Use the **no** form of this command to cancel the SAP specification and revert to the default SAP.

> **hpr sap** *sap*
> **no hpr sap**

Syntax	Description
sap	SAP value, in hexadecimal, used for automatic network routing frames. Valid hexadecimal values are even numbers in the range 0x02 to 0xFE. The default SAP value is 0xc8.

Default

The default SAP value is 0xc8.

Command Mode

APPN port configuration

Usage Guidelines

This command first appeared in Cisco IOS Release 11.3.

The SAP value is configured on the port and is used by all link stations that use that port.

Example

The following example specifies a SAP value of 0x02:

```
hpr sap 0x02
```

Related Commands

To locate documentation of related commands, you can search online at www.cisco.com.

show appn port
show appn rtp

hpr timers liveness

Use the **hpr timers liveness** APPN control point configuration command to specify how many seconds to wait for a packet to be received before initiating a path switch. Use the **no** form of this command to cancel the timers.

> **hpr timers liveness** *low-time medium-time high-time network-time*
> **no hpr timers liveness**

Syntax	Description
low-time	Time, in seconds, for a node to wait to send an HPR status request when no low-priority data traffic is present. The valid range is 1 to 180 seconds. The default time is 45 seconds.
medium-time	Time, in seconds, for a node to wait to send an HPR status request when no medium-priority data traffic is present. The valid range is 1 to 180 seconds. The default time is 45 seconds.
high-time	Time, in seconds, for a node to wait to send an HPR status request when no high-priority data traffic is present. The valid range is 1 to 180 seconds. The default time is 45 seconds.
network-time	Time, in seconds, for a node to wait to send an HPR status request when no network-priority data traffic is present. The valid range is 1 to 180 seconds. The default time is 45 seconds.

Defaults

The default for each of the four time values is 45 seconds.

Command Mode

APPN control point configuration

Usage Guidelines

This command first appeared in Cisco IOS Release 11.3.

Example

The following example sets the HPR liveness timers:

```
hpr timers liveness 180 120 60 30
```

Related Commands

To locate documentation of related commands, you can search online at www.cisco.com.

hpr retries
show appn node
show appn rtp

hpr timers path-switch

Use the **hpr timers path-switch** APPN control point configuration command to specify the amount of time allowed to attempt a path switch for an RTP connection. Use the **no** form of this command to cancel the specification.

> **hpr timers path-switch** *low-time medium-time high-time network-time*
> **no hpr timers**

Syntax

Syntax	Description
low-time	Time, in seconds, allowed to perform a path switch for a low-priority RTP connection. The valid range is 0 to 7200 seconds. The default is 480 seconds.
medium-time	Time, in seconds, allowed to perform a path switch for a medium-priority RTP connection. The valid range is 0 to 7200 seconds. The default is 240 seconds.
high-time	Time, in seconds, allowed to perform a path switch for a high-priority RTP connection. The valid range is 0 to 7200 seconds. The default is 120 seconds.

Syntax	Description
network-time	Time, in seconds, allowed to perform a path switch for a network-priority RTP connection. The valid range is 0 to 7200 seconds. The default is 60 seconds.

Defaults

The default time allowed to attempt a low-priority RTP connection is 480 seconds.

The default time allowed to attempt a medium-priority RTP connection is 240 seconds.

The default time allowed to attempt a high-priority RTP connection is 120 seconds.

The default time allowed to attempt a network-priority connection is 60 seconds.

Command Mode

APPN control point configuration

Usage Guidelines

This command first appeared in Cisco IOS Release 11.3.

Example

The following example sets the HPR path switch timers:

```
hpr timers path-switch 1200 600 300 120
```

interrupt-switched

Use the **interrupt-switched** APPN control point configuration command to specify that ISR should be processed at the interrupt level. Us the **no** form of this command to cancel the specification.

> **interrupt-switched**
> **no interrupt-switched**

Syntax Description

This command has no arguments or keywords.

Default
Disabled

Command Mode
APPN control point

Usage Guidelines
This command first appeared in Cisco IOS Release 11.0.

This command improves the performance of ISR routing. The command can be used only if segment size is the same on all nodes in the message path. Re-segmenting cannot be accomplished at the interrupt level. In addition, this command should only be used when routing between interfaces with similar speeds. This is because no pacing is done in the node when **interrupt-switched** is specified.

Example
The following example specifies that ISR should be processed at the interrupt level:

```
appn control-point CISCO.APPN1
 interrupt-switched
 complete
```

Related Commands
To locate documentation of related commands, you can search online at www.cisco.com.

appn control-point
show appn intermediate-session

lan-dest-address

Use the **lan-dest-address** APPN link station configuration command to specify the MAC address of the partner node. Use the **no** form of this command to return to the default.

> **lan-dest-address** *lan-addr* [*sap*]
> **no lan-dest-address**

Syntax	Description
lan-addr	12-byte hexadecimal number in the form *xxxx.xxxx.xxxx*.
sap	(Optional) 1-byte hexadecimal number in the range 04 to EC, and divisible by 4. The default SAP value is 04 (hexadecimal).

Defaults

No default lan-addr is specified.

The default SAP value is 04 (hexadecimal).

Command Mode

APPN link station configuration

Usage Guidelines

This command first appeared in Cisco IOS Release 11.0.

This command is required for interface types Token Ring, Ethernet, or FDDI. It is not allowed for other interface types.

Example

The following example sets the MAC address and SAP for a link to a partner node:

```
appn link-station LINK0001
 port ETHER1
 lan-dest-address 1234.cfe0.9745 08
 complete
```

Related Commands

To locate documentation of related commands, you can search online at www.cisco.com.

appn link-station
fr-dest-address
sdlc-dest-address
show appn link-station

limited-resource (APPN link station)

Use the **limited-resource** APPN link station configuration command to specify that the connection be taken down when no sessions are using it. Use the **no** form of this command to specify that the connection will remain active when no sessions are using it.

> **limited-resource**
> **no limited-resource**

Syntax Description

This command has no arguments or keywords.

Default

The value specified in the **appn port** command.

Command Mode

APPN link station configuration

Usage Guidelines

This command first appeared in Cisco IOS Release 11.0.

This command identifies a link that has a higher cost or is a switched connection and should not remain active if no resource is using the link. The **limited-resource** command issued at the APPN link station level overrides the same command issued at the APPN port level.

Example

The following example specifies that the link be taken down when no sessions are active:

```
appn link-station FRLINK34
 port FR1
 fr-dest-address 34
 limited-resource
 complete
```

Related Commands

To locate documentation of related commands, you can search online at www.cisco.com.

appn link-station
limited-resource (APPN port)
show appn link-station

limited-resource (APPN port)

Use the **limited-resource** APPN link station configuration command to specify that the link be taken down when no sessions are using the link. Use the **no** form of this command to specify that the link will remain active when no sessions are using the link.

>**limited-resource**
>**no limited-resource**

Syntax Description

This command has no arguments or keywords.

Default

The default is no limited resource.

Command Mode

APPN port configuration

Usage Guidelines

This command first appeared in Cisco IOS Release 11.0.

This command identifies a link that has a higher cost or is a switched connection and should not remain active if no resource is using the link. This command applies to all link stations accessed through this port. Specifying limited resources at the link station level overrides this command.

Example

The following example activates limited resource:

```
appn port FR0 serial 0/2
 limited-resource
 complete
```

Related Commands

To locate documentation of related commands, you can search online at www.cisco.com.

appn port
limited-resource (APPN link station)
show appn port

link-queuing

Use the **link-queuing** APPN link station configuration command to specify queuing options and parameters for the link station. Use the **no** form of this command to cancel the option.

> **link-queuing** {**priority** *level* | **custom** *queue-number*}
> **no link-queuing**

Syntax	Description
priority *level*	Priority level, indicated by one of the following keywords: **high**, **medium**, **normal**, **low**.
custom *queue-number*	Priority number used to specify custom queuing for the link station. The default is that no number is assigned.

Default

No default priority number is assigned.

Command Mode

APPN link station configuration

Usage Guidelines

This command first appeared in Cisco IOS Release 11.0.

Example

The following example specifies medium priority level queuing for the link station:

```
link-queuing medium
```

Related Commands

To locate documentation of related commands, you can search online at www.cisco.com.

show appn link-station

local-sap

Use the **local-sap** APPN port configuration command to specify the local service access point (SAP) to activate on the interface. Use the **no** form of this command to return to the default.

> **local-sap** *sap*
> **no local-sap**

Syntax

Syntax	Description
sap	Hexadecimal number in the range 04 to EC, and divisible by 4. The default is 04.

Default

The default local SAP is 04 (hexadecimal).

Command Mode

APPN port configuration

Usage Guidelines

This command first appeared in Cisco IOS Release 11.0.

Example

The following example specifies the local SAP:

```
appn port TR0 tokenring 0
 local-sap 44
 complete
```

Related Commands

To locate documentation of related commands, you can search online at www.cisco.com.

appn port
show appn port

locate-queuing

Use the **locate-queuing** APPN control point configuration command to enable the locate throttling feature on this control point and prevent multiple broadcast locate searches to the same destination LU. Use the **no** form of this command to disable the locate throttling feature.

> **locate-queuing**
> **no locate-queuing**

Part
II

Command Reference

Syntax Description

This command has no arguments or keywords.

Default

Locate queuing is disabled.

Command Mode

APPN control point configuration

Usage Guidelines

This command first appeared in Cisco IOS Release 11.3.

When the **locate-queuing** command is enabled, it is applied at the network node server only for locate search requests from its end node.

Example

The following example enables the locate throttling feature:

```
locate-queuing
```

Related Commands

To locate documentation of related commands, you can search online at www.cisco.com.

appn control-point
negative-caching
show appn directory
show appn node

max-cached-entries

Use the **max-cached-entries** APPN control point configuration command to specify the maximum number of cached directory entries. Use the **no** form of this command to return to the default.

> **max-cached-entries** *number*
> **no max-cached-entries**

Syntax

number

Description

Maximum number of cached directory entries. The valid range is 0 to 32,767. The default is 255.

Default

255 cached directory entries

Command Mode

APPN control point configuration

Usage Guidelines

This command first appeared in Cisco IOS Release 11.0.

This command enables you to balance memory usage and performance. A large number requires more memory, but reduces the number of network broadcasts. Cached directory entries are created as nodes learn locations of other network resources. This command affects cached entries only. A value of zero still allows location of node, but broadcasts are required.

Example

The following example specifies the maximum number of cached directory entries:

```
appn control-point CISCO.ROUTER
 max-cached-entries 100
 complete
```

Related Commands

To locate documentation of related commands, you can search online at www.cisco.com.

appn control-point
show appn node

max-cached-trees

Use the **max-cached-trees** APPN control point configuration command to specify the maximum number of cached class of service routing trees. Use the **no** form of this command to return to the default.

> **max-cached-trees** *number*
> **no max-cached-trees**

Syntax

number

Description

Maximum number of cached class of service routing trees. The valid range is 0 to 32,767. The default is 20.

Default

20 class of service routing trees

Command Mode

APPN control point configuration

Usage Guidelines

This command first appeared in Cisco IOS Release 11.0.

This command allows you to balance memory usage and performance. Each cached tree represents all paths through the network for a class of service. If you specify a lower number, fewer will be caches and longer processing time may be required to calculate the paths through the network and select a route.

Example

The following example specifies the maximum number of cached topology trees:

```
appn control-point CISCO.ROUTER
 max-cached-trees 5
 complete
```

Related Commands

To locate documentation of related commands, you can search online at www.cisco.com.

appn control-point
show appn node

maximum-memory

Use the **maximum-memory** APPN control point configuration command to specify the maximum amount of memory available to APPN. Use the **no** form of this command to cancel the specification.

maximum-memory *bytes*
no maximum-memory

Syntax	Description
bytes	Maximum amount of memory (in bytes) available to APPN. The valid range is 3,000,000 to 64,000,000 bytes. The default is that APPN has access to all memory.

Default

The default is that APPN has access to all memory.

Command Mode

APPN control point configuration

Usage Guideline

This command first appeared in Cisco IOS Release 11.0.

This command ensures that APPN will not monopolize the memory of the device and that other protocols being routed will have memory available.

Example

The following example specifies the maximum amount of memory available to APPN as 16,000,000 bytes (16 MB):

```
appn control-point CISCO.APPN1
 maximum-memory 16000000
 complete
```

Related Commands

To locate documentation of related commands, you can search online at www.cisco.com.

appn control-point

max-link-stations

Use the **max-link-stations** APPN port configuration command to specify the maximum number of active link stations allowed on this port. Use the **no** form of this command to return to the default.

> **max-link-stations** *number*
> **no max-link-stations**

Syntax	Description
number	Number in the range 1 to 255. Must be greater than or equal to the sum of **reserved-inbound** and **reserved-outbound**. The default is media dependent.

Default

The default is media dependent:

Ethernet—255
FDDI—255
Frame Relay—255
QLLC—1
RSRB—255
SDLC—1
Token Ring—255

Command Mode

APPN port configuration

Usage Guidelines

This command first appeared in Cisco IOS Release 11.0.

For leased negotiable lines, the maximum value is 1.

For leased primary lines, not multidrop, the maximum value is 1 and inbound is 0.

For leased secondary lines and switched lines, the maximum value is 1.

Example

The following example sets the maximum link stations:

```
appn port TR01 tokenring 0/1
 max-link-stations 10
 complete
```

Related Commands

To locate documentation of related commands, you can search online at www.cisco.com.

appn port
reserved-inbound
reserved-outbound
show appn port

max-rcv-btu-size

Use the **max-rcv-btu-size** APPN port configuration command to specify the desired maximum receive BTU. Use the **no** form of this command to return to the default.

> **max-rcv-btu-size** *size*
> **no max-rcv-btu-size**

Syntax

Syntax	Description
size	Maximum receive BTU (in bytes), in the range 99 to 5107. The default is 1024 bytes.

Default

1024 bytes

Command Mode

APPN port configuration

Usage Guideline

This command first appeared in Cisco IOS Release 11.0.

The BTU specifies a maximum message size at the physical layer, similar to the MTU in TCP/IP. Do not confuse BTU with MAXRU, which is session related.

Example

The following example sets the maximum BTU value to 500:

```
appn port TR11 tokenring1/1
 max-rcv-btu-size 500
 complete
```

Related Commands

To locate documentation of related commands, you can search online at www.cisco.com.

appn port
show appn port

minimum-memory

Use the **minimum-memory** APPN control point configuration command to specify the minimum amount of memory available to APPN. Use the **no** form of the command to cancel the specification.

minimum-memory *bytes*
no minimum-memory

Syntax

bytes

Description

Maximum amount of memory (in bytes) available to APPN. The valid range is 1,000,000 to 64,000,000. The default is 1,000,000 bytes.

Default

The default is 1,000,000 bytes.

Command Mode

APPN control point configuration

Usage Guidelines

This command first appeared in Cisco IOS Release 11.0.

This command ensures that APPN will always have a specified amount of memory. Memory that is dedicated to APPN will not be available for other processing.

Example

The following example reserves 10,000,000 bytes (10 MB) of memory for APPN:

```
appn control-point CISCO.APPN1
 minimum-memory 10000000
 complete
```

Related Commands

To locate documentation of related commands, you can search online at www.cisco.com.

appn control-point
maximum-memory

negative-caching

Use the **negative-caching** APPN control point configuration command to specify that the negative caching feature is enabled on this control point. Use the **no** form of this command to disable the negative caching feature.

> **negative-caching** [**time**] *time* [**threshold**] *threshold-value*
> **no negative-caching**

Syntax	Description
time *time*	Length of time, in seconds, that the negative cache entry will remain in the directory database. This timer determines how long a resource is considered unreachable. The range is 0 to 3600 seconds. The default is 60 seconds.
threshold *threshold-value*	Number of locate searches to be rejected. When this threshold expires, the negative cache entry will be removed from the directory database. The range is 0 to 1000 searches. The default is 20 searches.

Defaults

Negative caching is disabled.

The default time is 60 seconds.

The default threshold is 20 locate searches.

Command Mode

APPN control point configuration

Usage Guidelines

This command first appeared in Cisco IOS Release 11.3.

When negative caching is enabled, it is applied at the network node server only for locate search requests from its end node.

Example

The following example configures the negative caching feature to specify that requests for unreachable resources will be retained in the directory database for 30 seconds or until 10 locate search requests have been made:

```
negative-caching time 30 threshold 10
```

Related Commands

To locate documentation of related commands, you can search online at www.cisco.com.

appn control-point
locate-queuing
show appn directory
show appn node

node-row

Use the **node-row** APPN class of service configuration command to specify a node description or node row, and associated weights defined for this class of service. Use the **no** form of this command to delete a previous node row description.

> **node-row** *index* **weight** *weight* **congestion** {**yes** | **no**} {**yes** | **no**} **route-additional-resistance** *min max*
> **no node-row** *index*

Syntax	Description
index	Specifies which row is being entered. The valid range is one to eight.
weight *weight*	Weight assigned to a node, given the characteristics identified in the remainder of the row. The weight of row n must be less than the weight of row $n + 1$. The valid range is 0 to 255.
congestion	Minimum and maximum congestion tolerance for the node row.
yes yes	Only yes. Only congested transmission groups match this row.
no yes	Yes or no. Congestion does not affect class of service row.
no no	Only no. Only noncongested transmission groups match this row. The default is no no.

Syntax

route-additional-resistance
min max

Description

Minimum and maximum additional resistance value for the row. The value is compared to the same parameter defined in the CP for each network node and exchanged on the topology database updates. The valid range for minimum and maximum is 0 to 255. The default range for minimum and maximum is 0 0.

Defaults

No default node row is specified.

No default weight is specified.

The default congestion tolerance is no no.

The default route additional resistance is 0 0.

Command Mode

APPN class of service configuration

Usage Guidelines

This command first appeared in Cisco IOS Release 11.0.

You can define up to eight rows. Each row represents the characteristics of a node that meets the requirements for this class of service and defines a weight for the node that will be used in calculating the cost of a total route.

If the congestion maximum is set to "no," the congestion minimum must also be set to "no."

Example

The following example defines an APPN class of service with one node row:

```
appn class-of-service #SECURE
 node-row 1 weight 5 congestion no no route-additional-resistance 0 255
 tg-row 1 weight 30 byte 0 255 time 0 255 capacity 0 255 delay 0 255 security 200 255
 user1 0 255 user2 0 255 user3 0 255
 complete
```

Related Commands

To locate documentation of related commands, you can search online at www.cisco.com.

appn class-of-service
show appn class-of-service

null-xid-poll

Use the **null-xid-poll** APPN port configuration command to specify that the null XID should be used to poll the remote node associated with this APPN port. Use the **no** form of the command to cancel the specification.

> **null-xid-poll**
> **no null-xid-poll**

Part II

Command Reference

Syntax Description

This command has no arguments or keywords.

Default

XID3 negotiation is used to poll remote devices.

Command Mode

APPN port configuration

Usage Guidelines

This command first appeared in Cisco IOS Release 11.2.

The **null-xid-poll** command permits PU 2.0 devices that connect in with XID0 to build a dynamic link station. It is no longer necessary to configure a link definition. When this command is used, the router expects its partner to reveal its identity first by responding with either XID3 or XID0.

This feature works in a mixed environment of PU 2.0 and PU 2.1 devices where the same APPN port is shared by both types of devices. By default, XID3 is used to poll the devices. When a PU 2.0 device responds with XID0, the link is created and established dynamically. PU 2.1 devices are not affected by this change and go through the XID3 negotiation as usual.

Some care must be exercised when configuring **null-xid-poll**: If two Cisco APPN network node routers connect across ports configured with **null-xid-poll**, the APPN connection will fail because both routers expect the other to respond first using either XID0 or XID3. Similar behavior may occur when a port configured with **null-xid-poll** attempts communication with a front-end processor configured for XID polling. You only need to configure **null-xid-poll** when dealing with a PU 2.0 device that does not respond gracefully to the XID3 poll.

Example

The following example specifies that null XID should be used to poll the remote nodes associated with the APPN port FDDI0:

```
appn port FDDI0 fddi 0
 null-xid-poll
 complete
```

Related Commands

To locate documentation of related commands, you can search online at www.cisco.com.

appn port

owning-cp

Use the **owning-cp** APPN partner LU location configuration command to specify the name of the CP that owns the partner LU. Use the **no** form of this command to delete the definition.

> **owning-cp** *netid.cpname*
> **no owning-cp**

Syntax

netid.cpname

Description

Fully qualified network name. A fully qualified name is a string of one to eight characters, a period, and another string of one to eight characters. The following characters are acceptable:
A–Z, a–z
0–9
$ # @
The first character of either string must not be a number.

Default

No default name is assigned.

Command Mode

APPN partner LU location configuration

Usage Guidelines

This command first appeared in Cisco IOS Release 11.0.

The *netid.cpname* argument must be unique in the network and must match the name specified as control point on the specific node.

Example

The following example sets the owning CP name:

```
appn partner-lu-location CISCO.LU000012
 owning-cp CISCO.CP00001
 complete
```

Related Commands

To locate documentation of related commands, you can search online at www.cisco.com.

appn partner-lu-location
show appn directory

port (APPN connection network)

Use the **port** APPN connection network configuration command to specify the ports that have visibility to the connection network. Use the **no** form of this command to delete the definition.

> **port** *portname*
> **no port** *portname*

Syntax

portname

Description

Type A name. A Type A character string contains one to eight of the following characters:
A–Z, a–z
0–9
$ # @

Default

No default port name is assigned.

Command Mode

APPN connection network configuration

Usage Guidelines

This command first appeared in Cisco IOS Release 11.0.

Up to five ports can be specified by repeating the command. Port names must be previously defined by the **appn port** command.

Example

The following example specifies an APPN connection network with one port:

```
appn connection-network CISCO.CN1
 port TR0
 complete
```

Related Commands

To locate documentation of related commands, you can search online at www.cisco.com.

appn connection-network
appn port
show appn connection-network

port (APPN link station)

Use the **port** APPN link station configuration command to specify the port that can be used to access the link station. Use the **no** form of this command to delete the definition.

>**port** *portname*
>**no port**

Syntax	Description
portname	Type A name. (Required when defining a new link station; optional on subsequent changes to the link station.) A Type A character contains one to eight of the following characters: A–Z, a–z 0–9 $ # @

Default

No default port is specified.

Command Mode

APPN link station configuration

Usage Guidelines

This command first appeared in Cisco IOS Release 11.0.

The *portname* argument must be a value defined in a previous **appn port** command. The **port** command is required to define an APPN link station.

Example

The following example defines the port:

```
appn link-station FDDILINK
 port FDDI0
 lan-dest-address 0200.0000.cfbd
 complete
```

Related Commands

To locate documentation of related commands, you can search online at www.cisco.com.

appn link-station
appn port
show appn link-station

ppp-dest-address

Use the **ppp-dest-address** APPN link station configuration command to specify the remote SAP of a node across a PPP interface. Use the **no** form of this command to return to the default.

> **ppp-dest-address** *sap*
> **no ppp-dest-address**

Syntax   Description

Syntax	Description
sap	Service access point of the remote node. The default is 04 hexadecimal.

Default

The default SAP is 04 hexadecimal.

Command Mode
APPN link station configuration

Usage Guidelines
This command first appeared in Cisco IOS Release 11.1.

The command should be specified only if the APPN port used by the link station is a PPP port.

Related Commands
To locate documentation of related commands, you can search online at www.cisco.com.

appn link-station
show appn link-station

propagation-delay (APPN link station)
Use the **propagation-delay** APPN link station configuration command to specify the amount of inherent delay of the connection. Use the **no** form of this command to return to the default.

> **propagation-delay** {**minimum** | **lan** | **telephone** | **packet-switched** | **satellite** | **maximum**}
> **no propagation-delay**

Syntax	Description
minimum	No delay.
lan	Less than 480 microseconds delay.
telephone	Between 480 and 49,152 microseconds delay.
packet-switched	Between 49,152 and 245,760 microseconds delay.
satellite	Greater than 245,760 microseconds delay.
maximum	Maximum delay allowed.

Default
The value specified in the **appn port** command.

Command Mode
APPN link station configuration

Usage Guidelines

This command first appeared in Cisco IOS Release 11.0.

The inherent delay is used in route selection by comparing this value to the value requested for a particular class of service. This value supersedes any value specified on the **appn port** command. Propagation delay is used by the node to determine the least cost route for APPN intermediate sessions.

Example

The following example specifies a delay of less than 480 microseconds:

```
appn link-station FRLINK12
 port FR1
 propagation-delay lan
 complete
```

Related Commands

To locate documentation of related commands, you can search online at www.cisco.com.

appn link-station
show appn link-station

propagation-delay (APPN port)

Use the **propagation-delay** APPN port configuration command to specify the propagation delay of the link. Use the **no** form of this command to return to the default.

> **propagation-delay** {**minimum** | **lan** | **telephone** | **packet-switched** | **satellite** | **maximum**}
> **no propagation-delay**

Syntax	Description
minimum	No delay.
lan	Less than 480 microseconds delay.
telephone	Between 480 and 49,152 microseconds delay.
packet-switched	Between 49,152 and 245,760 microseconds delay.
satellite	Greater than 245,760 microseconds delay.
maximum	Maximum delay allowed.

Part II

Command Reference

Default

The default is media dependent:

Ethernet—**lan**
FDDI—**lan**
Frame Relay—**packet-switched**
QLLC—**packet-switched**
RSRB—**packet-switched**
SDLC—**telephone**
Token Ring—**lan**

Command Mode

APPN port configuration

Usage Guidelines

This command first appeared in Cisco IOS Release 11.0.

This command applies to all link stations accessed through this port. Specifying propagation delay at the link station level overrides this command. The value of propagation delay is used by the node to determine the least cost route for APPN intermediate sessions.

Example

The following example specifies a delay of less than 480 microseconds:

```
appn port FR1 Serial1/1
 propagation-delay lan
 complete
```

Related Commands

To locate documentation of related commands, you can search online at www.cisco.com.

appn port
show appn port

pu-type-20

Use the **pu-type-20** APPN link station configuration command to indicate that the downstream PU whose dependent LU request is propagated through the link is a PU type 2.0. Use the **no** form of this command or omit this command to indicate that the downstream PU is a type 2.1.

> **pu-type-20**
> **no pu-type-20**

Syntax Description

This command has no arguments or keywords.

Default

The downstream PU is defined as a PU type 2.1.

Command Mode

APPN link station configuration

Usage Guidelines

This command first appeared in Cisco IOS Release 11.0.

This command is normally used in conjunction with the **dlur-dspu-name** link-station configuration command.

Example

The following example indicates that the downstream PU is a PU type 2.0:

```
appn link-station LINK0001
 port TR0
 lan-dest-address 1000.4521.9812
 pu-type-20
 dlur-dspu-name PU009812
 complete
```

Related Commands

To locate documentation of related commands, you can search online at www.cisco.com.

appn link-station
dlur-dspu-name
show appn link-station

reserved-inbound

Use the **reserved-inbound** APPN port configuration command to specify the number of link stations (out of **max-link-stations**) to be reserved for inbound links (partner initiates). Use the **no** form of this command to return to the default.

> **reserved-inbound** *number*
> **no reserved-inbound**

Syntax	Description
number	Number in the range 0 to 255. The default is 0.

Default

No link stations are reserved for inbound links.

Command Mode

APPN port configuration

Usage Guidelines

This command first appeared in Cisco IOS Release 11.0.

The total of **reserved-inbound** plus **reserved-outbound** must be less than or equal to the maximum number of link station allowed on the port. This value is configured using the **max-link-stations** command.

Example

The following example sets the number of link stations reserved for inbound links to 50:

```
appn port TR0 tokenring 0
 reserved-inbound 50
 complete
```

Related Commands

To locate documentation of related commands, you can search online at www.cisco.com.

appn port
max-link-stations
reserved-outbound
show appn port

reserved-outbound

Used the **reserved-outbound** APPN port configuration command to specify the number of link stations (of **max-link-stations**) to be reserved for outbound link stations where this node initiates the connection. Use the **no** form of this command to return to the default.

        reserved-outbound *number*
        no reserved-outbound

Syntax

Description

number   Number in the range 0 to 255. The default is 0.

Default

No link stations are reserved for outbound links.

Command Mode

APPN port configuration

Usage Guidelines

This command first appeared in Cisco IOS Release 11.0.

The total of **reserved-inbound** plus **reserved-outbound** must be less than or equal to the maximum number of link station allowed on the port. This value is configured using the **max-link-stations** command.

Example

The following example sets the number of link stations reserved for outbound links to 50:

```
appn port TR1 tokenring 1
 reserved-outbound 50
 complete
```

Related Commands

To locate documentation of related commands, you can search online at www.cisco.com.

appn port
max-link-stations
reserved-inbound
show appn port

retry-limit (APPN link station)

Use the **retry-limit** APPN link station configuration command to specify the number of times a link station attempts reactivation after failure. Use the **no** form of this command to specify the default.

> **retry-limit** {*retries* | **infinite** [*interval*]}
> **no retry-limit**

Syntax	Description
retries	Number of reactivation attempts. The valid range is 0 to 255 (0 equals infinite retries). The default is 5.
infinite	Infinite retries.
interval	(Optional) Amount of time allowed between reactivation attempts (in seconds). The valid range is 0 to 32,767 seconds. The default is 30 seconds.

Defaults

The default number of retries is 5.

The default amount of time is 30 seconds.

Command Mode

APPN link station configuration

Usage Guidelines

This command first appeared in Cisco IOS Release 11.0.

This value supersedes any value specified in the **appn port** command.

Example

The following example specifies 25 retries for APPN link station LINK12:

```
appn link-station LINK12
 port FDDI1
 lan-dest-address 4000.0211.4567
 retry-limit 25
 complete
```

Related Commands

To locate documentation of related commands, you can search online at www.cisco.com.

appn link-station
show appn link-station

retry-limit (APPN port)

Use the **retry-limit** APPN port configuration command to specify how many times a line will attempt reactivation after failure. Use the **no** form of this command to delete the previous definition.

> **retry-limit** {*retries* | **infinite**} [*interval*]
> **no retry-limit**

Syntax	Description
retries	Number of reactivation attempts. The valid range is 0 to 255 (0 equals infinite retries). The default is 5.
infinite	Infinite retries.
interval	(Optional) Amount of time allowed between reactivation attempts (in seconds). The default is 30 seconds.

Defaults

The default number of retries is 5.

The default amount of time is 30 seconds.

Command Mode

APPN port configuration

Usage Guidelines

This command first appeared in Cisco IOS Release 11.0.

This command applies to all link stations accessed through this port. Specifying a retry limit at the link station level overrides this command.

Example

The following example specifies 25 retries:

```
appn port ETHER0 ethernet 0
 retry-limit 25
 complete
```

Related Commands

To locate documentation of related commands, you can search online at www.cisco.com.

appn port
show appn port

role (APPN link station)

Use the **role** APPN link station configuration command to specify the link station role used in XID negotiations. Use the **no** form of this command to return to the default.

> **role** {**negotiable** | **primary** | **secondary**}
> **no role**

Syntax	Description
negotiable	The link station can be the primary or secondary end of the link station connection.
primary	The link station is the primary end of the link station connection.
secondary	The link station is the secondary end of the link station connection.

Default

The value specified in the **appn port** command.

Command Mode

APPN link station configuration

Usage Guidelines

This command first appeared in Cisco IOS Release 11.0.

This command overrides the value specified on the port definition.

Example

The following example sets the role to primary:

```
appn link-station LINK44
 port ETHER1
 lan-dest-address 0200.98ab.de23
 role primary
 complete
```

Related Commands

To locate documentation of related commands, you can search online at www.cisco.com.

appn link-station
show appn link-station

role (APPN port)

Use the **role** APPN port configuration command to specify the link station role used in XID negotiations for all link stations defined through this port. Use the **no** form of this command to return to the default.

role {**negotiable** | **primary** | **secondary**}
no role

Syntax	Description
negotiable	The link station can be the primary or secondary end of the link station connection.
primary	The link station is the primary end of the link station connection.
secondary	The link station is the secondary end of the link station connection.

Default

The default role is **negotiable**.

Command Mode

APPN port configuration

Usage Guidelines

This command first appeared in Cisco IOS Release 11.0.

This command applies to all link stations accessed through this port. Specifying a role at the link station overrides this command.

Example

The following example sets the role to primary:

```
appn port FDDI0 fddi 0
 role primary
 complete
```

Related Commands

To locate documentation of related commands, you can search online at www.cisco.com.

appn port
show appn port

route-additional-resistance

Use the **route-additional-resistance** APPN control point configuration command to specify an arbitrary value for the local node. Use the **no** form of this command to return to the default.

> **route-additional-resistance** *number*
> **no route-additional-resistance**

Syntax   Description

number   Arbitrary value in the range of 0 to 255. The default is 128.

Default

The default resistance value is 128.

Command Mode

APPN control point configuration

Usage Guidelines

This command first appeared in Cisco IOS Release 11.0.

The route additional resistance value is included in topology updates and is used by network nodes to select a least-cost path associated with a particular class of service. You use this command to assign an arbitrary value and to indicate preference or nonpreference for particular nodes in route paths.

Example

The following example specifies a route additional resistance value of 200:

```
appn control-point CISCO.ROUTER
 route-additional-resistance 200
 complete
```

Related Commands

To locate documentation of related commands, you can search online at www.cisco.com.

appn control-point
show appn node

rsrb-virtual-station

Use the **rsrb-virtual-station** APPN port configuration command to configure APPN for remote source-route bridging. Use the **no** form of this command to delete the configuration.

> **rsrb-virtual-station** *mac-address local-ring bridge-number target-ring*
> **no rsrb-virtual-station**

Syntax	Description
mac-address	Virtual MAC address on which APPN resides.
local-ring	Virtual ring number on which the APPN station resides. The valid range is 1 to 255.
bridge-number	Bridge number connecting the local virtual ring and the RSRB target virtual ring. The valid range is 1 to 15.
target-ring	Target ring through which the local ring bridges data. The valid range is 1 to 255.

Default

No defaults are defined.

Command Mode

APPN port configuration

Usage Guidelines

This command first appeared in Cisco IOS Release 11.0.

Example

The following example defines an APPN port that uses RSRB as a transport protocol:

```
appn port rsrb
 rsrb-virtual-station 1234.1234.1234 50 1 60
 complete
```

Related Commands

To locate documentation of related commands, you can search online at www.cisco.com.

appn port
show appn port

safe-store-cycle

Use the **safe-store-cycle** APPN control point configuration command to specify the number of cache instances to be saved. Use the **no** form of this command to delete the previous definition.

> **safe-store-cycle** *number*
> **no safe-store-cycle**

Syntax	Description
number	Number of cache instances to be saved. The valid range is 1 to 99. The default is 2.

Default

The default is 2.

Command Mode

APPN control point configuration

Usage Guidelines

This command first appeared in Cisco IOS Release 11.0.

The file naming convention used for the cache instances is

> *control-point-name*.d*nn*

where *nn* is a number in the range from 00 to the cycle number specified. The files that will be generated in the example are:

> **APPN1.d00**
>
> **APPN1.d01**
>
> **APPN1.d02**
>
> **APPN1.d03**

Example

The following example specifies that three cache instances will be saved:

```
appn control-point CISCO.APPN1
 safe-store-host ip-address 171.69.44.1 directory appnsafe
 safe-store-cycle 3
 complete
```

Related Commands

To locate documentation of related commands, you can search online at www.cisco.com.

appn control-point

safe-store-host

Use the **safe-store-host** APPN control point configuration command to specify the IP host address and the file path for safe store. Use the **no** form of this command to delete the previous definition.

> **safe-store-host ip-address** *address* **directory** *path*
> **no safe-store-host**

Syntax	Description
ip-address *address*	Host IP address.
directory *path*	File path for safe store.

Default
No defaults are assigned.

Command Mode
APPN control point configuration

Usage Guidelines
This command first appeared in Cisco IOS Release 11.0.

Some TFTP hosts might require you to create the file entries in advance. Refer to the **safe-store-cycle** command reference entry for the file naming convention.

Example
The following example specifies that the IP host address and the file path where the database will be stored:

```
appn control-point CISCO.APPN1
 safe-store-host ip-address 171.69.44.1 directory appnsafe
 safe-store-cycle 3
 complete
```

Related Commands
To locate documentation of related commands, you can search online at www.cisco.com.

appn control-point

safe-store-interval

Use the **safe-store-interval** APPN control point configuration command to specify how often the directory database is stored to permanent media. Use the **no** form of this command to delete the previous definition.

> **safe-store-interval** *interval*
> **no safe-store-interval**

Syntax	Description
interval	Interval in minutes between storage of the directory database to permanent media. The valid range is 0 to 32,767 minutes. The default is 20 minutes.

Default
20 minutes

Command Mode
APPN control point configuration

Usage Guidelines
This command first appeared in Cisco IOS Release 11.0.

This command allows you to balance processor usage with potential performance savings. A longer interval reduces the processor cycles used to save data, but potentially reduces the validity of the data due to less frequent updates.

Example
The following example specifies that the database will be stored to permanent media every 30 minutes:

```
appn control-point CISCO.APPN1
 safe-store-host ip-address 171.69.44.1 directory appnsafe
 safe-store-interval 30
 complete
```

Related Commands
To locate documentation of related commands, you can search online at www.cisco.com.

appn control-point

sdlc-dest-address

Use the **sdlc-dest-address** APPN link station configuration command to specify the local address of the partner node for nonswitched SDLC. Use the **no** form of this command to return to the default.

> **sdlc-dest-address** *address*
> **no sdlc-dest-address** *address*

Syntax	Description
address	Two-digit hexadecimal number in the range of 00 to FE.

Default

No default address is assigned.

Command Mode

APPN link station configuration

Usage Guidelines

This command first appeared in Cisco IOS Release 11.0.

This command is optional if the interface type is switched SDLC. It is not allowed for other interface types.

Example

The following example assigns address F1:

```
appn link-station LINK12
 port SDLC1
 sdlc-dest-address f1
 complete
```

Related Commands

To locate documentation of related commands, you can search online at www.cisco.com.

appn link-station
show appn link-station

sdlc-sec-addr

Use the **sdlc-sec-addr** command to configure APPN for SDLC. Use the **no** form of this command to delete the configuration.

> **sdlc-sec-addr** *sdlc-address*
> **no sdlc-sec-addr**

Syntax	Description
sdlc-address	SDLC secondary address. The valid range is 00 to FE (hexadecimal). The default is 00.

Default

The default address is 00.

Command Mode

APPN port configuration

Usage Guidelines

This command first appeared in Cisco IOS Release 11.0.

Example

The following example defines a port with a local SDLC address of 2.

```
appn port serial 1
 sdlc-sec-addr 2
 complete
```

Related Commands

To locate documentation of related commands, you can search online at www.cisco.com.

appn port
show appn port

security (APPN link station)

Use the **security** APPN link station configuration command to specify the security level of the connection. Use the **no** form of this command to delete the previous definition.

> **security** *security-level*
> **no security**

Syntax	Description
security-level	One of the following keywords:

- **nonsecure**
- **public-switched**
- **underground-cable**
- **secure-conduit**
- **guarded-conduit**
- **encrypted**
- **guarded-radiation**

The default is the value specified in the **appn port** command.

Default

The default value specified in the **appn port** command.

Command Mode

APPN link station configuration

Usage Guidelines

This command first appeared in Cisco IOS Release 11.0.

The security level is used in route selection.

Example

The following example sets the security level to encrypted:

```
appn link-station LINK12
 security encrypted
 complete
```

Related Commands

To locate documentation of related commands, you can search online at www.cisco.com.

appn link-station
show appn link-station

security (APPN port)

Use the **security** APPN port configuration command to specify security level of the connection. Use the **no** form of this command to delete the previous definition.

> **security** *security-level*
> **no security**

Syntax	Description
security-level	One of the following keywords:

- **nonsecure**
- **public-switched**
- **underground-cable**
- **secure-conduit**
- **guarded-conduit**
- **encrypted**
- **guarded-radiation**

The default is **nonsecure**.

Default

The default security is **nonsecure**.

Command Mode

APPN port configuration

Usage Guidelines

This command first appeared in Cisco IOS Release 11.0.

The command applies to all link stations accessed through this port. Specifying security at the link station level overrides this command.

Example

The following command sets the security level to encrypted:

```
appn port TR0 tokenring 0
 security encrypted
 complete
```

Related Commands

To locate documentation of related commands, you can search online at www.cisco.com.

appn port
show appn port

service-any

Use the **service-any** APPN port configuration command to specify that this port will create dynamic transmission groups for outbound or inbound links. Use the **no** form of this command to specify that the link station must be defined through configuration commands.

>**service-any**
>**no service-any**

Syntax Description

This command has no arguments or keywords.

Default

The default state is **service-any**.

Command Mode

APPN port configuration

Usage Guidelines

This command first appeared in Cisco IOS Release 11.0.

Specifying **no service-any** serves as a security mechanism to control who may or may not connect to the local node.

Example

The following example deactivates service any:

```
appn port FDDI0 fddi0
 no service-any
 complete
```

Related Commands

To locate documentation of related commands, you can search online at www.cisco.com.

appn port
show appn port

serving-nn

Use the **serving-nn** APPN partner LU location configuration command to specify the name of the network node server servicing the partner LU. Use the **no** form of this command to return to the default.

> **serving-nn** *netid.cpname*
> **no serving-nn**

Part
II

Command Reference

Syntax

netid.cpname

Description

Fully qualified network name. A fully qualified name is a string of one to eight characters, a period, and another string of one to eight characters. The following characters are acceptable:
A–Z, a–z
0–9
$ # @
The first character of either string must not be a number.
The default is the CP name of the local network node.

Default

The CP name of the local network node.

Command Mode

APPN partner LU location configuration

Usage Guidelines

This command first appeared in Cisco IOS Release 11.0.

The **serving-nn** may be specified as null if the LU name is specified as null. This specification indicates a wildcard definition for all LUs.

Example

The following example specifies the name of the network node server for the partner LU
CISCO.APPN1:

```
appn partner-lu-location CISCO.LU000012
 serving-nn CISCO.APPN1
 complete
```

Related Commands

To locate documentation of related commands, you can search online at www.cisco.com.

appn partner-lu-location
show appn directory

show appn class-of-service

Use the **show appn class-of-service** EXEC command to display the APPN classes of service defined
to the local node.

> **show appn class-of-service [brief | detail]**

Syntax	Description
brief	(Optional) Short display of APPN classes of service.
detail	(Optional) Long display of APPN classes of service.

Command Mode
EXEC

Usage Guidelines

This command first appeared in Cisco IOS Release 11.0.

Sample Displays

The following is sample output from the **show appn class-of-service** command:

```
Router# show appn class-of-service

Number of class of service definitions       7
     APPN Classes of Service
        Name     Trans. Pri.   Node Rows   TG Rows
      --------   -----------   ---------   -------
```

```
1> #CONNECT   Medium          8          8
2> CPSVCMG    Network         8          8
3> SNASVCMG   Network         8          8
4> #INTER     High            8          8
5> #INTERSC   High            8          8
6> #BATCH     Low             8          8
7> #BATCHSC   Low             8          8
```

The following is sample output from the **show appn class-of-service detail** command. This example shows just one part of one table. There could be up to eight node rows and eight TGs and multiple tables. This shows, however, the correspondence between the configuration commands and **show** commands.

```
Router# show appn class-of-service detail

Number of class of service definitions    8
1> Class of service name                   #connect
     Transmission priority                 Medium
     Number of node rows                   8
     Number of TG rows                     8
1.1> Node row weight                       5
       Congestion min                      no
       Congestion max                      no
       Route additional resistance min     0
       Route additional resistance max     31
.                                          .
.                                          .
1.1>TG row weight                          30
       Cost per connect time min           0
       Cost per connect time max           0
     Cost per byte min                     0
     Cost per byte max                     0
     Security min                          Nonsecure
     Security max                          Maximum security
     Propagation delay min                 0 microseconds (minimum)
     Propagation delay max                 384 microseconds (local area network)
     Effective capacity min                4 megabits per second
     Effective capacity max                604 gigabits per second
     User defined parameter 1 min          0
     User defined parameter 1 max          255
     User defined parameter 2 min          0
     User defined parameter 2 max          255
     User defined parameter 3 min          0
     User defined parameter 3 max          255
```

Table 22-1 describes significant fields shown in the display.

Table 22-1 *show appn class-of-service detail* Field Descriptions

Field	Description
Class of service name	Administratively assigned name for this COS.
Transmission priority	Relative priority this COS will receive when transmitting out of this node.
Number of node rows	Number of node rows associated with this COS.

Continues

Table 22-1 *show appn class-of-service detail Field Descriptions (Continued)*

Field	Description
Node of TG rows	Number of TG rows associated with this COS.
Node row weight	Weight assigned to this node given the characteristics identified in the remainder of this row.
Congestion min	If set to "yes," this node row will be chosen only if the node is congested. If set to "no," this node row may be chosen if the node is congested. If the congestion maximum is set to "no," the congestion minimum must also be set to "no."
Congestion max	If set to "yes," this node row may be chosen if the node is congested. If set to "no," this node row will never be chosen for this COS.
Route additional resistance min	Minimum route additional resistance for this node row.
Route additional resistance max	Maximum route additional resistance for this node row.
TG row weight	Weight associated with this TG given the characteristics identified in the remainder of this row.
Cost per connect time min	Minimum acceptable value for cost per connect time for this TG row.
Cost per connect time max	Maximum acceptable value for cost per connect time for this TG row.
Cost per byte min	Minimum acceptable value for cost per byte for this TG row.
Cost per byte max	Maximum acceptable value for cost per byte for this TG row.
Security min	Minimum acceptable value for security for this TG row.
Security max	Maximum acceptable value for security for this TG row.
Propagation delay min	Minimum acceptable value for propagation delay for this TG row.
Propagation delay max	Maximum acceptable value for propagation delay for this TG row.
Effective capacity min	Minimum acceptable value for effective capacity for this TG row.
Effective capacity max	Maximum acceptable value for effective capacity for this TG row.
User defined parameter 1 min	Minimum value for a network-unique TG characteristic—parameter 1.
User defined parameter 1 max	Maximum value for a network-unique TG characteristic—parameter 1.
User defined parameter 2 min	Minimum value for a network-unique TG characteristic—parameter 2.
User defined parameter 2 max	Maximum value for a network-unique TG characteristic—parameter 2.
User defined parameter 3 min	Minimum value for a network-unique TG characteristic—parameter 3.
User defined parameter 3 max	Maximum value for a network-unique TG characteristic—parameter 3.

Related Commands

To locate documentation of related commands, you can search online at www.cisco.com.

appn class-of-service
class-of-service

show appn connection-network

Use the **show appn connection-network** EXEC command to display the APPN connection networks defined to the local node.

Part
II

Command Reference

show appn connection-network [brief | detail]

Syntax	Description
brief	(Optional) Short display of APPN connection networks.
detail	(Optional) Long display of APPN connection networks.

Command Mode

EXEC

Usage Guidelines

This command first appeared in Cisco IOS Release 11.0.

Sample Displays

The following is sample output from the **show appn connection-network brief** command:

```
Router# show appn connection-network brief

Connection network definitions                    2
     APPN Connection Networks
          Resource Name    Attached Ports   First Port Name
     ----------------      --------------    ---------------
     1> NETA.CN                  2           TR0
                                             ABCDEFGH
     2> NETADDDD.WWWWEEEE        1           TR0
```

The following is sample output from the **show appn connection-network detail** command:

```
Router# show appn connection-network detail

Connection network definitions                    1

1>Connection network name                  NETA.CONNECT
```

```
Effective capacity                    15974400 bits per second
Cost per connect time                 0
Cost per byte                         0
Propagation delay                     384 microseconds (local area network)
User defined parameter 1              128
User defined parameter 2              128
User defined parameter 3              128
Security                              Nonsecure
Attached ports                        1

1.1>Port name                         TR0
```

Table 22-2 describes significant fields shown in the display.

Table 22-2 *show appn connection-network detail* Field Descriptions

Field	Description
Connection network name	Fully qualified name of the connection network.
Effective capacity	Bit rate for the connection network.
Cost per connect time	Relative cost of this connection network's TG.
Cost per byte	Cost-per-byte of transmitting a byte over this TG.
Propagation delay	Inherent delay of the connection network
User defined parameter 1	Value for a network-unique TG characteristic — parameter 1.
User defined parameter 2	Value for a network-unique TG characteristic — parameter 2.
User defined parameter 3	Value for a network-unique TG characteristic — parameter 3.
Security	Security level for this connection network.
Attached ports	Number of ports associated with the connection network.
Port Name	Port supporting this connection network.

Related Commands

To locate documentation of related commands, you can search online at www.cisco.com.

appn connection-network

show appn directory

Use the **show appn directory** EXEC command to display negative cache entries and the remaining time and threshold-count values.

> **show appn directory**

Syntax Description

This command has no arguments or keywords.

Command Mode

Privileged EXEC

Usage Guidelines

This command first appeared in Cisco IOS Release 11.0.

Sample Displays

The following is sample output from the **show appn directory** command:

```
Router1# show appn directory

    Total directory entries              4
        APPN Directory Entries
            Resource Name       Owning CP Name        NN Server           Entry Type
            ----------------    --------------        -----------         ----------
    1> NETA.ROUTER1            NETA.ROUTER1           NETA.ROUTER1        Home
    2> NETA.EN1                NETA.EN1               NETA.ROUTER1        Register
    3> NETA.EN2                NETA.EN2               NETA.ROUTER2        NCache
    4> NETA.EN3                                                           NCache
```

The following is sample output from the **show appn directory detail** command:

```
Router2# show appn directory detail

    Total directory entries              4

1>LU name                        NETA.ROUTER1
   Owning CP name                NETA.ROUTER1
   Network node CP name          NETA.ROUTER1
   LU entry type                 Home
   Register Resource             No
2>LU name                        NETA.EN1
   Owning CP name                NETA.EN1
   Network node CP name          NETA.ROUTER1
   LU entry type                 Register
   Register Resource             No
3>LU name                        NETA.EN2
   Owning CP name                NETA.EN2
   Network node CP name          NETA.ROUTER2
   LU entry type                 NCache
   Register Resource             No
   NCache time Remaining         2
   NCache count Remaining        5
4>LU name                        NETA.EN3
```

```
Owning CP name
Network node CP name
LU entry type                     NCache
Register Resource                 No
NCache time Remaining             0
NCache count Remaining            10
```

In these examples, two negative cache entry type entries are found in the directory database table. Notice that the NETA.EN2 resource was entered as a cache entry previously, so its Owning CP Name and NN Server information are known. On the other hand, NETA.EN3 was not found on the APPN network during a previous locate search, so the corresponding information for that resource is empty.

Related Commands

To locate documentation of related commands, you can search online at www.cisco.com.

appn partner-lu-location
central-resource-registration

show appn dlur-lu

Use the **show appn dlur-lu** EXEC command to display all active SSCP dependent LUs known to DLUR.

> **show appn dlur-lu** [**pu** *pu-name*] [**brief** | **detail**]

Syntax | Description

Syntax	Description
pu *pu-name*	Eight-character Type-A string of a specific PU.
brief	(Optional) Short display of the APPN directory database.
detail	(Optional) Long display of the APPN directory database.

Command Mode
EXEC

Usage Guidelines
This command first appeared in Cisco IOS Release 11.0.

Sample Displays
The following is sample output from the **show appn dlur-lu** command:

```
Router# show appn dlur-lu

APPN DLUR-LU:
     LU Name   PU Name   DLUS Name   PLU Name
     -------   -------   ---------   ----------
   1> SJDRLU11  BEAGLE    NETA.CPAC   NETA.TSO0005
```

The following is sample output from the **show appn dlur-lu detail** command:

```
Router# show appn dlur-lu detail

LU name                          SJDRLU11
PU name                          BEAGLE
Dependent LU Server Name         NETA.CPAC
LU location                      Remote
NAU address                      2
PLU name                         NETA.TSO0005
```

Table 22-3 describes the fields in this output.

Table 22-3 *show appn dlur-lu Field Descriptions*

Field	Description
LU name	Logical unit name of the active SSCP dependent LUs supported by DLUR.
PU name	Physical unit name of the active SSCP dependent LU.
DLUS name	Fully qualified name of the DLUS providing SSCP services for the SSCP dependent LU.
LU location	Always identifies the LUs as remote LUs.
NAU address	Network addressable unit of the LU.
PLU name	When the SSCP dependent LU has an active session, the name of the primary LU name will be displayed.

Related Commands

To locate documentation of related commands, you can search online at www.cisco.com.

backup-dlus (APPN control point)
dlur
dlus (APPN control point)
show appn dlur-pu
show appn dlus

show appn dlur-pu

Use the **show appn dlur-pu** EXEC command to display all active SSCP dependent PUs known to DLUR.

show appn dlur-pu [**dlus** *dlus-name*] [**brief** | **detail**]

Syntax

Syntax	Description
dlus *dlus-name*	(Optional) 17-character Type-A string of a specific DLUS.
brief	(Optional) Short display of the APPN directory database.
detail	(Optional) Long display of the APPN directory database.

Command Mode

EXEC

Usage Guidelines

This command first appeared in Cisco IOS Release 11.0.

Sample Displays

The following is sample output from the **show appn dlur-pu** command:

```
Router# show appn dlur-pu

APPN DLUR-PU:
       PU Name  Active DLUS  Defined DLUS  Backup DLUS
       --------  -----------  ------------  -----------
    1> BEAGLE    NETA.CPAC
```

The following is sample output from the **show appn dlur-pu detail** command:

```
Router# show appn dlur-pu detail

PU name                          BEAGLE
Defined DLUS name
Backup DLUS name
Physical unit (PU) Node ID       05D00010
PU location                      Downstream
Active DLUS name                 NETA.CPAC
ANS support                      Continue
PCID                             D6DB11281AF90044
Fully qualified CP name          NETA.WONDER
```

Table 22-4 describes the fields in this output.

Table 22-4 *show appn dlur-pu detail* Field Descriptions

Field	Description
PU name	Physical unit name of active SSCP dependent PUs.
Defined DLUS name	DLUS name specified with the **dlus** (APPN link station) configuration command.
Backup DLUS name	DLUS name specified with the **backup-dlus** (APPN link station) configuration command.
PU Node ID	IDBLK and IDNUM of the PU.
PU Location	Always identifies the PU as downstream.
Active DLUS name	Fully qualified name of the DLUS providing SSCP services for the PU.
ANS support	Identifies whether DLUR will keep active LU-LU sessions (Continue) when the connection to the DLUS is lost or whether DLUR will tear down active LU-LU sessions (Stop).
PCID	Procedure correlation identifier used to distinguish encapsulated traffic associated with this PU.
Fully qualified CP name	Fully qualified CP name of the CP which generated the PCID above.

Related Commands

To locate documentation of related commands, you can search online at www.cisco.com.

backup-dlus (APPN control point)
dlur
dlus (APPN control point)
show appn dlur-lu
show appn dlus

show appn dlus

Use the **show appn dlus** EXEC command to display all LUs known to DLUR.

show appn dlus [brief | detail]

Syntax	Description
brief	(Optional) Short display of the APPN directory database.
detail	(Optional) Long display of the APPN directory database.

Command Mode

EXEC

Usage Guidelines

This command first appeared in Cisco IOS Release 11.0.

Sample Displays

The following is output from the **show appn dlus** command:

```
Router# show appn dlus

APPN DLUS:
     DLUS Name    State    # Active PUs
     ---------    -----    ----------
   1> NETA.CPAC   ACTIVE            1
```

The following is sample output from the **show appn dlus detail** command:

```
Router# show appn dlus detail

Dependent LU Server Name              NETA.CPAC
Is this default DLUS?                 Yes
Is this default backup DLUS?          No
Pipe State                            Active
Number of active PUs                  1
Pipe statistics
# of REQACTPU requests sent           1
# of REQACTPU responses received      1
# of ACTPU requests received          1
# of ACTPU responses sent             1
# of REQDACTPU requests sent          0
# of REQDACTPU responses received     0
# of DACTPU requests received         0
# of DACTPU responses sent            0
# of ACTLU requests received          1
# of ACTLU responses sent             1
# of DACTLU requests received         0
# of DACTLU responses sent            0
# of SSCP_PU MUs received             0
# of SSCP_PU MUs sent                 0
# of SSCP_LU MUs received             4
# of SSCP_LU MUs sent                 5
```

Table 22-5 describes the displays in this output.

Table 22-5 *show appn dlus detail* *Field Descriptions*

Field	Description
DLUS name	Fully qualified DLUS name.
default DLUS	Identifies the DLUS as the node default DLUS.
default backup DLUS	Identifies the DLUS as the node backup default DLUS.
Pipe State	Identifies the state of the DLUS-DLUR connection.
Number of active PUs	Total number of active PUs.
REQACTPU sent/rcvd	Number of REQACTPU requests sent to the DLUS and the number of REQACTPU responses received from DLUS.
ACTPU rcvd/sent	Number of ACTPU responses sent to the DLUs and the number of ACTPU requests received from the DLUS.
REQDACTPU rcvd/sent	Number of REQDACTPU requests sent to the DLUS and the number of REQDACTPU responses received from the DLUS.
DACTPU sent/rcvd	Number of DACTPU responses sent to the DLUS and the number of DACTPU requests received from the DLUS.
ACTLU rcvd/sent	Number of ACTLU responses sent to the DLUS and the number of ACTLU requests received from the DLUS.
DACTLU rcvd/sent	Number of DACTLU responses sent to the DLUS and the number of DACTLU requests received from the DLUS.
SSCP PU MUs rcvd/sent	Number of SSCP PU MUs sent and received from the DLUS.
SSCP LU MUs rcvd/sent	Number of SSCP LU MUs sent and received from the DLUS.

Part II

Command Reference

Related Commands

To locate documentation of related commands, you can search online at www.cisco.com.

backup-dlus (APPN control point)
dlur
dlus (APPN control point)

show appn intermediate-session

Use the **show appn intermediate-session** EXEC command to display information about the SNA sessions that are currently being routed through the local node.

> **show appn intermediate-session** [**pcid** *pcid*] [**name** *lu-name*] [**brief** | **detail**]

Syntax	Description
pcid *pcid*	(Optional) Filter by procedure correlation identifier (PCID). PCID is a 16-byte hexadecimal number.
name *lu-name*	(Optional) Filter by fully qualified LU name.
brief	(Optional) Short display of APPN intermediate session information.
detail	(Optional) Long display of APPN intermediate session information.

Command Mode

EXEC

Usage Guidelines

This command first appeared in Cisco IOS Release 11.0. The following keywords and arguments first appeared in Cisco IOS Release 11.1: **pcid** *pcid*, **name** *lu-name*.

Sample Displays

The following is sample output from the **show appn intermediate-session** command:

```
Router# show appn intermediate-session

Number of intermediate sessions         1
     APPN Intermediate Sessions
       PCID (hex)       Primary LU Name    Secondary LU Name    Mode      COS
    ----------------   ----------------   -----------------    --------  --------
   1> C6D328B0922EE4FF  NETA.MARGE          NETA.APU             #INTER    #INTER
```

The following is sample output from the **show appn intermediate-session detail** command:

```
Router# show appn intermediate-session detail

Number of intermediate sessions         2

1>Procedure correlator ID (PCID) X'SS3321E8934CF101'
Primary LU name NETA.LISA
Secondary LU name NETA.BART
Mode name #INTER
Class of service name #INTER
Primary side adjacent CP name            NETA.PATTY
  Secondary side adjacent CP name          CISCO.MARGE
  Primary side link name                   PATTY
  Secondary side link name                 MARGE
PCID generator CP name                   NETA.PATTY
```

```
2>Procedure correlator ID (PCID) X'DD3321E8944CF101'
Primary LU Name NETA.LISA
Secondary LU Name NETA.BART
Mode name SNASVCMG
Class of service name SNASVCMG
Primary side adjacent CP name          NETA.PATTY
  Secondary side adjacent CP name        CISCO.MARGE
  Primary side link name                 PATTY
  Secondary side link name               MARGE
PCID generator CP name                 NETA.PATTY
```

Part
II

Command Reference

Table 22-6 describes the fields shown in this display.

Table 22-6   *show appn intermediate-session detail Field Descriptions*

Field	Description
Procedure correlator ID (PCID)	PCID for this session.
Primary LU name	Primary LU name for this session.
Secondary LU name	Secondary LU name for this session.
Mode name	Mode used by this session.
Class of service name	Class of service used by this session.
Primary side adjacent CP name	Fully qualified name of the adjacent CP on the primary side.
Secondary side adjacent CP name	Fully qualified name of the adjacent CP on the secondary side.
Primary side link name	Link name used on the primary side.
Secondary side link name	Link name used on the secondary side.
PCID generator CP name	Fully qualified CP name that generated the PCID.
Session interrupt switched	Specifies is this session is processed at interrupt-level.

Related Commands

To locate documentation of related commands, you can search online at www.cisco.com.

show appn connection-network

show appn link-station

Use the **show appn link-station** EXEC command to display information about the APPN link stations active on or defined to the local node.

show appn link-station [**name** *link-station-name*] [**port** *port-name*] [**brief** | **detail**]

Syntax

name *link-station-name*

port *port-name*

brief

detail

Description

(Optional) Filter by link station name.

(Optional) Filter by port name.

(Optional) Short display of active APPN links. Brief is the default display.

(Optional) Long display of active APPN links with more information.

Command Mode

EXEC

Usage Guidelines

This command first appeared in Cisco IOS Release 11.0. The following keywords and options first appeared in Cisco IOS Release 11.1: **name** *link-station-name*, **port** *port-name*.

Sample Displays

The following is sample output from the **show appn link-station brief** command:

```
Router# show appn link-station brief

Number of active links 1
APPN Logical Links
        Link Name  State     Port Name  Adjacent CP Name   Node Type
        ---------  --------  ---------   ----------------   -----------
    1>  ROSEBUD    Active    TOK0        NETA.APU           Learn
    2>  HOST       Inactive  FDDI0                          Learn
    3>  DOWNSTR    Inactive  RSRB                           Learn
    4>  CANE       Inactive  FDDI0                          Learn
```

The following is sample output from the **show appn link-station detail** command:

```
Router# show appn link-station detail

Number of links                   1

1>Link name                       ROSEBUD
    Port name                     TOK0
    Interface name                TokenRing0
    Destination DLC address (remote SAP)  1111.2222.3333 (04)
    Link state                    Active
    Deactivating link             No
    Max send frame data (BTU) size  0
    Adjacent node CP name         NETA.APU
```

```
Adjacent node type                  Learn
CP-CP session support               Yes
Link station role                   Negotiable
Line type                           Shared access transport facility
Transmission group number           0
Effective capacity                  100000000 bits per second
Cost per connect time               0
Cost per byte                       0
Propagation delay                   384 microseconds (local area network)
User defined parameter 1            128
User defined parameter 2            128
User defined parameter 3            128
Security                            Nonsecure
HPR supported                       Yes
HPR RTP support level               (CF¦RTP¦Base)
HPR local SAP                       0xC8
HPR remote SAP                      0xC8
HPR ERP used                        No
HPR ANR label                       0x8003
Queuing Type                        Default
Primary DLUS Name
Backup DLUS Name
Downstream PU Name
Retry link station                  No
```

Table 22-7 describes significant fields shown in the display.

Table 22-7 *show appn link-station* *Field Descriptions*

Field	Description
Link name	Name of the link station.
Port name	Port this link station is using.
Interface name	Interface used by this link.
Destination DLC address (remote SAP)	Data-link control address of the partner node and its SAP.
Link state	State of the link.
Deactivating link	Indicates if the link is deactivating.
Max send frame data (BTU) size	Maximum BTU size this link can support.
Adjacent node CP name	Name of the partner node for the link station.
Adjacent node type	Node type of the partner node of this link.
CP-CP session support	Specifies whether CP-CP sessions can be supported.
Link station role	Specifies the role the link uses in XID negotiation.
Line type	Specifies the line type.
Transmission group number	Transmission group assigned to this link.

Continues

Table 22-7   *show appn link-station Field Descriptions (Continued)*

Field	Description
Effective capacity	Bit rate of this link.
Cost per connect time	Relative cost of this link.
Cost per byte	Cost per byte of transmitting over this link.
Propagation delay	Specifies the inherent delay of the link.
User defined parameter 1	Value for a network-unique transmission group characteristic—parameter 1.
User defined parameter 2	Value for a network-unique transmission group characteristic—parameter 2.
User defined parameter 3	Value for a network-unique transmission group characteristic—parameter 3.
Security	Security level of the link.
HPR supported	Indicates whether or not HPR is supported over the link station.
HPR RTP support level	Specifies the level of HPR support: CF—Control flows over RTP tower is supported. RTP—RTP tower is supported. Base—Only base HPR is supported.
HPR local SAP	Value for the local SAP used by HPR traffic.
HPR remote SAP	Value for the remote SAP used by HPR traffic.
HPR ERP used	Indicates whether or not the link level error recovery protocol is used.
HPR NCE label	ANR string that represents the network connection end point
Queuing Type	Indicates if a special queuing algorithm has been configured for this link station. Can be default, priority, custom, or fair.
Primary DLUS Name	If the DLUR feature is configured, this specifies the control point name of the corresponding DLUS.
Backup DLUS Name	If the DLUR feature is configured, this specifies the control point name of the corresponding backup DLUS.
Downstream PU Name	If this link is to a PU 2.0 type device, this field specifies the PU name of the remote node.
Retry link station	Indicates if the retry feature has been configured for this link and specifies the number of retries and the retry interval in seconds.

Related Commands

To locate documentation of related commands, you can search online at www.cisco.com.

appn link-station

show appn mode

Use the **show appn mode** EXEC command to display information about the APPN modes defined to the local node.

>**show appn mode**

Syntax Description

This command has no arguments or keywords.

Command Mode

EXEC

Usage Guidelines

This command first appeared in Cisco IOS Release 11.0.

Sample Display

The following is sample output from the **show appn mode** command:

```
Router# show appn mode

Number of modes                 8
     APPN Modes
     Name       Associated COS
     --------   --------------
  1>            #CONNECT
  2> #BATCH     #BATCH
  3> #BATCHSC   #BATCHSC
  4> #INTER     #INTER
  5> #INTERSC   #INTERSC
  6> CPSVCMG    CPSVCMG
  7> SNASVCMG   SNASVCMG
  8> CPSVRMGR   SNASVCMG
```

Table 22-8 describes significant fields shown in the display.

Table 22-8   *show appn mode* Field Descriptions

Field	Description
Name	Mode name.
Associated COS	Class of service.

Related Commands

To locate documentation of related commands, you can search online at www.cisco.com.

appn mode

show appn node

Use the **show appn node** EXEC command to display information about the local APPN control point.

> **show appn node**

Syntax Description

This command has no arguments or keywords.

Command Mode

EXEC

Usage Guidelines

This command first appeared in Cisco IOS Release 11.0.

Sample Display

The following is sample output from the **show appn node** command:

```
Router# show appn node

Network name                          NETA
  Control point (CP) name             BARNEY
  Node ID (for XID)                   X'07700000'
  Route additional resistance         128
  Maximum directory cache entries     255
  Current directory cache entries     0
```

```
   Directory save interval                2
Maximum sessions per RTP connection        65535
hpr timers liveness (low/med/hi/net)        1/1/1/1
Maximum RTP retries (low/med/hi/net)       6/6/6/6
Path switch timer (low/med/hi/net)         480/240/120/60
Locate-queue Enabled                       Yes
Total locate-q found count                 2
Negative-caching Enabled                   Yes
Total negative-cache match count           30
```

Table 22-9 describes significant fields shown in the display.

Table 22-9 *show appn node Field Descriptions*

Field	Description
Network name	Network name for this node.
Control point (CP) name	Control point name for this node.
Node ID (for XID)	Eight-digit hexadecimal node ID value for this node.
Route additional resistance	Arbitrary value associated with the cost of sessions passing through this node.
Maximum directory cache entries	Maximum number of cached directory entries.
Current directory cache entries	Current number of cached directory entries
Directory save interval	Time (in minutes) between directory safe stores.
Maximum sessions per HPR connection	Indicates the value configured for hpr max-sessions.
HPR timers liveness	Indicates the values configured for hpr timers liveness. The four values are for low-, medium-, high-, and network-priority packets.
Maximum HPR retries	Indicates the values configured for hpr retries. The four values are for low-, medium-, high-, and network-priority packets.
Path switch timer	Indicates the values configured for hpr timers path-switch. The four values are for low-, medium-, high-, and network-priority packets.
Locate-queue Enabled	Indicates whether or not the locate queuing feature has been enabled.
Negative-caching Enabled	Indicates whether or not the directory negative caching feature has been enabled.

Related Commands

To locate documentation of related commands, you can search online at www.cisco.com.

appn control-point

show appn port

Use the **show appn port** EXEC command to display information about the APPN ports active on the local node.

> **show appn port** [**port** *port-name*] [**brief** | **detail**]

Syntax

Description

port *port-name*   (Optional) Filter by port name.

brief   (Optional) Short display of APPN port definitions.

detail   (Optional) Long display of APPN port definitions.

Command Mode

EXEC

Usage Guidelines

This command first appeared in Cisco IOS Release 11.0. The **port** keyword first appeared in Cisco IOS Release 11.1. The output display changed in Release 11.2 to incorporate information about the HPR feature.

Sample Displays

The following is sample output from the **show appn port** command:

```
Router# show appn port

Number of ports                         2
     APPN Ports
     Name      State     SAP    HPR-SAP    Interface
     --------  --------  ---    -------    ------------
  1> TOK0      Active    x04      xC8      TokenRing0
  2> TOK1      Active    x04      xC8      TokenRing1
```

The following is sample output from the **show appn port detail** command:

```
Number of ports                         2

1>Port name                           TOK0
  Interface name                      TokenRing0
  Port State                          Active
  SAP                                 X'04'
  Link station role                   Negotiable
  Limited resource                    No
  Max frame send data (BTU) size      2000
```

```
Maximum receive BTU size              2000
Effective capacity                    16000000 bits per second
Cost per connect time                 0
Cost per byte                         0
Propagation delay                     384 microseconds (local area network)
User defined parameter 1              128
User defined parameter 2              128
User defined parameter 3              128
Security                              Nonsecure
Total available link stations         65535
Number reserved for inbound link stations    0
Number reserved for outbound link stations   0
HPR supported                         Yes
HPR SAP                               X'C8'
Allow dynamic link stations (service any)    Yes
Retry link stations                   No
```

Table 22-10 describes significant fields shown in the display.

Table 22-10   *show appn port detail* Field Descriptions

Field	Description
Port name	Name of this port.
Interface name	Interface used by this port.
Port State	Current state of this port.
SAP	Default service access point for links on this port.
Link station role	Specifies the role link stations used in XID negotiation.
Limited resource	Specifies if links on this port should be taken down when no sessions are using the link.
Max send frame data (BTU) size	The largest size allowed for basic transmission units sent through this port.
Maximum receive BTU size	The largest size allowed for basic transmission units received through this port.
Effective capacity	Bit rate of this port.
Cost per connect time	Relative cost of the links on this port.
Cost per byte	Cost per byte of transmitting a byte over the links on this port.
Propagation delay	Specifies the inherent delay of the port.
User defined parameter 1	Value for a network-unique transmission group characteristic— parameter 1.
User defined parameter 2	Value for a network-unique transmission group characteristic— parameter 2.
User defined parameter 3	Value for a network-unique transmission group characteristic— parameter 3.

Continues

Table 22-10   *show appn port detail Field Descriptions (Continued)*

Field	Description
Security	Security level of this port.
Total available link stations	The maximum number of link stations supported for this port.
Number reserved for inbound link stations	Of the total available link stations, the number reserved for inbound connections.
Number reserved for outbound link stations	Of the total available link stations, the number reserved for outbound connections.
HPR supported	Indicates whether or not HPR is supported over the port.
HPR SAP	Service access point for HPR frames on this port.
Allow dynamic link stations (service any)	Indicates if this port will accept incoming connections from remote nodes without requiring a link-station definition at the local node.
Retry link stations	Specifies the number of times and the time between retries that the node will retry links that have failed before giving up.

Related Commands

To locate documentation of related commands, you can search online at www.cisco.com.

appn port

show appn rtp

Use the **show appn rtp** EXEC command to display information about the RTP connections.

> **show appn rtp [brief | detail]**

Syntax	Description
brief	(Optional) Short display of APPN RTP connections.
detail	(Optional) Long display of APPN RTP connections.

Command Mode

EXEC

Usage Guidelines

This command first appeared in Cisco IOS Release 11.2.

Sample Displays

The following is sample output from the **show appn rtp** command:

```
Router# show appn rtp

TCID                Partner Node     COS
----------------    ------------     ------
0000000012345678    NETA.LISA        #BATCH
```

The following is sample output from the **show appn rtp detail** command:

```
Router# show appn rtp detail

Number of RTP connections                        1
Local TCID                          X'8000000000EBF6E8'
  Local CP name                       NETA.APPN2
  Remote NCEID                        X'8280'
  Remote TCID                         X'8000000000000000'
  Remote CP name                      NETA.FRANS
  Class of service name               SNASVCMG
  Liveness timer                      60 seconds
  Short request timer               1 milliseconds
  Path switch timer                   60 seconds
  Total bytes sent                    153
  Total bytes received                0
  Minimum send rate                   0
  Current send rate                   2208 Kilobits/second
  Maximum send rate                   9830 Kilobits/second
  Round trip delay time               4000 microseconds
  ANR string                          X'C60080008280FF00'
  Route                               NETA.APPN2          <-tg21->
                                      NETA.FRANS
```

Table 22-11 describes significant fields shown in the display.

Table 22-11   *show appn rtp detail Field Descriptions*

Field	Description
Local TCID	Connection ID that uniquely identifies this connection. It is a 16-digit hexadecimal number.
Local CP name	Control point name of the local node.
Remote NCEID	ANR label that represents the network connection end point at the remote node.
Remote TCID	Unique connection ID that the remote node uses to identify this connection.
Remote CP name	Control point name of the remote node.

Continues

Table 22-11 *show appn rtp detail Field Descriptions*

Field	Description
Class of service name	Name of the class of service used for packets flowing over this connection.
Liveness timer	Value configured for HPR timers liveness.
Short request timer	Calculated value for the timer used to wait for acknowledgment of HPR status request packets.
Path switch timer	Value configured for HPR timers path switch.
Total bytes sent	Running count of the amount of data sent over this connection.
Total bytes received	Running count of the amount of data received over this connection.
Minimum send rate	Minimum send rate allowed for this connection.
Current send rate	Calculated value for the current optimal send rate for this connection.
Maximum send rate	Maximum send rate allowed for this connection.
Round trip delay time	Measured round-trip delay for an HPR status request packet.
ANR string	HPR routing string put in the NHDR of each packet sent over this connection.
Route	Control point name and transmissions group number representing each hop through intermediate nodes for the route taken by packets sent or received over this connection.

Related Commands

To locate documentation of related commands, you can search online at www.cisco.com.

hpr max-sessions
hpr retries
hpr timers liveness
hpr timers path-switch

show appn session

Use the **show appn session** EXEC command to display information about the SNA LU 6.2 sessions, such as CP-CP sessions; that originate from the local node.

show appn session [pcid *pcid*] [**name** *lu-name*] [**brief | detail**]

Syntax

pcid *pcid*

name *lu-name*

brief

detail

Description

(Optional) Filter by procedure correlator identifier (PCID). PCID is a 16-byte hexadecimal number.

(Optional) Filter by fully qualified LU name.

(Optional) Short display of APPN session information.

(Optional) Long display of APPN session information.

Command Mode

EXEC

Usage Guidelines

This command first appeared in Cisco IOS Release 11.0. The following keywords and arguments first appeared in Cisco IOS Release 11.1: **pcid** *pcid*, **name** *lu-name*.

Sample Displays

The following is sample output from the **show appn session** command:

```
Router# show appn session

Number of sessions                        4
      APPN Endpoint Sessions
      PCID (hex)          Local LU Name      Partner LU Name    Mode      COS
      ----------------    ---------          ---------------    -------   --------
  1>  C6D328B0912EE4FF    NETA.BART          NETA.MARGE         CPSVCMG   CPSVCMG
  2>  F1DBABC818AB53AC    NETA.BART          NETA.APU           CPSVCMG   CPSVCMG
  3>  F37F3BE237DE7242    NETA.BART          NETA.MARGE         CPSVCMG   CPSVCMG
  4>  C21BFDC300ED68DB    NETA.BARNEY        NETA.LISA          #INTER    #INTER
```

The following is sample output from the **show appn session detail** command:

```
Router# show appn session detail

Number of sessions                        4

4>LU name                                 NETA.BARNEY
   Partner LU name                        NETA.LISA
   Mode name                              #INTER
   Class of service name                  #INTER
   Link name                              *OverHPR
   HPR RTP PCID                           X'8877665544332211'
   Send maximum RU size                   1920
   Receive maximum RU size                1920
   Send pacing window                     2
```

```
Receive pacing window                    8
Pacing type                              Adaptive
Outbound destination address (DAF)
Outbound origin address (OAF)
OAF-DAF assignor indicator (ODAI)
FID5 Session ID                          X'8123456712345678
Procedure correlator ID (PCID)           X'C21BFDC300ED68DB'
PCID generator CP name                   NETA.BARNEY
Session ID                               X'000000000093B198'
Conversation group ID                    133
```

Table 22-12 describes significant fields shown in the display.

Table 22-12 *show appn session detail* *Field Descriptions*

Field	Description
LU name	Fully qualified name of the local LU.
Partner LU name	Fully qualified name of the partner LU.
Mode name	Mode used by this session.
Class of service name	Class of service used by this session.
Link name	Link this session traverses.
HPR RTP PCID	Procedure correlator identifier.
Send maximum RU size	Maximum RU size that can be sent on this session.
Receive maximum RU size	Maximum RU size that can be received on this session.
Send pacing window	Current send pacing window size.
Receive pacing window	Current receive pacing window size.
Pacing type	Type of pacing used by this session.
Outbound destination address (DAF)	Session routing destination address.
Outbound origin address (OAF)	Session routing origin address.
OAF-DAF assignor indicator (ODAI)	Defines which session partner chose the addresses (DAF and OAF) for a session. Together with the DAF and OAF values, the ODAI forms the local form session identifier (LFSID). The DAF and OAF values used in the transmission header (TH) in one direction are reversed in the other direction.
FID5 Session ID	If this session is activated using HPR instead of the OAF, DAF, ODAI session identifier, the session is identified by this eight-byte hexadecimal value.
Procedure correlator ID (PCID)	PCID used by this session.
PCID generator CP name	Fully qualified CP name which generated this PCID.

Table 22-12 *show appn session detail Field Descriptions (Continued)*

Field	Description
Session ID	Local session ID.
Conversation group ID	Conversation group ID for this session.

show appn topology

Use the **show appn topology** EXEC command to display the contents of the APPN topology database.

show appn topology [**name** *cp-name*] [**brief** | **detail**]

Syntax	Description
name *cp-name*	(Optional) Filter by fully qualified CP name.
brief	(Optional) Short display of APPN topology information.
detail	(Optional) Long display of APPN topology information.

Command Mode
EXEC

Usage Guidelines
This command first appeared in Cisco IOS Release 11.0.

Sample Displays
The following is sample output from the **show appn topology** command:

```
Number of network nodes              3
    APPN Topology Entries
    Resource Name      Type        TG#  Dest. Node        TG Type   TG Status
    ------------       -----------  ---  --------------    -------   ---------
1> NETA.BARNEY         Network Node
    1>                               0   NETA.CN           Intermed  Active
    2>                               0   NETA.CN1          Intermed  Active
    3>                               21  NETA.R2CP0389     Intermed  Active
    4>                               21  NETA.BART         Intermed  Active
```

The following is a sample output from the **show appn topology detail** command:

```
Router# show appn topology detail

Number of network nodes               6

1>Network node CP name                NETA.MAGGIE
Node type                             Network Node
Route additional resistance     128
Congested?                      No
Quiescing?                      No
ISR depleted?                   No
Time left in topology           15
Current FRSN                    29
Resource Sequence Number        4
Last FRSN sent                  0
Last FRSN received              0
Node HPR Level                  RTP
Number of TGs                   2

1.1>TG partner CP name                NETA.BARNEY
Transmission group number       21
TG partner node type            Real
Tg Type                         Endpoint
TG Status                       Active
Quiescing?                      No
Topology                        Network
Effective capacity              16 megabits per second
Cost per connect time           0
Cost per byte                   0
Propagation delay               384 microseconds (local area network)
User defined parameter 1        128
User defined parameter 2        128
User defined parameter 3        128
Security                        Nonsecure
Time left in topology           15
Current FRSN                    29
Resource Sequence Number        4
HPR enabled                     Yes
HPR RTP level                   RTP
```

Table 22-13 describes significant fields shown in the display.

Table 22-13 *show appn topology Field Descriptions*

Field	Description
Network node CP name	Fully qualified name of the resource.
Node type	Resource type of this node.
Route additional resistance	Arbitrary number associated with the cost of using this node.
Congested?	Specifies whether or not the node is capable of processing requests.
Quiescing?	Specifies whether or not the node is stopping.

Table 22-13 *show appn topology* *Field Descriptions (Continued)*

Field	Description
ISR depleted?	Specifies whether or not the node is capable processing additional ISR requests.
Number of TGs	Number of transmission groups associated with the network node.
TG partner CP name	Partner node's fully qualified name.
Transmission group number	Transmission group number.
TG partner node type	Resource type for the partner of this transmission group.
TG Type	Type of transmission group: intermediate or endpoint.
TG Status	Status of the transmission group.
Quiescing?	Specifies whether or not the transmission group is in the process of stopping.
Topology	Topology type: local or network.
Effective capacity	Bit rate of the transmission group.
Cost per connect time	Relative cost of the transmission group.
Cost per byte	Cost per byte of transmitting over the transmission group.
Propagation delay	Specifies the inherent delay of the transmission group.
User defined parameter 1	Value for a network-unique transmission group characteristic—parameter 1.
User defined parameter 2	Value for a network-unique transmission group characteristic—parameter 2.
User defined parameter 3	Value for a network-unique transmission group characteristic—parameter 3.
Security	Security level of the transmission group.
Time left in topology	The number of days that APPN will wait before removing this node from the topology database.
Current FRSN	The current flow-reduction sequence number for this resource. This value is used to reduce topology exchange between two NNs if they temporarily lose contact.
Resource Sequence Number	The current resource sequence number for this resource. This number is used by APPN to prevent loops when exchanging topology information.
HPR enabled	Specifies if this node or transmission group support HPR.

Continues

Table 22-13 *show appn topology* *Field Descriptions (Continued)*

Field	Description
HPR RTP level	Specifies the level of HPR support for this node or transmission group:
	Base—HPR base support only.
	RTP—Supports the HPR RTP feature tower.
	CF—Supports the HPR control flows feature tower.

smds-dest-address

Use the **smds-dest-address** APPN link station configuration command to specify the SMDS address of the partner node. Use the **no** form of this command to return to the default.

> **smds-dest-address** *smds-addr* [*sap*]
> **no smds-dest-address**

Syntax	Description
smds-addr	Eight-byte hexadecimal number in the form HD.DD.DD.HH.
sap	One-byte hexadecimal number in the range 04 to EC, and divisible by four.

Defaults

No default *smds-addr* is specified.

The default SAP is 04 (hexadecimal).

Command Mode

APPN link station configuration

Usage Guidelines

This command first appeared in Cisco IOS Release 11.1.

This command is required for interface types Token Ring, Ethernet, or FDDI. It is not allowed for other interface types.

Example

The following example sets the MAC address and SAP for a link to a partner node:

```
appn link-station LINK0001
 port ETHER1
 smds-dest-address 11.22.33.44 08
 complete
```

Related Commands

To locate documentation of related commands, you can search online at www.cisco.com.

appn link-station
fr-dest-address
sdlc-dest-address
show appn link-station
smds address

tg-number

Use the **tg-number** APPN link station configuration command to specify the transmission group number for the connection. Use the **no** form of this command to delete the previous definition.

> **tg-number** *number*
> **no tg-number**

Syntax

number

Description

Number in the range 0 to 255. The default is 0.

Default

Transmission group number is 0.

Command Mode

APPN link station configuration

Usage Guidelines

This command first appeared in Cisco IOS Release 11.0.

If zero, the transmission group number is negotiable.

Example

The following example sets the transmission group number to 10:

```
appn link-station LINK4
 port ETHER1
 lan-dest-address 0200.6f8e.1a3b
 tg-number 10
 complete
```

Related Commands

To locate documentation of related commands, you can search online at www.cisco.com.

appn link-station
show appn link-station

tg-row

Use the **tg-row** APPN class of service configuration command to specify a transmission group description, or transmission group row, and associated weight for the row. Use the **no** form of this command to delete the previous definition.

> **tg-row** *index* **weight** *weight* **byte** *min max* **time** *min max* **capacity** *min max*
> **delay** *min max* **security** *min max* **user1** *min max* **user2** *min max* **user3** *min max*
> **no tg-row** *index*

Syntax	Description
index	Specifies which row is being entered. The valid range is one to eight.
weight *weight*	Weight assigned to a transmission group, given the characteristics defined in the remainder of the row.
byte *min max*	Minimum and maximum cost-per-byte values, compared with the **cost-per-byte** command on the port or link station command.
time *min max*	Minimum and maximum cost-per-connect-time values, compared with the **cost-per-connect-time** command on the port or link station command.
capacity *min max*	Minimum and maximum capacity values, compared with the **effective-capacity** command on the port or link station command.
delay *min max*	Two values compared with the **propagation-delay** command.

Syntax	Description
security *min max*	Value compared with the security command. The minimum and maximum are specified with one the defined values, in ascending order:
user1 *min max*	Number in the range 1 to 255.
user2 *min max*	Number in the range 1 to 255.
user3 *min max*	Number in the range 1 to 255.

Default

There is no default provided. A minimum of one transmission group row must be provided or the configuration will fail.

Command Mode

APPN class of service configuration

Usage Guidelines

This command first appeared in Cisco IOS Release 11.0.

The characteristics of transmission groups in the topology database are compared to the characteristics in each row. A weight is assigned which determines a low-cost route for a session. You can define from one to eight transmission group rows.

Example

The following example defines an APPN class of service with one transmission group row:

```
appn class-of-service #SECURE
 node-row 1 weight 5 congestion no no route-additional-resistance 0 255
 tg-row 1 weight 30 byte 0 255 time 0 255 capacity 0 255 delay 0 255 security 200 255
 user1 0 255 user2 0 255 user3 0 255
 complete
```

Related Commands

To locate documentation of related commands, you can search online at www.cisco.com.

appn class-of-service
show appn class-of-service

transmission-priority

Use the **transmission-priority** APPN class of service configuration command to specify the transmission priority for the class of service. Use the **no** form of this command to delete the previous definition.

> **transmission priority** *priority*
> **no transmission priority**

Syntax

priority

Description

One of the following keywords:

- **network**
- **high**
- **medium**
- **low**

Default

The default priority is **medium**.

Command Mode

APPN class of service configuration

Usage Guidelines

This command first appeared in Cisco IOS Release 11.0.

The value **network** is reserved for control traffic and cannot be specified for LU-LU sessions. High, medium, and low reflect the priority that traffic for an individual application should receive when congestion begins to build and queues form.

Example

The following example defines an APPN class of service with a transmission priority of high:

```
appn class-of-service #SECURE
 transmission-priority high
 node-row 1 weight 5 congestion no no route-additional-resistance 0 255
 tg-row 1 weight 30 byte 0 255 time 0 255 capacity 0 255 delay 0 255 security 200 255
 user1 0 255 user2 0 255 user3 0 255
 complete
```

Related Commands

To locate documentation of related commands, you can search online at www.cisco.com.

appn class-of-service
show appn class-of-service

user-defined-1 (APPN link station)

Use the **user-defined-1** APPN link station configuration command to specify the relative value for a network-unique transmission group characteristic. Use the **no** form of this command to return to the default.

> **user-defined-1** *value*
> **no user-defined-1**

Syntax	Description
value	Number in the range 0 to 255 used to specify the relative value. The default is the value specified in the **appn port** command.

Default

The value specified in the **appn port** command.

Command Mode

APPN link station configuration

Usage Guidelines

This command first appeared in Cisco IOS Release 11.0.

This command can be used to specify a user defined characteristic of this link. The value of a network unique transmission group characteristic is used in route selection.

Example

The following example defines an APPN link station with a **user-defined-1** value of 200:

```
appn link-station LINK17
 port TOKEN1
 lan-dest-address 1000.4455.abcd
 user-defined-1 200
 complete
```

Related Commands

To locate documentation of related commands, you can search online at www.cisco.com.

appn link-station
show appn link-station

user-defined-1 (APPN port)

Use the **user-defined-1** APPN port configuration command to specify the relative value for a network-unique transmission group characteristic. Use the **no** form of this command to return to the default.

> **user-defined-1** *value*
> **no user-defined-1**

Syntax

Syntax	Description
value	Number in the range 0 to 255 used to specify the relative value. The default is 128.

Default

The default is 128.

Command Mode

APPN port configuration

Usage Guidelines

This command first appeared in Cisco IOS Release 11.0.

This command is specified for defined transmission groups (with the **appn link-station** command) if the command has not been specified at that level. This command also specifies the value for dynamically created transmission groups. The cost is used in route selection for a particular class of service.

Example

The following example defines a port with a **user-defined-1** value of 50:

```
appn port ETHER1
 user-defined-1 50
 complete
```

Related Commands

To locate documentation of related commands, you can search online at www.cisco.com.

appn port
show appn port

user-defined-2 (APPN link station)

Use the **user-defined-2** APPN link station configuration command to specify the relative value for a network-unique transmission group characteristic. Use the **no** form of this command to return to the default.

> **user-defined-2** *value*
> **no user-defined-2**

Syntax	Description
value	Number in the range 0 to 255 used to specify the relative value. The default is the value specified in the **appn port** command.

Default

The value specified in the **appn port** command.

Command Mode

APPN link station configuration

Usage Guidelines

This command first appeared in Cisco IOS Release 11.0.

This command can be used to specify a user defined characteristic of this link. The value of a network unique transmission group characteristic is used in route selection.

Example

The following example defines an APPN link station with a **user-defined-2** value of 200:

```
appn link-station LINK17
 port TOKEN1
 lan-dest-address 1000.4455.abcd
 user-defined-2 200
 complete
```

Related Commands

To locate documentation of related commands, you can search online at www.cisco.com.

appn link-station
show appn link-station

user-defined-2 (APPN port)

Use the **user-defined-2** APPN port configuration command to specify the relative value for a network-unique transmission group characteristic. Use the **no** form of this command to return to the default.

> **user-defined-2** *value*
> **no user-defined-2**

Syntax	Description
value	Number in the range 0 to 255 used to specify the relative value. The default is 128.

Default

The default is 128.

Command Mode

APPN port configuration

Usage Guidelines

This command first appeared in Cisco IOS Release 11.0.

This command is specified for defined transmission groups (with the **appn link-station** command) if the command has not been specified at that level. This command also specifies the value for dynamically created transmission groups. The cost is used in route selection for a particular class of service.

Example

The following example defines a port with a **user-defined-2** value of 50:

```
appn port ETHER1
 user-defined-2 50
 complete
```

Related Commands

To locate documentation of related commands, you can search online at www.cisco.com.

appn port
show appn port

user-defined-3 (APPN link station)

Use the **user-defined-3** APPN link station configuration command to specify the relative value for a network-unique transmission group characteristic. Use the **no** form of this command to return to the default.

> **user-defined-3** *value*
> **no user-defined-3**

Syntax

Syntax	Description
value	Number in the range 0 to 255 used to specify the relative value. The default is the value specified in the **appn port** command.

Default

The value specified in the **appn port** command.

Command Mode

APPN link station configuration

Usage Guidelines

This command first appeared in Cisco IOS Release 11.0.

This command can be used to specify a user defined characteristic of this link. The value of a network unique transmission group characteristic is used in route selection.

Example

The following example defines an APPN link station with a **user-defined-3** value of 200:

```
appn link-station LINK17
 port TOKEN1
 lan-dest-address 1000.4455.abcd
 user-defined-3 200
 complete
```

Related Commands

To locate documentation of related commands, you can search online at www.cisco.com.

appn link-station
show appn link-station

user-defined-3 (APPN port)

Use the **user-defined-3** APPN port configuration command to specify the relative value for a network-unique transmission group characteristic. Use the **no** form of this command to return to the default.

> **user-defined-3** *value*
> **no user-defined-3**

Syntax	Description
value	Number in the range 0 to 255 used to specify the relative value. The default is 128.

Default

The default is 128.

Command Mode

APPN port configuration

Usage Guidelines

This command first appeared in Cisco IOS Release 11.0.

This command is specified for defined transmission groups (with the **appn link-station** command) if the command has not been specified at that level. This command also specifies the value for dynamically created transmission groups. The cost is used in route selection for a particular class of service.

Example

The following example defines a port with a **user-defined-3** value of 50:

```
appn port ETHER1
 user-defined-3 50
 complete
```

Related Commands

To locate documentation of related commands, you can search online at www.cisco.com.

appn port
show appn port

vdlc

Use the **vdlc** APPN port configuration command to identify which ring group the APPN VDLC port uses and, optionally, which virtual MAC address is used as the local MAC address identifying this APPN port. Use the **no** form of this command to delete the configuration.

> **vdlc** *ring-group* [**vmac** *vdlc-mac-address*]
> **no vdlc** *ring-group* [**vmac** *vdlc-mac-address*]

Syntax	Description
ring-group	Ring group number matching the number you specified with the **source-bridge ring-group** command. The valid range is 1 to 4095.
vmac *vdlc-mac-address*	(Optional) Virtual MAC address used as the local MAC address identifying this APPN port.

Default

No defaults are defined.

Command Mode

APPN port configuration

Usage Guidelines

This command first appeared in Cisco IOS Release 11.2.

Use the **appn port vdlc** command to define a VDLC port before using the **vdlc** command.

The virtual MAC address must be defined in either the **source-bridge ring-group** command or in the **vdlc** command. If a virtual MAC address is defined in the **source-bridge ring-group** command, providing a virtual MAC address in the **vdlc** command is optional.

To avoid an address conflict on the virtual MAC address, use a locally-administered address in the form 4000.*xxxx.xxxx*.

Examples

The following example defines an APPN port that uses VDLC. The **vdlc** subcommand specifies both the ring group (100) and the virtual MAC address (4000.3745.0000) to be used as the local MAC address identifying this port.

```
appn port VDLCPORT vdlc
 vdlc 100 vmac 4000.3745.0000
 complete
```

The following example defines an APPN port that uses VDLC. The MAC address to be used as the local MAC address identifying this virtual port is the MAC address specified in the **source-bridge ring-group** command. The **vdlc** subcommand only specifies the ring group.

```
source-bridge ring-group 100 4000.3745.0000
dlsw local-peer peer-id 172.18.3.111
dlsw remote-peer 0 tcp 172.18.3.125
!
interface ethernet 0
 ip address 172.18.3.111 255.255.255.0
 loopback
 media-type 10BaseT
!
interface TokenRing 0
 no ip address
 ring-speed 16
!
appn control-point NETA.BART
 complete
!
appn port VDLC vdlc
 vdlc 100
 complete
!
appn port TR0 TokenRing 0
 complete
```

Related Commands

To locate documentation of related commands, you can search online at www.cisco.com.

appn port
show appn port

verify-adjacent-node-type

Use the **verify-adjacent-node-type** APPN link station configuration command to specify that the adjacent node type must be verified as a requirement of link activation. Use the **no** form of this command to return to the default.

verify-adjacent-node-type {**learn** | **len** | **nn**}
no verify-adjacent-node-type

Syntax
Description

learn	Any adjacent node type is accepted.
len	Only LEN adjacent node type is accepted.
nn	Only NN adjacent node type is accepted.

Default

The default node type is **learn**.

Command Mode

APPN link station configuration

Usage Guidelines

This command first appeared in Cisco IOS Release 11.0.

If the adjacent node type is LEN, the **cp-cp-sessions-supported** command must specify no.

If the adjacent node type is LEN, the **adjacent-cp-name** must be specified.

There is no verification for type EN.

Example

The following example specifies that any adjacent node type is accepted:

```
appn link-station NN4
 port ETHER1
 lan-dest-address 0200.5672.3212
 verify-adjacent-node-type nn
 complete
```

Related Commands

To locate documentation of related commands, you can search online at www.cisco.com.

appn link-station
show appn link-station

wildcard

Use the **wildcard** APPN partner LU location configuration command to specify this entry as a "wildcard." Use the **no** form of this command to return to the default of no "wildcard".

> **wildcard**
> **no wildcard**

Syntax Description

This command has no arguments or keywords.

Default

The default is **no wildcard**.

Command Mode

APPN partner LU location configuration

Usage Guidelines

This command first appeared in Cisco IOS Release 11.0.

A wildcard entry serves any LU whose name matches the configured name up to the length of the configured name. Without an LU name and wildcard specified, the entry services all LUs.

Example

The following example defines a wildcard that represents any LU that starts with LU2, such as LU21, LU221, LU234, and so on:

```
appn partner-lu-location LU2
 owning-cp CISCO.CP2
 wildcard
 complete
```

Related Commands

To locate documentation of related commands, you can search online at www.cisco.com.

appn partner-lu-location
show appn directory

x25-dest-address

Use the **x25-dest-address** APPN link station configuration command to specify the local address of the partner node for QLLC. Use the **no** form of this command to delete the specification.

          x25-dest-address [pvc | svc] *address*
          no x25-dest-address

Syntax	Description
pvc	(Optional) Uses X.25 permanent virtual circuit.
svc	(Optional) Uses X.25 switched virtual circuit.
address	X.25 destination link station address.

Default

No default address is specified.

Command Mode

APPN link station configuration

Usage Guidelines

This command first appeared in Cisco IOS Release 11.0.

The *address* argument must be a valid X.121 address. This address must match that assigned by the X.25 network service provider.

Example

The following example configures the X.25 destination address:

```
appn link-station QLLC
 port QLLC1
 x25-dest-address 170090
 complete
```

Related Commands

To locate documentation of related commands, you can search online at www.cisco.com.

appn link-station
show appn link-station

x25-subaddress

Use the **x25-subaddress** APPN port configuration command to configure APPN over QLLC. Use the **no** form of this command to delete the configuration.

> **x25-subaddress** [**pvc** | **svc**] *address*
> **no x25-subaddress**

Syntax	Description
pvc	(Optional) Uses X.25 permanent virtual circuit.
svc	(Optional) Uses X.25 switched virtual circuit.
address	X.25 subaddress from which data is received.

Default

No default address is assigned.

Command Mode

APPN port configuration

Usage Guidelines

This command first appeared in Cisco IOS Release 11.0.

The *address* argument must be a valid X.121 address. This address must match that assigned by the X.25 network service provider.

Example

The following example configures the X.25 subaddress from which data is received:

```
appn port QLLC1 Serial0/1
 x25-subaddress svc 0001121
 complete
```

Related Commands

To locate documentation of related commands, you can search online at www.cisco.com.

appn port
show appn port

xid-block-number

Use the **xid-block-number** APPN control point configuration command to specify the first three digits of the node identifier for the local node. Use the **no** form of this command to return to the default.

> **xid-block-number** *number*
> **no xid-block-number**

Part
II

Command Reference

Syntax	Description
number	Three-digit hexadecimal number in the range 000 to FFF. The default is 077.

Default

The default is 077 (hexadecimal).

Command Mode

APPN control point configuration

Usage Guidelines

This command first appeared in Cisco IOS Release 11.0.

A unique ID is required for links to older versions of VTAM.

Example

The following example specifies XID block number 456:

```
appn control-point CISCO.ROUTER
 xid-block-number 456
 complete
```

Related Commands

To locate documentation of related commands, you can search online at www.cisco.com.

appn control-point
show appn node

xid-id-number

Use the **xid-id-number** APPN control point configuration command to specify the last five digits of the node ID for the local node. Use the **no** form of this command to delete the previous definition.

> **xid-id-number** *number*
> **no xid-id-number**

Syntax	Description
number	Five-digit hexadecimal number in the range 00000 to FFFFF.

Default

The default is 00000 (hexadecimal).

Command Mode

APPN control point configuration

Usage Guidelines

This command first appeared in Cisco IOS Release 11.0.

The XID ID and block numbers are included in XID exchanges and alert information, and are required for communicating with older versions of VTAM.

Example

The following example specifies XID ID number 0cab7:

```
appn control-point CISCO.ROUTER
 xid-id-number 0cab7
 complete
```

Related Commands

To locate documentation of related commands, you can search online at www.cisco.com.

appn control-point
show appn node

Configuring Cisco Database Connection

This chapter describes how to configure the Cisco Database Connection feature. For a complete description of the Database Connection commands in this chapter, refer to Chapter 24, "Cisco Database Connection Commands." To locate documentation of other commands that appear in this chapter, search online at www.cisco.com.

The Database Connection feature enables Cisco routers to implement IBM's distributed relational database architecture (DRDA) level 3 over the Transmission Control Protocol/Internet Protocol (TCP/IP). The Cisco router with Database Connection exists in the TCP/IP network and clients use the Database Connection IP address and port on the router to connect to the IBM host system that exists in the Systems Network Architecture (SNA) network.

When Database Connection is configured on a router, client-based Open Database Connectivity (ODBC) applications can connect to IBM's family of IBM D2 relational databases, which include:

- DB2 for OS/390 (MVS)

- DB2 for Virtual Machine (VM)

- DB2 for Virtual Storage Extended (VSE) (SQL/DS)

- DB2 for OS/400

- DB2 Universal Server (AIX, HP-UX, UNIX, Solaris, Windows NT, Windows 95, OS/2, SCO OpenServer)

The router with Database Connection converts DRDA packets over TCP/IP to DRDA packets over Advanced Program-to-Program Communications (APPC, LU 6.2) and then routes them to DB2 databases. Database Connection runs as a TCP/IP daemon on the router, accepting DRDA client connections over TCP/IP. When a client connects to the database on an IBM mainframe host, Database Connection allocates an APPC conversation over SNA to an IBM server, and acts as a gateway between DRDA over TCP/IP and DRDA over APPC.

Figure 23-1 illustrates how the Cisco router configured with the Database Connection feature enables the exchange of database information between ODBC client applications running DRDA in a TCP/IP network and a DRDA-based IBM system that accesses DB2 relational data.

Figure 23-1 *Cisco Router Configured with the Database Connection Feature*

When configured on a router, the Database Connection feature enables desktop applications to access data in remote databases located on IBM hosts. Database Connection receives database access messages from the client over a TCP/IP link. Database Connection converts the messages to SNA and transmits them to the host using APPC services provided by Cisco IOS Advanced Peer-to-Peer Networking (APPN) software.

Figure 23-2 shows a user working with a spreadsheet application on a PC and accessing database information from a remote relational database management system (RDBMS) on an IBM host. When the user seeks data from the RDBMS system on the IBM host, the spreadsheet application sends SQL statements to the remote host system and retrieves the data.

Figure 23-2 *StarSQL PC Client User Accessing Database Information from Mainframe*

To use the Database Connection feature, the following prerequisites must be met:

- Clients in your network are installed with either StarSQL software or ODBC driver software from another vendor.

- Cisco IOS Release 11.3(2)T software is configured on your router.

- DB2 is configured on your network.

The following DB2 software packages are supported:

- DB2 MVS (versions 2.3, 3.1, 4.1, and 5.1)

- SQL/DS (VM & VSE) v3.3 and later

- DB2/400 (OS/400) v2r2 and later

- DB2 Common Server (Universal Database) for DB2/AIX, DB2/2, DB2/NT v2.1 and later

The Database Connection feature is supported on the following platforms and is available in the specified Cisco IOS Release software images:

- Cisco 4500 series routers (c4500-aejs-mz)

- Cisco 4700 series routers (c4500-aejs-mz)

- Cisco 7200 series routers (c7200-aejs-mz)

- Cisco 7500 series routers (rsp-aejsv-mz)

Database Connection Configuration Task List

To configure the Database Connection feature on a Cisco router, perform the tasks in the following sections:

- Define an APPN Control Point

- Define an APPN Port

- Define an APPN Link Station

- Define an APPN Mode

- Define an APPN Partner Logical Unit Location

- Configure the Database Connection Server

- Configure Database Connection for StarSQL License

- Start and Stop APPN Ports and Link Stations

- Monitor and Maintain Database Connection

See the end of this chapter for the section "Database Connection Configuration Examples."

Define an APPN Control Point

An APPN control point definition is required to use APPN. This definition adds the fully qualified control point name for the node, which is a combination of a network identifier and a control point name. The network identifier must be the same as other network nodes in the APPN subnetwork attached to this node. The control point name identifies this node uniquely within the particular subnetwork.

To define an APPN control point, use the following command in global configuration mode:

Command	Purpose
appn control-point *netid.cpname*	Defines an APPN control point.

Entering this command takes you from global configuration mode into APPN control point configuration mode.

Define an APPN Port

An APPN port definition associates APPN capabilities with a specific interface that APPN will use. Each interface that will be used for APPN communications requires an APPN port definition statement. Associate a port with a specific interface by using the following command in global configuration mode:

Command	Purpose
appn port *portname interface*	Defines an APPN port associated with an interface.

Define an APPN Link Station

A link station is a representation of the connection or potential connection to another node. In many cases, if the partner node is initiating the connection, a link station definition is not necessary. It will be built dynamically when the partner node initiates the connection. You must define a link station if you want this node to initiate APPN connections with other nodes. In addition, you may define a link station to specify attributes of an APPN connection regardless of which node initiates the connection.

To define an APPN logical link, use the following command in global configuration mode:

Command	Purpose
appn link-station *linkname*	Defines an APPN logical link.

Entering this command takes you from global configuration mode into APPN link station configuration mode. From the APPN link station configuration mode, you must associate the link station with an APPN port that it will use.

To associate a link station, use the following command in APPN link station configuration mode:

Command	Purpose
port *portname*	Associates a link station with the APPN port that it will use.

Define an APPN Mode

Use an APPN mode definition to associate a mode name received on an APPN search or session request with a class of service (CoS) known to this node. Most APPN nodes will supply the CoS to their network node server, so mode definition may not be required in many APPN networks. However, if the node is providing network node services to an end node that does not supply a CoS, or if the node is providing network node services for a low-entry networking (LEN) node, mode definitions may be required for each mode that is used by the partner node.

Cisco provides standard predefined mode definitions for modes that are commonly used in an APPN network. The predefined mode names are:

- blank mode
- #BATCH
- #BATCHSC
- #INTER
- #INTERSC
- CPSVCMG
- SNASVCMG

You can change a predefined mode or define a new mode.

To define an APPN mode, use the following command in global configuration mode:

Command	Purpose
appn mode *modename*	Defines an APPN mode.

Entering this command takes you from global configuration mode into APPN mode configuration mode. Within this mode, you must assign a class of service to the mode definition.

To assign a CoS to the mode definition, use the following command in APPN mode configuration mode:

Command	Purpose
class-of-service *cosname*	Associates a class of service with the defined mode.

Use the following commands to allow for the addition, removal, or completion of configuration items within the APPN mode configuration mode:

Command	Purpose
no *command*	Negates or restores the default value for a configuration command.
complete	Completes the APPN mode definition, return to global configuration mode, and update the APPN subsystem.
no complete	Allows modifications to a previously completed APPN mode definition.
exit	Exits APPN class of service definition dialog without completing the definition and without updating the APPN subsystem.

Define an APPN Partner Logical Unit Location

Defining the APPN partner logical unit (LU) location is optional for the Database Connection feature. The APPN directory stores names of resources and their owners. Usually, this information is learned dynamically via APPN searches. However, you may wish to manually define the location of specific resources. Doing so can improve network performance by allowing directed APPN searches to travel straight to the owning control point without the need for an initial broadcast search for the resource. However, APPN is known for its dynamic capabilities, not its need for system definition. For this reason, and for easier manageability, it is good practice to define location names only when necessary.

If you do not use APPN in your SNA environment, you must configure an APPN partner LU location and specify the destination LU and D2 for Database Connection in the router configuration.

When a LEN node is attached to an APPN network node, all destination resources that reside on the LEN node must be defined on the network node to be reachable via the APPN network.

To define a partner LU location, use the following command in global configuration mode:

Command	Purpose
appn partner-lu-location *netid.luname*	Specifies the partner resource name.

Specifying the partner resource name takes you from the global configuration mode into the APPN partner LU location configuration mode.

You must configure an owning control point for each partner LU configured. The owning control point is the control point name for the LEN, end node, or network node on which the resource resides.

To specify the name of the control point owning the partner LU, use the following command in APPN partner LU location configuration mode:

Command	Purpose
owning-cp *netid.cpname*	Specifies the name of the control point owning the partner LU.

If this node is not the network node server for the resource, you may also configure the network node server name. To reduce APPN searching, the network node server operand must be coded and must be the current server for the resource.

If this node is the network node server for the resource being defined, do not configure a network node server.

To specify the name of the network node server for the resource, use the following command in APPN partner LU location configuration mode:

Command	Purpose
serving-nn *netid.cpname*	Specifies the name of the network node server for the resource.

A partial name wildcard partner LU is a definition that applies to all resources that match a partial name. For example, a definition for location NETA.PE, which is specified as a wildcard definition, serves as an entry for NETA.PEANUT and NETA.PENNY, but not NETA.PUMKIN. Be careful when using partial name wildcards because they can easily cause network problems if resources that match the partial name do not actually exist in the specified location.

A full wildcard partner LU definition is specified by defining a partner LU location without specifying a resource name and specifying the wildcard option. Full wildcards answer positively to any search for any resource in the network. Only one full wildcard definition can exist in an APPN network. Full wildcards are sometimes used when the APPN subnetwork is small and an attached LEN node is the gateway to a large connected network. Full wildcard definitions reduce APPN performance and can cause a variety of network problems. Hence, use of full wildcard definitions should be avoided.

To specify a partial name or full wildcard partner LU, use the following command in APPN partner LU location configuration mode:

Command	Purpose
wildcard	Specifies the entry as a partial-name wildcard or a full wildcard.

Use the following commands to allow for the addition, removal, or completion of configuration items within the APPN partner LU location configuration mode:

Command	Purpose
no *command*	Negates or restores the default value for a configuration command.
complete	Completes the APPN partner LU definition, returns to global configuration mode, and updates the APPN subsystem.
no complete	Allows modifications to a previously completed APPN partner LU definition.
exit	Exits APPN partner LU definition dialog without completing the definition and without updating the APPN subsystem.

Configure the Database Connection Server

To configure a Database Connection server on a Cisco router, use the following command in privileged EXEC mode:

Command	Purpose
dbconn server *server-name* **[ipaddress** *ip-address*] **[port** *port-number*] **[rdbname** *rdbname*] **[rlu** *remote-lu*] **[mode** *mode*] **[tpname** *tp-name*] **[idle-timeout** *minutes*] **[window-size** *bytes*]	Configures a Database Connection server.

When a client attempts to connect to a Database Connection server, the server's port, IP address, and remote database name (RDB name) determine whether that connection is accepted or not. By default, the port for Database Connection servers is 446.

You can configure Database Connection servers and specify any of the options used by the servers when accepting connections.

Configure Database Connection for StarSQL License

If you are using StarSQL or StarSQL Pro software, use the following command in privileged EXEC mode to configure the Database Connection license for StarSQL clients:

Command	Purpose
dbconn license *license-key*	Configures a Database Connection license key.

The license key is available from StarQuest Software, Inc. Skip this task if you are not using StarSQL or StarSQL Pro products.

Start and Stop APPN Ports and Link Stations

APPN port and link station definitions are started automatically when the APPN subsystem starts. However, configuration commands will not take effect on an APPN port or link when it is active. To start or stop an APPN port or link station, use the following commands in privileged EXEC mode:

Command	Purpose
appn stop link-station *linkname*	Deactivates the specified APPN link.
appn stop port *portname*	Deactivates the specified APPN port.
appn start link-station *linkname*	Activates the specified APPN link.
appn start port *portname*	Activates the specified APPN port.

Monitor and Maintain Database Connection

To monitor and maintain Database Connection configured on a router, use one or more of the following commands:

Command	Purpose
show dbconn server	Displays a summary of each Database Connection server.
show dbconn server *server-name*	Displays a detailed status of the specified Database Connection server.
show dbconn connection	Displays the status of each connection.
show dbconn connection *connection-id*	Displays a detailed status of the specified Database Connection connection.
show dbconn connection server *server-name*	Displays the status of the Database Connection connection server.
show dbconn connection user *userid*	Displays the status of a user connected to the Database Connection.
show dbconn connection rdbname *rdb-name*	Displays a status of each connection that matches the specified RDB name.
show dbconn ports	Displays information on all ports through which Database Connection servers are accepting connections.

Command	Purpose
show dbconn license	Displays the status of dbconn license for StarSQL.
clear dbconn connection *connection-id*	Breaks the specified client connection to the server.
dbconn ping *server-name* [**rdbname** *rdbname]* [**userid** *userid*] [**password** *password*]	Connects to the relational database on the IBM system for troubleshooting.
debug dbconn {*appc* | *config* | *drda* | *event* | *tcp* | *all*}	Enables debugging.
show debugging	Displays current status of debugging for Database Connection.

Database Connection Configuration Examples

The following sections provide Database Connection configuration examples:

- Database Connection Servers with IP Addresses Configuration Example

- Database Connection Servers with IP Addresses, RDB Names, and Ports Configuration Example 1

- Database Connection Servers with IP Addresses, RDB Names, and Ports Configuration Example 2

- Server Selection by IP Addresses, RDB Names, and Ports Configuration Example

- Database Connection with Channel Interface Processor and DB2 on VTAM Example

Database Connection Servers with IP Addresses Configuration Example

Figure 23-3 shows a Database Connection configuration where the Database Connection servers are configured to listen on port 446 (by default) for IP addresses specified for these servers in the router's configuration for Database Connection. When a client attempts to make a connection, a Database Connection server accepts the connection if the IP address specified in its configuration matches the IP address to which the client wants to connect.

In this illustration, Servers A and B are configured with IP addresses 172.0.10.2 and 172.0.45.3. Servers A and B accept any connection that targets their IP addresses. Server C accepts any connection that targets any IP address of router on the target port of 446 and an RDB name of IOWA.

Figure 23-3 *Database Connection Servers' Configuration with IP Addresses*

The following are the configurations for servers Server A, Server B, and Server C in the Cisco router's configuration:

```
dbconn server SERVERA ip-address 172.0.10.2 rdbname nevada
dbconn server SERVERB ip-address 172.0.45.3
dbconn server SERVERC rdbname iowa
```

Database Connection Servers with IP Addresses, RDB Names, and Ports Configuration Example 1

When a client request comes in for a server and multiple servers are configured in the router, the three configured attributes of IP address, RDB name, and port determine which server is chosen for the connection. When a server is selected for a connection, the client remains associated with that server for the duration of that connection. The APPC attributes configured for that server are used to connect to the IBM system. If a server is unconfigured while active connections exist, the active connections with that server will break.

Only one Database Connection server can be configured with a unique combination of IP address, port, and RDB name. If a situation arises where multiple servers in a router meet the criteria for accepting a client connection, the Database Connection server that meets the most specific criteria accepts the connection. For example, Servers A and B inFigure 23-4 are listening on port 446 for client connections that match their IP address of 161.55.122.80. Server A is configured to accept RDB name NEVADA and Server B is configured to accept any RDB name. A client connecting to port 446 for RDB name NEVADA matches the criteria for both servers. In this situation, Server A is selected to accept the connection because its configuration includes a specific RDB name NEVADA as compared to Server B whose configuration accepts any RDB name.

Figure 23-4 *Database Connection Server Configuration with IP Address and RDB Name Defined*

Database Connection Servers with IP Addresses, RDB Names, and Ports Configuration Example 2

The IP address and port specified for a server in a router's configuration also determine which server accepts a connection. For example, Server C is configured to listen on any local IP address on port 446 and RDB name IOWA. Server D is configured to listen for IP address 145.56.180.34 on port 446 and RDB name IOWA. When a client attempts to connect to IP address 145.56.180.34 on port 446 for RDB name IOWA, both servers meet the criteria in accepting the connection. In this case, Database Connection selects a connection based on the IP address first, then the port, and finally, the RDB name.

Server Selection by IP Addresses, RDB Names, and Ports Configuration Example

If multiple servers in a router meet the criteria for accepting a client connection, the Database Connection server that meets the most specific criteria accepts the connection. In Figure 23-5, the Cisco router contains four server configurations. All four servers listen for client connections on port 446 by default. Both Servers A and B are configured with the same IP address, 161.55.122.80. Servers A and C are configured to accept RDB name NEVADA. Servers B and D are configured to accept any RDB name.

If a client connects to IP address 161.55.122.80 on port 446 and sends RDB name NEVADA in the DRDA data stream, all four servers match the criteria for accepting the client connection. However, Server A will be selected to accept the connection because it meets the most specific criteria for IP address, RDB name, and port. If Server A was not configured, Server B would be the second choice because it meets the criteria for the IP address and port. The IP address specified in a server always has the highest precedence when matching a connection to a server.

Figure 23-5 *Database Connection Server Configurations with IP Addresses, RDB Names, and Default Port*

The following is the configuration for Servers A, B, C, and D in the Cisco router:

```
hostname routera
!
enable password allie

dbconn server SERVERA ip-address 161.55.122.80 rdbname NEVADA
dbconn server SERVERB ip-address 161.55.122.80
dbconn server SERVERC rdbname NEVADA
dbconn server SERVERD
```

Database Connection with Channel Interface Processor and DB2 on VTAM Example

Figure 23-6 illustrates a Cisco router with a Channel Interface Processor (CIP) that is configured with Database Connection. The CIP is networked and connected to VTAM on the mainframe. DB2 is configured on VTAM.

Figure 23-6 *Cisco Router with CIP and Connection to DB2 on VTAM*

The configuration in Figure 23-6 uses router commands to configure APPN over CIP and CSNA via RSRB. Note that the source-bridge ring-group of 100 matches the source bridge of 10 2 100 for interface Channel 13/2 to enable APPN to run over RSRB. In addition, the destination LAN address used by the APPN link station MVS1 corresponds to the virtual MAC address used by the adapter for Channel 13/2.

In the VTAM host definitions, the variable CONNTYPE=APPN is optional but recommended if you use APPN in your SNA environment. If CP to CP is set to YES and CONNTYPE is set to APPN, this configuration enables the Cisco router to establish CP to CP sessions with VTAM. By allowing CP to CP sessions, you gain the benefit of APPN's dynamic features such as the availability of directory and topology for locating resources and calculating optimal routes.

Configuration Example for Router Smoke

```
!
version 11.3
service password-encryption
service udp-small-servers
service tcp-small-servers
!
hostname smoke
!
enable password 7 11051807
!
microcode CIP flash slot0:cip22-14
microcode reload
ip subnet-zero
no ip routing
!
dbconn server BUDDHA rdbname DB2510 rlu STARW.DSNV510 mode LU62STAR
!
```

```
interface TokenRing0/0
 mac-address 4000.2222.0501
 ip address 10.10.22.1 255.255.255.0
 no ip route-cache
 no ip mroute-cache
 early-token-release
 ring-speed 16
 multiring all
!
interface TokenRing0/1
 mac-address 4000.1111.0501
 ip address 198.147.235.196 255.255.255.224
 no ip route-cache
 no ip mroute-cache
 early-token-release
 ring-speed 16
 multiring all
!
source-bridge ring-group 100
!
interface Channel13/0
  no ip address
  no keepalive
  shutdown
!
interface Channel 13/1
  no ip address
  no keepalive
  csna F010 38
!
interface Channel 13/2
  no ip address
  no keepalive
  lan TokenRing 1
    source bridge 10 2 100
    adapter 1 4000.0190.2001
!
appn control-point STARW.SMOKECP
  xid-block-number 05E
  xid-id-number 00002
  complete
!
appn mode LU62STAR
  class-of-service #INTER
  complete
!
appn port TOK1 TokenRing0/1
  complete
!
appn port TOK0 TokenRing0/0
  complete
!
appn port SRB rsrb
  rsrb-virtual-station 4000.2222.3333 50 1 100
  complete
!
```

```
appn link-station MVS1
 port SRB
 lan-dest-address 4000.0190.2001
 adjacent-cp-name NETA.MVS1
 complete
!
appn link-station BUDDHA
 port TOK1
 lan-dest-address 4000.0200.0448
 retry-limit infinite
 complete
!
appn partner-lu-location STARW.DSNV510 / DB2 APPL
  owning-cp STARW.BUDDHA / VTAM NetID
  complete
!
appn routing
ip default-gateway 198.147.235.12
no ip classless
logging monitor informational
!
line con 0
 exec-timeout 0 0
line aux 0
 transport input all
line vty 0 4
 exec-timeout 0 0
 password 7 11051807
 login
!
```

Sample VTAM Host Definitions

```
>Switched Major Node
 000042 P0202    PU    ADDR=C1,                   Router SMOKE
X
 000043                IDBLK=05E,
X
 000044                IDNUM=00002,
X
 000045                PUTYPE=2,
X
 000046                MAXDATA=1456,
X
 000047                USSTAB=STARSNA,
X
 000048                MODETAB=AGWTAB,
X
 000049                CPNAME=SMOKECP,
X
 000050                CONNTYPE=APPN
 000051 *
 000052 L02T0201 LU    LOCADDR=000,               Independent LU
X
```

```
 000053                    MODETAB=AGWTAB,
X
 000054                    MAXSESS=1024,
X
 000055                    DLOGMOD=LU62STAR,PACING=1,VPACING=1
```

Sample DB2 APPLID

```
DB2 APPL
 000100 DSNAPPL   VBUILD TYPE=APPL
 000200 DSNV510   APPL   APPC=YES,          X
 000300                  AUTH=ACQ,          X
 000400                  AUTOSES=1,         X
 000500                  DMINWNL=2048,      X
 000600                  DMINWNR=2048,      X
 000700                  DSESLIM=4096,      X
 000800                  EAS=65535,         X
 000900                  MODETAB=AGWTAB,    X
 001000                  SECACPT=ALREADYV,  X
 001100                  SRBEXIT=YES,       X
 001200                  VERIFY=NONE,       X
 001300                  VPACING=1,         X
 001400                  SYNCLVL=SYNCPT,    X
 001500                  ATNLOSS=ALL
```

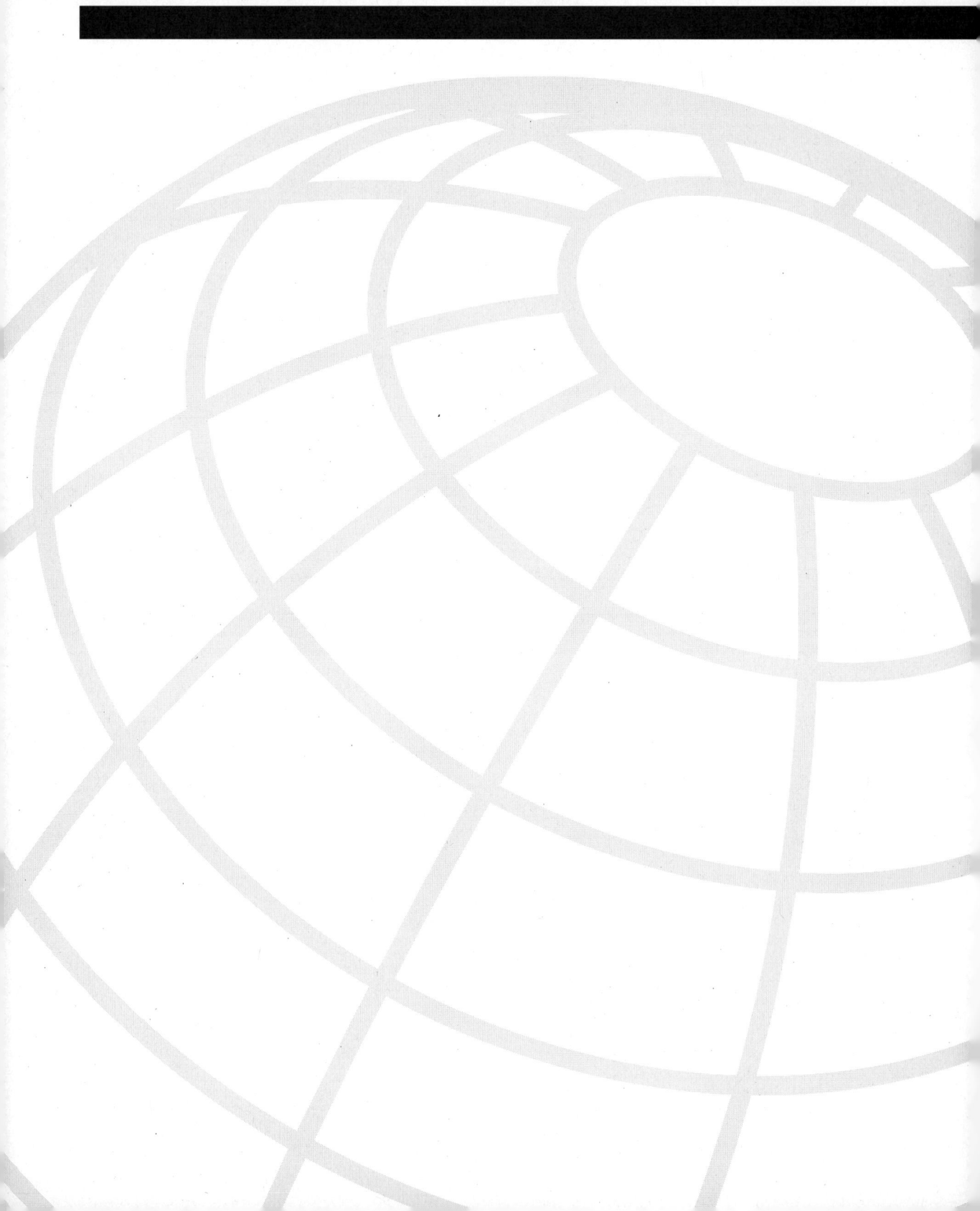

Cisco Database Connection Commands

Use the commands in this chapter to configure and monitor the Cisco Database Connection feature. For Cisco Database Connection configuration information and examples, refer to Chapter 23, "Configuring Cisco Database Connection."

clear dbconn connection

Use the **clear dbconn connection** privileged EXEC command to break a client connection.

clear dbconn connection *connection-id*

Syntax

connection-id

Description

Client connection identification number.

Command Mode

Privileged EXEC

Usage Guidelines

This command first appeared in Cisco IOS Release 11.3(2)T.

Examples

In the following example, the client connection 786A7c is cleared:

```
Router# clear dbconn connection 786A7C

Connection 786A7C cleared
```

Related Commands

To locate documentation of related commands, you can search online at www.cisco.com.

show dbconn connection

dbconn license

Use the **dbconn license** privileged EXEC command to configure the Database Connection license for StarSQL clients. Use the **no** form of this command to remove the license.

> **dbconn license** *license-key*
> **no dbconn license**

Syntax

license-key	License key obtained from StarQuest Software, Inc. The license determines the maximum number of StarSQL connections to a Cisco router configured with Database Connection. The license key is a 32-character hexadecimal string and is not case sensitive.

Command Mode

Privileged EXEC

Usage Guidelines

This command first appeared in Cisco IOS Release 11.3(2)T.

A Database Connection license is required if you use StarSQL clients.

Examples

In the following example, a StarSQL license is configured for StarSQL client connections:

```
dbconn license F66F84ABF809AF020HE0RC33KJH0MQ89
```

Related Commands

To locate documentation of related commands, you can search online at www.cisco.com.

show dbconn license

dbconn ping

Use the **dbconn ping** EXEC command to check whether or not the Database Connection servers are connecting to the relational databases on the IBM systems.

dbconn ping *server-name* [**user** *user-id*] [**password** *password*] [**rdbname** *rdbname*]

Syntax

Syntax	Description
server-name	Name of the Database Connection server.
user-id	(Optional) User ID used to connect to the IBM system. If no user ID is specified, the **ping** connection is made without APPC security. The IBM system's security settings determine whether or not the **ping** can succeed.
password	(Optional) Password used to connect to the IBM system.
rdbname	(Optional) The name of the relational database. If RDB name is not specified, the RDB name configured for the server is used.

Command Mode

EXEC

Usage Guidelines

This command first appeared in Cisco IOS Release 11.3(2)T.

Sample Output

The following is sample output from the **dbconn ping** command:

```
Router# dbconn ping canopus

RDB named NEVADA on database server CANOPUS successfully contacted!
Database server product id is QSQ03020, DB2 for OS/400 V3R2
Elapsed time was 00:00:00
```

Related Commands

To locate documentation of related commands, you can search online at www.cisco.com.

show dbconn server

dbconn server

Use the **dbconn server** Privileged EXEC mode command to configure a Database Connection server in a Cisco router. Use the **no** form of this command to unconfigure and disable the server.

> **dbconn server** *server-name* [**ipaddress** *ip-address*] [**port** *port-number*]
> [**rdbname** *rdbname*] [**rlu** *remote-lu*] [**mode** *mode*] [**tpname** *tp-name*]
> [**idle-timeout** *minutes*] [**window-size** *bytes*]
> **no dbconn server**

Syntax

Syntax	Description
server-name	Name of the Database Connection server. Server names are user-defined strings up to 16 characters.
ipaddress *ip-address*	(Optional) IP address used by the Database Connection server to receive a connection. When a connection arrives, this IP address is used for matching and selecting the server from multiple configured servers.
port *port-number*	(Optional) The port used to listen for connections. If no port is specified, the default is 446.
rdbname *rdbname*	(Optional) The remote database name on host. When a connection arrives, this name is used to identify and select the appropriate server from multiple configured servers. The string is used to match the RDB name sent by the client in the DRDA data stream at connect time. The default RDB name is an asterisk (*), which indicates that this Database Connection server serves any remote database.
rlu *remote-lu*	(Optional) APPC remote LU used to allocate the connection to the IBM system. An example is NETA.S103B345. If no remote LU is specified, the default is the configured server name which is set to uppercase and truncated to eight characters. An RLU need not be qualified with a NET ID. If you omit the NET ID, the NET ID of the router's APPN control point is used to fully qualify the LU name.
mode *mode*	(Optional) APPC mode used to allocate the conversation to the IBM system. If no mode is specified, the default is #INTER.
tpname *tp-name*	(Optional) APPC remote transaction program name used to allocate the conversation to the IBM system. If no TP name is specified, the default is the architected DRDA TP name \x076DB.

Syntax	Description
idle-timeout *idle-timeout*	(Optional) Time in minutes to wait for an idle client. If there is no activity from the client for this amount of time, the connection is forcibly broken. The time spent in waiting for a response from the IBM system is not counted, only idle time in between client requests is counted. The maximum is 1440 minutes (24 hours). If no idle timeout is specified, the default is 0 (zero) for no timeout.
window-size *bytes*	(Optional) This value is used for the TCP receive window size. If no window size is specified, the default is 4K (4096 KB).

Command Mode
Privileged EXEC

Usage Guidelines
This command first appeared in Cisco IOS Release 11.3(2)T.

You can configure more than one Database Connection server per router. For each IBM database system in your network, you can configure a Database Connection server in the router configuration.

If you do not specify a port number, DRDA clients in a TCP/IP network expect to use port 446 by default.

Examples
In the following example, a Database Connection server is configured:

```
dbconn server coffee rdbname COFFEE rlu PARIS.COFFEE match idle-timeout 20 window-size 16
```

Related Commands
To locate documentation of related commands, you can search online at www.cisco.com.

clear dbconn connection
dbconn ping
show dbconn server
show dbconn ports

show dbconn connection

Use the **show dbconn connection** EXEC command to display the status of connections made to Database Connection servers.

> **show dbconn connection** [*connection-id*] [**server** *server-name*] [**user** *user-id*]
> [**rdbname** *rdb-name*]

Syntax

Syntax	Description
connection-id	(Optional) Display status for specified connection.
server *server-name*	(Optional) Display connection information for specified server.
user *user-id*	(Optional) Display connections for specified user ID.
rdbname *rdb-name*	(Optional) Display connections for specified RDB name.

Command Mode

EXEC

Default

Displays all connections if you do not specify *connection-id*.

Usage Guidelines

This command first appeared in Cisco IOS Release 11.3(2)T.

Sample Displays

The following is sample output from the **show dbconn connection** command:

```
Router# show dbconn connection

ID        Server       Userid     ClientIPAddress Connect   Idle
6127E428 SERVERA       ALLIE      198.999.989.36  00:01:26  00:01:12
6127D34C SERVERB       BRIAN      198.999.989.84  00:00:48  00:00:41
```

The following is sample output from the **show dbconn connection** command for a specified connection:

```
Router# show dbconn connection 6127E428

connection id 6127E428
  connection state is active
  server is WILLOW
  rdbname is KINGSTON
  userid is JSMITH
```

```
client name is ARIES
local ip-address is 198.999.999.5
local port is 446
client ip-address is 198.999.999.53
client port is 1067
connect time 00:03:51
idle time 00:03:37 (client)
508 bytes received from client
9644 bytes received from host
client is licensed StarSQL
```

Table 24-1 describes significant fields shown in the display.

Table 24-1   *show dbconn connection* Field Descriptions

Field	Description
connection id	Identification number of the connection made by a StarSQL client to the Database Connection server.
connection state	Status of the connection made by a StarSQL client.
server	Name of the Database Connection server.
rdbname	Name of the relational database on the IBM system.
userid	User ID of the user connected through a port to the Database Connection server.
client name	Name of the client system.
local ip-address	IP address of the Database Connection server in the router to which the client connects.
local port	Port in the Database Connection server through which the client connects.
client ip-address	IP address of the client connected to the Database Connection server.
client port	Port used by the client to connect to the Database Connection server.
connect time	Time when connection was made by the client to the Database Connection server.
idle time	Amount of time that the active client connection has been idle.

Related Commands

To locate documentation of related commands, you can search online at www.cisco.com.

show dbconn license
show dbconn ports
show dbconn server

show dbconn license

Use the **show dbconn license** EXEC command to display the status of licensed StarSQL connections made to Database Connection servers.

>   **show dbconn license**

Syntax Description

This command has no arguments or keywords.

Command Mode

EXEC

Usage Guidelines

This command first appeared in Cisco IOS Release 11.3(2)T.

Sample Display

The following is sample output from the **show dbconn license** command:

```
Router# show dbconn license

Database Connection is licensed for unlimited connections, 2 licensed connections in use
```

Related Commands

To locate documentation of related commands, you can search online at www.cisco.com.

dbconn license
show dbconn connection
show dbconn ports
show dbconn server

show dbconn ports

Use the **show dbconn ports** EXEC command to display information on all ports that are being used by Database Connection to receive connections.

>   **show dbconn ports**

Syntax Description

This command has no arguments or keywords.

Command Mode

EXEC

Usage Guidelines

This command first appeared in Cisco IOS Release 11.3(2)T.

Sample Display

The following is sample output from the **show dbconn ports** command:

```
Router# show dbconn ports

Port  State
446   listening
447   listening
```

Table 24-2 describes significant fields shown in the display.

Table 24-2 *show dbconn ports Field Descriptions*

Field	Description
Port	Port number
State	Listening or disabled status

Related Commands

To locate documentation of related commands, you can search online at www.cisco.com.

show dbconn connection
show dbconn license
show dbconn server

show dbconn server

Use the **show dbconn server** EXEC command to display the status of Database Connection servers.

        show dbconn server [*server-name*]

Syntax	Description
server-name	(Optional) Specific server for which status should be displayed.

Command Mode

EXEC

Usage Guidelines

This command first appeared in Cisco IOS Release 11.3(2)T.

Sample Displays

The following is sample output from the **show dbconn server** command:

```
Router# show dbconn server
Server          Port  IPAddress       RDBName       State      NumConn
SERVERA         446   0.0.0.0         MATTY         enabled    0
SERVERB         446   0.0.0.0         SCU_DSNM      enabled    4
SERVERC         446   0.0.0.0         DSN4          enabled    0
SERVERD         446   0.0.0.0         MKTG          enabled    0
SERVERE         446   0.0.0.0         ABBY          enabled    6
SERVERF         446   0.0.0.0         DB2510        enabled    0
SERVERG         446   0.0.0.0         ELLE          enabled    3
SERVERH         446   0.0.0.0         SUNSET        enabled    0
SERVERI         446   0.0.0.0         NELL          enabled    1
SERVERJ         446   198.989.999.32  SAMPLE        enabled    0
SERVERK         446   0.0.0.0         DB2410        enabled    0
SERVERL         446   0.0.0.0         SQLDS         enabled    0
SERVERM         446   0.0.0.0         STELLA        enabled    1
SERVERN         446   10.10.19.4      OAK           enabled    2
SERVERO         447   0.0.0.0         DB2510        enabled    0
```

The following is sample output from **show dbconn server** command where the database server **willow** is specified:

```
Router# show dbconn server willow

server willow
  server state is enabled (accepting connections)
  ip-address is 10.10.11.4
  port is 446
  rdbname is MATTY
  rlu is STARW.MATTY
  mode is LU62STAR
  tpname is DB2
  idle-timeout is 1 minute
  window-size is 4096 bytes
  database server name is DB2
  database product id is SQL05000
  number of connections is 2000
  number of licensed StarSQL connections is 200
```

Table 24-3 describes significant fields shown in the display.

Table 24-3 *show dbconn server* *Field Descriptions*

Field	Description
server	Server name.
server state	Current state of the server (enabled or disabled).
ip-address	IP address accepted by the Database Connection server.
port	Port number through which the Database Connection server accepts a client connection.
rdbname	Name of the remote database accessed by the Database Connection server.
rlu	Remote SNA LU used when connecting to the database server.
mode	SNA mode used when connecting to the database.
tpname	SNA transaction program name used for DRDA server on the database system.
idle-timeout	Maximum length of time allowed for inactive connections to the Database Connection server.
window-size	TCP receive window size.
database server name	System name returned by the database server. Field shows none until first contact.
database product ID	Database product ID. Field shows none until first contact.
number of connections	Number of all ODBC clients currently connected to the Database Connection server.
number of StarSQL connections	Number of licensed StarSQL clients currently connected to the Database Connection server.

Related Commands

To locate documentation of related commands, you can search online at www.cisco.com.

show dbconn connection
show dbconn ports

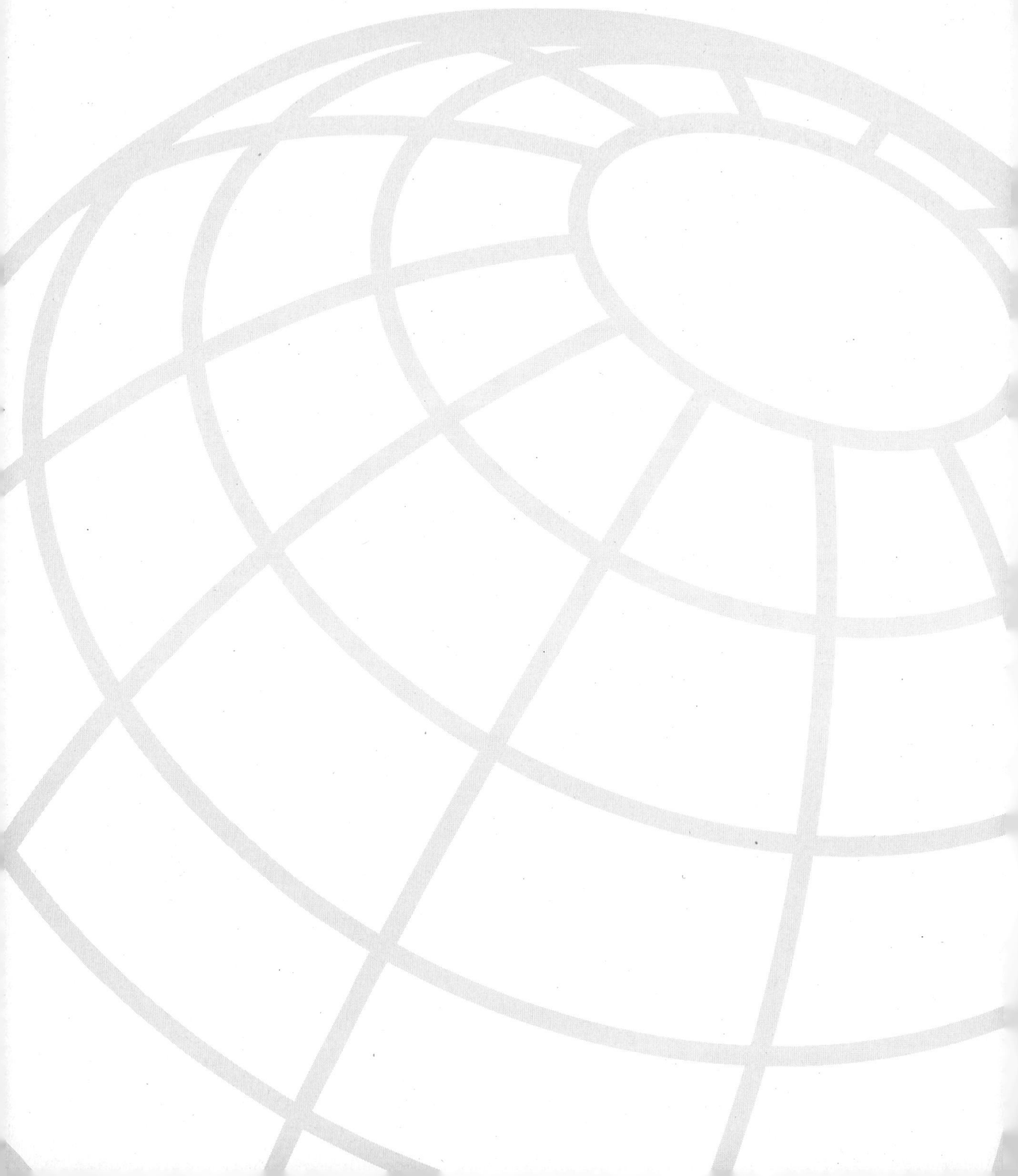

Configuring NCIA Client/Server Topologies

This chapter describes native client interface architecture (NCIA) support for Systems Network Architecture (SNA) devices. NCIA server and the NCIA client/server model extends the scalability of NCIA I, the earlier NCIA implementation, by minimizing the number of central-site remote source-route bridging (RSRB) or data-link switching plus (DLSw+) peer connections required to support a large number of NCIA clients. For a complete description of the NCIA client/server commands mentioned in this chapter, refer to Chapter 26, "NCIA Server Configuration Commands." To locate documentation of other commands that appear in this chapter, search online at www.cisco.com.

Cisco's NCIA server feature implements RFC 2114, Data Link Switch Client Access Protocol.

NCIA Server Session to Local Token Ring Using DLSw+ Local Switch

The network configuration shown in Figure 25-1 includes NCIA clients that connect to a front-end processor (FEP) on a Token Ring through a local router (the NCIA server). The virtual ring is used in conjunction with DLSw+ local switch. The routing information field (RIF) of each circuit is terminated on the virtual ring. Figure 25-2 shows a logical view of an NCIA server session using a DLSw+ local switch (connected to a local Token Ring). In addition to Token Ring, an NCIA server also supports Ethernet, Synchronous Data Link Control (SDLC) Protocol, and Qualified Logical Link Control (QLLC) network connections, as well as Channel Interface Processor (CIP) connections through a DLSw+ local switch. For more information on the different media types that a DLSw+ local switch supports, refer to Chapter 9, "Configuring Data-Link Switching Plus."

Figure 25-1 *NCIA Server Session to Local Token Ring Using DLSw+ Local Switch*

Figure 25-2   *Logical View of NCIA Server Session to a Local Token Ring Using DLSw+ Local Switch*

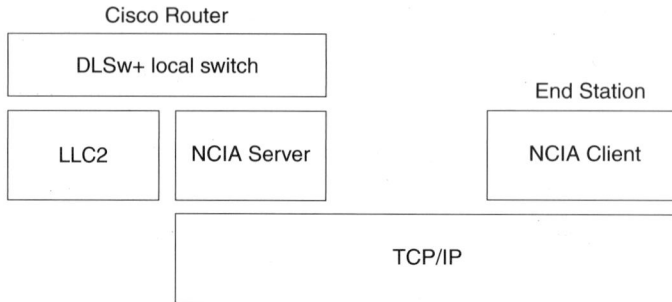

Configuration Task List

To configure an NCIA server session connected to a local Token Ring, perform the tasks in the following sections:

● Define a Source-Bridge Ring Group for DLSw+

● Define a DLSw+ Local Peer for the Router

● Configure an NCIA Server on the Router

For a configuration example, see the section "NCIA Server Session to Local Token Ring Using DLSw+ Local Switch Example" at the end of this chapter.

Define a Source-Bridge Ring Group for DLSw+

In DLSw+, the source-bridge ring group specifies the virtual ring that will appear to be the last ring in the RIF. This ring is transparent to the NCIA client. From the host's point of view, all NCIA clients look like stations sitting on the virtual ring. To define a source-bridge ring group for DLSw+, use the following command in global configuration mode:

Command	Purpose
source-bridge ring-group *ring-group* [*virtual-mac-address*]	Defines a ring group.

Define a DLSw+ Local Peer for the Router

Defining a DLSw+ local peer for a router enables DLSw+ local switch. You specify all local DLSw+ parameters as part of the local peer definition. To define a local peer, use the following command in global configuration mode:

Command	Purpose
dlsw local-peer [**peer-id** *ip-address*] [**group** *group*] [**border**] [**cost** *cost*] [**lf** *size*] [**keepalive** *seconds*] [**passive**] [**promiscuous**] [**biu-segment**]	Defines the DLSw+ local peer.

Configure an NCIA Server on the Router

Configuring an NCIA server on a router enables the router to perform two roles:

●   Establish TCP/NDLC sessions with clients for the purpose of sending and receiving data.

●   Use the standard interface (CLSI) to communicate with other software modules in the router, such as APPN, DLSw+, and downstream physical unit (DSPU), and act as the data intermediary between them and the clients of the NCIA server.

To configure an NCIA server, use the following command in global configuration mode:

Command	Purpose
ncia server *server-number server-ip-address server-virtual-mac-address virtual-mac-address virtual-mac-range* [**inbound-only**] [**keepalive** *seconds*] [**tcp_keepalive** *minutes*]	Configures the NCIA server.

NCIA Server Session with DLSw+

In the network configuration shown in Figure 25-3, the NCIA server uses DLSw+ to connect its clients to the FEP through a remote router. Figure 25-4 shows a logical view of the NCIA Server session with DLSw+.

Figure 25-3   *NCIA Server Session with DLSw+*

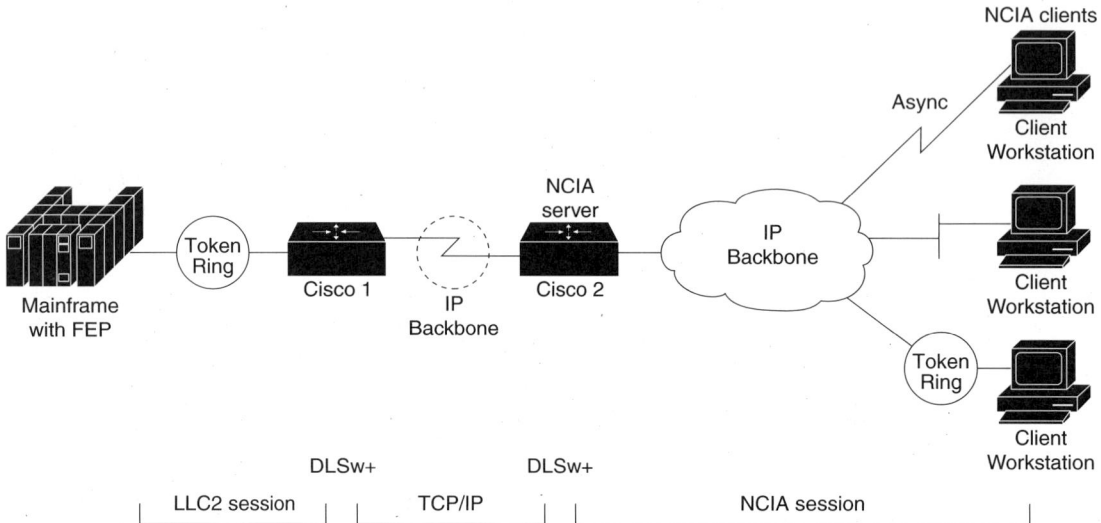

Figure 25-4   *Logical View of NCIA Server with DLSw+*

DLSw+ Configuration Task List

To configure an NCIA server session connected to a remote router using DLSw+, perform the tasks in the following sections:

- Define a Source-Bridge Ring Group for DLSw+

- Define a DLSw+ Local Peer for the Router

- Define a DLSw+ Remote Peer

- Configure an NCIA Server on the Local Router

For a configuration example, see the section "NCIA Server Session with DLSw+ Example" at the end of this chapter.

Define a Source-Bridge Ring Group for DLSw+

The source-bridge ring can be shared between DLSw+ and SRB/RSRB. In DLSw+, the source-bridge ring group specifies the virtual ring that will appear to be the last ring in the RIF. Because RIFs are terminated at the router, there is no correlation between the ring-group number specified in DLSw+ peers. The numbers can be the same for management simplicity, but they do not have to be. To define a source-bridge ring group for DLSw+, use the following command in global configuration mode:

Command	Purpose
source-bridge ring-group *ring-group* [*virtual-mac-address*]	Defines a ring group.

Define a DLSw+ Local Peer for the Router

Defining a DLSw+ local peer for a router enables DLSw+. You specify all local DLSw+ parameters as part of the local peer definition. To define a local peer, use the following command in global configuration mode:

Command	Purpose
dlsw local-peer [**peer-id** *ip-address*] [**group** *group*] [**border**] [**cost** *cost*] [**lf** *size*] [**keepalive** *seconds*] [**passive**] [**promiscuous**] [**biu-segment**]	Defines the DLSw+ local peer.

Define a DLSw+ Remote Peer

To configure TCP encapsulation on a remote peer, use the following command in global configuration mode:

Command	Purpose
dlsw remote-peer *list-number* **tcp** *ip-address* [**backup-peer** *ip-address*] [**bytes-netbios-out** *bytes-list-name*] [**cost** *cost*] [**dest-mac** *mac-address*] [**dmac-output-list** *access-list-number*] [**dynamic**] [**host-netbios-out** *host-list-name*] [**inactivity** *minutes*] [**keepalive** *seconds*] [**lf** *size*] [**linger** *minutes*] [**lsap-output-list** *list*] [**no-llc** *minutes*] [**priority**] [**tcp-queue-max** *size*] [**timeout** *seconds*]	Defines a TCP encapsulation remote peer.

Configure an NCIA Server on the Local Router

Configuring an NCIA server on the local router enables the router to perform two roles:

● Establish TCP/NDLC sessions with clients to send and receive data.

● Use the standard interface (CLSI) to communicate with other software modules in the router, such as APPN, DLSw+, and DSPU, and act as the data intermediary between them and the NCIA clients.

To configure an NCIA server, use the following command in global configuration mode:

Command	Purpose
ncia server *server-number server-ip-address server-virtual-mac-address virtual-mac-address virtual-mac-range* [**inbound-only**] [**keepalive** *seconds*] [**tcp_keepalive** *minutes*]	Configures the NCIA server.

NCIA Server Session with DSPU

In the network configuration shown in Figure 25-5, the NCIA server uses DSPU to connect its clients to the FEP through a remote router. Figure 25-6 shows a logical view of the NCIA server session with RSRB/DLSw+ and DSPU.

Figure 25-5 *NCIA Server Session with DSPU*

Figure 25-6 *Logical View of NCIA Server with DSPU*

DSPU Configuration Task List

To configure an NCIA server session connected to a remote router using DSPU, perform the tasks in the following sections:

- Define a DSPU Upstream Host

- Explicitly Define DSPU

- Define Dedicated LU

- Configure the NCIA Server as the Underlying Transport Mechanism

For a configuration example, see the section "NCIA Server Session with DSPU Example" at the end of this chapter.

Define a DSPU Upstream Host

To define a DSPU host over Token Ring, Ethernet, Fiber Distributed Data Interface (FDDI), RSRB, or virtual data-link control (VDLC) connections, use the following command in global configuration mode:

Command	Purpose
dspu host *host-name* **xid-snd** *xid* **rmac** *remote-mac* [**rsap** *remote-sap*] [**lsap** *local-sap*] [**interface** *slot/port*] [**window** *window-size*] [**maxiframe** *max-iframe*] [**retries** *retry-count*] [**retry-timeout** *retry-timeout*] [**focalpoint**]	Defines a DSPU host over Token Ring, Ethernet, FDDI, RSRB, or virtual data-link control connections.

Explicitly Define DSPU

To explicitly define a DSPU over Token Ring, Ethernet, FDDI, RSRB, VDLC, or NCIA connections, use the following command in global configuration mode:

Command	Purpose
dspu pu *pu-name* [**rmac** *remote-mac*] [**rsap** *remote-sap*] [**lsap** *local-sap*] [**xid-rcv** *xid*] [**interface** *slot/port*] [**window** *window-size*] [**maxiframe** *max-iframe*] [**retries** *retry-count*] [**retry-timeout** *retry-timeout*]	Explicitly defines a DSPU over Token Ring, Ethernet, FDDI, RSRB, VDLC, or NCIA connections.

Define Dedicated LU

To define a dedicated logical unit (LU) or a range of dedicated LUs for an upstream host and DSPU, use the following command in global configuration mode:

Command	Purpose
dspu lu *lu-start* [*lu-end*] {**host** *host-name host-lu-start*	**pool** *pool-name*} [**pu** *pu-name*]	Defines a dedicated LU or a range of dedicated LUs for a DSPU.

Configure the NCIA Server as the Underlying Transport Mechanism

To configure the NCIA server as the underlying transport mechanism, use the following command in global configuration mode:

Command	Purpose
dspu ncia [*server-number*]	Configures the NCIA server as the underlying transport mechanism.

To enable a local service access point (SAP) on the NCIA server for use by DSPUs, use the following command in global configuration mode:

Command	Purpose
dspu ncia enable-pu [**lsap** *local-sap*]	Enables local SAP for DSPUs.

NCIA Server Session with RSRB

The network configuration shown in Figure 25-7 includes NCIA clients that connect to a FEP on a Token Ring through a remote router. Figure 25-8 shows a logical view of the NCIA Server session with RSRB (to a remote Token Ring). Because DLSw+ is the latest technology provided by Cisco, Cisco does not encourage using the NCIA Server feature with RSRB. If the router on the host side is running DLSw+, RSRB should not be used. Support for the NCIA Server feature with RSRB is provided to encourage RSRB users to migrate to DLSw+.

Figure 25-7   *NCIA Server Session with RSRB*

Figure 25-8   *Logical View of NCIA Server Session with RSRB (Remote Token Ring)*

RSRB Configuration Task List

To configure an NCIA server session connected to a remote Token Ring using RSRB, perform the tasks in the following sections:

- Define a Source-Bridge Ring Group for DLSw+ and RSRB
- Identify the Remote Peer (TCP Connection)
- Define a DLSw+ Local Peer for the Local Router
- Configure an NCIA Server on the Router
- Configure an RSRB Ring for the NCIA Server on the Local Router

For a configuration example, see the section "NCIA Server Session with DLSw+ Example" at the end of this chapter.

Define a Source-Bridge Ring Group for DLSw+ and RSRB

The source-bridge virtual ring can be shared between DLSw+ and SRB/RSRB. In DLSw+, the source-bridge ring group specifies the virtual ring that will appear to be the last ring in the RIF. Because RIFs are terminated at the router, the ring group numbers specified in commands to set up DLSw+ peers can be different. The ring group numbers can be the same for management simplicity, but they do not have to be.

To define a source-bridge ring group for DLSw+, use the following command in global configuration mode:

Command	Purpose
source-bridge ring-group *ring-group* [*virtual-mac-address*]	Defines a ring group.

Identify the Remote Peer (TCP Connection)

In our implementation, whenever you connect Token Rings using non-Token Ring media, you must treat that non-Token Ring media as a virtual ring by assigning it to a ring group. Every router that you want to exchange Token Ring traffic must be a member of this same ring group. For more information about defining a ring group, see the "Define a Ring Group in SRB Context" section of Chapter 3, "Configuring Source-Route Bridging."

To identify the remote peers, use the following command in global configuration mode:

Command	Purpose
source-bridge remote-peer *ring-group* **tcp** *ip-address* [**lf** *size*] [**tcp-receive-window** *wsize*] [**local-ack**] [**priority**]	Identifies the IP address of a peer in the ring group with which to exchange source-bridge traffic using TCP.

Specify one **source-bridge remote-peer** command for each peer router that is part of the virtual ring. Also, specify one **source-bridge remote-peer** command to identify the IP address of the local router.

NCIA server supports only RSRB pass-through mode. Local acknowledgment is not supported.

Define a DLSw+ Local Peer for the Local Router

Defining a DLSw+ local peer for the local router enables DLSw+. You specify all local DLSw+ parameters as part of the local peer definition. To define a local peer, use the following command in global configuration mode:

Command	Purpose
dlsw local-peer [**peer-id** *ip-address*] [**group** *group*] [**border**] [**cost** *cost*] [**lf** *size*] [**keepalive** *seconds*] [**passive**] [**promiscuous**] [**biu-segment**]	Defines the DLSw+ local peer.

Configure an NCIA Server on the Router

Configuring an NCIA server on a router enables the router to perform two roles:

- Establish TCP/NDLC sessions with clients for the purpose of sending and receiving data.

- Use the standard interface (CLSI) to communicate with other software modules in the router, such as APPN, DLSw+, and DSPU, and to act as the data intermediary between them and the NCIA clients.

To configure an NCIA server, use the following command in global configuration mode:

Command	Purpose
ncia server *server-number server-ip-address server-virtual-mac-address virtual-mac-address virtual-mac-range* [**inbound-only**] [**keepalive** *seconds*] [**tcp_keepalive** *minutes*]	Configures the NCIA server.

Configure an RSRB Ring for the NCIA Server on the Local Router

Configuring an RSRB ring to associate with the NCIA server on the local router provides the virtual ring that connects the DLSw+ ring within the local router and the target ring between the local router and the remote router.

To configure an RSRB ring for the NCIA server on the local router, use the following command in global configuration mode:

Command	Purpose
ncia rsrb *virtual-ring local-bridge local-ring ncia-bridge ncia-ring virtual-mac-address*	Defines the NCIA/RSRB interface.

Monitor and Maintain an NCIA Server Network

You can monitor and maintain the operation of an NCIA server network. To display information about the state of the NCIA server feature and perform maintenance tasks, use the following commands in EXEC mode:

Command	Purpose
show ncia server [*server-number*]	Shows the status of the NCIA server.
show ncia client [**sap-list**] [*ip-address*]	Shows the status of the NCIA client.
clear ncia client [*ip-address*]	Terminates an NCIA client connection.
show ncia circuits [*id-number*]	Shows the status of an NCIA circuit.
clear ncia circuit [*id-number*]	Drops an NCIA circuit.
clear ncia client registered [*ip-address*]	Terminates the active connection to the specified client and releases all control blocks of the registered client.
ncia stop	Stops an NCIA server.
ncia start	Restarts an NCIA server.

NCIA Server Configuration Examples

The following sections provide NCIA server configuration examples:

- NCIA Server Session to Local Token Ring Using DLSw+ Local Switch Example
- NCIA Server Session with DLSw+ Example
- NCIA Server Session with DSPU Example
- NCIA Server Session with RSRB Example

NCIA Server Session to Local Token Ring Using DLSw+ Local Switch Example

Figure 25-9 illustrates the use of DLSw+ local peer with an NCIA server session to a local Token Ring.

Figure 25-9   *NCIA Server Session to Local Token Ring Using DLSw+ Local Switch*

The following is a configuration file for the network example shown in Figure 25-9:

```
source-bridge ring-group 44
dlsw local-peer
ncia server 1 10.2.20.4 4000.3174.0001 4000.0000.0001 128
!
interface token ring 0
 ring-speed 16
 source-bridge 21 3 44
```

NCIA Server Session with DLSw+ Example

Figure 25-10 illustrates the use of DLSw+ with an NCIA server session.

Figure 25-10 *NCIA Server Session with DLSw+*

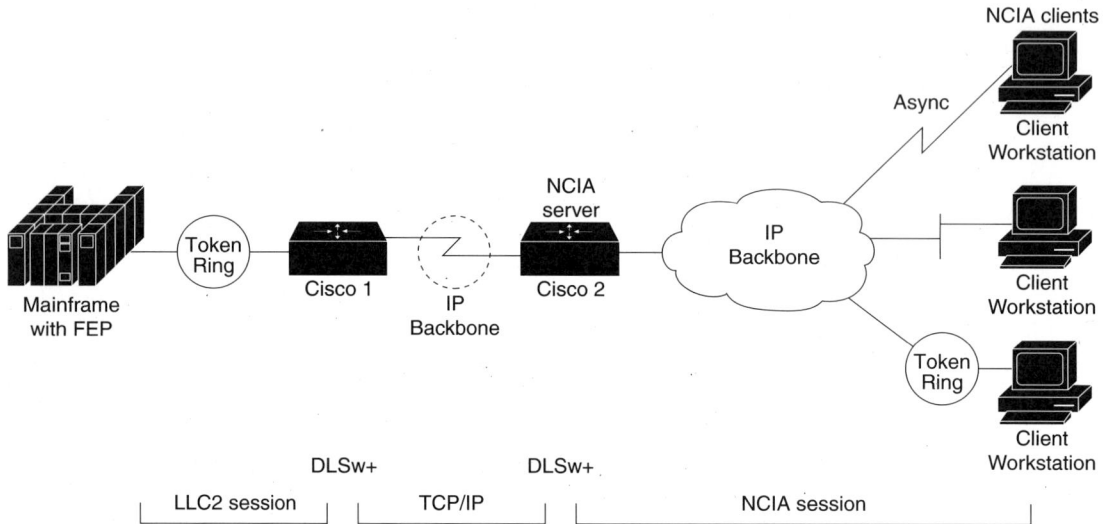

The following is a configuration file for the network example shown in Figure 25-10:

```
source-bridge ring-group 44
dlsw local-peer peer-id 10.2.20.4
dlsw remote-peer 0 tcp 10.2.20.3
ncia server 1 10.2.20.4 4000.3174.0001 4000.0000.0001 128
```

NCIA Server Session with DSPU Example

Figure 25-11 illustrates an NCIA server session with RSRB/DLSw+ and DSPU.

Figure 25-11 *NCIA Server Session with RSRB/DLSw+ and DSPU*

The following is a configuration file for the network example shown in Figure 25-11:

```
ncia server 1 10.2.20.4 4000.3745.0001 4000.0000.0001 128
!
dspu ncia 1
dspu ncia enable-pu lsap 8
!
dspu host HOST-9370 xid-snd 11100001 rmac 4000.1060.1000 rsap 4 lsap 4
!
dspu pu CISCOPU-A xid-rcv 01700001
dspu lu 2 6 host HOST-9370 2
!
interface TokenRing 0
 ring-speed 16
 llc2 xid-retry-time 0
 dspu enable-host lsap 4
 dspu start HOST-9370
```

NCIA Server Session with RSRB Example

Figure 25-12 illustrates the use of RSRB with an NCIA server session.

Figure 25-12 *NCIA Server Session with RSRB*

The following is a configuration file for router Cisco 2 for the network example shown in Figure 25-12:

```
source-bridge ring-group 44
source-bridge ring-group 22
source-bridge remote-peer 22 tcp 10.2.20.3
source-bridge remote-peer 22 tcp 10.2.20.4
dlsw local-peer
ncia server 1 10.2.20.4 4000.3174.0001 4000.0000.0001 128
ncia rsrb 22 2 33 4 44 1111.1111.2222
```

NCIA Server Configuration Commands

This chapter describes the commands you use to configure native client interface architecture (NCIA) client/server support for Systems Network Architecture (SNA) devices. For NCIA server configuration tasks and examples, refer to Chapter 25, "Configuring NCIA Client/Server Topologies."

Cisco's NCIA server feature implements RFC 2114, Data Link Switch Client Access Protocol.

clear ncia circuit

Use the **clear ncia circuit** privileged EXEC command to drop a specified NCIA circuit.

> **clear ncia circuit** [*id-number*]

Syntax	Description
id-number	(Optional) Number assigned to identify the circuit. If no circuit ID number is specified, the command drops all circuits.

Command Mode

Privileged EXEC

Usage Guideline

This command first appeared in Cisco IOS Release 11.2.

If no circuit ID number is specified, the command drops all circuits.

Example

The following example clears the active NCIA circuit identified as 791F8C:

```
clear ncia circuit 791F8C
```

Related Commands

To locate documentation of related commands, you can search online at www.cisco.com.

show ncia circuits

clear ncia client

Use the **clear ncia client** privileged EXEC command to terminate a specified active client connection.

> **clear ncia client** [*ip-address*]

Syntax

ip-address	(Optional) IP address of the client. If no IP address is specified in the command, the command terminates all active client connections.

Command Mode

Privileged EXEC

Usage Guideline

This command first appeared in Cisco IOS Release 11.2.

If no IP address is specified in the command, the command terminates all active client connections.

Example

The following example terminates the active connection to the client identified by the IP address 10.2.20.126:

```
clear ncia client 10.2.20.126
```

Related Commands

To locate documentation of related commands, you can search online at www.cisco.com.

show ncia client

clear ncia client registered

Use the **clear ncia client registered** privileged EXEC command to release the control block of a specified registered client after terminating the active connection to it.

> **clear ncia client registered** [*ip-address*]

Syntax	Description
ip-address	(Optional) IP address of the registered client. If no IP address is specified in the command, the command releases the control blocks of all registered clients after terminating any active connections to them.

Command Mode

Privileged EXEC

Usage Guidelines

This command first appeared in Cisco IOS Release 11.2.

If no IP address is specified in the command, the command releases the control blocks of all registered clients after terminating any active connections to them.

Example

The following example terminates the active connection to the registered client identified by the IP address 10.2.20.126 and releases its control block:

```
clear ncia client registered 10.2.20.126
```

Related Commands

To locate documentation of related commands, you can search online at www.cisco.com.

show ncia client

ncia

Use the **ncia** privileged EXEC command to stop and start an NCIA server.

ncia {start | stop}

Syntax	Description
start	Starts the NCIA server when it has been stopped using the **ncia stop** command.
stop	Stops the NCIA server. When the server is stopped, all clients are disconnected, all circuits are dropped, and no clients can connect to the server.

Command Mode

Privileged EXEC

Usage Guidelines

This command first appeared in Cisco IOS Release 11.2.

As soon as the NCIA server is configured, it begins running. If an NCIA server is configured and the configuration is stored in the NVRAM of the router, when the router boots up, the server is automatically started. Issuing the **ncia start** command when a server is already running causes the router to display the following message:

```
NCIA server is running already!
```

Example

The following example stops an active NCIA server:

```
ncia stop
```

Related Commands

To locate documentation of related commands, you can search online at www.cisco.com.

ncia server

ncia client

Use the **ncia client** global configuration command to configure an NCIA client on a Cisco router. Use the **no** form of this command to remove the configuration.

> **ncia client** *server-number client-ip-address virtual-mac-address* [**sna** | **all**]
> **no ncia client** *server-number client-ip-address virtual-mac-address* [**sna** | **all**]

Syntax	Description
server-number	Number assigned to identify the server. Currently, the server number must be configured with a value of 1.
client-ip-address	IP address of the client.
virtual-mac-address	Virtual MAC address of the client.
sna	(Optional) NCIA client only supports SNA traffic.

Syntax	Description
all	(Optional) NCIA client supports all types of traffic. If you do not specify **all** as the supported traffic type when you configure an NCIA client, the client only supports SNA traffic.

Default

No NCIA client is configured.

Command Mode

Global configuration

Usage Guidelines

This command first appeared in Cisco IOS Release 11.2.

You must use the **ncia server** command to configure an NCIA server on the router before using the **ncia client** command to configure an NCIA client.

The purpose in configuring a client is so the NCIA server can connect outward to a client. When an end station on the LAN side tries to connect to a client, the end station sends an explorer. When the server receives this explorer, the server tries to match the MAC address in the client database. If it finds a match, the server then connects to that client. If the ability for the server to connect outward to clients is not needed, there is no reason to configure any clients.

Each client is assigned a MAC address from the pool created by the **ncia server** command. There are two exceptions to this guideline:

- A MAC address outside the pool created by the **ncia server** command can be defined in the **ncia client** command.

  When a client configured with a MAC address outside the pool connects to the server, the client's configured MAC address is used rather than allocating a new one from the pool.

- If a client has its own MAC address, it uses that address.

  The MAC address is recognized during the "capability exchange" period when the client establishes a session with the NCIA server. Normally, it is not necessary to configure any client. The server accepts a connection from any unconfigured client. If the unconfigured client does not have its own MAC address, a MAC address from the pool will be assigned to it. If the unconfigured client has its own MAC address, that MAC address is used. If the client has its own MAC address and it is configured using the **ncia client** command, the two MAC addresses must match; otherwise, the connection will not be established.

Part
II

Command Reference

If you do not specify **all** as the supported traffic type when you configure an NCIA client, the client only supports SNA traffic.

Example

The following example configures an NCIA client on a router:

```
ncia client 1 10.2.20.5 1111.2222.3333
```

Related Commands

To locate documentation of related commands, you can search online at www.cisco.com.

ncia server
dlsw local-peer

ncia rsrb

Use the **ncia rsrb** global configuration command to configure an RSRB ring to associate with an NCIA server on a Cisco router. Use the **no** form of this command to remove the configuration.

> **ncia rsrb** *virtual-ring local-bridge local-ring ncia-bridge ncia-ring*
>   *virtual-mac-address*
> **no ncia rsrb**

Syntax	Description
virtual-ring	RSRB ring group number. This number corresponds to the ring-number parameter defined by a **source-bridge ring-group** command.
local-bridge	Number of the bridge connecting the virtual ring and the local ring.
local-ring	Number of the virtual ring connecting the virtual ring and the NCIA ring.
ncia-bridge	Number of the bridge connecting the local ring and the NCIA ring.
ncia-ring	NCIA ring group number. This number corresponds to the ring-number parameter defined by a **source-bridge ring-group** command.
virtual-mac-address	Local ring virtual MAC address.

Default

No RSRB ring is configured.

Command Mode

Global configuration

Usage Guidelines

This command first appeared in Cisco IOS Release 11.2.

You must use the **ncia server** command to configure an NCIA server on the router before using the **ncia rsrb** command to configure an RSRB ring to associate with the server.

Example

The following example configures a virtual ring to associate with an NCIA server on a Cisco router:

```
source-bridge ring-group 22
source-bridge ring-group 44
ncia rsrb 44 4 33 3 22 1111.1111.2222
```

Related Commands

To locate documentation of related commands, you can search online at www.cisco.com.

ncia server
source-bridge ring-group

ncia server

Use the **ncia server** global configuration command to configure an NCIA server on a Cisco router. Use the **no** form of this command to remove the configuration.

> **ncia server** *server-number server-ip-address server-virtual-mac-address*
> *virtual-mac-address virtual-mac-range* [**inbound-only**] [**keepalive** *seconds*]
> [**tcp_keepalive** *minutes*]
> **no ncia server**

Syntax	Description
server-number	Number assigned to identify the server. Currently, the server number must be configured with a value of 1.
server-ip-address	IP address used to accept the incoming connection, or to make an out-going connection.
server-virtual-mac-address	MAC address of the server.
virtual-mac-address	The first MAC address of the virtual MAC address pool.

Part II

Command Reference

Syntax	Description
virtual-mac-range	The range of virtual MAC addresses that can be assigned to the client. The valid range is 1 to 4095. This number sets the upper limit on the number of contiguous MAC addresses that make up the MAC address pool.
inbound-only	(Optional) When **inbound-only** is configured, the NCIA server cannot make an outgoing connection.
keepalive *seconds*	(Optional) Keepalive interval in seconds. The valid range is 0 to 1200. Setting the value to 0 turns the **keepalive** off.
tcp_keepalive *minutes*	(Optional) TCP keepalive processing interval in minutes. The valid range is 0 to 99 minutes. Setting the value to 0 stops TCP from sending keepalive packets when an NCIA client is idle. If no **tcp_keepalive** value is set, the default waiting period for TCP keepalive packets is 20 minutes.

Default

No NCIA server is configured.

Command Mode

Global configuration

Usage Guidelines

This command first appeared in Cisco IOS Release 11.2.

Before configuring an NCIA server, you must use the **dlsw local-peer** command to configure a DLSw+ local peer on this router. Depending on your network design, you may need to use the **ncia client** command to configure an NCIA client on this router (optional), or use the **ncia rsrb** command to configure an RSRB ring to associate with this router (optional).

If you use the **inbound-only** option, there is no need to configure any NCIA clients (the server does not make outgoing connections).

In a DSPU configuration, before a client can establish a connection to a downstream PU, such as a PC or workstation, the MAC address of the server (*server-virtual-mac-address*) must be defined at the PC or workstation as the destination MAC address. This MAC address appears as the server MAC address in the output of the **show ncia circuits** command.

Example

The following example configures an NCIA server on a Cisco router:

```
ncia server 1 10.2.20.4 4000.3174.0001 4000.0000.0001 128 keepalive 0 tcp_keepalive 0
```

Related Commands

To locate documentation of related commands, you can search online at www.cisco.com.

dlsw local-peer
ncia client
ncia rsrb

show ncia circuits

Use the **show ncia circuits** privileged EXEC command to display the state of all circuits involving this MAC address as a source and destination.

> **show ncia circuits** [*id-number*]

Syntax	Description
id-number	(Optional) Number assigned to identify the circuit. If no ID number is specified, the command lists information for all circuits.

Command Mode

Privileged EXEC

Usage Guidelines

This command first appeared in Cisco IOS Release 11.2.

Use the **show ncia client** command to list the active circuits by circuit ID number, then use a specific circuit ID number in the **show ncia circuits** command.

Sample Display

The following is sample output from the **show ncia circuits** command:

```
Router# show ncia circuits

IP              State                    ID       Mac              SAP CW  GP
10.2.20.125     START_DL_RCVD   (Client)10000000  1000.0000.0001   4   0   0
                                (Server)163D04    4000.1060.1000   4   10  0
```

Table 26-1 describes significant fields shown in the display.

Table 26-1 *show ncia circuits* Field Descriptions

Field	Description
IP	IP address of the client.
State	Communication state of the circuit.
ID	Circuit ID number. The server circuit ID is used by the server to identify a circuit. Use this ID in the **show ncia circuits** command. The client circuit ID is for information only.
Mac	Client MAC address is the MAC address used by the client; server MAC address is the MAC address used by the host. In a DSPU configuration, the server MAC address is the one defined in the **dspu ncia** command as *server-virtual-mac-address*.
SAP	Local address (LSAP), specified in the **dspu enable-pu** command
CW	Current Window, the number of packets that can be increased or decreased for each Increment or Decrement operation.
GP	Granted Packets, the number of packets the client or server is permitted to send to the other.

show ncia client

Use the **show ncia client** EXEC command to display the status of the NCIA client.

   show ncia client [**sap-list**] [*ip-address*]

Syntax	Description
sap-list	(Optional) Display the SAPs supported by the client. If the **sap-list** option is not specified, the command does not display SAP list information.
ip-address	(Optional) Client IP address. If no IP address is specified, the command lists information for all clients.

Command Mode
EXEC

Usage Guidelines
This command first appeared in Cisco IOS Release 11.2.

Use the **show ncia server** command to list the active clients by IP address, then use a specific IP address in the **show ncia client** command.

Sample Displays

The following are sample outputs from the **show ncia client** command:

```
Router# show ncia client

IP            State  MacAddr        Flags   Num SAP   PktRxd  PktTxd  Drop
10.2.20.123       4  1000.0000.0011 0x0800     3         27      36    0
    Circuit[1] : 791F8C
10.2.20.126       4  1000.0000.0011 0x0800     1         28      58    0
    Circuit[2] : 793500

Router# show ncia client sap-list 10.2.20.123

IP            Num SAPS  Sap List
10.2.20.123       3     4 8 c
```

Table 26-2 describes significant fields shown in the display.

Table 26-2 *show ncia client* Field Descriptions

Field	Description
IP	IP address of the client.
State	Communication state of the client. Possible values are: 0 CLOSED—Read and write pipe closed 1 OPEN_WAIT—Active open 2 CAP_WAIT—Waiting for a cap exchange request 3 CAP_NEG—Waiting for a cap exchange req/rsp 4 OPENED—Both pipes opened 5 BUSY—WAN Transport is congested 6 CLOSE_WAIT—Close connection 7 SHUTDOWN_PENDING—TCP, HOST or router shutdown
MacAddr	MAC address of the client.
Flags	Current operational status of the client. Possible values are: 0x0100—Client is configured 0x0200—Client is registered (a client connects to the server to register itself, and then disconnects) 0x0800—Client is active
Num SAP	The number of SAPs supported by this client. 0 indicates this client supports all SAPs.
PktRxd	Number of packets transmitted downstream from the server toward a client workstation.

Continues

Table 26-2   *show ncia client Field Descriptions (Continued)*

Field	Description
PktTxd	Number of packets the server received from a downstream client workstation.
Drop	Number of packets that should have been transmitted to a downstream client, but dropped by the server because the TCP connection has failed. Normally, no packets should be dropped.
Circuit[*n*]	The bracketed decimal indicates the order of the circuit in the list. The hexadecimal circuit ID is used by the server to identify a circuit. The circuit ID can be used to query circuit status in the **show ncia circuits** command.
SAP List	The list of SAPs supported by this client. A client can specify a maximum of 16 SAPs. If the "Num SAP" field is 0, no SAPs are displayed in this field.

show ncia server

Use the **show ncia server** EXEC command to display the state of the NCIA server.

show ncia server [*server-number*]

Syntax	Description
server-number	(Optional) NCIA server number. If no server number is specified, the command lists information for all servers.

Command Mode
EXEC

Usage Guidelines
This command first appeared in Cisco IOS Release 11.2.

Sample Display

The following is sample output from the **show ncia server** command:

```
Router# show ncia server

NCIA Server [1]:
    IP address: 10.2.20.4
    Server Virtual MAC address: 4000.3174.0001
    Starting MAC address: 1000.0000.0001
    MAC address range: 128
    Flags: 0x02
    Number of MAC addresses being used: 0
```

Table 26-3 describes significant fields shown in the display.

Table 26-3 *show ncia server Field Descriptions*

Field	Description
NCIA Server	Server number. Currently, only a single NCIA server is supported.
IP Address	Server IP address, used to accept incoming connections.
Server Virtual MAC Address	Virtual MAC address that represents this server.
Starting MAC Address	Virtual MAC address that begins the virtual MAC address pool range.
MAC Address Range	Virtual MAC address range that can be assigned to the NCIA client. This number sets the upper limit on the number of contiguous MAC addresses that make up the MAC address pool.
Flags	Current operational status of the NCIA server: 0x01: NCIA server is configured 0x02: NCIA server is running 0x03: NCIA server is configured and is running
Number of MAC addresses being used	Number of MAC addresses in the MAC address pool that have been assigned to clients. This number reflects connected clients that do not have their own MAC addresses and must be assigned one from the MAC address pool.

Configuring Cisco Mainframe Channel Connection Adapters

This chapter describes how to configure the Cisco Mainframe Channel Connection (CMCC) family of adapters. These adapters include the Channel Interface Processor (CIP) for Cisco 7500 and Cisco 7000 series routers, and the ESCON Channel Port Adapter (ECPA) and the Parallel Channel Port Adapter (PCPA) for Cisco 7200 series routers.

NOTE   In this chapter, references to Channel Port Adapter (CPA) correspond to both the ECPA and the PCPA.

For hardware technical descriptions and information about installing the router interfaces, refer to the hardware installation and maintenance publication for your product. For a complete description of the CMCC adapter commands in this chapter, refer to Chapter 28, "Cisco Mainframe Channel Connection Adapter Commands." To locate documentation of other commands that appear in this chapter, you can search online at www.cisco.com.

Cisco's Mainframe Channel Connection Adapters

The CMCC adapter family supports the IBM channel attachment and includes the following products:

- CIP on the Cisco 7000 and Cisco 7500 series routers

- ECPA on the Cisco 7200 series routers

- PCPA on the Cisco 7200 series routers

All CMCC adapters support the full range of channel software applications available in Cisco IOS software. (See Figure 27-1.)

Figure 27-1 *Cisco Mainframe Channel Connection Adapters*

CIP

The CIP for the Cisco 7000 and Cisco 7500 series is designed for high-end network environments that demand high-performance, high-port density, and high-capacity solutions.

The CIP provides support for the IBM ESCON Channel Adapter (ECA) and Bus-and-Tag Parallel Channel Adapter (PCA) channel-attached interfaces from Cisco 7000 series routers to IBM mainframes and in most cases, it eliminates the need for a separate front-end processor (FEP).

A single CIP can support up to two physical channel interfaces in any combination of either PCA or ECA. The CIP's Parallel channel interface is provided by the PCA, and the ESCON channel interface is provided by the ECA. Each CIP is preconfigured with the appropriate channel adapters at manufacturing time.

The Cisco 7000 and Cisco 7500 series routers support online insertion and removal (OIR), which allows you to install or remove CIPs while the system is operating.

Benefits

The key benefits of the CIP are as follows:

- Maximum throughput for every application—For the individual applications supported on the CIP, the CIP offers maximum throughput. For example, the number of users supported for TCP/IP offload is 10,000 and the number of LLC2 session supported is 8000.

- Scalability—The CIP supports up to 22 channel connections on Cisco 7000 and Cisco 7500 series router platforms.

- Multiple interface support—The CIP supports multiple ESCON and Bus-and-Tag channel interfaces.

- Higher memory capacity—The CIP offers a high memory capacity of 128 MB that can be useful for software applications utilizing a high number of sessions. An example of such an application is the TN3270 server.

- Port density—The CIP contains two channel interfaces, as compared to the CPA which offers one channel interface.

CPA

The CPA is available for the Cisco 7200 series routers. The CPA expands the value of Cisco's IBM channel solution by providing channel connectivity to mid-range mainframe configurations. The CPA is a standard single-width port adapter supporting ESCON or Parallel channel interfaces to IBM mainframes.

The only differences between CMCC software applications running on the CIP and a CPA are performance and capacity. The performance difference is based upon differences in the internal bus architecture of a CIP versus a CPA, and the capacity difference is based on the difference in maximum memory configurations (128 MB for CIP and 32 MB for CPA).

Each CPA provides a single channel interface for Cisco 7200-series routers. In some situations, this eliminates the need for a separate front-end processor (FEP). The CPA contains a single I/O connector.

The Cisco 7200-series router supports OIR, which allows you to install or remove port adapters while the system is operating.

Benefits

The key benefits of CPA are as follows:

- Cost-effective—Both a CPA and Cisco 7200-series router provide industry-leading price performance.

- Simplified migration path—The CPA and CIP microcode support the same features and applications, enabling seamless migration for network expansion.

- Flexibility—The Cisco 7200 series router platform provides a great number of features and capabilities that can be used in conjunction with a CPA.

ECPA

An ECPA is classified as a high-speed port adapter providing a single ESCON physical channel interface. Current Cisco 7200 configuration guidelines recommend using no more than three high-speed port adapters in a single Cisco 7200 router.

PCPA

A PCPA provides a single parallel channel physical interface supporting both 3.0 and 4.5 MBps data transfer rates.

Differences Between the CIP and CPA

Table 27-1 illustrates the differences between the CMCC adapters.

Table 27-1 *Differences Between the CIP and the CPA*

Product Differences	CIP	ECPA	PCPA
Router Platform	Cisco 7500 Cisco 7000 with RSP7000	Cisco 7200	Cisco 7200
Channel Interfaces	ESCON Parallel	ESCON	Parallel
Maximum Number of Interfaces	2	1	1
Maximum Memory	128 MB	32 MB	32 MB
Cisco IOS Release Support	Cisco IOS 10.2 and above	Cisco IOS 11.3(3)T and above	Cisco IOS 11.3(3)T and above
Virtual Port Adapter	2	0	0

Supported Environments

The CMCC adapters provide support for the environments discussed in the following sections:

- TCP/IP Environments Using CLAW

- TCP/IP Offload Environments

- IP Host Backup Environment

- TN3270 Server Environments

- Cisco SNA Environments

- Cisco MultiPath Channel Environments

TCP/IP Environments Using CLAW

TCP/IP mainframe protocol environments for IBM operating systems Multiple Virtual Storage (MVS) and Virtual Machine (VM) are supported. This support includes TCP/IP-based applications such as terminal emulation (Telnet), File Transfer Protocol (FTP), Simple Mail Transfer Protocol (SMTP); and Network File System (NFS), a distributed file access system. In addition, Internet Control Message Protocol (ICMP) and User Datagram Protocol (UDP) are supported.

Cisco IOS implements the Common Link Access to Workstation (CLAW) channel protocol to transport data between the mainframe and a CMCC adapter in TCP/IP environments. Each CLAW connection requires two devices out of a maximum of 256. Although this allows for a maximum of 128 CLAW connections per interface, a maximum of 32 CLAW connections per interface is recommended.

The CLAW packing feature enables the transport of multiple IP packets in a single channel operation and significantly increases throughput performance between a mainframe and a CMCC adapter. Currently, IBM's TCP/IP stack does not support the CLAW packing feature.

The CLAW packing feature requires changes to the mainframe CLAW driver support. In partnership with Cisco Systems, Interlink Computer Science has made the corresponding CLAW driver change to Cisco IOS for S/390 Release 2 and Interlink TCPaccess 5.2. Customers must make the necessary changes to their host configurations in order to enable the CLAW packing feature.

TCP/IP Offload Environments

TCP/IP mainframe protocol environments for IBM operating systems MVS, VM, and Transaction Processing Facility (TPF) are supported.

The TCP/IP offload feature for CMCC adapters delivers the same function as the TCP/IP offload function on the 3172 Interconnect Controller (Model 3), but with increased performance.

IP Host Backup Environment

You can connect multiple mainframes to a single CMCC adapter using a ESCON. Often, these mainframes run using the ESCON Multiple Image Facility (EMIF), which permits the physical machine to be divided into multiple logical partitions (LPARs). By defining an unused partition on another mainframe, a user can move the operating system from a failed mainframe or mainframe partition to the unused partition. By having multiple paths to each device, the move is accomplished without changing the mainframe software. This function also permits moving an IP stack between multiple operating system images.

On the CMCC adapter, each IP connection is treated as a physical device. The CMCC adapter does not support multiple active paths to a single IP connection (or device). Prior to IP Host Backup, the router configuration had to be changed whenever the mainframe operating system was moved from one mainframe or LPAR to another. The IP Host Backup feature permits the mainframe operating system to be moved from one mainframe to another without requiring a change to the router configuration at the time of the move.

NOTE   IP Host Backup does not provide single system image or automatic failover to a waiting
backup application. Host operator action on the mainframe is required in these instances.

TN3270 Server Environments

The TN3270 server feature on a CMCC adapter card provides mapping between an SNA 3270 host and
a TN3270 client connected to a TCP/IP network as shown in Figure 27-2. Functionally, it is useful to
view the TN3270 server from two different perspectives: SNA functions and Telnet Server functions.

- SNA Functions

  From the perspective of an SNA 3270 host connected to the CMCC adapter, the TN3270 server is
  an SNA device that supports multiple PUs, with each PU supporting up to 255 logical units (LUs).
  The LU can be Type 1, 2, or 3. The SNA host is unaware of the existence of the TCP/IP extension
  on the implementation of these LUs.

  The LUs implemented by TN3270 server are dependent LUs. To route these dependent LU sessions
  to multiple VTAM hosts connected to the TN3270 server in the CMCC adapter card, rather than
  routing in the VTAM hosts, the TN3270 server implements a SNA session switch with end node
  dependent LU requester (DLUR) function. Using the DLUR is optional so that the TN3270 server
  can be used with VTAM versions prior to version 4.2, which provide no Advanced Peer-to-Peer
  Networking (APPN) support.

  SNA session switch allows you to eliminate SNA subarea routing between hosts of TN3270 traffic
  by establishing APPN links with the primary LU hosts directly.

- Telnet Server Functions

  From the perspective of a TN3270 client, the TN3270 server is a high-performance Telnet server
  that supports Telnet connections, negotiation and data format. The server on the CMCC adapter
  card supports Telnet connection negotiation and data format as specified in RFC 1576 (referred to
  as "traditional TN3270") and RFC 1647 (referred to as "TN3270E").

Figure 27-2   *TN3270 Implementation*

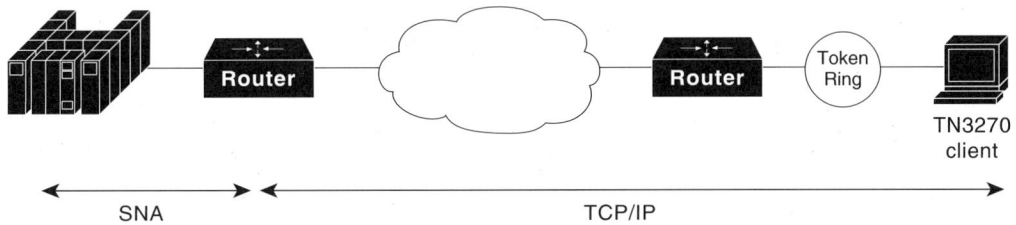

Unless the TN3270 server uses a Token Ring connection to a front-end processor (FEP) as its host connection, it will require CSNA or CMPC support. For this reason, TN3270 configuration issues and tasks begins in the section "Configure TN3270 on a CMCC Adapter," later in this chapter.

NOTE   To enable the TN3270 server feature, you must have a CMCC adapter installed in a Cisco 7000 with RSP7000, Cisco 7500 series router, or a Cisco 7200 router.

Cisco SNA Environments

The CSNA feature provides support for SNA protocols over both ESCON and Parallel interfaces to the IBM mainframe. As an IBM 3172 replacement, a CMCC adapter supports the External Communications Adapter (XCA) feature of Virtual Telecommunications Access Method (VTAM), which allows VTAM to define Token Ring devices attached to the 3172 as switched devices.

In SNA environments, support for the XCA feature of VTAM allows the CMCC adapter to provide an alternative to FEPs at sites where NCP is not required for SNA routing functions.

By providing CLS and the Logical Link Control type 2 (LLC2) protocol stack on the CMCC adapter card, all frames destined to the CMCC adapter or from the CMCC adapter card are switched by the router. The presentation of LAN media types allows the CSNA feature to take advantage of current source-route bridging (SRB), remote source-route bridging (RSRB), data-link switching plus (DLSw+), Source-Route Translational Bridging (SR/TLB), internal SDLC-LLC2 translational bridging (SDLLC), Qualified Logical Link Control (QLLC) services and APPN.

The CSNA feature supports the following communication through a Cisco 7000 with RSP7000, Cisco 7500, and Cisco 7200 series router:

● Communication between a channel-attached mainframe running VTAM and a LAN/WAN attached Physical Unit (PU) 2.0 SNA node

● Communication between a channel-attached mainframe running VTAM and a LAN/WAN attached PU 2.1 SNA node

● Communication between a channel-attached mainframe running VTAM and a LAN/WAN attached PU 5/4 SNA node

● Communication between two mainframes running VTAM channel-attached to the same CMCC adapter card or different CMCC adapter cards in a Cisco 7000 with RSP7000, Cisco 7500 series router, or a Cisco 7200 router

The CSNA feature provides SNA connectivity through Media Access Control (MAC) addresses configured for internal MAC adapters on the Cisco 7000 with RSP7000, Cisco 7500 series router and the Cisco 7200 series router. These internal MAC adapters correspond to XCA major node definitions in VTAM, providing access points (LAN gateway) to VTAM for SNA network nodes. The internal MAC adapters are configured to exist on internal LANs located on a CMCC adapter card. Each CMCC adapter card can be configured with multiple internal Token Ring LANs. Each internal Token Ring LAN must be configured to participate in source-route bridging. There is a maximum limit of 18 internal MAC adapters per CMCC adapter. The internal MAC adapter is an emulation of LAN adapters in an IBM 3172 Interconnect Controller.

Cisco MultiPath Channel Environments

The CMPC feature provides support for APPN connections using both High Performance Routing (HPR) and Intermediate Session Routing (ISR). It supports the VTAM Transport Resource List (TRL) major node and the VTAM Local SNA major node.

The CMPC feature can be used to establish an APPN connection between VTAM and the following APPN nodes:

● Another VTAM channel attached to the same CMCC adapter

● Another VTAM channel attached to a different CMCC adapter in the same router

● TN3270 server DLUR in the same CMCC adapter

● An APPN network node (NN) in the router with the CMCC adapter

● Other APPN nodes external to the CMCC adapter and router with the CMCC adapter: CS/2, AS/400, other LAN or WAN attached VTAM nodes

The CMPC feature isolates VTAM from the actual network topology. The MPC protocol is terminated on the CMCC adapter and converted to LLC protocols. Once converted to LLC protocols other Cisco features are used to connect VTAM to other APPN nodes in the network. CMPC can be used with DLSw+, RSRB, SR/TLB, SRB, SDLLC, QLLC, ATM LAN emulation, and FRAS host to provide connectivity to VTAM.

CMCC Adapter Interface Configuration Task List

You can perform the tasks in the following sections to configure and maintain IBM channel attach interfaces.

Some CMCC adapter software features are configured on a *virtual port*. On the CIP adapter cards installed in a Cisco 7000 with RSP 7000 or a Cisco 7500 series router, there are up to two physical ports, numbered 0 and 1, and a virtual port, numbered 2. However, on the CPA installed in a Cisco 7200 series router, the single physical port and the virtual port are configured using the same port number ID, number 0.

Not all tasks are required. Your CMCC adapter image may be preloaded. You must select an interface, after which you configure the features you want supported on that interface.

NOTE   You can configure a CMCC adapter interface for any or all of the supported environments. If you want only CSNA support, for example, you need not configure TCP/IP support.

- Load the CMCC Adapter Microcode Image
- Select the Interface
- Configure TCP/IP CLAW or CLAW Packing Support
- Configure TCP/IP Offload Support
- Configure TN3270 on a CMCC Adapter
- Configure CSNA Support
- Configure the CMCC Adapters for IP Host Backup
- Select Host System Parameters
- Monitor and Maintain the Interface
- Configure TN3270 on a CMCC Adapter

See the end of this chapter for "CMCC Interface Configuration Examples."

Because the TN3270 server configuration is performed after an interface is configured for CSNA support, TN3270 configuration issues and tasks are addressed separately from the interface configuration tasks. The TN3270 configuration task list begins in the section "TN3270 Configuration Task List," later in this chapter.

Load the CMCC Adapter Microcode Image

This section provides information on loading the microcode images for the CIP and CPA.

CIP Microcode Image

Beginning with Cisco IOS Software Release 11.1, the CIP microcode (or CIP *image*) no longer is bundled with Cisco IOS software. You must have Flash memory installed on the Route Switch Processor (RSP) card to use the IBM channel attach features in Cisco IOS Software Release 11.1 and later.

The CIP image is preloaded on Flash cards for all Cisco 7000 with RSP7000 and Cisco 7500 series routers ordered with the CIP option for Cisco IOS Software Release 11.1 and later. Use the commands in this section if you are upgrading the CIP image in your router.

To prepare the CIP, use the following commands beginning in privileged EXEC command mode:

Step	Command	Purpose
1	**enable**	Enters the privileged EXEC mode command interpreter.
2	**copy tftp flash** **copy tftp slot0:** (Flash card) **copy tftp slot1:** (Flash card on 7500 series router) **copy tftp bootflash:** (onboard Flash on 7500 series router)	Copies the CIP image from a server to the Flash memory. Use the appropriate command for your system. You must be running Cisco IOS Release 11.1 or later prior to executing a **copy tftp** command.
3	**configure terminal**	In privileged command mode, enters router configuration mode and specifies that the console terminal will be the source of the configuration subcommands.
4	**microcode cip flash bootflash:***cipxxx-yy* or **microcode cip flash slot** *n:cipxx-yy*	Configures your router to load the Flash image to the CIP: • Enters global configuration mode and specifies that the CIP microcode load from a Flash card in router slot *n* or from embedded Flash. • Loads the image from Flash to the CIP card.
5	**microcode reload**	Forces a microcode reload in router configuration mode.
6	**end**	Exits configuration mode.
7	**copy running-config startup-config**	Saves the running configuration as the new startup configuration in NVRAM.
8	**show controllers cbus**	Exits configuration mode and display images loaded on the CIP card.

Step	Command	Purpose
9	**show running-config**	Verifies the contents of the configuration file.
10	**show microcode**	Shows the microcode images for downloadable hardware.

CPA Microcode Image

The CPA microcode image is preloaded on Flash memory cards for Cisco 7200 series routers for Cisco IOS Release 11.3(3)T and later. You may be required to copy a new image to Flash memory when a new microcode image becomes available. Use the commands in this section if you are upgrading or loading a microcode image other than the default.

To prepare the CPA, use the following commands beginning in privileged EXEC command mode:

Step	Command	Purpose
1	**enable**	Enters the privileged EXEC mode command interpreter.
2	**copy tftp:**_filename_ [**bootflash**	**slot0:**	**slot1:**]_filename_	Copies the CPA microcode image from a server to either of the Flash memory cards. The source of the file is **tftp:**_filename_.
3	**configure terminal**	In privileged command mode, enters router configuration mode and specifies that the console terminal will be the source of the configuration subcommands.
4	**microcode** {**ecpa**	**pcpa**} _filename_	To load the microcode from an individual microcode image that is stored as a file on a Flash memory card, enter the **microcode** command, the processor type, the specific memory location of the CPA microcode image, and the exact argument for _filename_.
5	**microcode reload** or **microcode reload** {**all**	{ { **ecpa**	**pcpa** } **slot** _number_}}	Loads the specified CPA image from router configuration mode or Forces a microcode reload in privileged EXEC mode, without entering global configuration mode.
6	**end**	Exits configuration mode.
7	**copy running-config startup-config**	Saves the running configuration as the new startup configuration in NVRAM.

Step	Command	Purpose
8	**show controllers channel** *slot/port*	Verifies that the correct microcode is loaded according to the new instructions. The display indicates the currently loaded and running microcode version for each CPA display software and hardware information for the CPAs in your router.
9	**show running-config**	Verifies the contents of the configuration file.
10	**show microcode**	Shows the microcode images for downloadable hardware.

Select the Interface

Before you configure your channel attach interface, you must select the interface. Use the following command in global configuration mode:

Command	Purpose
interface channel *slot/port*	Selects the channel attach interface and enters interface configuration mode.

Use the **show extended channel** EXEC commands to display current CMCC adapter status. This command provides a report for each interface configured to support IBM channel attach.

Configure TCP/IP CLAW or CLAW Packing Support

The following sections describe how to configure CLAW support. This feature is configured on the physical interface. All tasks, except for configuring other interface support are required.

● Assign an IP Address

● Configure the IBM Channel Attach Interface

● Select a Data Rate for the Parallel Channel Interfaces

● Configure Other Interface Support

See the section "Select Host System Parameters" for guidelines on matching interface configuration values with host system values.

Assign an IP Address

You must assign an IP address to the channel interface so that it can communicate with other devices (or tasks) on the network. The IP address you assign to the interface must be in the same subnetwork as the hosts with which you wish to communicate.

To assign an IP address, use the following command in interface configuration mode:

Command	Purpose
ip address *address mask*	Assigns an IP address and network mask to the selected interface.

Configure the IBM Channel Attach Interface

You must define the devices, or tasks, supported on the interface. Some information you need to perform this task is derived from the following host system configuration files: MVSIOCP, IOCP, and the TCPIP configuration. Refer to the section "Select Host System Parameters" for guidelines on matching interface configuration values with host system values.

To configure an IBM channel interface, use the following command in interface configuration mode:

Command	Purpose
claw *path device-address ip-address host-name device-name host-app device-app* [**broadcast**] [**backup**]	Defines the CLAW parameters for this device.

The CLAW Packing feature requires changes to the mainframe CLAW driver support. In partnership with Cisco Systems, Interlink Computer Science has made the corresponding CLAW driver change to Cisco IOS software for S/390 Release 2 and Interlink TCPaccess 5.2. Configuration parameters in the host TCP/IP applications must change to enable the CLAW packing feature.

See the section "CMCC Interface Configuration Examples" for samples of **claw** commands for different configurations.

Select a Data Rate for the Parallel Channel Interfaces

When you configure a Parallel channel attach interface, you must define a data rate of either 3 MBPS or 4.5 MBPS.

To select a data rate, use the following command in interface configuration mode:

Command	Purpose
channel-protocol [s | s4]	Defines the Parallel data transfer rate.

Configure Other Interface Support

To enhance the usefulness of IBM channel attach support, you can further define how the interface and the router interoperate by using the following commands in interface configuration mode:

Step	Command	Purpose
1	**ip route-cache same-interface**	Includes fast switching support for multiple IP datagram applications running on the same CMCC adapter, as required.
2	**no ip redirects**	Always include this command when configuring host-to-host communications through the same interface.

Configure TCP/IP Offload Support

The following sections describe how to configure the IBM channel attach interface for TCP/IP offload support. All tasks, except for configuring other interface support, are required:

● Assign an IP Address

● Configure the IBM Channel Attach Interface

● Select a Data Rate for the Parallel Channel Interfaces

● Configure Other Interface Support

See the section "Select Host System Parameters" for guidelines on matching interface configuration values with host system values.

Assign an IP Address

You must assign an IP address to the channel interface so that it can communicate with other devices (or tasks) on the network. The IP address you assign to the interface must be in the same subnetwork as the hosts with which you wish to communicate.

To assign an IP address, use the following command in interface configuration mode:

Command	Purpose
ip address *address mask*	Assigns an IP address and network mask to the selected interface.

Configure the IBM Channel Attach Interface

You must define the devices, or tasks supported on the interface. Some information you need to perform this task is derived from the following host system configuration files: MVSIOCP, IOCP, and the

TCP/IP configuration. Refer to the section "Select Host System Parameters" for guidelines on matching interface configuration values with host system values.

To configure the IBM channel interface, use the following command in interface configuration mode:

Command	Purpose
offload *path device-address ip-address host-name device-name host-app device-app host-link device-link* [**broadcast**] [**backup**]	Defines the offload parameters for this device.

See the section "CMCC Interface Configuration Examples" for samples of **offload** commands for different configurations.

Select a Data Rate for the Parallel Channel Interfaces

When you configure a Parallel channel attach interface, you must define a data rate of either 3 MB per second or 4.5 MB per second.

To select a data rate, use the following command in interface configuration mode:

Command	Purpose
**channel-protocol [s	s4]**	Defines the Parallel data transfer rate.

Configure Other Interface Support

You can further define how the interface and the router interoperate. You can use the following commands in interface configuration mode to enhance the usefulness of IBM channel attach support:

Step	Command	Purpose
1	**ip route-cache same-interface**	Includes autonomous switching support for multiple IP datagram applications running on the same CMCC adapter, as required.
2	**no ip redirects**	Always include this command when configuring host-to-host communications through the same ESCON interface.

Configure CSNA Support

The following sections describe how to configure the IBM channel attach interface for CSNA support. This procedures requires the configuration of both the physical and virtual interfaces. The last task, "Configure an Internal Adapter's Link Characteristics," is optional. All other tasks are required.

- Select a Data Rate for the Parallel Channel Interfaces
- Configure the Subchannel Information
- Configure the Internal LAN
- Configure the Source Bridge
- Configure Internal Adapters
- Name the Internal Adapter
- Configure an Internal Adapter's Link Characteristics

Select a Data Rate for the Parallel Channel Interfaces

When you configure a Parallel channel attach interface, you must define a data rate of either 3 MBps or 4.5 MBps.

To configure the data rate, use the following command in interface configuration mode:

Command	Purpose
channel-protocol [s | s4]	Defines the Parallel data transfer rate.

Configure the Subchannel Information

To define an SNA subchannel supported by the CSNA feature, use the following command in interface configuration mode for the physical channel interface:

Command	Purpose
csna *path device* [**maxpiu** *value*] [**time-delay** *value*] [**length-delay** *value*]	Defines the CSNA subchannel device.

Configure the Internal LAN

To configure an internal LAN, use the following commands beginning in global configuration mode:

Step	Command	Purpose
1	**interface channel** *slot/port*	Selects the virtual interface.
2	**lan tokenring** *lan-id*	Selects the internal LAN interface and enters internal LAN configuration mode.

Configure the Source Bridge

Select the bridging characteristics for the internal LAN. Use the following commands in internal LAN configuration mode:

Command	Purpose
source-bridge *local-ring bridge-number target-ring*	Selects SRB for the selected LAN interface.

Configure Internal Adapters

To select or configure an internal adapter, use the following command in internal LAN configuration mode:

Command	Purpose
adapter *adapno mac-address*	Selects the internal adapter to configure.

Name the Internal Adapter

Select a name for the internal adapter. Use the following command in internal adapter configuration mode:

Command	Purpose
name *name*	Selects a name for the internal adapter.

Configure an Internal Adapter's Link Characteristics

To configure the LLC link characteristics of an internal adapter, use the following optional commands in internal adapter configuration mode:

Command	Purpose
llc2 N1 *bytes*	Maximum size of an I-frame in bytes.
llc2 N2 *retry-count*	Maximum retry count.
llc2 Nw *window-size-increase*	Increases the window size for consecutive good I-frame received (zero is disabled).
llc2 ack-delay-time *milliseconds*	Maximum time for incoming I-frames to stay unacknowledged.
llc2 ack-max *frame-count*	Maximum number of I-frames received before an acknowledgment must be sent.
llc2 idle-time *milliseconds*	Frequency of polls during periods of idle traffic.
llc2 local-window *frame-count*	Maximum number of I-frames to send before waiting for an acknowledgment.
llc2 recv-window *frame-count*	Receives window.
llc2 t1-time *milliseconds*	Specifies amount of time to wait for an acknowledgment to transmit I-frames.
llc2 busy-time *milliseconds*	Amount of time to wait while the other LLC2 station is in a busy state before attempting to poll the remote station.
llc2 tpf-time *milliseconds*	Amount of time to wait for a final response to a poll frame before resending the original poll frame.
llc2 trej-time *milliseconds*	Amount of time to wait for resending a rejected frame before sending the reject command.

Configure the CMCC Adapters for IP Host Backup

The following sections describe how to configure the IBM channel attach interface for IP Host Backup support. With IP Host Backup, you can configure a backup group for each CLAW or offload device, one path at a time, or you can specify a group of IP host paths and then configure which CLAW or offload IP addresses are used with those paths. Using the second method, specifying paths, provides a shortcut to the one at a time method.

- Configure a CLAW IP Host Backup Group
- Configure an Offload IP Host Backup Group
- Configure an IP Host Backup Group Using Paths

Configure a CLAW IP Host Backup Group

You must define the devices, or tasks, supported on the interface. Some information you need to perform this task is derived from the following host system configuration files: MVSIOCP, IOCP, and the TCPIP configuration.

To configure the CLAW IP Host Backup, use the following command in interface configuration mode:

Command	Purpose
claw *path device-address ip-address host-name device-name host-app device-app* [**broadcast**] **backup**	Defines the CLAW parameters for this device.

See the section "Configuration Tasks" for samples of **claw** commands for different configurations.

Configure an Offload IP Host Backup Group

You must define the devices, or tasks supported on the interface. Some information you need to perform this task is derived from the following host system configuration files: MVSIOCP, IOCP, and the TCP/IP configuration.

To configure the Offload IP Host backup, use the following command in interface configuration mode to configure an Offload device (read and write subchannel) for communication with a mainframe TCP/IP stack in Offload mode:

Command	Purpose
offload *path device-address ip-address host-name device-name host-ip-link device-ip-link host-api-link device-api-link* [**broadcast**] **backup**	Defines the offload parameters for this device.

See the section "Configuration Tasks" for samples of **offload** commands for different configurations.

Configure an IP Host Backup Group Using Paths

You can define a backup group by specifying a path, or group of paths, that are used as the IP Host Backup. Under the backup group, you can have multiple backup connections defined that all use the same IP address.

To configure the IP Host Backup using paths, use the following commands beginning in interface configuration mode:

1	Command	Purpose
2	**path** *path* [[*path* ...]]	Defines the backup path, or paths, for this group and enter IP Host Backup configuration mode.
3	**claw** *device-address ip-address host-name device-name host-app device-app* [**broadcast**]	Defines the CLAW parameters for this device.
4	**offload** *path device-address ip-address host-name device-name host-ip-link device-ip-link host-api-link device-api-link* [**broadcast**]	Alternatively, you can define the offload parameters for this device.
5	**exit**	Exits IP Host Backup configuration mode and return to interface configuration mode.

Select Host System Parameters

This section describes how to correlate values found in the VM and MVS system I/O configuration program (IOCP) files with the fields in the **claw**, **csna**, **cmpc**, and **offload** interface configuration commands. In addition, for CLAW and Offload, you will need configuration information from the host TCP/IP application configuration file. Refer to the following IBM operating system manuals for specific IOCP configuration statement details:

- *Transmission Control Protocol/Internet Protocol TCP/IP Version 2 Release 2.1 for MVS: Planning and Customization*, SC31-6085 (or later version)

- *Transmission Control Protocol/Internet Protocol TCP/IP Version 2 Release 2 for VM: Planning and Customization*, SC31-6082 (or later version)

Values from the Host IOCP File

When you define CLAW or offload parameters, you must supply path information and device address information to support routing on an IBM channel. The path information can be simple, in the case of a channel directly attached to a router, or more challenging when the path includes an ESCON director switch or multiple image facility support.

The *path* argument is a concatenation of three hexadecimal numbers that represent the values listed in Table 27-2.

Table 27-2 *CLAW Path Argument Values*

CLAW Path Argument Breakdown	Values	Description
Path	01–FF	For a directly attached ESCON channel or any Parallel channel, this value is 01 unless the system administrator has configured another value.
		For a channel attached through an ESCON director switch, this value will be the path that, from Cisco IOS software point of view, exits the switch and attaches to the host.
Channel logical address	0–F	For a Parallel channel, this value is 0. For a directly attached ESCON channel, the value may be non-zero.
		If the host is running in Logical Partition (LPAR) mode and the CHPID is defined as shared, this is the partition number associated with the devices configured in the IOCP.
		The default for this part of the path argument is 0.
		Otherwise, the channel logical address associated with the channel is defined in the IOCP.
Control unit logical address	0–F	For a Parallel channel, this value is 0. For a directly attached ESCON channel, the value may be non-zero.
		If this value is specified in the IOCP, match that value here.
		Otherwise, the control unit logical address is specified in the IOCP CNTLUNIT statement for the host channel in the CUADD parameter.

In Figure 27-3, two host systems connect to the ESCON director switch on paths 23 and 29. The channels both exit the switch on path 1B and attach to Router A.

Figure 27-3   *System with an ESCON Director Switch and a Directly Attached Channel*

Note that the path between Host A and Host B is dynamically switched within the ESCON director. A third host is attached directly to Router B through path 42.

The IOCP control unit statements would look similar to the following examples:

- Host A

```
CNTLUNIT CUNUMBER=0001, PATH=(23), LINK=1B, UNITADD=((00,64)), UNIT=SCTC, CUADD=F
```

- Host B

```
CNTLUNIT CUNUMBER=0002, PATH=(29), LINK=1B, UNITADD=((00,64)), UNIT=SCTC, CUADD=A
```

- Host C

```
CNTLUNIT CUNUMBER=000A, PATH=(42), UNIT=SCTC, UNITADD=((00,64))
```

The system administrator can provide you with the values. For example the ESCON director ports 15 and 19 in Figure 27-3 are the channel attachments from the ESCON director to each host. Given these values, the **claw** command *path* argument for the two channel attachments to Router A becomes:

```
claw 150F
claw 190A
```

The **offload** command *path* argument for the two channel attachments to Router A becomes:

```
offload 150F
offload 190A
```

The **claw** command *path* argument for the directly attached channel to Router B is easy to determine:

```
claw 0100
```

Similarly, the **offload** command *path* argument for the directly attached channel to Router B is as follows:

```
offload 0100
```

Next, determine the **claw**, **csna**, **cmpc**, or **offload** command *device-address* argument value, which is shown as 00 in the UNITADD parameter for all three devices. Based on the above example, this value can be any even value.

The UNITADD parameter in the CNTLUNIT macro of the IOCP file defines the valid range for device addresses. In the example above, a UNITADD parameter of (00,64) means that the first valid device address is 00 and the number of devices is 64 for a range of 00 to 63. In the hexadecimal notation used by channel configuration commands this translates to a range of 00 to 3F.

The **claw** (or **offload**) commands now become:

● Router A (for the **claw** command)

```
claw 150F 00
claw 190A 00
```

● Router A (for the **offload** command)

```
offload 150F 00
offload 190A 00
```

● Router B (for the **claw** command)

```
claw 0100 02
```

● Router B (for the **offload** command)

```
offload 0100 02
```

Values from the Host TCP/IP File

The remainder of the **claw** and **offload** command arguments are derived from the DEVICE, LINK, and HOME statements in the host TCP/IP configuration files. The **csna** and **cmpc** configuration commands include only path and device. The statements will be similar to the following:

● Host A

```
DEVICE EVAL CLAW 500 VMSYSTEM C7000 NONE  20  20 4096 4096
LINK EVAL1 IP 0 EVAL
HOME 198.92.2.12    EVAL1
```

● Host B

```
DEVICE EVAL CLAW 600 STSYSTEM C7000 NONE  20  20 4096 4096
LINK EVAL1 IP 0 EVAL
HOME 198.92.2.13    EVAL1
```

- Host C

```
DEVICE EVAL CLAW 700 RDUSYSTM C7000 NONE  20  20 4096 4096
LINK EVAL1 IP 0 EVAL
HOME 198.92.2.14    EVAL1
```

The DEVICE statement lists the *host-name* and *device-name* values to use, which follows the CLAW 500 entry in the DEVICE statement.

The LINK statement links the device name, EVAL, to EVAL1. The IP address for EVAL1 appears in the HOME statement.

Based on this example, you can supply the remainder of the arguments for the sample **claw** commands:

- Router A

```
claw 150F 00 198.92.2.12 VMSYSTEM C7000 TCPIP TCPIP
claw 190A 00 198.92.2.13 STSYSTEM C7000 TCPIP TCPIP
```

- Router B

```
claw 0100 02 198.92.2.14 RDUSYSTM C7000 TCPIP TCPIP
```

Similarly, the sample **offload** commands are as follows:

- Router A

```
offload 150F 00 198.92.2.12 VMSYSTEM C7000 TCPIP TCPIP TCPIP API
offload 190A 00 198.92.2.13 STSYSTEM C7000 TCPIP TCPIP TCPIP API
```

- Router B

```
offload 0100 02 198.92.2.14 RDUSYSTM C7000 TCPIP TCPIP TCPIP API
```

Example of a Derived Value

When you have a directly attached channel, the system administrator may provide you with a system IODEVICE ADDRESS that you can use. In this case, you must work backwards through the IOCP file to locate the proper *device-address* argument value for the **claw** command.

In this first example, the IODEVICE ADDRESS value is 800. Using this number, you locate the IODEVICE ADDRESS statement in the IOCP file, which points you to the CNTLUNIT statement that contains the *device-address* argument value for the **claw**, **csna**, **cmpc,** or **offload** command:

```
IODEVICE ADDRESS=(0800,256),CUNUMBR=(0012),UNIT=SCTC
**** Address 800 points to CUNUMBR 0012 in the following statement

CNTLUNIT CUNUMBR=0012,PATH=(28),UNIT=SCTC,UNITADD=((00,256))
**** The device-address is the UNITADD value of 00
```

From this example, the **claw** command would be similar to the following:

```
claw 0100 00 197.91.2.12 CISCOVM EVAL TCPIP TCPIP
```

In the next example, the system administrator has given you an IODEVICE ADDRESS of 350, which does not correspond exactly to a value in the IOCP file. In this instance, you must calculate an offset *device-address* argument value for the **claw** or **offload** command:

```
IODEVICE ADDRESS=(0340,64),CUNUMBR=(0008),UNIT=SCTC
IODEVICE ADDRESS=(0380,64),CUNUMBR=(0009),UNIT=SCTC
**** Address 350 (340 + 10) is in the range covered by CUNUMBER 0008

CNTLUNIT CUNUMBR=0008,PATH=(24),UNIT=SCTC,UNITADD=((40,64)),SHARED=N, X
**** The device-address is the UNITADD value of 40, offset by 10
**** The device-address to use is 50
```

From this example, the **claw** command would be similar to the following:

```
claw 0100 50 197.91.2.12 CISCOVM EVAL TCPIP TCPIP
```

NOTE   In the IOCP examples for the IODEVICE and CNTLUNIT statements, UNIT=SCTC is the usual value for ESCON channels. Parallel channels will have UNIT=3088 in the CNTLUNIT statement and UNIT=CTC in the IODEVICE statement.

CAUTION   When you are running MVS, you must disable the missing interrupt handler (MIH) to avoid introducing errors into the CLAW algorithm. Refer to the IBM publication *Transmission Control Protocol/Internet Protocol TCP/IP Version 2 Release 2.1 for MVS: Planning and Customization* (publication SC31-6085 or later) for information on disabling the MIH.

Monitor and Maintain the Interface

You can perform the tasks in the following sections to monitor and maintain the interfaces:

- Monitor Interface Status
- Clear and Reset an Interface
- Shut Down and Restart an Interface
- Run CMCC Adapter Interface Loopback Diagnostics
- Configure CMCC Adapter Core Dump

Monitor Interface Status

The software allows you to display information about the interface, including the version of the software and the hardware, the controller status, and statistics about the interfaces. The following table lists some of the interface monitoring commands. To display the full list of **show** commands, enter **show ?** at the EXEC prompt.

Perform the following commands in EXEC mode to display information associated with each command. All commands are applicable to all CMCC adapter interfaces (CIP and CPA), unless it is mentioned that they are specific to a particular CMCC adapter. Commands are listed in alphabetic order.

Command	Purpose
show controllers cbus	Displays the cbus internal state for the Cisco 7000 with RSP7000 and Cisco 7500 series routers. Also included in the display is CIP-specific information such as the currently loaded microcode, currently loaded microcode application segments, and load metrics.
show controllers channel [*slot/port*]	Displays CPA-specific information, including the currently loaded microcode.
show extended channel *slot/port* **backup** [*ip-address*]	Displays information about CLAW and offload commands for each backup group.
show extended channel *slot/port* **cmpc** [*path* [*device*]]	Displays information about each CMPC subchannel configured on the specified CMCC adapter interface.
show extended channel *slot/port* **connection-map llc2**	Displays the number of active LLC2 connections for each SAP and the mapping of the internal MAC adapter and the SAP to the resource that activated the SAP.
show extended channel *slot/port* **csna** [**admin** | **oper** | **stats**] [*path* [*device*]]	Displays information about the CSNA subchannels configured on the specified CMCC adapter interface.
show extended channel *slot/port* **llc2** [**admin** | **oper** | **stats**] [*lmac* [*lsap* [*rmac* [*rsap*]]]]	Displays information about the LLC2 sessions running on the CMCC adapter interfaces.
show extended channel *slot/port* **max-llc2-sessions**	Displays information about the number of LLC2 sessions supported on the CMCC adapter.
show extended channel *slot/port* **icmp-stack** [*ip-address*]	Displays information about the ICMP stack running on the CMCC adapter interfaces.
show extended channel *slot/port* **ip-stack** [*ip-address*]	Displays information about the IP stack running on the CMCC adapter interfaces
show extended channel *slot/port* **llc2** [**admin** | **oper** | **stats**] [*lmac* [*lsap* [*rmac* [*rsap*]]]]	Displays information about the LCC2 sessions running on the CMCC adapter interfaces.
show extended channel *slot/port* **packing names** [*path* [*device*]]	Displays CLAW packing names and their connection state.

Command	Purpose
show extended channel *slot/port* **packing stats** [*path*[*device*]]	Displays CLAW packing statistics.
show extended channel *slot/port* **statistics** [*path* [*device*]] [**connected**]	Displays information about CMCC adapter interfaces for diagnostic purposes.
show extended channel *slot/port* **subchannel** [**connected**]	Displays information about the CMCC adapter interfaces
show extended channel *slot/port* **tcp-connections** [[*loc-ip-addr* [*loc-port* [*rem-ip-addr* [*rem-port*]]] [**detail** | **summary**]	Displays information about the TCP sockets on a channel interface.
show extended channel *slot/port* **tcp-stack** [*ip-address*]	Displays information about the TCP stack running on the CMCC adapter interfaces.
show extended channel *slot/port* **tg** [**oper** | **stats**] [**detailed**] [*tg-name*]	Displays configuration, operational, and statistics information for CMPC transmission groups configured on a specified CMCC adapter internal LAN interface.
show extended channel *slot/port* **tn3270-server**	Displays current configuration parameters and the status of the PUs defined in each TN3270 server.
show extended channel *slot/port* **tn3270-server client-ip-address** *ip-address* [**disconnected** | **in-session** | **pending**]	Displays information about all clients at a specific IP address.
show extended channel *slot/port* **tn3270-server dlur**	Displays information about the SNA session switch.
show extended channel *slot/port* **tn3270-server dlurlink** *name*	Displays information about the DLUIR components.
show extended channel *slot/port* **tn3270-server nailed-ip** *ip-address*	Displays mappings between a nailed client IP address and nailed LUs.
show extended channel *slot/port* **tn3270-server pu** *pu-name*	Displays the PU configuration parameters, statistics, and all the LUs currently attached to the PU.
show extended channel *slot/port* **tn3270-server pu** *pu-name* **lu** *locaddr* [history]	Displays information about the TN3270 server LUs running on CMCC adapter interfaces.
show extended channel *slot/port* **udp-listeners** [*ip-address*]	Displays information about the UDP listener sockets on the CMCC adapter interfaces.
show extended channel *slot/port* **udp-stack** [*ip-address*]	Displays information about the UDP stack running on the CMCC adapter interfaces.
show interfaces channel *slot/port* **accounting**	Displays the number of packets for each protocol type that has been sent through the channel interface.
show version	Displays the hardware configuration, software version, names and sources of configuration files, and boot images.

Clear and Reset an Interface

To clear the interface counters shown with the **show interfaces** command, use the following command in EXEC mode:

Command	Purpose
clear counters [*type slot/port*]	Clears interface counters for router.

NOTE   This command will not clear counters retrieved using SNMP, but only those seen with the EXEC **show interfaces** command.

To clear the counters associated with application features configured on the CMCC adapters, use the following command in EXEC mode:

Command	Purpose
clear extended counters channel *slot/port* [**csna** | **icmp-stack** | **ip-stack** | **llc2** | **statistics** | **tcp-connections** | **tcp-stack** | **tg** | **tn3270-server** | **udp-stack**]	Clears counters for application features configured on CMCC adapters.

NOTE   This command will not clear counters retrieved using SNMP, but only those seen with the EXEC **show extended channel** commands.

Use the following command in EXEC mode to clear and reset interfaces. Under normal circumstances, you do not need to clear the hardware logic on interfaces.

Command	Purpose
clear interface *type slot/port*	Resets the hardware logic on an interface.

Shut Down and Restart an Interface

You can disable an interface. Doing so disables all functions on the specified interface and marks the interface as unavailable on all monitoring command displays. This information is communicated to other network servers through all dynamic routing protocols. The interface will not be mentioned in any routing updates. On the CMCC adapter with ESCON interface, a command is sent to the host to inform it of the impending shutdown. On the CMCC adapter's Parallel interface, the **shutdown** command disables the adapter card's transceivers and the interface stops responding to all commands.

For the following reasons, it is recommended that channel interfaces be shut down:

- For a CMCC adapter's ESCON interface, you may want to change the interface type of a Cisco 7000 with RSP7000 or Cisco 7500 port online. To ensure that the system recognizes the new interface type, shut down the interface, then reenable it after changing the interface. Refer to your hardware documentation for more details.

- If you want to reload the router.

- If, prior to reloading the microcode, you want to shut down the interface.

- If you want to power off the router.

- If it is recommended that channel interfaces be shut down.

To shut down an interface and then restart it, use the following commands in interface configuration mode:

Step	Command	Purpose
1	**shutdown**	Shuts down an interface.
2	**no shutdown**	Reenables an interface.

To check whether an interface is disabled, use the EXEC command **show interfaces**. An interface that has been shut down is shown as administratively down in the **show interfaces** command display.

Run CMCC Adapter Interface Loopback Diagnostics

The CMCC adapter does not provide software loopback support. You can use special loopback wrap plugs to perform hardware loopback with the ESCON and Parallel channel interfaces. Hardware loopback information is included in the hardware installation notes for the CMCC adapters.

Configure CMCC Adapter Core Dump

To obtain the output of a CMCC adapter core dump, use the following commands in global configuration mode:

Step	Command	Purpose
1	**ip domain-name** *name*	Configures the router FTP services.
	ip name-server *address*	
	ip ftp username *name*	
	ip ftp password *password*	
2	**exception slot** [*slot*] *protocol//:host/filename*	Configures the CMCC adapter core dump feature.

NOTE   The exception slot command is only supported on the Cisco 7000 with RSP7000 and Cisco 7500 series routers. On the Cisco 7200 series routers, only FTP is supported.

While the router is running, you can use the **write** EXEC command to write the contents of a CMCC adapter that is not halted.

Command	Purpose
write	Writes the contents of a CMCC adapter.

NOTE   The output obtained by the **exception slot** command can be interpreted by a qualified Cisco technical support person.

Configure TN3270 on a CMCC Adapter

The following sections describe additional features of TN3270 server support on the CMCC adapter.

- Dynamic LU Allocation

- Formation of LU Model Type and Number

- Specific LU Allocation

- SNA Switching—End Node DLUR

- Multiple Hosts Support

- IP Type of Service and Precedence Setting

You will also need to understand the following information before proceeding with TN3270 configuration tasks:

- VTAM Host Configuration Considerations for Dynamic LU Allocation
- LU Address Mapping
- TN3270 Configuration Modes

Dynamic LU Allocation

This will be the most common form of request from TN3270 clients emulating a TN3270 terminal. The user typically wants to specify emulating a particular terminal type and normally is not interested in what LOCADDR or LU name is allocated by the host, as long as a network solicitor logon menu is presented. The server will perform the following on such a session request:

- Form an EBCDIC string based on the model type and number requested by the client (see "Formation of LU Model Type and Number" on the algorithm used). This string is used as a field in a Reply product set ID (PSID) network management vector transport (NMVT).

- Allocate a LOCADDR from the next available LU in the generic LU pool. This LOCADDR is used in the NMVT.

- Send the formatted Reply PSID NMVT to VTAM.

When VTAM receives the NMVT, it will use the EBCDIC model type and number string to look up an LU template under the LUGROUP. For example, the string "327802E" will find a match in the sample configuration shown in Table 27-5. An ACTLU will be sent and a terminal session with the model and type requested by the client can be established.

Formation of LU Model Type and Number

VTAM requires a model type and number from the Reply PSID NMVT to use as a key to look up in the LU group to find an LU template. The model type is a four character string; the model number is a two or three character string. The server will accept the following formats of terminal type string from the client:

- IBM-<XXXX>-<Y>[-E]: This will be formatted as "XXXX0Y"or "XXXX0YE" in the model type and number field in the Reply PSID NMVT.

- IBM-DYNAMIC: This will result in "DYNAMIC" being put in the model type and number field. The VTAM configuration will need to have "DYNAMIC" defined as a template in the LU group. In fact "IBM-ZZ..Z," where "ZZ..Z" does not match the preceding syntax, will be forwarded as "ZZ..Z."

NOTE	The "E" in the model string refers to 3270 Extended Datastream. It has no connection with the "E" in "TN3270E".

- Any other string is forwarded as is.

- In all cases, the string forwarded is translated from ASCII to EBCDIC and truncated at seven characters.

Clients that do not support TN3270E typically require a 3270 datastream on the SSCP-LU flow. Clients that are TN3270E compliant will typically utilize the SNA Character Set (SCS) on the SSCP-LU session. In order to accommodate these two classes of clients, the TN3270 server directs them to different LUGROUP entries at the host. To make this as easy as possible, the SCS requirement is also encoded into the model string sent to the host. Following the previously described terminal type string formats accepted by the server, this additional condition is applied: If the client has negotiated TN3270E support, the character "S" is overlaid on the fifth character of the string, or appended if the string is less than five characters. See Table 27-3.

Table 27-3 *Examples of Model String Mapping*

String from Client (ASCII)	BIND-IMAGE Requested?	String to Host (EBCDIC)
IBM-3278-4	No	327804
IBM-3279-5E	No	327905E
IBM-3279-3-E	Yes	3279S5E
IBM-DYNAMIC	Yes	DYNASIC
ABC	Yes	ABCS
ABCDEFGH	Yes	ABCDSFG

Specific LU Allocation

A TN3270E client can request a specific LU name by using the TN3270E command CONNECT as documented in RFC 1647. The name requested must match the name by which the TN3270 server knows the LU (see the section "LU Names in the TN3270 Server"), and the host must have activated the LU (with ACTLU).

LU Names in the TN3270 Server

Where SNA session switching is configured (that is, on DLUR PUs) the TN3270 server learns the LU names from the ACTLUs.

For direct PUs, a "seed" name can be configured on the PU. TN3270 server uses this name in conjunction with the LOCADDRS to generate names for the LUs. It is best to use the same naming convention as the host.

SNA Switching—End Node DLUR

An end node DLUR function is implemented as part of the TN3270 server. The purpose of the DLUR is to allow the routing of TN3270 LUs to multiple VTAM hosts to be performed in the CMCC adapter card rather than on the VTAM hosts. This feature is especially important with the new multi-CPU CMOS mainframe, which comprises up to 16 CPUs that appear as separate VTAMs.

The implementation of TN3270 server LUs under DLUR also allows the server to learn about the LU names on the ACTLU, which greatly simplifies the configuration to support specifically requestable LUs such as printers.

Multiple Hosts Support

The TN3270 server supports access to multiple hosts via the configuration on a PU basis (Table 27-4). PUs connected to different hosts/applications can be configured with different IP address.

Table 27-4 *Direct PU Configuration in Router*

Command	PU Name	Idblk	IP-address	Type	Adapter number	Lsap	RMAC	RMAC	Lu-seed	Lu-name
PU	X1	05D30001	192.195.80.40	tok	1	4	RMAC	4100.cafe.0001	lu-seed	TN3X1###
PU	X2	05D30002	171.69.176.43	tok	1	8	RMAC	4100.cafe.0002	lu-seed	TN3X2###

From the **pu (direct)** TN3270 configuration command values shown in Table 27-4, PU X2 establishes a link to a host at SAP 4 (the default) on MAC address 4100.cafe.0002. A client connecting to IP address 171.69.176.43 is allocated an LU from that PU and is routed to that host.

Note that by using the DLUR function, all the LUs in the server can be defined and owned by a controlling VTAM. When a client requests an application residing on a different VTAM host, the controlling VTAM will issue the request to the target host which will send a BIND directly to the client. All LU-LU data will then flow directly between the target host and the client without needing to go through the controlling VTAM.

IP Type of Service and Precedence Setting

The TN3270 server supports IP type of service (ToS) precedence setting. ToS is used in router networks to make routing decisions for the generated IP packets. The TN3270 server generates packets that comply to IP ToS and IP precedence values. (Refer to RFC 1349 for a description of IP ToS and IP precedence.)

Cisco implementation of IP precedence allows values of 0 to 7 while ToS allows values from 0 to 15. You must choose appropriate values for TN3270 screens and printers consistent with your organization's policy.

At the protocol level, IP precedence allows a router network to discriminate between different types of traffic by giving different priorities to them. IP ToS allows router networks to discriminate between different types of traffic by giving different routing characteristics to them. Precedence and ToS values complement one another and provide flexibility in managing your network traffic.

In TN3270 server, two types of TN3270 clients connect: interactive screens or printers. Screens are interactive while printers need bulk data transfer. IP ToS and IP precedence allows you to discriminate between those two types of sessions and assign different precedence values to the interactive connection and the bulk data connection.

IP ToS and IP precedence values can be specified either at the TN3270 server command level or on the individual PU command level. Values can be specified on both levels, in which case siftdown will be used to determine value on individual PU. Siftdown is used when you configure values in TN3270 server configuration mode that apply to all entities in the server, yet you still can configure individual PUs at the PU configuration mode to alternative values. PU values not specifically changed use the values configured at the TN3270 server configuration mode. This flexibility provides a powerful, yet efficient, way to manage the values.

VTAM Host Configuration Considerations for Dynamic LU Allocation

Other non-Cisco implementations of TN3270 support depend on predefined, static pools of LUs to support different terminal types requested by the TN3270 clients. The CMCC adapter TN3270 server implementation removes the static nature of these configurations by using a VTAM release 3.4 feature, dynamic definition of dependent LU (DDDLU). (Refer to the VTAM operating system manuals for your host system, under the descriptions for LUGROUP for additional information.) DDDLU dynamically requests LUs using the terminal type provided by TN3270 clients. The dynamic request eliminates the need to define any LU configuration in the server to support TN3270 clients emulating a generic TN3270 terminal.

To support DDDLU, the PUs used by the TN3270 server have to be defined in VTAM with LUSEED and LUGROUP parameters as shown in Table 27-5.

Table 27-5 *VTAM Host Values Defining LUSEED and LUGROUP*

```
Example VTAM host values defining LUSEED and LUGROUP name parameters:

TN3270PU     PU          .                          *   define other PU parameters
                         IDBLK=05D,
                         IDNUM=30001,

                         LUSEED=TN3X1###,            *   define the seed component of the
                                                         LU names created by DDDLU (e.g.
                                                         LOCADDR 42 will have the name
                                                         TN3X1042)

                         LUGROUP=AGROUP             *   define the LU group name
*
TN3X1100     LU          LOCADDR=100,               *   define a terminal which requires
                         MODETAB=AMODETAB               a specific LU name
*
TN3X1101     LU          LOCADDR=101,               *   define a printer which requires a
                         DLOGMODE=M3287CS               specific LU name


Example VTAM host values defining LUGROUPname, AGROUP:

AGROUP       LUGROUP                                *   define LU group to support
                                                        various terminal types

327802E      LU          USSTAB=USSXXX,             *   define template to support IBM
                         LOGAPPL=TPXP001,               3278 terminal model 2 with
                         DLOGMOD=SNX32702,              Extended Data Stream. Note that
                         SSCPFM=USS3270                 the USS messages in USSXXX should
                                                        be in 3270 datastream.

3278S2E      LU          USSTAB=USSYYY,             *   define template to support IBM
                         LOGAPPL=TPXP001,               3278 terminal model 2 with
                         DLOGMOD=SNX32702,              Extended Data Stream, for TN3270E
                         SSCPFM=USSSCS                  clients requesting BIND-IMAGE.

327805       LU          USSTAB=USSXXX,             *   define template to support IBM
                         LOGAPPL=TPXP001,               3279 terminal model 5
                         DLOGMOD=D4C32785,
                         SSCPFM=USS3270

@            LU          USSTAB=USSXXX,                 this is the default template to
                         LOGAPPL=TPXP001,               match any other terminal types
                         DLOGMOD=D4A32772,
                         SSCPFM=USS3270
```

With the configuration shown in Table 27-5 defined in the host, the ACTPU sent by VTAM for the PU TN3270PU will have the "Unsolicited NMVT Support" set in the system services control point (SSCP) capabilities control vector. This allows the PU to dynamically allocate LUs by sending network management vector transport (NMVT) with a "Reply Product Set ID" control vector.

After the TN3270 server sends a positive response to the ACTPU, it will wait for VTAM to send ACTLUs for all specifically defined LUs. In the sample configuration shown in Figure 27-5, ACTLUs will be sent for TN3X1100 and TN3X1101. The server sends a positive response and sets SLU DISABLED. The LOCADDR of these LUs are put into the specific LU cache and reserved for specific LU name requests only.

To allow sufficient time for the VTAM host to send all the ACTLUs, a 30-second timer is started and restarted when an ACTLU is received. When the time expires, it is assumed all ACTLUs defined in VTAM for the PU have been sent. All LUs that have not been activated are available in a generic LU pool to be used for DDDLU unless they have been reserved by the configuration using the **generic-pool deny** TN3270 configuration command.

After the VTAM activation, the server can support session requests from clients using dynamic or specific LU allocation.

LU Address Mapping

Logical unit (LU) address mapping allows a client IP address to be mapped, or "nailed," to one or more LU local addresses on one or more physical units (PUs) by means of router configuration commands. You can control the relationship between the TN3270 client and the LU.

Clients from traditional TN3270 (non-TN3270E) devices can connect to specific LUs, which overcomes a limitation of TN3270 devices that cannot specify a "CONNECT LU." LU nailing is useful for TN3270E clients because you can perform the configuration at the router, providing central control, rather than at the client.

Handling Large Configurations

The largest size nonvolatile random-access memory (NVRAM) planned for the Cisco 7000, Cisco 7500 and Cisco 7200 series routers is 128 KB. The maximum number of nailing commands that can be stored in a 128 KB NVRAM is approximately 4000. However, large configurations may map as many as 10,000 IP addresses to LUs.

To maintain a configuration file that exceeds 128 KB, there are two alternatives. The configuration file can be stored compressed in NVRAM. Or, the configuration file can be stored in Flash memory that is either internal Flash or on a PCMCIA card.

LU Nailing and Model Matching

The "model matching" feature of the CMCC TN3270 server is designed for efficient use of dynamic LUs. Each client specifies a terminal model type at connection. When a non-nailed client connects and does not request a specific LU, the LU allocation algorithm attempts to allocate an LU that operated with that terminal model the last time it was used. If no such model is available, the next choice is an LU that has not been used since the PU was last activated. Failing that, any available LU is used; however, for dynamic LUs only, there is a short delay in connecting the session.

Where a client or set of clients is nailed to a set of more than one LU, the same logic applies. If the configured LU nailing maps a screen client to a set of LUs, the LU nailing algorithm attempts to match the client to a previously used LU that was most recently used with the same terminal model type as requested by the client for this connection. If a match is found, that LU is used. If a match is not found, any LU in the set that is not currently in use is chosen. If there is no available LU in the set, the connection is rejected.

For example, the following LUs are nailed to clients at address 192.195.80.40, and LUs BAGE1004 and BAGE1005, which were connected but are now disconnected:

```
lu    name    client-ip:tcp        nail state     model    frames in out    idle for
1     BAGE1001 192.195.80.40:3822   Y    P-BIND    327904E  4       4        0:22:35
2     BAGE1002 192.195.80.40:3867   Y    ACT/SESS  327904E  8       7        0:21:20
3     BAGE1003 192.195.80.40:3981   Y    ACT/SESS  327803E  13      14       0:10:13
4     BAGE1004 192.195.80.40:3991   Y    ACT/NA    327803E  8       9        0:0:7
5     BAGE1005 192.195.80.40:3997   Y    ACT/NA    327805   8       9        0:7:8
```

If a client at IP address 192.195.80.40 requests a terminal model of type IBM-3278-5, LU BAGE1005 will be selected over BAGE1004:

```
lu    name    client-ip:tcp        nail state     model    frames in out    idle for
1     BAGE1001 192.195.80.40:3822   Y    P-BIND    327904E  4       4        0:23:29
2     BAGE1002 192.195.80.40:3867   Y    ACT/SESS  327904E  8       7        0:22:14
3     BAGE1003 192.195.80.40:3981   Y    ACT/SESS  327803E  13      14       0:11:7
4     BAGE1004 192.195.80.40:3991   Y    ACT/NA    327803E  8       9        0:1:1
5     BAGE1005 192.195.80.40:4052   Y    ACT/SESS  327805   13      14       0:0:16
```

TN3270 Configuration Modes

The TN3270 configuration modes and router command prompts are described in the following sections and displayed in Figure 27-4. The TN3270 server can be configured only on the virtual interface of a CMCC adapter.

Some configuration commands create entities on the CMCC adapter. For most of these, the command changes to the mode associated with that entity (for example, a PU). In general, the parameters provided to create the entity come in two sets: those that identify the specific instance of the entity (for example, a PU name) and those that merely set operating parameters. To return to the mode later, the same command is used but with only the first set of parameters. The tasks in this section clarify how to return to a command mode without necessarily creating a new entity.

To create a DLUR LSAP and enter DLUR LSAP configuration mode, use the following command in TN3270 DLUR configuration mode:

Command	Purpose
lsap token-adapter 1 84	Creates a DLUR LSAP and enter DLUR LSAP configuration mode.

To return later to the DLUR LSAP configuration mode on the same entity, use the following command in TN3270 DLUR configuration mode:

Command	Purpose
lsap token-adapter 1	Enters DLUR LSAP configuration mode on the same LSAP.

To remove an entity, the same identification parameters are needed. Use the following command beginning in TN3270 DLUR configuration mode:

Command	Purpose
no lsap token-adapter 1	Removes a previously defined DLUR LSAP entity.

TN3270 configuration modes described in this section include the following:

- TN3270 Server Configuration Mode
- DLUR Configuration Mode
- DLUR SAP Configuration Mode
- PU Configuration Mode
- Commands Allowed in Multiple Modes

Figure 27-4 *TN3270 Configuration Modes*

```
┌──────────────┐                        Prompt:
│   TN3270     │
│configuration │                        tn3270-server>
│    mode      │
└──────────────┘

        ┌──────────────┐                Prompt:
        │ TN3270 DLUR  │
        │configuration │                tn3270-dlur>
        │    mode      │
        └──────────────┘

                ┌──────────────┐        Prompt:
                │TN3270 DLUR SAP│
                │ configuration │       tn3270-dlur-lsap>
                │    mode       │
                └──────────────┘

        ┌──────────────┐                Prompts:
        │  TN3270/PU   │
        │TN3270 DLUR PU│                tn3270-pu>
        │configuration │                tn3270-dlur>
        │    mode      │
        └──────────────┘
```

Use TN3270 PU configuration mode when the TN3270 server is attached to a non-APPN host.

Use TN3270 DLUR PU configuration mode when the TN3270 server is attached to an APPN host.

TN3270 Server Configuration Mode

From interface configuration mode, **tn3270-server** command puts you in TN3270 server configuration mode. The following prompt appears:

```
tn3270-server>
```

DLUR Configuration Mode

From TN3270 server configuration mode, the **dlur** command puts you in DLUR configuration mode. The following prompt appears:

```
tn3270-dlur>
```

DLUR SAP Configuration Mode

From DLUR server configuration mode, **lsap** command puts you in DLUR SAP configuration mode. The following prompt appears:

```
tn3270-dlur-lsap>
```

PU Configuration Mode

There are two paths to PU configuration mode: from the TN3270 server configuration mode or from the DLUR configuration mode. In either mode, the **pu** command puts you in PU configuration mode.

From TN3270 configuration mode, the **pu** command to create a new PU is

> **pu** *pu-name idblk-idnum ip-address type adapno lsap* [**rmac** *rmac*]
> [**rsap** *rsap*] [**lu-seed** *lu-name-stem*]

From DLUR configuration mode, the **pu** command to create a new PU is

> **pu** *pu-name idblk-idnum ip-address*

From either mode, to return to PU configuration mode on PU pu-name the command is

> **pu** *pu-name*

The following prompts appear, depending on which mode you are in:

```
tn3270-pu>
tn3270-dlur-pu>
```

Commands Allowed in Multiple Modes

The following commands are valid in TN3270 configuration mode, or in either variation of PU configuration mode:

- **generic-pool** {**permit** | **deny**}

- **idle-time** *seconds*

- **ip precedence** {**screen** | **printer**} *value*

- **ip tos** {**screen** | **printer**} *value*

- **keepalive** *seconds*

- **shutdown**

- **tcp-port** *port-number*

- **unbind-action** {**keep** | **disconnect**}

Values entered in PU configuration mode override settings made in TN3270 configuration mode. In addition, the **no** form of these commands entered in PU configuration mode will restore the command value entered in TN3270 command mode.

TN3270 Configuration Task List

The following sections describe how to configure TN3270 server support on a CMCC adapter's virtual interface. Not all tasks are required. Refer to "TN3270 Configuration Examples" for configuration examples.

Task List for Multiple APPN Hosts

When the host site uses APPN and the TN3270 server can reach multiple hosts, we recommend you use DLUR and configure your PUs under DLUR. In this instance, perform the following tasks:

● Configure SNA Support

● Configure TN3270 Server

● Configure IP Precedence

● Configure IP ToS

● Configure DLUR

● Configure SAPs under DLUR

● Configure PUs under DLUR

● Configure LU Nailing

● Monitor the TN3270 Server

NOTE	You can also use DLUR to reach a mix of APPN and non-APPN hosts. The host owning the PUs must be an APPN network node that also supports the subarea (that is, an interchange node). When an SLU starts a session with any of the APPN hosts, it can use session switching to reach that host directly. When it starts a session with a non-APPN host, the traffic will be routed through the owning host.

Task List for Non-APPN Hosts

When the host site does not use APPN, you configure your PU parameters for a directly-connected host. In this instance, perform the following tasks:

- Configure SNA Support
- Configure TN3270 Server
- Configure IP Precedence
- Configure IP ToS
- Configure PU Parameters on the TN3270 Server
- Configure LU Nailing
- Monitor the TN3270 Server

Configure SNA Support

Host connectivity must be configured prior to configuring TN3270 support. This is accomplished in one of three ways:

- Configure CSNA support. Refer to the section "Configure CSNA Support."
- Configure CMPC support. Refer to the section "Configure CMPC Support."
- Configure Token Ring Attachment to a FEP. Refer to the section "TN3270 Configuration Examples."

After the host connection is configured, begin the TN3270 configuration.

Configure TN3270 Server

This task is required. To establish a TN3270 server on the internal LAN interface on the CMCC adapter, use the following commands beginning in global configuration mode:

Step	Command	Purpose
1	**interface channel** *slot/port*	Selects the channel attach internal LAN interface and enter interface configuration mode.
2	**tn3270-server**	Specifies a TN3270 server on the internal LAN interface and enters TN3270 configuration mode.
3	**maximum-lus** *max-number-of-lu-allocated*	(Optional) Configures maximum number of LUs allowed.
4	**client** [*ip* [*ip-mask*]] **lu maximum** *number*	(Optional) Configures LU session limits for each client IP address or IP subnetwork address.

Step	Command	Purpose
5	**timing-mark**	(Optional) Configures transmission of a WILL TIMING-MARK.
6	**tcp-port** *port-nbr*	(Optional) Assigns a TCP port other than the default of 23. This command is also available in PU configuration mode.
7	**idle-time** *num-of-seconds*	(Optional) Specifies the idle time for server disconnect. This command is also available in PU configuration mode.
8	**keepalive** *num-of-seconds*	(Optional) Specifies the maximum time allowed between keepalive marks before the server disconnects. This command is also available in PU configuration mode.
9	**unbind-action** {**keep** | **disconnect**}	(Optional) Specifies whether the TN3270 session will disconnect when an UNBIND command is received. This command is also available in PU configuration mode.
10	**generic-pool** {**permit** | **deny**}	(Optional) Selects whether "left-over" LUs can be used from a generic LU pool. This command is also available in PU configuration mode.
11	**ip precedence** {**screen** | **printer**} *value*	(Optional) Specifies the precedence level for IP traffic in the TN3270 server.
12	**ip tos** {**screen** | **printer**} *value*	(Optional) Specifies the ToS level for IP traffic in the TN3270 server.

When you use the **tn3270-server** command, you enter TN3270 configuration mode and can use all other commands in the task list. You can later override many configuration values you enter in TN3270 configuration mode from PU configuration mode. On IBM host systems, these types of commands are often referred to as "sift down" commands because their values can sift down through several levels of configuration and can be optionally altered at each configuration level.

Configure IP Precedence

To configure IP precedence, use the following command in TN3270 server or TN3270 PU configuration mode:

Command	Purpose
ip precedence {**screen** | **printer**} *value*	Configures the IP level.

Use the **no ip precedence screen** or the **no ip precedence printer** commands to return the precedence value to a default of 0.

Configure IP ToS

To configure IP ToS, use the following command in TN3270 server or TN3270 PU configuration mode:

Command	Purpose
ip tos {**screen**	**printer**} *value*	Configures the IP ToS delay level.

Use the **no ip tos screen** or the **no ip tos printer** commands to return the precedence value to a default of 0.

Configure PU Parameters on the TN3270 Server

This task is required when configuring PUs that do not use DLUR. The first command, **pu rmac rsap lu-seed** command is required. All other commands are optional. To configure PU parameters for the TN3270 server, use the following commands beginning in TN3270 configuration mode:

Command	Purpose
pu *pu-name idblk-idnum ip-address type adapno lsap* [**rmac** *rmac*] [**rsap** *rsap*] [**lu-seed** *lu-name-stem*]	Enters PU configuration mode and create or delete PUs with direct host links.
tcp-port *port-nbr*	(Optional) Assigns a TCP port other than the default of 23. This command is also available in TN3270 configuration mode.
idle-time *num-of-seconds*	(Optional) Specifies the idle time for server disconnect. This command is also available in TN3270 configuration mode.
keepalive *num-of-seconds*	(Optional) Specifies the maximum time allowed between keepalive marks before the server disconnects. This command is also available in TN3270 configuration mode.
unbind-action {**keep**	**disconnect**}	(Optional) Specifies whether the TN3270 session will disconnect when an UNBIND command is received. This command is also available in TN3270 configuration mode.
generic-pool {**permit**	**deny**}	(Optional) Selects whether "left-over" LUs can be used from a generic LU pool. This command is also available in TN3270 configuration mode.
ip precedence {**screen**	**printer**} *value*	(Optional) Specifies the precedence level for IP traffic in the TN3270 server.

Command	Purpose
ip tos {**screen**	**printer**} *value*	(Optional) Specifies the ToS level for IP traffic in the TN3270 server.

When you use the **pu** command, you enter PU configuration mode and can use all other commands in this task list. Configuration values you enter in PU configuration mode will override other values entered while in TN3270 configuration mode. In addition, you can enter PU configuration mode from DLUR configuration mode when configuring PUs that are connected by means of DLUR.

If you are configuring PUs for directly connected hosts, you need not perform any additional configuration tasks.

Configure DLUR

This task is required when configuring DLUR connected hosts. To configure DLUR parameters for the TN3270 server, use the following commands beginning in TN3270 configuration mode:

Step	Command	Purpose
1	**dlur** *fq-cpname fq-dlusname*	Creates a DLUR function in the TN3270 server and enter DLUR configuration mode.
2	**dlus-backup** *dlusname2*	(Optional) Specifies the fallback choice for the DLUR DLUS.
3	**preferred-nnserver** *NNserver*	(Optional) Specifies the preferred network node (NN) server.
4	**client** [**printer**] **ip** *ip-address* [*mask*] **lu** *first-locaddr* [*last-locaddr*]	(Optional) Configures the IP address and nail type and specifies the locaddr range.

Configure SAPs under DLUR

To configure SAPs under the DLUR function, use the following commands beginning in DLUR configuration mode:

Step	Command	Purpose
1	**lsap** *type adapno* [*lsap*]	Creates a SAP function under DLUR and enter DLUR SAP configuration mode.
2	**vrn** *vrn-name*	(Optional) Identifies an APPN virtual routing node (VRN).

Step	Command	Purpose
3	**link** *name* [**rmac** *rmac*] [**rsap** *rsap*]	(Optional) Creates named links to hosts. A link should be configured to each potential NN server. (The alternative is to configure the NN servers to connect to DLUR.) If VRN is used, it is not necessary to configure links to other hosts. Do not configure multiple links to the same host.
4	**client** [**printer**] **ip** *ip-address* [*mask*] **lu** *first-locaddr* [*last-locaddr*]	(Optional) Configures the IP address and nail type and specifies the locaddr range.

Configure PUs under DLUR

This task is required when configuring DLUR connected hosts. To configure PUs under the DLUR function, use the following commands beginning in DLUR configuration mode:

Step	Command	Purpose
1	**pu** *pu-name idblk-idnum ip-address*	Creates a PU function under DLUR and enters PU configuration mode.
2	**tcp-port** *port-nbr*	Assigns a TCP port other than the default of 23.
3	**idle-time** *num-of-seconds*	Specifies the idle time for server disconnect.
4	**keepalive** *num-of-seconds*	Specifies the maximum time allowed between keepalive marks before the server disconnects.
5	**unbind-action** {**keep** | **disconnect**}	Specifies whether the TN3270 session will disconnect when an UNBIND command is received.
6	**generic-pool** {**permit** | **deny**}	Selects whether "left-over" LUs can be used from a generic LU pool.
7	**ip precedence** {**screen** | **printer**} *value*	(Optional) Specifies the precedence level for IP traffic in the TN3270 server.
8	**ip tos** {**screen** | **printer**} *value*	(Optional) Specifies the ToS level for IP traffic in the TN3270 server.
9	**client** [**printer**] **ip** *ip-address* [*mask*] **lu** *first-locaddr* [*last-locaddr*]	(Optional) Configures the IP address and nail type and specify the locaddr range.

The **pu** command entered in DLUR configuration mode has different parameters than when it is entered from TN3270 configuration mode.

Configure LU Nailing

To configure LU nailing, use the following command in TN3270 PU configuration mode:

Command	Purpose
client [**printer**] **ip** *ip-address* [*mask*] **lu** *first-locaddr* [*last-locaddr*]	Configures the IP address and nail type and specifies the locaddr range.

The **client** command allows a client with multiple TN3270 connections from the same IP address to nail their screen connections to LUs that are configured as screen LUs at the host and to nail printer connections to LUs that are configured as printers at the host. When the connection is made, a device type of "328*" is matched to a printer definition and any other device type is matched to a screen definition.

Monitor the TN3270 Server

The following table lists the monitoring commands specific to the TN3270 server. To display the full list of **show** commands, enter **show ?** at the EXEC prompt.

Use the following commands in privileged EXEC mode:

Command	Purpose
show extended channel *slot/port* **tn3270-server**	Displays the current server configuration parameters and the status of the PUs defined in each server.
show extended channel *slot/port* **tn3270-server client-ip-address** *ip-address* [**disconnected** | **in-session** | **pending**]	Displays information about all clients at a specific IP address.
show extended channel *slot/port* **tn3270-server** *pu-name*	Displays the PU configuration parameters, statistics and all the LUs currently attached to the PU.
show extended channel *slot/port* **tn3270-server pu** *pu-name* **lu** *locaddr* [*history*]	Displays information about the TN3270 server LUs running on a CMCC adapter interface.
show extended channel *slot/port* **tn3270-server nailed-ip** *ip-address*	Displays mappings between a nailed client IP address and nailed LUs
show extended channel tn3270-server *pu-name* **lu** *lu-number* [**history**]	Displays the status of the LU.
show extended channel tn3270-server client-ip-address *ip-address*	Displays the information about LUs that are defined under an IP address.
show extended channel *slot/port* **tn3270-server dlur**	Displays information about the SNA session switch.

Command	Purpose
show extended channel *slot/port* **tn3270-server dlurlink** *name*	Displays information about the DLUR components.

Configure CMPC Support

Cisco MultiPath Channel (CMPC) is Cisco Systems's implementation of IBM's MultiPath Channel (MPC) feature. CMPC allows VTAM to establish Advanced-Peer-to-Peer Networking (APPN) connections using both High Performance Routing (HPR) and Intermediate Session Routing (ISR) through a channel-attached router platforms.

With CMPC, Cisco 7000 with RSP7000, Cisco 7500, and Cisco 7200 series routers can be deployed in Parallel MVS systems complex (sysplex) configurations.

CMPC can be used to establish an APPN connection between VTAM and the following APPN nodes:

- Another VTAM channel attached to the same CMCC adapter

- Another VTAM channel attached to a different CMCC adapter in the same router

- TN3270 server DLUR in the same CMCC adapter

- APPN network node (NN) in the router with the CMCC adapter

- Other APPN nodes external to the CMCC adapter and router with the CMCC adapter: CS/2, AS/400, other LAN or WAN attached VTAM hosts

One read subchannel and one write subchannel are supported for each MPC transmission group. The read subchannel and write subchannel may be split over two physical channel connections on the same CMCC adapter.

CMPC insulates VTAM from the actual network topology. The MPC protocols are terminated on the CMCC adapter and converted to LLC protocols. After they are converted to LLC protocols, other Cisco features can be used to connect VTAM to other APPN nodes in the network. CMPC can be used in conjunction with DLSw+, RSRB, SR/TLB, SRB, SDLLC, QLLC, ATM LAN emulation, and FRAS host to provide connectivity to VTAM.

CMPC supports connections to PU 2.1 nodes: APPN NN, APPN EN, and LEN. Subarea connections are not supported.

The CMPC feature coexists on a CMCC adapter with the TCP/IP Offload, IP Datagram, TN3270, and CSNA features.

CMPC Requirements

The following are minimum host system requirements to support CMPC:

- VTAM V4.2+, for MPC APPN ISR connections
- VTAM V4.3+, for MPC APPN HPR connections

CMPC Configuration Overview

To configure the CMPC feature, you must configure the host VTAM parameters and the CMCC adapter. The CMPC Configuration Examples for CMPC show the VTAM configuration parameters and the router configuration commands for each example.

The following guidelines will help you prepare for CMPC configuration:

- A CMPC link uses two subchannels: one read and one write. Some IBM implementations of MPC allow multiple read and multiple write subchannels. CMPC will not support multiple read and write subchannels. Only one read subchannel and one write subchannel can be configured for each CMPC link. A CMPC link is also referred to as a CMPC transmission group.

- Multiple CMPC links can be configured between the host and the CMCC adapter in the Cisco 7500, 7000, or 7200 series router.

- The two subchannels in a CMPC link need not be adjacent devices. Either channel may be the read subchannel and either channel may be the write subchannel. The two subchannels can be on separate channel process IDs in the host.

- The two subchannels must be connected to the same CMCC adapter, however they do not have to be connected to the same physical channel interface. In other words, it is possible to connect a read subchannel to channel interface 0, while the write subchannel is connected to the channel interface.

- Only APPN connections will be supported across CMPC. For this reason when TN3270 server is configured with CMPC, it must be configured as an APPN end node with DLUR.

- You must know what device addresses you will be using and the associated channel path statements.

- You must know whether or not you will use HPR.

- To configure the LLC2 interface for the CMCC adapter, you will need to choose a local MAC address and a local SAP address.

- You must know the remote MAC address and remote SAP of the LLC2 peer with which the CMPC communicates.

- You must know how to configure source-bridge ring groups on the CMCC adapter.

- On the router, the combination of one read subchannel definition, one write subchannel definition, and a transmission group definition, associated by a unique *tg-name*, makes up a CMPC transmission group specification.

To help clarify the configuration process, refer to Figure 27-5, which shows the CMPC link between the VTAM host, the router, and CMCC adapter card, and the communication to the LLC2 end point. The read and write addresses defined in the VTAM host correspond to the read and write paths defined for CMPC. CMPC communicates with the LLC2 stack, which communicates to the end point of the connection by means of the IEEE 802.2 link.

Figure 27-5 *Logical View of CMPC Link*

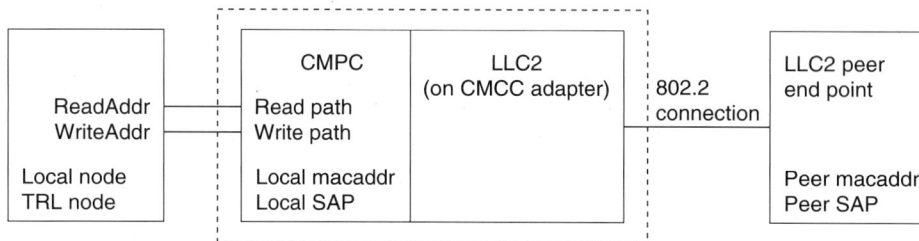

Configuration Tasks

This section describes the following configuration tasks associated with the CMPC feature. The first two tasks are performed on the VTAM host. The remaining tasks are performed on the router. All tasks are required.

● Configure the VTAM Transport Resource List Major Node

● Configure the VTAM Local SNA Major Node

● Configure the CMPC Subchannels

● Configure the CMPC Transmission Groups

● Configure the CMCC Adapter Internal LAN for CMPC

Configure the VTAM Transport Resource List Major Node

To configure MPC on the host, define the Transport Resource List (TRL) major node. See the following IBM documents for details on how to configure the TRL major node:

● *VTAM Resource Definition Samples*, SC31-6554

● *VTAM Operation*, SC31-6549

● *VTAM Network Implementation Guide*, SC31-6548

The following is an example of a typical configuration:

```
LAGTRLA  VBUILD TYPE=TRL
LAGTRLEA   TRLE  LNCTL=MPC,MAXBFRU=8,REPLYTO=3.0,              X
READ=(2F0),                                                    X
WRITE=(2F1)
```

In this example, device 2F0 has been configured for read and 2F1 has been configured for write. The command to activate the TRL should be issued before activating the Local node. If your TRL data set was named LAGTRLA, the activate command would be as follows:

v net,act,id=lagtrla,update=add

The ID parameter refers to the name of the data set containing the TRL definition.

Note that "update=add" is preferred and is the default for later versions of VTAM. The argument "update=all" can cause inactive TRLEs to be deleted unexpectedly from ISTTRL. However, "update=all" must be used if you change an active TRL data set and wish the changes to become active. The following commands are useful for displaying the current list of TRLEs:

d net,trl
d net,id=isttrl,e
d net,trl,trle=trle_name

Configure the VTAM Local SNA Major Node

To configure the MPC channel link on the VTAM host, define the local SNA major node.

The following is an example of a typical configuration:

```
LAGLNA   VBUILD TYPE=LOCAL
 LAGPUA   PU  TRLE=LAGTRLEA,                                   X
              ISTATUS=ACTIVE,                                  X
              XID=YES,CONNTYPE=APPN,CPCP=YES,HPR=YES
```

The TRLE parameter in the local node refers to the label on the TRLE statement from the TRL major node LAGTRLA. Also, if you do not want to run HPR set the HPR parameter to "NO." The local SNA major node must be activated after the TRL node has been activated. If your local node data set was named LAGLNA, the activate command is as follows:

v net,act,id=laglna

Configure the CMPC Subchannels

To define a CMPC read subchannel and CMPC write subchannel, use the following commands in interface configuration mode on a CMCC adapter physical interface:

Step	Command	Purpose
1	**cmpc** *path device tg-name* **read**	Configures the CMPC read subchannel.
2	**cmpc** *path device tg-name* **write**	Configures the CMPC write subchannel.

These statements define the subchannel addresses that CMPC will use to connect to the host and correspond to the definitions in the TRL major network node on the host. Specifically, the last two hexadecimal digits in the read parameter match the device value configuration in the **cmpc** command. The last two hexadecimal digits in the write parameter match the device value in the **cmpc** command.

Use the **no cmpc** *path device* command to remove the definition of a subchannel.

Configure the CMPC Transmission Groups

To define a CMPC transmission group by name and specify its connection to the LLC2 stack, use the following command in interface configuration mode on a CMCC adapter virtual interface:

Command	Purpose
tg *tg-name* **llc** *type adaptno lsap* [**rmac** *rmac*] [**rsap** *rsap*]	Defines the CMPC transmission group name.

The **tg** command defines an LLC connection with a complete addressing 4-tuple. The *lsap*, *rmac*, and *rsap* are specified explicitly by parameters. The *lmac* is the LMAC of the adapter referred to by the *type* and *adaptno* parameters.

The *tg-name* must match the name given in the **cmpc** command issued in the physical interfaces on the same CMCC adapter.

Use the **no tg** command to remove a CMPC transmission group from the configuration, which will deactivate the named CMPC transmission group.

To change any parameter of the **tg** statement, the statement must be removed by using the **no tg** *tg-name* command.

Configure the CMCC Adapter Internal LAN for CMPC

Configuring CMPC support on the CMCC adapter internal LAN is similar to configuring CSNA support. Many of the configuration tasks are the same. To configure the internal LAN adapter on the CMCC adapter to support CMPC, perform the following tasks:

● Configure the CMCC Adapter Internal LANs

● Configure SRB

● Configure Internal Adapters

● Configure the Internal Adapter and Its Link Characteristics

● Configure the Internal Adapter and Its Link Characteristics

Configure the CMCC Adapter Internal LANs

To select a CMCC adapter internal LAN interface, use the following commands beginning in global configuration mode:

Step	Command	Purpose
1	**interface channel** *slot/port*	Selects the virtual interface.
2	**lan tokenring** *lan-id*	Selects the internal LAN interface and enters internal LAN configuration mode.

Use the **no lan** command to disconnect all LLC2 sessions established through all internal LAN interfaces configured on a particular internal LAN.

Up to 18 internal adapters can be configured on a CMCC adapter.

Configure SRB

Select the bridging characteristics for Token Ring and FDDI, or Ethernet. Use the following command in internal LAN configuration mode:

Command	Purpose
source-bridge *local-ring bridge-number target-ring*	Selects SRB for the selected LAN interface.

Configure Internal Adapters

To select or configure an internal adapter, use the following command in internal LAN configuration mode:

Command	Purpose
adapter *adapno mac-address*	Selects the internal adapter to configure.

Name the Internal Adapter

Select a name for the internal adapter. Use the following command in internal adapter configuration mode:

Command	Purpose
name *name*	Selects a name for the internal adapter.

Naming an internal adapter is optional.

Configure the Internal Adapter and Its Link Characteristics

To configure the link characteristics of the internal LAN adapter, use the following commands in internal LAN configuration:

Command	Purpose
llc2 N1 *bytes*	Maximum size of an I-frame in bytes.
llc2 N2 *retry-count*	Maximum retry count.
llc2 Nw *window-size-increase*	Increases the window size for consecutive good I-frame received (zero is disabled).
llc2 ack-delay-time *milliseconds*	Maximum time for incoming I-frames to stay unacknowledged.
llc2 ack-max *frame-count*	Maximum number of I-frames received before an acknowledgment must be sent.
llc2 idle-time *milliseconds*	Frequency of polls during periods of idle traffic.
llc2 local-window *frame-count*	Maximum number of I-frames to send before waiting for an acknowledgment.
llc2 recv-window *frame-count*	Receives window.
llc2 t1-time *milliseconds*	Specifies amount of time to wait for an acknowledgment to transmit I-frames.

Command	Purpose
llc2 busy-time *milliseconds*	Amount of time to wait while the other LLC2 station is in a busy state before attempting to poll the remote station.
llc2 tpf-time *milliseconds*	Amount of time to wait for a final response to a poll frame before resending the original poll frame.
llc2 trej-time *milliseconds*	Amount of time to wait for resending a rejected frame before sending the reject command.

Configuring LLC parameters is optional. Default values are used when no parameters are configured.

CMCC Interface Configuration Examples

The following sections include examples to help you understand some aspects of interface configuration:

- CPA Microcode Load Example

- IP Address and Network Mask Configuration Example

- CLAW Configuration Example

- CLAW Packing Configuration Examples

- Offload Configuration Example

- CSNA Configuration Example

- TN3270 Configuration Examples

- Configure TN3270 DLUR with CMPC Host Connection

- Static and Dynamic LUs with LU Nailing Configuration Example

- Removing LU Nailing Definitions Example

- Configuring Different Values for Precedence and ToS Example

- Overriding Configured Values Example

- Configure IP Host Backup Example

- CMPC Configuration Examples for CMPC

CPA Microcode Load Example

The following example copies a new image to Flash memory:

```
router#copy tftp:xcpa26-2 slot0:xcpa26-2

Address or name of remote host []? neptune
Translating "neptune"...domain server (10.20.30.10) [OK]
Destination filename [xcpa26-2]?
Accessing tftp://neptune/xcpa26-2...
Loading motto/xcpa26-2 from 10.20.30.10 (via FastEthernet0/0): !
  Expanding slot0:xcpa26-2_kernel_xcpa (343148 bytes):
!!!!!!!!!!!!!!!!!!!!!!!!!!!!!!!!!!!!!!!!!!!!!!!!!!!!!!!!!!!!!!!!!!!
  Expanding slot0:xcpa26-2_seg_802 (237848 bytes):
!!!!!!!!!!!!!!!!!!!!!!!!!!!!!!!!!!!!!!!!!!!!!!!!!!!!
  Expanding slot0:xcpa26-2_seg_cmpc (319960 bytes):
!!!!!!!!!!!!!!!!!!!!!!!!!!!!!!!!!!!!!!!!!!!!!!!!!!!!!!!!!!!
  Expanding slot0:xcpa26-2_seg_csna (89856 bytes): !!!!!!!!!!!!!!!!!!!
  Expanding slot0:xcpa26-2_seg_eca (461424 bytes):
!!!!!!!!!!!!!!!!!!!!!!!!!!!!!!!!!!!!!!!!!!!!!!!!!!!!!!!!!!!!!!!!!!!!!!!!!!!!!!!!!!!!!!
!!!
  Expanding slot0:xcpa26-2_seg_offload (80344 bytes): !!!!!!!!!!!!!!!!!!!
  Expanding slot0:xcpa26-2_seg_pca (69376 bytes): !!!!!!!!!!!!!!!
  Expanding slot0:xcpa26-2_pseg_push (15936 bytes): !!!
  Expanding slot0:xcpa26-2_seg_tcpip (158896 bytes): !!!!!!!!!!!!!!!!!!!!!!!!!!!!!!!!!!
  Expanding slot0:xcpa26-2_seg_tn3270 (601784 bytes):
!!!!!!!!!!!!!!!!!!!!!!!!!!!!!!!!!!!!!!!!!!!!!!!!!!!!!!!!!!!!!!!!!!!!!!!!!!!!!!!!!!!!!!
!!!!!!!!!!!!!!!!!!!!!!!!!!!!!
[OK - 2387456/4774912 bytes]
2387456 bytes copied in 110.588 secs (21704 bytes/sec)
router#
```

After copying a CMCC ucode image to flash memory, a directory command of the flash device displays the following:

```
Router#dir slot0:

Directory of slot0:/
    1  -rw-           1   Aug 18 1998 12:29:12   xcpa26-2
    2  -rw-      344438   Aug 18 1998 12:29:12   xcpa26-2.kernel_xcpa
    3  -rw-      237848   Aug 18 1998 12:29:37   xcpa26-2.seg_802
    4  -rw-      319960   Aug 18 1998 12:29:56   xcpa26-2.seg_cmpc
    5  -rw-       89856   Aug 18 1998 12:30:15   xcpa26-2.seg_csna
    6  -rw-      461424   Aug 18 1998 12:30:20   xcpa26-2.seg_eca
    7  -rw-       80344   Aug 18 1998 12:31:03   xcpa26-2.seg_offload
    8  -rw-       69376   Aug 18 1998 12:31:07   xcpa26-2.seg_pca
    9  -rw-       15936   Aug 18 1998 12:31:11   xcpa26-2.seg_push
   10  -rw-      158896   Aug 18 1998 12:31:12   xcpa26-2.seg_tcpip
   11  -rw-      601784   Aug 18 1998 12:31:32   xcpa26-2.seg_tn3270
```

```
7995392 bytes total (5614116 bytes free)
```

The following example loads the microcode from an individual microcode image that is stored as a file in Flash memory:

```
Router(config)# microcode ecpa slot0:xcpa26-2
Router(config)# microcode reload
```

IP Address and Network Mask Configuration Example

The following example assigns an IP address and network mask to the IBM channel attach interface on the router:

```
ip address 197.91.2.5 255.255.255.0
```

CLAW Configuration Example

The following example configures the IBM channel attach interface to support a directly connected device:

```
claw 0100 00 197.91.2.2 VMSYSTEM C7000 TCPIP TCPIP
```

CLAW Packing Configuration Examples

The following example configures the IBM channel attach interface to support CLAW packing on HOSTA and HOSTC and the nonpacked version of CLAW on HOSTB:

```
interface Channel0/0

  ip address 172.18.4.49 255.255.255.248
  no keepalive
  claw C010 F2 172.18.4.50 HOSTA RTRA PACKED PACKED
  claw C020 F4 172.18.4.52 HOSTB RTRA TCPIP TCPIP
  claw C030 F6 172.18.4.53 HOSTC RTRA PACKED PACKED
```

The following is an example of a CLAW definition in the host configuration file for IOS/390:

```
000100 *----------------------------------------------
000200 * Member: IOS390R2.V510.PARM(TCPCFGxx)
000300 * Description: TCP task group configuration
000400 *----------------------------------------------
000500
000600 * Define the virtual medium
000700
000800 MEDIA VIRTUAL MTU(4096) NAME(LOOPBACK)
000900
001000 * Define the physical medium
001100
001200 MEDIA CLAW    MTU(4096) NAME(ROGCLAW) ASSIST
001300
```

```
001400 * Define the host
001500
001600 NETWORK IPADDRESS(172.18.4.50)
001700        SUBNET(255.255.255.248)
001800
001900 *
002000
002100 CLAW DEVADDR(8f2)
002200        BUFSIZE(32768)
002300        IBUF(5)
002400        OBUF(5)
002500        RESTART(60)
002600        HOSTNAME(HOSTA)
002700        WSNAME(RTRA)
002800        START
002900        PACKED
003000
003100 * Define gateway
003200
003300 ROUTE DEST(0.0.0.0) ROUTE(172.18.4.49)
003400
003500 * Define the transport pr
003600
003700 TCP   MAXRCVBUF(131072)
003800        MAXSNDBUF(131072)
003900        DEFRCVBUF(131072)
004000        DEFSNDBUF(131072)
004100        DELAYACK(2)
004200        FASTRX(3)
004300        MAXRXMIT(18)
004400        MINDEV(90)
004500        PORTUSE(1:4095)
004600        PORTASGN(4096:8191)
004700
004800 UDP   MAXRCVBUF(64000)005200        PORTUS
004900        MAXSNDBUF(64000)
005000        DEFRCVBUF(64000)
005100        DEFSNDBUF(64000)005300        PORTAS
005200        PORTUSE(1:4095)
005300        PORTASGN(4096:8191)
005400
005500 RAW   MAXRCV
005600        MAXSND
005700
```

Offload Configuration Example

The following example consists of the mainframe host profile statements, buffer poolsize recommendations, and router configuration statements for the network shown in Figure 27-6.

Figure 27-6 *Offload Network Configuration Block Diagram*

Host Profile Statements

```
; Device statement
DEVICE OFF CLAW 762 CISCOVM CIP1 NONE 20 20 4096 4096
!
; Link Statements (both needed)
LINK OFFL OFFLOADLINK1 1 OFF
LINK MEMD OFFLOADAPIBROAD 162.18.4.59 OFF OFFL
!
; Home Statement
; (No additional home statements are added for offload)
!
!
```

```
; Routing information (if you are not using the ROUTED SERVER)
GATEWAY
; NETWORK FIRST HOP  DRIVER   PCKT_SZ   SUBN_MSK       SUBN_VALUE
162.18        =      MEMD     4096      0.0.255.248    0.0.4.56
DEFAULTNET    =      MEMD     1500      0
!
;START statements
START OFF
!
```

Router Configuration Statements

The following statements configure the offload feature in the router. When you configure a host-to-host communication through the same channel interface, include the **no ip redirects** and **ip route-cache same-interface** commands:

```
interface Channel0/0
 ip address 162.18.4.57 255.255.255.248
 no ip redirects
 ip route-cache same-interface
no keepalive
 offload C300 62 162.18.4.59 CISCOVM CIP1 TCPIP TCPIP TCPIP API
```

CSNA Configuration Example

The following configuration is an example of configuring CSNA on a Cisco 7500 router with a CIP. Figure 27-7 illustrates this configuration example.

Figure 27-7   *CIP CSNA Internal LAN Network Diagram*

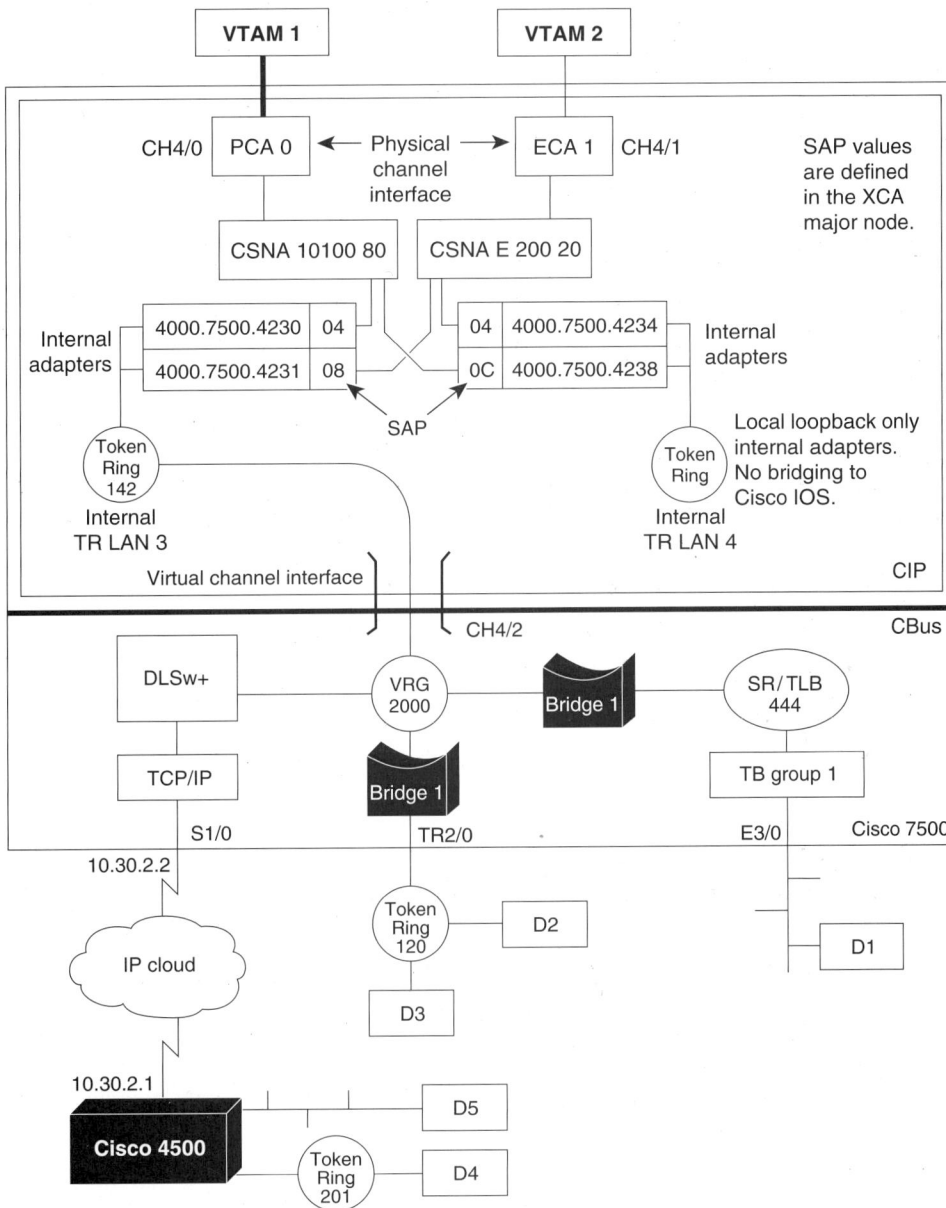

```
source-bridge ring-group 2000
source-bridge transparent 2000 444 1 1
dlsw remote-peer 0 tcp 10.30.3.1
dlsw local-peer peer-id 10.30.2.2
!
interface serial 1/0
 ip address 10.30.2.2 255.255.255.128
 clockrate 56000
!
interface tokenring 2/0
 mac-address 4000.7500.0200
 no ip address
 ring-speed 16
 source-bridge 120 1 2000
 source-bridge spanning
!
interface ethernet 3/0
 mac-address 0200.ae00.c000
 no ip address
 bridge-group 1
!
interface channel 4/0
 no ip address
 no ip directed-broadcast
 no keepalive
 csna 0100 80
!
interface channel 4/1
 no ip address
 no ip directed-broadcast
 no keepalive
 csna E200 20 maxpiu 65535 time-delay 100
!
interface channel 4/2
 no ip address
 no ip directed-broadcast
 no keepalive
 max-llc2-sessions 2500
 lan TokenRing 3
  source-bridge 142 1 2000
  adapter 0 4000.7500.4230
   llc2 local-window 1
   llc2 ack-max 1
  adapter 1 4000.7500.4231
 lan TokenRing 4
  adapter 7 4000.7500.4234
  adapter 8 4000.7500.4238
!
bridge 1 protocol ieee
```

ECPA CSNA Configuration Example

The following configuration is an example of configuring CSNA on a Cisco 7200 router with a ECPA. Figure 27-8 illustrates this configuration example.

Figure 27-8   *ECPA CSNA Translational Bridging Configuration Example*

```
source-bridge ring-group 2000
source-bridge transparent 2000 444 1 1
dlsw remote-peer 0 tcp 10.30.3.1
dlsw local-peer peer-id 10.30.2.2
!
interface serial 1/0
 ip address 10.30.2.2 255.255.255.128
 clockrate 56000
!
interface tokenring 2/0
 mac-address 4000.7500.0200
 no ip address
 ring-speed 16
 source-bridge 120 1 2000
 source-bridge spanning
!
interface ethernet 3/0
 mac-address 0200.ae00.c000
 no ip address
 bridge-group 1
!
interface channel 4/0
 no ip address
 no ip directed-broadcast
 no keepalive
 csna E200 30 maxpiu 65535
 CSNA E200 40 maxpiu 65535
 max-llc2-sessions 2500
 lan TokenRing 3
  source-bridge 142 1 2000
  adapter 0 4000.7500.4230
   llc2 local-window 1
   llc2 ack-max 1
  adapter 1 4000.7500.4231
 lan TokenRing 4
  adapter 7 4000.7500.4234
  adapter 8 4000.7500.4238
!
bridge 1 protocol ieee
```

TN3270 Configuration Examples

The following configuration has three PUs using DLUR and two more with direct connections.

The initial CIP configuration is as follows:

```
interface Channel2/2
 ip address 10.10.20.126 255.255.255.128
 no ip redirects
 no ip directed-broadcast
 no keepalive
```

```
lan TokenRing 0
 source-bridge 223 1 2099
 adapter 0 4100.cafe.0001
  llc2 N1 2057
 adapter 1 4100.cafe.0002
  llc2 N1 2057
```

Configuration dialog to configure the TN3270 function follows:

```
! HOSTA is channel-attached and will open SAP 8 on adapter 0.
! HOSTB is reached via token-ring
! HOSTC is channel-attached non-APPN and will open SAP 4 on adapter 0.

! enter interface configuration mode for the virtual interface in slot 2
router(config)#int channel 2/2

! create TN3270 Server entity
router(config-if)#tn3270-server

! set server-wide defaults for PU parameters
router(cfg-tn3270)#keepalive 0
router(cfg-tn3270)#unbind-action disconnect
router(cfg-tn3270)#generic-pool permit

! define DLUR parameters and enter DLUR configuration mode
router(cfg-tn3270)#dlur SYD.TN3020 SYD.VMG

! create PUs under DLUR
! Note that the first two share an IP address
router(tn3270-dlur)#pu pu0 05d99001 10.10.20.1
router(tn3270-dlur-pu)#pu pu1 05d99002 10.10.20.1
router(tn3270-dlur-pu)#pu pu2 05d99003 10.10.20.2

! create a DLUR LSAP and enter DLUR LSAP configuration mode
router(tn3270-dlur-pu)#lsap token-adapter 1

! specify the VRN name of the network containing this lsap
router(tn3270-dlur-lsap)#vrn syd.lan4

! create a link from this lsap
router(tn3270-dlur-lsap)#link hosta rmac 4100.cafe.0001 rsap 8
router(tn3270-dlur-lsap)#link hostb rmac 4000.7470.0009 rsap 4
router(tn3270-dlur-lsap)#exit
router(tn3270-dlur)#exit

! create direct pus for the non-APPN Host
! note that they must use different lsaps because they go to the same Host
router(cfg-tn3270)#pu pu3 05d00001 10.10.20.5 tok 1 24 rmac 4100.cafe.0001 lu-seed
pu3###
router(tn3270-pu)#pu pu4 05d00002 10.10.20.5 tok 1 28 rmac 4100.cafe.0001 lu-seed
pu4###
router(tn3270-pu)#end
```

The resulting configuration from the initial configuration and the configuration dialog follows:

```
interface Channel2/2
 ip address 10.10.20.126 255.255.255.128
 no ip redirects
 no keepalive
 lan TokenRing 0
  source-bridge 223 1 2099
  adapter 0 4100.cafe.0001
   llc2 N1 2057
  adapter 1 4100.cafe.0002
   llc2 N1 2057
  tn3270-server
   pu PU3       05D00001 10.10.20.5    token-adapter 1  24 rmac 4100.cafe.0001 lu-seed
   PU3###
   pu PU4       05D00002 10.10.20.5    token-adapter 1  28 rmac 4100.cafe.0001 lu-seed
   PU4###
   dlur SYD.TN3020 SYD.VMG
    lsap token-adapter 1
     vrn SYD.LAN4
     link HOSTB    rmac 4000.7470.0009
     link HOSTA    rmac 4100.cafe.0001 rsap 08
    pu PU0       05D99001 10.10.20.1
    pu PU1       05D99002 10.10.20.1
    pu PU2       05D99003 10.10.20.2
```

Configure TN3270 DLUR with CMPC Host Connection

The following example shows a DLUR PU with a CMPC host connection:

```
interface Channel0/0
 no ip address
 no keepalive
 cmpc C010 E5 LPAR1TG READ
 cmpc C010 E6 LPAR1TG WRITE
 cmpc C020 00 LPAR2TG READ
 cmpc C020 01 LPAR2TG WRITE
!
interface Channel0/2
 ip address 172.18.5.1 255.255.255.224
 no keepalive
 lan TokenRing 0
  source-bridge 100 1 8
  adapter 0 4000.4040.0000 ! for cmpc
  adapter 1 4000.6060.0000 ! TN3270 server
  adapter 2 4000.7070.0000
  tn3270-server
   maximum-lus 20000 ! optional
   idle-time 64800 ! optional
   timing-mark ! optional
   tcp-port 24 ! optional
   client 10.10.10.0 255.255.255.0 lu maximum 10000 ! optional
   dlur NETA.TN3270CP NETA.CPAC
```

```
    dlus-backup NETA.MVS2 ! optional
    preferred-NNserver NETA.CPAC ! optional
    lsap token-adapter 1 04 ! TN3270 server uses cmcc adapter 1 and sap=04
      link LINK1 rmac 4000.4040.0000 rsap 08 ! link to cmpc on adapter 0
    lsap token-adapter 2 04
      link LINK2 rmac 4000.7070.0000 rsap 08 ! link to cmpc on adapter 2
    pu TNPU1 0175 4321 172.18.5.2
!
tg LPAR1TG llc token-adapter 0 08 rmac 4000.6060.0000 rsap 04 ! rsap optional
tg LPAR2TG llc token-adapter 2 08 rmac 4000.7070.0000 ! rsap=04 by default"
```

Static and Dynamic LUs with LU Nailing Configuration Example

The following example shows a direct PU and a DLUR PU configured with the same listening point. The PUs are configured with the same nailed client IP address.

```
tn3270-server
  pu PU1 05D18081 172.28.1.82 token-adapter 1  24 rmac 4100.cafe.0001 lu-seed PU3###
  client ip 192.195.80.40 lu 1 10
  dlur
  pu PU2 05D190B3 172.28.1.82 token-adapter 1  28 rmac 4100.cafe.0001 lu-seed PU4###
  client ip 192.195.80.40 lu 1 10
```

Assuming each PU has three static LUs, which are ACTLU enabled and not connected, then these LUs are the first to be nailed. That is, the first six connections from client IP address 192.195.80.40 use the static LUs and subsequent connections use the remaining dynamic LUs.

Removing LU Nailing Definitions Example

In the following example, locaddrs 1 to 50 are reserved for all remote screen devices in the 171.69.176.0 subnet.

```
interface channel 2/2
  tn3270-server
  pu BAGE4
  client ip 171.69.176.28 255.255.255.0 lu 1 50
```

To remove a nailing definition, the complete range of locaddrs must be specified as configured. So, for the example above, the following command would remove the LU nailing definition.

```
no client ip 171.69.176.28 255.255.255.0 lu 1 50
```

If an attempt is made to remove a subset of the range of configured locaddrs then the command is rejected.

```
no client ip 171.69.176.28 255.255.255.0 lu 1 20
% client ip 171.69.176.28 lu not matched with configured lu 1 50
```

Configuring Different Values for Precedence and ToS Example

The following example changes IP precedence and IP ToS to different values under the TN3270 server for both the screen and printer. Note that any PUs defined under this configuration will inherit these values unless the corresponding parameter is specifically changed for that PU.

```
interface channel 3/2
tn3270-server
  ip precedence screen 6
  ip precedence printer 3
  ip tos screen 8
  ip tos printer 4
```

Overriding Configured Values Example

In the following example, the PU PUS1 uses the IP ToS precedence screen and printer values from the values provided in TN3270 server configuration mode. PUS2 uses the IP ToS screen and printer values defined in TN3270 server configuration mode. However, different values for IP precedence are provided for PUS2 under PU configuration mode.

```
interface channel 3/2
tn3270-server
  ip precedence screen 6
  ip precedence printer 3
  ip tos screen 8
  ip tos printer 4
  pu PUS1     05D18009 172.28.1.101    token-adapter 0  AC rsap 08
  pu PUS2     05D18071 172.28.1.99     token-adapter 0  A4 rmac 4000.7470.00e7
   ip precedence screen 7
   ip precedence printer 0
```

Configure IP Host Backup Example

Figure 27-9 shows the backup connection occurring between System B mainframe3 when mainframe 2 fails.

Figure 27-9   *IP Host Backup Configuration*

The intent of this backup configuration is that the system named A will be loaded on one of the mainframes in LPAR1 on that mainframe. The DASD for that system will be shared among all the mainframes but only one of them will ever IPL the system at one time. The same holds for LPAR2 and LPAR3.

The ESCON director has the following connections:

● A Cisco 7500 series router with a CIP connected to port C5

● Mainframe1 connected to C0

● Mainframe2 connected to C1

● Mainframe3 connected to C2

The following examples show how to configure IP Host Backup for three mainframe hosts, Mainframe 1, Mainframe 2, and Mainframe 3, as shown in Figure 27-9. Each mainframe is configured for at least three logical partitions (LPARs).

Excerpts from the host TCP/IP profiles show how the host might be configured. Excerpts from the router configuration show how the IP Host Backup configuration statements are configured.

Host TCP/IP Profiles

The DEVICE and HOME statements in the nine TCP/IP profiles are similar to the following:

```
LPAR1 (mainframes 1, 2, 3):
DEVICE CIP1 CLAW 630 LPAR1 CIP1 NONE 20 20 4096 4096
LINK CIP1L IP 0 CIP1
HOME
 198.92.5.2 CIP1L

LPAR2 (mainframes 1, 2, 3):
DEVICE CIP1 CLAW 730 LPAR1 CIP1 NONE 20 20 4096 4096
LINK CIP1L IP 0 CIP1
HOME
 198.92.5.3 CIP1L

LPAR3 (mainframes 1, 2, 3):
DEVICE CIP1 CLAW 830 LPAR1 CIP1 NONE 20 20 4096 4096
LINK CIP1L IP 0 CIP1
HOME
 198.92.5.4 CIP1L
```

Router Configuration

On the router, the CIP is located in slot 3 and port 1 is connected to the ESCON director. The **path** commands define the group of paths that are used as the IP Host Backup.

```
interface channel 3/1
 ip address 198.92.5.1 255.255.255.128
 path c010 c110 c210
   claw 30 198.92.5.2 lpar1 cip1 tcpip tcpip
 path c020 c120 c220
   claw 30 198.92.5.3 lpar2 cip1 tcpip tcpip
 path c030 c130 c230
   claw 30 198.92.5.4 lpar3 cip1 tcpip tcpip
```

CMPC Configuration Examples for CMPC

This section provides sample configurations for the CMPC feature. Throughout these configuration samples, a Cisco 7500 router with an RSP is used to illustrate the configurations. The configurations also apply to a Cisco 7000 router with an RP or an RSP installed. All SAP values are written in hexadecimal form.

Refer to the following configuration examples to see how different networked systems can be configured:

● Connecting VTAM to a Remote PC with Communications Server/2 Example

● Connecting VTAM to the APPN NN on the CIP Example

● Connecting Two VTAM Nodes Using Two CIPs in the Same Router Example

● Connecting VTAM to the APPN NN on a Remote Router with DLUR Example

● TN3270 Server DLUR Running on the Same CIP Example

Connecting VTAM to a Remote PC with Communications Server/2 Example

Figure 27-10 shows the physical components for this example. Figure 27-11 shows the various parameters for each component in the configuration example.

Figure 27-10 *Topology for VTAM-to-Remote PC with Communications Server/2*

In Figure 27-10, the following activity occurs:

- VTAM connects to the CMPC driver on the CIP.

- The CMPC driver converts the data to an LLC data stream and passes the data to the LLC2 stack on the CIP.

- The LLC2 stack on the CIP passes the data to the bridging code on the RSP.

- The bridging code on the RSP passes the data to the APPN network.

Figure 27-11 *Parameters for VTAM-to-Remote PC with Communications Server/2*

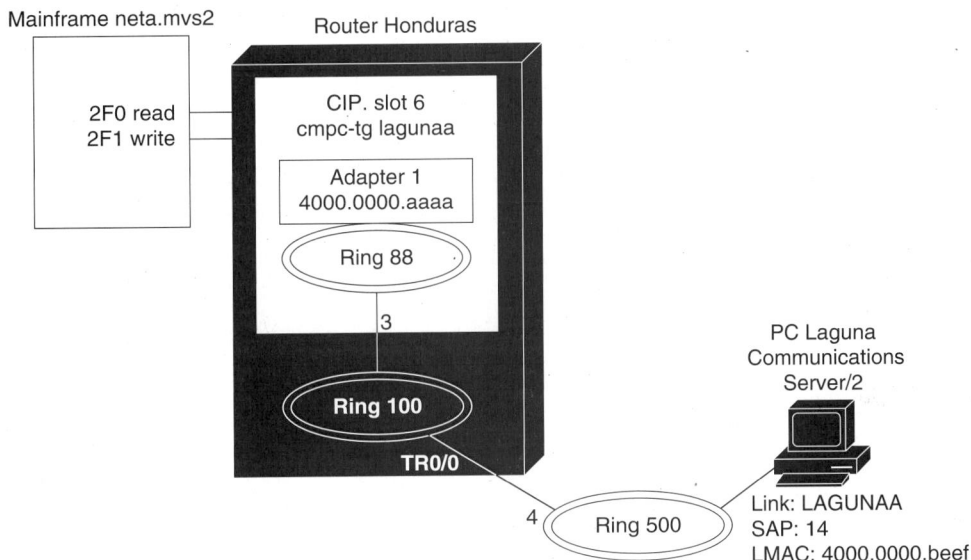

The example in Figure 27-11 shows CMPC running on the CIP and communicating with a PC running Communications Server/2. APPN is not running on the router. It is only running in VTAM and on the PC.

The configuration examples for the VTAM host and the router follow.

TRL Node LAGTRLA on MVS2

```
LAGTRA     VBUILD TYPE=TRL
LAGTRLA    TRLE  LNCTL=MPC,MAXBFRU=8,REPLYTO=3.0,              X
                 READ=(2F0),                                   X
                 WRITE=(2F1)
```

Local Node LAGLNA on MVS2

```
LAGNNA     VBUILD TYPE=LOCAL
LAGPUA  PU    TRLE=LAGTRLA,                                    X
              ISTATUS=ACTIVE,                                  X
              XID=YES,CONNTYPE=APPN,CPCP=YES,HPR=YES
```

Configuration for Honduras Router

```
source-bridge ring-group 100
!
interface TokenRing0/0
 no ip address
 ring-speed 16
 source-bridge 500 4 100
!
interface Ethernet1/0
 ip address 172.18.3.24 255.255.255.0
!
interface Channel6/1
 no ip address
 no keepalive
 cmpc C020 F0 LAGUNAA READ
 cmpc C020 F1 LAGUNAA WRITE
!
interface Channel6/2
 no ip address
 no keepalive
 lan TokenRing 0
  source-bridge 88 3 100
  adapter 1 4000.aaaa.aaaa
 tg LAGUNAA  llc token-adapter 1  18 rmac 4000.0000.beef rsap 14
```

Activate the Configuration

To activate the configuration, issue the following commands from MVS2:

```
v net,act,id=lagtrla,update=add
v net,act,id=laglna
```

Connecting VTAM to the APPN NN on the CIP Example

Figure 27-12 shows the physical components for this example. Figure 27-13 shows the various parameters for each component in the configuration example.

Figure 27-12 *Topology for VTAM-to-APPN NN Connection on the CIP*

In Figure 27-13, the following activity occurs:

- VTAM connects to the CMPC driver on the CIP.

- The CMPC driver converts the data to an LLC data stream and passes the data to the LLC2 stack on the CIP.

- The LLC2 stack on the CIP passes the data to the LLC2 stack on the RSP.

- The LLC2 stack on the RSP passes the data to APPN on the RSP.

- APPN on the RSP sends the data to the APPN network.

Figure 27-13 *Parameters for VTAM-to-APPN NN Connection on the CIP*

The configuration illustrated in Figure 27-13 is more complex because you must configure APPN on the router. There are many different ways to configure APPN. The example is a simple APPN configuration in which SRB is used to connect the APPN NN on the RSP to VTAM and the token-ring attached PC.

It is possible to connect directly to the Token Ring port, an option not shown in the example.

When configuring APPN on the router, you must type the **complete** command before exiting an APPN configuration subsection. If you need to change an APPN configuration subsection, you must type the **no complete** command before you can change the subsection. Remember to type **complete** before exiting the subsection. The router ignores the new APPN configuration commands until you type the **complete** command.

Configuration for TRL Node LAGTRLB

```
LAGTRB    VBUILD TYPE=TRL
LAGTRLB   TRLE  LNCTL=MPC,MAXBFRU=8,REPLYTO=3.0,          X
                READ=(2F2),                                X
                WRITE=(2F3)
```

Local SNA Major Node LAGLNB

```
LAGNNB    VBUILD TYPE=LOCAL
LAGPUB    PU    TRLE=LAGTRLB,                              X
                ISTATUS=ACTIVE,                            X
                XID=YES,CONNTYPE=APPN,CPCP=YES
```

Honduras Router

```
interface Channel6/1
 no ip address
 no keepalive
 cmpc C020 F2 LAGUNAB READ
 cmpc C020 F3 LAGUNAB WRITE
!
interface Channel6/2
 no ip address
 no keepalive
 lan TokenRing 0
  source-bridge 88 3 100
  adapter 2 4000.bbbb.bbbb
 lan TokenRing 2
 tg LAGUNAB  llc token-adapter 2  20 rmac 4000.0000.bbbb rsap 24
!
!
appn control-point NETA.HONDURAS
    complete
!
appn port RSRBPORT rsrb
  local-sap 24
  desired-max-send-btu-size 4096
  max-rcv-btu-size 4096
  rsrb-virtual-station 4000.0000.bbbb 61 2 100
  complete
!
appn link-station LAGUNAB
  port RSRBPORT
  lan-dest-address 4000.0000.beef 14
  complete
router eigrp 109
 network 172.18.0.0
```

Activate the Configuration

After all configurations are in place, the following commands can be used to start up the links. On the MVS system, use the following commands:

```
v net,act,id=lagtrlb,update=add
v net,act,id=laglnb
```

On the router, use the following command from the global configuration mode:

```
appn start
```

Connecting Two VTAM Nodes Using Two CIPs in the Same Router Example

Figure 27-14 shows the physical components for this example. Figure 27-15 shows the various parameters for each component in the configuration example.

Figure 27-14 *Topology for VTAM-to-VTAM Connection*

In Figure 27-15, the following activity occurs:

- VTAM on Mainframe 1 passes MPC data to the CMPC driver on CIP 1.

- The CMPC driver on CIP 1 passes the data to the LLC2 stack.

- LLC2 sends the data to CIP 2 in the same router via IEEE 802.2.

- The LLC2 stack on CIP 2 passes the data to the CMPC driver on CIP 2, which passes the data to VTAM on Mainframe 2.

The CIPs could be in different routers or both VTAM connections could be to the same CIP.

Figure 27-15 shows parameters for VTAM-to-VTAM connection.

Figure 27-15 *Parameters for VTAM-to-VTAM Connection*

Cisco 7500

Differing solutions can be configured for the example shown in Figure 27-15. For example, you can have two CIPs in different routers connected via LLC2. You can also configure host connections going into the same CIP card rather than two separate CIP cards.

mvs2trlc

```
MVS2TRC  VBUILD TYPE=TRL
MVS2TRLC TRLE  LNCTL=MPC,MAXBFRU=8,REPLYTO=3.0,              X
               READ=(2F4),                                   X
               WRITE=(2F5)
```

mvs2lnc

```
MVS2NNC   VBUILD TYPE=LOCAL
MVS2PUC   PU     TRLE=MVS2TRLC,                                            X
                 ISTATUS=ACTIVE,                                          X
                 XID=YES,CONNTYPE=APPN,CPCP=YES
```

cpactrlc

```
CPACTRC   VBUILD TYPE=TRL
CPACTRLC  TRLE   LNCTL=MPC,MAXBFRU=8,REPLYTO=3.0,                         X
                 READ=(840),                                             X
                 WRITE=(841)
```

cpaclnc

```
CPACNNC   VBUILD TYPE=LOCAL
CPACPUC   PU     TRLE=CPACTRLC,                                           X
                 ISTATUS=ACTIVE,                                         X
                 XID=YES,CONNTYPE=APPN,CPCP=YES
```

Router

```
interface Channel4/1
 no ip address
 no keepalive
 cmpc C010 40 CPACC READ
 cmpc C010 41 CPACC WRITE
!
interface Channel4/2
 no ip address
 no keepalive
 lan TokenRing 0
  source-bridge 43 5 100
  adapter 3 4000.0000.cccc
 tg CPACC     llc token-adapter 3  34 rmac 4000.cccc.cccc rsap 30
!
interface Channel6/1
 no ip address
 no keepalive
 cmpc C020 F4 MVS2C READ
 cmpc C020 F5 MVS2C WRITE
!
interface Channel6/2
  lan TokenRing 0
  source-bridge 88 3 100
    adapter 3 4000.cccc.cccc
 tg MVS2C     llc token-adapter 3  30 rmac 4000.0000.cccc rsap 34
```

Activate the Configuration

On the MVS system MVS2, use the following commands to activate the configuration:

```
v net,act,id=mvs2trlc,update=add
v net,act,id=mvs2lnc
```

On the MVS system CPAC, use the following commands to activate the configuration:

```
v net,act,id=cpactrlc,update=add
v net,act,id=cpaclnc
```

Connecting VTAM to the APPN NN on a Remote Router with DLUR Example

Figure 27-16 shows the physical components for the DLUS-to-DLUR configuration. Figure 27-17 shows the various parameters for each component in the configuration example.

Figure 27-16 *Topology for VTAM-to-APPN NN on a Remote Router with DLUR Connection*

Figure 27-17   *Parameters for VTAM-to-APPN NN on a Remote Router with DLUR Connection*

In the example shown in Figure 27-17, DLUS is running on the MVS host. DLUR is running on a remote Cisco 4000 router. The connection from MPC to the APPN stack on the Cisco 4000 is via LLC2. There is no NN on the Cisco 7500. The PC is running Communications Server/2.

mvs2trld

```
MVS2TRD  VBUILD TYPE=TRL
MVS2TRLD TRLE  LNCTL=MPC,MAXBFRU=8,REPLYTO=3.0,              X
               READ=(2F7),                                   X
               WRITE=(2F6)
```

mvs2lnd

```
MVS2NND  VBUILD TYPE=LOCAL
MVS2PUD  PU    TRLE=MVS2TRLD,                                 X
               ISTATUS=ACTIVE,                                X
               XID=YES,CONNTYPE=APPN,CPCP=YES
```

Additional Configuration for Router Honduras

```
interface Channel6/1
 cmpc C020 F6 CONFIGD WRITE
 cmpc C020 F7 CONFIGD READ
!
interface Channel6/2
 lan TokenRing 0
  source-bridge 88 3 100
  adapter 4 4000.dddd.dddd
  tg CONFIGD  llc token-adapter 4  40 rmac 4000.0000.dddd rsap 44
```

Router Dustin

```
source-bridge ring-group 84
interface Ethernet0
 ip address 172.18.3.36 255.255.255.0
 media-type 10BaseT
!
interface TokenRing0
 no ip address
 ring-speed 16
 source-bridge 500 2 84
!
appn control-point NETA.DUSTIN
  dlus NETA.MVS2
  dlur
  complete
!
```

```
appn port RSRBPORT rsrb
  local-sap 44
  desired-max-send-btu-size 4096
  max-rcv-btu-size 4096
  rsrb-virtual-station 4000.0000.dddd 94 5 84
  complete
!
appn link-station LAGUNAD
  port RSRBPORT
  lan-dest-address 4000.0000.beef 14
  complete
!
appn link-station MVS2D
  port RSRBPORT
  lan-dest-address 4000.dddd.dddd 40
  complete
```

Activate the Configuration

On the MVS2 system, use the following commands to activate the configuration:

```
v net,act,id=mvs2trld,update=add
v net,act,id=mvs2lnd
```

On the router Dustin, use the following command from the global configuration mode:

```
appn start
```

TN3270 Server DLUR Running on the Same CIP Example

Figure 27-18 shows the physical components for this example. Figure 27-19 shows the various parameters for each component in the configuration example.

Figure 27-18   *Topology for VTAM-to-TN3270 Server DLUR Running on the Same CIP Connection*

In Figure 27-19, the following activity occurs:

● The TN3270 server on the CMCC adapter takes on the role of an APPN EN running DLUR.

● The APPN NN in VTAM communicates with the CMPC driver over the channel.

● The CMPC driver on the CMCC adapter passes the data to the LLC2 stack on the CIP via a fast-path loopback driver to the TN3270 server on the CIP.

● The TN3270 server converts the 3270 data stream to a TN3270 data stream and forwards the packets to the IP TN3270 clients in the IP network.

The TN3270 server does not have to be in the same CMCC adapter as the CMPC driver.

Figure 27-19 *Parameters for VTAM-to-TN3270 DLUR Running on the Same Connection*

The following configurations apply to the example shown in Figure 27-19.

mvs2trle

```
MVS2TRE   VBUILD TYPE=TRL
MVS2TRLE TRLE   LNCTL=MPC,MAXBFRU=8,REPLYTO=3.0,
                READ=(2F8),
                WRITE=(2F9)
```

mvs2lne

```
MVS2NNE   VBUILD TYPE=LOCAL
MVS2PUE PU     TRLE=MVS2TRLE,
               ISTATUS=ACTIVE,
               XID=YES,CONNTYPE=APPN,CPCP=YES
```

swlagtn

```
SWLAGTN  VBUILD TYPE=SWNET,MAXGRP=10,MAXNO=10,MAXDLUR=10
LAGTNPU PU      ADDR=01,                                                    X
                MAXPATH=1,                                                  X
                IDBLK=017,IDNUM=EFEED,                                      X
                PUTYPE=2,                                                   X
                MAXDATA=4096,                                               X
                LUGROUP=TNGRP1,LUSEED=LAGLU##
```

tngrp1

```
TNGRP1E  VBUILD TYPE=LUGROUP
TNGRP1   LUGROUP
DYNAMIC  LU     DLOGMOD=D4C32XX3,                                           X
                MODETAB=ISTINCLM,USSTAB=USSTCPIP,SSCPFM=USS3270
@        LU     DLOGMOD=D4C32784,                                           X
                MODETAB=ISTINCLM,USSTAB=USSTCPIP,SSCPFM=USS3270
```

Additional Router Configuration for Router Honduras

```
interface Channel6/1
 cmpc C020 F8 CONFIGE READ
 cmpc C020 F9 CONFIGE WRITE
!
interface Channel6/2
 lan TokenRing 0
  source-bridge 88 3 100
  adapter 5 4000.eeee.eeee
  adapter 6 4000.0000.eeee
 tn3270-server
  dlur NETA.HOND327S NETA.MVS2
   lsap token-adapter 6  54
    link MVS2TN   rmac 4000.eeee.eeee rsap 50
   pu TNPU      017EFEED 172.18.1.218
  tg CONFIG  llc token-adapter 6 50 rmac 4000.eeee.eeee rsap 54
```

Activate the Configuration

On the MVS system, use the following commands to activate the configuration:

```
v net,act,id=mvstrle,update=add
v net,act,id=mvslne
v net,act,id=swhondpu
v net,act,id=swlagtn
v net,act,id=swhondcp
v net,act,id=tngrp1
```

On the router Honduras, use the following command from TN3270 configuration mode:

```
no shutdown
```

Cisco Mainframe Channel Connection Commands

Use the commands in this chapter to configure and monitor the Cisco Mainframe Channel Connection (CMCC) products which include the Channel Interface Processor (CIP) and the Channel Port Adapter (CPA). For hardware technical descriptions and for information about installing the router interfaces, refer to the hardware installation and maintenance publication for your particular product.

NOTE Unless otherwise specified, all commands in this chapter are supported on the Cisco 7000 with RSP7000, Cisco 7500 and the Cisco 7200 series routers.

For interface configuration information and examples, refer to Chapter 27, "Configuring Cisco Mainframe Channel Connection Adapters."

adapter

Use the **adapter** internal LAN configuration command to configure internal adapters. Use the **no** form of this command to remove an internal adapter.

adapter *adapter-number* [*mac-address*]
no adapter *adapter-number* [*mac-address*]

Syntax	Description
adapter-number	Number in the range 0 to 31 that uniquely identifies the internal adapter (relative adapter number) for all internal LANs of the same type on the CMCC adapter. When configuring CSNA, this value corresponds to the ADAPNO parameter defined in the Virtual Telecommunications Access Method (VTAM) Extended Communications Adapter (XCA) Major Node.
mac-address	(Optional) Media Access Control (MAC) address for this internal adapter. This is a hexadecimal value in the form *xxxx.xxxx.xxxx*.

Default
This command has no defaults.

Command Mode

Internal LAN interface configuration

Usage Guidelines

This command first appeared in Cisco IOS Release 11.0.

This command is valid only on the virtual channel interface. Internal adapters are used to provide LAN gateway MAC addresses for the following CMCC adapter features: CSNA, CMPC, and TN3270-Server.

Up to 18 internal adapters can be configured on a CMCC adapter. Internal adapters are configured on internal LANs. The only limit to the number of internal adapters you can configure on a single internal LAN is the limit of up to 18 total internal adapters per CMCC.

When removing an internal adapter configuration command or modifying an existing internal adapter, the *mac-address* parameter is not required. When in internal adapter configuration mode, the router prompt appears as follows:

router(cfg-adap-*type n-m*)#

In this syntax, *type* is the internal LAN type, *n* is the lan-id, and *m* is the adapter-number.

Example

Following is an example:

```
interface channel 1/2
 lan tokenring 20
  adapter 3 4000.7500.0003
  adapter 4 4000.7500.0004
 lan tokenring 10
  source-bridge 100 1 2000
  adapter 1 4000.7500.1111
```

Related Commands

To locate documentation of related commands, you can search online at www.cisco.com.

lan
llc2
name
source-bridge
show extended channel lan
show extended channel llc2
show extended channel connection-map llc2

channel-protocol

Use the **channel-protocol** interface configuration command to define a data rate of either 3 megabytes per second or 4.5 megabytes per second for Parallel Channel Interfaces.

channel-protocol [s | s4]

Syntax	Description
s	(Optional) Specifies a data rate of 3 megabytes per second.
s4	(Optional) Specifies a data rate of 4.5 megabytes per second.

Part
II

Command Reference

Default
If no value is specified, the default data rate for the PCA is 3 megabytes per second.

Command Mode
Interface configuration

Usage Guidelines
This command first appeared in Cisco IOS Release 10.2.

This command is valid on Parallel Channel Interfaces.

Example
The following example specifies a data rate of 4.5 megabytes per second for the interface:

```
channel-protocol s4
```

claw

Use the **claw** interface configuration command to configure a CLAW device (read and write subchannel) for communication with a mainframe TCP/IP stack in IP Datagram mode. This command can also be used to configure individual members of a CLAW backup group for the IP Host Backup feature.

claw *path device-address ip-address host-name device-name host-app device-app*
    [broadcast] [backup]
no claw *path device-address*

Syntax	Description
path	Hexadecimal value in the range 0000 to FFFF. This value specifies the logical channel path and consists of two digits for the physical connection (either on the host or on the ESCON director), one digit for the channel logical address, and one digit for the control unit logical address. If the path is not specified in the IOCP, the default values for channel logical address and control unit logical address is 0.
device-address	Hexadecimal value in the range 00 to FE. This is the unit address associated with the control unit number and path as specified in the host IOCP file. The device address must have an even value.
ip-address	IP address specified in the HOME statement of the host TCP/IP application configuration file.
host-name	Host name specified in the device statement in the host TCP/IP application configuration file.
device-name	CLAW workstation name specified in the device statement in the host TCP/IP application configuration file.
host-app	Host application name as specified in the host application file. If connected to the IBM TCP host offerings, or if the CLAW packing feature is not enabled on the mainframe TCPIP stack, this value will be **tcpip**, which is the constant specified in the host TCP/IP application file. When attached to other applications, this value must match the value hard coded in the host application. **PACKED** is another value that can be used for the *host-app* parameter to enable the CLAW packing feature.
device-app	CLAW workstation application specified in the host TCPIP application. If connected to the IBM TCP host offerings, or if the CLAW packing feature is not enabled on the mainframe TCPIP stack, this value will be **tcpip**, which is the constant specified in the host TCP/IP application file. When attached to other applications, this value must match the value hard coded in the host application. **PACKED** is another value that can be used for the *device-app* parameter to enable the CLAW packing feature.
broadcast	(Optional) Enables broadcast processing for this subchannel.
backup	(Optional) Enables this CLAW connection to be used as part of a backup group of CLAW connections for the specified IP address.

Default

This command has no defaults.

Command Mode

Interface configuration

Usage Guidelines

This command first appeared in Cisco IOS Release 10.2. The **packed** and **backup** options for this command first appeared in Cisco IOS Release 12.0.

This command defines information that is specific to the hardware interface and the IBM channels supported on the interface. When used with the **path** command, the **claw** command provides a quick way to configure a CLAW backup group.

CLAW devices are used to switch IP packets between a mainframe and a channel-attached router.

At most, 128 statements can be configured per interface because each interface is limited to 256 subchannels. Each CLAW device uses a read channel and a write channel. There is also a restriction of 64 unique paths.

A limit of 32 CLAW device configuration commands is recommended.

Duplicate IP addresses are invalid for nonbackup configurations.

Duplicate IP addresses are permitted if they appear within a backup group of only **claw** or **offload** interface configuration commands. All configuration commands in one backup group must specify the **backup** keyword.

You can use the **path** interface configuration command to specify a number of paths that belong to a backup group. In that case, a **claw** IP host backup configuration command is used that needs no *path* variable or **backup** keyword.

Examples

The following example shows how to enable IBM channel attach routing on channel interface 3/0, which is supporting an ESCON direct connection to the mainframe:

```
interface channel 3/0
ip address 172.18.4.49 255.255.255.248
claw c020 F4 172.18.4.52 HOSTB RTRA TCPIP TCPIP
```

The following example shows how to enable CLAW packing:

```
interface Channel 3/0
ip address 172.18.4.49 255.255.255.248
claw c010 F2 172.18.4.50 HOSTA RTRA PACKED PACKED
```

The following example shows how an IP host backup group is specified using the **backup** keyword:

```
interface Channel3/0
 no ip address
 no keepalive
 no shutdown
 claw 0100 C0 10.30.1.2 CISCOVM EVAL TCPIP TCPIP backup
 claw 0110 C0 10.30.1.2 CISCOVM EVAL TCPIP TCPIP backup
 claw 0120 C0 10.30.1.2 CISCOVM EVAL TCPIP TCPIP backup
 claw 0110 C2 10.30.1.3 CISCOVM EVAL TCPIP TCPIP
```

Related Commands

To locate documentation of related commands, you can search online at www.cisco.com.

claw (backup)
offload
path
show extended channel packing names
show extended channel packing stats
show extended channel subchannel
show extended channel statistics

claw (backup)

Use the **claw (backup)** configuration command to configure a CLAW device (read and write subchannel) for communication with a mainframe TCP/IP stack in Offload mode. This command can also be used to configure individual members of a CLAW backup group for the IP Host Backup feature.

> **claw** *device-address ip-address host-name device-name host-app device-app*
> [**broadcast**]
> **no claw** *device-address*

Syntax   Description

path   Hexadecimal value in the range 0000 to FFFF. This value specifies the
                       logical channel path and consists of two digits for the physical connection
                       (either on the host or on the ESCON director), one digit for the channel
                       logical address, and one digit for the control unit logical address. If the
                       path is not specified in the IOCP, the default values for channel logical
                       address and control unit logical address is 0.

device-address   Hexadecimal value in the range 00 to FE. This is the unit address
                       associated with the control unit number and path as specified in the host
                       IOCP file. The device address must have an even value.

Syntax	Description
host-name	Host name specified in the device statement in the host TCP/IP application configuration file.
device-name	CLAW workstation name specified in the device statement in the host TCP/IP application configuration file.
host-app	Host application name as specified in the host application file. When connected to the IBM TCP host offerings, this value will be **tcpip**, which is the constant specified in the host TCP/IP application file. When attached to other applications, this value must match the value hard coded in the host application.
device-app	CLAW workstation application specified in the host TCPIP application. When connected to the IBM TCP host offerings, this value will be **tcpip**, which is the constant specified in the host TCP/IP application file. When attached to other applications, this value must match the value hard coded in the host application.
broadcast	(Optional) Enables broadcast processing for this subchannel.

Default

This command has no defaults.

Command Mode

IP host backup configuration

Usage Guidelines

This command first appeared in Cisco IOS Release 12.0.

This command defines information that is specific to the hardware interface and the IBM channels supported on the interface.

CLAW devices are used to switch IP packets between a mainframe and a channel-attached router.

At most, 128 statements can be configured per interface because each interface is limited to 256 subchannels. Each CLAW device uses a read channel and a write channel. There is also a restriction of 64 unique paths.

A limit of 32 CLAW device configuration commands is recommended.

Duplicate IP addresses are invalid for non-backup configurations.

Duplicate IP addresses are permitted if they appear within a backup group of only **claw** or **offload** interface configuration commands. All configuration commands in one backup group must specify the **backup** keyword.

You can use the **path** interface configuration command to specify a number of paths that belong to a backup group. In that case, a **claw** IP host backup configuration command is used that needs no *path* variable or **backup** keyword.

Examples

The following examples show two methods for entering the same IP host backup group information. The first group of commands is the long form, using the **claw** interface configuration command. The second group is the shortcut, using the **path** interface configuration command and a **claw** IP host backup configuration command.

Long form:

```
claw c000 00 198.92.10.5 sysa router1 tcpip tcpip backup
claw c100 00 198.92.10.5 sysa router1 tcpip tcpip backup
claw c200 00 198.92.10.5 sysa router1 tcpip tcpip backup
```

Shortcut form:

```
path c000 c100 c200
  claw 00 198.92.10.5 sysa router1 tcpip tcpip
```

Related Commands

To locate documentation of related commands, you can search online at www.cisco.com.

claw
offload
path
show extended channel packing names
show extended channel packing stats
show extended channel subchannel
show extended channel statistics

clear extended counters

Use the **clear extended counters** EXEC command to clear the extended interface counters associated with CMCC features.

> **clear extended counters** [**channel** *slot/port* [**csna** | **icmp-stack** | **ip-stack** |
> **llc2** | **statistics** | **tcp-connections** | **tcp-stack** | **tg** | **tn3270-server** | **udp-stack**]]

Syntax   Description

Syntax	Description
channel	(Optional) Specifies a channel interface.
slot	(Optional) Slot number.
port	(Optional) Port number.
csna	(Optional) Clears CSNA feature counters.
icmp-stack	(Optional) Clears ICMP stack counters.
ip-stack	(Optional) Clears IP stack counters.
llc2	(Optional) Clears LLC2 counters.
statistics	(Optional) Clears subchannel statistic counters.
tcp-connections	(Optional) Clears TCP connection counters.
tcp-stack	(Optional) Clears TCP stack counters.
tg	(Optional) Clears TG counters.
tn3270-server	(Optional) Clears TN3270 Server counters.
udp-stack	(Optional) Clears UDP stack counters.

Command Mode
Privileged EXEC

Usage Guidelines
This command first appeared in Cisco IOS Release 11.3.

This command is valid on both the physical and virtual channel interfaces. To clear counters for a selected CMCC feature, you must specify the channel interface on which the feature is configured or running.

Counters displayed using the **show extended channel** EXEC command are cleared using this command.

Entering any form of this command will prompt the user for a confirmation before clearing any counters. A "CLEAR-5-EXT_COUNT" message is displayed to indicate successful completion of the command.

These counters will be cleared in the show commands and remain uncleared when obtained via the SNMP interface.

Example

The following is an example of the command:

```
clear extended counters
```

Related Commands

To locate documentation of related commands, you can search online at www.cisco.com.

show extended channel csna
show extended channel icmp-stack
show extended channel ip-stack
show extended channel lan
show extended channel llc2
show extended channel statistics
show extended channel tcp-connections
show extended channel tcp-stack
show extended channel tg
show extended channel tn3270-server
show extended channel udp-stack

client (lu limit)

Use the **client** TN3270 configuration command to limit the number of LU sessions that can be established from a client IP address. Use the **no** form of this command to remove a single LU limit associated with a particular IP address.

> **client** [*ip* [*ip-mask*]] **lu maximum** *number*
> **no client** [*ip* [*ip-mask*]] [**lu maximum** *number*]

Syntax	Description
ip	(Optional) IP address of the client. The *ip* value is optional when setting the maximum number of LU sessions. If no IP address is specified, then the limit is applied to all clients.
ip-mask	(Optional) IP network mask for the client. The default is 255.255.255.255
number	(Optional and ignored in **no** form of the command) Maximum number of LU sessions. The allowed value is from 0 to 65,535.

Default

The default is that there is no limit on the number of concurrent sessions from one client IP address.

In the **no** form of this command, the default *number* is 65,535.

Command Mode

TN3270 configuration

Usage Guidelines

This command first appeared in Cisco IOS Release 12.0.

This command is valid only on the virtual channel interface. An instance of the **client** (lu limit) command on a given **tn3270-server** is uniquely identified by the *ip-mask* and the logical AND of the *ip-address* with that mask. For example, if the command is entered as the following:

```
client 10.1.1.62 255.255.255.192 lu maximum 2
```

It will be stored (and subsequently displayed by **write term**) as:

```
client 10.1.1.0 255.255.255.192 lu maximum 2
```

The maximum specified on the command can be changed simply by reissuing the command with the new value. It is not necessary to remove the command first.

When you use the **no client** command, only the corresponding **client lu maximum** statement is removed, as identified by the IP address and IP address mask combination. You cannot use **no client** to specify an unlimited number of LU sessions.

For example, if a service bureau has 8000 clients and each client IP address is limited to four LU sessions, you will never need more than 32,000 concurrent LU definitions even when the service is running at 100 percent capacity.

Examples

The following example limits all clients to a maximum of two LU sessions:

```
client lu maximum 2
```

The following example limits a client at IP address 10.1.1.28 to a maximum of three LU sessions:

```
client 10.1.1.28 lu maximum 3
```

The LU limit can be applied to different subnets as shown in the following example. The most exact match to the client IP address is chosen. Clients with IP addresses that reside in the subnet 10.1.1.64

(those with IP addresses in the range of 10.1.1.64 through 10.1.1.127) are limited to a maximum of 5 LU sessions while other clients with IP addresses in the subnet 10.1.1.0 are limited to a maximum of 4 LU sessions.

```
client 10.1.1.0  255.255.255.0 lu maximum 4
client 10.1.1.64 255.255.255.192 lu maximum 5
```

The following example prevents an LU session for the client at IP address 10.1.1.28:

```
client 10.1.1.28 lu maximum 0
```

Related Commands

To locate documentation of related commands, you can search online at www.cisco.com.

maximum-lus

client (lu nailing)

Use the **client** TN3270 PU configuration mode command to define a range of locaddrs to be reserved for remote devices. Use the **no** form of this command to cancel this definition.

> **client** [**printer**] **ip** *ip-address* [*ip-mask*] **lu** *first-locaddr* [*last-locaddr*]
> **no client** [**printer**] **ip** *ip-address* [*ip-mask*] **lu** *first-locaddr* [*last-locaddr*]

Syntax	Description
printer	(Optional) Specifies that a client connection from the nailed IP addresses will be nailed to one of the specified LUs only if the client-session negotiates a model type of 328*n*, where *n* is any alphanumeric character. Moreover, it ensures that a printer matching the IP address condition can only use an LU nailed as a printer LU.
	If the **printer** keyword is not specified for any **client** statement that has this IP address set, all model types can use this range of LUs.
ip-address	Specifies remote client IP address.
ip-mask	(Optional) The mask applied to the remote device address. Multiple client IP addresses in the same subnet can be nailed to the same range of *locaddrs*.
first-locaddr	Defines a single *locaddr* to nail.
last-locaddr	(Optional) Defines the end range of inclusive *locaddrs* to be nailed from *first-locaddr* to *last-locaddr*.

Default

No LUs are nailed. They are all available to any client.

Command Mode

TN3270 PU configuration mode

Usage Guidelines

This command first appeared in Cisco IOS Release 11.3.

This command is valid only on the virtual channel interface. Multiple statements can be configured for one IP address or nail type either on one PU or multiple PUs. But each LU can only appear in one client statement.

A client with a nailed IP address can request one of the nailed LUs via the TN3270 device name. If the requested LU is not available, then the connection is rejected.

A client with a nailed IP address cannot request an LU outside the range of nailed LUs for its type (screen or printer).

A client with a nonnailed IP address cannot request an LU that is configured as nailed.

The command will be rejected if some of the *locaddrs* are already nailed. If the *locaddrs* are currently in use by other remote clients, the nailing statement will take effect only when the *locaddr* is made available.

To cancel the definition, the **no client** form of the command must be entered exactly as the **client** command was originally configured. If a range of *locaddrs* was specified, to cancel this definition the whole range of *locaddrs* must be specified. There is no way to cancel only one *locaddr* if a whole range of *locaddrs* was configured.

Examples

In the following example, *locaddrs* 1 to 50 are reserved for remote devices in the 171.69.176.0 subnet:

```
interface channel 2/2
 tn3270-server
 pu BAGE4
  client ip 171.69.176.28 255.255.255.0 lu 1 50
```

In the following example, *locaddrs* 1 to 40 are reserved for screen devices in the 171.69.176.0 subnet, while 41 to 50 are reserved for printers in that subnet:

```
interface channel 2/2
 tn3270-server
 pu BAGE4
  client ip 171.69.176.28 255.255.255.0 lu 1 40
  client printer ip 171.69.176.28 255.255.255.0 lu 41 50
```

In the following example, there is an attempt to cancel a definition but this is rejected because it does not specify the full range of locaddrs and the second attempt fails to specify the correct nail type:

```
interface channel 2/2
 tn3270-server
  pu BAGE4
  client printer ip 171.69.176.50 255.255.255.0 lu 1 100
  no client printer ip 171.69.176.50 255.255.255.0 lu 1
  %Invalid LU range specified
  no client ip 171.69.176.50 255.255.255.0 lu 1 100
  %client ip 171.69.176.50 nail type not matched with configured nail type printer
```

Related Commands

To locate documentation of related commands, you can search online at www.cisco.com.

pu (direct)
pu (DLUR)

cmpc

Use the **cmpc** interface configuration command to configure a CMPC read subchannel and a CMPC write subchannel. Use the **no** form of this command to remove a subchannel definition and to deactivate the transmission group.

> **cmpc** *path device tg-name* {**read** | **write**}
> **no cmpc** *path device*

Syntax	Description
path	Hexadecimal value in the range 0000 to FFFF. This value specifies the logical channel path and consists of two digits for the physical connection (either on the host or on the ESCON director), one digit for the channel logical address, and one digit for the control unit logical address. If the path is not specified in the IOCP, the default values for channel logical address and control unit logical address is 0.
device	Hexadecimal value in the range of 00 to FF. This is the unit address associated with the control unit number and path as specified in the host IOCP file.
tg-name	The name of the CMPC transmission group. The maximum length of the name is eight characters.
read	The same value read , as specified in the TRL major node.
write	The same value write, as specified in the TRL major node.

Default
No default is specified.

Command Mode
Interface configuration

Usage Guidelines
This command first appeared in Cisco IOS Release 11.3.

Each **cmpc** configuration command in a given CMPC transmission group specifies the same transmission group name. The corresponding **tg** command specifies the same transmission group name. Together, the **cmpc** and **tg** commands make up the transmission group specification.

The **cmpc** command defines the read/write subchannel addresses that CMPC uses to connect to the host. The command corresponds to the definitions in the TRL major node on the host. Configure the CMPC command on a CMCC adapter physical interface. Configure one read subchannel and one write subchannel. If CMPC is configured on a CMCC adapter with two physical interfaces, the read and write CMPC subchannels may be configured on separate physical interfaces.

The **no cmpc** command deactivates the CMPC subchannel. If the transmission group is used for a non-HPR connection, all sessions using the TG will be terminated immediately. If the transmission group is an HPR connection, all sessions using the transmission group will be terminated if no other HPR connection is available to the host.

Example
The following example configures a read and a write subchannel on path C020 for the CMPC transmission group named CONFIGE:

```
cmpc C020 F8 CONFIGE READ
cmpc C020 F9 CONFIGE WRITE
```

Related Commands
To locate documentation of related commands, you can search online at www.cisco.com.

tg
show extended channel cmpc
show extended channel tg
show extended channel subchannel
show extended channel statistics

csna

Use the **csna** interface configuration command to configure SNA support on a CMCC physical channel interface. This command is used to specify the path and device/subchannel on a physical channel of the router to communicate with an attached mainframe. Use the **no** form of this command to delete the CSNA device path.

> **csna** *path device* [**maxpiu** *value*] [**time-delay** *value*] [**length-delay** *value*]
> **no csna** *path device*

Syntax	Description
path	Hexadecimal value in the range 0000 to FFFF. This value specifies the logical channel path and consists of two digits for the physical connection (either on the host or on the ESCON director), one digit for the channel logical address, and one digit for the control unit logical address. If the path is not specified in the IOCP, the default values for channel logical address and control unit logical address is 0.
device	Hexadecimal value in the range 00 to FF. This is the unit address associated with the control unit number and path as specified in the host IOCP file.
maxpiu *value*	(Optional) Maximum channel I/0 block size in bytes that is transmitted across the physical channel from the CMCC adapter to the attached mainframe. The range is 4096 to 65,535 bytes. The default is 20,470 bytes.
time-delay *value*	(Optional) Number of milliseconds a host-bound SNA frame may be delayed in order to maximize the channel I/0 block size. The range is 0 to 100 ms. The default is 10 ms.
length-delay *value*	(Optional) Amount of SNA frame data in bytes the CSNA subchannel accumulates before transmitting the accumulated channel I/0 block to the attached mainframe. The range is 0 to 65,535 bytes. The default is 20,470 bytes.

Defaults

maxpiu *value*: 20470 (0x4ff6) bytes
time-delay *value*: 10 ms
length-delay *value*: 20470 (0x4ff6) bytes

Command Mode

Interface configuration

Usage Guidelines

This command first appeared in Cisco IOS Release 11.0.

The parameters **maxpiu**, **time-delay** and **length-delay** control the characteristics of host-bound traffic for the CSNA subchannel. The channel protocol used by CSNA allows multiple SNA frames to be blocked into one channel I/0 block, reducing the channel bandwidth utilization and mainframe and CMCC adapter process utilization.

The **maxpiu** parameter allows you to set the maximum size of a host-bound channel I/0 block.

The **time-delay** parameter instructs the CSNA subchannel to delay sending the channel I/0 block for the specified time in milliseconds, from the time the first SNA packet is blocked. This can increase the network latency for an SNA packet by up to the specified time delay.

The length-delay parameter instructs the CSNA subchannel to delay sending the channel I/0 block until it contains the number of bytes specified by the length-delay parameter. An accumulated block is sent to the mainframe if one of the following conditions is true:

● The time-delay expires

● The channel I/0 block reaches the length-delay size

● Channel I/0 block reaches the maxpiu size

A time-delay value of 0 instructs the CSNA subchannel to send SNA packets to the mainframe as soon as they are received from the network. A length-delay value of 0 instructs the CSNA subchannel to ignore this parameter.

The **no csna** command deactivates and removes the CSNA subchannel configuration. It also deactivates all LLC2 sessions established over the subchannel.

Example

The following example shows CSNA, offload, and CLAW configured on a channel interface. CSNA has no dependencies to CLAW, Offload, or CMPC.

```
interface channel 1/0
 no ip address
 no keepalive
 offload c700 c0 172.18.1.127 TCPIP OS2TCP TCPIP TCPIP TCPIP API
 claw C700 c2 172.18.1.219 EVAL CISCOVM AAA BBB
 csna c700 c4
 csna c700 c5 maxpiu 65535 time-delay 100 length-delay 65535
 csna c700 c6 maxpiu 65535 time-delay 100
```

Related Commands

To locate documentation of related commands, you can search online at www.cisco.com.

lan
adapter
show extended channel csna
show extended channel connection-map llc2
show extended channel subchannel
show extended channel statistics

dlur

Use the **dlur** TN3270 configuration command to enable the Systems Network Architecture (SNA) session switch function on the CMCC adapter, or to enter dependent logical unit requester (DLUR) configuration mode. Use the **no** form of this command to disable the SNA session switch function and discard all parameter values associated with the SNA session switch.

> **dlur** [*fq-cpname fq-dlusname*]
> **no dlur**

Syntax

Syntax	Description
fq-cpname	(Optional) Fully qualified control point (CP) name used by the SNA session switch and the logical unit (LU) name for the DLUR function. This name must be unique among APPN nodes in the network including other *fq-cpname* values specified on all other TN3270 servers running under Cisco IOS software.
fq-dlusname	(Optional) Fully qualified name of the primary choice for the dependent LU server (DLUS). This is the name of an LU, usually a CP, in an APPN host. The *fq-dlusname* value can be repeated and shared across servers.

Default

No DLUR function is enabled.

Command Mode

TN3270 configuration

Usage Guidelines

This command first appeared in Cisco IOS Release 11.2.

This command is valid only on the virtual channel interface. If the SNA session switch function is already enabled, the **dlur** command with no arguments puts you in DLUR configuration mode. The session switch function implements an End Node DLUR.

Several parameters in the DLUR configuration mode consist of fully qualified names, as defined by the APPN architecture. Fully qualified names consist of two case-insensitive alphanumeric strings, separated by a period. However, for compatibility with existing APPN products, including VTAM, the characters "#" (pound), "@" (at), and "$" (dollar) are allowed in the fully qualified name strings. Each string is from one to eight characters long; for example, RA12.NODM1PP. The portion of the name before the period is the NETID and is shared between entities in the same logical network.

The **no dlur** command hierarchically deletes all resources defined beneath it.

Example

The following example performs two functions: It enters DLUR configuration mode and it enables the DLUR function and defines the LU name for the DLUR as SYD.TN3020 and the primary choice for DLUS as SYD.VMG. Note that the NETID portion of both names is the same:

```
dlur SYD.TN3020 SYD.VMG
```

Related Commands

To locate documentation of related commands, you can search online at www.cisco.com.

dlus-backup
lsap
preferred-nnserver
pu (DLUR)

dlus-backup

Use the **dlus-backup** DLUR configuration command to specify a backup DLUS for the DLUR function. Use the **no** form of this command to remove a backup DLUS name.

> **dlus-backup** *dlusname2*
> **no dlus-backup**

Syntax	Description
dlusname2	Fully qualified name of the backup DLUS for the DLUR.

Default
No backup DLUS is specified.

Command Mode
DLUR configuration

Usage Guidelines
This command first appeared in Cisco IOS Release 11.2.

This command is valid only on the virtual channel interface. Only one backup DLUS can be specified per CMCC adapter. If the backup DLUS specified in the **dlus-backup** command is in use when a **no dlus-backup** is issued, the connection is not torn down.

Several parameters in the DLUR configuration mode consist of fully qualified names, as defined by the APPN architecture. Fully qualified names consist of two case-insensitive alphanumeric strings, separated by a period. However, for compatibility with existing APPN products, including VTAM, the characters "#" (pound), "@" (at), and "$" (dollar) are allowed in the fully qualified name strings. Each string is from one to eight characters long; for example, RA12.NODM1PP. The portion of the name before the period is the NETID and is shared between entities in the same logical network.

Example
The following example specifies SYD.VMX as the backup DLUS:

```
dlus-backup SYD.VMX
```

Related Commands
To locate documentation of related commands, you can search online at www.cisco.com.

dlur

exception slot

Use the **exception slot** global configuration command to provide a core dump of a CMCC adapter. This command is only supported on the Cisco 7000 with RSP7000 and Cisco 7500 series. Use the **no** form of the command to disable the core dump.

> **exception slot** [*slot*] *protocol://host/filename*
> **no exception slot** [*slot*] *protocol://host/filename*

Syntax	Description
slot	(Optional) Slot number of the CMCC adapter. If no *slot* is specified, all installed CMCC adapters will output a core dump when they halt unexpectedly.
protocol	Protocol for transferring the file. Currently, the only allowed value is FTP.
host	Name or IP address of the host that receives the core dump information.
filename	Filename on the host that receives the core dump information. The maximum name length is 31 characters. When written to the host, *slot* is automatically appended, where *slot* is the slot number.

Part
II

Command Reference

Default

This command has no defaults.

Command Mode

Global configuration

Usage Guidelines

This command first appeared in Cisco IOS Release 11.2.

You must configure FTP services on the router before you can create a CMCC adapter core dump.

Do not exceed your host limits on filename length. An additional two characters are added to the filename, *.slot*, where *slot* is the slot number.

Example

The following example shows how to configure a router to perform a CMCC adapter core dump. Assuming the CIP is installed in slot 3, the filename `cipdump.3` will be written to the host.

```
ip domain-name cisco.com
ip name-server 168.69.161.21
ip ftp username tech1
ip ftp password tech1
exception slot ftp://168.18.2.196/cipdump
```

Related Commands

To locate documentation of related commands, you can search online at www.cisco.com.

ip domain-name
ip name-server
ip ftp username
ip ftp password

generic-pool

Use the **generic-pool** TN3270 configuration command to specify whether or not left-over LUs will be made available to TN3270 sessions that do not request a specific LU or LU pool through TN3270E. Use the **no** form of this command to selectively remove the permit or deny condition of generic pool use.

> **generic-pool** {**permit** | **deny**}
> **no generic-pool**

Syntax	Description
permit	Left-over LUs should be made available to TN3270 users wanting generic sessions. This value is the default.
deny	Left-over LUs should not be given to a generic pool. The physical unit (PU) is not automatically fully populated with 255 LOCADDR definitions. The default is the value configured in TN3270 configuration mode.

Defaults

In TN3270 configuration mode, generic pool use is permitted.

In PU configuration mode, the default is the value currently configured in TN3270 configuration mode.

Command Modes

TN3270 configuration

PU configuration

Usage Guidelines

This command first appeared in Cisco IOS Release 11.2.

This command is valid only on the virtual channel interface.

A left-over LU is defined as one for which all of the following conditions are true:

● The system services control point (SSCP) did not send an ACTLU during PU start-up; and

● The PU controlling the LU is capable of carrying product set ID (PSID) vectors on network management vector transport (NMVT) messages, thus allowing dynamic definition of dependent LU (DDDLU) operation for that LU.

All LUs in the generic pool are, by definition, DDDLU capable.

Values entered for **generic-pool** in TN3270 configuration mode apply to all PUs for that TN3270 server but can be changed in PU configuration mode.

In PU configuration mode, a **no generic-pool** command will restore the **generic-pool** value entered in TN3270 command mode.

In TN3270 configuration mode, the **no generic-pool** command reverts to the default, which permits generic pool use.

The command takes effect immediately. If **generic-pool deny** is specified on a PU, no further dynamic connections to it will be allowed. Existing sessions are unaffected, but as they terminate, the LUs will not become available for dynamic connections.

Similarly, if **generic-pool permit** is specified, any inactive LUs are immediately available for dynamic connections. Moreover, any active LUs that were dynamic previously (before **generic-pool deny** was issued) return to being dynamic.

Example

The following example permits generic LU pool use:

```
generic-pool permit
```

Related Commands

To locate documentation of related commands, you can search online at www.cisco.com.

client (lu nailing)

idle-time

Use the **idle-time** TN3270 configuration command to specify how many seconds of LU inactivity, from both host and client, before the TN3270 session is disconnected. Use the **no** form of this command to cancel the idle time period and return to the default.

> **idle-time** *seconds*
> **no idle-time**

Syntax	Description
seconds	Idle time in seconds, from 0 to 65,535. A value of 0 means the session is never disconnected.

Defaults

The default in TN3270 configuration mode is that the session is never disconnected (0).

The default in PU configuration mode is the value currently configured in TN3270 configuration mode.

Command Modes

TN3270 configuration

PU configuration

Usage Guidelines

This command first appeared in Cisco IOS Release 11.2.

The **idle-time** command is valid only on the virtual channel interface, and can be entered in either TN3270 configuration mode or PU configuration mode. A value entered in TN3270 mode applies to all PUs for that TN3270 server, except as overridden by values entered in PU configuration mode.

A **no idle-time** command entered in PU configuration mode will restore the idle-time value entered in TN3270 command mode.

The **idle-time** command affects currently active and future TN3270 sessions. For example, if the **idle-time** value is reduced from 900 seconds to 600 seconds, sessions that have been idle for between 600 and 900 seconds are immediately disconnected.

NOTE   For the purposes of idle-time logic, TIMING-MARKs generated by the keepalive logic do not constitute "activity."

Examples

The following command sets an idle-time disconnect value of 10 minutes:

```
idle-time 600
```

The following command entered in TN3270 configuration mode sets the default idle-time disconnect value to 0, or never disconnect:

```
no idle-time
```

Related Commands

To locate documentation of related commands, you can search online at www.cisco.com.

keepalive
timing-mark

interface channel

Use the **interface channel** global configuration command to specify a channel attach interface and enter interface configuration mode.

        interface channel *slot/port*

Syntax	Description
slot	Slot number where the CMCC adapter is located.
port	Inteface where the CMCC adapter is located.

Default

This command has no defaults.

Command Mode

Global configuration

Usage Guidelines

This command first appeared in Cisco IOS Release 10.2.

Example

The following example shows how to enter interface configuration mode for a CIP in slot 2 and begin configuring port 0:

```
interface channel 2/0
```

Related Commands

To locate documentation of related commands, you can search online at www.cisco.com.

channel-protocol
claw
cmpc
csna
lan
max-llc2-sessions
offload
path
tg
tn3270-server

ip precedence

Use the **ip precedence** command to specify the precedence level for IP traffic in the TN3270 server. Use the **no** form of this command to remove the precedence value.

> **ip precedence** {**screen** | **printer**} *value*
> **no ip precedence** {**screen** | **printer**}

Syntax	Description
screen	Specifies the precedence is for screen devices.
printer	Specifies the precedence is for printer devices.
value	Sets the precedence priority. A value between 0 and 7, with 7 being the highest priority. The default is 0.

Default

The default is a precedence value of 0 for both screens and printers.

Command Modes

TN3270 server configuration mode

TN3270 PU configuration mode

Usage Guidelines

This command first appeared in Cisco IOS Release 11.3.

This command is valid only on the virtual channel interface. Precedence values applied in TN3270 PU configuration mode override values applied in TN3270 server configuration mode.

You can enter new or different values for IP precedence without first using the **no** form of this command.

During initial Telnet negotiations to establish, or bind, the session an IP precedence value of 0 and IP TOS value of 0 is used. These values are used until the bind takes place. When the session is a type 2 bind, the TN3270 client is assumed to be a screen; otherwise, the client is assumed to be a printer.

Example

The following example assigns a precedence value of 3 to printers:

```
ip precedence printer 3
```

Related Commands

To locate documentation of related commands, you can search online at www.cisco.com.

ip tos

ip tos

Use the **ip tos** command to specify the ToS level for IP traffic in the TN3270 server. Use the **no** form of this command to remove the ToS value.

> **ip tos** {**screen** | **printer**} *value*
> **no ip tos** {**screen** | **printer**}

Syntax	Description
screen	Specifies the ToS is for screen devices.
printer	Specifies the ToS is for printer devices.
value	Sets the ToS priority. A value between 0 and 15. The default is 0.

Default

The default is a ToS value of 0 for both screens and printers.

Command Modes

TN3270 server configuration mode

TN3270 PU configuration mode

Usage Guidelines

This command first appeared in Cisco IOS Release 11.3.

This command is valid only on the virtual channel interface. ToS values applied in TN3270 PU configuration mode override values applied in TN3270 server configuration mode.

The default ToS values for screen and printer are 0. However, RFC 1349 recommends different default values. Specifically, the RFC recommends a default minimize screen delay value of 8 and a default maximize printer throughput value of 4. You must configure these values using the **ip tos** command if you want to comply to the defaults as stated in the RFC.

Table 28-1 shows the values described in RFC 1349.

Table 28-1   *ToS Defined Values*

Value	Definition	Action
0	All normal	Use default metric.
8	Minimize delay	Use delay metric.
4	Maximize throughput	Use default metric.
2	Maximize reliability	Use reliability metric.
1	Minimize monetary cost	Use cost metric.
Other	Not defined	Reserved for future use.

During initial Telnet negotiations to establish, or bind, the session, an IP precedence value of 0 and IP ToS value of 0 is used. These values are used until the bind takes place. When the session is a type 2 bind, the TN3270 client is assumed to be a screen; otherwise the client is assumed to be a printer.

When you use the **no** form of the command, the ToS value is either set to 0 for that configuration mode or the value set at a previous (higher) configuration mode is used. For example, if you are at the TN3270 PU configuration mode and issue a **no ip tos screen** command, any value you configured previously at the TN3270 server configuration mode will take effect.

You can enter new or different values for ToS without first using the **no** form of this command.

Example

In the following example, the TN3270 server TOS screen value is set to 10 and a specific PU ToS screen value is set to 0:

```
interface channel 3/2
  tn3270-server
   ip tos screen 8
   ip tos printer 4
  pu PUS2
   ip tos screen 0
```

Related Commands

To locate documentation of related commands, you can search online at www.cisco.com.

ip precedence

keepalive

Use the **keepalive** TN3270 configuration command to specify how many seconds of inactivity elapse before transmission of a DO TIMING-MARK to the TN3270 client. Use the **no** form of this command to cancel the keepalive period and return to the default.

keepalive *seconds*
no keepalive

Syntax

	Description
seconds	Number of seconds, from 0 to 65,535. A value of 0 means no keepalive signals are sent. The default is 1800 seconds (30 minutes).

Defaults

The default in TN3270 configuration mode is 1800 seconds (30 minutes).

The default in PU configuration mode is the value currently configured in TN3270 configuration mode.

Command Modes

TN3270 configuration

PU configuration

Usage Guidelines

This command first appeared in Cisco IOS Release 11.2.

The **keepalive** command is valid only on the virtual channel interface. This command can be entered in either TN3270 configuration mode or PU configuration mode. A value entered in TN3270 mode applies to all PUs for that TN3270 server, except as overridden by values entered in PU configuration mode. A **no keepalive** command entered in PU configuration mode will restore the **keepalive** value entered in TN3270 command mode.

If the client does not reply within 30 minutes of the transmission of the DO TIMING-MARK, the TN3270 server disconnects the TN3270 session. The DO TIMING-MARK is a Telnet protocol operation that does not affect the client operation.

If the IP path to the client is broken, the TCP layer will detect the failure to acknowledge the DO TIMING-MARK and initiate disconnection. This action will usually take much less than 30 minutes.

The keepalive command affects currently active and future TN3270 sessions. For example, reducing the value to a smaller nonzero value will cause an immediate burst of DO TIMING-MARKs on those sessions that have been inactive for a period of time greater than the new, smaller value.

Examples

The following example sets keepalive disconnect value of 15 minutes (900 seconds):

```
keepalive 900
```

The following example entered in TN3270 configuration mode sets the keepalive disconnect value to 1800 seconds, the default:

```
no keepalive
```

Related Commands

To locate documentation of related commands, you can search online at www.cisco.com.

idle-time
timing-mark

lan

Use the **lan** interface configuration command to configure an internal LAN on a CMCC adapter interface and enter the internal LAN configuration mode. Use the **no** form of the command to remove an internal LAN interface.

> **lan** *type lan-id*
> **no lan** *type lan-id*

Syntax	Description
type	Interface type for this internal LAN: **tokenring**.
lan-id	A number 0 to 31 that uniquely identifies this internal LAN on this CMCC adapter. This value must be unique between all internal LANs of the same interface type on a CMCC adapter.

Default
This command has no defaults.

Command Mode
Interface configuration

Usage Guidelines
This command first appeared in Cisco IOS Release 11.0.

This command is valid only on the virtual channel interface. All internal adapters configured on the internal LAN must be removed first before the internal LAN can be removed.

A CMCC internal LAN can be configured as a SRB LAN. This allows LLC packets to be bridged between the CMCC adapter and IOS, providing a means to link the internal LAN to IOS SNA features such as SRB, DLSw+, RSRB, SDLLc, QLLC, APPN, and SR/TLB.

An internal LAN can only be configured on a virtual channel interface of a CMCC adapter. You enter the internal LAn configuration mode by issuing the command for an internal LAN that already exists or when you configure an internal LAN for the first time. In the internal LAN configuration mode, the router prompt appears as follows:

router (cfg-lan-*type n*) #

In this syntax, *type* is the specified internal LAN type and *n* is the specified *lan-id*.

Example
The following example shows how to configure an internal LAN Token Ring with a LAN ID of 20 on the channel interface 1/2:

```
interface channel 1/2
 lan tokenring 20
```

Related Commands

To locate documentation of related commands, you can search online at www.cisco.com.

adapter
show extended channel lan
source-bridge

link

Use the link DLUR SAP configuration command to define and activate a link to a host. Use the **no** form of this command to delete the link definition.

> **link** *name* [**rmac** *rmac*] [**rsap** *rsap*]
> **no link** *name*

Syntax   Description

name   Link name, from one to eight alphanumeric characters. The first
                      character must be alphabetic. The name must be unique within the
                      DLUR function.

rmac   (Optional) Remote MAC address of the form *xxxx.xxxx.xxxx* in
                      hexadecimal. If not specified, a loopback link to another SAP on
                      the same internal LAN adapter is assumed.

rsap   (Optional) Remote SAP address, 04 to FC in hexadecimal. The
                      rsap value must be even and should be a multiple of 4, but this
                      requirement is not enforced. The *rsap* value default is 04.

Defaults

No DLUR link is defined.

The default remote SAP address is 04 (hexadecimal).

Command Mode

DLUR SAP configuration

Usage Guidelines

This command first appeared in Cisco IOS Release 11.2.

This command is valid only on the virtual channel interface. The combination of *rmac* and *rsap* must be unique within the DLUR SAP function. These values can only be changed by deleting the link definition, using the **no link** command, and recreating the link definition.

For a link via a channel on this CMCC adapter, the TN3270 server and the hosts should open different adapters. Using different adapters avoids any contention for SAP numbers, and is also necessary if you configure duplicate MAC addresses for fallback CSNA or CMPC access to the host.

Examples

The following example defines a link name and a remote SAP address:

```
link LINK5 rsap 08
```

The following example shows different adapter numbers configured on the same internal LAN to avoid SAP contention. The host uses SAP 4 on Token Ring adapter 0.

```
lan tokenring 0
 adapter 0 4000.0000.0001
 adapter 1 4000.0000.0002
tn3270-server
 dlur ...
 lsap token-adapter 1
  link HOST rmac 4000.0000.0001 rsap 4
```

Related Commands

To locate documentation of related commands, you can search online at www.cisco.com.

adapter
dlur
lan
lsap

lsap

Use the **lsap** DLUR configuration command to create a SAP in the SNA session switch, or to enter DLUR SAP configuration mode. Use the **no** form of this command to delete a SAP and all SNA session switch links using the internal LAN interface.

> **lsap**
> **lsap** *type adapter-number* [*lsap*]
> **no lsap** *type adapter-number* [*lsap*]

Syntax	Description
type	Internal adapter type on the CIP card, which corresponds to the value specified in the **lan** internal LAN configuration command. The currently supported type is **token-adapter**.
adapter-number	Internal adapter interface on the CIP card, which is the same value specified in the **adapter** internal LAN configuration command.
lsap	(Optional) Local SAP number, 04 to FC, in hex. The value must be even and should normally be a multiple of four. It must be unique within the internal adapter in that no other 802.2 clients of that adapter, in the router or in a host, should be allocated the same SAP. The default value is C0.

Default

The default value for *lsap* is hexadecimal C0.

Command Mode

DLUR configuration

Usage Guidelines

This command first appeared in Cisco IOS Release 11.2.

The **lsap** command is valid only on the virtual channel interface. If the SAP in the SNA session switch function is already created, the **lsap** command with no arguments puts you in DLUR SAP configuration mode.

The **lsap** command can be entered only in DLUR configuration mode.

The **lsap** command uses values that are defined in two other commands: the **lan** internal LAN configuration command and the **adapter** internal LAN configuration command. The **lan** *type* and **adapter** *adapter-number* values configured on the CMCC internal LAN interface are used in the **lsap** command. However, the **lan** *type* keyword is a little different. Where the *type* on the **lan** command is **tokenring**, the corresponding *type* on **lsap** is **token-adapter**. This emphasizes that the number that follows is an **adapter** number, not a **lan** number.

The **no lsap** command hierarchically deletes any links using it. Any sessions using those links are lost.

Example

The following example defines an adapter type, an adapter number, and a local SAP:

```
lsap token 0 B0
```

Related Commands

To locate documentation of related commands, you can search online at www.cisco.com.

adapter
dlur
lan

max-llc2-sessions

Use the **max-llc2-sessions** interface configuration command to specify the maximum number of LLC2 sessions supported on the CMCC adapter. Use the **no** form of this command to remove the current value and change back to the default value.

> **max-llc2-sessions** *number*
> **no max-llc2-sessions** *number*

Syntax   Description

number   A value in the range 0 to 6000 LLC sessions. If this command is not configured, the default is 256.

Default

The default number of sessions is 256.

Command Mode

Interface configuration

Usage Guidelines

This command first appeared in Cisco IOS Release 11.0.

This command is valid only on the virtual channel interface. A value of 0 indicates that the maximum number of LLC2 sessions is limited to 6000, however the memory on the CMCC adapter required to support 6000 sessions is not preallocated. If you do not configure this parameter on the CMCC adapter, then the limit of LLC2 sessions is 6000 with enough memory preallocated to support 256 sessions.

This command will fail if there is not enough memory currently available on the CMCC adapter to support the specified number of LLC2 sessions.

Example

The following example limits the maximum number of LLC2 sessions to 212:

```
max-llc2-sessions 212
```

maximum-lus

Use the **maximum-lus** TN3270 configuration command to limit the number of LU control blocks that will be allocated for TN3270 server use. Use the **no** form of this command to restore the default value.

> **maximum-lus** *number*
> **no maximum-lus**

Syntax	Description
number	Maximum number of LU control blocks allowed. The allowed range is 0 to 32,000. However, the practical upper limit for concurrently operating TN3270 sessions depends on the hardware and usage characteristics. The default is 2100.

Default

Because of the license structure, the default is 2100, which represents the limit of the lower-priced license (2000) plus a 5 percent buffer. If you configure a value greater than the default, a license reminder is displayed.

Command Mode

TN3270 configuration

Usage Guidelines

This command first appeared in Cisco IOS Release 11.2.

The **maximum-lus** command is valid only on the virtual channel interface. Although the value may be varied at any time, reducing it below the current number of LU control blocks will not release those blocks until a PU is inactivated by DACTPU or by using the **no pu** command.

If the number of LUs in use reaches 94% of the current setting of **maximum-lus**, a warning message is displayed on the console. To prevent redundant messages, the threshold for generating such messages is raised for a period.

The TN3270 server attempts to allocate one LU control block for each LU activated by the hosts. In the case of dynamic definition of dependent LU (DDDLU) the control block is allocated when the client requests the LU, in anticipation of an ACTLU from the SSCP host.

By limiting the number of LU control blocks allocated, you can make sure enough memory is available to support other CMCC functions. The control blocks themselves take about 1K bytes per LU. During session activity, a further 2K per LU may be needed for data. On a CIP, 32 MB of memory will support 4000 LUs. To support more than 4000 LUs, we recommend 64 MB of memory. On an XCPA, 8 MB of memory supports 1000 LUs.

Example

The following example allows 5000 LU control blocks to be allocated:

```
maximum-lus 5000
```

Related Commands

To locate documentation of related commands, you can search online at www.cisco.com.

client (lu limit)
pu (direct)
pu (DLUR)

name

Use the **name** internal adapter configuration command to give a name to the internal adapter. Use the **no** form of the command to remove the name assigned to an internal adapter.

> **name** *name*
> **no name** *name*

Syntax	Description
name	Name that identifies this internal adapter. Consists of up to eight characters that does not include blanks.

Default

This command has no defaults.

Command Mode

Internal adapter configuration

Usage Guidelines

This command first appeared in Cisco IOS Release 11.0.

Example

The following example assigns a name to an internal adapter interface:

```
name VTAM_B14
```

Related Commands

To locate documentation of related commands, you can search online at www.cisco.com.

adapter

offload

Use the **offload** interface configuration command to configure an offload device (read and write subchannel) for communication with a mainframe TCP/IP stack in offload mode. This command can also be used to configure individual members of an Offload backup group for the IP Host Backup feature. Use the **no** form of this command to cancel the offload task on the CMCC adapter.

> **offload** *path device-address ip-address host-name device-name host-ip-link*
> *device-ip-link host-api-link device-api-link* [**broadcast**] [**backup**]
> **no offload** *path device-address*

Syntax	Description
path	Hexadecimal value in the range 0000 to FFFF. This value specifies the logical channel path and consists of two digits for the physical connection (either on the host or on the ESCON director), one digit for the channel logical address, and one digit for the control unit logical address. If the path is not specified in the IOCP, the default values for channel logical address and control unit logical address is 0.
device-address	Hexadecimal value in the range 00 to FE. This is the unit address associated with the control unit number and path as specified in the host IOCP file. The device address must have an even value.
ip-address	IP address specified in the host TCP/IP application configuration file.
host-name	Host name specified in the device statement in the host TCP/IP application configuration file.
device-name	CLAW workstation name specified in the device statement in the host TCP/IP application configuration file.

Syntax	Description
host-ip-link	CLAW host link name for the IP link as specified by the host application. For IBM VM and VMS TCP/IP stacks, this value is **tcpip**. When used with other applications, this value must match the value coded in the host application.
device-ip-link	CLAW workstation link name for the IP link as specified by the host application. For IBM VM and MVS TCP/IP stacks, this value is **tcpip**. When used with other applications, this value must match the value coded in the host application.
host-api-link	CLAW host link name for the API link as specified by the host application. For IBM VM and MVS TCP/IP stacks, this value is **tcpip**. When used with other applications, this value must match the value coded in the host application.
device-api-link	Offload link name for the API link as specified by the host application. For IBM VM and MVS TCP/IP stacks, this value is **api**. When used with other applications, this value must match the value coded in the host application.
broadcast	(Optional) Enables broadcast processing for this subchannel.
backup	(Optional) Enables this offload connection to be used as part of a backup group of offload connections for the specified IP address.

Default

This command has no defaults.

Command Mode

Interface configuration

Usage Guidelines

This command first appeared in Cisco IOS Release 11.0. The **backup** option first appeared in Cisco IOS Release 12.0.

Offload devices provide IP connectivity to a mainframe while at the same time offloading a large part of the TCP/IP processing to the CMCC adapter. Not every mainframe TCP/IP stack supports offload.

The **offload** command uses the same underlying configuration parameters as does the **claw** command.

Examples

The following example shows how to enable IBM channel attach offload processing on a CMCC adapter's physical channel interface which is supporting a directly connected ESCON channel:

```
interface channel 3/0
ip address 198.92.0.1 255.255.255.0
offload 0100 00 198.92.0.21 CISCOVM EVAL TCPIP TCPIP TCPIP API
```

The following example shows how an IP host backup group is specified using the **backup** keyword:

```
interface Channel3/0
 no ip address
 no keepalive
 shutdown
 offload 0100 C0 10.30.1.2 TCPIP OS2TCP TCPIP TCPIP TCPIP API backup
 offload 0110 C0 10.30.1.2 TCPIP OS2TCP TCPIP TCPIP TCPIP API backup
 offload 0120 C0 10.30.1.2 TCPIP OS2TCP TCPIP TCPIP TCPIP API backup
 offload 0110 C2 10.30.1.3 TCPIP OS2TCP TCPIP TCPIP TCPIP API
```

Related Commands

To locate documentation of related commands, you can search online at www.cisco.com.

offload (backup)
path
show extended channel icmp-stack
show extended channel ip-stack
show extended channel statistics
show extended channel subchannel
show extended channel tcp-connections
show extended channel tcp-stack
show extended channel udp-listeners
show extended channel udp-stack

offload (backup)

Use the **offload** IP Host Backup configuration mode to configure a backup group of Offload devices. Along with the path command, the **offload** command provides a quick way to configure an Offload backup group. Use the **no** form of this command to cancel the offload task on the CMCC adapter.

> **offload** *device-address ip-address host-name device-name host-ip-link device-ip-link host-api-link*
>   *device-api-link* [**broadcast**]
> **no offload** *path device-address*

Syntax	Description
device-address	Hexadecimal value in the range 0000 to FFFF. This value specifies the logical channel path and consists of two digits for the physical connection (either on the host or on the ESCON director), one digit for the channel logical address, and one digit for the control unit logical address. If the path is not specified in the IOCP, the default values for channel logical address and control unit logical address is 0.
ip-address	Hexadecimal value in the range 00 to FE. This is the unit address associated with the control unit number and path as specified in the host IOCP file. The device address must have an even value.
host-name	Host name specified in the device statement in the host TCP/IP application configuration file.
device-name	CLAW workstation name specified in the device statement in the host TCP/IP application configuration file.
host-ip-link	Host link name for the IP link as specified by the host application. For IBM VM and MVS TCP/IP stacks, this value is **tcpip**. When used with other applications, this value must match the value coded in the host application.
device-ip-link	Workstation link name for the IP link as specified by the host application. For IBM VM and MVS TCP/IP stacks, this value is **tcpip**. When used with other applications, this value must match the value coded in the host application.
host-api-link	Host link name for the API link as specified by the host application. For IBM VM and MVS TCP/IP stacks, this value is **tcpip**. When used with other applications, this value must match the value coded in the host application.
device-api-link	Offload link name for the API link as specified by the host application. For IBM VM and MVS TCP/IP stacks, this value is **api**. When used with other applications, this value must match the value coded in the host application.
broadcast	(Optional) Enables broadcast processing for this subchannel.

Default

This command has no defaults.

Command Mode

IP host backup configuration

Usage Guidelines

This command first appeared in Cisco IOS Release 12.0.

Offload devices provide IP connectivity to a mainframe while at the same time offloading a large part of the TCP/IP processing to the CMCC adapter. Not every mainframe TCP/IP stack supports offload.

The **offload** command uses the same underlying configuration parameters as does the **claw** command.

Examples

The following examples show two methods for entering the same IP host backup group information. The first group of commands is the long form, using the **offload** interface configuration command. The second group is the shortcut, using the **path** interface configuration command and an **offload** IP host backup configuration command.

Long form:

```
offload c000 00 198.92.10.5 sysa router1 tcpip tcpip tcpip api backup
offload c100 00 198.92.10.5 sysa router1 tcpip tcpip tcpip api backup
offload c200 00 198.92.10.5 sysa router1 tcpip tcpip tcpip api backup
```

Shortcut form:

```
path c000 c100 c200
  offload 00 198.92.10.5 sysa router1 tcpip tcpip tcpip api
```

Related Commands

To locate documentation of related commands, you can search online at www.cisco.com.

offload
path
show extended channel icmp-stack
show extended channel ip-stack
show extended channel statistics
show extended channel subchannel
show extended channel tcp-connections
show extended channel tcp-stack
show extended channel udp-listeners
show extended channel udp-stack

path

Use the **path** interface configuration command to specify one or more data paths for the IP host backup.
Use the **no** form of this command to delete a single path.

> **path** *path* [[*path*]...]
> **no path** *path*

Syntax	Description
path	Hexadecimal value in the range 0000 to FFFF. This value specifies the logical channel path and consists of two digits for the physical connection (either on the host or on the ESCON director), one digit for the channel logical address, and one digit for the control unit logical address. If the path is not specified in the IOCP, the default values for channel logical address and control unit logical address is 0.

Part
II

Command Reference

Default

This command has no defaults.

Command Mode

Interface configuration

Usage Guidelines

This command first appeared in Cisco IOS release 12.0.

Up to 16 *path* values can be specified in the **path** command.

The path command places you in IP host backup configuration mode, where you can enter additional
commands to define backup groups for CLAW and offload connections.

Examples

The following examples show two methods for entering the same IP host backup group information.
The first group is the long form, using the **offload** interface configuration command. The second group
of commands is the shortcut, using the **path** interface configuration command and a **offload** IP host
backup configuration command.

Long form:

```
offload c000 00 198.92.10.5 sysa router1 tcpip tcpip backup
offload c100 00 198.92.10.5 sysa router1 tcpip tcpip backup
offload c200 00 198.92.10.5 sysa router1 tcpip tcpip backup
```

Shortcut form:

```
path c000 c100 c200
  offload 00 198.92.10.5 sysa router1 tcpip tcpip
```

Related Commands

To locate documentation of related commands, you can search online at www.cisco.com.

claw (backup)
offload (backup)

preferred-nnserver

Use the **preferred-nnserver** DLUR configuration command to specify a preferred network node (NN) as server. Use the **no** form of this command to remove the preference.

> **preferred-nnserver** *name*
> **no preferred-nnserver**

Syntax   Description

name   A fully qualified name of an NN.

Default

This command has no defaults.

Command Mode

DLUR configuration

Usage Guidelines

This command first appeared in Cisco IOS Release 11.2.

The **preferred-nnserver** command is valid only on the virtual channel interface. Fully qualified names consist of two case-insensitive alphanumeric strings, separated by a period. However, for compatibility with existing APPN products, including VTAM, the characters "#" (pound), "@" (at), and "$" (dollar) are allowed in the fully qualified name strings. Each string is from one to eight characters long; for example, RA12.NODM1PP. The portion of the name before the period is the NETID and is shared between entities in the same logical network.

When no preferred server is specified, the DLUR will request NN server support from the first suitable node with which it makes contact. If refused, it will try the next one, and so on.

If a preferred server is specified, then DLUR will wait a short time to allow a link to the preferred server to materialize. If the preferred server is not found in that time, any suitable node can be used, as above.

DLUR will not relinquish the current NN server merely because the preferred server becomes available.

Example

The following example selects SYD.VMX as the preferred NN server:

```
preferred-nnserver SYD.VMX
```

Related Commands

To locate documentation of related commands, you can search online at www.cisco.com.

dlur

pu (direct)

Use the **pu** TN3270 configuration command to create a PU entity that has its own direct link to a host, or to enter PU configuration mode. Use the **no** form of this command to remove the PU entity.

> **pu** *pu-name idblk-idnum ip-address type adapter-number lsap* [**rmac** *rmac*]
> [**rsap** *rsap*] [**lu-seed** *lu-name-stem*]
> **no pu** *pu-name*

Syntax	Description
pu-name	Name that uniquely identifies this PU.
idblk-idnum	This value must match the IDBLK-IDNUM value defined at the host. The value must be unique within the subarea; however, the TN3270 Server cannot tell which remote hosts are in which subareas and does not enforce the unique value requirement.
ip-address	IP address that the clients should use as host IP address to map to LU sessions under this PU.
type	Internal adapter type on the CIP card, which corresponds to the value specified in the **lan** internal LAN configuration command. The currently supported type is **token-adapter**.
adapter-number	Internal adapter interface on the CIP card, which is the same value specified in the **adapter** internal LAN configuration command.

Syntax	Description
lsap	Local SAP number in hexadecimal, ranging from 04 to FC. The value must be even and must be unique within the internal adapter so that no other 802.2 clients of that adapter, in the router or in a host, should be allocated the same SAP. Other direct links from TN3270 server direct PUs may use the same value on the internal adapter as long as the remote MAC or SAP is different.
rmac *rmac*	(Optional) Remote MAC address. The remote MAC address of the form *xxxx.xxxx.xxxx* hexadecimal, specifying the MAC address of the remote host. If not specified, a loopback link to another SAP on the same internal LAN adapter is assumed.
rsap *rsap*	(Optional) Remote SAP address. The remote SAP address is a one- or two-character hexadecimal string, ranging from 04 to FC, specifying the SAP address of the remote host. The default is 04.
lu-seed *lu-name-stem*	(Optional) Provides an LU name that the client can use when a specific LU name request is needed. The format can be *x...x*## or *x...x*### where *x..x* is an alphanumeric string. When ## is specified, it is replaced with the LU LOCADDR in hexadecimal digits to form the complete LU name. When ### is specified, decimal digits are used, padded with leading zeroes to make three characters. The first *x* must be alphabetic and the entire string, including the # symbols, must not exceed eight characters.

Defaults

No PU is defined.

The default remote SAP address is 04 (hexadecimal).

Command Mode

TN3270 configuration

Usage Guidelines

This command first appeared in Cisco IOS Release 11.2.

The **pu** *pu-name* command is valid only on the virtual channel interface. If the PU is already created, the **pu** *pu-name* command with no arguments puts you in PU configuration mode, where you can modify an existing PU entity.

The **pu** (direct) command uses values that are defined in two other commands: the **lan** internal LAN configuration command and the **adapter** internal LAN configuration command. The **lan** *type* and **adapter** *adapter-number* values configured on the CIP internal LAN interface are used in the **pu** command.

For a link via a channel on this CMCC adapter, the TN3270 server and the hosts should open different adapters. Using different adapters avoids any contention for SAP numbers, and is also necessary if you configure duplicate MAC addresses for fallback CSNA or CMPC access to the host.

Examples

The following example configures the TN3270 server to be active, and has one PU, CAPPU1, trying to connect in. An LU seed using hexadecimal digits is defined.

```
tn3270-server
pu CAPPU1 05D18101 10.14.20.34 token-adapter 3 rmac 4000.0501.0001 lu-seed CAP01L##
```

The following example shows different adapter numbers configured on the same internal LAN to avoid SAP contention. The host uses SAP 4 on token ring adapter 0.

```
lan tokenring 0
 adapter 0 4000.0000.0001
 adapter 1 4000.0000.0002
tn3270-server
 pu PU1 05d00001 10.0.0.1 token-adapter 1 8 rmac 4000.0000.0001 rsap 4
```

Related Commands

To locate documentation of related commands, you can search online at www.cisco.com.

adapter
lan
tn3270-server
show extended channel tn3270-server

pu (DLUR)

Use the **pu (DLUR)** configuration command to create a PU entity that has no direct link to a host or to enter PU configuration mode. Use the **no** form of this command to remove the PU entity.

> **pu** *pu-name*
> **pu** *pu-name idblk-idnum ip-address*
> **no pu** *pu-name*

Syntax	Description
pu-name	Name that uniquely identifies this PU.
idblk-idnum	This value must match the *idblk-idnum* value defined at the host. The value must be unique within the subarea; however, the TN3270 server generally cannot tell which remote hosts are in which subareas, so the server only enforces uniqueness within the set of DLUR PUs.
ip-address	IP address that the clients should use as host IP address to map to LU sessions under this PU.

Default

No PU is defined.

Command Mode

DLUR configuration

Usage Guidelines

This command first appeared in Cisco IOS Release 11.2.

If the PU is already created, the **pu** *pu-name* command with no arguments puts you in PU configuration mode. In this mode, you can modify an existing PU DLUR entity.

A typical usage for the IP address is to reserve an IP address per host application. For example, clients wanting to connect to TSO specify an IP address that will be defined with PUs that have LOGAPPL=TSO.

Example

The following example defines define three PUs. Two of the PUs share the same IP address and the third PU has a separate IP address:

```
pu p0   05D99001 192.195.80.40
pu p1   05D99002 192.195.80.40
pu p2   05D99003 192.195.80.41
```

Related Commands

To locate documentation of related commands, you can search online at www.cisco.com.

dlur

show controllers channel

Use the **show controllers channel** EXEC command to display CPA-specific information, including the currently loaded microcode.

show controllers channel [*slot/port*]

Syntax	Description
slot	(Optional) The slot number.
port	(Optional) The interface number.

Command Mode
EXEC

Usage Guidelines
This command first appeared in Cisco IOS Release 11.3T.

Sample Display
The following is sample output from the **show controllers channel** command:

```
Router> show controllers channel 5/0
ECPA 5, hardware version 1.0, microcode version 26.0
    Mailbox commands: 0 forevers, 0 max elapsed usecs
    Microcode loaded from flash slot0:xcpa26-0_kernel_xcpa
    Loaded:seg_eca       Rev. 0    Compiled by cip-release on 01-Apr-98
    EPROM version 1.0, VPLD version 1.1
    ECA0: hw version 255, microcode version C50602D1
    Load metrics:
      Memory    sram 2964552/4096K, dram 11552952/16M
      CPU       1m  0%, 5m  0%, 60m  0%
      DMA       1m  0%, 5m  0%, 60m  0%
      ECA0      1m  0%, 5m  0%, 60m  0%
 Interface Channel5/0
 Hardware is Escon Channel
  HW Registers control status=0x0001EC07  LED control=0x00045DD5
  HW Poll Register 4B05D4E0:[00000001]
  Free buffer queues
    queue=0 max_entries=128 size=600 head=39 ring=4B095F00
    queue=1 max_entries=32 size=4520 head=31 ring=4B095E40
    queue=2 max_entries=64 size=4520 head=63 ring=4B096140
  Tx Queues
    queue=0 head=0 tail=0 tx_cnt=0 tx_pakcnt=0
    max_entries=128 type=1 poll_index=0 ring=4B0963C0
    fspak buffers swapped out=0
    queue=1 head=31 tail=31 tx_cnt=0 tx_pakcnt=0
```

```
    max_entries=32 type=2 poll_index=1 ring=4B096280
    fspak buffers swapped out=0
 Rx Queues
    max_entries=221 poll_index=3 head=57 ring=4B096800
    max packets per interrupt count = 0
```

show extended channel backup

Use the **show extended channel backup** privileged EXEC command to display information about the CLAW and offload commands for each backup group configured on CMCC channel interfaces.

show extended channel *slot/port* **backup** [*ip-address*]

Syntax	Description
slot	Slot number.
port	Port number.
backup	Display all CLAW or OFFLOAD commands associated with the backup group.
ip-address	(Optional) Display information about all devices in the backup group defined by *ip-address*.

Command Mode
Privileged EXEC

Usage Guidelines
This command first appeared in Cisco IOS Release 12.0.

Sample Display
The following is sample output from the **show extended channel backup** command:

```
Router#show extended channel 0/1 backup

Mode     Path Device IP Address: 80.11.198.2
OFFLOAD  E200   50  CISCOVM RISPIX   TCPIP    TCPIP    TCPIP    API
OFFLOAD  E300   50  CISCOVM RISPIX   TCPIP    TCPIP    TCPIP    API
Last statistics 4 seconds old, next in 6 seconds
```

Related Commands

To locate documentation of related commands, you can search online at www.cisco.com.

claw (backup)
offload (backup)
path

show extended channel cmpc

Use the **show extended channel cmpc** privileged EXEC command to display information about each CMPC subchannel configured on the specified channel interface.

show extended channel *slot/port* **cmpc** [*path* [*device*]]

Syntax	Description
slot	Slot number.
port	Physical channel interface port number.
path	(Optional) The logical channel path.
device	(Optional) A 2-digit hexadecimal value that specifies a device address of the CPMC subchannel. If specified, only status for that CMPC device will be displayed. If not specified, status for all CMPC devices for the specified path will be displayed.

Command Mode

Privileged EXEC

Usage Guidelines

This command first appeared in Cisco IOS Release 11.3.

This command is valid only on the CMCC adapter physical interfaces.

Sample Display

The following is sample output on a Cisco 7500 router from the **show extended channel cmpc** command:

```
Router# show extended channel 3/0 cmpc c020

     Path Dv  TGName   Dir   Bfrs  Status
CMPC C020 46  MVS2ISRA READ  10    Active
```

```
CMPC C020 47  MVS2ISRA  WRITE  16  Active
CMPC C020 4A  MVS2ISR1  READ   7   Active
CMPC C020 4B  MVS2ISR1  WRITE  16  Active
CMPC C020 4C  MVS2ISR2  READ   7   Active
CMPC C020 4D  MVS2ISR2  WRITE  16  Active
CMPC C020 4E  MVS2TN    READ   0   Inactive
CMPC C020 4F  MVS2TN    WRITE  0   Inactive
```

Table 28-2 describes the fields shown in the display.

Table 28-2 *show extended channel cmpc Field Descriptions*

Field	Description
Path	CMPC channel path configured.
Dv	CMPC subchannel device configured.
TGName	Transmission group name configured for the CMPC subchannel.
Dir	Identifies this CMPC subchannel as READ or WRITE.
Bfrs	On the read subchannel, this is the number of 4 KB-size pages that VTAM has allocated for each Read. This will match the MAXBFRU value configured in the VTAM TRL major node. On the write subchannel, this is the maximum number of 4 KB pages VTAM can write to the CMCC adapter for a single channel I/O. The value will always be 16 for the write subchannel because the CIP always allows VTAM to write up to 64 KB per channel I/O.
Status	State of the CMPC subchannel. Valid values are: • **Shutdown**—CMCC adapter interface for this CMPC subchannel is shutdown. In this state, the Bfrs value is not available and will be displayed as zeros. • **Inactive**—CMPC subchannel is not active. • **XID2 Pending**—XID2 handshaking in progress. • **Active**—XID2 exchange completed; CMPC subchannel is active.

Related Commands

To locate documentation of related commands, you can search online at www.cisco.com.

cmpc
tg

show extended channel connection-map llc2

Use the **show extended channel connection-map llc2** privileged EXEC command to display the number of active LLC2 connections for each SAP and the mapping of the internal MAC adapter and the SAP to the resource that activated the SAP.

show extended channel *slot/port* **connection-map llc2**

Syntax	Description
slot	Slot number.
port	Port number.
connection-map llc2	Displays a connection map of LLC2 connections.

Command Mode

Privileged EXEC

Usage Guidelines

This command first appeared in Cisco IOS Release 11.0(3).

The **show extended channel connection-map llc2** command is valid only on the virtual channel interfaces.

Sample Display

The following is sample output from the **show extended channel connection-map llc2** command:

```
Router# show extended channel 1/2 connection-map llc2

LAN Token  0 Adapter   0 4000.7000.0747
 Local SAP=08 LLC2 Connections=4   CSNA Port=1 Path=C200 Device=60
 Local SAP=0C LLC2 Connections=4   CSNA Port=1 Path=C200 Device=60
 Local SAP=10 LLC2 Connections=2   CSNA Port=1 Path=C200 Device=60
 Local SAP=14 LLC2 Connections=0   CSNA Port=1 Path=C200 Device=60

LAN Token  1 Adapter   1 4000.7000.0767
 Local SAP=08 LLC2 Connections=3   CSNA Port=1 Path=C200 Device=61
 Local SAP=0C LLC2 Connections=3   CSNA Port=1 Path=C200 Device=61
 Local SAP=10 LLC2 Connections=2   CSNA Port=1 Path=C200 Device=61
 Local SAP=14 LLC2 Connections=2   CSNA Port=1 Path=C200 Device=61

LAN Token  2 Adapter   2 4000.7000.0737
 No SAPs open on this interface

 Total : SAPs opened = 8     Connections active = 20
```

show extended channel csna

Use the **show extended channel csna** privileged EXEC command to display information about the CSNA subchannels configured on the specified CMCC interface.

show extended channel *slot/port* **csna** [*path* [*device*]] [**admin** | **oper** | **stats**]

Syntax	Description
slot	Slot number.
port	Port number.
path	(Optional) A hexadecimal value in the range of 0x0000 – 0xFFFF. This specifies the data path and consists of two digits for the physical connection (either on the host or on the ESCON Director switch), one digit for the control unit address, and one digit for the channel logical address. If not specified, information is displayed for all CSNA subchannels configured on the selected interface.
device	(Optional) A hexadecimal value in the range of 0x00 – 0xFE. This is the unit address associated with the control unit number and path as specified in the host IOCP file. If not specified, information is displayed for all CSNA subchannels configured with the specified path on the selected interface.
admin	(Optional) Displays configured values for CSNA channel devices. If neither **admin**, **oper**, or **stats** is specified, **admin** is the default.
oper	(Optional) Displays operational values for CSNA channel devices.
stats	(Optional) Displays statistics for CSNA channel devices.

Command Mode

Privileged EXEC

Usage Guidelines

This command first appeared in Cisco IOS Release 11.0(3).

The information that is displayed by this command is generally useful for diagnostic tasks performed by technical support personnel only.

Sample Displays

The following is sample output from the **show extended channel csna** command. Three examples are provided, one for each type of output as specified by the **admin**, **oper**, and **stats** keywords.

The following example displays the configured values for all CSNA devices on interface channel 1/0:

```
Router# show extended channel 1/0 csna admin

     Path Dv  maxpiu      time-delay   length-delay
CSNA C200 60  64000       100          64000
CSNA C200 61  64000       100          64000
CSNA C200 62  64000       100          64000
```

Table 28-3 describes the fields shown in the display.

The following example displays operational data for all CSNA devices configured on interface channel 1/0. The channel interface must be up (no shut) for this information to be displayed.

```
Router# show extended channel 1/0 csna oper

     Path Dv Status      SlowDown  maxpiu      time-delay   length-delay
CSNA C200 60 setupComplet off       64000       100          64000
CSNA C200 61 setupComplet off       64000       100          64000
CSNA C200 62 setupComplet off       64000       100          64000
```

Table 28-3 describes the fields shown in the display.

The following example displays CSNA statistics for subchannel path c200, device 60. The channel interface must be up (no shut) for this information to be displayed. If the maxpiu value is reconfigured while the CSNA subchannel is active (setupComplete) then the maxpiu value displayed by the oper keyword is the old, operational value.

```
Router# show extended channel 1/0 csna c200 60 stats

CSNA      C200 60
Blocks Transmitted =    38979079  Received =    38979075
Bytes  Transmitted =   79251477K  Received =       13554
Slow downs Sent =           0  Received =           0
Txd by maxpiu     : Blocks =         0  Bytes =           0
Txd by time-delay : Blocks =       222  Bytes =       12522
Txd by length-delay: Blocks =         0  Bytes =           0
```

Table 28-3 describes the fields shown in the display.

Table 28-3   *show extended channel csna Field Descriptions*

Field	Description
Path	Path from the CSNA configuration.
Dev	Device address from the CSNA configuration.

Continues

Table 28-3 *show extended channel csna Field Descriptions (Continued)*

Field	Description
Status	State of the CSNA device. One of the following values: • **closed** —Subchannel is closed. • **pendingOpen** —An Open Subchannel command has been received from VTAM. • **open** —Subchannel is open. • **pendingSetup** —VTAM has queried CIP for all configured MAC adapters. • **setupComplete** —All internal MAC adapter information has been responded to the CIP. The CSNA subchannel is operational. • **pendingClose** —A Close Subchannel command has been received from VTAM. • **unknown** —Current state of the CSNA subchannel cannot be determined.
SlowDown	Status of flow control for the CSNA device. • **off** —Subchannel is normal (both CSNA and VTAM are able to send data. • **sent** — CSNA has put VTAM into a slow down state for this CSNA subchannel. • **received** —VTAM has put the CSNA subchannel into a slow down state. • **both** —Both VTAM and the CSNA subchannel are in a slow down state. • **unknown** —Current state of flow control on this CSNA subchannel cannot be determined.
maxpiu	Maximum size of a channel i/o block that the CSNA subchannel can send to the host. This value may differ from the configured maxpiu value if the value is reconfigured while the CSNA subchannel is active (setupComplete). CSNA blocks SNA frames into channel i/o blocks which must not exceed the maxpiu value. A length-delay value less than the maxpiu value can cause the channel i/o blocks to be limited to the lower value. The maxpiu value may be reconfigured while the subchannel is operational but the new maxpiu value does not take effect until the subchannel is reinitialized (in other words, until the XCA major node is recycled). In this case, the maxpiu value displayed with the **admin** keyword will be the new, configured value while the maxpiu displayed by the **oper** keyword will be the old, operational value.

Table 28-3 *show extended channel csna Field Descriptions (Continued)*

Field	Description
time-delay	CSNA blocks SNA frames destined for VTAM for time-delay milliseconds from the time the first SNA frame within a channel i/o block is blocked for transmission. This can increase the overall throughput of CSNA by minimizing the number of channel i/o operations. However, blocking can induce response time latency of a transaction by up to the time-delay value. If time-delay=0, CSNA ignores length-delay and puts each frame into the channel i/o block for transmission to the host. Even with a time-delay=0, CSNA may still block frames while waiting for a previous channel i/o to complete.
length-delay	CSNA blocks SNA frames destined for VTAM when the current block reaches the length-delay value in size (bytes). This will increase the chance of using larger block sizes for CSNA channel i/o. SNA frames are blocked up to either time-delay milliseconds or until the block reaches the length-delay size, at which time CSNA starts the channel i/o.
	The length-delay is ignored if it is larger than the maxpiu value. It can be used to force CSNA blocking to generate smaller i/o blocks than specified by maxpiu. In general, however, larger blocks result in better channel throughput and efficiency. A value of zero causes the length-delay value to be ignored; blocking is then controlled by the maxpiu and time-delay parameters.
Blocks Transmitted	Number of channel i/o blocks sent to VTAM from this CSNA subchannel.
Blocks Received	Number of channel i/o blocks received from VTAM by this CSNA subchannel.
SlowDowns Sent	Number of times CSNA put VTAM into a slow down (flow control) for this subchannel device.
SlowDowns Received	Number of times VTAM put CSNA into a slow down (flow control) for this subchannel.
Txd by maxpiu Blocks/Bytes	Number of channel i/o blocks and bytes transmitted to VTAM by this CSNA subchannel because the size of the channel i/o block reached the maxpiu. value configured for this subchannel.
Txd by time-delay Blocks/Bytes	Number of channel i/o blocks and bytes transmitted to VTAM by this CSNA subchannel because blocking time-delay configured for this subchannel expired.
Txd by length-delay Blocks/Bytes	Number of channel i/o blocks and bytes transmitted to VTAM by this CSNA subchannel because blocking length-delay configured for this subchannel was reached.

Related Commands

To locate documentation of related commands, you can search online at www.cisco.com.

csna

show extended channel icmp-stack

Use the **show extended channel icmp-stack** EXEC command to display information about the Internet Control Message Protocol (ICMP) stack running on the CMCC channel interfaces.

show extended channel *slot/port* **icmp-stack** [*ip-address*]

Syntax	Description
slot	Slot number.
port	Port number.
ip-address	(Optional) IP address specified by the **offload** interface configuration command or the **tn3270-server pu** command.

Command Mode

EXEC

Usage Guidelines

This command first appeared in Cisco IOS Release 11.0.

The **show extended channel icmp-stack** command is valid on both physical and virtual channel interfaces.

Sample Display

The following is sample output from the **show extended channel icmp-stack** command:

```
Router#show extended channel 0/1 icmp-stack

ICMP Statistics for IP Address 80.11.198.2
  InMsgs        : 3         InErrors        : 0        InDestUnreachs: 0
  InTimeExcds   : 0         InParmProbs     : 0        InSrcQuenchs  : 0
  InRedirects   : 0         InEchos         : 3        OutEchoReps   : 3
  OutTimestamps : 0         OutTimestampReps: 0        OutAddrMasks  : 0
  OutAddrMaskReps: 0
ICMP Statistics for IP Address 80.11.198.3
  InMsgs        : 1         InErrors        : 0        InDestUnreachs: 0
  InTimeExcds   : 0         InParmProbs     : 0        InSrcQuenchs  : 0
```

```
InRedirects    : 0        InEchos         : 1        OutEchoReps  : 1
OutTimestamps  : 0        OutTimestampReps: 0        OutAddrMasks : 0
OutAddrMaskReps: 0
```

Related Commands

To locate documentation of related commands, you can search online at www.cisco.com.

offload
offload (backup)
tn3270-server

show extended channel ip-stack

Use the **show extended channel ip-stack** EXEC command to display information about the IP stack running on CMCC channel interfaces.

> **show extended channel** *slot/port* **ip-stack** [*ip-address*]

Syntax	Description
slot	Slot number.
port	Port number.
ip-address	(Optional) IP address specified by the **offload** interface configuration command or the **tn327-server pu** command.

Command Mode

EXEC

Usage Guidelines

This command first appeared in Cisco IOS Release 11.0.

The **show extended channel ip-stack** command is valid on both physical and virtual channel interfaces.

Sample Display

The following is sample output from the **show extended channel ip-stack** command:

```
Router#show extended channel 0/1 ip-stack

IP Statistics for IP Address 80.11.198.2
    Forwarding      : no        DefaultTTL       : 64       InReceives    : 165
    InHdrErrors     : 0         InAddrErrors     : 0        ForwDatagrams: 0
    InUnknownProtos: 0          InDiscards       : 0        InDelivers    : 165
    OutRequests     : 157       OutDiscards      : 0        OutNoRoutes   : 0
    ReasmTimeout    : 60        ReasmReqds       : 0        ReasmOKs      : 0
    ReasmFails      : 0         FragOKs          : 0        FragFails     : 0
    FragCreates     : 0         RoutingDiscards: 0
IP Statistics for IP Address 80.11.198.3
    Forwarding      : no        DefaultTTL       : 64       InReceives    : 77
    InHdrErrors     : 0         InAddrErrors     : 0        ForwDatagrams: 0
    InUnknownProtos: 0          InDiscards       : 0        InDelivers    : 77
    OutRequests     : 78        OutDiscards      : 0        OutNoRoutes   : 0
    ReasmTimeout    : 60        ReasmReqds       : 0        ReasmOKs      : 0
    ReasmFails      : 0         FragOKs          : 0        FragFails     : 0
    FragCreates     : 0         RoutingDiscards: 0
```

Related Commands

To locate documentation of related commands, you can search online at www.cisco.com.

offload
offload (backup)
tn3270-server

show extended channel lan

Use the **show extended channel lan** EXEC command to display the internal LANs and adapters configured on a CMCC adapter.

> **show extended channel** *slot/port* **lan** [*tokenring* [*lan-id* [*adapno*]]]

Syntax	Description
slot	Slot number.
port	Port number.
tokenring	(Optional) Specifies CMCC internal LAN type to be displayed.
lan-id	(Optional) Specifies the CMCC internal LAN number to be displayed.
adapno	(Optional) Specifies the CMCC internal adapter number on the selected internal LAN to be displayed.

Default

Display all internal LANs and adapters on the selected channel interface.

Command Mode

Privileged EXEC

Usage Guidelines

This command first appeared in Cisco IOS Release 11.0.

This command is valid only on the virtual channel interface.

Sample Display

The following is sample output from the **show extended channel lan** command:

```
Router#show extended channel 3/2 lan

Lan TokenRing 0
        Adapno Mac Address      Name      Vcnum
            0 4000.1111.1112              544
           20 4000.1111.2200              564
           30 4000.3030.0101              574
Lan TokenRing 1
        source-bridge 207 1 2002
        Adapno Mac Address      Name      Vcnum
            1 4000.2222.2222              545
Lan TokenRing 2
        source-bridge 50 1 1500
        Adapno Mac Address      Name      Vcnum
            2 4000.3333.2222              546
Lan TokenRing 5
        source-bridge 112 1 3000
        Adapno Mac Address      Name      Vcnum
            5 4000.1234.5656              549
Lan TokenRing 9
        source-bridge 111 1 3000
        Adapno Mac Address      Name      Vcnum
            9 4000.9999.1111              553
Lan TokenRing 10
        source-bridge 110 1 3000
        Adapno Mac Address      Name      Vcnum
           10 4000.aaaa.1111              554
Lan TokenRing 20
        source-bridge 20 1 2002
        Adapno Mac Address      Name      Vcnum
           21 4000.2020.2020              565
```

Part
II

Command Reference

Related Commands

To locate documentation of related commands, you can search online at www.cisco.com.

adapter
lan

show extended channel llc2

Use the **show extended channel llc2** EXEC command to display information about the LLC2 sessions running on the CMCC adapter interfaces.

show extended channel *slot/port* **llc2** [**admin** | **oper** | **stats**]
[*lmac [lsap [rmac [rsap]]]*]

Syntax	Description
slot	Slot number.
port	Port number.
admin	(Optional) Shows configured values. This is the default.
oper	(Optional) Shows operational values for:
	• Internal adapters
	• SAPs opened on the internal adapters
	• LLC2 connections on the internal adapters
stats	(Optional) Shows statistics for:
	• Internal adapters
	• SAPs opened on the internal adapters
	• LLC connections on the internal adapters
lmac	(Optional) Local MAC address.
lsap	(Optional) Local SAP address, 0 to 256.
rmac	(Optional) Remote MAC address.
rsap	(Optional) Remote SAP address, 0 to 256.

Command Mode

EXEC

Usage Guidelines

This command first appeared in Cisco IOS Release 11.0(3).

The **show extended channel llc2** command is valid on virtual channel interfaces.

To specify LLC information for internal adapters:

- Specify the *lmac* to get information for a specific internal adapter.

- Omit the *lmac* parameter to display information for all internal adapters on the specified channel interface.

To display LLC information for SAPs opened on an internal adapter:

- Specify the *lmac* and *lsap* parameters to display information for a particular SAP.

- Specify the *lmac* parameter and '*' to display information for all SAPs opened on the specified channel adapter.

To display information for LLC2 connections on a channel interface:

- Specify the *lmac*, *lsap*, *rmac*, and *rsap* parameters to display information for a particular active LLC2 connection.

- Specify the *lmac*, *lsap*, and *rmac* parameters to display information for all LLC2 connections active between the specified remote MAC address and the specified local SAP opened on the specified internal adapter.

- Specify the *lmac* and *lsap* parameters, and '*' to display information for all LLC2 connections active on the specified local SAP and the specified internal adapter and any remote MAC address the connections are active with.

- Specify the *lmac*, '*' for the local SAP, and *rmac* to display information for all LLC2 connections active between the specified internal adapter and the remote MAC address.

- Specify the *lmac*, '*' for the local SAP, and '*' for the remote MAC address to display information for all active LLC2 connections on the specified internal adapter.

Sample Displays

The following is sample output from the **show extended channel llc2** command. Three examples are provided, one for each type of output as specified by the **admin**, **oper**, and **stats** keywords.

The following sample displays the configured values for all LLC2 connections on channel 2/2:

```
Router# show extended channel 2/2 llc2 admin

   Lan Token adapter   0 0004.0004.0004
 t1-time  = 1000  tpf-time  = 1000  trej-time = 3200  tbusy-tim = 9600
 idle-time =60000  local-win =    7  recv-wind =    7  N2       =    8
 N1    = 1033 ack-delay = 100 ack-max  =  3 nw    =   0
```

Table 28-4 describes the fields shown in the display.

Table 28-4 *show extended channel llc2 admin* *Field Descriptions — All LLC2 Connections*

Field	Description
t1-time	Length of time the CMCC LLC2 link station waits for an acknowledgment to a transmitted I-frame before polling the remote LLC2 station.
tpf-time	Amount of time the CMCC LLC2 link station waits for a final response to a poll before resending the original poll frame.
trej-time	Amount of time the CMCC LLC2 link station waits for a correct frame after sending a reject command to a remote LLC2 station.
tbusy-time	Amount of time the CMCC LLC2 link station waits before repolling a busy LLC2 station.
idle-time	Frequency of polls during periods of idle traffic.
local-win	Maximum number of I-frames that the CMCC LLC2 link station connection can send to the remote LLC2 station without receiving an acknowledgment.
recv-wind	Maximum number of I-frames that the CMCC LLC2 link station connection can receive without receiving an acknowledgment.
N2	Number of times the CMCC LLC2 link station connection will resend an unacknowledged I-frame.
N1	Maximum size of LLC frames supported by the CMCC LLC2 link station. The maximum size LLC frame supported on the CMCC is controlled by other factors including the largest interface MTU between the CMCC and the remote network device, and configured values at VTAM and at the end station.
ack-delay	Maximum amount of time the CMCC LLC2 link station allows received I-frames to remain unacknowledged. The CMCC LLC2 connection will acknowledge received I-frames within the ack-delay time.
ack-max	Maximum number of I-frames the CIP LLC2 link station receives before sending an acknowledgment.
Nw	Working send window size. When I-frames sent by the CMCC are rejected by the remote LLC2 station, the CMCC LLC2 connection reduces its working send window size to 1. Then, for every subsequent I-frame sent by the CMCC LLC2 connection that is positively acknowledged by the remote LLC2 station, the CMCC LLC2 connection increases its working send window by the Nw value until the working send window reaches the configured local-window value.

The following sample displays the operational values for all LLC2 connections on channel 2/2:

```
Router#show extended channel 5/2 llc oper

  LAN Token  0 Adapter   0 4000.1010.2020
      Open SAPs=1
      Max SAPs Opened=1
```

Open SAPS is the number of SAPs currently opened on this internal MAC adapter. *Max SAPs Opened* is the number of SAPs concurrently opened on this internal MAC adapter since the last reset of the channel adapter of channel interface.

The following sample displays operational information for the specified SAP opened on a CMCC internal adapter:

```
Router#show extended channel 5/2 llc stat

LAN Token  0 Adapter   0 4000.1010.2020
    PDUsIn    =    223339   PDUsOut     =      9564
    OctetsIn  =   6949875   OctetsOut   =    307448
    TESTCmdsIn =   213293   TESTRspsOut =         2
    LocalBusies=        0   UnknownSAPs =         0
```

Table 28-5 describes the fields shown in the display. These statistics are available on the adapter because when LLC2 connections are deactivated, users can no longer retrieve the information per LLC2 connection.

Table 28-5 *show extended channel llc2 stat Field Descriptions — All LLC2 Connections*

Field	Description
PDUsIn	Protocol Data Units received by the internal adapter.
PDUsOut	Protocol Data Units sent by the internal adapter.
OctetsIn	PDU bytes received by the internal adapter.
OctetsOut	PDU bytes sent by the internal adapter.
TESTCmdsIn	Number of TEST commands received destined for this MAC address.
TESTRspsOut	Number of TEST responses sent by this MAC address reponding to TEST commands received.
Local Busies	Number of times LLC2 connection stations on this adapter entered a busy state, send RNRs to the remote LLC2 station.
UnknownSAPs	Number of frames received that are destined for a SAP that does not exist on this adapter.

The following sample displays operational information for the specified SAP opened on the internal adapter, 4000.1010.2020 configured on channel interface 5/2:

```
Router#show extended channel 5/2 llc2 oper 4000.1010.2020 04

  LAN Token  0 Adapter   0 4000.1010.2020
    Local SAP=04
      Open Connections=2
  Max Connections Opened=2
```

The following table describes the fields shown in the display:

Field	Description
Open Connections	Number of LLC2 connections active on the SAP.
Max Connections	Highest number of LLC2 connections concurrently active on that SAP since the SAP has been active.

The following sample displays statistics for the specified SAP on the internal adapter, 4000.1010.2020 configured on channel interface 5/2:

```
Router#show extended channel 5/2 llc2 stats 4000.1010.2020 04

  LAN Token  0 Adapter   0 4000.1010.2020
    Local SAP=04
      TESTRspsIn     =        0  TESTCmdsOut    =        0
      XIDCmdsIn      =       14  XIDCmdsOut     =       16
      XIDRspsIn      =        4  XIDRspsOut     =        0
      UIFramesIn     =        0  UIFramesOut    =        0
      UIOctetsIn     =        0  UIOctetsOut    =        0
      ConnectOk      =        2  ConnectFail    =        0
      DiscNorm       =        0  DiscByTmr      =        0
      DiscByFRMRSent =        0  DiscByFRMRRcvd =        0
      DMsInABM       =        0  SABMEsInABM    =        0
```

Table 28-6 describes the fields shown in the display. All statistics for SAPs are based on the time the SAP was last opened.

Table 28-6 *show extended channel llc2 stats* *Field Descriptions — Specified Interface*

Field	Description
TESTRspsIn	Number of TEST responses received on this SAP for TEST commands sent by VTAM (connect out).
TESTCmdsOut	Number of TEST commands sent by this SAP to explore for a remote MAC address (VTAM connect out).
XIDCmdsIN	Number of XID commands received by this SAP from a remote link station.
XIDCmdsOut	Number of XID commands sent by this SAP to a remote link station.

Table 28-6 *show extended channel llc2 stats Field Descriptions — Specified Interface*

Field	Description
XIDRspsIN	Number of XID responses received by this SAP from a remote link station.
XIDRspsOut	Number of XID responses sent by this SAP to a remote link station.
UIFreamesIn	Number of Unnumbered I-frames received by this SAP from a remote link station.
UIFramesOut	Number of Unnumbered I-frames sent by this SAP to a remote link station.
UIOctetsIn	Number of Unnumbered I-frame bytes received by this SAP from a remote link station.
UIOctetsOut	Number of Unnumbered I-frame bytes sent by this SAP to a remote link station.
ConnectOk	Number of successful LLC2 connection attempts on this SAP.
ConnectFail	Number of LLC2 connections that failed.
DiscNorm	Number of normal LLC2 connection disconnections.
DisByTmr	Number of LLC2 connections disconnected due to the CMCC LLC2 link station not getting responses to polls from the remote LLC2 station, typically due to the remote station being powered off or a severe network failure/congestion. The CMCC LLC2 stack generates an event each time it detects this condition. The event can be configured to generate a NetView alert, SNMP trap, and a router console message.
DiscByFRMRSent	Number of times a CMCC LLC2 connection disconnected after detecting a protocol violation and sending a FRNR to the remote LLC2 station.The CMCC LLC2 link station generates an event each time it detects this condition. The event can be configured to generate a NetView alert, SNMP trap, and a router console message.
DiscByFRMRRcvd	Number of times the CMCC LLC2 connection disconnected after the remote LLC2 station detected a protocol violation and sent a FRMR to the CMCC LLC2 link station.The CMCC LLC2 stack generates an event each time it detects this condition. The event can be configured to generate a NetView alert, SNMP trap, and a router console message.
DMsInABM	Number of times the CMCC LLC2 link station went into disconnect mode after receiving a DM. The CMCC LLC2 stack generates an event each time it detects this condition. The event can be configured to generate a NetView alert, SNMP trap, and a router console message.
SABMEDsInABM	Number of times the CMCC LLC2 link station went into disconnect mode after receiving a SABME from the LLC2 station. The CMCC LLC2 stack generates an event each time it detects this condition. The event can be configured to generate a NetView alert, SNMP trap, and a router console message.

Part II

Command Reference

The following sample displays operation information for the specified CMCC link station:

```
Router#show extended channel 5/2 llc2 oper 4000.1010.2020 04 4000.1234.1030 18

  LAN Token   0 Adapter    0 4000.1010.2020
    Local SAP=04 Remote MAC=4000.1234.1030 Remote SAP=18  State=normal
       t1-time   = 1000  tpf-time  = 1000  trej-time = 3200  tbusy-tim = 9600
       idle-time =60000  local-win =    7  recv-wind =    7  N2        =    8
        N1-Send   = 4105  N1-Rcv    = 4105  ack-delay =  100  ack-max   =    3
Nw         =    0  Ww        =    7
       Last Ww Cause = neverInvoked
       Connection Time: 17:50:11
       Last modified: never
```

Table 28-7 explains parameters in use by the LLC2 connection. These parameters are the ones configured on the internal adapter 4000.0000.0001 at the time the LLC2 connection was established. If the LLC2 parameters on the internal adapter are changed while this connection is active, the connection will not reflect the changes to the adapter.

Table 28-7 *show extended channel llc2 Field Descriptions — Internal LAN Adapter*

Field	Description
State	• aDM
	• setup
	• conn
	• normal
	• busy
	• reject
	• await
	• awaitBusy
	• awaitReject
	• discConn
	• reset
	• error
	• pendDiscRsp
	The descriptions for each state can be found in Section 7.8.3, IOS 8802-2 : 1989, ANSI/IEEE Std 802.2 - 1989.
t1-time	Length of time the CMCC LLC2 link station waits for an acknowledgment to a transmitted I-frame before polling the remote LLC2 station.
tpf-time	Amount of time the CMCC LLC2 link station waits for a final response to a poll before resending the original poll frame.
trej-time	Amount of time the CMCC LLC2 link station waits for a correct frame after sending a reject command to a remote LLC2 station.

Table 28-7 *show extended channel llc2 Field Descriptions — Internal LAN Adapter (Continued)*

Field	Description
tbusy-tim	Amount of time the CMCC LLC2 link station waits before repolling a busy LLC2 station.
idle-time	Frequency of polls during periods of idle traffic.
local-win	Maximum number of I-frames that the CMCC LLC2 link station can send to the remote LLC2 station without receiving an acknowledgment.
recv-wind	Maximum number of I-frames that a CMCC LLC2 link station can receive without receiving an acknowledgment.
N2	Number of times a CMCC LLC2 link station will resend an unacknowledged I-frame.
N1-Send	Largest frame size this CMCC LLC2 link station is allowed to send.
N1-Rcv	Largest frame size this CMCC LLC2 link station can receive.
ack-delay	Maximum amount of time the CMCC LLC2 link station allows received I-frames to remain unacknowledged. The CIP LLC2 connection will acknowledge received I-frames within the ack-delay time.
ack-max	Maximum number of I-frames a CMCC LLC2 link station receives before sending an acknowledgment.
Nw	Working send window size. When I-frames sent by a CMCC LLC2 link station are rejected by the remote LLC2 station, the CMCC LLC2 link station reduces its working send window size to 1. Then, for every subsequent I-frame sent by the CMCC LLC2 connection that is positively acknowledged by the remote LLC2 station, the CMCC LLC2 link station increases its working send window by the Nw value until the working send window reaches the configured local-window value.
Ww	Current working window size for this LLC2 link station. This is the current number of unacknowledged I-frames that this LLC2 link station will send.
Last Ww Cause	Last event that caused the working window to change values. Valid values are: • neverInvoked — This LLC2 station has not detected a condition to change the working window from the initial value at activation time. • lostData — The current working window value was changed due to loss of data by the remote LLC2 link station • macLayerCongestion — The current working window value was changed due to the remote end station sending this LLC2 link station a RNR frame.
Connection Time	Length of time this LLC2 connection has been active.
Last modified	Length of time since one of the LLC2 parameters for this connection was last modified.

The following sample displays statistics for the CMCC LLC2 link station connection between LMAC 4000.1010.2020 LSAP 04 and RMAC 4000.1234.1030 RSAP 18:

```
Router#show extended channel 5/2 llc2 stats 4000.1010.2020 04 4000.1234.1030 18

  LAN Token  0 Adapter  0 4000.1010.2020
    Local SAP=04 Remote MAC=4000.1234.1030 Remote SAP=18
      LocalBusies     =        0  RemoteBusies    =         0
      IFramesIn       =        1  IFramesOut      =         1
      IOctetsIn       =       19  IOctetsOut      =        21
      SFramesIn       =        0  SFramesOut      =         0
      REJsIn          =        0  REJsOut         =         0
      RetransmitsOut  =        0  WwCountChanges  =         0
```

Table 28-8 describes the fields shown in the display.

Table 28-8 *show extended channel llc2 Field Descriptions — Statistics*

Field	Description
LocalBusies	Number of times the CMCC LLC2 link station entered the busy state. This occurs for a CMCC LLC2 link station when there are *n* I-Frames received from the remote LLC2 station on the CMCC queued to be sent over the channel to VTAM. Where n is 2 times the recv-wind. The CMCC LLC2 link station will also enter into busy state whenever it receives a flow control command from VTAM.
RemoteBusies	Number of times the remote LLC2 link station entered into busy state.
IFramesIn	Number of LLC2 Information Frames received by the CMCC LLC2 link station from the remote link station.
IFramesOut	Number of LLC2 Information Frames sent by the CMCC link station to the remote link station.
IOctetsIn	Number of LLC2 Information Frame bytes received by the CMCC LLC2 link station from the remote link station.
IOctetsOut	Number of LLC2 Information Frame bytes sent by the CMCC link station to the remote link station.
SFramesIn	Number of LLC2 supervisory frames received by the CMCC link station from the remote link station. These include RRs, RNRs and REJs.
SFramesOut	Number of LLC2 supervisory frames sent by the CMCC link station to the remote link station. These include RRs, RNRs and REJs.
REJsIn	Number of LLC2 REJ frames received by the CMCC link station from the remote link station. This indicates the number of times the remote link station detected dropped I-Frames sent from the CMCC LLC2 station.
REJsOut	Number of LLC2 REJ frames sent by the CMCC link station to the remote link station. This indicates the number of times the CMCC link station detected dropped I-Frames sent by the remote link station.

Table 28-8 *show extended channel llc2 Field Descriptions — Statistics (Continued)*

Field	Description
RetransmitsOut	Number of I-Frames the CMCC link station was required to retransmit.
WwCountChanges	Number of times the CMCC LLC2 link station changed its working send window (local-win). Refer to Nw in Table 28-7 for a description of when the LLC2 link stations working send window is changed.

Related Commands

To locate documentation of related commands, you can search online at www.cisco.com.

adapter

show extended channel max-llc2-sessions

Use the **show extended channel max** privileged EXEC command to display information about the number of LLC2 sessions supported on the CMCC adapter.

show extended channel *slot/port* **max-llc2-sessions**

Syntax	Description
slot	Slot number.
port	Port number.
max-llc2-sessions	Displays the maximum number of LLC2 sessions supported on the CMCC adapter.

Command Mode

Privileged EXEC

Usage Guidelines

This command first appeared in Cisco IOS Release 11.0(3).

This command is valid only on the virtual channel interface.

Sample Display

The following is sample output from the **show extended channel max-llc2-sessions** command:

```
Router# show extended channel 1/2 max-llc2-sessions

Administrative max-llc2-sessions = 1000
Operational max-llc2_sessions = 1000
Highest concurrent LLC2 sessions = 30
LLC2 session allocation failures = 0
```

Table 28-9 describes the fields shown in the display.

Table 28-9 *show extended channel max-llc2-sessions Field Descriptions*

Field	Description
Administrative max-llc2-sessions	Maximum number of LLC2 sessions configured.
Operational max-llc2-sessions	Maximum number of LLC2 sessions configured on the CMCC adapter. This value l differs from the value for the administrative max-llc2-sessions if the maximum number of LLC2 sessions is decreased by configuring a new value while the CMCC adapter's virtual interface is up. If the CMCC adapter's virtual interface is reset (shut / no shut), both the administrative and operational max-llc2-sessions numbers will match.

Highest concurrent llc2 sessions	Highest number of LLC2 sessions active concurrently since the CMCC adapter LLC2 was started. When the CMCC adapter llc2 is initiated, the following message displays:
	
	`%CIP1-6-MSG: %MSG802-6-LLC_START: Starting LLC-2 with`
	`a session capacity of 1000`

LLC2 session allocation failure	Number of times network devices tried to establish an LLC2 connection with the CMCC adapter and failed because the operational max-llc2-sessions limit was reached when the connection was attempted.

Related Commands

To locate documentation of related commands, you can search online at www.cisco.com.

adapter
show extended channel connection-map llc2

show extended channel packing names

Use the **show extended channel packing names** EXEC command to display CLAW packing names and their connection state.

> **show extended channel** *slot/port* **packing names** [*path* [*device-address*]]

Syntax	Description
slot	Slot number.
port	Port number.
path	Hexadecimal value in the range 0000 to FFFF. This value specifies the logical channel path and consists of two digits for the physical connection (either on the host or on the ESCON director), one digit for the channel logical address, and one digit for the control unit logical address. If the path is not specified in the IOCP, the default values for channel logical address and control unit logical address is 0.
device-address	Hexadecimal value in the range 00 to FE. This is the unit address associated with the control unit number and path as specified in the host IOCP file. The device address must have an even value.

Command Mode
EXEC

Usage Guidelines
This command first appeared in Cisco IOS Release 12.0.

Sample Display
The following is sample output from the **show extended channel packing names** command:

```
Router# show extended channel 3/0 packing names
Path: C010  Devices: F2,F3 CLAW Link: 1

    Sublink          Link Names
       0                CONTROL
       1             IP        IP
       2             CKSUM     CKSUM

Path: C030  Devices: F6,F7 CLAW Link: N

    Sublink          Link Names
 DISCONNECTED           CONTROL
 DISCONNECTED        IP        IP
 DISCONNECTED        CKSUM     CKSUM
```

Table 28-10 describes the fields shown in the display.

Table 28-10   *show extended channel packing names* Field Descriptions

Field	Description
Path	The path from the CLAW configuration. It indicates which port on the switch is used by the channel side of the configuration.
Devices	The device address for each device. One CLAW connection requires two devices. You need only specify the even address.
CLAW Link	The established CLAW link number used for all CLAW packing messages. A number value indicates that a CONTROL sublink is connected. "N" indicates that a control sublink is disconnected.
Sublink	• DISCONNECTED indicates that a sublink connection for a particular link name is not established. • 0 indicates that the CONTROL sublink is established. • 1–15 indicates the negotiated sublink number for each application pair.
Link Names	The name used to represent the type of traffic that flows over a particular sublink. • CONTROL indicates the sublink used to transport CLAW packing control messages. • IP indicates the sublink used to transmit IP datagrams whose TCP checksum is handled by the host. CKSUM indicates the sublink used to transmit IP datagrams that use the CMCC checksum assist feature.

Related Commands

To locate documentation of related commands, you can search online at www.cisco.com.

claw
offload

show extended channel packing stats

Use the **show extended channel packing stats** EXEC command to display CLAW packing statistics.

show extended channel *slot/port* **packing stats** [*path* [*device-address*]]

Syntax	Description
slot	Slot number.
port	Port number.
path	(Optional) Hexadecimal value in the range 0x0000 to 0xFFFF. This specifies the data path and consists of two digits for the physical connection (either on the host or on the ESCON Director switch): one digit for the control unit address, and one digit for the channel logical address. If not specified, the control unit address and channel logical address default to 0.
device-address	(Optional) Hexadecimal value in the range 0x00 to 0xFE. This value is the unit address associated with the control unit number and path as specified in the host IOCP file. For CLAW and offload support, the device address must have an even value.

Command Mode

EXEC

Usage Guidelines

This command first appeared in Cisco IOS Release 12.0.

Sample Display

The following is sample output from the **show extended channel packing stats** command:

```
Router# show extended channel 3/0 packing stats

Path: C010 Devs: F2,F3 CLAW Link: 1  Read Blks: 4584      Wrt Blks: 15054
                Packets            Bytes              Drops
Linkname      Read    Write     Read     Write     Read    Write    Err C
CONTROL          4        2      128        64        0        0      0 Y
IP               5        5      500       500        0        0      0 Y
CKSUM         4694    93584   187854  53889648        0        0      0 Y
  Total:      4703    93591   188482  53890212        0        0      0
```

Part
II

Command Reference

```
Path: C030 Devs: F6,F7 CLAW Link: N  Read Blks: UNKNOWN    Wrt Blks: UNKNOWN
                 Packets            Bytes              Drops
Linkname    Read     Write      Read     Write      Read     Write    Err C
CONTROL        0        0          0        0          0        0       0 N
IP             0        0          0        0          0        0       0 N
CKSUM          0        0          0        0          0        0       0 N
   Total:      0        0          0        0          0        0       0
```

Table 28-11 describes the fields shown in the display.

Table 28-11 *show extended channel packing stats* Field Descriptions

Field	Description
Path	The path from the CLAW, offload, or CSNA configuration.
Devs	The device address for each device. One CLAW connection requires two devices. You need only specify the even address.
CLAW Link	The established CLAW link number used for all CLAW packing messages. A number value indicates that a CONTROL sublink is connected. "N" indicates that a control sublink is disconnected.
Read Blks	The number of CLAW channel blocks read.
Write Blks	The number of CLAW channel blocks written.
Linkname	The name used to represent the type of traffic that flows over a particular sublink. • CONTROL indicates the sublink used to transport CLAW packing control messages. • IP indicates the sublink used to transmit IP datagrams whose TCP checksum is handled by the host. CKSUM indicates the sublink used to transmit IP datagrams that use the CMCC checksum assist feature.
Packets Read Write	The total number of packets read and written for each sublink.
Bytes Read Write	The total number of bytes read and written for each sublink.
Drops Read Write	The total number of dropped read and write packets for each sublink.
Err	The number of errors. Each error produces an error message at the router console.
C	Connection state of a sublink. "Y" indicates connected. "N" indicates not connected.
Total	The total for each of the recorded statistics.

Related Commands

To locate documentation of related commands, you can search online at www.cisco.com.

claw
offload

show extended channel statistics

Use the **show extended channel statistics** EXEC command to display statistical information about subchannels on the physical interface of a CMCC adapter. This command displays information that is specific to the interface channel devices. The information is generally useful only for diagnostic tasks performed by technical support personnel.

show extended channel *slot/port* **statistics** [*path* [*device-address*]] [**connected**]

Syntax	Description
slot	Slot number.
port	Port number.
path	(Optional) Hexadecimal value in the range 0x0000 to 0xFFFF. This specifies the data path and consists of two digits for the physical connection (either on the host or on the ESCON Director switch): one digit for the control unit address, and one digit for the channel logical address. If not specified, the control unit address and channel logical address default to 0.
device-address	(Optional) Hexadecimal value in the range 0x00 to 0xFE. This value is the unit address associated with the control unit number and path as specified in the host IOCP file. For CLAW and offload support, the device address must have an even value.
connected	(Optional) For each backup group, only display information about the active subchannel or the first subchannel defined in the group if none are active.

Command Mode

EXEC

Usage Guidelines

This command first appeared in Cisco IOS Release 10.2.

Sample Displays

The following is sample output for the **show extended channel statistics** command from a CMCC adapter configured with CLAW, Offload, CSNA, and CMPC:

```
Router#show extended channel 0/1 statistics E010

Path: E010  -- ESTABLISHED
```

Dev	Connects	Command Retries	Cancels	Selective Reset	System Reset	Device Errors	CU Busy
D0	4459	4459	0	0	0	0	0
D1	4950	0	0	0	0	0	0
D2	2529	2526	0	0	0	0	0
D3	2600	0	0	0	0	0	0
D9	2211	0	0	0	0	0	0
DA	4048	2024	0	0	0	0	0

Dev-Lnk	Blocks Read	Blocks Write	Bytes Read	Bytes Write	Dropped Blk Read	Dropped Blk Write	Memd wait	Con
D0-00	0	0	0	0	0	0	0	Y
D0-01	5017	0	1215457	0	0	0	0	Y
Total:	5017	0	1215457	0	0	0	0	
D1-00	0	0	0	0	0	0	0	Y
D1-01	0	5039	0	1247307	0	0	0	Y
Total:	0	5039	0	1247307	0	0	0	
D2-00	0	0	0	0	0	0	0	Y
D2-01	0	0	0	0	0	0	0	Y
D2-02	2671	0	661621	0	0	0	0	Y
Total:	2671	0	661621	0	0	0	0	
D3-00	0	0	0	0	0	0	0	Y
D3-01	0	0	0	0	0	0	0	Y
D3-02	0	2680	0	653285	0	0	0	Y
Total:	0	2680	0	653285	0	0	0	
D9-00	0	2214	0	223418	0	0	0	Y
DA-00	2024	0	124587	0	0	0	0	Y
Path E010								
Total:	9712	9933	2001665	2124010	0	0	0	

```
   Last statistics 5 seconds old, next in 5 seconds
```

Table 28-12 describes the fields shown in the display.

Table 28-12   *show extended channel statistics Field Descriptions*

Field	Description
Path	The path from the CLAW, offload, CMPC, or CSNA configuration.
Dev	The device address for each device. For CLAW and offload, you get two device addresses. In the configuration statement, you only specify the even address. Both CSNA and CMPC get one device.
Connects	The number of times the channel started a channel program on the device.
Command Retries	The number of times the CMCC adapter either had no data to send to the channel (for the read subchannel) or the number of times the CMCC adapter had no buffers to hold data from the channel (for the write subchannel). Every command retry that is resumed results in a connect. A command retry may be ended via a cancel.
Cancels	The host requested any outstanding operation to be terminated. It is a measure of the number of times the host program was started.
Selective Reset	Selective reset affects only one device, whereas a system reset affects all devices on the given channel. It is a reset of the device. On VM this will occur whenever you have a device attached and issue a CP IPL command.
System Reset	The number of times the system Initial Program Load (IPL) command was issued. The command is always issued when the ECA is initialized and when the channel is taken off line.
Device Errors	Errors detected by the ESCON or Parallel inteface due to problems on the link. This value should always be 0.
CU Busy	The number of times the adapter returned a control unit busy indication to the host. This occurs after a cancel or reset if the host requests an operation before the CMCC adapter has finished processing the cancel or reset.
Dev-Lnk	The first number is the device address. The second number is the logical link. Link 0 is always used for CLAW control messages. For IP datagram mode, link 1 is for actual datagram traffic.
	For offload, link 2 is for API traffic. For CSNA and CMPC, the Dev-Lnk is not relevant.
Blocks Read/Blocks Write	A count of channel blocks that are read and written from the mainframe.
Bytes Read/Bytes Write	Bytes is the sum of the bytes in the blocks.
Dropped Blk Read/Write	If the route processor sends data to the CMCC adapter faster than it can send it to the channel, then the block is dropped. High values mean the host is not running fast enough. There are drops on write, too. A write drop will occur if the CMCC adapter fails to get a router processor buffer *n* times for a given block. See Memd wait counter.

Continues

Table 28-12 *show extended channel statistics Field Descriptions (Continued)*

Field	Description
Memd wait	The number of times the CMCC adapter could not obtain a buffer.
Con	For link 0, connect of Y means the system validation has completed. For all other links, it means the connection request sequence has completed. Con is an abbreviation for connected. For CSNA devices, a value of Y is displayed when the CSNA device status becomes setupComplete. For all other states, the Con shows a value of N.

The following is sample output for the CSNA path, using the **show extended channel statistics** command:

```
Router# show extended channel 0/1 statistics E200

Path: E200  -- ESTABLISHED
             Command            Selective   System   Device      CU
Dev  Connects Retries  Cancels   Reset      Reset    Errors     Busy
 D0   217440  108293      1        0          0        0          0
 D1    59530   19800      1        0          0        0          0
 D2     1065     252      2        0          0        0          0
 D3     1329      16      2        0          0        0          0
 D4     1066     251      2        0          0        0          0
 D5      887      29      2        0          0        0          0
 DA     1073      17      2        0          0        0        373
 DB      410     174      2        0          0        0          0
 DC     1154      14      2        0          0        0        459
 DD      254      17      2        0          0        0          0
              Blocks             Bytes         Dropped Blk  Memd
Dev-Lnk  Read      Write    Read       Write    Read    Write  wait Con
 D0-00  109096   109095 237799616    880468      0       0      0   Y
 D1-00   19877    19875   160688   237876362     0       0      0   Y
 D2-00       9    12842      801    52554701     0       0      0   Y
 D3-00    1315        8 30378114       1052      0       0      0   Y
 D4-00       9    12842      801    52554701     0       0      0   Y
 D5-00     860        8 17003956       1052      0       0      0   Y
 DA-00     687        8 14617852       1052      0       0      0   Y
 DB-00       9     3578      801    14613989     0       0      0   Y
 DC-00     682        8 14513604       1052      0       0      0   Y
 DD-00       9     3594      801    14679517     0       0      0   Y
Path E200
Total:  132553   161858 314477034 373163946     0       0      0
    Last statistics 3 seconds old, next in 7 seconds
```

Related Commands

To locate documentation of related commands, you can search online at www.cisco.com.

claw
cmpc
csna
offload

show extended channel subchannel

Use the **show extended channel subchannel** EXEC command to display information about the CMCC adapter physical interfaces. This command displays information that is specific to the interface channel connection. The information displayed is generally useful only for diagnostic tasks performed by technical support personnel.

show extended channel *slot/port* **subchannel** [**connected**]

Syntax	Description
slot	Slot number.
port	Port number.
connected	(Optional) For each backup group, only display information about the active subchannel or the first subchannel defined in the group if none are active.

Command Mode
EXEC

Usage Guidelines
This command first appeared in Cisco IOS Release 10.2.

Sample Display

The following is sample output from the **show extended channel subchannel connected** command used on a CMCC adapter configured for CLAW, Offload, CSNA, and CMPC:

```
Router#show extended channel 0/1 subchannel

Channel0/1: state up
  Flags: VALID ESCON LOADED ENABLED SIGNAL
  Link: DD, Buffers 0, CRC errors 0, Load count 4
  Link Incident Reports
    implicit 0, bit-error 0, link failed 0,
    NOS 0, sequence timeout 0, invalid sequence 0
  Neighbor Node - VALID
    Class: Switch          Type Number : 009032      Tag: DD
    Model: 002             Manufacturer: 000
    Plant: 02              Sequence    : 000000011123
  Local Node - VALID
    Class: CTCA-standalone Type Number : C7500        Tag: 1
    Model: 2               Manufacturer: CSC
    Plant: A               Sequence    : 76027714
                                                                      Last
  Mode      Path Device                                               Sense
  CLAW      E010 D0    10.50.1.11        CISCOMVS DUBLIN    TCPIP    TCPIP   0080
  CLAW      E010 D1    10.50.1.11        CISCOMVS DUBLIN    TCPIP    TCPIP   0080
  OFFLOAD   E010 D2    10.50.1.2         CISCOMVS MPC1OF    TCPIP    TCPIP   0080
                                         TCPIP    API
  OFFLOAD   E010 D3    10.50.1.2         CISCOMVS MPC1OF    TCPIP    TCPIP   0080
                                         TCPIP    API
  CMPC      E010 D9    PC1-789 WRITE                                         0080
  CMPC      E010 DA    PC1-789 READ                                         0080
  CSNA      E200 D0    maxpiu 20470 time-delay  10 length-delay 20470       0000
  CSNA      E200 D1    maxpiu 20470 time-delay  10 length-delay 20470       0000
  CMPC      E200 D2    PC1-7F2 WRITE                                        0000
  CMPC      E200 D3    PC1-7F2 READ                                         0000
  CMPC      E200 D4    PC1-7F4 WRITE                                        0000
  CMPC      E200 D5    PC1-7F4 READ                                         0000
  CMPC      E200 DA    PC1-7FA READ                                         0000
  CMPC      E200 DB    PC1-7FA WRITE                                        0000
  CMPC      E200 DC    PC1-7FB READ                                         0000
  CMPC      E200 DD    PC1-7FB WRITE                                        0000
  Last statistics 0 seconds old, next in 10 seconds
```

Table 28-13 describes the fields shown in the display.

Table 28-13 *show extended channel subchannel* *Field Descriptions*

Field	Description
Channel*x/y*: state	The state can be up, down, or administratively down.
Flags	• BUF_WAIT—State that a device can get into when the mainframe attempts to write data to the CMCC adapter and the CMCC adapter has no buffers for all of the write operation.
	• BUSY—Transient state that a device can get into during processing of various resets.
	• CMD_RETRY—State that a device can get into if the mainframe attempts to write data to the CMCC adapter when the CMCC adapter has no buffers for it or if the mainframe performs a read operation and the CMCC adapter does not have any data to send.
	• ENABLED—The interface is allowed to send and receive datagrams.
	• ESCON—The channel interface is an ESCON interface.
	• FBL_WAIT—State that a device can get into when the mainframe attempts to write data to the CMCC adapter and the CMCC adapter has no buffers for all of the write operation.
	• GO-OFF—The CMCC adapter is trying to gracefully shut down the channel interface. This state should not persist for more than a few seconds. (Not applicable to the virtual channel interface.)
	• INVALID—All displays for virtual channel interfaces should contain this flag. On physical channel interfaces, it indicates a problem with the CMCC adapter microcode.
	• LOADED—The channel firmware for the physical channel interface is loaded. The channel firmware is only loaded if the interface configuration contains at least one device configuration statement and is not shut down. This flag matches the state of the "loaded" LED. (Not applicable to the virtual channel interface.)
	• LOVE—A love note indicating an interface state change (up-down or down-up) is pending on this interface. This state should not persist for more than a few seconds.

Continues

Part II

Command Reference

Table 28-13   *show extended channel subchannel* *Field Descriptions (Continued)*

Field	Description
Flags (continued)	• OFFLINE—For an ESCON channel interface, this flag indicates that no mainframe has established an ESCON logical path corresponding to the paths specified in any device configuration statement (claw, offload, csna, or cmpc). For a Parallel channel interface, this flag indicates that the x'0100' path is not defined in any device configuration statement or SIGNAL is not present.
	• ONLINE—For an ESCON Channel interface, this indicates that at least one mainframe has established an ESCON logical path corresponding to the paths specified in one of the device configuration statements (claw, offload, csna, or cmpc). For a Parallel Channel interface, this flag indicates that the x'0100' path is defined in at least one device configuration statement and SIGNAL is present.
	• RQC_PEND—The CMCC adapter is attempting to send status to the channel on this interface. This state should not persist for more than a few seconds. (Not applicable to the virtual channel interface.)
	• SIGNAL—For an ESCON channel interface, this flag indicates that light is detected. For a Parallel channel interface, this flag indicates that the "operational out" signal is detected. This flag matches the state of the "signal" LED. It will only be set if the LOADED flag is set as well. (Not applicable to the virtual channel interface).
	• STAT_PEND—Indicates that the CMCC adapter has status to present for this device. The indication is cleared when the mainframe accepts the status.
	• SUSPEND—Indicates that the CMCC device task has decided to suspend data transfer for a particular device.
	• VALID—A physical interface is installed. All displays for physical channel interfaces should contain this. This flag matches the state of the "present" LED.
Link: xx	The Director Port number the physical channel is connected to. If the physical channel is direct connected, then this value is host dependent.
Buffers	Number of times the CMCC adapter has dropped a packet bound for the route processor because no packet switching buffer was available on the route processor.
CRC errors	Number of CRC errors detected on the channel for ESCON. Number of parity errors detected on the channel for Parallel.
Load count	For a CMCC physical channel interface, this is the number of times the channel adapter microcode has been loaded.

Table 28-13 *show extended channel subchannel* *Field Descriptions (Continued)*

Field	Description
Link Incident Reports	Link Incidents are errors on an ESCON channel. These errors are reported to the host operating system and are recorded here for additional information.
	• Implicit incidents—A recoverable error occurred in the ECA.
	• Bit errors—The bit error rate threshold was reached. The bit error rate threshold is 15 error bursts within 5 minutes. An error burst is defined as a time period of 1.5+/-.5 seconds during which one or more code violations occurred. A code violation error is caused by an incorrect sequence of 10 bit characters.
	• Link failed—A loss of synchronization or light has occurred.
	• NOS—The channel or switch transmitted the Not Operational Sequence.
	• Sequence timeout—Occurs when a connection recovery timeout occurs or when waiting for the appropriate response while in the transmit off-line sequence (OLS) state.
	• Invalid Sequence—Occurs when a UD or UDR is recognized in the wait for offline sequence state. UD is an unconditional disconnect and UDR is an unconditional disconnect response
Neighbor node	Describes the channel or switch.
	• VALID—Shows information has been exchanged between the router and channel or switch.
	• Class—Switch or channel depending on whether the connection is a switched point-to-point connection or a point-to-point connection.
	• Type number—Describes the model of switch or processor.
	• TAG—Describes the physical location of the connector.
	• Model—A further classification of type.
	• Manufacturer—Describes who made switch or processor.
	• Plant and sequence—Manufacturer specific information to uniquely define this one device.

Continues

Part
II

Command Reference

Table 28-13 *show extended channel subchannel Field Descriptions (Continued)*

Field	Description
Local node	Describes the router.
	• VALID—Shows information has been exchanged between the router and channel or switch.
	• Class—Will be CTCA.
	• The type number and model—Defines the router.
	• The tag—The slot and port where the channel interface processor resides.
	• Manufacturer—Will always be CSC (for Cisco Systems).
	• Plant—The location where the CMCC adapter was manufactured.
	• Sequence—The base Ethernet address assigned to the route processor (RP).
Mode	CLAW, offload, CSNA, or CMPC.
Last sense	Two bytes of sense data transmitted to the host at the time of the last unit exception. Normally, the value will be 0000 if no unit exception has occurred, or 0080 to indicate that a resetting event has occurred. Resetting events occur whenever an ESCON device starts, unless the first command is a 0x02 read command. The CLAW read subchannel always starts with a 0x02 read command so a resetting event will not occur.

Related Commands

To locate documentation of related commands, you can search online at www.cisco.com.

claw
cmpc
csna
offload

show extended channel tcp-connections

Use the **show extended channel tcp-connections** EXEC command to display information about the Transmission Control Protocol (TCP) sockets on a channel interface.

> **show extended channel** *slot/port* **tcp-connections** [[*loc-ip-addr* [*loc-port*
> [*rem-ip-addr* [*rem-port*]] [**detail** | **summary**]

Syntax	Description
slot	Slot number.
port	Port number.
tcp-connections	Specifies TCP connections display.
loc-ip-addr	(Optional) Local IP address. IP address of the local connection endpoint. Restricts the output to those connections with a matching local IP address.
loc-port	(Optional) Local TCP port. This is the TCP port of the local connection endpoint. Restricts the output to those connections with a matching local TCP port. An asterisk (*) is a wildcard that matches every port.
rem-ip-addr	(Optional) Remote IP address. IP address of the remote connection endpoint. Restricts the output to those connections with a matching remote IP address.
rem-port	(Optional) Remote TCP port. TCP port of the remote connection endpoint. Restricts the output to those connections with a matching remote TCP port.
detail	(Optional) Prints detailed information about every matching connection.
summary	(Optional) This is the default. Prints a summary of all matching connections.

Command Mode

EXEC for **summary** and Privileged EXEC for **detail**.

Usage Guidelines

This command first appeared in Cisco IOS Release 11.0.

The **show extended channel tcp-connection** command is valid on both physical and virtual channel interfaces. If no IP addresses or TCP ports are specified, all TCP connections are displayed in a summary for the specified interface.

The command displays detailed information about a large number of sessions that can take a long time. Consider restricting the output by IP address and TCP port to connections of interest.

Part II

Command Reference

Sample Display

The following is sample output for the **show extended channel tcp-connections detail** command:

```
Router#show extended channel 0/1 tcp-connections detail

Local IP Addr   Port   Remote IP Addr   Port    State      In Bytes   Out Bytes
80.11.198.2     21     0.0.0.0          0       listen        0           0
80.11.198.2     21     172.18.48.194    38668   establish     62         298
80.11.198.2     23     0.0.0.0          0       listen        0           0
80.11.198.2     23     172.18.48.194    38666   establish    124       11966
80.11.198.2     1025   0.0.0.0          0       listen        0           0
80.11.198.2     1025   172.18.48.194    38705   closeWait     24          1
80.11.198.3     7      0.0.0.0          0       listen        0           0
80.11.198.3     9      0.0.0.0          0       listen        0           0
80.11.198.3     19     0.0.0.0          0       listen        0           0
80.11.198.3     21     0.0.0.0          0       listen        0           0
80.11.198.3     23     0.0.0.0          0       listen        0           0
80.11.198.3     23     172.18.48.194    38667   establish     85         446
```

The following is sample output for the **show extended channel tcp-connections summary** command:

```
Router# show extended channel 0/1 tcp-connections summary

TCP Connections=12  Input Bytes=     294  Output Bytes=     13049
```

Related Commands

To locate documentation of related commands, you can search online at www.cisco.com.
pu (direct)
pu (DLUR)
offload
show extended channel tcp-stack

show extended channel tcp-stack

Use the **show extended channel tcp-stack** EXEC command to display information about the TCP stack running on CMCC adapter interfaces.

> **show extended channel** *slot/port* **tcp-stack** [*ip-address*]

Syntax	Description
slot	Slot number.
port	Port number.
tcp-stack	Specifies **tcp stack** display.
ip-address	(Optional) IP address specified by the **offload** interface configuration command or the **tn327-server pu** command.

Command Mode

EXEC

Usage Guidelines

This command first appeared in Cisco IOS Release 11.0.

The **show extended channel tcp-stack** command is valid on both physical and virtual channel interfaces. If no *ip-address* argument is specified, then information is displayed for all IP addresses configured on the specified interface.

Sample Display

The following is sample output from the **show extended channel tcp-stack** command:

```
Router#show extended channel 0/1 tcp-stack

TCP Statistics for IP Address 80.11.198.2
   RtoAlgorithm: vanj      RtoMin     : 1000      RtoMax     : 64000
   MaxConn    : -1         ActiveOpens : 1        PassiveOpens: 17
   AttemptFails: 0         EstabResets : 0        CurrEstab  : 5
   InSegs     : 181        OutSegs    : 147       RetransSegs : 0
   InErrs     : 0          OutRsts    : 0
TCP Statistics for IP Address 80.11.198.3
   RtoAlgorithm: vanj      RtoMin     : 1000      RtoMax     : 64000
   MaxConn    : -1         ActiveOpens : 0        PassiveOpens: 1
   AttemptFails: 0         EstabResets : 0        CurrEstab  : 6
   InSegs     : 25         OutSegs    : 23        RetransSegs : 0
   InErrs     : 0          OutRsts    : 0
```

Related Commands

To locate documentation of related commands, you can search online at www.cisco.com.

offload
pu (direct)
pu (DLUR)
show extended channel tcp-connections

show extended channel tg

Use the **show extended channel tg** EXEC command to display configuration, operational information, and statistics information for CMPC transmission groups configured on the specified CMCC adapter's virtual interface.

show extended channel *slot/port* **tg** [**oper** | **stats**] [**detailed**] [*tg-name*]

Syntax	Description
slot	Slot number.
port	Port number.
oper	(Optional) Operational parameters for the CMPC transmission group values.
stats	(Optional) Statistical values for the CMPC transmission group.
detailed	(Optional) Additional LLC information about the CMPC transmission group.
tg-name	(Optional) Information for the specified *tg-name*.

Command Mode

EXEC

Usage Guidelines

This command first appeared in Cisco IOS Release 11.3.

The **show extended channel tg** command is valid only on the virtual channel interface. If *tg-name* argument is not specified, information about all *tgs* configured on the specified interface is displayed.

If neither the **oper** or **stats** arguments are specified, operational values are displayed.

Sample Displays

The following is sample output from the **show extended channel tg oper** command:

```
Router# show extended channel 3/2 tg oper detailed MVS2-TG1

CMPC-TG: MVS2-TG1 Status: ACTIVE
    Adapter:token   1  RMAC:4000.4040.1996        LSAP:04       RSAP:04
    TGN     :21         Local CP: NETA.MVS2        Remote CP: NETA.CALEB
    MaxIn   :4105       MaxOut  :4105
    HPR     :NO         HPR LSAP:04                HPR RSAP :00
    RIF     :0830.1FF1.0041.00A0
Connection LLC2 Information:
    t1-time   = 1000  tpf-time  = 1000  trej-time = 3200  tbusy-tim = 9600
    idle-time =60000  local-win =    7  recv-wind =    7  N2        =    8
    N1-Send   = 1033  N1-Rcv    = 1033  ack-delay =  100  ack-max   =    3
    Nw        =    0  Ww        =    7
    Last Ww Cause = other
    Connection Time: 00:00:00 UTC Jan 1 1970
    Last modified: 00:00:00 UTC Jan 1 1970
```

Table 28-14 describes the fields shown in the display.

Table 28-14 *show extended channel tg oper* *Field Descriptions*

Field	Description
Status	Connection status of the CMPC transmission group. Valid values are:
	• **Shutdown**—CMCC virtual interface is shutdown. In this state, all nonconfigurable values will not be displayed and the LLC connection operational values displayed when the detailed argument is specified also are not displayed.
	• **Inactive**—CMPC transmission group is reset ready to activate.
	• **LocatingRemoteLinkStation**—Exploring network for configured CMPC transmission group peer.
	• **RemoteLinkStationLocated**—CMPC transmission group network peer found. Waiting for connection negotiation to start.
	• **XID3Negotiation**—XID negotiation in progress.
	• **PendingActive**—Connect station pending.
	• **Active**—CMPC transmission group connection active.
Adapter	Identifies the CMCC adapter's internal MAC adapter configured for this CMPC transmission group. The MAC address configured for this adapter is the local MAC address for the CMPC transmission group LLC connection.
RMAC	Remote MAC address configured for the CMPC transmission group LLC connection.
LSAP	Local SAP configured for the CMPC transmission group LLC connection.
RSAP	Remote SAP configured for the CMCP transmission group LLC connection.
TGN	Transmission group number for this CMPC transmission group LLC connection. This value is extracted from the XID3 negotiation exchange.
Local CP	Control point name for VTAM. The name is extracted from XID3s received from VTAM.
Remote CP	Control point name for the remote node connected by this CMPC transmission group. The name is extracted from XID3 received from the remote node.
MaxIn	Maximum PIU the remote node is allowed to send to VTAM. The value is the max PIU field in the XID3s received from VTAM.
MaxOut	Maximum PIU VTAM is allowed to send to the remote node. The value is the lowest of the max PIU field in the XID3 received from the remote node, the LF (length field) size in the RIF and the CMCC virtual interface MTU size.
HPR	Valid values are YES and NO. If HPR is active on this CMPC transmission group, then the value will display YES.

Continues

Part II

Command Reference

Table 28-14 *show extended channel tg oper Field Descriptions (Continued)*

Field	Description
HPR LSAP	Local SAP value used for HPR traffic. This value will be the same as the configured local SAP value.
HPR RSAP	Remote SAP value used for HPR traffic. This value is extracted from the XID3s during the connection negotiation between VTAM and the remote node.
RIF	Routing information field. If the CMPC transmission group LLC connection is established using source-route bridging, then the RIF used for the connection is displayed here.

The following is sample output on a Cisco 7500 router from the **show extended channel tg stats** command:

```
Router# show extended channel 3/2 tg stats detail MVS2-TG1

CMPC-TG:MVS2ISR1
   IFramesIn    :51          IFramesOut   :41
   IBytesIn     :4378        IBytesOut    :51803
   UIFramesIn   :0           UIFramesOut  :0
   UIBytesIn    :0           UIBytesOut   :0
   TESTRspsIn   :1           TESTCmdsOut  :1
   XIDCmdsIn    :3           XIDCmdsOut   :3
   XIDRspsIn    :0           XIDRspsOut   :0
   ConnectReqs  :2           ConnectInds  :0
   ConnectRsps  :2           ConnectCnfms :0
   DISCReqs     :1           DISCInds     :0
   SweepReqsIn  :0           SweepReqsOut :0
   SweepRspsIn  :0           SweepRspsOut :0
   Wraps        :0
   LastSeqNoIn  :9           LastSeqNoOut :7
   LastSeqNoFailureCause     : None
TimeSinceLastSeqNoFailure : never
   LLC2 Connection Statistics:
   LAN Token  0 Adapter   1 4000.cdcd.cdcd
     Local SAP=04 Remote MAC=4000.4040.1996 Remote SAP=04
       LocalBusies     =        0  RemoteBusies    =        0
       IFramesIn       =       51  IFramesOut      =       41
       IOctetsIn       =     4378  IOctetsOut      =    51803
       SFramesIn       =        0  SFramesOut      =        0
       REJsIn          =        0  REJsOut         =        0
       RetransmitsOut  =        0  WwCountChanges  =        0
```

Table 28-15 describes the fields shown in the display.

Table 28-15 *show extended channel tg stats Field Descriptions*

Field	Description
IFramesIn	Number of connection-oriented PIUs received by this CMPC transmission group from the remote network node.
IFramesOut	Number of connection-oriented PIUs sent by this CMPC transmission group to the remote network node.
UIFramesIn	Number of connectionless PIUs (HPR frames) received by this CMPC transmission group from the remote network node.
UIFramesOut	Number of connectionless PIUs (HPR frames) sent by this CMPC transmission group to the remote network node.
TestRspsIn	Number of TEST responses received for this CMPC transmission group.
TestCmdsOut	Number of TEST commands sent by this CMPC transmission group to the configured remote MAC address.
XidCmdsIn	Number of XID commands received for this CMPC transmission group.
XidCmdsOut	Number of XID commands sent by this CMPC transmission group.
XidRspsIn	Number of XID responses received for this CMPC transmission group.
XidRspsOut	Number of XID responses sent by this CMPC transmission group.
SweepReqsIn	Number of CMPC sweep requests received from VTAM on this CMPC transmission group.
SweepReqsOut	Number of CMPC sweep requests sent to VTAM on the CMPC transmission group.
SweepRspsIn	Number of CMPC responses received from VTAM on this CMPC transmission group.
SweepRspsOut	Number of CMPC responses sent to VTAM on this CMPC transmission group.
IBytesIn	Number of bytes for connection-oriented PIUs received by this CMPC transmission group from the remote network node.
IBytesOut	Number of bytes for connection-oriented PIUs sent by this CMPC transmission group to the remote network node.
UIBytesIn	Number of bytes for connectionless PIUs received by this CMPC transmission group from the remote network node.
UIBytesOut	Number of bytes for connectionless PIUs sent by this CMPC transmission group to the remote network node.
ConnectReqs	Number of connect requests received from the host by this CMPC transmission group.

Continues

Table 28-15 *show extended channel tg stats Field Descriptions (Continued)*

Field	Description
ConnectInds	Number of connect indications sent to the host by this CMPC transmission group.
ConnectRsps	Number of connect responses received from the host by this CMPC transmission group.
ConnectCnfms	Number of connect confirms sent to the host by this CMPC transmission group.
DISCReqs	Number of disconnect requests received from the host by this CMPC transmission group.
DISCInds	Number of disconnect indications sent to the host by this CMPC transmission group.
Wraps	The number of times the sequence numbers wrapped for this CMPC transmission group.
LastSeqNoIn	The sequence number on the last CMPC data block sent to the host from this CMPC transmission group.
LastSeqNoOut	The sequence number on the last CMPC data block received from the host for this CMPC transmission group.
LastSeqNoFailureCause	The cause of the last sequence number failure for this CMPC transmission group. Valid values are as follows: • None—No sequence number failures have occurred on this CMPC transmission group since it was configured or the interface was last "no shut." • Block—The sequence number failure occurred on a MPC data block received from the host for this CMPC transmission group. • Sweep—The sequence number failure occurred on a sweep command received from the host for this CMPC transmission group.
TimeSinceLastSeqNoFailure	Time since the last CMPC sequence number failure for this CMPC transmission group. If there have been no failures, "never" is displayed.

The following is sample output on a Cisco 7500 router from the **show extended channel tg stats** command when the interface is shut down:

```
Router# show extended channel 3/2 tg stats detail MVS2-TG1

CIP LLC-TG:MVS2ISR1 -Statistics Not Available
```

Related Commands

To locate documentation of related commands, you can search online at www.cisco.com.

cmpc
tg

show extended channel tn3270-server

Use the **show extended channel tn3270-server** EXEC command to display current server configuration parameters and the status of the PUs defined for the TN3270 server.

show extended channel *slot/port* **tn3270-server**

Syntax	Description
slot	Slot number.
port	Port number.

Command Mode

EXEC

Usage Guidelines

This command first appeared in Cisco IOS Release 11.2.

Sample Display

The following is sample output from the **show extended channel tn3270-server** command:

```
Router# show extended channel 3/2 tn3270-server

<current stats> < connection stats >  <response time(ms)>
server-ip:tcp        lu in-use  connect disconn fail   host     tcp
172.28.1.106:23      510    1       12      11    0      54      40
172.28.1.107:23      511    0        0       0    0       0       0
172.28.1.108:23      255    0        0       0    0       0       0
total               1276    1
configured max_lu 20000
idle-time   0             keepalive 1800       unbind-action disconnect
tcp-port   23             generic-pool permit no timing-mark
dlur MPX.GOANCP                            status SHUT
dlus MPX.NGMVMPC

name(index)     ip:tcp           xid    state    link  destination     r-lsap
EXT2(1)         172.28.1.106:23  05D18092 ACTIVE  tok 0  4000.7470.00e7  08 04
PUS10(2)        172.28.1.107:23  05D19010 ACTIVE  tok 0  4000.7470.00e7  08 2C
PUS11(3)        172.28.1.107:23  05D19011 ACTIVE  tok 0  4000.7470.00e7  08 28
```

```
PUS12(4)     172.28.1.108:23     05D19012 ACTIVE    tok 0   4000.7470.00e7 08 24
PUS9(5)      172.28.1.109:23     05D18509 SHUT      tok 0   4001.3745.1088 04 40
SDTF(7)      172.28.1.107:23     12345678 ACTIVE    tok 0   0800.5a4b.1cbc 04 08
TEST(8)      172.28.1.106:23     05D18091 ACTIVE    tok 0   4000.7470.00e7 08 30
INT1(6)      172.28.1.106:23     05D18091 SHUT      dlur
```

Table 28-16 describes significant fields in the display. Those fields not described correspond to configured values.

Table 28-16 *show extended channel tn3270-server* Field Descriptions

Field	Description
server pickup	IP address and TCP port number, listening point, configured on one or more PUs.
lu *number*	Total number of LUs available for this listening point.
in-use *number*	Number of LUs currently in use.
connect *number*	Total number of connect ins since the TN3270 feature was started.
disconn *number*	Total number of disconnects since the TN3270 feature was started.
fail *number*	Total number of failed connects since the TN3270 feature was started.
response time, host *number*	The average response time from the host across all sessions through this server IP address. This is measured from sending CD to the host to receiving the reply.
response time, tcp *number*	Average response time from the clients on this server IP address. This is measured only when TIMING MARKs are sent. If **no timing-mark** is configured, they are only sent on special occasions, such as Bind.
idle-time *number*	Configured idle-time for this PU.
keepalive *number*	Configured keepalive for this PU.
unbind-action *type*	Configured unbind action for LUs on this PU.
tcp-port *number*	Configured TCP port number.
generic-pool *type*	Configured generic-pool for LUs on this PU.
dlur *fq-cpname*	Configured fully qualified DLUR CP name.
status *status-value state-value*	Shows the status of the DLUR-DLUS pipe followed by the state of the pipe. Possible values for the status are: RESET—The pipe is reset. PND-ACTV—The pipe is pending active. ACTIVE—The pipe is active. PND-INAC—The pipe is pending inactive. OTHER—Status is an undefined value. WAIT—Waiting for status from the CMCC adapter. SHUT—The TN3270 server is shut down. NOTKNOWN—Status cannot be obtained.

Table 28-16 *show extended channel tn3270-server Field Descriptions (Continued)*

Field	Description
dlus *fq-dlusname*	Currently active DLUS.
name *pu-name*	This is the name of the PU as configured.
ip:tcp *ip-addr:tcpport*	IP address and TCP port number configured for the PU.
xid *number*	Configured XID - idblk and idnum.
STATE *value*	Possible STATE values and their meanings are: • SHUT—The PU is configured but in shut state. • RESET—The link station of this PU is not active. • TEST—PU is sending a TEST to establish link. • XID—TEST is responded, XID is sent. • P-ACTPU—The link station is up but no ACTPU is received. • ACTIVE—ACTPU is received and acknowledged positively. • ACT/BUSY—Awaiting host to acknowledge the SSCP-PU data. • WAIT—Waiting for PU status from CMCC adapter. • OTHER—PU in undefined state. • P-RQACTPU-R—DLUR PU is pending request ACTPU response. • P-ACTIVE—ACTPU received by DLUR but not yet passed to PU. • P-DACTPU—PU is pending DACTPU. • UNKNOWN—State cannot be obtained.
LINK *type*	LINK type is either internal adapter type and internal adapter number or dlur if it is a SNA Session Switch PU.
DESTINATION *mac-address or PU-name*	If a direct PU, then it is the destination MAC address, otherwise, it is the name of the partner PU.
R-LSAP *number number*	Remote and local SAP values.

show extended channel tn3270-server client-ip-address

Use the **show extended channel tn3270-server client-ip-address** EXEC command to display information about all clients at a specific IP address.

> **show extended channel** *slot/port* **tn3270-server client-ip-address** *ip-address*
> [**disconnected** | **in-session** | **pending**]

Part
II

Command Reference

Syntax	Description
slot	The slot number.
port	The port number.
ip-address	IP address of the client.
disconnected	(Optional) Shows all clients with *ip-address* in disconnected state. Disconnected state refers to an LU session state of ACTIVE or INACTIVE. In this case, the *ip-address* refers to the client that last used the LU.
in-session	(Optional) Shows all clients with *ip-address* in active session state. Active session state refers to an LU session state of ACT/SESS.
pending	(Optional) Shows all clients with *ip-address* in pending state. Pending session state refers to an LU session state of P-SDT, P-ACTLU, P-NTF/AV, P-NTF/UA, P-RESET, P-PSID, P-BIND, P-UNBIND, WT-UNBND, WT-SDT or UNKNOWN.

Command Mode

EXEC

Usage Guidelines

This command first appeared in Cisco IOS Release 11.2.

The **show extended channel tn3270-server client-ip-address** command is valid only on the virtual channel interface. Note that this command does not show information about LUs that have never been connected.

Sample Displays

The following is sample output from the **show extended channel tn3270-server client-ip-address** command. The example shows only active sessions because no other session types exist at this client IP address.

```
Router# show extended channel 3/2 tn3270-server client-ip 192.195.80.40

lu    name    client-ip:tcp        nail state    model   frames in out   idle for
1     PUS11001 192.195.80.40:3169    Y   ACT/SESS 327804   5        5       0:5:47

pu is PUS11, lu is DYNAMIC type 2, negotiated TN3270
bytes 155 in, 1758 out; RuSize 1024 in, 3840 out; NegRsp 0 in, 0 out
pacing window 0 in, 1 out; credits 0 in, queue-size 0 in, 0 out
```

The following is sample output using the **disconnected** argument:

```
Router# show extended channel 2/2 tn3270 client-ip 10.14.1.21 disconnected

Total 2 clients found using 10.14.1.21
```

The following is sample output using the **in-session** argument:

```
Router# show extended channel 2/2 tn3270 client-ip 10.14.1.21 in-session

Note: if state is ACT/NA then the client is disconnected

lu   name   client-ip:tcp       nail state    model   frames in out   idle for
3    PU1L03 10.14.1.21:35215      N   ACT/SESS 327804    317    316     0:0:1

pu is PU1, lu is DYNAMIC type 2, negotiated TN3270
bytes 12167 in, 225476 out; RuSize 2048 in, 1536 out; NegRsp 0 in, 0 out
pacing window 0 in, 1 out; credits 0 in, queue-size 0 in, 0 out
Note: if state is ACT/NA then the client is disconnected

lu   name   client-ip:tcp       nail state    model   frames in out   idle for
4    PU1L04 10.14.1.21:35216      N   ACT/SESS 327804    317    316     0:0:1

pu is PU1, lu is DYNAMIC type 2, negotiated TN3270
bytes 12167 in, 225476 out; RuSize 2048 in, 1536 out; NegRsp 0 in, 0 out
pacing window 0 in, 1 out; credits 0 in, queue-size 0 in, 0 out
Note: if state is ACT/NA then the client is disconnected
Total 2 clients found using 10.14.1.21
```

The following is sample output using the **pending** argument:

```
Router# show extended channel 2/2 tn3270 client-ip 10.14.1.21 pending

Total 2 clients found using 10.14.1.21
```

Table 28-17 describes significant fields in the display.

Table 28-17 *show extended channel tn3270-server client-ip-address* Field Descriptions

Field	Description
lu *locaddr*	LOCADDR of the LU.
name *lu-name*	If the PU is directly connected, then the name shown is the one generated by the seed. If DLUR, then only the unqualified portion is shown. The NETID portion will be the same as the current DLUS.
client-ip:tcp *ip-address:port*	Client's IP address and TCP port number.
nail	Status of LU nailing, either Y or N.

Continues

Table 28-17   *show extended channel tn3270-server client-ip-address* Field Descriptions *(Continued)*

Field	Description
state *lu-state*	The LU state and their meanings are:
	• UNKNOWN—LU in an undefined state.
	• INACTIVE—LU did not receive ACTLU.
	• ACT/NA—LU received ACTLU and acknowledged positively.
	• P-SDT—LU is bound, but there is no SDT yet.
	• ACT/SESS—LU is bound and in session.
	• P-ACTIU—Telnet connects in and is waiting for ACTLU.
	• P-NTF/AV—Awaiting host notify-available response.
	• P-NTF/UA—Awaiting host notify-unavailable response.
	• P-RESET—Awaiting a buffer to send DACTLU response.
	• P-PSID—Awaiting NMVT Reply PSID response.
	• P-BIND—Waiting for host to send bind.
	• P-UNBIND—Awaiting host unbind response.
	• WT-UNBND—Waiting for client to acknowledge disconnection.
	• WT-SDT—Waiting for client to acknowledge SDT.
model *model*	IBM 3278 model type of client; blank if STATIC LU.
frames in *number*	Number of frames sent inbound to the host.
frames out *number*	Number of frames sent outbound from the host.
idle for *time*	Time the client has been idle. The time is in HH:MM:SS.
pu is *pu-name*	Name of the PU.
lu is *type*	Whether LU is DYNAMIC or STATIC.
negotiated *type*	Whether client is TN3270 or TN3270E.
bytes in / out *number/number*	Total number of bytes sent to/received from the host.
RuSize in / out *number/number*	RU size as configured in the bind.
NegRsp in / out *number/number*	Number of SNA negative responses sent to/received from the host.
pacing window in / out *number/number*	SNA pacing window as configured in the bind.
credits in *number*	Number of frames that can be sent inbound without requiring an isolated pacing response.
queue size in *number*	Indicates the number of SNA frames waiting to be sent to the host that are blocked and are waiting for a pacing response.
queue-size out *number*	SNA frames not yet acknowledged by an isolated pacing response by the TN3270 server.

Related Commands

To locate documentation of related commands, you can search online at www.cisco.com.

client (lu nailing)

show extended channel tn3270-server dlur

Use the **show extended channel tn3270-server dlur** EXEC command to display information about the SNA session switch.

Part
II

Command Reference

show extended channel *slot/port* **tn3270-server dlur**

Syntax	Description
slot	The slot number.
port	The port number.

Command Mode

EXEC

Usage Guidelines

This command first appeared in Cisco IOS Release 11.2.

The show extended channel tn3270-server dlur command is valid only on the virtual channel interface.

Sample Display

The following is sample output from the **show extended channel tn3270-server dlur** command:

```
Router# show extended channel 3/2 tn3270-server dlur

dlur MPX.GOANCP
current dlus MPX.NGMVMPC              dlur-dlus status ACTIVE
preferred dlus MPX.NGMVMPC           backup dlus MPX.NGMVMPB
preferred server MPX.NGMVMPA
lsap token-adapter   0 5C      vrn MPX.LAN4          status ACTIVE
link P390                 remote 4000.7470.00e7 08  status ACTIVE
```

Table 28-18 describes significant fields in the display.

Table 28-18   *show extended channel tn3270-server dlur Field Descriptions*

Field	Description
dlur *fq-luname*	Fully qualified CP name used by the SNA session switch and the LU name for the DLUR function configured as the *fq-cpname* on the dlur statement.
current dlus *fq-luname*	Name of the currently active DLUS, either the primary DLUS or the backup DLUS.
dlur-dlus status *dlur-status*	Possible values for the status of the DLUR-DLSU pipe and their meanings are: • RESET—The pipe is reset. • PND-ACTV—ThE pipe is pending active. • ACTIVE—The pipe is active. • PND-INAC—The pipe is pending inactive. • OTHER—Status is an undefined value. • WAIT—Waiting for status from the CMCC adapter. • SHUT—The TN3270 server is shut down. • NOTKNOWN—Status cannot be obtained.
preferred dlus *fq-luname*	Name of the DLUS as configured on the DLUR statement.
backup dlus *fq-luname*	Name of the DLUS that is used if the preferred DLUS is unavailable.
preferred server *fq-luname*	Fully qualified name of the preferred network node server.
lsap	Configured value for the local SAP on the configured internal adapter. Token-adapter specifies the type of internal adapter used.
vrn *fq-name*	Name of the connection network as configured by the vrn statement for this LSAP and internal adapter pair.
lsap...status status	Possible *sap-status* values and their meanings are: • ACTIVE—The SAP is open. • INACTIVE—Not connected to the adapter. • PDN-ACTV—SAP activation in progress. • PND-INAC—SAP deactivation in progress. • OTHER—Status is an undefined value. • WAIT—Waiting for status from the CMCC adapter. • SHUT—The TN3270 server is shut down. • NOTKNOWN—Status cannot be obtained.
link *name*	Name of the configured link. If not a configured link, then the name is an invented name, @DLUR*nn*.

Table 28-18 *show extended channel tn3270-server dlur Field Descriptions (Continued)*

Field	Description
remote *mac sap*	Remote MAC and SAP for this link.
link...status *status*	Possible *link-status* values and their meanings are:

- ACTIVE—Link is active.
- INACTIVE—Not connected to host.
- PND-ACTV—Link activation in progress.
- PND-INAC—Link deactivation in progress.
- OTHER—Status is an undefined value.
- WAIT—Waiting for status from the CMCC adapter.
- SHUT—The TN3270 server is shut down.
- NOTKNOWN—Status cannot be obtained.

show extended channel tn3270-server dlurlink

Use the **show extended channel tn3270-server dlurlink** EXEC command to display information about the DLUR components.

show extended channel *slot/port* **tn3270-server dlurlink** *name*

Syntax	Description
slot	Specifies a particular CMCC adapter in the router where slot is the slot number.
port	The port number.
name	Name of the SNA session switch link to be displayed.

Command Mode
EXEC

Usage Guidelines
This command first appeared in Cisco IOS Release 11.2.

The **show extended channel tn3270-server dlurlink** command is valid only on the virtual channel interface.

Sample Display

The following is sample output from the **show extended channel tn3270-server dlurlink** command:

```
Router# show extended channel 3/2 tn3270-server dlurlink P390

lsap token-adapter  0 5C  vrn MPX.LAN4              status ACTIVE
link P390                 remote 4000.7470.00e7 08  status ACTIVE
partner MPX.NGMVMPC       tgn 1                     maxdata   1033
```

Table 28-19 describes significant fields in the display.

Table 28-19   *show extended channel tn3270-server dlurlink* *Field Descriptions*

Field	Description
lsap...vrn...status *status*	Possible *lsap-status* values and their meanings are: • ACTIVE—The SAP is open. • INACTIVE—Not connected to the adapter. • PDN-ACTV—SAP activation in progress. • PND-INAC—SAP deactivation in progress. • OTHER—Status is an undefined value. • WAIT—Waiting for status from the CMCC adapter. • SHUT—The TN3270 server is shut down. • NOTKNOWN—Status cannot be obtained.
link *name*	Name is an invented name, @DLUR*nn*, if not a configured link.
link...status *status*	Possible link-status values and their meanings are: • ACTIVE—The SAP is open. • INACTIVE—Not connected to the adapter. • PDN-ACTV—SAP activation in progress. • PND-INAC—SAP deactivation in progress. • OTHER—Status is an undefined value. • WAIT—Waiting for status from the CMCC adapter. • SHUT—The TN3270 server is shut down. • NOTKNOWN—Status cannot be obtained.
partner *name*	CP name of the remote node for this link.
tgn *tg-number*	Transmission group number for this link. Because the SNA session switch only supports 1 transmission group per pair of CP names, it is typically 0 or 1.
maxdata *maxdata*	Maximum frame size allowed on this link.

Related Commands

To locate documentation of related commands, you can search online at www.cisco.com.

dlur

show extended channel tn3270-server nailed-ip

Use the **show extended channel tn3270-server nailed-ip** EXEC command to display mappings between a nailed client IP address and nailed LUs.

show extended channel *slot/port* **tn3270-server nailed-ip** *ip-address*

Syntax	Description
slot	The slot number.
port	The port number.
ip-address	Remote client IP address.

Command Mode

EXEC

Usage Guidelines

This command first appeared in Cisco IOS Release 12.0.

The **show extended channel tn3270-server nailed-ip** command is valid only on the virtual channel interface.

Sample Displays

The following is sample output from the **show extended channel tn3270-server nailed-ip** command:

```
Router# show extended channel 3/2 tn3270-server nailed-ip 172.28.0.0
172.28.1.0  255.255.255.192    pu BAGE1  lu 1     50
172.28.1.80 255.255.255.248    pu BAGE2  lu 100   200    printer
172.28.1.83                    pu BAGE3  lu 1     60     printer
172.28.1.82                    pu BAGE1  lu 100   200
```

Table 28-20 describes significant fields in the display.

Table 28-20 *show extended channel tn3270-server nailed-ip* *Field Descriptions*

Field	Description
172.28.1.0	IP address of the nailed client.
255.255.255.192	Network mask for the range of configured nailed clients.
pu BAGE1	PU name under which the **client** command was configured.
lu 1 50	LU LOCADDR range showing first LOCADDR and last LOCADDR. There need not be a last LOCADDR if only a single LOCADDR rather than a range is configured.
printer	Type of device being nailed to the LOCADDRs. If printer is specified, only clients which are printers are nailed to the LOCADDRs. If screen is specified, only clients that are screens are nailed to the LOCADDRs. If neither is specified, both screens and printers can use the LOCADDRs. A printer client is any client with a device type of "328*". A screen client is a client with any other device type.

Related Commands

To locate documentation of related commands, you can search online at www.cisco.com.

client (lu nailing)

show extended channel tn3270-server pu

Use the **show extended channel tn3270-server pu** EXEC command to display the PU configuration parameters, statistics and all the LUs currently attached to the PU.

> **show extended channel** *slot/port* **tn3270-server pu** *pu-name*

Syntax   Description

slot   Specifies a particular CMCC adapter in the router where *slot* is the slot number.

port   The port value for a TN3270 server will always be 2.

pu-name   PU name that uniquely identifies this PU.

Command Mode
EXEC

Usage Guidelines

This command first appeared in Cisco IOS Release 11.2.

The **show extended channel tn3270-server pu** command is valid only on the virtual channel interface. The display shown depends on whether the PU is a direct PU or a SNA session switch PU.

Sample Displays

The following is sample output from the **show extended channel tn3270-server pu** command for a direct PU named BAGE1:

```
Router# show extended channel 3/2 tn3270-server pu BAGE1

name(index)     ip:tcp          xid      state    link    destination    r-lsap
BAGE1(1)        172.28.1.82:23  05D18081 ACTIVE   tok 0   4000.7470.00e7 08 10
idle-time   0       keepalive 1800      unbind-act discon   generic-pool perm
bytes 560 in, 3765 out; frames 20 in, 27 out; NegRsp 0 in, 0 out
actlus 12, dactlus 0, binds 2

lu    name       client-ip:tcp      nail     state       model    frames in out    idle for
1     BAGE1001 never connected      Y     ACTIVE                 1       1        4:50:44
2     BAGE1002 never connected      Y     ACTIVE                 1       1        4:50:44
3     BAGE1003 192.195.80.40:2077   N     ACT/SESS    327804    5       5        5:4:36
4     BAGE1004 192.195.80.40:2644   Y     ACTIVE      327804    5       5        0:36:7

client ip          mask              nail-type  lu first  lu last
192.195.80.40   255.255.255.0        screen       1          2
192.195.80.40   255.255.255.0        printer      4
```

The following is sample output from the **show extended channel tn3270-server pu** command for a SNA session switch PU:

```
Router# show extended channel 3/2 tn3270-server pu INT1

name(index)     ip:tcp           xid      state   link   destination    r-lsap
INT1(5)         172.28.1.106:23  05D18091 ACTIVE  dlur   MPX.GOAN1

idle-time   0       keepalive   0       unbind-act discon   generic-pool perm
bytes 50 in, out; frames 87 in, 2 out; NegRsp 3 in, 0 out
actlus 2, dactlus 0, binds 0

lu    name    client-ip:tcp       state   model   frames in out   idle for
1     GOAN1X01 never connected    ACTIVE            1       1      0:32:14
2     GOAN1X02 never connected    ACTIVE            1       1      0:32:14
```

Table 28-21 describes significant fields in the display.

Table 28-21   *show extended channel tn3270-server pu* *Field Descriptions*

Field	Description
name (index) *pu-name* (*index*)	Name and index of the PU as configured.
ip:tcp *ip-addr:tcpport*	IP address and TCP port number configured for the PU.
xid *number*	Configured XID - idblk and idnum.
state *pu-state*	Possible state values and their meanings are as follows: • SHUT—PU is configured but in shut state. • RESET—Link station of this PU is not active. • TEST—PU is sending a TEST to establish link. • XID—TEST is responded, XID is sent. • P-ACTPU—Link station is up but no ACTPU is received. • ACTIVE—ACTPU is received and acknowledged positively. • ACT/BUSY—Awaiting host to acknowledge the SSCP-PU data. • WAIT—Waiting for PU status from CMCC adapter. • UNKNOWN—Direct PU in undefined state. • P-RQACTPU-R—PU is pending request ACTPU response. • P-ACTIVE—DLUR PU and direct PU states disagree. • P-DACTPU—PU is pending DACTPU. • OTHER—State is an undefined value.
link *type*	LINK type is either internal adapter type and internal adapter number or dlur if it is a SNA Session Switch PU.
destination *mac-address or pu-name*	If a direct PU, then it is the destination MAC address, otherwise, it is the name of the partner PU.
r-lsap *number number*	Remote and local SAP values.
idle-time *number*	Configured idle-time for this PU.
keepalive *number*	Configured keepalive for this PU.
unbind-act *type*	Configured unbind action for LUs on this PU.
generic-pool *type*	Configured generic-pool for LUs on this PU.
bytes in / out *number/number*	Total number of bytes sent to/received from the host for this PU.
frames in / out *number/number*	Total number of frames sent to/received from the host for this PU.
NegRsp in / out *number/number*	Total number of SNA negative responses sent to/received from the host.
actlus *number*	Total number of ACTLUs received from the host.

Table 28-21 *show extended channel tn3270-server pu* Field Descriptions *(Continued)*

Field	Description
dactlus *number*	Total number of DACTLUs received from the host.
binds number	Total number of BINDs received from the host.
lu *number*	LOCADDR of the LU.
name *lu-name*	Name of the TN3270 LU.
client-ip:tcp *ip-addr:tcpport*	Client's IP address and TCP port number.
nail	Status of LU nailing, either Y or N.
state *lu-state*	The LU states and their meanings are: • UNKNOWN—LU in an undefined state. • INACTIVE—LU didn't receive ACTLU. • ACT/NA—LU received ACTLU and acknowledged positively. • P-SDT—LU is bound but there is no SDT yet. • ACT/SESS—LU is bound and in session. • P-ACTLU—Telnet connects in and is awaiting ACTLU. • P-NTF/av—Awaiting host notify-available response. • P-NTF/UA—Awaiting host notify-unavailable response. • P-RESET—Waiting for a buffer to send DACTLU response. • P-PSID—Waiting for NMVT Reply psid response. • P-BIND—Waiting for host to send bind. • P-UNBIND—Awaiting host unbind response. • WT-UNBND—Waiting for client to acknowledge disconnection. • WT-SDT—Waiting for client to acknowledge SDT.
model *model*	IBM 3278 model type of client.
frames in *number*	Number of frames sent inbound to the host.
frames out *number*	Number of frames sent outbound from the host.
idle for *time*	Time the client has been idle. The time is in HH:MM:SS.
client ip	Remote client IP address.
mask	Current network mask.
nail-type	LU nailing type, screen or printer.
lu first	First LU address in the range.
lu last	Last LU address in the range, if one is specified in the **client** configuration command.

Related Commands

To locate documentation of related commands, you can search online at www.cisco.com.

pu (direct)
pu (DLUR)

show extended channel tn3270-server pu lu

Use the **show extended channel tn3270-server pu lu** EXEC command to display information about the TN3270 server LUs running on CMCC adapter interface.

> **show extended channel** *slot/port* **tn3270-server pu** *pu-name* **lu** *locaddr* [**history**]

Syntax	Description
slot	Specifies a particular CMCC adapter in the router where *slot* is the slot number. The port value for a TN3270 server will always be 2.
port	The port value for a TN3270 server will always be 2.
pu-name	PU name that uniquely identifies this PU.
locaddr	LU LOCADDR that uniquely identifies the LU.
history	(Optional) Displays the LU trace history.

Command Mode

EXEC

Usage Guidelines

This command first appeared in Cisco IOS Release 11.2.

The **show extended channel tn3270-server pu lu** command is valid only on the virtual channel interface.

Sample Displays

The following is sample output from the **show extended channel tn3270-server pu lu** command for a direct PU:

```
Router# show extended channel 3/2 tn3270 pu ext2 lu 3

lu    name     client-ip:tcp          state    model    frames in out   idle for
3     EXT2003  171.69.176.77:3829     ACTIVE   327902E  8       9        0:4:43

pu is EXT2, lu is DYNAMIC type 0, negotiated TN3270
bytes 203 in, 2954 out; RuSize 0 in, 0 out; NegRsp 1 in, 0 out
pacing window 0 in, 1 out; credits 0 in, queue-size 0 in, 0 out
```

The following is sample output from the **show extended channel tn3270-server pu lu** command for a SNA session switch PU:

```
Router# show extended channel 3/2 tn3270 pu int1 lu 1

lu    name     client-ip:tcp          state    model    frames in out   idle for
1     GOAN1X01 171.69.176.77:3828     ACTIVE            4       4        0:4:51

pu is INT1, lu is STATIC type 0, negotiated TN3270E
bytes 74 in, 1219 out; RuSize 0 in, 0 out; NegRsp 0 in, 0 out
pacing window 0 in, 0 out; credits 0 in, queue-size 0 in, 0 out
```

The following is sample output from the **show extended channel tn3270-server pu lu history** command:

```
Router# show extended channel 3/2 tn3270 pu pus20 lu 1 history

lu    name     client-ip:tcp          state    model    frames in out   idle for
1     PUS20001 192.195.80.40:2480     ACT/SESS 327804  5       4        0:0:8

pu is PUS20, lu is DYNAMIC type 2, negotiated TN3270
bytes 155 in, 1752 out; RuSize 1024 in, 3840 out; NegRsp 0 in, 0 out>pacing window 0
in, 1 out; credits 0 in, queue-size 0 in, 0 out
traces:
        Client connect req
        Reply PSID pos rsp
        actlu req
        bind req
        sdt req
OUT len=12    2Dxxxxxxxx456B80000D0201
IN  len=25    xxxxxxxxxx45EB80000D0201000000
OUT len=53    2Dxxxxxxxx466B800031010303B1
IN  len=10    2D0001010646EB800031
OUT len=10    2D00010106476B8000A0
IN  len=10    2D0001010647EB8000A0
OUT len=1677  2Cxxxxxxxx010381C07EC7114040
IN  len=9     2C0001010001838100
```

Table 28-22 describes significant fields in the display.

Table 28-22 *show extended channel tn3270-server pu lu Field Descriptions*

Field	Description
LU *locaddr*	LOCADDR of the LU.
NAME *lu-name*	Name of the TN3270 LU.
CLIENT-IP:TCP *ip-addr:tcpport*	Client's IP address and TCP port number.
STATE *lu-state*	The LU state and their meanings are: • UNKNOWN—LU in an undefined state. • INACTIVE—LU didn't receive ACTLU. • ACT/NA—LU received ACTLU and acknowledged positively. • P-SDT—LU is bound but there is no SDT yet. • ACT/SESS—LU is bound and in session. • P-ACTIU—Telnet connects in and is awaiting ACTLU. • P-NTF/AV—Awaiting host notify-available response. • P-NTF/UA—Awaiting host notify-unavailable response. • P-RESET—Waiting for a buffer to send DACTLU response. • P-PSID—Waiting for NMVT Reply psid response. • P-BIND—Waiting for host to send bind. • P-UNBIND—Awaiting host unbind response. • WT-UNBND—Waiting for client to acknowledge disconnection. • WT-SDT—Waiting for client to acknowledge SDT.
MODEL *model*	3278 model type of client; blank if STATIC LU.
FRAMES IN *number*	Number of frames sent inbound to the host.
FRAMES OUT *number*	Number of frames sent outbound from the host. .
IDLE FOR *time*	Time the client has been idle. The time is in HH:MM:SS.
PU IS *pu-name*	Name of the PU.
LU IS *type*	Whether LU is DYNAMIC or STATIC.
NEGOTIATED *type*	Whether client is TN3270 or TN3270E.
BYTES IN / OUT *number/number*	Total number of bytes sent to/received from the host.
RUSIZE IN / OUT *number/number*	RU size as configured in the bind.

Table 28-22 *show extended channel tn3270-server pu lu Field Descriptions (Continued)*

Field	Description
NEGRSP IN / OUT *number/number*	Number of SNA negative responses sent to/received from the host.
PACING WINDOW IN / OUT *number/number*	SNA pacing window as configured in the bind.
CREDITS IN *number*	Number of frames that can be sent inbound without requiring an isolated pacing response.
QUEUE SIZE IN *number*	If non-zero, indicates the number of SNA frames waiting to be sent to the host which are blocked, waiting for a pacing response.
QUEUE SIZE OUT *number*	SNA frames not yet acknowledged by an isolated pacing response by the TN3270 server.

Related Commands

To locate documentation of related commands, you can search online at www.cisco.com.

pu (direct)
pu (DLUR)

show extended channel udp-listeners

Use the **show extended channel udp-listeners** EXEC command to display information about the User Datagram Protocol (UDP) listener sockets running on the CMCC adapter interfaces.

show extended channel *slot/port* **udp-listeners** [*ip-address*]

Syntax	Description
slot	Slot number.
port	Port number.
udp-listeners	Specifies UDP listener port display.
ip-address	(Optional) IP address specified by the **offload** interface configuration command or the **tn3270-server pu** command.

Command Mode
EXEC

Usage Guidelines

This command first appeared in Cisco IOS Release 11.0.

The **show extended channel tn3270-server udp-listeners** command is valid on both physical and virtual channel interfaces.

Sample Display

The following is sample output from the **show channel udp-listeners** command:

```
Router#show extended channel 0/1 udp-listeners

UDP Listener: IP Address 80.11.198.3      LocalPort 7
UDP Listener: IP Address 80.11.198.3      LocalPort 9
UDP Listener: IP Address 80.11.198.3      LocalPort 19
```

Related Commands

To locate documentation of related commands, you can search online at www.cisco.com.

offload
pu (direct)
pu (DLUR)

show extended channel udp-stack

Use the **show extended channel udp-stack** EXEC command to display information about the UDP stack running on the CMCC adapter interfaces.

show extended channel *slot/port* **udp-stack** [*ip-address*]

Syntax	Description
slot	Slot number.
port	Port number.
udp-stack	Selects UDP stack display.
ip-address	(Optional) IP address specified by the **offload** interface configuration command or the **tn3270-server pu** command.

Command Mode

EXEC

Usage Guidelines

This command first appeared in Cisco IOS Release 11.0.

The **show extended channel udp-stack** command is valid on both physical and virtual channel interfaces.

Sample Display

The following is sample output from the **show extended channel udp-stack** command:

```
Router# show extended channel udp-stack

rispix#show extended channel 0/1 udp-stack
UDP Statistics for IP Address 80.11.198.2
   InDatagrams : 6          NoPorts     : 6
   InErrors    : 0          OutDatagrams: 0
UDP Statistics for IP Address 80.11.198.3
   InDatagrams : 6          NoPorts     : 6
   InErrors    : 0          OutDatagrams: 1
```

Related Commands

To locate documentation of related commands, you can search online at www.cisco.com.

offload
pu (direct)
pu (DLUR)

show interfaces channel

Use the **show interfaces channel** privileged EXEC command to display information about the CMCC adapter interfaces. This command displays information that is specific to the interface hardware. The information displayed is generally useful for diagnostic tasks performed by technical support personnel only.

show interfaces channel *slot/port* [**accounting**]

Syntax	Description
slot	Slot number.
port	Port number.
accounting	(Optional) Shows interface accounting information.

Command Mode

Privileged EXEC

Usage Guidelines

This command first appeared in Cisco IOS Release 10.2.

Sample Display

The following is sample output from the **show interfaces channel** command:

```
Router# show interfaces channel 3/0

Channel3/0 is up, line protocol is up
  Hardware is cxBus IBM Channel
  Internet address is 198.92.1.145, subnet mask is 255.255.255.248
  MTU 4096 bytes, BW 0 Kbit, DLY 0 usec, rely 255/255, load 1/255
  Encapsulation CHANNEL, loopback not set, keepalive not set
  ECA type daughter card
  Data transfer rate 12 Mbytes  Number of subchannels 1
  Last input never, output never, output hang never
  Last clearing of "show interface" counters 0:00:04
  Output queue 0/0, 0 drops; input queue 0/75, 0 drops
  Five minute input rate 0 bits/sec, 0 packets/sec
  Five minute output rate 0 bits/sec, 0 packets/sec
    0 packets input, 0 bytes, 0 no buffer
    Received 0 broadcasts, 0 runts, 0 giants
    0 input errors, 0 CRC, 0 frame, 0 overrun, 0 ignored, 0 abort
    0 packets output, 0 bytes, 0 underruns
    0 output errors, 0 collisions, 0 interface resets, 0 restarts
```

Table 28-23 describes the fields shown in the display.

Table 28-23 *show interfaces channel Field Descriptions*

Field	Description
Channel... is {up | down | administratively down}	Indicates whether the interface hardware is currently active (whether synchronization is achieved on an ESCON channel, or whether operational out is enabled on a parallel channel) and whether it has been taken down by an administrator.
line protocol is {up | down | administratively down}	Indicates whether the software processes that handle the line protocol think the line is usable (that is, whether keepalives are successful).
Hardware is	Hardware type.
Internet address is	IP address and subnet mask.
MTU	Maximum transmission unit of the interface.

Table 28-23 *show interfaces channel Field Descriptions (Continued)*

Field	Description
BW	Bandwidth of the interface in kilobits per second.
DLY	Delay of the interface in microseconds.
rely	Reliability of the interface as a fraction of 255 (255/255 is 100% reliability), calculated as an exponential average over 5 minutes.
load	Load on the interface as a fraction of 255 (255/255 is completely saturated), calculated as an exponential average over 5 minutes. The calculation uses the value from the **bandwidth** interface configuration command.
Encapsulation	Encapsulation method assigned to interface.
loopback	Indicates whether loopbacks are set or not.
keepalive	Indicates whether keepalives are set or not.
daughter card	Type of adapter card.
Data transfer rate	Rate of data transfer.
Number of subchannels	Number of subchannels.
Last input	Number of hours, minutes, and seconds since the last packet was successfully received by an interface. Useful for knowing when a dead interface failed.
Last output	Number of hours, minutes, and seconds since the last packet was successfully transmitted by an interface.
output hang	Number of hours, minutes, and seconds (or never) since the interface was last reset because of a transmission that took too long. When the number of hours in any of the "last" fields exceeds 24 hours, the number of days and hours is printed. If that field overflows, asterisks are printed.
Last clearing	The time at which the counters that measure cumulative statistics (such as number of bytes transmitted and received) shown in this report were last reset to zero. Note that variables that might affect routing (for example, load and reliability) are not cleared when the counters are cleared. These asterisks (***) indicate the elapsed time is too large to be displayed. 0:00:00 indicates the counters were cleared more than 2^{31}ms (and less than 2^{32}ms) ago.
Output queue, drops input queue, drops	Number of packets in output and input queues. Each number is followed by a slash, the maximum size of the queue, and the number of packets dropped due to a full queue.
Five minute input rate, Five minute output rate	Average number of bits and packets transmitted per second in the last 5 minutes.

Continues

Table 28-23 *show interfaces channel* *Field Descriptions* *(Continued)*

Field	Description
packets input	Total number of error-free packets received by the system.
bytes input	Total number of bytes, including data and MAC encapsulation, in the error free packets received by the system.
no buffer	Number of received packets discarded because there was no buffer space in the main system. Compare with ignored count. Broadcast storms on Ethernets and bursts of noise on serial lines are often responsible for no input buffer events.
broadcasts	Total number of broadcast or multicast packets received by the interface.
runts	Number of packets that are discarded because they are smaller than the medium's minimum packet size.
giants	Number of packets that are discarded because they exceed the medium's maximum packet size.
input errors	Total number of no buffer, runts, giants, CRCs, frame, overrun, ignored, and abort counts. Other input-related errors can also increment the count, so that this sum may not balance with the other counts.
CRC	Number of code violation errors seen on the ESCON interface, where a received transmission character is recognized as invalid. On a parallel interface, the number of parity errors seen.
frame	Number of packets received incorrectly having a CRC error and a noninteger number of octets. This value is always 0.
overrun	Number of times the serial receiver hardware was unable to hand received data to a hardware buffer because the input rate exceeded the receiver's ability to handle the data. This value is always 0.
ignored	Number of received packets ignored by the interface because the interface hardware ran low on internal buffers. These buffers are different than the system buffers mentioned previously in the buffer description. Broadcast storms and bursts of noise can cause the ignored count to be incremented.
abort	Illegal sequence of one bits on a serial interface. This usually indicates a clocking problem between the serial interface and the data link equipment. This value is always 0.
packets output	Total number of messages transmitted by the system.
bytes	Total number of bytes, including data and MAC encapsulation, transmitted by the system.

Table 28-23 *show interfaces channel* *Field Descriptions* *(Continued)*

Field	Description
underruns	Sum of all errors that prevented the final transmission of datagrams out of the interface being examined. Note that this may not balance with the sum of the enumerated output errors, as some datagrams may have more than one error, and others may have errors that do not fall into any of the specifically tabulated categories.
output errors	Number of output errors.
collisions	Number of collisions detected. This value is always 0.
interface resets	Number of times an interface has been completely reset. This can happen if packets queued for transmission were not sent within several seconds. On a serial line, this can be caused by a malfunctioning modem that is not supplying the transmit clock signal, or by a cable problem. If the system notices that the carrier detect line of a serial interface is up, but the line protocol is down, it periodically resets the interface in an effort to restart it. Interface resets can also occur when an interface is looped back or shut down.
	On the CMCC adapter, this may occur if the host software is not requesting data.
restarts	Number of times the controller was restarted because of errors.

Part
II

Command Reference

shutdown

Use the **shutdown** interface configuration command to shut down an interface or the virtual interface on the CMCC adapter when you are in interface configuration mode. The **shutdown** command also shuts down TN3270 entities, such as PU, DLUR, and DLUR SAP, depending on which configuration mode you are in when the command is issued. Use the **no** form of this command to restart the interface or entity. The entity affected depends on the mode in which the command is issued.

shutdown
no shutdown

Syntax Description

This command has no arguments or keywords.

Default

The interface or entity is enabled.

Command Modes

CMCC adapter interface configuration

TN3270 configuration

PU configuration

DLUR configuration

DLUR SAP configuration

Usage Guidelines

This command first appeared in Cisco IOS Release 10.2 for channel interface configuration. This command was first supported in Cisco IOS Release 11.2 for TN3270, PU, DLUR, and DLUR SAP.

In channel interface configuration mode, the command applies to the entire CMCC adapter.

In TN3270 configuration mode, the command applies to the whole TN3270 Server.

In PU configuration mode, the command applies to the DLUR or direct PU.

In DLUR configuration mode, the command applies to the whole DLUR subsystem.

In DLUR SAP configuration, mode the command applies to the local SAP.

Example

The following example issued in TN3270 configuration mode shuts down the entire TN3270 server:

```
shutdown
```

tcp-port

Use the **tcp-port** TN3270 configuration command to override the default TCP port setting of 23. Use the **no** form of this command to restore the default.

> **tcp-port** *port-number*
> **no tcp-port**

Syntax	Description
port-number	A valid TCP port number in the range of 0 to 65,534. The default is 23, which is the IETF standard. The value 65,535 is reserved by the TN3270 server.

Defaults

In TN3270 configuration mode, the default is 23.

In PU configuration mode the default is the value currently configured in TN3270 configuration mode.

Command Modes

TN3270 configuration

PU configuration

Usage Guidelines

This command first appeared in Cisco IOS Release 11.2.

The **tcp-port** command is valid only on the virtual channel interface, and it can be entered in either TN3270 configuration mode or PU configuration mode. A value entered in TN3270 mode applies to all PUs for that TN3270 server, except as overridden by values entered in PU configuration mode. The **tcp-port** command affects only future TN3270 sessions.

The **no tcp-port** command entered in PU configuration mode removes the override.

Example

The following example entered in TN3270 configuration mode returns the TCP port value to 23:

```
no tcp-port
```

Related Commands

To locate documentation of related commands, you can search online at www.cisco.com.

pu (direct)
pu (DLUR)

tg

Use the **tg** interface configuration command to define LLC connection parameters for the CMPC transmission group. Use the **no** form of this command to remove the specified transmission group from the configuration, which also deactivates the transmission group.

> **tg** *name* **llc** *token-adapter adapter-number lsap* [**rmac** *rmac*] [**rsap** *rsap*]
> **no tg** *name*

Syntax	Description
name	The name of the CMPC transmission group. The maximum length of the name is eight characters. This must match the name specified on the **cmpc** statements.
llc	Specifies that this TG is connected to the LLC stack on the CMCC adapter card.
token-adapter	Internal adapter type on the CMCC adapter card. The currently supported type is token-adapter.
adapter-number	Internal adapter number on the CMCC adapter card, which is the same value specified in the **adapter** internal LAN configuration command.
lsap	Local SAP number, 04 to FC, in hexadecimal. The value must be even and should normally be a multiple of four. It must be unique within the internal adapter in that no other IEEE 802.2 clients of that adapter, in the router or in a host, can use the same SAP.
rmac *rmac*	(Optional) Remote MAC address of the form *xxxx.xxxx.xxxx* in hexadecimal. If not specified, a loopback link to another SAP on the same internal LAN adapter is assumed.
rsap *rsap*	(Optional) Remote SAP address, 04 to FC in hexadecimal. The *rsap* value must be even and should be a multiple of 4, but this requirement is not enforced. The *rsap* value default is 04.

Defaults

The *lsap* and *rsap* values default to 04.

Command Mode

Interface configuration

Usage Guidelines

This command first appeared in Cisco IOS Release 11.3.

The **tg** command is valid only on the virtual channel interface. This command defines an LLC connection with a complete addressing 4-tuple. The *lsap*, *rmac*, and *rsap* are specified explicitly by parameters. The *lmac* is the local MAC address of the adapter referred to by the *type* and *adapter-number* parameters.

To change any parameter of the **tg** command, the existing TG must be removed first by using **no tg** *name*.

The **no tg** command removes the CMPC transmission group from the configuration. If the transmission group is used for a non-HPR connection, all sessions using the TG will be terminated immediately. If the transmission group is an HPR connection, all sessions using the transmission group will be terminated if no other HPR connection is available to the host.

Example
The following example configures a transmission group name and includes the *rmac* and *rsap* parameters:

```
tg LAGUNAA  llc token-adapter 1  18 rmac 4000.0000.beef rsap 14
```

Related Commands
To locate documentation of related commands, you can search online at www.cisco.com.

adapter
cmpc
lan

tn3270-server

Use the **tn3270-server** interface configuration command to start the TN3270 server on a CMCC adapter or to enter TN3270 configuration mode. Use the **no** form of this command to remove the existing TN3270 configuration.

> **tn3270-server**
> **no tn3270-server**

Syntax Description
This command has no arguments or keywords.

Default
No TN3270 server function is enabled.

Command Mode
Interface configuration

Usage Guidelines

This command first appeared in Cisco IOS Release 11.2.

The **tn3270 sever** command is valid only on the virtual channel interface. Only one TN3270 server can run on a CMCC adapter. It will always be configured on a virtual channel interface.

The **no tn3270-server** command shuts down TN3270 server immediately. All active sessions will be disconnected and all DLUR and PU definitions deleted from the router configuration. To restart a TN3270 server, you must reconfigure all parameters.

Example

The following example starts the TN3270 server and enters TN3270 configuration mode:

```
tn3270-server
```

timing-mark

Use the **timing-mark** TN3270 configuration mode command to select whether a WILL TIMING-MARK is transmitted when the host application needs an SNA response (definite or pacing response). Use the **no** form of this command to turn off WILL TIMING-MARK transmission except as used by the keepalive function.

> **timing-mark**
> **no timing-mark**

Syntax Description

This command has no arguments or keywords.

Default

No WILL TIMING-MARKS are transmitted except by keepalive.

Command Mode

TN3270 configuration

Usage Guidelines

This command first appeared in Cisco IOS Release 11.2.

If **timing-mark** is configured the TN3270 server will send WILL TIMING-MARK as necessary to achieve an end-to-end response protocol. Specifically, TIMING-MARK will be sent if any of the following are true:

- The host application has requested a pacing response.

- The host application has requested a Definite Response, and either the client is not using TN3270E, or the request is not Begin Chain.

The use of the **timing-mark** command can degrade performance. Some clients do not support **timing-mark** used in this way. Therefore, **timing-mark** should only be configured where both of the following are true:

- All clients support this usage.

- The application benefits from end-to-end acknowledgment.

Example

The following example enables TIMING-MARK transmission:

```
timing-mark
```

Related Commands

To locate documentation of related commands, you can search online at www.cisco.com.

idle-time
keepalive

unbind-action

Use the **unbind-action** TN3270 configuration command to select what action to take when the TN3270 server receives an UNBIND. Use the **no** form of this command to restore the default.

unbind-action {**keep** | **disconnect**}
no unbind-action

Syntax	Description
keep	No automatic disconnect will be made by the server upon receipt of an UNBIND.
disconnect	Session will be disconnected upon receipt of an UNBIND.

Part II

Command Reference

Defaults

In TN3270 configuration mode, the default is disconnect.

In PU configuration mode the default is the value currently configured in TN3270 configuration mode.

Command Modes

TN3270 configuration

PU configuration

Usage Guidelines

This command first appeared in Cisco IOS Release 11.2.

The **unbind-action** command is valid only on the virtual channel interface. This command can be entered in either TN3270 configuration mode or PU configuration mode. A value entered in TN3270 mode applies to all PUs for that TN3270 server, except as overridden by values entered in PU configuration mode. The **unbind-action** command affects currently active and future TN3270 sessions.

The **no unbind-action** command entered in PU configuration mode removes the override.

The **unbind-action** command affects currently active and future TN3270 sessions.

Example

The following example prevents automatic disconnect:

```
unbind-action keep
```

vrn

Use the **vrn** DLUR SAP configuration command to tell the SNA session switch the connection network to which the internal adapter interface on the CMCC adapter belongs. Use the **no** form of this command to remove a network name.

> **vrn** *vrn-name*
> **no vrn**

Syntax

Description

vrn-name

Fully qualified name of the connection network.

Default
The adapter is not considered to be part of a connection network.

Command Mode
DLUR SAP configuration

Usage Guidelines
This command first appeared in Cisco IOS Release 11.2.

The **vrn** command is valid only on the virtual channel interface. This command is used to discover routes without having to configure all possible links.

A connection network is also known as a shared-access transport facility (SATF). This means, at the MAC level, that all nodes in the network can reach each other using the same addressing scheme and without requiring the services of SNA session routing. A bridged LAN (whether source-route or transparent) is an example. Such a network is represented in the APPN topology as a kind of node, termed a virtual routing node (VRN).

To make use of this function, all APPN nodes must use the same VRN name for the SATF.

Refer to the VTAM operating system documentation for your host system for additional information regarding the VTAM VNGROUP and VNNAME parameters on the PORT statement of an XCA major node.

Several parameters in the DLUR configuration mode consist of fully qualified names, as defined by the APPN architecture. Fully qualified names consist of two case-insensitive alphanumeric strings, separated by a period. However, for compatibility with existing APPN products, including VTAM, the characters "#" (pound), "@" (at), and "$" (dollar) are allowed in the fully qualified name strings. Each string is from one to eight characters long; for example, RA12.NODM1PP. The portion of the name before the period is the NETID and is shared between entities in the same logical network.

Example
The following example sets a VRN name:

```
vrn SYD.BLAN25
```

Related Commands
To locate documentation of related commands, you can search online at www.cisco.com.

dlur
adapter
lan
lsap

Configuring the Airline Product Set

This chapter describes how to configure the Airline Product Set (ALPS). For a complete description of the ALPS commands in this chapter, refer to Chapter 30, "Airline Product Set Configuration Commands." To locate documentation of other commands that appear in this chapter, you can search online at www.cisco.com.

ALPS is a tunneling mechanism that transports airline protocol data across a Cisco router-based TCP/IP network to an X.25-attached mainframe. This feature provides connectivity between agent set control units (ASCUs) and a mainframe host that runs the airline reservation system.

Figure 29-1 shows the basic ALPS topology and the protocols implemented in the feature. Three major components provide the end-to-end transportation of airline protocol traffic across the network: the Airline Control (ALC) protocol, the TCP-based transport protocol, and the access to the mainframe, Airline X.25 (AX.25) or exchange of mixed traffic over X.25 (EMTOX).

Figure 29-1 *ALPS Architecture*

ASCU – agent set control unit
EMTOX – exchange of mixed traffic over X.25
CPE – customer premises equipment
AX.25 – Airline X.25

Cisco's ALPS feature provides an end-to-end solution for airlines and central reservation systems.

The ALPS feature is integrated in Cisco IOS software and allows airlines to replace their existing hardware and software with Cisco routers. For customers who already use Cisco routers, this feature allows them to consolidate networking overhead and functionality.

The ALPS feature is supported on the following platforms:

- Central customer premises equipment (CPE) routers:
    - Cisco 25xx series
    - Cisco 36xx series
    - Cisco 4500
    - Cisco 4700
    - Cisco 7200
    - Cisco 7500
- Remote CPE routers
    - Cisco 2520, 2521, 2522, and 2523
    - Cisco 2600 series
    - Cisco 3600 series
    - Cisco 4500
    - Cisco 4700

NOTE The Cisco 4500 and Cisco 4700 platforms must have a high-density, low-speed serial card installed. 16 low-speed ports are usable for performing the remote CPE functions.

ALPS Configuration Task List

Perform the tasks in the following sections to configure and maintain the ALPS feature:

- Configure the Remote CPE Routers
- Configure the Central CPE Router
- Monitor the ALPS Feature

See the end of this chapter for the section "ALPS Configuration Examples."

Configure the Remote CPE Routers

Perform the tasks in the following sections to configure the ALPS feature on the remote CPE routers:

- Specify the ALPS Local Peer IP Address
- Specify the ALPS Remote Peer IP Address
- Customize the Service Messages
- Specify the ALPS Circuit
- Specify Each ASCU

Specify the ALPS Local Peer IP Address

You must identify an IP address as an ALPS local peer on the remote CPE. Only one ALPS local peer is permitted on a router.

To specify the ALPS local peer IP address, use the following commands in global configuration mode:

Step	Command	Purpose
1	**alps local-peer** *ip-address*	Specifies an IP address to use as the ALPS local peer on the remote CPE.
2	**alps keepalive** [**interval** *time*] [**retry** *count*]	Enables TCP keepalives for ALPS TCP peer connections.

Specify the ALPS Remote Peer IP Address

You must also specify in the remote CPE configuration the IP addresses of ALPS peers that exist on the central CPE router. The peer connection may be either permanent or dynamic (established on demand).

To specify the IP addresses that exist on the central CPE, use the following command in global configuration mode:

Command	Purpose
alps remote-peer *ip-addr* [**dynamic** [*inact-timer*]] [**tcp-qlen** [*num*]]	Specifies the IP addresses of ALPS peers that exist on partner CPE routers.

Customize the Service Messages

You can customize the contents of the service message list. To specify the service message number and the content of the message, use the following command in global configuration mode:

Command	Purpose
alps service-msg-list *list* **number** *number msg*	Specifies service message numbers and content.

Specify the ALPS Circuit

An ALPS circuit is a communication path across a TCP connection for one or more ASCUs. The ALPS circuit must have a configured association with an ALPS remote peer to establish a connection to the host. Additionally, an ALPS circuit configuration may specify a different remote peer as a backup peer to the host. Configuration for an ALPS circuit also includes X.25 connection information to be passed to the central CPE router when the circuit is established. ALPS circuits may be multiplexed across a single TCP connection.

To specify an ALPS circuit, use the following commands, beginning in global configuration mode:

Step	Command	Purpose
1	**alps circuit** *name*	Specifies an ALPS circuit at the remote CPE and enters ALPS circuit submode.
2	**alps primary-peer** *ip-addr* [**backup-peer** *ip-addr*]	Specifies the primary TCP peer and an optional backup peer for this ALPS circuit.
3	**alps local-hld** *loc-hld* **remote-hld** *rem-hld*	Specifies the local and remote HLDs for this ALPS circuit.
4	**alps connection-type permanent** *retry-timer*	Specifies that this circuit should be established when the circuit is enabled.
5	**alps lifetime-timer** *timer*	Specifies how long messages can be queued in the ALPS circuit queue.
6	**alps hostlink** *number* {**ax25** *lcn* | **emtox** *x121-addr*} [**winout** *val1*] [**winin** *val2*] [**ops** *val3*] [**ips** *val4*]	Specifies the information required to establish an X.25 virtual circuit at the central CPE.
7	**alps service-msg-interval** *seconds*	Specifies the interval between the transmission of a service message to an ASCU and the transmission of a "PLEASE RETRY' message. The "PLEASE RETRY" message is transmitted only to ASCUs that use circuits with a dynamic connection type.
8	**alps service-msg-list** *list*	Defines the service message list to be used for this circuit.
9	**alps enable-circuit**	Enables the circuit to be activated.

Specify Each ASCU

Each ASCU must be configured within the context of the serial interface configuration. ASCU addressing information and association with an ASCU circuit must be configured. Timers, maximum frame sizes, and retry values are optional configuration parameters for each ASCU. Appropriate default parameters are used for unspecified parameters.

To specify an ASCU, use the following commands, beginning in global configuration mode:

Step	Command	Purpose
1	**interface** *type number*	Configures an interface and enters interface configuration mode.
2	**encapsulation alc**	Specifies that the ALC protocol will be used on the serial interface.
3	**alps t1** *delay*	Specifies the timeout delay between the transmission of an ALC poll message and the receipt of the first character of the poll message response.
4	**alps t2** *delay*	Specifies the timeout delay between receipt of the first character of the response to a poll message and the receipt of a Go Ahead message.
5	**alps n1** *errors*	Specifies the threshold of consecutive errors logged before an ASCU is declared to be down.
6	**alps n2** *polls*	Specifies the number of polls that must be correctly replied to before an ASCU is declared to be up.
7	**alps servlim** *polls*	Specifies the number of polls of the ASCU UP list allowed between two successive polls of the ASCU DOWN list.
8	**alps ascu** *id*	Specifies a physical ASCU identity (the ASCU interchange address value for ALC) and enters ALPS ASCU submode.
9	**alps default-ckt** *name*	Specifies the ALPS circuit that this ASCU uses.
10	**alps a1-map** *a1-value* **a2-map** *a2-value*	Specifies the A1 and A2 logical ASCU identification information.
11	**alps retry-option [resend | reenter]**	Specifies the retry option when an ALC message with a bad cyclic check character (CCC) is received.
12	**alps max-msg-length** *value*	Specifies maximum input message length.
13	**alps error-display** *number1 number2*	Specifies where error messages are displayed.
14	**alps enable-ascu**	Begins polling the ASCU.

Configure the Central CPE Router

Perform the tasks in the following sections to configure the ALPS feature on the central CPE router:

● Specify the ALPS Host Local Peer Address

● Specify AX.25

● Specify EMTOX

Specify the ALPS Host Local Peer Address

You must identify an IP address to use as the ALPS local peer IP address. Only one ALPS host local peer is permitted on a router. The promiscuous option, which allows any remote CPE to connect, is recommended at the remote CPE.

To specify the ALPS host local peer address, use the following command in global configuration mode:

Command	Purpose
alps local-peer *ip-address* [**promiscuous**]	Specifies the IP address of the local peer.

Specify AX.25

For AX.25 to be enabled on an X.25 interface, the ALPS host high-level designator (HLD) and hostlink number must be configured and AX.25 must be specified on an X.25 serial interface. At circuit-establishment time, the remote CPE router forwards the host HLD, the logical channel number (LCN), and the hostlink number for the permanent virtual circuit (PVC), to be used for the ASCU group.

To configure AX.25 on an X.25 interface, use the following commands, beginning in global configuration mode:

Step	Command	Purpose
1	**interface** *type number*	Configures an interface and enters interface configuration mode.
2	**encapsulation x25 ax25**	Specifies a serial interface as an X.25 device.
3	**alps host-hld** *num* **host-link** *num* **ax25** [**damp-tmr** *value*] [**life-tmr** *value*]	Enables ALPS on the X.25 interface.

Specify EMTOX

For EMTOX to be enabled on an X.25 interface, the host HLD and the hostlink number must be configured and EMTOX must be specified on an X.25 serial interface. At circuit-establishment time, the remote CPE router forwards the X.121 address to be used as the calling address in the X.25 call and the host HLD and the hostlink number. If the host performs a call out, a correlation between the X.121 called address and a remote CPE peer IP address must be configured.

To configure EMTOX on an X.25 interface, use the following commands, beginning in global configuration mode:

Step	Command	Purpose
1	**interface** *type number*	Configures an interface and enters interface configuration mode.
2	**encapsulation x25**	Specifies a serial interface as an X.25 device.
3	**alps host-hld** *num* **host-link** *num* **emtox** [**life-tmr** *value*]	Enables ALPS on the X.25 interface.
4	**alps translate** *x.121-addr ip-addr*	Maps an X.121 address to an IP address on a remote peer.

Monitor the ALPS Feature

To monitor the status of the ALPS feature, use the following commands in EXEC mode:

Command	Purpose
show alps ascu [*interface id*] [**detail**]	Displays the status of the ALPS ASCU.
show alps circuits [**name** *name*] [**detail**]	Displays the status of the ALPS circuits.
show alps peers [**ipaddress** *addr*] [**detail**]	Displays the status of the ALPS remote peers.
show interfaces *type number*	Displays P1024B information.

ALPS Configuration Examples

Figure 29-2 shows a simple router topology for the ALPS feature. The configuration for this topology follows.

Figure 29-2 *Router Topology for ALPS*

HLD – high-level designator
IA – interchange address

Remote CPE Configuration Example

```
alps local-peer 172.22.0.90
alps keepalive interval 60
alps remote-peer 172.22.0.91
alps remote-peer 172.22.0.92 dynamic 60
alps service-msg-list 1 number 2 NETWORK DOWN
!
alps circuit CKT1
alps primary-peer 172.22.0.91 backup-peer 172.22.0.92
alps local-hld 4B10 remote-hld 5C00
alps connection-type permanent 30
alps lifetime-timer 3
alps hostlink 3 ax25 120 winout 3 winin 3
alps service-msg-interval 3
alps service-msg-list 1
alps enable-circuit
!
alps circuit CKT2
alps primary-peer 172.22.0.91 backup-peer 172.22.0.92
alps local-hld 4B10 remote-hld 5C00
alps hostlink 3 ax25 1500 winout 4 winin 5
alps enable-circuit
!
```

```
alps circuit CKT3
alps primary-peer 172.22.0.91
alps local-hld 4B10 remote-hld 5C00
alps connection-type permanent 30
alps lifetime-timer 6
alps hostlink 3 ax25 905
alps enable-circuit
!
interface serial 1
ip address 172.22.0.90 255.255.255.0
!
interface serial 2
encapsulation alc
alps t1 3
alps t2 6
alps n1 3
alps n2 2
alps servlim 20
!
alps ascu 51
alps default-ckt CKT1
alps a1-map 40 a2-map 2D
alps retry-option resend
alps max-msg-length 1950
alps error-display 6d 78
alps enable-ascu
!
alps ascu 44
alps default-ckt CKT1
alps a1-map 40 a2-map 2E
alps max-msg-length 590
alps error-display 6d 78
alps enable-ascu
!
alps ascu 7E
alps default-ckt CKT2
alps a1-map 40 a2-map 2F
alps retry-option re-send
alps max-msg-length 2000
alps error-display 6d 78
alps enable-ascu

interface serial 3
encapsulation alc
alps t1 5
alps t2 6
alps n1 1
alps n2 2
alps servlim 20
!
alps ascu 4B
alps default-ckt CKT3
alps a1-map 63 a2-map 41
alps retry-option re-send
alps max-msg-length 1960
```

```
alps error-display 6d 78
alps enable-ascu

alps ascu 66
alps default-ckt CKT2
alps a1-map 40 a2-map 21
alps max-msg-length 3800
alps error-display 6d 78
alps enable-ascu
```

Central CPE Configuration (Main) Example

AX.25 Host

```
alps local-peer 172.22.0.91 promiscuous
interface serial 0
encapsulation x25 ax25
x25 ltc 1600
alps host-hld 4B10 host-link 3 ax25
```

EMTOX Host

```
alps local-peer 172.22.0.91 promiscuous
interface serial 0
encapsulation x25
alps host-hld 4B20 host-link 3 emtox 1114235
alps translate 88845* 172.22.0.90
```

Central CPE Configuration (Backup) Example

AX.25 Host

```
alps local-peer 172.22.0.92 promiscuous
interface serial 0
encapsulation x25 ax25
x25 ltc 1600
alps host-hld 4B10 host-link 3 ax25 nonstd-ps 240
```

EMTOX Host

```
alps local-peer 172.22.0.92 promiscuous
interface serial 0
encapsulation x25
alps host-hld 4B20 host-link 3 emtox 1114235
```

Airline Product Set Configuration Commands

Use the commands in this chapter to configure and monitor the Airline Product Set. For Airline Product Set configuration information and examples, refer to Chapter 29, "Configuring the Airline Product Set."

alps a1-map a2-map

Use the **alps a1-map a2-map** ALPS ASCU submode command to specify the A1 and A2 logical ASCU identification information.

alps a1-map *a1-value* **a2-map** *a2-value*

Syntax	Description
a1-value	A1 logical ASCU identification. A hexadecimal number in the range 0x00 to 0x7F, except 0x10, 0x16, and 0x17.
a2-value	A2 logical ASCU identification. A hexadecimal number in the range 0x00, 0x10, 0x16, 0x17, 0x40, 0x50, 0x51, 0x52, and 0x53.

Default

No values are predefined.

Command Mode

ALPS ASCU submode

Usage Guidelines

This command first appeared in Cisco IOS Release 11.3T.

Example

The following example specifies the A1 identification as 40 and the A2 identification as 20:

```
alps a1-map 40 a2-map 20
```

Related Commands

To locate documentation of related commands, you can search online at www.cisco.com.

show alps ascu

alps ascu

Use the **alps ascu** interface configuration command to specify a physical ASCU identity. Use the **no** form of this command to remove the ASCU from the interface and delete any messages queued for transmission to the ASCU or the network.

> **alps ascu** *id*
> **no alps ascu** *id*

Syntax	Description
id	ASCU interchange address. Valid range is between 41 and 7E, except 43, 44, 47, 50 to 57, 60, 64, and 7B.

Default

No values are predefined.

Command Mode

Interface configuration

Usage Guidelines

This command first appeared in Cisco IOS Release 11.3T.

If an ASCU already exists on the interface, the **alps ascu** command initiates the ALPS ASCU submode for that ASCU. If the ASCU does not exist, an ASCU is created and the ALPS ASCU submode is initiated.

Example

The following example specifies the interchange address as 4B:

```
alps ascu 4B
```

Related Commands

To locate documentation of related commands, you can search online at www.cisco.com.

show alps ascu

alps circuit

Use the **alps circuit** global configuration command to specify an ALPS circuit at the remote CPE across a TCP/IP connection. Use the **no** form of this command to remove the circuit definition from the configuration, send a close message on the ALPS circuit, and delete any queued messages for the circuit.

> **alps circuit** *name*
> **no alps circuit** *name*

Syntax	Description
name	Name given to identify an ALPS circuit.

Default

No values are predefined.

Command Mode

Global configuration

Usage Guidelines

This command first appeared in Cisco IOS Release 11.3T.

Entering this command causes a circuit control block to be created. the command also initiates the ALPS circuit submode. If the circuit already exists, the only action is the initiation of the ALPS circuit submode.

Note that this command is used to statically create an ALPS circuit at the remote CPE. ALPS X.25 circuits (at the central CPE) are always dynamically created and are never created using this command.

Example

The following example specifies the name of the ALPS circuit at the remote CPE as CKT1:

```
alps circuit CKT1
```

Related Commands

To locate documentation of related commands, you can search online at www.cisco.com.

show alps circuits

alps connection-type permanent

Use the **alps connection-type permanent** ALPS circuit submode command to specify that this circuit should be established when the circuit is enabled.

> **alps connection-type permanent** *retry-timer*
> **no alps connection-type permanent** *retry-timer*

Syntax   Description

retry-timer   Specifies the maximum interval between consecutive attempts to establish
                       a circuit in the event of a failure. The default for retry-timer is 30 seconds
                       and the range is 1 to 180 seconds.

Default

The default is 30 seconds.

Command Mode

ALPS circuit submode

Usage Guidelines

This command first appeared in Cisco IOS Release 11.3T.

Example

The following example specifies that the circuit is established when enabled and that the CPE will retry the connection every 30 seconds in the event of a failure:

```
alps connection-type permanent 30
```

Related Commands

To locate documentation of related commands, you can search online at www.cisco.com.

show alps circuits

alps default-ckt

Use the **alps default-ckt** ALPS ASCU submode command to specify the ALPS circuit that this ASCU uses.

alps default-ckt *name*

Syntax	Description
name	Name given to identify an ALPS circuit on the remote CPE.

Default
No values are predefined.

Command Mode
ALPS ASCU submode

Usage Guidelines
This command first appeared in Cisco IOS Release 11.3T.

Example
The following example specifies that ALPS circuit to be used is CKT1:

```
alps default-ckt CKT1
```

Related Commands
To locate documentation of related commands, you can search online at www.cisco.com.

show alps circuits

alps enable-alarms ascu

Use the **alps enable-alarms ascu** global configuration command at the remote CPE to enable alarms for the ALPS ASCUs. Use the **no** form of this command to disable alarms for the ALPS ASCUs.

alps enable-alarms ascu [*interface id*]
no alps enable-alarms ascu

Syntax	Description
interface id	(Optional) ASCU identifier. Enable alarms for the specified ASCU.

Default

If no interface and interchange address combination is specified, then alarms (SYSLOG messages and SNMP traps) are enabled for all ALPS ASCUs.

Command Mode

Global configuration

Usage Guidelines

This command first appeared in Cisco IOS Release 11.3T.

If an interface and interchange address combination is specified, then the alarms are enabled only for the ASCU matching that combination. Up to eight **alps enable-alarms ascu** commands can be entered to allow a set of ALPS ASCUs to be monitored. ALPS ASCU alarms are only generated at the remote CPE.

Example

The following example enables alarms for ALPS ASCU 42 on serial interface 1:

```
alps enable-alarms ascu Serial1 42
```

Related Commands

To locate documentation of related commands, you can search online at www.cisco.com.

show alps ascu

alps enable-alarms circuit

Use the **alps enable-alarms circuit** global configuration command to enable alarms for the ALPS circuits. Use the **no** form of this command to remove the circuit definition from the configuration.

> **alps enable-alarms circuit** *name*
> **no alps enable-alarms circuit** *name*

Syntax	Description
name	Name given to identify an ALPS circuit on the remote CPE.

Default

No values are predefined.

Command Mode

Global configuration

Usage Guidelines

This command first appeared in Cisco IOS Release 11.3T.

If a valid circuit name is specified, then the alarms are enabled only for the circuit matching the name. Up to eight **alps enable-alarms circuit** commands can be entered to allow a subset of ALPS circuits to be monitored. ALPS circuit alarms are generated at both the remote (ALC) CPE and the central (X.25) CPE.

Example

The following example enables alarms for the ALPS circuit named CKT1:

```
alps enable alarms circuit CKT1
```

Related Commands

To locate documentation of related commands, you can search online at www.cisco.com.

show alps circuits

alps enable-alarms peer

Use the **alps enable-alarms peer** global configuration command to enable alarms for the ALPS peers. Use the **no** form of this command to remove the circuit definition from the configuration, send a close message on the ALPS circuit, and delete any queued messages for the circuit.

> **alps enable-alarms peer** *ip-address*
> **no alps enable-alarms peer** *ip-address*

Syntax	Description
ip-address	IP address of the remote peer for which alarms are enabled.

Default

No values are predefined.

Command Mode

Global configuration

Usage Guidelines

This command first appeared in Cisco IOS Release 11.3T.

If an IP address is specified, then the alarms are enabled only for the remote peer matching the IP address. Up to eight **alps enable-alarms peer** commands can be entered to allow a set of ALPS peers to be monitored. ALPS peer alarms are generated at both the remote and the central CPE.

Example

The following example enables alarms for the ALPS peer at IP address 172.22.0.91:

```
alps enable alarms peer 172.22.0.91
```

Related Commands

To locate documentation of related commands, you can search online at www.cisco.com.

show alps peers

alps enable-ascu

Use the **alps enable-ascu** ALPS ASCU submode command to move the previously defined ASCU from the inactive poll list to the active poll list. This move results in the protocol handler polling the ASCU and rendering it ready for handling terminal traffic. Use the **no** form of this command to remove the ASCU from the active poll list to the inactive poll list. This action prevents the ASCU from being polled, rendering it not ready for handling terminal traffic.

> **alps enable-ascu**
> **no alps enable-ascu**

Syntax Description

This command has no arguments or keywords.

Default

No values are predefined.

Command Mode

ALPS ASCU submode

Usage Guidelines

This command first appeared in Cisco IOS Release 11.3T.

Example

The following example moves the ASCU to the active poll list:

```
alps enable-ascu
```

Related Commands

To locate documentation of related commands, you can search online at www.cisco.com.

show alps ascu

alps enable-circuit

Use the **alps enable-circuit** ALPS circuit submode command to enable the circuit to be activated when data is received from an ASCU. Use the **no** form of this command to disable the circuit.

> **alps enable-circuit**
> **no alps enable-circuit**

Syntax Description

This command has no arguments or keywords.

Default

The circuit is disabled by default.

Command Mode

ALPS circuit submode

Usage Guidelines

This command first appeared in Cisco IOS Release 11.3T.

Example

The following example specifies the circuit to be activated when data is received from an ASCU:

```
alps enable-circuit
```

Related Commands

To locate documentation of related commands, you can search online at www.cisco.com.

show alps circuits

alps error-display

Use the **alps error-display** ALPS ASCU submode command to specify where error messages about service availability or network problems are displayed. Use the **no** form of this command to return to the default values.

> **alps error-display** *number1 number2*
> **no alps error-display** *number1 number2*

Syntax	Description
number1	For ALC, specifies the terminal address where these service messages are to be sent. Valid numbers are hexadecimal numbers in the range 0x40 to 0x7F. The default address is 0x72.
number2	For ALC, specifies the screen line number where service messages are to be displayed. Valid numbers are hexadecimal numbers in the range 0x40 to 0x7F. The default screen line number is 0x66.

Defaults

The default terminal address for ALC is 0x72.

The default screen line for ALC is 0x20.

Command Mode

ALPS ASCU submode

Usage Guidelines

This command first appeared in Cisco IOS Release 11.3T.

Example

The following example specifies that error messages are displayed at terminal address 6d, on screen line number 78:

```
alps error-display 6d 78
```

Related Commands

To locate documentation of related commands, you can search online at www.cisco.com.

show alps ascu

alps host-hld host-link

Use the **alps host-hld host-link** interface configuration command to enable ALPS on the X.25 interface. Use the **no** form of this command to disable ALPS on the X.25 interface.

> **alps host-hld** *hld* **host-link** *num* {{**ax25** [**damp-tmr** *value*]} | {**emtox** *x.121*}}
>   [**life-tmr** *value*]
> **no alps host-hld** *hld* **host-link** *num* {{**ax25** [**damp-tmr** *value*]} | {**emtox** *x.121*}}
>   [**life-tmr** *value*]

Syntax	Description
hld	Host high-level designator. A hexadecimal number in the range 101 to 7f7f.
num	Host-link identifier. A number in the range 1 to 255.
ax25	Specifies airline X.25 implementation of X.25.
damp-tmr *value*	(Optional) Specifies the AX.25 PVC damping timer. The *value* argument is the length of time that a PVC can be inactive before it is destroyed and the corresponding ALPS circuits are closed. The default is 10 seconds.
emtox	Specifies EMTOX implementation of X.25.

Syntax	Description
x.121	X.121 address of the EMTOX host (called address on calls to the EMTOX host).
life-tmr *value*	Specifies the maximum amount of time (in seconds) that a message may be queued for transmission to the host X.25 system before it is discarded. The *value* argument is time (in seconds).

Default

The default damping timer value is 10 seconds.

Command Mode

Interface configuration

Usage Guidelines

This command first appeared in Cisco IOS Release 11.3T.

Example

The following example enables ALPS on an X.25 interface, using the airline X.25 implementation:

```
alps host-hld 4B10 host-link 3 ax25
```

Related Commands

To locate documentation of related commands, you can search online at www.cisco.com.

encapsulation x25

alps hostlink

Use the **alps hostlink** ALPS circuit submode command to specify information required to establish an X.25 virtual circuit at the central CPE. Use the **no** form of this command to remove the circuit definition from the configuration, send a close message on the ALPS circuit, and delete any queued messages for the circuit.

> **alps hostlink** *number* {**ax25** *lcn* | **emtox** *x121-addr*} [**winout** *val1*] [**winin** *val2*]
> [**ops** *val3*] [**ips** *val4*]
> **no alps hostlink** *number* {**ax25** *lcn* | **emtox** *x121-addr*} [**winout** *val1*] [**winin** *val2*]
> [**ops** *val3*] [**ips** *val4*]

Syntax	Description
number	Interface at the host CPE. Decimal number in the range 1 to 255.
ax25	Specifies airline X.25 implementation of X.25.
lcn	Local channel number for AX.25 connections.
emtox	Specifies EMTOX implementation of X.25.
x121-addr	X.121 address for EMTOX connections.This is the X.121 calling address for X.25 call packets sent from the central CPE to the EMTOX host.
winout *val1*	(Optional) Specifies the X.25 transmit window The *val1* argument is a decimal number in the range 1 to 7.
winin *val2*	(Optional) Specifies the X.25 receive window. The *val2* argument is a decimal number in the range 1 to 7.
ops *val3*	(Optional) Specifies the maximum output packet size. The *val3* argument is one of the following numbers: 128, 240, 256, 512, 1024, 2048, or 4096.
ips *val4*	(Optional) Specifies the maximum input packet size. The *val4* argument is one of the following numbers: 128, 240, 256, 512, 1024, 2048, or 4096.

Default
If no values are specified, the default values at the X.25-attached central CPE are used.

Command Mode
ALPS circuit submode

Usage Guidelines
This command first appeared in Cisco IOS Release 11.3T.

Example
The following example establishes an X.25 virtual circuit at the central CPE. The configuration specifies airline X.25 implementation. The host CPE interface is 3, the local channel number for airline X.25 connections is 120, and the X.25 transmit window is 3.

```
alps hostlink 3 ax25 120 winout 3 winin 3
```

Part
II

Command Reference

Related Commands

To locate documentation of related commands, you can search online at www.cisco.com.

alps circuit
show alps circuits

alps idle-timer

Use the **alps idle-timer** ALPS circuit submode command to specify (for dynamic circuits) the length of time that can elapse before an idle circuit is disabled. Use the **no** form of this command to return to the default idle-timer value.

> **alps idle-timer** *timer*
> **no alps idle-timer** *timer*

Syntax	Description
timer	Length of time that can elapse before an idle circuit is brought down. The range is 10 to 600 seconds. The default is 60 seconds.

Default

The default length of time that can elapse before an idle circuit is brought down is 60 seconds.

Command Mode

ALPS circuit submode

Usage Guidelines

This command first appeared in Cisco IOS Release 11.3T.

Example

The following example specifies that an idle circuit is maintained for 90 seconds before it is disabled:

```
alps idle-timer 90
```

Related Commands

To locate documentation of related commands, you can search online at www.cisco.com.

alps circuit
show alps circuits

alps keepalive

Use the **alps keepalive** global configuration command to enable TCP keepalives for ALPS TCP peer connections. A TCP keepalive request will be sent to the remote peer if the TCP connection to the remote peer is silent for a time period larger than the interval specified. The TCP connection to the ALPS host will be closed when a count equal to the retry count specified is missed consecutively. Use the **no** form of this command to disable keepalives for ALPS.

> **alps keepalive** [**interval** *time*] [**retry** *count*]
> **no alps keepalive** [**interval** *time*] [**retry** *count*]

Syntax	Description
interval *time*	(Optional) Interval for keepalive requests. The *time* argument is the keepalive interval, in the range of 10 to 300 seconds. The default is 30 seconds.
retry *count*	(Optional) Indicates how many times keepalive requests will be sent before the connection is closed. The *count* argument is the retry count, in the range 1 to 10. The default is 3 retries.

Default

The default keepalive interval is 30 seconds.

The default retry count is 3.

Command Mode

Global configuration

Usage Guidelines

This command first appeared in Cisco IOS Release 11.3T.

Example

The following example specifies that a TCP keepalive request will be sent to the remote peer if the TCP peer connection is idle for 60 seconds. The connection will be closed after 3 consecutive keepalive requests are sent.

```
alps keepalive interval 60 retry 8
```

Related Commands

To locate documentation of related commands, you can search online at www.cisco.com.

alps local-peer

alps lifetime-timer

Use the **alps lifetime-timer** ALPS circuit submode command to specify the maximum amount of time messages can be queued in the ALPS circuit queue awaiting transmission to the central CPE. Use the **no** form of this command to return to the default lifetime-timer value.

> **alps lifetime-timer** *timer*
> **no alps lifetime-timer** *timer*

Syntax   Description

timer   Length of time, in seconds, that a message can be queued. The range is
                 1 to 20 seconds. The default is 4 seconds.

Default

The default length of time that a message can be queued in the ALPS circuit queue is 4 seconds.

Command Mode

ALPS circuit submode

Usage Guidelines

This command first appeared in Cisco IOS Release 11.3T.

Messages that exceed the timer limit are discarded.

Example

The following example specifies that a message remains in the ALPS circuit queue for no longer than 3 seconds:

```
alps lifetime-timer 3
```

Related Commands

To locate documentation of related commands, you can search online at www.cisco.com.

alps circuit
show alps circuits

alps local-hld remote-hld

Use the **alps local-hld remote-hld** ALPS circuit submode command to specify the local and remote HLDs (in hexadecimal) to use for this ALPS circuit. Use the **no** form of this command to remove the definition from the configuration.

> **alps local-hld** *loc-hld* **remote-hld** *rem-hld*
> **no alps local-hld** *loc-hld* **remote-hld** *rem-hld*

Syntax	Description
loc-hld	Local HLD to use for ALPS circuit. Hexadecimal number in the range 0x0101 to 0x7F7F.
rem-hld	Remote HLD to use for ALPS circuit. Hexadecimal number in the range 0x0101 to 0x7F7F.

Default

No values are predefined.

Command Mode

ALPS circuit submode

Usage Guidelines

This command first appeared in Cisco IOS Release 11.3T.

Example

The following example specifies the local HLD as 4b10 and the remote HLD as 5c00:

```
alps local-hld 4B10 remote-hld 5c00
```

Related Commands

To locate documentation of related commands, you can search online at www.cisco.com.

alps circuit
show alps circuits

alps local-peer

Use the **alps local-peer** global configuration command to specify the IP address of the local peer. Use the **no** form of this command to remove all subsequent ALPS configuration commands from the router.

> **alps local-peer** *ip-address* [**promiscuous**]
> **no alps local-peer** *ip-address* [**promiscuous**]

Syntax   Description

ip-address   IP address of the local peer.

promiscuous   (Optional) Keyword specified at the central CPE to accept incoming TCP connections from any remote CPE.

Default

No values are predefined.

Command Mode

Global configuration

Usage Guidelines

This command first appeared in Cisco IOS Release 11.3T.

Example

The following example specifies the local peer IP address as 172.22.0.91 and specifies that the CPE accepts incoming TCP connections from any CPE:

```
alps local-peer 172.22.0.91 promiscuous
```

Related Commands

To locate documentation of related commands, you can search online at www.cisco.com.

show alps peers

alps max-msg-length

Use the **alps max-msg-length** ALPS ASCU submode command to specify maximum input message length. Use the **no** form of this command to return to the default maximum input message length.

> **alps max-msg-length** *value*
> **no alps max-msg-length** *value*

Syntax	Description
value	Maximum input message length. The range is 1 to 3840. The default is 962 characters.

Default

The default maximum input message length is 962 characters.

Command Mode

ALPS ASCU submode

Usage Guidelines

This command first appeared in Cisco IOS Release 11.3T.

Example

The following example specifies that the maximum length of a message is 1000 characters:

```
alps max-msg-length 1000
```

alps mpx

Use the **alps mpx** ALPS circuit submode command to specify the multiplexing and the ASCU identification header for this circuit. Use the **no** form of this command to remove the definition from the configuration.

> **alps mpx** {**group** | **single**} **hdr** {**a1a2** | **none**}
> **no alps mpx** {**group** | **single**} **hdr** {**a1a2** | **none**}

Syntax	Description
group	Specifies that multiple ASCUs will be multiplexed on the ALPS circuit.
single	Specifies that only one ASCU will use this circuit.
hdr	Specifies the ASCU identification header for the circuit.
a1a2	ASCU identification via A1, A2.
none	No ASCU identification.

Default

The default for multiplexing is **group**.

The default header is **a1a2**.

Command Mode

ALPS circuit submode

Usage Guidelines

This command first appeared in Cisco IOS Release 11.3T.

If **alps mpx group** is specified, multiple ASCUs will be multiplexed on this ALPS circuit. If **alps mpx single** is specified, then only one ASCU uses this ALPS circuit. If **alps mpx single hdr none** is specified, the A1 and A2 ASCU identification information is not added to the front of data frames sent across this circuit, and it is assumed that it does not exist in frames received on this circuit. The exclusion of ASCU identification should only be specified when the EMTOX protocol is used.

alps n1

Use the **alps n1** interface configuration command to specify the threshold of consecutive errors logged before an ASCU is declared down. Use the **no** form of this command to reassert the default number of consecutive errors before declaring an ASCU down.

> **alps n1** *errors*
> **no alps n1** *errors*

Syntax   Description

errors   Error count limit. The valid range is 1 to 30 errors. The default is 30 errors.

Default

The default error count is 30 errors.

Command Mode

Interface configuration

Usage Guidelines

This command first appeared in Cisco IOS Release 11.3T.

The error count limit is a threshold value. If the ASCU state is UP and the error count threshold is exceeded, the ASCU state changes to DOWN and it is moved to the inactive poll. If alarms are enabled for the ASCU, a SYSLOG message is displayed and an SNMP notification is sent to the SNMP network management station.

Example

The following example specifies that an ASCU is declared down when the error count exceeds 1:

```
alps n1 1
```

Related Commands

To locate documentation of related commands, you can search online at www.cisco.com.

alps ascu
show alps ascu

alps n2

Use the **alps n2** interface configuration command to specify the number of polls that must be correctly replied to before an ASCU is declared up. Use the **no** form of this command to reassert the default number of polls that must be correctly replied before an ASCU is declared up.

> **alps n2** *polls*
> **no alps n2** *polls*

Syntax

Syntax	Description
polls	Number of polls that must be correctly replied to. The valid range is 1 to 30 polls. The default is 30 polls.

Default

The default number of polls that must be correctly replied to is 30.

Command Mode

Interface configuration

Usage Guidelines

This command first appeared in Cisco IOS Release 11.3T.

If the ASCU state is DOWN and the reply threshold is exceeded, the ASCU state changes to UP and the ASCU is moved to the active poll list. If alarms are enabled for the ASCU, a SYSLOG message is displayed and an SNMP notification is sent to the SNMP management station.

Example

The following example specifies that 2 polls must be correctly replied to before the ASCU is declared up:

```
alps n2 2
```

Related Commands

To locate documentation of related commands, you can search online at www.cisco.com.

alps ascu
show alps ascu

alps poll-pause

Use the **alps poll-pause** interface configuration command to specify the minimum interval, in milliseconds, between initiations of the polling cycle. Use the **no** form of this command to revert to the default interval.

> **alps poll-pause** *msec*
> **no alps poll-pause**

Syntax   Description

msec   Minimum interval between polls, in microseconds.The valid range is
                   10 to 1000 microseconds. The default interval is 50 microseconds.

Default

The default minimum interval is 50 microseconds.

Command Mode

Interface configuration

Usage Guidelines

This command first appeared in Cisco IOS Release 11.3T.

Example

The following example sets a 200-microsecond minimum interval between polls.

```
alps poll-pause 200
```

Related Commands

To locate documentation of related commands, you can search online at www.cisco.com.

alps ascu

alps primary-peer

Use the **alps primary-peer** ALPS circuit submode command to specify the primary TCP peer and, optionally, a backup TCP peer for this ALPS circuit. Use the **no** form of this command to remove the definition from the configuration.

> **alps primary-peer** *ip-addr* [**backup-peer** *ip-addr*]
> **no alps primary-peer** *ip-addr* [**backup-peer** *ip-addr*]

Syntax

Syntax	Description
ip-addr	IP address specified in the **alps remote-peer** command.
backup-peer	(Optional) Backup TCP peer for the ALPS circuit.
ip-addr	IP address specified in the **alps remote-peer** command.

Default

No values are predefined.

Command Mode

ALPS circuit submode

Usage Guidelines

This command first appeared in Cisco IOS Release 11.3T.

Example

The following example specifies a primary peer at IP address 172.22.0.91 and a backup peer at IP address 172.22.0.92:

```
alps primary-peer 172.22.0.91 backup-peer 172.22.0.92
```

Related Commands

To locate documentation of related commands, you can search online at www.cisco.com.

alps circuit
show alps peers

alps remote-peer

Use the **alps remote-peer** global configuration command to specify the IP address of a peer connection to the partner CPE. Use the **no** form of this command to remove the definition from the configuration.

> **alps remote-peer** *ip-addr* [**dynamic** [*inact-timer*]] [**tcp-qlen** [*num*]]
> **no alps remote-peer** *ip-addr* [**dynamic** [*inact-timer*]] [**tcp-qlen** [*num*]]

Syntax	Description
ip-addr	IP address of the peer.
dynamic	(Optional) Allows the TCP connection to the host peer to be opened only when there is data to be transferred to the host reservation system.
inact-timer	(Optional) Length of inactivity, in seconds, after which the connection is closed. The range is 10 to 300 seconds. The default is 60 seconds.
tcp-qlen	(Optional) Specifies a default number of packets in the queue.
num	(Optional) Number of packets allowed in the queue. The range is 26 to 100 packets. The default is 50 packets.

Default
The default is length of inactivity is 60 seconds.

The default number of packets is 50.

Command Mode
Global configuration

Usage Guidelines
This command first appeared in Cisco IOS Release 11.3T.

Issuing the **no alps remote-peer** command causes the following to occur:

- Destruction of the TCP connection
- Notification to the remote TCP peer that this connection is aborted
- Notification to the ALPS circuits using this TCP peer that the connection is closed

Example

The following example specifies a peer connection at IP address 172.22.0.92 and allows the TCP connection to be opened only when there is data to be transferred:

```
alps remote-peer 172.22.0.92 dynamic 60
```

Related Commands

To locate documentation of related commands, you can search online at www.cisco.com.

alps local-peer
show alps peers

alps retry-option

Use the **alps retry-option** ALPS ASCU submode command to configure the CPE to transmit a message to the ASCU when a message with a bad cycle check character (CCC) is received from an ASCU. Use the **no** form of this command to reassert the default action of no retry.

> **alps retry-option** {**resend** | **reenter**}
> **no alps retry-option**

Syntax	Description
resend	Specifies the retry option as resend. This option causes an indicator LED to signal the operator at the ASCU to resend data.
reenter	Specifies the retry option as reenter. This option causes a service message to signal the operator at the ASCU to reenter data.

Default

The default retry option is no retry.

Command Mode

ALPS ASCU submode

Usage Guidelines

This command first appeared in Cisco IOS Release 11.3T.

Example

The following example specifies that an indicator LED signals the ASCU to resend data:

```
alps retry-option resend
```

Related Commands

To locate documentation of related commands, you can search online at www.cisco.com.

alps ascu
show alps ascu

alps service-msg-interval

Use the **alps service-msg-interval** ALPS circuit submode command to specify the interval between transmission of a service message to an ASCU and transmission of a "PLEASE RETRY" message. Use the **no** form of this command to remove the definition from the configuration.

> **alps service-msg-interval** *seconds*
> **no alps service-msg-interval** *seconds*

Syntax

Syntax	Description
seconds	Interval, in seconds, between consecutive transmissions of service messages from the remote CPE to the ASCU. The range is 1 to 20 seconds. The default interval is 4 seconds.

Default

The default interval between consecutive transmissions of service messages from the remote CPE to the ASCU is 4 seconds.

Command Mode

ALPS circuit submode

Usage Guidelines

This command first appeared in Cisco IOS Release 11.3T.

The "PLEASE RETRY" message is transmitted only to ASCUs that use circuits with a dynamic connection type.

Example

The following example specifies an interval of 3 seconds between transmission of service messages from the CPE to the ASCU:

```
alps service-msg-interval 3
```

Related Commands

To locate documentation of related commands, you can search online at www.cisco.com.

alps circuit
alps service-msg-list

alps service-msg-list

Use the **alps** service-msg-list ALPS circuit submode command to define the service message list to be used for this circuit. Use the **no** form of this command to remove the list from the circuit configuration, thus issuing no service messages until another list is configured.

> **alps service-msg-list** *list*
> **no alps service-msg-list** *list*

Syntax	Description
list	The service message list to be used for this circuit. The valid numbers are 1 to 8.

Default

No values are predefined.

Command Mode

ALPS circuit submode

Usage Guidelines

This command first appeared in Cisco IOS Release 11.3T.

Example

The following example specifies that message list 1 is used for this circuit:

```
alps service-msg-list 1
```

Related Commands

To locate documentation of related commands, you can search online at www.cisco.com.

alps circuit
alps service-msg-interval

alps service-msg-list number

Use the **alps service-msg-list number** global configuration command to define the service message identity and its contents for a service message list. Use the **no** form of this command to remove a service message number from the service message list configuration.

> **alps service-msg-list** *list* **number** *number msg*
> **no alps service-msg-list** *list* **number** *number msg*

Syntax	Description
list	The service message list to be used for this circuit. The valid numbers are 1 to 8.
number	Specifies a list number.
number	List number. The valid numbers are 1 to 8.
msg	Contents of a service message.

Default

The default service message is used if no service message list number is specified.

Command Mode

Global configuration

Usage Guidelines

This command first appeared in Cisco IOS Release 11.3T.

Example

The following example specifies the text of message list 1, message number 2:

```
alps service-msg-list 1 number 2 "Turn off the terminal NOW."
```

alps servlim

Use the **alps servlim** interface configuration command to specify the number of cycles of the active poll list to execute before polling the next ASCU on the inactive poll list. Use the **no** form of this command to reassert the default number of cycles through the normal (active) poll list allowed before the slow poll list is processed.

> **alps servlim** *polls*
> **no alps servlim** *polls*

Syntax	Description
polls	Number of polls of the ASCU UP list. The valid range is 1 to 30 polls. The default is 30 polls.

Default

The default number of polls of the ASCU UP list allowed between two successive polls of the ASCU DOWN list is 30 polls.

Command Mode

Interface configuration

Usage Guidelines

This command first appeared in Cisco IOS Release 11.3T.

Example

The following example specifies that 5 polls of the ASCU UP list are allowed between 2 successive polls of the ASCU DOWN list.

```
alps servlim 5
```

Related Commands

To locate documentation of related commands, you can search online at www.cisco.com.

alps n1
alps n2
alps t1
alps t2

alps t1

Use the **alps t1** interface configuration command to specify the timeout delay between polling and response. Use the **no** form of this command to reassert the default poll timeout value of 0.5 seconds.

> **alps t1** *delay*
> **no alps t1** *delay*

Syntax

Syntax	Description
delay	Timeout delay, in seconds, between polling and response. The valid range is 1 to 10 tenths of a second (.1 to 1 second). The default is 5 tenths of a second (.5 second).

Default

The default timeout delay between polling and response is 5 tenths of a second (.5 second).

Command Mode

Interface configuration

Usage Guidelines

This command first appeared in Cisco IOS Release 11.3T.

Example

The following example specifies a .5-second time-out delay between polling and response:

```
alps t1 5
```

Related Commands

To locate documentation of related commands, you can search online at www.cisco.com.

alps n1
alps n2
alps servlim
alps t2

alps t2

Use the **alps t2** interface configuration command to specify the timeout delay between receipt of the first character of an I/P sequence solicited by a poll and receipt of a Go Ahead (GA) sequence. Use the **no** form of this command to reassert the default timeout value of 6 seconds.

> **alps t2** *delay*
> **no alps t2** *delay*

Syntax

Description

delay   Timeout delay, in seconds, between receipt of first character of an I/P sequence solicited by a poll and receipt of GA sequence. The valid range is 1 to 10 seconds. The default is 6 seconds.

Default

The default timeout delay between receipt of first character of an I/P sequence solicited by a poll and receipt of GA sequence is 6 seconds.

Command Mode

Interface configuration

Usage Guidelines

This command first appeared in Cisco IOS Release 11.3T.

Example

The following example specifies a timeout delay of 8 seconds between receipt of the first character of an I/P sequence solicited by a poll and receipt of GA sequence:

```
alps t2 8
```

Related Commands

To locate documentation of related commands, you can search online at www.cisco.com.

alps n1
alps n2
alps servlim
alps t1

alps translate

Use the **alps translate** interface configuration command to map an X.121 address to an IP address of a remote peer. Use the **no** form of this command to remove mapping from the configuration.

> **alps translate** *x.121-addr ip-addr*
> **no alps translate** *x.121-addr ip-addr*

Syntax

Syntax	Description
x.121-addr	X.121 address to be mapped to an IP address of a remote peer.
ip-addr	IP address of the remote peer.

Default

No values are predefined.

Command Mode

Interface configuration

Usage Guidelines

This command first appeared in Cisco IOS Release 11.3T.

The X.121 address is compared to the Called Address on inbound X.25 call packets to determine if the call should be accepted. The X.121 address may have an asterisk (*) at the end to indicate that "all X.121 addresses prefixed with the address before the *".

Example

The following example maps all X.121 addresses prefixed with the address 88845 to the remote peer IP address 172.22.0.90:

```
alps translate 88845* 172.22.0.90
```

Related Commands

To locate documentation of related commands, you can search online at www.cisco.com.

encapsulation x25

clear alps circuits

Use the **clear alps circuits** EXEC command to remove configured ALPS circuits.

clear alps circuits [**ipaddr** *address* | **name** *string*]

Syntax	Description
ipaddr *address*	(Optional) Clear ALPS circuits for peer with specified IP address.
name *string*	(Optional) Clear ALPS circuits for peer with specified name.

Default

If no IP address or name is specified, the command clears all ALPS circuits.

Command Mode

EXEC

Usage Guidelines

This command first appeared in Cisco IOS Release 11.3T.

Example

The following example clears the ALPS circuit named CKT1:

```
clear alps circuits name CKT1
```

Related Commands

To locate documentation of related commands, you can search online at www.cisco.com.

alps circuit
show alps circuits

clear alps counters

Use the **clear alps counters** EXEC command to clear all counters relevant to the ALPS feature.

clear alps counters

Syntax Description

This command has no arguments or keywords.

Default

No values are predefined.

Command Mode

EXEC

Usage Guidelines

This command first appeared in Cisco IOS Release 11.3T.

Example

The following example clears all counters for the ALPS feature:

```
clear alps counters
```

Related Commands

To locate documentation of related commands, you can search online at www.cisco.com.

show alps ascu
show alps circuits
show alps peers

encapsulation alc

Use the **encapsulation alc** interface configuration command to specify that the ALC protocol will be used on the serial interface. Use the **no** form of this command to remove ALC protocol handling from the serial interface, and return the default encapsulation (HDLC) to the interface.

> **encapsulation alc**
> **no encapsulation alc**

Syntax Description

This command has no arguments or keywords.

Default

No values are predefined.

Command Mode

Interface configuration

Usage Guidelines

This command first appeared in Cisco IOS Release 11.3T.

The **encapsulation alc** command causes any ASCU configuration to be removed from the interface. As each ASCU defined on the interface is removed, it is also unlinked from the ASCU circuit it belongs to. All data frames queued for transmission to the ASCU are destroyed.

This encapsulation command must be entered prior to any ASCU configuration. Note that all timer and counter values are applicable to all ASCUs on the interface.

Example

The following example specifies that the ALC protocol is used:

```
encapsulation alc
```

Related Commands

To locate documentation of related commands, you can search online at www.cisco.com.

show interfaces

show alps ascu

Use the **show alps ascu** EXEC command to display the status of the ALPS ASCU.

           show alps ascu [*interface id*] [**detail**]

Syntax	Description
interface id	(Optional) Combined interface and interchange address. If specified, only the status of that ASCU is displayed.
detail	(Optional) Long display of output.

Command Mode

EXEC

Usage Guidelines

This command first appeared in Cisco IOS Release 11.3T.

Sample Displays

The following is sample output from the **show alps ascu** command:

```
Router# show alps ascu

interface   dlc    ia    a1    a2    circuit    pkt_tx    pkt_rx    state
--------------------------------------------------------------------------------
Serial6     ALC    42    24    49    AX_CKT     105       105       UP
Serial6     ALC    46    46    52    EM_CKT     0         0         UP
```

The following is sample output from the **show alps ascu detail** command:

```
Router# show alps ascu detail

ascu 42 on i/f Serial6, dlc = ALC, state = UP
    default-circuit = AX_CKT, a1 = 24, a2 = 49
    retry_option = resend, max_msg_len = 962
    err_disp_terminal = 0, err_disp_line = 0
    pkt_tx = 105, byte_tx = 1050, pkt_rx = 105, byte_rx = 1050

ascu 46 on i/f Serial6, dlc = ALC, state = UP
    default-circuit = EM_CKT, a1 = 46, a2 = 52
    retry_option = reenter, max_msg_len = 962
    err_disp_terminal = 0, err_disp_line = 0
    pkt_tx = 0, byte_tx = 0, pkt_rx = 0, byte_rx = 0
```

Related Commands

To locate documentation of related commands, you can search online at www.cisco.com.

alps ascu

show alps circuits

Use the **show alps circuits** EXEC command to display the status of the ALPS circuits. If a circuit name is specified, then only the status of that circuit will be displayed; otherwise, the status of all circuits will be displayed.

show alps circuits [**name** *name*] [**detail**]

Syntax

Syntax	Description
name *name*	(Optional) If specified, only the status of that circuit is displayed.
detail	(Optional) Long display of output.

Command Mode

EXEC

Usage Guidelines

This command first appeared in Cisco IOS Release 11.3T.

Sample Displays

The following is sample output from the **show alps circuits** command:

```
Router# show alps circuits

name       pri_peer       curr_peer      dlc      state    pkt_tx   pkt_rx
- - - - - - - - - - - - - - - - - - - - - - - - - - - - - - - - - - - - - - - - - - -
AX_CKT     172.18.3.141   172.18.3.141   AX25     OPEN     57       57
EM_CKT     172.18.3.141   172.18.3.141   EMTOX    OPEN      0        0
```

The following is sample output from the **show alps circuits detail** command:

```
Router# show alps circuits detail

AX_CKT: dlc = AX25, peer = 172.18.3.141, state = OPEN, uptime = 00:00:00
    i/f = Serial2, host_link = 1, host_hld = 700, remote_hld = 145
    lcn = 33, nonstd_240 = TRUE
    damping_tmr = 10, lifetime_tmr = 4
    pkt_tx = 57, byte_tx = 1311, pkt_rx = 57, byte_rx = 1311
    src_corr = 5063224, dst_corr = 88D990
    drops_q_overflow = 0, drops_lifetime_exceeded = 0, drops_vc_reset = 0
    ascus: (24,49),

EM_CKT: dlc = EMTOX, peer = 172.18.3.141, state = OPEN, uptime = 00:00:00
    i/f = Serial3, host_link = 3, host_hld = 1200, remote_hld = 145
    lcn = 1, host_x121 = 22233, remote_x121 = 44005
    damping_tmr = 0, lifetime_tmr = 4
    pkt_tx = 0, byte_tx = 0, pkt_rx = 0, byte_rx = 0
    src_corr = 502F220, dst_corr = 88DBF8
    drops_q_overflow = 0, drops_lifetime_exceeded = 0, drops_vc_reset = 0
    ascus: (46,52),
```

The following is sample output from the **show alps circuits** command:

```
Router# show alps circuits

name        pri_peer        curr_peer       dlc      state    pkt_tx    pkt_rx
- - - - - - - - - - - - - - - - - - - - - - - - - - - - - - - - - - - - - - - - -
AX_CKT   172.18.3.27     172.18.3.27     ALC      OPEN     105       105
EM_CKT   172.18.3.27     172.18.3.27     ALC      OPEN     0         0
```

The following is sample output from the **show alps circuits detail** command:

```
Router# show alps circuits detail

AX_CKT: dlc = ALC, conn_type = DYN, state = OPEN, uptime = 00:00:00
        pri_peer = 172.18.3.27, sec_peer = 0.0.0.0, curr_peer = 172.18.3.27
        local_hld = 145, remote_hld = 700
        ax25:  hostlink = 1, lcn = 33
        lifetime_tmr = 4, idle_tmr = 60, retry_tmr = 0
        pkt_tx = 105, byte_tx = 2415, pkt_rx = 105, byte_rx = 2415
        src_corr = 9A1760, dst_corr = 50333C8
        drops_q_overflow = 0, drops_ckt_disabled = 0
        drops_lifetime_tmr = 0, drops_invalid_ascu = 0
        ascus:  (24,49),

EM_CKT: dlc = ALC, conn_type = PERM, state = OPEN, uptime = 00:00:00
        pri_peer = 172.18.3.27, sec_peer = 0.0.0.0, curr_peer = 172.18.3.27
        local_hld = 145, remote_hld = 1200
        emtox: hostlink = 3, x121 = 44005
        lifetime_tmr = 4, idle_tmr = 60, retry_tmr = 10
        pkt_tx = 0, byte_tx = 0, pkt_rx = 0, byte_rx = 0
        src_corr = 9A18D4, dst_corr = 8FB520
        drops_q_overflow = 0, drops_ckt_disabled = 0
        drops_lifetime_tmr = 0, drops_invalid_ascu = 0
        ascus:  (46,52),
```

Related Commands

To locate documentation of related commands, you can search online at www.cisco.com.

alps circuit

show alps peers

Use the **show alps peers** EXEC command to display the status of the ALPS remote peers. If an IP address is specified, than only the status of that peer will be displayed; otherwise, the status of all peers will be displayed.

> **show alps peers** [**ipaddress** *addr*] [**detail**]

Syntax	Description
ipaddress *addr*	If specified, only the status of that circuit is displayed.
detail	(Optional) Long display of output.

Command Mode
EXEC

Usage Guidelines
This command first appeared in Cisco IOS Release 11.3T.

Sample Displays
The following is sample output from the **show alps peers** command:

```
Router# show alps peers

local_peer : ip_address = 172.18.3.141

ip_address     type     create     state     pkt_tx     pkt_rx
- - - - - - - - - - - - - - - - - - - - - - - - - - - - - - - - - - - - - - - - - - - - - - - - - -
172.18.3.27    PERM     LEARN      OPENED       1          1
```

The following is sample output from the **show alps peers detail** command:

```
Router # show alps peers detail

local_peer : ip_address = 172.18.3.141

TCP: 172.18.3.27, type = PERM, create = ADMIN, state = OPENED, uptime = 00:08:21
   pkt_tx = 0, byte_tx = 0, pkt_rx = 0, byte_rx = 0
   drops_giants = 0, drops_q_overflow = 0, drops_peer_down = 0, drops_ver_mismatch = 0
   active_ckts: CKT1, CKT2
```

Related Commands
To locate documentation of related commands, you can search online at www.cisco.com.

alps primary-peer
alps remote-peer

show interfaces

Use the **show interfaces** EXEC command to display ALC information.

show interface *type number*

Syntax	Description
type	Interface type
number	Port number

Command Mode

EXEC

Usage Guidelines

This command first appeared in Cisco IOS Release 10.0.

Sample Display

The following output shows ALC information for the serial 2 interface:

```
Router# show interface s2

Serial2 is up, line protocol is up
Hardware is CD2430
MTU 1500 bytes, BW 115 Kbit, DLY 20000 usec, rely 255/255, load 1/255
Encapsulation ALC, loopback not set
Full-duplex enabled.
      ascus in UP state: 42, 46
      ascus in DOWN state:
      ascus DISABLED:
Last input never, output never, output hang never
Last clearing of "show interface" counters never
Queueing strategy: fifo
Output queue 0/40, 0 drops; input queue 0/75, 0 drops
5 minute input rate 0 bits/sec, 0 packets/sec
5 minute output rate 0 bits/sec, 0 packets/sec
0 packets input, 0 bytes, 0 no buffer
Received 0 broadcasts, 0 runts, 0 giants
0 input errors, 0 CRC, 0 frame, 0 overrun, 0 ignored, 0 abort
0 packets output, 0 bytes, 0 underruns
0 output errors, 0 collisions, 3 interface resets
0 output buffer failures, 0 output buffers swapped out
DCD=down  DSR=down  DTR=down  RTS=down  CTS=down
```

Ethernet Type Codes

Table A-1 lists known Ethernet type codes. You can use these type codes in transparent bridging and , source-route bridging access lists for filtering frames by protocol type. For configuration information on filtering by protocol type, refer to the following two sections:

- "Filter Transparently Bridged Packets" in Chapter 1, "Configuring Transparent Bridging."
- "Secure the SRB Network" in Chapter 3, "Configuring Source-Route Bridging."

Table A-1   *Ethernet Type Codes*

Hexadecimal	Description (Notes)
0000-05DC	IEEE 802.3 Length Field
0101-01FF	Experimental; for development (conflicts with 802.3 length fields)
0200	Xerox PARC Universal Protocol (PUP) (conflicts with IEEE 802.3 length fields)
0201	Xerox PUP Address Translation (conflicts with IEEE 802.3 length fields)
0400	Nixdorf Computers (Germany)
0600	Xerox XNS IDP
0660-0661	DLOG (Germany)
0800	DOD Internet Protocol (IP) *[1] #[2]
0801	X.75 Internet
0802	NBS Internet
0803	ECMA Internet
0804	CHAOSnet
0805	X.25 Level 3
0806	Address Resolution Protocol (for IP and CHAOS)
0807	XNS Compatibility
081C	Symbolics Private
0888-088A	Xyplex
0900	Ungermann-Bass (UB) Network Debugger
0A00	Xerox IEEE 802.3 PUP
0A01	Xerox IEEE 802.3 PUP Address Translation

Continues

Table A-1 *Ethernet Type Codes (Continued)*

Hexadecimal	Description (Notes)
0BAD	Banyan VINES IP
0BAE	Banyan VINES Loopback
0BAF	Banyan VINES Echo
1000	Berkeley trailer negotiation
1001-100F	Berkeley trailer encapsulation for IP
1600	VALID system protocol
4242	PCS Basic Block Protocol
5208	BBN Simnet Private
6000	DEC unassigned
6001	DEC Maintenance Operation Protocol (MOP) Dump/Load Assistance
6002	DEC MOP Remote Console
6003	DEC DECnet Phase IV Route
6004	DEC Local Area Transport (LAT)
6005	DEC DECnet Diagnostics
6006	DEC Customer Protocol
6007	DEC Local-Area VAX Cluster (LAVC), SCA
6008	DEC unassigned
6009	DEC unassigned
6010-6014	3Com Corporation
7000	Ungermann-Bass (UB) Download
7001	UB diagnostic/loopback
7002	UB diagnostic/loopback
7020-7029	LRT (England)
7030	Proteon
7034	Cabletron
8003	Cronus VLN
8004	Cronus Direct
8005	HP Probe protocol
8006	Nestar
8008	AT&T

Table A-1 *Ethernet Type Codes (Continued)*

Hexadecimal	Description (Notes)
8010	Excelan
8013	Silicon Graphics diagnostic (obsolete)
8014	Silicon Graphics network games (obsolete)
8015	Silicon Graphics reserved type (obsolete)
8016	Silicon Graphics XNS NameServer, bounce server (obsolete)
8019	Apollo Computers
802E	Tymshare
802F	Tigan, Inc.
8035	Reverse Address Resolution Protocol (RARP) (Stanford)
8036	Aeonic Systems
8038	DEC LANBridge Management
8039-803C	DEC unassigned
803D	DEC Ethernet CSMA/CD Encryption Protocol
803E	DEC unassigned
803F	DEC LAN Traffic Monitor Protocol
8040-8042	DEC unassigned
8044	Planning Research Corporation
8046-8047	AT&T
8049	ExperData (France)
805B	Versatile Message Translation Protocol RFC 1045 (Stanford)
805C	Stanford V Kernel, production
805D	Evans & Sutherland
8060	Little Machines
8062	Counterpoint Computers
8065-8066	University of Massachusetts at Amherst
8067	Veeco Integrated Automation
8068	General Dynamics
8069	AT&T
806A	Autophon (Switzerland)
806C	ComDesign

Continues

Table A-1   *Ethernet Type Codes (Continued)*

Hexadecimal	Description (Notes)
806D	Compugraphic Corporation
806E-8077	Landmark Graphics Corporation
807A	Matra (France)
807B	Dansk Data Elektronik A/S
807C	University of Michigan
807D-807F	Vitalink Communications
8080	Vitalink TransLAN III Management
8081-8083	Counterpoint Computers
809B	Kinetics EtherTalk (AppleTalk over Ethernet)
809C-809E	Datability
809F	Spider Systems, Ltd.
80A3	Nixdorf Computers (Germany)
80A4-80B3	Siemens Gammasonics, Inc.
80C0-80C3	Digital Communications Association (DCA), Inc.
80C1	DCA Data Exchange Cluster
80C4	Banyan VINES IP
80C5	Banyan VINES Echo
80C6	Pacer Software
80C7	Applitek Corporation
80C8-80CC	Intergraph Corporation
80CD-80CE	Harris Corporation
80CF-80D2	Taylor Instrument
80D3-80D4	Rosemount Corporation
80D5	IBM SNA Services over Ethernet
80DD	Varian Associates
80DE	Integrated Solutions Transparent Remote File System (TRFS)
80DF	Integrated Solutions
80E0-80E3	Allen-Bradley
80E4-80F0	Datability
80F2	Retix

Table A-1 *Ethernet Type Codes (Continued)*

Hexadecimal	Description (Notes)
80F3	Kinetics AppleTalk Address Resolution Protocol (AARP)
80F4-80F5	Kinetics
80F7	Apollo Computer
80FF-8103	Wellfleet Communications
8107-8109	Symbolics Private
8130	Hayes Microcomputer Products, Ltd. (formerly Waterloo Microsystems, Inc.)
8131	VG Laboratory Systems
8132-8136	Bridge Communications, Inc.
8137	Novell NetWare IPX (old)
8137-8138	Novell, Inc.
8139-813D	KTI
8148	Logicraft, Inc.
8149	Network Computing Devices
814A	Alpha Micro
814C	SNMP
814D-814E	BIIN
814F	Technically Elite Concepts, Inc.
8150	Rational Corporation
8151-8153	Qualcomm, Inc.
815C-815E	Computer Protocol Pty, Ltd.
8164-8166	Charles River Data Systems, Inc.
817D-818C	Protocol Engines, Inc.
818D	Motorola Computer X
819A-81A3	Qualcomm, Inc.
81A4	ARAI Bunkichi
81A5-81AE	RAD Network Devices
81B7-81B9	Xyplex
81CC-81D5	Apricot Computers
81D6-81DD	Artisoft, Inc.
81DE-81E0	Hewlett Packard

Continues

Table A-1 *Ethernet Type Codes (Continued)*

Hexadecimal	Description (Notes)
81E6-81EF	Polygon, Inc.
81F0-81F2	Comsat Laboratories
81F3-81F5	Science Applications International Corporation (SAIC)
81F6-81F8	VG Analytical, Ltd.
8203-8205	Quantum Software Systems, Ltd.
8221-8222	Ascom Banking Systems, Ltd.
823E-8240	Advanced Encryption Systems, Inc.
827F-8282	Athena Programming, Inc.
8263-826A	Charles River Data Systems
829A-829B	Institute for Industrial Information Technology, Ltd.
829C-82AB	Taurus Controls, Inc.
82AC-838F	Walker Richer & Quinn, Inc.
8390	LANSoft, Inc.
8391-8693	Walker Richer & Quinn, Inc.
8694-869D	Idea Courier
869E-86A1	Computer Network Technology Corporation
86A3-86AC	Gateway Communications, Inc.
86DB	SECTRA - Secure Transmission AB
86DE	Delta Controls, Inc.
86DF	USC-ISI
86E0-86EF	Landis & Gyr Powers, Inc.
8700-8710	Motorola, Inc.
8711-8720	Cray Communications
8725-8728	Phoenix Microsystems
8739-873C	Control Technology, Inc.
8755-8759	LANSoft, Inc.
875A-875C	Norland
875D-8766	University of Utah Dept. of Computer Science
8780-8785	Symbol Technologies, Inc.

Table A-1 *Ethernet Type Codes (Continued)*

Hexadecimal	Description (Notes)
8A96-8A97	Invisible Software
9000	Loopback (Configuration Test Protocol)
9001	3Com (Bridge) XNS Systems Management
9002	3Com (Bridge) TCP/IP Systems Management
9003	3Com (Bridge) loop detect
FF00	BBN VITAL LANBridge cache wakeups
FF00-FF0F	ISC-Bunker Ramo

1. An asterisk (*) indicates the current connection in various informational displays.
2. A pound sign (#) is a delimiting character for configuration commands that contain arbitrary text strings.

INDEX

A

access expressions, defining, 211–212
access filtering
    SR/TLB, example, 199–200
    NetBIOS, example, 203, 204
access lists
    assigning to interfaces, 84
    bridging (table), 1453
    Ethernet type codes (table), 1453
    extended, filtering MAC addresses, 26
    MAC, 65
    protocol type, 28
    SRB, Ethernet type codes (table), 1453
    type code, 67–68
access-expression command, 211–212
accessing
    link stations, 1046
    local resources, 470–472
    remote databases, 1122
access-list command, 63–68, 213–214
activating
    ALPS circuits, 1419
    APPN links, lxvi–lxvii
    APPN routing, 989
activation window (DSPU), modifying, 813
ACTLU (active logical unit), lxxiv
ACTPU (active physical unit), lxxiv
adapter addresses (LNM), configuring, 168
adapter command, 1271–1272
adapter interfaces (CMCC)
    TCP stack, displaying statistics, 1358–1359
    TN3270 servers LUs, displaying information, 1380–1383
    UPD stack, displayig statistics, 1384
adapters
    CMCC (Cisco Mainframe Channel Connection), lxxx
        CIP, lxxxi, 1184
        CLAW, 1186–1187
        clearing, 1210
        CMPC (Cisco Multipath Channel), lxxxvi, 1190

adapters, Continued
        comparing CIP and CPA, lxxxii, 1186
        configuration task list, 1190
        connection networks, specifying, 1396–1397
        core dumps, 1212, 1290–1292
        CPA, lxxxi, lxxxii, 1185
        CSNA, support, 1189–1190
        DLUS backups, specifying, 1289
        internal LANs, configuring, 1300–1302
        IP host backup, lxxxiii, 1187, 1200, 1202
        LLC2 sessions, setting maximum, 1305
        loopback diagnostics, 1211
        microcode, loading, 1191–1194
        restarting, 1211
        statistics, monitoring, 1208–1212
        TCP/IP offload, lxxxiii
        TN3270 servers, support, lxxxiv, 1188
    internal (IBM channel attach), configuring, 1199
    internal MAC, 1190
adding static RIF cache entries (SRB), 196–197
addresses
    Bisync, contention interfaces, example, 564
    comparing QLLC conversion and SDLLC, lvi
    IP, assigning to CLAW, 1194
    LUs, mapping, 1218
    MAC
        assigning to bridge-group virtual interface, xxviii
        packet filtering, 25–29
    NAU (network addressable unit), lxii
    network, assigning to bridge-group virtual interface, xxviii
    serial interfaces, prioritizing traffic, 532–533
    TICs, caching (DLSw+), xlii
    VTRA (virtual Token Ring address), li
adjacent nodes (APPN), verifying, 1113
adjacent-cp-name command, 977
administrative filtering
    configuring, 24–29
    LAT service announcements, configuring, 30–32
adplex protocol (BSTUN), 552

E

O

P

T

CCIE Professional Development

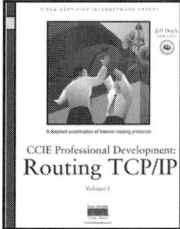

Routing TCP/IP, Volume I
Jeff Doyle, CCIE
1-57870-041-8 • **AVAILABLE NOW**

This book takes the reader from a basic understanding of routers and routing protocols through a detailed examination of each of the IP interior routing protocols. Learn techniques for designing networks that maximize the efficiency of the protocol being used. Exercises and review questions provide core study for the CCIE Routing and Switching exam.

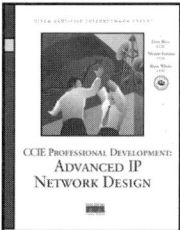

Advanced IP Network Design
Alvaro Retana, CCIE; Don Slice, CCIE; and Russ White, CCIE
1-57870-097-3 • **AVAILABLE NOW**

Network engineers and managers can use these case studies, which highlight various network design goals, to explore issues including protocol choice, network stability, and growth. This book also includes theoretical discussion on advanced design topics.

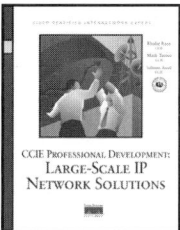

Large-Scale IP Network Solutions
Khalid Raza, CCIE; Salman Asad, CCIE; and Mark Turner
1-57870-084-1 • **AVAILABLE NOW**

Network engineers can find solutions as their IP networks grow in size and complexity. Examine all the major IP protocols in-depth and learn about scalability, migration planning, network management, and security for large-scale networks.

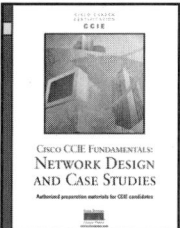

Cisco CCIE Fundamentals: Network Design and Case Studies, Second Edition
Cisco Systems, Inc.
1-57870-167-8 • **AVAILABLE SEPTEMBER 1999**

This two-part reference is a compilation of design tips and configuration examples assembled by Cisco Systems. The design guide portion of this book supports the network administrator who designs and implements routers and switch-based networks, and the case studies supplement the design guide material with real-world configurations. Begin the process of mastering the technologies and protocols necessary to become an effective CCIE.

CISCO SYSTEMS
CISCO PRESS

www.ciscopress.com

Cisco Career Certifications

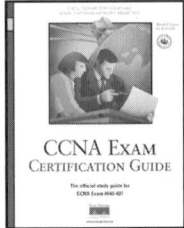

CCNA Exam Certification Guide
Wendell Odom, CCIE

0-7357-0073-7 • AVAILABLE NOW

This book is a comprehensive study tool for CCNA Exam #640-407 and part of a recommended study program from Cisco Systems. *CCNA Exam Certification Guide* helps you understand and master the exam objectives. Instructor-developed elements and techniques maximize your retention and recall of exam topics, and scenario-based exercises help validate your mastery of the exam objectives.

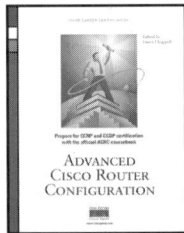

Advanced Cisco Router Configuration
Cisco Systems, Inc., Edited by Laura Chappell

1-57870-074-4 • AVAILABLE NOW

Based on the actual Cisco ACRC course, this book provides a thorough treatment of advanced network deployment issues. Learn to apply effective configuration techniques for solid network implementation and management as you prepare for CCNP and CCDP certifications. This book also includes chapter-ending tests for self-assessment.

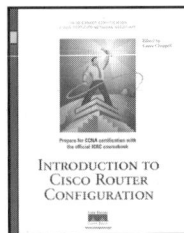

Introduction to Cisco Router Configuration
Cisco Systems, Inc., Edited by Laura Chappell

1-57870-076-0 • AVAILABLE NOW

Based on the actual Cisco ICRC course, this book presents the foundation knowledge necessary to define Cisco router configurations in multiprotocol environments. Examples and chapter-ending tests build a solid framework for understanding internetworking concepts. Prepare for the ICRC course and CCNA certification while mastering the protocols and technologies for router configuration.

Cisco CCNA Preparation Library
Cisco Systems, Inc.; Laura Chappell; and Kevin Downes, CCIE

1-57870-125-2 • AVAILABLE NOW • CD-ROM

This boxed set contains two Cisco Press books—*Introduction to Cisco Router Configuration* and *Internetworking Technologies Handbook*, Second Edition—and the *High-Performance Solutions for Desktop Connectivity* CD.

CISCO SYSTEMS

CISCO PRESS

www.ciscopress.com

Cisco Press Solutions

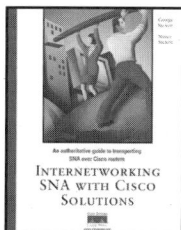

Internetworking SNA with Cisco Solutions
George Sackett and Nancy Sackett
1-57870-083-3 • AVAILABLE NOW

This comprehensive guide presents a practical approach to integrating
SNA and TCP/IP networks. It provides readers with an understanding of
internetworking terms, networking architectures, protocols, and
implementations for internetworking SNA with Cisco routers.

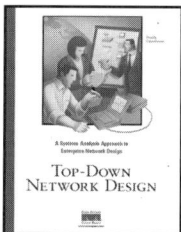

Top-Down Network Design
Priscilla Oppenheimer
1-57870-069-8 • AVAILABLE NOW

Building reliable, secure, and manageable networks is every network
professional's goal. This practical guide teaches you a systematic method for
network design that can be applied to campus LANs, remote-access networks,
WAN links, and large-scale internetworks. Learn how to analyze business and
technical requirements, examine traffic flow and Quality of Service requirements, and select protocols and technologies based on performance goals.

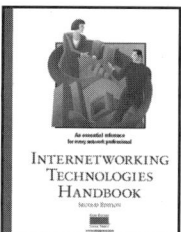

Internetworking Technologies Handbook, Second Edition
Kevin Downes, CCIE; Merilee Ford; H. Kim Lew; Steve Spanier; Tim Stevenson
1-57870-102-3 • AVAILABLE NOW

This comprehensive reference provides a foundation for understanding and
implementing contemporary internetworking technologies, providing you with
the necessary information needed to make rational networking decisions.
Master terms, concepts, technologies, and devices that are used in the
internetworking industry today. You also learn how to incorporate networking
technologies into a LAN/WAN environment, as well as how to apply the OSI
reference model to categorize protocols, technologies, and devices.

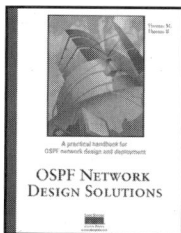

OSPF Network Design Solutions
Thomas M. Thomas II
1-57870-046-9 • AVAILABLE NOW

This comprehensive guide presents a detailed, applied look into the workings
of the popular Open Shortest Path First protocol, demonstrating how to
dramatically increase network performance and security, and how to most
easily maintain large-scale networks. OSPF is thoroughly explained through
exhaustive coverage of network design, deployment, management, and
troubleshooting.

CISCO SYSTEMS

CISCO PRESS

www.ciscopress.com

Cisco Press Solutions

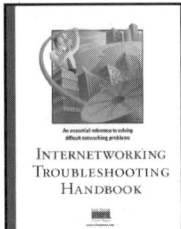

Internetworking Troubleshooting Handbook

Kevin Downes, CCIE; H. Kim Lew; Spank McCoy;
Tim Stevenson; Kathleen Wallace

1-57870-024-8 • AVAILABLE NOW

Diagnose and resolve specific and potentially problematic issues common to
every network type with this valuable reference. Each section of the book is
devoted to problems common to a specific protocol. Sections are subdivided
into symptoms, descriptions of environments, diagnosing and isolating problem
causes, and problem-solution summaries. This book aims to help you reduce
downtime, improve network performance, and enhance network reliability
using proven troubleshooting solutions.

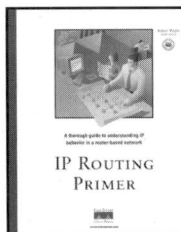

IP Routing Primer

Robert Wright, CCIE

1-57870-108-2 • AVAILABLE NOW

Learn how IP routing behaves in a Cisco router environment. In addition to
teaching the core fundamentals, this book enhances your ability to troubleshoot
IP routing problems yourself, often eliminating the need to call for additional
technical support. The information is presented in an approachable,
workbook-type format with dozens of detailed illustrations and real-life
scenarios integrated throughout.

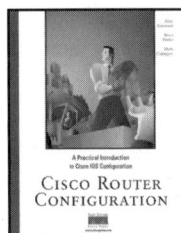

Cisco Router Configuration

Allan Leinwand; Bruce Pinsky; Mark Culpepper

1-57870-022-1 • AVAILABLE NOW

An example-oriented and chronological approach helps you implement and
administer your internetworking devices. Starting with the configuration
devices "out of the box," this book moves to configuring Cisco IOS for the
three most popular networking protocols used today: TCP/IP, AppleTalk, and
Novell Internetwork Packet Exchange (IPX). You also learn basic administrative and management configuration, including access control with TACACS+
and RADIUS, network management with SNMP, logging of messages, and time
control with NTP.

For the latest on Cisco Press resources and Certification and
Training guides, or for information on publishing opportunities, visit
www.ciscopress.com.

Cisco Press

Staying Connected to Networkers

We want to hear from **you**! Help Cisco Press **stay connected** to the issues and challenges you face on a daily basis by registering your book and filling out our brief survey.

Complete and mail this form, or better yet, jump to **www.ciscopress.com** and do it online. Each complete entry will be eligible for our monthly drawing to **win a FREE book** from the Cisco Press Library.

Thank you for choosing Cisco Press to help you work the network.

Name _____

Address _____

City _____ State/Province _____

Country _____ Zip/Post code _____

E-mail address _____

May we contact you via e-mail for product updates and customer benefits?
- ❏ Yes
- ❏ No

Where did you buy this product?
- ❏ Bookstore
- ❏ Online retailer
- ❏ Mail order
- ❏ Computer store
- ❏ Office supply store
- ❏ Class/Seminar
- ❏ Electronics store
- ❏ Discount store

- ❏ Other _____

When did you buy this product? _____ Month _____ Year

What price did you pay for this product?
- ❏ Full retail price
- ❏ Discounted price
- ❏ Gift

How did you learn about this product?
- ❏ Friend
- ❏ Catalog
- ❏ Magazine ad
- ❏ School
- ❏ Store personnel
- ❏ Postcard in the mail
- ❏ Article or review
- ❏ Professional Organization
- ❏ In-store ad
- ❏ Saw it on the shelf
- ❏ Used other products

- ❏ Other _____

What will this product be used for?
- ❏ Business use
- ❏ Personal use
- ❏ School/Education

- ❏ Other _____

How many years have you been employed in a computer-related industry?
- ❏ 2 years or less
- ❏ 3-5 years
- ❏ 5+ years

CISCO SYSTEMS

CISCO PRESS

www.ciscopress.com

Which best describes your job function?

- ❏ Corporate Management
- ❏ Network Design
- ❏ Marketing/Sales
- ❏ Professor/Teacher
- ❏ Systems Engineering
- ❏ Network Support
- ❏ Consultant
- ❏ IS Management
- ❏ Webmaster
- ❏ Student

- ❏ Other _____

What is your formal education background?

- ❏ High school
- ❏ College degree
- ❏ Vocational/Technical degree
- ❏ Masters degree
- ❏ Some college
- ❏ Professional or Doctoral degree

Have you purchased a Cisco Press product before?

- ❏ Yes
- ❏ No

On what topics would you like to see more coverage?

_____

_____

Do you have any additional comments or suggestions?

_____

_____

Cisco IOS 12.0 Bridging and IBM Network Solutions   1-57870-162-7

Cisco Press

201 West 103rd Street
Indianapolis, IN 46290
www.ciscopress.com

Place
Stamp
Here

Cisco Press
Customer Registration
P.O. Box 189014
Battle Creek, MI 49018-9947